Sam Miller

with a foreword by William Dalrymple

Somerset Books • London

First edition 2012

Published by Blue Guides Limited, a Somerset Books Company
Winchester House, Deane Gate Avenue, Taunton, Somerset TA1 2UH
www.blueguides.com
'Blue Guide' is a registered trademark.

ISBN 978-1-905131-53-2

A CIP catalogue record of this book is available from the British Library.

Distributed in the United States of America by
W.W. Norton & Company, Inc.
500 Fifth Avenue, New York, NY 10110.

Your views on this book would be much appreciated. We welcome not only specific comments, suggestions or corrections, but any more general views you may have: how this book enhanced your visit, how it could have been more helpful. Blue Guides authors and editorial and production team work hard to bring you what we hope are the best-researched and best-presented cultural, historical and academic guide books in the English language. Please write to us by email (editorial@blueguides.com), via the comments page on our website (www.blueguides.com) or at the address given above. We will be happy to acknowledge useful contributions in the next edition, and to offer a free copy of one of our titles.

Series editor Annabel Barber

Produced for Blue Guides by Thameside Media. Typesetting, interior page layouts and copy editing by Thameside Media. Proofreader Peter Bently. Maps and plans by Thameside Media, © Blue Guides 2012.

Illustrations: p. 1 Ashoka Pillar four-lion capital © Malgorzata Kistryn/Shutterstock; p. 100 Isa Khan Tomb, Delhi © Scott Norsworthy/Shutterstock; p. 137 Jantar Mantar Observatory, Jaipur © Jeremy Richards/Shutterstock; p. 139 Jal Mahal Jaipur, © Oksana Perkins/Shutterstock p. 210 Taj Mahal at sunset © Luciano Mortula/Shutterstock; p. 292 Golden Temple, Amritsar © Boris Stroujko/Shutterstock; p. 355 Thikse Monastery near Leh © Upadhyay/Shutterstock; p. 453 Carving at Khajuraho © Neale Cousland/Shutterstock; p. 543 Victoria Memorial (west side), Kolkata © Dr Ajay Kumar Singh/Shutterstock; p. 703 Hampi ruins © Juhku/Shutterstock; p. 819 Meenakshi Temple, Madurai © VLADJ55/Shutterstock.

Cover image research, editing and pre-press: Hadley Kincade
Cover photo: Khajuraho: ©istockphoto.com/oversnap
Spine photo: ©istockphoto.com/hanoded.

Author's acknowledgements:
Thank you to all those who helped me in a variety of ways during the writing of this book. In particular: Lucy Peck, John Keay, Francis Wacziarg, Aman Nath, Priya Paul, Varsha Hoon, Penny Richards, Shantum Seth, Natalia Leigh, William Crawley, Tom Crawley, William and Olivia Dalrymple, Eleni Philon, Paul Stafford, Benedict Leigh, Gautham Subramaniam, Abhishek Madhukar, Andrew Whitehead, William and Anjali Bissell, Ferzina Banaji, Anuradha Goyal, Harpreet Kaur, Sachin Mulji, Richard Holkar, Toby Sinclair, Jonty Rajagopalan, the late Tony Mango, Veeresh Malik, Neeta Das, Rajiv Saurastri, Surinder and Umi Dewan, Jivi Sethi, Shireen Vakil Miller, Zubin Miller, Roxana Miller, Naoshirvan Vakil, Ferida and Noni Chopra, Naval Chopra, Saira Menezes, Annie Dare, Altaf Hussain, Sidharth Bhatia, Valeria Corvo, Karuna Nundy, Nadir Bilimoria, Pheroza and Vijay Singh, Pia Chugani, Raj Kumar Sharma, Pan Singh Bisht, Clementina Lakra, Dipika and Gautam Mehra, Sameera and Syed Zaidi, Christine and Aman Rai, Viva Kermani, Jeroo Mango, Jane and Karl Miller, Subir Bhaumik, Gopal Gandhi, Indivar Mukhopadhyay, Madhup Mohta, Binoo Joshi, Naresh Fernandes, Ran Chakrabarti.

Material prepared for press by Anikó Kuzmich
Printed in Hungary by Dürer Nyomda Kft., Gyula.

ISBN 978-1-905131-53-2

Sam Miller is the Country Director, India, for the BBC World Service Trust, the international NGO arm of the BBC. He has lived and worked in India for much of the last two decades and is a former BBC Delhi correspondent. His first book, *Delhi: Adventures in a Megacity*, was published in 2009.

William Dalrymple is the author of a number of books, including *The Last Mughal: the Fall of a Dynasty, Delhi, 1857* and *Nine Lives* (Bloomsbury). www.williamdalrymple.com.

CONTENTS

THE GUIDE

MAPS & PLANS

Site plans

FOREWORD

by William Dalrymple

In his book *Landscape and Memory*, Simon Schama writes of his conviction that history not only shapes but becomes embedded in a landscape—in the land and the rocks and the water. For millennia, armies have been crashing through the Himalayan passes to attempt the conquest of India; and for as long as history records, India has been the scene of their clashes. Aryans, Persians, Scythians, Kushans, Huns, Turks and Mughals have all debouched through here, most of them sooner or later coming to grief in a similar manner to the last of the foreign invaders, the British. All over India lie the monuments left by the subcontinent's palimpsest of dynasties. Each in turn has raised its palaces and its great citadels; each in turn has seen its fortunes ebb and its monuments crumble. The British painted and celebrated the ruins of the Delhi sultans and the Mughals in their letters and travelogues, while never seeming to realise that they themselves were subject to the same inexorable historical laws which levelled the domes and vaults of the dynasties that predated them. Perhaps inevitably, it took a Frenchman to see the hubris of the British: when Clemenceau saw the dome of Lutyens's Viceregal Palace in Delhi rising above the crumbling vestiges of the Mughals he gasped and said: 'Ah! This will make the most magnificent ruin of them all.' He had a point: only 17 years after it was opened, the British left India for ever.

Yet alongside all these monuments to secular ambition and power, there has always been in India a parallel monumental landscape of the sacred and the holy. As the great Sanskritist, Diana Eck, puts it: 'Considering its long history, India has had but a few hours of political and administrative unity. Its unity as a nation, however, has been firmly constituted by the sacred geography it has held in common and revered: its mountains, forests, rivers, hilltop shrines.' For Hindus, as for many Indian Buddhists, Muslims, Christians and Sikhs, India is a Holy Land. The actual soil of India is thought by many rural Hindus to be the residence of the divinity and, in villages across India, it is worshipped and understood literally to be the body of the Goddess, while the features of the Indian landscape—the mountains and forests, the caves and outcrops of rock, the mighty rivers—are all understood to be her physical features. She is *Bharat Mata*, Mother India, and in her temple in Benares (Varanasi) she is worshipped not in the form of an idol but manifested in a brightly-coloured map of India. Her landscape is not dead but alive, dense with sacred significance.

This idea of India as a sacred landscape predates classical Hinduism, and, most importantly, is an idea which in turn was passed on to most of the other religions that came to flourish in the Indian soil. Just as the sacredness of the landscape percolated from pre-Vedic and tribal folk cults into classical 'Great Tradition' Hinduism, so in the course of time the idea slowly trickled from Hinduism into Buddhism, Sikhism, Indian Islam and even Indian Christianity. As a result, for example, nowhere else in Islam are there so many Sufi shrines where individual pilgrims can come and directly gain access to the divine through the intercession of the saint of a particular village or *mohalla*. Mosques are everywhere in Islam, but Sufi shrines are, in a very specific way—and very like Hindu *tirthas*—fords linking one world with the next. They are places where, thanks to the intervention of a great saint, you can cross over from the realm of the human to the realm of the divine, a place where prayers are somehow simply more likely to be answered. The Indian Sufi tradition, and the distance it has at times travelled from the strictures of pure koranic orthodoxy, is typical of the diversity of views and faiths and competing ideas that have always coexisted: 'In India,' writes the Nobel Prize-winner Amartya Sen, heterodoxy 'has always been the natural state of affairs.' Indeed India's genius, argues Sen, derives from this diversity, and from the way that its different orthodoxies have always been challenged by each other.

As a microcosm of modern India, Delhi is paramount. Of the great cities of the world, only Rome and Cairo can even begin to rival it for the sheer volume and density of its historic remains; yet in Delhi, as elsewhere in South Asia, familiarity has bred not pride but contempt. Every year, a few more ruins disappear. According to historian Pavan Verma, the majority of the buildings he recorded in *Mansions at Dusk* only six years ago no longer exist. On every side, rings of new suburbs are springing up, full of call centres, software companies and apartment blocks, all rapidly rising on land that only two years ago was billowing winter wheat. Shah Jahan's great Shalimar Garden, where Aurangzeb was crowned, now has a municipal housing colony on its land. The changes in Delhi reflects the growth of the Indian economy in general: measured by purchasing power parity, India is already on the verge of overtaking Japan to become the third largest economy in the world. This fast-emerging middle-class India has its eyes firmly fixed on the coming century. Everywhere there is a profound hope that the country's rapidly rising international status will somehow compensate for a past often perceived as one long succession of invasions and defeats at the hands of foreign powers. The result is a tragic neglect of its magnificent heritage. There is little effective legislation protecting ancient monuments, no system whatsoever of architectural listing, and the rich array of domestic and colonial architecture is entirely unprotected by law. In the competition between development and heritage, it is the latter that gives way. All of this makes Sam Miller's remarkable guide all the more valuable; and for his masterful work of celebrating and recording and directing us to the best of India's monuments, we owe him a huge debt. India still receives a fraction of the world's travellers: only five million visited in 2010, compared to the eleven million who visited tiny, monumentless Singapore, or the 77 million who visited France. Mass tourism, a threat in many countries, remains only a dream in India, and as a result travellers can play a positive role, highlighting the value—economic and otherwise—of the country's magnificent heritage. I road-tested this guide pre-publication on a trip around the little-visited state of Madhya Pradesh and can vouch for its accuracy, wit, discrimination and remarkable comprehensiveness. Other guide books may give fuller advice on the night club scene of Goa or the pubs of Bangalore; but there exists in print no better one-volume guide to India's architectural legacy, and how to get to see it. I have been waiting many years for a guide like this, and look forward to packing it in my rucksack for many trips to come.

New Delhi 1st July 2011.

INTRODUCTION

India's size, its billion-plus population, its long, complex history and its huge variety of cultural, religious and ethnic traditions make it feel more like a continent than a country. It is impossible to 'know' India in much the same way that it is impossible to 'know' Europe. Many visitors will fall in love with a particular area of India, to which they will return repeatedly, or find a specific architectural or artistic tradition that captivates them. Others will come back to India to explore, gradually, the whole enormous country, learning that wherever they go, there is still more to visit, if only they could tarry a little longer.

Foreign visitors have been touring India for more than 2,000 years, and many first-timers return dazzled and awestruck, and sometimes a little confused. The earliest foreign visitor to describe India was Megasthenes, a diplomat of Greek origin, who gave a vivid and mainly trustworthy account of life in north India in the 3rd century BC. He described the caste system and the geography of India with great accuracy. But, like so many others after him, he also repeats fantastic tales: he speaks of gold-digging ants, of humans with eight-toed feet that point backwards, and tribes of people whose ears are large and long enough to wrap around themselves to sleep in. None of this was true, of course, but for centuries India has been a land of hyperbole—the mysterious, mystic East where all is possible. And it is not always easy to reconcile different versions of the truth. Today, guides at major tourist attractions will spin stories because that's what they think tourists want to hear, or because they're repeating tales from their local oral tradition. If one were to believe every guide (and quite a few guidebooks), one would think that every fort had a secret tunnel to a far-off city, that every piece of inlaid mirror-work was a secret signalling device or every ruler cut off the arms of (or blinded or executed) the builders of a beautiful monument. In fact, the truth is often more interesting.

It is the aim of this book to be a reliable guide to the great monuments and artworks of India by putting them in their historical and cultural context—the first full *Blue Guide to India*, and the first modern attempt to compile an all-India guidebook that specialises in Indian history and culture. This book also aims to encourage visitors to look at the familiar and the famous in new ways, and to explore some magnificent but less well-known monuments before they get swamped by mass tourism.

Sam Miller

HIGHLIGHTS OF INDIA

So rich is India in art and great cultural and historic buildings that it can be hard to know where to begin. Perhaps with those great mausolea of the Mughal era—the Taj Mahal and Humayun's Tomb; or the erotic carvings at the Hindu temples of Khajuraho and Konarak; or the deserted city of Hampi; the ancient Buddhist sites of Sanchi and Sarnath; the even more ancient cave paintings of Bhimbetka; the great palace-forts of Rajasthan; the Victorian buildings of those teeming megacities of British India, Kolkata and Mumbai; the rock-cut caves of Elephanta, Ajanta and Ellora; the living temples of Madurai and Tanjore; or the magnificent early Muslim architecture of Sultanate Delhi and Ahmedabad. Each of these is an introduction to an important facet of India's culture and history. This guidebook seeks to provide authoritative information about all of these places, but it also seeks to direct visitors to some of the less well known: the forgotten hill-forts of Maharashtra; the ruined Rajasthani city of Bhangarh and the equally ruinous southern fortress of Gingee; the great mosques of Jaunpur and Dholka; and the Greek-influenced Nara Nag temples in Kashmir.

NORTHERN INDIA

Delhi: India's capital and, historically, the most important of India's major cities. It contains an extraordinary collection of mainly Muslim monuments, dating back as far as the 12th century, and has no fewer than three UNESCO World Heritage Sites: the Red Fort, Humayun's Tomb and the Qutb Minar.

Rajasthan: A state famous for its princely cities and desert landscapes. The state capital, Jaipur, is a superb 18th-century example of a planned city, and is easy to reach from Delhi. Udaipur, Jodhpur and Jaisalmer are spectacular older urban centres, while Ajmer contains India's most popular Muslim shrine.

Uttar Pradesh: India's most populous state is home to its most famous monument, the Taj Mahal. The state capital, Lucknow, has some fine Islamic architecture, while Varanasi, on the River Ganges, is the best-known and prettiest of India's Hindu temple towns.

Uttarakhand: This mountainous state (formerly called Uttaranchal) is easily accessible from Delhi, and includes the temple towns of Rishikesh and Hardwar, as well as several hill-stations.

Haryana: This small state, neighbouring Delhi, is little visited by tourists and offers fine opportunities for getting off the beaten track. **Chandigarh**, its modern capital, which it shares with Punjab, was designed by the Swiss-born Modernist architect Le Corbusier.

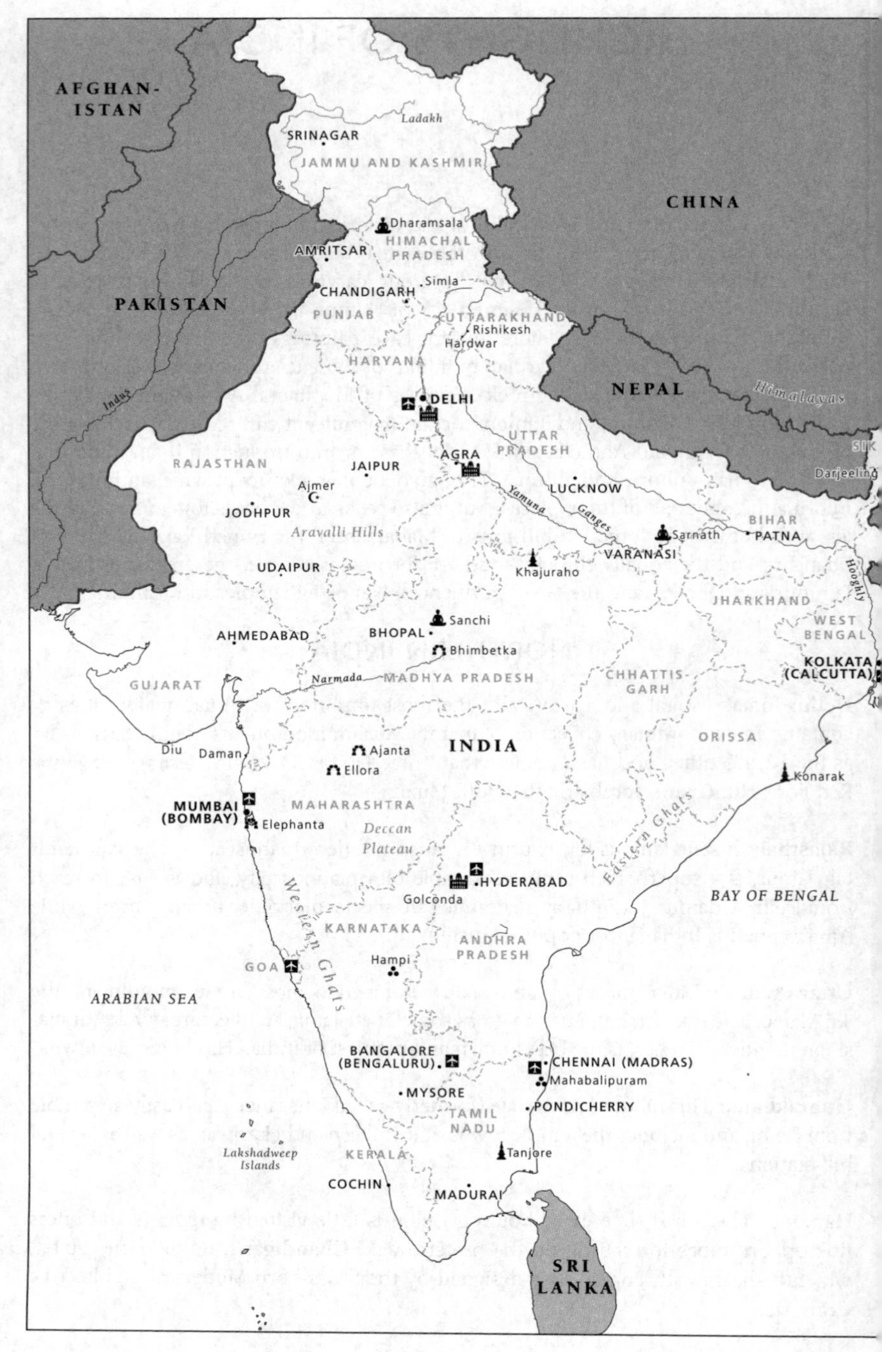
AFGHAN-
ISTAN
PAKISTAN
CHINA
NEPAL
SRI
LANKA
INDIA
Ladakh
SRINAGAR
JAMMU AND KASHMIR
Dharamsala
HIMACHAL
PRADESH
AMRITSAR
Simla
CHANDIGARH
PUNJAB
UTTARAKHAND
Rishikesh
Hardwar
HARYANA
DELHI
Himalayas
UTTAR
PRADESH
AGRA
RAJASTHAN
JAIPUR
LUCKNOW
Darjeeling
Ajmer
JODHPUR
Yamuna
Ganges
BIHAR
Sarnath
PATNA
Aravalli Hills
VARANASI
UDAIPUR
Khajuraho
Hooghly
JHARKHAND
Indus
Sanchi
WEST
BENGAL
BHOPAL
AHMEDABAD
Bhimbetka
KOLKATA
(CALCUTTA)
GUJARAT
Narmada
MADHYA PRADESH
CHHATTIS-
GARH
ORISSA
Diu
Daman
Ajanta
Ellora
Konarak
MUMBAI
(BOMBAY)
MAHARASHTRA
Elephanta
Deccan
Plateau
Eastern Ghats
HYDERABAD
Western Ghats
BAY OF BENGAL
Golconda
KARNATAKA
ANDHRA
PRADESH
Hampi
GOA
ARABIAN SEA
BANGALORE
(BENGALURU)
CHENNAI (MADRAS)
Mahabalipuram
MYSORE
PONDICHERRY
TAMIL
NADU
Lakshadweep
Islands
KERALA
Tanjore
COCHIN
MADURAI

Punjab: The state is best known for the holiest Sikh shrine, the Golden Temple, in the city of Amritsar. Punjab is India's only Sikh-majority state, and also has some interesting—and little-visited—princely palaces.

Himachal Pradesh: Simla, once the summer capital of British India, is the capital of this mountainous state. The hill-station of Dharamsala is home to the Dalai Lama and a large Tibetan community.

Jammu and Kashmir: India's only Muslim-majority state is best known for the beautiful Kashmir Valley, but a growing number of visitors travel to the arid Ladakh region, with its Buddhist temples and spectacular landscapes.

WESTERN & CENTRAL INDIA

Gujarat: The main city, Ahmedabad, has superb medieval Muslim architecture. Other parts of the state have some very fine Hindu and Jain buildings, and there are two former Portuguese coastal enclaves at Daman and Diu.

Madhya Pradesh: This land-locked state has some of India's finest fortresses and wildlife parks, as well as the erotic temple carvings of Khajuraho, the great Buddhist stupa of Sanchi and the cave paintings of Bhimbetka. The smaller neighbouring state of **Chhattisgarh** is little visited, largely because of a long-running insurgency.

Maharashtra: Mumbai, India's most populous city, is the capital of this western state, which also has some fine hill-forts and the superb cave temples of Elephanta, Ajanta and Ellora. *Contd overleaf*

For a key to the map symbols, see back page.

NB: The external boundaries of India on this map have not been authenticated and may be incorrect.

EASTERN INDIA

Bihar: Often ignored by Western tourists, this state has several of India's most important Buddhist sites, making it a major attraction for East Asian visitors. Neighbouring **Jharkhand** state has few foreign visitors.

West Bengal: The state capital, Kolkata, was once the capital of British India and consequently has some fine architecture from the colonial period. Other attractions include Darjeeling, a British-period hill-station and major tea-growing centre.

Orissa: This coastal state is best known for the great Sun Temple at Konarak, but also has many other important Hindu and Buddhist buildings, as well as some fine beaches and wildlife parks.

Sikkim: This largely Buddhist Himalayan mountain state has spectacular scenery and many Buddhist monasteries.

The northeastern states: Among the seven small northeastern states, only Assam receives much international tourist traffic, much of which is directed to the wildlife parks.

SOUTHERN INDIA

Goa: Once a Portuguese colony, this state has India's best-known beach resorts and some very fine colonial-period buildings.

Karnataka: As well as the modern metropolis of Bangalore, Karnataka has important Hindu, Jain and Muslim buildings, the magnificent ruined city of Hampi and the royal palaces of Mysore.

Andhra Pradesh: The capital, Hyderabad, and the fortress of Golconda were the headquarters of India's richest princely state, while other parts of Andhra Pradesh have important Hindu and Buddhist monuments.

Tamil Nadu: The state is best known for its enormous Hindu temples, most of them still used for worship. There are also the superb ancient shrines and rock carvings of Mahabalipuram, as well as the former French enclave of Pondicherry.

Kerala: This coastal state has fine beaches, sea-forts, lush landscapes and the fascinating port-city of Cochin (officially Kochi).

The Andaman and Nicobar islands: These islands—best accessed via the Tamil Nadu capital, Chennai—are mainly visited for their beaches and natural beauty.

GEOGRAPHY

Geographically, India can be described as the land south of the Himalayan peaks, and bordered to the northwest and northeast, respectively, by the watersheds of the great rivers, the Indus and the lower Brahmaputra. India's maritime borders are defined to the southwest and southeast, respectively, by the Arabian Sea and the Bay of Bengal. Most of this territory is part of the modern-day nation-state of India, but the geographical land border is surrounded, and sometimes intruded on, by six other nations: Pakistan, China, Nepal, Bhutan, Bangladesh and Burma. India's modern borders are largely confined to the subcontinent, but there are also three isolated island groups, the Andaman Islands and Nicobar Islands in the Bay of Bengal (both closer to Burma than to the Indian mainland), and the Lakshadweep Islands (closer to the Republic of the Maldives than to the Indian mainland).

India takes the shape of a ragged quadrilateral, a part-polished diamond. It is known as a subcontinent because its desert and mountain borderlands cut it off from the rest of the Eurasian landmass. It juts out, pointing southwards, from the rest of the continent, to the place from where it came. For, 100 million years ago, if modern geological theories are to be believed, the Indian subcontinent was an enormous island, resting on a subterranean continental plate, heading northwards towards Eurasia. About 50 million years ago, the two continental plates crashed into each other, buckling the landmasses to create the world's highest mountain range, the Himalayas. Fossils of ocean creatures can still be found high in the mountains. Three great rivers would begin to flow from the newly-formed Himalayas into the Indian Ocean: the Indus, from which the name India is derived, but which barely enters its modern frontiers; the Ganges, which cuts a great west–east gash across the subcontinent before debouching into the Bay of Bengal; and the Brahmaputra, which begins north of the Himalayas in China and heads east before reversing its direction and emptying itself into the same enormous delta fed by the Ganges.

Some parts of the subcontinent are even older. The low-lying Aravalli Hills, for example, that run from southern Rajasthan northwards to Delhi, were created almost 500 million years ago. The enormous Deccan Plateau, which covers much of south and central India, consists of solidified overlapping lava flows (known as the Deccan traps), which were formed while India was still an island, some 65 million years ago. The volcanic explosions that created the Deccan Plateau are thought by some scientists to have triggered the extinction of the dinosaurs. The whole southern part of India has been likened to a weather-worn table, sloping down to the east, with a ridge to the west and a steep drop towards the sea. All the major rivers of southern India flow to the east, into the Bay of Bengal.

HISTORY

There are few places in the world where controversies about the history of a country play such a major role in modern political life. Even issues of ancient history—such as the identity of the first Indians, of the people of the Indus Valley civilisation and of the 'Aryan invaders'—divide academics, politicians and many ordinary people in India along partisan lines. Hindu nationalists tend to argue that the tales told in Hindu religious texts should be taken literally, and that Indian culture, languages and tradition all originated in India. Many south Indians argue that they were the original Indians, and that the northerners are outsiders. Historians who challenge political and religious orthodoxies face intense criticism and have sometimes been threatened, while visitors should expect to be told untruths by politically-motivated guides. History is a major battleground of modern Indian politics.

Prehistory (before 2500 BC)

There is great uncertainty about the early human settlement of India. The earliest migrants to India are thought likely to have reached the subcontinent by a coastal route from the Middle East, though there is no scientific consensus on this—as with so many issues related to prehistoric India. There is some evidence of human presence from more than 75,000 years ago, prior to the Toba super-volcano, which many scientists see as the most important single event in early human history and migration. The eruption at Mount Toba in Indonesia took place about 73,000 years ago and, as well as creating a volcanic winter and wiping out most of the human race, it also caused the first major non-African 'ethnic' division in the world—between the humans who had already moved from Africa through India into East Asia (and would go on to become the first populations of the Americas and Australia) and those who remained in Africa, the Middle East and Europe.

Objects such as hand-axes, blades, choppers and scrapers—all made of stone—are found at Palaeolithic sites in many areas of western and central India. They date back at least 30,000 years and possibly much further. The earliest major prehistoric site in India, though, is in the central state of Madhya Pradesh, at the Bhimbetka caves, which have spectacular rock paintings. The caves were originally used by pre-agricultural hunter-gatherers, though they continued to be occupied into the modern period. Agriculture seems to have first developed in the Indus Valley, now in Pakistan, where wheat and legumes were harvested on the floodplains perhaps as early as 8,000 years ago. However, there is evidence that agriculture may not have reached the rest of the subcontinent, which had much greater tree cover and less easily tilled soil, until as recently as 1000 BC.

Indus Valley civilisation (flourished c. 2500–c. 1900 BC)

The Indus Valley (or Harappan) civilisation emerged in what is now southern Pakistan about 5,000 years ago—the time when, thousands of miles away, the first pharaohs were ruling in ancient Egypt. In the early 20th century, excavations at Harappa and Mohenjo-

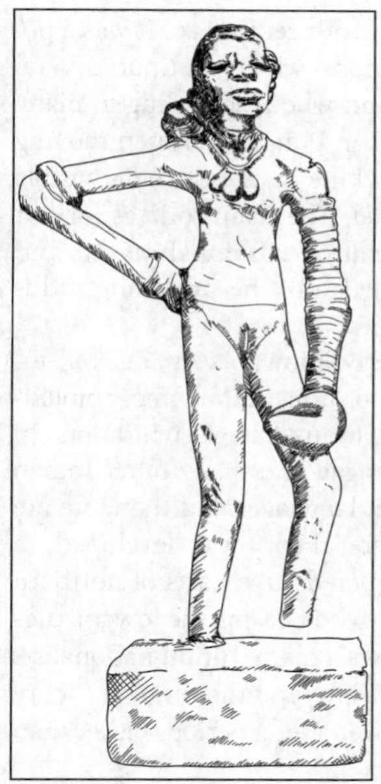

Third-century BC bronze statuette from Mohenjo-daro dubbed the 'Dancing Girl'. Her left arm is enmeshed in bangles, while her left leg is raised, perhaps in a dance posture. The statue is part of the collection of the National Museum in New Delhi.

daro revealed the existence of complex settlements close to the River Indus. More sites have since been discovered, several of them within India's modern frontiers, and not close to the Indus, including Lothal and Dholavira in Gujarat, and Kalibangan in Rajasthan.

The excavations revealed that the cities themselves had been carefully planned, sometimes with massive fortified walls. They were divided in a grid-like pattern, with standardised street, plot and brick sizes. Some houses had interior courtyards—and there were clear hierarchies in the size and position of residential areas. There were also shops, granaries, bathing pools, wells and covered drains. The inhabitants grew wheat, mustard, sesame, peas and dates, and had domesticated many animals, including the camel, the buffalo and the elephant. They used wheeled transport and, indeed, may have been the first people in the world to do so.

Copper and bronze were the main metals used by the Harappans, and the best-known piece of Harappan art, the 'dancing girl of Mohenjo-daro', is also of bronze. They made wheel-thrown pottery, woven cotton cloth and fine jewellery, and had a written language that has still not been deciphered despite numerous attempts—in part because each inscription is less than 17 characters long. A team of Finnish computer scientists and ethnolinguists have found evidence of similarity to the Dravidian language family of southern India, but an agreed translation of the Harappan inscriptions still seems far off, and some argue that the inscriptions are not a language at all, but a set of symbols similar to heraldic devices or traffic signs—perhaps representing the names of individuals.

Harappans traded with Sumer (a Harappan seal was discovered in Ur in modern-day Iraq) and with southern India, and built ships. Little is known about the people themselves, and there is much controversy about their origins. It is probable, but far from certain, that ethnically and linguistically they were not Indo-European, unlike the Indo-Aryans whose arrival seems to postdate the collapse of the Indus Valley civilisation. The most likely hypothesis is that the Harappans were Dravidians, related to the dominant communities of modern-day southern India, and that a change in the course and behaviour of the River Indus led to floods that destroyed many of their cities.

The Vedic Age (c. 1500–c. 600 BC)

The Vedic Age, named after the Sanskrit religious texts known as the *Vedas*, is the shorthand often used for the period after the decline of the Indus Valley civilisation until the consolidation of India's northern kingdoms in the 6th century BC. It was a period of important religious, linguistic and cultural innovations, which continue, several millennia later, to play a major role in Indian society—and when, according to many accounts, the Indo-Aryans settled in northern India, first in Punjab and then moving into the Ganges plain. The roots of modern Hinduism and the caste system are visible in the *Vedas*—of which the best-known text is the *Rigveda*. The main sources for our knowledge of the Vedic Age are textual, in the form of orally-transmitted prayers and stories, only written down much later, while our knowledge of the preceding Indus Valley civilisation is almost entirely archaeological.

It is thought likely that Indo-European settlers, formerly known as 'Aryans' but today as Indo-Aryans, brought their language and culture to India at this time, coinciding with, but probably not causing, the decline of the Indus Valley civilisation. In the 18th century it was realised that Sanskrit, Hindi, Bengali and many other Indian languages share a common ancestor with most European languages and therefore are Indo-European in origin. Consequently an 'Aryan' invasion theory was developed, in which 'Aryans' from the west were thought to have conquered large parts of northern India, subduing the existing darker-skinned Dravidians—who became the lower castes under the Hindu caste system. This theory is unproven, with many Hindu nationalists claiming that the 'Aryans' were indigenous to India. Supporters of the original theory now argue in favour of a gradual, less violent migration over a long period, rather than a dramatic, single, all-conquering invasion.

During the early Vedic Age, there appear to have been no big cities, and most of the buildings were constructed of wood—and partly for this reason no major archaeological Vedic sites have been discovered, though a significant amount of pottery has been excavated. During this period, northern India is seen as shifting from the Bronze Age to the Iron Age. For the first time, iron ploughs pulled by draught animals were used on the previously untilled lands of the Ganges plain—the start of serious agriculture in northern India. Huge areas of jungle, across modern Uttar Pradesh and Bihar, were cut down for agriculture—and large iron deposits were found in southern Bihar.

The Indo-Aryan settlers are thought to have brought horses and chariots with them, as well as their new gods and belief in reincarnation. Brahmins, the name given to the priestly caste, were the dominant social group for much of the Vedic Age—and Brahmanism and the caste system spread gradually to southern India. This was the time at which the great religious-historical epics of Hinduism, the *Ramayana* and the *Mahabharata*, were composed; the great battles and moral debates are thought to reflect the politics of the Vedic Age, and growing Indo-Aryan dominance in northern India.

The birth of new religions and the Mauryan Empire (c. 600–c. 200 BC)

By c. 600 BC, north India was consolidated into a number of kingdoms, most of which had distinct urban centres. A small-scale cash economy had developed, and India's earliest coins, with punch-marked inscriptions, date from this period. A number of specialised urban professions had also emerged. The most powerful of the kingdoms were Kosala, with its capital Sravasti in what is now eastern Uttar Pradesh, and Magadha, with its early capital Rajagriha in what is now Bihar. It was an environment in which two extraordinary princes would grow up, adopt a life of asceticism, launch new social movements, and profoundly influence Indian religious and secular life in a way that survives today. They were Siddhartha Gautama (c. 563–483 BC), later known as the Buddha, and Mahavir (c. 549–477 BC), the founder of Jainism. These two were the key Indian figures in what is often known as the Axial Age. Among their near-contemporaries were Confucius and Socrates. The ideas and practices of the Buddha and Mahavir were a response to the materialism and violence of their times, and also, arguably, a revolt by members of the warrior Kshatriya caste, to which they both belonged, against the monopoly held by the priestly Brahmin caste over spiritual and philosophical life. The deep influence left by both Buddhism and Jainism on India's heritage is obvious to visitors to most parts of India in the form of monasteries, stupas and fine carvings—although the most impressive Buddhist and Jain monuments date to a period long after their founders had died.

In 320 BC, Chandragupta Maurya (c. 340–298 BC) took power in the kingdom of Magadha, and founded the Mauryan Empire which would eventually—under his grandson Ashoka—rule most of the subcontinent. As a young man, Chandragupta, apparently the son of a shepherd, is said to have met Alexander the Great as he camped on the River Indus, inspiring Chandragupta to build his great Indian empire. Alexander had turned back at the borders of modern-day India, but he left behind a succession of smaller Indo-Greek kingdoms which ruled parts of India's western borders.

We know more about the court of Chandragupta Maurya than that of any other Indian ruler until the 14th-century Sultanate period. This is because of two ancient texts: one purportedly written by Chandragupta's chief advisor, known as Kautilya or Chanakya; the other by Megasthenes, a visiting Greek ambassador. It was only proved in the 19th century that the king described by Megasthenes, whom he calls Sandrocottus, was the same as Chandragupta. Megasthenes' writings, only parts of which have survived, are the earliest foreign travellers' eyewitness descriptions of India.

Chandragupta ruled his empire from Pataliputra (modern-day Patna in the state of Bihar), and historians believe it was then the most populous city in the world. Pataliputra stretched for more than 12km along the southern bank of the Ganges. It had its own sophisticated municipal government run by city elders and employing government officials with a list of functions that seems very modern: overseeing the water supply, collecting taxes, protecting consumer rights, ensuring unadulterated goods were sold, looking after foreign visitors, and collecting statistics. After 20 years in power Chandragupta abdicated in favour of his son, Bindusara, and is said to have become a Jain ascetic, starving himself to death at Shravana Belagola in the southern state of Karnataka—which is today one of the most important Jain sites in India. Bindusara would reign as Mauryan emperor for 20 years, and was succeeded after his death—following a four-year power struggle between his relatives—by one of his sons, Ashoka, who had been governor of the Hindu pilgrimage city of Ujjain in central India.

Ashoka the Great (c. 304–232 BC), the grandson of Chandragupta, is one of the few figures in Indian history who is universally admired. He created an enormous empire that stretched from Bengal to Afghanistan and included large parts of southern India. Later in his reign he renounced war—appalled by the blood that had been shed in his final battle, over the Kalinga Kingdom in Orissa—and thereafter attempted to spread Buddhism throughout the subcontinent and beyond, sending envoys to Thailand, Sri Lanka, the Middle East, Greece and North Africa. His period of rule was one of exceptional artistic creativity—arguably the first in India's history. The glorious four-headed, eight-legged lion, bursting forth from a smooth sandstone pillar, which can be seen at Sarnath near Varanasi, is one of India's iconic pieces of art, visible on every government letterhead and every modern coin.

Between two empires (c. 200 BC–AD 320)

The Mauryan Empire began to disintegrate not long after the death of Ashoka—and it was not until the emergence of the Gupta Empire more than 500 years later that northern India was reunited. In the long interim period, several smaller kingdoms emerged in the north, often with rulers of foreign origin. Buddhist art and architecture flourished, and the greatest surviving stupa at Sanchi, in central India, dates to this period, as do many of the rock-cut temples of western India. Some of the Indo-Greek kingdoms survived in the northwest—and these became the sources of that great flourishing of Indo-Greek syncretic art known as Gandhara sculpture (*see p. 36*). One of the early Indo-Greek kings, Menander—known in India as Milinda—who ruled Punjab c. 150 BC, was converted to Buddhism by the monk Nagasena. Their dialogues, entitled *Questions of Milinda*, were written down and have survived as a key text of Buddhism. Several other Greeks converted to Buddhism—including an ambassador called Heliodorus, who erected the inscribed pillar that bears his name in central India. Some historians have speculated about whether key ideas from Buddhism influenced the birth of Christianity, and suggested that Greek travellers may have been the transmission route for Buddhist ideas to the Middle East.

The northwestern frontier remained a key migration route, with Scythians (known as Shakas in India) from Central Asia, Parthians from Persia and Kushans from western China entering what is now Pakistan, adopting Sanskrit titles and sometimes converting to Buddhism. The Kushan king Kanishka (flourished c. AD 100) was a convert to Buddhism who controlled parts of northern and central India—the earliest Mathura carvings in red sandstone date from his reign. The first Jewish and Christian communities almost certainly established themselves in this period, in coastal settlements in southern India—while politically the south was in the control of three powerful Hindu dynasties: the Cholas, the Cheras and the Pandyas. There was also extensive trading with the Roman Empire, as finds of hoards of coins and amphorae along the coast of India demonstrate. The main exports to Rome were pepper, cinnamon and other spices, and an ivory statuette carved in India was found at Pompeii during excavations in the 1930s.

The Early Classical Age and the Gupta Empire (AD 320–c. 700)

The middle years of the first millennium AD are widely known as India's Classical Age—a period of great artistic, literary, scientific and philosophical creativity—when most of northern India was once again reunited, this time under the Gupta Empire. This was the period when the great frescoes of Ajanta were painted, when the Iron Pillar at the Qutb Minar was forged, when the *Kama Sutra* was written, when Indian mathematicians became the first to use a 'zero', when Indian astronomers demonstrated that the earth spun on its own axis. The name of the empire's founder, Chandra Gupta I, is very similar to that of the founder of the previous great empire, Chandragupta Maurya, more than 600 years earlier—but there is not thought to be any connection. Chandra Gupta and his successors built an empire that encompassed not only their homeland on the Gangetic Plain, but also Bengal, Gujarat and large parts of the Deccan Plateau, and whose influence spread much further still. India had been looking east for several centuries; and during the first half of the first millennium AD it developed important trading and cultural relations with China and the countries of South Asia. Indian travellers took Hinduism, Buddhism and Sanskritic culture to Burma, Thailand, Vietnam and Indonesia. The Indonesian island of Bali remains the only Hindu outpost beyond South Asia, apart from those created by more modern migration. Buddhism, on the other hand, has been much more successful in East Asia than in the land of its birth.

New invaders, this time nomadic White Huns, defeated the Guptas in the early 6th century, and the empire fell apart and was replaced by several smaller kingdoms. There was a brief reintegration of old Gupta territories, under King Harsha Vardhana in the 7th century. Harsha ruled from Thanesar, north of Delhi, and later from Kannauj, in central Uttar Pradesh. One of the main rivals to Harsha's kingdom was the Chalukya Dynasty, which controlled large parts of central India, mainly towards the western coast, but which also reached the Bay of Bengal. The Chalukyas built the magnificent temples at Badami, Aihole and Pattadakal in northern Karnataka. Their great southern rivals were the Pallavas, who were responsible for the rock carvings at Mahabalipuram on the coast of modern Tamil Nadu.

The Late Classical Age (c. AD 700–1192)

The era known as the Late Classical Age is no less important than the earlier period, but it was not dominated by one figure or empire—and therefore Indian history in this period is really the histories of particular regions. It remained a time of exceptional artistic creativity—encompassing the spectacular art and architecture of the southern Chola and Chalukya dynasties, as well as the extraordinary rock-cut and free-standing Hindu temples of Elephanta, Bhubaneswar, Kashmir and Gujarat. For the early part of this period, Kannauj, in modern-day Uttar Pradesh, was the most important Indian city, fought over by three separate dynasties: the Rashtrakutas from central India (who built the great Ellora caves); the Palas from the east; and the Gurjara-Pratiharas from the west. Islam also appeared in the subcontinent, gradually at first, with Muslim traders active along the west coast. In the same period, in the far south, the Chola Empire was at its height—and the great Brihadishwara Temple in Tanjore was built (*see p. 807*). The Cholas invaded Sri Lanka, the Maldives and Malaysia, sent missions to China, Cambodia and Burma, and raided north India—the first major southern incursion into the north of the country.

The Sultanate period (AD 1192–1526)

The first Muslim to lead an army into India was Mahmud of Ghazni in AD 1000. He mounted a series of raids on the country, with the aim of plundering the fabled wealth of India. No figure in Indian history has been more demonised than Mahmud of Ghazni—who did not come to settle or to convert but simply to plunder. He destroyed temples, killing many thousands of Hindus and stole whatever his army could lay its hands on—though recent reassessments suggest that Mahmud's own historians exaggerated his actions.

Mahmud's incursions, however, were raids and not conquests, and Muslim rule in northern India only really began in 1192 with the arrival, from what is now Afghanistan, of the armies of Muhammad of Ghor, whose general, Qutbuddin Aibak, became the sultan of Delhi. Qutbuddin Aibak was a slave, and for this reason the dynasty he founded became known as the Mamluk or Slave Dynasty. Among the Slave sultans was Aibak's granddaughter Razia (reigned 1236–40), one of India's, and Islam's, first female rulers; she was described by contemporaries as both wise and inspirational. The Slave Dynasty extended its control over large parts of north India, but left few monuments except the extraordinary Qutb Minar and its magnificent ruined mosque in South Delhi. The Slave Dynasty relied heavily on the small group of families that had come with the Ghorid army to Delhi in 1196, and it was only with the successor dynasties—the Khiljis (1290–1320) and the Tughlaqs (1320–1413)—that the ruling class began to be Indianised.

The Tughlaq period is one that has left an indelible mark on Indian architecture—defining a style that was later known as Sultanate. Under the Tughlaqs, the empire was ruled through a series of local governors in the more distant regions—in Gujarat, Jaunpur, Bengal and the Deccan—each of which developed a distinctive style of 'provincial' Sultanate architecture. At various points in the 14th and 15th centuries, these provinces also declared their independence from Delhi. Both the Khiljis and the Tughlaqs raided far into southern India, and in turn were attacked from the north by the Mongols. The second Tughlaq sultan, Muhammad bin Tughlaq, even briefly moved his capital from Delhi to Daulatabad in modern-day Maharashtra. Muhammad bin Tughlaq was one of the most controversial figures ever to rule in India. He was sophisticated and cultured, but his cruelty became legendary. He was succeeded by his cousin Feroze Shah Tughlaq, who restored many older buildings and moved two ancient Ashoka pillars to Delhi.

In 1398, the ease with which foreign armies could enter India from the west was demonstrated once again, when the Mongol forces under Timur (better known in the West as Tamerlane) rampaged through Delhi, killing and plundering. Timur is also said to have kidnapped Delhi architects and artisans to help build the city of Samarkand in Central Asia. The Tughlaq Sultanate collapsed in on itself, and was replaced by the Sayyid (1414–51) and then the Lodi (1451–1526) dynasties. The territory controlled by the Delhi Sultanate had shrunk, and the Lodis moved their capital from Delhi to Agra. The Lodis, like the Tughlaqs, left a deep mark on Indian architecture—particularly with their tombs and mosques in Delhi.

Throughout the Sultanate period, Hindu kingdoms continued to flourish in the south, along the eastern coast and in Rajasthan. The Ganga Dynasty in Orissa was responsible for the extraordinary Sun Temple at Konarak and many other fine Hindu shrines. Hindu warriors fleeing the advance of the Sultanate forces gathered in northern Karnataka and in 1336 founded a new city, Vijayanagar, now best known as the ruined city of Hampi. In Rajasthan, several major hill-forts were constructed or refortified, including those at Jodhpur, Jaisalmer, Kumbhalgarh and Chittorgarh—and the region saw the emergence of a series of semi-independent kingdoms, most of them ruled by members of the warrior Rajput caste.

Towards the end of the Sultanate period, the number of European travellers to India increased—in large part because of the opening up of a sea route around the Cape of Good Hope. Most of the travellers were traders and explorers, though Christian missionaries soon followed. The most famous of the early travellers was Vasco da Gama, the Portuguese explorer who landed near Calicut on the coast of Kerala in 1498; he returned five years later to build a small fort further south along the Kerala coast in Cochin. Over the next 30 years, the Portuguese built fortified settlements at Goa, Bassein (Vasai) in Maharashtra and Diu in Gujarat.

The Mughal period (1526–1707)

The Lodi Dynasty was eventually overthrown by a new set of Muslim invaders from the west, the Mughals, whose artistic and architectural reputation remains undimmed by time. They were responsible for many of India's most famous buildings, including the Taj Mahal, the two Red Forts (in Agra and Delhi) and Humayun's Tomb. The first Mughal emperor was Babur, followed by his son Humayun and grandson Akbar. Akbar was succeeded by Jehangir, Shah Jahan and then Aurangzeb. Officially, the Mughal Empire lasted until 1857, but it went into decline after the death of Aurangzeb in 1707. The Mughals normally called themselves Timurids, descendants of the Mongol leader Timur, who briefly conquered Delhi at the end of the 14th century, rather than Mughal, a Persianisation of 'Mongol'. Timur's attack on Delhi, and the concessions he extracted from its ruler, gave the Mughal emperors their much cherished but rather dubious claim to being the rightful sovereigns of northern India.

Babur (1483–1530), the first of the Mughal emperors, was descended from two great Mongol commanders: Ghengis Khan, on his mother's side, and Timur, through his father. Born in what is now Uzbekistan, he conquered much of Afghanistan while still a young man. After a series of smaller attacks, he invaded India and defeated the Lodi Sultanate, killing Sultan Ibrahim Lodi at the Battle of Panipat, north of Delhi, in 1526. Babur's army is thought to have been one-tenth the size of the Lodi forces, but it had far superior artillery, being equipped with cannon and matchlock guns. Babur established himself in Agra, the former Lodi capital, which remained his base until his death in 1530. He wrote a remarkable autobiography, the *Baburnama*, which contains an extraordinary amount of detail about his life and his brief reign as Mughal emperor in India. He is candid about his dislike of India, in what must rank as one of the most negative descriptions ever given of the country. 'Hindustan is a country that has few pleasures to recommend it. The people are not handsome. They have no idea of the charms of friendly society, of frankly mixing together, or of familiar intercourse. They have no genius, no comprehension of mind, no politeness of manner, no kindness or fellow-feeling, no ingenuity or mechanical invention in planning or executing their handicraft works, no skill or knowledge in design or architecture; they have no horses, no good flesh, no grapes or musk-melons, no good fruits, no ice or cold water, no good food or bread in their bazars, no baths or colleges, no candles, no torches, not a candlestick…' He does make some concession to the country, though: 'The chief excellency of Hindustan is that it is a large country and has an abundance of gold and silver.' Although he died in Agra, Babur's body was returned to his beloved Kabul for burial. One of the few surviving buildings from Babur's reign, the Babri Mosque in Ayodhya, was demolished in 1992 by Hindu activists who believed it was constructed on the site of an ancient temple marking the birthplace of the Hindu god Rama.

Humayun (1508–56), the second Mughal emperor, lost and then regained his father's newly-won Indian empire. He officially reigned for 26 years, but only ruled in Delhi for ten. He is best known today for the magnificent Delhi tomb in which he was buried. Babur divided his empire between his two eldest sons: Humayun, who received the new Indian territories, and Kamran Mirza, who ruled territory stretching from Kabul to Lahore. Humayun was immediately challenged by other Muslim rulers in Gujarat and Bengal, and was eventually driven out of Delhi for 15 years by the forces of Sher Shah Suri.

Sher Shah Suri (1486–1545) was a former Lodi warlord of Afghan origin who drove the Mughals out of north India in 1540 and founded a short-lived dynasty. Suri was an able administrator and helped create the infrastructure that would be so important to the later Mughals. He rebuilt the Grand Trunk Road across northern India, created a provincial bureaucracy and introduced the silver coins known as rupayas, precursor of the modern rupee. He was also responsible for two of India's least-heralded but most impressive pieces of funerary architecture: his own tomb at Sasaram in Bihar, and his grandfather's tomb at Narnaul in Haryana—as well as the great mosque inside Delhi's Purana Qila, or Old Fort. He died in an accidental explosion inside the fort of Kalinjar.

Having been driven out of Delhi and without the support of his brother Kamran, Humayun took refuge in Persia. In 1555, however, he returned to Delhi, defeated Sher Shah Suri's descendants, and moved into Delhi's Purana Qila, or Old Fort, which he had begun building 20 years earlier, but which Sher Shah Suri had completed. Within a year, Humayun was dead, having tumbled down the stone steps of his library inside the fort.

Akbar (1542–1605) is regarded as the greatest of the Mughal emperors, a reputation that rests on his success in unifying and extending the empire, on his architectural innovations—including the tomb of his father, Humayun, and the city of Fatehpur Sikri—and the spirit of religious enlightenment that marked most of his rule. He was the first Mughal emperor to be born in the subcontinent (though his actual birthplace, Umarkot, is now in Pakistan), under the protection of a Hindu prince who was providing refuge for Humayun. He succeeded to the imperial throne in Delhi at the age of 13, and for the first four years of his reign the empire was under the control of his guardian, Bayram Khan, who consolidated Mughal power in northern India. In the early 1560s, Akbar lifted discriminatory laws against Hindus, and among his many wives was the Hindu daughter of a Rajput prince from Rajasthan.

Under Humayun, most of the Mughal nobility were non-Indian Muslims mainly from Central Asia, but by the 1580s the majority were Indian—many of them Hindus. Akbar gradually extended the empire, conquering or gaining the allegiance of much of modern-day Rajasthan and Gujarat, and then expanding into central and eastern India, as well as Kashmir. He also recaptured the Mughals' ancestral lands in Afghanistan. Towards the end of his life, Akbar tried to push further into central and southern India, but was unable to bring the Deccan sultanates under Mughal control.

Akbar moved his capital several times, building a new city at Fatehpur Sikri and enormous fortresses in Agra, Lahore and Allahabad. He invited members of various religions, including Jesuits from Portuguese-ruled Goa, to take part in religious debates, and eventually started his own religion, in which he played a central role, and which some Muslims saw as idolatrous. Akbar, unlike the other Mughals, is thought to have been illiterate, but this did not inhibit his activities as a patron of the arts and as a reforming head of government. He created a centralised bureaucracy, which introduced standardised weights and measures, and proper land and revenue records were compiled for the first time. In Akbar's final years, his son Salim—later to become the emperor Jehangir—challenged his rule. They were eventually reconciled, however, on the understanding that Salim would be his successor.

Jehangir (1569–1627), whose name means 'World Conqueror', ruled the Mughal Empire for 22 years, following the death of his father Akbar in 1605. He was less tolerant than his father and had a reputation for drunkenness. One of his first acts on taking power was to subdue a revolt by his own son Khusrau, whom he ordered to be blinded. Militarily, Jehangir got bogged down in central India and in the hills of northern India. He also lost control of Afghanistan to the Persian emperor Shah Abbas. His favourite wife, Nur Jahan, and his father-in-law, Itimad ud-Daula (whose exquisite tomb in Agra is probably the most important architectural achievement of Jehangir's rule), both played a major role in running the Mughal Empire.

The reign of **Shah Jahan** (1592–1666), or 'King of the World', is often seen as the golden age of the Mughals, when the empire expanded deep into southern India, when the Taj Mahal and a new capital city at Delhi were built, and when European visitors were entranced and awestruck by the riches and the rituals of the Mughal court. Shah Jahan is now best remembered for his love of his favourite wife, Mumtaz, for whom he built the Taj Mahal as a tomb. He had a complex relationship with the rest of his family, rebelling against his father, Jehangir, and almost certainly ordering the death of two of his brothers. Before succeeding to the imperial throne, and when he was known simply as Khurram, he proved himself on the battlefield, winning important victories in what is now Rajasthan. Once emperor, Shah Jahan extended the empire into central India, defeating the Ahmednagar Sultanate and forcing the sultans of Golconda and Bijapur to accept Mughal supremacy. These two new vassal states, which continued to show real independence, pushed into the south of India—and, at least on paper, the Mughal Empire reached deep into modern-day Karnataka and northern Tamil Nadu. Sustaining Mughal control over the southern part of the empire became a major drain on the empire's resources. Shah Jahan's third son and eventual successor, Aurangzeb, was based in central India and led costly wars against the empire's errant vassal states. The emergence of the great Maratha leader Shivaji, from the late 1640s, provided more problems for the overstretched empire in the hills of western Maharashtra.

Shah Jahan was personally more involved in projecting the glory of his empire closer to home. First the Taj Mahal and then the new capital in Delhi were built. The new walled city, then known as Shahjahanabad and now as Old Delhi, was laid out to the north of the 14th-century Tughlaq ruins known as Feroze Shah Kotla. The new city was an innovative piece of town planning, with the Red Fort as its citadel overlooking the River Yamuna—this became Shah Jahan's seat of government.

In 1657, Shah Jahan fell seriously ill. This set off a struggle for power among his four sons, but principally between Dara Shikoh, Shah Jahan's oldest son and designated successor, and his third son, Aurangzeb. Aurangzeb and Dara Shikoh could not have been more different. Aurangzeb was a conservative and intolerant Muslim, while Dara Shikoh—like his great-grandfather Akbar—encouraged dialogue with other religions, and once said that 'the essential nature of Hinduism is identical with that of Islam.' To some orthodox Muslims this was heresy. Dara Shikoh was captured by Aurangzeb's forces, taken through the streets of Delhi in chains, and executed. His execution represented a victory for Islamic orthodoxy and, ever since, people have wondered how different the history of the Mughal Empire, and India, would have been if Dara Shikoh had succeeded Shah Jahan. Some of Dara Shikoh's admirers believe India might have entered into a period of great innovation and discovery, similar to the European Enlightenment more than a century later. As for Shah Jahan's fourth son, Murad, he was beheaded, and his second son, Shuja, disappeared in Burma—probably murdered on the orders of Aurangzeb. Shah Jahan himself was held captive in Agra Fort until his death in 1666.

Aurangzeb (1618–1707), the last of the great Mughal emperors, ruled over more of India than any of his predecessors—yet his long reign is largely remembered as the beginning of the end of the Mughal Empire. He over-extended the empire, and became obsessed with controlling the south of India; he was much harsher than his predecessors towards Hindus and Sikhs, and his reputation in modern India is as a temple-destroyer and Hindu-hater. Aurangzeb declared himself emperor in 1658, with his father Shah Jahan still alive, and went on to rule India for almost 50 years. He was driven by a conservative view of Islam, reimposed discriminatory taxes on Hindus, and built many new mosques—sometimes, as in Varanasi, on the site of former temples. He ordered the execution of the ninth Sikh guru, Tegh Bahadur Singh, and he caused a major revolt by the princely states of Udaipur and Jodhpur by interfering in their internal politics. One of his sons, Akbar, rebelled and declared himself emperor before fleeing to Persia. The last 20 years of Aurangzeb's rule were dominated by his military campaigns in the south, where, from his base in the city named in his honour, Aurangabad, he finally ended the rule of the Bijapur and Golconda sultans and integrated their territory into the Mughal Empire. But he could never defeat the Marathas, with Shivaji and his successors gradually—and despite many setbacks—building a new confederacy which would become a major force in the 18th century.

The European presence in the subcontinent expanded rapidly during the 17th century, with first Surat and then Chennai (Madras), Mumbai (Bombay) and Kolkata (Calcutta) becoming British trading centres; and there were a series of firmly established Portuguese settlements down the western coast of India. The French, the Dutch and the Danes also had trading outposts—north of Kolkata on the Hooghly River and in coastal India.

The Mughal Empire collapses (1707–57)

Aurangzeb's death in 1707 led to a long-running succession crisis involving several of his sons, grandsons and great-grandsons. There were six Mughal emperors in the next 12 years, during which time revolts in Rajasthan and the Punjab severely weakened the empire, and a Maratha army reached the outskirts of Delhi. Muhammad Shah, who became Mughal emperor in 1719, provided some stability by ruling for almost 30 years, but his reign was deeply troubled and Delhi was invaded by the Marathas in 1737, by Persians under Nadir Shah in 1739, and by Afghans under Ahmed Shah Abdali in a series of raids from the 1740s to the 1760s. The Mughal emperor still officially controlled large parts of India—but a series of powerful governors in Bengal, Hyderabad and Avadh (in modern Uttar Pradesh) were now, in practice, independent of Delhi. The Marathas had become the major force in central India, and Europeans were emerging as the key powers in the south, the east and along most of India's long coastline.

In 1717, the British East India Company had been granted an imperial *firman*, or directive, by the Mughal emperor, allowing it to operate in Mughal territories and thereby gaining for Britain a clear advantage over the other European powers. The objective, at this stage, was profit rather than colonisation. East India Company traders were able to make fortunes largely by selling Indian cotton and other textiles to the West. But they recognised other opportunities available to them, as they began imposing taxes on areas under their control. Gradually, the East India Company built a powerful army as a way of protecting its business interests and the increasing number of British settlements along the Indian coast. Growing Anglo-French rivalry in southern India led to the Carnatic Wars (named after the area in southern India now known as Karnataka) between the two European powers and to the capture of Madras (now Chennai) by the French in 1746—it was restored to the British almost three years later.

The Anglo-French rivalry in India would continue for more than half a century, with the next major outbreak of fighting in the second (1748–54) and third (1756–63) Carnatic Wars. These wars were often fought alongside and on behalf of local forces, but were also an extension of continuing Anglo-French disputes in Europe and North America. The greatest domestic challenge to growing British expansionism was in Bengal, where the local nawab, Siraj ud-Daula, officially still a Mughal vassal, captured Calcutta (now Kolkata) from the British. A group of British residents was incarcerated in a small room that became known as the Black Hole of Calcutta, where a majority of the captives are thought to have died of suffocation. The British regrouped under Robert Clive (later known as Clive of India), recapturing Calcutta and then defeating Siraj ud-Daula at the Battle of Plassey in 1757—the event from which the period of British domination of India is often dated.

British expansion (1757–1857)

Under the leadership of Robert Clive and later Warren Hastings, the British gradually—by negotiation and by force of arms—acquired large tracts of territory in northern India. They defeated the Mughal army at Buxar in 1764, and obtained a second *firman* from the emperor, granting the British effective control over most of modern-day West Bengal and Bihar and parts of Uttar Pradesh. In 1774, Calcutta was officially made the Indian headquarters of the British East India Company—and the company began to build the administrative infrastructure that would turn it into a capital city. A series of wars was fought by the British over several decades against the southern kingdom of Mysore—led by Hyder Ali and then his son Tipu Sultan—often with French support, until the final defeat of Tipu Sultan at the Battle of Srirangapatnam (Seringapatam) in 1799.

A second series of wars was fought against the Marathas, who had been dominant in central India, and British forces only fully defeated them in 1818. The British strategy was, wherever possible, to control much of India through compliant local princes who would ensure a continuous supply of revenue to the British. Conquest and annexation were seen as expensive, and Britain's activities in India were still being run as a business that was supposed to be not only self-financing, but profitable; taxation as well as trade was becoming an important source of revenue. Many East India Company men made great fortunes, and some British settlers integrated themselves into Indian society, marrying local women and adopting local customs. So did many European mercenaries, including such important figures as Claude Martin in Lucknow and George Thomas in Hansi, both of whom set themselves up as local potentates and patrons of art.

But the British and Europeans did not come in search of wealth only; some were missionaries and others were scholars—serious Western interest in Indian archaeology and early history can be dated from this period. William Jones, an East India Company employee, pointed out the similarities between most European languages and the main languages of northern India; and James Prinsep, another company servant, deciphered the Ashoka inscriptions found in many parts of the country.

By the 1820s, the British were firmly entrenched in India. They began to behave less like businessmen and explorers, and more like autocratic rulers. They asserted what they believed was their right to rule, as well as what they saw as their duty to civilise. There were attempts to eradicate child marriage and widow burning (or *sati*), for which they found natural allies among Indian reformers, particularly in Bengal. They continued to expand, defeating the Sikh kingdom of Punjab and extending their control over modern-day Pakistan, as well as Kashmir in the north and Assam in the east. Annexation of territory previously controlled by local princes became common—most controversially in the 1850s with the small territory of Jhansi and the larger kingdom of Avadh (known by the British as Oudh) with its capital, Lucknow. Avadh had become a major artistic and architectural centre, the flamboyance of which is still visible in many buildings in Lucknow, but its rulers had, according to the British, become too wasteful and untrustworthy.

The 1857 Uprising

The rebellion of 1857 is described in modern Indian school textbooks as the First War of Independence, and was known by the British as the Indian Mutiny or the Sepoy (soldier) Mutiny. The Uprising would eventually affect large areas of northern India, particularly Delhi, Lucknow and Kanpur—and at one point seemed to be a serious threat to British rule. It briefly brought together a heterogeneous mixture of discontented soldiers, members of deposed royal families, religious zealots and ordinary peasants and city dwellers. The spark for the rebellion seems to have been the rumoured use of beef and pork fat in new cartridges issued to the army, the ends of which soldiers were expected to bite off with their teeth before ramming them down their rifle barrels. This offended both Hindus (for whom the cow is sacred), and Muslims (for whom the pig is profane) in the British army.

This appears to have caused the first act of rebellion, when a soldier called Mangal Pandey, based in the eastern town of Barrackpore, attacked and wounded a British officer. Pandey was then executed. In the summer of 1857, under the rather unwilling leadership of Mughal emperor Bahadur Shah Zafar (whose empire barely stretched beyond Delhi), the British were driven out of several of their north Indian strongholds. But large parts of the country did not respond to the call for rebellion, and by September 1857 the Delhi Uprising had been defeated, and the last Mughal was a prisoner of the British, destined to an exile's death in Burma. British vengeance for what they still saw as a mutiny was bloodiest in Delhi. The Uprising spluttered on into 1858, but the defeat in Delhi and the recapture of Lucknow by the British ended any real hope of a rebel victory. The most celebrated leader of the revolt, the Rani of Jhansi, died in a hail of British bullets in Gwalior, while another prominent figure, Nana Sahib, the adopted son of the last ruler of the Maratha confederacy, fled to Nepal.

The consolidation of British rule (1858–1930)

Only in 1858 did the British government formally take control of all of the East India Company's Indian possessions. And although Britain's Queen Victoria took the title of Queen of India, she did not assume the title of Empress until the 1870s. The British realised that their policy of annexation had been dangerous, and now attempted to maintain weak and pro-British local princes in power in many parts of India, often conspiring in the overthrow of any prince who showed too much independence. They increased the percentage of British troops in the Indian Army to make further mutinies less likely, and began building a railway network to make the rapid movements of large numbers of troops possible. The railways would also play a major economic role and, arguably, by making internal travel easier, helped create a sense of India's geographical unity among early nationalists. Rail travel also helped encourage migration from the interior into the main cities and, with British encouragement, many migrants also went much further afield, to the plantations of the Caribbean, Africa, Southeast Asia and Fiji. A few Indians went to Britain to study and work, including most famously Mohandas Gandhi, later to be known as Mahatma ('Great Soul'), who trained as a barrister in London in the 1880s and later practised in South Africa.

The Indian National Congress, which would eventually lead the country to independence in the 20th century, was formed in 1885. Several of its early presidents were in fact British, and it began more as a reformist pressure group than as the political movement into which it evolved. Congress, as it became known, lobbied strongly and successfully for Indian representation on local councils; while reformers in general stressed the importance of educating an Indian elite that could play a greater role in government. In 1911, the visiting king-emperor George V announced that Delhi would replace Calcutta as the capital of British India, and an entirely new city, New Delhi, was built to the south of the one constructed 250 years earlier by the Mughal emperor Shah Jahan. This was the heyday of British rule in India, remembered for its tiger hunts, cricket matches and durbars—a time when junior civil servants, fresh from Britain, would suddenly find themselves in charge of hundreds of thousands of people.

Opposition to British rule grew gradually during the early years of the 20th century, and there was a series of attacks on British officials. Most Indians supported the British during the First World War, and more than two million Indian soldiers and support staff travelled overseas to fight against Germany and its allies. However, many Indians also objected to their lack of self-rule, and believed that the imperial government was arbitrarily restricting their right to protest. In 1919, a large number of unarmed demonstrators in the Sikh holy city of Amritsar were fired on by imperial troops, and many were killed. The 'Jallianwala Bagh Massacre' helped recruit many Indians to what was now being seen as a freedom struggle. Mahatma Gandhi had assumed leadership of this movement, and committed himself and his supporters to a non-violent campaign against the iniquities of British rule. Others preached and practised violent resistance; while many of the princely families who were allowed by the British to accumulate fabulous wealth and construct enormous new palaces seemed happy with the status quo.

Road to Independence (1930–47)

It was not until 26th January 1930 that Congress formally declared itself in favour of 'complete self-rule' or independence. A few weeks later, Gandhi led the 'Salt March' from Ahmedabad to Dandi on the coast of Gujarat, ceremonially challenging the British monopoly on salt—and attracting international media attention to the Indian freedom struggle. At Dandi, he picked up a handful of saline mud, boiled it in water, and created illegal salt. Thousands of others copied him—and so began a campaign of civil disobedience. Gandhi and many of his followers were arrested.

Throughout much of the 1930s there were complex multi-party negotiations which led to limited self-rule, though this fell well short of most Indian nationalist aspirations. The nationalist camp was divided, however. Some Muslims, headed by Muhammad Ali Jinnah, the leader of the Muslim League and the future founder of Pakistan, had growing concerns about the prospect of Hindu majority rule; while the nationalist leader from Bengal, Subhash Chandra Bose, felt that Congress should confront the imperial government more directly. Gandhi and his core group of supporters, who now included Jawaharlal Nehru, the future prime minister of India, refused to condone violence and believed in negotiation and peaceful non-cooperation.

In 1939, Congress was unhappy that there was no consultation about India's entry into the Second World War. Britain promised dominion status for India once the war was over, but this was dismissed by Gandhi as 'a post-dated cheque on a failing bank'. The Quit India movement was launched by Congress in 1942, and Gandhi, Nehru and many other nationalist leaders were imprisoned. Subhash Chandra Bose had by this time escaped from India, and travelled to Berlin and Tokyo to get Axis support against the British. With Japanese backing he formed the Indian National Army, or INA, which fought alongside the Japanese in northeast India—the only part of mainland India that saw fighting during the war. More than two million Indian soldiers fought on the Allied side, with more than 80,000 fatalities—but the casualties were far higher in the Bengal famine of 1943, when, with the British authorities distracted by the war, more than two million people died.

Independence and Partition (1947)

With the war over and a new Labour government in power in London, it was clear that Indian independence was very close. But the main parties—Congress, the Muslim League, the princes and the British government—could not agree on the details. In early 1947, the British decided to speed up their withdrawal and sent Lord Mountbatten to India as the last viceroy. Britain's Indian empire was to be partitioned—the majority-Muslim parts of the country, in the northwest and northeast, were to form a single new country, called Pakistan. British India became, on 15th August 1947, the newly independent nations of India and Pakistan. It was a time for celebration in Delhi, where Prime Minister Jawaharlal Nehru led the festivities with his famous 'tryst with destiny' speech, but it was also a time of great tragedy. In the panic and confusion of Partition, many millions of people lost their homes as Hindus and Sikhs fled into India, and millions of Muslims fled to Pakistan. There was widespread violence, including a series of massacres on both sides of the new border. Hundreds of thousands of people were killed in the conflict, the memory of which still traumatises communities in both countries. The former kingdom of Kashmir became a battleground. Its Hindu ruler eventually opted for India—though the majority of the population was Muslim—and a brief war led to the division of Kashmir between the two countries, in a way that satisfied none of the parties involved.

The Nehru years (1947–64)

Nehru's long reign as prime minister of India began with the tragedy of Partition. Not long after, in January 1948, his mentor and ally, Mahatma Gandhi, was assassinated by a Hindu extremist who believed that Gandhi had been too generous towards Pakistan. Nehru and his Congress party were able to provide many years of stable democratically-elected government and slow but solid economic growth. He was unable to resist the growth of sometimes violent regional language movements within India, demanding separate statehood—and several new monolingual states were created to replace the British territorial divisions. Southern India was divided into the four states that exist today: Karnataka, Andhra Pradesh, Tamil Nadu and Kerala. Bombay state was divided into Marathi-speaking Maharashtra and Gujarati-speaking Gujarat.

Under Nehru's leadership, India became an important player in international affairs, spearheading the non-aligned movement with Sukarno of Indonesia, Nasser of Egypt, Nkrumah of Ghana and Tito of Yugoslavia. He earned Chinese hostility by giving sanctuary to the Dalai Lama and thousands of his Tibetan followers, and in 1961 Indian forces successfully invaded Goa and took control of it and other smaller territories from the Portuguese—the last European outposts in the subcontinent. Nehru's final years were overshadowed by India's defeat in a war with China in 1962, and the great apostle of non-alignment was forced to seek arms from the United States. In 1965, the year after Nehru's death, Pakistan attempted to inflict a similar defeat on India, but was driven back. Nehru's successor, Lal Bahadur Shastri, was able to claim a moral victory, but died in Tashkent, in the Soviet Union, the day after signing the peace treaty with Pakistan in January 1966.

The Indira years (1966–84)

Shastri was succeeded as prime minister by Nehru's only child, Indira (who had married Feroze Gandhi, a Parsi journalist unrelated to Mahatma Gandhi). Indira was seen by senior Congress party politicians as a weak leader whom they could manipulate, 'a dumb doll' as one of them famously put it. She proved them wrong. Gradually she forced out the Congress's 'Old Guard', split the party in 1969, adopted more left-wing policies and trounced the opposition in elections in 1971. In the same year, under her leadership, India defeated Pakistan, while helping Bangladesh, formerly East Pakistan, obtain its independence. In 1974, India announced its nuclear capability with underground nuclear tests in the Rajasthan desert.

Indira Gandhi's successes seemed to encourage her to be more authoritarian, and when a court found her guilty of electoral malpractice in 1975 she declared a state of emergency. Many did not believe that democracy would survive in India. Mrs Gandhi arrested many of her opponents and introduced censorship. Many day-to-day decisions were taken by her younger son, Sanjay, on whom many of the excesses of the emergency—such as slum clearances and forced sterilisation—were blamed. Two years later, Indira Gandhi called a general election which, to her surprise, she lost. India had its first non-Congress prime minister, Morarji Desai. But the opposition was unable to unite behind Desai, or his successor, and Mrs Gandhi swept back to power in 1980. Four years later she was dead, assassinated at her Delhi residence by two of her Sikh bodyguards. She had angered many Sikhs by sending the army into their holiest shrine, the Golden Temple at Amritsar in Punjab, to flush out Sikh separatists who had taken refuge there.

Rajiv and after (1984–)

Following the death of Mrs Gandhi, the leadership of the country passed immediately to her elder son, Rajiv. Her younger, more politically experienced son Sanjay, who had played such a controversial role during the state of emergency in 1975, had died while flying a stunt plane. Rajiv was, at first, rather unwilling to enter politics. He promised clean, modern government, but quickly got embroiled with secessionist movements in Punjab, Assam and neighbouring Sri Lanka. The optimism of his early days dissipated quickly, and some of his former allies turned against him—accusing his administration of corruption. He was voted out of office in 1989, marking the end of Congress dominance of the Indian political system. All governments since have been run by multi-party coalitions.

During the election campaign of 1991 Rajiv Gandhi, like his mother, was assassinated. His killer was a Sri Lankan Tamil female suicide bomber who objected to India's military involvement in the Sri Lankan civil war in the 1980s. A new minority Congress government was voted into power; it liberalised India's economy and set in motion a period of economic growth. But the early 1990s also saw serious Hindu-Muslim violence that followed the destruction of a 16th-century mosque in Ayodhya, as well as secessionist movements in Kashmir, Punjab and the northeast, which continued to cost many lives—though Punjab Sikh militancy began to die down in the mid-1990s. In the late 1990s, the largest opposition group, the Bharatiya Janata Party, took power at the head of a coalition government for the first time. Under its veteran leader, Atal Behari Vajpayee, the government took a more combative international role—testing nuclear weapons once again in the face of almost universal criticism from around the world, and fighting an undeclared war with Pakistan in the Kargil area of Kashmir. It also brought in controversial new anti-terrorism laws in the wake of an attack on the Indian parliament in 2001, and the following year India and Pakistan once again came close to war. Continued Hindu-Muslim tension led to a further outbreak of violence in Gujarat in 2002, in which about 2,000 people, most of them Muslim, were killed.

A minority Congress government came to power in 2004. Rajiv Gandhi's Italian-born widow Sonia refused the post of prime minister and instead India had Manmohan Singh, a Sikh economist, as its first non-Hindu head of government. He continued with the previous government's economic reform, and overall the first decade of the new millennium proved to be a period of rapid economic growth in many areas, with a booming IT services sector leading the way. India sought to play a larger role on the international stage: it demanded membership of the United Nations Security Council, insisting it should be treated on a par with China; and some nationalistic Indians even declared, a little prematurely, the advent of 'the Indian century'.

Modern India

Modern India is the world's second most populous country, with more than 1.2 billion inhabitants. It is expected to overtake China in the 2020s. India's most populous state, Uttar Pradesh, has a population of more than 180 million, larger than all but five of the world's countries.

India also proudly declares itself to be the world's largest democracy, with a president as its head of state and a prime minister as head of government. Under the Indian constitution, the president—who is elected by an electoral college of MPs and members of state assemblies—has a largely ceremonial role. Real power rests with the lower house of the Indian parliament, the Lok Sabha, all but two of whose members are directly elected (two Anglo-Indian representatives are nominated by the president). Normally, the party leader with the support of the largest number of MPs is invited to form a government and to demonstrate that they can command majority support in a parliamentary vote. The maximum term of each Lok Sabha is five years, though general elections have frequently been called early. There is also a less powerful upper house of parliament, the Rajya Sabha, whose members are either indirectly elected or nominated.

The two largest political parties are the centrist Congress Party and the mainly-Hindu BJP, or Bharatiya Janata Party. There are many other political groupings, including two powerful communist parties, and a variety of caste, state and religious parties.

India has a written constitution which has been the country's supreme law since its promulgation on 26th January 1951, on which day India became a republic. Republic Day is celebrated annually on 26th January, while 15th August is Independence Day. The Supreme Court of India is both the highest court of appeal and the guardian and interpreter of the constitution. However, most parts of the constitution can be amended by a two-thirds majority in both houses of parliament, and there have been more than 90 constitutional amendments since 1951.

India has 28 states and seven union territories. Each state has its own chief minister and state assembly. The union territories are smaller or less well-developed administrative units, and have less autonomy than the states. State governments have a wide range of powers, set out in the constitution. But direct rule from Delhi (known as president's rule) can be imposed on states when they are deemed not to be functioning effectively. India also has a well-established system of local government, which goes down to village level.

Despite the recent rapid growth of the services and manufacturing sectors, India is still a predominantly agricultural economy, dependent in many parts of the country on traditional farming methods. The economic performance of the country continues to depend heavily on the monsoon rains—and there is a high level of endemic poverty, particularly in rural areas. This has led to large-scale migration to the cities, the basic services of which are often severely stretched. India has a large middle-class population, mainly located in the big and medium-sized cities which have prospered in recent years—the country has a larger number of dollar billionaires, approximately 60, than its overall economic performance would suggest. IT services and English-language call centres are among the businesses that have grown rapidly in recent years, to the benefit of a number of growing cities such as Bangalore, Hyderabad, Pune and Gurgaon.

The most widely-spoken language in India is Hindi—with more than 400 million mother-tongue speakers in the northern 'Hindi belt'. Hindi is also widely understood in other parts of India, except in the far south. India has 22 officially-recognised languages, of which Telugu, Bengali, Marathi, Tamil and Urdu are each spoken by more than 50 million people; there are hundreds of other languages and dialects. English is widely understood at airports, railway stations, hotels, restaurants and major tourist sites across the country. There are many English-language daily newspapers, weekly magazines and TV news channels.

Movies and cricket are national obsessions. India's film industry is the most prolific in the world. The best-known are Bollywood films—Hindi-language movies made in Mumbai—but several other cities have booming film industries in a wide range of languages. Cricket is the most important sport in India, and a billion-dollar business. The best-known figures in India, visible on advertising hoardings throughout the country, are leading cricketers such as Sachin Tendulkar and Mahendra Singh Dhoni.

ARCHITECTURE & THE ARTS

The size and diversity of India have led to the emergence of many interconnected and overlapping artistic, architectural and cultural traditions. Some have been inspired by the two most important faiths in the country, Hinduism and Islam. But other factors have often been as important, including climate, available natural resources and older folk traditions—and, in more recent times, Western influences. All of these elements make India's cultural traditions some of the richest and most complex found anywhere in the world.

Early art and architecture

Cave paintings: the earliest surviving cultural artefacts in India are cave paintings. Those in the rock shelters of Bhimbetka (*see p. 416*) in Madhya Pradesh are the best-known and the most impressive—and the earliest paintings here date back to c. 5500 BC. Although as old as some European cave paintings, those in India represent more of a continuing tradition—this largely Stone Age art form continued to be practised until close to the present day. So some cave paintings in India are actually comparatively recent, or are overpaintings of earlier works. The earliest figurative art that is found in these caves tends to show scenes involving stick-like humans and more realistic animals. The bodies of the animals are sometimes filled in with geometric patterns. In later paintings, the human figures were made more realistic and shown in a variety of active poses: running, riding, dancing or hunting. The paints used are from local mineral sources—with red (from ferrous minerals such as haematite) and white (from clay). Either a finger or the stem of a plant was used as a brush.

Harappan art: the Harappan, or Indus Valley, civilisation, which is thought to have flourished more than 4,000 years ago, left behind a large range of artefacts that have been excavated over the last 150 years from Harappan sites in India and Pakistan. Although the best-known sites are Mohenjo-daro and Harappa in Pakistan, artefacts from both of these places, as well as from a number of Indian sites, can be seen in museums in India, with a superb collection in the National Museum in Delhi. There are also several important Harappan sites in India, including Lothal and Dholavira in Gujarat. Among the excavated objects are a huge number of clay tablets—some bearing symbols that are thought to be a written language, hitherto undeciphered, but others, probably used as seals, bearing images of humans, animals and god-like figures. Some decorated pottery and fine, mostly figurative sculpture, carved from stone or made from copper or terracotta, have been found from this period. Hundreds of small trinkets and toys have also been excavated. Harappan cities were laid out on a grid system, and there is evidence of the ancient equivalent of zoning—with a central citadel, granary, bathing area, workshops and very different residential areas for different social classes. Many of the buildings used sun-dried or kiln-fired bricks, but not enough has survived for us to know much about the external appearance of the key buildings—though they may have had wooden superstructures. Little evidence of decorative architectural features has survived, though some patterned floor tiles have been found. Ruined staircases imply that some buildings were two-storey or at least had roof terraces.

The Vedic period: this is usually dated from the collapse of the Harappan civilisation (c. 1500 BC) to the birth of the Buddha (c. 560 BC). It is a period that left behind almost no art or architecture. But we know from the main literary sources of the period, the *Vedas*, that palaces were adorned with wall-paintings and wood carvings. It is believed that so little has survived because the main construction material was wood, though decorated pottery fragments have been recovered from a number of sites, including the Purana Qila in Delhi, a possible site for Indraprastha, one of the major cities described in the Hindu epic, the *Mahabharata*.

Early Buddhist art and architecture

The Mauryan period (c. 320–232 BC) saw the first great flowering of Indian art, and some quite extraordinary pieces of carved, finely-polished Chunar sandstone have survived relatively intact—they can be seen at museums in Delhi, Sarnath and Patna. These include a number of cylindrical **sandstone columns**, mainly dating from the rule of Ashoka the Great; inscribed with royal edicts, they are found in several places in north India. The finest of these are at sites connected with the Buddha, and have carved stone capitals with exquisitely detailed animal figures on top. The four-headed lion capital, with its elegant animal frieze—now in the museum at Sarnath near Varanasi—has become India's national emblem, used widely on coins, banknotes and government documents. The detail on the Mauryan capitals have similarities to earlier Persian sculptures found in Persepolis in modern-day Iran, and it is thought possible that some Persian artisans may have fled the armies of Alexander the Great and settled in India. The main city of the Mauryan Empire, Pataliputra, now Patna, has a few column stumps—possibly a ruined palace—that are *in situ*; while Patna Museum (*see p. 599*) has several fine stone carvings of human figures from the Mauryan period. The Buddha himself is never portrayed in early Buddhist art and is represented by symbols: an empty throne, an umbrella or footprints.

Among the sparse architectural remains of the Mauryan period are India's earliest **rock-cut caves**, which mark the start of a great architectural and aesthetic tradition that lasted for more than 1,000 years; later examples of rock-cut caves can be found all over the country. These caves were hand-cut from bare rock, inch by inch, using simple iron tools; they would have taken many years to complete. They were used by ascetics as places of meditation and retreat during the monsoon, and their shape and the use of the pointed ogival arch suggests they were built in the style of earlier shelters constructed out of wood. The finest of the early rock-cut caves are at Barabar, south of Patna (*see p. 607*), with polished stone interiors, and in the case of the Lomas Rishi cave, the stone entrance has been carved with a frieze of elephants, and a *trompe l'oeil* geometric pattern that resembles a bamboo lattice screen—in a wooden building, such a screen would allow daylight to enter and air to circulate.

The next major development in Indian architecture, in the mid-2nd century BC, is the ***chaitya* hall**—a horseshoe-shaped rock-cut cave used as a place of worship by Buddhists. The *chaitya* hall would be cut into a sheer rockface, and its creation would have involved far more planning than the Mauryan rock-cut caves, because the interior contained important architectural features—normally two rows of columns parallel to the sides of the cave and a small internal stupa, which the monks could circumambulate. The entrances were usually pointed ogival arches, much larger than the Mauryan cave openings, through which more air and light could enter, and were surrounded by figurative carvings in low relief. Post-holes inside and outside most surviving *chaitya* halls indicate that there was a wooden superstructure. Nearby are smaller square or rectangular chambers used as living quarters by monks. They often have a series of tiny inner rooms with raised surfaces used as beds, and would probably have been covered with straw or other vegetation. The *chaitya* halls are most widespread in the modern-day state of Maharashtra, and the one at Bhaja—between Mumbai and Pune—is probably the most impressive and complete *chaitya* hall from the early period. The nearby Karli cave is a more ornate version from the late 1st or early 2nd century AD, with superb internal and external sculpture.

Another major development from this period is the elaborately decorated **Buddhist stupa**, or relic-mound. The stupa, almost equivalent to European burial mounds, or tumuli, dates back to at least the start of the early Buddhist period, and portions of the ashes of the Buddha himself are said to have been buried in a number of different stupas. But by the 2nd century BC, stupas as an architectural form had been transformed from a simple pile of earth into a richly decorated, dome-shaped mound, surrounded by intricately carved and interlocking stone railings. The earliest surviving railings are from Bharhut in Madhya Pradesh, but the site was dismantled in the 19th century—and most of the carvings are now in Kolkata's Indian Museum (*see p.* 552). The stone-carved railing panels show scenes from the life of the Buddha, and have names and sometimes figures of lay donors who paid for the railings. Aesthetically the most impressive intact stupa is at Sanchi, north of Bhopal, and its decorative elements date to the 1st century AD. It has a stone carved railing surrounding it and four superbly carved gates, or *toranas*, with crossbars and uprights, covered with panels showing battle scenes, events from the life of the Buddha (though the Buddha himself is still unrepresented), as well as stand-alone sculptures of animals and humans, sometimes used as brackets.

The Gandhara and Mathura styles

In about the late 1st century AD, there was a major but gradual theologicial and aesthetic shift in Indian Buddhism, which led to the emergence of a very different artistic tradition based on free-standing stone sculptures, often of the Buddha himself. There are also many stone-cut friezes of the life of Buddha, and of other forms of the Buddha, known as *bodhisattvas*. Previously the Buddha was not represented, but the newly dominant Mahayana school of Buddhism was less monastic and more devotional than the other branch of Buddhism. There were strong influences from outside, most notably from Greco-Roman art and architecture—which played a major role in the development of what became known as Greco-Buddhist or Gandhara sculpture. Some coins of this period have Greek inscriptions and the earliest examples of representations of the Buddha. Under the Kushan king Kanishka, a broad swathe of territories from Afghanistan to the plains of modern-day Uttar Pradesh were united, including both Gandhara and Mathura—and this facilitated the emergence of what are now known as the Gandhara and Mathura styles of Indian art.

Gandhara sculpture of the Buddha with flowing robes, topknot and solar disc.

Although the territory of Gandhara is in modern-day Afghanistan and Pakistan, many **Gandhara sculptures** were excavated in undivided British India, and so several Indian museums (and others around the world) have superb examples of Gandhara art. Particularly impressive are the collections in Mumbai, Chandigarh and Delhi. Most Gandhara sculptures are carved from grey schist stone. Among the distinctive features of Gandhara art are the way the flowing robes of the Buddha are exquisitely carved in stone—a feature that is thought to have come from a Greco-Roman tradition that survived in the Greek principalities that endured in the region. Other repeated features include the top-knot on the Buddha's head, with a solar disc behind. The arms were often added later, and placed in a particular gesture, or *mudra*, which denotes a specific action of the Buddha.

The **Mathura style** of sculpture is named after the town of Mathura (*see p. 225*), in which the god Krishna is said to have been born. However, the main surviving examples of art from Mathura are not Hindu, but Buddhist or secular statues, carved from red sandstone. Some of the statues are larger than life-size, and have a similar attention to detail of hair and clothing as Gandhara statues—though the Mathura Buddhist figures tend to be wearing lighter clothing, a reflection of the warmer climate. The secular statues are of members of the Kushan royal family and wear heavy clothing, which reflects their Central Asian origins. No buildings, apart from a large plinth, survive from this period, but many fine statues have been excavated and are in the museums in Mathura and Delhi. Sarnath, near Varanasi, also has some fine Mathura sculptures. There are also a few sculptures of Hindu gods from Mathura, though it is only from the Gupta period that a large variety of stone representations of Hindu deities have been found.

The Gupta period

By the early 4th century AD, a new style—strongly influenced by Mathura sculpture—had emerged in the plains of eastern Uttar Pradesh and Bihar. Under the Guptas, who ruled from Ashoka's old capital at Pataliputra (now Patna), sculpture became more refined and delicate—though some of the statues were more than life-size. Clothes were portrayed clinging to the body in a way that shows the anatomical proportions of the subject. Statues tended to show the Buddha as heavy-lidded, eyes almost closed, in a state of meditation. Although most of the statues are carved out of stone, there are also fine Gupta statues cast in bronze and copper, as well as carved from ivory. There are also, for the first time, large numbers of carvings and statues of Hindu deities. The rock-temple at Udayagiri, near Bhopal, dates from the early 5th century and has enormous rock-cut images of Vishnu in his boar avatar, Varaha, surrounded by other deities—a style that would later become associated with Shaivite cave-temples around the country. A huge free-standing statue of Varaha at Eran (*see p. 424*), also near Bhopal, dates from this period too. Some representations show Varaha purely in animal form, others depict him with a human body and a porcine head.

Also from this period are some of the earliest surviving free-standing **Hindu temples**—particularly in Madhya Pradesh, in areas where stone for construction was widely available. It is from the Gupta period that the most commonly encountered Hindu temple design can be first seen. This design is based on a square inner sanctuary housing a statue of a god, often with a connected assembly area, all of which is raised above the ground on a stone plinth—partly to avoid flooding during the monsoon. Many of the temples had some kind of *shikhara*, or curvilinear tower over the inner sanctum, and some had a surrounding corridor so devotees could circumambulate the idol. The doorway usually had a series of multiple frames, often heavily decorated with carvings, and widespread use was made of the horseshoe-shaped *gavaksha* motif. In the case of the Dasavatara Temple in Deogarh, south of Jhansi, there are also some of the earliest stone panels, with superb relief carvings of Hindu gods.

The earliest surviving **Indian paintings**—apart from prehistoric cave art—mainly date from the Gupta period, and are at their most impressive in the famous caves of Ajanta. Adorning a series of internal, chisel-cut walls are superb, lushly-depicted paintings largely showing scenes from the Buddhist *Jataka* tales. The walls were coated with a mix of clay, straw, dung and animal hair, covered with a thin lime plaster, and the outlines of the painting were drawn with the plaster still wet. Some of the images, such as two lovers seated under a canopy, are the earliest examples of subjects that became much-repeated motifs in Indian painting, particularly miniatures, until the 19th century.

The post-Gupta period in western India

The period after the fall of Guptas in about AD 550 saw a number of smaller Hindu states refining and challenging ideas about how Hindu temples should be built, and many of the great early Shiva shrines date from the post-Gupta era. The Chalukya Dynasty built the temples of Aihole and Pattadakal, which for a modern-day visitor feel like testing grounds for temple design. The architecture experiments with curved and rectangular-shaped buildings, with closed and open assembly areas, or *mandapas*, and with small squat *shikharas*, or towers, while the same dynasty also built the rock-cut temples of Badami to a more traditional design. Rock-cut temple architecture and carving was not, however, being replaced by free-standing temples—and from this period comes the great Shaivite temple of Elephanta, on an estuarine island close to modern Mumbai, with its superb panels showing scenes from the story of Shiva.

In fact, in the 8th century the Rashtrakuta Dynasty took the art and architecture of rock-cut temples to its apogee, with the building (or rather excavation) of the enormous Kailashnath Temple at Ellora (*see p. 524*). This involved the removal of approximately 85,000 cubic metres of rock. It demanded, as the art historian Roy Craven points out, 'the most sophisticated planning, since it depended not on what was added, as in conventional architecture, but on what was removed'. Once excavated, the result was a temple that appeared to be free-standing, but which was actually cut out of the bedrock by artisans working with chisels.

Elsewhere in India, distinctive regional styles of Hindu architecture were emerging. In Orissa, the earliest surviving temples come from this period—they have several of the key elements of what later became known as the Orissan style: the almost vertical tower that curves in sharply at the top, the long rectangular assembly halls and detailed external carvings. In Kashmir, the great Sun Temple at Martand made use of the trefoil design, and Hellenistic influences can be seen in the use of fluted Corinthian columns, pediments and moulded cornices. Elsewhere, such as in Gujarat and Rajasthan, the temple design was closer to that of the Guptas—of which the Harihara I Temple at Osiyan in central Rajasthan is a particularly fine example, with subsidiary shrines at each of the four corners of the plinth on which the main temple sits.

Early art and architecture of southern India

It is an unsolved mystery why so little early art or so few buildings have survived in Tamil Nadu and Kerala from the period before the 7th century. According to some accounts, wood was the main construction material—and this has simply decayed over the centuries. Others point to the problems of cutting into granite, the main stone available in Tamil Nadu. Whatever the truth, suddenly, from the 7th century AD there are some quite extraordinary works of mature Hindu architecture and art which have survived at Mahabalipuram. These include not only fine examples of rock-cut and free-standing temples, and superb rock-cut friezes of unsurpassed quality, but, even more extraordinary from the point of view of architectural history, a series of temples cut from single rocks, the Pancha Ratha, that have been made to look like built structures.

The early Chola period in northern Tamil Nadu is marked by free-standing Hindu shrines of a modest scale, and it was not until the early 11th century that the dramatically impressive Chola architectural style emerged, with the construction of the Brihadishwara temples at Tanjore and Gangaikondacholapuram. These temples were designed on a massive scale, with huge towers, and were intended to inspire awe, as creations of a powerful empire rather than as simple places of devotion. Deep niches on the temple exterior were used

Chola-period bronze sculpture of Shiva as Nataraja, the Lord of the Dance.

for fine stone carvings, representing a limited range of well-known stories related mainly to Shiva and his associated deities—though there are also depictions of Vishnu and his avatars.

The most famous works of art from the Chola period are the bronze religious icons made by the lost-wax, or *cire perdue*, method. Bronze-casting in India dates back to the early historical period—but neither before nor since the Cholas have bronzes of such grace and delicacy been cast. The lost-wax method involves first making a model out of wax, which is then encased in a clay mould. The mould is heated, allowing the wax to run out, and then molten bronze is poured in. The mould is allowed to cool, then broken to reveal the bronze, ready for finishing and polishing. The most famous images are of Shiva as Nataraja, the Lord of the Dance, but other key figures in the Hindu pantheon are also represented.

The *gopura*, an immense, sloping, multi-tiered gateway, only began to emerge as the most distinctive feature of southern Indian temple architecture in the 12th century, with the Nataraja Temple at Chidambaram as the best-known example—though they existed in a far smaller and rudimentary form several centuries earlier. The *gopura*, covered in religious statues, came to replace the sanctuary and the tower as the main artistic feature of the south Indian temple. The second key feature of the southern temple was a series of compounds of diminishing size, nestled inside each other.

The later Hindu period

The 10th to the 13th centuries, just before and during the appearance of the first Islamic buildings in India, saw a great flowering of Hindu (and Jain) art and architecture. This period saw the construction of many of India's most important surviving temples in Gujarat, Khajuraho and Orissa. In this era, Hindu temple design and decoration was at its most vivacious and innovative—and the great erotic Hindu carvings of Konarak, in Orissa, and at Khajuraho remain some of India's most beautiful and best-known works of art. In Orissa, temple architecture became more distinctive, with the pyramid-shaped roofs of the *mandapa* as the key feature of later shrines, as well some incredibly lissom relief carvings, almost in the round, on the external walls of temples. In the south, the softness of the soapstone used in the Hoysala period as a construction material made possible the intricately detailed and varied sculptures still visible at the great temples of Halebid and Belur in modern-day Karnataka.

From the 14th century onwards, partly as a result of Muslim rule, Hindu art and architecture in north India went into decline. However, further south, particularly in Hampi (*see p. 694*) and other areas ruled by the Vijayanagar Empire, the great traditions of Hindu architecture and artistic innovation survived. Carved pillars of extraordinary complexity and artistic refinement are typified in the late Vijayanagar period by mini-columns cut out of, but still attached to, the main columns (known as 'cut-out colonettes'). The dazzlingly detailed figurative carving visible at the Srirangam (*see p. 813*) and Vellore (*see p. 794*) temples in Tamil Nadu would influence the art and sculpture of the Nayak dynasties that followed.

Islamic architecture

From the late 12th century until the mid-18th century, Muslim architectural and artistic influences dominated in large parts of India. Many visitors associate Muslim architecture in India with the Mughals of the 16th and 17th centuries, though it predates them by more than 300 years—and the surviving mosques, tombs, fortresses and palaces of the **Sultanate period** (c. 13th to the early 16th century) include some of India's finest buildings. It was the period when the arch, the dome and the minaret tower all became widespread in India—architectural features that would play a major role in almost all forms of later construction in the country. Much of the earliest Muslim architecture in India, visible at the Qutb Minar and the neighbouring mosque in South Delhi, as well as at Ajmer, is a spectacular hybrid. Old temple masonry was reused, and many of the artisans were Hindus, whose exceptional stoneworking skills were no longer used to make images of gods, but to carve calligraphy, patterns and other decorative features on the walls of mosques and tombs. In fact the true arch, with a keystone, is not found in the earliest Muslim buildings; instead the traditional corbels, or overlapping stepped stones, seen in Hindu structures were used. The true arch is thought to have been first used in the late 13th century in Balban's tomb in Delhi.

The 14th century is marked by the distinctive sloping walls of Tughlaq architecture—most famously at Tughlaqabad Fort in Delhi (*see p. 89*) and the nearby tomb of Ghiyasuddin Tughlaq (*see p. 90*). In the 15th century, the architecture of the Lodi Dynasty was typified by octagonal tombs, some of them with small mini-pavilions on their roofs. The Lodi style continued to survive into the Sher Shah Suri and Mughal periods.

The 14th century outside the Delhi region saw the emergence of what became known later as the 'provincial styles' of Muslim architecture—typified, for instance, by the ornate minarets and stone-cut tracery work of Gujarat, or the high entrances to the prayer halls in the mosques of Jaunpur. In the Deccan, the Bahmanids built tombs with higher walls than usual, and made wide use of coloured, glazed tiles. Bijapur has high arches in its palaces, while its most famous tomb, the Gol Gumbaz, has what was then one of the world's largest unsupported domes. The Deccan tradition of distinctive Islamic architecture continued long into the Mughal period, and is marked by high bulbous domes and decorated parapets.

Some of India's finest military architecture is also from this period—typified by large enclosures with enormous fortress walls, which change direction frequently to make defence easier, and which usually have a citadel either at the centre or at the highest point of the enclosed area.

The **Mughal period** is often seen as the heyday of India's architectural history, particularly because of the iconic status of the Taj Mahal. Earlier Mughal buildings tend to be red, while later ones are white, reflecting a transition from sandstone, with some marble inlay, to entire buildings clad in marble. The great Mughal tombs are set in formal gardens—Humayun's enormous mausoleum in Delhi is the prototype—and many of them used double domes, so that the dimensions of the interior domed ceiling did not dictate the shape of the outer dome that formed the roof. Humayun's Tomb was built in the reign of Akbar, who was also responsible for the city of Fatehpur Sikri, with its numerous palaces, its enormous triumphant mosque gateway, as well as several of India's greatest fortresses. It was the 17th-century rule of Shah Jahan that saw the construction of the buildings that are now seen as defining the Mughal style. These include the Taj Mahal and several other fine buildings in the Red Forts of Agra and of Delhi, structures renowned not only for their elegance of design but also for their fine decorative workmanship. The increasing impact of European techniques and design is visible in the coloured stone inlay work on the external walls of the Taj Mahal. It was during the same period that a new Mughal capital was laid out, named Shahjahanabad after the emperor, but now better known as Old Delhi.

The Mughal palaces had clearly demarcated zones that were public or private, and the private zones were divided into the *mardana* (men's quarters) and *zenana* (women's quarters). There were outer courtyards for addressing the public or to review troops, and smaller inner courtyards, sometimes with running water, that would be used for entertainment. Rooftops could be used for sleeping in the hot weather. The architectural scheme and functions were replicated in many Rajasthani palaces.

Miniature paintings

Miniatures are most closely associated with the Mughal and Rajasthani artistic traditions, but many of the themes and styles are derived from earlier illustrated Hindu and Jain palm-leaf manuscripts, with paper coming into use by the late 14th century. The Mughal miniature emerged as an important artform during the reign of Akbar, when it was used as a way of illustrating story books, but it also became a way of recording life at the Mughal court, as well as of immortalising imperial triumphs. The last of the great Mughals, Aurangzeb, was more conservative and did little to encourage his ancestors' love of miniatures—but by that time many other less important royal courts, particularly in Rajasthan, were encouraging the painting of miniatures, drawing on traditional local religious and secular stories as subject matter.

Hindu revivalism and late Mughal architecture

Some historians date the revival of Hindu architecture in north India to the rule of Akbar, the most ecumenical of the Mughal emperors. In Rajasthan and nearby principalities, the Rajput style emerged, derived both from Mughal and much older Hindu traditions—and it applied to cities as well as buildings. The style was ornate, with balconies, projecting windows, arches, enclosed courtyards and separate quarters for men and women, and it made wide use of locally-available marble. Udaipur, for instance, is largely a 17th-century city, while Jaipur was built in the early 18th century. There was also a revival of temple-building in the 18th century, in which the Maratha queen, Ahilyabai Holkar, was a major figure—and many of the important shrines that are still in use, such as those in Varanasi, date from this period. Meanwhile, Muslim architecture in the 18th century and into the British period became more flamboyant, almost Rococo in style. The best examples are the early 19th-century buildings of Lucknow.

European influences on art and architecture

The earliest European buildings in India are along the west coast, where Portuguese fortifications and churches from the 16th century survive, while there are also fine Dutch funerary monuments from the 17th century. Some fine 18th-century British buildings survive in Kolkata and Chennai. Almost all early British churches are modelled loosely on St Martin-in-the-Fields, in London's Trafalgar Square, for the reason that it was described in detail in a popular book on architecture of the time. Neoclassical government buildings and residences were built, sometimes as close copies of existing British buildings—such as Government House in Kolkata, which was modelled on Kedleston Hall in Derbyshire. By the late 19th century, other imperial styles had emerged, as evident in the neo-Gothic Victoria Terminus in Mumbai and in a new hybrid architectural style, rather clumsily referred to as Indo-Saracenic—it combined European and Indian neo-Mughal and Rajput styles. Many of the most flamboyant late 19th- and early 20th-century royal palaces, such as those at Mysore and Vadodara, were built in this style, by Indian craftsmen following the directions of British architects and engineers. The final years of British rule were marked by a slightly more restrained classicism, albeit with important Indian motifs, such as the remarkable buildings of New Delhi, designed by Lutyens and Baker. The most influential architects of the post-independence period were Modernists from Europe and America; they included Le Corbusier, who designed much of Chandigarh, the new capital of Punjab.

Modern art and architecture

India has a flourishing modern art scene which draws on European and Indian cultural traditions. The dominant figure of the late 19th century was Raja Ravi Varma, who used European oil painting techniques in a series of portraits and stylised images of sari-clad women and Hindu deities. Varma's style remains a powerful influence, particularly in popular religious imagery and in film posters—there are large collections of Varma's work in Vadodara and Trivandrum. Important artists of the 20th century include the Indo-Hungarian painter Amrita Sher-Gil (with a large collection at the

National Gallery of Modern Art in Delhi, *see p. 121*) and the Bengali polymath Rabindranath Tagore. Leading artists of the independence period include the enormously successful and often controversial M.F. Hussain, as well as many other painters, sculptors and installation artists who have contributed to a very lively contemporary arts scene. Indian architecture has also attempted to draw on both traditional and Western design and engineering techniques, particularly in Delhi. The best-known contemporary architects are Charles Correa (responsible for the British Council and the Crafts Museum in Delhi) and Raj Rewal (who designed the Pragati Maidan exhibition centre in Delhi).

Other cultural traditions

A wide range of artistic, cultural and craft traditions survives in almost every part of India.

Crafts: India has an extraordinary variety of traditional craft products, including metalwork, woodwork, tribal painting, papier-mâché objects, lacquerware, jewellery and textiles. They are widely available to buy, though it is advisable to take local advice about cost and quality. The Crafts Museum in Delhi and the Calico Museum (for textiles) in Ahmedabad have particularly fine collections.

Dance: There are eight different schools of Indian classical dance, most of which originated in a religious setting—usually a temple—as a way of recounting stories about the Hindu gods. Originating from Tamil Nadu, Bharatnatyam is internationally the best-known form of Indian classical dance, while Kathakali, from Kerala, involves the use of elaborate costumes. Odissi dance is from Orissa, and has a distinctive emphasis on the independent use by dancers of their head, upper body and lower body to express themselves. Kathak dance is mainly performed in northern India, and is most closely associated with Mughal rule. It was widely disparaged during the British period as the seductive dance of courtesans, but there has been a more recent revival of Kathak. Among the more popular folk dances are Bhangra, from Punjab, which began as a harvest celebration and became popular in Britain in the 1990s, and a wide variety of tribal dances from Rajasthan.

Music: Internationally, Indian classical music is most closely associated with the sitar, the stringed instrument that was brought to Western audiences in the 1960s, largely by its best-known modern performer, Ravi Shankar. In fact, there is a large variety of instruments, vocal styles and playing techniques, descriptions of which date back to the earliest Hindu texts. There are two major streams of Indian classical music: the mainly northern, Hindustani style, in which the drum known as the *tabla* is normally used to keep time; and the mainly southern, Carnatic music, in which the vocal style usually plays a more important role. The most popular forms of music in India are film songs, which make use of a wide range of Indian classical and folk styles, as well as music from a variety of Western traditions. Normally, songs are not performed by actors, who instead lip-synch to the vocalisations of what are known as playback singers.

Film: India's film industry is the most prolific in the world. The best known are Bollywood films—Hindi-language movies made in Mumbai—but several other cities have booming film industries in a wide range of languages. Almost all popular films contain extended song and dance sequences. The Indian film industry dates back to the start of the 20th century, and internationally its most famous director is Satyajit Ray, best known for *Pather Panchali*, the first of the Apu Trilogy of films, which appeared in the 1950s.

Literature: The earliest surviving Indian literature is in Sanskrit, and includes the *Vedas* and the great Hindu epics, the *Mahabharata* and the *Ramayana*, while the oldest secular writing, from about 2,000 years ago, is Tamil-language verse known as Sangam poetry. The Sanskrit poet and dramatist Kalidasa (c. 5th century AD) is arguably the greatest of the early Indian writers, and is often referred to as the Indian Shakespeare. The late 19th century saw the emergence of a distinctive Bengali-language literature, and Rabindranath Tagore won the 1913 Nobel Prize for Literature. Urdu and Hindi literature also flourished in the period, and Prem Chand—best known for writing about village life in northern India—emerged as the most influential writer of the inter-war years. The leading figures in the first phase of Indian writing in English was R.K. Narayan, whose series of short books set in the fictional town of Malgudi had a large Indian and international readership. From the late 1970s, a new generation of Indian writers in English emerged, including Salman Rushdie, Vikram Seth, Amitav Ghosh, Rohinton Mistry and Arundhati Roy—all of whom have been enormously successful internationally.

RELIGION

India has been the birthplace of no fewer than four important religions—Hinduism, Buddhism, Jainism and Sikhism—and has been a land in which Islam, Christianity, Judaism and Zoroastrianism have all developed their own local identities. More generally, India has a reputation as a country where religion suffuses every part of life. Like almost everything else one says about India, this is only partly true. India is also home to a powerful rationalist movement, largely in the south of the country; there are also many for whom religious observance and ritual are far more important than religious or spiritual belief.

A veteran BBC India correspondent, Gerald Priestland, once controversially observed: 'Contrary to the belief of many Westerners, India is not a profoundly spiritual country but a profoundly materialist one. The object of most religious practice is to ensure material success.' Undoubtedly, some visitors to India are surprised and disappointed by the extent of overt materialism on open display in many places and on many occasions. In some Hindu and Jain temples, and in some Muslim shrines, the custodians will try, rather aggressively, to relieve foreign visitors of large sums of money. Many Indians, from across the social spectrum, are extremely materialistic—but the opposite, as usual, can also be true. And in the holy cities and elsewhere, there are ascetics who have shed all their worldly belongings, sometimes including their clothes, in favour of a life of poverty and abstinence.

Traditionally, India has tolerated an extraordinarily wide variety of religious beliefs and practice. Hinduism, in particular, has historically been the least dogmatic of all religions. This tolerance has been strained in recent years—as some politicians and religious leaders have encouraged people to see religion, more than language or culture or nationality, as their key to self-identity. This has led to the rise of political parties that predominantly represent members of one religious group, and, in its worst form, to riots and pogroms that have targeted members of a particular religion.

India is overwhelmingly Hindu. According to government census statistics, more than 80 percent of the population is Hindu, with just over 13 percent belonging to the largest religious minority, Muslims, two percent each of Christians and Sikhs, and less than one percent each of other religions. These percentage figures do not tell the whole story. Although Muslims are a small minority, they account for more than 140 million people nationally, making India—after Indonesia and Pakistan—the country with the third highest number of Muslims. Additionally, several of the northeast states have a Christian majority, while Jammu and Kashmir is majority Muslim and Punjab is majority Sikh. Similarly, the vast majority of India's 70,000 Zoroastrians, or Parsis—one of the smallest minority groups—live in one city, Mumbai. Moreover there is an astonishing level of diversity within each religious group. The census data reflect the large divisions between, for instance, Shaivite and Vaishnavite Hindus, or Shia and Sunni Muslims, or the enormous array of

Christian denominations—and this is just as true for religions such as Buddhism, Jainism and Parsi Zoroastrianism.

HINDUISM

Hinduism is the hardest of all religions to define, and can be difficult for outsiders to understand. It has no agreed set of core beliefs, no supreme deity or hierarchy of gods, no canonical text and no central authority. Hinduism is, ultimately, best defined as what Hindus believe and practise. Even the word Hinduism is a relatively modern coinage, popularised by Europeans in the 18th century, and many Hindus will use other phrases such as *sanatan dharma* (close in meaning to 'eternal path') to describe their religion. Some will argue that Hinduism is not really a religion, but a way of life, or a culture—and ultimately define Hinduism as Indian-ness.

There are, however, beliefs and practices that most Hindus have in common—and that are widely held as being the essence of Hinduism. A long list of these would include a belief in the cyclical nature of time, in reincarnation, in a pantheon of gods—among whom Shiva, Vishnu, two avatars of Vishnu (Rama and Krishna) and a variously-named female goddess (Kali, Durga, Devi, Shakti) are currently the most popular. Historically, the caste system has played an important role—though many would argue that it is not intrinsic to Hinduism. Very few Hindus eat beef. Fire and water play an important role in many rituals. Most Hindus worship in temples, go on pilgrimages and are cremated. Hindus share a number of common festivals, including Diwali, Holi and Dussehra, though the names and importance of each of these varies across India and between different communities. Worship normally takes the form of *darshan*—the viewing of a statue, image or other representation of a god. And then there are the philosophical underpinnings of Hindus, which often seem esoteric to foreigners and deserve a more thorough explanation than will be possible here. These philosophies can also seem quite obscure to a lot of Indians, and it is often more important to understand how Hinduism has been interpreted and practised, and how it has been reflected in art and architecture.

THE HINDU TRINITY

Visitors are often taught, especially in guide books, about the Hindu trinity, or *trimurti*: Brahma, the Creator; Vishnu, the Preserver; and Shiva, the Destroyer. However, as the historian A.L. Basham points out: 'Early Western students of Hinduism were impressed by the parallel between the Hindu trinity and that of Christianity. In fact the parallel is not very close, and the Hindu trinity, unlike the Holy Trinity of Christianity, never really "caught on". All Hindu trinitarianism tended to favour one god of the three.' Most Hindus are in fact henotheistic—meaning they mainly worship one god, but recognise the existence of others.

HISTORY OF HINDUISM

Hinduism is one of the world's oldest religions, dating back at least three and half thousand years, and almost certainly much further. Most historians believe an early form of Hinduism, known as Vedic Brahmanism, was brought to the country by Indo-European or Indo-Aryan migrants in the period c. 1500 BC—although others claim to have identified specifically Hindu images on objects recovered from archaeological excavations in the Indus Valley.

THE MOHENJO-DARO SEAL

A broken stone seal found at Mohenjo-daro in modern-day Pakistan provides the strongest evidence of a Hindu god being worshipped in pre-Vedic India. The image of the god-like figure, sitting in a yogic posture, displaying his erect penis, with a tricorn headdress, surrounded by animals, has many similarities to images of Rudra, an early version of Shiva. Others argue that the similarities are coincidental, and that without additional evidence—perhaps from the as-yet undeciphered text on the seal—the identification of the image with Rudra is unjustified.

Some of the evidence of a non-Indian origin for Hinduism comes from early Hindu texts themselves, as well as from an excavation in Bogazköy in northern Turkey in 1909—where a peace treaty between the Hittites and the Mitannis from c. 1400 BC refers to the gods Indra, Mitra and Varuna—all key figures in the early Hindu pantheon.

In the earliest Hindu texts, the best-known modern-day Hindu gods are all but absent and—as with Greco-Roman and Egyptian polytheism—the prominence and distinguishing characteristics of different gods changes over time. In the *Rigveda*, the earliest of the Hindu sacred texts, Vishnu and Shiva (in the form of Rudra) play a minor role, while the war-and-weather god Indra and the fire-god Agni are the most important deities. The basic fourfold caste division, which became an important feature of Hinduism, is mentioned in the *Rigveda*.

The next major development in the history of Hinduism is the composition of the great epics, the *Ramayana* and the *Mahabharata*, both of which are widely presumed to be based on real events. Many of the place names, geographical descriptions and social structures are accurate. The great Battle of the *Mahabharata* has been tentatively dated to c. 1000 BC. Gods take on overtly human forms in both epics: Rama as the princely hero of the *Ramayana*, Krishna as the charioteer in the *Mahabharata*.

With the emergence of Buddhism and Jainism, sometimes known as the Shramanic religions, in the 6th century BC, Hinduism entered a period of change and crisis. Buddhism and Jainism both had founders who were not members of the Brahmin priestly caste. They were both from princely families who challenged Brahmin orthodoxy and developed ascetic, unritualistic, individual-centred philosophies.

Buddhism, during the time of Ashoka the Great (304–232 BC), became the main religion of the Mauryan Empire, which covered most of modern-day India, as well as Pakistan and Afghanistan. As Buddhism was gradually transformed from a godless religion to one with a pantheon of *bodhisattvas*, or enlightened beings, it began to resemble Hinduism. And ultimately Hinduism would incorporate parts of Buddhism, and the Buddha himself would become an avatar of the Hindu god Vishnu. During the Gupta Empire, Buddhism was still the main religion, but one that appeared to be evolving back into Hinduism; and the priestly Brahmin caste appears to have retained or resumed its dominance over spiritual matters and religious ritual. Animal sacrifice, which played an important role in Vedic Brahmanism, had almost disappeared. Many of the earliest surviving Hindu temples come from this period—when Shiva, Vishnu, Surya (the sun-god) and Devi (the generic name for a female goddess) were the main objects of worship.

Devotional cults began to emerge from the middle of the first millennium—particularly around Shiva, Vishnu (and his avatars Krishna and Rama), and the female goddess. Devotees, or *bhaktis*, would form a special emotional and personal relationship with 'their' god, without denying the existence of other gods. The *bhakti* movement was a challenge to Brahmin domination by positing a personal relationship with a god, unmediated by a priest—but often encouraged by a poet or spiritual leader. The *bhakti* movement rose as the influence of Buddhism fell. At a similar time, Tantric beliefs (*see p. 58*) began to take hold as an esoteric cult which drew elements from both Hinduism and Buddhism.

The next great test of Hinduism came from Islam, which first reached India towards the end of the first millennium—though at no point did Islam come close to challenging Hinduism as the majority religion of India. The earliest Muslims in India seemed more interested in trade or plunder than in conversion, though many temples were destroyed by Muslim invaders. The Muslim rulers of India were from families that had migrated originally from Afghanistan, Persia or Central Asia, and few made any attempt to convert Hindus—partly out of a desire to keep themselves separate from the Indian masses. There were, however, significant conversions from Hinduism in the lands that are now Pakistan and Bangladesh, as well as in Kashmir. Some Hindus found the mystical branch of Islam known as Sufism very attractive—and to this day many visitors to Sufi shrines are practising Hindus, just as many Muslims will take part in Hindu festivals.

Throughout the Muslim period, under both Sultanate and Mughal rule, independent and feudatory Hindu kingdoms thrived—in the south, in Orissa, Maharashtra and Rajasthan—and functioned as very effective patrons of sacred Hindu art and architecture.

The European arrival in India presented a new challenge to Hinduism, with Christian missionaries attempting to make converts from a religion that they often considered savage and depraved. Other Europeans made more serious attempts to understand Hinduism and its complex history. One reaction in India was the emergence of Hindu monotheism and a variety of reform movements, such as the Brahmo Samaj—which campaigned against practices such as *sati*, or widow immolation, and child marriage. The Arya Samaj (founded 1875) used the original *Vedic* texts of Hinduism to reject child marriage, Untouchability and a number of other practices which they saw as un-Hindu and immoral. In the 19th and 20th centuries, there was a great flourishing of Hindu sects, and more recently of New Age groups with strong Hindu influences. These ranged from the public-service oriented Ramakrishna Mission to the Theosophist followers of J. Krishnamurti; Sri Aurobindo, the teacher of 'integral yoga' who founded Auroville; and on to the more modern swamis and gurus who were so popular in the West in the 1960s and 70s. The 20th century also saw a long and inconclusive debate about the caste system within Hinduism, with Mahatma Gandhi leading a campaign to eradicate Untouchability. The lawyer and writer of the Indian constitution, B.R. Ambedkar, did not believe that Hinduism could reform, and led a large number of former 'Untouchables' away from Hinduism and into Buddhism. Many other former 'Untouchables' in south India converted to Christianity.

A new, more political form of Hinduism also emerged in the early 20th century, with the formation of the Hindu Mahasabha—partly as a response to Muslim separatism. The key figure in the rise of Hindu nationalism was Veer Savarkar, who coined the idea of Hindutva, or 'Hindu-ness', according to which anyone born in India, and for whom India was the holy land, was a Hindu. His ideas inspired a wide range of Hindu activism—from the killers of Mahatma Gandhi, who thought he was appeasing Muslims, to the leading Hindu political party in modern India, the Bharatiya Janata Party, or BJP. One of the main objectives of Hindu nationalists in recent years has been the destruction of mosques which they maintain were built on key Hindu religious sites—in 1992 they destroyed the 16th-century Babri Mosque in Ayodhya, which they said was built on the ruins of a temple marking the birthplace of the god Rama.

Most modern Hindus can be described as either Vaishnavite or Shaivites—that is followers of either Vishnu or Shiva—though many would not actually use those terms themselves. Additionally, there are not many Vishnu temples, and most Vaishnavites are actually devotees of one of his avatars or incarnations, most commonly Rama or Krishna, or of Narayan, the name used for Vishnu in south India. Similarly, some Shaivites are actually devotees of other members of Shiva's family, such as his son, the elephant-god Ganesha, or one of the forms of his consort, Parvati. Some Hindus say that there are 320 million gods—only the major gods are listed below.

MAJOR HINDU GODS & HOW TO RECOGNISE THEM

Most of the major Hindu gods have key attributes that make them easily identifiable. Each of them has, for example, a 'vehicle' that usually takes the form of an animal on which they ride: Shiva is normally portrayed riding a bull, Nandi; while Vishnu rides the man-eagle Garuda. Other key distinguishing features include their hair (Shiva's is usually matted) and head-dress; the number of arms they have; what they are carrying in their hands; and their companions.

NAMING THE GODS

When speaking the names of the gods, it is normal not to pronounce the final 'a' where it forms a separate syllable, so Shiva is pronounced 'Shiv', and Rama is pronounced 'Raam'. It is also usual to add an honorific title—in English it is common to say Lord Shiv, or Lord Ram; in Indian languages the most common forms are either Sri as a prefix (as in 'Sri Ram') or –ji as a suffix (as in 'Shivji').

Vishnu

Vishnu is traditionally described as 'the Preserver', in contrast to Shiva, 'the Destroyer'. He is usually portrayed with four arms, carrying a conch shell, a mace, a discus and a lotus. He wears a crown. His vehicle is the man-eagle **Garuda**. His main consort, **Lakshmi** (*see p. 55*), is often standing next to him, or massaging his feet. The multi-headed serpent **Ananta**, meaning endless, is often seen alongside Vishnu, sometimes coiled up as a seat for the god, or with its many heads forming a kind of halo behind him. Vishnu is also known as **Narayan**. He is mentioned as a minor god in the earliest Hindu sacred text, the *Rigveda*. Although he has benevolent and protective attributes, he is best known today through his avatars. In mainstream Hinduism, there are ten of these avatars, or forms in which Vishnu descended to earth from Baikunth, his heavenly home (avatar literally means 'descent' in Sanskrit). Other versions of the story of Vishnu list as many as 22 avatars. Vishnu's traditional ten avatars are sometimes all seen together on wall carvings and are normally listed in historical and evolutionary order (*see below*).

The British geneticist J.B.S. Haldane (1892–1964), who became an Indian citizen and died in Bhubaneswar, pointed out how the order of Vishnu's avatars was echoed by Darwin's theory of the descent of man from animals. The first three avatars of Vishnu also all played important roles in early Hindu tales of a great deluge—in a way that echoes the biblical flood.

The ten avatars of Vishnu

Matsya, a fish, is sometimes represented as a merman, with the full body of a fish, out of whose mouth the upper torso of man with four arms emerges. There is thought to be only one Matsya temple in India, near Tirupati in southern Andhra Pradesh.

Kurma, a tortoise, is sometimes represented with the head of a man and the body of a tortoise or turtle. Kurma temples are also very rare—the best-known is one near Srikakulam in northern Andhra Pradesh.

Varaha, a boar, is usually represented with the head of a boar and the body of man with four arms, and carrying Vishnu's traditional accessories. Images of Varaha are much more common than Matsya and Kurma. There are very fine Varaha images at Khajuraho, and several Varaha temples in south India.

Narasimha, a lion, is usually represented with the head of a lion and the body of a man, sometimes with lion claws. Narasimha is a popular deity, particularly in southern India, where he is seen as a demon-killer and symbol of divine anger. There is a superb colossal statue of a seated Narasimha at Hampi.

Vamana, a dwarf, is usually represented as a small man with a paunch, often carrying an umbrella. As the diminutive Vamana, Vishnu tricked the demon-king Bali into granting him a kingdom the breadth of three strides. Vishnu then transformed himself from a dwarf into a giant. His first stride covered the earth, the second covered the skies and finally, stepping on Bali's head, he was able to reach into the heavens. The best-known Vamana temple is at Khajuraho.

Parashuram, literally 'Rama-with-an-axe', is depicted as an axe-wielding Brahmin warrior, who kills members of the Kshatriya warrior caste who have become too powerful.

Rama is the king of Ayodhya and hero of the Hindu epic the *Ramayana*. Some of his devotees see him as a separate god, and not an avatar of Vishnu (*see opposite*).

Krishna is one of Hinduism's most popular gods in his own right (*see opposite*).

Buddha was integrated into the Vaishnavite tradition long after his death, at a time when Buddhism was beginning to decline in India as a major force.

Kalki, the future incarnation of Vishnu, is a god who is yet to be born. Kalki is normally shown with a white horse and brandishing a sword. His appearance in the world is thought to presage the ending of the current Dark Age, or Kalyug. Jaipur has India's best-known Kalki temple.

Shiva

Shiva is traditionally described as the 'Destroyer', but he is a much more complex figure than that epithet suggests. Typically, he carries a trident, and has matted hair and a third eye in the middle of his forehead. His sacred 'vehicle' is the bull **Nandi**, and he is often accompanied by his main consort, **Parvati** (*see overleaf*), and his sons—the elephant-god **Ganesha** (*see overleaf*) and the war-god **Kartikeya** (who goes under several other names—*see overleaf*). Unlike Vishnu, who is transformed into something or someone new with each avatar, Shiva has a range of 'aspects' that represent different sides of his character. The only non-anthropomorphic aspect of Shiva is when he becomes a body part, such as his own phallus. The best known of all of Shiva's many manifestations is as a phallus-like object called a **lingam**—usually a stone object of worship placed in the central sanctuary of thousands of temples across India. Among the key aspects of Shiva is **Nataraja**, or Lord of the Dance, where a dancing, swirling Shiva stands on the head of a dwarf who symbolises ignorance. Other aspects include the androgynous **Ardhanarishwara**, where he is half-man and half-woman, split down the middle, and the fearsome **Bhairava**, with a dog as his vehicle, who is invoked by devotees who wish to destroy their enemies. Shiva is also shown in much gentler aspects, as a householder teasing Parvati, or as **Pashupati**, the Lord of Creatures. The most famous shrine is probably Viswanath Temple in Varanasi, which is where Shiva came to earth after leaving his mountain home to marry Parvati, and where he brought the goddess Ganga down his matted hair to earth as the River Ganges—and made Parvati jealous. The Hindu rock caves at Ellora and Elephanta contain superb examples of

Shaivite sculpture; and some of the best Chola bronzes from Tamil Nadu show various aspects of Shiva—most famously as Nataraja. Shiva is not named in the earliest Hindu texts, though **Rudra**, a howling storm-god, bears many of his characteristics. Devotional worship of Shiva appears to be only about 1,500 years old.

Brahma

Though he is traditionally described as the 'Creator', that role does not give Brahma the pre-eminence among the gods that one might expect—and he does not command a large following among Hindu devotees. He is typically shown with four heads and four arms, one hand carrying a book representing the *Vedas*, the early Hindu sacred texts. His other hands sometimes hold a rosary, a spoon and a vessel of holy water. His vehicle is a swan or goose, **Hamsa**, and he is often accompanied by his wife **Saraswati**, the goddess of learning (*see overleaf*). There are very few Brahma temples—the best known is in Pushkar in Rajasthan. The god Brahma is not to be confused with Brahman (the Hindu concept of an infinite and transcendent reality) or with Brahmin (the priestly caste), though all are drawn from the same Sanskrit root.

Rama

Also known as **Ram** or **Ramachandra**, Rama is the hero of the epic *Ramayana* and the king of ancient Ayodhya, where he is said to have reigned for 11,000 years. He is the popular god-king, whose period of rule is known as Ram Rajya, a shorthand description still in use in India to describe perfect government. He is also the seventh avatar of Vishnu. Typically he is shown with a crown, carrying a bow and a quiver of arrows, and is often accompanied by his consort **Sita**. There are not many Rama temples, though shrines throughout the land are covered with scenes from the *Ramayana*. The best-known Rama temple is the one in Hampi (*see p. 701*). In recent years, there have been controversial attempts to build a Rama temple on the site of a mosque at Ayodhya that was demolished in 1992, and which some Hindus say had been built on the site of a temple marking Rama's birthplace.

Krishna

The eighth avatar of Vishnu, Krishna is also the narrator of the *Bhagavad Gita*, a Hindu philosophical work that forms part of the epic *Mahabharata*. Krishna also plays the role of a charioteer to the *Mahabharata's* most important character, **Arjuna**. Typically, Krishna is portrayed as a very young man, often painted blue, playing a flute, sometimes surrounded by cows. He is often shown in the company of pretty cowherd girls, or *gopis*, whom he used to tease by stealing their clothes while they were bathing. One of the *gopis*, **Radha**, is his main consort. The most important Krishna temple is in Mathura, his birthplace—but there are many others, such as the Jagannath Temple in Orissa, Dwarkadish Temple in Gujarat and a large number of Hare Krishna temples around the world. According to some Hindu texts, Krishna was born in 3228 BC, and his death, 125 years later in the Gujarati town of Dwarka, marks the beginning of Kalyug, the Dark Age.

Ganesh/Ganesha/Ganapati

Ganesha is the elephant-god, one of the best-known and most popular deities in the Hindu pantheon. He is instantly recognisable from his elephant head and pot-belly. His 'vehicle' is a mouse, and he is normally described as a bachelor. Ganesha is traditionally held to be the son of Shiva and Parvati. Every Indian child learns the story of how Ganesha got his elephant head. Parvati asked him to guard her while she bathed, then Shiva (whom Ganesha had not met) appeared and chopped off his head when barred from entering. Parvati explained to Shiva that he had just decapitated his own son, and a distraught Shiva gave him the head of a passing elephant. Ganesha is also known as **Vighneshvara**, the 'Lord of Obstacles', and is worshipped as a remover of obstacles, though traditionally he also places obstacles in the paths of those who need to be stopped. There are Ganesha temples in many parts of the country, and he is often also venerated at Shiva temples. His image can also be seen in millions of homes across India. As Ganapati, he is particularly venerated in the western state of Maharashtra.

Ganesha, the elephant-god, son of Shiva, is usually shown with a large belly and his trunk turned to his left.

Kartikeya

Kartikeya, or **Skanda**, is the war-god, and son of Shiva and Parvati. He is also usually identified with the popular south Indian god **Murugan** (also known as **Subramaniam**). Kartikeya is normally shown holding a spear and riding a peacock. He once was a popular god in north India, but there are now almost no temples devoted to his worship. As Murugan in southern India, though, he is one of the most popular deities.

Hanuman

Hanuman is the popular and characterful monkey-deity who plays a central role in the *Ramayana*, helping to rescue Sita (*see p. 53*) from the demon-king Ravana. Because of his role in the *Ramayana*, he is most closely associated with Rama. There are Hanuman temples throughout India.

Indra

Indra is the early Vedic god of war and weather, and probably the most important god in early Hinduism. His role has diminished in recent centuries, but images of Indra are seen in many early rock-cut temple carvings. He is normally shown carrying a small hand-held weapon called a *vajra*, and his mount is an elephant.

Agni

The early Vedic god of fire, Agni normally has two heads and several arms, and rides a ram.

Surya

Surya is the early Vedic sun-god. He is normally shown with a high crown and being pulled in a chariot led by seven horses. Three of India's most important and beautiful temples—at Konarak in Orissa, Modhera in Gujarat, and Martand in Kashmir—were dedicated to Surya, but none of them is still in use as a place of worship. However, millions of Indians perform the *Surya Namaskar*, or 'sun salutation' prayer, every day, some of them doing it as a yogic exercise.

GODDESSES

Lakshmi/Laxmi

Goddess of wealth and the consort of Vishnu/Narayan (*see p. 51*), Lakshmi is typically portrayed with four arms and seated or standing on a lotus flower. Her 'vehicle' is an owl, but this is rarely depicted in painting or carvings. She often has gold coins spilling from one of her hands and is sometimes surrounded by elephants. Lakshmi is a very popular god throughout India, and seen as a bringer of good fortune. There are several Mahalakshmi (Great Lakshmi) temples, the most famous of which is in Mumbai.

Parvati

Parvati is the consort of Shiva (*see p. 52*) and, according to some Hindu texts, the gentle form of the **Shakti**, the divine feminine force, of whom **Durga** and **Kali** are more ferocious forms (*see overleaf*). She is normally portrayed bare-breasted, with two arms when at Shiva's side, though when alone she is sometimes shown with four arms. In the south she is known as **Meenakshi**, the fish-eyed goddess, and the famous Meenakshi Temple in Madurai is dedicated to her.

Saraswati

The goddess of knowledge and art, Saraswati is also the consort of Brahma (*see p. 53*). She is usually shown with four arms, playing a stringed musical instrument called the *veena*. Paintings of Saraswati often depict her beside a river, as a reference to the River Saraswati. Referred to in the earliest Hindu texts, the disappearance of this ancient river has long puzzled archaeologists.

Durga

Durga is the ten-armed demon-fighting goddess, often described as an avatar of Parvati, and a consort of Shiva (*see p. 52*). She rides a lion or tiger, and carries a large number of weapons. The most common image of Durga shows her killing the demon **Mahishasura**, who is usually shown disguised as a water-buffalo. Durga Puja is Bengal's most popular Hindu festival, when the streets are filled with people as images of Durga and other gods are taken down to the river for immersion.

Kali

Kali is usually described as the goddess of death and destruction, though many of her devotees say that this over-emphasises the negative aspects of Hinduism's most fearsome deity. She is usually depicted as black (*kali* means black), her lips red with blood and her tongue hanging out of her mouth, and she is often garlanded with skulls. She usually has four arms—one holding a human head, another a bowl to catch the dripping blood, and the remaining two holding a sword and a trident. Sometimes she is shown as **Mahakali**, with ten heads, ten arms and ten legs. She is normally described as an avatar of Parvati and Durga, and Shiva is her consort (*see p. 52*). The best-known Kali temple is Kalighat in south Kolkata.

SACRED HINDU TEXTS

The *Vedas*

The four *Vedas* are the earliest sacred texts of Hinduism, thought to have been brought by Indo-Europeans who migrated to India more than three millennia ago. They mainly consist of a series of short prayers and hymns. The best-known text is the *Rigveda*, in which the main gods are Indra and Agni, and where there are many prayers to the ritual drink, *soma*—which has not been identified, but appears from the text to have had hallucinogenic properties.

The *Ramayana*

One of the two great epics of Hindu sacred literature, the *Ramayana* tells the story of Rama, prince of Ayodhya. It is a heavily moral tale, which most Indians know well, and scenes from it are painted or carved on temples across the country—it has also been seen by historians as an attempt to legitimise monarchical rule. The *Ramayana* tells of how Rama wins the hand of Sita by breaking the divine bow of Shiva. In the next key episode, Rama, Sita and Rama's brother Lakshman go into exile in the forest, forced out of Ayodhya by the intrigues of Rama's stepmother. The heart of the story is about how Rama's wife Sita is then kidnapped by the ten-headed demon-king Ravana (or Ravan), who lives in Lanka. With the help of Lakshman, the monkey-god Hanuman and his monkey army, Sita is set free. She is then tested by Rama to be certain that she remained chaste while in captivity. The modern town of Ayodhya in central Uttar Pradesh and the country of Sri Lanka are widely believed to be the original Ramayana sites, and the undersea causeway between India and Sri Lanka is believed by some Hindus to be the bridge built by Hanuman's army of monkeys to allow Rama and Lakshman to cross into Ravana's territory. There are several alternative versions of the story, and some south Indians even revere Ravana as a hero.

The *Mahabharata*

The *Mahabharata* is the other great epic of Hindu sacred literature—and is now thought to predate the *Ramayana*. Even longer than the *Ramayana*, it tells the story of the great battles between the Pandavas and the Kauravas. The Pandavas are five princely brothers: Yudhishtara, Bhima, Arjuna and the twins Nakula and Sahadeva. The first three are the best known today: pious Yudhishtara for his truthfulness; huge Bhima for his strength; and the archer Arjuna for his great skill in battle. They all marry the same woman, Draupadi, whom Arjuna 'wins' in an archery contest. The god Krishna makes a series of appearances as Arjuna's charioteer. The Kauravas, the cousins of the Pandavas, are made up of King Dhritarashtra's 100 sons, of whom the most important is Duryodhana. Among famous scenes is the one where Yudhishtara loses Draupadi to the Kauravas in a game of dice. When the Kauravas attempt to remove her sari, it has become, thanks to Krishna's intervention, endless—and her honour is saved. The centrepiece of the book is the great Battle of Kurukshetra, which the Pandavas, helped by Krishna, eventually win. But by the end of the book all the main characters are dead—including Krishna, whose demise is said to mark the beginning of the current dark age, or Kalyug, that started in 3102 BC. A number of geographical place names in the *Mahabharata* have been identified with historical sites in India. They include: the battlefield of Kurukshetra, in modern-day Haryana; the city of Indraprastha, which is identified with the Purana Qila in Delhi; and the city of Hastinapura, which is near Meerut in modern-day Uttar Pradesh.

The *Bhagavad Gita* forms part of the *Mahabharata*, though it is often read as a separate text, and referred to as 'the *Gita*'. It consists of a conversation between Krishna and Arjuna which has come to function as a concise guide to Hindu philosophy. Other key early Hindu texts included the *Brahmanas*, the *Upanishads* and the *Puranas*.

KEY CONCEPTS IN HINDUISM

Dharma (or ***Dhamma***) is a central concept in Hinduism and Buddhism. It means 'righteous path', or 'path of duty'—but it also means, in the context of an individual, his or her religion. It literally means 'that which upholds', and is often translated, imprecisely, as 'law'.

Karma is often translated as 'destiny', but this is an oversimplification. Karma really expresses the idea that one's actions have consequences even in future lives, so that beneficial results will come out of beneficial actions, and harmful results will come from harmful actions.

Atma is usually translated by the word 'soul'. In Hinduism the soul is immortal, unlike the body. Mahatma, meaning 'great soul', was the name given to Mohandas Gandhi by his followers.

Samsara is the cycle of individual rebirth or reincarnation of the *atma*, or soul, that is decided by one's karma.

Caste is a complex subject in Hinduism, and is often confused by the way the English word 'caste', taken from Portuguese, conflates two different but connected concepts: *varna* and *jati*. There are many hundreds of *jatis*, for which the closest English-language equivalent is probably 'clan'; these play a bigger role in social organisation than *varnas*. *Varna* describes the traditional fourfold division of Hindu society, with the priestly Brahmins, the warrior Kshatriyas, the merchant Vaishyas, and the farming Sudras. In the earliest Hindu sacred text, the *Rigveda*, each *varna* represented part of the body of the creator god, Brahma—so the Brahmins were the mouth (or the head), the Kshatriyas were the arms, the Vaishyas were the thighs and the Sudras were the feet. A fifth group, once known as 'Untouchables', were outside this caste framework, and were seen as ritually impure—Gandhi renamed them Harijans (children of god), but they are now most commonly known as Dalits (the oppressed) in modern India. *Jati* is the key factor in how most Hindus define their relationship to each other. Normally, Hindus marry within their *jati*, but not within their *gotra*, or sub-clan.

Darshan literally means 'sight' or 'viewing', and describes the act of worship of a Hindu devotee before the idol or symbol of a deity.

Puja is a religious ceremony, usually consisting of an invocation or prayer and an offering to the gods. A *pujari* is a Hindu priest, normally a Brahmin, who conducts *pujas*.

Kalyug means 'Black Age'. According to Hindu philosophy, time is cyclical, and passes through a repeating pattern of ages, or *yug*. We are currently in the Kalyug (or Kali Yuga), which began 5,000 years ago, and will continue for another 426,000 years. Then the cycle will restart, with the Satya or Krita Yug, followed by the Treta Yug and the Dwapara Yug, before a new Kalyug begins. The Satya Yug is the highest point of the cycle, when everyone follows the path of righteousness, while the current Kalyug is the lowest point of the cycle, when people are most degenerate, and obsessed with the physical and material aspects of consciousness. The entire cycle takes 4,320,000 years.

Brahman is a term for the transcendent essence of reality. Not to be confused with the god Brahma or the priestly caste Brahmin, Brahman is an esoteric Hindu concept and can be hard to grasp. Other definitions include the 'soul of the world', and the Cosmic Spirit that is 'eternal, genderless, omnipotent, omniscient, omnipresent, and ultimately indescribable in human language'.

Shakti is described as the ultimate feminine power, the dynamic female form of Brahman. Sometimes, more prosaically, Shakti is described as the mother goddess—of which Parvati, Durga and Kali are all aspects.

Tantra is a form of Hinduism, with strong Buddhist influences, which emphasises control over one's own mind and body, including bodily fluids. Many practitioners of Tantra believe greater spiritual awareness and enlightment can come through carefully regulated sexual activity.

MAJOR HINDU FESTIVALS

The celebrations of the main festivals are determined by an ancient Hindu lunisolar calendar, so the dates vary each year within a broad time band, in the way that Easter varies in the Christian tradition. Several regions of India have their own calendars, and often celebrate New Year at different times.

Diwali (or **Deepawali**) is the 'Festival of Lights' (Oct/Nov), when houses, shops and public places are lit up by small oil lamps, candles or fairy lights. The festival is usually said to mark the return of the god Rama from exile, though some also say it commemorated the slaying of a demon by Krishna. The goddess Lakshmi is also often worshipped at Diwali as a bringer of wealth

Dussehra is the ten-day festive period (Sept/Oct, with marked regional variations) usually said to mark the victory of the god Rama over the demon Ravana. In northern India, public re-enactments of scenes from the *Ramayana* are staged over the nine nights, or *navaratri*, of Dussehra. The climax is the burning of an effigy of Ravana on the tenth day known as Vijay Dashami.

Holi (Feb/March), often referred to as the 'Festival of Colours', marks the defeat of the demoness Holika by Prahlad, a devotee of Vishnu. People celebrate Holi on the streets by throwing coloured powder and water at each other.

The **Kumbh Mela** (Jan) is a Hindu festival (*kumbh* means pitcher or pot, while a *mela* is a fair) that takes place every four years at either Hardwar, Ujjain, Allahabad or Nasik. The festival takes the form of a mass pilgrimage and immersion in sacred waters, and is said to be the largest gathering of people in the world. Every 12 years there is a Maha (or Great) Kumbh Mela at Allahabad. The next Maha Kumbh Melas are in 2012 and 2024.

Other widely-celebrated festivals include **Janmashtami** (Aug/Sept), which is Krishna's birthday, **Shivratri** (Feb/March), a special day of worship for Shiva, **Ramnavami** (March/April), which is Rama's birthday and **Raksha Bandhan** or **Rakhi** (Aug), which celebrates the relationship between brothers and sisters. Kites are flown in **Makar Sankranti** (Jan), which is often described as a harvest festival and which marks the end of winter in parts of northern India.

Major regional festivals include **Ganesh Chaturthi** (Aug/Sept), also known as **Ganpati**, mainly celebrated in western India, especially Mumbai, which marks the birthday of the elephant-god Ganesha. **Durga Puja** (Sept/Oct) is Kolkata's best-known festival—a celebration of the goddess Durga which takes place at the same time as Dussehra. **Chhath** (Oct/Nov) is a post-Diwali festival, dedicated to the sun-god Surya, and widely celebrated in Bihar. **Gangaur** (March/April) is Rajasthan's best-known regional festival, marking the worship of Gauri, the local version of Shiva's consort Parvati. **Pongal** (Jan) is the widely celebrated Tamil version of the harvest festival, Makar Sankranti, while **Onam** (Aug/Sept) is Kerala's most popular festival, marking the homecoming of the legendary King Mahabali. Several other harvest festivals are celebrated in India, including **Baisakhi** (April), which is most closely associated with Punjab.

BUDDHISM

Buddhism, founded in the middle of the 1st millennium BC, was a major Indian religion for almost 2,000 years, and had an enormous impact on the art, architecture and culture of India. It had practically died out as a living faith in India by the 13th century AD, surviving only in the mountain borderlands, but has now re-established itself as a minor but significant religion drawing much of its support from former Hindu 'Untouchables' who converted to Buddhism in the 20th century.

Buddhism's founder, Siddhartha Gautama (c. 563–483 BC, though some recent historians now say he probably lived more recently, in the 4th century BC), was from a princely family in northern India, though he was born in Lumbini, just over the modern-day border with Nepal. He became a beggar when he realised that material success was not a satisfactory goal in life. Through meditation and self-denial he was, according to early Buddhist texts, able to achieve enlightenment—sitting under a tree in Bodhgaya, which is today an important Buddhist site. He became known as the Buddha—literally 'the one who has achieved enlightenment'. Thereafter he was an itinerant preacher, challenging the Brahmin priesthood with his innovative ideas. He rejected the existence of early Hindu gods and the caste system, and developed such concepts as the 'Four Noble Truths' and the 'Eightfold Path' (*see box below*).

At Sarnath, now one of India most important Buddhist sites, he gathered a group of his first five followers, the *sangha*, and gradually the new faith grew—with monks and nuns and lay members joining the *sangha* from all castes and races. More than 200 years after the death of the Buddha, the Mauryan emperor Ashoka converted to Buddhism and it became, in effect, the state religion. The Ashoka rock and pillar edicts, scattered across the subcontinent, in Delhi, Orissa, Gujarat and many other places, still testify to the proselytising zeal of the later Mauryan period. Ashoka sent Buddhist envoys to Sri Lanka, China, Southeast Asia, the Middle East and several Mediterranean countries.

For the following millennium, Buddhism was probably the dominant faith in the subcontinent. In that time, it underwent major changes and a series of schisms. The Buddha himself began to be worshipped, and the earliest carved images of the Buddha date back approximately to the 1st century AD. Rich Buddhist patrons emerged who

THE BUDDHA'S NEW IDEAS

The Four Noble Truths are that suffering is the key feature of human life; that suffering results from craving worldly things; that release from suffering can be achieved only by eliminating cravings; and that the way to give up cravings is to follow the Eightfold Path. This path consists of: right understanding, right intentions, right speech, right conduct, right livelihood, right effort, right awareness and right concentration. Successfully following this path will lead to an absence of craving, the state of nirvana.

donated large sums of money for religious buildings, and Buddhism began to lose the egalitarianism which was so important in the early period. Greek kingdoms in what is now Pakistan were deeply influenced by Buddhism, and inspired the extraordinary mix of European and Indian art that is known as Gandhara sculpture. The largest of the many schisms is reflected today in the division between **Theravada Buddhism** (the oldest surviving branch of Buddhism which dominates in Sri Lanka and Southeast Asia) and **Mahayana Buddhism** (which dominates in China and the northeast of Asia). The most obvious difference to anyone visiting ancient Buddhist sites is that most Mahayana Buddhists usually believe in a pantheon of Buddhas and *bodhisattvas*, who are all worthy of veneration. For some Theravada Buddhists, this is too close to Hindu-style idol worship. Both Tibetan and Zen Buddhism, the two forms of the religion best known in the West, belong to the Mahayana branch of Buddhism. Most branches of Buddhism reject the concept of a deity.

By the end of the 1st millennium AD, Buddhism was dying out in the land of its birth. Many of its ideas were integrated into Hinduism, which had re-emerged in a number of different forms to become the dominant religion. The Buddha had been transformed into an avatar of the Hindu god Vishnu. The arrival of Islam dealt a death blow to a faith that was almost moribund. The great Buddhist university at Nalanda in Bihar did survive until the end of the 12th century AD, when it was sacked by Muslim forces of the Delhi sultan. Small pockets of Buddhism survived on the Ladakh plateau, in the Himalayas and in the northeast—but in the plains Buddhism had disappeared. Foreign Buddhists would occasionally come on a pilgrimage to the key sites of the life of the Buddha, but many of these had become ruins or disappeared entirely.

In the 19th century, the British began the systematic, but not always very careful, excavation of the major Buddhist sites. This led to a growth in interest in Buddhist history around the world, particularly from Buddhist countries, which began building rest-houses and modern stupas at ancient Buddhist locations. In the 1950s in India, the neo-Buddhist movement emerged under the leadership of the lawyer B.R. Ambedkar. He was a former Hindu 'Untouchable' and led his followers into the Buddhist faith, in the belief that it was the most egalitarian and least caste-conscious of religions. A little later, the first large influx of Tibetan Buddhist refugees arrived in India, bringing their distinctive brand of Buddhism to settlements in various parts of the country. From the 1960s there was also a growing interest in Buddhism among Western visitors, as well as an increasing number of Asian Buddhists who came on pilgrimage to visit key Buddhist sites across India. The Buddha is said to have been born, achieved enlightenment and died on the same day of the year, and it is commemorated as the festival of **Vesakha** or **Buddha Jayanti** (May/June) in many areas of India.

KEY CONCEPTS OF BUDDHISM

Mahayana Buddhism is the main form of Buddhism practised in China and East Asia. Mahayana literally means 'greater vehicle', in contrast to the Hinayana (or 'lesser vehicle'), which was the polemical name the Mahayana branch gave to other schools. The first references to Mahayana Buddhism date to about 1,000 years ago, and it became a major branch of the religion in India around the 5th century AD. Mahayana Buddhist art tends to reflect a belief in the importance of *bodhisattvas* as part of a Buddhist pantheon. Mahayana has undergone a series of further schisms, and such varied sects as **Zen**, **Tantric Buddhism**, **Pure Land Buddhism** and **Tibetan Buddhism** all belong to the Mahayana branch.

Theravada Buddhism is the main form of Buddhism practised in Sri Lanka and Southeast Asia. Theravada literally means the 'teaching of the elders'. It is the older and smaller of the two major branches of Buddhism, and appears to have emerged from an early schism (c. 250 BC) during the reign of Emperor Ashoka. Theravada puts greater emphasis on monasticism, and less of an emphasis on the *bodhisattvas* than Mahayana.

Bodhisattva means 'enlightened being' and refers to one of a series of followers of the Buddha who have achieved enlightenment and have an almost saint-like status among some branches of Buddhism. The word is also used to describe incarnations of the Buddha. Important *bodhisattvas* included Avalokiteshwara, Manjushri, Tara and Maitreya; their carved images are key motifs of Indian Buddhist art. Some Buddhists consider the present Dalai Lama to be a *bodhisattva*.

Avalokiteshwara is the best-known and probably the most popular of the Mahayana *bodhisattvas*. He is normally represented with either four or 1,000 arms, and symbolises compassion. His name means 'the Lord who looks down', and he is also known as Padmapani, the 'lotus bearer'.

Manjushri is the *bodhisattva* of wisdom, and one of the most important figures in the Mahayana Buddhist pantheon. He is normally shown carrying a sword and a sacred text.

Tara is the generic name for a group of female *bodhisattvas*, who form part of the Mahayana Buddhist pantheon. Most of the 'Taras' are described in terms of their colour: 'Green Tara' is associated with enlightened activity, for example, and 'Black Tara' is associated with power.

Maitreya is the *bodhisattva* of the future—a Buddhist near-equivalent of a Messiah. He will be the successor to the Buddha, will achieve complete enlightenment and teach the true path, or *dharma*. He is often depicted seated, with his hands crossed and wearing a crown. He is sometimes shown as part of a triad, alongside the Buddha and Avalokiteshwara. Unlike the other Mahayana *bodhisattvas*, Maitreya is also an important figure in Theravada Buddhism, though more as an aspect of the Buddha than as a different being.

JAINISM

Jainism and Buddhism emerged as important faiths in India at about the same time, in the middle of the 1st millennium BC. Both religions have no gods, have prominent founders and place a strong emphasis on personal consciousness and on asceticism. Jainism was always a minority religion, unlike Buddhism which played a dominant role for more than 1,000 years. But when Buddhism all but died out in India around the 13th century AD, Jainism survived and, in some places, thrived. Jain art and architecture have been a major influence on Indian art and architecture as a whole. The Jain temples at Ranakpur in Rajasthan and Shatrunjaya in Gujarat, and the colossal statue at Shravana Belagola in Karnataka are among India's most important and impressive monuments. Today, Jainism has more than 4,000,000 followers in India (less than 0.4 percent of the population). Many have proved very successful in business, and the community has an influence that outweighs its numerical importance.

Most accounts of Jainism begin with Mahavir (c. 549–477 BC), who was born into a princely family in what is now Bihar in northern India, but spent most of his adult life as a naked ascetic, meditating and preaching. According to Jain tradition, Mahavir was the 24th, and last, in a long line of *tirthankars*, or 'ford-makers'—the Jain equivalent of prophets. The *tirthankars* achieved perfect wisdom by breaking all bonds with the material world. Mahavir's immediate predecessor was Parusnath, who is thought to have lived in the 9th century BC, and the line of *tirthankars* goes back to Adinath, to whom the great Ranakpur Temple is dedicated. Many Jain temples contain almost identical white stone carvings of all the *tirthankars*.

Mahavir's message was one of self-liberation through meditation and the casting off of sensual pleasures. Jains believe in the sanctity of all forms of life and are vegetarians. Many devout Jains wear a face mask to stop themselves from swallowing flying insects. Jain monks and nuns take five vows: to commit themselves to non-violence; to tell the truth; to remain chaste; not to take anything that has not been properly given to them; and to avoid worldly attachments. They will sweep the floor with a fly-whisk or small broom when they walk to prevent themselves killing insects accidentally. Jain monks of the smaller **Digamber** (literally 'sky-clad') sect wear no clothes. The monks of the larger **Svetamber** ('white-clad') sect wear white clothes.

The birthday of Mahavir, known as **Mahavir Jayanti** (March/April), is widely celebrated by Jains.

SIKHISM

Sikhism is the religion founded by Guru Nanak (1469–1539), and whose male followers wear distinctive turbans and beards. The religion draws important elements from Hinduism (such as reincarnation) and Islam (monotheism and the central role played by a single holy book). There are ten Sikh gurus who played a major part in the development of the faith—which is today numerically the most important religion in the northern state of Punjab. The most important Sikh building is the Golden Temple in the holy city of Amritsar, but there are Sikh pilgrimage sites and *gurudwaras* (temples) in many parts of northern India and in Pakistan. Sikh means 'learner' or 'disciple'.

Guru Nanak taught that there was only one God, Waheguru, a transcendent deity who exists in everything—and therefore was very different from the human-like gods of Hinduism, the faith into which the first Sikh guru was born. Guru Nanak rejected social divisions based on caste (though these would re-emerge in later Sikhism), and also rejected the extreme asceticism of Jain monks. Under the first three gurus, Sikhism grew gradually in the Punjab, without major incident or controversy. The third guru, Ram Das, began constructing the pool at Amritsar and appointed his son Arjan as his successor; all future gurus would be descendants of Arjan. Under Guru Arjan, Sikhism began to expand more rapidly. The first version of Sikhism's holy book, the *Adi Granth* ('original book') was compiled, and the Mughal emperor Akbar discussed religion and politics with Guru Arjan. Amritsar was growing into an important settlement, and a temple was constructed in the centre of the pool built by Ram Das. To Akbar's less liberal successor, Jehangir, the Sikhs had become a threat. Jehangir accused Guru Arjan of supporting his rebel brother Khusrau, and imposed an enormous fine. Guru Arjan refused to pay, and was tortured and murdered by Mughal forces in 1606.

The martyrdom of the Guru Arjan brought about a fundamental transformation of Sikhism, which then became a martial religion. Guru Hargobind, Arjan's son and successor, began building the military strength of the Sikhs. By the second half of the 17th century—with the conservative and intolerant Emperor Aurangzeb on the Mughal throne, and the proselytising ninth guru Tegh Bahadur attempting to expand Sikhism beyond the Punjab—a major confrontation developed. Tegh Bahadur was arrested and told to perform a miracle to prove his nearness to God. When he failed to do this, he was ordered to convert to Islam. He refused and was beheaded on the road known as Chandni Chowk in Old Delhi. His successor, the tenth guru, Gobind Singh, created the **Khalsa**, the Sikh brotherhood, according to which all adult male Sikhs were to leave their hair uncut, to call themselves Singh ('lion') and to carry a sword. He also compiled the final version of the Sikh holy book, the *Granth Sahib*, and appointed the book rather than a relative or follower as his eternal successor, the 11th guru.

At the end of the 18th century, a new Sikh leader emerged, Ranjit Singh. He led what became known as the **Sikh Empire**, which by 1820 included all of the Punjab and

DULEEP SINGH

Duleep Singh (1838–93) was the last Sikh maharaja of the Punjab. He was deposed when just 11 years old, and was later sent to London to meet Queen Victoria, who received the Kohinoor diamond as a 'gift' from him. Duleep Singh settled down in Britain, living the life of a country gentleman and becoming famous for his shooting parties; he was known as the Black Prince of Perthshire. Late in life, he turned against the British and tried to encourage the Russian tsar to invade India and restore the Sikh Empire. He died in Paris. Two of his daughters, princesses Catherine and Sophia, became prominent suffragettes.

the Kashmir valley. The British, who had encouraged Ranjit Singh, eventually turned against his successors, and his youngest son, Duleep Singh, was deposed in 1849 after a series of battles known as the Anglo-Sikh wars.

The Partition of India at independence from Britain in 1947 meant the division of the Punjab, the Sikhs' historical homeland. Large numbers of Sikhs were among the hundreds of thousands of victims of Partition violence, and almost no Sikhs remained in the Pakistan region of the Punjab, cutting off the Sikh community from several of their most important shrines. In the 1980s, a Sikh separatist movement emerged in the Indian Punjab, and the government of Prime Minister Indira Gandhi ordered the army into the Golden Temple complex, where Sikh militants had taken sanctuary. A few months later, Mrs Gandhi was shot dead by two of her Sikh bodyguards. By the mid-90s, the separatist movement had lost strength, and today Punjab state is peaceful and safe for visitors. In 2004, Dr Manmohan Singh became India's first Sikh prime minister.

Among the key Sikh festivals are **Guru Nanak's birthday** (November) and **Baisakhi** (April), which marks the foundation of the Khalsa in 1699.

ISLAM

The impact of Islam on Indian society and culture has been enormous. From the late 12th to the mid-19th centuries, a series of Muslim dynasties ruled much of north India, and often extended their empires well beyond the north. The influence of the Mughals is world famous, with the Taj Mahal and Humayun's Tomb among their most impressive memorials. However, the earlier Sultanate period of Muslim rule has left its own deep aesthetic mark on Indian architecture. The Qutb Minar in Delhi is the most renowned example from this time; but the less well-known medieval mosques and tombs of Kashmir, Bengal, Jaunpur, Gujarat and the Deccan all bear witness to how Islamic styles were integrated, in so many different ways, with local architectural and artistic traditions. At the time of independence in 1947, Pakistan (including the area of East Pakistan which is now Bangladesh) was created as a homeland for South Asia's Muslims, but many Muslims decided to stay in India; they currently form about 14 percent of the population, easily the largest minority group. There is one Muslim-majority state, Jammu and Kashmir, while significant Muslim minorities are present in all the major states of India.

Islam is the monotheistic religion founded by the Prophet Muhammad in the early 7th century. It draws on Jewish and Christian traditions, and the three religions have many prophets in common. Abraham and Moses, Jesus and Mary are all important figures in Islam's holy book, the Koran. The first authenticated Muslim incursion into the subcontinent was in the 8th century, when Arab forces reached the southern part of what is now Pakistan. However, according to oral tradition in Kerala, a local king, Cheruman Perumal, was the first Indian to convert to Islam, while the Prophet Muhammad was still living. He is said to have travelled to Mecca, and died as he was returning home. His companions are believed to have built the first mosque in India, at Cranganore in Kerala.

The first major Muslim raids on the Indian heartland were by the forces of Mahmud of Ghazni, in modern-day Afghanistan, in the early 11th century. The Ghaznavid attacks were almost annual affairs, with large raiding parties plundering the fabled wealth of India. Many temples were sacked, including, in 1026, the great Shiva temple at Somnath. The raid reached as far west as Bahraich, in what is now central Uttar Pradesh. Mahmud's son-in-law, Salar Masud, died in battle just north of Bahraich in 1033. His tomb is probably the oldest authenticated Muslim grave in India and is an important pilgrimage site, though the oldest buildings at the site belong to the later Tughlaq period. The earliest invaders did not make serious attempts to convert non-Muslims to Islam or to build permanent settlements. Ghaznavid accounts of the invasions describe the killings of huge numbers of infidels and Muslim heretics in a way that is formulaic and repetitive, suggesting that much of it may have been invented. The Ghaznavids seem to have run something closer to a protection racket, and allowed existing non-Muslim rulers to remain in power, so long as they paid a sufficient tribute.

Muslim rule in India can be dated from 1192, when the army of Muhammad of Ghor captured Delhi from Prithviraj Chauhan. Like the Ghaznavids, the Ghorids were also from modern-day Afghanistan, and Muhammad of Ghor left behind several of his Turkic-origin generals, who had once been his slaves, or Mamluks, and so the Slave or Mamluk Dynasty was born. They built the Qutb Minar and, next to it, what is probably the oldest surviving mosque in India (though some historians make that claim for a ruined mosque at Bhadreshwar in Gujarat). The earliest Muslims are all thought to have belonged to the majority Sunni sect of Islam, and were keen not to dilute their mainly Turkic leadership group by allowing conversions from other religions. The most important task of the new rulers was to remit funds back to Muhammad of Ghor, but when he died the most senior general, Qutbuddin Aibak, became sultan of Delhi—a move that signalled his independence from the Ghorid leaders in Afghanistan. Early Sultanate coins show Hindu gods, and the Sanskrit-derived Devanagari script—an indication that they were not attempting to turn India into an Islamic country. They did destroy temples, but, as some historians have pointed out, new Hindu rulers would often do the same with the temples of their defeated Hindu rivals.

Many early Indian Muslims were, in fact, converted by itinerant Sufi mystics—Muslim preachers whose relationship with mainstream Islam was often somewhat detached. This gave Islam in India a distinctly unorthodox flavour, and encouraged the mingling of religious and cultural traditions. The first of the great Indian Sufis was Moinuddin Chishti, born in modern-day Afghanistan, and founder of the **Chishti order of Sufis**. His shrine in Ajmer in Rajasthan is the most important Muslim pilgrimage site in India. Chishti preached a tolerant, mystical, anti-materialist form of Islam which would have not seemed very foreign to many Indians. He and his successors won many converts; they also had many other followers who did not convert to Islam but nevertheless continued to visit Sufi shrines and pay reverence to the Sufi saints, almost as if they were Hindu gods. Islam was also attractive to some Hindus who were consigned to a lower social position by the caste system, and in the most extreme case, in Kashmir, almost all non-Brahmins converted to Islam.

DEOBAND & BAREILLY

Two distinct schools of thought emerged among South Asian Sunni Muslims, named after the towns in northern India in which they first emerged. The Deobandis, from Deoband, are more austere and conservative, while the Barelvis, from Bareilly, are more liberal, closer to Sufism, and believe in the importance of Muslim saints, or *pirs*, as objects of devotion and as a means of getting closer to God. Barelvis see the Prophet Muhammad as semi-divine, an 'omnipresent light', and their mosques and tombs tend to be more ornate than those of Deobandis.

His successor as head of the Chishti order was Qutbuddin Bakhtiyar, whose shrine is near the Qutb Minar in south Delhi. Several other Sufi mystics from the order left their mark on Sultanate Delhi, and sometimes clashed with the sultan. There was a great influx of Muslim scholars and preachers in the 13th and 14th centuries. They came partly because they were fleeing the Mongols who had invaded several other Muslim lands and partly because the court in Delhi, and a series of provincial sultanates, welcomed them. India also attracted Muslims from the countries to the west; they came to India to seek their fortunes, or to develop a successful military or political career. In many ways this pattern would be echoed in the 18th and 19th centuries with European migration to India.

Under the Mughals, Islam took a variety of distinctive forms—most famously a period of tolerance and religious dialogues under Akbar, and of intolerance and conservatism under Aurangzeb. Akbar came under a number of influences, including Sufism and Shia Islam, as well as non-Muslim traditions. Early in his adult life, Akbar married a Hindu Rajput wife, celebrated Hindu festivals and lifted discriminatory taxes against Hindus. But Akbar also went much further than mere tolerance: he was fascinated by religion, and presided over a series of discussions and debates between members of different faiths in his new city of Fatehpur Sikri—built alongside a Sufi shrine of the Chishti order. The participants included Sunni, Shia and Ismaili Muslims, Jain monks, Christian priests, and a very wide range of Hindus, including Vaishnavites, Shaivites, and numerous ascetics, mendicants and living saints. Akbar promulgated his own religion, **Din Ilahi**, usually translated as the 'divine faith', but more literally the 'religion of God', a synthesis of Islam and Hinduism, and with some borrowings from Christianity, Jainism and Zoroastrianism. It never attracted much of a following, but it represented a genuine attempt to find common ground between religions, as well as to boost Akbar's own temporal and spiritual status as the founder of a faith. In his religion, Akbar was presented as the Insaan-i Kamil (the 'perfect man').

Some orthodox Muslims found Akbar's attitude towards Islam deeply troubling. A religious *fatwa* was issued, calling on all Muslims to rebel and support the claims to the throne of Akbar's half-brother Hakim. But Akbar's position was strong: he had the support of most of the Hindu princes, and the rebellion petered out. Akbar's immediate successors, Jehangir and Shah Jahan, tended to be a little more orthodox in public—though privately Jehangir sought advice from a Hindu hermit, and happily ate pork and drank wine during Ramadan.

Aurangzeb made a serious attempt to reunite the different strands of Islam that had developed in South Asia under a more conservative, traditional banner, and led the fight against what he saw as heresy and Hindu idolatry. The attempt was ultimately a failure, and many suffered along the way, including Aurangzeb's older brother Dara Shikoh, a religious scholar and builder of the Pari Mahal in Kashmir. He argued that 'the essential nature of Hinduism is identical with that of Islam', and was murdered on the orders of his brother. So was Tegh Bahadur, the ninth Sikh guru. Some well-known Hindu temples were destroyed, punitive taxes on Hindus were reintroduced, alcohol and opium were outlawed, and the imperial court no longer employed singers and dancers. However, in the 18th century, Islam became even more diffuse, with the emergence of several powerful Muslim kingdoms, often led by Shia descendants of Persian fortune seekers. The Shia rulers had a number of practices that set them apart from the Sunni majority: for instance Muharram, the period of mourning for the Prophet's grandsons, was marked as a major religious occasion, with processions through the streets and the construction of special buildings known as *imambaras*. The Shia rulers took extravagance and ostentation to a new level, but their courts were also centres of Islamic learning, attracting poets, scholars, calligraphers and Shia theologians from other parts of the Muslim world.

During the Uprising of 1857, there was an attempt by some Muslims to convert what began as a mutiny into a religious war—with the last Mughal emperor, Bahadur Shah Zafar, as the leader of a *jihad* against the British. But many Muslims also supported the British, and others were keen to ally with Hindus against the colonial powers. In the years after the Uprising, new divisions emerged among Muslims: some, such as Sir Syed Ahmed Khan, who founded what became the Aligarh Muslim University, saw themselves as modernisers; while others preached a return to more conservative Muslim values.

By the 20th century, there was growing concern among some Muslims about Hindu assertiveness, and this contributed to the emergence of Muslim separatism, which eventually culminated in the creation of Pakistan. Many Muslims fled India at Partition, but huge numbers also remained behind and India still maintains one state with a Muslim majority, Jammu and Kashmir. The separatist movement that emerged there in the late 1980s was largely secular, but gradually took on a more anti-Hindu and orthodox Muslim form. Many Hindus were forced out of the Kashmir valley, and conservative Muslim groups have attempted to close down cinemas and alcohol shops, and to force women to cover their heads.

India's powerful Hindu nationalist parties tend to be very suspicious of Muslims—some of whom they accuse of being secret supporters of Pakistan. Muslims have suffered disproportionately in the religious rioting that has erupted sporadically in different parts of the country. While a few Indian Muslims have responded with violence, this has been very much the exception, and the culture of Islam in India remains largely tolerant, if sometimes very conservative on social and gender issues.

JESUS IN ISLAM

Jesus, or Isa, is the second to last of the Muslim prophets, before Muhammad, and, according to the Koran, he was not killed or crucified, but raised to heaven by God. He is often referred to as Ibn Maryam, or son of Mary. Mary, as in the New Testament, is a virgin when she gives birth to Jesus, but the setting is quite different—under a palm tree, rather than in a manger.

KEY CONCEPTS OF ISLAM IN INDIA

Sunni Islam is the majority sect of Islam, to which most Indian Muslims belong. The split with **Shia Islam**, the largest minority sect, dates back to the years following the death of the Prophet Muhammad. The dispute, essentially over who should succeed the Prophet, led to open warfare and the **Battle of Karbala** in AD 680, at which the Prophet's grandson Hussain was killed. Shias consider the Prophet's son-in-law, Ali, and his grandsons Hussain and Hassan to be his true successors, or *imams*, rather than the Sunni caliph who was victorious at Karbala. Shias and Sunnis follow identical versions of the Muslim holy book, the Koran or Qur'an.

There are several other smaller sects of Islam with a significant following in India. The **Ismailis** are a branch of Shi'ism which follows a different order of *imams* as successors to the Prophet Muhammad. According to Ismailis, there were just seven *imams*, of whom Ismail ibn Jafar was the last. The main branch of Shi'ism believes there were 12 *imams*. The largest branch of the Ismailis are followers of the Aga Khan, while another smaller group are the **Bohras**, who are concentrated in Gujarat and Mumbai. The **Ahmadis** or **Qadianis** are a sect which calls itself Muslim, but does not believe that Muhammed was the final prophet of Islam. Instead, they say the 19th-century religious leader Mirza Ghulam Ahmed, based in Qadian in the Indian Punjab, was the last of the prophets. Ahmadis believe Jesus, or Isa, did not die on the cross, but escaped to Kashmir where he preached and was buried in a tomb in the heart of old Srinagar.

Sufism is a way of practising Islam that cuts across the traditional sectarian boundaries, though most of its followers are Sunni. It has strong mystical elements, and helps and encourages its followers to attain a spiritual closeness to God. There are several Sufi orders—the Chishti order, founded by the 13th-century Sufi Moinuddin Chishti, is the most important in South Asia.

The Five Pillars of Islam are accepted by most sects of Islam, though sometimes in slightly different forms and with some additional pillars. The Five Pillars are as follows:

1 The *shahadah* is the creed of Islam in which believers testify that 'there is no God but God, and Muhammad is the messenger of God'. Some Shia Muslims add the phrase 'and Ali is beloved of God'.

2 *Salah*, or prayer, is performed facing towards Mecca, which is why all South Asian mosques are aligned to the west. Traditionally, Muslims pray five times a day.
3 *Zakah* is the practice of charitable giving.
4 *Sawm* (fasting) is practised during daylight hours during the holy month of Ramadan.
5 *Hajj* is the pilgrimage to the holy city of Mecca in Saudi Arabia.

Masjid is the Arabic and Urdu word for a mosque, literally meaning 'place of prostration', and is commonly used in Indian English. A Jama Masjid, or Friday Mosque, is usually the main mosque in a particular area, where a large congregation gathers on a Friday, the Muslim weekly holiday, and will listen to an *imam*, *maulana* or *maulvi* preaching a sermon.

Islamic prophets: in Islam, Muhammad is the last (or 'seal') of the prophets, most of whom are immediately recognisable to those brought up in the Jewish or Christian traditions—and are all venerated in Islam. For instance, Musa is Moses, Ibrahim is Abraham, Daud is David and Isa is Jesus.

MUSLIM FESTIVALS & COMMEMORATIONS

Muharram is a month in the Islamic calendar, particularly associated with Shia ceremonies marking the anniversary of the death of the Prophet Muhammad's grandson Hussain at Karbala. For Shias it is a period of mourning, and in some places devotees flagellate themselves during public processions as part of the remembrance of the death of Hussain.

Ramadan is the name of the month in the Islamic calendar when Muslims fast between dawn and dusk. It is often referred to as Ramazan in the subcontinent.

Eid or **Id** (pronounced 'eed') means festival—and refers to either of two important religious festivals in the Islamic calendar. **Eid ul-Fitr** ('festival of the breaking of the fast') takes place at the end of Ramadan, and lasts three days. The Islamic calendar is based on the phases of the moon, and Eid ul-Fitr is celebrated when the new moon is spotted that marks the beginning of a new month. **Eid ul-Adha** ('festival of the sacrifice') is better known as **Bakri Eid** ('goat festival') in South Asia. Large numbers of goats are sacrificed on Eid ul-Adha, which commemorates the day on which the prophet Ibrahim (the Judeo-Christian Abraham) nearly killed his eldest son, Ismail (Ishmael), for whom God substituted a goat at the last minute. In Jewish and Christian tradition the would-be sacrificial victim was Abraham's second son, Isaac. In Muslim tradition, all Arabs, and therefore the Prophet Muhammad, were descendants of Ismail.

CHRISTIANITY IN INDIA

Christians form India's third largest religious group, after Hindus and Muslims, and number about 25 million. Christians live in almost every part of the country, but the biggest populations are in the southern states of Kerala, Tamil Nadu and Goa. They are the majority group in three small northeastern states: Meghalaya, Nagaland and Mizoram; and there are many Christians in India's central tribal belt.

There are very few sources for the early history of Christianity in India, which therefore relies largely on local oral tradition. There were certainly Christian communities in south India in the first few centuries after the death of Christ, and most Indian Christians date the arrival of their faith in India to as early as AD 52. On that date, according to local tradition, the apostle Thomas made landfall at Kodungallur (formerly known as Cranganore) in modern-day Kerala, and then lived and preached the gospel at Mylapore, not far from Chennai (formerly Madras). He was then said to have been murdered by priests, presumably Hindus, in AD 72. Many Kerala Christians continue to identify themselves as **St Thomas Christians** or **Nasranis** (probably derived from Nazarenes, meaning from Nazareth). Other Christian traditions also speak of Thomas travelling to and living in north India, and of another apostle, Bartholomew, visiting India. More obscure and unauthenticated traditions have Jesus surviving the crucifixion and eventually moving to, and dying in, Kashmir.

By the 6th century AD, **Syrian Christians** from the Middle East were travelling regularly to Kerala as missionaries and traders, and their South Asian brethren adopted Syriac as the liturgical language, which is still in use by Syrian Orthodox congregations in Kerala.

The next major impetus to the growth of Christianity was the arrival of the Portuguese in 1498, though the French missionary Jordanus had lived and preached in India more than 150 years earlier. The Portuguese encouraged Christian missionary activity, and in particular the mass conversions carried out by St Francis Xavier in Goa and various other places along the coast of western India.

ST FRANCIS OF GOA

Francis Xavier (1506–52) was a Jesuit missionary who in ten years travelled to India, Sri Lanka, Indonesia, the Philippines, China and Japan. He is regarded as having converted more people to Christianity than anyone except St Paul. He is reputed to have performed miracles wherever he went: raising the dead, turning salt water fresh, speaking in tongues, floating on air and restoring withered limbs. Goa was Francis Xavier's base—and his mummified body can be seen in the Bom Jesus Basilica in Old Goa.

The Portuguese also introduced the Latin Rite and converted some of the early Kerala Christians to Roman Catholicism. The Inquisition was introduced in 1560, originally as a means of countering heresy, but soon becoming a tool of forced conversion—thousands of people were brought to trial, and several dozen executed.

The first Protestant missionary is thought to have been a German, Bartholomäus Ziegenbalg, who arrived in 1708 in the Danish enclave of Tranquebar, in modern-day Tamil Nadu. There he established a printing press and translated the New Testament into Tamil. At the end of the 18th century another Danish enclave, Serampore in Bengal, became the home of the most famous of the missionaries, the British Baptist William Carey—and he was followed by many more missionaries from a variety of Protestant denominations. American Baptists were particularly successful in gaining converts to Christianity in the northeast, while in many other parts of the country missionaries became key providers of education and health services. Most converts were drawn from tribal people and former Untouchables, now known as Dalits.

Foreign and local Christians still play an important role in health care and education, and, until her death in 1997, Mother Teresa—an ethnic Albanian nun born in the former Yugoslav republic of Macedonia—was the world's most famous missionary. She founded the Missionaries of Charity in Kolkata in 1950, best known for providing refuge and care for the dying. Many Hindu nationalists are opposed to Christian missionaries, whom they accuse of 'forcibly converting' Hindus; disputes over missionary activities have led to conflict in several states, including Gujarat and Orissa.

JUDAISM IN INDIA

There are only a few thousand Jews living in modern India, but there are several distinct communities that claim Jewish heritage in different parts of the country. Best known are the **Cochin Jews**, who now number less than 50. The fine synagogue in Old Cochin is a reminder of what was once a vibrant community of several thousand, divided into Black Jews and White Jews, depending largely on the colour of their skin. Both groups claimed to have been the first Jews in India, and would usually date their arrival to AD 72, two years after the Roman destruction of the Second Temple in Jerusalem (though some date their arrival to the time of King Solomon, possibly a whole millennium earlier). The earliest definite reference to the Jews of Cochin is from the 10th century AD.

The largest Jewish community in India are the **Bene Israel** ('Sons of Israel'), who are thought to number about 4,000. They are Marathi-speakers and have lived for many centuries in western India, near Mumbai. According to Bene Israeli tradition, they are all descended from seven men and seven women shipwrecked off the western coast of India. Cut off from other Jews, they became assimilated with the rest of the local population, retaining only a few traditions such as the Jewish Sabbath and circumcision. From the mid-18th century onwards, they came back into contact with other Jewish communities and adopted mainstream Jewish traditions and rituals.

The most recent Jewish migrants to India were the Arabic-speaking Baghdadi Jews, who came not only from Iraq but also from other parts of the Middle East, mainly as traders and businessmen. Most of them settled in Mumbai and Kolkata in the 19th century, and many were very successful in business—they built several fine synagogues that are little used today. The best known of the Baghdadi Jewish families are the Sassoons, after whom a library, a school and the main fishing docks in Mumbai are named. Most Baghdadi Jewish families have now left India.

THE BAGHDADI JEWISH SASSOONS

The founder of the Sassoon business dynasty was David Sassoon of Baghdad, who moved to Mumbai in 1832, creating a trading empire that became a major force in India, China, Southeast Asia and Britain. Although he did not speak English, he became a British citizen, and was buried in the graveyard of the synagogue in Pune. His grandson married a Rothschild and became a British MP; and one of his great-grandsons was the poet Siegfried Sassoon (*see also p. 474*).

There are two other communities that claim to be descendants of the Lost Tribes of Israel, dispersed, according to the Bible, after the destruction of the northern kingdom of Israel in the 8th century BC. The **Mizo Jews**, or **Bnei Manashe**, are a community of about 5,000 people living in the states of Mizoram and Manipur, close to the Burmese border. They claim to be members of the Lost Tribe of Manesseh, but retained very few, if any, Jewish traditions until they were 'rediscovered' in the 1970s. More than 1,000 Mizo Jews have migrated to Israel. The **Telugu Jews**, or **Bene Ephraim** ('sons of Ephraim'), are an even smaller group, who rediscovered their Jewish roots in the 1980s. They live near Guntur in the southern state of Andhra Pradesh, and have not been granted the level of recognition as Jews that Israel has accorded to the Mizos.

Tens of thousands of young Israelis come as tourists to India every year, often after completing military service. In some places—particularly Dharamsala and Manali in the northern state of Himachal Pradesh—there are so many Israelis that shop signs and menus are written in Hebrew, and there is a small makeshift synagogue on the outskirts of Dharamsala.

ZOROASTRIANISM IN INDIA

India has about 70,000 Zoroastrians, known as **Parsis**, as descendants of migrants from Persia (or Pars); most of them live in Mumbai. The Parsi community, though only a tiny percentage of the Indian population, is very affluent and influential.

The Parsis are followers of the Prophet Zarathustra (or Zoroaster), who is thought to have lived in Central Asia at some point between 1100 and 600 BC. The religion is monotheistic, with Ahura Mazda as the one God. Zoroastrian theology is complex, and most Parsis will tell you, more simply, that their religion preaches 'good thoughts, good words, good deeds'. Parsis are sometimes incorrectly portrayed as fire-worshippers, partly because their shrines, or agiaries, are known as fire-temples in English. The most important agiaries have permanently burning fires, before which Parsis pray—but they are worshipping God, not the fire. The religion is non-congregational, and priests do not deliver sermons in agiaries, but preside over key rituals such as the *navjote*, the coming-of-age ceremony, or at marriages and funerals. The liturgical language of Zoroastrianism is Avestan, which is no longer spoken—and most Parsis have either Gujarati or English as their mother tongue. Parsis are expected to marry within the community. There are major divisions within the community about whether Parsis who 'marry out', and their children, can still be Parsis. Orthodox Parsis wear a string around their waist, known as a *kusti*, and a cotton vest, known as a *sudrah*.

Parsis consider the elements earth, fire and water to be sacred, and not to be defiled by dead bodies. Therefore, traditionally, the corpses of Parsis are left in the open, in huge cylindrical buildings known as **Towers of Silence**, such as the one on Malabar Hill in Mumbai, where they can decay gradually and be picked clean by vultures. However, many Parsis now opt for cremation, and the scarcity of vultures has led to gruesome tales of rotting bodies inside the Towers of Silence.

PARSIS & VULTURES

The South Asian vulture population has become almost extinct in recent years. The cause is the widespread use of the drug Diclofenac on cattle, which results in renal failure in vultures that eat cattle flesh. A photograph smuggled out of a Tower of Silence showed piles of partially decomposed bodies and no vultures. Solar reflectors have been placed on the Towers of Silence to accelerate the speed of decomposition, and there are plans to construct a vulture aviary especially for the Parsi community.

HISTORY OF PARSI ZOROASTRIANS

The first of several waves of Zoroastrian migrants from Persia are thought to have arrived in India more than 1,000 years ago, fleeing religious persecution in their homeland. Until the 7th century AD, Zoroastrianism was the state religion of the Persian Sassanid Empire, but the arrival of Islam and end of the Sassanid Dynasty almost obliterated Zoroastrianism. The migrants became known as Parsis, literally 'from Pars', the province that also gave Persia its name. They settled in Gujarat and were allowed by the local Hindu rulers to keep their faith, so long as they agreed not to encourage non-Zoroastrians to convert. They adopted local dress and language, though their cuisine remains distinctive, with its extensive use of eggs and a large variety of lentils.

The earliest Parsi documents are a series of requests for advice on religious matters sent to Persian Zoroastrians between the 13th and 16th centuries. In the 17th century, educated Parsis began to move to the larger towns, Surat and then Mumbai, and became key figures in the banking and shipbuilding industries. The British openly favoured the Parsis, believing them to be more hard-working and honest than other Indians. The small Parsi community in Mumbai prospered, more Parsi migrants came from the countryside and a new wave of Zoroastrian migration from Persia got underway. The newcomers, who are still known as **Iranis**—and who often have Irani as a surname, are well-known for their restaurants in Mumbai. Many Parsis in Mumbai live in large Parsi-only housing estates, known as *baugs*.

Several of India's largest and best-known business houses are owned by Parsi families, such as the Tatas, the Wadias and the Godrejs. Famous Parsis include the novelist Rohinton Mistry, the rock star Freddie Mercury, the conductor Zubin Mehta, India's first field marshal, Sam Maneckshaw, and Indira Gandhi's husband, Feroze Gandhi.

BAHA'IS IN INDIA

The Baha'i faith is thought to be India's fastest growing religion, with more than two million adherents. The Baha'i Mandir, or Lotus Temple, in Delhi has become a major visitor attraction, and probably India's best-known modern building.

The Baha'i faith was founded in Persia in 1863 by Baha'ullah, a follower of a Persian mystic called the Bab ('gateway'), who was executed for apostasy by the Tehran government in 1850. Baha'ullah declared himself to be the Promised One, or Messiah of all religions. The core principles of the Baha'i faith are normally summarised as the unity of God, religion and mankind. The first Baha'i teacher came to India in the 1870s and gained its first converts. It remained a largely urban religion until the 1950s, when large numbers of rural, usually low-caste Hindus in central India converted to the faith. By the time the Lotus Temple in Delhi was inaugurated in 1986, India had become the country with the largest population of Baha'is in the world.

DELHI

In geographical terms, Delhi (*map 2 C3*) is the triangular area sandwiched between the River Yamuna and a rocky escarpment known as the Ridge—though the modern city spills far beyond these limits. Delhi occupies an important strategic position on the broad and fertile Gangetic plain separating the Himalayas from the deserts of Rajasthan. Historically, Delhi is one of the world's great cities, containing an astonishing array of forts, tombs, mosques and government buildings constructed over the last 1,000 years. The Indian capital has also become a brashly intimidating modern megacity, with over 15 million inhabitants. Ancient monuments that just 50 years ago were surrounded by jungle or farmland have been enveloped by urban sprawl—and some are occupied by squatters or dwarfed by modern developments.

Over the last millennium, Delhi has been sacked and rebuilt, deserted and resettled several times, and its many rulers constructed a series of overlapping cities in the area now occupied by the Indian capital. Tourist literature traditionally talks of the seven cities of Delhi, but historians have made the case for several more. Its centre of gravity has changed markedly over the centuries, as if it were a city on wheels. Its earliest buildings are in the south of modern Delhi. The city then crept slowly northwards into what is now known as Old Delhi. The course of the Yamuna has changed over the centuries, and for that reason several buildings that were built on its western bank, such as the Red Fort, the Purana Qila and Humayun's Tomb, are now several hundred metres away from the river. In British times, the centre of gravity began moving steadily southwards again, with the construction of New Delhi in the first half of the 20th century.

For all these reasons, Delhi can, at times, feel overwhelming in its historical and architectural complexity. In Mehrauli, for instance—the area around Delhi's most distinctive and most visited monument, the Qutb Minar—one can find historically or architecturally important buildings from each of the last ten centuries. And among the monuments for which this city is famous are no less than three entirely separate UNESCO World Heritage Sites—the early Sultanate Qutb Minar, Humayun's Tomb from the early Mughal period and the later Mughal Red Fort—as well as dozens more major ruins and monuments. Delhi is also a cornucopia of minor ruins—an official guide lists more than 1,000 of them—that can be a source of delight and wonder to anyone who casually wanders or drives through its streets.

HISTORY OF DELHI

Delhi's history divides naturally into five major historical periods, several of which have further subdivisions.

Pre-Islamic period (before AD 1192)

The earliest historical sites in Delhi date back to the lower Palaeolithic period, and Stone Age tools have been found which are now in the National Museum. There is also archaeological evidence, mainly in the form of excavated pottery fragments, indicating that parts of modern Delhi were settled in the late Harappan period. The earliest extant built structures are the pre-Islamic fortifications and other minor ruins in the south of Delhi, built when this area was ruled by the Hindu Tomar and Chauhan dynasties. The Tomar Dynasty is believed to have built the original walls of the citadel of Lal Kot in Mehrauli; and Prithviraj Chauhan, the last Hindu king of Delhi—and hero of the north Indian epic poem the *Prithviraj Raso*—extended the citadel. The city's period of great architectural creativity began with the capture of Delhi by the army of Muhammad of Ghor (in modern-day Afghanistan) in 1192. He appointed one of his officers, Qutbuddin Aibak, as the new ruler of Delhi. For the next 665 years, Delhi was run by a series of Muslim dynasties.

Sultanate period (1192–1526)

Most of the great buildings of South Delhi were constructed during the Sultanate period, which is normally subdivided according to the ruling dynasties.

Slave Dynasty (1192–1290): Delhi in this period was ruled by a series of sultans selected from a small group of Afghan families left behind in India by Muhammad of Ghor's army (*see p. 20*). The first two rulers, Qutbuddin Aibak and Iltutmish, had been Muhammad of Ghor's slaves as well as high-ranking army officers, and their origins gave their name to the dynasty (they are also known as Mamluks, from the Arabic word for slave). Qutbuddin Aibak occupied the pre-Islamic citadel at Lal Kot and began to build his own city in the area now known as Mehrauli (*see p. 85*).

This period saw the first flowering of Islamic architecture in India, and the building of Delhi's most distinctive monument, the Qutb Minar. Other buildings from this period include several built close to the Qutb Minar. Also of the period but further afield are Delhi's oldest Muslim mausoleum, the tomb of Sultan Garhi, and the tomb of Sultan Razia, Delhi's only female sultan.

Khilji Dynasty (1290–1320): The last sultan of the Slave Dynasty was overthrown by an Afghan nobleman, Jalaluddin Khilji, in 1290. The Khiljis were riven by internal divisions and only ruled Delhi for 30 eventful years. In 1296, Jalaladdin was murdered by his nephew Alauddin Khilji, who built a new citadel on an army camping ground outside the old city. The new city, some of the walls of which still stand, was called Siri. These walls were strong enough to save Delhi from a Mongol invasion in 1303. After the death of Alauddin Khilji in 1316, there were four years of bloody infighting between members of the Khilji family, until one of Alauddin's former officers, Ghiyasuddin Tughlaq, intervened in 1320.

Tughlaq Dynasty (1320–1414): We know more about the Tughlaq period of Delhi's history than any other pre-Mughal dynasties, partly because the Arab traveller Ibn Battuta left a remarkable account of life at the court of Muhammad bin Tughlaq in the 1330s. The Tughlaqs were great builders and movers, and constructed three of Delhi's traditional seven cities, as well as mosques, hunting lodges and *madrasas*, which can be found in many parts of modern Delhi.

Ghiyasuddin, the first Tughlaq ruler, constructed the enormous fortress of Tughlaqabad, whose towering walls still stand in South Delhi. His son and successor, Muhammad bin Tughlaq, was famously capricious—a ruler who could be very generous and outrageously cruel. Muhammad bin Tughlaq moved the capital 5km away to Jahanpanah. Furious about a perceived insult from some of Delhi's residents, he abandoned the city in 1327. As many as half a million inhabitants were said to have been sent away to a new capital, Daulatabad, several hundred kilometres to the south. According to Ibn Battuta, only two people remained in Delhi: a cripple and a blind man. The sultan ordered the cripple to be thrown out of the city from a giant catapult, while the blind man was to be dragged out of the city. Ibn Battuta tells how 'he fell to pieces on the road, and all of him that reached Daulatabad was his leg'. The sultan ordered everyone back to Delhi a few years later.

He was succeeded as sultan of Delhi by his cousin Feroze Shah Tughlaq, who was responsible for the construction of a fortress and other buildings at the site now known as Feroze Shah Kotla, 10km north of Jahanpanah, though it seems likely that Jahanpanah still served as his capital. Feroze Shah also built a number of hunting lodges and mosques—and moved two of Ashoka's pillars to Delhi from elsewhere in north India. Feroze Shah was arguably Delhi's first conservationist, restoring many old buildings and tombs. The political situation deteriorated after Feroze Shah's death in 1388, and ten years later the invading army of the Mongol leader Timur (better known in the West as Tamerlane) met little resistance as it captured and despoiled the city. Timur's army soon left; but his descendants would return 128 years later. They would become known as the Mughals, though they continued to describe themselves as Timurids, or descendants of Timur.

Sayyid Dynasty (1414–51): The Sayyids are Delhi's forgotten dynasty, and have left behind no important buildings in the city, apart from a couple of tombs. Contemporary sources indicate that they built a new city in the area now occupied by New Friends Colony.

Lodi Dynasty (1451–1526): The Lodi Dynasty moved their capital from Delhi to Agra; and Delhi declined in importance in this period. However, Delhi remained an important city, and the Lodis used parts of South Delhi as a kind of necropolis, and left behind dozens of beautiful tombs and mosques.

Mughal Period 1526–1857

The Mughal emperors were responsible for a large number of important buildings in Delhi, including Humayun's Tomb and the Red Fort Complex. In 1526, the first

Mughal emperor, Babur, invaded northern India, defeating the Lodis. He installed himself in Agra—which he disliked, complaining about the lack of gardens and the hot Indian summers.

Humayun (1530–56): Humayun began and ended his reign as Mughal emperor in Delhi. But for many years in the middle of his reign he was in exile, replaced as ruler of Delhi by a nobleman of Afghan origin called Sher Shah Suri. Humayun began building the citadel now known as the Purana Qila, or Old Fort, but it was completed by Sher Shah. Humayun returned in 1555 and died a year later, falling down the steps of his library in the Purana Qila. He would later be immortalised in Delhi's most gracious and architecturally important building, Humayun's Tomb.

Akbar (1556–1606): Akbar the Great used Agra as his capital rather than Delhi, and then decided to build a new capital at Fatehpur Sikri. For these reasons, apart from Humayun's Tomb, there are few other major monuments in Delhi that date from Akbar's long reign as Mughal emperor. His son and successor, **Jehangir (1605–28)**, rarely visited Delhi, and there are no major buildings remaining from his reign in the city.

Shah Jahan (1628–58): Shah Jahan restored Delhi as the leading city of north India by laying out and building a huge new capital, Shahjahanabad, to the north of the former Sultanate citadels. Shahjahanabad is now known as Old Delhi, and has been continuously occupied since the middle of the 17th century. The Red Fort, the Jama Masjid and several other buildings survive from the earliest period, and the street plan is essentially the same as that laid out by Shah Jahan's architects. Shah Jahan was deposed by Aurangzeb, his son and successor, and spent his last eight years imprisoned in Agra Fort. He did not get another chance to see the new city that he had built.

Aurangzeb (1658–1703): Aurangzeb completed some of his father's plans for Delhi, but spent much of his time away on military campaigns or in the other great cities of the Mughal Empire. Aurangzeb was famously austere, and did not approve of frivolity in architecture. However, the Moti Masjid, or Pearl Mosque, inside the Red Fort Complex was completed under Aurangzeb, as was the beautiful Zinat-ul Masjid, set into the city walls 700m south of the Red Fort.

Later Mughal period (1703–1857): The succession to Aurangzeb was not clear, and the Mughal Empire fell into a gradual decline from which it never recovered. However, there are a number of important buildings from this later period—including the Jantar Mantar Observatory, Safdarjung's Tomb and the Zafar Mahal in Mehrauli. Delhi fell prey to a series of invading armies. In 1739, the Persian emperor Nadir Shah plundered the city, leaving, according to estimates, as many as 120,000 people dead on the streets of Shahjahanabad. He also took away Shah Jahan's Peacock Throne and the Kohinoor diamond. In 1788, an Afghan warlord took the emperor Shah Alam prisoner in the Red Fort and blinded him. The Marathas of central India came to Shah Alam's rescue and were the most powerful force in Delhi until they were in turn defeated by the British in 1803.

Officially, the Mughal Empire was still supreme in north India. But the British gradually strengthened their position with the appointment of a 'Resident', who began to play a leading role in the politics of Delhi. The first British buildings date from this period. By the time Bahadur Shah Zafar became emperor in 1837, there was little left of the Mughal Empire in geographical terms, apart from Delhi, but the old ways lived on in the culture, etiquette and rituals of the Mughal court. This was all destroyed in the Great Uprising of 1857, known to the British as the Indian Mutiny, and to modern-day Indian schoolchildren as the First War of Independence. Bahadur Shah Zafar, who supported the Uprising, was exiled to Burma, and the British took full control of Delhi.

British period (1857–1947)

The British rampaged through Delhi after the 1857 rebellion, killing thousands and driving most inhabitants out of the city. Eventually the citizens were allowed to return, but Delhi became, in the second half of the 19th century, little more than a sleepy backwater, outranked by several other cities in British India. Then, in 1911, the visiting King George V announced that Delhi would replace Calcutta as India's capital. The next 20 years saw the building of New Delhi, a planned colonial city built on scrub and agricultural land to the south of Shahjahanabad. The British did not get much time to enjoy the new 'second city of the empire', for India gained its independence in 1947.

Post-Independence (after 1947)

Delhi, which had a population of less than a million at independence, is now one of the largest cities in the world. It became a new home for huge numbers of Hindu and Sikh refugees from the part of the Punjab allotted to Pakistan, and since then has continued to attract migrants from the rest of India. It now has over 15 million inhabitants—more than 20 million if you include its suburbs which spill over into neighbouring states. Delhi has spread far beyond its traditional geographical borders—across the Ridge and over the Yamuna. The ruins of the ancient cities of South Delhi have been encircled by newer versions of the city—which have, on the whole, been architecturally undistinguished. One well-known Delhi architect described the predominant style, particularly for government-constructed housing, as 'matchbox', and derided as 'Punjabi Baroque' recent attempts by the affluent of South Delhi to fuse several Western styles in a single over-ornate building. In recent years, the city has begun to improve its infrastructure, with the building of a metro network, dozens of flyovers and new measures to reduce traffic pollution. Numerous international companies have expatriate workers based in Delhi and the nearby suburb of Gurgaon, and foreigners are no longer objects of curiosity. However, they are a major source of income—for beggars and for tourist guides in particular—and no one should expect their stay in Delhi to be hassle-free.

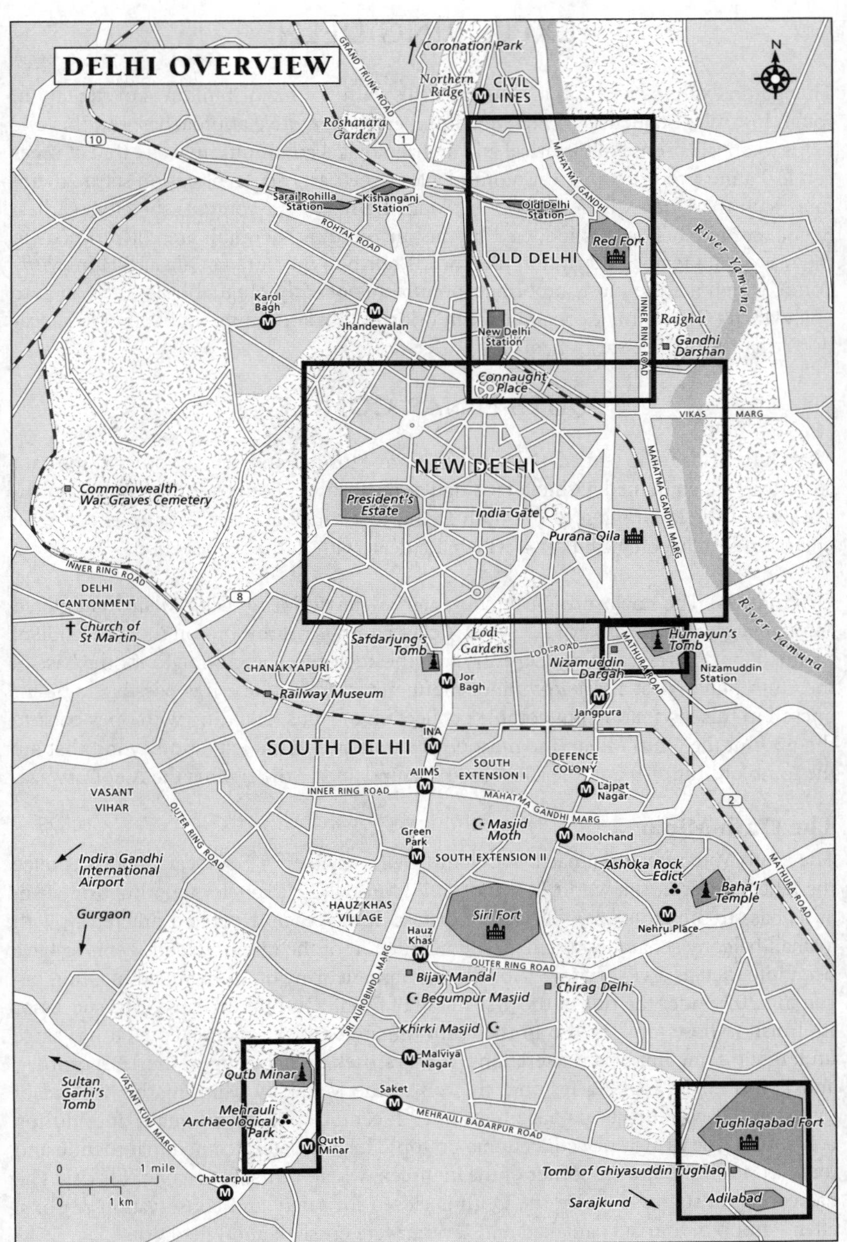
DELHI OVERVIEW
N
Coronation Park
GRAND TRUNK ROAD
Northern Ridge
CIVIL LINES
Roshanara Garden
10
1
MAHATMA GANDHI
Sarai Rohilla Station
Kishanganj Station
Old Delhi Station
ROHTAK ROAD
Red Fort
River Yamuna
OLD DELHI
Karol Bagh
Jhandewalan
INNER RING ROAD
Rajghat
New Delhi Station
Gandhi Darshan
Connaught Place
VIKAS MARG
NEW DELHI
MAHATMA GANDHI MARG
Commonwealth War Graves Cemetery
President's Estate
India Gate
Purana Qila
INNER RING ROAD
DELHI CANTONMENT
8
Church of St Martin
Safdarjung's Tomb
Lodi Gardens
LODI ROAD
Humayun's Tomb
River Yamuna
Nizamuddin Dargah
MATHURA ROAD
Nizamuddin Station
CHANAKYAPURI
Jor Bagh
Railway Museum
Jangpura
INA
SOUTH DELHI
SOUTH EXTENSION I
DEFENCE COLONY
AIIMS
VASANT VIHAR
Lajpat Nagar
INNER RING ROAD
MAHATMA GANDHI MARG
2
OUTER RING ROAD
Masjid Moth
Green Park
Moolchand
SOUTH EXTENSION II
Indira Gandhi International Airport
Ashoka Rock Edict
MATHURA ROAD
Baha'i Temple
Gurgaon
HAUZ KHAS VILLAGE
Siri Fort
Nehru Place
Hauz Khas
SRI AUROBINDO MARG
OUTER RING ROAD
Bijay Mandal
Chirag Delhi
Begumpur Masjid
Khirki Masjid
Malviya Nagar
Qutb Minar
Sultan Garhi's Tomb
VASANT KUNJ MARG
Saket
Mehrauli Archaeological Park
MEHRAULI BADARPUR ROAD
Tughlaqabad Fort
Qutb Minar
0
1 mile
Chattarpur
0
1 km
Tomb of Ghiyasuddin Tughlaq
Sarajkund
Adilabad

For a detailed map of central New Delhi see p. 114, for Old Delhi see p. 108.

EXPLORING DELHI

This guide explores Delhi in a way that deals with the major buildings of the city in rough historical sequence. There are a number of alternative approaches, but this one helps establish a sense of historical and archaeological continuity, in a city that at times can feel almost too rich in great monuments of the past. The exploration starts, therefore, with the Qutb Minar complex in South Delhi, which contains the city's earliest major monuments, and is followed by the surrounding Mehrauli area. It proceeds to the rest of Sultanate South Delhi, then heads north to the Purana Qila and Humayun's Tomb, which are the most important monuments of early Mughal Delhi, and then to Shah Jahan's Old Delhi. It concludes with British Delhi and a number of other key locations that fall outside this schemata.

QUTB MINAR COMPLEX

The Qutb Minar, the ruined Quwwat-ul Islam Mosque and several other important structures are contained within a rectangular enclosure, 300m by 200m, in the northern part of the Mehrauli area of South Delhi. Just south of the enclosure is Mehrauli village and Archaeological Park—which are dealt with in the next section.

Orientation: The enclosure (*open daily sunrise–sunset; Metro: Qutb Minar*) is entered through a gate on the eastern side—the ticket booth is nearby, but on the other side of the road, next to the car park. On entry into the enclosure, head straight for the base of the Qutb Minar, past a series of minor monuments, from where it is possible to orient oneself in this fascinating but complex collection of ruins. Standing with one's back to the door of the Qutb Minar, the mosque is ahead and to the left, and beyond that are the tomb of Iltutmish and the Alai Minar; behind and to the right is the Alai Darwaza.

The Qutb Minar

The Qutb Minar has dominated the South Delhi skyline for 800 years, and was once the tallest tower in the world. It stands at 72.5m tall, its diameter tapering from 14m at its base to 3m at its apex. It has five distinct levels, each decorated differently, with a small balcony separating them. The construction of the Minar, which seems to have been intended as a victory tower for the triumphant army of Muhammad of Ghor, began in 1202 under the rule of the first sultan of Delhi, Qutbuddin Aibak. His successor Iltutmish (whose tomb is also in the Qutb Minar complex) completed it. It has since undergone some important alterations. It was struck by lightning in the 14th century, and Feroze Shah Tughlaq restored the top of the Minar by using marble instead of sandstone. It was further damaged in the 19th century by an earthquake and, during restoration, the British placed a cupola on top. This was later deemed inauthentic and removed to the southeast corner of the complex, where it sits, forlorn, to this day. The narrow spiral staircase inside the Qutb is closed for safety and conservation reasons, after a group of tourists panicked and several were crushed and killed.

The Qutb Minar is one of those rare historical buildings that is just as spectacular from close-up as from a distance. The detail of the red and grey sandstone walls is of the highest quality, and seems undamaged by time. The lowest level has 24 vertical ribs, which are alternately curved and angular, and horizontal belts of Islamic *naskh* calligraphy, with geometric and floral borders. Most elegant of all—and binoculars or a telephoto lens can be useful here—is the detailed carving under each balcony of the Minar. The higher levels of the Minar are a little simpler. The second one has only curved ribs, the third only angular ribs. The fourth and fifth levels are fully circular.

The inspiration for the Qutb Minar was probably the victory towers of Afghanistan, of which the Minaret of Jam is the most famous. However, the Qutb Minar is also quite clearly unlike any other contemporary building, both in its profile and its detail. In particular, the workmanship of the Qutb Minar is finer than other Islamic architecture of the time, and there is a strong case for local Hindu craftsmen having been responsible for much of the exterior work. The building may also have been used as a traditional minaret (from where a *muezzin* makes the call to prayer) and as a look-out tower. The Qutb Minar, which literally means 'axial tower', appears to have been dedicated to the Muslim saint Qutb Sahib, whose shrine is nearby in Mehrauli.

Quwwat-ul Islam Mosque

The construction of Delhi's earliest mosque (also known as the Qutb Mosque) began at the tail-end of the 12th century, slightly before the Qutb Minar. The basic structure of the mosque appears to have been completed during the reign of the first sultan. It was extended by the second sultan, Iltutmish, and again by the Khilji sultan, Alauddin, in the early 14th century. This makes the layout of these fascinating ruins quite complex to decipher. The mosque has not been in use for prayer for several centuries.

The original mosque consisted of a large walled courtyard with colonnades on three sides and a prayer hall on the west that has an ancient pillar (*see overleaf*) in the centre.

Most of the columns in the colonnades were salvaged from Hindu temples, and Hindu motifs, such as bells, cows, leaves and ropes are clearly visible. An inscription on the eastern portal says that the mosque was built with material from 27 demolished Hindu and Jain temples. Some of the carvings on the stonework merit close inspection, and among the unlikely decorations to be found on the mosque building are human figures, a horse (under the exterior frame of the small door in the northwest corner of the mosque) and a small frieze showing the birth of Krishna (high up beneath a waterspout on the eastern wall).

The first addition to the mosque was a spectacular interior façade of five arches (four of which survive), along the courtyard wall of the mosque, next to the prayer hall. The façade doesn't align properly with the pre-existing colonnades, and the junctions between the two are an amusing example of botched 12th-century building work. From a distance the arches look genuine, but on closer examination they have no keystone and are built with the kind of corbelling used traditionally by Hindu builders. The outer colonnades of the mosque and the extension to the façade were added later, during the rule of Iltutmish, and the Hindu influence is visibly less—the decoration is geometric rather than floral. The calligraphy has also changed: the curvaceous *naskh* script has been replaced by the rectilinear *kufic* script. Alauddin Khilji planned a further huge expansion of the mosque, but only completed the Alai Darwaza (*see opposite*). He did begin construction work, but the work stopped at his death in 1315—which is why parts of the Qutb Minar complex seem like an ancient building site. Many of the foundations laid by Alauddin's builders are still visible, and it is possible to make out the ground plan of what would have been the largest mosque in South Asia.

The most widely-used named for the mosque, Quwwat-ul Islam, or Might of Islam, appears to be a recent corruption of an older name, Qubbat-ul Islam, or Sanctuary of Islam.

The Iron Pillar

The mosque may have been the first building to be erected in the Qutb Minar Complex, but it is not the oldest structure there. The 7m tall inscribed iron pillar that stands in the middle of the mosque courtyard dates back to at least the 4th century. According to the inscription on the pillar, it was erected by a king called Chandra on Vishnupada Hill. Chandra is probably the Gupta emperor Chandragupta II, but Vishnupada Hill has not been located with any certainty. The pillar, which has been identified as a staff of the Hindu god Vishnu, was probably once surmounted by an image of the eagle-god Garuda, Vishnu's vehicle, and was shifted to this area before the Islamic invasion. The pillar itself is a testament to early Indian metallurgical skills, involving techniques of casting iron that were not in use until the 19th century in Europe. Experts are still unsure about exactly how the pillar was cast and why it doesn't rust. Popular tradition holds that anyone who can stand with their back to the pillar and link their hands around it will be blessed with good fortune. However, railings have now been placed around the pillar, and it can no longer be hugged.

Tomb of Iltutmish

The other important early Sultanate building in the Qutb Minar complex is the lavishly decorated tomb of the second Slave Dynasty sultan, Iltutmish, built in 1235. From the outside, the mausoleum is relatively simple, but inside there is a riot of calligraphic and geometric decoration. The three *mihrabs* are of particularly high quality. Iltutmish was actually buried underneath the building in a chamber accessed by a grille-covered staircase on the northern side of the building. Almost certainly, there was once a dome over the building—it was probably India's first domed building. The square profile of the tomb is transformed near the ceiling into an octagon by the use of corbelled squinches, presumably intended to support the dome. The relatively thin walls of the tomb, and the weakness of the corbelled arches, would have made it hard to support the dome's weight.

Alai Darwaza

This gateway was built in 1305 during the reign of the Khilji sultan Alauddin, as part of his plans to double the size of the Qutb Minar Mosque. None of the rest of his proposed buildings—except a *madrasa* to the east of the mosque—was completed. The Alai Darwaza shows how much Islamic architecture had changed since the early Sultanate period. Unlike the older buildings, it used genuine keystone arches and marble inlay and is covered with a low dome, which in turn is capped with a white mini-dome.

Alai Minar

Only an enormous stump remains of a tower begun by Sultan Alauddin that was to have been more than twice as high as the Qutb Minar. The vertical ribs, which would have been faced with stone like the Qutb Minar, are visible—and so, through an opening in the rubble wall, is the inner core of the tower, around which the staircase would have been built.

The other minor structures in the Qutb Minar complex are largely **garden enclosures** and **rest-houses** from the later Mughal period, when Mehrauli was a summer retreat.

MEHRAULI ARCHAEOLOGICAL PARK

To the south and west of the Qutb Minar complex are dozens of tombs, mosques, stepwells and fortifications from the pre-Islamic, Sultanate, Mughal and British periods that belong to what is now known as the Mehrauli Archaeological Park. Only some of them are actually within the park south of the Qutb Minar; others are surrounded by modern buildings in Mehrauli village; while some stand alone in scrubland or forest on either side of the village. This area of approximately 4km^2 in South Delhi probably has a greater number and diversity of separate historically or architecturally significant monuments than any other place in the world. An official listing records more than 440 structures—which come from every period of Indian history since the 10th century—and could keep a determined visitor busy for many days.

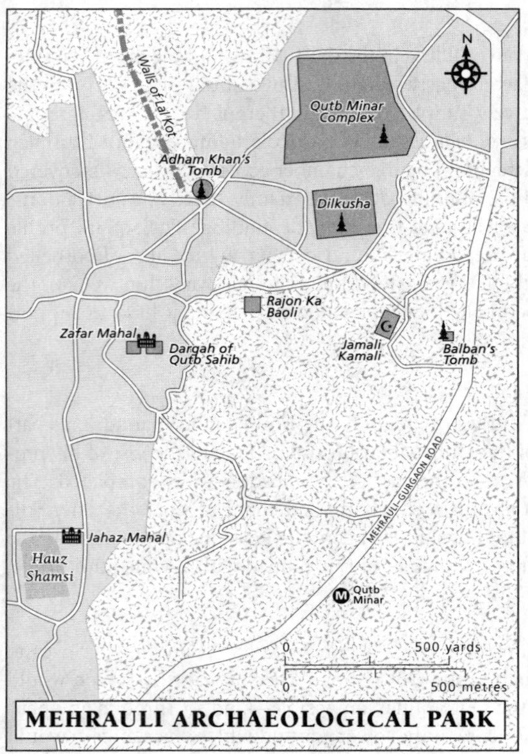

It can feel like an enormous archaeological jigsaw puzzle. The key to making sense of the puzzle is understanding the historical role of just three of the most important structures in Mehrauli. First, the pre-Islamic walls of **Lal Kot**, which provided a ready-made fortified citadel when Muslim invaders took over Delhi in the late 12th century. Second, the **Qutb Minar**, built within the walls of Lal Kot and around which a new city was built. The third structure is the 13th-century shrine, or *dargah*, of the Muslim saint **Qutb Sahib**, which ensured that the area around the Qutb Minar continued to thrive as a place of pilgrimage and a site for the building of tombs and mosques, long after the political centre of power moved elsewhere in Delhi. In fact, by the 19th century, Mehrauli was a village in the countryside—a place where Mughal emperors would retreat in the summer or go for hunting expeditions; where British officials would build country homes; and where thousands of pilgrims would visit the *dargah*. Only in the last 50 years has rapid urbanisation reabsorbed Mehrauli into the city.

Zafar Mahal

This charming and ramshackle late Mughal palace, which backs onto the *dargah*, was built in the early 19th century around an older mosque and tomb. It was rebuilt a little later by the last Mughal emperor, Bahadur Shah Zafar, to allow elephants inside; he used it as his summer palace. There is a small cemetery containing the graves of several later Mughals. The empty grave in the middle was intended for Bahadur Shah Zafar, but he was exiled to Burma after the Uprising of 1857 and buried in Rangoon in 1862.

Dargah of Qutb Sahib

The shrine of the 13th-century Muslim saint Khwaja Qutbuddin Bakhtiyar, also known both as Qutb Sahib and as Kaki, is a major Sufi pilgrimage centre, similar to the

Nizamuddin shrine 9km to the northeast. Qutb Sahib was born in Persia and came to India during the reign of Iltutmish, the second sultan of Delhi. He became a disciple of Khwaja Moinuddin Chishti of Ajmer, and after Chishti's death became one of the most influential Sufi leaders in India. The busy *dargah* enclosure contains a large number of tombs, including those of the royal families of Jhajjar and Loharu, small principalities with feudal ties to the Mughal Empire. The railings and canopy surrounding the grave of Qutb Sahib himself were constructed in British times—until the 19th century, it had been a simple mound of earth.

Adham Khan's Tomb

This large early Mughal tomb, constructed in 1562, stands on a raised platform abutting the walls of Lal Kot, on the main road running through Mehrauli village. It is one of the last of the octagonal tombs that proliferated earlier in Sultanate Delhi under the Lodi Dynasty. Adham Khan was the son of Akbar's wet-nurse, Maham Atgah, and according to Mughal tradition was therefore the emperor's foster brother. Adham Khan was politically ambitious, and was involved in the killing of a rival—for which Akbar had him thrown from the walls of Agra Fort as a form of execution. Adham Khan's mother died soon after. Akbar is said to have regretted ordering her son's execution and so agreed to the building of the tomb. In the British period, the tomb was used as a private residence, a post office and a police station. It is known locally as the Bhul Bhulaiyan.

Hauz Shamsi

This 13th-century tank or reservoir stands at the southern end of Mehrauli village. The tank was once much larger, and the pretty domed pavilion (1311) on the western side originally stood in the middle of it. Next to the main road is a small U-shaped building, the 15th-century Jahaz Mahal, or Ship Palace. For the later Mughals, this area became a kind of pleasure garden, with other early 19th-century pavilions, and an artificial waterfall, the remains of which can be seen (look behind the wood store) on the other side of the road from the tank.

Rajon ka Baoli

This is arguably Delhi's finest step-well, with a mosque and tomb attached. This late Lodi *baoli*, or step-well, constructed in 1506, has four levels and a series of arcades and small rooms. Step-wells like this were not just water sources, but places of refuge from the summer heat and the monsoon rains.

Dilkusha

This former 16th-century tomb has a strange history. It was built as the tomb of Adham Khan's brother, Quli Khan. It was purchased by the British Resident Sir Thomas Metcalfe during the 1830s, at a time when, as now, this area was a major tourist attraction; it also allowed him to follow the Mughal court when it moved to Mehrauli. He converted the tomb into a country house, which he called Dilkusha, or Heart's Delight, set in formal gardens. The tomb chamber was used as the dining room. He also created a lake and a boathouse. As if the scattered Sultanate ruins were not enough, he built a number of follies, including two ziggurats, which are close to the Qutb Minar car park.

Balban's Tomb

Balban was one of the most powerful of the Slave sultans, ruling Delhi from 1265 to 1287. This partly-ruined building is thought to be the first structure in India to have a true arch. There are three interlinked chambers. The central one is thought to contain Balban's grave, while the smaller one to the east may contain the grave of his son, Khan Shahid.

Jamali Kamali

This little-visited mosque and tomb are exquisite examples of 16th-century Islamic architecture. They were built in 1528–29 by the poet Sheikh Fazlullah, whose pen-name was Jamali. He was buried in the tomb when he died in 1535. The five-bayed mosque is in good condition, with a delicately carved *mihrab*. In the next courtyard, look out for the pretty blue tiles on the exterior of the small square tomb. You may need to find a watchman to open the door to the tomb, which is normally locked. The interior is beautifully decorated, and almost perfectly preserved. The detail of the ceiling is of exceptional quality, with ornate plasterwork patterns in red and blue. The walls are decorated with plasterwork inlaid with tiles. There are two graves in the tomb, and for years it was supposed that the second one belonged to someone called Kamali. It is now thought that the name of the mosque-tomb is alliterative, but the mysterious occupant of the second grave has not been identified.

The walls of Lal Kot

The overgrown western walls of Lal Kot are Delhi's earliest standing structures, 15m high in places and ignored in most tourist literature. They are slightly hard to access, and involve some climbing. The walls provide spectacular views of the Qutb Minar and much of South Delhi, and are excellent examples of pre-Islamic fortifications. They were probably built in the 11th century, though parts of them were extended in the early Sultanate period. There are two (in some places three) sets of walls, each of which can be walked along, separated by a dry moat. Some of the bastions and gates of this enormous fortress can be still be made out amid the thorn and creepers that threaten to engulf it. Within the walls is a huge reservoir that is now empty. Nearby are archaeological excavation pits which reveal the existence of large unidentified masonry buildings. Outside the walls are an *idgah*, a *dargah* and some Muslim graves. The inner walls are most easily accessed through, unfortunately, a rubbish dump, from behind Adham Khan's tomb. The outer walls are best accessed from the *idgah* on the western side of Mehrauli village.

THE REST OF SOUTH DELHI

Much of the rest of South Delhi is also full of impressive architecture and monuments. These are spread out over a wide area and include one of India's earliest Muslim tombs

(Sultan Garhi), the city's most imposing fortress (Tughlaqabad), its most famous modern building (the Baha'i Lotus Temple), as well as some exquisite mosques and tombs from the Sultanate and Mughal periods, including those in the popular Lodi Gardens. Historically, Sultanate Delhi spread north and east from the Qutb, and the remains of the second, third and fourth cities of Delhi—Siri, Tughlaqabad, Jahanpanah—can be found amidst the urban sprawl that has enveloped the south of the city over the last 50 years.

Tughlaqabad Fort

The walls of the former city of Tughlaqabad (*open sunrise–sunset; Metro: Tughlaqabad*) are Delhi's most impressive and most intimidating fortifications. The enormous sloping walls of the fort extend for more than 6km, and enclose two smaller fortified areas containing the remains of a large palace complex and the inner citadel. The interior of these enclosures consists largely of ruined buildings and large open spaces. Typically for Tughlaq-period architecture, the fort is notable for its enormous scale, its proportions and its clean profile rather than for any artistic detail.

Tughlaqabad Fort was built in just two years (1321–23) during the brief reign of Ghiyasuddin. It seems to have been deserted not long after completion, possibly because of a lack of water or because Ghiyasuddin's son, Muhammad bin Tughlaq, believed the fort was cursed. The construction work was undertaken at an extraordinary speed by the Tughlaq army, whose commanders were each assigned a section of the fortifications to build. The walls, faced with dressed grey quartzite stones, slope steeply away from the exterior foundations—a feature that distinguishes most Tughlaq architecture. There are huge rounded bastions, often two storeys high, at regular intervals along the wall. The battlements have lancet windows for archers. The modern entrance to the Fort is from the south, on the other side of the road from a stone causeway that leads to Ghiyasuddin's Tomb (*see overleaf*). On entering the Fort, the remains of the palace complex are visible to the left. Ahead is a deep cleft in the rock, where stone for the fort buildings was probably quarried, and to the right is the pathway that leads up to the citadel. In order to make sense of the fort complex as a whole it is best to visit the citadel first, from where, on a clear day, excellent views of the rest of South Delhi can be had.

The **citadel**, built high on a rocky outcrop, contains a small undecorated mosque; close by is a lengthy underground passage (take a torch), with rooms leading off it. Local guides may tell you that this is a medieval shopping mall, or that it once contained treasure—but the rooms, cool in the hottest days of summer, were probably used for storage. Ibn Battuta, writing in the 1330s, records that Ghiyasuddin dug a huge hole in the ground, which he filled with molten gold, so it is not surprising that treasure-hunters have been searching Tughlaqabad ever since. Beyond the far exit of the passage is another staircase leading downwards. This was a secret route out of the citadel, and the concealed exit, disguised as a large drain outlet, can be seen on returning to the main road below. The highest point of the citadel is a mound called the Burj Mandal, which is surfaced and probably had a small building on its summit. Most of the other ruins in the citadel are thought to be from the Mughal period.

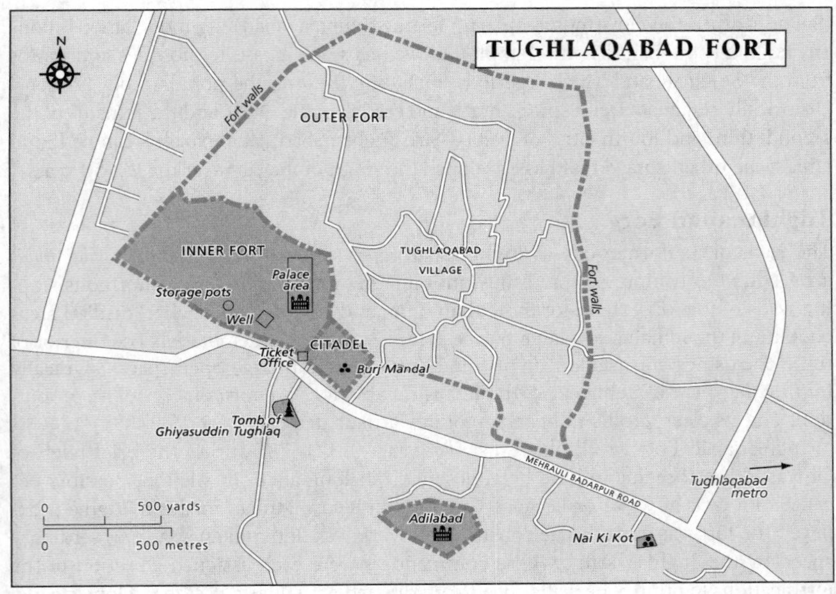

Return down the steps to the palace area, where the desolate ruins of what was once a series of cloistered courtyards and two-storey buildings are visible. Some of the doorways and niches have the remains of patterned plasterwork, suggesting that the palace was not always as austere as it now seems. Near the outer wall is a huge square well and beyond that are some strange beehive-shaped underground rooms, open at the top but without any way in. These are rumoured to have been dungeons, but are more likely to have have been used for storage. There are more of these beehive rooms near the western and northern gates. From the northern gate there are good views of the rest of the former city of Tughlaqabad, and the lines of ancient streets can be made out through the undergrowth.

Tomb of Ghiyasuddin Tughlaq

The exquisite and architecturally important tomb of Ghiyasuddin Tughlaq, set within its own fortified enclosure, is approached by a stone causeway across the busy road opposite the entrance to Tughlaqabad Fort. Ghiyasuddin died in 1324 in mysterious circumstances, possibly murdered on the instructions of his son. The tomb, which is in almost perfect condition, has the steeply sloping walls typical of most Tughlaq architecture and is made of finely cut sandstone and marble. The three doorways each have a series of diminishing curved and straight frames, a syncretic style of design which became an important feature of Islamic architecture in India.

Adilabad Fort

This smaller fort sits high on the hill on the other side of the road from Tughlaqabad, overlooking what was once a large reservoir. Access is via a rocky goat-path on the south side. The walls of the dam that created the reservoir are visible on the ascent. Inside are two sets of walls, those of the exterior recently restored. The purpose of the Adilabad Fort is not clear. Originally it was thought to have been used as the temporary headquarters when Tughlaqabad was built, but Adilabad is now thought to have been constructed a few years later. Some 800m beyond is another very small fortification, called **Nai ki Kot**, or Barber's Fort, on a rocky outcrop. The walls are in good condition and the plinth of an octagonal sandstone building, perhaps a pavilion, can be seen inside.

Surajkund

The large man-made reservoir at Surajkund in the far south of modern Delhi (*Metro: Badarpur*) almost certainly marks the site of an important older settlement that predates Lal Kot. The reservoir, which was probably built in the early 11th century, has a stepped semicircular embankment. The area around Surajkund is used for cultural and handicraft fairs, and is a popular picnic place. Further south, in **Anangpur**, is a large dam, 7m high, that dates to the same period. Also nearby are the ruined foundations of the walls of Anangpur Fort (a short walk from Anangpur village), just visible as they wind their way around a small hill overlooking a ravine.

Siri Fort

Siri Fort (*Metro: Hauz Khas*) was built in 1303 by the first ruler of the Khilji Dynasty, Alauddin, to defend Delhi—successfully—against the first Mongol invasion. Large chunks of the 5km walls and foundations are still standing, and it is possible to walk most of the length of the walls through residential neighbourhoods and parkland. The easiest access points are from Khel Gaon Marg, where the western walls are clearly visible from the main road, and from E Block, Panchsheel Park, where the southern walls have been excavated and the 5m high remains of a major gateway to the fort can be visited.

Bijay Mandal

This intriguing building (*Metro: Hauz Khas*) is probably the remains of Muhammad bin Tughlaq's great 1,000-pillared palace, described by the 14th-century traveller Ibn Battuta. If so, it would be the heart of the fourth city of Delhi, known as Jahanpanah. The evidence is not conclusive and it is likely that there was considerable rebuilding here in the later Sultanate period. The existing Bijay Mandal consists of a two-storey octagonal tower attached to a pillared hall, with a few other smaller buildings, and broken columns lying around. Bijay Mandal is easiest to reach from a road that runs through the Sarvodya Enclave area of South Delhi.

Begumpur Masjid

This fine mid-14th-century building was probably the main mosque for the fourth city of Delhi, Jahanpanah, and is close to Bijay Mandal, the putative pillared palace of

Muhammad bin Tughlaq (*Metro: Hauz Khas*). It has an enormous arcaded courtyard, with an unusually high central two-storeyed prayer hall. It is (just about) possible to climb onto the highest part of the roof and get good views of South Delhi and of the possible layout of Jahanpanah.

Khirki Masjid

Slightly younger than Begumpur, the Khirki Mosque, on the north side of Press Enclave Road near Saket (*Metro: Saket*), is one of Delhi's most fascinating Sultanate buildings. Built like a small fort, with a stepped entrance gate, it is very unusual in being covered. The roof is constructed with clusters of small domes—and there are four open areas that function as skylights. Additional light comes in from the lattice windows (*khirki* means window) on three sides of the building. The side with the prayer hall and the *mihrab* has no windows, and a torch is useful for inspecting the interior; superb photographs can be taken from the roof. Some 500m to the east of the mosque, further along Press Enclave Road, are the remains of a 14th-century bridge and sluice-gate, the seven-arched Satpula.

Chirag Delhi

The area around the *dargah* of the 14th-century Muslim saint Roshan, Chirag Delhi is full of buildings from the 14th to 18th centuries. The *dargah* itself remains an important place of pilgrimage, similar to Mehrauli and Nizamuddin. And among the buildings to be found in Chirag Delhi is an unusual square tomb, perhaps that of Bahlol Lodi, the first of the Lodi rulers of Delhi.

Hauz Khas

The Hauz Khas area of South Delhi (*Metro: Green Park or Hauz Khas*) has a number of impressive tombs and other buildings from the Tughlaq and Lodi periods. The most important are the ruins of a *madrasa*, or Islamic college, and the tomb of Feroze Shah Tughlaq. The *madrasa*, with its many small domes, is a particularly impressive multi-storeyed building, with lots of rooms built around the southeast corner of the reservoir. These ruins, along with some other pretty Sultanate buildings, overlook a reservoir built under the Khiljis, in what is now known as Hauz Khas village, which is full of antique shops and small restaurants.

Masjid Moth and the tombs of South Extension

Masjid Moth is one of Delhi's prettiest mosques, hidden away in the backstreets of South Extension Part II (*Metro: AIIMS*). It was built in the early 16th century, not long before the Mughals ended the Lodi Dynasty. Note the unusual series of wall niches running vertically up the columns separating the bays of the mosque. On the other side of the Inner Ring Road, in South Extension Part I, are some very interesting Lodi tombs in a range of different styles. The **tomb of Darya Khan Lohani**, a senior administrator, takes the form of a large plinth, with the cenotaph at its centre, open to the skies, and pretty pillared *chattris* (pavilions) at each corner. The nearby tomb of Bara Khan ke

Gumbad is an imposing three-storey edifice, with unusual sets of triple niches on the sides of each doorway. Also nearby, in the 'village' of Kotla Mubarakpur, is the tomb of Mubarak Shah, the second ruler of the Sayyid Dynasty (*see p. 78*)—along with the tomb of his nephew Muhammad Shah in Lodi Gardens, these are the only significant Sayyid monuments in Delhi.

Lodi Gardens

The gardens, which are one of Delhi's prettiest places for a walk or a picnic, are a 20th-century creation, when a village that surrounded tombs of the Lodi and Sayyid dynasties was cleared by the British and its inhabitants relocated. The park was first known as Lady Willingdon Gardens, after the wife of the viceroy. In the 1960s—by which time it was known as Lodi Gardens—the lake was built and many of the trees were planted. The tombs made an excellent introduction to the architecture of the late Sultanate period.

Orientation: Most visitors approach from Lodi Road, to the south of the gardens. Visible through the trees from the road is the splendid tomb of Muhammad Shah. A little further in and to the right is a complex of tombs, and at the north end of the gardens is the tomb of Sikander Lodi, the last of Delhi's major pre-Mughal buildings.

The octagonal **tomb of Muhammad Shah** is the finest surviving building of the Sayyid period of rule in Delhi, and dates back to the mid-15th century. Its array of upper-storey *chattris* and turrets make the tomb look circular.

The **Bara Gumbad** and **Sheesh Gumbad** are a pretty group of buildings in the centre of Lodi Gardens, with some fine external and internal decoration (especially the smaller domed building, Sheesh Gumbad). The two domed buildings, which are imperfectly aligned, are thought to have been built as tombs, though the larger one has no evidence of a cenotaph. The other buildings form a mosque, in which the three domes are grouped together in an unusual fashion over the inner bays, rather than being placed evenly over the first, central and last bays. The large walled **tomb of Sikander Lodi** is the last major Lodi building in Delhi. In the western wall is a wall mosque. The mausoleum is octagonal—but lacks the roof *chattris* of several similar tombs.

Safdarjung's Tomb

This curious and extravagant 18th-century tomb (*open dawn–dusk; Metro: Jor Bagh*) has almost as many detractors as admirers. It was built in the 1750s and is certainly the city's best example of late Mughal tomb architecture. Its layout is similar to the great tomb of Humayun 4km to the east, but it is a smaller, more compact building, almost frivolous by comparison. Unlike Humayun's Tomb, there is considerable surviving internal decoration on the entrance gate and inside the tomb. Inside is the cenotaph of a member of the royal family of Avadh, Safdarjang, who was an enormously influential figure under a series of less well-known Mughal emperors.

Sultan Garhi's Tomb

This unusual tomb complex (*open daily 9–5*) is one of the earliest surviving Muslim mausolea in India, and is some distance from the rest of the monuments of the Slave Dynasty. Set amid the ruins of a later village, this large walled compound looks at first sight more like a mosque or a small fort. The body buried here is believed to be Nasiruddin Mahmud, the eldest son of Iltutmish, the second Slave sultan. He predeceased Iltutmish, and this tomb is usually dated to 1231. The tomb was repaired by Feroze Shah Tughlaq in the second half of the 14th century.

Visitors to the tomb complex enter up a staircase through a raised gateway, inscribed with koranic verses and a cleverly designed false arch, similar to the one seen at the Qutb, but with a single stone acting as a false key to the arch. The inner gate has a lintel and further inscriptions around the frame. The open courtyard has galleries running round its sides. Unusually, there is a flat-roofed underground tomb chamber, which projects upwards above the ground, and has some carved stonework taken from pre-Muslim buildings. Originally, a cenotaph—possibly with a small pavilion—would have stood on the roof of the chamber. The grave itself is approached down a staircase on the north side of the octagonal chamber. The tomb has become a modern-day place of worship for local people, Muslims and Hindus. There is a small wall mosque at the back of the complex—the marble columns are thought to be a 14th-century Tughlaq addition.

Ashoka Rock Edict

This rock-cut inscription from the 4th century BC is by far the oldest *in situ* monument in Delhi (the two Ashoka pillars in the north of the city were originally constructed at the same time, but were brought to Delhi only in the 14th century). The edict was one of many that have been found across the country, and was inscribed on the orders of Ashoka the Great—the Buddhist emperor who, 24 centuries ago, ruled most of India. The presence of the rock edict suggests that Delhi was on an important trade route at the time of Ashoka. The edict itself commands all people to spread the word of Buddhism, reminding them that 'even a humble man who exerts himself can attain heaven'. The edict was written in the ancient Brahmi script and only discovered in 1965; not much of the inscription survives. It can be found not far from the Baha'i Temple (*see below*; *Metro: Nehru Place*), in a small park in the East of Kailash locality, protected by a small concrete roof.

Baha'i Temple / Lotus Temple

This spectacular piece of modern architecture, popularly known as the Lotus Temple, is now one of Delhi's most popular visitor attractions (*Metro: Nehru Place*). The temple, completed in the 1980s, is built in the shape of a half-open lotus, to a design reminiscent in its colour and style of the Sydney Opera House. The architect, Fariborz Sabha, is an Iranian Baha'i. The temple is a place of worship for members of the Baha'i religion, which was founded in Iran in the 19th century, but all are welcomed here. There is a small museum about the Baha'i religion on the left as you enter the temple complex. (*For more on the religion, see p. 75.*)

EARLY MUGHAL DELHI: HUMAYUN'S TOMB & PURANA QILA

There are two outstanding Delhi buildings from the early Mughal period. Both of these monumental 16th-century buildings were constructed on the banks of the River Yamuna, which has since moved more than 1km to the east. The earliest of the buildings, the Purana Qila, or Old Fort, was begun during the reign of Emperor Humayun but completed by members of the short-lived Sher Shah Suri Dynasty that temporarily dislodged the Mughals from Delhi. The second building, the spectacular garden tomb of Humayun, was built early in the reign of his son Akbar, a little further south, close to the old pilgrimage village of Nizamuddin. The *dargah*, or Sufi Muslim shrine, at Nizamuddin is still a major pilgrimage site—and the 'village', with its collection of interesting buildings from the 13th to the 19th centuries, is a fascinating place to explore.

PURANA QILA

The dramatically imposing walls of the Purana Qila (Old Fort) rank with Tughlaqabad as Delhi's most impressive fortifications. Inside are a very fine mosque and the remains of what may be the oldest Delhi of them all. Local tradition holds this to be the site of Indraprastha, a huge city described in the Hindu epic the *Mahabharata* as being 'as beautiful as a new heaven', with grand palaces, lakes and pavilions. Pottery fragments show that this site was probably first settled some 3,000 years ago, but excavations have not revealed traces of any large buildings. The fort was built during the reigns of the Mughal emperor Humayun (1530–40 and 1555–56) and the short-lived Sher Shah Suri Dynasty (1540–55) and it is not clear which ruler was responsible for which parts of the building. Much of the interior of the fort is empty, though it contained a village called Indrapat until the early 20th century, and became a long-stay refugee camp in the aftermath of Partition in 1947. Now its only occupants stay in the small tree-fringed temple complex, which is supposed to mark the site of the original temple of Indraprastha. Concerts are occasionally held at the southern end of the fort.

Orientation: The modern entrance to the Purana Qila is by the West Gate (*open sunrise–sunset*). To the left is a boating lake, which was once the moat. The walls run for 2km around the fort but are much lower on the far side of the fortifications, which once overlooked the river. There are pretty domed pavilions (*chattris*) on the battlements that served as decoration and as sentry posts. The West Gate has large sloping bastions on either side, the southern retaining its small domed pavilion on its roof. The gate itself has two small canopied balconies. Note the hexagram symbols above the larger door arch, and some pretty tiles on the balcony and above the arrow slits at the top of the gateway. Ahead and very slightly to the left on entering the fort is the single-domed Qila-i Kuhna Mosque and further to the right is the octagonal Sher Mandal building. There are two other gates, now closed, to the Purana Qila. Both are designed as two-storey gates, possibly allowing entrance by boat at the lower level, and by drawbridge at the upper level. (The exteriors of both gates are worth studying—the south gate can be seen from within the grounds of Delhi zoo, while the north, or Forbidden, gate can be seen at the other end of the boating lake.)

Qila-i Kuhna Mosque: This early 16th-century mosque is widely acclaimed as a superb example of mosque architecture, arguably the best in Delhi. Its basic design—with five bays and single dome—is relatively simple, and it is the quality of the carved stonework and inlay that makes this mosque special. Notice how different stones have been used to great effect around the archway of the central bay and on the *mihrab*, or prayer niche, inside the mosque. Beyond the mosque is a series of subterranean chambers built into what was the river-facing wall of the fort.

Sher Mandal: This two-storeyed octagonal sandstone building has been described as a library and an observatory, and was possibly both. While coming down from the roof of this building, Emperor Humayun tripped on his robe and fell down the stairs, dying from his injuries three days later. Witnesses say Humayun had climbed onto the roof to observe Venus rising in the evening sky, and on hearing the call of the *muezzin* from Qila-i Kuhna Mosque hurried down the very steep steps too quickly.

Beyond the Sher Mandal the ground slopes downwards, past the remains of a Mughal-period bathhouse and excavations which showed that this site was settled many centuries earlier. The foundations of small mud-brick buildings can be seen here, if the terrain is not too overgrown, which date from the 2nd and 3rd centuries AD.

Buildings close to the Purana Qila

On the other side of the main road from the Purana Qila are more buildings from the early Mughal period. The **Lal Darwaza**, or Red Gate, is thought to have been built in the time of Sher Shah Suri (1540s), and may have formed part of the outer walls of a city briefly known as Delhi Sher Shahi. The remains of shops on either side of the street leading up to the gateway can still be seen. Note the unusual red sculpted panels on either side of the gate and the intersecting yellow arches above them. Next to the Lal Darwaza is a mosque known as the **Khair ul-Munazil**, which literally means 'the most beautiful of houses'. It was built in the 1560s by Akbar's wet-nurse Maham Angah, mother of Adham Khan, whose elegant octagonal tomb is in Mehrauli. The gateway to the mosque has an unusual half-domed recess. The mosque courtyard has two-storeyed cloisters that served as a *madrasa*.

HUMAYUN'S TOMB

The enormous, elegant mausoleum of Humayun, set in 30 acres of gardens, is the crowning glory of early Mughal architecture. It is one of those rare buildings, like the Taj Mahal, to which the usual hyperbolic superlatives do not seem to do justice. It has to be visited to see how the combination of the immensity of this sandstone structure with a seemingly perfect architectural balance gives this tomb an ineffable beauty.

History: Humayun was the second Mughal emperor, the least successful of the early Mughals and now chiefly remembered for his tomb. He officially ruled the Mughal Empire from the death of his father, Babur, in 1530 until his own death, 26 years later. However, he spent little time in Delhi, having been defeated in battle by the Afghan general Sher Shah Suri, whose dynasty lasted 15 years. During this time Humayun was in exile, wandering about northern India, Afghanistan and Persia. He recaptured Delhi in 1555, and within six months he was dead, having fallen down the steps of his library in the Purana Qila (*see opposite*). One of his wives, Hamida, and his son and successor, Akbar, commissioned his tomb, which was completed in 1571.

It is often described as the first of the great Indian tombs to have a Persian-style *char-bagh*, a garden divided into four quarters, which became the hallmark of so much Mughal architecture and design—though there is some doubt about the original layout of the garden. The architect of the *char-bagh* was almost certainly a Persian called Mirak Mirza Ghiyas, who had also worked in the Central Asian city of Bukhara. It represents a revolution in funerary architecture in India—just compare it with the slightly earlier Isa Khan tomb in the same complex (*illustrated on p. 100*) to see the difference.

The mausoleum also became a burial ground for later, lesser Mughals, whose cenotaphs can be seen on the plinth and inside the main building. During the Uprising of 1857, the last of the Mughal emperors, Bahadur Shah Zafar, fled from the Red Fort to Humayun's Tomb. The British captured him and his family and shot dead two of his sons. In 1947, like the Purana Qila, Humayun's Tomb became a refugee camp for the victims of Partition. More recently, a major conservation project led to the restoration of the garden's watercourses and a lowering of the lawns. Part of the complex is now used for Sufi music concerts and occasional state dinners for visiting dignitaries.

Orientation: Humayun's Tomb (*open daily sunrise–sunset*) sits within a large walled compound, outside which are other important and interesting Mughal and Sultanate buildings, and inside which are some of Delhi's prettiest gardens.

Visitors approach the tomb complex from the west, past the distinctive blue-domed Sabz Burj Tomb in the centre of a roundabout, into the car park and ticket office area. Humayun's Tomb is just 400m away, but the view is obscured by an outer and inner gate. On the right, before the small outer gate, is the impressive octagonal Tomb of Isa Khan (*see overleaf*). Beyond the outer gate is a walled garden with a small tomb on the right. On approaching the second inner gate, there is a path to the right which leads to several other buildings, including a mosque, a tomb and another gate to the Humayun's Tomb complex. The entrance gate to the garden of the tomb has, like several buildings in the complex, two hexagrams—the shape that is usually thought of today as the Jewish Star of David, but which is also known as the Seal of Solomon. Inside the gate is a small museum describing the restoration of the garden, but at this point most visitors are too awestruck by their first clear view of the tomb to pay the museum much attention.

The mausoleum

The mausoleum itself consists of a low plinth, on which stands a huge square platform, chamfered at each corner, its sides 93m long. On the platform is a large white-domed building containing the tomb, its striking façade constructed out of red sandstone inlaid with white marble. The mausoleum stands within a large walled garden, carefully laid out in a six-by-six pattern, with watercourses running along the dividing paths, and small pools on the four cardinal axes.

Pass through the inner gate, head past the water pool, and climb the steep 6m high stairs onto the platform. The exterior of the mausoleum is, by the standards of later Mughal tombs, austere. Turn right to find the entrance to the tomb on the south side.

Inside the tomb

Inside is a lobby chamber with a decorated ceiling. Beyond the lobby is the simple cenotaph of Emperor Humayun, whose actual body was buried on the level below, in a crypt accessible through one of the bays in the platform—but which is normally closed to the public. There are *jali* screens and the marble floor is patterned, but, that apart, the original interior decoration of the tomb has disappeared. According to the 17th-century Italian traveller Niccolò Manucci, there were 'many paintings and stones of various kinds, and the roof of the dome is gilded.' Note how the interior of the dome

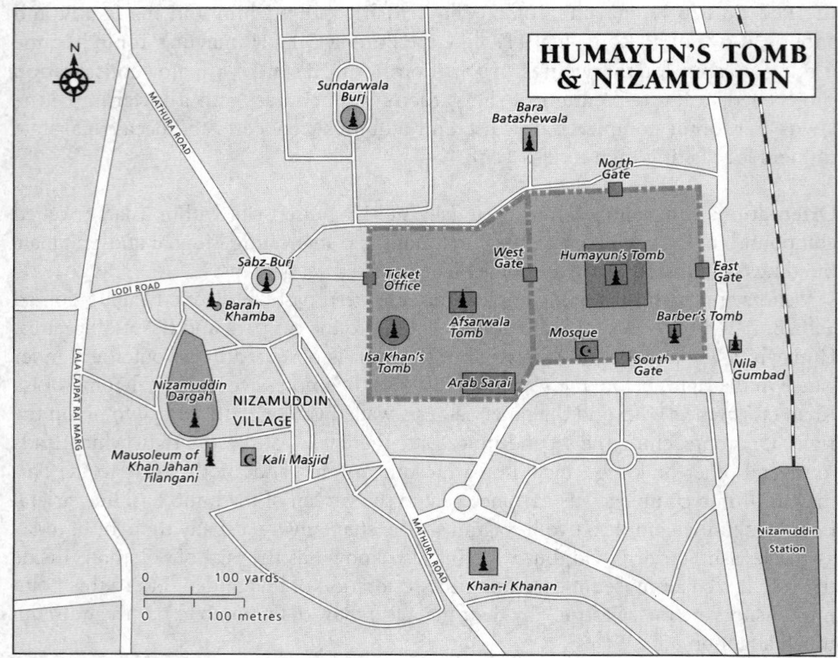

is different from its exterior shape: in fact there are two domes, one on top of the other, with a space in between. There are seven other chambers, apart from the lobby and the tomb room, several of which contain other cenotaphs. In the northwest corner is that of Humayun's wife, Hamida, who was the driving force behind the construction of the tomb; and in the southwest corner are the cenotaphs of the 18th-century emperor Bahadur Shah and his wife. The entire upper part of the mausoleum is laid out in a square pattern with bevelled corners, the shape known as the Baghdad octagon, with alternating very long and very short sides. This shape is repeated inside in the form of four outer Baghdad octagons, grouped around a central chamber, which is also enclosed in a similar octagon.

The rest of the compound

There are excellent views of the entire compound from the platform, and it is worth surveying the area from here before returning to ground level. The external gate opposite the entrance to the tomb, on the south side of the compound, is the original main gateway, long since closed. Near the gate is a small mosque and on the left is a building known as the **Barber's Tomb**, which according to tradition is the grave of Akbar's barber, one of the most important and trusted servants in Mughal times. Note how the east wall is much lower than the others, with a small pavilion at its centre. This was where the river once flowed, and where boats carrying royal visitors to the tomb complex would be moored. The area is now a tangle of railway lines and roads. On the northeast side is a modern Sikh temple.

OTHER BUILDINGS IN THE TOMB COMPLEX

Isa Khan's Tomb and Mosque

This pretty, octagonal mausoleum, to the right of the ticket office on entering the complex, predates Humayun's Tomb by about 25 years and, architecturally, represents the late flowering of an older style of tomb design. Isa Khan was a senior minister during the Sher Shah Suri interregnum, when Humayun was in exile. The building is similar in style to Sher Shah Suri's own tomb in Sasaram, Bihar, as well as to several Sultanate tombs in Delhi, with triple bays on each of its eight sides, an arcaded verandah, projecting eaves, and a cluster of *chattris* and other protuberances surrounding the squat dome, giving the top half of the mausoleum a pyramid-like appearance. The three-bayed mosque has some surviving tiling on its exterior.

Afsarwala Tomb and Mosque

This small tomb and mosque complex, set in the corner of a large walled garden, is accessed through a doorway on the right just before the main entrance to the Humayun's Tomb compound. Afsar comes from the English word officer, and suggests the tomb was that of an important soldier. There are interesting views of Humayun's Tomb from the roof: this is one of the few places from where one can get a view of the tall drum that supports the dome of the tomb.

The mid-16th-century tomb of Isa Khan, one of the finest examples of funerary architecture built in the style of the late Sultanate period.

Arab Sarai

The Arab Sarai is now used as the name for the walled compound beyond the garden with the Afsarwala Tomb and Mosque, but it probably originally included the garden. This is thought to be where 300 Arabs who recited the Koran at Humayun's graveside stayed. It also appears to have been a marketplace, and the compound is divided up into a number of smaller rooms. There is also a fine gateway that local residents (with specially-issued passes) use to get in and out of the tomb complex.

BUILDINGS NEAR THE HUMAYUN COMPLEX

The area around the tomb complex has a number of other interesting buildings, including two that have become Delhi landmarks because they are next to major roads. The **Sabz Burj** is a small early Mughal tomb, with a tall stretched blue-tiled dome, in the middle of the roundabout near the entrance road to Humayun's Tomb. The large **Khan-i Khanan** is a tomb that stands next to the Mathura Road, which runs between the Humayun's Tomb complex and Nizamuddin. It is an impressive early 17th-century mausoleum, built for a Mughal nobleman and poet, but which was stripped of external decoration and stonework, allegedly for the construction of Safdarjung's Tomb. Its shape and design represent a mid-way stage between Humayun's Tomb and the Taj Mahal, and some experts believe that the latter building was consciously based on the Khan-i Khanan Tomb.

Slightly harder to find, but also very interesting, are the **Nila Gumbad** (blue-domed tomb), with its fine mosaic tilework, which is to the east of the main tomb complex, and some tombs in the Scouts' camp and nursery gardens to the north of Humayun's tomb. These include the unusual **Bara Batashewala**, an early 17th-century tomb, consisting of a sunken burial chamber with eight interlinked chambers beneath a flat roof. Also notice the fine plasterwork decoration on the small **Sundarwala Burj**, a tomb inside the government nursery.

NIZAMUDDIN

The area known as Nizamuddin is named after Sheikh Nizamuddin Aulia, a Muslim saint who died in 1325, and was a disciple of the branch of Sufi Islam founded by Moinuddin Chishti of Ajmer in Rajasthan. Like the Sufi *dargah*, or shrine complex, in Mehrauli, the grave of Sheikh Nizamuddin Aulia has been a place of pilgrimage for many centuries. Around the Nizamuddin *dargah* there are many other tombs and mosques dating from the 14th to the 20th centuries.

The *dargah* is still an important place of pilgrimage, and not only for Muslims. It attracts visitors of all faiths, and Thursday is thought to be the most auspicious day to pay homage to Nizamuddin. Every Thursday after sunset, *qawwali* musicians play music and sing in the central courtyard of the shrine. Visitors are welcome at the performance.

Approaching the *dargah*

The *dargah*, in the area known as Nizamuddin West, is approached along a broad bustling road, with lots of street vendors. The road narrows as it nears the entrance to the *dargah*. To the left, through a Mughal gateway, a quick detour takes visitors to the 17th-century **Chausath Khamba Mausoleum**, a fine white-marble pillared hall built by the son of the Mughal nobleman Atgah Khan, whose tomb is inside the *dargah*. Chausath Khamba means '64 columns', for once an accurate count. Next to the Chausath Khamba is the **tomb of Ghalib**, the great 19th-century Delhi poet who was an eloquent witness to the death of the Mughal Empire in 1857 and the rise of imperial Britain. On returning to the main road, it is possible to take another quick detour to the right to the ruins of the 13th-century **Lal Mahal** (Red Palace), which is probably the oldest building in the Nizamuddin area. Beyond the Lal Mahal is the 15th-century **Barah Khamba Tomb**. The name Barah Khamba means '12 columns' and is presumed to be a reference to the number of double columns around the central chamber. It is not known who was buried here.

THE NIZAMUDDIN DARGAH

The *dargah* itself is a fascinating complex of more than a dozen buildings and shrines, of which the most important are the grave of Nizamuddin himself, the Jamaat Khana Mosque, and the tombs of Atgah Khan and the poet Amir Khusro. Many of the buildings have been heavily restored and altered over the centuries, as is often the case with living pilgrimage sites, and in the later Mughal period many royal princes and princesses were buried here. The original simple **grave of Nizamuddin**, who died in the early 14th century, is now surrounded by later Mughal structures, including 16th-century screens, a 17th-century wooden canopy, and marble pillars and a striped dome from the early 19th century. Note the mother-of-pearl inlay in the wooden canopy. The actual grave is covered with a green cloth, over which devotees scatter rose petals.

The **Jamaat Khana Mosque** is immediately behind the grave of Nizamuddin. It was built before Nizamuddin died in 1325 and was possibly originally intended as his mausoleum. However, many religious Muslims insist on being buried in the open, and it is said that, as a result, the building was instead transformed into a mosque by the addition of side chambers. It is thought to have been constructed during the reign of Alauddin Khilji (died 1316), who was also responsible for the very similar Alai Darwaza near the Qutb Minar.

Near the Nizamuddin grave and the mosque are small screened compounds containing Mughal cenotaphs. These include the **grave of Jahanara**, the daughter of Emperor Shah Jahan, who became his closest companion after the death of Mumtaz Mahal. Jahanara asked that her grave be covered in grass, and her marble cenotaph has been constructed so as to allow grass to grow on it. On either side of her cenotaph are the graves of children of later Mughal emperors. Immediately beside this compound is the screened enclosure containing the **grave of Muhammad Shah Rangila** (died 1748), the Mughal ruler during the sacking of Delhi by the Persian emperor Nadir Shah, who took the Peacock Throne and the Kohinoor diamond back with him. Just south of these enclosures is the 17th-century **Tomb of Amir Khusro**, the 13th–14th-century poet and disciple of Nizamuddin.

The other major building in the Nizamuddin *dargah* complex is the **Tomb of Atgah Khan**, a nobleman whose wife was one of Akbar's wet-nurses. Atgah Khan was murdered by Adham Khan, the son of another of Akbar's wet-nurses—and whom Akbar himself then killed (Adham Khan's much larger tomb is in Mehrauli). Atgah Khan's tomb has some very fine carved marble and sandstone, with a painted plasterwork ceiling.

Other buildings near the Nizamuddin Dargah

Just to the south of the *dargah* complex is a walled enclosure known as **Kotla Nizamuddin**, inside of which is the **Mausoleum of Khan Jahan Tilangani**, Feroze Shah Tughlaq's prime minister, who died in 1368. It is Delhi's earliest octagonal tomb, but is difficult to inspect properly, as it is occupied by families who have lived there for generations; some stucco decoration is visible on the outside walls, however. Next to the Kotla Nizamuddin enclosure is the partially ruined **Kali Masjid**, or Black Mosque, which was completed in 1370 and is one of the seven Delhi mosques built by Feroze Shah Tughlaq.

THE RED FORT & OLD DELHI

Delhi's famous Red Fort is part of a 17th-century planned city, now known as Old Delhi or Shahjahanabad, built by the Mughal emperor Shah Jahan. In the late 17th century, Shah Jahan's Delhi was one of the world's largest cities. The city went into gradual decline, as it was sacked by a series of invading armies in the 18th century. The British took control of Delhi at the start of the 19th century though the Mughal emperor, known by the British as the 'King of Delhi', remained the *de jure* authority in the city. After the failed Uprising of 1857, Delhi was evacuated and many buildings destroyed. It became a minor city under the British for more than 50 years, until 1911 when they decided to shift the capital from Calcutta to Delhi. Until the British began building a new capital city immediately to its south, Old Delhi was Delhi. The traditional ways and culture of Old Delhi took a further blow in 1947, when many Muslim families left for Pakistan. Today, Old Delhi has a cluttered, neglected feel to it, a tiny part of a rapidly expanding megacity—but it remains an extraordinary place to explore. It has also become much easier to visit thanks to the new underground Metro.

There are also some older pre-Mughal buildings in and close to Old Delhi, including the fascinating ruins of the 14th-century Tughlaq fifth city of Delhi, known as Feroze Shah Kotla. And the memorials to Mahatma Gandhi and other 20th-century leaders are situated on the green lawns of Rajghat, opposite the Red Fort and the walls of Old Delhi, on land that was once the riverbed of the Yamuna, now flowing further east.

THE RED FORT

After the Taj Mahal, Delhi's Red Fort (*open 9–6 Tues–Sun*), or Lal Qila, is the most famous of Emperor Shah Jahan's buildings. The imposing red sandstone walls on the land side of the fort are intact, as are its more modest riverside walls; and the fort contains some important late Mughal architecture. The moat that surrounded the land side of the fort has been filled in.

History: From the mid-17th century (construction started in 1638) until the Mughal Empire was formally overthrown in 1857, the Red Fort was the main residence of the emperor. His private quarters were in the eastern part of the fort, which then overlooked the river. The Red Fort was designed to impress visitors with its size and grandeur, but it proved hard to defend. The fort was sacked several times by invading armies in the 18th century, until the British took *de facto* control of Delhi in 1803. The Mughal Empire continued to exist in name, and many of the old rituals and traditions survived until 1857, but the emperor had little real power.

The last of the Mughal emperors, Bahadur Shah Zafar, was put on trial here by the British after the 1857 Uprising (also known as the Mutiny), to which he had rather unwillingly lent his name. He was exiled to Burma, where he died in 1862. The British turned large parts of the Red Fort into a barracks, destroying some Mughal buildings. The Indian Army took over most of the fort at Independence in 1947. On 15th August, India's Independence Day, the prime minister delivers his annual speech to the nation from the ramparts of the Red Fort, and the national flag is raised. The fort was only officially relinquished by the Indian Army in 2003, though the mosque, gardens and most of the remaining palaces had been open to the public since British times. The fort was declared a UNESCO World Heritage Site in 2007.

Orientation: Access to the Red Fort is from the western **Lahori Gate**, where the walls are at their most impressive, more than 30m high. A large part of the area on the Old Delhi side of the fort was once full of buildings, but they were cleared by the British after 1857. The Lahori Gate is aligned perfectly with the main east–west street of Old Delhi, known as Chandni Chowk. The actual gate is obscured by a defensive barbican erected by Shah Jahan's son (and jailer) Aurangzeb. Note the modern lift installed to allow the prime minister easy access to the ramparts for the Independence Day speech. Immediately inside is a covered market place, the **Chatta Chowk**, a rarity in India and based on a Persian design. To the left of the market place, and now closed off, were the public areas of the fort, with workshops and stables, and congested streets and alleyways similar to the rest of the city outside. To the right, also closed off, was where the most junior members of the imperial family stayed—often, by the end of the Mughal period, in conditions of great poverty. Directly ahead is the **Naubat Khana**, or Naqqar Khana (drum house), where musicians used to play and where visitors had to dismount before entering the inner sanctum of the fort.

Diwan-i Am

Through the archway of the Naubat Khana is a large open area that leads, at the far end, to the Diwan-i Am, where the emperor used to meet members of the public. This large covered rectangular cloister is supported by octagonal columns and cusped arches. In an alcove on a raised platform at the back of the hall an imperial throne (probably not the Peacock Throne, which would have been in the Diwan-i Khas) once stood under the elegant marble canopy. The canopy partially conceals some superb stone inlay work in the niche behind. The black panels that make up this fine wall decoration, most of them portraying birds, were probably imported from Italy, and use the *pietra dura* technique (highly polished cut stones of different hues) that was so effective at the Taj Mahal. The top panel shows the mythological Greek musician Orpheus playing on his lyre. The very fine white marble inlay that surrounds the panels is thought to be the work of local craftsmen. The throne alcove is aligned with the Lahori Gate and Chandni Chowk and, until Aurangzeb erected the outer bastion of the gate, the emperor seated on his throne would have had a direct line of sight into Shahjahanabad.

To enter the private quarters of the palace, which once overlooked the river, walk behind the Diwan-i Am. To the south, where there are now no buildings from Shah Jahan's time, were the palaces of the *zenana*—the private quarters of the women of the imperial household.

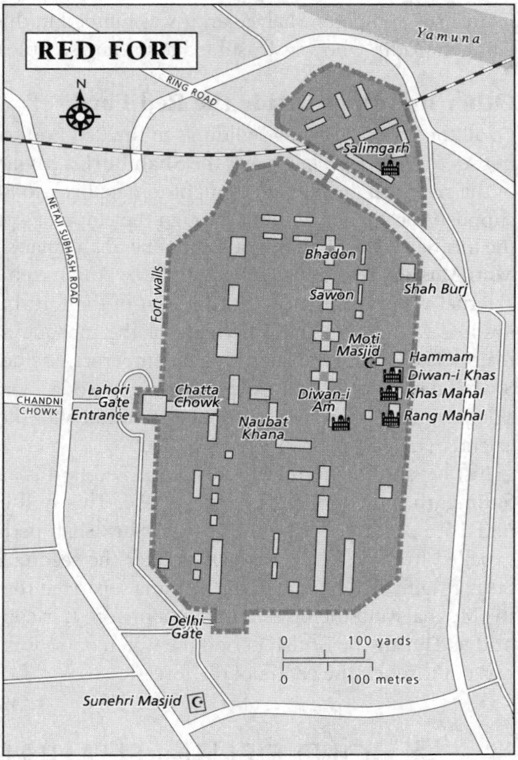

Rang Mahal

This open palace is directly behind the Diwan-i Am, beyond a small garden with a square pool. In Shah Jahan's time, the Rang Mahal (Coloured Palace) was seen as the most beautiful of the Red Fort buildings. A small stream, known as the Nahar-i Bahisht, or 'canal of paradise', passed alongside the entire eastern side of the fort. The palace's central chamber has a marble floor beautifully carved in the shape of a flattened lotus flower, with a fountain in the middle. At each end of the Rang Mahal are smaller partly-enclosed chambers, decorated with inlaid glass.

Khas Mahal

To the north of the Rang Mahal is the smaller Khas Mahal (Private Palace), which were the emperor's private rooms. A small octagonal tower on the outer wall overlooks what was, in Shah Jahan's time, the western bank of the River Yamuna. The Khas Mahal has perforated *jali* marble screens of exceptional quality. Note the depiction of the scales of justice on one of the northern screens.

Diwan-i Khas

The emperor would meet his ministers and senior advisers in the Diwan-i Khas, which also contained the famous Peacock Throne—taken from here, along with the Kohinoor diamond, by the invading Persian army of Nadir Shah in 1739. The floral marble inlay is of high quality. On the walls of the Diwan-i Khas are inscribed the words of the 14th-century Delhi poet Amir Khusro: 'If there be heaven on earth, this is it, this is it, this is it.' In 1787, Emperor Shah Alam II was blinded in this hall by the plundering warlord Ghulam Qadir, who was frustrated at finding so little treasure in the fort.

Other buildings inside the Red Fort

Of all the other surviving buildings in the Red Fort, only two, the **Hammam**, or bath-house (*closed to the public*), and the **Shah Burj**, a pavilion and tower at the northern end of the river-facing wall, are thought to date back to Shah Jahan's time. The water that supplied the stream running through the emperor's private quarters was pumped into the fort here. The Shah Burj also became Shah Jahan's favourite place of work. The tiny **Moti Masjid** (Pearl Mosque) was built by Aurangzeb as his own private mosque—the external walls are aligned with the rest of the fort, but the internal layout faces west, towards Mecca. On the other side of the mosque are some gardens and pavilions, mainly laid out by the later Mughal emperors, including the last of the line, Bahadur Shah Zafar, who died in exile in Burma in 1862. Some experts believe the two pool-side pavilions, known as **Sawon** and **Bhadon** after the two rainy months in the Hindu calendar, date from Shah Jahan's period.

Just beyond the northern walls of the Red Fort is a smaller, older fortification called **Salimgarh**, now reopened to the public. This well-built fort was constructed in the mid-16th century, during the 15-year Sher Shah period, when the Mughals had been expelled from Delhi. It was named after the second ruler of the dynasty, Salim Shah Suri. Originally, a branch of the Yamuna separated the Red Fort from Salimgarh, which the Mughals and the British used as a prison. It is connected to the Red Fort by a foot-bridge. During the British period the watercourse was covered by a road, and a railway was cut through the centre of the fort.

OLD DELHI—SHAHJAHANABAD

History: On maps of the late 19th century, what is now known as Old Delhi is described as Modern Delhi, to distinguish it from the early Mughal and Sultanate versions of the city further to the south. Shahjahanabad, or the Walled City, as Old Delhi is also known, was a planned urban area enclosed within 9km long walls. The Red Fort, overlooking the river, was the citadel and the seat of imperial government. On a mound 500m away from the walls of the fort was the other great building of Shah Jahan's new city, the main mosque, the Jama Masjid. A major east–west road, Chandni Chowk, was constructed with a canal running down its centre and an arcaded bazaar on both sides. A road heading south out of the fort towards the ruins of earlier Mughal and Sultanate Delhi was also built. Eight city gates were constructed along the walls. The city was placed under the control of the *kotwal* (magistrate), divided into 12 *thanas* (districts) under the control of *thanadars*, and further subdivided into *mohallas*. Many of these divisions were settled by a particular vocational or ethnic group, such as washermen, needle-makers, Punjabis or Marwaris. Parts of Shahjahanbad are still known by the predominant trade or occupation of that area. Large *havelis*, or mansions with interior courtyards, were built, at first by Mughal nobles or by princely families allied to the Mughal Empire, then later by rich traders.

Orientation: The basic layout of the walled city remains as it was in Mughal times, though the building of railway lines in the British colonial period resulted in the northern part of Old Delhi being detached from the rest of the city. The western walls of the city were destroyed at the same time. However, large portions of the walls, four of the gates, many mosques and other religious buildings, and a few *havelis* survive from Mughal times.

Today Old Delhi can be a confusing place to visit. Many of its streets are very narrow and the buildings high, making it hard to orient oneself. Vehicular access to many parts of Old Delhi is extremely difficult, and the Metro is recommended as a means of getting to and from Old Delhi. Chandni Chowk Metro station deposits visitors in the commercial centre of the walled city, and it is still relatively easy to access the areas close to the Red Fort and the Jama Masjid by vehicle.

Jama Masjid (Friday Mosque)

The 17th-century Jama Masjid (*open daily 8–6; normally closed to non-Muslims from 12.30–2; closed Fri 11–2*) is Delhi's largest and most important mosque. It was built, along with dozens of smaller mosques, as part of the new city constructed by the Mughal emperor Shah Jahan. By the mid-19th century the area between the fort and the mosque had become built up, but it was cleared of all buildings by the British after the 1857 Uprising. The mosque itself, completed in 1656, was constructed on a natural rise in the land, and it stands 10m above the rest of the city. It has three gates with steep stone steps leading up to an enormous square paved courtyard, empty but for a large pool for washing before prayers. The ceremonial eastern gate, facing the Red Fort—through which the emperor would enter—is now closed. The public enter from the northern or southern gates. Unusually, the mosque's arcades are open on both sides so that the city can be seen from the courtyard of the mosque. Note also how the main mosque building has been built out into the courtyard, and that the two minarets are not therefore in a corner of the complex but very much inside it. One of the three-storeyed minarets is usually open and can be climbed, and there are exceptional views over Old Delhi from the top.

South of the Jama Masjid

Head south from the Jama Masjid (with the famous Old Delhi landmark, Karim's Restaurant, on the left) towards Turkman Gate. On the right, in the backstreets, are Old Delhi's most important pre-Mughal buildings—all of them Muslim. These include: the unimpressive tomb of Sultan Razia, Delhi's only female ruler, who died in 1240; the shrine of Shah Turkman, a 13th-century Sufi saint; and the **Kalan Masjid** (1387), one of the seven mosques built during the rule of Feroze Shah Tughlaq. The mosque gateway, with distinctive Tughlaq sloping walls, is approached up a stone staircase. The interior has been heavily restored and painted, but the external structure is intact. Ask for access to the mosque roof, with its 28 small domes that cover the prayer hall and

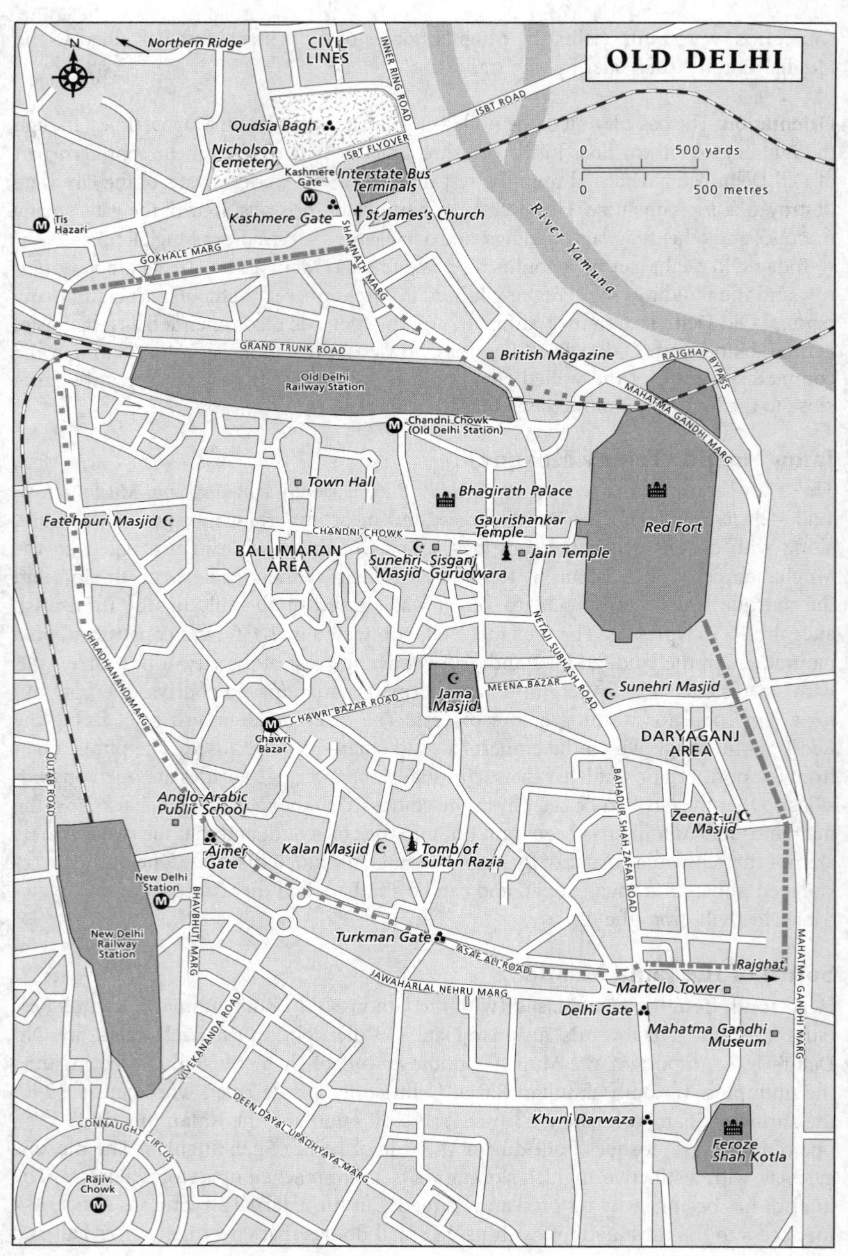

OLD DELHI
N
Northern Ridge
CIVIL LINES
INNER RING ROAD
ISBT ROAD
Qudsia Bagh
Nicholson Cemetery
ISBT FLYOVER
Kashmere Gate
Interstate Bus Terminals
0 500 yards
0 500 metres
Tis Hazari
Kashmere Gate
St James's Church
River Yamuna
SHAMNATH MARG
GOKHALE MARG
GRAND TRUNK ROAD
British Magazine
RAJGHAT BYPASS
Old Delhi Railway Station
MAHATMA GANDHI MARG
Chandni Chowk (Old Delhi Station)
Town Hall
Bhagirath Palace
Fatehpuri Masjid
Gaurishankar Temple
Red Fort
CHANDNI CHOWK
BALLIMARAN AREA
Sunehri Masjid
Sisganj Gurudwara
Jain Temple
NETAJI SUBHASH ROAD
SHRADHANAND MARG
Jama Masjid
MEENA BAZAR
Sunehri Masjid
CHAWRI BAZAR ROAD
Chawri Bazar
DARYAGANJ AREA
QUTAB ROAD
BAHADUR SHAH ZAFAR ROAD
Anglo-Arabic Public School
Zeenat-ul Masjid
Ajmer Gate
Kalan Masjid
Tomb of Sultan Razia
New Delhi Station
BHAVBHUTI MARG
Turkman Gate
ASAF ALI ROAD
Rajghat
New Delhi Railway Station
JAWAHARLAL NEHRU MARG
Martello Tower
Delhi Gate
MAHATMA GANDHI MARG
Mahatma Gandhi Museum
VIVEKANANDA ROAD
DEEN DAYAL UPADHYAYA MARG
CONNAUGHT CIRCUS
Khuni Darwaza
Feroze Shah Kotla
Rajiv Chowk

the cloisters. **Turkman Gate** itself, still intact and with octagonal turrets on either side, is 300m southeast of the Kalan Masjid. About 600m to the east of the mosque is **Ajmer Gate**, which now serves as an unusually distinguished traffic island.

Just beyond Ajmer Gate is one of Delhi's finest 18th-century buildings, known as the **Anglo-Arabic Public School** (formerly Delhi College). It was built as an Islamic school, or *madrasa*, attached to the mosque and tomb of Ghaziuddin Khan, a Mughal courtier, whose son became the first nizam of Hyderabad, southern India's most important princely state. The two-storeyed cloisters surround a large courtyard. Behind the school buildings are the three bulbous white domes of the red sandstone mosque and, to the left, the open tomb, protected by high marble screens.

South of the Red Fort: Daryaganj

This part of Old Delhi, known as Daryaganj, has two fine 18th-century mosques, the small **Sunehri Masjid** (Golden Mosque)—one of three with the same name in Old Delhi—and the larger **Zeenat-ul Masjid**. The Sunehri Masjid is the only significant building close to Red Fort that the British did not demolish after 1857. Further south, along the river walls of Old Delhi, is the Zeenat-ul Masjid, also known as the Ghata Masjid, built by Emperor Aurangzeb's daughter Zeenatunnisa. It is beautifully proportioned, and has three very pretty black and white striped domes. After the failed Uprising of 1857, this mosque was converted into a bakery and only restored as a place of worship in the early 20th century. The mosque formed the backdrop for several scenes in the 1962 Merchant Ivory movie *The Householder*. Further south is the **Delhi Gate**, so named because in Shah Jahan's time it led to what was then thought of as historical Delhi. It has become, like Ajmer Gate, a traffic island. To the east of Delhi Gate, alongside the southern walls of Shahjahanabad, is a very small free-standing fortification, or **Martello Tower**, erected by the British. Four hundred metres further down the road, beyond the modern cricket stadium of the same name, is the entrance to Feroze Shah Kotla, the important remains of a late Tughlaq city fortification (*see overleaf*).

Around Chandni Chowk

Eastern Chandni Chowk: This part of Old Delhi is very busy, and remains the city's commercial heart. Start at the eastern (Red Fort) end of Chandni Chowk. The first building on the south side is a Jain temple and an adjoining Jain-run bird hospital, which allows visitors (there are several interesting older Jain temples just to the south, in the back alleys off Chandni Chowk). Immediately next door is the 18th-century **Gaurishankar Hindu Temple**, and 300m further, on the same side of the road, is the much modernised 17th-century Sikh **Sisganj Gurdwara**, or temple, which marks the site where the ninth Sikh guru, Tegh Bahadur, was beheaded on the orders of Emperor Aurangzeb. Just beyond the Gurdwara is the **Sunehri Masjid**, or Golden Mosque—on its first-floor platform the invading Persian emperor, Nadir Shah, supervised the massacre of tens of thousands of Delhi-ites on a single night in 1739. In 1857, after the collapse of the Uprising, Chandni Chowk was once again strewn with corpses—so many of them that the horses of the British victors could not be ridden down the street without stepping on the dead.

On the other side of the road from the mosque and gurdwara, down a small back street, is the **Palace of Begum Samru**, also known as the **Bhagirath Palace**. Begum Samru was the rich Indian widow of a European mercenary called Walter Reinhardt, who was nicknamed Sombre (or Samru) because of his dark complexion. Begum eventually became the ruler of the princely state of Sardhana in Uttar Pradesh (*see p. 228*) and built a large European-style mansion in Delhi. The columns of the façade, and at the back of the building, are still clearly visible. The front rooms of the palace were turned into a bank not long after Begum Samru's death (see the old Lloyds Bank signage on the top of the building), and the palace still houses offices of the Central Bank of India. The rest of the building is a huge electrical goods market.

Central and western Chandni Chowk: On the north side of Chandni Chowk, about 300m after the Sunehri Masjid, is the colonial-period **town hall**, built in 1864 on the site of a group of 17th-century buildings known as Jahanara's Sarai, after the daughter of Shah Jahan. It is an impressive two-storey building, constructed in the European Classical style, with Corinthian capitals and arched openings.

On the southern side of Chandni Chowk, just beyond the town hall, is the area known as **Ballimaran**, which contains some of Old Delhi's best surviving *havelis*, or mansions built around a courtyard. Those that survive are mainly from the 19th century and, as many are no longer the property of one family, there is usually open access to the courtyard, offering a nosy visitor a chance to see some interesting domestic architecture by simply walking the streets of Ballimaran.

In a prominent position, marking the western end of Chandni Chowk, is Old Delhi's second most important mosque, the **Fatehpuri Masjid**, built by one of Shah Jahan's wives, Fatehpuri Begum, in 1650. It is a single-domed red sandstone building that was sold by the British to a Hindu trader for 40,000 rupees after the Uprising of 1857, and restored to Muslim worshippers 20 years later.

North of the Red Fort

Prior to the fall of the Mughal Empire in 1857, the British had a foothold in the part of the walled city north of the Red Fort, near Kashmere Gate. There was intense fighting in this area during the Uprising of 1857. The area includes some early 19th-century colonial bungalows and **St James's Church**, built in 1836. This is Delhi's earliest intact church, and was constructed by Colonel James Skinner, a half-Scottish, half-Indian mercenary, who eventually led an irregular cavalry regiment, known as Skinner's Horse, under the British. This fine church was built by army engineers to an unusual design. The elegant Florentine dome rises over the nave, where the congregation sits, rather than, as is more common, over the crossing or chancel. On the north side of the church is the Skinner family's private burial ground.

South of the church is the **former British Residency**, now an archaeology office within the grounds of a university. Part of the building is thought to have been the library of Dara Shikoh, Shah Jahan's oldest son, who was murdered on the orders of his brother and future emperor, Aurangzeb. Behind the church, away from the main road, is the **former home of the British Deputy Resident** in the early 19th century; it is now owned by the railways. Its basement contains rooms thought to be from Shah Jahan's period, when this was the palace of his leading general, Ali Mardan Shah, who built the canals that served Shahjahanabad.

A little to the north of the church, before the huge overground Metro station, are the ruins of **Kashmere Gate**, originally the largest of the city's gateways. The gate was badly damaged during the 1857 rebellion. Further down the road towards the Red Fort, on the traffic island, are the remains of the **British Magazine**, also badly damaged in 1857.

BUILDINGS & MONUMENTS CLOSE TO OLD DELHI

Feroze Shah Kotla

The 14th-century ruins of Feroze Shah Kotla (*open dawn–dusk*), just outside the walls of the much more recent Old Delhi, are a fascinating jumble of buildings. This was the citadel of Feroze Shah Tughlaq, who was one of north India's more benign rulers of the Sultanate period. Feroze Shah was a builder and rebuilder of cities and monuments, and constructed the new city of Ferozabad, the fifth city of Delhi, here on the banks of the Yamuna—though it seems that the Jahanpanah in South Delhi may have continued to function as the Tughlaq capital. Ferozabad was the first of the cities to have been built along the river, guaranteeing a source of water and an easy means of transport. The rest of Feroze Shah's city does not survive, probably having been destroyed in the building of Old Delhi—but the *Kotla* (small fortress) remains, with its high walls, old mosque and *madrasa*, and its Ashoka Pillar. According to a contemporary, there were five palaces inside the citadel—all now gone. Despite the impressive scale of the walls, (note the loop-holes for arrows), they were probably intended more for show than for military purposes—there is no evidence of a walkway along the top of the walls from which the building could have been defended.

Inside the main gate there are the remains of guard houses. The citadel is now largely a peaceful, open green area. Straight ahead, towards the riverside walls, are the two key surviving structures, a pyramid-like building on which a tall stone pillar stands, and, slightly to its right, Feroze Shah's Jama Masjid, or Friday Mosque.

Ashoka Pillar building: This unusual three-storeyed stepped building, possibly a palace built in the 1350s, containing many small chambers, was almost certainly constructed specially for the 13m Ashoka Pillar that sits on its summit. Feroze Shah had this pillar (its estimated weight is 27 tonnes) brought by boat from Topra, more than 200km away. Another pillar brought to Delhi by Feroze Shah stands on the Ridge, near the Mutiny Memorial. The pillar is one of many originally erected by Emperor Ashoka in the 3rd century BC, and is inscribed with seven of his edicts aimed at encouraging the spread of Buddhism and good government. It would have had a sculpture, probably of an animal, on its capital. The Brahmi script of the inscriptions could no longer be understood in Feroze Shah's time, and later a legend spread that this was the victory column of Alexander the Great, who reached the River Indus a few decades before the birth of Ashoka. The script, which is still astonishingly clear after more than 2,000 years, was eventually deciphered in the 19th century.

Feroze Shah's Mosque: Despite being in ruins, Feroze's Shah Jama Masjid (1350s) is still a place of pilgrimage and worship. On Thursdays, large numbers of people gather here to pray, and to ask favours or beg forgiveness of the *djinns*, or genies, that they believe inhabit these ruins. Notice the long tunnel-like passage that runs along the back of the western wall of the mosque. The *djinns* are believed to inhabit the arched chambers beneath the mosque. In 1759 the Mughal emperor Alamgir II was murdered on the orders of his chief adviser while visiting Feroze Shah Kotla to meet a Sufi preacher.

Khuni Darwaza: On the main road, near the road leading to Feroze Shah Kotla, is a 16th-century gate known as the Khuni Darwaza, or Bloody Gateway. It was given this name in 1857, because this was where three Mughal princes were killed by the British in the aftermath of the failed Uprising. The gate is thought to have been originally built by Sher Shah Suri in the 1540s.

Rajghat

The area east of Feroze Shah Kotla and Old Delhi, which was once the course and floodplain of the River Yamuna, is now a huge peaceful park, known as Rajghat, with memorials to many of India's 20th-century leaders. Furthest south is the **place of Mahatma Gandhi's cremation (Gandhi Darshan)**. It is marked by a simple monument in black marble in an open-air sunken garden. Visiting dignitaries are often brought here, and there are usually queues of Indian tourists and children waiting to pay tribute to the 'Father of the Nation'. Among the other leaders cremated here, and for whom memorials have been constructed, are India's first three post-independence prime ministers—Jawaharlal Nehru, Lal Bahadur Shastri and Nehru's daughter, Indira Gandhi. There are also memorials to her two sons, Rajiv, a former prime minister who, like his mother, was assassinated, and Sanjay, who died in a plane accident.

There is a **Mahatma Gandhi Museum** diagonally opposite his memorial on the other side of the road. It contains some of his old pocket-watches, a pair of spectacles, two of his teeth (extracted in 1936), the shawl he was wearing on the day of his assassination and one of the bullets that killed him.

WEST OF OLD DELHI

To the west of Old Delhi are several little-visited buildings that are of historical importance. **Qadam Sharif** is a 14th-century shrine containing what is believed to be the footprint of the Prophet Muhammad, as well as the tomb of Atgah Khan, the son of Feroze Shah Tughlaq, the ruler of Delhi and large parts of north India from 1351 to 1388. It is hard to find, near the Jai Hind School, in a poor area of the city called Nabi Karim, just outside what were the western walls of Shahjahanabad. The footprint is locked away, but the simple tomb, set in a two-storeyed pavilion, is enclosed within a colonnaded structure, surrounded on all sides by more modern buildings. About 600m to the northwest is the **Shahi Idgah**, a large walled open-air mosque used at times when very large numbers of Muslims gather for prayer; it was built in the early 18th century, during the reign of Emperor Aurangzeb. There is an interesting old Muslim cemetery opposite the Idgah.

Delhi's earliest surviving Christian place of worship, the 18th-century **Eremao Armenian Chapel**, can be found 200m northwest of Kishanganj railway station. The chapel is being used a place of residence, but the main building is intact and a number of graves, with the distinctive Armenian script, can be seen nearby. Several Indian cities had small communities of Armenian Christian traders during Mughal times.

NEW DELHI

In 1911, the city of Delhi was a parochial place with a population of less than 250,000, most of whom lived in the old walled city, built by the Mughal emperor Shah Jahan more than a quarter of a millennium earlier. Since the Uprising of 1857, and the death of the Mughal Empire, Delhi had been a much diminished city. Then, on 12th December 1911, the visiting British King-Emperor George V announced that the capital of British India, and the second city of the British Empire, would be transferred from Calcutta to Delhi—or rather to an unbuilt New Delhi. What followed were more than two decades of construction on largely scrub and agricultural land situated between Shah Jahan's city and the much older tombs and ruins of Sultanate Delhi. It was intended as a magnificent new city that would inspire among Britain's Indian subjects a sense of awe for an empire that was expected to endure for centuries. But in 1947, not long after the city was completed, the British left, in something of a hurry, and New Delhi became the home of the government of independent India.

A planned city

New Delhi was carefully planned on an enormous scale, with huge government buildings, broad open streets and smaller residences set in large gardens for India's rulers. The great buildings of this city are undeniably monumental, and the name of the chief architect, Edwin Lutyens, has been immortalised in what is now, rather inaccurately, known as Lutyens' Delhi. Lutyens was, in fact, the architect for only a very few of New Delhi's buildings, and his colleague Herbert Baker, with whom Lutyens later fell out, played as important a role in drawing up the plans for the new city.

When it was chosen, the site for the new capital was on the southern edge of the existing urban area. But today, Lutyens' Delhi has been encircled by more modern development, and is at the heart of a megacity. Architects, historians and the people of the city continue to disagree about whether New Delhi was a triumph or failure of urban planning. It is certainly impressive as a place to visit, but it is also quite forbidding and deserted. The long ceremonial avenue, formerly Kingsway and now known as Rajpath, only really comes into its own on Republic Day, when processions

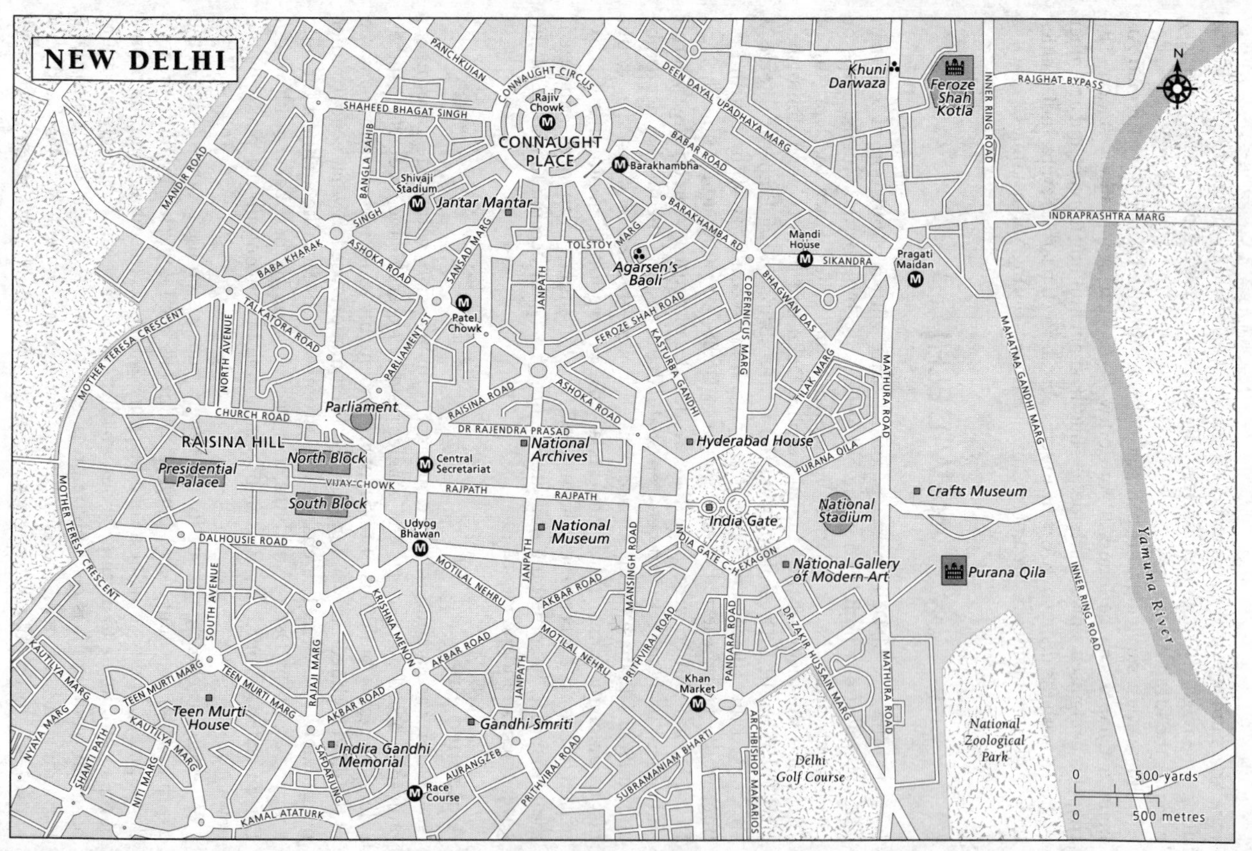

NEW DELHI
N
PANCHKUIAN
CONNAUGHT CIRCUS
Rajiv Chowk
CONNAUGHT PLACE
SHAHEED BHAGAT SINGH
DEEN DAYAL UPADHAYA MARG
Khuni Darwaza
Feroze Shah Kotla
INNER RING ROAD
RAJGHAT BYPASS
BABAR ROAD
Barakhambha
BANGLA SAHIB
Shivaji Stadium
Jantar Mantar
MANDIR ROAD
SINGH
BARAKHAMBA RD
INDRAPRASHTRA MARG
TOLSTOY MARG
Agarsen's Baoli
Mandi House
SIKANDRA
Pragati Maidan
BABA KHARAK
ASHOKA ROAD
SANSAD MARG
Patel Chowk
JANPATH
FEROZE SHAH ROAD
COPERNICUS MARG
BHAGWAN DAS
TALKATORA ROAD
MOTHER TERESA CRESCENT
NORTH AVENUE
PARLIAMENT ST
KASTURBA GANDHI
TILAK MARG
MATHURA ROAD
MAHATMA GANDHI MARG
Parliament
RAISINA ROAD
CHURCH ROAD
DR RAJENDRA PRASAD
RAISINA HILL
National Archives
Hyderabad House
PURANA QILA
North Block
Central Secretariat
Presidential Palace
VIJAY CHOWK
RAJPATH
Crafts Museum
South Block
National Stadium
India Gate
Udyog Bhawan
National Museum
DALHOUSIE ROAD
MANSINGH ROAD
INDIA GATE C-HEXAGON
National Gallery of Modern Art
Purana Qila
MOTILAL NEHRU
AKBAR ROAD
INNER RING ROAD
Yamuna River
SOUTH AVENUE
KRISHNA MENON
PRITHVIRAJ ROAD
PANDARA ROAD
DR ZAKIR HUSSAIN MARG
KAUTILYA MARG
TEEN MURTI MARG
RAJAJI MARG
Khan Market
Teen Murti House
Gandhi Smriti
NYAYA MARG
SHANTI PATH
NITI MARG
SAFDARJUNG
Indira Gandhi Memorial
AURANGZEB
SUBRAMANIAM BHARTI
ARCHBISHOP MAKARIOS
Delhi Golf Course
National Zoological Park
Race Course
KAMAL ATATURK
0
500 yards
500 metres

of marching soldiers and military vehicles pass by in front of enormous crowds. The rest of the time the centre of Delhi—one of the most populous cities in the world—is remarkably empty, except for a few picnickers near India Gate. It feels very different from the rest of Delhi.

LUTYENS

Best known for designing British country houses and their gardens, and with little experience of town planning, Edwin Lutyens (1869–1944) was a surprise choice for the building of New Delhi. He was, however, married to the daughter of a former British viceroy and this may have swung the decision in his favour. Lutyens was famously stubborn—particular over architectural matters—and well known for irritating puns, such as giving a friend of his called Monty the nickname Carlo.

MAIN BUILDINGS & DISTRICTS

The most important buildings of New Delhi—the President's Palace, the Central Secretariat and Parliament—are in daily use and not normally open to the public. They are architecturally interesting, particularly as an attempt to mix Indian and European design styles, and so are still worth a close inspection from outside. There are several museums that should be visited in this area, as well as the 20th-century commercial centre of New Delhi, still widely known as Connaught Place. New Delhi also has a few interesting pre-British structures that survived the building of the new capital: they include the 18th-century observatory known as Jantar Mantar, a very fine step-well and a 14th-century hunting lodge.

Rajpath

This avenue is the main axis around which the rest of New Delhi was planned. It runs from the old National Stadium in the east to Raisina Hill in the west, where the presidential palace now sits. It is actually aligned at its eastern end with the northernmost wall of the early Mughal Purana Qila, or Old Fort, but this view is normally hidden by trees and the stadium. Rajpath itself is a broad ceremonial avenue, more than 3.5km in length, with well-kept lawns and ponds on either side of the tarmac.

India Gate

Towards the eastern end of Rajpath is the monumental gateway known as India Gate, originally called the All-India War Memorial Arch and modelled on arches of ancient Rome and the Arc de Triomphe in Paris. Unlike the Arc de Triomphe, however, India Gate has no statuary and is topped by a small flattened dome on its roof—the only indigenous architectural feature on the building. The early drawings of the arch show small Indian-style pavilions placed in front of it, but they were never built. About 150m to the east, set in a rectangular pond, is a tall canopied plinth, or *chattri*, more than 22m high, the pillars, dome and eaves of which are distinctively Indian architectural features. This originally contained an enormous statue of King George V, which was moved in the 1960s to the site of the 1911 Delhi Durbar at Coronation Park in North Delhi (*see p. 123*).

The road system around India Gate is a perfect hexagon. It was originally known as Princes Park, because, on the outer side of the hexagon, space was allotted for the palaces of India's most important princely families, whose names they still bear. The most impressive of them, the well-preserved and Lutyens-designed Hyderabad House, on the northeast of the hexagon, is now used by the Indian Foreign Ministry for meetings and formal occasions, while the neighbouring Baroda House is used as the Railways office. Jaipur House, on the southeast of the hexagon, can be visited by the public, since it houses the National Gallery of Modern Art (*see p. 121*).

A kilometre to the west is where New Delhi's north–south axis, Janpath (formerly Queensway) intersects with Rajpath. On the northwest corner of the intersection are the National Archives, and on the southeast corner is the National Museum, which has the best collection of antiquities in the country (*see p. 120*).

Raisina Hill and Vijay Chowk

Proceeding westwards for another 2.5km towards the Presidential Palace, one reaches Vijay Chowk, a large open area with six fountains at the foot of Raisina Hill. On the northern side is the circular Parliament building. Note how most of the Presidential Palace disappears from view as one proceeds up Raisina Hill. This was a result of a geometrical miscalculation of the gradient by the architects.

Presidential Palace

The enormous Presidential Palace, or Rashtrapati Bhavan, sits on top of Raisina Hill. The interior of the building, built as the Viceregal Palace (the residence of the British viceroy), is not accessible to the public, though in February and March some of its superb formal gardens are open to visitors. It is possible, throughout the year, to go up to the main front gates and get a close look at Delhi's most important building of the British colonial period—a hybrid of classical and Indian influences. The palace, which has 340 rooms, is largely laid out as a monumental two-storey building, constructed out of red and cream sandstone. It has a distinctive tall dome, loosely based on the shape of the Buddhist stupa at Sanchi (*see p. 418*), which covers the main durbar hall, and the building is fronted by a long colonnade, with a broad stone staircase leading up to the main entrance. Among the other Indian features are the small pavilions, or *chattris*, set into the roof eaves on either side of the dome. Mahatma Gandhi called for the building to be converted into a hospital after Independence. It became instead the home of the Indian president, who plays a largely symbolic role in the Indian political system, and the palace is little used except for grand state occasions.

Jaipur Column

The tall column in the central courtyard, which obstructs one's view of the Presidential Palace, is loosely based on Trajan's Column in Rome. It was a gift from the maharaja of Jaipur, who owned much of the land on which New Delhi was built, but was constructed to a design specified by Lutyens. The white sandstone shaft has a steel tube running through it to support the bronze lotus and glass star at its apex.

North and South Block

These grandiose, unimaginatively-named, almost identical buildings, known collectively as the Central Secretariat, appear from Rajpath to flank the Presidential Palace, though in fact they are set more than 300m in front of it. Designed by Herbert Baker, they are slightly more traditionally Classical in design than the Presidential Palace, each having a Florentine dome (though with Indian-style *jali* screens) and projecting wings with colonnaded porticoes. But like the Presidential Palace, the buildings are almost entirely constructed from red and cream sandstone, and use pavilions, or *chattris*, as an ornamental feature. In order to deal with the heat of the Indian summer, Baker used deep-set windows in thick walls with a central cavity—whereas Lutyens, in the Presidential Palace, used wide verandahs and cross ventilation. The buildings are used by government departments—'North Block' has become a kind of shorthand for the Finance Ministry, while 'South Block' is the home of the Foreign and Defence ministries. On the road between the two buildings are the four dominion columns—gifts from Australia, Canada, New Zealand and South Africa. Note the supercilious imperial inscription around the main gate of North Block: 'Liberty will not descend to a people. A people must raise themselves to liberty. It is a blessing that must be earned before it can be enjoyed.'

Parliament

This building was an afterthought, as a democratically-elected chamber was not a high imperial priority when the plans for New Delhi were being laid out. It was

LUTYENS' BAKERLOO

Herbert Baker was an experienced architect and town planner who had worked on colonial buildings in South Africa. He was also an old friend of Lutyens, who recommended that he be recruited for the building of New Delhi. But they quarrelled over the construction of the Secretariat buildings, designed by Baker, which Lutyens felt partially blocked the view of his own creation, the Viceregal Palace, and made it seem less important. In best punning form, Lutyens declared this to be his 'Bakerloo', a reference, of course, to Napolean's defeat at the Battle of Waterloo; though the joke is funnier if one also knows that Bakerloo is the name of the London Underground line that links Waterloo Station and Baker Street. The two friends did not speak for five years following the dispute.

placed in a relatively insignificant location at the foot of North Block—as if to symbolise the executive's supremacy over the legislature. It is a circular, colonnaded building; inside are one circular and three semicircular chambers, and three courtyards. The second storey is a later addition that almost entirely obscures the dome on the inner circular chamber.

THE REST OF NEW DELHI

New Delhi is much more than Rajpath and the government buildings on Raisina Hill. Lutyens and his colleagues laid out a large number of civic, religious, commercial and residential buildings north and south of Rajpath. Most important was Connaught Place, the new commercial centre for Delhi, but elsewhere there were law courts, an Anglican cathedral and even a Jewish cemetery, as well as about 4,000 bungalows. There are also three important pre-British buildings that have survived—a hunting lodge and a step-well from the 14th century, and an extraordinary 18th-century observatory. The roads were laid in a complex pattern of hexagons and triangles, and trees were planted according to a carefully drawn-up plan, for which 13 tree varieties were short-listed for the main avenues. Akbar Road, for instance, is an avenue of *imli*, or tamarind, trees; many of the trees were chosen primarily for their appearance, though, and have not fared well in the Delhi climate. However, more native tree species have been planted since, and New Delhi, with its broad avenues and large lawns, is one of the greenest city centres in the world.

Connaught Place

Often considered to be Delhi's city centre, CP (as Connaught Place is more commonly known; officially Rajiv Chowk) was named after George V's uncle, the Duke of Connaught. It became the commercial centre of New Delhi and was completed in the 1930s. It takes the form of a series of concentric circles surrounding a central park, under which two Metro lines now pass. This park is circumscribed by the Inner Circle—a circular colonnade in Palladian style, which contains shops and homes and is said to be inspired by Bath's Royal Crescent and Circus. The Outer Circle is built to a similar design.

Jantar Mantar

Built in 1724, this extraordinary observatory (*open daily dawn–dusk*) is one of Delhi's strangest sights. Surrounded by modern tower blocks not far from Connaught Place, this bizarre collection of stone-built astronomical instruments is set in a well-kept park. It is one of five observatories across India built by Maharaja Jai Singh, the founder of Jaipur, who was unhappy with the poor quality of existing astronomical information. The observatories at Jaipur, Varanasi and Ujjain survive; the one at Mathura no longer exists. Jantar Mantar literally means 'calculation instrument', but has come to be a Hindi equivalent of 'Abracadabra'. The building closest to the entrance is the Misra Yantra, or 'mixed instrument', and has a number of purposes, including telling the time in other parts of the world and calculating the time of sunrise. The tallest of the buildings, with a tall staircase which one can climb, is the Samrat Yantra, and is a sophisticated sundial—the time being read from the shadow on either of the neighbouring curved quadrants. The two bowl-like instruments beyond the Samrat Yantra are the Jai Prakash Yantras, which were used for calculating the height and azimuth of the sun. The two circular enclosed buildings at the rear of the site, known as the Ram Yantra, are for measuring the positions of heavenly bodies.

Agarsen's Baoli

Hidden away on a backstreet off Hailey Road (close to Kasturba Gandhi Marg and Tolstoy Marg), this pretty 14th-century step-well is probably the oldest building in New Delhi. Agarsen is thought to have been a local chieftain. The neighbouring mosque is from a slightly later period.

Teen Murti House

This large Classical building of 1930 was constructed as Flagstaff House, the residence of the British commander-in-chief, and aligned some 1.5km to the south of the Presidential Palace. On Independence it became the home of India's first prime minister, Jawaharlal Nehru, who died here in 1964. It then became a library and thereafter a museum dedicated to the life of India's longest-serving prime minister. In the grounds of the house is a modern planetarium and a 14th-century hunting lodge known as the **Kushak Shikargah**, built on a high plinth which was once part of an embankment. The hunting lodge was one of several constructed by Feroze Shah Tughlaq.

Indira Gandhi Memorial

This typical New Delhi bungalow of the 1930s, at 1 Safdarjang Lane, was home to Indira Gandhi, daughter of Jawaharlal Nehru and prime minister for more than 15 years. In 1984, she was killed by two of her Sikh bodyguards in the grounds of the bungalow, because she ordered an army operation to flush out separatists from Sikhism's holiest shrine, the Golden Temple in Amritsar. Her former home is now an interesting, if macabre, museum dedicated to her life and that of her son Rajiv Gandhi, who succeeded her as prime minister. He was also assassinated—by Tamil separatists from Sri Lanka. The museum displays a wide range of Indira and Rajiv's personal belongings, as well as the clothes they were wearing when they were killed.

Gandhi Smriti, Birla House

A large 1930s house on Tees January Marg was where Mahatma Gandhi stayed on his last visits to Delhi. And it was here in 1948 that he was shot dead by a Hindu chauvinist, Nathuram Godse, who thought Gandhi had been too generous towards the newly-formed nation of Pakistan. The spot where Gandhi was killed, in the garden, is marked by a headstone. Gandhi's room is kept much as it was, and his few possessions are on display.

The National Museum

This museum (*open Tues–Sun 10–5; camera fee payable*) on Janpath, close to the intersection with Rajpath, has India's most important collection of historical artefacts. More specifically, it houses the country's best collections of Harappan objects and miniature paintings, and has superb stone carvings from many of India's most important archaeological sites. Unfortunately, the labelling is inadequate for a museum of such distinction, the chaotic upper floors are ignored by many visitors, and many important works are kept in storage.

The entrance lobby of the building—a three-storey circular structure—has a small selection of interesting sculptures, including, at the centre, a very fine 13th-century statue of the sun-god Surya, taken from the great Konarak Temple in Orissa.

A long passageway lined with carvings leads to the main part of the museum—with the **Harappan Gallery** immediately on the left. The best-known object in the entire museum, a superb bronze figurine of a dancing girl (*illustrated on p. 15*), just 10.5cm high, is in a cabinet on the right. The figurine, probably 4,000 years old, was excavated at Mohenjo-daro, now in Pakistan. Note the small seals, with undeciphered writing, in a neighbouring cabinet. The Harappan Gallery has a large collection of pottery, often finely decorated, as well as some superb terracotta figures of animals and humans. The next gallery (Gallery 5) has some fine stone carving and terracotta pieces from the Mauryan period (c. 300 BC), as well as fragments from the important Buddhist sites of Sanchi and Amaravati.

Gallery 6 has the museum's important collection of **Gandhara carvings and stucco heads**, as well as some very early pieces of Hindu statuary—including a 2nd-century AD Shiva lingam with four heads, from Mathura. The finest of the early Mathura carvings is a 2nd-century statue of the pot-bellied Kuber, god of wealth, with the Central Asian facial features of the ruling Kushan Dynasty. Galleries 7 and 8 have more fine statues from Mathura, mainly from the later Gupta period.

Gallery 9 has the world's best collection of **Tamil bronzes** outside Tamil Nadu, including two particularly fine Natarajas, in which Shiva is portrayed as the Lord of the Dance, as well as an unusual early bronze of the child Krishna killing a snake. The **medieval art gallery** (Gallery 10) has some early wooden carvings—and in the far left corner, a very fine stone image of a resting woman and baby believed to have been carved in Bengal during the Pala period. The **Buddhist art gallery** (Gallery 11) has some very fine painted textiles from Central Asia, dated to the 9th century, which were collected by the renowned Hungarian-born archaeologist Aurel Stein in the early 20th century.

The Museum's superb collection of **miniature paintings**, spread out over several galleries, includes some very fine examples from the Mughal period, including famous images of the first Mughal emperor, Babur, visiting Gwalior, and his grandson Akbar taking part in a hunt. There are also some unusual Mughal miniatures with Christian themes, including one of Emperor Jehangir looking at a picture of the Madonna and another that depicts the Nativity. There are also large collections of Rajasthani and Pahari miniatures and, at the end of the final gallery, some fascinating half-complete miniatures, which help explain the painting process. A door part-way through the miniatures gallery leads, via an uninteresting exhibition about coins (the main coin gallery is upstairs), to a large **gallery for decorative arts**. Here, the large inlaid wooden figure of Garuda, the mount of Vishnu, is one of the most memorable exhibits. Outside, along the walls of the circular corridor, and in the central garden, are many interesting sculptures—including an enormous sleeping 16th-century Vijayanagar-period Vishnu brought from Hampi. Note also the finely carved 12th-century stone door lintel from Warangal in Andhra Pradesh.

There are many more stone carvings displayed in the corridors of the upper floors. The first floor has galleries devoted to maritime history, tribal India, coins and more Central Asian antiquities, while the second floor has a fine armoury, the exhibits of which include a sword, a dagger and body armour that belonged to the Mughal emperor Aurangzeb; an ornate bow that belonged to the last of the Mughals, Bahadur Shah Zafar; and a wide range of handheld, knuckleduster-style weaponry.

The National Gallery of Modern Art or NGMA

This gallery (*open Tues–Sun 10–5*) is in the imposing Jaipur House, on the south side of India Gate. The house was built in the 1930s as the Delhi residence of the maharajas of Jaipur. The main building is now used for temporary exhibitions, while the new block at the back is purpose-built for India's best collection of art from the mid-18th century to the present. There is an interesting collection of Company School miniatures—paintings in the hybrid Indian-European style of painting that flourished in the early 19th century—as well as some fine landscapes by Thomas Daniell. There are important paintings from all the major names of Indian painting of the last two centuries, including Raja Ravi Varma, some fine oils by the inter-war Indo-Hungarian artist Amrita Sher-Gil, and modern stars ranging from S.H. Raza to Subodh Gupta.

Other Delhi museums

Delhi has a number of other museums. These include: the much-loved **Crafts Museum** (*open Tues–Sun 10–5*), just north of the Purana Qila, devoted to the art and crafts of India and where one can see artisans at work; the interesting **Railway Museum** (*open 9.30–5 Tues–Sun*) in Chanakyapuri, with several well-maintained 19th-century carriages and locomotives; and the unexpectedly fascinating **Sulabh International Toilet Museum** (*open Mon–Sat 10–5*) in Mahavir Enclave II, north of the airport.

NORTH DELHI

The little-visited area north of the old city was once the heart of British Delhi. It is studded with interesting monuments, including some of the city's earliest colonial buildings, the remains of three Mughal formal gardens, some of the key sites of the 1857 Uprising, as well as the bizarre memorial to the 1911 Coronation Durbar. North Delhi is physically dominated by the Ridge—the northernmost tip of the Aravalli hill range, which starts in southern Rajasthan and flattens out just before it reaches the River Yamuna. Until the early 19th century the area between the northern Ridge and the river had orchards and gardens. The British kept many of the gardens and turned it into the area known as Civil Lines, with several large country-house style residences. The army cantonment was built on the other side of the Ridge, where the main campus for Delhi University is now situated.

Civil Lines

While New Delhi was being built, Civil Lines served as the administrative centre of Britain's Indian Empire. But, with the completion of the new planned city and the growth of Delhi to the south, Civil Lines gradually became less important. Unfortunately, the two most important British buildings in Civil Lines—**Metcalfe House** (1835) and the **Secretariat** (1912)—are closed to the public. The Secretariat is now the Delhi State Assembly building, while Metcalfe House—a Palladian mansion built by, and named after, the long-term British Resident Sir Thomas Metcalfe—is now used for defence research.

Qudsia Bagh (1748) consists of a large peaceful garden just above Kashmere Gate at the northern fringe of Old Delhi, and contains an interesting, partially ruined three-bayed mosque and a gateway, both decorated flamboyantly in the Lucknow style—similar in conception but not execution to Safdarjang's Tomb in South Delhi. The rectangular building in the centre of the park is thought to have been a pavilion which was converted by the British into a residence. Qudsia Bagh originally stretched to the banks of the Yamuna and included the area now occupied by the enormous Interstate Bus Terminal. Qudsia herself was a former dancing girl who became the wife of Emperor Muhammad Shah.

Just west of Qudsia Bagh is **Nicholson Cemetery**, where many of the British who died in the 1857 Uprising are buried, among them the famously brutal General John Nicholson, who was killed during the final, successful British assault on Delhi. A little north of Nicholson Cemetery is the Neoclassical **Maiden's Hotel** (1900–07), now owned by the Oberoi group—and which was, for more than half a century, Delhi's smartest hotel.

The Northern Ridge

There are a number of interesting sites on the crest of the Ridge, several of which are associated with the 1857 Uprising. The **Mutiny Memorial** (1863) is a sandstone Gothic spire erected on the Ridge to commemorate those soldiers, British and Indian, who died fighting against the rebels in 1857. Note the small plaque placed in recent times at the foot of the memorial that says: 'The "enemy" of the inscriptions on this monument were those who rose against colonial rule and fought bravely for national liberation in 1857.' Three hundred metres north of the Mutiny Memorial is a smoothly polished sandstone **Ashoka Pillar** (3rd century BC). The 9m high pillar is one of many originally erected by Emperor Ashoka, and is inscribed with six of his edicts aimed at encouraging the spread of Buddhism and good government. This pillar originally stood in the town of Meerut, 60km to the northeast. Like Delhi's other Ashoka Pillar, at

Feroze Shah Kotla, it was brought here by the 14th-century ruler Feroze Shah Tughlaq. This pillar was broken into five pieces in an accidental explosion in the 18th century, then clumsily reconstructed and placed in its current setting by the British in 1867.

A little further north, beyond the largely modern Hindu Rao Hospital—which incorporates parts of a fine early 19th-century British mansion (a key British military position in 1857)—is a large step-well, and a tall ruined building with extremely steep staircases known as **Pir Ghaib** (14th century BC), which was thought to have been used as a hunting lodge and an observatory by Feroze Shah Tughlaq. This is also thought to be where the Meerut Ashoka Pillar was originally moved to. Further north along the Ridge, in the middle of the road, is a building known as **Flagstaff Tower** (1828), to which British women and children were evacuated during the 1857 Uprising, and from where they eventually fled into the Indian countryside.

West of the Ridge

On the other side of the Ridge, not far from the Mutiny Memorial, is the **Roshanara Garden** (1650), commissioned by Roshanara, the daughter of Mughal emperor Shah Jahan. Her pretty tomb, a converted pavilion, is on the eastern side of the gardens. Five kilometres to the northwest is another Mughal Garden. Like the more famous gardens in Kashmir and in Lahore, it is named **Shalimar Bagh** (1653). This garden was built for Akbarabadi Begum, one of Shah Jahan's wives, and contains a pavilion known as the Sheesh Mahal, which is thought to be the site of Emperor Aurangzeb's coronation in 1658. The gardens were used as a country retreat by British Residents in the early 19th century.

Coronation Park

In Delhi's far north, well beyond the Ridge, is the extraordinary Coronation Park—the almost-forgotten site of the 1911 Durbar, at which George V announced that Delhi would replace Calcutta as the capital of British India. In 1911, more than 100,000 people gathered here to attend the Durbar; today there is barely a soul. An obelisk marks the site, and in the neighbouring park are a few marble busts of former British senior officials, grouped in a semicircle around an enormous 22m statue of George V, towering over this forlorn wasteland. The statue used to be under the large canopy next to India Gate on Rajpath, but was moved in the 1960s. Originally, imperial planners had intended to build New Delhi here, well to the north of the Old City, but it was deemed too marshy and malarial; instead the new city was built where it stands today, some 12km to the south.

Delhi Cantonment

Still used by the armed forces, the Cantonment area of southwest Delhi was laid out by the British in the early 20th century. It is home to the architecturally interesting fortress-like Garrison **Church of St Martin** (1931) and the well-maintained **Commonwealth War Graves Cemetery**, near Brar Square.

PRACTICAL INFORMATION

Delhi, along with Mumbai, is one of the two main entry points for foreign visitors to India, and is well-connected to the rest of the country. It can be a little overwhelming for first-time visitors, and some prefer, therefore, to head off to a smaller, quieter place before undertaking an exploration of what is historically and architecturally one of the great cities of the world. Even though Delhi has a large resident population of foreigners—mainly in the south of the city and in Gurgaon, just over the state border in Haryana—foreigners still get hassled in the main tourist areas of the city. Beggars congregate at areas where newcomers are likely to be—near monuments, in Connaught Place, near the railway stations—and there are lots of tricks played on visitors. Most famous is the 'shit on shoe scam', in which a shoeshine man approaches an unwary tourist, pointing to his or her shoe, and at the large lump of foul-smelling substance that an accomplice has placed on it. The shoeshine man then demands a large sum of money to clean it off.

GETTING THERE

• **By air:** Delhi's main airport is **Indira Gandhi International Airport**, situated near Palam in southwest Delhi, 15km from Connaught Place. There are flights to Delhi from more than 100 locations around the world. The airport has undergone a major modernisation programme, and there are new, comfortable international and domestic terminals. Domestic and international flights share the same infrastructure and runways, but have separate terminals on opposite sides of the airport complex. Flights are often delayed in late December and early January because of heavy fog.

The modern **international terminal**, opened in 2010, now caters to more foreign visitors than any other Indian airport. All arriving international travellers need to fill in an immigration form, part of which also has a separate customs declaration, which must be handed over after luggage collection. There are foreign exchange facilities inside the terminal building. It is easiest and safest if you ask your hotel to send a car for you. The driver will normally be inside the terminal after the customs check, holding up a notice board with your name on it—though it is useful to get the driver's mobile number in advance. There is also a pre-paid taxi booth inside the terminal building which is recommended. Do not hire a taxi outside the airport building—there are numerous reports of travellers being robbed. The airport Metro, which goes to Connaught Place and New Delhi railway station, is recommended. There is a regular shuttle bus to the domestic terminal, 8km away by road.

The modern **domestic terminal**, opened in 2009, caters to flights from a growing number of domestic airlines, and direct connections are available to all major domestic airports. The pre-paid taxi booth is inside the terminal, while the waiting area for drivers is just outside and can be very congested. Again, do not take an unlicensed taxi. There is a shuttle to the international terminal.

• **By train:** Delhi is a major railway hub, and trains provide a cheap, slow and usually comfortable way of travelling to many historically important sites and tourist centres in northern India. There are also many very long-distance trains—particularly to destinations in the south, where the journey can take more than 24hrs. Delhi has two major, and several minor, railway stations. The busiest of them, and the one most used by visitors, is **New Delhi Railway Station**, which is just north of Connaught Place, and can be approached from either the Ajmer Gate side (on the east) or the Paharganj side (on the west). Check with your travel agent which side you are leaving or departing from if you want to avoid walking on a footbridge above all the platforms to your train. Pre-paid taxis are available on both sides of the station, and the Metro is connected to the station.

About 3km to the north is **Delhi Railway Station** (usually referred to as Old Delhi railway station), which is in one of the most crowded parts of the old city. Night trains to Pathankot (for Dharamsala) and to Kathgodam (for Naini Tal and Almora) as well as a number of middle-distance trains in north India go from Old Delhi. Several trains to southern India start at, or go through, **Nizamuddin Railway Station**, which is in the area of the same name, 6km southeast of Connaught Place, and which is easier to access for those staying in South Delhi. **Sarai Rohilla Station**, 4km northwest of Connaught Place, has trains to several key Rajasthan towns, including Bikaner, Udaipur, Jodhpur and Jaisalmer.

• **By bus or coach:** Delhi is also a major road travel hub, and there are bus services, of very varied standards, to most parts of north India. However, for most places, if you need to use public transport rather than a hire car, a plane or train journey will be much more comfortable and faster. The main bus stand for the city is the **Interstate Bus Terminal (ISBT)** at Kashmere Gate on the north side of Old Delhi. There are also important bus stands at Bikaner House near India Gate (for Jaipur), at Sarai Kale Khan near Nizamuddin, and at Majnu ka Tila in North Delhi (for Dharamsala).

• **By car:** Travelling outside the evening rush hour (6–8pm) can make an enormous difference to the speed at which you reach your destination and the city. And starting early (before 7am) can make an even larger difference to the speed at which you leave Delhi, particularly if you're not close to the highway you need. The main entrance/exit routes are the NH8 Jaipur Highway (for Rajasthan), which passes close to the airport and Gurgaon; the NH2 Mathura Road (for Agra), which passes through Faridabad; and the NH1 Grand Trunk Road (for Chandigarh) which passes through north Delhi.

GETTING AROUND

• **Metro:** The city's new urban railway system, known as the **Delhi Metro**, is the best way of travelling around Delhi. It now reaches most parts of the city. There are three major lines: two of them east–west, and one north–south. The main interchanges are at Connaught Place, Kashmere Gate and Central Secretariat. The Metro is particularly useful for travelling to crowded areas of the city, such as Old Delhi. Entry is by token, purchased for a particular journey at the ticket office. The token is then brushed over the sensor at the entrance, and then swallowed by the exit gate at the end of your journey. It is also possible to buy top-up travel cards and one- or three-day passes.

• **Taxis:** Although widely available in Delhi, taxis are often difficult to hail on the street. Instead, get one from your hotel, ring the nearest stand or phone one of several numbers for radio cabs (*Delhi Cab: 011 44333222; Easy Cab: 011 43434343; Quick Cab: 011 45333333*) well in advance of your departure time. Most taxis have meters. If—as often happens—your driver tells you the meter is broken, agree the fare in advance. For sightseeing it is often best to hire a taxi or a car for a half-day (normally 4hrs) or a day (8hrs), for a pre-agreed fee.

• **Rickshaws:** This is the most widely available form of transport in Delhi. **Auto-rickshaws** can be hailed on the street. They have meters that often do not work—and therefore a fare should be agreed on in advance. **Cycle-rickshaws** are available at a number of Delhi's less affluent or more crowded locations. They are often found outside metro stations and are suitable for short journeys. Agree the fare in advance.

• **Buses:** Delhi's buses have a poor reputation—a crowded, unreliable means of transport in which single women are often harassed. There are exceptions, such as the new **Bus Corridor** (known at **BRT** or **Bus Rapid Transport**), and it is best to get local advice.

• **Cycling:** Bicycle lanes were introduced in Delhi in 2008, but the network remains small—and other road users are very unsympathetic towards cyclists.

• **Walking:** In some parts of Delhi, such as the old city, Connaught Place, Nizamuddin and Mehrauli, it is easiest to get around on foot. The lack of pavements can make walking rather exasperating and dangerous in some places, but it is possible. The best map to use is the excellent **Eicher City Map**.

ACCOMMODATION

Delhi has a large number of very comfortable luxury hotels. Many of the major chains, including the Taj, Oberoi, Hyatt, Meridien, Shangri-La and Sheraton, are represented in the city. The exquisite **Imperial Hotel** (*$$$; theimperialindia.com; T: 011 2334 1234*) on Janpath, close to Connaught Place, built in the 1930s to an Art Deco design, has a distinctly colonial feel, beloved by those who feel nostalgic about British rule. The more modern **Park Hotel** (*$$$; theparkhotels.com; T: 011 2374 3000*), with its strong sense of contemporary interior design, is nearby, opposite the 18th-century Jantar Mantar observatory. The **Oberoi Hotel** (*$$$; oberoidelhi.com; T: 011 2436 3030*) is near Humayun's Tomb, and has very pretty views over the Delhi Golf Course. Make sure you get a room on the Golf Course side, otherwise you overlook a flyover. Even closer to Humayun's Tomb is the city's most exclusive hotel, the **Aman New Delhi** (*$$$; amanresorts.com; T: 011 4363 3333*), where every room has its own plunge pool. If you want to be near the old city, the best place is one of Delhi's oldest hotels, the **Oberoi Maidens** (*$$$; maidenshotel.com; T: 011 2397 5464*), a handsome colonial mansion in Civil Lines.

It is hard to find cheaper comfortable hotels in Delhi, but a number of attractive guest houses have sprung up in recent years. Try the **Amarya guest houses** (*$$; amaryagroup.com; Amarya Haveli T: 011 4175 9268; Amarya Garden T: 011 4656 2735*). The Haveli is in Hauz Khas Enclave, while the Garden is in Defence Colony. Another option is **Colaba guest house** (*$$; T: 011 4067 1773; colabahouse.com*) in Safdarjung Enclave.

FOOD

Delhi is a wonderful city for food-lovers, with a huge variety of cuisine from all over India, and abroad. Until recently, most good restaurants were only in the 5-star hotels, but now it is possible to find good food in market areas all over the city. Delhi is best known for its **north Indian cuisine**—curries, kebabs, naans, dal—which has become the food most often identified with India in the rest of the world. Historically, Delhi is most closely associated with **Mughlai cuisine**—the food of the Mughal emperors, who ruled Delhi for more than 300 years. The great texts of the Mughal period have descriptions of the rich meat-based meals eaten by the emperors, in which vegetables play a very small role ('radish-eater' was an insult of the time).

Typically, Mughlai food, with a heavy emphasis on meat dishes, is richer and creamier than the north Indian Punjabi and Avadhi cuisine, but the boundaries between these cuisines has largely dissolved into what has become north Indian food—with its kebabs, biryanis, kormas and 'tandoori everything'. In traditional Mughlai food, nuts and fruits are used in sauces with meat, or cooked with rice and meat to make a pilau. Many different dals are eaten too. According to folklore, when imprisoned by Aurangzeb, Shah Jahan was told that he could have his favourite food every day for the rest of his life. He chose dal, because it could be cooked in so many different ways. Lots of different unleavened breads were used in Mughlai cuisine, and sweet dishes—such as the rice pudding known as *firni*—were eaten after the main meal, and the chewing of *pan*, betel nut wrapped in a leaf, was common as a digestive.

The best-known Mughlai restaurant in Delhi is **Karims** (*$; karimhoteldelhi.com; T: 011 2326 9880; no credit cards*) a large, basic non-air-conditioned restaurant close to the Jama Masjid in the old city. The owners are descendants of Mughlai cooks who set up this restaurant in 1913, and many of their meat and chicken dishes are named after Mughal emperors. Among the signature dishes are *Badshahi Badam Pasanda*—mutton cooked in almonds and spices—and many regulars love the brain *masala*. There are several other more luxurious restaurants that serve a broad selection of north Indian food. Highly recommended is **Punjabi by Nature** (*$$; T: 011 4151 6666; punjabibynature.in*) in Vasant Lok market in South Delhi, with the *Raan-e Punjab*, a marinated leg of lamb, as its signature dish. Excellent kebabs are available at the **Bokhara** (*$$$; T: 011 2611 2233*) at the Maurya Sheraton in the diplomatic area, Chanakyapuri, and the **Great Kebab Factory** (*$$; T: 011 2677 9191*) at the Radisson Hotel near the international airport.

For other Indian food try the Defence

Colony market for South Indian vegetarian at **Sagar** (*$; T: 011 2433 3658*), with superb *dosas* and *thalis*, and excellent Indian seafood, cooked in the Mangalorean style, at **Swagath** (*$$; T: 011 2433 7538; swagath.in*) with their speciality dish: crab with butter, pepper and garlic. **Oh Calcutta!** (*$$; T: 011 2646 4180*), next to the Park Royal Hotel near the Lotus Temple, has very good Bengali food, while **Andhra Bhavan** (*$; T: 011 2338 2031*), near India Gate, has a canteen-style lunch with the best Andhra food in north India.

There is also some excellent **international food**, including several of India's best Italian restaurants. Try **Baci** (*$$; T: 011 4150 7445*) in Sunder Nagar, or **Diva** (*$$; T: 011 2921 5673*) in Greater Kailash-II. The **Sakura**, in the Hotel Nikko near Connaught Place, has good Japanese food, while **Nanking** (*$$; T: 011 26138936*), in Vasant Kunj, has excellent Chinese—including dim sum on Sunday lunch.

FURTHER READING & VIEWING

• **Books:** There are enough books on Delhi to fill several bookshelves. The best guide to the monuments of Delhi is *Delhi: A Thousand Years of Building* by Lucy Peck (Roli 2005), while the most comprehensive anthology is H.K. Kaul's *Historic Delhi* (OUP India 2004), which includes very entertaining and accessible selections from the writings of the medieval Moroccan traveller Ibn Battuta, the Mongol warlord Timur, the first Mughal emperor, Babur, as well as Edward Lear and Mark Twain. Khushwant Singh's anthology *City Improbable* (Penguin India 2001) is more contemporary, and contains pieces by travel writers Jan Morris and William Dalrymple. *City of Djinns* by William Dalrymple (Penguin 2004) is a classic piece of nostalgic travel writing set in Delhi of the early 1990s. Sam Miller's idiosyncratic *Delhi: Adventures in a Megacity* (Jonathan Cape and Penguin India 2009) is more up-to-date and 'disturbingly funny' according to one reviewer, while *Delhi Metropolitan* (Penguin India 2008) by Ranjana Sengupta is an insider's view of the modern city.

Twilight in Delhi (Rupa 2008) by Ahmed Ali, set in Old Delhi before Independence, is probably the classic Delhi novel. But others include two superb novels both set and written in a slightly later period in Old Delhi: *The Householder* (Norton 2002) by Ruth Prawer Jhabvala and *Clear Light of Day* (Vintage 2001) by Anita Desai. Contemporary novels include the bestselling *One Night at the Call Centre* (Black Swan 2007) by Chetan Bhagat.

• **Films:** The first of the Merchant Ivory films, *The Householder* (1963), is probably the quintessential Delhi movie, starring Shashi Kapoor and Leela Naidu in a comic portrayal of two newlyweds in an arranged marriage getting to know each other in their small flat in Old Delhi. More recently, Mira Nair's *Monsoon Wedding* (2001) and Deepa Mehta's *Fire* (1996) are both set in Delhi, and were successful in the West and India. The 2009 Hindi movie *Delhi-6* was less well-received critically, but has beautiful images of Old Delhi.

RAJASTHAN

Rajasthan (*maps 2 and 3*) is India's largest state and contains many of the country's best-known tourist locations. These range from medieval desert fortress cities like Jaisalmer to ornate modern palaces, and include exquisite Jain and Hindu temples, extraordinary street murals, the important Muslim pilgrimage site of Ajmer, and the great royal cities of Jaipur, Jodhpur and Udaipur. Despite its popularity, Rajasthan is large and varied enough for visitors to find fascinating places away from the tourist crowds.

Rajasthan is also one of India's poorest states, with low literacy rates, particularly among women, and high levels of infant mortality. The old feudal system is partially intact, and many of the large number of former princely families continue to play an important role in politics. Others have diversified into tourism, which plays a major part in Rajasthan's economy.

The long, low Aravalli mountain range, which runs from Delhi to Mt Abu in the south of Rajasthan, bisects the state from northeast to southwest. The arid western and northern parts of Rajasthan are dominated by the great Thar Desert, which stretches across the international border into Pakistan. Summer temperatures are extremely high, often more than 46°C. On winter nights, the temperatures dip rapidly and the desert can feel very cold. The less visited, more populous southeastern part of the state is a little cooler, has higher rainfall and an all-year river, the Chambal.

HISTORY OF RAJASTHAN

Rajasthan's many former princely states retain a strong sense of their individual history and heritage—arguably more so than in any other part of India. As a political entity, Rajasthan has rarely been united during its complex history, and is essentially a modern creation. This account of the region's general history needs to be read alongside the more specific histories, particularly of the most important principalities: Jodhpur, Udaipur and Jaipur.

Rajasthan's unforgiving climate, and in particular the availability of water, has played a major role in dictating where humans built their settlements. Stone Age tools found along the banks of several river beds indicate that parts of Rajasthan have been inhabited for at least 50,000 years. The earliest excavated permanent settlements come from the pre-Harappan and Harappan periods, reaching back about 6,000 years. In southern Rajasthan, what has become known as the Ahar culture (after the area near Udaipur where many early finds were made) flourished at this time, and the distinctive black and red Ahar pottery has been found at dozens of sites, along with a wide variety of copper artefacts. The most important of these sites is on the outskirts of Udaipur. Kalibangan, in the far north of the state, is the best known of the Harappan excavation sites in Rajasthan. It dates back about 4,000 years and reveals clear cultural and technological affinities with other Harappan sites, including Harappa itself, less than 100km away in Pakistan. In the 3rd century BC, Mauryan rule spread as far as Rajasthan—though the only major monuments from this period are the Buddhist ruins at Bairat. Rajasthan remained a border territory for the series of empires that succeeded the Mauryas, and several tribes driven by invaders from their homelands in Punjab and elsewhere would settle there. Both the Guptas (4th–5th century) and the White Huns (6th century) controlled parts of Rajasthan.

The early Rajput period

The arrival of the Rajputs, possibly in the 7th century, began a period of domination by leaders from a single community, which partially continues to this day. It now seems that the Rajput clans actually came from a number of different places and only later became inter-related, and that not all of them originally belonged to the Kshatriya warrior caste.

RAJPUT GENEALOGY

Traditionally, there are 36 Rajput clans. Their right to rule was based on long family trees demonstrating their descent from either the sun (*surya*) or the moon (*chandra*). Most of the modern princely families of Rajasthan still describe themselves as Suryavanshi (from the race of the sun) or as Chandravanshi (from the race of the moon). The family trees and celestial emblems that can be seen in many princely palaces, bear witness to the importance of this tradition. Another group of Rajput clans, the Agnivansh, claim to have been descended from a sacred fire on Mt Abu in the south of the state.

Among the early Rajput dynasties were the Gurjara Pratiharas, whose capital was, for a time, at Kannauj in Uttar Pradesh. Their descendants played an important role in later dynasties too. Among the important architecture from the very early pre-Muslim Rajput period are temples at Osiyan, Abhaneri, Jagat, Mt Abu and Badoli. The earliest structures at Chittor also date from this period.

Muslim incursions

By the 11th century, the emergence of new trade routes across the desert, and Muslim incursions from the west, had increased the military and economic importance of Rajasthan. Strategic hilltops were fortified, and became the administrative centres for the emergent Rajput dynasties. In the late 12th century, the armies of Muhammad of Ghor defeated the most powerful of the Rajput kings, Prithviraj, who ruled Delhi as well as parts of eastern and central Rajasthan around Ajmer. The victors remained in India, creating the Delhi Sultanate which, despite repeated attempts, was never able to subdue fully the Rajput principalities. This period, from the 13th to the 15th century, became the heroic age of Rajput legend, when many great tales of Rajput valour and self-sacrifice were composed and passed down through the generations by storytellers and poets. It is not always easy to disentangle myth from reality, and visitors will be told stories that should not always be interpreted literally.

The early 14th century saw famous sieges at the great fortresses of Ranthambore and Chittorgarh that resulted in victory for the Delhi Sultanate (by then under the rule of the Khilji Dynasty) over the Rajput armies. In both cases, the women of the fort committed *jauhar*—they are said to have chosen, *en masse*, death by burning rather than capture and the likelihood of becoming part of the Sultan's harem. The men also refused to surrender, and are said to have fought on the battlefield until they were all killed. The Khiljis were unable to hang on to their new fortresses, and during the later Sultanate period the weakened political leadership in Delhi was less involved in Rajasthan. Ajmer, however, developed into an important Muslim pilgrimage centre, and was under Sultanate control for much of the period. At the same time, smaller principalities in Rajasthan were being swallowed up by larger ones, and this period saw the emergence of two of the great rival Rajput dynasties, the Rathores of Marwar and the Sisodias of Mewar; their royal descendants later became better known by the names of their capital cities, Jodhpur and Udaipur respectively.

Mughal impact

Mughal rule in north India was destined to have a major impact on all the Rajput kingdoms. A large Rajput army was defeated at Khanua near Bharatpur by the first emperor, Babur, in 1527. During the reign of Akbar, almost all the Rajput kingdoms were incorporated into the Mughal Empire and, in return for their loyalty to the emperor, their rulers were allowed to remain in power. The exception was Mewar, which did not succumb, despite being defeated on the battlefield (its capital, Udaipur, was occupied by Akbar's army). Only under Akbar's successor, Jehangir, would Mewar accept a watered-down version of Mughal suzerainty. During Akbar's rule, the kingdom of Amber (later to be known as Jaipur) became one of the leading Rajput states, and its ruler, Raja Man Singh, was one of Akbar's most important generals and advisors. Several Rajput princesses became wives of leading Mughals—at least 25 marriages between Muslim Mughal princes and Hindu Rajput princesses have been recorded from this period.

Under Akbar's successors, many Rajput princes attended the Mughal court and took senior positions in the imperial army—getting caught up in the family feuds that marked so much of the Mughal period. As the Mughal Empire began to fall apart in the early 18th century, the princely states began to assert their independence and show off their wealth. The city of Jaipur was laid out, not far from the old fortifications at Amber, and the Lake Palace at Udaipur was built, as were the water palaces at Deeg, by the maharaja of Bharatpur, one of the few non-Rajput rulers in the region. The other non-Rajput rulers were the maharajas of Dholpur—like Bharatpur, a Hindu Jat (from a farming caste)—and the Muslim nawabs of Tonk.

BRITISH TALES OF RAJPUT CHIVALRY

James Tod was a British army officer who served in Rajputana as a political agent and compiled a history of the region called *Annals & Antiquities of Rajas'than* (1829) to which every subsequent historian, and most Rajput royalty, are indebted. The book, still a stirring read, relates many of the great medieval tales of Rajput chivalry, and did much to foster the modern image of the princes of Rajasthan. The maharana of Udaipur later renamed a village Todgarh in his honour.

The British period

For a long period the Marathas were the biggest threat to the independence of the Rajasthan kingdoms, but it was eventually the British, in the early 19th century, who took gradual control. Most of the kingdoms remained officially independent, but signed treaties with the British that placed them under British protection and, in most cases, required them to pay an annual tribute. The princely states of Rajputana, as they came to be known, all signed agreements with the East India Company. By the 1830s, the British agent based in Ajmer, which was ruled directly by the British, had become the most powerful individual in Rajasthan. He was supported by four British Residents, one each based in Jodhpur, Udaipur, Jaipur and Dholpur (later moved to Bharatpur).

Although some Rajasthani troops rebelled during the Uprising of 1857, none of the important princes gave their active support to the rebellion. The British rewarded the princes well, reducing their debts and allowing some of them to accumulate great wealth. As under the Mughals, several of the states raised regiments to support the imperial army, most notably Bikaner's 'camel corps'. Under the British, Udaipur outranked the other kingdoms, receiving a 19-gun salute, whereas Jodhpur, Jaipur and several others received only a 17-gun salute.

Modern Rajasthan

At the time of Independence, all of the princes agreed (though they had little real choice) to join India, and the present state of Rajasthan, with Jaipur as its capital, was formed in 1956. The princely families remain very influential in Rajasthan: some have joined the modern political world, others have turned to tourism as a way of maintaining their luxurious palaces and lifestyles; their princely titles, officially abolished in 1971, are still widely used. Politically, Rajasthan has alternated between periods of Congress and BJP rule, but has seen little of the Hindu-Muslim violence that has affected other states.

The main language of Rajasthan is Rajasthani, which is very similar to Hindi. The best-known dialect is Marwari, originally spoken in the area around Jodhpur. The word Marwari is also widely used by other Indians to refer to a community of successful Rajasthani business families, most of whom actually come from the Shekhawati region of northern Rajasthan, not from Marwar.

Names and titles

Place names and titles in Rajasthan can be a little confusing, and not all the rulers were maharajas. Marwar is the region around Jodhpur, formerly ruled by the Rathore family who were styled as the maharajas of Jodhpur. Another branch of the Rathore family ruled the Bikaner area. Mewar is the region around Udaipur (and the old capital at Chittorgarh), formerly ruled by the Sisodia family, who were styled as the maharanas of Udaipur. Dhoondhar is the old name of the region around Jaipur (and the old capital at Amber); it was formerly ruled by the Kachhwaha family, who were styled as the maharajas of Jaipur. Kota's ruler was a maharao; Jaisalmer's was a maharawal, Pratapgarh's was a maharawat and Tonk's a nawab.

EASTERN RAJASTHAN

The eastern part of Rajasthan has Jaipur—the state capital, largest city in the region and one of India's most important tourist destinations. There are also a number of smaller, less-visited former principalities, such as Alwar, Karauli and Kishangarh. There are two important pilgrimage sites: one Hindu (Pushkar) and one Muslim (Ajmer). It has three of India's best-known nature parks: a bird sanctuary at Bharatpur and two tiger sanctuaries, at Ranthambhore and at Sariska near Alwar. Each of the parks has, nearby, little-visited buildings of genuine cultural and historical importance. This part of Rajasthan, despite the large number of tourists who come here to visit Jaipur and Pushkar, also has some hidden gems: the water palaces of Deeg, the deserted city of Bhangarh and the medieval mosques of Bayana. For Dholpur, the easternmost part of Rajasthan, see the Madhya Pradesh section of the guide, where it is listed because of its proximity to the city of Gwalior and its distance from the main Rajasthan tourist routes.

JAIPUR

With a population of more than 2,500,000, Jaipur (*map 3 D1–2*) is a large, modern, bustling city. But its old 18th-century heart—the geometrically-planned walled city built by Maharaja Jai Singh—has largely survived and, despite the tourist crowds and the ubiquitous touts and scamsters, remains a fascinating and superb example of Rajput urban architecture and design.

History: Jaipur is the newest of Rajasthan's great royal cities. It was built in the early 18th century by Maharaja Jai Singh II and replaced the former capital of the Rajput Kachhwaha Dynasty at the nearby fortress of Amber—the Jaipur princely state was also often referred to as Amber, or as Dhoondhar, the old name of the region around Jaipur. Compared to the ruling families of Jodhpur and Udaipur, the Kachhwahas were relative newcomers to the top rank of Rajasthani royalty. In the 16th century, the Kachhwahas of Amber had allied themselves closely to the Mughal emperor Akbar, who married an Amber princess, and Raja Man Singh became one of Akbar's most important advisors and

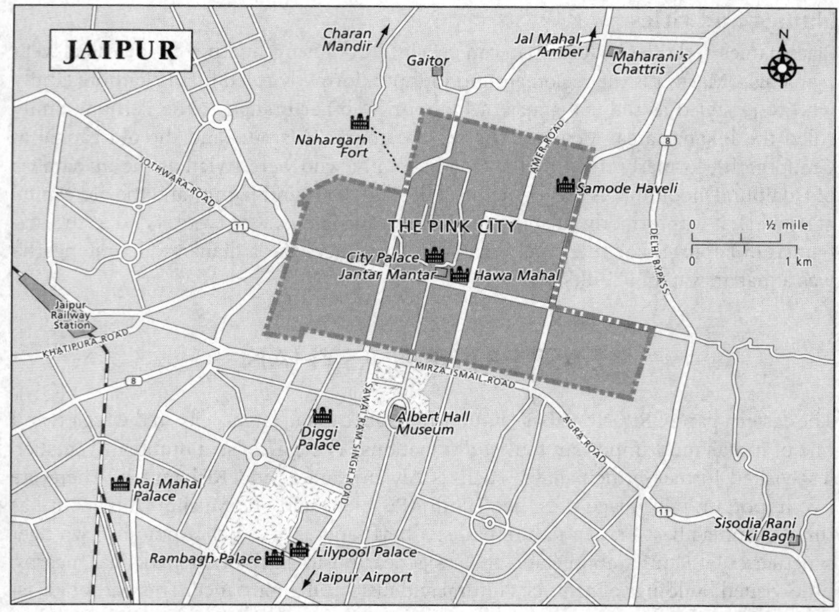

generals. By the time of Maharaja Jai Singh II (ruled 1700–43) of Amber, the Kachhwahas were one of the leading Rajput royal families, and one of the richest. According to Jaipur historians, Jai Singh, while still a child, had been given the special title 'Sawai', meaning one-and-a-quarter, by the Mughal emperor Aurangzeb, who was impressed by his alertness and courage. The implication was that the Jaipur maharaja was 25 percent more important than his fellow Rajput princes. Jai Singh married princesses from the Udaipur and Jodhpur royal families, while his daughter married the maharaja of Jodhpur—all ways of securing a close relationship with the region's other leading kingdoms and of improving his status among his peers. He was, by the time of his death in 1743, the most respected of the Rajput princes, and had vastly increased his state's territory.

Jai Singh was deeply interested in mathematics and astronomy, building five 'Jantar Mantar' observatories: in Delhi, Varanasi, Mathura, Ujjain and Jaipur. The observatory is at the heart of Jai Singh's walled city, next to his royal palace, and these were among the first buildings to be constructed in Jaipur. The most famous building in the city, the Hawa Mahal, or Wind Palace, was not built until 1799 and was the work of Jai Singh's grandson, Maharaja Pratap Singh, during whose reign (1778–1803) Jaipur was repeatedly threatened by Maratha armies. In 1818, Jaipur came under British protection and paid an annual tribute of 800,000 rupees to the East India Company. It supported the British during the Uprising of 1857 and was rewarded with the territory of Kot Kasim, taken from a rebel prince. It was only in the late 19th century that the buildings in the walled city were given the distinctive pink wash—for the benefit of the visiting future King Edward VII—that earned Jaipur its modern soubriquet, the Pink City. Maharaja Madho Singh (ruled 1880–1922) was the first of the Rajput princes to visit Britain, when he attended King Edward VII's coronation in 1902. In the 1930s, Jaipur became the focus of the anti-colonial and pro-democracy movement called the Praja Mandal, led by the Gandhian industrialist Jamnalal Bajaj, which successfully campaigned for a representative government for Jaipur. At Independence, the state of Jaipur joined the Indian Union, and the city of Jaipur later became the capital of the new state of Rajasthan.

THE PINK CITY

The Walled City of Jaipur, now known as the Pink City, was laid out according to strict geometric principles and in accordance with early Hindu ideas about the layout of the universe. The plan, drawn up by the Bengali scholar Vidhyadhar Bhattacharya, was originally based on a three-by-three grid of squares, or *chowkries*. However the northwest square could not be built on, because it contains the hill on which Nahargarh stands, so this square was shifted to the southeast. The central square and the one behind it are occupied by the palace complex, while the other squares were assigned to different professions and activities. Hindu and Jain businessmen occupied the area immediately in front of the palace, while the square in the middle left position was for courtiers, and the middle right square was for royal temples and priests. There are several gates, or *pols*, that connect the walled city with the rest of Jaipur. The city's buildings used to be in a range of colours, but were turned pink in 1876, when the maharaja decided to repaint Jaipur in honour of the visit of the Prince of Wales (later King Edward VII). Since then, all buildings inside the walls, except those within the royal compound, have to be painted pink.

Orientation: Jaipur is surrounded by hills on its northern and eastern sides. The oldest part, the walled Pink City, is on the north side of modern Jaipur. Further to the north, on the nearest hilltop, and visible from many places in the city, is Nahargarh, or Tiger Fort. The New City, largely a 19th- and early 20th-century creation, is south of the Pink City, and has the Albert Hall Museum, the Rambagh Palace and a number of other royal buildings. The airport is to the south of the modern city, while the railway station is to the west. Travellers by road coming from Delhi approach Jaipur from the northeast, passing the old capital Amber on the right (west) as they near the Rajasthani capital.

The City Palace

In the centre of the walled city, the City Palace contains Jaipur's two most distinctive buildings, the Hawa Mahal and the Jantar Mantar observatory, and a number of palaces, some of which are open to the public.

Hawa Mahal: The external façade of the five-storeyed red sandstone Hawa Mahal (or Wind Palace, *open Tue–Sun 9–4.30*) is at the southern end of the eastern wall of the City Palace compound, and consists of dozens of little windows, projecting slightly, each with gently curving arches. Built in 1799, Hawa Mahal was designed as a *zenana* (a palace for the women of the royal household) and the windows were intended to allow cool air to circulate, and to allow the princesses and their retinue to watch street processions without being seen. Note the pretty eaves and roof of the maharajah's high school opposite. The entrance to the Hawa Mahal is from the side, through a gateway on Tripolia Bazaar, the main east–west street of the walled city. The interior is less extraordinary than the façade, but still well worth visiting, and prettily maintained. The top storeys have fine views over the royal compound and surrounding city.

The rest of the buildings in the City Palace compound, including the Jantar Mantar, are entered from the **Sireh Deori Gateway**, 250m north of the Hawa Mahal façade and just beyond the old town hall. Immediately within is a large courtyard, which used to house the palace guard. Straight ahead is one of two entrances to the palace buildings, while to the left, the road passes through another gateway which leads to the Jantar Mantar and to the second, main entrance to the palaces.

Jantar Mantar: The extraordinary Jantar Mantar complex (*open daily 9.30–4.30*) consists of a large walled compound containing 16 different stone-built astronomical instruments. Jantar Mantar literally means 'calculating instrument', though the words have become a Hindi equivalent of 'abracadabra'. It was built on such a large scale to ensure precise measurements of the positions of the stars and other heavenly bodies—essential for the drawing up of horoscopes by Hindu astrologers, who still use the information to help believers make decisions about marriage and other key occasions. Construction began in 1728, after the similar complex in Delhi had been completed (*see p. 118*). Guides are available if you wish to learn the scientific purpose of each instrument, and the instruments have informative labelling. Among the more impressive buildings are the 27m high **Samrat Yantra**—like a stairway to heaven—and the two concave spheres of the **Jai Prakash Mantra**, faced with white marble and serving as a map of the heavens. Note how the shadow of the crosswire shows the position of the sun on the marble facing and which sign of the zodiac it is passing through.

The main **Virendra Pol** entrance to the rest of the City Palace (*open 9.30–5*) is opposite the gate leading to the Jantar Mantar and leads into a large courtyard. The two-storey **Mubarak Mahal** (1890) at the centre of the courtyard was a royal guest house, and now houses an interesting textiles and garments museum. In the far right corner of the courtyard is the armoury museum, which, as well as having a fine collection of weapons, has some unusual sporting equipment, including a ball that contains a light for playing polo at night. Note also the paintings in the lobby of the armoury: they include an image of heaven that resembles a maharaja's palace. The **Rajendra Pol** gateway on the right side of the courtyard, guarded by two marble elephants, leads through to a smaller courtyard with a central pavilion that originally functioned as the public assembly hall, or **Diwan-i Am**, until the end of the 18th century, when it was converted into the private assembly hall, or **Diwan-i Khas**. Note the two enormous

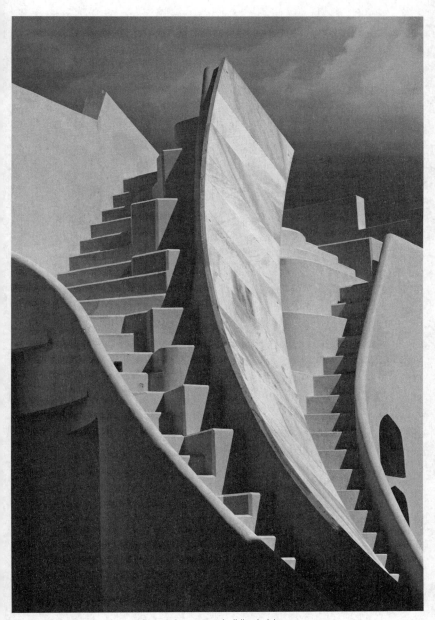

The early 18th-century Jantar Mantar observatory building in Jaipur.

silver urns, made by melting down 14,000 coins and used by Maharaja Madho Singh to carry sacred water from the Ganges during his trip to London in 1902. A gate to the right leads to the public assembly hall, known as the **Sabha Niwas** (note the superb painted cloth *pichwai*, showing Krishna playing his flute), as well as the **Carriage Museum**, a small café and the second entrance/exit to the City Palace. A gate to the left leads deeper into the residential area of the palace and the innermost courtyard, the **Pritam Niwas Chowk** (note the pretty painted door with its peacock feather and rose petal motifs). This is overlooked by the original seven-storeyed palace building, known as the **Chandra Mahal**, with the women's quarters, the *zenana*, on its left. It is possible to visit the Chandra Mahal by purchasing a ticket back at the Rajendra Pol for an exorbitant Rs2500. The interior of the palace is interesting and well maintained, but not dramatically different from palace buildings you will find in other Rajasthani cities. Inside the verandah area are murals, including royal portraits, painted by European artists in the 1940s. The downstairs double height reception hall has been furnished in a European style—notice the peepholes on the upper level which allowed the women of the palace to view what was happening down below. There are several more decorated palace rooms on the upper storeys of the building.

Gaitor: 1.5km north of the City Palace, at a place known as Gaitor (*open daily 9.30–4.30*), on the lower slopes of the hill, are pretty marble *chattris* that are memorials of the maharajas of Jaipur. The oldest ones, including that of Jai Singh, the founder of Jaipur, are in the compound at the back. The **Maharani's Chattris**, the memorials of the women of the royal household, are in a park opposite the Holiday Inn hotel on the Delhi Road, 2km northeast of the City Palace.

The New City

Outside the Walled City are a large number of palaces—no other city in India has quite so many palaces as Jaipur. This was partly because of the wealth and prodigality of the ruling Kacchawaha Dynasty, but also because many of Jaipur's feudatory states (such as Samode, Bissau and Diggi) have their own palaces in Jaipur. Most of them are in the New City, though the pretty Samode Haveli is just to the northeast of the City Palace. Many of these palaces are now hotels, including the enormous **Rambagh** (1920), 3km south of the City Palace, which was the main royal residence from 1925 to 1957. It was designed by Sir Samuel Swinton Jacob on the site of an older garden and guest house, and has a particularly fine Neoclassical indoor swimming pool. The Neoclassical **Raj Mahal** (1729), 4km southwest of the City Palace, was originally built as a garden palace and was then the British Residency, becoming the main royal residence from 1959 to 1976, when it was also turned into a hotel. Two other palaces remain in the hands of the royal family: **Moti Dhoongri**, a tiny hill-fort built like a Scottish castle, 1km east of Rambagh, and **Lilypool** (1930s) in the Rambagh grounds (though there is currently no public access). Among the palaces of the minor princely states, **Diggi Palace** (1881), 2km southwest of the City Palace, is the best known, largely because it hosts the Jaipur Literature Festival each January.

The New City also has a large number of municipal buildings, of which the **Albert Hall** (1876–87) is a fine example of Indo-Saracenic architecture, as well as being one of India's best museums. Named after the visiting Prince of Wales, the Albert Hall was designed by Sir Samuel Swinton Jacob. In many ways it still feels like a Victorian museum, with its old turnstiles, huge historical murals and display cases full of anthropological figurines showing different Indian castes, ethnic groups and professions—and even yogic postures. There is an Egyptian mummy and a collection of European and East Asian porcelain. The Indian exhibits include a superb collection of 19th-century Indian pottery and metalwork, and some very fine Rajput miniatures. There are also fine carvings from the area near Jaipur, including an unusual triple-headed Brahmini (11th or 12th century), the female form of Brahma, as well as several pieces from Abhaneri (*see p. 156*). In a separate room on the ground floor is one of the world's most valuable carpets, the 17th-century 'Jaipur garden carpet' from Kerman in modern-day Iran.

The **Sisodia Rani ki Bagh**, or Sisodia Queen's Garden (*open daily 8–8*), is a garden palace surrounded by hills and located just outside Jaipur on the Agra Road, 5km east of the City Palace. It was built in 1710 for a princess from Udaipur's Sisodia Dynasty, who was married to Maharaja Jai Singh, the founder of Jaipur. She did not want to live in the main palace in Amber, so the Sisodia Rani ki Bagh was built for her. The external paintings on the palace depict courtly and religious themes, including episodes from the life of Krishna. The interior has been modernised tastefully, and the garden and its ponds and fountains are well maintained. There is a pretty painted temple, just opposite the garden, and there is a much larger garden complex, Vidhyadhar ka Bagh, on the other side of the road.

The 18th-century Jal Mahal, or Water Palace, in the Man Sagar, Jaipur.

The **Jal Mahal**, or Water Palace, is a pretty building of the 1750s with fine cupolas and archways, positioned in the large lake known as Man Sagar, on the road to Amber. It is connected to the shore by a causeway which is often covered by water during the rainy season.

Nahargarh, or Tiger Fort

High on a hill on the north side of Jaipur and visible from most parts of the city, this fort is only 1.5km from the City Palace, as the crow flies. There is a steep winding footpath up to the fort, but most visitors take the Amber Road and then turn left up into the hills before veering back to Nahargarh—a distance of more than 15km. The road splits: the left path leads to a large open step-well and the way to Jaipur; the right path leads into the heart of Nahargarh and the unusual Madhvendra Palace. The fort was built in the 1730s, after the construction of Jaipur, while the palace was built in the 1880s as a summer retreat for Maharaja Madho Singh and his wives. The palace has nine almost identical two-storeyed apartments, all of them prettily painted and decorated, using a special polished plasterwork known as *arayish*. There was one apartment for each of Madho Singh's wives, all grouped round a long central courtyard. There are superb views of Jaipur from the east- and south-facing apartments.

CHARAN MANDIR

On the road between Nahargarh and Jaigarh is a striking yellow-painted building, the Charan Mandir. Built in the style of the tallest of the buildings at Jantar Mantar (the Samrat Yantra), it has served both as a watchtower and as a temple, containing what is said to be a footprint of Krishna.

JAIGARH

The long, narrow 17th-century fortress of Jaigarh sits on the ridge above Amber Fort and contains what is thought to be the largest wheeled cannon in the world. It is approached by the same road that leads towards Nahargarh, but instead of turning left, head right once you've reached the top of the hill. The fort (*open 9–5*) is entered through the Dungar Gate and a large courtyard with an underground water tank. Cars can go no further than the second courtyard, which has an armoury and several small temples. A path on the right leads to the great Jaivana cannon and the cannon foundry (*see opposite*)—but straight ahead are the main palace buildings, beginning with the Subhat Mahal Pavilion.

The 17th-century **Lakshmi Vilas Palace**, protected from the elements by an undignified tin roof, has a pretty internal balcony with cusped arches and some delicate painted patterns on its walls. Beyond is a maze of rooms and passageways, leading to another courtyard, which has a pavilion that overlooks the well-maintained, Mughal-style **Char-bagh Gardens**, surrounded by a raised walkway, from which there are superb bird's-eye views of Amber Fort and of the fortifications on the nearby hills. There is also another small palace building, the Lalit Mahal, on the west side of the fort near the gardens. Return to the large courtyard with a car park, and follow the signs to the **cannon foundry**, where cannon were manufactured from the 17th to the 19th centuries. Note the huge oxen-pulled wheel that gradually bored the deep cylindrical hole in the cannon. The enormous **Jaivana Cannon** is set slightly apart from the main fort on a bastion overlooking the gateway, through which the old path down to Amber Fort passes (it can still be used by pedestrians). The 6m long cannon is decorated with floral and animal designs, and could fire cannonballs weighing as much as 50kg.

AMBER FORT

Pronounced locally without the 'b', as, approximately, 'aam-air', Amber (*map 3 D1*) preceded Jaipur as the capital of the Kachhwaha Dynasty's state, known as Dhoondhar. The superb Amber Fort was elegantly designed as a series of beautifully decorated palace courtyards that ascend a steep hill overlooking a strategic route from Delhi to Rajasthan. Nearby are ruins of older buildings—a reminder that this was an ancient stronghold of Meena tribal chiefs until 1037, when the Kachhwaha Dynasty set up their first capital here—though none of the ruins dates to the pre-Kachhwaha period. The construction of Amber Fort began in 1592 under Maharaja Man Singh, but most of its palaces were built in the reign of Jai Singh I. Both rulers were close allies of the Mughal Empire, and there is a strong Mughal influence in the architecture and art of Amber Fort.

Orientation: There are three routes to Amber Fort. The most popular with tourists is the old ceremonial route that starts at the bottom of the hill close to the Delhi–Jaipur road. It is a short, steep walk uphill to the Suraj Pol Gate; while elephants (about Rs600 per two-person elephant) are available on a broader path next to this route. A ride in a shared jeep is available (about Rs100) up the back roads of Amber, past the ruins of the old capital, through the Chand Pol Gate. It is also possible to come down the broad path from Jaigarh and enter Amber Fort through the Suraj Pol. Both the Suraj Pol and the Chand Pol lead into the first and largest of the palace courtyards, the Jaleb Chowk.

The outer fort: So named because it faces the rising sun, the 3-storey **Suraj Pol** (Sun Gate) is the eastern entrance to Amber Fort (*Jaleb Chowk: open sunrise to sunset; rest of the fort: open 9.30–5.30*). It was the main ceremonial entrance, with guard-rooms at the side, and leads into the enormous **Jaleb Chowk**. This courtyard was used as a parade ground for the maharaja's troops and as a stable for his elephants and horses. On the far side is the **Chand Pol** (Moon Gate), which was the route into the palace for commoners. Above the gate is the **Naubat Khana** (*open 8–10am*), where drums and other instruments would have been played. Near the Chand Pol is the ticket office for the rest of Amber Fort. Steep steps lead up to the Singh Pol (Lion Gate).

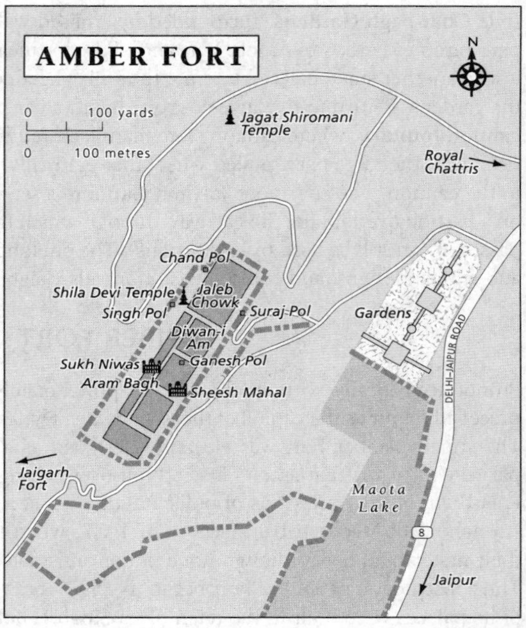

On the right of the gate is the 17th-century **Shila Devi Temple** (*closed 12–4; no leather items allowed*), the family shrine of the Kachhwahas, with fine 20th-century silver relief-work on the door. It contains some fine marble screens, and a stone slab ('shila devi' means 'slab-goddess') that is considered to be a representation of the goddess Kali. It was brought by Maharaja Man Singh from Jessore, now in Bangladesh, where he fought a victorious campaign on behalf of the Mughal emperor Akbar in 1604. The **Singh Pol** is the entrance to the imperial quarters of the fort, with well-restored murals of flowers and birds.

Inside is a second courtyard containing the **Diwan-i Am**, or public assembly hall—a large pavilion open on three sides, where the maharaja would meet his subjects. Note the use of alternating slabs of red sandstone and cream-coloured marble on the ceiling, sandstone columns on the outside and marble ones inside, as well as the elephant-head brackets on top of the columns. The colonnaded area to the right of the Diwan-i Am is known as Sattais Kacheri (or '27 courts') and is where 27 of the maharaja's leading officials would run the government. There are marvellous views from here of the gardens and lake near the main road. A door on the right leads through to the **Hammam**, or royal baths.

The inner fort: The heavily decorated **Ganesh Pol** (1640), or Ganesh Gate, separated the public and private areas of the fort. Note the image of Ganesha, the elephant-god, above the cusped arch, and the perforated screens on the upper floors, through which the women of the palace could watch what was happening in the courtyard. On the left in the next courtyard is the **Sheesh Mahal**, or Mirror Palace, which also served as the Diwan-i Khas, or private assembly hall. It has some superbly intricate mirror work and inlay, with lots of Mughal-style motifs of jugs, vases and other vessels. The nearby royal latrines have some excellent views over the surrounding countryside. A sunken Mughal-style garden, known as the **Aram Bagh** (Garden of Leisure), fills much of the rest of the courtyard. On the right (west) is the Sukh Niwas

(House of Peace) used by the maharaja's wives. Note how the water channel flows from the Sukh Niwas into the Aram Bagh. The final courtyard contains the private apartments of the maharaja and his wives, and is the oldest part of the palace, dating to 1599. In the centre of the courtyard is a pavilion known as the **Baradari** (literally '12 doors' or archways). Note the delicate floral paintings on the first floor, as well as some finely decorated interiors. Steps lead to the upper storeys of the Sheesh Mahal and the Ganesh Pol.

If you leave Amber Fort by the Chand Pol, you pass several half-ruined buildings that predate the fort; they include the Narsingha Temple and the Rajtilak ki Chattri, which was used as a location for royal marriages. A little further down the hill is the fascinating **Jagat Shiromani Temple** (early 17th century), dedicated to Krishna, with a superb *torana*, or entrance archway, and some very fine external and interior decoration. The lower levels of the exterior have friezes of elephants, cows and courtly scenes, and some fine relief carvings higher up. The upper levels of the interior (go up the steep steps to the left on entering) have excellent religious paintings. Note, at the far end of the upper area, a painting of Matsya, the fish incarnation of Vishnu, and the event known as the Samudra Manthan, or churning of the ocean, with gods and demons pulling on either end of an enormous snake. The image in the subsidiary shrine facing the main temple is of Garuda, the man-eagle and vehicle of Vishnu.

Next to the main Jaipur–Delhi road, at the foot of the fort, are the Maota Lake and some very well-maintained Mughal-style gardens, as well as some minor palaces. About 1km further, on the side of the Delhi–Jaipur road, are the **royal *chattris***—memorials of the maharajas of Amber.

FURTHER NORTH OF JAIPUR

Neemrana

Some 133km northeast of Jaipur and close to the main road to Delhi (which is 110km away), Neemrana (*map 3 D1*) was the capital of a former small feudatory state, which was part of the kingdom of Jaipur. Neemrana's spectacular fort is now one of India's best-known heritage hotels. There is an interesting *baoli* (step-well) in fields near the village, and the ruins of some fortifications further up the hill, above the palace.

Samode

Samode (*map 3 D1*), 33km north of Jaipur, was the capital of one of Jaipur's former feudatory states. It is best known for its pretty 19th-century palace-hotel, nestled in the rocky Arvalli Hills above the town. The family of the former ruler of Samode, who had the title rawal, still live in part of the palace, which was used for shooting the 1980s TV series *The Far Pavilions*. There are some fine wall-paintings inside. There is a small fort further up the hill, behind the palace, and a Mughal-style garden, known as Samode Bagh, 4km to the south.

Kuchaman

Kuchaman (*map 3 C1*), 97km northwest of Jaipur, is the capital of a small former princely state that was a distant part of the kingdom of Jodhpur, more than 200km away. It has a handsome medieval fort, now a hotel, with some interesting 19th-century murals depicting religious and erotic themes.

WEST OF JAIPUR

Ajmer

Surrounded by rocky hills 125km southwest of Jaipur, the town of Ajmer (*map 3 C2*) is home to India's most important Muslim shrine: the *dargah*, or tomb, of the 13th-century Sufi saint Moinuddin Chishti. It is also the site of India's oldest and most impressive mosques. The tomb continues to draw huge numbers of pilgrims, not all of them Muslim, from all over India and beyond.

History: Ajmer has an important pre-Islamic history which goes back to at least the 12th century, and probably a lot earlier. By the 11th century, Ajayraj of the Hindu Chauhan Dynasty built his new capital here, naming it Ajaymeru—later contracted to Ajmer. He fortified the hilltop now occupied by the Taragarh Fort. It was from Ajmer that the last Hindu ruler of Delhi, Prithviraj Chauhan, was captured by the forces of Muhammad of Ghor in 1193, at the same time that Moinuddin Chishti settled in the town. The city was captured by Rana Kumbha of Chittorgarh in the 1430s, and passed under the control of the sultan of Malwa and then the maharaja of Jodhpur. Ajmer was one of Emperor Akbar's earliest conquests, in 1557, the first year of his reign; it became an important Mughal city, with a royal residence, and emerged as a major centre of pilgrimage. Akbar is said to have walked barefoot from Agra to Ajmer in thanksgiving for the birth of Salim, later known as Jehangir. Jehangir and his son Shah Jahan both stayed for long periods in Ajmer, and the city saw the first meeting between a British envoy and a Mughal emperor in 1616. In the 18th century, with the Mughal Empire disintegrating, the rulers of Jodhpur and the Marathas vied for control over Ajmer. The city was ceded to the British in 1818 by Daulat Rao Scindia of Gwalior. Unlike almost all of the rest of Rajasthan, Ajmer came under direct British rule, and its importance grew when the British opened Mayo College to provide a Western education for Indian princes. Ajmer is now once again best known as a pilgrimage town.

Orientation: The town of Ajmer is built around a lake, the Ana Sagar, and surrounded by rocky hills and outcrops of the Aravalli range. The hill-fort of Taragarh looms above the town, and at the foot of Taragarh, between the hill and the lake, are the *dargah* and the 12th-century mosque that make Ajmer so special. The *dargah* and the mosque are normally approached from the lakeside, but cars are allowed only as far the old Delhi Gate to the north of the *dargah*, from where it is another 600m on foot or by cycle-rickshaw. There is an alternative road, which takes a winding route over the hills, and allows vehicular access close to the old mosque and less than 300m from the *dargah*.

The old footpath up Taragarh Hill is close to both the mosque and the *dargah*, and is still widely used by pilgrims.

The *dargah* of Moinuddin Chishti: India's most important Muslim pilgrimage site is positioned close to a cleft between two hills in the old city and consists of a large walled complex (*open 5am–9pm; shoes are not allowed, and carry a hat or scarf to cover your head; cameras are not allowed, but there are facilities to leave valuables to the right of the main gate*). Enter the *dargah* complex through the high gateway, with pretty tracery windows on each side. On the right, in the first courtyard is Akbar's Mosque (c. 1570), with its unusually high central arch, painted a very modern green and blue and with a marble floor. Note the *minbar*, or pulpit, above the main *mihrab*, as well as the doors either side of the *mihrab*. The second courtyard has two *degs*, or copper cauldrons, set into stepped plinths, into which money, rice and other foodstuffs are thrown in order to provide meals for the poor.

The third courtyard contains the heavily decorated white-domed tomb of Moinuddin Chishti, with marble external columns, gold-covered walls and silver doors. The hereditary servants of the mosque, known as *khadims*, sit and stand outside its doors asking for donations for special prayers. The porch was a 17th-century addition, commissioned by Emperor Shah Jahan's daughter, Jahanara Begum. Inside, beneath a canopy, surrounded by a silver railing and covered in silk and velvet cloths, is the cenotaph of Moinuddin Chishti. Here, there are usually long queues of pilgrims, many of whom scatter rose petals over the grave. It can be very crowded inside, and do expect to be asked for a donation. Attached to the far side of the tomb are two smaller compounds: the one on the east contains the grave of Chishti's daughter Bibi Hafiz Jamal; the one on the west is a separate prayer area for women, said to have been built by another of Shah Jahan's daughters, Chimni Begum—it contains her grave. The *dargah* complex also houses mosques built during the reigns of Shah Jahan and Aurangzeb, and the large pool known as the Victoria Tank, the roof of which was built by the British after the visit of Queen Mary in 1911.

MOINUDDIN CHISHTI

Known as Khwaja Sahib to his followers, Moinuddin Chishti (1141–1230) was the founder of the Chishti order of Sufis in South Asia. He was born in Sistan in modern-day Iran and became a religious scholar. The Prophet Muhammad is said to have appeared in a dream and told him to travel to India, where, after stopping in Lahore, he settled in Ajmer. Here he developed his distinctive brand of Sufi Islam, which emphasised toleration, public service and anti-materialism, and which uses music and poetry as a means of conveying its ideas. Chishti's death anniversary is marked by a major festival known as the Ajmer Urs in the Islamic lunar month of Rajab. Delhi's two most famous Sufi shrines, in Nizamuddin and Mehrauli, were founded by followers of Moinuddin Chishti.

Arhai Din ka Jhompra Masjid: This superb building dating to 1200 is one of India's oldest mosques, and one of the few major surviving buildings from the Slave Dynasty period outside Delhi. It is normally approached from the *dargah*, which is 300m further north, though it is possible to take the hill road almost to the main gate of the mosque. The origin of the name of the mosque is disputed. The phrase 'Arhai Din ka Jhompra' literally means 'two-and-a-half days hut', which suggested to some that it took only two-and-a-half days to build; others believe that the two-and-a-half days refer to a fair that used to be held here. The mosque was built during the rule of Qutbuddin Aibak, the first sultan of Delhi; it is contemporaneous with, similar in design to, and larger than, the great Quwwat-ul Islam Mosque next to the Qutb Minar in Delhi.

The mosque, which sits on a high plinth nestled into the lower level of a rock hillside, is approached by a stone staircase from the east. The gateway has small covered side pavilions, used by the mosque watchman. Note the koranic inscription on the thick lintel, and the use of corbelled ogee arches. The internal façade of the gateway uses carved pillars as decoration rather than to support the structure. The large courtyard was once surrounded by arcades, most of which have now disappeared. The impressive seven-bayed façade, with a high central arch, was built slightly later than the rest of the mosque, in about 1230, by Aibak's successor Iltutmish. Note the stumps of thin minarets rising above the arch, and also how the arches of the two outer bays have a simple corbelled arch while the other bays have multi-foil lobed arches. The stone-carved calligraphy work and geometric patterns on the central arches are in superb condition and of unusual depth. The multi-domed roof of the large assembly area of the mosque is supported by columns—largely taken from Jain and Hindu temples—which are resting on top of one another. Note how three columns have been stacked to support the central part of the mosque building. Look carefully at the uppermost part of the columns, where defaced human and animal figures can be made out—and temple debris can be seen where the southern wall of the mosque has partially collapsed, exposing the old stonework.

Akbar's Fort: The fort (1570) is 700m northeast of the *dargah*, on the road towards the railway station. It consists of a fortified compound, with four imposing octagonal corner bastions; inside is a single large square sandstone palace building, which now houses the **Ajmer Museum** (*open daily 10–4.30*). Note the fine stone tracery work on the main gateway, as well as the pretty look-out balconies. From the gates, there are good views of the hillside fortifications above Ajmer. Inside are well-maintained gardens and the palace where, on 10th January 1616, Emperor Jehangir received the British ambassador Sir Thomas Roe, representing James I of England—the first formal contact between the British and the Mughal emperor. Two hundred and forty-two years later, Britain sent the last Mughal emperor into exile. The recently renovated museum has some interesting Hindu and Jain sculptures from the neighbouring region, including several important sculptures and other stone carvings from the Vishnu temples of Baghera, to the southeast of Ajmer.

Mughal pavilions: The Anasagar Baradari (1637) are a series of white marble Mughal pavilions constructed along the southeastern embankment of Anasagar lake, which was itself excavated in the 12th century. The five pavilions were part of a Mughal pleasure garden known as Daulat Bagh, completed by Emperor Shah Jahan and begun by his father Jehangir; they were used as homes and offices in British times, and have since been restored. Note the long overhanging eaves which provide protection from the sun, and the decorative multi-shaped niches inside the pavilions.

Other buildings in Ajmer: There are several other interesting buildings from the Mughal and British periods in Ajmer, including the 18th-century **Badshah Haveli**, close to Akbar's Fort, which probably served as a guest house; the old **British Residency** on a small hill overlooking the lake; the impressive neo-Mughal **Nasiyan Jain Temple** (1865), 350m north of Akbar's Fort, and popularly known as the **Red Temple**; and **Mayo College** (1875), set up by the British to provide a Western education for sons of Indian princes—it was named after a viceroy and consciously modelled on Eton. It continues to function as one of India's most prestigious schools. The enormous main college building, with its white marble façade, is one of the most ostentatious Indo-Saracenic structures in the country. It has a superbly ornate central tower and a series of small, domed pavilions on the rooftop. Call in advance for permission to visit (*T: 0145 2661154*).

Around Ajmer

The main hill above Ajmer, known as **Taragarh**, was fortified by the 11th century and possibly earlier. It became, in the Sultanate and Mughal periods, a key military base, and was much fought over. Now it is largely visited by pilgrims coming to the ***dargah* of Miran Shah**, an early 13th-century governor of Ajmer, who was killed by Rajput warriors. Most of the pilgrims make the long walk up the hill behind the Dargah of Moinuddin Chishti, but there is a winding road that goes to the top—head south of Ajmer for 5km on the Udaipur Road (NH8) and then turn right. Note the impressive fortifications on the left just before the road ends. The views from the top are superb, and there are other parts of the ruined fort that can be visited, mainly on the far side of the hill (walk through the more modern *dargah* complex from where the road ends), including old gateways, and a system of stone acqueducts for raising water to the top of the hill.

The pretty 16th-century **Kharwa Fort**, 35km southwest of Ajmer, is the residence of the former rulers of Kharwa, a feudatory state under Jodhpur, and sits on a hillock overlooking the village of the same name. It is now open to visitors if you call in advance (*T: 01462 265432*), and has some interesting wall-paintings and hunting trophies. The town of **Merta**, 65km northwest of Ajmer, is an important pilgrimage town because the popular 16th-century female mystic and follower of Krishna, Meerabai, was born here. There are two ruined forts, several temples and the small **Meerabai Museum**.

Pushkar

This small temple town (*map 3 C2*) is best known for its camel fair, which is held annually in late October or November, and it is very popular with young Western travellers who congregate here in the winter months. But it is also an ancient Hindu pilgrimage centre, and contains one of the few temples in India dedicated to the creator-god, Brahma. It has more than 400 other temples, many of them grouped around an almost square lake at the centre of the town. According to one version of the story of Pushkar's origins, Brahma killed a demon with a lotus blossom which floated to earth at the site of Pushkar Lake. None of its temples appear particularly old, partly because they have been heavily restored, but also because some of them were destroyed by the Mughal army of Emperor Aurangzeb in the late 17th century. Note the memorial plaques inlaid into the ground around the lake and paid for by visiting pilgrims. Be sure to take off your shoes near the lake. A priest or temple worker will often attempt to charge visitors large sums for tying a red thread (nicknamed the 'Pushkar passport') around one's wrist. Despite what you may be told, this is not compulsory, but agreeing to wear one in return for a small tip will stop other over-enthusiastic locals doing the same thing.

Kishangarh

Kishangarh (*map 3 C2*) is the capital of the small former princely state of the same name. This pretty town is 100km southwest of Jaipur, on the road to both Ajmer and Pushkar (both about 30km away). It has a fine fortress, and a palace hotel. Kishangarh was founded in 1603 by Kishan Singh, a younger son of the maharaja of Jodhpur, and was strongly supported by Delhi's Mughal rulers, partly because of its proximity to the key Muslim pilgrimage site at Ajmer. In the 18th century the Kishangarh school of painting developed, for which the town is still best known, though there are few examples to be seen in the town itself, unless one can gain access to the private collection of the royal family (ask at the Phool Mahal Hotel).

Kishangarh Fort: The main fort (17th century), surrounded by a narrow deep moat, is in the heart of the town, with just the Phool Mahal, or flower palace, separating it from the lake. The fort has three outer gates, well defended by high bastions, which lead into a large courtyard with stables for horses and elephants, and barracks built into the outer walls. Note the old horse carriages in the arcades beneath the well-defended wall of the inner citadel containing the old royal palace. High up on the inner walls is a delicately carved stone balcony. The entrance to the palace within the citadel is at the far end and to the left, and passes through two more gateways. The outer gateway has paintings of elephants and soldiers, as well as old cannon, and look for more murals inside the gateway. On the right is a small Krishna temple and a pretty tiled arched gateway, before the second large entrance gate, which leads through into the main palace courtyard. Ahead is a small platform from where the maharaja used to address his courtiers, and the larger pillared verandah is still used for marriages and other ceremonies by the former royal family. Above and to the left are *zenana* quarters, a maze of rooms used by the women of the family. The 'First Maharani's Room' (the maharaja usually had several wives) has a small pool with a fountain and pretty paintings on the cupboards.

The Phool Mahal: Originally a flower market, this long narrow building of 1870 stands on a spit of land between the fort and the lake. It was turned into a palace in the 19th century by Maharaja Prithvi Singh, and has since been converted into a hotel; it affords superb views over the lake. Note the ruined former royal guest house on what appears to be an island on the lake, but which is in fact connected by a causeway on the other side. Visible but inaccessible beyond the pretty swimming pool and pavilions in the palace gardens are the royal memorials, or *chattris*. Up on the nearby hill is a Hanuman temple inside the walls of a small fort. The former royal family now live at the Majella Palace, a converted hunting lodge which is closed to the public.

Roopangarh Fort: The impressive 17th-century fort and palace at Roopangarh (*map 3 C2*), which stand side by side in the town of the same name, 25km to the north of Kishangarh, also belong to the former royal family of Kishangarh. Roop Singh, after whom the buildings are named, led a breakaway principality, which was later subsumed by Kishangarh.

SOUTH OF JAIPUR

Ranthambore

Up in the Aravalli Hills, 115km southeast of Jaipur and 10km east of the town of Sawai Madhopur, Ranthambore (*map 3 D2*) is now best known as the site of one of India's leading wildlife reserves, which has seen recent increases in its tiger population. But it also has one of India's most impressive forts, on a hill overlooking the entrance to the reserve. The fort dates back to at least the 11th century, and one of Prithviraj Chauhan's sons based himself here after the defeat of his father's forces at the hands of Muhammad of Ghor, who then established the Delhi Sultanate. The fort changed hands many times until it eventually became, in 1753, part of the princely state of Jaipur, when it began to be used as a base for hunting expeditions in what is now the wildlife park.

Visiting Ranthambore: Most visitors to Ranthambore organise their early morning or pre-sunset visits to the wildlife park through their hotel, which can provide jeeps or buses for travelling around the reserve. Ask your hotel to ensure that you have extra time (at least 2hrs) to visit the fort. It is possible to visit the fort at any of time of day, and to go there in a taxi or hired car, or on foot, even when the gates of the park are closed.

Ranthambore Fort: The fort is approached via a narrow valley with an impressively fortified gateway which effectively cuts off the wildlife park and fort from the outside world. There are good views of the 13th-century walls of the fort, high overhead, from the road. At the foot of the fort (*open daily dawn–dusk*) there is a large car park with the gates to the wildlife reserve on the left and, on the right, the steep footpath leading up to the fort, which passes through a series of gateways. On top is a large plateau, with several groups of surviving buildings and a choice of directions in which to head. On the right, along the walls, are a number of palace buildings from which there are some superb views of the main lake of the wildlife reserve; further on is a pool with a pretty pavilion and a Muslim *dargah*, or holy tomb. There are Jain and Hindu temples nearby. If instead you go straight ahead at the top, climbing slightly, you reach a multi-pillared *chattri*, or memorial, on a high plinth. Beyond are the largest surviving palace buildings (*normally closed to the public*) and a footpath that goes past further ruins and a large water tank to reach the **Hanuman Temple**, which continues to attract large numbers of devotees. On the far side of the temple, a path leads down to another gate to the fort. Back near the first gateway, if you head left, you reach a two-storeyed Hindu temple with a spire and a sanctuary, but decorated as if it were a palace.

Within the wildlife park there are small hunting lodges and other buildings not usually open to the public; they include the 1930s pillared rest-house known as **Jogi Mahal**, which overlooks the lake.

Indergarh

The small town of Indergarh (*map 3 D2*), 55km south of Ranthambore on the highway to Kota, has a fairytale fort-palace, with dozens of buildings in a large walled compound clinging to the side of a hill. The fort is deserted, but there are plans to develop it into a hotel. Look for the 'Contact here, to visit the fort' sign written in large letters on the side of a house leading up to the fort. The watchman lives here, and will let you into the compound, which is full of tumble-down palace buildings with pretty pavilions, balconies and cupolas, some lovely wall-painting, and mirror-work decoration.

Tonk

The town of Tonk (*map 3 D2*), 80km south of Jaipur on the Bundi road, was the capital of a small principality of the same name. Tonk was the only Rajasthani princely state with a Muslim ruler, the Nawab of Tonk—a relatively recent creation, by the British in 1817. The old **Tonk Palace** is in the centre of the modern town, unimpressive by Rajasthani standards, and inhabited by the descendants of the last nawab. Ask to see the old durbar hall at the far end of the palace. Next to it is the **Sunehri Kothi**, a two-storey building used by the nawab as a meeting hall, and superbly decorated inside and out. The upstairs room is covered in mirror-work and paintings. (*Ask for permission to go inside the Sunehri Kothi from the Arabic-Persian research institute on the other side of the road. The institute also has some very fine external decoration.*)

Madhopur

The village of Madhopur (*map 3 D2*), 40km southeast of Jaipur, has a handsome 17th-century hill-fort with impressive walls. It is now a hotel.

EAST OF JAIPUR

Bharatpur

Bharatpur (*map 5 A1*) is best known for its **Keoladeo Bird Sanctuary**, which starts on the southern edge of the modern city and was once the site of many royal duck shoots. It has been starved of water in recent years, and the overall number of birds and number of different species has declined rapidly. Bharatpur was, until Independence, a medium-sized principality. Unusually for Rajasthan, the maharaja of Bharatpur did not belong to the warrior Rajput caste, but was a Jat—a caste usually associated with farming. The principality was founded in the 18th century, and its best-known ruler was Maharaja Suraj Mal, who moved the capital from Deeg to Bharatpur; he also sacked the city of Agra, taking away many jewels and weapons. His successor raided Delhi in the 1760s and carried off the metal gates that still stand at the northern entrance to Bharatpur Fort. Today, Suraj Mal's descendants live in an ornate Edwardian palace on the northern outskirts of the city, where uninvited visitors can get no further than the main gate. But the little-visited old fort, known as **Lohagarh** (Iron Fort), at the centre of the city, has high fortified walls and several old palaces and monuments, as well as a very impressive royal bathhouse.

Lohagarh Fort is surrounded by a moat with two access bridges and is, unlike so many forts in Rajasthan, inhabited and part of the main town. Entering from the northern gate, the old town hall—a fine three-storeyed structure with arched galleries—is on the left. Head to the right and ask for the museum, which is inside the newest of the palaces, the **Khas Mahal**, and contains an impressive collection of poorly-labelled ancient Hindu and Jain sculptures, an armoury and some specimens of the sentimental European pottery of which so many maharajas were fond. From the roof you can get a good view of the other important buildings in Bharatpur. On the right side of the main courtyard is a passageway that leads to the royal baths, which are formed from a series of interconnected rooms. The first chamber has fine fluted columns and lobed arches, and a central cusped pool. The second chamber has painted spandrels and multi-coloured floor tiles, but finest of all is the octagonal third chamber, which has an ornate dome (notice the steam vent at its centre) and small bathing rooms off each side of the octagon.

The nearby palace known as **Kishori Mahal** is very run-down but still a fascinating building to wander through. It contains government offices, and the land records for Bharatpur district are piled high in the inner archways of the palace, wrapped up in brightly coloured cloth bags. On the hill next to the Khas Mahal—known as Fateh Burj, or Victory Tower—are an iron pillar and two small pavilions, commemorating the successful defence of Bharatpur against the British in the early 19th century. Note the series of cartoon-like paintings on the roof of the smallest building.

Deeg

Deeg (*map 5 A1*, also known as Dig) was the summer capital of the Bharatpur royal family, and here they created a charming series of water palaces, set amid gardens with two artificial lakes. The main entrance is from the north and leads directly to the first palace, Gopal Bhavan, overlooking the western lake. Gopal Bhavan has two storeys on the land side and four storeys on the lake side. Inside is a small museum (*no shoes and no photographs*) which shows the palace as it was when last used in the early 1950s. Among the less expected exhibits are a dartboard and an elephant's foot that has been turned into a receptacle for crystal decanters. Note also the large curtain-like fans, which would have been pulled back and forth by servants using long ropes. On the upper floor are two adjacent dining rooms: one European in style, the other Indian, with a low-level table made out of stone. There are several other palaces set amidst the gardens. Note the pretty squashed-cushion quoins used as a decorative feature in several areas; the water maze near Kishan Bhavan; and the bathing pool next to Nand Bhavan.

Beyond the water palaces is a huge crumbling old fortress, with the broken remains of a palace inside, occupied by welcoming office workers. Note the elephant spikes on the gate to the fort. It is possible to walk around the walls of the forts, and there are excellent views of the water palaces. Several cannon are *in situ* on the walls, including, unusually, one that still sits on its full gun carriage in the southwest corner.

Kaman

North of Deeg by 20km is the town of Kaman (*map 5 A1*). Like Deeg, it was once part of Bharatpur state. It has one of India's oldest mosques, known as the Chaurasi Khamba, or Eighty-four Pillars. The partially restored four-storey façade of an old fort palace overlooks the modern town, and behind the fort on the far side of the hill, where the terrain dips, is the mosque, which is thought to have been built in the earliest years of the Delhi Sultanate (probably in 1204). It is an unusual design, with pretty open colonnades on two sides. There are some finely carved pillars—mainly re-used Hindu temple stonework, though the human images have been partly defaced. The mosque is the oldest in India to have a surviving *minbar*, or pulpit, and a separate women's area in the prayer hall. Note the complex figurative carving on a stone beam under the women's area and in the small arched ceiling over the women's entrance on the side of the mosque.

Karauli

This little-visited former princely state deserves to be on more tourist itineraries. It is easy to reach from either Agra or Jaipur, 60km south of the highway that connects both these cities (*map 5 A2*), and it is a good place to stay en route to the tiger reserve at Ranthambore. Karauli has good accommodation at a palace hotel and a fascinating old city palace; it also has pretty temples, *chattris* and a fine step-well. The princely state is one of Rajasthan's oldest, dating back to the 14th century, and the royal family claim descent from the Hindu god Krishna. The Karauli maharaja supported the British during the Uprising of 1857 and sent troops to free the maharaja of Kota, whose own soldiers had mutinied.

The **City Palace** (*open daily 8–6*), one of the prettiest in Rajasthan, was built in the 18th century on the highest part of the old walled city overlooking the river. The large public courtyard has some spectacular decorated façades. Ahead is a superb painted and tiled gateway, capped by three tiers of overhanging rooms, with perforated jali-style windows and a curved bangaldar-style roof. This gateway leads to a garden and the ancient but heavily restored, **Madan Mohan Temple**—on the left is a small, uninteresting museum. The entrance to the main palace is on the right, through a gateway over which are some pretty balconies. The superbly decorated inner courtyard has a fine painted durbar hall. Ask the guards to show you around the residential quarters, where many of the rooms are painted, often with images of battle scenes from the life of Krishna, or decorated with mirror-work. There is an upstairs courtyard, which was used for musical and dance performances—note the fountains with the old water pipes embedded in columns. Ask to see the gymnasium at the back of the palace, with its old-fashioned wrestling pit. The older parts of the palace are less decorated, and use bare red sandstone on most of their surfaces. It is possible to walk down just beyond the city walls to the river, and visit the **Shahi Kund**—a very fine example of a Rajasthani step-well, with a pretty underground cloister. The royal *chattris* of the Karauli princes are nearby.

The **Bhanwar Vilas Palace** (1938), to the southeast of the walled city, is now a comfortable heritage hotel with a pretty central courtyard set in spacious grounds. There are also the impressive ruins of a three-storey *shikargah*, or hunting lodge, 1km to the south of the Bhanwar Vilas Palace. There are several interesting, little-visited hill-forts in the area around Karauli, including the 12th-century **Timangarh Fort**, 33km to the northeast, and the great **Mandrael Fort**, 30km to the southeast, close to the River Chambal, where Arjun Pal, the 14th-century founder of Karauli, is said to have had his base.

Bayana

During the 12th to the 15th centuries, Bayana (*map 5 A1*) was an important centre under the Delhi Sultanate, but it is now an obscure town 25km south of the main Agra–Jaipur highway. There are two unusual and similar mosque-like buildings from the Sultanate period that share a wall. The building on the right is known as the **Ukha Mandir**, or Ukha Temple, and dates to the early 13th century. It was built as a mosque, reusing masonry from an older temple, and then converted into a temple. Note how the main prayer niche is now part of the temple's circumambulatory passage, and the raised women's prayer area is a home. On the left is the later red sandstone **Ukha Masjid** (1320), which is still a mosque, and with a pretty entrance arch that makes use of sandstone of different colours. Unusually the side colonnades have two storeys. To the far right of the two buildings is the bottom half of an unfinished free-standing cylindrical minaret (1520). There are tombs, pavilions, water tanks, *chattris* and other buildings scattered throughout the town, and in and around the impressive hill-fort on the south side.

THE ALWAR REGION

The former princely state of Alwar (*map 3 D1*) is 110km northeast of Jaipur and 130km south of Delhi, and has some fine forts, palaces and tombs.

Delhi–Alwar Road: The most popular route to Alwar is from Delhi, and the road journey takes about three hours (take the Dharuhera Road, not the old Sohna–Alwar Road). Once beyond Delhi's seemingly endless urban sprawl, this is a lovely journey, particularly in the early months of the year when the bright yellow mustard flowers are in bloom. The road closely follows the low ridge of the geologically impressive Aravalli range of hills, whose ancient rocks twist and turn as they emerge through the surface soil. Note the crumbling Muslim tombs on the eastern side of the road near **Tijara**, and a fascinating hill-fort, now being converted into a hotel, on the far side of the same town. Further south along the road is the derelict fort of **Kishangarh**—the group of small temples and pavilions on the west side of the road near an incline as it passes through the Aravallis. And the tombs and forts of **Bahadurpur** can be seen about 15km before Alwar.

History: The region around Alwar, known as Mewat, has witnessed many battles, and the hill-forts scattered all over the former principality are a reminder of its strategic importance. The state became independent only in the 18th century; most of its lands had previously been part of Jaipur, and the first maharaja, Pratap Singh, was a member of a minor branch of the Jaipur royal family. He had ruled Jaipur as the regent during the childhood of Maharaja Prithvi Singh, and used the opportunity to create his own independent state. His son, under military threat from Jaipur and the Marathas, asked the British East India Company for help, and Alwar became one of the first of the large Rajput states to sign a treaty with the British. The state had a series of ruthless and unpredictable rulers for large periods of the 19th and 20th centuries. Maharaja Jey Singh became famous for refusing to shake hands with the British unless he was wearing gloves, and for using a Rolls-Royce car as a city garbage van. He also set fire to his polo pony after a disappointing match. In the 1920s and 30s there were peasant uprisings and major Hindu-Muslim clashes, and Alwar was the most volatile of the Rajasthan kingdoms. The British eventually removed Jey Singh from power, and in 1937 he died in exile in Paris. The Alwar princely family always aspired to join the ranks of the great kingdoms of Rajasthan, with their ancient traditions and legendary wealth, but they were sometimes treated as parvenus. This partly explains why from the 18th to the 20th centuries there were several rapid spurts of extremely costly royal construction work, which saw the building of the imposing fort, high up on the hill above the city, the fascinating city palace sheltered by the lower slopes of the same hill, as well as several other important monuments.

Alwar city

Alwar Fort, or Bala Qila (Young Fort), whose walls extend around the large hilltop that overshadows the city of Alwar 300m below, has the deserted **Nikumbh Palace** and several other ruined buildings on its summit. The 18th-century stone walls replaced much older 10th-century mud-brick fortifications. Because it contains police communications equipment, the palace can be visited only with the generally forthcoming permission of the superintendent of police in Alwar City. It is possible to visit the rest of the large hilltop without permission, and the views are spectacular. The fortified area of the hill is entered by a road that runs through the Jai Pol, or Victory Gate. Note the steep fortifications with their stone staircases following the switchback contours of the hill. A few hundred metres above the Jai Pol is a derelict mosque, which appears at first sight to be no more than a dome on the side of the road. But there is another level below, with three arched bays and some minor traces of decoration. Continue towards the palace and, on the right, is one of the old gates of the fort leading down to Alwar by a different, steeper route. The views from the walls near the gate are exceptional. Turn to the right for the palace, where, if you have permission, you can visit a neglected early 19th-century building with pretty balconies and windows and some faded wall-paintings. At the other end of the ridge on which the palace sits is another palace, built in the European style; though more modern, it is in an even more advanced state of decay than Nikumbh Palace.

Alwar City Palace (Vinay Vilas) is an impressive edifice in a beautiful location, scarred by having been used as government offices for many years. The interior walls of the huge palace courtyard are in good condition, and major restoration work is underway. The red and yellow sandstone canopied balconies, or *jharokas*, overlooking the courtyard are particularly fine. The gilded marble throne of Alwar is usually locked away in the durbar hall behind the marble pavilions at the back of the courtyard, though a guide may point out a peep-hole through which it can just be seen. The **museum** (*open Tues–Sun 10–5*) is interesting, but poorly laid out. Amongst its treasures are two 11th-century bluestone carvings: one of Shiva as Nataraja, the Lord of the Dance, with his foot resting on the head of a dwarf; the other is of Vishnu, in his third avatar as the boar Varaha. There is also an illustrated 60m scroll of the *Mahabharata*, and a fine armoury with a good collection of swords, shields, guns for use on camelback and a sword with a pistol concealed in its hilt. Outside is the sandstone and marble *chattri* of Maharaja Bhakhtawar Singh and his wife Moosa Rani, who committed *sati* on his death in 1815. The interior is richly decorated with relief carvings of scenes from the Hindu epics. The large pool next to the *chattri* has excellent views of the nearby palace fortifications, built into the hillside, as well as of the fort above.

The impressive five-storey **tomb of Fateh Jung**, one of Emperor Shah Jahan's ministers, who died in 1647, is on the eastern side of Alwar. Unusually for a Mughal tomb it has a small *chattri* placed on its large white dome. The exterior wall of the tomb has some fine geometric and calligraphic carving.

Near Alwar

To the north of the city is the strange **Moti Dhoogri**, a large fortified area set up on a hill which once had a palace within. Little remains of the palace, destroyed by Maharaja Jey Singh, who was apparently searching for buried treasure, but there are two well-tended Muslim graves.

The enormous, sprawling **Vijay Mandir Palace**, 10km north of Alwar, overlooking the lake known as Vijay Sagar, was largely constructed in the 20th century. It has an unusual lighthouse-like watchtower, and the main building has an impressive array of neo-Mughal domes. The palace is currently closed to the public, but it can be viewed, at a distance, from the lakeside.

On the far side of the hill under which Alwar was built, 16km by road from the city, is **Siliserh**, a large man-made lake with a small over-restored, under-maintained palace on the waterside. About 10km east of Alwar, on the road towards Ramgarh, is the pretty 14th-century hill-fort of **Kesroli**, built on a rocky outcrop above the plains; it is now a hotel.

The wildlife park of **Sariska**, south of Alwar, was a former royal hunting estate, now sadly devoid of the tigers for which it was famous. There are several interesting buildings in and around the park. **Sariska Palace**, on the northern side of the park, was a 19th-century royal hunting lodge and is now a luxury hotel, while the overgrown 17th-century **Kankwadi Fort**, 35km southwest of Alwar on a hilltop in the heart of the park, was where Dara Shikoh, the son of Emperor Shah Jahan, was imprisoned in 1659 by his brother, the future Emperor Aurangzeb. Note the walled staircase leading down to the lake, providing access to water for those living in the fort. South of Kankwadi are the crumbling **Neelkanth temples**, which are thought to date back to the 9th century; in the vicinity there are impressive fortifications. The nearby village of **Tehla** has a small hill-fort.

BETWEEN ALWAR & JAIPUR

This area, east of the Delhi–Jaipur highway, is little visited but has some fascinating historical sites. **Bairat** (*map 3 D1*), 68km northeast of Jaipur and just 16km east of the Delhi-Jaipur highway, is an important early Buddhist site from the Mauryan period; it is situated 3km southwest of the modern town of Viratnagar (which was in fact the original name for Bairat). The 3rd-century BC circular shrine that enclosed a stupa is more than 8m in diameter and is thought to be India's earliest surviving built (rather than rock-cut) structure. There are ruined monasteries nearby. **Bhandarej**, 65km east of Jaipur, just 10km beyond Dausa on the south side of the Jaipur–Agra road, has an interesting fort in the centre of the village and a step-well on the south side.

Abhaneri

The village of Abhaneri (*map 3 D1*), 85km east of Jaipur and just to the north of the Jaipur–Agra road, has a spectacular 9th-century multi-tiered step-well, known as the **Chand Baoli**. Its complex geometric design and carved panels make it arguably the finest of Rajasthan's step-wells. Nearby are the sanctuary and assembly hall of the **Bharat Mata Temple** (9th century), with some carved panels depicting courtly scenes from the Pratihara period.

Bhangarh

This deserted 16th-century city, midway between Alwar and Jaipur and 10km south of the town of Ajabgarh, is one of India's most extraordinary historical sites (*map 3 D1*). It is little-visited because it is widely believed to be haunted. It was built in the late

16th century by Madho Singh, the younger brother of Man Singh, the ruler of Amber, but was deserted by the 18th century. The ruined city, which is approached along a deserted, partially-restored market street with stone-built shops and homes, is set in a cleft in some rocky hills. There are several temples, some of them grouped around a pond, and a large palace slightly further up the hill. There are many outlying buildings and fortifications, and it is easy to spend several hours visiting Bhangarh.

NORTHERN RAJASTHAN

The north of Rajasthan has traditionally been less visited than other parts of the state. The great Rajasthani cities are elsewhere (and so are the airports), and Bikaner was the only major principality and urban centre in the region. Historically, the region was divided up into lots of mini-states, some of them very small indeed, that owed allegiance to either Jaipur, Bikaner or Jodhpur (and sometimes more than one of them at the same time). However, the 'discovery' of the painted *havelis* of Shekhawati in the 1980s led to a tourist boom for this part of Rajasthan and the gradual emergence of a tourist infrastructure. Shekhawati's wall-paintings, the fort and *havelis* of Bikaner, as well as camel-riding in the desert, have placed northern Rajasthan firmly on the tourist map.

THE SHEKHAWATI REGION

The name Shekhawati comes from a 15th-century military leader called Rao Shekha, whose descendants and followers became known as the Shekhawats. In the 18th century, Sardul Singh emerged as the most important of the Shekhawati leaders. He was a small-time landowner who took over the lands of Parsurampura, where his beautifully decorated cenotaph still stands. He became a key adviser to the nawab of Jhunjhunu, the main town in Shekhawati, and seized power when the nawab died. Sardul Singh's estates were eventually divided up among five sons, and then further subdivided. By the 19th century there were dozens of minor princes in the Shekhwati region, vassals of one or other maharaja, and almost all of them built palaces or forts—some still occupied, some derelict, others transformed into heritage hotels. Also in the 19th century, men from Shekhawati began travelling to the great cities of British India, Calcutta and Bombay, in search of work. Many of them were very successful, and some of the best-known business families of modern India, including the Birlas, Goenkas and Poddars, came from this small arid area of Rajasthan. These businessmen became known as Marwaris, although most of them did not actually come from Marwar (the area around Jodhpur) but from Shekhawati. In the early days, the women and the children of the family would remain in Shekhwati, living in the *havelis*, the women often in *purdah*. But with success and modernity many of the families followed their menfolk to the cities and left the *havelis* deserted, but for a watchman. Today the families return occasionally to their ancestral homes, often for a religious festival or ceremony, but the rest of the time the homes are empty; while some are firmly locked, others offer a welcome to passing visitors.

Orientation: There is no best way of visiting Shekhawati (*map 3 D1*). It will partly depend on where you are coming from and where you are based. Visitors arriving from Delhi usually approach Shekhawati from Baggar and Jhunjhunu; those coming from Jaipur usually go first to Nawalgarh, and those coming from Bikaner pass through Fatehpur. Each of these entry points provides a good introduction to the wall-paintings of the Shekhawati region. Nawalgarh and Mandawa are good bases, with a range of accommodation in both places. Most of the area known as Shekhawati falls within Jhunjhunu district, but some interesting wall-paintings can also be found in the neighbouring districts of Sikar and Churu.

THE WALL-PAINTINGS OF SHEKHAWATI

The tradition of wall-painting in the region goes back to at least the 18th century, and the surviving work from the early period is largely religious. By the middle of the 19th century, however, secular wall-painting was becoming popular. For the next 80 years or so, until about the 1930s, well-off families competed with each other to have the best wall-paintings on the external walls and internal courtyards of their homes, known as *havelis*. They often chose modern subject matter, including trains, cars, telephones and gramophones, with the intention of showing the sophistication of the *haveli* owners, and there are many entertaining paintings of India's British rulers, overdressed and stern-faced. Other *havelis* carry genealogical, historical and sometimes erotic paintings. Some of the painters came to Shekhawati from Jaipur, where they had worked on the building and decorating of the new city. They used a combination of dry and wet fresco techniques, and painted in a folk style that showed a mixture of Mughal miniature and European influences but developed an almost cartoon-like feel. The earlier works used natural colours, but imported artificial colours from Germany gave the later paintings a wider spectral range.

There are at least 15 towns or villages where wall-paintings can be seen; and there are many hundreds of *havelis*, most of which will have some interest for the visitor. Many travellers ask their hotel or guest house to arrange a guide. Otherwise it is quite easy to wander the streets of many of the towns and find the *havelis* for oneself—local people are usually helpful. Do not be shy about going inside the courtyards of the *havelis*; most of the locals are used to visitors, and will tell you if you are not welcome or if they want a small fee.

Jhunjhunu

Jhunjhunu is the district headquarters and feels a bit like any other busy Rajasthani market town, with crowded streets and unplanned construction work. However, it does have, a little hidden away, some very fine frescoes and *havelis*, and a controversial temple.

There is a tumble-down 18th-century palace called the **Khetri Mahal** in the centre of the old town, with superb views over the rest of Jhunjhunu, and with traces of floral decoration inside wall-niches. Nearby are several interesting *havelis*, including three that were owned by different branches of the Modi family. The **Modi Haveli**, next to Nehru bazaar, is particularly attractive, with wall-paintings depicting a row of European soldiers wearing bowler hats, and a car being steered by a man standing up in the driving seat. Note how many painters, in Jhunjhunu and elsewhere, use trains as a horizontal decoration above window frames, or to mark the division between different floors of a building. Jhunjhunu also has a **Sati temple**—one of the country's richest and most-visited. *Sati*, or *suttee*, the burning of living widows after the death of their husbands, was abolished in the 19th century, but there have been occasional cases of *sati* over the last few decades, including a famous case in nearby Deorala in 1987. The folk tales and history of Rajasthan, and particularly of Shekhwati, have tended to glorify the act of *sati*. On the ceiling of this temple is a particularly bloody painting, telling the story of Rani Sati, the goddess who defeated her husband's enemies before throwing herself on his funeral pyre.

About 12km to the northeast is the small town of **Bagar**, with a fine *haveli* that has been converted into a hotel, a pretty tank with attached pavilions, and a huge gate erected for the visit of the maharaja of Jaipur in 1928.

Mandawa

Mandawa is probably the best known of the Shekhawati towns, partly because its tourist infrastructure developed earliest and it is in a central position for visiting other places. It is also smaller than the other main towns and is therefore more manageable to wander round on foot. However, success has been at a cost: antique shops are selling carvings stripped from old *havelis*, and tourism is now a major part of the economy, accounting perhaps for the interest in money shown by some guides and *haveli* watchmen. However, there are some superb *havelis* and a fine fort that is also a hotel. There are some particularly delightful paintings on the exterior of a *haveli* that has been converted into a bank—ask for the **State Bank of Bikaner & Jaipur** on the main road, and go through the door to the right of the bank. The paintings include a bizarre flying machine, a small boy using a wall telephone, several bicycles, a hang-glider and a body-builder who appears to be in a tug-of-war with an Edwardian car. The erotic paintings on the **Gulab Rai Ladia Haveli** in the south of town have been defaced, though images have survived next to an exterior wall bracket. Nearby is a lovely image of a crouching woman giving birth while a tiny maid mops her brow.

Dundlod, a small village 20km along the road from Mandawa to Nawalgarh, has an interesting fort and several painted *havelis*.

Nawalgarh

It is worth spending a few hours exploring this large town on foot. It has dozens of interesting *havelis*, with fine early 20th-century paintings. It is helpful, but not essential, to have a guide. The town and its fort were founded by Sardul Singh's son Nawal in the early 18th century, and it is now one of the biggest urban centres in Shekhawati.

One of the most beautiful *havelis*, the **Sekhsaria Haveli**, has been converted into a school. It has some superb and amusing paintings on the exterior and interior. Note the wan-faced European family, with a fearsome dog, sitting in a car, as well as the portraits of George V and Queen Mary, and a woman hard at work on a Singer sewing machine. The nearby **Hira Lal Sarawgi Haveli** has charming pictures of a train, with lots of differently-attired passengers leaning out of the carriage windows. There is also a man struggling with what appears to be a table fan, and a painting of an early dump truck. The best-known *havelis* are slightly to the west of the fort, and are known as **aath havelis** (eight *havelis*), although only six have survived.

Parsurampura

Some 20km south of Nawalgarh is the small village of Parsurampura, where the **cenotaph** of the 18th-century Shekhawati leader Sardul Singh can be visited. The shrine, in a walled compound, is historically and culturally important because it contains some of the earliest surviving paintings in the region, and the quality is extremely high. On the inside of the dome of Sardul Singh's 12-sided *chattri*, painted in red and black, are tales from the Hindu epic, the *Ramayana*. Using a peacock feather, so as not to damage the paintwork, the watchman will point out key scenes from the tale of Rama and Sita, the monkey-god Hanuman and the demon Ravana.

Nearby is the very pretty **Shamji Sharaf Haveli**, with a lovely picture of woman looking into a mirror while having her hair dressed, and a European man sitting on a very mis-shapen bicycle while smoking a pipe. There is also a temple with some incomplete ceiling paintings, showing how the painters would first sketch outline figures. Local people tell visitors that the artist's hands were chopped off so that the paintings on Sardul Singh's shrine would remain the best, but the artist then continued with his work by using his feet.

Just outside the village is a small fort, still occupied, which has some interesting paintings, including a *trompe l'oeil* of a clock in the main hall, forever stuck at 3.20.

Fatehpur

This large town (*map 3 C1*), 20km west of Mandawa, is on the route from Shekhawati towards Bikaner and Jaisalmer. Along the main north–south road are several interesting painted buildings, with images of Hindu gods in modern settings. Radha and Krishna are shown being chauffeured by another god in a 1920s stretched limousine and in a flying car, complete with rotary blades and wings.

There are several other towns and villages in Shekhawati that are worth visiting, including Mukundgarh, Bissau, Churu, Mahansar, Ramgarh, and Lakshmangarh, the last of these with an imposing fort and more erotica.

BIKANER

Bikaner (*map 3 C1*) was one of the largest and most important princely states of Rajputana. It is now Rajasthan's fourth largest city, sitting on the northeastern edge of the Thar Desert.

Bikaner contains one of the prettiest of Rajasthan's large forts, a modern palace in the Indo-Saracenic style, and an unusual Jain temple. The old walled city is fascinating to wander through, and contains hundreds of old *havelis* with some of India's best street architecture.

History: Bikaner was founded in 1488 by Rao Bika, the second son of the founder of Jodhpur, Rao Jodha. Bika had a complicated relationship with his father and his brothers, and the rivalry between Bikaner and Jodhpur, which often descended into open warfare, lasted until the 19th century. During Mughal times, the rulers of Bikaner played major roles as vassals, commanders and senior advisers at the courts of all Mughal emperors from Akbar until the mid-18th century. Bikaner was important to the Mughals because it lay on one of the main routes to their Afghan homelands, and was also an important trading post. By the 19th century, the Bikaner maharajas were firmly allied with the British East India Company, and gained a reputation for being reform-minded—introducing a proper legal code and state-run schools, and building canals that have made farming possible in spite of the proximity to India's largest desert. One of the best-known Bikaner rulers, Maharaja Ganga Singh (ruled 1887–1943), personally led his celebrated Camel Corps on various British military campaigns, and was one of the signatories, on behalf of the Indian princes, of the Versailles Peace Treaty.

Junagarh Fort

The old fort of Bikaner, known as Junagarh, is, unlike most of Rajasthan's big forts, not built on a hill. It was founded in 1588 on a site 500m northeast of the old city, and is an almost perfect rectangle. Junagarh (*open daily 10–4.30*) is entered from the Suraj Pol (Suraj Gate), which leads through a series of further gates and then into the fort complex and car park. Tourist cars are allowed inside, but this means many visitors fail to notice the impressive multiple defences, including a moat, the *sati* handprints on the wall to the left of the first interior gate and the two little temples inside the final interior gate.

Orientation: Before purchasing your ticket in the covered area to the left, it is best to orient yourself inside Junagarh. Ahead and to your left (with your back to the gate) is a beautiful façade of windows and galleries that conceal the warren of palace rooms to which visitors are given access. Directly left is the main **fort museum**, and ahead and slightly to the right is a small **crafts museum**. The rest of the fort is out of bounds and largely empty.

From the ticket office, visitors are ushered up a steep ramp into the first of three courtyards, around which are the palace rooms—most are quite small. The first and least significant courtyard is built of red sandstone. The second is a mixture of red sandstone and white marble (with a large pool at one end), and the final one is almost entirely marble and coloured tiling. Among the rooms on view are the **Diwan-i Khas**, where the maharaja, seated on a silver chair, would meet his ministers. This room is richly decorated in gold leaf, now protected by Plexiglass. The most sumptuous room of them is all the 17th-century **Anup Mahal**, with ornately lacquered walls and mirror-work, and a plush recessed alcove created for Maharaja Anup Singh, after whom the room is named. The pretty 19th-century **Badal Mahal**, or Cloud Palace, has an old-fashioned water dispenser, and is painted with rain clouds and lightning—a very rare phenomenon in the deserts of northern Rajasthan. The 18th-century **Chandra Mahal** (Moon Palace) is covered with a mosaic of coloured glass, while the 19th-century **Chattra Mahal**, has a spectacular painted ceiling, with images from the story of Krishna, and mirrors in which the maharaja is said to have been able to see what was happening elsewhere in the palace.

Much of the rest of the palace is devoted to a **museum** in the vast public rooms of the complex. The star exhibits include a sandalwood throne that Rao Bika took from Jodhpur—said to be the oldest item of wooden furniture in India—and a First World War biplane (pieced together from two derelict biplanes given to the maharaja by the British).

Two kilometres away is the new palace, called **Lallgarh**, which was begun in 1902. It was designed by one of the most prolific British architects in India, Sir Samuel Swinton Jacob, in the Indo-Saracenic style, a marrying of Indian and European architectural traditions. Part of the palace is now a luxury hotel, and there is a fine indoor swimming pool with stained-glass windows and marble benches. The erstwhile royal family live in another part of the palace. There is also a museum, with modern memorabilia of the former rulers.

Bikaner old city

The old walled city of Bikaner contains dozens of old *havelis*, some of them with superb exterior carvings. Others have wall-paintings, more realistic than those of Shekhawati, but with similar subject matter, such as trains. A walk through the old city is recommended, as are visits to the **Bhanwar Niwas Haveli**, now a hotel, and the rest of the nearby **Rampuria havelis**. The old city also has the interesting 15th-century **Jain Bhandasar Temple**, more ornately decorated than most, with painted friezes showing great cities, battles and tortures, and with excellent views of Bikaner and the desert beyond.

Around Bikaner

Near Bikaner are several other places of interest including **Devikund**, 8km east of the city, where the pretty sandstone and marble cenotaphs of the Bikaner royal family can be visited, and **Bhand Sagar**, 5km to the southwest, with its medieval Hindu and Jain temples. **Gajner**, 30km west of Bikaner, has a nature reserve (good for deer, wild boar and birds) and a royal hunting lodge, where visitors can stay. Camel-lovers would be advised to visit the **National Research Centre on Camels** (*open to the public in the afternoons*) which is at Jorbeer, 8km east of the city. Rat-admirers will enjoy the **Karni Mata Temple**, an important place of pilgrimage in Deshnoke, 30km south of Bikaner, where large numbers of rats are fed by the faithful; it is said to be auspicious if a rare white rat runs across your feet. **Kolayat** is a popular Hindu pilgrimage town with temples set around a lakeside oasis in the desert, south of Gajner, 50km from Bikaner.

KALIBANGAN

The little-visited town of Kalibangan (*map 2 A2*), in the far north of Rajasthan, 180km from Bikaner, contains one of India's most important prehistoric sites, dating back to the Harappan and pre-Harappan periods of the Indus Valley Civilisation (c. 3000–2000 BC). Kalibangan is less than 100km from Harappa in Pakistan, the site which gave its name to these periods of history. The excavated mounds have revealed a grid-like street layout, with mud-brick houses, the remains of a citadel, a cemetery, fire altars and numerous smaller objects, including toys, figurines, bangles and copper arrowheads and fishhooks. Many archaeologists believe the site was deserted in about 1750 BC because of the drying up the River Ghaggar, the bed of which is still traceable. There is a small museum (*open Sat–Thur 9–5*).

WESTERN RAJASTHAN

Western Rajasthan contains two of India's most popular tourist attractions: the great fortress cities of Jodhpur and Jaisalmer, whose size and beauty alone make them objects of awe. Both, in different ways, have also played critical roles in the history of Rajasthan and the wider region—and because so much from the past has survived to this day, modern visitors can get a very tangible sense of what life was once like in these cities. The region also has a number of other important sites, including the old Marwar capital of Mandore, the Hindu temples at Osiyan and the enormous fort at Nagaur.

JODHPUR

Jodhpur (*map 3 B2*) is Rajasthan's second largest city (pop. 1,000,000), situated on the eastern edge of the great Thar Desert. It has a well-connected airport and good road connections to the other major cities of Rajasthan—and most visitors to Jaisalmer will travel via Jodhpur. Despite its size, the city is still dominated visually by two enormous royal buildings, the towering 15th-century hill-fort of Mehrangarh and the gargantuan 20th-century Umaid Bhavan Palace.

History: The city was founded in 1459 by Rao Jodha, whose name it still bears. Jodha was the chief of the Rathore Dynasty, who claimed descent from the god Rama via the ancient kings of Kannauj, in modern-day Uttar Pradesh, who were overthrown by Muslim invaders in the 12th century. Rao Jodha moved the capital of his state, known as Marwar, from Mandore, 7km to the north. His son Rao Bika founded the rival city of Bikaner a generation later, and besieged Jodhpur, eventually carrying off the family heirlooms from Kannauj in return for lifting the siege. The distrust between Jodhpur and Bikaner lasted several centuries, and a similar rivalry marked Jodhpur's relationships with its other large neighbours, Udaipur and, later, Jaipur.

Jodhpur's most powerful 16th-century ruler, Maldeo Singh, is chiefly remembered for throwing his own father to his death from the roof of Mehrangarh, Jodhpur's royal fort, and incurring the enmity of both the Mughal and Sher Shah dynasties, which ruled in Delhi. However, in the popular folk traditions of Jodhpur, Maldeo Singh was also a great hero, who won many battles and built many forts.

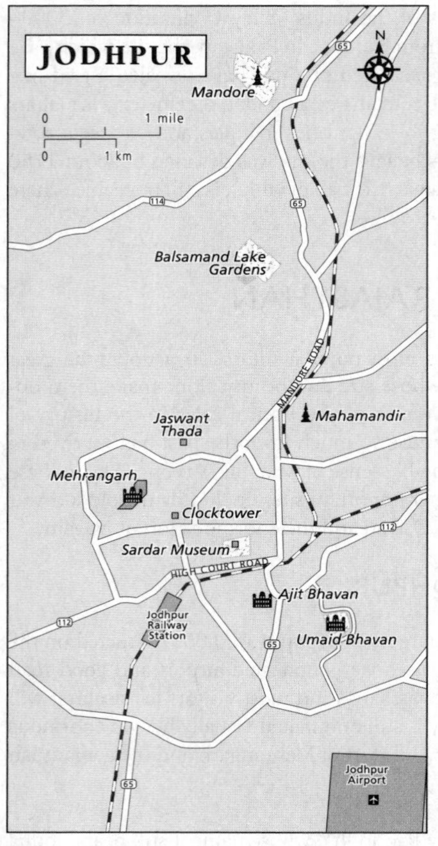

In 1583, Maldeo Singh's son Udai acknowledged Mughal supremacy over Jodhpur, and Udai Singh's daughter was married to the future emperor Jehangir—she would later be best remembered as the mother of Emperor Shah Jahan, who constructed the Taj Mahal. Under Aurangzeb, the Mughal army occupied Jodhpur, and full control of the city was not regained until after Maharaja Ajit Singh's death. This occurred in 1724, when, in a continuation of Jodhpur parricidal tradition, Ajit Singh was murdered by one of his sons—67 women of the *zenana* then committed *sati*, burning themselves to death on his funeral pyre.

In the early 19th century the chief threats to Jodhpur's independence were the Marathas and the British, who each separately overthrew Maharaja Man Singh, and then saw him return to the royal throne. His successor supported British forces during the 1857 Uprising, though some Jodhpur nobles rebelled and were defeated. The British played an increasing role in the affairs of Jodhpur, and for many years Sir Pratap Singh, a son of a Jodhpur maharaja but never a maharaja himself, was the regent of the state. He also popularised the riding breeches now known as jodhpurs. Maharaja Umaid Singh, who ruled from 1918 to 1947, constructed the Umaid Bhavan Palace, the last of India's great royal buildings, completed in 1944 just three years before Jodhpur formally lost its independence and became part of the Indian Union.

Mehrangarh Fort-Palace

Jodhpur has what is probably Rajasthan's grandest and most visitor-friendly fort-palace (*open daily 9–5*), with cafés, a lift (it is a hard but worthwhile uphill climb) and an excellent audio guide. Mehrangarh also has one of the most imposing fortifications to be found anywhere in the world. On visiting Jodhpur in 1888, Rudyard Kipling described 'the splendours of a Palace that might have been built by Titans and coloured by the morning sun.' The fort is built high up on a hill, with 36m walls that tower over the busy city below. Most of Mehrangarh is in very good condition, and gives a palpable sense of the past and present roles of the erstwhile royal family of one of India's most important principalities. Seventeen generations of the Rathore Dynasty have lived here, and most of the rulers added to or altered the existing buildings.

The approach to the fort: From the car park, walk through a series of seven *pols*, or gates, always uphill, along a broad, paved pathway that turns sharply to the left (from where there is a route down into the old town) and then the right, in a way that made the fort easier to defend. Near the **Jai Pol** (Victory Gate), the walls are scarred by marks made by cannon balls during a failed attempt by Jaipur's forces to capture the fort in 1808. To commemorate the lifting of the siege of Mehrangarh, Jai Pol and new outer fortifications were constructed. A little further on are two small post-holes in the wall on the left that mark the outer limit of the original fort constructed by Rao Jodha in 1459. Beyond, just before entering the interior of the fort, are the wall plaques bearing the handprints in relief of women—wives, concubines and servants—who committed *sati* on the death of a maharaja.

Ground floor: Inside the fort are a series of interconnected palaces and apartments arranged around small courtyards. Note the pretty balconies with *jali* screens carved out of pink, and sometimes yellow, sandstone. In the first courtyard is the **coronation throne of Jodhpur**, a surprisingly unostentatious marble seat resting on a plinth. In neighbouring rooms are an **armoury** and two galleries containing palanquins (litters) and howdahs (the passenger's compartment on an elephant). Note the silver howdah presented by the Mughal emperor Shah Jahan to Maharaja Jaswant Singh in the 17th century, and the 20th-century palanquin in which the maharani of Jodhpur was carried on a trip to England—and was able to remain in *purdah*. The museum sections are periodically rearranged, but look out for an unusual sword-pistol, four painted camel-bone carpet weights, a garishly dressed silver effigy of the Hindu goddess Gauri (an incarnation of Parvati, the consort of Shiva) and some wood-and-ivory dumbbells used by the women of the palace.

Upper floors: Upstairs are the richly-decorated 18th-century **Phool Mahal** (Flower Palace) and the even more ornate 19th-century **Takhat Mahal**, with coloured glass balls hanging from the wooden-beamed ceiling and an original cloth *pankha* (fan) attached to ropes once pulled by *pankhawallahs*. The views from the higher apartments of Mehrangarh are exceptional, and from here you can see many of the blue-painted Brahmin houses of the old city, beyond the ramparts of the fort. The rooms in the *zenana* include the **Jhanki Mahal** (Palace of Glimpses), with its wide range of diverse *jali* screen carvings and an unparalleled collection of royal cradles. Look out for the particularly fine mirrored swinging cradle and its small peacock statuettes with tails made of glass.

The rest of Jodhpur

Less than 1km from Mehrangarh is **Jaswant Thada** (1899), the large white marble cenotaph of Maharaja Jaswant Singh II, who died in 1895; it is surrounded by smaller, more recent memorials. With the death of Jaswant Singh, the royal cremation ground was moved from Mandore to this site.

The main landmark in the new city, which extends to the east of Mehrangarh, is the 19th-century **clock tower**. Many of the houses in the old city to the south and southwest are painted blue—originally the colour denoted the home of Jodhpur's Brahmins, and it is believed locally that the colour wards off mosquitoes.

Umaid Bhavan (1925–43) is arguably the most impressive of India's many 20th-century royal palaces, and is now a luxury hotel—though part of the building is still occupied by the former royal family. About 3km southeast of Mehrangarh, it is an enormous domed Neoclassical sandstone building, designed by Henry Lanchester, one the most successful British architects of the early 20th century. It was named after Maharaja Umaid Singh, and it was one of a series of public works projects designed to give employment to the poor after a major famine. Non-guests will need to pay a fee (redeemable against food or drink) to enter the parts of the building used as a hotel. There is also a small museum (*open daily 9–5*) containing some of the royal family's possessions.

Ajit Bhavan (1929), on the airport road, was another royal palace built at a similar time for the maharaja's younger brother, Sir Ajit Singh, and which Lanchester also helped design, albeit in a markedly different, neo-Rajput style.

The purpose-built **Sardar Museum** (*open Tues–Sun 10–4.30*), on the east side of Jodhpur, opened in 1935. It has a small collection of Hindu and Jain sculpture and temple pieces, including two pillars from Mandore with panels illustrating stories relating to Krishna. The museum is set in some pretty gardens, with a much older *baoli*, or step-well, and it backs onto the handsome high court building. The **Mahamandir**, or Great Temple, is an important 19th-century shrine dedicated to Shiva on the north side of Jodhpur.

Near Jodhpur

Just 4km north of Jodhpur on the road to Mandore is **Balsamand** (12th century), an artificial lake that supplied water to Mandore and later Jodhpur. Part of the old aqueducts have survived, and run through the pretty gardens that were first laid out in the 17th century and redesigned as an English-style garden in the 1920s. The pretty sandstone palace close to the dam was built in the mid-19th century. Note the fine columned *baoli*, or step-well near the entrance gate. The whole area has been turned into a luxury hotel, and non-guests will need to pay an entrance fee, redeemable against food or drink.

Mandore, 2km beyond Balsamand, is best known for the *chattris* memorialising the rulers of Marwar up until the 1890s, but it was also, until the mid-15th century, the capital of Marwar. The main road into Mandore leads to a car park from where visitors can wander among the *chattris* marking the cremation sites of the maharajas of Jodhpur. Unlike most royal *chattris*, which are open pavilions, almost all of those at Mandore resemble Hindu temples. Each has a nameplate, saying to which maharaja it belongs, next to the steps leading up to the plinth. The *chattri* of Maharaja Ajit Singh (1679–1724) is particularly fine, with elegant carvings on the inside of the domed roof. At the back is the *chattri* of Maharaja Takhat Singh (ruled 1843–73), which looks like a small fortress, with turrets and a very pretty inner courtyard. To the left of the *chattris* is an enclosure with the *zenana* building and water garden used by royal female visitors from Jodhpur as a summer palace, and built during the reign of Maharaja Ajit Singh. Note the much-restored rock-cut images of gods and heroes in the nearby colonnade.

Steps lead up through partly ruined buildings to the old **Mandore Fort**. Near the top, the path on the right leads inside the old fort, while the path on the left leads, after a walk of a further 800m, to another group of *chattris* at Panchkund. The lower part of the fort walls is largely intact, and inside are the remains of several buildings, including the plinth of a large temple from which there are fine views of the rest of Mandore. The very pretty **Panchkund *chattris*** (*open daily 9–5*), which can also be approached by car by taking a left on the road that leads from Balsamand to Mandore, are built to a more traditional design, as open pavilions. These are memorials to female members of the royal family.

OSIYAN

The temple town of Osiyan (also Osian, *map 3 B2*), 50km to the north of Jodhpur, has fine Hindu and Jain shrines from the 8th to the 12th centuries.

The Sachiyay Mata Temple

Osiyan's largest shrine, the Sachiyay Mata Temple (11th–12th century), stands on a fortified hillock with small rounded bastions in the centre of the town, and attracts large numbers of devotees to the main shrine, dedicated to the mother goddess. It is approached by steps that lead up from the main market, passing under a series of ornamental arches, and with subsidiary shrines on either side. The upper part of the temple complex has superb external carvings, particular on the tower of the main shrine. There are also smaller twin shrines on the left with almost identical external Vaishnavite images, including: Vishnu's boar avatar, Varaha; Vishnu as the giant Trivikrama, his leg raised high as he crosses the three heavens; and Vishnu with his consort Lakshmi.

Osiyan's other temples are in two groups, the southern and the western, and some of the shrines can be hard to find, so it is advisable to obtain local assistance.

Southern group of temples

About 250m to the south of the Sachiyay Mata Temple is the southern group of temples (8th–9th century). These temples had partially collapsed, and have been reassembled. There are **three shrines** here—two next to the road and the other 300m further out of the town—dedicated to Harihara, a combination of Shiva and Vishnu, normally recognisable from the vertical line that is drawn down the centre of the top of the god's head, separating the squared-off headdress of Vishnu from the matted locks of Shiva. There are some fine carvings around the Harihara temples—look in particular for a superb image of Krishna killing the horse-demon, as well as a number of village and domestic scenes. There is also a small **Vishnu temple** on the other side of the road, and a modernised **Shiva temple**, still used for worship.

Western group of temples

These shrines are even more spread out to the west of the Sachiyay Mata Temple. The largest is the **Jain temple** dedicated to Mahavir. It is much restored, but has a superb ornate doorway (in the courtyard) which was erected in 1015, an impressively complex tower over the sanctuary, a finely decorated ceiling and some intricate sandstone carvings. A pretty **Vishnu temple** (9th century) 250m to the northeast has some interesting external carvings, the finest of which shows Vishnu riding his vehicle, the man-eagle Garuda. Around 150m behind the Jain temple is the **Pippala Devi Temple**, dedicated to a form of the goddess Durga, who is seen killing the demon buffalo Mahishasura in one of the external recesses. Note also unusual carvings of extremely long-armed women. The nearby **Surya Temple** has some of Osiyan's finest carvings, including another image of Durga killing Mahishasura—in which, unusually, the buffalo is shown with a human-like demon figure escaping from its severed neck. Pass through the pretty courtyards behind the Surya Temple to reach a dilapidated 8th-century ***baoli*** (step-well), with carved columns and brackets.

NAGAUR

The great city-fortress of Nagaur (*map 3 C1*), 120km northeast of Jodhpur, is one of Rajasthan's key historical sites. It was founded as a mud-fort in the 4th century, though its imposing stone walls date from the early Muslim period in the 12th century. Also known as Ahhichatragarh (or 'fort of the hooded cobra'), it switched hands many times, and was seen by Delhi's rulers as strategically critical to controlling Rajasthan. Most of the surviving buildings date from the 16th to 18th centuries, during which time there were periods of Mughal and Jodhpur rule. Emperor Akbar captured the fort in 1557, and even held court in Nagaur in 1570, when he received the maharaja of Jodhpur. It was later fought over by different factions of the Jodhpur royal family. Part of it is now being converted into a hotel, and this will help attract more tourists to this interesting city, which already hosts an annual camel fair and occasional music festivals.

Nagaur Fort

The Fort is approached from a walled market area in the heart of the city, dominated by the impressive Tripolia clock tower. The entrance to the actual fort (*open daily 9–5*) is through the Hathi Pol, or Elephant Gate, in the southeast corner of the fort, which is half-hidden near some shops and leads to three more gates and other defensive features. Vehicles are allowed inside the fort. Inside, the **Shah Jahan Mosque** (*normally closed to visitors*) is straight ahead, but turn right and then left to enter the main palace area.

The large inner courtyard area served as the **Diwan-i Am**, or public audience area, overlooked by a pretty balcony from which the ruler addressed his subjects. Head through the small gateway to the right of the balcony and enter a hall with columns, cusped arches and wall-paintings, which leads to another courtyard. The stairs next to the hallway lead up to more rooms, used at one point as the *zenana*, or women's palace, and which have fine paintings of courtly scenes, including ones depicting life in the *zenana*, as well as images from the story of Krishna. On the left of the courtyard beyond a long colonnaded hall is the two-storey **Diwan-i Khas**, or private assembly hall, with more fine paintings and water channels and fountains inside the double-height main hall. At the back of the Diwan-i Khas is the **Hammam**, or palace bathhouse, with its roof vents to let out the steam.

The flower beds outside in the garden have an underground water supply which is partly visible. Towards the back of the open area are a pretty pavilion and a large square pond with a smaller two-storey pavilion in the middle. On the right is the **Akbari Mahal**, or Akbar's Palace, which is believed to have been used by the Mughal emperor when he came here in 1570, and which has more paintings. There is a pretty courtyard behind the palace (*normally closed to visitors*), visible through the *jali* screen windows. Further to the right, heading back towards the entrance, is the **Krishna Temple**, which looks more like a palace apartment than a shrine, but has lots of Krishna images painted on the walls—including a version of the story in which Krishna steals the cowgirls' clothes when they are bathing. The **Bakht Singh Mahal**, named after an 18th-century ruler of Nagaur, has more paintings and fine views from the roof.

The rest of Nagaur

There are several other interesting little-visited sites in Nagaur. The high minarets of the 16th-century **Akbari Masjid**, or Akbar Mosque, are visible from most parts of the city. A closer inspection of the mosque, 400m east of the fort, reveals some surviving blue tiling on the minarets. The extraordinary Sufi **Darwaza**, 800m north of the fort, is a large ornate high-arched gateway to a Sufi shrine, almost every inch of which is covered with floral and calligraphic carvings. The **Bare Pir Dargah**, another Islamic shrine, 400m southeast of the fort, overlooks a lake and has the 15th-century tomb of a Sultanate-period governor of Nagaur, as well as a small museum. The **Chattri Amar Rao** is a memorial to Amar Rao, a Jodhpur prince still remembered in Rajasthani folklore for his bravery and foolhardiness. There are several pretty sandstone pavilions, raised high on a fortified plinth overlooking a lake, 800m east of the fort. Amar Rao's father, Maharaja Gaj Singh, chose Amar's younger brother as the next in line to the Jodhpur throne, and Amar Rao died while at the Mughal court, where he had gone to complain about his father's decision to Emperor Shah Jahan.

JALORE

The little-visited town of Jalore (*map 3 B3*), 120km southwest of Jodhpur and an easy day-trip from Rohet or Luni (both less than 90km away), has one of Rajasthan's most historically important hill-forts. The **fort**, which dates back to at least the 8th century, is high up on the hill that overlooks the old walled town. It was captured in a famous siege of 1311 by the forces of the Delhi Sultanate, and later became a key outpost of the kingdom of Jodhpur. The steep footpath to the top (*at least 45 minutes' walk*) is best approached by road from the Lal Kot gate on the far side of town. The walk takes you past a Hindu temple, several Muslim graves, old defensive walls and a series of gates that lead to a rocky plateau with a group of temples and a mosque, all of which are still in use. To the left are some half-ruined palace buildings, with a series of courtyards and colonnades with pretty cusped arches. At the far end of the plateau is the *dargah* of Malik Shah, with a painted interior to the shrine. There are superb views from the hillock above the *dargah*.

THE FORT-PALACES OF MARWAR

Within a 150km radius of Jodhpur are an extraordinary number of often very fine forts and palaces, most of them belonging to Jodhpur's feudatory states. The most historically important is at Nagaur, but there are many others that are of architectural and historical interest. A large number have been converted into luxury hotels (*see Accommodation, p. 201*), sometimes being partly ruined in the process. It is usually possible for non-guests to enter and look around if they're happy to spend a bit of money at the restaurant. Such places include the over-restored 16th-century **Khimsar Fort**, 85km to the northeast of Jodhpur on the road to Nagaur (though the oldest portion of the fort has been left as it was); **Nimaj Palace**, 120km east of Jodhpur on the Ajmer road (*map 3 C2*). To the south of Jodhpur, and much closer to the city, are **Rohetgarh** (38km from Jodhpur; *map 3 C2*), with its pretty *chattris* close to the lake and the impressive 18th-century **Chanwa Fort** in Luni (33km from Jodhpur, *map 3 B2*).

JAISALMER

The great fort-city of Jaisalmer (*map 3 A1*), like the Taj Mahal, is a place of almost shocking beauty, perhaps a psychological trick played on us by the effect of sunlight (and moonlight) on huge stone edifices. There is an elusive, evanescent quality to both these very different places, a quality which survives despite their fame and the instant recognition factor that they both command. The walls, turrets and bastions of Jaisalmer Fort are of golden sandstone, and they shimmer like a mirage rising out of the Thar Desert. The fort is not Jaisalmer's only attraction, however. There are several interesting Jain temples, some beautiful *havelis*, as well as camel safaris in the desert.

It is not easy to get to Jaisalmer (though the roads, built for and by the Indian Army, are among the best in the country), a journey through hundreds of kilometres of scrubby deserts that makes one's first distant view of the fort even more breathtaking and welcoming. But all is not idyllic in Jaisalmer. The crowds of tourists have spawned hordes of touts, not quite as aggressive as those at Agra, but harder to escape in such a small place. The fort walls are beginning to crumble too—weakened in part by the excessive use of water by visiting tourists used to running water rather than bucket baths. There have been calls to have the fort emptied of its inhabitants, or for all its hotels to be moved beyond its walls. Jaisalmer claims to be unique in India because it is a living fort, though in fact Bharatpur and several other places can all claim the same. None of them, though, is nearly as impressive: here there are more than 3,000 people residing permanently inside its walls, and many more overnight visitors in high season (November to March). Be prepared: Jaisalmer gets bitterly cold on winter evenings, and uncomfortably hot on summer days.

History: Jaisalmer was founded in the 12th century by Rawal Jaisal (rawal and maharawal are the local equivalents of raja and maharaja) of the Bhatti Dynasty, which traces its line to the Hindu god Krishna, and which had ruled previously from nearby Lodrava. The old capital had been captured during the invasion of India by Muhammad of Ghor, and so a new location was chosen on top of Trikuta Hill, which would prove easier to defend. In the late 13th century, the Muslim Khilji Dynasty, rulers of Delhi, took eight years to capture Jaisalmer. When the Khilji forces were finally victorious, the women and children of Jaisalmer performed *jauhar*, sacrificing their lives by fire or sword rather than being taken captive. The fort was retaken by the Bhattis a few years later, and at about this time the Ghadsi reservoir was excavated, providing the desert city with enough water for it to grow in population—though, until recently, the water had to be carried to the fort in pots and buckets.

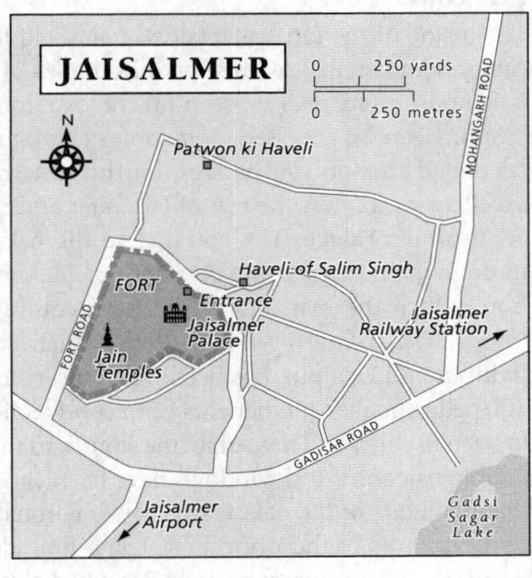

Jaisalmer became an important trading town, and also attracted large numbers of Jain preachers and pilgrims, who built the temples that are found today inside the fortifications. There were further confrontations with Delhi during the Tughlaq and early Mughal periods, but in the 16th century the rulers of Jaisalmer recognised the suzerainty of the Mughal emperor Akbar. By the 18th century, Jaisalmer's prime ministers, or *dewans*, had become more powerful than its titular rulers, and this period saw the growth of the city outside the fort walls, where several impressive *havelis* were constructed. The 19th century saw a close alliance with the British, who gradually took greater control of the state. The desert caravan routes that had been so fundamental to Jaisalmer's economy became less important as maritime trade from Bombay (present-day Mumbai) and the Gujarat seaports grew in importance. Jaisalmer also suffered from recurrent droughts and famine.

The Partition of India at the time of Independence meant that Jaisalmer was isolated in a bulge on the India-Pakistan border, which has been closed to almost all trade and travel ever since. The city became a little-visited desert outpost that remained strategically important because of its proximity to Pakistan. A proper metalled road to Jaisalmer was constructed only in the 1950s, and it was not until after the 1965 Indo-Pakistani War that the city was finally connected to the Indian railway network. Jaisalmer was 'rediscovered' in the 1970s, partly because of *Sonar Kella*, or *Golden Fort*, a film made by the great Indian director Satyajit Ray, which was partly set in Jaisalmer. The city has since become one of India's major tourist attractions.

Orientation: The dominating presence of the fort makes it easy to find one's way about Jaisalmer. The walled city circles the fort, which is built on a large rocky outcrop on the southwest side of Jaisalmer. The fort itself, which is shaped like an arrowhead, has 99 bastions and a total length of more than 1km. It is not possible to walk along the walls, because they are blocked or dangerous in some places, and also used as a latrine by local residents.

Jaisalmer Fort

The inside of the fort has retained many old features (despite the plethora of internet cafés and giftshops), with superb examples of the stone carving for which this region is famous, which can be seen on the exteriors walls of houses. At several points the bastions can be accessed, sometimes through hotels and restaurants. An impressive decorated cannon can be seen on the easternmost bastion, and from here there are excellent views over the rest of Jaisalmer and beyond into the desert.

Jaisalmer Palace: The entrance to the palace is on your left as you enter the fort through the main gate. Set on steps outside the palace is the small white marble throne from which the maharawal (the local equivalent of a maharaja) used to review his troops. The palace (*open daily 9–6*), which is much smaller than its counterparts in Jodhpur and Udaipur, has been well conserved (having suffered serious damage in the 2001 earthquake) and benefits from good audio guides, available at the ticket gate. The first small courtyard has some fine stone and marble work. Notice in particular how the marble balconies and windows have been carved so that they resemble wood. Among the highlights of the palace are a silver coronation throne; a well-presented exhibition of the stamps of the princely states; a fine idol of Lord Rama, unusual for having a beard; the mirror mosaics of the Rang Mahal (Colour Palace); and the pretty European wall-tiles in the Sarvottam Vilas. In an alcove in the Rang Mahal is a charming portrait of an unidentified European woman. Exceptional views of Jaisalmer and the desert can be had from the roof of the palace, where a small stone sundial and an astrological measuring instrument are also to be found.

Elsewhere in the fort: The fort also contains a number of fine Hindu and Jain temples. The finest of these is probably the temple dedicated to Chandraprabha, the eighth Jain *tirthankar* (or saviour). The quality of the stone carving—on the column, the friezes and the ceiling—is particularly high. Make sure you go upstairs to inspect the ceiling carvings more closely. There is also the interesting but heavily restored Laxminath Hindu temple, with some friezes and carving that were probably taken from older temples. Note how some devotees first visit the prettier and smaller Shiva temple on the other side of the road.

Jaisalmer's *havelis*

Back in Jaisalmer town there are several fine *havelis*—and a walk through the older parts of the town will show how even quite modest homes used beautifully carved stone as part of their exterior architecture. The most impressive of the *havelis* is the 19th-century **Patwon ki Haveli**, which is in fact a complex of five separate *havelis* owned by five brothers. The exterior stonework is magnificent. Internally, the most interesting *haveli* is the tallest, furthest from the fort, and now under the ownership of the Rajasthan government. Look up as you enter this six-storey building constructed around an inner courtyard and you'll see some wall-paintings. On the third floor is a painting showing a battle being fought with European soldiers; also notice the mirror-work around the window frames, the original wooden cupboards and the decorated wooden red-and-gold ceiling on the fourth floor. It is worth visiting the **Salim Singh Haveli** too—Singh was the *dewan*, or prime minister, of Jaisalmer for several decades in the late 18th and early 19th centuries. He was a figure of terrible cruelty who also built a *haveli* that is particularly interesting for its unusual external design, with an ornately carved cantilevered look-out tower at its summit.

Around Jaisalmer

There are several other places around Jaisalmer which are easy to visit. Avoid the government museum unless you like unlabelled fossils and bits of sculpture. The museum itself is hard to miss, for it has a fighter plane parked outside its door. Instead, head for **Gadsi Sagar**: this 14th-century reservoir has been critical to Jaisalmer's survival, and, until recently, the women of the fort used to make a daily trips down to it to fetch water. There are some pretty pavilions and gateways on the waterfront. Jaisalmer has several other reservoirs with small palaces, temples and pavilions, including **Amar Sagar** and **Mool Sagar**, to the west of the city, and **Bara Bagh**, with its rows of royal memorials bearing carved ceilings and equestrian images of Jaisalmer's rulers, 5km to the north of the city.

Not far from Amar Sagar, some 25km to the northwest of Jaisalmer, is the heavily-restored Jain temple at **Lodrava** (*map 3 A1*), the site of the major town in the region before the building of Jaisalmer in the 12th century. The lower parts of the temple are largely original, but most of the upper parts are all too obviously recent. The *torana*, or formal entrance gateway, is particularly impressive—and notice the animal cage. Anyone who signs up for a camel safari is likely to be taken to several other deserted towns and forgotten temples. None is of great historical significance, but they do look very fetching amid the sand dunes.

About 50km northeast of Jaisalmer is the fine desert fortress of **Mohangarh** (*map 3 B1*), built of sandstone and with some fine decorative carved stone panels.

POKHARAN

This small town (*map 3 B1*) sits at the point where two main roads join en route to Jaisalmer from Jodhpur and Bikaner. It is best known as the site of India's controversial nuclear tests in 1974 and 1998, which drew criticism from around the world, but the actual underground detonation site is 20km away from the town. Pokharan, which was part of the old Jodhpur state, has a 14th-century red sandstone fort. The fort contains a palace, which has limited public access, but also a small hotel. Scattered among the rooms around the large courtyard at the back of the fort is a small, almost empty museum. Up on a hill behind the railway line (which visitors will need to walk across) are some pretty royal memorials, with fine eaved domes and carved columns.

KIRADU TEMPLES

The 11th-century Kiradu temples (*map 3 B2*), 40km northwest of the city of Barmer, deep in the deserts of western Rajasthan, are fine, little-visited examples of Hindu architecture from the Pratihara period—when this area was ruled by Parmar chieftains. Note the very fine carved stone reliefs on the temple plinths, with images of elephants, horses and courtly scenes.

SOUTHERN RAJASTHAN

Southern Rajasthan is dominated by the former state of Mewar and its spectacular capital city, Udaipur. But this is a region rich in Rajput heritage, and many of the other princely cities, such as Kota, Bundi and Dungarpur are well worth a visit too. South of Udaipur is the hill-station of Mt Abu, which is also an important Jain pilgrimage centre, while, to the north, Ranakpur has arguably the finest Jain temples in the country. Chittorgarh (Chittor) and Kumbhalgarh, to the east and north of Udaipur respectively, are two of the most impressive hilltop fortresses in the country, both of which have played an important role in the history of the region. And this is a perfect place for getting off the beaten track, with small palace hotels at Bhainsrorgarh, Bijaipur, Ghanerao and Narlai, for instance, scattered across some quite breathtaking countryside.

UDAIPUR

Of all the urban centres of the subcontinent, Udaipur (*map 3 C3*) comes closest to the Western romantic image of what an Indian city should be like. And, so long as the monsoon rains have been good and the lakes are filled with water, Udaipur is undeniably a spectacular city. The enormous main palace complex overlooks Lake Pichola, with its two smaller island palaces, and there is yet another palace high up on a hill, on the other side of the lake. The city hasn't grown too fast, and is smaller and easier to wander around than its two great rival cities in Rajasthan: Jaipur and Jodhpur.

History: The Sisodia Dynasty of Mewar, which had its capital at Udaipur, has long considered itself the premier Rajput royal family. The dynasty claims descent from the sun, and, a little more recently, from an 8th-century warrior, Bappa Rawal, who established himself at the hill-fortress of Chittorgarh—the capital of Mewar until the 16th century. In 1559, Udaipur was founded by and named after Maharana Udai Singh (maharana being the local equivalent of maharaja) as the new capital of the kingdom of Mewar. The old capital, Chittorgarh, was deemed too vulnerable, whereas Udaipur was surrounded by hills and lakes and stood further from the Mughal forces based in the plains of north India. Just a few years later, Chittorgarh was captured by the Mughal army of Emperor Akbar. Unlike the other Rajput princes, the rulers of Udaipur refused to accept Mughal suzerainty, even when, in 1576, Udaipur city was also captured.

For several decades, Udaipur fought for independence from the Mughals, and in 1615 a peace treaty was agreed, under which the ruler of Udaipur would not have to attend the Mughal court and would not have to marry Udaipur princesses into the imperial family, as so many other Rajput dynasties had done. But Udaipur still had to acknowledge Mughal supremacy by sending a thousand cavalry to serve in the Mughal army, and by ensuring that the heir apparent attended the Mughal court. The Mughal-Udaipur relationship was further tested when the future emperor Shah Jahan rebelled against his father Jehangir and sought refuge in Udaipur. He stayed at the Jagmandir Palace, the domed pavilion of which, with its inlaid white marble, is said to have inspired the Taj Mahal.

During the rule of the Mughal emperor Aurangzeb, relations with the imperial court worsened—partly because Maharana Raj Singh married a Rajput princess from the state of Kishangarh whom Aurangzeb had wanted as a bride. The maharana refused to send troops to serve in the Mughal army, and eventually, in 1679, Aurangzeb attacked, and Udaipur was taken once again. The new maharana, Jai Singh, supported the unsuccessful rebellion of Aurangzeb's son Prince Akbar before eventually agreeing a peace treaty with the emperor. With the decline of the Mughal Empire in the 18th century, the greatest threat to the independence of Udaipur (and the other Rajput states) were the Marathas, particularly the rulers of Gwalior and Indore (in modern-day Madhya Pradesh), whose forces frequently invaded the state and extracted large sums of money from its rulers.

By the early 19th century, the Marathas had been eclipsed by the British, and in 1818 Udaipur, like many other Rajput states, came under the protection of the British East India Company. Udaipur supported Britain during the Uprising of 1857, though noble families from the state assisted the rebel leader Tantia Tope, who fled to the region. Ever-conscious of Udaipur's status, Maharana Fateh Singh (1885–1930) insisted that the British should recognise his precedence over fellow princes. He famously did not turn up at two successive British durbars, in 1903 and 1911, because he would have been outranked by other rulers, and he repeatedly fell out with the British. His successor did support the British more actively, at a time when the freedom movement was growing in strength, and shortly before Indian Independence in 1947 the maharana agreed to constitutional reform and a representative assembly. As one of the largest

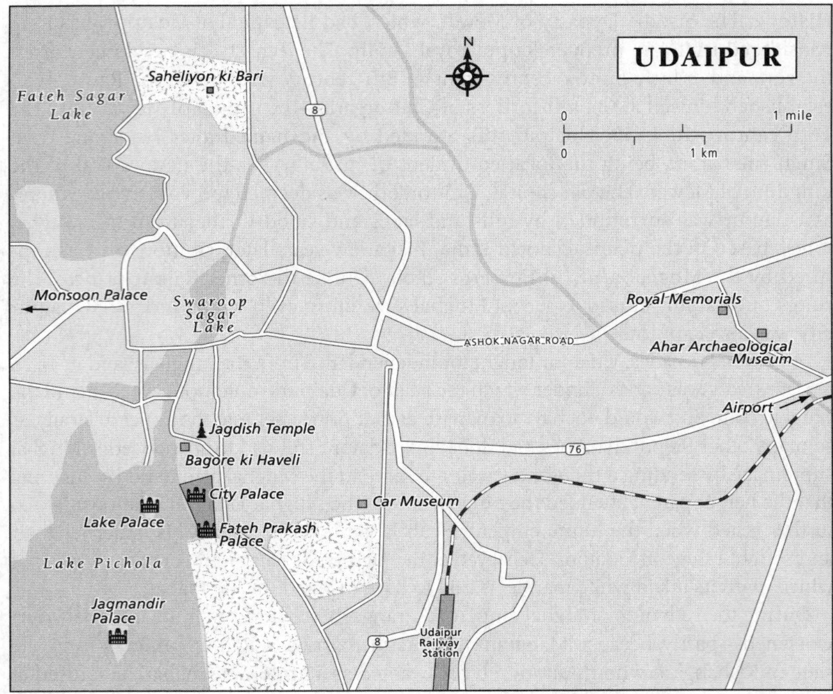

principalities, Udaipur originally planned to form its own state, but then agreed to join the other Rajput princes in forming Rajasthan.

Orientation: Udaipur's key landmark is pretty Lake Pichola, artificially created in the 14th century. Overlooking its eastern banks is the city palace and many other royal buildings, as well as two island palaces surrounded, if the monsoon has been adequate, by the waters of Lake Pichola. To the north and east of the city palace is the old city of Udaipur. Further to the east is the modern heart of the city and its main railway station, with the airport way out beyond Udaipur's easternmost suburbs—and the royal memorials at Ahar. To the north of Lake Pichola are two other lakes, the smaller Swaroop Sagar and the large Fateh Sagar. To the west of Lake Pichola, and visible from almost every part of Udaipur, is Bansdara Hill, with the Sajjangarh (Monsoon Palace) on its summit.

Udaipur City Palace complex

Part of the enormous City Palace complex overlooking Lake Pichola is open to the public. Most visitors approach the City Palace from the north, through the Bari Pol, or Great Gate, though guests of the palace hotels on the south side of the complex have a separate entrance. Visitors pay separately to enter the **complex** (*open daily 8am–10pm*) and the **museum** (*open daily 9–4.30*) but from the same ticket office. Packages involving trips to Jagmandir Island can also be bought.

The oldest parts of the complex date back to 1567, when Maharana Udai Singh founded the city as the new capital of Mewar, and subsequent rulers have added many buildings in a mixture of architectural styles. Some parts of the palaces have been converted into hotels while the central part of the complex is now a large museum.

Outer buildings of the City Palace: Visitors coming from the north or south gates arrive in a large courtyard known as **Manek Chowk**, with shops, restaurants and arcades looking out of the city on the east side and impressive multi-storey walls of the City Palace on the west side. Note the pretty upper level balconies and carvings, as well as the large sun emblem of the Udaipur royal family on the façade. To reach the City Palace museum go up through the door with a royal crest overhead, and past the old **Armoury** on the right, which has an impressive collection of weaponry, including swords mounted with tiny pistols, as well as trumpets captured from the army of the first Mughal emperor, Babur, at the Battle of Bayana in 1527. The armoury, with its extra-thick walls, is also one of the oldest buildings in the City Palace, dated to 1569. Just opposite is the large durbar hall, or **Sabha Shiromani**, which is normally closed. Continue down into a second smaller courtyard (which can also be reached by a separate vehicular gate from Manek Chowk). The entry to the main part of the City Palace museum is by the gate on the near right (northeast door), while the government museum is also entered from this courtyard.

City Palace Museum: Stairs lead up from the entrance of the City Palace Museum to the first of several courtyards. On the right is a display of paintings and armour relating to the early rulers of Mewar, including Rana Pratap, whose horse, Chetak, was disguised in battle as a small elephant by the addition of a fake trunk. To the left, stairs lead up to the Chandra Mahal, with a huge marble basin that used to be filled with coins to give to the poor. Beyond is a pretty courtyard with trees, a pond and arcades round the side—there is a good view over the city from the windows. Beyond the courtyard is a series of 17th-century rooms, with fine mirror-work decoration and early 19th-century wall-paintings depicting festival and court scenes in Udaipur, with many of today's surviving buildings clearly recognisable, including the two island palaces of Lake Pichola. The next small courtyard, built in the 18th century, has largely 19th-century decoration, including some fine blue tilework (note the image of Joseph leading Jesus and Mary into Egypt on the back of an ass) and the original plans for the construction of the hill-top Monsoon Palace of Sajjangarh, intended to be a 13-storey building. The well-signposted but roundabout route through the palace continues, past the **Moti Mahal** (or Pearl Palace), with its coloured glass and mirror-work, to the suite of rooms used by Maharana Bhupal Singh, who ruled Udaipur at the time of Independence. Eventually you reach the **Mor Chowk**, or Peacock Court, with superb late 19th-century wall-mounted peacock mosaics. The final parts of the museum pass through the private apartments of the last maharani of Udaipur, and into a large ground-floor gallery of paintings, before ending up in the **Lakshmi Chowk**, the main courtyard of the *zenana* (women's quarters).

Other buildings in the complex: The nearby **Government Museum** (*open 9.45–5.15*) is undergoing renovation, and has a small collection of paintings, arms, coins and some religious sculpture, including a particularly fine 6th-century Shiva head.

The Shiv Niwas and Fateh Prakash Palace, on the southern side of the City Palace complex, are both now hotels. However the Fateh Prakash Palace has opened its **Crystal Gallery** (*open 9–7; Rs500; no cameras*) to the more affluent members of the general public, with its unusual collection of 19th-century crystal furniture manufactured in Britain, each piece inscribed with the Udaipur royal crest. Visitors to the gallery are also allowed to see the enormous durbar hall, and the 18th-century 1,802-piece Danish porcelain set, known as the Flora Danica.

Around the complex: Opposite the City Palace complex are two more palaces which have been built on islands in Lake Pichola. The white marble **Jag Niwas** (1746), built by Maharana Jagat Singh and now better known as the **Lake Palace**, is currently one of India's most exclusive hotels, and according to many, has the best location of any hotel in the country. It is hard for non-guests to visit the Lake Palace, and the hotel boat service won't allow you across without a reservation for a room or a meal.

The older **Jagmandir Palace** (1550s), famous as the refuge of the future Mughal emperor Shah Jahan, is open to the public. Boats leave every hour, on the hour, for the hour-long trip to the palace, and pass close to the Lake Palace and other smaller islands on the way. The boats leave from Rameshwar Ghat, on the south side of the City Palace. In 1623, Shah Jahan, then known as Prince Khurram, stayed at the Jagmandir Palace with Mumtaz Mahal and their children, after falling out with his father Emperor Jehangir. Shah Jahan learnt of the death of his father while staying here and proclaimed himself emperor. The inlay work and the dome on the Gul Mahal Pavilion are said to have provided inspiration for the Taj Mahal. Most of the other buildings on the island are from the 18th century. The island served once again as a place of refuge in 1857, when British families fleeing the Uprising took shelter here.

The rest of Udaipur

Just 150m north of the outer gate to the City Palace is Udaipur's most important Hindu shrine, the **Jagdish Temple** (1640), the exterior of which is covered with carved stone images of gods, musicians, dancers and animals. It is dedicated to Vishnu, and there is a statue of Vishnu's vehicle, the man-eagle Garuda, in the small pavilion facing the main shrine. Behind the temple, overlooking the lake at Gangaur Ghat, is the **Bagore ki Haveli** (*open 10–5.30*), the 18th-century home of one of Udaipur's prime ministers. It has been restored, and turned into a venue for music and dance performances.

One of India's best-maintained collections of vintage cars can be seen at the purpose-built garages of the **Car Museum** (*open 9–9*) at another royal property, the Garden Hotel, 1km east of the City Palace. The collection also includes old carriages and a range of modern solar-powered vehicles.

The **Saheliyon ki Bari** is a pretty garden close to the Fateh Sagar lake, 3km north of the City Palace, which was laid out in the early 18th century. The inner walled garden, with its central pond and fountain, was used by female members of the royal family as a day palace in the summer. At the back of the outer garden is another pool, with marble elephants that spout water from their trunks.

The royal *chattris*, or memorials, are at **Ahar**, 4km east of the City Palace. There are two main compounds: one on the main road for the maharanas who ruled Udaipur and another, with dozens of smaller memorials, for other members of the family. The memorial for Amar Singh (d. 1620) is particularly impressive—note the two stone carvings under the dome of the memorial: a four-faced lingam-like image, and a square stone bearing images of women, said to be Amar Singh's wives committing *sati*. The area of raised scrubland just opposite the *chattris* is Ahar, the site of the ancient capital of Mewar. The nearby **Ahar Archaeological Museum** (*open Tues–Sun 9.45–5.15*), on the airport road, has an impressive collection of material, some of it dating back 4,000 years. Particularly interesting are unusual 10th-century stone carvings of the first (fish) and second (tortoise) avatars of Vishnu, recovered from the site.

The 19th-century **Sajjangarh**, or Monsoon Palace, is set high on Bansdara Hill on the western side of Udaipur, and has superb views over the city and the surrounding countryside. Sajjangarh (*open daily dawn–dusk*) is approached from an entrance gate, 3.5km west of the city palace, that leads to a long, steep, winding road that climbs through a forest reserve to the palace, 335m above the lakes below. Sajjangarh was commissioned by Maharana Sajjan Singh as a 13-storey summer palace, but when he died the plans were scaled back to just four storeys. It is possible to climb to the top of the palace by taking the spiral staircase just on the left of the main entrance.

NORTH OF UDAIPUR

There are a number of impressive historical and religious sites north of Udaipur, on both sides of the main ridge of the Aravalli Hills. The countryside here is very pretty and thickly forested. Some places that are very close on the map are actually quite difficult to travel between. For instance, the Jain temple at Ranakpur and the fortress of Kumbhalgarh—just 11km as the crow flies—are more than 50km apart by road. For this reason, it is not really possible to do the key sites as a day trip, and instead it is advisable to stay in some of the comfortable accommodation in this area. There are several interesting forts and palaces north of Udaipur, most of which belonged to feudatory states, and several of which have now been converted into hotels. These include the unspoilt Ghanerao Palace, at the foot of the hill on which Kumbhalgarh sits, and the 17th-century Narlai hunting lodge, which sits in the shadow of huge, bare rock (that can be climbed) surrounded by temples. Both are close to Ranakpur, while nearer to Udaipur is the towering 18th-century Devigarh Fort-Palace.

Ranakpur

Rajasthan's best-known Jain temple is nestled into the side of a tree-covered hill, at Ranakpur (*map 3 C3*), 60km north of Udaipur. The main **Adinath Temple** (*open daily 12–5; camera fee payable; no leather items; legs and shoulders should be covered*) is a short walk from the car park. It is a square building, completed in 1439 and commissioned by two brothers, Dhanasha and Ratnasha, both dignitaries who served the Mewar royal family. The temple was later abandoned, and then heavily restored in the 19th century. It was constructed out of white marble, and raised on a high plinth with four corner towers and an entrance on each side—though all but one is closed. The lower part of the exterior is largely unadorned, though each entrance gate has a carved door frame with images of guardians and saviours cut into the marble. Above are dozens of small and large towers that give the temple its impressive profile. Note the carved elephants on the parapets above the main entrance, as well as the dragon-like heads cut into the entrance steps.

Inside is a complex multi-storey building, supported by 1,444 finely carved columns, with images of dancers, musicians and guardians. There are dozens of small shrines around the periphery of the temple, and the large Chaumukh (or four-faced) images of the first Jain *tirthankar*, or saviour, Adinath, are in the main sanctuary. Some of the finest stonework is on the inside of the domes, with some remarkably complex floral, figurative and geometric designs. On the balcony area above the entrance is an elephant with riders who are thought to represent the benefactors of the temple.

Parusnath and Neminath temples: There are several other 15th-century shrines nearby, including a very small one, finely carved but without an idol, on the south (right) side of the main temple. The others include, to the west of the main shrine, nearer the car park: the raised **Parusnath Temple**, dedicated to the 23rd Jain saviour, with some fine external carvings including images of amorous couples; and the **Neminath Temple**, dedicated to the 22nd Jain saviour. About 100m south of the Jain sacred area, on the main road just before the river, is a Hindu temple, the **Surya Mandir**, dedicated to the sun-god. Surya is usually shown being pulled by a team of seven horses, and note how the sculptor has used this to compose a group of strange stretched horses that became the key motif of the external carvings.

Kumbhalgarh

Kumbhalgarh (*map 3 C3*) is one India's finest hill-forts, with superb defensive fortifications, commanding the summit of one of the highest peaks of the Aravalli Hills, 65km north of Udaipur. It was built by the 15th-century ruler of Mewar, Rana Kumbh, and gained the reputation of being impregnable—indeed it was never captured by force, despite sieges by the armies of Gujarat, Malwa and the Mughals. It was widely used as a palace by the royal family of Udaipur, and is said to have contained, at one point, 365 Hindu and Jain temples.

Orientation: The 15th-century fort is normally approached by road, but it is also possible to trek with a guide from the village of Ghanerao, 10km up the hillside to Kumbhalgarh. The car park and ticket office are just outside the main walls. Tickets are only needed for the palace buildings (*open daily 9–5*) and the rest of the fortress, including the temples, can be visited at any time. On entering the fort, the citadel is on the left, the dam and some minor temples are straight ahead, while the main temples are on the right. The fort walls and temples are lit up soon after dusk, and a visit at this time is highly recommended—ask locally for precise timings.

The citadel and the palaces: The road to the fort is well defended with a series of outer gates (there is a fine step-well just beyond the Hulla Gate) before one reaches the enormous walls and circular bastions that encompass the fortress. The main walls are said to be wide enough to accommodate eight horses riding abreast. A path to the left leads sharply upwards, past a Ganesha temple, to the inner citadel and its palaces, through several more gates and past ruined buildings. Just before the **Pagda Pol** (or Stirrup Gate), where the maharaja would dismount his horse, keep left to view the impressive western façade of the palace—it is actually possible to walk around the entire palace structure along an overgrown path. Also just next to the Pagda Pol are steps leading to the room in which Rana Pratap, the most renowned of the Mewar rulers, was born in 1540. Inside the Pagda Pol are several outbuildings, and the partially ruined **Kumbha Palace**. The final ascent leads to the **Badal Mahal**, or Cloud Palace, with a pretty inner courtyard, surrounded by rooms and verandahs, with lots of 19th-century paintings of elephants. In the near right corner are the royal toilets, where the latrine holes lead to a huge drop inside the octagonal corner towers of the palaces. In the far left corner are steps up to the roof—and quite superb views of the rest of Kumbhalgarh, the Aravalli Hills and the plains below. A staircase also leads down and connects to another smaller courtyard with more paintings.

The Kumbhalgarh temples: The compound just to right of the main gate of Kumbhalgarh contains the **Vedi Temple** (1457), built as part of the original fort. It is a striking building, constructed to an unusual design, set within its own compound, and consists of a finely decorated three-storey assembly hall separated from the triple-towered shrine at the back of the compound. The **Neelkanth Temple**, dedicated to Shiva, is 100m behind the Vedi Temple, and was built to a more classical design, but with a columned verandah surrounding the building. Further on are smaller Hindu temples and three simply decorated Jain temples. Take a left, down a path that leads away from the fort walls for about 400m to reach the interesting **Golerao temples**—a group of nine Hindu and Jain shrines, with some very fine external carvings.

The Sun Temple: From the foot of the citadel, walk downhill towards the enormous stone embankment that once created a large lake in Kumbhalgarh, to reach a footpath leading to the red-domed Sun Temple, on a hilltop to the left. It is possible to walk across the dam to reach the main groups of temples on the right (east) side of the fort.

Eklingji

The 15th-century Eklingji Temple (*map 3 C3*), 20km north of Udaipur, is the most important shrine of the Udaipur royal family. It is situated in a narrow gorge in a small compound, and inside is a four-faced marble image of Shiva. Like Nathdwara, the Eklingji Temple has irregular opening hours.

Nagda

The superb and little-visited 10th-century Sas Bahu temples at Nagda (*map 3 C3*) are just 4km southwest of Eklingji, beside a small lake. Sas and Bahu mean 'mother-in-law' and 'daughter-in-law' respectively, and are names often given by locals to two adjacent temples of different sizes. The **Sas Temple** is the larger one, with a ruined tower and the remains of ten subsidiary shrines on its plinth. Both temples were dedicated to Vishnu, and there are many carved images of Vishnu riding the man-eagle Garuda—though there are also image of Shiva, Parvati and Ganesha. The Sas Temple has some deliberately comic erotica carved in relief on the exterior (near side), including an image of a woman covering her face in shock at the sexual activity she is witnessing. The entrance and the interior are also richly decorated with carvings, partly with elaborate friezes of scenes from the *Ramayana*. The smaller **Bahu Temple** has an unusual detached entrance archway, with simple cylindrical columns, as well as an open assembly hall. Note the fine image of three-headed Brahma on the exterior of the temple. Nagda was the ancient capital of the Mewar region, before Chittorgarh and Udaipur, and there are other ruined buildings in the countryside around the Sas Bahu temples.

Nathdwara

The **Srinathji Temple** in Nathdwara (*map 3 C3*), 40km north of Udaipur, is one of Rajasthan's most important shrines. The black marble image of Srinathji, a form of Krishna, was brought here from Mathura in 1699 to save it from the army of the Mughal emperor Aurangzeb. The opening hours of the temple are very irregular: it is often open for half an hour, then closed for the next hour and a half, though the temple authorities have become more relaxed about allowing non-Hindus to enter. Nathdwara is also known for its cloth paintings known as *pichwais*, in which images of Krishna were painted onto a large piece of material that would hang behind the idol.

Rajsamand Lake

This artificial lake, 57km north of Udaipur, created in the 1660s, has pretty waterside terraces and pavilions (*map 3 C3*). On a hill overlooking Rajsamand, which means 'royal lake', is the **Dayal Singh Jain Mandir**, a fort-like shrine with carved animals on its roof, while in the nearby town of **Kankroli** is the impressive Dwarkadhish Shrine, built like a Rajasthani palace and dedicated to Krishna.

Deogarh

The impressive 17th-century **Deogarh Fort-Palace** (*map 3 C2*), 110km northeast of the city of Udaipur, is the home of the former rulers of the feudatory state of Deogarh—historically part of Udaipur. The fort-palace is now a hotel and has some interesting 18th-century wall-paintings, stained-glass windows, tile-work and a small family temple. **Badnore**, with its multi-storeyed medieval fortress and the better-maintained Jal Mahal Water Palace, is another 50km northeast, towards Ajmer.

SOUTH OF UDAIPUR

Jagat

The small elaborate **Ambika Mata Temple** in Jagat (*map 3 C3*), 30km southeast of Udaipur, is one of the finest surviving Hindu shrines from the 10th-century Pratihara period. Note the many female deities in the niches around the exterior of the temple, many of which are forms of Durga (*see p. 56*). Higher up the walls are representations of musicians and amorous couples. The attractive **Karni Fort**, 42km southeast of Udaipur, has an 18th-century palace, now a hotel, within its older stone walls.

Jaisamand Lake

Also known as Dhebar Lake, Jaisamand (*map 3 C3*) is 45km southeast of Udaipur. It is one of India's largest artificial water bodies, and was built during the reign of Maharaja Jai Singh in the late 17th century. On the western bank of the lake is a long series of marble steps with pretty domed pavilions and sculptures of elephants. There is a small palace at either end of the steps, and more royal buildings on the hills overlooking the lake.

Rishabdeo

The town of Rishabdeo (*map 3 C3*), 55km south of Udaipur, has a 14th-century Jain temple with some fine carved stone figures. It is dedicated to Rishabdeo, another name for the first Jain saviour, Adinath.

Dungarpur

This former princely state in the far south of Rajasthan, 80km south of Udaipur, has two remarkable palaces set in a spectacular location, at the southern end of the Aravalli Hills. One of the palaces is a comfortable and unusual hotel, while the other has an extraordinary secret cupboard full of 18th-century erotica. The town of Dungarpur (*map 4 D1*) lies at the base of a series of hills on the edge of a large lake. It makes an excellent and little-visited escape from the crowds of Udaipur.

History: Dungarpur was ruled from the 14th century until 1947 by the elder branch of the Sisodia Dynasty, which also ruled Udaipur. Dungarpur became a vassal state of the Mughal Empire under Emperor Akbar in 1577, after a defeat at the Battle of Haldighati. There were repeated attempts by the Udaipur rulers to take control of Dungarpur, and, after the Mughal Empire began to wither in the 18th century, the Marathas emerged as the major force in the region, exacting tribute from the Dungarpur rulers. Like many Rajput kingdoms, Dungarpur eventually sought protection from the British, and, after 1818, the British became the effective overlords of the state.

Udai Bilas Palace: Now a hotel, the modern Udai Bilas Palace is a most unusual synthesis of Indian and European styles, and beautifully situated, overlooking the large lake at the heart of modern Dungarpur. There is a small island close by, with a Shiva temple that is lit at night. The palace is built around a small 17th-century Durga temple, with the sanctuary and idol hidden behind a curtain in the banqueting room. The temple's spire is built into the wall of the fabulous Art Deco *zenana chowk*, now used as the main dining room. Note the extraordinary dining table with its long central pool, which gets transformed into a whirlpool while guests are eating dessert, and which creates an optical illusion that the centre of the pool is deeper than the ends. The lake-side façade, built of local blue stone, dates from the mid-19th century, along with the **Ek Thambia Mahal**, or One Pillar Palace, an unusual, beautifully decorated tower in the centre of a courtyard, surrounded by a pool (ask for access to the tower, and climb the spiral staircase to the top). This was created as a pleasure garden in the 1860s, when the older Juna Mahal was still the main residence. The rest of the courtyard and the other parts of the palace date from the 1930s, which explains the Art Deco feel to the modern wings.

The Juna Mahal: The Old Palace (*open daily 9–5; tickets only available at the Udai Bilas Palace*), as it is otherwise known, is on the opposite side of the hill from the Udai Bilas Palace. Ask locally for directions—there are two routes: one through pretty wooded countryside; the other through the town. The Juna Mahal is well looked after and has very helpful signage. It is one of India's oldest surviving royal palaces, with parts dating back to the 13th century, and it remained a royal residence until the mid-20th century.

Ground floor: From the car park, enter the courtyard for a good view of the seven-storey main building. This courtyard was used as a stable for elephants and also contains a step-well which is thought to have been part of the original 13th-century building. Enter the inner courtyard, known as the Jambua Chowk, which has some fine carved friezes on the interior walls. Steps lead down to a series of bat-filled basement rooms. The main public rooms of the palace are also accessed from the inner courtyard, including the large durbar hall to the left, which has colourful murals, and, next to the window, the area where the ruler would sit while holding court.

Upper floors: Most of the first floor rooms are locked, but the second floor has a superbly decorated audience chamber and adjoining rooms with spectacular murals, many from the early British period. There is a very amusing picture of the British Resident, as well as some fine mirror-work, mosaics and coloured glass, and entire walls inlaid with willow-pattern dinner plates. Note the large old-fashioned human-operated ceiling fan with images of Queen Victoria and Prince Albert. The third floor has several more rooms, including a pretty screened terrace called the Jali ka Mahal and the Raniji ka Kamra, or the Queen's Room, with a large mural showing the Gangaur procession, which is such an important part of Rajasthani tradition. The fourth floor has a set of rooms known as the Shiv Niwas Mahal, containing some more colourful murals, including a particularly fine painting of a battle scene (the only one portrayed at the Juna Mahal) from the 1880s. But the highlight of the visit to Juna Mahal is hidden away inside a cupboard: an extraordinary cartoon-strip-like series of superbly painted erotic miniature murals from the early 18th century. By the British period, such images were considered pornographic, and so the then rulers covered them up by putting doors in front of the alcove in which they were painted. There are two further levels of terraces from which there are excellent views of the town and the lake (though the Udai Bilas cannot be seen from here), as well as the fortifications on top of the hill.

Vijaygarh: It is a short walk from the Juna Mahal—or a very quick journey in a four-wheel drive vehicle—to the upper fortifications, known as Vijaygarh, with their ancient walls, 19th-century guest houses and superb views over the Dungarpur region.

WEST OF UDAIPUR

Mount Abu

One hundred kilometres west of Udaipur, Mt Abu (*map 3 B3*) is Rajasthan's only hill-station, with small hotels, boat trips on the lake and pretty walks, as well as the superb medieval Jain temples at nearby Dilwara. It provides a welcome escape from the summer heat of the plains, though winter nights can be very cold. This enormous granite outcrop, rising more than 1200m above sea level, at the southern end of the Aravalli range of hills, has been considered a sacred mountain for many centuries. There are dozens of unusual rock formations and oddly-shaped crags throughout the area, and many have been given nicknames, such as the Toad and the Nun, because of their supposed resemblance to an enormous crouching toad and to a veiled woman, respectively.

History: Mt Abu was developed as a hill-station in the 19th century by the British, who leased it from the princely state of Sirohi. It was later used as a sanatorium for British troops and as the summer residence of the British agent to the states of Rajputana; after Independence, it became a residence for the governor of Rajasthan. It is also a place of pilgrimage for Hindus belonging to the modern Brahma Kumari sect, who have their headquarters here.

Orientation: The only vehicular route up to Mt Abu, which is 1165m above sea level, is from Abu Road to the south, which also has the nearest railway station. The hill-station has been built around a lake—known as the Nakki Talao ('nakki' refers to the fingernails of the god who is said to have created the lake by digging into the ground with his bare hands)—and a large polo ground. The hill-station's main 19th-century buildings, including St Saviour's Church, the former Lawrence School (now a police training college) and the former British Residency, are grouped close to Raj Bhavan (the Governor's House) overlooking the mountain.

Mount Abu Museum: This museum (*open Tues–Sun 9.15–5.15*), close to Raj Bhavan, has an interesting collection of sculpture, arms and textiles gathered from different parts of Sirohi district. There are some fine stone carvings of Hindu gods, many of them excavated from Chandrawati, close to Abu Road, which was once the most important city in the region. Many of Rajasthan's princely states had small palaces or homes here, and several have been turned into hotels, including the impressive Jaipur House (1897) with fantastic early morning views over the lake.

The Christian Cemetery: The interesting cemetery is in a narrow strip of land that runs between Sophia School and the Tibetan market. It has the graves of the baby son of the British explorer Francis Younghusband, and of the diarist and educationalist Honoria Lawrence. Her husband, Henry Lawrence, died four years after her in the 1857 siege of Lucknow.

Around Mount Abu

The four main Dilwara temples, 2.5km northeast of Mount Abu, are superb examples of medieval Jain art and architecture, and older than the larger Ranakpur Temple north of Udaipur. On entering the temple complex (*open to non-Jains daily noon–6; photography not allowed; useful guidebook on sale at the small bookstall*), the first building on the left is the **Parusnath Temple** (1458), the most recent and tallest of the four main shrines. It is also the only one made of sandstone and not marble. It is dedicated to the penultimate Jain saviour, Parusnath, and four entrances to the inner sanctuary each have a statue of him in white marble.

Straight ahead is the superb **Vimal Vasahi Temple** (1032) the oldest and most elaborate of the shrines. It was built by and named after Vimal Shah, a minister of Bhima Dev, the Solanki Dynasty ruler of Gujarat. Outside the entrance of the temple is a later addition: a small pavilion known as the Hastishala, or Elephant Hall (1147–59), in which a heavily restored statue of Vimal Shah is surrounded by marble elephants. Inside, the temple takes the form of a courtyard, with small shrines around the inner walls and a large central shrine housing a large image of Adinath, the first Jain saviour. The finest carvings in the temple are on the ceilings, under the dome over the assembly hall to the main sanctuary, and more particularly on the underside of the parapet roof in front of the subsidiary shrines. The latter carvings, in white marble, are some of the finest examples of Jain art, and include among the subject matter gods normally associated with Hinduism—a reminder of how entangled the history of both religions has been. Among the most interesting carved panels over the shrines (which are numbered) are those of the goddess Ambika (shrine 20), Krishna (shrine 41) and Narasimha, the lion avatar of Vishnu (shrine 49).

To the right (north) of the Vimal Vasahi Temple is the **Luna Vasahi Temple** (1230), built to a similar design by two brothers, both ministers of the Solanki ruler Bhima Dev II, in memory of a deceased third brother called Luna. The carving is richer and denser than in the older temple, but is not as lively, and the superb ceiling carvings are not replicated. Note how there is only one shrine on the wall. The Luna Vasahi Temple is dedicated to the 22nd Jain saviour, Neminath. The fourth shrine at Dilwara, raised up on a plinth and unfinished, is known as the **Pittalhar Temple** (14th century) because of the enormous brass ('*pittal*') statue of Adinath, the first Jain saviour.

About 5km northeast of Dilwara is the ruined **Achalgadh Fort**, one of 32 built by Rana Kumbh of Chittorgarh in the 14th century. There are two interesting Jain shrines here, and a Hindu temple said to contain a toenail of Shiva. Some 35km north of Mount Abu is the little-visited town of **Sirohi**, the capital of the former princely state of the same name, with a pretty fort palace, which is currently not open to the public.

EAST OF UDAIPUR

Chittorgarh

The mightily impressive hill-fortress of Chittor, usually known as Chittorgarh (*map 3 C3*), or Chittor Fort, is, in historical terms, arguably the most important site in Rajasthan. The enormous fortified hilltop plateau, 100km east of Udaipur, has come to symbolise, in Rajput tradition, great bravery in the face of defeat, as well as the antiquity of Rajput rule in this part of India.

History: Chittorgarh is believed to have been founded in the early 8th century, by Bappu Rawal, ancestor of the rulers of Udaipur and Dungarpur, and it was the original capital of Mewar, the old alternative name for the former princely state of Udaipur. It was conquered three times after long sieges, which remain key events in Rajput history and folklore. The first sack of Chittorgarh was in 1303, and followed a seven-month siege by the forces of the Sultan of Delhi, Alauddin Khilji. It was more than 20 years before a member of the deposed royal family recaptured the fortress.

Chittorgarh's most famous ruler was Rana Kumbha (reigned 1433–68), during whose reign Mewar became the pre-eminent power in this region, defeating the sultans of Gujarat and Malwa, and building the Rana Kumbha Palace, the extraordinary Victory Tower and the great fortress (110km to the west) that bears his name, Kumbhalgarh. The second sack of Chittorgarh was in 1535 by Bahadur Shah, the sultan of Gujarat, and for the second time the women of the fortress committed *jauhar*, or mass suicide, rather than be captured by the invaders—though this time the fort was quickly retaken. The third and final sack of Chittorgarh was by the Mughal army of Emperor Akbar in 1568, after a five-month siege in which the defence was led by two young local chieftains, Jaimal and Patta, whose feats of bravery became the subject of ballads that are still sung in Rajasthan. Again there was a *jauhar* and the Mughals occupied Chittorgarh. They did not relinquish the fortress until 1615, by which time Udaipur was the undisputed capital of Mewar.

Orientation: The fortress of Chittorgarh sits high on a plateau, 180m above the plains, and its walls and its distinctive victory tower are visible from afar. It occupies a long narrow piece of land, 5km from north to south, and just 800m from west to east. It is approached from the modern town, and there is a road that leads through a series of gates to the top of the fortress—this is in fact the old back route to the fort, which had its main entrance on the east side. Tickets (*open daily dawn–dusk*) are available from the ticket office near the Rana Kumbh Mahal, and will need to be shown at the Vijay Stambh and Padmini's Palace. Chittorgarh is poorly signposted, and you may need to get directions locally.

Prior to reaching the base of the fort, most travellers cross the limestone bridge over the Gambhiri River, which is believed to have been built by the forces of the sultan of Delhi following the first siege of the fortress in 1303. Note how the bridge has nine pointed arches, and, for no obvious reason, one that is semicircular. The steep 1.5km road up to Chittorgarh passes through seven well-defended gates, known as *pols*, most of them very impressive and in good condition. Note how they are set at right angles to the main walls, and have spiked wooden doors and watchtowers. Several memorials along the road mark the places where Rajput leaders fell defending the fort: the most important of which is just beyond the Bhairon Pol, and which commemorates the death of Jaimal at the hands of Akbar during the third siege of Chittorgarh in 1567. The lower gates are built to a largely functional design, while the upper gates are more ornately decorated, with carved friezes of animals and humans, and carved corbelled archways.

Rana Kumbh Palace: On arriving at the top of the plateau, head right past some old inner defensive walls to the ticket office near the entrance to the Rana Kumbh Palace, Chittorgarh's most extensive and most confusing monument. The palace, still four storeys high in places, was built in the mid-15th century, during the reign of Rana Kumbh (1433–68), and is largely in ruins. It is useful to have a guide here to make sure you see the most important parts of the palace, though many of their stories are invented, and the purpose of many of the buildings remains unclear.

The palace is accessed through a small entrance in its northern wall, though the older formal entrance is from the east, facing the original gateway at the top of the ancient main route up to Chittorgarh. The northern wall entrance takes you directly inside the inner part of the old palace, from where Rana Kumbh ruled Chittorgarh, and where there is a columned area and a high terrace to the left. There is no public access to the furthest part of the terrace, with its ornate 'sun window' facing the rising sun. Behind the buildings immediately in front of you is a large grassy courtyard, with a modern seating area for the sound and light show—from here, it is easier to orient oneself.

As you head towards the courtyard, you will pass some inaccessible underground chambers, where Queen Padmini is said to have burnt herself to death during the first siege of Chittorgarh in 1303 (though the current building did not exist then). Note the original entrances to the palace on the eastern side of the courtyard, and the columned area underneath the walls of the inner palace, with a single large pillar with a very beautifully carved capital next to the end wall. This columned area is thought to have served as the council chamber, and the part of the courtyard beneath the sun window was where Rana Kumbha's subjects would have gathered to pay homage. Beyond the western side of the courtyard is a jumbled series of evocative ruined buildings, some with traces of paintwork and other decoration, which were probably the main living area for the royal family, or possibly the separate home of the heir apparent.

Jain Temple: The unusual Sringar Chauri Jain Temple (1448) is opposite the entrance to the Rana Kumbha Mahal and was later covered by an enormous wall. The parts of the wall adjoining the temple have now been removed, and it is possible to see the fine external carvings, including friezes of warriors, musicians and maidens, and visit the inner sanctum which once held a statue of the 16th Jain *tirthankar*, Shantinath.

Museum: The Government Museum (*open Tues–Sun 9.45–5.15*) is inside the modern Fateh Prakash Palace (1930s) and has an interesting collection of sculpture and armoury

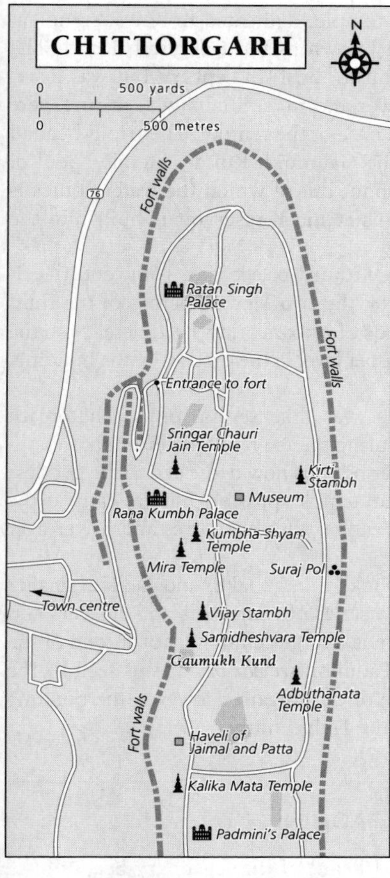

from Chittorgarh and the neighbouring area. The exhibits include a statue of Ganapati that dates back to the 8th century.

Kumbha Shyam Temple: This elaborate and well-maintained temple, dedicated to Krishna, is on the road south towards the now visible Vijay Stambh (Victory Tower). It is a 15th-century building constructed on the ruins of an 8th-century temple. The temple is thought to have originally been dedicated to Varaha, the boar avatar of Vishnu, and there is an old carving of Varaha set into the rear wall of the sanctuary. The plinth, wall niches and some of the columns are almost certainly part of the older shrine, while the high tower and the elaborate roof above the *mandapa*, or assembly hall, are of later origin. The smaller, neighbouring Mira Temple is where the celebrated 16th-century mystic poet and Krishna devotee Mirabai worshipped.

Vijay Stambh: The spectacular nine-storey Vijay Stambh (1448), or Victory Tower, dominates the western skyline of Chittorgarh. The tower is more than 37m high, significantly taller than Chittorgarh's older Kirti Stambh (*see overleaf*), and was built to commemorate Rana Kumbha's victories over the sultans of Malwa and Gujarat. Note the statues of lions on the third storey, and how the eighth storey from the top has an extended balcony overhanging the lower floors. It is possible to go inside the tower (watch your head as you enter), and climb up its unusual spiral staircase, which on alternate storeys aligns itself with either the exterior or the core of the building. There are fine views from the balconies and window on each storey of the tower, and some superb internal and external carvings. The tower is dedicated to Vishnu, and sculptures of his avatars are in prominent places—though other Hindu deities can also be seen, including a superb panel of a bearded Brahma sitting on a bench with his consort Saraswati on his knee, and their vehicle, the goose Hamsa, beneath the bench. There is also a very striking but worn image of the lion avatar of Vishnu, Narasimha, killing the demon Hiranyakashipu.

The area around the Vijay Stambh is rich in monuments, including a fine gateway, and several temples, small shrines and *sati* stones, marking the old Chittorgarh royal cremation ground, known as the Mahasati.

Samidheshvara Temple: This impressive temple, dedicated to Shiva, stands at the top the stairs leading down to the pool known as the Gaumukh Kund. The temple is thought to have originally been built in the 11th century, but was heavily restored in the 15th century, when its tower and pyramidal *mandapa* roof were constructed. Note the fine friezes around the base of the temple. The triple-headed Shiva in the temple sanctuary is modern. The Gaumukh Kund—literally, pool of the cow's mouth—is so called because the spout out of which the water comes is thought to resemble the mouth of a cow. This artificial reservoir is built into the outer walls of Chittorgarh.

***Haveli* of Jaimal and Patta:** This three-storey ruined palace is of 16th century origin. Local tradition holds that Jaimal and Patta, the two Mewari heroes of the third siege of Chittorgarh, who both died at the hands of Akbar's army, lived here. Note the remains of pretty blue-coloured tiling on the upper level of the exterior of the building, near the two small balconies.

Kalika Mata Temple: This ancient temple was, like several other Chittorgarh shrines, heavily restored in the 15th century, during the reign of Rana Kumbh; the upper part of the structure dates from the latter period. It is now dedicated to the goddess Kali, but it was almost certainly originally a sun temple, possibly built as early as the 8th century—note the images of the sun-god, Surya, with his horses and driver over the main doorway.

Padmini's Palace: This pretty palace overlooks a large lake, and faces a smaller building on an island. The palace consists of a series of courtyards and cloisters and was probably used as a pleasure garden. There is a large ceiling mirror in one of the rooms, showing how the reflection of Queen Padmini (*see box below*) was seen by the sultan of Delhi in 1303, prior to the first siege of Chittorgarh. However, the building was almost certainly originally constructed in the 15th century.

THE STORY OF PADMINI

According to local tradition, Alauddin had heard of the legendary beauty of Padmini, the queen of Chittor, and demanded to see her. He was allowed to enter the fort, but, because of the custom of *purdah* among Rajput women, only allowed to see her reflection in a pool of water. He was so struck by her beauty, so the story goes, that he had the king of Chittor kidnapped, and demanded that Padmini hand herself over to him in return for her husband. She pretended to agree but, instead, sent a small army of men to Alauddin disguised as the queen and her retinue. The Chittorgarh army was defeated, however, and the women of Chittorgarh, led by Padmini, committeed *jauhar*, or ritual suicide by fire, in an underground cavern. The story of Padmini was first written down in the 16th century, and most historians argue that she was a romantic invention of the bards of Rajasthan.

Continue south past a number of other minor buildings, gateways, shrines, memorials and reservoirs—many of them overgrown and uncared for—until, after about 1.25km, the road swings round and starts heading north close to the eastern walls of Chittorgarh. (If you're on foot, or in a hurry, it is possible to cut through to the eastern wall along the road close to the Kalika Mata Temple.)

Adbuthanata Temple: The first major monument (there are many interesting minor ones) that one meets on the eastern side of Chittorgarh is this incomplete 15th-century temple. The temple, which is dedicated to Shiva, has lost its *mandapa* roof and the top of its tower, but the surviving carvings of deities and dancing girls are of a very high quality. Note the small figure of Ganesha, the elephant-god son of Shiva, over the main doorway, and the triple-headed stone carving of Shiva in the sanctuary. North of the temple is the Suraj Pol, or Sun Gate, which was the original entrance gateway to Chittorgarh, and from which a stone stairway leads down to the plains below.

The Kirti Stambh: Some 200m further north of the Suraj Pol is the Kirti Stambh, or Tower of Fame (1301), which inspired the later and taller Vijay Stambh. It is in fact an unusual Jain temple, dedicated to the first *tirthankar*, Adinath. This 24.5m six-storey temple has four large naked standing images of Adinath on the lowest level, and hundreds more tiny carvings of the *tirthankar* on the upper levels. Note the pretty columned pavilion on top of the tower. Access to the interior of the tower is not allowed. Next to the Kirti Stambh is a recently restored Jain temple (14th century) with some fine external carvings.

Ratan Singh Palace: Continue north to the far end of the Chittorgarh plateau where the road once again swings round and one reaches the large Ratan Singh Palace (c. 1530) overlooking a reservoir. The palace is the most recent of Chittorgarh's major buildings and contains the important Ratneshwar Mahadeva Temple, dedicated to Shiva. The palace consists of a series of courtyards, partially ruined two- and three-storey buildings and a complex maze of rooms, some of which were in more recent use. Note, in comparison to the earlier Rana Kumbha Palace, the widespread use of the arch form. The temple has some fine exterior carvings. There are small niches containing statues of deities that have been set into the wall of the reservoir outside the palace.

Shahpura

About 85km north of Chittorgarh is Shahpura (*map 3 C2*), with an attractive 18th-century palace, now a hotel, that can be used as a stopover on the way to Jaipur. It has a fine step-well and several old temples.

SOUTHEASTERN RAJASTHAN

Southeast Rajasthan is the most fertile and least tourist-heavy part of the state, and includes three important former princely states: Kota, Bundi and Jhalawar.

KOTA

The large industrial city of Kota (*map 3 D3*) in southeastern Rajasthan is the capital of the former princely state of the same name. It is less spectacular than most of Rajasthan's other princely capitals, but parts of the old city overlooking the River Chambal are very pretty, as is the lake, Kishore Sagar. Kota was formed in the 1630s as a breakaway state from Bundi, its rulers belonging to a junior branch of the Bundi royal family. Bundi and Kota fought several wars over the following century, and in the early 19th century Jhalawar state was formed as a breakaway state from Kota, headed by Kota's former prime minister. Kota was the part of Rajasthan most severely affected by the Uprising of 1857, and the pro-British maharaja was detained by his own troops, eventually being freed by soldiers sent by the maharaja of Karauli.

Orientation: The old walled city is on the south side of modern Kota on the east bank of the Chambal. The modern palaces, now heritage hotels, are in the north of the city. In between is a large lake, Kishore Sagar, with the old royal *chattris* on its northern bank. To reach the old Garh Palace it is necessary to go round the old city and enter by its southern gate.

The Garh Palace

The fort palace, which dates back to the 13th century, is in a large compound at the southern tip of the old city. Parts of the palace are out of bounds—one of the buildings is occupied by the Albert Einstein school—but the fine painted façades can be seen from the main courtyard. Enter a smaller courtyard which leads to the **Rao Madho Singh Museum** (*open daily 10–4.30*), housed in part of the palace and which has pretty wall-paintings and decorations. Among the museum exhibits are a silver howdah, a large collection of swords, a fan that runs off kerosene and a 1930s washing machine. The **Raj Mahal** has some very fine murals, depicting religious and courtly scenes. The private galleries are upstairs via a well-hidden staircase—you will need to ask the guard to let you in, and buy a separate ticket. There are more superb murals in rooms spread over three rooms. Note the amusing portraits of Westerners near the light switch on the left in the room full of small paintings covered in glass. The walled city has several other interesting buildings, including the **Palkiya Haveli**, a traditional city mansion built around a courtyard and which is now a heritage hotel.

Around Kishore Sagar

The distinctive feature of Kota's central lake, Kishore Sagar, is a pretty two-storey palace, known as the **Jagmandir** (1740), which sits on an island (*no public access*). Just to the north of the lake, and next to a bastion of the fort, is the **Sarbagh**, with its memorial *chattris* to members of the Kota royal family, including one to Kota's best-known modern ruler, Umed Singh, maharaja for 51 years until his death in 1940. Note also some more *chattris* in the overgrown park on the other side of the road from Sarbagh. Further east by about 600m is a small **archaeological museum**, with mainly Hindu sculpture from the region.

North Kota

On the northern side of Kota are two former palaces, both converted into hotels. **Brijraj Bhawan** (1830, modernised 1909), a former British residency and royal guest house, is in a pretty position overlooking a small island in the river. The British Resident and his two sons were killed here during the 1857 Uprising. The larger palace, **Umed Bhavan** (1904), was designed by Swinton Jacob, and is built in the Indo-Saracenic style with a tall clock tower.

NEAR KOTA

Badoli

The exquisite ancient temples of Badoli (*open daily dawn–dusk; map 3 D3*), also known as Baroli, are 4km east of Bhainsrorgarh Fort on the Kota–Chittorgarh road. There is a pretty park close to the road with some minor Shiva temples, one of them set in a water pond, but the main temple complex, which dates from the 10th century, is a little further on over a footbridge. The main **Ghatesvar Temple**, dedicated to Shiva, is probably the finest surviving building from the late Pratihara period, and has a superb separate assembly area, or *mandapa*, with a pyramidal roof. Both the temple and the *mandapa* have fine external carvings, though the image of Shiva dancing that stood in the recess at the rear of the temple has been stolen. The left recess has a fine image of Shiva dancing beneath an elephant skin, while the right recess shows a skeletal Chamunda. Note also the fine carvings of animals next to the tower of the main temple, as well as the superb workmanship on the pillar capitals and ceiling of the entrance to the sanctuary. Unusually, in the sanctuary there is a large stone shaped like an inverted pot, or *ghata* (giving the temple its name), which plays the role of the lingam. There are several other smaller temples, and ruined temple pieces nearby.

Bhainsrorgarh

The town of Bhainsrorgarh (*map 3 D3*), 40km southwest of Kota, has one of Rajasthan's prettiest forts, overlooking the River Chambal; it is now a hotel. The 18th-century fort has pretty memorial *chattris* next to the river. **Hinglajgarh** is an extraordinary overgrown fort, dating back to at least the 5th century. It is, in fact, just over the border in Madhya Pradesh, but is best approached from Bhainsrorgarh, 40km to the northeast. The fort is surrounded by forests, and there are lots of ruined buildings, pretty water tanks and superb carvings and statues, though many of the best pieces are to be found in museums in Indore and Bhopal, in Madhya Pradesh.

Kota–Jhalawar Road

The road from Kota to Jhalawar passes next to a large fortified hunting lodge, or *shikargah*, known as **Dara Mahal**, 43km southeast of Kota. This area is still thickly forested, but note how the main railway line from Delhi to Mumbai passes behind the lodge. Inside the *shikargah* are several buildings, and a small Shiva temple. Note the other old buildings, one on top of the hill, and several others by the roadside, a few hundred metres further on towards Jhalawar.

JHALAWAR

This town (*map 3 D3*), 72km southeast of Kota, is the capital of the former princely state of the same name. It was one of the most recently formed princely states, having broken away from Kota in 1838, and was named after the Jhala Dynasty, which became its rulers. The Jhalas had previously been the hereditary *dewans*, or prime ministers, of Kota, and often the effective rulers of the state. There are some fine temples, an important fort, some unusual palaces, a fine museum and comfortable palace hotels in, or near, Jhalawar.

Jhalawar Fort-Palace

The old fort-palace is in the centre of town—and in poor condition after having been used as government offices for years, and then vandalised. The façades are very pretty, and the brightly-coloured interior paintings and mirror-work are impressive, but in dire need of conservation. In the grounds of the palace is an old theatre of the 1920s.

Archaeological Museum

Just outside the fort-palace is an archaeological museum that was established in 1915 by the maharaja of Jhalawar. It has some very fine Hindu sculptures, including a superb triple-headed Vishnu (with a human, boar and lion face) riding on his vehicle, Garuda. Note also the hermaphrodite form of Shiva, Ardhanarishwara, in which, unusually, both sets of genitalia are shown. There is also a very fine statue of Shiva and Parvati seated on the bull Nandi.

Prithvi Vilas

Known locally as the Durbar ki Kothi, this palace is an attractive Indo-Saracenic building, complete with its own square moat and nearby Sati temple. It has been converted into a comfortable hotel, with the former royal family still living in the building.

The Rain Basera

One of India's unlikeliest palaces, this decrepit former royal summer house built entirely out of wood overlooks a lake just north of Jhalawar. The maharaja of Jhalawar spotted the house at an industrial exhibition in Lucknow, and had it dismantled and brought here as his retirement home.

NEAR JHALAWAR

Jhalrapatan

This walled temple village (*map 3 D3*), known locally as 'Patan', is 6km south of Jhalawar, which it predates by many centuries. The **Surya Mandir** (11th century), or Sun Temple, is in the heart of the village, and has some superb external and internal carvings. The idol in the sanctuary and the front roof are 19th-century additions to the temple, which was probably built during the Parmar Dynasty. It is possible to get close to the external carving by pushing open the broken gate on the left side of the temple. The temple has several tiers of decorative and figurative friezes, including one consisting entirely of elephants. Above the elephants is a frieze showing humans, sometimes singing and dancing, as well some amusing erotica on the left side of the temple. Note the image of a shocked woman holding her hands over her face, while another woman consorts with two partners at once. The temple was not in fact dedicated to the sun-god Surya, but to Vishnu, as is made clear by the Vaishnavite image on the exterior, including carvings of Narasimha and Varaha, Vishnu's lion and boar avatars respectively. The nearby **Chandrabhaga temples** are next to the river of the same name, and date from the 8th to the 14th centuries.

Gagraon

This large river fortress (*map 3 D3*), founded in the 7th century, is 5km northeast of Jhalawar and visible from many places in the town. The long, narrow fort overlooks the confluence of two rivers, the Ahu and Kalisindh, and its impressive walls are largely intact. It has recently been over-restored, with romantically ruined palaces given a more modern touch.

Buddhist caves

Around the town of Bhawani Mandi (*map 3 D3*), 45km southeast of Jhalawar, are three groups of early Buddhist caves—the finest in Rajasthan. Ask for the villages of **Kolvi**, **Vinayaka** and **Hathygod** for the caves that have rock-cut stupas, and carvings of human figures and deities.

BUNDI

Just 34km northwest of Kota, Bundi (*map 3 D3*) is the capital of the former princely state of the same name, and its superb forts and step-wells have become a major visitor attraction in recent years. It is a good example of how one of Rajasthan's most attractive locations has not been ruined by tourism.

History: The princely state of Bundi is one of Rajasthan's oldest, dating back to at least the 14th century. It once incorporated Ranthambore, Kota and Jhalawar—a region still sometimes referred to as Hadoti. Bundi was split into two kingdoms by the Mughal emperor Shah Jahan in 1630, with a junior branch of the family ruling what became Kota state. It has often been said that Bundi never fully recovered from the partition of the Hadoti region. The rivalry between Bundi and Kota lasted almost until Indian Independence in 1947. Bundi has a long artistic tradition, and the Bundi school of painting—of which there are several fine examples in the Chitra Sala (*see overleaf*)—dates to the16th century. Mark Twain and Rudyard Kipling are among the more famous 19th-century visitors to Bundi, as well as James Tod, the first English-language historian of Rajasthan, who was the guardian of the infant maharaja of Bundi in the 1820s. Kipling wrote that the Garh Palace in Bundi, 'is such a palace as men build for themselves in uneasy dreams—the work of goblins rather than of men.'

Orientation: The oldest parts of Bundi are nestled inside a horseshoe-shaped valley. The exquisite fort known as the Garh Palace occupies the lower part of the hillside, with a large man-made rectangular lake at the bottom, while on top of the hill is the older fortress of Taragarh. Many of the step-wells are in the built-up area of modern Bundi, just to the south of the old city, while to east of the city is the lake, Jait Sagar.

Bundi Fort-Palace

The spectacular **Garh Palace**, or fort-palace (1580 and later), is a series of off-white palace buildings within a large fortified compound that runs down the slope of the hillside. There is a car park near the ticket office (*open daily 8–5.30; bring a torch to look at the paintings*), just outside the main gate to the complex. Tickets are not needed for the Chitra Sala, or for Taragarh further up the hill.

The lower fort: The large courtyard immediately inside the gate was used as a stables and a garrison. Note the huge arched masonry pier, known as the Bhim Burj, on which a large cannon once stood. It is a short, steep walk up to the Hathi Pol (Elephant Gate) of the **Chatra Mahal** (named after the 17th-century maharaja, Chatra Singh), past a café and shops on your right—go past the turning to the Chitra Sala. The arch over the gate is created by the trunks of two carved elephants, and leads into a cloistered courtyard. Note the projecting balcony on the first floor, aligned with the gateway, from where the maharaja would greet his subjects. Take the stairs on the left and walk past the marble seat on the balcony into another courtyard with a pool in the centre. To the left is a covered area leading to several more rooms with some fine paintings and decoration, as well as superb views over the town of Bundi, and some of its smaller palaces and mansions. Note the elephant brackets in the covered area on the right. Steps take you up to the next level, which has another smaller courtyard and more side rooms with fine paintings, particularly in the **Badal Mahal**, or Cloud Palace.

The upper fort: Return to the Elephant Gate, head down for 10m, and then take a left uphill, for the finest of all the Bundi paintings in the **Chitra Sala**, or Painting Hall. To reach it, pass through a landscaped garden, with a square pond, each side with a small projecting balcony; the gallery is at the back, up some stairs (*push hard on the steel mesh gates if they are closed—public access is allowed*) and inside another courtyard that contains wall-paintings from the late 18th and early 19th centuries. Most of them use the distinctive blue and turquoise of Bundi painting of this period, and many depict the life of Krishna. Two images in particular are among the most famous works of Rajasthani art. These are the paintings of Krishna sitting in a tree, having stolen the clothes of the cowgirls while they bathe, and a fine map-like image of the fortified Srinathji Temple at Nathdwara (*see p. 182*).

Taragarh: To reach Bundi's oldest fort (1342), which is set on the hilltop, continue upwards from the entrance to the Chitra Sala complex, through the Garh

Palace, as the path rapidly becomes narrower and more overgrown (*open sunrise to sunset*). After passing through a gate that marks the end of the Garh Palace, turn right, walking alongside the wall on level ground until you reach a footpath leading up the hill again (straight ahead is an old watchtower). Many of the buildings inside the high walls of Taragarh are in poor condition, but there are two water tanks and an old palace with two courtyards that have some surviving paintings. To the far right is a tower, used as a flagstaff and now occupied by the police, so therefore out of bounds. The views of Bundi from Taragarh are superb. There is a road that leads up to the nearby TV tower and is an alternative route to Taragarh—less scenic but also less exhausting.

The rest of Bundi

Just to the south of the Garh Palace, close to the Surang Gate, is a **museum** (*open daily 9–5*), named after Maharao Raja Bahadur Singh. It is set in a palace next to the lake, and has an unremarkable collection of stuffed animals, weapons and some photos of the last maharaja with Errol Flynn, Frank Sinatra and Ava Gardner, as well as Milton Reynolds, whom, we are informed, invented the ball-point pen. It is worth wandering around the area near the Surang Gate, where there are several older buildings, some of which have been converted into hotels.

The finest of Bundi's many step-wells, the **Raniji ki Baoli** (1699), or Queen's Step-well, is in the centre of modern Bundi, 1km south of the Garh Palace, and is just outside the southern walls of the old city. The step-well is marked by pretty, narrow-pillared kiosks above ground-level. Ask the watchman to open the gate leading down the steps, under the superbly carved stone arches and pillar capitals surmounted by elephants. On the walls leading down to the water are relief panels carved in stone. Most of the images are avatars of Vishnu. Head south down the side street from the Raniji ki Baoli for another fine step-well, the **Dhai-Bhau ki Kund**, the geometric design of which is remarkably complex—and next to which are two pretty memorial *chattris*.

Further out of town, just off the Kota Road, is the **Chaurasi Khambon**, or '84 pillars'—a fine memorial *chattri*, raised up on a plinth, with relief carvings in panels of elephants, horses and cows. Note how the sculptor has portrayed some of the elephant riders so that they just fit within the rectangular frame of the panels.

The closest part of the attractive lake, **Jait Sagar**, is just 600m east of the Garh Palace, as the crow flies, but about twice that distance by foot or cycle rickshaw through the most congested part of old Bundi. For car travellers, the easiest route is to go around the Taragarh Hill, and drive to the far side of Jait Sagar. **Sukh Mahal** is a small palace where Rudyard Kipling once stayed (it is also known as Kipling's House) on the side of Jait Sagar closest to Bundi, next to the dam that created the lake. **Kshar Bagh** is a large garden entered from the roadside, with the memorial *chattris* of the Bundi maharajas. Note the relief panels on *chattri* plinths, similar to those at Chaurasi Khambon in southern Bundi.

About 5km northwest of Bundi is the pretty **Phool Sagar**, or Flower Lake, with a palace in which the former royal family still lives. Permission is needed to enter.

Bijolia and Menal

The old walled town of **Bijolia** (*map 3 D3*) is 50km west of Bundi on the road to Chittorgarh, with several pretty temples around a man-made pond called the Mandakini Kund. The most important is the **Uddeshwar Temple**, dedicated to Shiva, with some fine carvings on the outer wall. Some 15km west of Bijolia is the village of **Menal** (*map 3 D3*), with some 9th–11th-century temples set in a compound near a waterfall. The main **Mahanaleshavara Temple**, dedicated to Shiva, has some fine carved panels depicting gods, and a pyramidal roof to the assembly hall.

PRACTICAL INFORMATION

GETTING THERE

Rajasthan's three best-known cities—Jaipur, Jodhpur and Udaipur—are well-connected by air to Mumbai and Delhi. Jaipur also has regular flights from Kolkata and Chennai.

There are good train services from Delhi to Jaipur, including an early morning Shatabdi service via Alwar (2½hrs) to Jaipur (5½hrs) and on to Ajmer (6½hrs); and from Delhi to Kota (8hrs) on the Delhi–Mumbai line that first runs through Bharatpur (3½hrs) and Sawai Madhopur—for Ranthambore (5hrs). Other cities are less well connected from Delhi, though there are night trains to Udaipur, Jodhpur, Jaisalmer and Bikaner. Other trains to Rajasthan include the rather slow Agra–Jaipur service (6hrs), but taking this line makes it hard to visit the many interesting places en route, and the Ahmedabad–Udaipur route (7hrs).

By road the main entry points to Rajasthan are: from Delhi to Jaipur, with Neemrana (*see Accommodation, p. 200*) as a good lunch or night stop; and from Ahmedabad to Udaipur. Both routes are major highways. The road from Agra to Jaipur is also a highway, and it is easy to visit Fatehpur Sikri, Bharatpur, Deeg and Karauli by taking smaller roads off the main Agra-Jaipur route. The old Delhi-Alwar road is in poor condition, and travellers should instead travel by the Jaipur highway to Dharuhera, and then take the smaller road via the outskirts of Tijara to Alwar.

GETTING AROUND

There are regular flights connecting Jaipur, Jodhpur and Udaipur, though many travellers prefer to do these journeys by road and visit important sites en route. Jaisalmer airport has had occasional periods when there have been commercial flights—check with your travel agent.

Internal rail services include Jaipur–Jodhpur (5½hrs) and Jodhpur–Jaisalmer (6hrs). Otherwise travel to Jaisalmer is by a good road from Bikaner (265km) or Jodhpur (225km). Udaipur is poorly connected by train with the other main cities.

The southeastern part of Rajasthan, around Kota and Bundi, suffers from not having an airport, which is one of the reasons why it receives fewer visitors. However, there are good roads to Bundi and Kota from Jaipur and Udaipur.

It is easy and, by Western standards, very cheap to hire cars (with drivers). Some visitors do this in Delhi, but they can be hired in any of the many cities. Car hire from **Rajputana Tours** (*T: 0941 4121359 / 9950320539*) in Jodhpur is recommended. An auto- or cycle-rickshaw is recommended for the urban areas, though many of the major sites can be visited on foot.

ACCOMMODATION

Eastern Rajasthan

• **Ajmer and around:** The best hotel in Ajmer is the modern **Man Singh Palace** (*$$; T: 0145 2425702; mansingh-hotels.com*); in Pushkar, it is the modern **Hotel Jagat Palace** (*$$; T: 0145 2772001; hotelpushkarpalace.com*). Kishangarh (30km east of Ajmer, and 35km east of Pushkar) has the enchanting and unpretentious **Phool Mahal** (*$$; T: 0145 2772226; royalkishangarh.com*), a 19th-century palace overlooking the lake. There is a fort-palace that also belongs to the former royal family of Kishangarh, at **Roopangarh Fort** (*$$; T: 01497 220217, royalkishangarh.com*), 25km to the north.

• **Alwar and around:** The area around Alwar has several fine hotels. The **Amanbagh** (*$$$; T: 01465 223333; amanresorts.com/amanbagh*), near Ajabgarh, 50km southwest of Alwar and 55km east of Jaipur, was constructed on the site of a former hunting lodge of the Maharaja of Alwar, and is one of India's most luxurious hotels, run by the Aman group. The 14th-century **Kesroli Hillfort** (*$$; T: 01468 289352; neemranahotels.com/kesroli*) has been converted into a superb small hotel by the Neemrana group, and is highly recommended. It is said to be the oldest heritage site in India at which visitors can stay, and is surrounded by very pretty countryside. Bharatpur has two heritage hotels: the slightly run-down 19th-century **Laxmi Vilas Palace** (*$$; T: 05644 231199; laxmivilas.com*), close to the nature reserve, and **The Bagh** (*$$$; T: 05644 225415; thebagh.com*), a pretty hotel laid out across several buildings, some old, some new, in a 200-year-old walled pleasure garden. There is one good hotel in Karauli, the 1930s **Bhanwar Vilas Palace** (*$$; T: 0141 2290763 or 094140 54257; karauli.com*).

• **Jaipur**: This city has a huge number of heritage and modern hotels, from the very cheap to the extremely expensive, and everything in between. The very grand **Rambagh Palace** (*$$$; T: 0141 2211919; tajhotels.com*) in Jaipur's New City, and 3.5km south of the City Palace, is one of India's best known hotels, run by the Taj group, and was the main royal palace in the city for the middle years of the 20th century. The 19th-century **Samode Haveli** (*$$$; T: 0141 2632407; samode.com*) is a pretty former palace within the old city, just 1km from the City Palace, and which was the Jaipur home of the royal family of Samode, one of Jaipur's feudatory states. Also recommended is **Diggi Palace** (*$$; T: 0141 2373091; hoteldiggipalace.com*), which, like the more upmarket Samode Haveli, was the Jaipur home of one of Jaipur's feudatory states. Built in the 1860s, it is in the New City, about 2km south of the City Palace.

• **Kuchaman:** there is a comfortable hotel inside **Kuchaman Fort** (*$$; T: 092140 40882; the kuchamanfort.com*)

• **Neemrana: Neemrana Fort** (*$$$; T: 01494 246006; neemranahotels.com/neemrana*), the flagship hotel of the Neemrana group, is a beautiful 15th-century fort, situated just off the Delhi–Jaipur highway, 132km from Jaipur and 105km from Delhi. Despite recent enlargements, it remains one of Rajasthan's most eclectic and interesting hotels.

• **Ranthambore:** The proximity of India's best-known tiger reserve means Ranthambore has a large number of comfortable hotels. These include the very comfortable tented accommodation at **Sher Bagh** (*$$$; T: 07462 252120 sherbagh.com*), and the even more luxurious and expensive tents at the adjoining **Aman-i Khas** (*$$$; T: 07462 252052; amanresorts.com/amanikhas*). If you want something cheaper and with solid walls, there is the **Castle Jhoomar Baori** (*$$; T: 07462 220495; jhoomarbaori@rtdc.in*), a former royal hunting lodge now run as a hotel by the state tourism department.

• **Samode:** 30km north of Jaipur, Samode has two heritage hotels. The **Samode Palace** (*$$$; T: 01423 240014; samode.com*) is a fine fort-palace, set in the hills, with an ornate 19th-century interior which has been turned into a comfortable hotel. The **Samode Bagh** (*$$; T: 01423 240235; samode.com*) has luxury tents in a Mughal-style garden.

Northern Rajasthan

• **Bikaner:** The **Bhanwar Niwas Haveli** (*$$; T: 0151 2529323; bhanwarniwas.com*) is a very grand 1930s *haveli*, in exceptional condition, which is slightly hard to find in the backstreets of the old city. Good food and excellent service. The *haveli* is a marvellous base for wandering through the old city. It has a good-as-new 1927 Buick in its forecourt, with a (working) horn shaped liked a dragon running along the front fender on the driver's side. The **Lallgarh Palace** (*$$$; T: 0151 2540201; lallgarhpalace.com*) is part of the vast Edwardian palace built by the Maharaja Ganga Singh, and named after his father Lall Singh. Beautiful and spacious, with an exquisite period swimming pool.

• **Shekhawati:** The Shekhawati region has a number of good hotels, though the major hotel chains are not represented here. In Mandawa, **Hotel Castle Mandawa** (*$$$; T: 01592 223124; mandawahotels.com*) is probably the best-known hotel in Shekhawati, inside a fascinating fort. It has a slightly trumped-up medieval atmosphere and unexciting food. Nearby is the more authentic and simpler **Hotel Mandawa Haveli** (*$$; T: 01592 223088; hotelmandawa.free.fr*). In Nawalgarh, **Apani Dhani** (*$$; T: 01594 222239; apanidhani.com*) has a series of eco-friendly traditional thatched huts on the outskirts of Nawalgarh. No air-conditioning, but very comfortable, with superb local vegetarian food and extremely helpful management. The handsome **Piramal Haveli** (*$$; T: 01592 221220; neemranahotels.com*) in Bagar is run by the Neemrana group, with the usual high quality service and food.

Western Rajasthan

• **Jaisalmer:** Here, there is a wide range of accommodation, including hotels that are inside the fort. Some environmental groups oppose the presence of hotels in the fort, because of the water management problems they cause, and appeal to visitors to boycott these hotels. If you choose to stay inside the fort, the **Hotel Killa Bhawan** (*$$-$$$; T: 02992 251204; killabhawan.com*), built into the ramparts, provides a range of accommodation from the simple to the luxurious, in a spectacular location. Outside the fort, but in the old city, is the **Mandir Palace Hotel** (*$$; T: 02992 252788; welcomheritagehotels.com*), a former royal palace with some beautiful stonework. The enormous **Fort Rajwada** (*$$$; T: 02992 253233; fortrajwada.com*), modern but built in a traditional style, is probably Jaisalmer's most luxurious hotel.

• **Around Jaisalmer:** Even more comfortable and expensive than the hotels in Jaisalmer is **The Serai** (*$$$; T: 011 4606 7608; the-serai.com*), a desert camp 28km east of the city. The **Fort in Pokharan** (*$$; T: 02994 222274; fortpokaran.com*), 100km east of Jaisalmer, has a small hotel which is a useful stopover for those who do not want to do the full drive to Jaisalmer in one day.

• **Jodhpur:** The city's leading hotel, run by the Taj group, is the luxurious **Umaid Bhawan** (*$$$; T: 0291 251 0101; tajhotels.com*), an enormous 20th-century palace (*see p. 166*). Other comfortable Jodhpur hotels include **Ajit Bhawan** (*$$$; T: 0291 2513333*), also a 20th-century palace, while other heritage accommodation includes the 19th-century **Pal Haveli** (*$$; T: 0291 3293328l; palhaveli.com*), between the fort and the clock tower. The **Bal Samand Lake Palace** (*$$$; T: 0291 2572321 jodhanaheritage.com*) overlooks a lake just to the north of Jodhpur and is surrounded by pretty gardens.

Around Jodhpur: There are many other forts and palaces around Jodhpur that have been converted into hotels, including, to the south of the city, the laid-back **Rohetgarh** (*$$; T: 02936 268531; rohetgarh.com; 38km from Jodhpur*), where travel writers Bruce Chatwin and William Dalrymple have been long-stay guests. It has a good reputation for its horse safaris. There is also the imposing **Fort Chanwa Luni** (*$$$; T: 02931 284216; fortchanwa.com; 33km from Jodhpur*). To the north is **Khimsar Fort** (*$$$; T: 01585 262345; khimsarfort.com; 85km from Jodhpur*), a little too modernised for some tastes, but very comfortable, while inside Nagaur Fort is the **Royal Camp** (*$$$; T: 0291 2572321; welcomheritagehotels.com; 120km northeast of Jodhpur*) run by the WelcomHeritage group, with 20 luxury tents—work is underway to convert part of the fort itself into a hotel. To the east is the highly recommended **Chhatra Sagar** (*$$$; T: 02939 230118; chhatrasagar.com; 120km from Jodhpur*) luxury tented accommodation overlooking a lake. The nearby **Nimaj Palace** (*$$; T: 02939 230022; nimajpalace.com*), run by members of the same extended family, is nearby, if you prefer solid walls. There is only very basic accommodation in Osiyan: contact **Prithviraj Saraswat** (*T: 09413 279747*), known as Babloo, for more information and for help in exploring the town. Outside Osiyan, amid the sand dunes, is **Reggie's Camel Camp** (*$$$; T: 0291 2437023; camelcamposian.com*).

Southern Rajasthan

• **Chittorgarh:** Though there are no comfortable places to stay in Chittorgarh itself, **Fort Bassi** (*$$, T: 01472 225321, bassifortpalace.com*), 20km northeast of Chittorgarh, and the **Castle Bijaipur**

(*$$$, T: 01472 240099, castlebijaipur.com*), 40km to the east, are both luxurious heritage hotels inside 16th-century forts. Shahpura Bagh, 80km north of Chittorgarh, has the comfortable **Palace Hotel** (*$$$; T: 09828 122012; shahpurabagh.com*).

• **Dungarpur:** The only comfortable hotel in Dungarpur is the superb **Udai Bilas Palace** (*$$; udaibilaspalace.com; T: 02964 230808 or 93146 53967*), with its mixture of Art Deco and traditional Rajput architecture, and one of India's most distinctive swimming pools, overlooking the lake.

• **Mount Abu:** Here there are a large number of comfortable hotels, some of them former summer palaces of Rajasthan princes. **Jaipur House** (*$$$ in main palace, $$ in outhouse; T: 02974 235176*), the summer residence of the maharaja of Jaipur, built in 1897, has fine views over the lake. **Kishangarh House** (*$$; T: 02974 238092; royalkishangarh.com*), belonging to the Kishangarh royal family, is also recommended.

• **Udaipur:** There are probably more heritage hotels here than in any other city in India. The best-known is the superbly located **Lake Palace** (*$$$; T: 0294 2428800; tajgroup.com*), run by the Taj group and accessed by private boat from the lakeside south of the City Palace. Of the two luxury hotels within the city palace, the **Fateh Prakash Palace** (*$$$; T: 0294 2528016; hrhhotels.com*) has the best views of the lake. For cheaper accommodation within walking distance of the City Palace, try the 19th-century **Rang Niwas Palace Hotel** (*$$; T: 0294 2523890; rangniwaspalace.com*), which belongs to a junior branch of the royal family.

Around Udaipur: There is a huge variety of heritage hotels of which the 18th-century fort-palace **Devigarh** (*$$$; T: 02953 289 211; deviresorts.com*), 27km north of the city on the Jodhpur road, is probably the most impressive and luxurious. Further to the north, close to Ranakpur, are the slightly run-down but very atmospheric 17th-century **Ghanerao Royal Castle** (*$$; T: 02934 284035; ghaneraoroyalcastle.com*), from where it is possible to trek to Kumbhalgarh, and the **Rawla Narlai** (*$$$; T: 02934 260443; rawlanarlai.com*), a 17th-century royal hunting lodge. The most comfortable accommodation near Kumbhalgarh is the **Aodhi** (*$$$; T: 02954 242341; hrhhotels.com*), a modern resort hotel owned by the Udaipur royal family. **Deogarh Mahal** (*$$$; T: 02904 252777; deogarhmahal.com*), 110km north of Udaipur, is another popular heritage hotel, and one that commands great loyalty from its many regular visitors.

Southeastern Rajasthan

• **Bundi:** Now turned into a comfortable hotel, the **Haveli Braj Bhushanjee** (*$$; T: 0747 2442322; kiplingsbundi.com*) is the former home of the prime ministers of Bundi, in the heart of the old city, close to the Garh Palace.

• **Kota:** The pretty family-run **Palkiya Haveli** (*$$; T: 0744 328797; palkiyahaveli@yahoo.com*) is a heritage building in the heart of the old city. There are two palaces in the north of the city (*see p. 193*). The smaller **Brijraj Bhawan** (*$$; T: 0744 2450057; brijraj@dil.in*) overlooks the river, while the larger **Umed Bhavan Palace** (*$$; 0744 2325262; welcomheritagehotels.com*) is set in pretty grounds.

Around Kota: The **Prithvi Vilas Palace** (*$$; T: 07432 231347 or 098913 49555*) in Jhalawar, known locally as Durbar ki Kothi, is to the east of the town, and is a comfortable palace hotel, with the former royal family living in the same building. The **Bhainsrorgarh Fort** (*$$$; T: 01475 232006; bhainsrorgarh.com*) is a small, comfortable hotel within the fort-palace of Bhainsrorgarh, spectacularly located overlooking the River Chambal.

FOOD

Rajasthani cuisine is predominantly vegetarian, with a wide range of cereals as the staple food. Among the most common dishes are *dal batti*, wheat dumplings eaten with a lentil curry, and *gatta curry*, which are balls made of chickpea flour cooked in a spicy stew. A wide range of vegetables are eaten, including the locally available 'desert greens'. Made up of five different herbs, seeds and berries, *panchkuta* is particularly distinctive and tasty. Popular meat dishes include *lal maas* (literally 'red meat'), a mutton curry with red chillies.

• **Jaipur:** The city's most venerable restaurant is the **LMB** (*$$; T: 0141 2565844; hotellmb.com*) inside the hotel of the same name on Johori Bazaar in the Pink City. It has excellent Rajasthani vegetarian food. For tasty fusion food try **Flow** (*$$; T: 0141 2374044; thefarmjaipur.com/flow*), a café-restaurant at the back of the Diggi Palace Hotel.

• **Jodhpur and Jaisalmer:** The best-located restaurant in Jodhpur is the outdoor **Mehran Terrace** (*evenings only 7–10.30; reservations advised, T: 0291 2555389*) within the grounds of Mehrangarh Fort, which serves vegetarian and non-vegetarian Rajasthani thalis. For lunches and dinner, excellent Rajasthani vegetarian food is available at **Mid Town Restaurant** on Station Road. The **Desert Café**, just north of Osiyan on the Jaisalmer road, is recommended for its Rajasthani food, particularly *panchkuta*. Jaisalmer's restaurants seem to be more Italian than Indian, but the restaurant at the **Rang Mahal Hotel** is recommended for Rajasthani food.

• **Udaipur:** The city is better known for its superb restaurant locations than for its cuisine, though it is possible to have some excellent local food, Indian and international in style. The Lake Palace Hotel has three restaurants: the more formal rooftop **Bhairo**, serving 'Asian fusion'; the **Neel Kamal**, serving Indian and Rajastani specialities next to the lily pond, and the lakeside multi-cuisine **Jharoka**. Booking in advance is mandatory (*T: 0294 2428800*). **Ambrai**, in the Amet Haveli (*T: 0294 243 1085*), next to Hanuman Ghat, has good Rajasthani food, in a pretty location near Lake Pichola.

FURTHER READING & VIEWING

There is a huge amount of general tourist literature about Rajasthan, but the only good recent history is Rima Hooja's *A History of Rajasthan* (Rupa, 2006), which is more more than 1200 pages long. The great 19th-century work on the region, James Tod's *Annals & Antiquities of Rajasthan*, was republished by Rupa in 2006. If you're staying in Jaipur for more than a day, Dharmendar Kanwar's *Jaipur: 10 Easy Walks* (Rupa, 2004) and Fiona Caulfield's *Love Jaipur* (Hardy's Bay, 2010) are both invaluable. *The Palaces of Rajasthan* (India Book House, 2005) by George Michell and *Stones in the Sand: The Architecture of Rajasthan* (Marg, 2002) by Giles Tillotson are both written by leading experts in the field. *The Raj* (Vintage, 2007) by Gita Mehta is a historical novel set in a princely state in Rajasthan during the British period, while the much-acclaimed *Cuckold* (Harper Collins, 2007) by Kiran Nargarkar is set in Chittorgarh in the Mughal period.

The best-known English-language film set in Rajasthan is the 1983 James Bond movie *Octopussy*, which was largely filmed in Udaipur, while the 1994 non-cartoon Disney version of *The Jungle Book* was shot partly in Mehrangarh Fort in Jodhpur. The critically acclaimed fantasy movie *The Fall* (2008) has key scenes in Jaipur, Jodhpur and inside the step-well at Abhaneri. Satyajit Ray's 1974 *Sonar Kella* (*The Golden Fort*) is a charming comedy, partly set in Jaisalmer. Huge numbers of Bollywood movies have been set in Rajasthan, including the 1971 classic *Reshma aur Shera*, and the ghost movie *Paheli* (2008).

UTTAR PRADESH

Uttar Pradesh, meaning 'North State' (*map 5*), is India's most politically important and populous state. If Uttar Pradesh (or UP, pronounced 'you-pee') were a nation, it would be the sixth most populous country in the world, with more than 170 million inhabitants. UP is home to several of India's most visited tourist sites, including the Taj Mahal and Varanasi. It is also home to a very wide range of other major historical and cultural attractions, modern and ancient—a melting pot of Hindu, Buddhist and Muslim traditions.

Geographically, Uttar Pradesh is set across the upper plain of the Ganges and its tributaries—a fertile land that has seen the rise and fall of many powerful empires. Several of the most famous sites pre-date recorded history. They include four of the most important Hindu holy places: Varanasi (the home of Shiva), Allahabad (the confluence of the Ganges and Yamuna rivers), Mathura (the birthplace of Krishna) and Ayodhya (the birthplace of Rama). There are several important Buddhist sites, including Sarnath, where the Buddha delivered his first sermon. Islam has also played an important role in this area for more than 900 years, and, in Jaunpur and Lucknow, UP has two of the finest and most distinctive collections of Muslim architecture to be found anywhere in the world. It has several deserted cities, including most famously Fatehpur Sikri, but also fascinating long-forgotten but once-important urban centres, such as Kaushambi and Kara, where tourists hardly venture. The British colonial period also left a deep mark on Uttar Pradesh, most famously as the scene of key battles of the 1857 Mutiny or Uprising—particularly in Kanpur, Lucknow and Jhansi.

Today UP is one of India's poorer states, ruled by regional parties that draw their strength from coalitions of different caste and religious groups. Recent chief ministers have been from the lower castes, and the traditional Hindu power hierarchy has been in large part overturned. The mountainous part of UP was turned into a separate state, Uttarakhand in 2000, and there are growing calls for Uttar Pradesh to be further divided.

This is India's Hindi-speaking heartland, part of what is known as the 'cow belt', and though UP may sound less romantic than Rajasthan or Kerala, it is very hard to make sense of India and its history without visiting its most populous state.

HISTORY OF UTTAR PRADESH

Several places in Uttar Pradesh are mentioned in the great Hindu epics the *Ramayana* and *Mahabharata*, and there seems little doubt that these lands, watered by the Ganges and its largest tributary, the Yamuna, have been settled for many thousands of years. Eastern UP, and the neighbouring state of Bihar, were the lands in which the Buddha lived and died five centuries before the Christian era. Two hundred years after the Buddha, Emperor Ashoka converted to Buddhism and created an empire that stretched across most parts of modern-day India, including Uttar Pradesh. Buddhism and various forms of what later came to be known as Hinduism vied for supremacy and popularity for more than a millennium, and, as Buddhism was dying in the country of its birth, a new challenge to traditional beliefs came from Muslim invaders. The first Muslim armies, which came in the 11th century, did not stay. But, by the end of the 12th century, a Muslim sultanate had been installed in Delhi and it controlled large parts of modern Uttar Pradesh. The Delhi Sultanate and later the Mughals remained the major force in the region until the 18th century, which saw the brief rise of the Shia Muslim nawabs of Avadh, based first in Faizabad and then in Lucknow. But by the end of the 18th century, the British were entrenching themselves in northern India, and took full control after the failed Uprising of 1857, during which there was fighting in many parts of UP. In 1902 the British created the administrative area they called the United Provinces of Agra and Oudh, which is largely the same as modern-day UP. At the time of Independence in 1947, the state was able to keep its initials, but changed its name to Uttar Pradesh, with the addition of three of the smaller princely states: Rampur, Varanasi and Tehri Garhwal.

AGRA & SOUTHWEST UTTAR PRADESH

This part of Uttar Pradesh, south of Delhi and close to the border with Rajasthan, contains India's most popular tourist attraction, the Taj Mahal. There is also a large number of other important buildings from the Mughal period, including the deserted royal city of Fatehpur Sikri, as well as the city of Mathura, where the Hindu god Krishna is said to have been born.

NB: For Jhansi, which is part of UP but almost surrounded by the neighbouring state of Madhya Pradesh, see the Madhya Pradesh chapter, p. 444.

AGRA

Agra (*map 5 A1*), a sprawling industrial city on the west bank of the River Yamuna, is home to India's most famous building, the Taj Mahal, constructed in the reign of the Mughal emperor Shah Jahan. Historically, Agra is the Mughal city. There are no significant pre-Mughal buildings, and only minor post-Mughal construction. The city's most important monuments represent the Mughal Empire at its apogee, under those great city-builders Akbar and Shah Jahan. The huge Red Fort, begun by Akbar and completed by Shah Jahan, is in itself a showcase of changing Mughal architecture, highlighting the shift from sandstone to marble as the key building material. But it is the garden tombs of the city—particularly the Taj Mahal, but also Akbar's mausoleum and the tomb of Itimad ud-Daula—that have caused many millions of visitors to draw breath and swear that they have never seen such beauty.

History: The city first became important in the late 15th century, when the rulers of the Lodi Dynasty of north India moved their capital from Delhi to Agra—the first of many such moves. The Lodis were defeated by the first Mughal emperor Babur in 1526

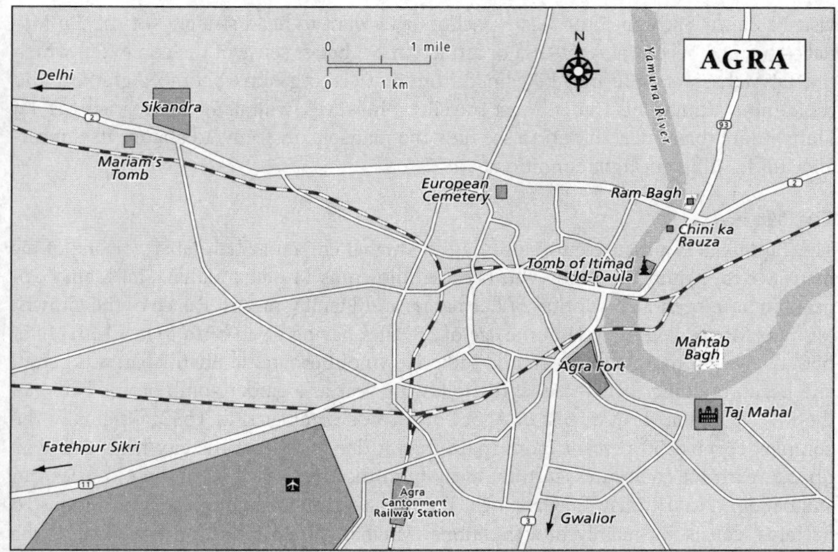

at the Battle of Panipat. Babur disliked Agra and complained about the hot climate and the lack of gardens. In 1530, Babur died in Agra, but his body was returned for burial to his favourite city, Kabul. His son, Humayun, moved the Mughals' Indian capital to Delhi, 180km upstream. It was Humayun's successor, Akbar, who then moved the capital back to Agra, starting the construction of the enormous fort which still dominates the centre of the city. Akbar later moved his capital again to nearby Fatehpur Sikri, and then to Lahore (in modern-day Pakistan), before returning to Agra in 1599. Akbar was eventually buried in Sikandra, on the outskirts of Agra, and his remarkable mausoleum is perhaps the city's most under-rated monument. Akbar's grandson, Shah Jahan, began building the Taj Mahal in 1632 as a memorial to his favourite wife, Mumtaz Mahal, and then spent his final years imprisoned by his own son Aurangzeb in Agra Fort. Thereafter, Agra—described by 17th-century foreign visitors as one of the largest and wealthiest cities in the world—played a diminished political role in the Mughal Empire. The city was overrun and sacked repeatedly in the 18th century, before coming under British control.

Agra is now a polluted, rather dirty city of more than one million people, a large number of whom are dependent on the tourist industry. Many visitors complain about the aggressive selling techniques used by local vendors, and, unfortunately, Agra has a reputation for harassing tourists which is unparalleled in India.

Orientation: Agra is well connected by rail, and many visitors come by train from Delhi. If you're travelling by road from Delhi, it makes sense to visit Sikandra, the site of Akbar's mausoleum, on your way into Agra. If you are coming by road from Jaipur, visit Fatehpur Sikri en route. Many visitors will want to head straight for the Taj Mahal—the most recent of Agra's major attractions. A better sense of the context in which the Taj Mahal was built may be gained from first visiting Akbar's tomb, Agra Fort and the tomb of Itimad ud-Daula. Most travellers, however, will also want to visit the Taj Mahal more than once, in part to see how the mausoleum seems to change its appearance under different light conditions.

Taj Mahal

The Taj Mahal is a mausoleum built by the Mughal emperor Shah Jahan for one of his many wives, Arjumand Bano, who became known as Mumtaz Mahal. 'Taj Mahal' appears to have been a corruption of her name, and literally means 'Palace of the Crown'. Mumtaz Mahal died in 1631 at the age of 38, after having given birth to her 14th child, 650km away from Agra in the central Indian town of Burhanpur. Shah Jahan was bereft, and began building the Taj Mahal the following year as a garden tomb on the banks of the River Yamuna, 1700m east of Agra Fort. It was completed in 1643. Originally, the complex covered 50 percent more space than it does now, but the city has swallowed up the rearmost enclosures, furthest away from the river—several of the old gates can still be found in the busy Taj Ganj area. Today, the rectangular complex covers about 16 hectares, consisting mainly of a traditional Mughal garden leading down towards the river, with the high-domed tomb and its four minarets at its furthest end, set on a plinth overlooking the Yamuna. Unusually for an imperial mausoleum the tomb is not set in the centre of the garden. Either side of the tomb are two other fine buildings, a mosque and a rest-house, which are worth close inspection. The tomb itself is in exceptional condition, despite the efforts of 19th-century graffiti artists, visitors who have gouged out the precious stones and the industrial pollution that Agra has suffered for many years.

The future Edward VII, visiting India in 1875–76, remarked that it was commonplace for every writer 'to set out with the admission that [the Taj Mahal] is indescribable, and then proceed to give some idea of it'. It is certainly even more of a pleasure to visit than to read or write about—and it is just as stunning on one's twentieth visit as on

MUMTAZ MAHAL

We know that Shah Jahan had a close relationship with Mumtaz Mahal, favouring her above his other wives, and openly declaring the strength of his attachment to her. This was unusual but not unprecedented. She came from a very powerful family, where women played an important role. Her aunt Nur Jahan was married to Shah Jahan's father, Emperor Jehangir, and in Jehangir's final years took many key decisions. Mumtaz's grandfather, Itimad ud-Daula, was, under Jehangir, probably the most influential person in the Mughal Empire. He was buried in an exquisite tomb in Agra that in its use of minarets, white marble and the *pietra dura* technique of stone inlay prefigured, on a much smaller scale, the Taj Mahal.

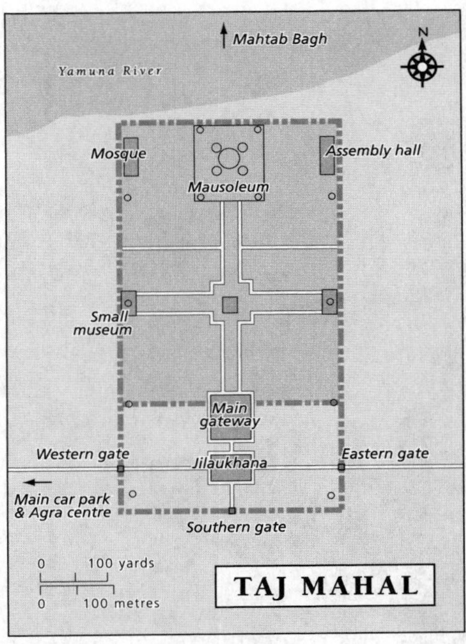

one's first. The Taj Mahal has been admired since it was created, and although it was undoubtedly a memorial to the undying love of Shah Jahan for Mumtaz Mahal, it was also a demonstration of the power, wealth and aesthetic values of the Mughal Empire. In the prescient words of Shah Jahan's court historian, Qazwini, the Taj Mahal would be a masterpiece for ages to come, and provide for 'the amazement of all humanity'. It was built to be visited. As one of its most recent historians, Ebba Koch, explains, the Taj Mahal was constructed 'with posterity in mind: we, the viewers, are part of its concept.'

For the Mughal poet Kalim, the Taj Mahal was a cloud, and for the Nobel Prize-winning polymath Rabindranath Tagore it was 'a teardrop on the cheek of time'. It is also worth remembering, amid the hyperbole, that the Taj Mahal is a building constructed largely out of oven-baked bricks faced with white marble, cut from the quarries of Makrana, 400km away in Rajasthan, and inlaid with precious stones. A British visitor described how it took 20,000 people to build. The name of the architect is not known, but it is certain that it was not originally a Hindu temple, as some guides will tell you. It is also clear that the Taj Mahal was not designed by an Italian called Geronimo, as many 19th-century Europeans believed. In fact there was an Italian called Jeronimo Veroneo who lived in Agra at that the time, but he was a jeweller. There is also no evidence, despite what you may be told, that the architect or the chief builders were maimed, blinded or killed on Shah Jahan's orders so they could never make something so beautiful again.

Orientation and visitor information: There are separate approach roads to the entrances, along which petrol- or diesel-powered vehicles are not allowed. It is possible to walk, but cycle rickshaws are also available, and some hotels arrange electric-powered vehicles for their customers. Be prepared for long queues at the ticket office in the middle of the day. The site is open Sat–Thur 6am–7pm, and closed on Fridays. It is open after dark, normally five days per month, around the New Moon, but not during Ramadan or on Fridays. Night viewing tickets can be bought from the Archaeological Survey of India, Agra Circle, 22 The Mall, Agra, between 10am and 6pm one day in advance. (Details on opening dates are available at asi.nic.in.)

The forecourt and main gate: Visitors enter the Jilaukhana, or forecourt, of the complex from one of the three gates, usually depending on which part of Agra they have just come from. Entry tickets are bought at these gates. The Jilaukhana was where important visitors would dismount from their horses or elephants. It has some low-lying buildings designed for people who worked at the complex, such as attendants, reciters of the Koran and guards. There are some minor tombs flanking the Jilaukhana, and there is inconclusive evidence that these may be the tombs of Shah Jahan's other wives. If sited anywhere else, the main gate would be seen as an object of great beauty. But here, for most visitors, it serves to frame one's first full view of the Taj Mahal, and tends to be ignored. However, the quality of the workmanship and the design is very fine, with a mixture of red sandstone and marble that is similar to the more richly decorated main gate at Akbar's tomb a few kilometres away, but without the minarets. Inside, the inlaid marble and white plasterwork is also of high quality. Note that there is no external dome; instead, the roof has a number of small *chattris* which function as gazebos, and a fringe of small decorative marble cupolas.

The Taj Mahal garden: Having passed through the gate, the full scale and majesty of the Taj Mahal complex becomes visible for the first time. Ahead is the mausoleum itself, with the sky as a backdrop, and, partially obscured by trees, a mosque to the left and a rest-house to the right. The view has barely changed from when the building was completed in the 1640s, though the formal gardens in between have changed a little—at one point the trees had grown so tall that the clear view of the main mausoleum was obstructed. The walled garden is a traditional Mughal *char-bagh*, divided into quarters. Running from the foot of the plinth of the gate to the plinth of the mausoleum is a water channel, in which a reflection of the mausoleum can be seen quite clearly. Midway down the water channel is a marble platform, often crowded with people having their photograph taken against the backdrop of the Taj. This is also the best place to see the layout of the whole complex, and to appreciate the central role that the garden and its water features play in the overall design. To the left and the right, built against the walls of the complex, are sandstone pavilions. The pavilion on the left houses a small museum, and is where the garden's water supply comes from (the waterworks can be inspected later by taking the path down towards the river before the western gate to the Taj complex). On the far left, just before the plinth of the mausoleum, is an unadorned square enclosure, which served as a temporary resting place for the body of Mumtaz Mahal while the Taj was being built.

Ahead is the mausoleum built on a high terrace overlooking the river, with its four tapering minarets, each with an octagonal lookout turret at the top. The minarets are tilted slightly outwards, probably as an optical effect, though visitors are also told that this is to protect the mausoleum from falling debris in case of an earthquake. Minarets were not used by the Mughals on tombs or on mosques until this period, and Shah Jahan's architects seem likely to have been inspired by the minarets on the main gate to Akbar's tomb just outside Agra, or by the glorious garden tomb of Itimad ud-Daula,

The formal gardens and shallow pool draw attention to the focal point, the Taj Mahal itself.

Mumtaz Mahal's grandfather, just 2km upstream from the Taj Mahal. The Taj Mahal's minarets are built around a spiral shaft, which forms a staircase (*no public access*), and are clad in curved blocks of white marble, jointed with black stone used as false mortar. There is also no access to the roof, and therefore some of details of the dome, the ornamental *chattris*, the gold finial and the *guldastas* (pinnacles shaped like a bunch of flowers) can only be seen from a distance. Like most Mughal tombs, it has a double dome, the one on the inside a very different shape and dimension from that on the outside—which was described at the time of building as guava-shaped.

The mausoleum exterior: From above, the main mausoleum is in the shape known as a Baghdad octagon, in which alternate sides are long and short, so that it has the appearance of a square with chamfered corners. On the face of each of the four larger sides of the octagon is a large monumental doorway, or *iwan*, flanked by four smaller *iwans*. The four smaller sides of the octagon each have just two of the smaller *iwans*, one above another. From a distance the building looks symmetrical, though the detail of the coloured inlay, the carved panels representing flowers and the koranic inscriptions all vary.

The mausoleum interior: The entrance to the mausoleum is from the south side—the side facing the gardens. There is a series of inner rooms that encircle the tomb chamber, which is also entered from the south side. The tomb chamber has the form, unlike the exterior of the mausoleum, of a perfect octagon, with each side equal in size (they vary by less than 2cm, in fact). There are two tiers of eight niches on each side of the octagon. Those facing north–south and east–west have full *jali* screens covering the whole area of the niche, and therefore let in more light than those on the diagonal axes, which only have little *jali*-style windows at the bottom of the niche. The cenotaphs (the actual graves are underneath, inaccessible to the public) are surrounded by an intricately-worked octagonal marble screen, inlaid with semi-precious stones in the technique known as *pietra dura*, introduced a short time earlier to India by European craftsmen. In fact this exquisite screen replaced an even more valuable one, made of enamelled gold, that Shah Jahan had originally placed in the tomb chamber. A careful examination of the *pietra dura* work shows that each flower is made up of as many as 100 separate pieces of perfectly joined inlay. The semi-precious stones include lapis lazuli from Afghanistan and jade from Burma.

Mumtaz Mahal's beautifully inlaid cenotaph lies at the centre of the mausoleum on a north–south axis. Squeezed in beside her is the cenotaph of Shah Jahan, an afterthought—as can be seen from the way it disrupts the geometric pattern of the marble flooring. In keeping with tradition, a small raised carving of a pen box on the cenotaph marks it as the tomb of a man. It was widely said, but unproven and most unlikely, that Shah Jahan had begun work on his mausoleum, a replica 'Black Taj', on the other side of the river. Instead, he is keeping his beloved wife company for eternity in a way that strengthens the romantic myth-making that surrounds the story of the Taj Mahal. Shah Jahan spent his last years in captivity, so he would not have had a chance to develop plans for his own mausoleum.

There is one other object in the tomb chamber that was not originally meant to be there: the bronze lamp inlaid with gold and silver, which hangs from the ceiling and was commissioned by the Viceroy Lord Curzon. The original was missing and this one was made in Cairo as a copy of a 14th-century lamp in the tomb of Sultan Baibars II.

The Taj Mahal mosque and assembly hall: Symmetrically placed on separate low sandstone plinths on either side of the mausoleum are a mosque and an assembly hall. The two buildings are identical, except that the mosque has different internal features that relate to its religious function—such as *mihrabs*, or prayer niches, and a separate area with a low screen where Shah Jahan would pray. Both buildings have three bays and three domes; the centre bay and dome larger than the side ones. Here, in deliberate contrast to the mausoleum, the main building material is sandstone, although the domes and the frames to the doorways are made of marble, and marble inlay is widely used elsewhere.

The quality of the internal decoration, although damaged in some places, is very high and represents a different kind of craftsmanship from that seen in the mausoleum. The main technique used on the upper levels of both is known as *sgraffito*, where white plaster is covered with a layer of red plaster and then incised to create the red and white design. On the lower walls there are floral designs in relief carved out of sandstone, which are also very fine, but more corroded than their marble equivalents in the mausoleum. Most of the rather naturalistic flowers depicted in the Taj Mahal complex are not images of real flowers, but thought to be stylised versions of European botanical drawings that had been brought to the Mughal court. Outside the assembly hall, or Mihman-i Khana (literally 'guest house'), is a copy of the outline of the finial from the roof of the Taj Mahal that has been cut into the sandstone. The black stone was inlaid in the 19th century, superimposed on an older representation of the finial.

On either side of both the mosque and the rest-house are two three-storey towers with marbled, domed *chattris*. Two of them also have important non-decorative functions. The one on the garden side of the mosque conceals a *baoli*, or step-well; while the one on the garden side of the rest-house contains a series of latrines. The two towers on the riverside each contained a staircase (now closed off) that led down to the Yamuna River.

Behind the Taj Mahal: By walking behind the Taj, it is possible to inspect the view across the Yamuna to the Mahtab Bagh (the supposed site for the Black Taj; *see below and overleaf*) and northwards up the river towards Agra Fort, from where Shah Jahan could watch the Taj Mahal being built, and where he spent his final years in captivity. Prior to that, Shah Jahan would normally visit the Taj Mahal by boat from Agra Fort.

Mahtab Bagh

Visiting the Mahtab Bagh, or Moonlight Garden (*open daily dawn–dusk; can be visited with the tomb of Itimad ud-Daula and Chini ka Rauza*) on the other side of the river, helps make sense of a key aspect of the aesthetics and design of the Taj Mahal, and importance of water in so much Mughal design. In Shah Jahan's time, the Yamuna was a much broader river, so the full glory of the mausoleum would have been reflected in its waters—as it still is during the monsoon season. Despite the shrinking of the river, there is still a quite magnificent view of the Taj Mahal from Mahtab Bagh.

There appears to have been formal gardens on this site since the time of the first Mughal emperor, Babur—Shah Jahan's great-great-grandfather. Recent excavations have revealed an octagonal pool with a delicate border of cusped arches. The gardens have now been restored, trees and flowers replanted, and it is now possible to see—just as intended—the grand scale of the Taj Mahal as an architectural exercise. Across the river, one notices for the first time the enormous size of the platform on which the mausoleum rests, high above the river. The ornate sandstone and marble wall, with doors and blind arches, is more than 8m high and 300m long. The doors led to rooms where the imperial family could rest and shelter before climbing the stairs to the mausoleum.

Some historians, who have wondered why the Taj Mahal is, unlike other Mughal tombs, at the end rather than the middle of a Mughal garden, have suggested that in fact the river should be seen as the east–west axis of the gardens. They argue that the Taj Mahal and the putative Black Taj—placed symmetrically on either side of the river, and joined by a bridge—would therefore have echoed the Mughal tradition of placing the tombs at the heart of a much larger formal garden.

THE LEGEND OF THE BLACK TAJ

The French traveller Jean-Baptiste Tavernier, visiting Agra shortly after the death of Shah Jahan, appears to be the source of the story that the former emperor had begun building his own mausoleum opposite the Taj, on the other side of the river. The legend grew that this was to be an identical building but constructed out of black rather than white marble—and in some more romantic versions that the two mausolea would be connected by a silver bridge. But there is no other evidence of any of this, apart from Tavernier's account, which is unusual given the amount of other source material about Shah Jahan's later years. Blackened stone was found at Mahtab Bagh, opposite the Taj Mahal, but this was later found to be discoloured, and recent excavations have revealed a formal garden with a large ornate pool where the Black Taj was supposed to stand. We may never know for sure where Shah Jahan wanted to be buried—but just possibly it was where he is in fact buried, next to his favourite wife.

Agra Fort

The Red Fort of Agra was built as a massive fortified citadel overlooking the banks of the Yamuna. It functioned as the headquarters of the Mughal Empire for those periods when Agra was the capital. The fort was constructed by the Mughal emperor Akbar on the site of an older Lodi-period mud-brick fortification, and reputedly contained, at one stage during Akbar's reign, 500 separate buildings, many built out of red sandstone. A European visitor who toured Akbar's fort in 1580 noted down the buildings he saw: 'mansions of his nobleman, the magazines, the treasury, the arsenal, the stables of the cavalry, the shops and huts of drug-sellers, barbers and all manners of common workmen.' Many of the non-imperial buildings were destroyed in colonial times. Additional palaces and courtyards, mainly in white marble, were constructed by Shah Jahan, who lived here with Mumtaz and his other wives. Shah Jahan was imprisoned by his son Aurangzeb in Agra Fort, from where he was able to gaze at the tomb he built for his wife, and in which he, too, would eventually be buried. In the 19th century, the fort was detached from its city hinterland by the building of a railway line and the destruction of the large octagonal courtyard that joined it to the main city mosque. Much of the fort is now occupied by the Indian Army and members of the public cannot enter by what was, in Akbar's time, the main public entrance, the Delhi gate. It remains, however, the most important secular Mughal building in India, and critical to understanding the development of 16th- and 17th-century Indian architecture. Like many other Mughal forts, it originally overlooked the river (a road now separates it from the Yamuna), and the palaces were constructed with a view over the water. The fort is in the shape of a semicircle, ringed by a moat and towering near-perpendicular walls with a circumference of about 2.5km.

Agra Fort orientation: Modern visitors enter by the southern Amar Singh Gate (*open daily dawn–dusk*), which is thought to have been the private entrance used by the imperial family. It is about 1.5km west of the Taj Mahal, back towards the heart of Agra city. The outermost part of the gate is decorated with fine sandstone carving and inlay, and the first courtyard has walls decorated with multi-coloured tiles. From a second courtyard, visitors proceed up a long ramp into the fort precincts. The top of the ramp is a good place to orientate oneself. Behind and to the right are the older palaces built by Akbar and Jehangir in sandstone, as well as a large stone bathing bowl; ahead and to the right are the marble palaces of Shah Jahan, while directly ahead are the half-obscured white domes of the Moti Masjid, or Pearl Mosque.

Jehangir's Hauz: Inside the fort is a bathing bowl, carved out of a single piece of stone and known as Jehangir's Hauz (or water tank). It has steps on the inside and outside, and is said to have been carried around India as part of the imperial convoy. It was dug out of a nearby courtyard in the 19th century. Beyond the bowl, in the nearest corner of the fort, are the remains of the two-storeyed **Akbari Mahal**, or Akbar's Palace. This is the oldest palace in the fort and is similar in design to the better-preserved Jehangiri Mahal, which, despite its name, was built by Akbar.

Jehangiri Mahal: This palace is on the other side of the courtyard from the Akbari Mahal, but the entrance door on this side is normally closed—it may be necessary to head back in the direction of the ramp to enter this masterpiece of 16th-century Mughal architecture. The Jehangiri Mahal consists of two main courtyards, one internal, the other against the fort walls, surrounded by dozens of smaller rooms. The sandstone carvings, particularly of the corbels supporting the roof beams, are of a very high quality. The rooms are all slightly different, with small *jali* screens, niches, and wall and ceiling carvings. The first set of rooms mainly uses the older trabeate (post-and-beam) style of architecture, while the riverside rooms use arches decoratively to support the roof. The entranceway is offset to ensure privacy for the palace inhabitants, and there is a concealed passageway around the internal room at the south side of the palace.

Khas Mahal: The next palace, the Khas Mahal, is very different, though, like the rest of the fort, it was built during the 17th-century reign of Emperor Shah Jahan. Constructed largely out of white marble, the Khas Mahal was built by Shah Jahan as a private palace and is thought to have contained the royal bedrooms. Some guides tell visitors that Shah Jahan lived here with Mumtaz Mahal. He did not: the Khas Mahal was not built until after Mumtaz died. The main pavilion, overlooking the river, housed the private quarters of Shah Jahan. There are two smaller pavilions on either side, with gently curving *bangla*-style roofs. The one on the right is said to have been used by Shah Jahan's favourite daughter and close companion of his later years, Jahanara. The one on his right was the Imperial Viewing Platform, known as the Bangla-i Darshan, where Shah Jahan appeared to the public, who gathered below at the foot of the riverside walls of the fort.

Anguri Bagh: The Khas Mahal overlooks a courtyard known as the Anguri Bagh (or Grape Garden), which is divided into four quarters in the traditional Mughal style. On the south side, visible through the window panes of a locked door, are the wooden doors of the tomb of India's early Muslim invader Mahmud of Ghazni. They ended up in Agra by accident in the 19th century, brought there in the mistaken belief that Mahmud, whose tomb is in Afghanistan, had taken them originally from the great Somnath Temple in Gujarat (*see p. 393*). The rest of the two-storeyed rooms around the Anguri Bagh are thought to have been the *zenana*, or women's quarters.

Musamman Burj: The most beautiful and most poignant of all the living spaces of Agra Fort is the Musamman Burj, or Octagonal Tower (also known as Shah Burj), which is beyond the Bangla-i Darshan pavilion. It was in the Musamman Burj that Shah Jahan spent the final years of his life, a captive in the palace he had built, able to stare down the river at the Taj Mahal, but not allowed to visit it—until his death, when he was entombed next to Mumtaz. Here, the craftsmanship of the fort is at its finest, with superb *pietra dura*, matching the marble inlay of the Taj. Note how the technique is used even on the floral decorations on the pool.

Machhi Bhavan: Beyond the Musamman Burj is another courtyard complex, known as the Machhi Bhavan, or Fish Building, presumably because it once contained a fishpond. In the southeast corner of the courtyard, on a raised platform, is the Diwan-i Khas, the private audience hall, with an enclosed room and a verandah. There are two stone thrones nearby, one carved out of marble, the other from black slate. The black throne has inscriptions that refer to Jehangir as heir apparent, and appear to date from a period when Jehangir had rebelled against his father, Akbar. The throne has a large crack, apparently caused by an overweight monarch from nearby Bharatpur who briefly seized the palace in the 18th century. The northeast corner of the Machhi Bhavan was once occupied by the imperial baths, which were taken apart by the British in the 19th century.

Diwan-i Am: The public counterpart to the Diwan-i Khas, the Diwan-i Am is to be found next to a much larger internal courtyard. Look for the elaborately decorated raised platform built into the covered part of the Diwan-i Am courtyard. This is where the emperor would sit. Behind is the door leading from the Machhi Bhawan.

The rest of the fort: To the north of the courtyard are the shimmering white domes of the Moti Masjid, or Pearl Mosque—currently closed to the public, as is, unfortunately the rest of the Agra Fort, which is occupied by the Indian Army. On leaving, it is worth driving or walking along the river side of the fort. From below one can see the profile of the main palaces, from the Akbar Mahal to the Diwan-i Khas, as they all overlook the river, from high up on the fort walls.

The tomb of Itimad ud-Daula and the Agra riverfront

Seventeenth-century Agra had a series of gardens along both banks of the River Yamuna. Some of these were pleasure parks for picnics and moonlight strolls, some were for army encampments; still others, like the Taj Mahal, were tombs to the great figures of the Mughal Empire, and the tomb of Itimad ud-Daula is one such garden. Itimad ud-Daula migrated from Persia, and became an adviser first to Akbar and then Jehangir. His daughter Nur Jahan married Jehangir, and his son Asaf Khan also became chief minister under Shah Jahan. It was Asaf Khan's daughter, born Arjumand Bano and later known as Mumtaz Mahal, who married Shah Jahan and whose death prompted the building of an even more spectacular tomb than that of her grandfather.

The word exquisite might have been invented for the tomb of Itimad ud-Daula. Much smaller than the Taj Mahal, it nevertheless has many similar qualities. It has four minarets, is set in a formal garden, is largely constructed from white marble, and has a very high quality of marble inlay work. This tomb predates the Taj Mahal by at least a decade (construction began in 1622), and it may have been seen as a chance to experiment with new techniques that would later be used at the larger tomb. Unlike the Taj Mahal, the tomb is at the centre of the formal garden, the *char-bagh*, and has a gently curving roof, the cross-section of which takes the form of a square rather than a circle.

Itimad ud-Daula's mausoleum: The tomb complex (*open dawn–dusk*) has four gates, the east one—through which one enters—two others to the left and right, which are both blind, and a fourth riverside gate, which functions as a pavilion and which has steps that allowed access to and from the Yamuna. The river gate has a fine painted ceiling with images of flowers, leaves and vases.

The tomb itself is built as a square divided into three sets of three rooms. The exterior has very fine marble inlay work and *jali* screens. Look up to see the intricate web-like vaulting inside the entrance doors. The centre room has the tombstones (though these may actually be another lower set of cenotaphs) of Itimad ud-Daula and his wife, and, as in the Taj Mahal, the woman's tomb takes centre place. The main cenotaphs, as at Akbar's tomb in Sikandra, are on the upper level of the tomb, and not accessible to the public. Tombs of members of the family are to be found in the other rooms on the ground floor.

There are several other garden tombs and river gardens that are worth visiting. **Chini ka Rauza**, or the Chinese tomb, has some fine decorated China tiles. The largely forgotten occupant of the tomb is Afzal Khan, a Persian nobleman who, like Itimad ud-Daula, moved to India to serve at the Mughal court. **Ram Bagh** is an interesting pleasure garden on the north side of Agra, built in the early 17th century, probably for Nur Jahan, the wife of Emperor Jehangir. There are small pavilions, which the British extended and used as guest houses.

The European Cemetery

The only significant late Mughal buildings in Agra are to be found, rather unexpectedly, in the European Cemetery. These are the tombs of Walter Reinhardt (d. 1782) and John Hessing (d. 1803), both of them European mercenaries who settled in India. Reinhardt became a rich landowner, but, because of his demeanour, was known as 'Sombre', this being Indianised to 'Samru'. His wife, Begum Samru—an Indian dancing girl before they married—inherited his estates and became an important political and social figure in early 19th-century India, and had palaces in Delhi and Sardhana (*see p. 228*). Reinhardt's octagonal tomb has a large bulbous dome and some fine external carving. Hessing, a Dutch soldier, helped the Maratha forces of Daulat Rao Scindia take Agra at the end of the 18th century, and was the commandant of Agra Fort when he died in 1803. His unmistakable tomb looks like a tiny red sandstone version of the Taj Mahal.

SIKANDRA

The mausoleum of the Mughal emperor Akbar is a little outside Agra, 10km northwest of the Red Fort, back towards Delhi in an area called Sikandra which is thought to have been important in Lodi times, and was probably named after Sikander Lodi, the second ruler of the dynasty. The tomb complex itself is captivating, not only because of the fine quality of the architecture, but also because of the serenity of the gardens. The crowds have not really discovered the tomb of the greatest of the Mughal emperors, and most visitors are more likely to have large numbers of deer, monkeys and peacocks for company rather than humans.

Akbar himself is thought to have chosen the site for his tomb. When he died in 1605, architects began the construction of a tomb, which his son and heir Jehangir so disliked that he had it pulled down. The new tomb, unlike the most famous Mughal mausolea in India, the Taj Mahal and Humayun's Tomb in Delhi, has no dome. The cenotaph on the upper level (*no public access*) is therefore open to the skies, in symbolic accordance with some conservative Islamic teachings that oppose burial in covered buildings.

Orientation: Sikandra is in the western suburbs of Agra, and is close to the main road to Delhi, 12km from the Taj Mahal. The tomb complex (*open daily dawn–dusk*) is approached from the south. It is marked on the map on p. 207.

Sikandra main gate: The main gate is both an architectural breakthrough and an aesthetic curiosity. Perched, slightly incongruously, on the superbly decorated sandstone gate are four white minarets, rather than the usual *chattris*, or small pavilions. It seems certain that the architects of the Taj Mahal were influenced by the minarets at Akbar's tomb, but they positioned the minarets on the plinth of Mumtaz's tomb rather than on the gate. The external and internal decoration on the gate is superb, with a mixture of floral and geometric patterns, and sandstone inlaid with coloured stones.

Sikandra mausoleum: As the visitor passes through the gate, the actual mausoleum becomes visible for the first time: a five-storey building, with the bottom four storeys largely made of sandstone and the top level, on which the cenotaph was placed, in marble. Unfortunately, the public are not allowed to visit the upper storeys. However, the tomb itself can be visited, by entering the tall ornate gateway, or *pishtaq*, of the mausoleum building, passing through a richly decorated vestibule, before descending a ramp into the tomb chamber. The chamber and the tomb are unadorned and dark, a skylight providing the only natural lighting. This room was once richly decorated, but despoiled in the 18th century, and later whitewashed. To either side of the vestibule entrance are smaller rooms with other tombs. An arcade of chambers runs around the whole building. A European who visited Sikandra in the 1640s described these chambers as being home to the 200 reciters of the Koran who stayed within the precincts of the tomb.

The mausoleum is set at the centre of a traditional Mughal *char-bagh*, with four equal parts divided by water channels. The other three massive gateways to the complex are false, with small real gates next to them. These gateways, particularly the one to the west (or left of the main gateway), are very impressive. They were designed as pavilions and guest houses, and the decorations on the squinches and upper walls are of the highest quality. Look for the sandstone panel on the east gate, with elephants and peacocks. Also near the east gate is an interesting *baoli*, or step-well, and an overgrown compound with a memorial to soldiers of the 42nd Royal Highlanders who died in an unexplained incident in 1864.

Outside the tomb complex is a small building known as the **Kanch Mahal**, or Glass Palace, which was probably a gateway to a nearby tomb. It has some fine coloured tiles (but no glass) and decoration on the side facing the mausoleum.

Mariam's Tomb

About 700m along the main road away from Agra, on the other side of the street is another unusual building, Mariam's Tomb (*open daily; map p. 207*). Mariam us-Zamani, or 'Mary of our times', was one of Akbar's wives, and the mother of Jehangir. Despite what guides may say, she was neither a Christian nor a European. Mariam, the Mary of the Bible and mother of Jesus, is also a deeply revered figured in Islam. The tomb is thought to be an extension of a pre-existing Lodi garden pavilion. Like Akbar's tomb, there is no dome, and the cenotaph is on the roof terrace. But Mariam's Tomb is a single-storey building, with strange oversize octagonal and rectangular roof *chattris*.

There are a number of other minor Mughal ruins along the road that separates the tombs of the husband and wife, Akbar and Mariam.

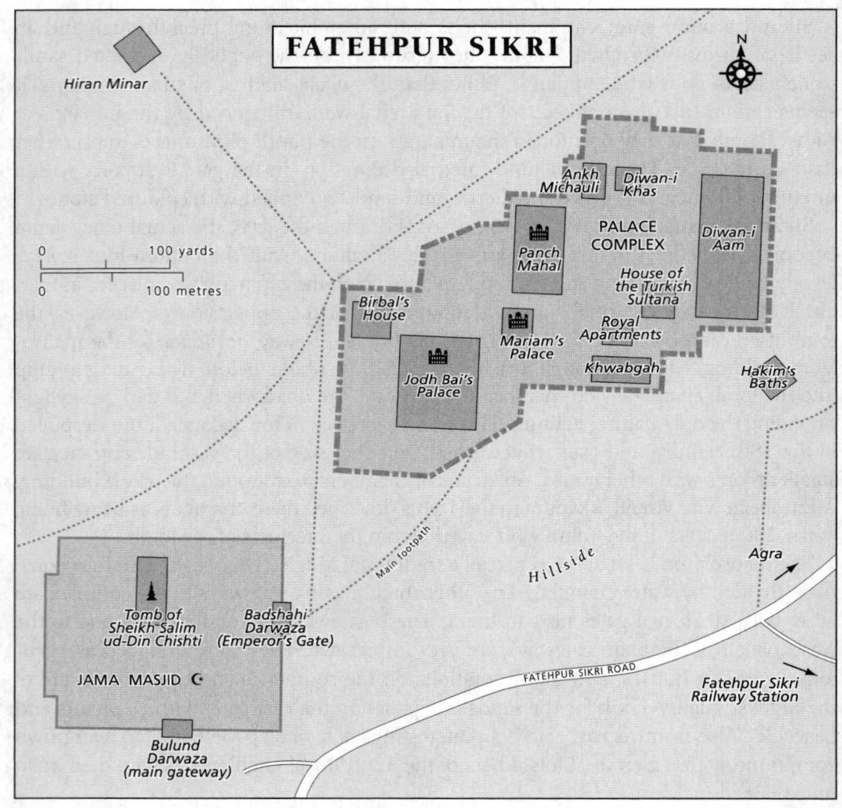

FATEHPUR SIKRI

More myths surround the extraordinary city of Fatehpur Sikri (*map 5 A1*) than any other Mughal capital. We do know that it was built by Emperor Akbar in the 1570s, and was deserted by him in 1585, for reasons that may never be entirely clear. Most of the important buildings have survived, and are largely intact. Indeed the condition of many of the buildings is so good that one feels Akbar might have just moved out. However, the purpose of many of the buildings in the royal complex is unclear, and, partly for this reason, tourist guides tell unsubstantiated stories of special mirrors used for signalling to lovers, of secret tunnels and of naked slave-girls used as the pieces of an enormous board-game.

Some of the names of the smaller palaces were invented in the 19th century, and are clearly misleading. Strictly speaking, it is also misleading to call Fatehpur Sikri a deserted city. For, although the palace was deserted, the spectacular mosque and its shrines remained an important place of pilgrimage; and the rest of the city, though smaller in population than in Akbar's time, has continued to exist without interruption since the 16th century. Fatehpur Sikri's location on the road from Agra to the great Sufi shrine at Ajmer meant that the city continued to be visited in the later Mughal period; just as today it is one of the main attractions in the Delhi-Agra-Jaipur tourist triangle.

History: Fatehpur Sikri existed long before Akbar's time, though it was then known as just Sikri. Akbar's grandfather Babur, the first Mughal emperor, visited Sikri and ordered the construction of a garden there. Later Akbar visited a Sufi holy man called Sheikh Salim ud-Din Chishti who was living in Sikri. Chishti predicted the birth of Akbar's long-awaited son and heir, and Akbar's wife, Mariam, remained in Sikri under Chishti's protection during her pregnancy. With the birth of the son, who would later become Emperor Jehangir, Akbar announced his decision to build a new city in Sikri. He prefixed the word Fatehpur, meaning 'city of victory', to the name of Sikri to celebrate the recent success of his military campaign in Gujarat.

At Fatehpur Sikri, Akbar held his famous discussions between clerics of many different faiths (*see p. 67*) in a building known as the Ibadat-khana, which has not been identified. The Mughal court did not remain at Fatehpur Sikri, however, for not long after completing the city, Akbar moved the imperial capital to Lahore—almost certainly because of the growing strategic importance to the Mughal Empire of their territories in what are now Pakistan and Afghanistan.

Tourist guides will often tell visitors that Akbar deserted the city because it ran out of water. This does not appear to be true, and the present-day village is supplied by the cisterns and wells installed during the time of Akbar's rule. The palace was not totally deserted either: Jehangir moved his court here for three months when Agra was struck by plague, and Emperor Muhammad Shah visited Sikri at the time of his coronation in 1709.

Orientation: Fatehpur Sikri (*open dawn–dusk*) is 38km west of Agra, and just inside the Uttar Pradesh border with Rajasthan. Most travellers visit Fatehpur Sikri from Agra, often en route to Jaipur, but the nearest big town is Bharatpur in Rajasthan, just 12km away. If you want to explore Fatehpur Sikri properly, the nearest good hotels are in Bharatpur.

The site is laid out on a low ridge running from the southwest (where the religious buildings are found) to the northeast (where the palace buildings were constructed). The necessity of the mosque facing westwards towards Mecca dictated the layout of the main building of the complex—and explains why the palace area takes the form of a series of courtyards and rectangular palaces that are off-set. To the south and west is the modern town of Sikri, with some interesting Mughal ruins; to the north is a dry reservoir that held the city's water supply. The city can be approached from either the palace side, on the east, or from the mosque side, to the southwest. This guide begins with the mosque's massive entrance gateway.

Bulund Darwaza

Entering Fatehpur Sikri via the main mosque provides visitors with the unforgettable spectacle of the enormous main gateway known as the Bulund Darwaza (Magnificent Gate) looming 50m over the road below. The steps leading up to the gate are very steep, and add to the intimidating sensation provided by the high gateway and the mosque walls. The gateway was in fact rebuilt after the Gujarat victory, and the original was smaller. Some architectural historians argue that its sheer size destroys the balance with the rest of the mosque. It is also out of alignment—as with several buildings in Fatehpur Sikri—with the key feature within the mosque, the shrine of Salim ud-Din Chishti. However, both in scale and in detail, the gateway is a very impressive building, and one that deserves close inspection. The inside of the arch carries the Arabic language inscription, 'Jesus, Son of Mary (on whom be peace) said: The World is a Bridge, pass over it, but build no houses upon it. He who hopes for a day, may hope for eternity; but the World endures but an hour. Spend it in prayer, for the rest is unseen.' The precise origin of the quotation is not clear, but it does not belong to the mainstream Christian tradition and is not in the Koran. It may be one of the sayings of Jesus, widely disseminated by Muslim holy men, for whom Jesus is a major prophet. It also clearly echoes the saying of the 11th-century Spanish theologian Petrus Alphonsi, a former Jew who grew up in Muslim Andalucia; he said, 'This world is, as it were, a bridge. Therefore, pass over it, only do not lodge there.'

Jama Masjid

The main mosque was for several centuries the largest in India (in the 19th century Bhopal's even larger Taj-ul Masajid was constructed), and its courtyard contains the marble Chishti shrine, as well as dozens of minor tombs. A covered gallery runs round the entire courtyard, with subtle variations in the architecture, using a mixture of arches, beams and corbelling to support the roof. The prayer hall has a large white dome, partly hidden by a tall gateway through which the faithful come to pray. The interior is richly decorated, particularly near the central *mihrab*. Note also how the prayer hall is divided up into smaller sections, with those at the end intended for women. There are also some unusual corbelled squinches that transform a square first-floor chamber into an octagon which supports a dome. The domed ceiling is then decorated with bands that radiate from the centre.

Tomb of Sheikh Salim ud-Din Chishti

This mausoleum was originally built in sandstone and reconstructed, in Jehangir's reign, in white marble. The marble *jali* screens are particularly fine, with some of the highest quality marble *jali*-work to be found anywhere in India. The Chishti tomb is still a place of pilgrimage, and attracts not only Muslims, but also people of other religions, particularly women who have difficulty conceiving. The larger red sandstone mausoleum is thought to contain the tomb of Chishti's grandson Nawab Islam Khan and other members of his family.

Fatehpur Sikri palace complex

Orientation: Visitors can reach the palace complex through the eastern gate of the mosque, known as the Badshahi Darwaza, or Emperor's Gate. From the ticket office, there are two routes: the most obvious way is to turn north directly into the heart of the residential quarters of the palace; but the second way, across an open area to the west, is marginally preferable, because it gives an opportunity to first explore the official government part of the palace.

Diwan-i Aam: By the taking the second route, heading west from the ticket office, visitors will enter the Diwan-i Aam, or public audience area, a large courtyard surrounded by a pillared verandah. This was where members of the public could meet, or at least see, the emperor, who would sit in the throne enclosure on the west side of the courtyard. The next courtyard contains a number of important buildings, some of which have disputed names and functions. The buildings include two of the finest specimens of early Mughal architecture: the Diwan-i Khas, and the Turkish Sultana's House.

The Diwan-i Khas: The building officially described as the Diwan-i Khas (literally, 'place of private audience') is a mysterious square sandstone building with a most unexpected interior. A finely decorated single column rises from the centre of the floor and supports four diagonal balustraded walkways that connect with the corners of the building. Note that at the floor level the column is square; it then becomes octagonal, then sixteen-sided, and finally circular. The capital of the column has 36 carved brackets, and the overall effect is breathtaking. With its bizarre walkways, the purpose of this room is far from clear, and there are no similar pieces of architecture found anywhere else. Among the theories that have been put forward are: that this was a treasury, which Akbar could inspect from above; that this was the discussion room for people of different religions, described by contemporary European visitors to Fatehpur Sikri; and that this was a religious building, full of symbolism that has not yet been fully decoded. It seems likely, though, that it did not function as a Diwan-i Khas, and that a neighbouring building, now named the Ankh Michauli, served this purpose.

Ankh Michauli: Guides will tell visitors that the Ankh Michauli is where Akbar would play hide-and-seek and blind man's bluff with women from the harem. Unfortunately, there is no evidence to support this charming tale—and the layout, with a central area for Akbar and two side rooms, suggests the Ankh Michauli was actually where the emperor would meet his ministers.

The northern part of the courtyard has squares marked out in the shape of a cross for the ancient game of *pachisi*, in which, according to tradition but not attributable to any contemporary sources, slave-girls were used as board pieces. In the middle of the courtyard are two buildings with incomplete colonnades that do not align. On the west side is a building known, for no clear reason, as the Girls School, which was probably used for storing water for the emperor and his family.

House of the Turkish Sultana: This small building on the eastern side of the centre of the courtyard has some exceptional sandstone carvings. The patterns on the exterior are largely floral, arboreal and geometric; inside are jungle scenes, with wild animals whose faces have been deliberately damaged, possibly under the more puritanical rule of Emperor Aurangzeb. Again the purpose of the room is not clear: Akbar did not have a Turkish wife, and the superb quality of the decoration suggests that this was a pavilion used by Akbar when visiting the nearby pool, known as the Anup Tulao.

Khwabgah: On the far side of the Anup Tulao is another strange construction, known as the Khwabgah (bedchamber), and this probably did serve as Akbar's private quarters. The front of the building and the mezzanine floor appear to have been a later additions, and there is currently no access to Akbar's bedroom. The lower half of the building may have been used as a library. Access for Akbar's wives and concubines would have been from the harem area via the covered passageway.

Panch Mahal: To the west of the courtyard is the part of the palace where the women of the imperial household would have lived: the *zenana*. However, the limits of the *zenana* are not clear, and the largest and most distinctive building in this area of the palace, the Panch Mahal, is probably too open to public gaze to have been used by Akbar's wives and concubines. The Panch Mahal is a palace with five (or *panch*) floors, each level smaller than the one below—from a distance, the building looks like a pyramid.

Jodh Bai's Palace: To the south of the Panch Mahal is an impressive building with a large courtyard, known as Jodh Bai's Palace, flanked by two smaller structures known as Mariam's Palace and Birbal's House. All of these names are misleading: Jodh Bai was the wife of Jehangir, not Akbar; and, although Birbal was one of Akbar's closest advisers, he would never have been allowed to stay in the women's quarters. It is possible that Akbar's mother—who, like one of his wives, was called Mariam—lived in the palace that now bears her name, but there is no evidence to suggest that she did so.

Jodh Bai's Palace is a typical example of *zenana* architecture, with a plain exterior, an ornate interior, off-set doorways to ensure privacy, screened walkways to allow its female occupants to see outside and full facilities for the women who lived within. Note the blue-glazed tiles on the ceiling, and the raised corridor leading northwards that may once have allowed the women of the *zenana* to visit the lake. The other two buildings are also worth visiting: **Mariam's Palace** for its painted interior, and **Birbal's House** for its asymmetric design, its wide eaves and its fine decorative carving.

Other buildings in Fatehpur Sikri

There are more than 30 other buildings in and around Fatehpur Sikri that are of architectural, aesthetic or historical interest—some of them in a state of advanced decay. Any visitor with the time to explore the city more would be advised to visit **Hakim's Baths** to the south of the Diwan-i Aam and the bizarre **Hiran Minar**, a 21m tower studded with fake elephant's tusks to the northwest of the palace complex.

BETWEEN DELHI & AGRA

The area between Delhi and Agra has a number of interesting historical sites that are seldom visited by foreign tourists and which are easy to access from either city.

MATHURA

The historically and religiously important city of Mathura (*map 5 A1*) sits on the eastern side of the Grand Trunk Road from Delhi to Agra, and was once more important than both of these more famous places. For Hindus, Mathura is a major pilgrimage centre because it is the birthplace of Krishna. In the 1st–3rd centuries it became one of the capitals of the Kushan Dynasty, which dominated north India. A famous headless statue of Kanishka, the greatest Kushan leader, is part of the superb collection at the Mathura Museum—one of numerous examples of what has become known as Mathura sculpture. Apart from the museum there is little to see from the Kushan period, but there are some interesting buildings from more recent times, as well as the waterfront overlooking the River Yamuna with innumerable temples, rest-houses and bathing *ghats*.

Mathura Museum

This museum (*open Tues–Sun 10.30–4.30*) is one of the most important in India and home to the superb headless King Kanishka (2nd century), with his sword, club and thick boots. Note also the extremely fine standing broad-shouldered carving of the Maitreya, the future Buddha, yet to come. The statue is in fine condition, its halo intact, and it is one of the earliest surviving images of a *bodhisattva*. There is also a broad range of red sandstone carved figures, friezes and architectural fragments from the Kushan and Gupta periods, including Jain, Buddhist, Hindu and secular pieces. The carved heads with pointed caps are thought to signify royal status. The collection of Gandhara art found locally is a testament to artistic traditions shared with an empire more than 800km away to the northwest.

Krishna Janambhoomi

The Krishna Janambhoomi, or Krishna's birthplace, is marked by a busy temple complex in the southern part of Mathura. Visitors are welcomed to the temple, which is modern but on part of the site of an older temple, destroyed in the 17th century, and which is said to mark the place where Krishna was born. Next to it is a large, attractive square pool known as the Potara Kund, where Krishna's baby clothes are said to have been washed; it was rebuilt by the maharaja of Gwalior in 1850.

Katra Masjid

On the north side of the temple is a three-domed mosque, known as the Katra Masjid (1669), built during the reign of the Mughal emperor Aurangzeb, after the destruction of the Kesava Deo Temple that stood on the site. Some Hindu activists have demanded the destruction of the mosque, and for this reason there is a heavy security presence.

The mosque can only be accessed from the east, by going round the entire complex to the main road running through Mathura, from where a footpath leads up to the mosque (no electronic items are allowed to be taken in). Note the use of sandstone slabs on the side walls of the mosque.

Other buildings in Mathura

About 1km to the east of the Krishna Janambhoomi, inside the old city, is the **Jama Masjid** (1661–64), raised above the crowded city streets, with four 40m high minarets and some pretty external decoration. The riverfront has the ruins of a 16th-century fort, the **Kans Qila**, which used to house the Mathura Jantar Mantar, one of five observatories set up by the maharaja of Jaipur in the 18th century. The British sold it off for scrap in the 1850s. The other four, in Jaipur, Delhi, Varanasi and Ujjain, all survive. Further south is the **Sati Burj**, a tall red sandstone tower, said to be a memorial to a Jaipur maharani who committed *sati* after the death of her husband. Along the riverfront are dozens of small shrines, and rest-houses often set up by princely families. Note the strange early 20th-century statues of a dwarflike Edward VII and Queen Alexandra outside Laskak Cottage, a rest-house for Kashmiri Hindus.

Mathura Cantonment

Five kilometres southeast of central Mathura, in the Cantonment area (turn left off the road to Agra), are two interesting 19th-century churches and a European cemetery. The Anglican **Christchurch** (1856), which served as the garrison church of what the British knew as Muttra, has a fine Italianate tower. Note the slots in the pews where soldiers rested their rifles while at prayer. The nearby Roman Catholic **Church of the Sacred Heart** (1870) was designed as a deliberate exercise in combining Eastern and Western styles of architecture, with a Mughal turret on the roof over the door and a Russian-style dome. Steps inside the unfinished minaret-like towers lead onto the roof. The nearby cemetery has an impressive variety of funerary architecture.

Vrindavan

The town of Vrindavan (*map 5 A1*, sometimes Brindavan), 10km north of Mathura, is also closely associated with Krishna. It is the site of the forest where the god, as a young cowherd, is said to have sported with the *gopis*, or cowgirls, and stolen their clothes—the subject of many Hindu miniature paintings. Historically, large numbers of widowed Hindu women, often abandoned by their families, have come to live here. This tradition lives on, with many women dressed in the white sari of the Hindu widow living on the streets or in hostels in the town. Mathura is the most important centre of the International Society for Krishna Consciousness—better known as the Hare Krishnas. It also has several striking late 16th-century Hindu temples, all dedicated to Krishna, built during the reign of the Mughal emperor Akbar. The red sandstone **Govindadeva Temple** (1590), dedicated to Krishna, has no external figurative carvings, but has very sharply moulded motifs and horizontal lines. The tower of the temple was destroyed in the late 17th century, during the reign of Akbar's less tolerant great-grandson Aurangzeb. The **Jagat Kishore Temple** (16th century), close to the river, has an unusual conical tower that makes the building look like a church, while the **Madan Mohan Temple**, on the west side of town, is built to a similar design.

Around Mathura and Vrindavan

Around Mathura and Vrindavan are several other locations connected with the story of Krishna, many of which have provided key images in Indian art. These include the hill of **Govardhan**, 21km to the west of Mathura, which the god is said to have lifted above his head to provide shelter to villagers and their animals from a great storm. About 20km southwest of Mathura is **Sonkh**, with the excavated ruins of one of India's oldest surviving Hindu shrines, a horseshoe-shaped temple dating from the 1st–3rd centuries. The village of **Mahaban**, 8km southeast of Mathura, has an old pillared hall, often referred to as Nanda's Palace, the home of Krishna's foster-father; it has served as both a mosque and a temple. (*All on map 5 A1.*)

ALIGARH

The city of Aligarh (*map 2 C3*, originally called Koil), 115km southeast of Delhi, is best known for the **Aligarh Muslim University** (AMU) founded in 1875 as the Mohammadan Anglo-Oriental College—in imitation of an unspecified Cambridge college, with handsome Victorian buildings and pretty gardens. To the northeast is the large moated **fortress**, after which the city was renamed in the early 19th century (Aligarh means High Fort). The fort dates back to the Lodi period, but much of the current building was constructed by French engineers working for the Marathas in the early 19th century. The triple-bayed **Jama Masjid** (1266–67) in the village of Jalali, 15km east of Aligarh, is one of India's oldest mosques, constructed during the reign of the Delhi sultan Balban. The two outer domes are 20th-century additions.

NORTHWEST UTTAR PRADESH: BETWEEN DELHI & THE HILLS

The plains of northwest Uttar Pradesh, between Delhi and the Himalayan foothills of the recently-formed state of Uttarakhand, have no major tourist sites. However, many travellers heading for the hills or Jim Corbett National Park pass through this region—and there some interesting towns and buildings to visit.

MEERUT

This large industrial city (*map 2 C2*), 65km northeast of Delhi, is best known as the place where some of the first major events in the 1857 Uprising took place. Soldiers mutinied against their British officers and headed towards Delhi. The mutiny took place while the British were attending evening service at **St John's Church** (1821), a fine Neoclassical building on the north side of the city. Some 200m north of the church is the fascinating **British Cemetery**, with a huge variety of funerary architecture, including cupolas, pyramids and obelisks. Among the tombs is that of the US-born British general David Ochterlony, who died here in 1825, and whose memorial column is one of Kolkata's best-known monuments (*see p. 545*).

SARDHANA

This town (*map 2 C2*), 20km northwest of Meerut, has an unusual European-style **palace** (1834) now a college, and the remarkable Roman Catholic Basilica of **Our Lady of Graces** (1822), a huge building designed by an Italian architect as a fusion of Mughal and Baroque architectural styles. They were built in the reign of Begum Samru of Sardhana, the Indian widow of a European adventurer and mercenary, Walter Reinhardt, known as 'Sombre' because of his gloomy disposition, an epithet which then was mispronounced as Samru. The Mughal emperor granted Reinhardt land in Sardhana, and he set himself up as a minor prince. There is also the **Begum's Old Palace**, now a seminary (between the church and the new palace), and a **European cemetery**, with several Mughal-style mausolea, near the bus stand.

KUCHESAR, UNCHAGAON & SAMBHAL

The well-travelled road to the Corbett National Park and the Kumaon Hills in the state of Uttarakhand passes close to several interesting places in Western Uttar Pradesh. Two minor fortresses—the 18th-century **Kuchesar Mud Fort**, 60km east of Delhi, and the 19th-century **Fort Unchagaon** (*map 2 C3*), 110km east of Delhi—have both been converted into hotels, while the town of **Sambhal** (*map 2 C3*), 130km east of the capital, has an attractive mosque which is one of the oldest Mughal buildings in the country. It was built, like the other surviving mosque from this period (in Panipat, Haryana), by the first of the Mughal emperors, Babur.

RAMPUR

The town of Rampur (*map 2 D2*, 180km east of Delhi, is the capital of the former princely state of the same name. There are several interesting royal buildings in Rampur, which was ruled from 1774 to 1947 by ethnically-Pashtun Shia Muslim nawabs, who originally came from the area close to the Afghanistan-Pakistan border—and who were known as Rohillas. Many Rohillas settled in this part of UP, which is often referred to as Rohilkand. Rampur's **old walled fort** is in the centre of town, and inside the **Hamid Mahal** (1905), a superb example of Indo-Saracenic palace architecture at its most exuberant, is the **Rampur Raza Library** (*open Sat–Thur 10–5*) with a collection of mainly Islamic manuscripts, many of them finely illustrated, as well as some miniature paintings. The new palace, built in the early 20th century, is in Khas Bagh, on the southern outskirts of Rampur.

BADAUN

The city of Badaun (*map 2 D3*, or Budaun), 200km east of Delhi, was an important centre during the early years of the Delhi Sultanate, and has one India's oldest mosques. The **Jama Masjid** (1222–24), on the west side of the city, was built to a similar design to the great Sultanate mosques in Delhi and Ajmer, but, following a fire, was much altered during the early Mughal period.

THE ROAD FROM DELHI TO HARDWAR

On the roads to the pilgrimage towns of Hardwar and Rishikesh, and the Uttarakhand capital, Dehra Dun, travellers pass through, or close to, some interesting places.

Deoband

The small town of Deoband (*map 2 C2*), midway between Muzaffarnagar and Saharanpur, 130km north of Delhi, gave birth to the conservative Deobandi school of Islam, seen by some as the inspiration for the Taleban movement. The **Dar-ul Uloom**, or House of Learning, founded in 1867, remains an important seminary, and conservatively-dressed visitors are free to wander around the main courtyard of the 19th-century Mughal-style building. The enormous 20th-century **Rashid Masjid** can accommodate 20,000 worshippers and is one of India's most impressive modern mosques.

Saharanpur

This town (*map 2 C2*), 62km southeast of Dehra Dun, was an important centre in the Mughal period, but little is left to be seen. There are the remains of the 18th-century **Ahmadabadi Fort** in the Nawabganj area (take the lane opposite the Vijay Talkies cinemas), into which modern dwellings and workshops have been built. There is also one of the country's earliest botanical gardens, started by the British in 1817, on the site of an older pleasure garden, and still known as **Company Bagh** (Company, after the East India Company, and Bagh meaning garden).

CENTRAL UTTAR PRADESH

LUCKNOW

Lucknow (*map 5 C1*) has been one of India's most important cities since 1775, when it became the capital of the kingdom of Avadh (or Oudh) and its famously pleasure-loving Muslim rulers, the nawabs. Today Lucknow has more than two million inhabitants and is the sprawling capital of India's most populous state, Uttar Pradesh. It nevertheless retains a genteel, civilised air, enhanced by its distinctive collection of 18th- and 19th-century buildings scattered across the city. Historians and architects have been deeply divided in their assessment of the almost Rococo architectural style

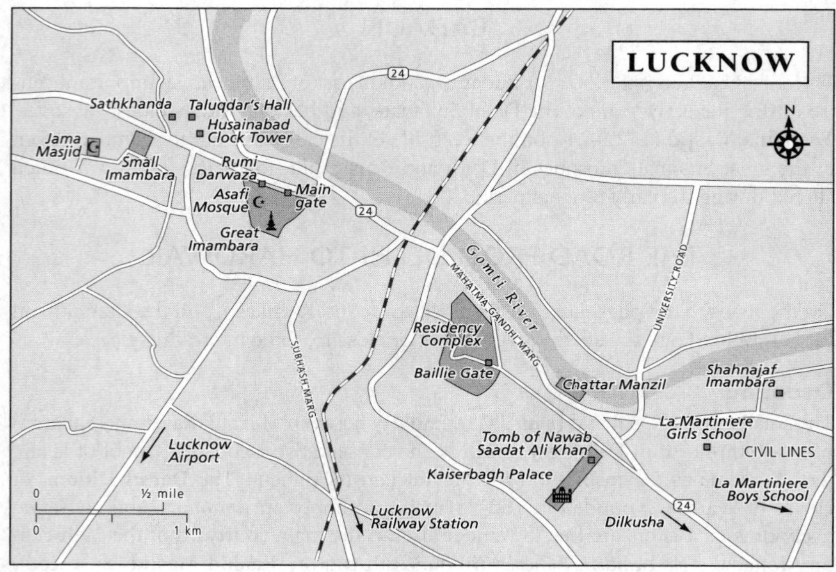

of Lucknow under the Shia Muslim nawabs. In the aftermath of the 1857 Uprising, in which several key events took place in Lucknow, it became commonplace to dismiss the city's architecture as decadent and hybrid. Today, there is a growing recognition of 'Nawabi' style as distinctive and refreshing, an important and fascinating fusion of different architectural and decorative traditions.

History: Until 1775, Lucknow was a medium-sized outpost of the weakening Mughal Empire. Since the early 18th century, it had been ruled by the nawabs of Avadh, from their capital Faizabad, 120km to the east. And, for a large part of the 18th century, the nawabs were as powerful as their titular overlords, the Mughal emperors. The nawabs themselves were relative newcomers—the first nawab, Saadat Khan, was a Persian nobleman who came to India in 1707, to serve the Mughals and to make his fortune. He did both successfully and his nephew, Safdarjung, whose famous tomb is in Delhi, became the *de facto* ruler of the Mughal empire. His son and heir Shuja ud-Daula was defeated by the British at the Battle of Buxar in 1764, but with British support was allowed to stay in power. The next nawab, Asaf ud-Daula, moved the capital to Lucknow, and the city saw a major spurt in the construction of palaces, public buildings and, most spectacularly, the Great Imambara—the most impressive of all Nawabi places of worship. Unlike Mughal architecture, which made great use of sandstone and marble, the main construction materials for the nawabs were bricks and stucco plaster. Most Nawabi buildings also have fish motifs placed over archways and other key architectural features.

Lucknow gradually replaced Mughal Delhi as the home of north Indian Muslim culture, attracting poets and artists, courtesans and master chefs. It became a place of legendary ostentation, where Europeans would seek, and often make, their fortunes. The most famous of the Europeans, a former French mercenary called Claude Martin, became the unofficial architectural adviser to Asaf ud-Daula, and was directly responsible for the unusual building that is now occupied by a school named after him, La Martiniere. The last nawab, Wajid Ali Shah, was exiled in 1856 by the British, who accused of him of maladministration and debauchery. A year later, the Uprising (known to the British as the Mutiny) reached Lucknow. The Residency, home to many of the British inhabitants of the city, was besieged for more than four months, and today is probably the most evocative of all the sites in India associated with the 1857 Uprising. After the Uprising, many important buildings in Lucknow were demolished, including large parts of all four city palaces. Lucknow played a diminished role in the politics of north India, with the growing importance of Allahabad as an administrative centre, and Kanpur as the commercial hub of what became the United Provinces (and later Uttar Pradesh). In 1920, Lucknow replaced Allahabad as the capital of United Provinces, and began to re-emerge as the major city of the region.

Orientation: Lucknow's major buildings—from the Small Imambara in the far west to La Martiniere in the southeast—all stand close to the southern bank of the Gomti, a navigable tributary of the Ganges. Many visitors start from the west, with major religious buildings—the Great and the Small Imambara—and what is left of the early Nawabi palaces. Heading east, one next can visit the ruins of the Residency, some of the other palaces and tombs of the nawabs, and then a scattering of other buildings, including some of the remaining private homes of Lucknow's richer inhabitants during the time of the nawabs.

The Great (or Bara) Imambara complex

This enormous religious complex is the earliest surviving major Nawabi building in Lucknow, dating from the 1780s. It was constructed partly as a means to give paid work to the poor at a time of famine. The actual *imambara* building is a Shia Muslim congregational hall, used at times of major religious festivals such as Muharram. The complex consists of two large courtyards: a square outer one, and the main courtyard, two sides of which are taken up by the *imambara* and the Asafi Mosque.

Outside the complex: Opposite the entrance to the outer courtyard, on the other side of the road, is a false northern gateway, which serves no purpose but symmetry. One hundred metres to the west is the fabulously ornate Rumi Darwaza (*see overleaf*), which was intended as the ceremonial entrance to the *imambara* complex. Originally, this area was once a long, rectangular walled court, but the missing gate, on the eastern side, was destroyed in 1857. Also demolished were Lucknow's oldest fortifications and palaces, known as the Machhi Bhavan (or Fish Palace), to the east of the Great Imambara.

The outer and inner gates: The outer gate of the Great Imambara has three entrances, each with a scalloped outer arch with Nawabi fish symbols, and a smaller inner arch, with a little canopied balcony, or *jharoka*. The roof of the gate itself has the ornate parapets and other decorative features that distinguish much Nawabi architecture. The ticket office to the complex is hidden away on the inner wall of the entrance gate. The large square outer courtyard, with its circular lawn, has an ornate inner gate leading towards the *imambara*. This gate also has three entrances topped by the fish emblem. Note the four mini-balconies that sit over the broad columns, which themselves contain small rooms.

The main courtyard: Pass through the inner gate into the main courtyard, and, unusually for a grand Muslim monument, you'll see an obviously unsymmetrical layout of the two major buildings, the mosque and *imambara*, both raised up on plinths accessed by steep steps. Straight ahead is the *imambara*, and to the right, at an angle to the rest of complex, is the triple-domed Asafi Mosque (*no entry for non-Muslims*) set on a high plinth. It is set at this strange angle to the rest of the courtyard in order for it to face Mecca—though it has never been fully explained why the whole complex was not therefore aligned in the same way. Part of the reason is that the *imambara* had to be fitted into an irregularly-shaped piece of land between the now demolished Machhi Bhavan Palace, on the east (the step-well attached to the *imambara* and some old walls are all that survive), and a small ravine with a stream that still exists, on the west.

The Great Imambara: Unless a special religious ceremony is underway, the Great Imambara is open to all visitors. The building, constructed out of brick and stucco, is divided into nine chambers. The cavernous central chamber has what was said to be, at the time of its construction, the largest unsupported concrete roof in the world. Set in the floor of this chamber is the simple sheet-covered tomb (aligned with Mecca, not the building) of Asaf ud-Daula (d. 1797), the nawab who commissioned the complex. For much of the year this building is relatively quiet, but it comes alive during the month of *Muharram*, when Shia Muslims mourn the martyrdom of Imam Hussain, the grandson of the Prophet Muhammad, killed at the Battle of Karbala in 680. The more valuable *tazias*, or portable shrines representing the grave of Hussein, which are carried through the streets, are kept here. On the second floor of the *imambara* is a maze of passageways entered from the east side of the building. Couples have to take a guide with them, a regulation introduced to stop them canoodling in the maze.

It is possible to walk around the back of the *imambara*, by heading through the pretty cusped archway with a sloping roof on the west side of the building. Note the 18th-century waste channels running down the side of the *imambara*, as well as the stream that runs beside the complex, which partly dictated the alignment of the buildings.

Rumi Darwaza

This single gateway near the Bara Imambara is a spectacular piece of early Nawabi architecture, and is probably the one building that is most closely associated with Lucknow. It was intended as a copy of the gateway known as the Sublime Porte in Istanbul, but bears little similarity, and the Lucknow building is far more ornate. This unique gate viewed from the west (i.e. the exterior entrance) consists of half of a domed building, cut vertically, and encrusted with extravagant decorative features and strange trumpet-like protuberances. 'Rumi' literally means 'Roman', but in Persian (the language of the Nawabi courts) this came to mean the Eastern Roman Empire which survived the fall of Rome, and the name was then transferred to its successor empire, ruled by the Ottomans.

Chota Imambara (Small Imambara)

The Chota Imambara, also known as the Husainabad Imambara, (after the Husainabad area of Lucknow) is 1km to the west of the Bara Imambara—on the northern side of the road connecting the two *imambaras* are the remains of another palace complex, the Daulat Khana (*see below*). Built more than 50 years later, in 1837, it shows much greater European influence, and has come to symbolise late Nawabi architecture. It has a fairy-tale quality and style, particularly when it is illuminated at night, that is immediately recognisable as early kitsch—but it is all the more interesting, even entertaining, for that reason.

The Chota Imambara has a walled rectangular outer enclosure, with a road that runs through it. The main gate is four-tiered and with a pitched gable, like a Portuguese church. Pass through the gate into the main *imambara* compound, 90m wide and 120m long. A long water pool, with a footbridge, bisects the compound and leads one's eye to the single-domed *imambara* at the far end. On either side are two almost identical buildings, deliberate miniature pastiches of the Taj Mahal. The one on the left is the tomb of the mother of Nawab Muhammad Ali Shah (not his daughter, as some guides insist). The actual *imambara*, has the nawab's own tomb. Note near the gateway two golden statues of women wearing rather skimpy dresses—unexpected images in an Islamic complex; and a winged golden fish, the emblem of the nawabs, on the trelliswork just before the pool starts. There is also a small mosque on the right of the complex (*no access to non-Muslims*).

The exterior of the *imambara* itself is covered in Arabic calligraphy, some of it in the form of pictograms; look for a leaf, on the front of the building, and what could be a bald-headed man on the upper level of the front side of the right wing of the building. The decoration on the roof is particularly ornate. Inside the *imambara*, as well as the nawab's grave, is a collection of 19th-century glassware, chandeliers, fancy lights, mirrors, lamps and a silver throne.

Near the *imambaras*

To the west of the Chota Imambara is the **Jama Masjid**, a large mosque also built in the reign of Muhammad Ali Shah. It was incomplete at the time of his death in 1842. The design of the *iwan*, or main doorway of the mosque, resembles the Rumi Darwaza.

To the east of the Chota Imambara on the north (river) side of the road are the remains of the **Daulat Khana Palace** complex, begun at the end of the 18th century and largely destroyed by the British after the 1857 Uprising. On the west side of the small lake, in dire need of restoration, is the unusual circular ziggurat-like building known as the **Sathkhanda** (or Seven-storey Tower), of which only four storeys were ever built, and from which Nawab Muhammad Ali Shah had intended to survey his domain. On the north side is the **Taluqdar's Hall**, built in 1840, which houses a collection of portraits of the nawabs, painted after the fall of the kingdom of Avadh. It contains a famous portrait of the last nawab, bearing his left nipple. From this building, pensions are still distributed to hundreds of surviving relatives of the last nawab. On the east side of the lake is the fine **Husainabad Clock Tower**, completed by the British in 1887, and said to be the tallest in India.

The Residency

This complex of ruined buildings (*open daily dawn–dusk*), set in a well-maintained park, is one of the eeriest memorials of British rule in India. The buildings have been left as they were after the failed 1857 Uprising, during which the British community in Lucknow (and some Indians) were besieged for 148 days.

Originally the term Residency referred just to the largest building, now housing a museum, where the Resident, the representative of the British East India Company, lived, built on flat Lucknow's highest hillock. But it came to mean the heart of the British part of the city, and specifically the area that was besieged during the Uprising. The complex, frozen in time, is a testament to the British obsession with military history, particularly glorious failures, and most Victorian schoolboys would have learnt the names of every building involved in the Siege of Lucknow.

Entrance area: The complex is entered through the Baillie Gate, built in the early 19th century as a guardhouse, at the start of the road up to the main Residency building. The forces of the first relief of Lucknow entered the compound here. Beyond the gate are the remains of houses on either side of the road. On the right are two memorials, both of them to the 'native officers and sepoys' who fought on the British side during the siege.

The approach to the Residency: The first building on the right is the **Treasury**, used during 1857 for making rifle cartridges. Immediately behind it is the **Banqueting Hall**, a large two-storeyed building that also served as the Council Chamber for the East Indian Company representatives. During the siege, it functioned as both a prison, for captive members of the Avadh and Mughal royal families, and as a hospital. Note the old British-style fireplaces, and the pretty inlaid marble fountain. On the other side of the road is the building known as **Dr Fayrer's House**, after the Residency's surgeon at the time of the siege. This large building has deep basements, known as *tykhanas*, designed for the hot weather, in which the women and children sheltered during the siege. A wall-plaque marks the place where Sir Henry Lawrence, the commander of the British forces, died. Note the remnants of yellow paint, and ornate plasterwork at the back of the house.

The Residency: The actual Residency, after which the whole complex would become known, is a late 18th-century three-storey building, constructed on the summit of a low hill, much added to in the 19th century, and reduced to a shell during the siege of 1857. A plaque in one room (next to hole in the wall) refers to 'Susanna Palmer—killed in this room by a cannon ball on the 1st July 1857, in her nineteenth year.' The underground *tykhanas* were places of shelter. The ruins of the Residency building now contain a small **museum** which tells the story of the siege of Lucknow.

THE SIEGE OF LUCKNOW

The siege began on 30th June 1857, with almost 3,000 people trapped inside the complex, many of them civilians. The civilian leader of the British, Sir Henry Lawrence (best remembered in India today for the two leading private schools named after him) was killed on the fifth day of the siege. When the first relief of the Residency took place in September, only 979 people were still alive. The relieving force, under General Havelock, was also trapped inside the complex, and the siege was not finally lifted until 17th November 1857.

Other buildings in the complex: Beyond the Residency building are the remains of **St Mary's Church** and the cemetery where unburied bodies were left during the siege. On the southern side of the complex is a series of other buildings, of which the **Begum Kothi** is the most interesting. It was given to the family of Emma Walters, the British wife of the eighth nawab, Nasir ud-Din Haider. The Begum Kothi compound includes an intact ornate arch, complete with Nawabi fish emblems, a small *imambara*, and a mosque which is still in use. It is the least ruined building in the Residency complex, and has the finest decoration.

Chattar Manzil

Northeast of the Residency is the palatial Central Drugs Research Institute (*no public access*) which actually was a Nawabi palace, first known as Farhad Baksh Palace, and now popularly known as the Chattar Manzil (or 'Palace of Umbrellas').

Kaiserbagh Palace

To the east of the Residency are the remains of Lucknow's most recent palace complex, the Kaiserbagh, which was completed in 1852. Kaiserbagh (the 'Kaiser' portion is taken from the name Caesar, like Czar, and the 'bagh' part means garden) was the last home of the last nawab, Wajid Ali Shah. It was built as an enormous palace complex—and was quickly derided by European architects and historians who judged it to be a tasteless and gigantic failure. Most of the buildings were demolished by the British, and it is only recently—through an examination of some of India's earliest photographs, in the form of panoramas of major Lucknow sites—that there has been a serious and more positive reassessment.

Some much altered buildings do survive, including the central two-storeyed former *imambara*, and it is possible to see traces of the best of Kaiserbagh on two of its surviving gates. The eastern gate is decorated with stucco and painted fish, and two angels carrying a crown, their legs twisted like rope. It has a quadrant arch, mimicking the summit of La Martiniere (*see overleaf*). The western gate has mermaids as well as angels and fish. These are the most recent surviving creations of the Nawabi architects.

Nawabi tombs

Integrated into the side of the Kaiserbagh complex, but standing in their own park in the heart of Lucknow, are two slightly older, impressive Nawabi tombs, both domed and built in the 1810s. The tomb of Nawab Saadat Ali Khan is more squat and square, with verandahs on each side, while the tomb of his wife, Khurshid Zadi, is narrower, with side towers that support tall handsome *chattris*, or pavilions, on the first floor.

Civil Lines

To the east of Kaiserbagh is the busy market area of Lucknow known as Hazratganj, and beyond that is the old Civil Lines, with a large number of interesting 19th-century buildings. These include the castle-like La Martiniere Girls' School (formerly the Khurshid Manzil), built in 1810 for Nawab Saadat Ali Khan by a British engineer. Also worth visiting is the pretty, green-domed Shahnajaf Imambara, built in the 1820s; it contains the tomb of Nawab Ghazi ud-Din Haider and three of his wives.

La Martiniere

The other important buildings of the Nawabi period in Lucknow are to the southeast, beyond the post-1857 British government buildings. The most remarkable of them is Constantia, now La Martiniere Boys' School, built on what was a lake next to the River Gomti. It was the home, and became the tomb, of Claude Martin, the French adventurer who played such an important role in Lucknow during the early Nawabi period. Because it is a functioning school, it doesn't encourage uninvited visitors (though they are usually allowed in). It is best to ring first (*T: 0522 2235415*), and anyone genuinely interested in the architecture of the period will be welcomed.

The five-storey building was begun in 1796, and is of a deliberately hybrid style. Its square central tower is topped by a quadrant arch, and is surrounded by statues of Greco-Roman goddesses and shepherdesses, some of them mounted on Indian-style *chattris*. There were also statues on the topmost level, but they were damaged in an earthquake and removed. Note the large heraldic lions that peer over the roof of the first floor, with niches intended for flaming torches. The interior of the college is in good condition, with some fine stucco plasterwork and particularly impressive ceilings in the chapel and the upstairs room.

The tomb of Martin is in the basement, and was badly damaged in the 1857 Uprising, when rebel soldiers took control of the building. The wings of the building are later additions, as is the tall tower opposite the building, which previously stood like a lighthouse in the middle of a lake. The embankment was built to prevent repeated flooding of the site. The steps leading up to the building are inscribed with the names of hundreds of La Martiniere old boys.

Behind La Martiniere is a small 1857 Uprising graveyard, as well as the mausoleum of one of Martin's favourite mistresses, seven of whom (three of them sisters) were provided for in his will. Two long-standing servants were also beneficiaries, and their descendants continue to work at the college.

Dilkusha

This fascinating but derelict European-style building (c. 1800) is situated beyond La Martiniere, in the Cantonment area. Dilkusha (which can be translated as 'heart's delight') was designed as a hunting lodge and country seat for Nawab Saadat Ali Khan by an amateur British architect and professional soldier called Major Gore Ousely. The building was based on Seaton Delaval, an English country house in Northumberland that was designed by Sir John Vanbrugh in the early 18th century.

Dilkusha's damaged condition allows visitors to see how Nawabi buildings were constructed; note, for instance, how the columns are made of curved bricks covered with carefully shaped plaster.

Bibiapur Kothi

Further into the Cantonment area, beyond the military dairy farm, is an even older European-style building (1780s), the Bibiapur Kothi, built during the reign of Nawab Asaf ud-Daula, and used as the temporary residence of new British Residents prior to receiving accreditation at the royal court. The roof has caved in, and the building is empty, but the fine two-storey façade is largely intact—in what was one of north India's earliest European-style buildings.

FAIZABAD

The city of Faizabad (*map 5 C1*) was once the capital of Avadh, close to the ancient Hindu temple town of Ayodhya. It contains two little-visited tombs deserving of wider attention, and an interesting riverside temple.

The mausoleum of Bahu Begum

Completed in 1816, this is an enormous multi-storeyed domed tomb, containing the grave of Bahu Begum, the widow of the third nawab of Avadh, Shuja ud-Daula. Bahu Begum, an affectionate name bestowed on Amat uz-Zahra by her husband's father, Safdarjang—who was for many years the *de facto* ruler of the Mughal Empire—literally means 'Princess Daughter-in-law'. She outlived her husband by 40 years, dying in her 80s in 1815. She had remained in Faizabad when her son, Asaf ud-Daula, moved the capital of Avadh to Lucknow. Bahu Begum became an important political figure and was fabulously rich in her own right. Alleged attempts by the then British governor-general in India, Warren Hastings, to extort money from her (and others) led to his impeachment on charges of corruption. He was eventually acquitted after a lengthy trial lasting some eight years.

The first entrance gate, aligned with the side of the tomb, brings the visitor into an outer courtyard, with galleries that have been turned into homes. The main gate, with its huge wooden doors, has pretty balconies and Nawabi fish emblems. Inside, one gets one's first partial view of the tomb, truncated by the tall palm trees that line the central path. The Mausoleum of Begum Bahu is loosely based on the Taj Mahal style of tomb design, with a larger lower plinth, and a square domed structure resting on it, but with two terraces, and a dome that looks as if it has been stretched upwards by an unseen hand.

The interior plasterwork is superb, and it is worth paying the small unofficial entrance 'fee' you may be asked for to gain access. Unusually, there are three internal domes on top of each other to give the mausoleum its great height. The space between the lowest and middle dome has particularly impressive painted plasterwork on the ceiling. There are large plinths at the corner of the structure, as if minarets were part of the original plan. Most of the garden is overgrown or used for agriculture, though it appears to have been intended as a Mughal-style *char-bagh*, with four quarters. It is frustratingly difficult to get a clear view of the whole tomb. The best views are those from the outer walls, which can be accessed via some stairs on the northwest corner of the complex.

Two kilometres northeast of the Mausoleum of Begum Bahu is the slightly smaller and earlier **Gulab Bari** (1775), the final resting place of the third nawab, Shuja ud-Daula, husband of Begum Bahu. It is a more compact mausoleum, has recently had some conservation work, and the carefully laid-out garden, with its four groups of parallel pools, is well maintained. The compound contains a mosque and an *imambara*.

The Cantonment area and Guptar Ghat

In the Cantonment area to the west of the city is a British-era **church**, which has been converted into a shopping mall for soldiers. The nave is an electronic goods shop, general groceries are sold from the transept, the apse is a tailor's shop and there is a small restaurant on the left of the aisle.

Guptar Ghat: Also worth visiting in Faizabad (to the north of the Cantonment area) is the riverside Guptar Ghat, where the Hindu god Rama is believed to have left the world of mortals. The site, on the banks of the River Saryu, is marked by an early 19th-century temple. The façade is asymmetrical, suggesting that the eastern wing was demolished at some stage. A passage with a painted ceiling runs through the west wing. Inside is a sanctuary with idols of Rama, and his wife Sita and brother Lakshman on either side. Note the stone carved images of Hanuman, Ganesha and other gods inset into the exterior wall of the inner sanctum. There is an interesting fort-like temple a little further up the river, as well as two stone-carved notices from the early 20th century declaring that shooting, fishing and the washing of dirty clothes is forbidden at Guptar Ghat.

AYODHYA

The town of Ayodhya (*map 5 C1*), sitting on the south bank of the River Saryu, just to the east of Faizabad, has played a major role in Indian ancient and modern history. Ayodhya is, according to Hindu scripture and tradition, where the god Rama was born. It is an attractive temple town, with hundreds of places of worship, and draws many pilgrims, but very few tourists. The crumbling 18th- and 19th-century buildings along its riverfront are particularly attractive (note the forgotten ruins of an old mosque), and perfect for a stroll at dawn or dusk.

The birthplace of Rama and the ruins of the Babri Masjid: The precise location of Rama's birthplace is the cause of a centuries-old controversy which led to a major political crisis and several thousand deaths in the early 1990s. In the 16th century, during the brief reign of the first Mughal emperor, Babur, a mosque was constructed in Ayodhya. According to some Hindus, an ancient temple that they say marked Rama's birthplace (or Ram Janambhoomi) stood on the same site previously and was destroyed to make way for the mosque. In 1992, Hindu extremists tore down the mosque, known as the Babri Masjid, with their bare hands and with crowbars, and placed idols of Rama and other gods on top of the ruins. More than 2,000 people, mainly Muslim, were killed in the riots that followed. It is possible to visit the site, which must be one of the most heavily defended places in all India. (NB: No electronic items are allowed in, and it is necessary to hand over a passport or other form of official identification. Visitors and devotees then queue in a snaking, caged corridor that eventually takes them close to the idols, in a makeshift temple, resting on the ruins of the mosque.)

BAHRAICH

This large town (*map 5 C1*), 105km northeast of Lucknow, near the Nepal border, was attacked by Mahmud of Ghazni in the 11th century, during one of the first Muslim invasions of India. His nephew (and son-in-law) Salar Masud died here in battle in 1033, and was buried in a grave just north of the town. This is the oldest identifiable Muslim grave site in northern India, although there are no extant buildings from the 11th century. The site is now the attractive Sufi **Dargah of Salar Masud**, an important place of pilgrimage for Muslims, and for people of other religions who come here to pray for good health, or the birth of a child. Note how devotees have nailed coins (some of them very old) to the door frame of the main tomb area, a practice believed to bring good luck. The *dargah* complex is an interesting place to wander round, with a mixture of buildings from the 14th century onwards. On the left side as you approach the *dargah*, there is an immaculate little **mosque** from the Nawabi period, with pretty bulbous domes, housing what is said to be a footprint and handprint of the Prophet Muhammad. The town also has a fine **clock tower** from the British period, with interesting Indian design features.

SRAVASTI

Some 2,500 years ago, Sravasti (*map 5 C1*), now overgrown and deserted, was, according to some estimates, the most populous city in the world. It was also the site of the Jethavana Monastery, where the Buddha delivered many sermons and is said to have walked on air. The city was deserted in the 12th century, but its 5km mud-and-brick walls are clearly visible amidst farmland and undergrowth. Parts of the city and the monastery area, just outside the old city walls, have been excavated, and a visit to the peaceful ruins of Sravasti makes an interesting day trip from Lucknow, 135km to the southwest. The site mainly attracts Buddhist visitors from East Asia and Sri Lanka.

The road into Sravasti brings visitors first to the **Jethavana Monastery** complex, in the area known as Seth, where dozens of buildings, including the monks' living quarters, and several temples have been excavated. The surviving walls are largely knee-high and undecorated, but they do give a sense of the layout of the complex where the Buddha is believed to have lived and preached during each rainy season for 24 years. Further along the road, through a gap in the ancient walls of Sravasti, is a later **Jain temple**—the most complete building in the area, with a domed canopy. Further inside the city walls, in an area known as Maheth, are two large excavated **stupas**, near to the old course of the river. A huge modern golden Buddha sits in a nearby park, dominating the horizon. A little further along the road towards Balrampur, on the right hand side of the road, is another stupa, of which only the very top has been excavated. The portion on top is worth visiting, to see the layout of the chambers, which had false wall columns as decoration, as well as a proper drainage system.

KANPUR

The large industrial city of Kanpur (*map 5 B2*) was known by the British as Cawnpore—as well as 'the Manchester of the East'. It lies 73km southwest of Lucknow on the river Ganges. It is best remembered for the Siege of Kanpur during the 1857 Uprising, in which many British residents of the city were killed. The red-brick **All Souls Memorial Church** (1862–76) in the southeast of city was erected on the site of the besieged British positions, and around the church are other memorials relating to the Uprising. The **Satichaura Ghat** on the river, where many of the British were killed while attempting to flee, is 1.25km north of the church next to a small Shiva temple. The other important site from 1857, the Bibighar, where dozen of bodies were thrown down a well, is now **Nana Rao Park**, named after one of the princely leaders of the Uprising—who is, in fact, better known as Nana Sahib. The village of **Bithur**, 17km north of Kanpur, was Nana Sahib's ancestral home. His palace was destroyed by the British after the Uprising, but the main *ghat* on the Ganges has an interesting Islamic arcade which is used as a temple.

KALPI

The town of Kalpi (*map 5 B2*), 70km southwest of Kanpur on the Yamuna, has the very fine medieval **Chaurasi Gumbad**, a Lodi-period tomb, the name of which means, literally, '84 domes'; there are, however, 'only' 45. The ruins of Kalpi's **old fort** are near the river.

BHITARGAON TEMPLE

This temple, 30km south of Kanpur in the village of Bhitargaon (*map 5 B2*), has one of the earliest examples of a Hindu shrine built from brick rather than stone, and which is covered with terracotta panels. The temple is thought to date from the 5th-century Gupta period. It is not clear who the temple was dedicated to, and there are images of both Shiva and Vishnu on the exterior panels.

KANNAUJ

One hundred kilometres west of Lucknow and close to the Ganges, Kannauj (*map 5 B1*) was the capital city of a series of Buddhist and Hindu empires between the middle and end of the first millennium. But almost nothing has survived from this period, apart from the foundation of excavated buildings on the east side of the modern town. Several of the major princely families of Rajasthan trace their origins to Kannauj. There is a fine **Jama Masjid** (Friday Mosque) from the 15th-century Sharqi Dynasty, which ruled Jaunpur (*see p. 250*), and several interesting sandstone tombs, including the impressive **Mausoleum of Sheikh Makhdum Jahaniya** (1470) and twin **17th-century tombs** of Baba Pir and his son Sheikh Mahdi.

EASTERN UTTAR PRADESH

VARANASI

Varanasi (*map 5 D2*, also called Benares, pop. 1,500,000) is both India's foremost Hindu pilgrimage town and a major destination for Western tourists seeking to find out more about Hinduism—and often about themselves. The city's modern identity has been largely built around these two groups of visitors. But Varanasi is also an important regional centre, and a major producer of saris.

For visitors, pilgrims or tourists, life pivots around the river and the famous *ghats*, or riverside landing places, that rise above the Ganges. Pilgrims come here to purify themselves, to atone for past sins by bathing in the river and by visiting the temple-homes of the gods. Others come here to die, or to cremate their loved ones—in public view along the Ganges. Tourists come here to traipse between the temples, wander along the *ghats*, take boat trips along the river, steep themselves in Hindu culture; some will stay here longer and learn about Indian music and dance, study ancient Hindu philosophy and religion, or learn Hindi and Sanskrit. Apart from the innumerable temples and *ghats*, Varanasi's other attractions include the Buddhist ruins at nearby Sarnath, the palace at Ramnagar, some interesting mosques and two of India's most important museums.

Geography and History: Varanasi sits on a bend in the Ganges, hugging its eastern bank for more than 5km, between the Varuna and Assi streams, the names of which when conjoined gave the city its current official moniker, according to the most popular theory. It was previously known as Kashi (the old Sanskrit name) and as Benares (a British corruption of Varanasi), and all three names are still in use today.

The city is built on higher land than the nearby plains, and the many stone staircases leading down to the river are often very steep. During the monsoon, the river rises dramatically, and anyone walking along the *ghats* will notice how carefully high flood marks have been recorded on buildings, and how temples and other low-lying buildings have sometimes been submerged beneath the swollen Ganges.

SHIVA IN VARANASI

Though many other gods and goddesses are worshipped here, Varanasi is the city of Lord Shiva for most Hindus. He is said to have left his mountainous retreat when he broke his vow of chastity to marry Parvati. Varanasi became his marital home, and the wild ascetic Shiva became a city-dweller. It was to Varanasi that he brought the goddess Ganga, the Ganges, down to earth—bearing her down in the matted locks of his hair. There are thousands of temples to Shiva in Varanasi, in a number of different guises: as Vishwanath (the Lord of the World), as Pashupati (the Lord of Creatures) and as Kala Bhairava (sometimes translated as the 'Black Terror'). Though there are many statues of Shiva, it is his lingam, or stylised phallus, that is almost always the main object of worship.

Varanasi is famous for being old, and the Mark Twain quote that it is 'older than legend' is a favourite phrase of many city guides. It is indeed very old, with evidence of continuous habitation for many thousands of years. However, the buildings are, by Indian standards, relatively young, and Varanasi as it is seen by modern visitors, is largely an 18th-century creation. Many of the Hindu idols and carvings do date back to earlier periods, though the oldest archaeological remains in the area are Buddhist and the best Hindu art can be seen, not in temples, but in the Varanasi Museum.

The older temples have all been demolished, largely by Muslim invaders, who first reached Varanasi in the late 12th century. Some Muslim rulers, such as the Mughal emperor Akbar, were less destructive, and indeed commissioned the building of new temples. But Akbar's great-grandson Aurangzeb had more temples destroyed in the late 17th century, and the city was largely built anew after that. Many of India's great princely families, as well as the city's own maharaja, played a large part in the rebuilding; and several *ghats* and pilgrim rest-houses still the bear the names of their royal sponsors. The British, in a smaller way, also contributed, creating what is still the administrative centre of the city, with some fine colonial-period architecture. The city also has a number of important mosques and has, to this day, a large Muslim population.

Orientation: The *ghats* stretch from Assi Ghat in the south (where the best riverside accommodation can be found) to Rajghat in the north. At Assi, the *ghats* are less steep, and vehicles can access the river front. Elsewhere it is necessary to walk to the *ghats*. The easiest part of the central part of the riverside area to reach is Dasashwamedh Ghat, which is the major bathing *ghat*, to which thousands of pilgrims come each day. Elsewhere it is necessary to find one's way, with the help of locals, through the narrow alleyways, known as *galis*—home to many more temples and occasional mosques. Small boats can be taken along the river from most of the *ghats*—and are particularly recommended at dawn and dusk.

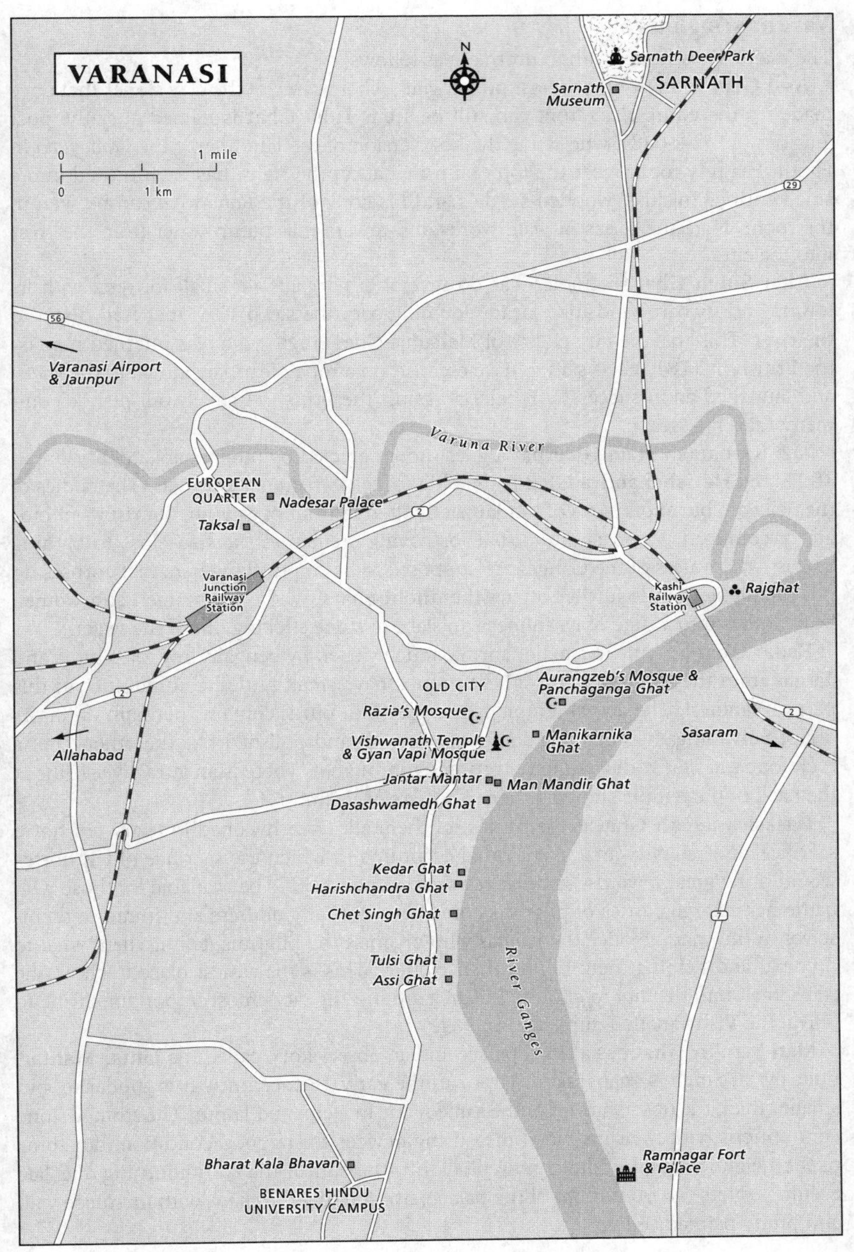
VARANASI
N
0
1 mile
0
1 km
Sarnath Deer Park
Sarnath Museum
SARNATH
29
56
Varanasi Airport & Jaunpur
Varuna River
EUROPEAN QUARTER
Nadesar Palace
2
Taksal
Varanasi Junction Railway Station
Kashi Railway Station
Rajghat
2
Aurangzeb's Mosque & Panchaganga Ghat
OLD CITY
Razia's Mosque
Allahabad
Vishwanath Temple & Gyan Vapi Mosque
Manikarnika Ghat
2
Sasaram
Jantar Mantar
Man Mandir Ghat
Dasashwamedh Ghat
Kedar Ghat
Harishchandra Ghat
Chet Singh Ghat
7
Tulsi Ghat
Assi Ghat
River Ganges
Bharat Kala Bhavan
Ramnagar Fort & Palace
BENARES HINDU UNIVERSITY CAMPUS

Varanasi's *ghats*

The major *ghats* from south to north are as follows:

Assi Ghat is the southernmost proper *ghat*, where some of the clay slopes that once made up the entire river front can still be seen. **Tulsi Ghat** is named after the poet Tulsidas (1532–1623), who wrote the first version of the Hindu epic the *Ramayana* in Hindi. His tiny room, near the top of Tulsi Ghat on the right, has been turned into a small shrine. Tulsidas' wooden sandals and his copy of the *Ramayana* can be seen in the room. Note the series of waterworks and towers that pump water from the river into the city.

Chet Singh Ghat resembles—as do several other *ghats*—a small fortress, with its towers and its bare sandstone façade looming over the steep steps that lead down to the river. This was the city palace of Maharaja Chet Singh, who was interned here by the British in 1781. He is said to have escaped on a rope of turbans down to the *ghats*, and launched an unsuccessful rebellion against the British. A small wall-plaque commemorates his escape.

The **Karnataka State Ghat** has a guest house erected by the maharaja of Mysore in 1904, and **Harishchandra Ghat** is the older of the two cremation *ghats*. The bodies of the dead are burnt on pyres of sandalwood, often in front of gawping tourists—photos are discouraged. Varanasi is unusual for having cremation *ghats* so close to bathing places—the waters of the Ganges are supposed to be so purifying here that corpses do not pollute it. A little further on are the **dhobi ghats**, where washermen and women beat clothes into a state of cleanliness on slabs of stone sticking out of the water.

Kedar Ghat is home to a major shrine, much visited by Bengalis from east India and Tamils from the south—both of these groups have small settled communities in this part of Varanasi. The actual temple is not very old, but it contains perhaps Varanasi's oldest Shiva lingam, since this one is not smooth and polished like the others, but a rock found *in situ*, with a white vein running through it. There is an attractive shrine at the back of the temple showing the ten avatars of Vishnu.

Dasashwamedh Ghat is the busiest of them all. Dasashwamedh means 'ten horse sacrifice' and refers to an ancient ritual according to which the sacrifice of ten horses would bring great rewards—similar rewards are now said to be available for those who bathe here. Large parties of pilgrims come here, partially undress and immerse themselves in the water. Notice the *pandas* who organise the pilgrims, telling them what to do next, and helping them to find their clothes. This is the easiest place to climb the steps back into the city to explore the area around the city's most important shrine to Shiva, the Vishwanath Temple (*see opposite*).

Man Mandir Ghat has a small palace and an observatory, called the **Jantar Mantar**, built by Jai Singh, a maharaja of Jaipur in the early 18th century. It is similar to, but smaller than, the observatories of the same name in Delhi and Jaipur. The strange stone contraptions with their inscribed measuring devices are in good condition, but some of the neighbouring buildings now block out the sun in the early morning and late evenings. Note the front room of the palace, overlooking the *ghats*, with its stucco wall and pretty painted ceiling.

Beyond the observatory is the second and largest of the cremation *ghats*: **Manikarnika Ghat**, which is also a bathing *ghat* and the terminus of a popular pilgrimage route known as the Panchatirtha—though many pilgrims prefer to bathe in the large tank, built high up above the cremation area. There are also several important temples on the *ghat*, including one that slipped down the side of the hill, and came to rest, slightly tilted, at the water's edge.

Panchaganga Ghat is dominated by a mosque, built by the last of the great Mughal emperors, Aurangzeb. He destroyed a Vishnu temple, which the 17th-century French traveller Jean-Baptiste Tavernier had described as the 'great pagoda' of Varanasi. The mosque has had its share of misfortune, losing both of its high front minarets, too narrow and unstable to support their weight. Inside, the triple-bayed mosque is in good condition, with some fine ceiling decoration—and the outer courtyard is one of the few peaceful places to be found along the *ghats*.

Beyong Panchaganga are a number of smaller and less-visited *ghats*, close to a Muslim part of the city, so less used by Hindu pilgrims and devotees. Beyond the double-decker road and rail bridge across the Ganges is a final *ghat*, called **Rajghat**, which was almost certainly the original site of Kashi, the first city of Varanasi. Here, next to a very pretty 18th-century tiled Muslim tomb belonging to one of Varanasi's ministers, are excavations that date back more than 2,000 years.

Vishwanath Temple and Gyan Vapi Mosque

Varanasi's most famous temple and mosque stand next to each other near to the area of the old city known as Chowk, though access is also relatively easy along narrow alleyways leading up from Dasashwamedh Ghat or Manikarnika Ghat, each about 400m away. The inner sanctum of the temple and interior of the mosque are accessible only to Hindus and Muslims respectively, though the outer precincts, including the Well of Knowledge, or Gyan Vapi, can be visited by everyone. There is heavy security at the site, and all bags, electronic equipment and even pens will need to be deposited in lockers in nearby shops.

The temple and the mosque share an uneasy and unhappy history. Neither is very old. The 17th-century mosque was built by the Mughal emperor Aurangzeb, destroying an older Vishwanath temple (Vishwanath is another name for Shiva), the ruins of which still stick out of its back wall. The new temple was then built slightly to the south of a mosque, on the other side of an ancient well—the Well of Knowledge—under the sponsorship of Queen Ahilyabai Holkar of Indore in the late 18th century. The gold for its spire was the gift of another princely ruler, the 19th-century Sikh king Ranjit Singh. The well has a grille to stop suicides, and is covered with a sheet to stop pilgrims throwing money into it. Devotees believe the well was built by Shiva himself to cool his overheated lingam. In recent years, Hindu extremists have demanded the destruction of the Gyan Vapi Mosque, and the rebuilding of the temple on what they say was its original site. But it appears likely that this was not the temple's original site, and that the correctly identified site is, in fact, now occupied by a different, much older mosque, named after Razia, a ruler of Delhi in the 13th century.

Razia Mosque

On the other side of the Chowk (or open area in the old city) from the temple-mosque complex, less than 100m to the north, is another mosque, largely forgotten and built on what is believed to be the site of the oldest of the Vishwanath temples. This is the Razia Mosque, which sits on the highest point in Varanasi, and which was constructed during the reign of Razia, a 13th-century female sultan of Delhi. It is a modest mosque, much added to, but it is almost certainly Varanasi's oldest surviving building. From its terraces, one gets good views across the Chowk, and, by peering over a wall, one can look down upon another quite modern temple, known as the Adi (or original) Vishwanath temple. If this were not confusing enough, there is a third Vishwanath temple at Mir Ghat, constructed by conservative Hindus who objected to Dalits (formerly known as Untouchables) being admitted to the main temple—a practice started in 1956.

The European Quarter

There are several interesting European-style buildings that date from the colonial period on the northwest side of Varanasi. The two-storeyed **Nadesar Palace** looks like a Georgian country home in the British countryside, and is now a luxury hotel. It was originally built in the late 18th century as the city's Residency for East India Company officials, and it was later purchased by the maharaja of Varanasi who used it as his city palace. A plaque records how, in 1799, the British magistrate of the city defended the building (with a spear) against a group of armed men led by the exiled nawab of Avadh, Wazir Ali. In the same year, Wazir Ali's men were responsible for the killing of the British Resident in Varanasi.

The Taksal, or mint, down a small alley opposite the entrance to Nadesar Palace, is a huge, long, two-storeyed building, now used as a showroom for arts and crafts. It was built as the home and factory of the early 19th-century British mint master James Prinsep. Prinsep was also an archaeologist, and is best remembered as such for deciphering the ancient Brahmi and Kharoshti scripts, which were used for inscriptions in the reign of Emperor Ashoka. The large exterior staircase is a 20th-century addition. Inside is a former dance hall and banqueting room. Notice the upper-level paintings of scenes from nature and a large number of famous Indian tourist sites, including the Qutb Minar in Delhi, the tower at Chittorgarh, the Taj Mahal and the *ghats* of Varanasi.

Bharat Kala Bhavan

This is Varanasi's main museum (*open Mon–Sat 11–4.30*), set in the well-planned campus of the early 20th-century Benares Hindu University—about 2.5km south of Assi Ghat. Although there are many statues, carvings and terracotta figures from the Varanasi area, this is a national museum with some excellent Mathura statues, including a heavily jewelled woman riding a griffin and a fine Chola bronze of Shiva dancing. Among the other major exhibits from the Varanasi area is a superb 4th-century carving of the youthful Krishna holding up a mountain above his head, which was found in a Muslim graveyard in the north of the city. There is also a very fine 11th-century carving of Shiva stabbing the demon Andhaka; he is shrouded by the skin of an elephant demon whom he has already killed. Look also for some naturalistic terracotta heads of women and an excellent display of Indian coinage, setting them clearly in historical context.

Ramnagar Fort and Palace

Ramnagar is the 18th-century home of the former maharajas of Varanasi, 3km south of Assi Ghat on the opposite bank of the Ganges. They are a comparatively recent royal family, made rajas by their overlords, the nawabs of Avadh, in the second quarter of the 18th century. The area was taken over by the East India Company in 1794, and did not achieve full statehood under the British until 1911. The maharaja did not, however, rule Varanasi city, which was kept under British control. Note how the rulers of Varanasi use the emblem of two fish, like their former Avadh overlords.

Public access is allowed to two of the main courtyards, a museum spread over several buildings and a temple overlooking the Ganges. The **museum** (*open daily 9–12 & 2–4.30*) is similar to many former maharajas' collections, and includes a 1927 Cadillac bearing the license plate '1' for Benares State, two kerosene-powered fans, special guns for shooting elephants and an impressively intricate astrological clock (in working order). One can look into the large **durbar hall**, with its coloured-glass windows, stucco ceilings and royal portraits. A series of underground staircases takes visitors to the riverfront of the palace, with a small **Shiva temple** which has a few pretty wall-paintings. The terrace round the temple has some excellent views of the river, the ornate palace façade and the ramparts of the fort.

SARNATH

The deer park at **Sarnath**, just outside Varanasi (*marked on map on p. 243*), is one of India's most important Buddhist sites. The Buddha himself preached here in about 527 BC. This was the site of his first sermon after having achieved Enlightenment at Bodhgaya in modern-day Bihar. Here he enunciated for the first time what became known as the Wheel of Law, and the four noble truths of Buddhism. At Sarnath, he also formed, from his five followers, the first Buddhist *sangha*, or company of monks. The ruins here are mainly of a later date, particularly the Ashokan period 200 years after the Buddha, and the 5th-century Gupta period.

On the approach to Sarnath is **Chaukhandi**, a 1,500-year-old Buddhist stupa with a Mughal tower constructed on its summit. The 16th-century octagonal brick tower, which has a good long-distance view of the main Sarnath stupa, was erected during the reign of Emperor Akbar in 1588 to commemorate the visit of his father, Humayun, more than a quarter of a century earlier.

The main Sarnath site

The site (*open daily dawn–dusk*) is approached from the south. Ahead to the north are the remains of monasteries, shrines, stupas and monastic cells, while to the east the site is dominated by the 30m high, finely decorated Dhamekh Stupa. On entering the site there are, to the right, the brick foundations of a monastery (known as **Monastery V**) with a typical Buddhist design, and ahead, a central square court, surrounded by small cells, with an entrance gate on the north side. Straight ahead are the circular remains of the 3rd-century BC **Dharmarajika Stupa**, which was reduced to its current state in the late 18th century on the orders of the ruler of Varanasi, who used the stones and bricks for new buildings.

Immediately to the north of the stupa are the main shrine and, to its left, a broken 3rd-century BC **Ashoka pillar**. The pillar was once surmounted by the superb four-headed lion capital, now in the Sarnath Museum, which is the modern emblem of India. The pillar bears an inscription in the Brahmi script threatening schismatic monks with expulsion.

The main shrine

According to the 7th-century Chinese pilgrim Xuan Zang, the main shrine was 60m high. Most of the shrine was constructed in the 3rd century on the remains of an older building, the carved stonework of which can still be seen in the stone walls. It is still possible to make out many of the features of this east-facing shrine, with a long entrance pathway marked by small stupas, a large entrance hall and an inner sanctum fenced in by four columns.

To either side of the inner sanctum were smaller shrines, as there were on the three external walls of the main building. The southern external shrine has a fine mini-stupa, and part of an older polished stone railing. Note the series of paired griffin faces low down on the western external wall of the building, on the right of the portal to the small western shrine. There is also a frieze of small seated Buddhas, using different hand gestures, on a western wall just north of the main shrine. Walk down the pathway, away from the shrine towards the main stupa, past a 19th-century covered **Jain shrine** on the south side. On the north side is a series of low walls with interesting Buddha, griffin and stupa motifs.

The Dhamekh Stupa

This stupa, more than 30m high, was mainly built in the 5th and 6th centuries, during the Gupta period. It has a richly decorated lower drum faced with carved stonework. There is a wide range of geometric and floral designs, and, on the south side, a human figure, seated on a lotus. Slightly to the left are two geese-like birds, one pecking at a plant, while a more upright bird can be seen sitting on a plant on the right.

On the northern side of the main Sarnath site are a number of other ruined brick monastery buildings, mainly from the 12th century, with intact columns and piles of unsorted carved stonework around them.

Sarnath Museum

The museum (*open Tues–Sun 10–5*), a little south of the main site, is one of India's most important, and contains the best-known piece of ancient sculpture in the country: the lion capital that once sat on top of the Ashoka pillar at the main site in Sarnath. In modern India, these four lions, staring and ferocious, are an iconic image found on all government documents, coins, banknotes and passports. The sculpture is made of polished sandstone, and is in good condition. Below the lions, the bottom of the capital consists of a fluted bell-shaped lower portion and an upper ring with reliefs of four animals (a galloping horse, a lion, a bull and an elephant) separated by spoked wheels. On the wall behind the lions are fragments of the wheel that was once positioned above the lions. In the same room is a huge standing Buddha, in the distinctive red sandstone of Mathura, an ancient gift to monasteries of Sarnath.

In the gallery to the left is a frieze showing different episodes from the Buddha's life, and an unusual panel showing a huge monstrous face, sandwiched between two flying geese. At the end of the galleries on the left side of the museum is the famous seated Buddha, in excellent condition, which is widely seen as the most perfect piece of sculpture from the 5th-century Gupta period. Note how carefully the thin drapery has been shaped, and how the sculptor has created a Buddha who does seem to be in a state of detachment. Below the Buddha are a wheel, two deer and some devotees, symbolising the sermon at the deer park in Sarnath. The museum also has fine specimens of Hindu art found at Sarnath, a reminder of the closely connected histories of Hinduism and Buddhism.

CHUNAR

Chunar (*map 5 D3*) is a large **fort** overlooking the Ganges, 25km southwest of Varanasi. Most of the fort is used as a police training centre. There is access to the buildings closest to the river ramparts, which tower 50m over the Ganges. It was in an important strategic position and was much fought over in the early years of the Mughal Empire, and was used as a base by Sher Shah Suri, who deposed the Mughal emperor Humayun. During the reign of Humayun's son Akbar, the building was refortified, and the Persian inscriptions to the right of the main external gate were added at this time. Later, in the 18th century, the British took control of the fort, using it as a garrison and a jail. Rani Jindan, the imprisoned mother of the deposed last Sikh maharaja of Punjab, escaped from here in 1849 dressed as a beggar.

There are several mainly 19th-century buildings in the fort, including the prison cells, with their metal gates that surround the main courtyard. There is a small **temple**, and it is believed that the fort was built on the site of a much older Hindu shrine. There are some pretty Hindu carvings in a heap outside the inner courtyard, while the step-well and the outer fortifications have carved stonework built into their walls. Sandstone for building has been excavated from this region for more than 2,000 years, and most of the pillars of Ashoka the Great (3rd century BC) were made of Chunar sandstone.

At the bottom of the road up to the fort is an old **British cemetery**, partially restored, that is used by local children as a cricket pitch. Most of the graves date back to the first half of the 19th century.

JAUNPUR

A visit to Jaunpur (*map 5 D2*) makes a good day trip from Varanasi, which is just 55km away. In the 15th century, Jaunpur was the capital of a powerful Muslim kingdom ruled by the Sharqi Dynasty. The main legacy of the Sharqis is a series of extraordinary and distinctive mosques that defy the norms of traditional Islamic architecture. Each has a huge towering *iwan*, or arched entrance, leading to the prayer area of the mosque. The arched entranceway is so large that it obscures the main dome of the mosque, so often the defining feature of such buildings. There is also a fine 14th-century fort in the centre of the city, as well as the high-arched 16th-century Mughal bridge across the Gomti River which runs through Jaunpur. All of the major monuments of the city are on the north side of the river.

History: Jaunpur was founded in the late 14th century as a dependency of the Tughlaq Sultanate in Delhi, and Feroze Shah Tughlaq gave its rulers the name Malik ush-Sharq, or King of the East. The fall of the Tughlaqs gave the Sharqis the opportunity to assert their independence, and several battles were later fought with the Lodi Dynasty, based in Delhi and Agra. In 1476, the Sharqis were overthrown by Sikander Lodi, whose forces destroyed Jaunpur's secular buildings but left the city's mosques intact. Today, Jaunpur is a busy city and district headquarters, on the main road between Varanasi and the state capital, Lucknow.

Atala Fort

The 14th-century Atala Fort dominates the northern bank of the Gomti as it passes through the centre of Jaunpur. The fort was built under the Tughlaq Dynasty, and has the familiar sloping walls of defensive Tughlaq buildings elsewhere. The two eastern gates are in good condition. The outer gate still has some of its original coloured inlaid tile, the larger inner gate has decorative niches, and its two side towers have large projecting balconies. Inside the fort is Jaunpur's oldest mosque, built in the 14th century, and more modest than the Sharqi mosques elsewhere in the city. The mosque reuses large numbers of older Hindu columns and stonework, presumably taken from temples.

There is also a large Turkish-style bath complex, or *hammam*, with pretty low-domed roofs, topped by ceiling vents. The complex consists of a series of entrance rooms, followed by an octagonal central chamber, with the main bathing rooms leading off each side. Almost all the decoration has disappeared (except at the far end of the entrance room), but most of the actual baths and the water channels are still intact.

Atala Mosque

About 250m north of the Atala Fort is the impressive Atala Mosque, completed in 1408 and the earliest of the major Sharqi buildings. It was the prototype for the later Jaunpur mosques, and is arguably the most successful architecturally. It was built on or close to the site of the old Atala Devi Temple, and masonry from the temple has been reused in the mosque. From the outside, the mosque does not appear particularly unusual, but, on entering the large courtyard, one is struck immediately by the distinctive towering arched entrance, or *iwan*, that stands in front of the prayer area. Either side of the main *iwan* are two more *iwans* leading to the side chambers of the prayer hall, each of which in turn has its own small dome.

The main entrance to the prayer hall through the largest *iwan* has a corbelled arch with some very fine carved stonework, and the quality of the interior masonry work is also very high. The mezzanine room in the northwest corner, intended for female worshippers, has superb carved ceilings. The unusual two-storeyed cloisters go round almost the entire courtyard. And on the outside of the mosque complex are rooms designed to serve as shops for traders. In this way, the mosque became the centre of activity for the entire community.

Jama Masjid

The Jama Masjid, or Friday Mosque, 1km north of Atala Fort, is Jaunpur's largest and most ambitious mosque, completed in 1478 by Husain Shah, the last of the Sharqi kings. Unlike the Atala mosque, the entire structure of Jama Masjid is built on a high plinth, 6m above the ground, and the compound is reached by climbing an imposing stone staircase. The tall entrance gates are copies in miniature of the main arched *iwan* inside the mosque, each with its own half-obscured dome. The main *iwan* is enormous—26m high—and almost as wide at its base, tapering slightly at the top to give the edifice an even more intimidating aspect. On either side of the gateway are long vaulted halls, unsupported from inside. As one architectural historian put it, they remind one of 'a military barracks rather than the wings of a congregational mosque.' Note how the cloisters have just one level on the interior, but, because of the plinth, two storeys on the exterior of the compound. Outside the compound, connected by a gate, is a tomb complex containing the graves of the Sharqi Dynasty.

Other Jaunpur mosques

Among the other Sharqi mosques in Jaunpur are the smaller **Lal Darwaza Mosque** (Red Gate Mosque), 3km to the northwest of Atala Fort, which makes wide use of Hindu temple pieces and copied Hindu motifs. The prettiest of all of the mosques is arguably the **Jhanjhiri Masjid**, 1.5km east of Atala Fort, set amid mustard fields not far from the river. Here, only the prayer hall and the gateway survive, with an almost cathedral-like look to them. The quality of the stonework decoration is very fine, particularly on the *jali* screens.

Zafarabad

In the town of Zafarabad, 8km southeast of Jaunpur, is a prototype of the Sharqi Mosque that is known as the **Bara Masjid**. It contains a large prayer hall, with more than 50 columns with Hindu motifs. The mosque has been modernised and painted in bright colours, and it is hard to make out the original features.

ALLAHABAD

The city of Allahabad (*map 5 C2*) sits at the junction (or *sangam*) of north India's two most important rivers, the Ganges and the Yamuna, and is the venue for the world's largest religious festival, the Maha Kumbh Mela. Allahabad contains the ancestral home of the Nehru/Gandhi Dynasty, which has dominated Indian politics since Independence. The city also has some very fine little-visited Mughal tombs and some interesting examples of public architecture from the British colonial period.

History: Allahabad, or 'city of God', was the name given by the Mughal emperor Akbar in 1584. The city was previously known as Prayag, or 'place of sacrifice', a name that is still widely used. Despite Allahabad's antiquity as a place of Hindu pilgrimage, there are no significant buildings from before the Mughal period. Under British rule, Allahabad was the capital of the United Provinces, before Lucknow was restored to its pre-eminent regional role in 1920. But the high court for what is now the state of Uttar Pradesh has remained in the city. Allahabad, now a large industrial city of more than one million people, also has a major military base.

Sangam

In Hindu tradition, the Sangam is actually the meeting place of three rivers, the invisible Saraswati joining the two visible rivers, the Ganges and the Yamuna. The point at which they meet is, for many Hindus, the single most holy place in the world. Every 12 years, the **Maha Kumbh Mela** (The Great Pitcher Festival) is held here, and tens of millions of people gather to bathe in the Sangam (2013 and 2025 are the next years for the celebration). Smaller festivals are held each year, attended by 'only' a few million people. Even at non-festival time, the sandy banks of the river, to the east of the city, are busy with thousands of pilgrims. Most of the temples are relatively modern, but it is still interesting to wander through the crowds and down to the waters of the Sangam. A boat can be hired to take visitors to where the rivers, which are usually different colours, merge along a very visible line.

Allahabad Fort

Overlooking the Sangam is Allahabad Fort, the largest of Akbar's three great forts, built in 1583. The other two are in Lahore and Agra. The Mughal emperor Shah Alam lived in Allahabad Fort, under British protection, from 1765 to 1771. Sadly it is occupied by the army, and it is not possible to see the buildings inside the complex (which include a *zenana* palace and an Ashoka pillar). Access is allowed, however, to a small **temple** just inside the walls. But the walls themselves and the gates of the fort are visible and impressive, though you may be stopped from taking photographs.

Khusrau Bagh

In the city itself, near Allahabad Junction railway station, is Khusrau Bagh—a large garden that houses three important Mughal tombs. This was once a pleasure garden used by Akbar's son Jehangir, when he rebelled against his father and based himself in Allahabad. Later, Jehangir's first wife, eldest son and daughter were all buried here, in separate and very different tombs.

On the furthest left is the **Tomb of Prince Khusrau**, after whom the garden is named. He rebelled against his father, Jehangir, who had him blinded (though Khusrau partially recovered his sight). Then he was almost certainly strangled on the orders of his younger half-brother, and future emperor, Shah Jahan. The double-storeyed white-domed tomb is square, with five bays on each side and some interesting painted interior plasterwork, including, unusually, a human figure—perhaps a prince, with wings.

The middle building is the **Tomb of Princess Nishan**, Khusrau's sister, and is the finest of the three. It is made of yellow and red sandstone, with a larger lower plinth concealing a multi-chambered basement—now used for storing bicycles, but which would once have housed the princess's grave, which has mysteriously disappeared. On the plinth rests the main structure of the tomb, with tall entrance archways, and a series of niches of different sizes on either side. There are four slender pavilions, or *chattris*, surrounding the dome. The interior decoration is very fine (even in the bat-infested basement), and the entrances have some excellent stonework and painting, with lots of floral and geometric imagery.

The third mausoleum, with open sides to the upper chamber, belongs to the mother of the two siblings, and is thought to predate the other tombs. This is the **Tomb of Man Bai**, the Rajasthani Hindu princess who married Emperor Jehangir and is believed to have committed suicide because of the differences between her husband, her son Khusrau and her father, the Raja of Amber. The tomb itself contains ten graves of other members of her family, but her cenotaph lies on the top level of the mausoleum, partially protected from the winds by finely carved scalloped screens. The fourth building, further to the right, with an octagonal base, is also thought to be a tomb.

Anand Bhavan

The ancestral home of the Nehru family, known as Anand Bhavan (*open Tues–Sun 9.30–5*), can be found in northeast Allahabad, in the 19th-century British period sector of the city. Motilal Nehru was a very rich and successful lawyer, and his son Jawaharlal was groomed for political leadership from an early age. He became the first prime minister of the newly independent India. This was the house in which he lived from the year 1900, when he was aged 11, and it is where his daughter Indira—another future prime minister—was born in 1917. Anand Bhavan (and a neighbouring second house called Swaraj Bhavan) has been turned into a memorial both to India's first family and to the Independence Movement in which they played such a prominent role. There are relics of everyday life, such as Motilal's spittoon and Jawaharlal's tennis racquet and electric shaver. Note the portable spinning wheels that Mahatma Gandhi encouraged freedom fighters to carry around with them—spinning was good for the soul, and would mean buying less fabric made in Britain.

British colonial buildings

Allahabad has a large number of other interesting buildings from the British period, particularly in the university area of the city. **Muir College** (completed 1886) is the best of them all, with its 60m sandstone minaret and a fine dome clad in glazed tiles. The façade has a series of arched bays, concealing a central arcaded courtyard. The college was designed by the British architect William Emerson, who was also responsible for the impressive **All Saints Cathedral**, which sits in the middle of a large roundabout in western Allahabad. **Allahabad Museum** (*open Tues–Sun 10.30–5*) has some fine Buddhist sculpture and terracotta figurines from Kausambi (*see below*), as well as later Hindu carvings from Gupta sites in Uttar Pradesh and from Khajuraho.

KAUSAMBI

This deserted site (*map 5 C2*, also called Kosam), 45km from Allahabad and overlooking the River Yamuna, was the location of one of India's most important ancient cities. When the Buddha visited Kausambi in the 6th century BC, it had already been in existence for several centuries, and it is mentioned as an important city in the Hindu epics. Kausambi was deserted more than 1,500 years ago, and, at first sight, the area seems to consist of little more than huge mounds of earth. But there are four interesting archaeological sites to be visited at Kausambi. Large numbers of carvings, statues, terracotta figurines, pottery fragments and coins were unearthed here. They have all been sent to museums and research institutes: Allahabad Museum has a fine collection of objects from the ruined city. In Kausambi it is possible to see the layout of parts of the city, a former palace, and the impressively-defended eastern gate, as well as piles of old pottery sticking out of the earth.

At the centre of Kausambi is a 4th-century BC **Ashoka pillar** (another pillar was taken from here to Allababad Fort in the time of the Mughal emperor Akbar). Close by are the foundations of several other buildings. To the east are two further, more interesting archaeological sites. The first is a **monastery** complex, built on the ruins of older foundations. There are lots of rooms, water courses and storage tanks here. Note the curved back wall to one of the shrines, and the row of column stumps on the rear back wall. The second site is the well-fortified remains of the **eastern gate**, with an exterior sentry-post. This has an outer and inner wall, with a narrow passage running through it. To the western side of Kausambi, with a fantastic view over the Yamuna, are the remains of an inner **citadel** and a **palace**. Parts of the citadel have been over-restored in recent times. The foundations of the palace and its lower walls are clearly visible, as are the carved lower edges of the stone door frames.

KARA

Kara (*map 5 C2*, Karadham on signposts) is a deserted and forgotten city overlooking the Ganges, 55km west of Allahabad. It was here that the early Sultanate ruler of north India, Jalaluddin Khilji, was murdered by Alauddin, his nephew and successor, in 1296. Until the Mughal period, when it was superseded by Allahabad, Kara was a major regional centre. Now there are only scattered ruins to bear witness to the city's importance.

To reach Kara, turn right off the Allahabad–Kanpur highway, as you pass through Sirathu. The first sign that this was once a major urban centre is an enormous, derelict **Muslim cemetery** on both sides of the road that leads to the ruins of **Kara Fort**. The fort stands on a large hill with spectacular views over the Ganges. One of the towers is still standing, and so are parts of the landside walls—but most of the fortifications have long since gone. On the hilltop are only two buildings of importance. One is a mysterious cylindrical **stepped tower**, with a curved staircase leading to its top; at some point the building served as a flagstaff, and was probably constructed as a cartographer's observatory in the early 19th century. Note the carving on the steps, suggesting this was once part of a very different building—perhaps a temple. The tower is solid, apart from a narrow passage on its southern side. At the foot of the western end of the fort overlooking a ruined riverside wharf is a small building that may have served as a **watchtower**. Next to the ruined wharf is a small temple complex, with a fine **Shiva temple**. At the foot of the eastern end of the fort is another ruined wharf, and an impressive **brick-built tower**, which may have served as a lighthouse. The area beyond the tower has the ruins of other buildings, tombs and wells.

NORTHEASTERN UTTAR PRADESH

GHAZIPUR

The town of Ghazipur (*map 5 D2*), on the north bank of the Ganges, 65km east of Varanasi, was once a major opium-trading centre. On the west side of town is the **Cornwallis Mausoleum** (1806), a fine Neoclassical building, with Doric pillars and a domed roof, erected to commemorate the death of the Marquess Cornwallis, the British governor-general who died here in 1805, and who is best remembered for his defeat by George Washington at Yorktown in 1781, during the American War of Independence. The building is said to have been influenced by, and is similar to, the mausoleum designed by the British architect Nicholas Hawksmoor at Castle Howard in Yorkshire.

BUDDHIST SITES IN NORTHEAST UTTAR PRADESH

Northeastern Uttar Pradesh has two important Buddhist sites close to the border with Nepal. The main city of the region is **Gorakhpur** (*map 5 D1*). It stands 240km east of Lucknow, and has comfortable basic accommodation. **Piprahwa** (*map 5 D1*) is 80km north of Gorakhpur, and is one of two rival sites for Kapilavastu, the capital of the princely state into whose royal family the Buddha was born 2,500 years ago. The other site is across the border in Nepal, not far from the Buddha's actual birthplace in Lumbini (*map 5 D1*). There is a ruined stupa, and the excavated walls of other buildings, including monasteries. It is possible to cross the border for the day at Sanauli if you have a Nepalese visa (and an Indian multi-entry visa), and visit Lumbini and the alternative Nepalese Kapilavastu site.

Kushinagar (*map 5 D1*, or Kusinagara), the site of the Buddha's death, known to Buddhists as his *parinirvana*, is 55km east of Gorakhpur. At the main part of the site is a stupa, the lower walls of an ancient monastery and a shrine containing a large reassembled 6m-long statue of the Buddha in the state of *parinirvana*. These structures are thought to date from around the 2nd century. About 1.5km to the east, at **Rambhar**, is another stupa, and further excavated buildings.

PRACTICAL INFORMATION

Uttar Pradesh is so large and varied that few travellers make a specific effort to tour the state as a whole, as they might with Rajasthan or Tamil Nadu. Visitors tend to be attracted to one particular part of the state—often Agra and the west, heading from there to either Jaipur in Rajasthan or Gwalior in Madhya Pradesh, as both are closer than other major sites in UP. Another popular traveller route that crosses state borders is between Varanasi in UP and Khajuraho in Madhya Pradesh.

GETTING THERE & GETTING AROUND

For western Uttar Pradesh, Delhi serves as the main airport. The state capital, Lucknow, is well connected to the rest of country by air, while there are also daily flights from Delhi to Varanasi and Allahabad in eastern Uttar Pradesh. There are good long-distance railway routes, with the main line from Delhi to Kolkata passing through the state. The Grand Trunk Road, now a major highway, runs from Delhi through Agra, Kanpur (for Lucknow), Allahabad and Varanasi.

Agra and western Uttar Pradesh

• **Agra:** It is possible to visit Agra from Delhi for the day, by train or by car, but this only allows time for the briefest of visits to the main sights. The Shatabdi train from New Delhi station at 6am is highly recommended; it takes just 2hrs, and is reliable and comfortable. The return Shatabdi train leaves Agra for Delhi at 8.18 pm. By road, the journey takes at least 3hrs, often more. Leave Delhi early to avoid heavy traffic on the way out of the city. Avoid flights to Agra—very few airlines operate here, and the flights are often delayed.

From Agra, some travellers will head on to the great fortress city of **Gwalior** (another 1½hrs by train or 2hrs by road), and then the palaces of **Orchha** (a further 1½hrs). But most will cross into Rajasthan, via Fatehpur Sikri, and visit **Jaipur** (5hrs by road), and 'do' the famous Delhi-Agra-Jaipur triangle. Alternative places to visit, nearer than Jaipur, include **Bharatpur** and **Deeg**. Those with their own transport might want to stay in Bharatpur. There is also an early morning train from Agra to Jaipur (7hrs) and **Jodhpur** (13hrs).

In **Agra**, the distances between key sites are too far apart to travel on foot. If you do not want to travel by car, it is possible to hire an auto-rickshaw for a half-day or day. Agree a rate in advance—your hotel should be able to advise you on the current rates.

Other parts of western UP are best reached by road from Delhi or Agra.

Central Uttar Pradesh

• **Lucknow:** The state capital is well-connected by air, rail and road to the rest of the country. There are several daily flights from Delhi, as well as connections to Kolkata and Mumbai. There are also good train services from Delhi to Lucknow (9hrs by the overnight Lucknow mail, or just 6½hrs by the early morning Shatabdi).

In Lucknow, auto-rickshaws are widely available—though it is possible to wander around the areas containing the *imambaras* as far as the Residency (it is about 2.5km between the Chota Imambara and the Residency). Unlike in Agra or Delhi, tourists are rarely the subject of unwanted attention. Taxis can be hired for longer trips around central Uttar Pradesh.

Eastern Uttar Pradesh

• **Varanasi and Allahabad:** The main airport for eastern UP is at Varanasi, with daily connections to Delhi, Lucknow and Kolkata. There are also less well-used airports at Allahabad and Gorakhpur. Allahabad is very well served by rail (7hrs from Delhi), while Varanasi is less well connected by train. Some visitors make the day-long road journey from Varanasi to either the temples of Khajuraho in Madhya Pradesh, or the Buddhist sites of southern Bihar.

Varanasi is a good city for walking, and boats along the river are widely available—but negotiate a price in advance.

ACCOMMODATION

Western Uttar Pradesh

• **Agra:** The city of the Taj Mahal has a large number of not very distinctive tourist hotels. The best (and most expensive) of the hotels is the Oberoi group's **Amarvilas**, which has superb views of the Taj Mahal from many bedrooms and the upstairs restaurant. (*$$$; T: 0562 2231515; amarvilas.com*). The Amarvilas is also close to the more peaceful eastern gateway to the Taj Mahal—the hotel provides golf carts to its customers so that visitors do not have to walk the final part of the entrance road, where petrol- and diesel-powered vehicles are not allowed. Other large chains with modern luxury hotels in the same area in southern Agra, close to the Taj Mahal, include the **Mughal** (formerly the Mughal Sheraton), run by ITC Welcomgroup (*$$$; T: 0562 2331701; itcwelcomgroup.in*) and the **Taj View** run by the Taj group (*$$$; T: 0562 2232 400-418; tajhotels.com*). The cheapest and oldest of the five-star hotels is the **Clarks Shiraz** (*$$$; T: 0562 2226121-27; hotelclarksshiraz.com*).

Among the mid-range hotels, there is none that stands out. But there are several on Fatehabad Road, not far from the Taj Mahal, including the **Mayur Tourist Complex**, which has individual cottages and green lawns (*$$; T: 0562 2332302, 2332310; email: info@mayurcomplex.com*).

• **Fatehpur Sikri:** This ancient site has basic accommodation and food. The best is probably **Goverdhan Tourist Complex** (*$; T: 05613 282643; fatehpursikriviews.com*). Most visitors stay in Agra, or in nearby Bharatpur, just across the border in Rajasthan.

• **En route from Delhi:** There are two heritage hotels that are useful places to break one's journey from Delhi through western UP: **Mud Fort Kuchesar** (*$$; T: 05736 273038; mudfortkuchesar.com*); and **Unchagaon Fort** (*$$; T: 9891458220*).

Central and Eastern Uttar Pradesh

• **Lucknow:** There are several comfortable places to stay in Lucknow. The top hotel is the **Taj Residency** (*$$$; T: 0522 2393939; tajhotels.com*), while the **Clarks Avadh** (*$$$; T: 0522 2620131-33; clarksavadh.com*) is closer to the old Nawabi city.

• **Varanasi:** It is possible to stay right next to the river in Varanasi. The **Hotel Ganges View** (*$$; T: 91542 2313218; hotelgangesview.com*), overlooking Assi Ghat, is very popular with regular visitors to Varanasi, so it is best to reserve well in advance. The neighbouring **Palace on the Ganges** (*$$$; T: 0542 2315050; palaceontheganges.com*) is also comfortable. The more luxurious hotels are away from the river, and include the historically important **Nadesar Palace** (*see p. 246*), run by the Taj group (*$$$; T: 0542 2503001; tajhotels.com*). There is also the slightly run-down **Pallavi International** (*$; T: 0542 2393012; pallavinternationalhotel.com*), which was the former residence of the royal family of the minor princely state of Hathwa Raj.

• **Allahabad and Gorakhpur:** The most comfortable hotel in Allahabad is the **Grand Continental** (*$$; T: 0532 2260631; birhotel.com*), while the best in Gorakhpur is **Clarks Inn** (*$$; T: 0551 2205015; clarksinn.in*).

FOOD

There is no distinctive Uttar Pradesh cuisine, and food traditions vary significantly across the state—particularly between Agra, Lucknow and Varanasi.

• **Agra:** One would expect Agra, as a former Mughal capital, to have excellent Mughlai food, but sadly Mughal culinary tradition has largely died out there, and the local cuisine is not particularly highly regarded. However, one local favourite is *kachori*, similar to a vegetable samosa, but in which cooked, spiced lentils, or sometimes chickpeas, are stuffed inside dough, which is then deep fried and served with potatoes and chutney. They are widely available at roadside stalls. At the other end of Agra's culinary spectrum are *pethas* (pronounced 'payta'): sweets made out of pumpkin and flavoured with rose water or saffron. **Ram Babu's Paratha Bhandar** ($) in the Belan Ganj area of Agra has excellent stuffed *parathas*—a kind of unleavened layered bread—which were chosen as Agra's culinary offering at the banquet in Delhi to celebrate the 50th anniversary of the Indian parliament.

Agra has a large number of not very distinctive tourist restaurants—mainly in the hotels—that are aimed at the bland end of the foreign palate. Of the top hotels, the ITC Mughal (still widely known by its old name, the Mughal Sheraton) probably has the best Indian food, with excellent kebabs, black dal and Indian naan and rotis at its **Peshawri** restaurant.

There is also a popular restaurant called **Zorba the Buddha** ($), in the Sadar Bazaar area, which is mainly used by backpackers, and has a mixed reputation.

• **Lucknow:** The state capital is home to Avadhi cuisine, best known for its superb kebabs. Avadhi cuisine is a little less rich than the Mughlai cuisine of Delhi, and it places greater emphasis on how the meat is prepared and cooked than on the sauces and marinades that accompany it. For some dishes, the container is sealed with a lid of dough, and then the contents are cooked very slowly. The pastry is then broken and discarded allowing the aroma of the food to escape as the diner sits down to eat. **Tunday's** in Aminabad is a very simple restaurant that is widely acknowledged as having Lucknow's best kebabs—try the very soft Galawat kebabs. It is not a place for vegetarians. At the top end, the **Faluknama** (*$$; T: 0522 2620131-33*) restaurant in the Clarks Avadh hotel has traditional Avadhi dishes.

• **Varanasi:** Best known for its vegetarian food, Varanasi offers especially good street snacks, known as *chaat*. Locals recommend **Kashi Chaat Bhandar** on Dasashwamedha Road, and other nearby shops, where a wide variety of Indian sweets is also available. Most visitors eat at hotels or at the large number of multi-cuisine restaurants for international and Indian tourists which have sprung up in recent years.

FURTHER READING & VIEWING

• **Agra:** There has been a recent spate of books about Agra and the Taj Mahal, which have gone a long way towards dispelling some of the myths that surround India's most famous building. The following are particularly recommended:

The Complete Taj Mahal by Ebba Koch (Thames & Hudson, 2006)—a beautifully produced coffee-table book, which is also a serious history of the Taj, written by the world's leading expert on Mughal architecture.

Taj Mahal by Giles Tillotson (Profile Books, 2008) is a well-written, intelligent history of the Taj Mahal. *Agra* by Lucy Peck (Lotus Roli, 2008) is a very detailed guidebook to Agra, and perfect for exploring the Mughal and colonial parts of the city, as well as its more famous buildings. It also has good coverage of Fatehpur Sikri.

Among the films with scenes set in Agra is *Garam Hawa* (1973), a thoughtful, beautifully shot Hindi-language film about the Partition of India. It is set in Agra, with the Taj Mahal and Fatehpur Sikri as a backdrop. *Bunti aur Babli* (2006) is an entertaining Bollywood movie, based around two lovable crooks, similar to Bonnie and Clyde, who attempt to sell the Taj Mahal to a businessman.

• **Lucknow:** There is an excellent anthology of Lucknow-related fiction and non-fiction called *Shaam-e-Awadh: Writings on Lucknow* (Penguin India, 2007), including selections from Rudyard Kipling, Mark Twain, V.S. Naipaul and William Dalrymple. The British author Rosie Llewellyn-Jones has also written several books about Lucknow, including *Engaging Scoundrels; True Tales of Old Lucknow* (OUP India, 2000). Several novels and short stories by the greatest Hindi writer of the 20th century, Prem Chand, are set in and around Lucknow.

The novel *The Gift of a Cow* (Indian Univ Press, 2002) is particularly recommended as a portrayal of country and town life in the 1930s.

The celebrated Satyajit Ray movie *The Chess Players* (1977) was based on the Prem Chand short story of the same name, which depicts the last days of the nawabs before the British took over in 1856.

• **Varanasi:** Diana Eck's *Banaras: City of Light* (Arkana, 2003) is an excellent historical and cultural guide to the city, while the second half of Geoff Dyer's entertaining novel *Jeff in Venice, Death in Varanasi* (Random House, 2009) is entirely set on the *ghats* along the Ganges. The novel *Water* (Penguin, 2006) by Bapsi Sidhwa is about child widows. It is set in Varanasi, and is based on the 2005 film of the same name by Deepa Mehta, a film that had to be shot in Sri Lanka because of objections by some local Hindus.

The 1956 film *Aparajito*, the second part of Satyajit Ray's magnificent *Apu Trilogy*, was partly shot on the *ghats* of Varanasi.

• **Allahabad:** *The Last Bungalow: Writings on Allahabad*, edited by A.K. Malhotra (Penguin India, 2006) is an interesting collection of fiction, non-fiction and poetry about Allahabad.

UTTARAKHAND

Uttarakhand (*map 2*) is one of India's newest and least populous states, formed in 2000 out of the hill districts of Uttar Pradesh. The state, with its capital at Dehra Dun, is better known for its beautiful mountainous countryside than for its architectural heritage. However, it does contain several important ancient Hindu pilgrimage sites and a number of interesting hill-stations built in the British period.

The state is divided into two regions: Garhwal, to the west, and Kumaon, to the east. Garhwal's main town is the state capital, Dehra Dun, while other important tourist sites include the hill-station of Mussoorie and the temple towns of Hardwar and Rishikesh. The main town in Kumaon is Naini Tal, and among the other tourist attractions are the hill-station at Almora and the ancient temples at Jageshwar. Large numbers of Indian tourists from Delhi and the plains head to the hills of Uttarakhand in May and June, and the hill-stations can get very overcrowded. Some of the more remote villages, often more than a day's trek from the nearest road, have fine traditional wooden domestic and temple architecture.

HISTORY OF UTTARAKHAND

The Ashoka rock inscriptions in the westernmost part of the state, at Kalsi, suggests that most of the low-lying areas of Uttarakhand were under the control of the Mauryan Empire in the 3rd century BC. However, the rest of Uttarakhand was, until the Sultanate period, divided into a number of smaller principalities, of which the best known are the Katyuri and Chand dynasties in Kumaon. Garhwal was plundered by Timur's Mongol invaders in 1399. By the early 16th century the Panwar Dynasty controlled most of Garhwal—and their descendants later became the maharajas of Tehri Garhwal. Under Emperor Akbar, the Mughal Empire extended to Hardwar, and in the late 17th century Guru Ram Rai, the leader of the Sikh Udasi sect, settled in the Doon Valley, founding what would later become Dehra Dun.

The late 18th century saw an invasion by Nepalese Gurkhas, who captured most of modern-day Uttarakhand, and were eventually defeated by the British in the Battle of Khalanga in 1814. The battle skills of the Gurkhas so impressed the British that Gurkha regiments became (and still are) part of the British and Indian armies. After 1814, the British took direct control of Kumaon, but the son of the maharaja of Garhwal, killed in battle by the Gurkhas, was reinstalled as the nominally independent maharaja of the smaller area known as Tehri Garhwal.

At Independence, the region became part of Uttar Pradesh, India's most populous state, but a long-running and largely peaceful separatist movement was successful in obtaining the creation of a breakaway state, first known as Uttaranchal, in 2000. The state's name was formally changed to Uttarakhand in 2006. The vast majority of Uttarakhandis are Hindu, though there are small Muslim and Sikh minorities in the low-lying areas of the state, and some Christians in the hill-stations. The state has a strong martial tradition, and the soldiers of the Garhwal Rifles and Kumaon Regiments are recruited and based in the state.

GARHWAL: WESTERN UTTARAKHAND

DEHRA DUN

Uttarakhand's capital (*map 2 C1*) is nestled into the Dun (pronounced and sometimes spelled 'Doon') Valley, set in the lowest of the Himalayan foothills. It therefore has a slightly lower temperature than the plains. To the north, looming over Dehra Dun, is the impressive first range of the Himalayas, with the hill-stations of Mussoorie and Landour at the summit. Dehra Dun—literally 'Camp of the Valley'—is today most closely associated with the Doon School, one of India's best-known private schools, and the enormous Forest Research Institute, to the west of the modern city. Dehra Dun originated, however, as a settlement around the Ram Rai Gurudwara, in the east of the city, in the late 17th century.

The Forest Research Institute

The institute (1924–29), set in enormous beautiful grounds on the western side of Dehra Dun, is one of India's finest Neoclassical buildings. The main red-brick façade, with its finely proportioned high-lanterned cupolas, Tuscan columns and simple pediments, is more than 300m long, and inside are six courtyards. The institute was originally housed in what is now the Doon School, 2km to the southeast, and the current building is a testament to the importance of forestry during the British period of rule. Timber was critical to many major industries, including construction and the railways, and a huge effort was put into ensuring a continuous supply of timber and other forest products.

There are six **exhibition rooms** (*open Mon–Fri 9–5.30*), with interesting, old-fashioned displays, many of them from the British period. Note in particular the enormous cross-section of a 700-year-old deodar tree, almost 3m across, with a timeline of Indian history. There is also an extraordinary collection of diseased trees—some with finger-sized holes made by woodworms and one in which another tree has grown inside it. Note the initials IFRI on the gutters of the building, standing for Imperial Forest Research Institute, and the wooden roof tiles. In the grounds is a **bamboo garden**, with more than 30 varieties of bamboo.

The **Guru Ram Rai Durbar** (1699–1756) is an unusual and finely decorated Sikh temple complex in the oldest part of central Dehra Dun, 300m north of the railway station. The complex was the home and *gurudwara* of Ram Rai, the oldest son of the seventh Sikh guru, Har Rai. Ram Rai quarrelled with his father by siding with Emperor Aurangzeb over an obscure reference to Muslims in the Sikh holy book, the *Guru Granth Sahib*. He was passed over as his father's successor, and instead his young brother became the eighth guru. Ram Rai then became the leader of the Udasin sect of Sikhs. The exterior of the complex, which is visible from afar because of its flagpole, has some superb 18th- and 19th-century murals, showing religious and secular images—including some amusing images of Western, presumably British, men and women. There are more fine paintings inside, both on the walls and on the minaret-like towers of the pretty main building, which resembles a Mughal-style tomb, set in a courtyard. Inside the building is the bed of Ram Rai. The four smaller buildings are a memorial to Ram Rai's four wives.

Other buildings in Dehra Dun

Among the other interesting buildings in Dehra Dun is the **Church of St Francis of Assisi**, which has murals painted by an Italian prisoner of war during World War II, and the **Indian Military Academy** (1922–32), a hybrid Tudor and Classical building, which serves as India's leading officer training school. It is also possible to drive through the extensive grounds of the **Survey of India**, while the **Doon School** is normally closed to visitors who do not have a connection with the school.

MUSSOORIE & LANDOUR

Mussoorie

This hill-station (*map 2 C1*) is located high on the mountainside above Dehra Dun, at 2,000m above sea level. It is very popular with Indian tourists, partly because it is the hill-station closest to Delhi. It is also home to several well-known boarding schools. Mussoorie is only about 15km from Dehra Dun, but the journey takes about an hour by road. Many of the older buildings have disappeared or are in a dilapidated state; however, there are some interesting churches—and, of course, some very fine views.

Mussoorie, named after the ubiquitous local shrub, the *mansur*, was first settled by the British in the 1820s. Among the earliest buildings were a brewery (1830), a school (1834), a bank (1836), a church (1836) and a library (1843). Many maharajas had summer homes here, and some of them survive—such as Kapurthala House, which is still a private residence. It was also a place of exile for members of the Afghan and Persian royal families during the 19th century.

The most impressive of Mussoorie's 19th-century buildings is situated near the top of the hill, above the town's main thoroughfare, The Mall. It is the recently restored **Christchurch** (1836), which has one of India's best examples of stained-glass windows. Note also the deodar tree planted by Mary, princess of Wales, in 1906 in the church garden, surrounded by a black railing. Nearby is the **Kasmanda Palace Hotel**, originally built as part of the church complex in 1836, then converted into a sanatorium, and which became the summer palace of the royal family of Kasmanda (from central Uttar Pradesh) in 1915. **The Mall** itself runs from the 19th-century library to the decaying façade of the defunct Picture Palace cinema. Other churches include the pretty, tower-less **Union Church** (1873). There is a fascinating multilevel cemetery on the road known as the Camel's Back, after a couple of hump-like outcrops of rock on the far side of Mussoorie's Gun Hill.

Landour

Just 250m higher than Mussoorie is the smaller hill-station of Landour. It is more exclusive and peaceful than Mussoorie, with which it is now contiguous, and, like its neighbour, was also first settled in the 1820s. It was used as a sanatorium for sick British soldiers, and those who did not survive are buried in the cemetery on the north side of the hill-station. Landour, named after the Welsh town of Llanddowror, retains a strong Anglo-Indian identity, and has several churches. Among them are: the well-restored **St Paul's Church** (1840), next to the area known as Char Dukan, or 'four shops'; the **Kellogg Presbyterian Church** (1903), on Landour's main hilltop road junction, which is used as a school for teaching Hindi to foreigners—except on Sunday mornings, when it still functions as a church; and the small hilltop **St Peter's Catholic Church** (1828), the oldest in the region, also recently restored, with a pretty Neoclassical façade. St Peter's is harder to find: take the steep road up to the left of the Kellogg Church, pass through the gate that says 'entry prohibited' (explain that you want to go to see the church if anyone stops you), and the church is just beyond the playing field.

At the eastern end of Landour is **Sister's Bazaar**—a group of buildings and shops named after the nuns who looked after the convalescent soldiers in the hill-station.

Everest House and Cloud End

There are two interesting 19th-century buildings, Everest House and Cloud End, that lie west of the hill-station. Set on a ridge 5km west of Mussoorie, **Everest House**, in Park Estate, is the former home of the man after whom the highest mountain in the world was named. Sir George Everest, who pronounced his name Eave-rist, was the surveyor general of India from 1830 to 1843, and was responsible for mapping most of the country. It was his successor as surveyor general, Andrew Scott Waugh, who surveyed Mt Everest, found it to be the highest in the world, and decided to name it after his predecessor. The simple whitewashed house, now deserted and very popular with local cattle, has a British-style fireplace and cornices. It is in a dramatic position, overlooking the Dun Valley, and has superb views to the south and to the north. On a neighbouring hillock is a small building which served as Everest's observatory. The house is approached directly by a track at the bottom of Hathipao Hill (only suitable for four-wheel drive vehicles). Alternatively, head towards Cloud End and turn left at the signboard for the 'Everest Camping Resort'; then it is a 15-minute walk from the end of the road.

Cloud End (1838) is a pretty but heavily restored house at the end of a spur, 7km west of Mussoorie, and one of the earliest British buildings in the area. It is now a small hotel. Cloud End was built by, and belonged to, the Swetenham family until the 1960s, and the traveller and diarist Fanny Parkes describes how she supervised the construction of the house in 1838, planning the living room windows so there would be excellent views of 'the Snowy Ranges'.

HARDWAR

Hardwar (*map* 2 *C2*), also spelled Haridwar—literally, the *dwar*, or door, of Hari (another name for Vishnu)—is an important Hindu pilgrimage town, situated at the point where the River Ganges, divided into several channels here, enters the great plains of northern India. Although the town is thought to have been settled for several thousand years, all the old buildings have disappeared or have been so heavily restored that there is little left to see. The town is one of the four sites, with Allahabad, Ujjain and Nasik, of the mass Hindu pilgrimage known as the Kumbh Mela. It is also the place where many north Indian Hindus come to immerse the ashes of their cremated relatives, and local priests, known as *pandas*, have an extraordinary collection of genealogical records of families who have been visiting Hardwar for key ceremonies over many generations.

The main bathing *ghat* at Hardwar is called **Har ki Pauri**, or 'footsteps of god', and many pilgrims come here to wash away their sins. This is also the head-point of the **Ganges Canal**, built in the 1840s to irrigate the lands known as the Doab, literally 'two waters', or the territory between the Ganges and the Yamuna. There are pretty views from the nearby hilltop temples: **Mansa Devi**, on the west bank; **Chand Devi**, on the east bank. Both are accessible by cable car.

RISHIKESH

Rishikesh (*map* 2 *C2*) is a popular Hindu pilgrimage town on the Ganges, 25km north and upstream of Hardwar. It is important as the gateway to the sources of the Ganges, and traditionally is noted as the site where Lakshman, the brother of Rama, crossed the river on a jute rope. It became internationally famous in the 1960s, when the Beatles stayed at the Maharishi Ashram, and it continues to attract a large number of often spaced-out Western visitors, who come here to stay at ashrams, and learn meditation and yoga techniques. There is also a growing number of tourists who come here to take part in white-water rafting and other forms of adventure tourism, a little further upstream from Rishikesh, and who base themselves in the town or on sandy beach camping sites beside the Ganges.

Like at Hardwar, the temples here are modern, but built on the site of ancient shrines. The eastern bank, with many popular temples and ashrams, is largely free from traffic and reached by huge suspended footbridges, known as Lakshman and Ram Jhula, after the brothers from the Hindu epic the *Ramayana* (a *jhula* is a swing).

To the south of Ram Jhula, on the east bank, are the ruins of the **Maharishi Ashram**, where the Beatles stayed in 1968 and studied transcendental meditation with Maharishi Mahesh Yogi. The ashram is now under the control of the Forestry Department, which originally owned the land, but it is possible to enter the site by heading to a small Ram temple overlooking the river and taking a footpath to the left which leads into the dilapidated complex, with its strange beehive-shaped places of meditation and prayer.

THE BEATLES & THE MAHARISHI

Controversy still surrounds The Beatles' visit to Rishikesh, where much of the *White Album* was written and composed. One of the accusations was that the Maharishi made a pass at the actress Mia Farrow or at another American visitor, and that John Lennon's response was the song *Sexy Sadie*, which he wrote as he was driven back to Delhi, and in which the words 'What have you done? You made a fool of everyone' were said to have been addressed to the Maharishi. Farrow later said the Maharishi wrapped his arms around her after a meditation session, but that she may have misinterpreted his intentions.

CHAR DHAM PILGRIMAGE SITES

To the north of Rishikesh are the Char Dham, four Hindu pilgrimage sites high up in the Himalayas—all at over 3000m above sea level—that mark the sources of the Ganges, and which are normally accessible from May to October. Getting to these involves long, uncomfortable journeys up into the Himalayas, more than compensated for by spectacular views and cool weather.

Yamunotri

The most westerly of the Char Dham is Yamunotri (*map 2 C1*), the source of the Yamuna, and the least visited—a day's journey north of Rishikesh. The final stretch of the journey involves a 5km walk to a small temple in the cleft of a mountainside. The temple is dedicated to the river goddess Yamuna, who is represented by a black marble idol—and there are hot springs nearby.

Gangotri

East of Yamunotri, and accessed by the same road out of Rishikesh, is Gangotri (*map 2 D1*), which lies close to the source of the most important branch of the Ganges, here known as the Bhagirathi. A road takes visitors right up to the 18th-century **temple**, dedicated to the river goddess Ganga. The temple was built by a Gurkha, General Amar Singh Thapa, and was restored by the maharaja of Jaipur in 1935. It is a further 19km trek, across difficult terrain, to **Gaumukh** (literally 'cow's mouth')—the mouth of the glacier which feeds the Ganges.

Kedarnath

Kedarnath (*map 2 D1*) and Badrinath (*see opposite*) are approached by a different road from Rishikesh, that splits at Rudraprayag. The road on the left heads to Kedarnath, the northernmost and, at over 3,500m, highest of the Char Dham. Getting there involves a long but straightforward 14km trek from the road-head at Gaurikund, where there are hot springs. There is also a mornings-only helicopter service from near Agastya Muni, near Rudraprayag. **Kedarnath Temple**, close to the source of the Madakini River and dedicated to Shiva, is the most impressive of the Char Dham shrines. Note the stone-carved Nandi (Shiva's vehicle, the bull) outside the door of the temple.

Badrinath

At Rudraprayag, take the road on the right to Badrinath (*map 2 D1*), the most easterly of the Char Dham, near the source of the Alak Nanda River. The brightly coloured **Badrinath Temple**, which is accessible by road, is dedicated to Vishnu, and there is a black stone idol of the god in a meditative posture in the sanctuary of the shrine. The head priest is always a Brahmin from Kerala, in the far south of India. Near Badrinath are several other pilgrimage sites, including **Joshimath** (*map 2 D1*), where the great 9th-century Hindu sage Shankaracharya died (Uttarakhand's main ski resort is close to here, at Auli), and the modern **Sikh shrine of Hemkund Sahib**, set in a spectacular location 18km from a road-head (*map 2 D1*), where the tenth guru, Gobind Singh, is thought to have meditated in a previous life. Near Hemkund is the **Valley of Flowers**, famous for its 300 varieties of beautiful wild flowers, which bloom during the monsoon in July and August.

LANSDOWNE

The cantonment town of Lansdowne (*map 2 C2*) also functions as a minor hill-station, midway between Dehra Dun and Naini Tal, the state's two most important centres. It was founded in 1887 during the rule of Viceroy Lord Lansdowne. There are two interesting churches on the peak known as Tiffin Top: the former **Anglican church** (now a reading room), and the **Catholic church** with stained-glass windows. There is also a small **war museum** (*open daily 9–12 & 3–6*), largely devoted to memorabilia of the Garhwal Rifles, the headquarters of which are in Lansdowne.

KUMAON: EASTERN UTTARAKHAND

NAINI TAL

This busy hill-station (*map 2 D2*) set around a lake is the main town of eastern Uttarakhand. The area was settled by the British in the 1840s, though the northern part of the town, known as Mallital (the southern part is called Tallital) was destroyed by a landslide in 1880, killing more than 150 people. The area affected was later levelled and is now known as The Flats. The oldest surviving building in the town is the neo-Gothic **Church of St John in the Wilderness** (1846), with some fine stained glass and interesting memorial tablets, while the impressive castle-like **Government House** (1899), now known as Raj Bhavan, serves as one of the homes of the governor of Uttarakhand (*open only when the governor is not in residence: Mon–Sat 11–1 & 2–4*). The **Naina Devi Temple** is built on the spot next to The Flats where the eye, or *naini*, of the goddess Sati is said to have fallen next to the lake, or *tal*. **Gurney House**, on Ayarpatta Hill on the west side of the town, is the former house of the tiger-hunting naturalist Jim Corbett, after whom the national park is named. It is a private house with a small museum, which is usually—but unpredictably—open to the public. There are three **British cemeteries**, one near the church, a second near Gurney House; the third, and largest, is 4km outside Naini Tal, on the road to Bhowali.

AROUND NAINI TAL

There are several other settlements near Naini Tal that date to the colonial period, including **Jeolikot**, 10km to the south, with some old bungalows and a British cemetery, and **Mukteshwar**, 40km northeast of Naini Tal, with a church and several government buildings connected with what was the Imperial Bacteriological Laboratory, now the Indian Veterinary Research Institute (IVRI). The main building of the IVRI is closed to the public, but Mukteshwar is still an interesting place to visit, and has superb views. **Ranikhet** is a pretty cantonment town, 45km north of Naini Tal, with the **Museum of the Kumaon Regiment** (*open Mon–Sat 9–5*) and the traditional British-period Ranikhet Club. The village of **Dwarahat**, 30km north of Ranikhet, has some interesting Hindu temples constructed from the 10th to the 12th centuries by the Katyuri and Chand dynasties. **Dunagiri**, 14km north of Dwarahat, has a popular 12th-century temple, dedicated to the form of the mother goddess known as Shakti. (*All on map 2 D2.*)

ALMORA

The other major hill-station in this part of Uttarakhand is Almora (*map 2 D2*), 65km northeast of Naini Tal. It is an older town, having been the stronghold of the Chand Dynasty, which dominated Kumaon for many centuries. The **Nand Devi Temple** in the Lala Bazar area dates from the Chand period, while the stone-built **Methodist Church** (1897), with its clock tower, is at the northern end of The Mall. The district jail in the heart of Almora was used by the British to imprison pro-Independence leaders, including the future prime minister, Jawaharlal Nehru.

AROUND ALMORA

Jageshwar (*map 2 D2*) is an important and unusual site, 33km northeast of Almora. It consists of the ruins of more than 100 Hindu temples from the 7th to the 18th centuries, all set in a pretty village in a valley. Jageshwar was a major religious centre during the Katyuri and Chand periods of rule in the Kumaon region. The largest groups of temples, mainly dedicated to Shiva, are in a large compound in the heart of Jageshwar. There is a small **museum** (*open Sat–Thur 10–5*) near the tourist rest home. There are more temples on the outskirts of the town, near the river.

To the north of Almora is: **Kausani**, 40km away, with its **Gandhi Ashram**, where the Mahatma composed a treatise on yoga; **Baijnath**, another 20km further north, with a group of attractive 8th–12th-century Katyuri-period temples; and **Bageshwar**, 20km east of Baijnath, with a 16th-century Shiva temple.

PRACTICAL INFORMATION

GETTING THERE

• **By air:** Uttarakhand is not well-served by air. There is one airport in the west of the state, called Jolly Grant, midway between Dehra Dun and Rishikesh, but it has only a couple of daily flights from Delhi, while the airport in the east, at Pantnagar, was not functioning for commercial flights at the time of writing. Most visitors from Delhi travel by train or road.
• **By train:** Rail travel is the most popular and probably the easiest way to reach the state. The key railway line in Garhwal terminates at Dehra Dun, having passed through Hardwar, with regular trains from Delhi (4½hrs to Rishikesh, 6hrs to Dehra Dun), while the rail terminus for Naini Tal and Almora is at Kathgodam. Taxis are available for hire at Kathgodam, including shared taxis to the main hill-stations. It is roughly 1½hrs' drive to Naini Tal, and 3hrs to Almora.
• **By road:** The main roads from Delhi to Uttarakhand are not very well maintained by the standards of other major highways. By road, Hardwar is about 5hrs from Delhi, 6hrs from Rishikesh and Dehra Dun, and 7hrs from Mussoorie and Naini Tal. (*See Uttar Pradesh chapter for places to visit en route.*)

GETTING AROUND

Most of Uttarakhand is mountainous, and served by winding hill roads. Be prepared for extensive delays caused by landslips and accidents, particularly in the rainy season. There is a morning helicopter service from near Rudraprayag to Kedarnath, but elsewhere there is no alternative to travelling by car, or on horseback or foot. If you're bringing a driver from Delhi, try to find one who has experience of driving in the hills—and it is best not to travel on hill roads at night. Some rental agencies charge higher rates per kilometre for the hills, partly because it is hard to travel far in a day.

ACCOMMODATION

• **Garhwal:** Mussoorie and the area north of Rishikesh have the best hotels in Garhwal. There are several former princely summer palaces in and around Mussoorie, including the comfortable **Kasmanda Palace** (*$$; kasmandapalace.com; T: 0135 2632424*), just off Mall Road in the heart of the hill-station; it is still owned by the former royal family of Kasmanda. Just 2km outside Mussoorie, on its own hilltop, is the **Claridges Nabha Residence** (*$$$; claridges-hotels.com; T: 0135 2631 426/427*), which belonged to the former maharaja of Nabha, a principality in Punjab. **Cloud End** (*see p. 264*) has also re-opened as a basic comfortable hotel (*$; cloudend.com; T: 0941 2050242*). Dehra Dun's most interesting hotel is **Shaheen Bagh** (*$$; T: 0120 2551963;*

shaheenbagh.com), in a traditional house on a ridge outside the city.

Five kilometres north of Rishikesh in Narendra Nagar is India's best-known spa hotel, the **Ananda** (*$$$, anandaspa.com; T: 01378 227500*) in the converted palace of the former maharaja of Tehri Garhwal. Also north of Rishikesh, 23km along the Rudraprayag road, is the unusual **Glasshouse on the Ganges** (*$$; neemranahotels.com; T: 01378 269224*), situated in a royal orchard, overlooking a sandy beach and the Ganges. The **Fairydale Resort** (*$$; T: 01386 262599; fairydalelansdowne.in*) is recommended in Lansdowne.

• **Kumaon:** There are many dozens of hotels in and around Naini Tal. Of these, the **Palace Belvedere** (*$$; T: 05942 237434; welcomheritagehotels.com*), a former home of the rajas of Awagarh, is in one of the best locations, above The Flats. In Ranikhet, the **Ranikhet Club** (*$$; T: 05966 226011; chevronhotels.com*) is an attractive 1860s hotel, which feels very British and club-like.

Kalmatia Sangam (*$$$; T: 05962 251176; kalmatia-sangam.com*), on a ridge above Almora, has British-style cottages with superb views of the Himalayas. The **Ramgarh Bungalows** (*$$; T: 05942 281156; neemranahotels.com*), set in pretty hills 30km from Naini Tal, are 19th-century British bungalows run by the Neemrana group of hotels.

FOOD

The staple food of the hills is *dal-bhaat*, or rice with lentils, in the morning, and *chapattis* with vegetables in the evenings. There are lots of local varieties of spinach that are widely eaten according to the season; meat is rarely consumed. Most restaurants serve the kind of basic food that is available throughout northern India. European-style food is widely available in the hill-stations and at Rishikesh. Mussoorie has good bakeries, and Landour has superb home-made cheddar cheese at Prakash Stores. The omelette rolls at Char Dukaan, in Landour, are also very popular. It is also possible to get fresh grilled or fried river trout in many parts of Uttarakhand.

FURTHER READING

Ruskin Bond, an Indian of British descent, who has lived in and around Mussoorie for more than 40 years, is one of India's best-loved writers, known particularly for his short stories and essays. The largely autobiographical *Landour Days* (Penguin India, 2005) is a charming introduction to his writing, and to the area where he lives. *The Man-eaters of Kumaon* (Oxford India, 1989), an international bestseller when it was first published in 1944, is one of several books by Jim Corbett, the great tiger-hunter and conservationist—after whom the Corbett National Park is named. Allen Sealy's novel *Red* (Picador, 2006), about a painter inspired by Matisse, is set in Dehra Dun. The Outlook Traveller guide to Uttarakhand, which is widely available in India, is the best guide to the state.

HARYANA

The north Indian state of Haryana (*map* 2) is little visited by tourists, despite its proximity to Delhi and Rajasthan. Many tourists actually pass through the state en route to Rajasthan, Punjab or the hills of Himachal Pradesh without stopping. In fact, it has some superb Islamic architecture, particularly at Narnaul and Thanesar, while Panipat and Kurukshetra were the sites of important battles. Kurukshetra was the site of the final conflict described in the Hindu epic the *Mahabharata*, and is an important place of pilgrimage. The central Haryana towns of Hansi, Hisar and Jhajjar also contain important Muslim buildings, as well as being part of a short-lived 'kingdom' ruled by the Irish mercenary-adventurer George Thomas in the 18th century. The state of Haryana shares its capital, Chandigarh (*see p. 282*), with the state of Punjab. The Delhi suburbs of Gurgaon, Faridabad and Najafgarh are all part of Haryana.

NORTHERN HARYANA: THE DELHI–CHANDIGARH ROAD

Most people travelling to the north of India go straight to Chandigarh, without stopping, but there are a number of important places to visit on the way—in part because the route largely follows the Grand Trunk Road, which historically was South Asia's most important highway. The road originally extended for more than 2500km from the Afghan frontier, through Lahore, Delhi and Agra to Bengal. It was constructed, for both military reasons and as a trade route, during the brief reign of Sher Shah Suri (1540–45), though some stretches of it are much older. Under the Mughals and the British, the road was critical for controlling a vast swathe of northern India.

Although the GT Road, as the Grand Trunk Road is often called, is now a modern highway—this stretch is officially NH1 (National Highway One)—one can still spot the thick stone or brick pillars covered with plaster, known as *kos minars*, when travelling along it. These were built in the Mughal period at regular intervals along the roadside, though they are often now dwarfed by the towering chimneys of more modern brick kilns. The *kos minars* functioned as milestones—a *kos* is about 3km, while a *minar* is a tower—and, though many of them are now missing or falling to pieces, dozens more survive, serving as reminders of the old Mughal route to their sometime capital in Lahore (in modern-day Pakistan) and their summer retreat in Kashmir.

The route from Delhi to Chandigarh, which runs parallel to the River Yamuna, also has a number of important monuments in the large and ancient towns that it connects.

PANIPAT

This industrial town (*map 2 C2*), 85km north of Delhi, was the site of three major battles and is home to one of India's oldest surviving Mughal buildings. It is widely believed to have been Paniprastha, one of five ancient cities of the Pandava brothers, who fought the Kauravas in the great Hindu epic the *Mahabharata*. The three battles of Panipat were much more recent. The earliest of them was fought in 1526 between the first Mughal emperor, Babur, and the last of the Delhi sultans, Ibrahim Lodi. It was a decisive victory for Babur over an ill-equipped army that had at least eight times as many soldiers.

Babri Masjid

The Babri Masjid, or Babur's Mosque, in Kabuli Bagh (Kabul Garden)—near the Kutani Road, on the outskirts of modern Panipat—was constructed soon after the battle. It is the oldest extant Mughal building in India. Its famous counterpart in Ayodhya, also known as the Babri Masjid, was destroyed by Hindu extremists in 1992. The Panipat Babri Masjid is a handsome, partially-ruined seven-bayed brick and sandstone mosque, set in the kind of garden that Babur maintained was lacking in India, and that made him so homesick for his former capital, Kabul. The mosque has been recently restored, and there are plans to beautify the surrounding area so that the nearby open sewer is less of an assault on one's eyes and nasal passages.

The **tomb of Ibrahim Lodi**, the ruler slain by the Mughals at the first Battle of Panipat is 2km to the west of the mosque, near the Tehsil office, in a public park. During the Mughal period, the tomb consisted of no more than a simple grave, and only after the British defeated the Mughals was the current tomb platform and the simple uncovered cenotaph erected.

Dargah of Bu Ali Qalandar

The Dargah of Bu Ali Qalandar, the shrine of a 12th-century Sufi saint originally from Azerbaijan, is in the heart of old Panipat. The shrine building is thought to date from the early 17th century, and the double three-arched entrance porch has some fine Mughal floral, geometric and calligraphic decorations on its walls and ceiling. The tiled interior of the tomb is more recent. Notice the small padlocks secured to parts of the tomb. They are placed there by pilgrims seeking the intercession of Bu Ali Qalandar—perhaps to cure an illness or bring about a change of fortune.

Kala Amb

Four kilometres east of Panipat, on the Sanauli road at Kala Amb, is a memorial site to all three battles of Panipat: the victory of Emperor Babur over the Lodis in 1526; the victory of the Mughal emperor Akbar over the forces of the Hindu General Hemu in 1556, which consolidated Mughal control over northern India; and, finally, the defeat of the marathas by the Afghan warlord Ahmad Shah Abdali (also known as Ahmad Shah Durrani) in 1761. The rather disappointing **Panipat Memorial Park** has been laid out at the site of the third battle, in which more than 60,000 soldiers are thought to have died. A small pillar erected in the British period marks the site of a famous black mango tree, which stood on the battlefield, and which gave 'Kala Amb' (literally 'black mango') its name. There is also a small museum, and some modern relief carving of battle scenes.

KARNAL

Karnal (*map 2 C2*), 30km north of Panipat on the GT Road, was an important garrison town for the British in the early 19th century. It was eventually abandoned because the area was so badly affected by malaria and other diseases. Turn off at the Liberty Chowk on the northern side of the modern town to visit the interesting old **British cemetery** at Karnal. This is also where the well-preserved **tower of the old garrison church** survives. It is possible to climb the tower for a good view over the surrounding countryside. The grave of the famously dilatory British commander-in-chief at the start of the 1857 Uprising, General George Anson, is among the overgrown tombs in the cemetery. General Anson died of cholera at Karnal while heading for Delhi, which had been captured by the rebels. His body was later disinterred, returned to England and reburied in Kensal Green Cemetery in London.

KURUKSHETRA

This pilgrimage town (*map 2 B2*), 35km north of Karnal (150km from Delhi) on the western side of the GT Road, is the site of the great final battle of the *Mahabharata*. According to this great Hindu epic, more than 3,000,000 soldiers died in the 18-day Battle of Kurukshetra—and only eleven people survived. The battle was fought between warring cousins: the five Pandava brothers (aided by the god Krishna) and the Kauravas. Scholars have used astronomical evidence in the text to come up with a number of possible dates for the battle, ranging from 5000 BC to 1500 BC, but no archaeological evidence has been found of a major conflict. The many temples and water tanks of Kurukshetra are a major pilgrimage site, partly because, prior to the great battle, the Pandava leader, Arjuna, and his charioteer, the god Krishna, held the conversation in verse known as the *Bhagavad Gita*. The *Gita*, as it known, forms part of the *Mahabharata*, and is one of the most important Hindu religious texts. More generally, the Kurukshetra area has taken on the status of a kind of Hindu holy land, and visitors to its mainly modern temples will hear tales of all the gods, and not just Krishna.

Brahma Sarovar

The **Brahma Sarovar**, 1,000m by 500m, is one of the largest artificial bathing tanks in India—notice the special partly-covered cubicles for women. It is said to be the place from which Brahma created the universe. There is also a well-restored 19th-century royal rest-house, with a very pretty façade; it previously belonged to the maharaja of Nabha, and stands next to the Sannehit Sarovar—a large water tank that some Hindus believe marks the home of the god Vishnu.

THANESAR

This town adjoining the western side of Kurukshetra has one of the finest and most unusual Muslim tomb complexes to be found anywhere in India. The 19th-century British traveller David Ross wrote that the tomb was, after the Taj Mahal, 'one of the most graceful of Muhammadan tombs'. A visit to this largely forgotten mausoleum is highly recommended. The site, signposted as Sheikh Chillie's tomb, is 2km west of the GT Road, on the eastern side of a large, ancient, partially excavated mound which was once a 7th-century citadel. The excavations reveal that this site has been settled for more than 2,000 years.

Orientation: The approach to the Thanesar site is from the west. A large walled garden, with a locked gate, described on a signboard as Harshavardhana's Park, is on the right (or north). The tomb complex is to the left, behind high brick walls, beyond the car park and the ticket office. Behind all of these buildings is the partially excavated mound, which also can be visited by walking around the tomb complex, or by a separate access gate on the northern side of the site.

The outer courtyard: The site is entered through steps that lead into a large cloistered courtyard, approximately 32m square, with a pool at its centre. The tomb itself is on a much higher level, and its marble dome can be seen up on the right. The courtyard and the rooms leading off it are thought to have been used as a *madrasa*, or religious school. Some of the rooms leading off the cloister are now in use as a **museum**, which sets out the history of the site. Implements and artefacts excavated at the site dating back to the 1st century AD are exhibited. On the northern side of the courtyard, a passage leads down to the actual graves, which are covered in silk cloth. Note the small ceiling apertures that allow sunlight into the chamber. The staircases onto the tomb platform are in the northwest and northeast corners of the courtyard.

The tomb platform: From the platform one gets a superb view of the octagonal tomb itself, raised slightly on its own plinth, with its butter yellow marble walls and its fine marble tracery screens. The backdrop to this view is the rest of the tomb platform, with its pretty cupolas and, behind that, the walled garden; the mound, with its excavated walls and rooms, is clearly visible from a distance.

The tomb: This has two cenotaphs. The raised one is thought to belong to Sheikh Cheheli, or Sheikh Chillie, a 17th-century Sufi, who, according to local tradition, played the role of spiritual advisor to Dara Shikoh, the oldest son of Emperor Shah Jahan. It is not known who the second cenotaph belongs to, or why there are more tombs in the grave chamber beneath than in the tomb. Balustrades once surrounded the plinth of the tomb, and the post-holes are still visible. Note the apertures on the side of the base of the tomb: these are the skylights, visible in the grave chamber beneath. Some of the cupolas have the remains of blue tiling, while the slightly larger pavilion, with an elongated *bangla*-style roof, has decorative relief panels in sandstone.

Formal garden: From the northern wall of the tomb platform, one gets an excellent and unusual bird's eye view of the formal Mughal-style garden. As with most Mughal gardens, it is divided into four parts, with a pool at its centre. Historians have struggled to date it precisely, and it may, in fact, be pre-Mughal. It certainly pre-dates the tomb complex, and was probably built during the rule of Sher Shah Suri in the 1540s. Note its water supply system, with excavations having clearly revealed terracotta pipes and a cistern close to the northwest corner of the mosque.

Excavated mound: To the west of the park, beyond the cistern, is the mound where four large areas have been excavated. The artefacts displayed in the museum in the tomb complex came from here—and it is possible, from the cleared areas, to see the walls, rooms and drainage systems of what may have been a garrison or palace. Historians believe the mound was almost certainly the citadel of the 7th-century Buddhist monarch Harsha Vardhana, who ruled large tracts of northern India from Thanesar, before moving his capital to Kannauj in modern-day Uttar Pradesh. Note the remains of the walls of the citadel, including part of a bastion, on the far side of the mound. The views of the tomb complex are superb from this area. Note also the fine small red mosque, the **Pathar Masjid**, in the grounds of the tomb complex. Normally locked, it is still possible to see its pretty fluted minaret stumps, as well as sandstone carvings on its pillars and under its eaves.

AMBALA

This cantonment town (*map 2 B1*), built after the British abandoned Karnal, is 42km north of Kurukshetra and just 40km from Chandigarh, the shared capital of Haryana and Punjab. At Ambala, the GT Road veers off northeast into Punjab, in the direction of Amritsar and the Pakistan border. The northern road (NH21) leads to Chandigarh, Simla and the hills of Himachal Pradesh. Just over a kilometre to the east of the GT Road, 3km before the junction with NH21 and next to the Air Force School, is the eerie half-ruined shell of a handsome Victorian Gothic church, one of the most impressive in India. **St Paul's Church**, which was consecrated just months before the 1857 Uprising, was attacked from the air by Pakistan in the 1965 war, and left in its current state, as a memorial to what the Indian authorities describe as the 'indiscriminate' bombing carried out by the Pakistanis.

Morni, situated 40km east of Chandigarh in the Morni Hills, is Haryana's only hill-station, with a recently restored ancient fortress, complete with large rounded bastions and battlements.

PINJORE

This small town (*map 2 C1*) at the northern tip of Haryana, near the rail terminus for the Simla line at Kalka, has some very pretty but over-restored 17th-century Mughal gardens called the **Pinjore Gardens** (*open daily 7am–10pm*). With functioning fountains and piped music, they create the impression of being on the set of a Hindi movie.

They were designed by Emperor Aurangzeb's foster brother Fidai Khan, and came under the control of Patiala, after whose ruler, Yadavindra, the gardens are sometimes now known. The design of the gardens, over seven levels, is similar to the Shalimar Gardens in Kashmir, though they slope down rather than up from the entrance. The gardens are lit at night.

WESTERN HARYANA

Western Haryana has a number of important and little-visited 14th-century buildings from the Tughlaq period. Before the 16th-century construction of the Grand Trunk Road, the main military and trade routes from Delhi into Punjab and towards Afghanistan went through this region. It is possible to visit this area on a long day trip from Delhi, Chandigarh or Patiala—or, alternatively, to stay overnight at the only good hotel in the region, just outside Hansi.

HANSI

The town of Hansi (*map 2 B2*) is 125km from Delhi and dates back to the pre-Islamic period. It was once a walled city, and the impressive southern **Barsi Gate** has survived in good condition. It was built in 1303, under the Khilji sultans of Delhi, and is excellent condition. It has some fine inlaid blue tiling above the entrance, and the gate is unusual for its period because of the two small relief carvings on either side of the wall showing human and animal figures. In the Sultanate period, koranic rules against the depiction of living things were normally interpreted strictly. Each panel shows a man with a sword and shield fighting a lion. Note how carefully the mane of the lion has been carved. It is possible to climb the stairs of either bastion and get a good view of the upper part of the gate, and make out, 500m to the north, the large mound of Hansi Fort.

Hansi Fort

This large open fort, constructed on a mound in the centre of old Hansi, is thought to have been founded by the last pre-Sultanate ruler of Delhi, Prithviraj Chauhan, in the 12th century. Most of its walls have crumbled away, and the brick-built gate is a late 18th-century addition, constructed by the Irish adventurer George Thomas. He briefly ruled a small kingdom, covering large parts of modern Haryana, from this fort. Among the buildings scattered across the huge flattened surface of the fort interior are a large pillared hall, an unusual water tank, supported internally by a series of arches, a mosque and a Muslim shrine. Notice the carved masonry work, which is part of the mosque building, though probably belonged originally to an older Hindu temple. There are some superb pieces of carved stone lying on the ground. Look out for a particularly fine row of carved geese, on the right hand side of the shrine, next to some plain graves.

HISAR

This town (*map 2 B2*, also known as Hissar), 150km west of Delhi and 25km west of Hansi, was founded in 1356 by Sultan Feroze Shah Tughlaq of Delhi on the site of a pre-Islamic settlement. Apart from Delhi, nowhere in India has such an impressive collection of Tughlaq buildings. Hisar Fort, in the centre of the modern town, dates from this period, as do the excavated palace, the fine mosque which can be visited within its precincts, and the strange Gurjari Palace, 200m away across the park outside the fort.

Hisar Fort

The fort is on the northern side of Hisar, close to NH10, the road which leads to Fatehabad. Large parts of the western walls of the fort survive, but there have also been many encroachments. Note the sloping walls which are typical of Tughlaq architecture. Head inside the main Talaqi Gate of the fort (note the extensive guard rooms). Straight ahead is the distinctive mosque, while to the left are the extensive ruins of Feroze Shah Tughlaq's four-storey palace.

Lat ki Masjid: The Lat ki Masjid, or Pillar Mosque, is an impressive building with a tall column, the lower portion of which is thought to have been an Ashoka pillar, carrying, like many others around the country, written edicts of the 3rd-century BC emperor Ashoka. The surface of the pillar is badly decayed, however, and it is not possible to make out any inscription. Experts believe this is the bottom half of the pillar, and the top half can be seen at the mosque in the nearby town of Fatehabad (*see overleaf*). The upper three levels of the pillar, made of red sandstone, are thought to have been erected during the Tughlaq period. The prayer hall and part of the northern side of the mosque survive. Some of the pillars in the mosque are finely carved and were probably taken from older Hindu temples. Note the deep excavated channel on two sides of the building which shows the original ground level inside the fort, and, therefore, just how high the mosque was originally raised above the ground. There is an elevated prayer area at the corner of the surviving walls, which was probably either used by the sultan himself or as a separate space where women prayed. Note also the small concealed passage near the raised prayer area, which may once have been part of a separate gate.

The small domed pavilion within the mosque walls was probably a tomb, but no grave survives—and it is unlikely to be a gateway because it is not aligned with the centre of the mosque.

Feroze Shah's Palace: The sprawling palace complex is on one's left as one enters Hisar Fort. It has been recently excavated and restored by the Archaeological Survey of India. Take a torch if you want to explore properly the maze of rooms and corridors spread over three storeys. The 14th-century chronicler Shams-i Siraj Afif, who said the palace had 'no equal in the world', also pointed out that 'the central apartment is very dark and the passages narrow, so that if the attendants did not guide the visitor, he would never be able to find his way out.' Sadly no decoration has survived in any of the rooms, and no artefacts have been found during the excavations. Note the carved columns on the far left of the palace, and the fallen pillars on the roof which once supported a fourth storey. The quality of the stonework is more refined on the upper storeys, and presumably this is where the royal apartments were.

Beyond the palace, overlooking the northern walls, are some rundown buildings from the British colonial period, complete with fireplaces and good views across to the Gujari Mahal.

Gujari Mahal

Very little is known for certain about this unusual and interesting 14th-century building, just 200m north of Hisar Fort. According to local tradition, it was the palace of Feroze Shah's lover Gujari, a milkmaid who refused to live with him in Delhi. There is a pavilion, with nine internal domes and some pretty carved pillars on the roof of the building. Note what was the old entrance to the building, now blocked up, between the two towers on the east side. The lower floor of the building is locked and consists of a large empty hall.

Jahaz Kothi and Jahaz Pul

These two neighbouring buildings, 1km east of the fort, are also worth a quick visit. Confusingly, the two names are used interchangeably for the two very different buildings. One is a 14th-century Tughlaq building, which was probably once a *madrasa* and is now a Jain temple. The second is a recently restored late 18th-century building constructed by the Irish adventurer George Thomas; it is now being turned into a local museum. 'Jahaz' is possibly a corruption of George; an alternative explanation is that *jahaz* is an Urdu word for 'ship', so perhaps locals, who are a very long way from the nearest sea, felt the building looked like a ship.

AGROHA

This ancient town (*map 2 B2*) lies halfway between Hisar and Fatehabad. Excavations, which are open to the public (you'll need to find the caretaker who is normally nearby), show that Agroha has been an important settlement since the 3rd century BC. The floors and lower walls of the fortifications, the shrines and residential accommodation have been exposed in the excavations. Some historians believe that the pillars at Hisar and Fatehabad were originally a single Ashoka pillar which stood in Agroha, which would therefore have been part of the Mauryan Empire. According to local tradition, this was the capital of the kingdom ruled by the legendary Hindu hero Maharaja Agarsen, many thousands of years ago—and there are many modern temples devoted to his memory.

FATEHABAD

This town (*map 2 B2*), 47km northwest of Hisar, was an important centre in the Tughlaq period. It was named after Feroze Shah Tughlaq's son Fateh Khan. There is a 5m high pillar outside a small 14th-century **Tughlaq Idgah**, or open air mosque, in the Old Police Lines, near Jauhar Chowk. Archaeologists believe the bottom part of the pillar, which is white and inscribed with Arabic text, was originally inscribed with Ashokan edicts, which were then chiselled off and replaced with the Arabic text in the Tughlaq period. This is thought to be the top half of the same pillar that is to be found in Hisar Fort (*see p. 277*); the sandstone upper part of the pillar was probably added by the Tughlaqs.

One hundred metres from the mosque, past some police buildings, are the ruined ramparts of the old citadel.

SOUTHERN HARYANA

NARNAUL

This little-visited town (*map 2 B3*) is on the route from Delhi to Shekhawati and the rest of northern Rajasthan. It has some architecturally important monuments, including a very pretty water palace, a superb tomb from the 16th century and an unusual example of 17th-century domestic architecture. Narnaul was a major administrative centre under the Mughals, and Akbar established a mint here.

Jal Mahal

On the southern outskirts of Narnaul, the Jal Mahal, or Water Palace, has been recently restored and is in good condition. A bridge takes visitors to a small two-storeyed palace with five rooftop *chattris*. When the artificial lake is full, the palace is totally surrounded by water. The palace has net vaulting over the entrance doorways, and some pretty geometric painted decoration. There is a pavilion on the side of the lake, next to a smaller feeder pool. To the west of the Jal Mahal is a large walled garden, with three tombs, an interesting gateway and two step-wells. The main tomb here, with modern protective fencing, contains the grave of Shah Quli Khan, one of Akbar's closest advisers, and governor of Narnaul. It echoes, in its use of grey and red sandstone, the magnificent mausoleum of Ibrahim Khan, 1km to the north.

Ibrahim Khan's Tomb

The splendid mausoleum is hidden away in the heart of the old town. Ibrahim Khan was the grandfather of Sher Shah Suri, who defeated the Mughal emperor Humayun, and whose brief dynasty ruled in Delhi for 15 years. Sher Shah was born in, or near, Narnaul, and the tomb over his grandfather's grave (c. 1540) is both very attractive and in excellent condition. It is a large two-storeyed square tomb, raised on a high plinth, with a white dome and octagonal *chattris* on the four corners of the roof. It is the mixture of colours—mainly grey and red—that makes the tomb so impressive from a distance. And from close up the quality of the carved stonework is remarkable. Note the carved corbelling over the main doorway, which prefigures some of the fine sandstone carving on the Jehangiri Mahal in Agra Fort. Traces of red paintwork are visible on the interior of the dome.

Opposite the mausoleum, across the narrow street, is the even older **Tomb of Pir Turkman**, a Sufi saint. It is part of complex of buildings from Tughlaq, Mughal and British times. The complex is quite derelict but interesting to wander around, as are the nearby streets, and there are several mosques and tombs that are inhabited, but their residents seems happy to show visitors around.

Birbal ka Chatta

To the northeast of Ibrahim Khan's Tomb by about 750m, in the backstreets of Narnaul, is another fascinating building. Known as **Birbal ka Chatta**, this five-storey residential complex was actually built sometime after the death of Birbal, Akbar's best-known adviser. It now seems that this crumbling edifice was constructed in the 17th century for the local chief, called Rai Mukand Das, and contains an elaborate arrangement of underground rooms, lit through a complex series of skylights which penetrate through the central courtyard of the building. There are also the remains of a suite of bathrooms, a sophisticated water supply system, pretty roof vaulting, a room with carved wooden columns and rafters, and decorated roof-top pavilions. About 1.5km further north, on the main road towards northern Rajasthan, there is a handsome 14th-century Muslim tomb, known as the **Chor Gumbad**.

JHAJJAR

The town of Jhajjar (*map 2 B3*), 55km west of Delhi, was, until the mid-19th century, a minor principality. Its ruler supported the 1857 Uprising, and was deposed and executed by the British. There are several interesting Mughal-style tombs, and a ruined palace and mosque on the eastern outskirts of the town.

FARRUKHNAGAR

The town of Farrukhnagar (*map 2 B3*), 45km southwest of Delhi and 7km west of the Sultanpur Bird Sanctuary, was, until the mid-19th century, a minor principality, much like nearby Jhajjar. And similarly also, Farrukhnagar's ruler supported the 1857 Uprising and was executed by the British. Several interesting late Mughal ruins have survived, including a palace, some *chattris* (with wall-paintings), tombs, a mosque (that is now a temple) and fortified town gateways.

PATAUDI

The town of Pataudi (*map 2 B3*), 60km southwest of Delhi, was the capital of the tiny princely state of the same name. The last two nawabs of Pataudi were both captains of the Indian cricket team, and the palace, built in 1935, is now a comfortable hotel.

PRACTICAL INFORMATION

GETTING AROUND

Haryana is easily accessible from Delhi or Chandigarh, and many of the key sites in the state make good day trips from either of these cities—or in the case of Narnaul, en route from Delhi to northern Rajasthan.

ACCOMMODATION & FOOD

Apart from Gurgaon, which really functions as a suburb of Delhi, with several 5-star hotels aimed at business travellers, Haryana has very few good places to stay. Two exceptions are: the beautiful **Sheikhpura Kothi** (*$$; T: 01663 24024; welcomheritagehotels.com*), a 19th-century European-style mansion set in pretty gardens, just outside Hansi on the Jind Road; and the 20th-century **Pataudi Palace** (*$$$; T: 0124 2672244; neemrana-hotels.com*), in Pataudi village, just off the Delhi-Jaipur highway, 60km southwest of Delhi—this is the former residence of the Pataudi royal family. There is no distinctive Haryana food, and Punjabi cuisine is widely available at roadside cafés, known as *dhabas,* in most parts of the state.

CHANDIGARH

Chandigarh (*map 2 B1 and on p. 285*), largely the creation of the 20th-century architect Le Corbusier, is India's most unusual city. It is determinedly modern in a way that now seems rather old-fashioned. Its signature buildings are made out of unadorned concrete, and most visitors tend to be derisive about its lack of colour and imagination—and yet it remains the city that many middle-class Indians aspire to live in during their retirement. Chandigarh is cleaner and less cluttered than other Indian cities, and people generally obey the rules when they are building a house or crossing the road. It is also in the unique position of being the shared capital of two states, Punjab and Haryana, but is not within the frontiers of either of them and enjoys the status of a separate Union territory, ruled by a governor appointed from Delhi. It is easy to reach by road, air or train and has become a gateway to the mountains of Kashmir and Himachal, and the plains of Punjab.

HISTORY OF CHANDIGARH

The construction of Chandigarh in the 1950s was a direct result of the division of the subcontinent into India and Pakistan at the time of Independence in 1947. The huge Punjab province was split between the two countries, and Pakistan was allotted the largest city and natural capital, Lahore. Indian Punjab needed a new capital, and although Simla played that role temporarily, it was transferred to the territory that would become the state of Himachal Pradesh. Some 114km square of largely agricultural land was set aside for a new capital. There were a number of small villages within the designated site, and the one called Chandigarh was selected as the name for the new city. Le Corbusier was not the first choice of architect, and an American team consisting of Albert Mayer and Matthew Nowicki developed the first plans for the new capital as a garden city. When Nowicki died in a plane crash, Mayer withdrew from the project, and Le Corbusier, already one of the best-known architects in world, was brought in.

Although Le Corbusier is usually credited with the creation of the city, he had a team of international and Indian architects working alongside him; they included his cousin Pierre Jeanneret and the British Modernist husband-and-wife team Maxwell Fry and Jane Drew. But, arguably, the key player in the early conception of the project was the prime minister, Jawaharlal Nehru, who called for the construction of the city as 'unfettered by the traditions of the past, a symbol of the nation's faith in the future'. When he saw the result, his response was a touch ambivalent: 'It hits you on the head and makes you think. You may squirm at the impact, but it makes you think and imbibe new ideas.'

The population of Chandigarh has grown far beyond what was intended and some of the buildings and parks have broken the rules set down by Le Corbusier for a truly modern city. However, the key elements remain, both as a testament to Modernism and to an idealised city in which people actually want to live. India has other planned state capitals, such as Bhubaneswar in Orissa and Gandhinagar in Gujarat, but none comes close to having the impact of Chandigarh. It also continues to serve as the shared capital of two states, though many politicians in Punjab insist that Chandigarh should be fully integrated into their state, as originally planned, and that Haryana should build its own capital.

LE CORBUSIER

The Swiss-born French architect and town planner Charles-Édouard Jeanneret (1887–1965) adopted the name Le Corbusier in the 1920s, before he was famous. It means the 'crow-like one' and is also a play on 'Lecorbésier', the name of one of his ancestors. He was an early Modernist, for whom reinforced concrete was the most important construction material: he did not believe that it should be covered with paint or plaster or hidden by ornamentation. One of the most distinctive elements of Le Corbusier's style—visible throughout Chandigarh—is that he raised many of his buildings off the ground on pillars, which he called pilotis. He also placed roof gardens on major buildings, as a way or replacing some of the green space that had been covered over. Although he designed many individual buildings, Chandigarh was his only major exercise in town planning to be implemented. He did, though, earlier in his career, design imagined cities, which were very influential with other town planners. Le Corbusier also designed two buildings in Ahmedabad (*see p. 368*). At Chandigarh, he took the Mayer/Nowicki plan and turned it into a Modernist experiment: he straightened its curved streets, focused less on creating integrated communities, and gave major buildings the undecorated monumentality for which he was so well known.

Orientation: The city has a rectilinear grid system of roads, which divide it into more than 60 numbered sectors. Sector 1, in the far northeast of the city, contains the main government buildings and the high court (known as the Capitol Complex), as well as the pretty Sukhna Lake and Chandigarh's most popular tourist attraction, the Rock Garden. There is a row of main sectors running southwest from the Rock Garden, numbered in order 4, 9, 17, 22 and 35. Sector 9 has the Chandigarh Secretariat, while Sector 17, about 2.5km southwest of the Rock Garden, serves as the city centre and has both the bus station and the Taj Hotel. The next two sectors to the southwest, 22 and 35, have lots more shops, restaurants and hotels. The railway station and the main road from Delhi are on the southeastern side of the city. Chandigarh has no Sector 13, but city planners insist this was not for superstitious reasons, but was omitted by chance.

The Capital Complex

The main Sector 1 buildings are the Secretariat, the Assembly Building and Chandigarh High Court, and represent the best and most interesting examples of Le Corbusier's work in India. You'll need permission to enter each of the buildings. A visit involves an unpredictable amount of queuing and waiting, but it is well worth it if you're interested in Modernist architecture. Permission is given readily when you show your passport at one of three sites in different parts of Chandigarh: The Tourism Department (*T: 0172 2740420 or dtour@chd.nic.in*) in the Additional Deluxe building in the Union Territory Secretariat in Sector 9 (take the inside slip road from Jan Marg); the Tourism Office (*T: 0172 703839*) in Sector 17 (next to the interstate bus terminal); and the Chandigarh College of Architecture (*T: 0172 2740572 or cca@chd.nic.in*) on the PEC Campus in Sector 12.

Once you've got your permission letters, you'll find that each of the buildings has slightly different rules. So, for the Secretariat, you'll be accompanied by a security officer and can use a camera, but you will need to leave your mobile phone at the desk; for the Assembly Building, you're not allowed to use a camera at all; and for Chandigarh High Court you'll need separate permission to use a camera (from the protocol officer on floor 2). The Secretariat and Assembly Building are accessed from a security checkpost on Jan Marg, which has a car park, and from where you have to walk approximately 400m through additional security checks. Chandigarh High Court is easier to access, so that members of the public can attend hearings, and there is a car park next to the building, close to the Rock Garden.

The Secretariat

The Secretariat, the largest and least fanciful building in the Capital Complex, is a rectangular block, more than ten times longer than it is wide, from which the modern city of Chandigarh is administered. It is very distinctively a Le Corbusier building, with unadorned concrete, strong horizontal lines, and tooth-like sunscreens on the windows. Early models show the lowest level of the building raised on pillars—some gaps between the pillars have now been filled in, but the upper levels still overhang the ground floor. Note the two ramps leading up to the roof, one on each side of the building, sticking out like fins. There are also little roof-top gardens, which Le Corbusier saw as a replacement for the green space his building took up on the ground. There are excellent views from the rooftop.

Assembly Building

The Assembly Building is just 100m to the northeast of the Secretariat; its distinctive rooftop protuberance is shaped like the cooling tower of a power station. The lower part of the building is to a typical Le Corbusier rectilinear design, but with a huge curved overhanging roof eave above two small square ponds. The extraordinary **Punjab State Assembly Chamber** is enclosed by the curved walls of the interior of the 'cooling tower', the roof funnel of which provides the only natural light. The interior is painted red and yellow, with yellow carpets, and large blackened sheets of raw cotton on its walls to absorb sound. The **Haryana State Assembly Chamber**, originally designed to house Punjab's Upper Chamber is built to a more traditional design, but has a yellow floor and brightly painted walls, two tapestries designed by Le Corbusier and a small rooftop pyramid allowing light inside.

Chandigarh High Court

Of all Chandigarh's modern buildings, the High Court is the most instantly recognisable, with its green, yellow and pink support pylons, and its broad sloping roof. Com-

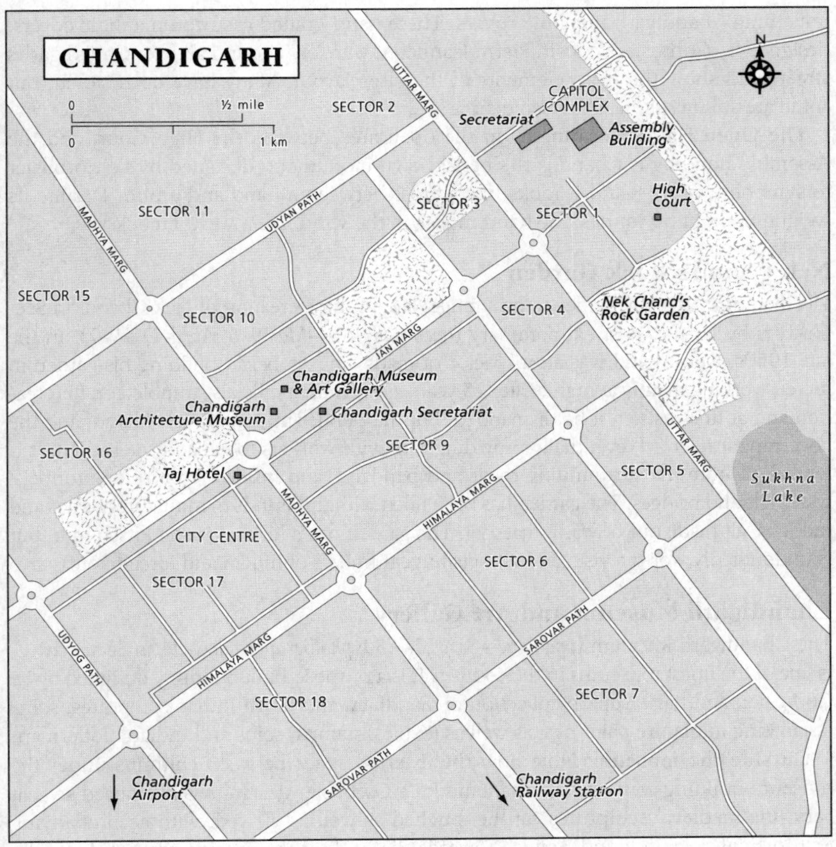

pleted in 1955, it is also Le Corbusier's most colourful creation in Chandigarh, and his least monumental monument. Nonetheless, it has proved controversial. The High Court judges were quick to defy Le Corbusier's plan that vehicles should approach the building along a sunken drive, and instead drove along paths intended for pedestrians and parked beneath the great arches of the building. The architect famously asked, 'What sort of judges are these who do not obey the traffic laws?' Several of the judges also had his cubist tapestries removed from the court rooms, to which Corbusier responded, 'They should confine themselves to be being judges of law not set themselves up as judges of art'. The tapestries are still there at the back of the courtrooms. It is possible to enter, even while the court is in session, but no photographs are allowed.

Just outside is the **High Court Museum**, where a pair of handcuffs worn by Nathuram Godse, the assassin of Mahatma Gandhi, is on display, as well as one of the few remaining Chandigarh manhole covers. These hand-crafted cast-iron manhole covers, designed by Corbusier's cousin Pierre Jeanneret, were once found all over Chandigarh's streets and show the main elements of the city's layout. Many have been stolen, but some are still *in situ* near the Secretariat.

The Open Hand Monument: In the open area between the High Court and the Assembly Building is Chandigarh's best-known monument, designed by Le Corbusier to symbolise peace—and it looks like a cross between a hand and a bird. Despite its weight of about 50 tonnes, the hand moves in the wind like a weathercock.

Nek Chand's Rock Garden

Of Chandigarh's many gardens, the strange, labyrinthine creation of Nek Chand, in Sector 1, is by far the most extraordinary (*open daily Nov–Mar 9–6; April–Oct 9–7*). In the late 1950s, Nek Chand was an inspector of roads, and he began building his garden in secret, working mainly at night. After 15 years, government officials stumbled on his creation and at first insisted it be dismantled. But the public supported Nek Chand, and the government relented, eventually providing him with workers to expand the garden. It is fenced off from the surrounding roads and parkland, and inside are corridors, tunnels, waterfalls and bridges. The garden has been filled with thousands of miniature statues and mosaics, all made out of waste material. The garden has a kind of rustic kitsch to it, but is undoubtedly worth a visit, and attracts huge numbers of Indian and foreign tourists.

Chandigarh Museum and Art Gallery

The Chandigarh Museum (*open Tues–Sun 10–4.30; photographs allowed*), in Sector 10-C, is one of the finest museums in the country. It is a purpose-built building, designed by Le Corbusier, and has a superb collection of Gandhara and north Indian sculptures, some fascinating miniature paintings, as well as textiles, stamps, coins and Indian modern art.

Outside the museum: Note how the external space between columns under the museum building, very much a trademark Le Corbusier design, has been used so that very fine medieval sculptures can be touched as well as viewed, with accompanying text in English, Hindi and Braille. Towards the back of the outside area, look for the excellent 9th-century standing Vishnu, with a male and a female attendant—the work is in pink sandstone, and comes from Agroha in Haryana.

Gandhara Collection: The most interesting exhibits in the museum are on the upper floor of this ramped building. They include India's share of the fabled Lahore collection of Gandhara sculpture, which was split between India and Pakistan at the time of Independence. The sculpture collection—mainly excavated during the British period from territory that is now in Pakistan—has some quite superb examples of Indo-Hellenic Buddhist art, in which the Greek influence is very marked. Note the fine detail on the clothing of the wonderfully naturalistic standing Buddha with a moustache (exhibit no. 2342). The extraordinary 2nd-century statue of the female *bodhisattva* Hariti (exhibit no. 1625), with three children, is the most celebrated of the Gandhara statues in Chandigarh. Hariti was a reformed demon, who used to feed other people's children to her own—of which she had several hundred—before the Buddha converted her into a protector of children.

Sanghol carvings: Among the other exhibits are some superb carved sandstone railings, mainly carrying reliefs of near-naked women, one of them holding a small child above her head. They were excavated in 1985 from close to the Buddhist stupa at nearby Sanghol in Punjab, and date back to the 1st century.

Harappan Exhibits: There are also some interesting Harappan remains, including pottery, figurines and jewellery dating back more than 3,000 years. The works were discovered just 1km from the museum in Sector 17 of Chandigarh, during the construction of an underground car park.

Other collections: Look out also for some fine 5th-century terracotta heads from Kashmir, and an excellent general introduction to miniature painting, with some good examples from the Mughal, Rajasthani and Pahari styles. Note particularly the unfinished 17th-century Mughal miniature of the Crucifixion of Jesus—an example of how Western iconography had begun to influence Mughal painting by this period.

Chandigarh Architecture Museum

This fascinating museum (*open Tues–Sun 10–5*), just 50m to the right of the main Chandigarh Museum and Art Gallery, is devoted to the planning and construction of the city. It contains early sketches, letters from Le Corbusier and models of buildings, and has excellent explanations of the philosophies that governed the layout of Chandigarh.

PRACTICAL INFORMATION

GETTING THERE

Chandigarh is just over 3hrs from Delhi by train (Shatabdi services leave from New Delhi at 7.40am and 5.15pm). It is 5hrs from Delhi by car. There are also several daily flights to Chandigarh from Delhi which take 50mins, as well as scheduled flights from Mumbai and Jammu. The road to Simla takes about 3½hrs, and there is also a 'toy' train that takes 5hrs.

GETTING AROUND

Chandigarh is spread out, so you will need a vehicle. Taxis, auto-rickshaws and cycle-rickshaws are widely available. Cycles can also be hired—and Chandigarh is one of the few cities in India where cycling is recommended (bikes are available at the Chandigarh Tourist Centre in Sector 17).

ACCOMMODATION

Chandigarh's best hotel is the **Taj** (*$$$; T: 0172 6613000; tajhotels.com*) in Sector 17-A. It is a large 21st-century structure, built in the style of Le Corbusier. The unusual **Kaptains Retreat** (*$$; T: 0172 5005594; nivalink.com/kaptainsretreat*), in Sector 35B, is owned by the former Indian cricketer Kapil Dev. It has ten rooms, is filled with cricket memorabilia, and is comfortable and centrally located.

PUNJAB

Apart from the Golden Temple in Amritsar, the holiest shrine of Sikhism, Punjab (*maps 1 and 2*) is a little-visited region. The Sikh separatist movement, which cost thousands of lives in the 1980s and early 90s, prevented the tourism infrastructure growing as fast as it had elsewhere, and Punjab is now trying to catch up. And there is plenty to see apart from the Golden Temple—in particular, the palaces of old princely states such as Patiala, Kapurthala and Faridkot; and the ruins of the medieval Sirhind, once the biggest city in the region. Its capital, the modern planned city of Chandigarh, is shared with the neighbouring city of Haryana, and covered on pages 282–87.

HISTORY OF PUNJAB

Punjab literally means 'five waters'—a reference to the five rivers (the Beas, Chenab, Jhelum, Ravi and Sutlej) that pass through this land and which then feed into the Indus. Historically, Punjab was much larger than the current Indian state. It included large parts of northern and central Pakistan, as well as the modern-day Indian states of Haryana and Himachal Pradesh. It was settled more than 4,000 years ago, and Alexander the Great reached its borders in 326 BC, though he may never have crossed into modern-day India. Islam reached here in the 12th century, and several towns in Punjab were important outposts of the Delhi Sultanate. In the 16th century, Sikhism, founded by Guru Nanak, began to be a major force in the region. Attempts to repress the new religion by the Mughal emperor Aurangzeb in the 17th century resulted in Sikhs taking to arms to defend themselves. In the early 19th century, the Sikh Empire of Ranjit Singh ruled over a huge swathe of territory, including Punjab and Kashmir.

Ranjit Singh was the son of a Punjabi Sikh landowner, who became the first maharaja of the Sikh Empire. He and his successors were defeated in a series of bloody battles with the British, however, and by the mid-19th century, Punjab was held by the British or a number of allied princes. Punjab was, in religious terms, very mixed, with large populations of Hindus, Sikhs and Muslims. This changed in 1947, in the bloody violence of Partition, when many hundreds of thousands of people were killed and more than 14,000,000 people are thought to have crossed the new border with Pakistan. Hindus and Sikhs headed for India, Muslims in the opposite direction. Partition, and the accompanying violence, was a deeply traumatic experience, and Punjabis of all communities suffered most. Almost all Muslims left the state, leaving behind their ancestral homes and mosques.

The borders of Indian Punjab have changed several times since Independence. In 1950, part of what is now Himachal Pradesh was detached as a separate administrative unit, and in 1956 the princely states in the region were integrated into Punjab. In 1966, under pressure from the Sikh political party, the Akali Dal, a new smaller state of Punjab was formed in which Sikhs and Punjabi speakers had a majority. The hill districts were given to Himachal Pradesh and the new state of Haryana (*see p. 271*) was created. Violence returned to Punjab in the 1980s, with the emergence of a movement campaigning for a separate homeland for Sikhs, led by small groups of armed militants. The Golden Temple became a focal point of the violence at one point, when the building was stormed by security forces seeking militants who were sheltering there (*see p. 290*). Thousands more died before the separatist movement was brought under control in the late 1990s.

Punjab is one of India's richest states, having benefited from what was known as the Green Revolution of the 1960s and 70s, which brought huge advances in agricultural productivity thanks to new crop varieties, improved canal irrigation and the greater availability of fertilisers. Punjab also has a strong industrial base, particularly in the central cities of Ludhiana and Jalandhar. The economy has also benefited from the remittances of the large Punjabi community that has settled in Britain and elsewhere.

RANJIT SINGH

Born in 1780, the son of a Sikh landowner, the one-eyed Ranjit Singh (he lost the other eye because of smallpox) had conquered Lahore before he had reached the age of 20. An astute military and political leader, and aided by European mercenaries, he became the first maharaja of the Sikh Empire, controlling most of Punjab, Kashmir and eventually Ladakh from his capital at Lahore (now in Pakistan). Ranjit Singh was fabulously rich: his golden throne is now in London's V&A Museum, while the Kohinoor diamond presented to him by the Afghan ruler Shah Shuja is now part of the British Crown Jewels in the Tower of London. His sons lost all their territory to the British in the Anglo-Sikh wars of the 1840s, and the last maharaja, Duleep Singh, was exiled to London (*see p. 64*).

AMRITSAR

Amritsar (pop. 1,000,000; *map 1 B3*) is home to Sikhism's holiest shrine, the Golden Temple, as well as Jallianwala Bagh, the best-known memorial to India's struggle for freedom from British colonial rule. It is also the nearest major city to the Pakistani border, and is just 50km from Lahore, Pakistan's second-largest city. It has an international airport, mainly used by Sikh pilgrims from all over the world.

History: Amritsar was founded in the 16th century by the fourth Sikh guru, Ram Das. The name, meaning 'lake of nectar', originally referred only to the large water tank which today surrounds the Golden Temple, but quickly came to refer to the settlement, which was originally called Ramdaspur, that grew up around the tank. In the 17th and early 18th centuries, the city was repeatedly fought over and plundered, as Sikhs battled against Mughal and then Afghan forces. It became part of Maharaja Ranjit Singh's Sikh

Empire in the early 19th century, and came under British control from the 1840s. It became part of the Indian state of Punjab in 1947, but lost a large part of its economic, religious and historical hinterland to Pakistan as a result of Partition, and many Sikh migrants moved into the area. In the 1980s, Amritsar became the focus of the Sikh separatist movement, as militants fortified the Golden Temple complex, which was then besieged by the Indian security forces (*see below*). Amritsar and the Golden Temple are safe and welcoming today, and attract large numbers of domestic and international tourists.

THE GOLDEN TEMPLE COMPLEX

History: The site for the Golden Temple was chosen by the third Sikh guru, Amar Das, shortly before he died. His son-in-law, the fourth guru, Ram Das, began excavating the large square tank in the late 1570s, and the foundation stone was laid by a Muslim preacher who was highly respected by the Sikhs. In the early 17th century, the fifth guru, Arjan Dev, collected the teachings of his predecessors and compiled them into the holy book known as the *Adi Granth* (original book). The extended version was later referred to as the *Guru Granth Sahib* (by which the holy book is given the status of a guru). At the same time, the first shrine was constructed on the site of the modern Golden Temple, the official name of which was, and still is, the Harmandir, or Temple of God. The holy book was first placed inside the Harmandir in 1604. The Akal Takht, or Eternal Throne, which is the building where the leadership council of the Sikhs sits, was also built in this period. With the death of Akbar in 1605, relations between the Mughal Empire and the Sikhs worsened, and Akbar's son Jehangir had Guru Arjan Dev tortured to death in Lahore. Almost 70 years later, in 1675, Jehangir's grandson Aurangzeb had Guru Arjan Dev's grandson Guru Tegh Bahadur executed in Delhi. In this period, and in the Afghan wars of the 18th century, the Golden Temple complex was often attacked and damaged.

The Golden Temple only took its current form in the early 19th century, when Maharaja Ranjit Singh restored the building, and had its dome covered in gold. Architecturally, the complex is a fascinating synthesis of Hindu and Islamic styles. In 1984, the Golden Temple complex became a battleground in a violent struggle between Sikh separatists lead by Jarnail Singh Bhindranwale and the Indian government. The army forced their way into the complex, killing many militants, including Bhindranwale, who were based inside, and major damage was caused to the Akal Takht. More than 500 people were killed within the precincts of the complex. A few months later, Prime Minister Indira Gandhi was shot dead by two of her Sikh bodyguards in revenge for the desecration of Sikhism's holiest shrine. The Akal Takht and other damaged buildings were repaired in the late 1980s.

Orientation: The Golden Temple complex is open 24hrs a day. It is particularly beautiful at dawn, and can be very hot during the daytime in the summer. The complex can be entered from any of its four sides, though visitors normally approach from the north. Most vehicles are not allowed to park close to the complex, and it is necessary

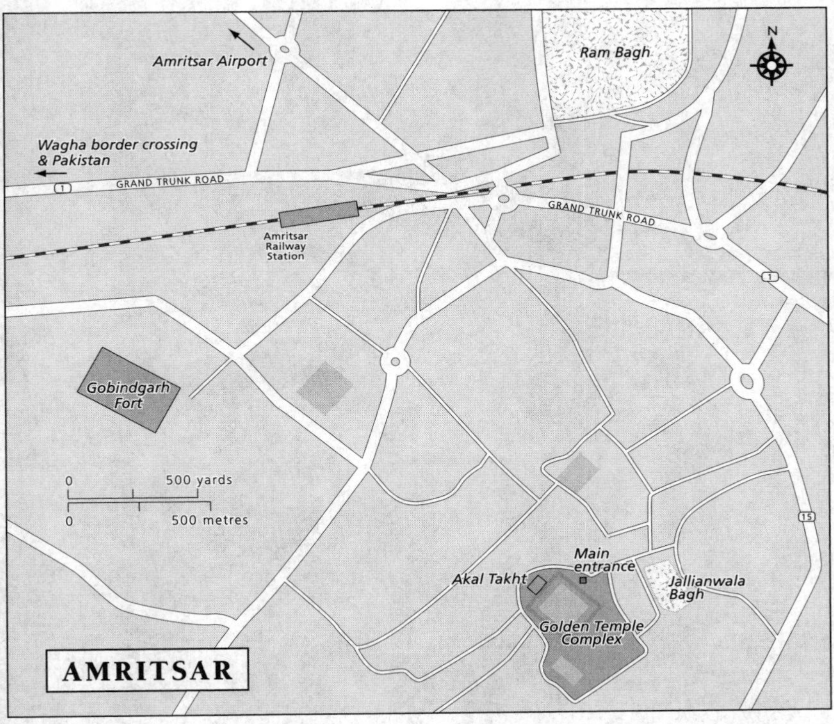

to walk or take a cycle rickshaw for the final 500m, passing close to the passageway that leads to Jallianwala Bagh (*see overleaf*). The main entrance, close to a clock tower, is set in the northern wall of the temple complex (there is a small museum above the main entrance). All are welcome to enter the complex, but visitors need to remove their shoes and socks and wear small cloths on their heads (hats are not normally acceptable). One can buy a small handkerchief-like cloth outside the temple, or wear one discarded by someone else at the entrance gate. Deposit your shoes in the special basement cloakrooms on the left of the entrance. Walk through the shallow pool of water as you enter the temple; one's feet have to be ritually clean before entering the holiest of Sikh shrines. Directly ahead of you is the Golden Temple itself, coated in gold—a near-island in a large square pool, with a causeway connecting it to the rest of the huge complex. The tall building on the right is the Akal Takht, while to the left are the huge eating halls and two tall minarets.

Parikrama

There is a marble walkway, called the Parikrama, that goes round the tank, and all are expected to walk in a clockwise direction. There are excellent views of the temple

from the walkway, and photography is allowed. Note how the marble walls and floors around the walkway are covered with inscriptions from donors—many of them members of the armed forces. Normally donors pay to have prayers read in their name. The two tall 18th-century **minarets** served as watchtowers, and just behind them is the large two-storey **Guru ka Langar**, or dining hall. Here simple and tasty vegetarian meals are given free to all, though donations are also welcome. Communal eating is an important part of Sikh culture, and was used as a way of symbolising that Sikhism did not retain the Hindu caste system (though in fact elements of the caste system have survived among Sikhs). As many as 40,000 meals are served here each day. Beyond the dining-hall, further away from the tank are rest-houses used by Sikh pilgrims. On the opposite side is a large prayer hall. Closer to the tank is a bathing area, part of which is covered for female bathers. At the opposite end of the tank, next to the causeway leading to the temple, is the five-storey **Akal Takht**, the seat of Sikh temporal authority, which became the headquarters of the militant forces in 1984, and was badly damaged when tanks entered the complex and shelled the building. The Sikh holy book, the *Guru Granth Sahib*, is stored here at night.

The Golden Temple

The temple itself, or Harmandir, is approached through a large marble gateway, decorated with gold, and with doors made of silver. This leads to the 60m marble causeway, with gilded lamps placed at regular intervals. The temple is a two-storey building with a small pavilion and *chattris* on its roof. Note the fine *pietra dura* inlay work on the marble lower part of the temple. The entire upper half of the temple is clad in gold, presented to the shrine by Maharaja Ranjit Singh, and is reputed to weigh more than 750 kilograms. The temple is open from four sides—a deliberate contrast with Hindu temples which usually only have one door. Inside, professional reciters chant from the holy book. Before dawn (about 4am in summer, 5am in winter), the original copy of the *Guru Granth Sahib* is ceremonially carried in a palanquin from the Akal Takht along the causeway to the Golden Temple, and is returned after dark (usually at 10pm). Throughout the day, pilgrims and tourists shuffle past, taking sweet food that has been blessed by a priest. It is sometimes possible to go upstairs when the crowds are not too great. On the first floor, Sikh men read out loud from the holy book, in what is known as the Akhand Path, or unbroken reading. A full reading of the *Guru Granth Sahib* takes about 48hrs. On the rooftop, pilgrims rest and meditate.

Other sights in Amritsar

Jallianwala Bagh: This is a national memorial in the form of a landscaped park, just 200m north of the Golden Temple complex. It was the scene of the killing of up to 2,000 Indians by British troops in 1919. The Jallianwala Bagh massacre was—along with the Salt March of 1930 and the Quit India movement of 1942—one of the critical

The Golden Temple in Amritsar.

milestones in India's struggle for independence from Britain. The details of the massacre have been learnt by generations of Indian schoolchildren.

THE JALLIANWALA BAGH MASSACRE

A large crowd had gathered in the open area of Jallianwala Bagh on the 13th April 1919. Some of those gathered were opponents of new legislation that allowed, among other things, detention without trial; others were farmers celebrating the festival of Baisakhi, and the Sikh New Year. The British had banned all public gatherings, and their troops, many of whom were Indian, were ordered to open fire on the crowd, causing many casualties. The exact numbers are disputed, and when the Duke of Edinburgh questioned the figure of 2,000 deaths, when visiting Amritsar in 1997, a major controversy erupted. The governor of Punjab at the time of the Jallianwala Bagh massacre, Michael O'Dwyer, was shot dead in London in 1940 by an Indian nationalist, Udham Singh, who was then executed.

The Jallianwala Bagh (*bagh* means park) is entered through a well-signposted narrow alleyway on the main road towards the Golden Temple. It was through this alley that the British forces reached the park, where they then opened fire. The bullet marks are still visible on a number of buildings. Many were shot dead in the park; others died when they jumped down the well at the back of the park.

Ram Bagh: This is a large park on the northern side of Amritsar, 2km north of the Golden Temple and close to the area of the city with many hotels. Among the 19th-century buildings in the park is the former summer residence of Maharaja Ranjit Singh (1780–1839), who lived the rest of the year in Lahore. The building is being restored, and will become (as it was previously) a museum.

Gobindgarh Fort: This large 18th-century fort, less than 1km east of the Golden Temple, is due to be vacated by the army and developed into a tourist site.

NEAR AMRITSAR

Wagha

The Wagha crossing point (*map 1 B3*) on the India-Pakistan frontier is just 30km from the centre of Amritsar. The crossing point itself has become a major tourist attraction because of a theatrical military ceremony involving soldiers from both countries, which takes place there every evening just before sunset. Foreign visitors are normally allowed to enter the VIP area to watch this strangest of spectacles.

Kapurthala

The capital of the former princely state of the same name, Kapurthala (*map 2 B1*) is 55km southeast of Amritsar, a short detour from the Grand Trunk Road. The closest big city, Jalandhar (*map 1 B1*), is less than 20km to the east. Kapurthala has some fine and unusual 19th- and 20th-century buildings, including the extraordinary French-influenced Jagatjit Palace and the Moroccan-influenced Moorish Mosque. The former maharajas, from the Sikh Ahluwalia Dynasty, were famed for their luxurious lifestyle, and for their dalliances with, and marriages to, Western showgirls.

The Jagatjit Palace: This enormous French-style palace was built by Maharaja Jagatjit Singh (1872–1949), who studied in France, and who called this building the Elysée, though it is modelled more closely on the palace of Fontainebleau. It is now the Sainik (Army) school. To get permission to enter the grounds and the palace, you need to get an official letter from the deputy commissioner's office, which is near the clock tower in the centre of Kapurthala, just 300m from the gates of the palace. This can take half an hour, and you need to hand the permission letter to a member of the school administration. You may also be expected to explain the purpose of your visit by phone from the school gatehouse. However, the effort is worthwhile.

The pink exterior of the building, completed in 1908, is both spectacular and unexpected, since most maharajas used indigenous, Mughal or British architectural styles for their palaces. Note the fine stucco plasterwork, and the copper-leaf tiling on the mansard roof. The most impressive room is the great hall, now in use as a library. Note the coloured-glass ceiling, and the fine woodwork around the doors and on the floor. There is also a small museum, in the drawing room, containing an assortment of furniture and memorabilia, as well as a Swiss music-box, busts of Churchill and Stalin, Buddhist prayer stones, an Egyptian stele with hieroglyphics, and the coffin cover of an Egyptian mummy. Ask to see the sumptuously decorated dining room, with its fine ceiling paintings, blue marble columns, exquisite gilding, and a Gobelins tapestry on the wall.

Moorish Mosque: About 800m east of the Kapurthala clock tower is another unexpected building: a mosque unlike any other in India. Its single minaret is an almost exact copy of the famous 12th-century Koutoubia Mosque minaret in Marrakesh, Morocco—the Moroccan royal family were friends of the Kapurthala ruler Jagatjit Singh. It was completed in 1930, in a ceremony presided over by Jagatjit Singh, a Sikh, and the Muslim ruler of the nearby state of Bahawalpur, now in Pakistan. Almost all Muslims from this part of Punjab left for Pakistan during the violence of Partition in 1947, and the mosque is now little used, but remains in excellent condition.

Other sights in Kapurthala

There are a number of other interesting buildings from Jagatjit Singh's long reign as maharaja in the city centre, including the district courts and, just opposite, a small **statue of a horse**, with the inscription, 'in memory of the charger "Sultana" on which His Highness the Maharaja Jagatjit Singh Sahib rode for 25 years'.

Villa Kothi (formerly Villa Buena Vista), 5km outside Kapurthala, beyond the cantonment, is the current home of the former royal family. It is a large yellow mansion in a vaguely Spanish style. Ask the guard if you can look around the grounds.

SOUTHERN PUNJAB

The area south of Amritsar is little visited and has a poor tourist infrastructure. Nevertheless, it has several interesting sites for those wanting to drive from Punjab to Rajasthan, or return from Amritsar to Delhi by an alternative route.

FEROZEPUR

Less than 80km south of Amritsar, this little-visited garrison town (*map 2 A1*) sits close to the border with Pakistan. It was not always so quiet. Locals remember the town bristling with foreigners until the border was closed in the 1960s. It is a very old city, named after Feroze Shah Tughlaq, the 14th-century sultan of Delhi—and it has a strong martial tradition. However, the oldest surviving buildings are from the British period, when this was an important cantonment. The great battles of the Sikh wars were fought around then, and the pretty **St Andrews Church** in the old cantonment area was built to commemorate the Sutlej campaign of 1845–46; the priest has marriage registers that go back to the 1850s. The nearby **St Joseph's Catholic Church** (known locally as **Lal Kurti**) dates from the 1880s, but was originally constructed in 1852, then burnt down five years later during the Uprising. There is a large Christian cemetery—overgrown, but full of the graves of soldiers, their wives and daughters, and still in use. The town has lots of other interesting buildings and memorials from the colonial period.

Near Ferozepur: the Pakistan border

Ferozepur's 19th-century fort, a few kilometres outside the town, on the road to the Pakistan border, is occupied by the army, but there are plans to vacate it. It is possible to go right up to the **Hussainiwala checkpost** on the border (*map 2 A1*), where every evening, just before sunset, Pakistani and Indian forces take part in a noisy, theatrical ceremony similar to the one at Wagah, near Amritsar. Note the stumps of the railway bridge across the Sutlej River, destroyed, according to locals, by the Indian Army to stop a Pakistani invasion. Next to the border post is a **memorial park**, marking the place where the British secretly buried the Indian nationalist Bhagat Singh, who was executed in 1931.

FARIDKOT

This town (*map 2 A1*), 105km south of Amritsar and 30km from Ferozepur, is the fascinating capital of the former princely state of the same name. Its many royal buildings are painted a distinctive green. The city took its name from a 13th-century Muslim Sufi saint, Baba Farid, who later became a deeply revered figure in Sikhism.

Baba Farid's shrine

This shrine is busy with pilgrims of all religions, though it is run by Sikh priests. On the left is an ancient tree on which Baba Farid is said to have wiped his hands, after having been forced to do manual labour by helping to build the ramparts of the town's fort. The local ruler, Choudhry Mokal Dev, had not recognised him as a holy man, but later renamed the town Faridkot in his honour. Baba Farid is recognised as one of the 15 Bhagats of Sikhism—that is non-Sikhs whose teachings are quoted in the holy book, or *Guru Granth Sahib.*

Other sights in Faridkot

The ramparts and green façade of Faridkot's **Qila Mubarak Fort** still dominate the centre of the city, though the current walls are thought to date to the 18th century. It was used as the official residence of the Faridkot royal family until 1898. The main entrance and several of the palace buildings have been restored, including a very pretty **Sheesh Mahal** (Glass Palace), and there are plans for a museum and exhibition of the Faridkot royal family's collection of vintage cars. Note the stucco birds that serve as brackets for the eaves and balconies of the palace façade. The handsome new palace, the **Raj Mahal**, was built to a French design in the 1880s, and is still occupied by the former royal family. It is closed to visitors, but you may be able to persuade the secretary of the royal family's Maharawal Khewa Ji's Trust to take you around the grounds. Among the other interesting buildings in the city is the neo-Gothic **Balbir Hospital**, which was once the main entrance gate to the Raj Mahal. There is also a fine 35m-high **clock tower**, constructed in 1902 as a memorial to Queen Victoria.

BHATINDA

This large town (*map 2 A1*), 55km south of Faridkot, is dominated by two buildings: an enormous power station and the ancient **Qila Mubarak Fort**. The impressive fort, which is thought to be more than 1,000 years old, has walls that tower above the centre of the city and are in good condition. The only female ruler of Delhi, the 13th-century Sultan Razia, was briefly imprisoned here. Inside the fort are a **Sikh temple** and meeting hall, as well as a small **palace** built into walls to the right of the main entrance. From the 18th century, the fort was part of the state of Patiala. The **Dargah of Ratan Baba**, a Sufi shrine marking the burial place of an early Hindu convert to Islam, has more Sikh and Hindu devotees than Muslims. Most Muslims left this area for Pakistan at the time of Independence.

EASTERN PUNJAB

PATIALA

Patiala (*map 2 B1*) was the capital of the former princely state of the same name, the most important in the Punjab region. The city (pop. 300,000) has several interesting forts and palaces, and efforts are underway to strengthen its tourist infrastructure. It has a beautiful palace hotel, which provides a good stopover close to the Delhi–Amritsar road, or for visiting nearby Sirhind and Thanesar (in Haryana).

History: Patiala was founded in 1757 by Ala Singh, a Sikh landowner who took advantage of the gradual collapse of the Mughal Empire. He allied himself with the Afghan invader Ahmad Shah Abdali, and was given the title raja. According to local tradition the name of his city came from 'Patti Ala', meaning 'lands of Ala'. The Mughal city of Sirhind had been the major centre of power in the area, and when it was destroyed in the 1760s (*see below*) it was transferred to Ala Singh, who persuaded Sirhind's inhabitants to found a new city. The Phulkian Dynasty—named after its ancestral leader, Phul, who also founded the ruling dynasties of the princely states Nabha and Jind—became a key ally of the East India Company, and supported the British in the Uprising of 1857. In the colonial period, Patiala became synonymous with good living and heavy drinking. A 'Patiala peg' is the name still used to describe a larger-than-normal shot of whisky. At Independence, the Punjab princely states were briefly united as one administrative area, called PEPSU (Patiala and East Punjab States Union), with Patiala as its capital. PEPSU was eventually integrated into Punjab. The current head of the Patiala royal family, Amarinder Singh, is one of Punjab's leading politicians.

Qila Mubarak

This extraordinary high-walled fortress (*open Tues–Sun 10.30–5*), which dates back to 1763, is in the heart of the busy market area of the old city. It is possible to drive through the large cusped entrance gates, with their pretty side pavilions, into the large inner courtyard. Ahead is the inner citadel, known as the **Qila Androon**, and on either side are former palaces; the one on the right houses a small museum. Note above the gateway of the inner citadel the single arched opening, from which the maharaja would preside over functions and festivities in the courtyard. There is no admission beyond the entrance corridor of the inner citadel because the ceiling is falling in, but there is an interesting walk along a path that runs round its walls. More palace buildings can be seen at the rear of the complex, as can some impressive 19th-century cannon.

The museum is inside a large **durbar hall**, set high on a plinth. It has a beautifully decorated 15m-high coffered ceiling, consisting of plaster-of-paris tiles set in a wooden frame, as well as some fine chandeliers. The hall contains a large collection of weapons, several portraits of members of the Patiala and the British royal families, and a 1903 Italian automobile. Sadly, it is the only well-maintained building in the entire complex.

Old Motibagh Palace

The enormous grounds of the maharaja of Patiala's Old Motibagh Palace (the 19th-century Pearl Garden Palace), 2km southwest of Qila Mubarak, are large enough to contain a full-size athletics arena, a velodrome, an Olympic-size swimming pool and many other sporting facilities. It is now the home of India's **National Institute for Sports**, and the old palace, one of the largest of all the royal residences, is taken up with classrooms, libraries and offices. The palace is a mixture of Rajput and Mughal styles, and constructed out of pink sandstone, much of which has been painted over. Show some identification, and you'll be allowed to wander around—but photography is not permitted within the grounds.

Sheesh Mahal

The smaller Sheesh Mahal, or Mirror Palace (*open Tues–Sun 10.30–5*), built in 1847, is actually part of Old Motibagh Palace, but is approached by a separate entrance, 500m beyond the gates of the sports institute. Outside the Sheesh Mahal is a slightly dilapidated 19th-century **formal garden**, with a large water tank, 300m long, two four-storey lookout towers and a suspension bridge across the tank. The **museum** contains some interesting 10th-century Hindu sculpture, including a very fine Vishnu head and a resting elephant. Other exhibits include a superb collection of miniatures from the 19th-century Patiala school of painting and, most bizarrely, a macramé-style Tibetan apron made of carved human bones. The actual Sheesh Mahal is a room decorated with mirror-work and paintings—visitors are not allowed to enter, but can peer through the door.

Baradari Palace

Probably the oldest building in Patiala is a Mughal *baradari* (rest-house), which a 19th-century maharaja incorporated into a palace that became known as Rajinder Kothi. It is in the centre of Patiala, not far from Mall Road, and is situated in the pretty Baradari Gardens. The building, which used to house the state archives, has recently been restored, and is now a heritage hotel called the Baradari Palace. There are a number of interesting municipal buildings from the late 19th and early 20th centuries near Mall Road, as well as the **Phul Cinema**—an excellent example of Art Deco architecture.

Bahadurgarh Fort

This impressive 19th-century circular fort, 5km outside Patiala on the Chandigarh road, is built on the site of a 17th-century Mughal fortification. It is now a police commando training camp, but you will almost certainly be allowed in if you ask politely and explain how interested you are in the history of the region. Bahadurgarh is unusually well defended for a fort on flat land, with a wide moat and two inner defensive fortifications. Inside is a large, crumbling palace spread around a vast courtyard with a pretty pool, all of which must once have been very beautiful. Look for the private bathing area in the palace, closest to the fort wall. You can still see the holes in the eaves of the overlooking courtyard from which water once spouted. Sadly, parts of the palace have been used for target practice and are very badly damaged. There is also a three-domed Mughal mosque with minarets.

SIRHIND

Sirhind (often pronounced Sarhind, *map 2 B1*) is just 3km north of the Grand Trunk Road and 40km west of Chandigarh. It is also known as Fatehgarh Sahib, after the nearby important Sikh temple. It is a place of pilgrimage for both Sikhs and Muslims, and has an interesting collection of Mughal ruins that are spread across the modern town and dotted around the surrounding countryside. The town was founded in the 14th century, and by the Mughal period had become the largest and most important city in the region, and a key stopover between the Mughal capitals of Delhi and Lahore. Wazir Khan, Sirhind's Mughal governor at the beginning of the 18th century, killed the younger sons of the tenth Sikh guru, Gobind Singh, by entombing them behind a brick wall on the site now occupied by the Fatehgarh Sahib Gurudwara. Sikh armies executed Wazir Khan, and repeatedly plundered Sirhind, which had been largely destroyed by the mid-18th century.

Mughal Gardens

Among the most impressive ruins are the Mughal gardens, known as Aam Khas Bagh (meaning public and private gardens). They were first constructed during the late 16th century, during the reign of Emperor Akbar, but extended by his son Jehangir and grandson Shah Jahan. On the left is the huge area consisting of a large water tank, with an arched walkway across the middle of it and small pavilions at either end. On the right are the private imperial gardens, complete with a bathing house and some small ruined palaces.

Fatehgarh Sahib

The Sikh temple of Fatehgarh Sahib, 2km north of the Mughal Gardens, is a handsome building with five golden domes that can be seen from most of the surrounding countryside. Just 200m north of the temple is the **Rauza Sharif**, the mausoleum of the conservative Sufi Muslim saint Sheikh Ahmed Sirhindi, popularly known as Mujaddid (the Renewer). He quarrelled with Emperor Akbar over the latter's liberal interpretation of Islam, and died in Sirhind in 1624. The actual mausoleum has some fine perforated stonework and carved marble pillars. There is access both to the cenotaphs of Sirhindi and his family and, down below, to the actual graves.

Other buildings in Sirhind

Set amid agricultural land to the west of Sirhindi's mausoleum are several dilapidated buildings from the Mughal period. Among them are the unusual ruins of one of the few surviving private residences from the Mughal period. This tall brick building, more than 20m high, is known as the **Jahaz Haveli**, or Ship Mansion, and was the home of a Mughal dignitary called Salabat Beg. Several hundred metres beyond the Jahaz Haveli are two handsome 17th-century domed mausolea, 300m apart, known as the **tombs of Ustad (teacher) and Shagird (pupil)**. The tomb of Shagird has the remains of some fine Mughal paintings of trees and flowers in one of its entrance portals. Several other buildings are worth visiting, including the strange **Lal Masjid**, or Red Mosque, which is taller than it is broad and situated near the Sikh temple, and the brick and stone **Sadna Qasai Mosque**, with the remains of unusually simple floral paintings, further along the railway lines in Choti Sirhind.

SANGHOL

This ancient, excavated settlement (*map 2 B1*), also known as Ucha Pind, lies just 8km north of Sirhind, close to the main Chandigarh–Amritsar road. The excavations at the main site, 500m south of the road, have revealed artefacts and buildings dating from the late Harappan period (c. 2000 BC) to the Gupta period (c. AD 320–550). Visitors to the site will see the base of a stupa and surrounding rooms, none higher than knee level. At the centre, the bones of an unknown Buddhist teacher were found in a soapstone casket. Some of the finds can be viewed in the small **Sanghol Museum** on the main road. They include Harappan pottery, and sculpture from the Kushana and Gupta periods—though some of the best pieces are in the Chandigarh Museum and Art Gallery (*see p. 286*).

ANANDPUR SAHIB

Anandpur Sahib (*map 2 B1*), 65km north of Chandigarh, is one of the holiest sites in Sikhism, founded by the ninth guru, Tegh Bahadur, in 1665. The town has several interesting *gurudwaras*. The head of the guru, executed on the orders of the Mughal emperor Aurangzeb in 1675, was brought here for cremation. The **Gurudwara Sisganj** was built on the cremation site. The largest of the *gurudwaras* is **Kesgarh Sahib**, where the tenth guru, Gobind Singh, founded the Khalsa—the military order of Sikhs, whose name means 'the pure'.

PRACTICAL INFORMATION

GETTING THERE

Punjab is well connected by air, rail and road to the rest of India. Amritsar has an international airport, mainly used by the large Punjabi diaspora in Europe and North America. Punjab also has India's only border crossing with Pakistan, at Wagah, just west of Amritsar, which is open to road and rail passengers. From Delhi, there are daily flights to Amritsar, as well as Chandigarh. The state is also well served by the rail network. There are two fast Shatabdi services leaving New Delhi railway station at 7.20am and 4.30pm, reaching Amritsar in less than 6hrs. Patiala is best reached by road from Chandigarh (1hr) or Delhi (4–5 hrs); there are also daily train services from Delhi.

GETTING AROUND

In the interior of Punjab, travel by hired car is recommended. The roads are among the best in India, and the state is bisected by the Grand Trunk Road, which runs from Ambala, just inside Haryana, through the large industrial cities of Ludhiana and Jalandhar, and on through to Amritsar.

ACCOMMODATION

The largest Indian hotel chains do not have much of a presence in Punjab, which has many unexciting mid-range hotels aimed at business travellers and foreign Punjabis returning on holiday. This is particularly true of Amritsar. One exception is the charming **Ranjit's**

Svaasa (*$$; T: 0183 2566618 or 3298840; svaasa.com/ranjit*), a former British guest house in the northern part of the city, which is also a spa resort, and has comfortable rooms and excellent food. Other more traditional hotels include the 4-star **Mohan International** (*$$; T: 0183 3010100*). Patiala has the superb **Baradari Palace** (*$$; T: 0175 2304433; neemranahotels.com*)—actually a former 19th-century palace, built round a Mughal rest-house. It is run by the Neemrana group. Many visitors to the eastern part of the state stay in Chandigarh.

FOOD

Traditionally Punjabi food included a lot of meat kebabs, but the departure of almost all Muslims at the time of Partition steered the cuisine of the state in a more vegetarian direction. Spinach, *paneer* (cottage cheese), *kali daal* (black lentils) and *rajma* (kidney beans) are all Punjabi staples, usually cooked with lots of *ghee* (clarified butter). The breads are particularly tasty—expecially *parathas*, which often come stuffed with cheese, potato or cauliflower. The best-known Punjabi food is *Sarson ka Saag* with *Makki ka Roti*. This is a seasonal dish, available in winter and spring, consisting of a delicious curry made of mustard leaves, which is eaten with cornbread. *Gajar ka Halwa*, a sweet dish made out of carrots, is also enormously popular. These dishes are available at the roadside cafés, known as *dhabas*, throughout the state.

The best-known and most popular Punjabi *dhaba* in Amritsar is the **Bhrawan da Dhaba** (*$, T: 0183 6941881*), opposite the town hall, and its 'sister' concern **Brothers**, which has international food as well. The **Ranjit Svaasa** (*see above*) can also provide Punjabi food on request. The Amritsari fish (marinated, battered and fried) and the stuffed *parathas* are recommended.

FURTHER READING & VIEWING

There are several books that deal with the violence of Partition in Punjab. Khushwant Singh's early novel *Train to Pakistan*, first published in 1956, is still in print and well worth reading. The book was turned into a film of the same name in 1998, directed by Pamela Rooks. The short stories of Saadat Hassan Manto are also recommended.

Khushwant Singh has also written a very readable *Illustrated History of the Sikhs*, updated in 2006, and *The Maharajah's Box* (1997), by Christy Lewis, tells the extraordinary story of the last maharaja of Punjab, Duleep Singh, who died in exile in France in 1893. The story of Duleep Singh is also the basis of the 2008 novel *The Exile*, written by Navtej Sarna.

The 1982 film *Gandhi* restages the Jallianwala Bagh massacre, and used the Golden Temple as a backdrop. The Golden Temple is also a backdrop for *Bride and Prejudice*, the 2004 Bollywood version of the Jane Austen novel with almost the same name.

HIMACHAL PRADESH

The northern hill state of Himachal Pradesh (*maps 1 and 2*) has some of India's prettiest landscapes and two of its most unusual cities: Simla, the former summer capital of British India; and Dharamsala, home to the Tibetan spiritual leader the Dalai Lama. There are several former princely states with some fine forts and palaces in the south and west, some lovely temples around Kulu and Manali, and some beautiful Buddhist monasteries in the remote northeastern parts of the state. Overall, Himachal has a good tourist and transport infrastructure, but the more mountainous districts are cut off from the rest of India for long periods during the winter.

Despite the ruggedness of the terrain, important trade routes have passed through Himachal Pradesh, including a key road to Tibet, which borders the eastern part of the state, and to Ladakh, which borders the north. Tibetan-style Mahayana Buddhism is the predominant religion in some parts of the thinly populated areas of Lahaul, Spiti and Kinnaur. The rest of the state is largely Hindu.

HISTORY OF HIMACHAL PRADESH

Himachal has been settled since the prehistoric era, but in political terms has not been unified until modern times. Tibetans and Mughals did lay claim to major parts of the territory, but its terrain ensured that local princes could retain a high level of independence. The Gurkhas of Nepal briefly extended their control as far as the Simla Hills in the south and Kangra in the north, but were defeated by the British in what became known as the Gurkha wars; they were forced to withdraw to the modern borders of Nepal under the Treaty of Sugauli (1816). In the early British period, the main external threat came from the Sikh Empire of Maharaja Ranjit Singh, but by the 1840s the British had consolidated their control over a large number of semi-independent small princely states, as well as territory they ruled directly, such as Simla and Dalhousie, and smaller parcels of land under the control of Patiala, the largest of the Punjab states. Simla rapidly grew in importance and became the summer capital of Britain's Indian Empire. Simla then became the temporary capital of Punjab—while Chandigarh was under construction—and eventually became the capital of the new separate state of Himachal Pradesh, which gained full statehood in 1971.

SIMLA

The former summer capital of British India, Simla (*map 2 C1*, officially Shimla) is set in the foothills of the Himalayas. It has lost some of its quaintness and charm, but remains a popular escape from Delhi and the heat of the plains. Nowhere in India boasts quite such an impressive range of colonial architecture, including government offices, a theatre, a railway station, hotels, churches, and numerous princely residences in a wide range of styles, from mock Tudor and neo-Gothic to Arts and Crafts and Art Deco—most of them still retain their very British names. The pedestrians-only upper part of the city is a lovely place for a stroll through Simla's history, and there are superb views of the surrounding hills and forests, and, on a clear day, of the snow-capped Himalayan peaks.

History: The origins of the name Simla are disputed, but it is usually said to have been named after the nearby shrine of the little-known Hindu goddess Shyamala—which is also the reason why the name has been officially changed to Shimla—though the two spellings and pronunciations are both in wide use. Simla's written history goes back no further than 1817, when two British officers, surveying the newly subjugated princely states, recently brought under British protection after the Gurkha wars, came upon 'Semla, a middling-size village' on a thickly wooded ridge.

Five years later, the first permanent building, Kennedy House, was constructed on the ridge by the British political agent Captain Charles Kennedy on a site that is now the car park of the State Assembly. In 1827 the British governor-general Lord Amherst came to Simla for two months to escape the heat of Calcutta, the capital of British India. Several more houses were built for a similar purpose, and Simla gained a reputation as a comfortable and pretty hill-station. By the middle of the century, there was a regular seasonal British population of 300, and at least 100 houses. Despite a distance of almost 1500km from Calcutta, Simla was chosen, in 1864, ahead of Darjeeling, as the summer capital—in part because it was in a more important strategic position, close to Punjab and the Afghan border, and because the local princes were friendly to British rule. By the 1860s it had also become the permanent headquarters of the British commander-in-chief, as well as the summer capital of Punjab province. By May each year, Simla was bursting at the seams. It still is.

The year 1903 saw the completion of one of the greatest feats of railway engineering anywhere in the world: the extraordinary winding Kalka–Simla line. And the annual migration got even quicker when, in 1911, the Indian capital was moved to Delhi. Simla continued to grow in importance, hosting key meetings on the long road to Indian Independence. The new government of India decided that it did not need the luxury or the inconvenience of a summer capital, and Simla became the temporary capital of Indian Punjab. In recent times, it has suffered the kind of unplanned growth and urban blight that has affected so many Indian cities, though few are as perilously constructed on the side of a hill. Several of its heritage buildings have burnt down, and only recently has a whole-hearted attempt to conserve Simla's past got underway.

Orientation: Simla was built on a series of hills and ridges that run from the Viceregal Lodge in the west to Christ Church in the east, and then curl round at the foot of Jakhu Hill (2,450m) to the south at Chota (or Little) Simla. The main ridge is, in fact, a major watershed. Rain that falls on the north side of the ridge eventually joins the Indus and enters the Arabian Sea near Karachi, while rain that falls on the south eventually joins the Ganges, and flows into the sea more than 2000km further east in the Bay of Bengal. The Mall is the main upper road, closed to all vehicles, and it also runs west to east, before heading south and downhill past Combermere Bridge towards Chota Simla. Another shorter road, with a large open public square sitting at the foot of Christ Church, is known as the Ridge. It runs uphill from Scandal Point, then descends into the market area of Lakhar Bazaar. Slightly to the south of the Mall, at a lower level, runs the Cart Road—the only part of Simla proper where cars and other vehicles are allowed. It is a short, steep walk up to the Mall from the Cart Road, but there is also a public lift near Combermere Bridge, and some of the hotels (including the Cecil and the Combermere) have private lifts. The railway station is just below the Cart Road, close to the Cecil.

Access to buildings: Many of Simla's heritage buildings are now government offices. If you want to look inside, walk in confidently but withdraw if asked to do so. If you seek permission from security officers, it will often be instinctively refused. If it is refused and you still want to see inside, ask to meet the 'in-charge', who will usually speak English and have a more relaxed attitude to visitors.

THE BRITISH IN SIMLA

Once a year, in March or April, hundreds of civil servants and their staff would make the journey across the Indian plains by train between Calcutta and Ambala, and then make the two-day trip to Simla by road—then, in October, they'd make the return journey. For the summer months, Simla was the heart of British India—a world of dances, amateur dramatics, tea-parties and picnics—its imported customs immortalised by Rudyard Kipling in *Plain Tales from the Hills*. In fact, there were always many more Indians than foreigners in Simla. Kipling, who spent several summers there in the 1880s, describes the Lower Bazaar as 'the crowded rabbit-warren that climbs up from the valley to the town hall at an angle of forty-five', a description that still holds true. He continued, 'here live those who minister to the wants of the glad city...grocers, oil-sellers, curio-vendors, firewood dealers, priests, pickpockets and native employees of the Government.'

Viceregal Lodge

The impressive former summer residence of the British viceroy is Simla's best-known building, now occupied by the Indian Institute of Advanced Affairs, and officially called the **Rashtrapati Niwas**. Completed in 1888, it rests on top of Observatory Hill at the western end of Simla. Visitors are welcome to wander around the grounds, and there are brief guided tours of parts of the ground floor.

The **grounds** are entered through a large green wooden gatehouse, with a road that sweeps up to a later addition (1927) to the main building, connected to it by a bridge.

The main building is constructed out of grey sandstone. Note the four-storey octagonal towers topped with cupolas, and the taller rectangular tower that conceals the building's water storage tanks. The building's façade retains the British royal coat of arms, as well as inscriptions commemorating the architects and engineers. There are a number of interesting features in the gardens on the far side of the Lodge, including a customised sundial which has lost its gnomon, a number of 'heritage trees' planted in the late 19th century, and the large plaque and coat of arms of Lord Minto, the viceroy who laid out these gardens in 1908.

Inside the lodge is an L-shaped **entrance hall**, with some very impressive wood panelling. Be sure to look up to see how the main staircase becomes a bridge across the entrance hall. The British coat of arms over the large teak fireplace has been replaced by the Indian Ashoka lion emblem; on the upper levels are display panels that bear the impression of weapons which have long been removed. At the end of the corridor is the **library**, the first part of which was the ballroom, and which retains the original chandeliers. The library also occupies the former dining room, which has blank spaces on the wall for the coats of arms of the governors-general and viceroys who governed British India from 1773 to 1858 and 1858 to 1948, respectively. The inscriptions, from the first governor-general, Warren Hastings, to the last viceroy, Lord Mountbatten, are still there. Three other small rooms are open to tourists. The old **morning room**, with its white silk wall coverings, is on the left of the entrance, and was the location for many important pre-Partition meetings. On the right of the entrance is the old **visitors' waiting room**, with a large portrait of a former vicereine, Lady Elgin, over the mantelpiece. The room has a superb ceiling made out of interlocking blocks of walnut wood. Next to it is the former **billiards rooms**, with a display of photographs relating to the history of the Viceregal Lodge.

The Mall

Much of the rest of historic Simla is best understood by dividing it up into easily walked sections along the Mall, starting from the Viceregal Lodge. The first two sections largely consist of government or former government buildings—this was the first part of Simla to be settled by the British. The next two sections cover the more public areas of Simla, including the theatre, the town hall and the main church. The final section follows the Mall downhill towards Chota Simla, past schools, princely homes and some government buildings.

Viceregal Lodge to the State Assembly

Heading east from the Viceregal Lodge, the first major building is a large modern hotel marking the site of Peterhof, the original residence of the viceroy, named after the summer palace of the Russian emperor Peter the Great. The original building burnt down in 1981. Uphill from Peterhof is Inverarm, a pretty 1860s building, housing the **Himachal State Museum** (*open Tues–Fri and Sun 10–1.30 & 2–5*). The focus of this small collection is paintings and sculptures from elsewhere in the state. Head downhill from the museum to the much-modernised **Cecil Hotel**, which opened in 1902 and

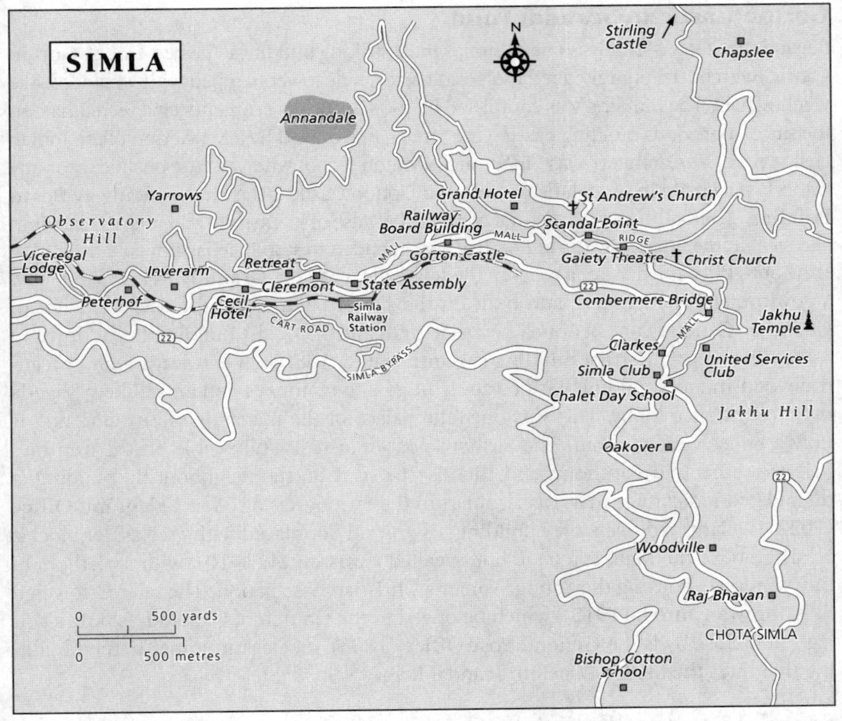

hosted many leaders of India's Independence movement when they were negotiating with the viceroy. Note how the building is built into the side of the hill, and has many floors that are below the level of the Mall. Kipling stayed in a cottage on this site when he first visited Simla. On the other side of the Mall is the Cecil Annexe, which is similar to how the main building used to look; note the pediments and scrolls on the upper façade, with a small blue urn standing in a niche. A track on the left (north) leads down to **Yarrows**, a 1913 building with strangely truncated wings and high chimneys, designed by one of the architects of New Delhi, Herbert Baker, in 1913. It was later used as a summer residence by Muhammad Ali Jinnah, the founder of Pakistan, and is now a training school for government accountants.

Continue along the Mall, past the Seventh-day Adventist church and sanatorium, and the early 20th-century **Retreat**—a building used by members of the viceroy's Executive Council, and which is now the army commander's residence. On the right is **Cleremont** (1927–28), home to offices of the labour minister, and then the **Vidhan Sabha**, or State Assembly, which opened in 1925 and functioned as the legislative assembly of India, during the summer months, until Independence. This was the site of Kennedy House, the first European building in Simla.

Gorton Castle to Scandal Point

Beyond the State Assembly is one of Simla's most striking buildings, the neo-Gothic **Gorton Castle**, with its steeply-raked red roofs and narrow side towers capped with what look like witches' hats. The building was completed in 1904 as the government's civil secretariat, on the site of a previous building bearing the same name owned by a Mr Gorton of the Indian civil service. The architect was Sir Samuel Swinton Jacob, who was responsible for many princely palaces in India. A little way beyond Gorton Castle is the unusual **Railway Board Building** (1896–97), an architectural curiosity because of its external and internal cast-iron and steel frame, prefabricated in Bombay and intended to stop it collapsing in a fire.

About 100m further on, a road on the left leads up to the **Grand Hotel** (1920s), now a government guest house, and built on the site of Bentinck Castle, the residence of Governor-General Lord Bentinck between 1828 and 1835; the building burnt down in 1922. The next important building is **Banthony** (c. 1880), an extravagant and eccentric wood-framed building with curious turret-like chimneys and an unlikely pagoda over its entrance lobby. This was once the palace of the maharaja of Sirmour, and is now a police control room. The Sirmour coat of arms is still visible on the iron railings that surround Banthony, and can also be seen on the neighbouring building, a dilapidated red cottage that was also part of the Sirmour estate. The **Telegraph Office** (1922) is a large red five-storey building, its ground floor faced with grey ashlar blocks. Nearby, above the Mall, is a large house called **Constantia** (1910), with a plethora of tiny windows, housing the Young Women's Christian Association. The tall red-towered **St Andrews Church** (1915), which belonged to the Church of Scotland, is now a college, and close by is the **General Post Office** (1883), an elegant timber-framed building that hugs the Mall, just before Scandal Point.

Scandal Point to the Gaiety Theatre

Scandal Point is the area where the road going eastwards splits: one part heads uphill to the large open space known as the Ridge; the other goes downhill, and continues to be known as the Mall. Scandal Point is often said to have got its name for its reputation as a meeting point—a place of gossip—but, according to one unsubstantiated but much-repeated story, a prince from Patiala swept away on horseback from this spot with the daughter of a viceroy. The open space on the Mall is dominated by the **town hall**, an Arts and Crafts building constructed in 1910, with a stone façade on the ground floor and elegant timber framed gables and windows on the upper floors. Note the unusual wooden spiral staircase in the entrance lobby. Go up the steps at the side to see how squat and cottage-like the building looks from the Ridge.

Next to the town hall is the **Gaiety Theatre**, which also straddles the steeply sloping space between the Ridge and the Mall. This Gothic stone building, which is the home of the Amateur Dramatic Club of Simla, began life in 1887 as the original town hall, also serving as library, police station (the police still occupy some rooms) and a theatre. Its top floor was badly constructed, and had to be removed in 1911; it was only recently restored. The theatre has served as the social centre of Simla for more than a century, and now has a second auditorium, and a club in the restored upper storey.

Christ Church and the Ridge

On the Ridge above the Gaiety Theatre and town hall is a large open area with a scattering of statues and a former bandstand that has been converted into a café—all of which is overshadowed by the majestic **Christ Church** (1844–57), the yellow tower of which dominates the Simla skyline. The church itself is well maintained, with a functioning organ, an upper gallery, some fine stained glass and a small gold plaque on the front pew to mark the seat of his 'H. E. The Viceroy'. The mock Tudor cottage at the foot of the church is the **library** (c. 1910), and still used for its original purpose. Behind the church is a footpath leading up the **Jakhu Temple**, dedicated to the monkey-god Hanuman, on Jakhu Hill—a 45-minute uphill walk.

Combermere Bridge to Chota Simla

Back on the Mall, the road dips downhill as its nears the ravine, largely obscured by a modern sports complex, which is spanned by Combermere Bridge, first constructed in 1828 under the supervision of the British commander-in-chief Lord Combermere, and rebuilt several times since then. This is where the Simla slope is at its steepest, and it is the site for the public lift down to the Cart Road.

A steep path up the hill, just past Combermere Bridge, leads to the very handsome, sprawling, wooden mansion which houses the **United Services Club**, known as the US Club. The Boundary Commission, which determined the borders of India and Pakistan in 1947, held many of its sittings here. Back down on the Mall, go gently downhill past the pretty Willow Banks Bakery, founded in 1876, to the timber-framed **Clarkes** (1898), one of Simla's oldest hotels, and the first to be owned by Mohan Singh Oberoi (the founder of the Oberoi chain), a penniless college drop-out who had worked as a desk-clerk at Cecil's at the other end of the Mall.

Beyond Clarkes is the **Chalet Day School** (1909), once part of the US Club (note the USC insignia), and built in the style of a Swiss chalet. Opposite is the tiny **Simla Club**, built by enclosing an old bandstand. Further downhill, in a narrow, less open stretch of the road, nicknamed the Khyber Pass, is a series of historically important buildings, which are usually not open to the public. On the right is the palatial and secluded **Oakover**, the official residence of the chief minister of Himachal Pradesh, and, until the 1970s, a home of the maharaja of Patiala. Just beyond Oakover, next to the rain shelter, is Simla's first cemetery—the last burial here was in 1841. On the left, is **Woodville**, now a heritage hotel, built as an Art Deco royal palace by the maharaja of Jubbal in 1938 on the site of a former home of the British commander-in-chief.

A little further ahead is Barnes Court (1879–86), now **Raj Bhavan**, the official home of the governor of Himachal Pradesh (*check locally whether there is access to the building, which has sporadically been open to the public in the past*). The main drawing room has been preserved as it was in 1972, when the Simla Agreement was signed here. The agreement brought a formal end to the 1971 Indo-Pakistan war over *bangla*desh, and was signed by Prime Minister Indira Gandhi on behalf of India, and President Zulfiqar Ali Bhutto for Pakistan—the latter accompanied by his teenage daughter and future Pakistani prime minister Benazir Bhutto. All three would meet violent ends. The road continues to **Chota Simla**, with a number of pretty residential houses and a fine mock-Tudor police station (late 19th century).

OTHER BUILDINGS IN SIMLA

North of Jakhu Hill

Chapslee (c. 1835) is an exquisite, unmodernised house beyond Lakhar Bazaar, on the north side of Jakhu Hill. It is occupied by a descendant of the royal family of Kapurthala, who lets out rooms to members of the public (*see Accommodation, p. 323*). It is one of Simla's oldest buildings and was known earlier as the Secretary Lodge, as it was the residence for the governor-general's private and military secretaries. The Edwardian and Victorian furniture and decorations are superb and in excellent condition—note the wood-panelled ceiling and the Gobelins tapestries. Next door is **Auckland House**, site of another former residence of a governor-general, and now a school. Beyond Chapslee, on top of Elysium Hill, the northernmost part of Simla, is **Stirling Castle**, a fine wooden building that could hardly be less like its Scottish namesake.

Annandale

This large, flat area is now occupied by a golf course, a helipad and a **museum of military history** on the northern side of Simla, a steep walk downhill from the Mall. During the colonial period, this was the venue for horse racing, cricket and polo matches, and fairs.

The Railway Station

Simla Railway Station is situated downhill from the Cecil Hotel and is the terminus of the Kalka–Simla Railway (completed 1903). The entire railway is a UNESCO World Heritage site—a distinction it shares with the mountain railways of the Nilgiris in south India and Darjeeling in the northeast. The length of the line is more than 96km, although the actual distance, as the crow flies, between Kalka and Simla is only 36km. The line has 917 curves, 988 bridges and viaducts and 102 tunnels—and is seen as one of the great feats of early railway engineering. The station was rebuilt in 1921, but the original locomotive turntable is still in place.

Bishop Cotton School

Below Chota Simla is Simla's most interesting and oldest educational institution, Bishop Cotton School (*visitors welcome, but call in advance T: 0177 2620880*). It started as the Bishop's School from 1859, but the foundation stone at its current site was laid on 16th September 1866. Its founder, Bishop George Cotton of Calcutta, died ten days later, and the school was renamed after him. It was the first Indian school to use the British prefect and house system. The main school buildings burnt down in 1905 and were rebuilt three years later. The neo-Gothic **Headmaster Lodge** is the only important building that survived. The well-maintained **chapel** has some very fine wood panelling and stained glass.

COTTON & SOCKS

Cotton's memory was preserved in other ways. He was the basis for the character of the 'young model master' in *Tom Brown's Schooldays*. And the phrase 'Bless my cotton socks' is thought to have originated in the woollen socks, donated by English church-goers, that Bishop Cotton blessed before he handed them out to the poor children in Simla. Bishop Cotton drowned after consecrating a cemetery in what is now Bangladesh. He slipped on a gangplank while getting onto a boat and was never seen again.

AROUND SIMLA

South of Simla

Chail: This small hill-station (*map 2 C1*), 45km southeast of Simla, was developed by a maharaja of Patiala in the early 20th century. It contains what is said to be the world's highest cricket ground and the maharaja's former palace, a 20th-century building which is now a government-run hotel.

Kasauli: This pretty hill-station (*map 2 C1*) is roughly halfway between Simla and Chandigarh. The 19th-century **Christ Church** is in the centre of the town, near the main bazaar. Note the sundial in the church garden, where the old spelling 'Kussowlie' is used. The exclusive **Lawrence School** (*T: 01792 261208 to visit*), just outside Kasauli in Sanawar, was founded in 1847 by Sir Henry Lawrence—who died in Lucknow during the Uprising of 1857. There is a pretty 19th-century chapel with stained glass in the school grounds and some interesting examples of colonial architecture.

Kuthar and Subathu: About 10km to the north of Kasauli is Kuthar, the capital of a very small princely state of the same name. The handsome **palace at Kuthar** has been restored recently, and there is some fine painting on the outer walls showing courtly scenes. Another 8km to the north is the cantonment at Subathu with a fascinating **cemetery** for the British garrison, established in 1827. Among those buried in the cemetery is Letitia, the infant daughter of Sir Henry Lawrence, founder of the Lawrence School, Sanawar. (*Both on map 2 C1.*)

Nahan: The town of Nahan (*map 2 C1*)—in the foothills, 135km south of Simla, but more easily accessed from Delhi or Chandigarh—is the capital of the small former princely state of Simoor. The **Royal Palace** at Nahan was recently renovated, while in the centre of the town there is the pretty **Rani Tal** (Queen's Lake) next to some well-maintained gardens. Eight kilometres north of Nahan is **Jaitak Fort**, the scene of an important battle between the British and the Gurkhas in 1810.

Paonta Sahib: Some 40km east of Nahan, near the border with Uttarakhand, is the Sikh holy town of Paonta Sahib (*map 2 C1*), which was the home of the tenth guru, Gobind Singh, and is where he composed the Sikh holy text known as the *Dasam Granth*.

West of Simla

Arki: The capital of the small former princely state of Baghal, Arki (*map 2 C1*) is midway between Nalagarh (*see below*) and Simla—approximately three hours by road from either place. The late 17th-century **fort-palace** of Arki overlooks the small town of the same name. A large part of the fort is now occupied by the security forces, but it is big enough to contain a small hotel, a private palace occupied by the former Raja of Baghal, and some superb wall-paintings. In the early 19th century, the fort was captured by the Gurkha General Amar Singh Thapa, who made it his headquarters for eight years, before being driven out by the British.

Arki's wall-paintings are in the **Diwan-i Khas**, or Royal Council Chamber, which is normally locked—but the watchman has the key. The two main rooms are entirely covered with coloured paintings, executed in the style of Pahari miniatures, common to the hill states of Himachal Pradesh. The paintings on the left wall of the first room are largely floral, with some images of the god Krishna in black, and a superb triptych of Indian cities in the window alcove, with Jaipur in the centre and Varanasi on the left; the location of the right one is unknown. The room on the right has an extraordinary array of religious and secular images: scenes from the life of Krishna and from the *Ramayana*, as well as pictures of gymnasts, wrestlers, foreign soldiers and giant birds. At the far end on the left is a series of erotic images, showing different sexual positions, and some imaginary vistas of European and Asian cities.

Nalagarh: This town (*map 2 B1*) is the capital of a small former princely state of the same name, situated in the low Himalayan foothills, 50km north of Chandigarh. The Mughal-style **palace** is inside a 15th-century **fort** built into the hillside overlooking Nalagarh, and has been turned into a comfortable hotel. The Chandrabansi Dynasty, which has ruled here since the 12th century, was briefly driven out by Gurkha armies from Nepal in the early 19th century, before being reinstated by the British in 1814. Nalagarh is often used as a stopover by travellers heading from Delhi to the hills of northern Himachal Pradesh.

Ramshahr and Ramgarh: The village of Ramshahr, 12km northeast of Nalagarh, was used as a summer capital of the state. It was the site of an important battle of the Gurkha wars, and the hilltop **Ramgarh Fort** was the scene of a three-year siege by the Gurkhas, which was ultimately successful. Ramgarh Fort—a steep uphill walk (or twisting, bumpy drive) from Ramshahr—is still an impressive fortification. The fort is normally locked, but the Nalagarh Palace Hotel staff can arrange for it to be opened, or otherwise ask for the caretaker, who stays in Ramshahr. Inside the fort, note the huge underground granaries and water tanks which enabled the Nalagarh forces to endure the siege for so long.

East of Simla

Mashobra: The area around the village of Mashobra (*map 2 C1*), 12km east of Simla, has several important colonial structures, including **Wildflower Hall**, the redeveloped former residence of the commander-in-chief (*see Accommodation, p. 323*), the large wooded **Retreat Building**, constructed in 1850 by the Raja of Koti and now used as a summer home by the president of India, and former **St Crispin's Church**, with its castellated tower.

Jabbal: This is the capital of the former princely state of the same name, 3½ hours' drive east of Simla along a poor road (*map 2 C1*). The multi-storeyed palace, with ancient and modern wings, is now a hotel. The nearby village of **Hatkoti** has several interesting old temples, with broad wooden slate-covered roofs that overhang the structure. The main **Hateshwari Shrine** is dedicated to the goddess Durga.

Northeast of Simla

The Kinnaur road: The road to Rampur from Simla, which is part of the old Hindustan–Tibet road (and eventually leads to the remote mountainous district of Kinnaur, *map 2 C1*), passes several villages with Himachal-style wooden Hindu temples, including **Manan**, with its finely painted Durga shrine, and **Balag**, which has an unusual Shiva temple, with a stone tower and a wooden assembly hall. **Sainj** has a 19th-century palace belonging to the minor princely state of Theog.

Rampur and Sarahan: These were the new and old capitals, respectively, of the former princely state of Bushahr. Rampur (*map 1 C3*) is 130km northeast of Simla on the Sutlej River, and has the handsome 20th-century **Padam Palace** opposite the bus stand, and several interesting temples. Another 20km east is Sarahan (*map 1 C3*), with some of Himachal's finest Hindu shrines, including the superb **Bhimakali Temple** (12th century; rebuilt early 20th century), dedicated to a form of Durga, within a palace complex. The twin-towered temple is constructed out of alternate layers of stone and wood to increase its resistance to earthquakes, and this gives its walls a striped appearance. The tower on the right leans as a result of an earthquake in 1905, and the left tower is now the main shrine. Note the particularly fine woodwork on the upper levels of the towers. Ask the caretaker of the palace for access to the drawing room with its painted ceiling.

KINNAUR, SPITI & LAHAUL

Beyond Bushahr is the district of Kinnaur, bordering Tibet. A small but growing number of tourists continue from mainly-Hindu Kinnaur into two of India's most remote areas, the mainly Buddhist Spiti and Lahaul, from where it is possible to drive, in summer, over the Rohtang Pass all the way to Manali (*see p. 319*). Permits are required for the journey between Kinnaur and Spiti (*see Practical Information, p. 322*).

Kinnaur

In Kinnaur, the picturesque **Sangla Valley** (*map 2 C1*) is the best-known tourist destination. Just north of the town of Sangla is the fine multi-storey **Kamru Fort**, a former stronghold of the rulers of Bushahr; there are several Hindu temples nearby too. The Kinnauri capital, **Rekong Peo** (*map 1 C3*), has a hilltop **Buddhist monastery**, and it is a long and interesting walk (12km) or short drive to **Kalpa**, which has several old Hindu temples.

Spiti

The best-known and most important tourist attraction in Spiti is the **Tibetan Buddhist *gompa*** at Tabo (*map 1 D3*). Still a working monastery, it dates back to the 10th century and is situated in a narrow green valley, next to the Spiti River, hemmed in by barren hills. The monastery, which has one of India's oldest Buddhist shrines still in use, has some very fine wall-paintings and carved woodwork, and is similar in conception to many Ladakhi *gompas*. The oldest part of the complex is the Sug La-khang, a prayer hall, with a large four-sided effigy of Vairochana—sometimes described at the Sun Buddha—at the back, and some interesting murals.

There are several more Buddhist monasteries, in even more spectacular locations than that at Tabo, on or close to the road leading towards Lahaul and the Rohtang Pass. These include the **fort-monastery** (16th century) in the small village of Dhankar (*map 1 C3*), which once served as Spiti's capital and sits on a promontory overlooking a cliff formed by high columns of rock. The **Ki Gompa**—12km north of Spiti's main town, Kaza (*map 1 C3*)—is the area's largest and most dramatically situated monastery.

Lahaul

More easily accessed from Ladakh or Manali, Lahaul (*map 1 C3*) also comes after Spiti on the long road that leads from Simla through Rampur and Kinnaur. Around Lahaul's main town, Keylong, are several interesting Buddhist monasteries, including the 12th-century **Khardong Monastery**, a two-hour walk from Keylong. There is also an eight-storey wood and stone **fort** at Gondla, 18km before Keylong, and the **Triloknath Temple**, close to the village of Udaipur, which was originally dedicated to Shiva and is now a Buddhist shrine.

NORTHERN HIMACHAL PRADESH

Among the main destinations in the north of Himachal Pradesh are the hill-stations of Dharamsala and Dalhousie, while the town of Manali, high up in the Kulu Valley, draws large numbers of visitors each summer.

DHARAMSALA

Dharamsala (*map 1 B3*, officially Dharamshala) is a hill-station in the north of the state, best known as the home of the Tibetan spiritual and political leader the Dalai Lama and the Tibetan government-in-exile. The main town sits at the foot of the magnificent Dhauladhar mountain range, and is the largest urban centre in the Kangra Valley. The part of Dharamsala known as McLeod Ganj, high above the main town, attracts an eclectic mix of visitors, with a changing seasonal population of Buddhist monks, Western hippies and Buddhists, former Israeli soldiers on long holidays, Indian tourists and local Himachalis. Many visitors use the names Dharamsala and McLeod Ganj interchangeably.

Originally built as a garrison town by the British army in 1849, Dharamsala's panoramic views and cool climate quickly transformed it into a popular hill-station, but few relics of this time remain—most of the older buildings were destroyed by an earthquake in 1905. Until the 1960s it was still best known as a military town, and thousands of Italian prisoners of war captured in North Africa were interned nearby during the Second World War. But today, Dharamsala's relatively recent Tibetan cultural heritage, as well as the spectacular countryside, act as the main draws for tourists.

Orientation: The lower, southern parts of Dharamsala consist of a largely modern Indian town, 1200m above sea level, while the upper part of the town, known as McLeod Ganj, is more than 500m higher, nestling in the foothills of the Dhauladhar mountain range. There is a very steep direct road (about 3km) leading from Dharamsala town to McLeod Ganj, and it goes past several important Tibetan buildings. Most vehicles are not allowed along this road without permission, but it is possible to walk up in about 40 minutes. There is a separate winding road (about 10km) open to normal vehicular traffic that connects the two communities. The key Tibetan buildings are at the southern, lower end of McLeod Ganj's main market, while on the northern side, roads and tracks head out towards neighbouring villages, such as Bhagsu and Dharamkot, and up the mountainside.

McLeod Ganj

McLeod Ganj (sometimes McLeodganj) is also known by some locals as Upper Dharamsala; it was named after a 19th-century British governor of Punjab, Donald McLeod. Almost all the buildings in McLeod Ganj date from the Tibetan arrival. Many visitors stay in small hotels in McLeod Ganj, and spend their time wandering around the markets, sitting in cafés, visiting temples, taking courses in Buddhism and walking in the spectacular countryside.

The Tsuglagkhang

The Tsuglagkhang complex of temples is at the southern end of McLeod Ganj's Temple Road and contains the residence and office of the Dalai Lama, as well as the most important of Dharamsala's Buddhist shrines. Tibetans usually translate Tsuglagkhang as 'central cathedral'. Passing through the main gates, visitors move clockwise through the temple complex. On the hill behind, shrouded by trees, is the off-limits private abode of His Holiness Tenzin Gyatso, the 14th Dalai Lama. Passing the entrance, upon climbing the steps, one sees two temples. On the right is the **Tsuglagkhang Temple**, dedicated to Avalokiteshwara, the Buddha of compassion (of whom the Dalai Lama is a reincarnation). Inside are the statues of Avalokiteshwara, the Sakyamuni Buddha (the historical Buddha) and Padmasambhava (the Indian monk who brought Buddhism to Tibet). They are flanked by the sacred scripts of, on the right, the Indian Buddhist masters in 225 volumes, known as the *Tangyur*; on the left are the 100 volumes of the teachings of Buddha himself, known as the *Kagyur*.

The temple to the left is the **Kalachakra** (1992), with its intricate murals of the *mandala*, or wheel of life. Further down is the Dalai Lama's temple: the **Namgyal Monastery**, where, on most afternoons, monks go to debate the Buddhist texts in a public and rather theatrical manner.

THE DALAI LAMA IN INDIA

In 1950 the Chinese army invaded Tibet, and began incorporating it into the People's Republic of China. In 1959, after an anti-Chinese rising, the Dalai Lama and many of his followers fled Tibet and sought refuge in India. This was granted by the then prime minister, Jawaharlal Nehru, souring Sino-Indian relations—and three years later the two countries were at war in a still-unresolved border dispute. The Dalai Lama moved first to the hill-station of Mussoorie (*see p. 263*), before setting up in the McLeod Ganj area of Dharamasala, which has been the home of the Tibetan government-in-exile ever since. Most of the 100,000 Tibetan refugees live elsewhere, scattered in settlements throughout India.

Gangchen Tyishong Square

Set around the stupa-dominated main square of Gangchen Tyishong, 3km downhill from McLeod Ganj and close to the main town of Dharamsala, is the home of the Tibetan government-in-exile. Around the square itself, numerous buildings bear the titles of departments of the Tibetan Government. Set back from the square, the **Library of Tibetan Works and Archives** (*open 9–5; closed Sun and 2nd and 4th Mon of month*) displays some aspects of traditional Buddhist architecture, with its carved wooden eaves, which are elaborately decorated. Many of Tibetan Buddhism's ancient surviving books and manuscripts can be found and studied here. The library also provides up-to-date information on the various cultural programmes taking place in the town. There is also a small **Tibet Museum** (*open Tues–Sun 9–5*).

Church of St John in the Wilderness

Little of significance remains from the time of British rule in Dharamsala, although this handsome church (1852–60) is worth visiting. It stands amid pine trees, 2km northwest of McLeod Ganj, along the main vehicular road to Dharamsala. Constructed out of granite, it seems oddly out of place in India. Note the grave of Viceroy Lord Elgin, who died just three years after the church's consecration. He was the son of the man who took what became known as the Elgin Marbles from the Parthenon in Athens to London. He asked to be buried in Dharamsala because it reminded him of his native Scotland.

Other places to visit in Dharamsala

The **Norbulingka Institute** (*open 9–5.30; closed Sun and 2nd Mon of month*) is 6km away, below Dharamsala. It was named after the summer residence of the Dalai Lama, and was founded in order to keep alive traditional Tibetan arts and crafts, such as *thangka* painting (using embroidery with silk painting) and metal sculpture.

There is also the **Kangra Art Museum** (*open Tues–Sun 10–5*) in the Kotwali Bazaar area of Dharamsala. It has a selection of Himachal paintings and carvings—a reminder of the indigenous local heritage, in contrast to the ubiquitous Tibetan cultural presence elsewhere in the area.

THE REST OF THE KANGRA VALLEY

The Kangra Valley (*map 1 C3*) is named after the town and fortress of Kangra (*map 1 B3*), which has been replaced by Dharamsala as the capital of the district. The valley's strategic importance and the legendary wealth of its temples led to a number of invasions. In 1009, Mahmud of Ghazni swept through the region; the Tughlaq sultans followed in the 14th century, and so did Akbar in 1566, occupying Kangra Fort. Under Emperor Jehangir, the small principalities of the valley were brought under Mughal control. In the late 18th century, under the leadership of Sansar Chand Katoch, a prince of Kangra, the small kingdoms of the valley briefly asserted their independence, until the Sikhs and then the British took full control of the valley. In 1905 the area was devastated by an earthquake, the destructiveness of which is still evident in some of the older monuments.

Kangra Fort

The impressive ruins of the Kangra Fort stand on a steep rock overlooking the Banganga Valley, 18km south of Dharamsala and 8km south of Gaggal Airport. The outermost gate was built in the 19th century, and the inner gates are progressively older. After a sharp turn, visitors pass through the Jehangiri Gate, named after the Mughal emperor. Inside are buildings from an earlier Hindu period, largely destroyed in the earthquake of 1905. Some of the stones in the walls are intricately carved and may have formed part of the temple. The **Brajesvari Devi Temple**, in Kangra town, is an important Hindu shrine dating back at least a millennium, though the old building was badly damaged in the earthquake, and the temple is almost entirely modern.

Masrur temples

These unusual ruined Hindu temples (9th–10th centuries), hewn out of bare rock, are located on a hill, along a winding road about 25km southeast of Kangra. The spires of the temples are badly worn, but several of them carry fine carvings, both decorative and figurative in a style that is similar to Ellora (*see p. 521*). The image of Shiva is carved on the lintel of the main shrine, while several other panels are now on display at the state museum in Simla.

Jwalamukhi Temple

The **Devi Temple** in Jwalamukhi (*map 1 B3*), 50km south of Dharamsala, is one of the most important Hindu pilgrimage sites in northern India. This impressive Hindu temple is located at the end of a bustling square, which is off-limits to vehicles with more than two wheels. The gilded dome was given by the Sikh ruler of Punjab, Maharaja Ranjit Singh. It is said that the tongue of the goddess Sati found its final resting place here.

Eastern Kangra Valley

The road from Dharamsala to Mandi passes near the pretty tea estates of Palampur, the former maharaja of Kashmir's summer palace at **Taragarh**—built in the 1930s and now a hotel—and the 13th-century stone Shiva temple at **Baijnath** (*map 1 C3*). Also nearby (17km south of Taragarh) is the small village of **Andretta**, which was home to one of India's most popular painters, Sardar Sobha Singh (1901–86), best known for his colourful and romanticised images of the Sikh gurus. There is a small museum, and some potteries scattered about the village, as well as the old house of Norah Richards (1876–1971), an Irish woman who attempted to set up Andretta as an artist's village, and who is often spoken of as the founder of Punjabi theatre.

CHAMBA VALLEY

The picturesque Chamba Valley (*map 1 B3*) is on the northern side of the Dhauladhar range of hills which separate it from Dharamsala and the Kangra Valley. Its main towns are the hill-station of Dalhousie, and Chamba itself, the old royal capital.

Dalhousie

The best-known tourist attraction in the valley is Dalhousie (*map 1 B3*), a hill-station first settled by the British in the 1850s, and named after the then governor-general of India. In the early 20th century, it became popular as a summer retreat from the city of Lahore, but went into decline when Lahore became part of Pakistan. There are several churches, of which **St John's** (1863) is the oldest. The old British cemetery can be reached by a track behind the bus stand.

Chamba

The town of Chamba (*map 1 B3*), 50km east of Dalhousie, was the capital of the former princely state of the same name—the royal family of which ruled the valley for almost a millennium. The **Lakshmi Narayan Temple** complex (14th century), on the north side of the town, is famous for its *shikhara* shrines—temples built with a high tower over the sanctuary and a small porch instead of an assembly hall. The shrines, mostly dedicated to Vishnu, have replaceable wooden hat-like roofs that protect the stone building. The **Akhand Chandi Palace** (1764) is just south of the complex, and is now a college, while the **Rang Mahal**, or Painted Palace, 300m to the southeast, also dates from the same period and is now a handicrafts centre. Some of the fine miniature paintings that used be in the Rang Mahal are now in the **Bhuri Singh Museum** (*open 10–5, closed Mon and 2nd Sat of month*), on Museum Road, along with royal memorabilia and woodcarvings. The **Chamunda Devi Temple** (11th century), on a hill on the southern outskirts of Chamba, is dedicated to Chamunda, a particularly fearsome form of the mother goddess; it has some fine carvings.

Bharmour

The village of Bharmour (*map 1 C3*), 65km east of Chamba, was the first capital of the region, and has several important early temples. The mainly wooden **Lakshana Devi shrine** (9th century) has some of Himachal's oldest surviving wood carvings. The tall, stone **Manimahesh Temple** (10th century), dedicated to Shiva, has some interesting brass statues.

MANALI & THE KULU VALLEY

Manali

The town of Manali (*map 1 C3*) sits close to the head of the Kulu Valley (sometimes spelled Kullu) and is a popular tourist resort which has grown rapidly in recent years. During the summer, the Rohtang Pass (3985m) north of Manali is open, allowing travellers to continue into Lahaul, Zanskar and Ladakh. Manali is an important trekking centre, and a place where young Westerners and many Indians come in the summer months to escape the heat of the plains. There are also dozens of interesting temples, mainly constructed out of wood, built in a range of styles appropriate to a location that sees a lot of rain and snow—styles include what has become known as 'pagoda', with tiers of roofs, and 'chalet', with a broad single roof.

Hadimba Temple: This temple, 2km northwest of the centre of Manali, near the village of Dunghri, is the town's oldest shrine. Unlike many of the area's other temples, boxed in by new developments, Hadimba is in its original forest setting, amongst cedar trees. An inscription dates the current wooden structure to 1553, though there was almost certainly a sacred shrine on the site long before. It is a popular pilgrimage place, where Hindus come to worship the form of the goddess Parvati known as Hadimba (or Hirma Devi). She is also often seen as an incarnation of Kali, and is said to have given the kingdom of Kulu to the forefathers of the rajas of Kulu. The temple is believed to have been built by Raja Bahadur Singh, son of Sidh Singh, who built Nagar Castle. The temple has a three-tiered pagoda structure. The three superimposed wooden roofs are crowned by a brass ball and the trident of Shiva. The outside of the temple is decorated with elaborate carvings in both a traditional Hindu (gods and goddesses, elephants and crocodiles) and western Himalayan folk style (knots, scrolls, plaitworks, stags). On the beams above the doorway are female dancers and isolated scenes from the Krishna story. Above the door are hung the horns of wild animals of the region—a form of offering to hill gods.

One enters the temple by climbing through a low door. The gloomy shrine inside houses a small gold statue of Hadimba and a large smooth sacrificial stone which slopes to the right and dips in the middle—into which the blood of the sacrificed animal flowed.

Jagat Sukh

This small village (*map 1 C3*), 10km south of Manali, on the old road along the east bank of the river, was formerly Nast, the ancient capital of Kulu before Nagar. The classical stone carvings of gods dotted around the village walls are a reminder of its former importance. The small **Sandhya Devi Temple** looks from a distance like another chalet-style Himachali temple. In fact, it has a finely carved 15th-century stone base, on which a 19th-century wooden structure has been built, with its own fine folk-art-style carvings.

Nagar

Nagar (or Naggar, *map 1 C3*) is a pretty town that rises up on the hillside above the less-used east bank road running alongside the Beas River from Manali to Kulu. It is a mixture of traditional Kulu architecture and colonial charm, although there has been a recent boom in the building of guest houses.

Nagar Castle: A steep climb from the main road brings you to the small centre of the town, dominated by Nagar Castle. It is not a castle in the European sense of the word, but a palatial Kulu-style chalet set around a courtyard. Thought to have been built in the 15th century by Raja Sidh Singh, it was used as the royal residence and state headquarters until the mid-17th century, when Raja Jagat Singh transferred the capital to Kulu, then still known as Sultanpur. It was used as a summer palace until 1846, when it was sold to the first assistant British commissioner. Since then the castle has been used as a courthouse, a school and now a hotel.

Extensive renovation in recent years has left the castle looking very clean and slightly at odds with the rest of Nagar's architecture, but the elaborate woodcarvings surrounding the outer walls are impressive. The castle was built in the timber-bonded, earthquake-proof style common in the valley. Alternate courses of dry stone and deodar beams meant that it withstood the 1905 earthquake. Inside, the British influence is clear, with staircases, fireplaces and chimneys. There is also a small shrine in the first courtyard: **Jagatipath Temple**, which is home to a sacred cracked stone slab. According to local tradition, the slab was carried from the cliff face of a hill near the base of the Rohtang Pass by *devtas*, or godlike beings, in the form of a swarm of bees. A young rani from the area felt homesick when she was brought to live in the castle, and the bees brought her the slab for comfort. Visitors are also told the story of a British official who made fun of the slab and died within a week.

NICHOLAS ROERICH

Nicholas Roerich (1874–1947) was a Russian artist, mystic and peace activist who inspired a cult-like following in the United States, and to whose life and work no fewer than four museums are devoted: in Nagar, New York, Moscow and Izvara, near St Petersburg. He was the leading force behind the first real attempt, in the 1930s, to get international support for the protection of sites of historic and cultural imporatance. The Roerich pact, as it was known, was a precursor to the work in this field that was undertaken by UNESCO after the Second World War. Roerich's poster-like paintings of colourful Himalayan landscapes are still popular and widely reproduced. He moved to India with his wife and two sons, one of whom, Svetoslav, became a well-known artist too—he also married the greatest Indian actress of her day, Devika Rani.

Roerich Art Gallery: This art gallery (*open Tues–Sun; closed for lunch*), 2km uphill from the castle, was founded in memory of the Russian painter Nicholas Roerich, who lived here from 1929 until his death in 1947. The gallery is in 'The Hall', built by a British colonel in the 1880s, and it houses about 60 of Roerich's paintings and some other family memorabilia. The house is set in an English-style garden, with wisterias and rose beds surrounding the lawns—and some snow-capped peaks in the distance. One hundred metres beyond the house, the Urusvati Himalayan Folk Art Museum has a collection of Himalayan folk art, more of Roerich's paintings and a small gallery of Russian folk art.

Other sites in Nagar

Dotted around the town are also a number of temples. The largest is the three-tiered pagoda-style **Tripuri Sundri Temple**, in an enclosure at the top of the town. More classical in design is the 11th-century **Gauri Shankar Temple**, with its fine stone carvings. Set in its own stone courtyard, just below the castle, on the way back to the main road, it is one of the oldest temples in the valley.

Kulu

Most travellers do not stop in Kulu (or Kullu, *map 1 C3*) on their way to Manali—though it is possible to visit the interesting **Raghunath Temple**, dedicated to Rama, which is annually the scene of one of the country's most impressive Dussehra celebrations. It is next to the palace of the former rulers of Kulu.

Four kilometres to the south of Kulu's Bhuntar Airport is one of the region's oldest temples, the **Vishveshwar Mahadeva Temple** (9th century), dedicated to Shiva and set in the village of Bajaura. It is a *shikhara* temple, with a tall tower over the sanctuary and external niches for stone-carved images of the Hindu gods Vishnu, Ganesha and Durga.

Mandi

The capital of a former princely state of the same name, Mandi (*map 1 C3*) stands at the junction where the road from Manali towards both Dharamsala and Simla divides. And that means that hundreds of travellers pass through it every day. There is the **Mandi Palace**, part of which is now a hotel, as well as the **Triloknath Temple** (1526), dedicated to Shiva.

PRACTICAL INFORMATION

OBTAINING PERMISSIONS

Foreigners travelling between Rekong Peo, in Kinnaur, and Tabo, in Spiti, need a permit, which can be picked up in government offices in several towns in the region; most of these offices are open 10–5, with a slightly unpredictable lunch break, and closed on Sundays and some Saturdays. You need three passport photos, two photocopies of the key pages of your passport, and the process normally takes no more than an hour. In Rekong Peo, the Kinnauri capital, go to the Sub-Divisional Magistrate's Offices, near the bus stand. In Kaza, the capital of Spiti, go to the Assistant District Commissioner's Office near the hospital. In Simla, go the Collectorate Building below the Mall.

GETTING THERE

Himachal Pradesh has three main airports, near Simla, Kulu and Dharamsala—all with regular flights from Delhi. For the southwest of the state, around Nalagarh and Nahan, Chandigarh is the nearest airport, and nearby Kalka the nearest major railway station.

Hill trains do go up to Simla and to Jogindernagar (from Pathankot in Punjab via Kangra town) in the Kangra Valley. There are four daily trains from Kalka—which is well connected to Chandigarh and Delhi—to Simla, a journey that takes 5hrs. The same journey by road is less picturesque and more hair-raising, but takes about 3hrs. Driving to Simla from Delhi takes about 8hrs.

GETTING AROUND

Himachal Pradesh is one of India's smaller states, but, because of its mountainous terrain, it often takes a very long time to cover relatively short distances. The road journey to Manali from Simla, for example, just 125km as the crow flies, can take more than 8hrs. Major journeys, such as the one from Simla through Kinnaur, Lahaul and Spiti, can take several days along hair-raising mountain roads. Be sure your driver has experience of the mountains, and carry provisions in case the roads are closed by landslips.

The easiest and quickest way of getting around the main tourist sites in Simla is on foot. If you want to get from one end of the town to the other, quickly, it is best to go down to the Cart Road, and take a rickshaw or taxi, and then you'll have a steep walk or lift-ride back up again.

ACCOMMODATION

• **Simla:** One of three Oberoi hotels in and around Simla, **The Cecil** (*$$$: T: 0177 280 4848; thececil.com*) is at the western end of the mall. **Clarkes** (*$$; T: 0177 2651010-15; clarkesshimla.com*), at the eastern end of the Mall, is not officially part of the Oberoi group, but is owned by the same family; it is slightly less luxurious, but more picturesque. **Woodville** (*$$; T: 0177 2623919, woodvillepalacehotel.com*) is a former royal residence (*see p. 309*) in the eastern part of the town. **Chapslee** (*$$$; T: 0177 2802542; chapslee.com*) is one of the most exquisite heritage hotels in the country, run by the descendants of the Kapurthala royal family (*see p. 310*).

• **Around Simla:** Another hotel owned by the Oberois, **Wildflower Hall** (*$$$; T: 0177 264 8585; wildflowerhall.com*) is one of the most luxurious hotels in the country; it is built on the site of the former residence of the British commander-in-chief. **Fort Nalagarh** (*$$; T: 01795 223179; thefort@nalagarh.com*) is a comfortable palace hotel on the hillside above the town of Nalagarh. It provides a good stopover on the way to Manali or Dharamsala. **Arki Palace Retreat** (*$; T: 01796 2206210; hotelpalaceretreat.com*), is a sleepy heritage hotel, with just four rooms, in the charming old fort in the town of Arki, between Nalagarh and Simla. The prettily situated **Chail Palace** (*$$; T: 01792 248141; thechailpalace.com*), in Chail, is run by the state tourism department. And the **Jubbal Palace** (*$$; T: 01781 252001*), in Jubbal, has excellent local cuisine.

• **Around Kinnaur and Spiti:** The most comfortable hotels in Kinnaur and Spiti are the **Banjara tented camps** (*$$; banjaracamps.com*) at Sangla (*T: 098169 59904*) and Kaza (*T: 094187 18123*).

• **Dharamsala and McLeod Ganj:** Dharamsala has dozens of hotels, though most of the ones in McLeod Ganj are small and homely rather than modern and luxurious. In McLeod Ganj, the **Chonor House** (*$$; T: 01892 221006; norbulingka.org*), decorated in traditional Tibetan style, is recommended. In Dharamsala, **Clouds End Villa** (*$$; T: 01892 222109; cloudsendvilla.com*) is a former residence of the raja of Kangra-Lambagraon, while **Grace Hotel** (*$$; T: 01892 223265; welcomheritagegrace.com*) is a 200-year-old home that belonged to the first chief justice of India.

• **Kangra and Chamba valleys:** Other hotels in the Kangra Valley include, near Palampur, **Taragarh** (*$$$; T: 01894 242034; taragarh.com*), a palace belonging to the former royal family of Kashmir. Dalhousie's comfortable **Grand View Hotel** (*$$; T: 01899 240760; grandviewdalhousie.in*) is in a British-period building, with, as you might expect, excellent views of the mountains.

• **Manali and the Kulu Valley:** Manali's most luxurious modern hotel is the **Highland Park** (*$$$; T: 01902 256501; highlandparkmanali.com*), 4km north of the town on the road to the Rohtang Pass, but many visitors prefer to stay closer to Manali. **Johnson Hotel** (*$$; T: 01902 253764; johnsonhotel.com*), which opened in 1917, is in the heart of the town. The 15th-century **Nagar Cas-**

tle (*$$; T: 01902 248316; hptdc.nic.in*), in the town of Nagar, has been converted into a hotel run by the state tourism department. Mandi's **Raj Mahal Palace Hotel** (*$$; T: 01905 222401; rajmahal.com*) is a comfortable, old-fashioned place to break a journey to Dharamsala or Manali.

FOOD

Traditional Himachali food uses lots of yoghurt, lentils and vegetables. *Sidu* is dumpling-like bread made from wheat flour. River fish, particularly local trout, are widely eaten, but Punjabi, North Indian and Tibetan food are easier to find than traditional Himachali cuisine. Ask at your hotel if you want to try Himachali food.

Traditionally, Simla was a place for British and Anglo-Indian food: kedgeree, bread-and-butter puddings, lamb cutlets; however, north Indian cuisine of a rather uninspiring kind has largely taken over. Some of the older hotels still serve the traditional dishes—**Clarkes**, for instance, still has excellent mulligatawny soup, and some very English fruit custards. Local river fish is also available—try downstairs at the **Combermere Hotel**.

Tibetan food is widely available in McLeod Ganj, as is a wide variety of popular Western dishes. The meat-filled dumplings known as *momos* are the ubiquitous Tibetan dish—now available throughout India—and there are many small Tibetan cafés, such as the **Peace Café** on Jogibara Road, serving *momos* and food such as *thukpa* (a Ladakhi dish, *see p. 359*).

In Manali, **Johnson's Café** at the Johnson Hotel serves English-style meals, including fish caught in the river that runs through the town. Tibetan food is also widely available in Manali. A small number of Italians live in Manali and Nagar, and have set up Italian restaurants.

FURTHER READING & VIEWING

Rudyard Kipling's *Kim* has some marvellous descriptions of Simla in the late 19th century. The best widely available study of colonial Simla is *Imperial Simla: The Political Culture of the Raj* by Pamela Kanwar (OUP India, 1990). Raaja Bhasin's *Simla On Foot: Ten Walks* (Rupa, 2007) is also recommended.

For Dharamsala, try Swati Chopra's travel book *Dharamsala Diaries* (Penguin India, 2007). For Manali, Christina Noble's *At Home in the Himalayas* (Fontana, 1991) is by a Scottish woman who lived there in the 1980s, while Imogen Lycett Green's *Grandmother's Footsteps* (Pan, 1997) is by the granddaughter of Penelope Betjeman, who died while trekking in the hills above Manali.

Staying On is a charming 1980s British TV movie, available on DVD, set in Simla; it is based on a Paul Scott novel of the same name, which was actually set in a rather different fictional hill-station. The 2001 Hindi movie *The Warrior*, an India-UK co-production, is largely set in Manali.

JAMMU & KASHMIR

India's most northerly state (*map 1*) was once a major tourist destination. The beautiful mountains, gardens and lakes of the Kashmir Valley had been a place of refuge from the burning summer sun of the Indian plains since Mughal times. But the valley had become, by the early 1990s, a battlefield, as Muslim separatists fought against the Indian security forces, and tens of thousands of people were killed. Tourism to the Kashmir Valley stopped. But gradually, in the new millennium, the security situation improved, and a trickle of visitors returned too. Meanwhile, tourists also began to travel in significant numbers to another part of the state which was largely unaffected by the troubles: Ladakh, which has a rich Buddhist heritage and a lunar-like mountain landscape.

The modern Indian state of Jammu and Kashmir is divided into three distinct parts: the Kashmir Valley, the Jammu region and Ladakh. Geographically and ethnically, these parts are markedly different from each other. Jammu has a majority Hindu population, and consists of the plains and the Himalayan foothills in the southern part of the state. The city of Jammu is the state's winter capital. The valley, also known historically as the Vale of Kashmir, is majority Muslim, surrounded by snow-capped hills and even today connected by only one proper road to the rest of India. The main city in the valley is Srinagar, which is the summer capital of Jammu and Kashmir. Ladakh has a mixed population of mainly Buddhists and Muslims, and is an arid plateau high up in the Himalayas. Its capital is Leh. India also claims, but does not administer, other parts of the historical kingdom of Kashmir that currently fall under Pakistani and Chinese control.

THE KASHMIR VALLEY

The Kashmir Valley is a place of almost legendary beauty—a paradise that, sadly, turned sour. It is best known for its mountains, gardens and lakes, a place where visitors come to trek, ski, fish, eat, shop and relax. But the valley is also home to less famous, but distinctively Kashmiri, Hindu and Muslim architectural traditions. South of Srinagar is the fascinating ruined Sun Temple of Martand, with its clear Hellenistic influences, while the ancient temple complex at Nara Nag nestles high in the Himalayas. Srinagar, meanwhile, has several of India's most unusual mosques and tombs from the pre-Mughal Muslim period, as well as the superb Mughal formal gardens that dominate the eastern banks of Srinagar's Dal Lake.

Kashmir's distinctiveness is something that the people of the valley are particularly proud of. Kashmiris look different—many of them have pale skin and green eyes. Their food is different, the way they dress and the buildings they create are distinctive and their own. Hindus from the valley almost all belong to the priestly Brahmin caste, and are known as Pandits.

HISTORY OF KASHMIR

Despite its apparent isolation, the Kashmir Valley is ringed by high mountain passes; it has been a crossroads and a place both of refuge and conquest for many centuries. Prehistoric human settlements have been discovered in the Kashmir Valley that date back more than 4,000 years, and the Kashmiri epic, the 11th-century *Rajatarangini* (*Chronicle of Kings*) by Kalhana tells of ancient battles between great kings of the past. Kashmir's earliest historically significant ruins—at Harwan—date from the 3rd or 4th century, when Buddhism was dominant in the valley. By the 8th century, Hinduism had reasserted itself, and, under powerful Hindu kings such as Lalitaditya (who commissioned the Sun Temple at Martand) and Adityavarman (responsible for the Avantipur temples), there was a great flourishing of Kashmiri culture and the development of a distinctive Kashmiri style of temple architecture. Under these kings, the population grew, as more of the Kashmir Valley came under cultivation through the improvement of irrigation and terracing techniques.

Muslim rule in Kashmir: Muslim rule first came to the valley in the mid-14th century, when Mir Shah founded a dynasty that controlled Kashmir for 200 years. Although some of the early Muslim rulers were iconoclasts and temple-destroyers, others adapted older Hindu and Buddhist construction techniques, using stone and wood, to build mosque and tombs. The greatest of the early Muslim rulers of Kashmir was Zain-ul Abedin, still known popularly as the Badshah (or Great King). He encouraged the return of Hindus to the valley, restored temples that had been damaged by his predecessors, and helped turn Kashmir into a place with a reputation for tolerance and learning. Srinagar grew, the Jama Masjid, or Friday Mosque, was enlarged, and the unusual cruciform tomb to the Badshah's mother was constructed.

Kashmir and the Mughals: After a long period of instability, the Mughals took control of Kashmir in 1586. It soon became a summer retreat for the imperial family, who would spend several weeks each year making the long journey from the Indian plains to the valley, before returning again a little later in the year. The Mughals built the fine formal gardens that overlook the eastern shores of Dal Lake, and in several other parts of the valley. As the Mughal Empire began to disintegrate, however, the valley was conquered by Afghans, who built the distinctive Hari Parbat hill-fort in Srinagar, and whose rule was marked by cruelty and extortion. Control of Kashmir then fell to the Sikh maharaja of Punjab, Ranjit Singh, who never visited the valley. One of his vassals, Gulab Singh of Jammu, a member of the mainly Hindu Dogra community, sided with the British during the Sikh wars of the 1840s. He was rewarded with the entire Kashmir Valley, Ladakh, and several other territories that are now under Pakistani administration. Maharaja Gulab Singh's descendants ruled until 1947, when the present state of Jammu and Kashmir became part of Independent India.

Kashmir at Partition: Kashmir's current problems largely date back to 1947, when the subcontinent was partitioned between mainly-Hindu India and mainly-Muslim

Pakistan. The Hindu maharaja of Kashmir originally wanted independence, but when Pakistani forces invaded the valley he chose to join India. The majority Muslim population was not consulted, and many Kashmiri Muslims continue to demand the right of self-determination. In 1947, Indian forces were able drive the Pakistani invaders out of most of the valley, but the larger historical kingdom of Kashmir was divided along a ceasefire line, separating many families and cutting key road links. India has not given up its claim to territory now controlled by Pakistan.

The dispute over Kashmir led to another war with Pakistan in 1965, and simmering discontent spilled over by the early 1990s into a full-scale guerrilla conflict, in which Muslim separatist forces controlled significant parts of the valley. Most Hindus left their ancestral homes. Tourism ground to an almost total halt, and it was not until relatively recently that visitors began to return to the valley, while a stop-start political dialogue got underway. Most of the valley is now safe, but it is always best to check with locals before travelling into more remote areas. Additionally, there continue to be long periods when strikes and curfews make visiting the valley very difficult—check the latest news from Kashmir before going there.

Despite the continuing heavy security presence, Kashmir remains a fascinating place to visit, and it is far from overrun by tourists. Accommodation is cheap, the food can be superb, and the valley's centuries-old reputation for romantic beauty lives up to most travellers' expectations.

Kashmir is also associated internationally with the kind of wool named after the region, but normally spelled cashmere. The shawl business, particularly in the fine variety of cashmere wool known as pashmina—which grows as an inner layer on a breed of Himalayan goats—is still a major source of income for Kashmiris. The finest wool of all, used to make the shawl known as the *shahtoosh*, is from the Chiru antelope. The antelope is an endangered species, and trade in the *shahtoosh* is now illegal.

MUGHAL JOURNEYS TO KASHMIR

The Mughal emperor Jehangir treated the Kashmir Valley as an enormous holiday home, and may have come here as many as 12 times. His son Shah Jahan came to the valley for four summers with the rest of his imperial court. But his son Aurangzeb, the most austere of the Mughals, only came once to the valley as emperor—an enormous logistical operation, witnessed by the French traveller François Bernier. Bernier described how it took 200 camels, 100 mules, 60 elephants and 100 porters to carry just the royal camping equipment. A duplicate set was necessary too, to be set up in readiness at the next campsite while the previous night's camp was being dismantled. The imperial party was accompanied by 100,000 horsemen, and great herds of goats and cattle to provide food for the travellers. The campsite would often be 10km in diameter.

EUROPEANS & KASHMIR

In the 17th century, the earliest European accounts of Kashmir were published, which echoed the Mughal romanticisation of the valley as heaven on earth—an isolated paradise, high in the mountains. Kashmir became a land of mystery and romance, epitomised in the 19th-century epic *Lalla Rookh*, by the Irish poet Thomas Moore, who never set foot in Asia:

Who has not heard of the Vale of CASHMERE,
With its roses the brightest that earth ever gave,
Its temples and grottos and fountains as clear
As the love-lighted eyes that hang over their wave?

SRINAGAR

Srinagar (*map 1 B1–2*) is India's most beautiful state capital, nestled into the northern corner of the Kashmir Valley, with snow-capped mountains visible from the city for much of the year. The city wraps itself around a series of lakes, is criss-crossed by canals and bisected by the meandering River Jhelum. It has two distinctive hills that dominate the skyline of the actual city: the smaller one, Hari Parbat, with an 18th-century yellow fortress on its summit; the larger one topped by the 5th-century Shankaracharya Hindu temple. The old city, consisting of mainly wooden buildings, stretches out on either side of the Jhelum and reaches to the banks of the largest of the waterbodies, the Dal Lake, which is studded with houseboats—Srinagar's unique alternative to hotels. The old city is an excellent place for a stroll, particularly close to the riverfront, with its charming painted wooden houses. The river was once spanned by a series of wooden bridges known in Kashmiri as *kadals*. The wooden Zaina Kadal, just north of the pretty Shah Hamadan Mosque, survives, but has been reinforced to take vehicular traffic.

Jama Masjid

Midway between the hill of Hari Parbat and the Jhelum stands Srinagar's magnificent Jama Masjid, or Friday Mosque (c.1400), a distinctive square building, with four tall pagoda-like towers rising from its walls. It was built by the Badshah's father in the early 15th century, and has been repeatedly damaged by serious fires—though it is thought to have always been reconstructed according to the original plan. The roof of the building, like so many in Kashmir, slopes steeply—as in other places around the world that experience heavy snowfall. Made out of wood, brick and stone, it consists of a large courtyard with raised water tanks and several trees, surrounded by high enclosed hallways on all four sides. The columns, beams and ceiling rafters are all constructed out of

wood, as are the *jali*-style windows at the back of the prayer area. Each column is made from the trunk of a single deodar tree. The mosque has an elongated *mihrab*, or prayer niche, in black marble. Note how the ceiling uses alternating patterns of north–south, and east–west facing rafters. The mosque is said to accommodate 33,333 people praying at one time, and each of the prayer places is marked in the four halls by the use of specially designed rugs and carpets. The tallest tower, above the main prayer area and the *mihrab*, has two small pavilions which function as minarets, from where the call to prayer is made.

The Tomb of Zein-ul Abidin's mother

This tomb (c. 1430) is one of Srinagar's most intriguing buildings. It is a Muslim mausoleum that looks more like a Byzantine church, with its multiple domes nested together, and it was built on the ruins of a Hindu temple. It stands in the middle of a Muslim cemetery overlooking the River Jhelum, just 400m southwest of the Jama Masjid. Zein ul-Abidin, better known as the Badshah, or Great King, is thought to be buried in the nearby enclosure, and it is his unnamed mother, wife of the temple-destroying Sultan Sikander, whose tiny cenotaph occupies the grand mausoleum. At the entrance to the cemetery, note the old Hindu gateway, with the triangular pediments and trefoils that are to be found on so much early Kashmiri Hindu architecture. The base of the temple and the low side walls of its small staircase are also of clearly Hindu origin, and the remains of carved idols can be made out on the side of the walls. The actual tomb building is cruciform—a reflection of the original shape of the temple. It is built of brick, studded with curious blue-glazed tiles, and has a cluster of five domes on its roof. The largest dome has unusual brick ribs, while the smaller domes have decorative arches.

Shah Hamadan Mosque

Srinagar's oldest Muslim building (1395), this attractive mosque is typical of the Kashmiri style, with a single green pagoda-like tower rising out of a green roof shaped like a step pyramid. The mosque is 700m south of the Jama Masjid, and overlooks the River Jhelum. The mosque is almost entirely built out of wood, except for the stone plinth and tiny bricks used to fill the gaps between the exterior wooden frames. Note how corbelled logs have been used to support the roof-eaves. Part of the exterior is painted with floral motifs, and the interior is richly decorated with carpets, painted walls and columns, and many chandeliers. Shah Hamadan was a 14th-century Muslim saint from Persia, who was one of the first Islamic preachers to come to the valley. Like the Jama Masjid, it has repeatedly been damaged by fire, and rebuilt to the original design.

Rozabal Mosque and Shrine

This small building, the date of which is unknown, officially contains the Tomb of Youza Asouph, a Muslim saint, but it is also known as the Tomb of Jesus, because of a legend that asserts that Jesus, rather than entering heaven after his resurrection, went to live in Kashmir.

JESUS IN KASHMIR

Similarities between Christianity and Buddhism, the discovery of ancient texts which have mysteriously disappeared and ancient legends about biblical figures visiting India have spawned a large number of theories about Jesus living in Kashmir. According to the book *Jesus Lived in India* by Horsten Kolger, Christ's 'missing years', between the ages of 12 and 30 in the biblical account of his youth, were spent in Kashmir, imbibing Buddhist philosophy. He is then said to have survived the crucifixion and returned to Kashmir, eventually to die at the age of 80. Other groups, including the heterodox Ahmeddiya sect of Islam, also believe he is buried in the small tomb.

Mughal Mosques

Srinagar also has two significant mosques from the Mughal period, both of which ignore the conventions of Kashmiri mosque building by being constructed out of stone and having no towers. The nine-bayed **Pathar Mosque** (1623) is on the western bank of the Jhelum, just opposite the Shah Hamadan Mosque. It was commissioned by Nur Jahan, the wife of Emperor Jehangir, to a traditional Mughal design, but with little decoration. It has a sloping roof over the bays, in the manner of other Kashmir mosques. The other mosque from the Mughal period is the **Akhund Mullah Masjid** (1649), on the southern slopes of Hari Parbat (*see below*), next to the footpath leading to the more modern Makhdoom Sahib shrine. This exquisite greystone mosque was built by Prince Dara Shikoh, the oldest son of Emperor Shah Jahan, for his spiritual mentor Akhund Mullah. Today the mosque is little visited and crumbling. Unusually, the mosque has an external compound which has been built into the side of the hill, and sits above a warren of small underground chambers, which can be accessed from a staircase in the compound.

Hari Parbat

This hill has a greatly restored and modernised Hindu temple, **Chakreshwar Mandir**, which is the closest one can get to the small Afghan **fort** on top of the hill. The fort is closed to the public and is occupied by the security forces. At the base of Hari Parbat are two gateways and some sections of an old city wall that date to the early Mughal period in Srinagar, when Emperor Akbar built a palace and a citadel on the hill.

Hazratbal

This modern white-domed mosque is regarded as Kashmir's holiest Muslim shrine, because it contains a single strand of the Prophet Muhammad's hair. The mosque stands on the side of Dal Lake, 3km northeast of Hari Parbat. The hair is inside a glass phial, which is usually kept in a small room above the *mihrab* of the mosque. In the 1960s, the hair was stolen, prompting large-scale demonstrations across the valley—until the hair reappeared just as mysteriously as it had vanished. There are lovely views from Hazratbal across Dal Lake towards the Mughal gardens at Shalimar and Nishat Bagh.

The **Sri Pratap Singh Museum** (*open Tues–Sun 10–4 summer, 10.30–4.30 winter*), on the south bank of the Jhelum near the modern bridge, has a fine collection of Hindu sculptures and other exhibits in a late 19th-century royal building. Particularly striking are the life-size 8th-century Hindu statues from Pandrethan, in the southern outskirts of Srinagar, including standing sculptures of Shiva and of Vishnu, a fine three-headed seated Shiva and an image of Bhairava with a skull on a stick. Note the triple-headed Vishnus from Avantipur with lions' faces on either side of the human image of Vishnu. There is a superb carving of Vishnu riding Garuda, with his consort Lakshmi on his knee, which was recovered from Verinag. There are also several early Buddhist sculptures, some terracotta tiles and, in the prettily decorated inner rooms, a small collection of Greek coins, and some fine textiles and miniature paintings.

Shankaracharya Temple

This ancient temple site sits on top of the forested hill at the southern end of Dal Lake, 3.5km southeast of Hari Parbat. Vehicles are allowed most of the way up the hill, but there is still a steep climb to the top. The high octagonal plinth of the temple is thought to date back to as early as the 5th century, but the main building was constructed in Mughal times. The temple itself is dedicated to Shiva, but named after Shankaracharya, a 9th-century Hindu philosopher-saint, who visited Kashmir. There are stunning views of Srinagar, Dal Lake and the surrounding mountains from the hilltop.

SRINAGAR'S MUGHAL GARDENS

The Mughals built at least a dozen formal gardens in Kashmir, of which four—all overlooking the eastern shores of Dal Lake—are in good condition and worth visiting. The Mughal emperors loved mountains and gardens, which reminded them of their Central Asian homeland. But they believed also in taming wildness, and the gardens have been carefully and geometrically designed. The Mughals would hold banquets in the gardens, and often camp out in them—a tradition that continued well into British times. The four gardens are each very different from each other: the Pari Mahal is a steeply raked garden, high up on the hillside; Chasma-i Shahi is a smaller garden, set around a natural spring; Nishat Bagh is huge, and sweeps down to the lakeside; while Shalimar Bagh has the finest buildings and is in excellent condition.

Pari Mahal

The unusual Pari Mahal, or Fairy Palace (1635), is a small fortified complex perched on the shoulder of a hill. This most magical of the Mughal gardens was originally built over seven levels, though only five now survive. It was built by Shah Jahan's oldest son, Dara Shikoh, who was also responsible for Srinagar's Akhund Mullah Mosque. Dara Shikoh was an erudite mystic, who preached a syncretic liberal form of Islam, friendly to Hinduism. He is thought to have used the Pari Mahal as a place of learning and religious debate, and possibly as an observatory. There are several interesting buildings, most of them needing restoration, either built into or on top of the retaining walls that separate the levels. The gardens themselves are well kept. Note the old bathhouse on the left as you enter the main gate, with its octagonal chimney to allow steam to escape. There are excellent views over Dal Lake and Srinagar.

Chashma-i Shahi

The small formal garden of Chashma-i Shahi, or Royal Spring (1632), is on the road up to Pari Mahal. It is laid out on three levels against a magnificent mountain backdrop. At the back of the garden is a natural spring. The garden was built for Emperor Shah Jahan, but has been extended and restored—only the internal wall and base of the two-storey pavilion are thought to be original.

Nishat Bagh

The spectacular Nishat Bagh, or Garden of Gladness (1632), is set on Dal Lake, its many terraces sweeping down the hillside for more than 500m. It was designed to be approached by boat, which is still possible, though a road now runs between the garden and Dal Lake. Nishat Bagh has fine views across the lake to the white-domed Hazratbal shrine. Note the small Mughal bridge on the causeway across the lake, constructed to allow boats through to Nishat Bagh. The upper terraces have octagonal stone benches, and there is a large pool with fountains at the top. This upper portion was designed for the women of the imperial family, and there were once several pavilions here. The building at the very top of Nishat Bagh has Mughal brickwork around its base with larger, more modern bricks higher up. Note that the stone arch of the exit gate has Mughal motifs, including an elephant and a vase, carved in relief. The gardens were commissioned by Emperor Jehangir's brother-in-law Asaf Khan.

Shalimar Gardens

Kashmir's best-known formal gardens (1616) are 2.5km north of Nishat Bagh, set away from Dal Lake, and originally accessed by a 1km-long canal that leads down to the waterside. Visitors now come by road. These beautiful, well-maintained gardens served as the royal camping ground during Emperor Shah Jahan's time, although they were originally built by his father Jehangir. A broad watercourse, with a row of central fountains, runs the length of these carefully designed gardens, which are neatly divided into squares and rectangles by terracing and footpaths. The gardens follow the contours of the hill, less steep than in the other nearby gardens, with shifts of level made possible by small cascades.

The Shalimar Gardens are divided into three parts, which in part echo the traditional layout of a Mughal palace. Members of the public were allowed into only the lowest level nearest the entrance. At the front of the second level is the Diwan-i Am, a public audience hall, where Emperor Shah Jahan would appear to his subjects. This is the much-restored pavilion through which the watercourse runs, swirling around the 'throne' and the stepping stones that have been placed in its path. Note the traditional Kashmiri teardrop motifs on the ceiling. Beyond the Diwan-i Am, but now no longer there, was the Diwan-i Khas, a private audience hall. This would have been the building from which the emperor worked, and where he met his advisors.

Beyond this, and past two gatehouses is the centrepiece of the gardens: the black marble pavilion surrounded by a water-basin with fountains. This was the *zenana* area, used by female members of the imperial family. Note the remains of a stone wall that cut right across the gardens—combined with the gate-houses, it ensured that the *zenana* was cut off from the rest of the garden. The roof and wall-paintings of the black pavilion have been restored, but the rest of this fine building is original, and arguably the best example of Mughal pleasure garden architecture. (Agra has, of course, some superb buildings in its many gardens, but most of these had a funerary purpose.) Note the little arched niches behind the waterfalls, above and below the pavilion. These would have had small lamps placed inside at night. The Shalimar

Gardens in Kashmir predate the famous Mughal gardens of the same name in Lahore, now in Pakistan, by about 25 years.

Harwan

Four kilometres beyond the Shalimar Gardens is the Buddhist site of Harwan (4th–5th centuries). Look out for the signboard on the main road running through the mainly Shia Harwan village. The site is a short walk uphill, between some houses and then through a water pumping station. The site is prettily located on a mountainside, with fine views over Dal Lake in the distance. Some historians believe that the fourth Buddhist council, in about AD 80, was held here, presided over by the Kushan emperor Kanishka. On the lower level are three excavated buildings. On the left is the monastery, with the foundation of a pyramid-like stupa in the middle and a residential building on the right, with a nearby pebble wall. Further up the hill is a horseshoe-shaped temple; it was decorated with tiles bearing images of goats, horses and dancing girls, but the tiles are now in storage. Ask the watchman to show you a few small pieces of tile that he has found on the site.

Beyond Harwan is the prehistoric site of **Burzahom**, where excavations have revealed a settlement that dates back at least 4,000 years. There are 11 megalithic menhirs at the site.

KASHMIR VALLEY: OUTSIDE SRINAGAR

The rest of the Kashmir Valley is better known for its outdoor pursuits—trekking, skiing, fishing, golf—than for its ancient monuments. But the partly-ruined Sun Temple at Martand, south of Srinagar, is a spectacular reminder of how far the influence of Greek architecture reached, and there are a number of other important monuments and attractions from the Buddhist, Hindu and Muslim periods of rule in Kashmir. The main centres, all easily reachable from Srinagar, are: Gulmarg to the west, which is best known for skiing and golf; Pahalgam to the east, which is good for trekking and for access to the Hindu Amarnath shrine; and Sonamarg to the northeast, which is on the road to Ladakh, and is becoming, again, a major trekking centre. Most of the valley's tourist sites have reopened and are safe to visit, but it is always sensible to take local advice before travelling.

SOUTH OF SRINAGAR

The road south of Srinagar towards the Banihal Pass and Jammu passes through a number of important historical locations. Just south of Srinagar, inside the Badami Bagh cantonment (*map 1 B2*), is the 12th-century Pandrethan Shiva Temple, currently out of bounds without army permission. Some 25km from Srinagar are the important Avantipur temples, accessible from the main road, and beyond them is the site of the formal Mughal gardens which spanned the River Jhelum at Bijbehara. No buildings remain, but there are some pretty gardens on the roadside. A left turn at the large commercial town of Anantnag takes you to the great Martand Sun Temple. Martand is easily visited, along with the Avantipur temples, on a half-day trip from Srinagar. Beyond Martand is Pahalgam, and the route to the Hindu pilgrimage site of Amarnath (where Shiva's lingam, or phallus, takes the form of a large column of ice inside a rock cave). Head straight at Anantnag, along the Jammu road, for more Mughal gardens and a few ruined Mughal buildings, at Achabal and Verinag.

The Avantipur temples

Avantipur (*map 1 B2*), overlooking the River Jhelum, was the capital of Kashmir under the Hindu monarch Avantivarman, who ruled here in the second half of the 9th century. The temples (9th century also) are all that is left of this ancient city. The two fascinating ruined temples, exactly 1km apart, are on the eastern side of the main Srinagar–Jammu highway, and are both visible from the road. They are younger but in a more ruinous state than the temple at Martand. However, the condition of the carvings is superior.

Avantiswami Temple: The southern, smaller temple is known as Avantiswami, and is dedicated to Vishnu. It is in better condition than the northern, larger Avantiswara Temple, simply because it was low-lying and buried beneath mud and silt for many centuries, before being excavated in British times. It is thought to have been the private shrine of the ruling family. The Avantiswami Temple once had a full peristyle colonnade surrounding its inner courtyard, like at Martand, with Classical Greek-style fluting and pediments, but the columns are now little more than stumps. The porch of the ruined gate has eroded carvings of the river godesses Yamuna (riding a turtle) and Ganga (riding a crocodile).

On the left as one passes through the gate into the courtyard, note a small relief carving of a man and woman kissing. The most important carvings are on the walls at the side steps leading up to the main sanctuary. Facing the gateway, at the end of each stair-wall are images of Vishnu, holding a bow above his head, with his two consorts. On the inside of each stair-wall are rich carvings showing a large group of people. Thought to be court scenes, they show, on the left, King Avantivarman with family and courtiers, and, on the right, the king's son Shankarvarman, surrounded by a similar group. There is a huge amount of broken masonry lying around the Avantiswami site, some of which is finely carved with images and motifs. Note four geometrically-placed platforms of smaller shrines, each at a diagonal to the corner of the main temple.

Avantiswara Temple: The northern, larger temple is known as Avantiswara, and is dedicated to Shiva. This was probably Avantipur's public temple, and, largely because it is on higher land, it has suffered greater damage and erosion. The design is in subtle ways different to the Avantiswami Temple. The Avantiswara Temple has four staircases leading up to the main sanctuary, and its smaller shrines are not separated from the main building. There are also lots of interesting architectural fragments scattered across the site, some of them with fine carved images.

Sun Temple at Martand

This beautiful ruined Hindu temple (8th century) is located on the side of a hill, up a winding road above the town of Mattan, about 50km southeast of Srinagar (*map 1 B2*). There is another, more modern Sun Temple in the same town, so do not be misled by locals who are less aware of the older one. The site at Martand consists of a large courtyard surrounded by a ruined peristyle colonnade, and a large temple in the centre, with numerous smaller shrines nearby. The colonnades are particularly striking, with fluted Doric columns, pediments and cornices that are all reminiscent of Greek architecture. There were Greek settlements further west in what is now Afghanistan. Note also the widespread use of the trefoil, or trilobe, on the colonnades, gateway and temple, which later became such an important motif of medieval architecture in Europe. Many of the temple carvings are severely eroded or damaged, but the location is superb, and the overall effect of this decaying temple, alone in the Kashmir hills, is very powerful. The Martand temple was built in the reign of the Hindu monarch Lalitaditya, who ruled Kashmir in the 8th century.

The courtyard is entered from the east, through a partially ruined gateway, with eroded relief sculptures of deities. The courtyard has a pool placed in front of the temple, which is served by a small stone-built watercourse entering the temple from the left corner. The main temple has the remains of its pyramid-shaped roof, supported by a corbelled trefoil arch, and some fine fluted pillars. Note the side porticoes, which must have served as secondary shrines, resting on the same plinth but half-detached from the main temple. There is also an eroded frieze of small relief carvings depicting musicians at knee-level all around the plinth. There are a few fine relief carvings a little higher up upon the southern walls, but the most important sculptures are all in the porch and the *mandapa*, or entrance chamber. Here, on the interior walls, are a profusion of eroded carvings of deities, including the river godesses Yamuna (riding a turtle) and Ganga (riding a crocodile).

NORTH OF SRINAGAR

North of Srinagar, the main road to Sonamarg (a major trekking centre, *map 1 B1*) and on to Ladakh, bears to the east, passing near the tranquil 20th-century Kher Bhawani Temple, one of the most important pilgrimage shrines for Kashmiri Hindus. Turn left off the Ladakh road for the dramatic Nara Nag temples at Wangath.

Nara Nag temples, Wangath

This group of ruined Hindu temples (c. 8th century) near the village of Wangath (*map 1 B1*) is spectacularly located, up a steep valley, close to the main Kashmir–Ladakh highway. These captivating grey granite shrines are surrounded by snow-capped hills, and the road up to the temples is very uneven. Most of the more than 15 temples are set inside two large compounds close to a fast-flowing river. The road up the valley ends at the first compound, where the largest of the temples has an aluminium roof for protection. Its four walls are largely intact, and the trilobes and pediments that typify the Kashmiri style of temple architecture are evident. Unusually for a Kashmiri temple, there are two entrances, which are opposite each other. Also note the way the large stone pieces that make up the temple are interlocked, like a carpenter's mortice-and-tenon joint. There are five smaller temples in the compound, which is constructed on a platform built out of the slope of the hill—the large size of the platform only becomes evident when heading to the second group of temples.

En route to the second group of temples is the base of an enormous rectangular pillared building, probably a refectory. Most of the column bases are still in place, with a socket for the insertion of the column shaft. The second group of temples—mainly Shiva shrines, complete with stone lingams—is also enclosed within a compound wall. Like the first group, these temples have no carvings, apart from the Classical-style flutings and pediments and overhanging lips of curved masonry. There are sockets cut into the rock leading up to the temple, suggesting the existence of an entrance porch. Note the large water tank carved out of a single boulder. Near the second group of temples is a natural spring, with a small Shiva shrine at the side of the water.

WEST OF SRINAGAR

The road west from Srinagar leads to **Baramullah** (*map 1 A1*) and the part of Kashmir under the control of Pakistan—the main route before 1947 into the valley. **Gulmarg** (*map 1 A2*), near Baramullah, is the valley's ski resort. It is possible to visit a number of historical sites in the area, including the ruins of Kashmir's 8th-century capital at **Parihaspura**, and the Hindu shrine at **Bunniyar**, one of the best preserved of the valley's ancient Hindu temples.

JAMMU

The little-visited Hindu-majority Jammu region extends from the plains of northern Punjab to the mountain range that cuts the Kashmir Valley off from the rest of India. Jammu is the part of the state from which the Dogri-speaking former royal family originated. The region still has a large percentage of its population from the Dogra ethnic community, though there are large numbers of Punjabi Hindus and Sikhs, as well as Hindus driven out of the Kashmir Valley at the start of the conflict there in the late 1980s and early 1990s.

Jammu City

The city of Jammu (*map 1 B3*) is the winter capital of the state of Jammu and Kashmir. It is often referred to as the 'city of temples' and is the base from which pilgrims travel to the Hindu holy site of Vaishno Devi, 40km to the northeast. The city sits on both sides of a deep gorge, through which the River Tawi runs. It has a number of 19th- and 20th-century buildings from its period as a royal capital.

Amar Mahal: The early 20th-century red-brick Amar Mahal is a former palace and now one of Jammu's two small royal museums. It is in a superb position overlooking the Tawi, set within a large compound. The **museum** (*open Tues–Sun 9–1 & 2–5*) has a very small collection of miniature paintings and oils of members of the royal family, and it is possible to gaze at the royal throne through a closed window.

Mubarak Mandi: The old royal centre, known as Mubarak Mandi (1880s) is 1.5km south of Amar Mahal, and there are numerous decrepit 19th-century buildings. The largest building, at the back of the central square, is the **Old High Court**, with its handsome arcades and octagonal domes. It was originally the headquarters of the army of the princely state of Jammu and Kashmir. Note the old sign that says 'Army Headquarters' above one of the entrance arches, while the upper level sign reads 'Foreign Department'. On the left side of the square are several former palace buildings, including the old royal courts and the durbar hall, which now houses part of the **Dogra Art Museum** (*open Tues–Sun 8–2 in summer, 10–4 in winter*), with two fine 9th-century triple-headed stone carvings from the Akhnoor archaeological site, northwest of Jammu. One of them is a *trimurti*, with Shiva in the middle, and Vishnu and a bearded Brahma on each side; the other shows three faces of the clean-shaven Vishnu. Note the pretty balconies in the durbar hall, as well other decorated palace rooms, particularly a fine marble hall, now in use as galleries for jewellery, arms, miniature paintings and modern art. A passageway between the Old High Court and the side of the square leads to several more interesting palace buildings, most of them now empty.

Other sights in Jammu

Jammu's most important temple is the pretty **Raghunath Mandir** (1857), in a large complex in the centre of the old town (*no cameras or phones*). The main temple is dedicated to Rama, and there are several subsidiary shrines. High on a cliff on the eastern bank of the river are the stone walls of the **Bahu Fort**, now a popular temple dedicated to the goddess Kali, with some pretty formal gardens that extend down the hillside.

Around Jammu

There are a number of interesting forts in the area around Jammu. The best known is **Bhimgarh Fort** (*map 1 B2*) at Reasi, 65km north of Jammu—a hill-fort that served as the headquarters of the rulers of Bhimgarh state, which lost its independence in the early 19th century. **Chingus Fort** (*map 1 A2*), a former Mughal *serai*, is 85km northwest of Jammu. The Mughal emperor Jehangir died near this riverside fortification, and his body was laid out in this fort prior to being taken to Lahore for burial.

LADAKH

Ladakh (*map 1 C1*) is the huge, sparsely populated area in the north of the Indian state of Jammu and Kashmir. It is a land of glaring paradoxes: a barren desert through which flows one of the world's great rivers, the Indus; it is one of the most remote places on earth, which historically was also a major trading post. Ladakh's extraordinary landscapes, and its Buddhist culture and history, have made it very popular with visitors in recent years, particularly among those who wish to escape the steamy summer heat of much of the rest of India. During the winter months, the land routes to Ladakh are closed, and few travellers visit the region. All visitors who arrive by air must acclimatise to the high altitude by resting for at least their first day.

Ladakh has its own microclimate, unconnected with the seasonal weather patterns seen elsewhere in India. Most of the Ladakh Plateau is above 3000m, and the mountains that cut it off from the rest of India are over 5000m high, creating a rain shadow. As a result, the monsoon rains rarely reach Ladakh, and its mountains are almost entirely barren. However, the River Indus, which rises in Tibet, and several of its tributaries, run through Ladakh, making agriculture and human settlement possible. Ladakh feels like nowhere else in India, and ethnically and culturally is closer to Tibet and Central Asia. Ladakh is sometimes referred to as Little Tibet or Western Tibet, and the Ladakhi language is closely related to Tibetan. The versions of Buddhism followed in Ladakh are very similar to Tibetan Buddhism, and the Tibetan spiritual and political leader the Dalai Lama is widely revered.

The population of Ladakh is less than 250,000, in an area the size of Scotland. It is made up of two districts. Leh is the eastern district, closer to Tibet, and named after the Ladakhi capital; it has a majority Buddhist population, and attracts the most visitors. Kargil is the western district, closer to Kashmir, and named after its main town; it has a majority Muslim population. The southern part of Ladakh is dominated by the Zanskar range of hills and the valley of the same name; the region has emerged as a centre for trekking. There are dozens of Buddhist shrines in Zanskar, which, while of no great historical significance, are often situated in spectacular locations. The Hungarian Tibetologist Alexander Csoma de Körös is said to have been the first European to visit Zanskar, which he did in 1823.

HISTORY OF LADAKH

The upper reaches of the River Indus have been settled for several thousand years. Prehistoric rock carvings near Kargil and Alchi have not been dated conclusively, but are possibly more than 15,000 years old. Buddhism first reached western Ladakh in the 1st or 2nd century (from which time the Mulbekh rock carving dates), almost certainly from Kashmir to the south. However, the modern heartland of Ladakhi Buddhism today, centred around Leh, appears not to have been affected at this time. And when the Vajrayana form of Buddhism reached Tibet in the 8th century—in what is known as the 'First Spreading', inspired by the Indian monk Padmasambhava (also known as Guru Rinpoche)—the faith does not seem to have reached the area around Leh then either.

It was not until about the 11th century, when Buddhism was all but dead in the rest of India, that Tibetan Buddhism made significant inroads in Ladakh, eventually replacing the ancient Tibetan Bon religion as the dominant faith. The best-known figure in what was called the 'Second Spreading' of Buddhism was Rinchen Tzangpo, who became known as the Lotsawa, or Great Translator. Rinchen, a Tibetan who visited India's holy Buddhist sites, founded several monasteries in the Ladakh region, including—according to local tradition, at least—those at Alchi and Lamayuru.

Islam in Ladakh: Islam is thought to have first reached Ladakh in the 14th century. The itinerant Persian Sufi preacher Sheikh Hamadani, who was the key figure in spreading Islam in Kashmir, visited Shey, 12km south of modern Leh. A small mosque marks the site, and is still a place of pilgrimage for Kashmiri Muslims. It was a Ladakhi by the name of Rinchen Shah who, in the 14th century, became the first Muslim ruler of Kashmir—a fact that Ladakhi Muslims are quick to point out to their Kashmiri brethren. However, Islam always remained a minority religion in this part of Ladakh, though Muslim migrants from Kashmir, Baltistan in modern Pakistan, and Kashgar in Central Asia all settled in the area around Leh.

The Namgyal Dynasty: Until the emergence of the 16th-century monarch Tashi Namgyal, Ladakh was divided as a political entity, with rival capitals at Shey (near Leh) and at Basgo (the site of some of Ladakh's most extraordinary ruins). Tashi Namgyal, ruthlessly efficient by reputation, put his older brother's eyes out in order to secure his succession. He united the kingdom of Ladakh, drove away Kashmiri Muslim invaders, and founded a dynasty, descendants of which still live in the palace at Stok, 8km south of Leh. Namgyal also built the temple that still stands on the rocky crag above Leh Palace.

Tashi Namgyal was childless, however, and his blind brother's sons succeeded him. The second of them, King Jamyang, was defeated by the Muslim rulers of Baltistan, and most of the monasteries of Ladakh were destroyed (Alchi survived because it was already deserted). Jamyang was captured, taken to Skardu, now in Pakistan, and married off to a Muslim princess. It is thought that he may have been expected to convert, but, on his return to Ladakh, with his wife and a cohort of Muslim retainers, he reasserted his Ladakhi Buddhist heritage. His son Sengge Namgyal, the 'lion king', built the palace at Leh, which replaced Shey as the capital. He also constructed many of the great monasteries of Ladakh, and expanded his kingdom into Zanskar and Spiti to the south, and Tibet to the east. Towards the end of his reign, his attempts to expand into Kashmir were checked by the Mughals, who exacted a promise of an annual tribute, which was never paid, and which became the basis of the Mughal claim to Ladakh. In 1667 his son Deldan, under pressure from the Mughal emperor Aurangzeb, erected the first mosque in Leh.

By the late 17th century, Ladakh had lost much of its independence, as Tibet and Kashmir attempted to control the region's growing caravan trade, linking Central Asia, Tibet, Kashmir, India and Baltistan. Carpets, cashmere wool, silk, apricots, spices, salt and saffron were carried over the mountains on pack-horses or Bactrian camels. In the 1830s, Zorawar Singh conquered Kashmir and then Ladakh on behalf of the Dogra Raja of Jammu Gulab Singh, building himself the fort on the outskirts of Leh, still occupied by the Indian army. Zorawar Singh was then killed in an attempted invasion of Tibet. Eventually, under the Treaty of Leh (1842), the Dogras took control of Ladakh, as part of what became the kingdom of Jammu and Kashmir, but renounced their claims to western Tibet. The royal family of Ladakh were pensioned off and sent to live in Stok. Soon, Western missionaries, explorers and surveyors began to arrive in Ladakh, which was being gradually opened up to the world.

After Indian Independence: Partition in 1947 was followed by the occupation of Kargil and other parts of Ladakh by Pakistani forces in 1948. Although these forces later withdrew, Ladakh was now cut off from its natural trading routes further down the Indus in Pakistan. The old northern trade route through China was closed from the late 1940s, and the Tibetan crises of the 1950s led to the closing of the still porous eastern border, as well as a large influx of refugees. Worse still, China effectively annexed the almost uninhabited eastern part of Ladakh, known as the Aksai Chin, during the India-China war of 1962. India closed off Ladakh to the outside world, only allowing tourists back into the area in 1974. Partly because of the effects of insurgency in the Kashmir Valley, there have been increasing calls in Ladakh for the region to be detached from the rest of Kashmir, and to have a separate status within India. However, Ladakh's remoteness—and the fact that the main road route into the region runs from Srinagar—continues to make it very dependent on Kashmir.

In the years since 1974, tourism has grown to play a major role in Ladakh. Hotels and guest houses have been built on agricultural land around Leh, and many young people have left their villages to work in tourism. Ladakh's economy is partly dependent on events in nearby Kashmir, and for a large part of the year the only land routes into Ladakh are closed or unreliable. The opening of the civil airport in the late 1970s has made a major difference, but Ladakh can still feel cut off from the rest of the world.

The main language of the region is Ladakhi, which is similar to Tibetan and is written in the Tibetan script. Urdu is the state language, and is widely understood, while most children now receive their education in English—which is widely spoken by people who work with tourists.

UNDERSTANDING LADAKHI BUDDHISM

The Buddhism that is followed in Ladakh (and some other mountainous parts of northern India, such as Sikkim) is quite different from the Buddhism that was once the dominant faith of the plains of India, the temple ruins of which can be visited today in places like Ajanta or Sanchi. In Ladakh, Buddhism is a living, changing religion—and one that can seem extremely complex and esoteric to outsiders. Some visitors are happy just to appreciate the obvious beauty of much Buddhist art and architecture, but others will want to explore the iconography and philosophy of Buddhism. Be prepared for confusing and obscure answers, depending on who you speak to. There is also a tradition of secrecy and self-censorship in Tibetan Buddhism, which is only gradually revealed to practising Buddhists.

The majority of Ladakh's population are practising Buddhists, belonging to one of the four major schools of Tibetan Buddhism, which is also known as Vajrayana Buddhism—Vajrayana meaning 'Vehicle of the Thunderbolt'. The key institution of this form of Buddhism is the *gompa*, which can mean anything from a small temple to a large monastery. Some of the larger monasteries, usually built into a hillside, have several hundred monks, sometimes with a separate nunnery. Small children get sent by their families to become novice monks, and it is commonplace to see young boys, dressed as monks, frolicking in the courtyard of a monastery, which serves as their school yard. The courtyard will often have prayer drums or wheels, to be spun (by monks or visitors alike) in a clockwise direction in a symbolic evocation of the Buddha's 'wheel of *dharma*', or 'righteous duty'.

THE FOUR ORDERS OF TIBETAN BUDDHISM

Nyingma: The oldest order, founded by Padmasambhava, of which the *Book of the Dead* is a key text. Ladakh's Thak-thok Monastery belongs to this order.
Kagyu: Many of Ladakh's monasteries belong to this order (or its Drug or Drigung subsects), which has a strong Tantric tradition and is headed by the Karmapa Lama.
Sakya: This is the least influential of the Buddhist orders in Ladakh, with just one small monastery at Matho.
Gelug: The newest of the orders, headed by the Dalai Lama, and very influential in Ladakh. The monks of the first three orders are sometimes known as the 'red-hats' and the Gelug are known as the 'yellow-hats', from the headwear they use on special occasions.

Ladakhi Buddhist temples

Within a Tibetan Buddhist monastery, the *du-khang* is the main temple, used as an assembly hall for daily ceremonies; it usually houses several idols, including different forms of Buddha—*bodhisattvas*—as well as statues and paintings of important historical figures in Tibetan and Ladakhi Buddhism. Among the most common forms of Buddha in the temples of Ladakh are: Avalokiteshwara, the 'Buddha of compassion' (usually with 11 heads, organised in a pyramid); and Maitreya, the 'Buddha of the future' (usually depicted stepping forwards). Also widely portrayed is the female form of Buddha, known as Tara, in one of a number of different aspects denoted by a colour—Green Tara and Blue Tara are probably the most common. The internal walls are often covered with a series of murals depicting a wide range of religious and secular themes, including pictures of the 1,000 Buddhas. Some of them—in sharp contrast to Indian Buddhism—depict monstrous figures, known as the 'protectors', or *dharmapalas*, often having sex with their female counterparts in an esoteric Tantric practice called *yab-yum*. The interiors of the temples have mattresses placed on the ground, behind low-level wooden reading desks. There are also musical instruments, including drums, cymbals and long trumpets that are used during ceremonies.

On the outside walls of most temples are paintings of four warriors, known as the Lords of the Four Quarters. Nearby there is usually a Wheel of Life, showing the life cycle endured by human beings until they attain enlightenment. The imagery is repeated, but in a wide range of very different styles; note the childbirth scene in the outer ring, and the stylised inner ring showing a rooster, a serpent and a pig, symbolising anger, desire and ignorance respectively.

Among the other temples to be found in most Ladakhi monasteries is the *gon-khang*, or the temple of the protectors, usually painted in red. The best-known protector, or *dharmapala*, is Mahakala (meaning the Great Black One), who is usually carrying a leopard skin, and shown trampling on the corpses of his enemies. Women are often barred from these temples, though this rule is generally relaxed when the faces of the statues have been covered up with scarves. According to one tradition, women who see the faces of the protectors will immediately become pregnant.

An even more ubiquitous feature of the monasteries are *chortens*, which are known as stupas in the rest of India. They are mound-like structures, usually with some kind of spire on top. They were often built as memorials, almost like a Muslim or Christian gravestone, to a dead holy person, whose ashes and relics may be buried within the *chorten*. Note also the apparently functionless chest-high dry stone walls, often near *gompas*, or connecting *chortens*. Many of the topmost stones are inscribed with the mystic Buddhist mantra 'Om Mani Padme Hum' ('Hail the Jewel in the Lotus'). Many Buddhist buildings are also adorned with prayer flags, and printed with sacred texts and invocations.

Visiting monasteries

This is very much part of the Ladakh tourism experience, but remember that most monasteries are living religious institutions. Respectful and properly dressed visitors are welcomed. In most cases this means that knees and shoulders should be covered up. Always remove your shoes before entering a temple, and follow any instructions about photography. Most allow photography within the outdoor precincts of the monastery, and permit photography without flash inside temples (though Alchi does not allow photography within its temples). Most monasteries will charge between 20 and 30 rupees for admission, and may charge for separate temples.

LEH

Leh (*map 1 C1*, pop. 30,000) is the capital of Ladakh, and is tucked into the northwestern corner of one of the region's larger valleys—the only one spacious enough for a commercial airport, which is 5km from the centre of the town. Just beyond the airport is the River Indus.

Orientation: The oldest parts of the town are high up on the rocky spur above modern Leh and include the 16th-century Namgyal Tsemo Temple. Halfway up the spur is the largest and most distinctive building, visible from most parts of town, the Leh Palace. The Main Market, with its travel agents, trekking shops, and Kashmiri handicraft sellers, is at the foot of the same spur. The Leh Old Town Conservation Project, run by the Tibet Heritage Fund (THF), has meant that many old buildings have been saved and restored in recent years, and your hotel or guest house should be able to give you a detailed map of the THF's Leh Heritage Walk.

Leh Palace

This large rambling eight-storey palace (*open daily dawn–dusk*), set into the hillside, can be approached by stone steps from the market area, or by a road that takes a longer route up the hill. The building was constructed out of mud-bricks and wood in about 1630, by Sengge Namgyal, Ladakh's most illustrious king. It has been unused since the royal family moved to Stok in the 1830s. The building is similar in design to the even larger Potala Palace in Lhasa, Tibet, which was built slightly later.

Leh Palace has recently undergone major restoration, and the walls that were damaged in the Dogra invasion of the 1830s have been repaired. There are dozens of empty rooms, a few with original painted wooden columns and crossbeams. One room has some faded wall-paintings, and is in use as an exhibition hall by the Archaeological Survey of India to display before-and-after photos of their conservation work. The royal family lived in the top floors of the building, and roofs were used for festivals and ceremonies.

Near the palace

Immediately below the road running up to the palace is a series of other important buildings. The spacious 19th-century **Soma Gompa** is the headquarters of the Ladakh Buddhist Association, and its courtyard is used for performances of traditional dance and music. Just beyond is the peaceful, well-lit, 17th-century **Chenrezig Gompa**, built as Leh's main monastic assembly hall, and dedicated to Chenrezig, the Tibetan name for Avalokiteshwara.

The most interesting of this group of buildings, just a few steps down the side of the hills, between the two *gompas*, is the **Red Chamba Lha-khang**, or Red Temple of Maitreya (the 'Buddha of the future'). The central part of the temple consists of a modern three-storey statue of Maitreya, but recent restorations have revealed some remarkable murals (previously hidden beneath whitewash) in the entrance porch and in the very narrow passage that runs round the side of the building. Some of the draughtsmanship is as exquisite as at Alchi, and the faces of the lesser *bodhisattvas*, surrounding the main Buddha, are particularly finely drawn. If the murals have been correctly dated to the 15th century, that would make the temple Leh's oldest building.

Tsemo Gompa

It is a tough 15-minute walk up the hill from Leh Palace to the Tsemo Gompa complex—though a slightly longer journey can be made via a very circuitous road route. The two temples here are usually open only early in the morning, before 8.30am, but the views make the trip worthwhile anyway. Traditionally, the temples and the ruined palace were seen as the oldest buildings in Leh, dating to the early 16th century and the reign of Tashi Namgyal, though earlier claims are now made for the Red Chamba

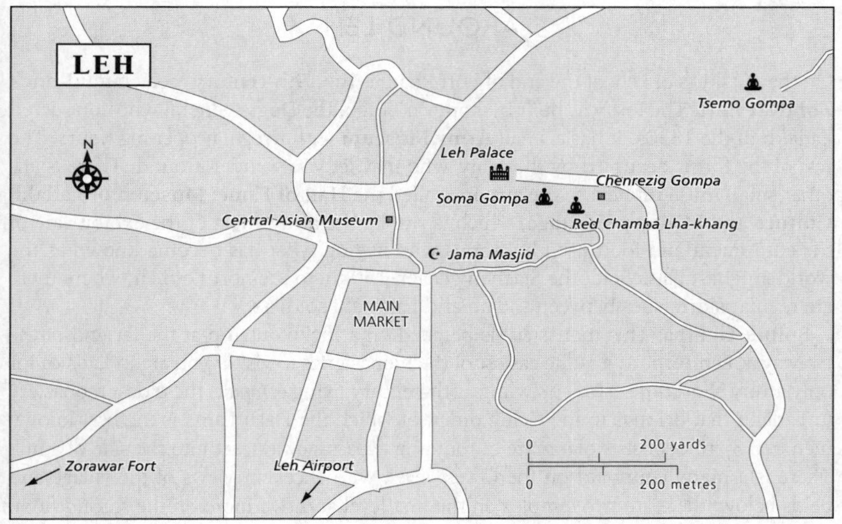

Lha-khang (*see above*). The lower building, painted white, is a **Maitreya temple**, with a large and charming gold-coloured statue of the 'Buddha of the future'. The Maitreya temple has bright but undistinguished wall-paintings, and very pretty images and designs on the ceiling.

Slightly further up the hill is the more interesting red-coloured **Gon-khang**, or temple of the protectors. The paintings here are older, and more finely drawn—but very dark and in need of restoration. On the left, at waist level, is what is thought to be a seated image of Tashi Namgyal. The faces of the statues of the protectors are normally covered, allowing women to visit this temple. Above the Gon-khang is the ruined **Palace of Tashi Namgyal**, which is usually closed, but a firm push on the door should open it. Be careful inside: the balconies are unlikely to bear the weight of a large human. In the top-most rooms are the remains of red-coloured circular murals, and carved wooden pillars and lintels.

Central Leh

The main market area of Leh is at the foot of the hill. On the northern side is a more Muslim-oriented area of the town, with four mosques. The largest is the two-storey **Jama Masjid**, with some particularly fine Central Asian carpets, which overlooks the central market area. The oldest and smallest mosque, 200m to the northeast, has been recently restored to a traditional design, and using some of the original pillars and stonework. Next to the old mosque is the new **Central Asian Museum**, recently built in the traditional style. Note the large old tree, wrapped in cloth, which is said to have grown from the twig that was used as a toothbrush by the founder of Sikhism, Guru Nanak.

AROUND LEH

On the outskirts of Leh, at the end of Fort Road, is the 19th-century moated mud-brick **Zorawar Fort**. The fort was built by Zorawar Singh, the Dogra general who conquered Ladakh in the 1830s. It has a small **Army Museum** with irregular opening hours. The rest of the fort is occupied by the army, who may let you wander around. There is another small museum next to the airport, called the **Hall of Fame: Museum of Ladakh Culture and Military Heritage**, which is run by the army. Most of the exhibits are of the equipment and food used by troops who live on what has become known as the world's highest battlefield, the Siachen glacier, 150km to the north of Leh, where there are regular skirmishes between Indian and Pakistani soldiers.

Spituk Gompa: This monastery is perched on a rocky outcrop at the far end of the runway at Leh Airport; it is the easiest of the monasteries to visit if you are in Ladakh for only a very short time. This sprawling 15th-century living *gompa* is the oldest monastery in Ladakh that belongs to the Gelug order, of which the Dalai Lama is the best-known member. Spituk consists of a maze of rooms and passageways, set into the side of a hill. There is a pretty courtyard on the lowest level, with excellent views of the village and fields below; there are two temples on the first level and two more on the second floor. A short walk further up the hill are fortifications that are thought to predate the monastery: a *chorten* covered in prayer flags and, the most interesting building, a red *gon-khang* temple to the protectors. Note the mixture of secular and religious wall-painting here, including a finely-painted series of women—one rides a horse, another a bird and one clutches a baby—all set amid scenes of cruelty, dismemberment and violence.

WEST OF LEH: THE ROAD TO KASHMIR

The main road from Leh westwards to Kargil, Kashmir and the rest of India follows the Indus for 70km, along what must be one of the most dramatically photogenic journeys in India, before climbing a series of high passes. Over the centuries, it is a route that has been used by many invading armies, trade caravans, and religious leaders and pilgrims. Several of Ladakh's most important sites, including the superb paintings at the Alchi Monastery and the extraordinary ruins of the former capital at Basgo, lie very close to this part of the Indus, while the spectacular living monastery at Lamayuru is just a few kilometres up into the mountains. Leaving Leh, one passes the side road to the pretty Phiyang Monastery, about 15km from Leh. It is a charming example of a living monastery, and is very welcoming of visitors. Though the building dates from the 16th century, most of the paintings are from modern times.

BASGO

The ruins of Basgo (*map 1 C1*), once the capital of western Ladakh, are visually stunning, and the temples inside have a fascinating history, as well as some beautiful and unusual wall-paintings. The site is just a few hundred metres from the main Kargil road, 30km west of Leh. Basgo is on the World Monuments Fund's endangered list, and parts of it look as though they are about to collapse. Fortunately the lack of rain means that these mud-brick buildings have survived for many centuries. It can take a while to realise that some the strange rock and mud formations, beneath the two towering buildings that still stand in Basgo, are actually the remains of the rest of the city.

History: Basgo is one of the more fertile places along this part of the Indus Valley, because of a series of mountain springs. Parts of Basgo date back to at least the 11th century, including a ruined temple on the valley floor and a strange *chorten* with a painted passage running through it. However, Basgo's heyday was in the 15th and 16th centuries, under the Namgyals, when its palaces and temples were built. It was the seat of Tashi Namgyal, who united Ladakh as one kingdom, and his nephew Jamyang Namgyal, who was captured by the Muslim rulers of Baltistan and returned to Basgo with a Muslim wife from the royal family there. The first undisputed European reference to Ladakh, by the early 17th-century Portuguese merchant Diogo D'Almeida, talks of Basgo as the capital. At about this period, the main towns of eastern Ladakh—Shey and Leh—became more important, and Basgo fell into decline. It was attacked in the 1830s by the Dogra army of Zorawar Singh, and many manuscripts were destroyed and jewels seized.

Orientation: From the car park, take the footpath towards the towers. The Serzang Temple, along with a small Maitreya temple, is in the left tower, while the large Maitreya temple, or Chamba Lha-khang, and the remains of the palace (*closed to visitors*) are on the right. To reach the Servang Temple, go through the wooden door of the left tower, turn right and visit the small Maitreya temple (which may once have been a mosque), and then head for the main temples. There is also a footpath—next to the monks' hut, between the two towers—which takes you down through the city ruins into the village.

Chamba Lha-khang, the main Maitreya temple

This three-storeyed temple to Maitreya, the 'Buddha of the future', is thought to have been built during the reign of King Tashi Namgyal in the late 16th century. As well as the tall statue of Maitreya, made of gilded clay, that extends up into the painted ceiling, there are also some of the best Buddhist paintings to be found anywhere in India—arguably, on a par with those at Alchi.

There is a strong secular theme to the murals, appropriately for what is a royal, rather than a monastery, temple. The religious paintings are largely on the upper levels of the temple, and at chest level there are astonishing and often amusing images that reflect ideas about 16th-century courtly life. Look in the right-hand corner closest to the entrance for an image of two men carrying a bed containing a bored-looking naked woman, who crouches on her front and is giving birth to a large boy who appears to be diving out of her womb; on a neighbouring bed, also carried high in the air, a man—presumably her husband and possibly King Tashi Namgyal—is sleeping through it all. This is thought to be a representation of the birth of the heir to the Basgo throne.

Elsewhere, there is a woman having a manicure, and a garden scene with ducks swimming in a pond. The left wall has a series of images from the life of the historical Buddha. Note in particular an image of the Buddha trying to pull a dead white elephant along the ground (he is said to have thrown an elephant killed by his cousin over the city walls). The other religious imagery is also quite different from that in other temples. Instead of a monster-like protector over the door, there is the beatific Vajrasattva Buddha; while the four guardians are not outside the door, but in a subsidiary position, to the left and beneath Vajrasattva.

Serzang Temple

Like Basgo's other two temples, Serzang is dedicted to Maitreya, the 'Buddha of the future'. It is known as the Serzang Temple because *serzang* means 'gold and copper' in Ladakhi, the material with which the exquisite Maitreya image is covered. This temple was completed in 1623. Note the pretty painted and carved series of seven architraves set inside each other, as well as the decorative ceiling of the temple.

Small Maitreya temple

This unusual small square temple, also known as the Chamchung shrine, is thought to have been built as a mosque by Gyal Khatun, the Muslim wife of King Jemyang Namgyal, in the early 17th century, and turned into a temple when she converted to Buddhism. It has a smaller Maitreya statue and some paintings of Mahakala protectors.

Likir

This beautifully situated monastery is at the head of a valley, 3km off the main Leh–Kargil road, just 10km after Basgo and 5km before the Alchi turning (*map 1 C1*). It is very much a living monastery, without the quality of paintings seen in Basgo and Alchi, but very atmospheric, with child monks running around the main courtyard. There has been a monastery on this site since the 12th century, but the current building was largely built in the 18th century, after the previous one burnt down. It is the seat of Ngari Rinpoche, whose current incarnation is the younger brother of the Dalai Lama. The main *du-khang*, or assembly temple, is in frequent use, and visitors are welcome to enter and sit round the sides during ceremonies. The lower, less-frequented *du-khang* has wild demonic images of decapitation and torture, in the more modern, almost cartoon-like, Tibetan style. There is a small museum with some fine *thangka* silk paintings, some superb 300-year-old lamas' hats, lots of accoutrements of daily life for a Buddhist monk and, for no obvious reason, an ammonite fossil from Germany.

Saspol

At Saspol (*map 1 C1*), before the bridge to Alchi, there is a small cave cut into a cliff face which has some quite superb Buddhist paintings—they rank with those of Basgo and Alchi. Yet this cave is hardly visited, and little is known about the paintings. It is quite an uphill scramble to get there. The position of the cave can be seen from the main road, marked by a large flag and a brown door on the half-collapsed rock face, just below a ruined fort. Follow the stream from the village to the house at the bottom of the hill. The cave is normally open, but its best to check at the house in case it has been locked, as the occupiers have the key. Do not go all the way to the monastery on the side of the hill, but head, by way of the rocky zigzag path, for the flag.

The small monastic cell is about 4m by 3m, and all the walls are covered by murals, some of which are in exceptional condition, and which are thought to date back to the 13th or 14th century. On the left of the door are the '1,000 Buddhas', followed by a richly illustrated Amitabha, or the 'Buddha in paradise', seated on a flower and surrounded by trees and plants. To his left is the 'Buddha of compassion', Avalokiteshwara, all in white and with 11 heads, piled-up pyramid fashion. Beneath and to the left are other *bodhisattvas*—note in particular two exquisitely drawn seated men, staring at their own hands. The central figure on the back wall is Sakyamuni, the historical Buddha. Look carefully at some of the smaller figures: there is a weaver, for instance, hard at work on his loom, in the upper left-hand corner of the rear wall; nearby is a man who appears to be levitating. To the left of Sakyamuni, most of the figures are of protectors, the *dharmapalas*, including some superb images of the dark-skinned, many-armed Mahakala and his consort having sex.

Other nearby caves have less interesting, more recent paintings on their façades. It is also possible to climb further up to the small ruined fort, and go up a staircase to a window from which there are fantastic views across to Alchi.

ALCHI

The former monastery at Alchi (*map 1 C1*), overlooking the River Indus, is the home to the best-known and broadest range of Buddhist art in Ladakh, as well as unquestionably the best examples of Ladakhi Buddhist statuary. A visit is highly recommended. Alchi is 55km from Leh, on the Kargil road. Take the bridge across the Indus at Saspol, and Alchi is a further 4km along the road—go through the village until you reach the car park, and then follow the signs to the monastery. The small monastery complex (*chos-khor* in Ladakhi) is peaceful and relaxed, and the perfect setting for exploring Ladakh's Buddhist heritage.

Alchi is the only monastery built at the time of 'Second Spreading' of Buddhism, led by the Great Translator Rinchen Tzangpo in the 11th century, to have survived relatively intact. It is no longer thought, however, that Rinchen Tzangpo actually founded Alchi. It is in such remarkable condition because it was abandoned as a monastery, for reasons that are not clear, in the 16th century, and remained, unlike many other *gompas*, unrenovated; the temples were still used as places of worship. The fact that the main route to Leh ran on the other side of the Indus Valley protected it from the destruction and plundering that affected many other monasteries.

Orientation: There are two routes from the car park: the direct one taken by most visitors, and the one that Buddhist pilgrims take, which circumambulates the monastery complex, giving fine views of the river—where it is possible to find large stones with prehistoric carvings on them. From the tourist entrance, pass between two buildings (the one on the left is the library) where you will see some *chortens*, with passages running through them. Pass to the left of both sets of *chortens*. On your left is the superb three-storey wooden Sumstek Temple, architecturally the most important building in Alchi. Ahead is the wooden door that leads to the inner part of Alchi. To the right is the path that comes from the pilgrims' entrance (notice the prayer wheels and stone carvings along the path to your right—even a modern vegetable-oil can has been converted into a prayer wheel). Beyond the wooden door is a small garden, and to the left is the entrance to the *du-khang* (main temple), which contains the best paintings in Alchi, while straight ahead is the entrance to another courtyard with two further temples, both of them worth visiting. No photographs are allowed inside any of the Alchi temples.

Sumstek Temple

This beautiful three-storey building (*sumstek* means three-storey) houses three extraordinary monumental *bodhisattva* statues set into recesses. The entrance to the Sumstek Temple has some superb decorative and figurative carving in wood, with seated Buddha images on the lintels, making the exterior of this temple quite unlike any other in Ladakh. The trefoil niches and the quality of the woodwork suggest a Kashmiri influence, but there is very little Kashmiri wood carving from such an early period with which it can be compared.

The interior is also quite different from most other Ladakhi temples, with a central *chorten* to be circumambulated. But the *chorten* feels like a minor feature of this temple compared with the enormous statues of, in clockwise order, Avalokiteshwara, Maitreya and Manjushri, their pensive faces half-concealed by the rafters of the upper storeys of the temple. The statues are all made of clay, but have been richly decorated and painted in the most exquisite manner, with exceptional and very different details on their clothing. Each figure is surrounded by smaller statues and paintings of celestial beings and *bodhisattvas*.

On the left of the group is Avalokiteshwara, the 'Buddha of compassion', white and four-armed, with distended ear-lobes. On the exquisitely shaped cloth that is draped round his lower body are paintings of temples and other buildings, thought to represent Buddhist places of pilgrimage. Avalokiteshwara is surrounded by divine beings and mythical creatures, many of them female, wearing crowns made of skulls. Note how modern devotees have hung necklaces and bracelets on the fingers of the statues.

In the centre is Maitreya, the 'Buddha of the future', dark brown and golden faced, and appearing to step out of the recess. His clothing has painted images from the life of the historical Buddha, referred to as Sakyamuni. If you have a torch, look carefully for Queen Maya clutching a tree and giving birth to the Buddha (on the inside of Maitreya's right thigh), the Buddha throwing a white elephant through the air (on the inside of his left thigh, near the knee) and the Buddha achieving enlightenment in spite of his attempted seduction by the four daughters of the evil Mara (top of the left leg). Note the four-armed flying goddesses that attend Maitreya high up in the recess, and nearby a wall frieze of geese.

On the right is Manjushri, often described as the 'Buddha of wisdom'. He is in the same pose as Avalokiteshwara, but dark brown and golden faced, like Maitreya. On his clothing are esoteric symbols and scenes from the Tantric Buddhist tradition, including representations of the 84 Tantric Buddhist masters in different yogic positions.

Du-khang

This unusual temple, though rather nondescript from the outside, is in fact much larger than the Sumstek shrine, and has Alchi's most impressive wall-paintings. Enter from the garden into a cloistered inner courtyard, now covered, which acts as an antechamber to the main temple. There is a series of columns that creates a kind of portico to the temple, as well as a roof for the *chorten*. There are interesting paintings on the walls of the antechamber. Note particularly the domestic scenes of people dancing and eating, on the left wall, as well as the ubiquitous frieze of geese; also look for an unusual painting of a large ship, more than 1300km from the nearest seaport. There are some smaller shrines at the back of the antechamber. In the left one, note the Avalokiteshwara statue, with his eleven heads piled up like a pyramid. On the right-hand side, within a small room, is a Maitreya, surrounded by a more modern style of painting than is seen elsewhere at Alchi.

The main temple contains some superb painting, including perhaps the most famous image from Ladakhi Buddhist art: a king and queen having a drink together, surrounded by courtiers. This image is just on the right, next to the entrance door, while a palm tree (of which there are none in Ladakh) can be spotted on the left. In religious terms, the most important paintings are the six elaborately geometric *mandalas*: a pair on the left wall, a pair on the right and one on either side of the door—each intended as an aid to prayer.

The recessed area at the back of the room is full of exuberant painted carvings, mainly in wood, like a Baroque altarpiece. At the centre is the four-headed *bodhisattva* Vairochana, the 'resplendent Buddha'—the most prominent of what are known as the five 'wisdom', or *dhyani*, Buddhas, whose statues are also displayed here. Note the exceptional detail on the celestial beings and animals that surround Vairochana, such as the eagle holding a rope in its beak (close to the ceiling), and the strange beast with the body of a serpent and trunk of an elephant.

Other temples at Alchi

The two other temples are in the next courtyard, and share a covered verandah and have an internal connecting window. On the left is the **Lotsawa Temple**, or Temple of the Translator, with richly-painted walls, badly cracked in places, and three statues in a glass cabinet. On the centre and right are two traditional *bodhisattvas*: Sakyamuni and Avalokiteshwara, respectively. But on the left is a statue of Rinchen Tzangpo, the 11th-century leader of the 'Second Spreading' of Buddhism. Note how the three idols seem to mimic the almost identical two-dimensional representation of the same three individuals on the wall behind, the only major difference being that Rinchen Tzangpo is looking respectfully at Sakyamuni, the historical Buddha. Note the fine portrait of a lama, with a jigsaw pattern on his garments, in the area above the small internal window. The neighbouring **Manjushri Temple** is thought to be older than its neighbour, and contains four statues showing the different gold, red, white and blue aspects of the 'Buddha of wisdom', Manjushri. Note the carving of a lion riding (and apparently eating) an elephant on the base of the frames that surround each statue.

Alchi village is an interesting place to spend an hour or two. Note the tall building, similar to Leh Palace, built into a rock face in the main village. It is possible to climb upon the rock and look down on what locals say was once a palace. In the highest part of Alchi village is a smaller temple complex called **Tsatsapuri**. It has been undergoing restoration, and has some paintings from slightly later than the main Alchi monastery.

TOWARDS KARGIL

Beyond Alchi heading west, the next major attraction on the Kargil road is the Lamayuru Monastery, but some visitors stop at the handsome 19th-century **Rizong Monastery**, set high in the hills and famous for its rigid monastic discipline. There is also a strange stone building sitting on a large rock overlooking the Indus, between Nurla and Khaltse, with the words Zorawar Outpost written on it in large yellow letters. It is thought to be more than 1,000 years old, and was used as a customs house by the Dogras after Zorawar Singh conquered Ladakh in the 1830s. Be very careful if you want to climb up: the only route is steep and slippery. After Khaltse, the road to Kargil leaves the Indus, and begins to climb very rapidly towards Lamayuru Monastery.

Lamayuru Monastery

The most spectacularly located of all the major Ladakhi *gompas*, Lamayuru (*map 1 C1*) is very much a living monastery, belonging to the Drigung subsect of the Kagyu order. It has existed since the time of the Great Translator, Rinchen Tzangpo, in the 11th century, but most of the buildings are much more recent. Drive up to the parking area and head upstairs through a small door into a courtyard, which leads to the double-chambered main temple, or *du-khang*. On the right is a window leading into a cave, where the 11th-century Indian Buddhist preacher Naropa spent many years meditating. The most interesting temple is one that's little visited and dedicated to Vairochana, the 'resplendent Buddha'. To reach it, you need to go back down the stairs, take the tunnel under the monastery, and then take more stairs down towards the village below. It is best to ask for a guide. There are some fine wall-paintings of *mandalas* here, and an unsupervised side room has some fearsome statues of the protectors, their faces for once not swathed in cloth. Take a torch.

Heniskot and Bodh Karbhu

After Lamayuru, the road to Kargil gets higher and even more rugged and barren—and reaches the highest point of the Srinagar–Leh road at the Fatu-La Pass, 4108m above sea level. The road then dips down to **Heniskot** (*map 1 C1*), a pretty village in a cleft in the hillside, with houses surrounding the ruins of the fort. It is a pleasant half-an-hour uphill walk. Next is **Bodh Karbhu** (*map 1 C1*)—notice the ruins of a seemingly inaccessible fort on a tall rock above the old town, on the other side of the river from the Leh–Kargil highway.

Mulbekh

Beyond another high pass, Namika-La (over 3700m), is the town of Mulbekh (*map 1 B1*), which has Ladakh's finest early Buddhist monument. Cut deep in a rock is a well-preserved 9m-high carving of Maitreya, the 'Buddha of the future', who is known as Chamba in Ladakhi. Note how finely the garments worn by Maitreya are represented, as is the small pot that he holds in his hand. A small temple has been built around it in recent times, covering up ancient inscriptions, and blocking a clear view of the carving. The best view of the entire statue is from the roof of the café opposite.

SOUTH OF LEH: THE ROAD TO MANALI

It is a long two-day drive to Manali in Himachal Pradesh, climbing over two passes higher than 5000m. However, the first part of the road is relatively gentle, and passes close to a number of very impressive monasteries and palaces. The road first touches Choglamsar, which is home to a large Tibetan refugee camp. A side road to the left takes one across the river to Stok Palace. Continue on the east bank of the Indus, for Shey, Thikse and the quickest road to the Hemis Monastery.

Stok Palace

This large and impressive four-storeyed building in the village of the same name is just 10km from Leh (*map 1 C2*). It is nestled prettily under a rocky spur, the view sadly disfigured by the erection of a TV tower. The palace is still the residence of the Namgyals, the former royal family of Ladakh, who moved here from their old palace in Leh in the 1830s. A few rooms set around a pretty two-storeyed courtyard have been set aside for an interesting museum (many other rooms are empty). Among the exhibits are the old throne of Ladakh, a series of 16th-century *thangkas* illustrating the life of the Buddha and some superb examples of the *perak*—the turquoise-studded headgear traditionally worn by Ladakhi women. Note the small trumpet made of a human thigh bone, described as 'a reminder of man's impermanence'. On the other side of the village (leave the village as if heading back to the Indus and turn right, following signs for Gyab-Thabo Heritage Home) is a fascinating traditional Ladakhi house, at least 300 years old, which has been turned into a museum. Do not confuse it with the less impressive traditional Ladakhi kitchen on display just next to the Stok Palace.

Shey

The old capital of eastern Ladakh, 14km south of Leh, is built on a large crag, with the oldest ruined buildings at the top, and the more modern palace complex further down (*map 1 C2*). According to local tradition, Shey was the ancient, pre-Tibetan capital of

Ladakh, and there are remains of some very old fortifications. It was deserted in the 1830s at the same time as Leh Palace. At the entrance to the palace, the first building you see is the Shey Temple, though the entrance is on the second floor. Inside is an enormous two-storey statue of Sakyamuni, the historical Buddha. The palace, undergoing restoration, is on the left, and at least one room has retained the original woodwork and ceiling frieze. It is a steep, rocky climb from here to the ruins of the old palace. The best route is from the far side of the temple, behind a room that the monks use as a temple of lights. The old palace is ruined, but many of its defensive features have survived. The views from the top are superb, particularly over the land just beyond Shey, on the Manali road, where there are huge numbers of white *chortens* covering a wide area.

Back on the road, just as it bends round the crags on which Shey is built, there is an impressive rock carving of the five *dhyani* or 'wisdom' Buddhas in different states of meditation. Each is portrayed standing on a lotus, which in turn rests on an animal. Beneath the animal are carvings of donors. Behind a *chorten* base, 50m back towards Leh, is a stone slab which also has a fine carving of a Buddha. In Shey village is what is believed to be Ladakh's oldest **mosque**, marking the site visited by the 14th-century Sufi preacher Sheikh Hamadan. The building, which attracts many Muslim pilgrims, is newly restored, with the wooden dome taken from the old Leh Mosque.

Thikse Monastery

This monastery is dramatically positioned at the top of the village (*map 1 C2*), which rises in tiers on a high hill overlooking the valley, 15km south of Leh on the east bank of the Indus. Despite being one of Ladakh's largest monasteries, Thikse is calm and well organised. As you enter the complex, the modern part of the temple is on the left, with a huge new statue of Maitreya, more than 10m high, consecrated by the Dalai Lama in 1980. Go up the steps from the courtyard to reach the older parts of the complex. On the left is the three-storey, brightly decorated *du-khang*, or main assembly temple, and a small inner chamber with a statue of Avalokiteshwara. To the right is the *gon-khang*, the protectors' temple, full of statues of monstrous creatures—their faces are covered and so women are allowed to enter this *gon-khang*.

From the windswept rooftop, there are some fantastic views, as well as three smaller rooms. The first one houses a library, full of manuscripts and small statues. The main statue in the library is Maitreya, with the two founders of the monastery at his side. The second room is a small temple, and the third is another temple for the monstrous creatures, into which women are not allowed. Thikse has its own museum, with a huge array of tea-making equipment, a luggage trunk decorated with a tiger skin that belonged to the head lama, and apron-like ritual objects made from human bones attached to each other by string, as well as bowls and drums made from human skulls.

Hemis Monastery

This large, lively monastery—set in a hidden valley, just a few kilometres from the town of Kura, on the Indus (*map 1 C2*)—is best known for the dance and drama festival that takes place in June or July, depending on the Tibetan calendar. For years, it was the

Thikse Monastery rises in tiers from the slopes of the Indus Valley.

only major monastic festival that took place in the summer, and therefore it attracted a large number of visitors to what became known as its 'devil-dances', when monks donned monstrous masks, and others dressed up as skeletons (monasteries elsewhere in the region have now switched their festivals to the summer).

Hemis does not have many high quality paintings or sculptures, but it is the largest and richest of the Ladakh monasteries, is very prettily situated and has a good museum. It was founded in the 1630s, during the reign of Sengghe Namgyal, and is part of the Kagyu order. The approach road to Hemis has lots of small *chortens*, and long stretches of *mani* wall: if you examine the wall closely you can see that devotees have inscribed holy words on the topmost stones. From the car park, head up the steps beside the four-storeyed monastery, at the top of which a monk will be waiting to sell you an entrance ticket. Inside is a large courtyard. The tall buildings on the right are the main temples. To your left are a series of wall-mounted painting fragments. Beyond them is the museum. Tucked into an alcove on your left is an enormous prayer drum, at least 3m high.

The **first temple** contains Hemis's famous rolled-up *thangka*, along the left wall, which is only unfurled every 12 years—the next time will be in 2016. Unusually the architecture is asymmetrical, with a secondary skylight to the left. Almost all the paintings are modern, except for a small patch in the rear right corner. The **second temple** was under restoration at the time of writing, but normally contains a large silver *chorten*, encrusted with turquoise. A **third temple** is approached via the stairs, close to the first temple, and has a large modern statue of Padmasambhava, the most influential figure in the 'First Spreading' of Buddhism to Ladakh, and to whom the Hemis Festival is dedicated.

Less visited, but the prettiest of the temples, is the **Lha-khang**, at the back of the complex. Head through a gate at the far end of the courtyard, turn right along a short tunnel and go straight ahead. Inside are some 16th-century paintings, including an image and a sculpture of an 11th-century Buddhist preacher, the bearded Naropa. Hemis has Ladakh's largest **museum**, which contains some very fine sculpture, and many *thangkas*, musical instruments, ornate saddles, and tiger and snow leopard skins. Look out for the beautiful conch shell with copper extensions, which is decorated with silver relief representations of two dragons and inlaid with turquoise and lapis lazuli.

Near Hemis

The area around Hemis has several other interesting monasteries. These include, in the valley directly opposite Hemis, on the other side of the Indus, **Chamrey Monastery** (another superbly situated *gompa*) and the unusual 16th-century **Thak-thok Monastery**. The main temple in Thak-thok is in a cave, where Padmasambhava is said to have meditated. It is the only Ladakh monastery belonging to the oldest of the Tibetan Buddhist orders, the Nyingma. The cave is black from the smoke of butter-lamps, but it is just possible to make out eight circles, four on each side wall, showing different manifestations of Padmasambhavana. The roof is so thick with the residue of butter smoke that devotees have been able to affix coins and banknotes without any adhesive. In the eaves of the entrance lobby are huge quantities of ancient manuscripts brought by refugee monks from Tibet. To the right of the main temple are steps leading down to several more caves, with the remains of an old kitchen.

On the road to Thak-thok are the ruins of an **ancient fort** which contain three small modern stupas. It is a five-minute uphill walk, and there are fine views from the ruins. Other monasteries near Hemis include **Stakna** and **Matho**, on the west bank of the Indus. The former is prettily situated on an isolated rock; the latter is the only representative of the Sakya order of Tibetan Buddhism in Ladakh.

PRACTICAL INFORMATION

For more than a decade, from the late 1980s to the early 2000s, the Kashmir Valley and some of the mountainous parts of Jammu were dangerous places for tourists to visit (Ladakh was not affected). The situation is now much improved, but there is still a huge security presence there and regular incidents of violence. Normal life continues to be disrupted by strikes, demonstrations and security clamp-downs. Foreigners are not normally targets, and visitors are much more likely to be inconvenienced than threatened. Check before you travel to Kashmir, though: your embassy should be able to advise you, and the BBC on radio, TV and the Internet continues to provide reliable coverage of the political and security situation in the valley. Once in Srinagar, your hotel will be able to advise you if there are any places where it is unsafe to go.

GETTING THERE

• **By air:** There are several daily flights to Srinagar from Delhi, all of which leave in the morning, and less regular flights from Mumbai, Chandigarh, Jammu and Leh. There are also regular flights from Delhi to Jammu. Security is often tighter than normal on flights to and from Jammu and Srinagar, and you may, for instance, not be allowed to carry batteries in your hand luggage. There is also tight security around each airport, and cars are often not allowed to go all the way to the entrance—so it is useful to have wheelable luggage, though there are usually porters around.

There are daily scheduled flights to Leh from Delhi, which usually leave very early in the morning. These are liable to postponement at short notice, depending on the weather in Leh—and sometimes are forced to turn back as they approach Leh Airport. It is a spectacular and slightly nerve-racking one-hour flight over the Himalayas. For the best view, ask for a window seat on the left-hand side of the plane.

• **By train:** There is currently no train service from the rest of India to Srinagar, though a railway is under construction and due to be completed in 2016. A service within the Kashmir Valley from Baramulla via Srinagar to Anantnag opened in 2009. Jammu is connected to the rest of the country by rail (12hrs from Delhi; 5½ from Amritsar). There is no railway anywhere in Ladakh.

• **By road:** The spectacular road between Jammu and Srinagar is open all year round, though heavy snowfall will occasionally close it. It is a full day's journey by bus, shared taxi or car. The only other motorable road to the Kashmir Valley is from Ladakh, but that is closed from October to April. The road to Muzaffarabad, which is under Pakistani control, is closed to tourists. In Srinagar, travellers are advised to hire taxis via their hotel or their houseboat.

The road routes to Ladakh are long and very beautiful. It takes two days by road from Srinagar in the Kashmir Valley, over the Zoji-La Pass, usually staying overnight in Dras or Kargil. The Zoji-La Pass is usually open from mid-April to November, but it can get blocked by landslides or snowfall at almost any time. It also takes two very long days from Manali in Himachal Pradesh, over the Rohtang Pass (*open June–Sept*), staying overnight in Keylong. The accommodation available en route is basic, but the journey on switchback mountain roads is spectacular, and a tribute to some extraordinary road-building skills. The quickest way of travelling within Ladakh is by private taxi. Leh has several good travel agencies that can arrange this for you. Rates are fixed by Ladakh's powerful taxi association, so it is probably not worth attempting to negotiate. (K-2 Adventures are in the Main Market; *T: 01982 252980 or 94191 79999*).

ACCOMMODATION

• **Srinagar:** The **Lalit Grand Palace** (*$$$; T: 0194 2501001; thelalit.com*), a former royal residence overlooking Dal Lake, is Srinagar's most luxurious hotel, but is a little outside the city. The comfortable **Broadway Hotel** (*$$$; T: 0194 2459001; hotelbroadway.com*) is better for exploring Srinagar. Many visitors prefer to stay on one of hundreds of houseboats on Dal Lake. Some of them are very comfortable, and the tradition of visitors staying in them dates back to the 19th century, when the maharaja would not allow foreigners to buy property: so instead they built houseboats. Among the best known is the long-established **Butt's Clermont Houseboats** (*$$; T: 0194 242 0325; buttsclermonthouseboats.com*), next to the Naseem Bagh Mughal garden on the west bank of Dal Lake. George Harrison, of the Beatles, was taught to play the sitar by Ravi Shankar in Butt's Houseboats.

• **Jammu:** The best place to stay in Jammu is the **Hari Niwas Palace** (*$$; T: 0191 2543303; hariniwaspalace.com*), a 19th-century heritage building overlooking the River Tawi, and next to the Amar Mahal Museum.

• **Ladakh:** The grandest place in Leh is the **Golden Dragon** (*$$; T: 01982 250786; thegranddragonladakh.com*), on the southern outskirts of the town, aimed in part at Bollywood film stars who come here for shoots. The nearby **Hotel Shangri-La** (*$; T: 01982 256050; 99069 75424; shangrilaladakh.com*) has more of a traditional Ladakhi feel, with wooden balconies, and a courtyard (often used for dances and music) on three sides, as well as a pretty garden. Many visitors stay in guest houses—private houses that have been converted into mini-hotels. Some of them are very comfortable, and give visitors a chance to meet Ladakhis and eat genuine Ladakhi food. **Harmony Guest House** (*$; T: 01982 252705 harmonyinleh.com*) is just off the Fort Road, and has traditional wooden ceilings, yak-hair stair carpets, a pretty garden and a very friendly owner, who cooks many of the meals herself.

Ule Tokpo Ethnic Resort (*$$; T: 01982 253640*), 12km from Alchi, on the Leh–Kargil road, provides comfortable accommodation in huts made of mud and canvas. Also recommended are **Himalayan Homestays** (*$; T: 01982 250953; himalayan-homestays.com*), if you'd like to stay in a Ladakhi home outside Leh. Facilities are clean but basic.

FOOD

• **Kashmir Valley:** Kashmiri Muslims have a distinctive and strongly carnivorous cuisine, with dozens of dishes not found outside the valley, except in Kashmiri homes and a few specialist restaurants. The traditional Kashmiri Muslim feast, known as *wazwan*, consists of as many as 36 different dishes. Mutton and rice are widely eaten, as is the local spinach-like vegetable, *haak*. The best-known meat dish is *goshtaba*, a succulent, lightly spiced ball of pounded mutton, while *yakhni* is a yoghurt-based curry, cooked with mutton or chicken. The best-known Kashmiri drink is *kahwa*, a green tea with saffron, cinnamon, cardamom, cloves and powdered nuts.

• **Ladakh:** Traditional Ladakhi food is based on wheat and barley, with no rice being grown in the region. Most Ladakhis are non-vegetarian. The staple food is *ngampe*, or *tsampa*, parched barley flour, which is often added to other dishes to make a soup or gruel. *Momos*, steamed dumplings usually stuffed with meat, are ubiquitous, but Ladakhis will tell you they are really Tibetan, not Ladakhi. The best-known Ladakhi dish is probably *thukpa*, a very tasty egg noodle soup with meat and vegetables. *Skyu*, a kind of pasta with meat or vegetables, is also very popular among Ladakhis, but not usually available at restaurants. Thick pieces of local *khambiri* bread are delicious when hot. Slice them open and insert butter or apricot jam. Apricots and apples are widely available. For Tibetan food, try **The Tibetan Kitchen** on Fort Road (*$; T: 01982/25 3071*). It gets very busy, so try to book a table in advance; alcohol is not served. **Summer Harvest**, also on Fort Road, has a reliable mix of Tibetan, Chinese, Indian and Western food.

The most popular drink in Ladakh is tea made with yak butter and salt, which many visitors take time to get accustomed to. The main alcoholic drink is *chang*, a beer made out of barley.

FURTHER READING & VIEWING

The best introductory book to Kashmir is Brigid Keenan's *Travels in Kashmir* (Permanent Black, 2006), first published in 1989. Basharat Peer's *Curfewed Night* (HarperCollins India, 2008) is a first-hand account of the period of militancy in Kashmir, when tourism virtually ceased. Also recommended is Andrew Whitehead's *A Mission in Kashmir* (Penguin India, 2008), a beautifully reconstructed retelling of an incident in 1947, when Pakistani raiders invaded the town of Baramullah in the Kashmir Valley. The first of V.S. Naipaul's books about India, *An Area of Darkness*, has some very funny and moving descriptions of Kashmir in the 1960s.

Janet Rizvi's *Ladakh: Crossroads of High Asia* (OUP, 1996) is a reliable, if rather dry, historical and cultural book about Ladakh. *A Journey in Ladakh: Encounters with Buddhism* (Mariner, 2001) by the British mystic Andrew Harvey was originally published in the early 1980s; it is an interesting account of Tibetan Buddhist spirituality.

Many mountain scenes in Bollywood movies are now shot in Ladakh, partly because of the troubles in Kashmir. The 2001 film *Samsara*, starring the Canadian-American actress Christy Chung, is set in Ladakh, and makes full use of its remarkable landscapes.

For a very impressive and scholarly picture gallery on the Sumstek Temple at Alchi go to www.univie.ac.at/itba—a website run by Vienna University.

GUJARAT

Gujarat (*map 4*), India's most westerly state, attracts relatively few international visitors, despite having some of the country's finest Hindu and Jain temples and the best collection of pre-Mughal Muslim architecture to be seen outside Delhi. It also has India's finest step-wells, its most important Harappan sites, some fascinating princely palaces and museums, as well as some excellent wildlife parks, unspoilt beaches and a superb cuisine. Moreover, Gujarat played a major role in the country's more recent history, as the main place from where Mahatma Gandhi led the Independence movement. It also has, arguably, the country's best roads, excellent flight connections and good hotels. Why then do visitors not come flocking to Gujarat? There are a number of very different possible reasons: it lacks a single world-famous monument or location that a traveller would put right at the top of the list of the places they most want to visit in India; additionally, the state's reputation suffered in the early years of the new millennium because of a major earthquake and serious inter-communal rioting, at a time when tourism was booming elsewhere. Finally, alcohol is prohibited in Gujarat, and only the top hotels can provide alcoholic drinks to their guests, and then only in their hotel rooms.

Geographically, Gujarat is largely comprised of the land between the deserts of Rajasthan and the Arabian Sea. It has a long sea coast that stretches more than 1650km from the border with Pakistan almost to Mumbai, broken by two major estuaries. Its westernmost region, Kutch, is almost an island, cut off from the rest of India by lagoons and salt flats, and the Gulf of Kutch. Gujarat's central coastal region is known as Saurashtra and is India's largest peninsula, bounded by the Gulf of Kutch to the west, the Arabian Sea to the south and the Gulf of Cambay (or Khambat) to the east. To the north and east of Saurashtra is Gujarat's industrial and commercial heartland, including the big cities of Ahmedabad, Vadodara (formerly Baroda) and Surat. Beyond, on the borders with the states of Madhya Pradesh and Maharashtra, is a large, underdeveloped rural belt mainly settled by tribal peoples.

HISTORY OF GUJARAT

Gujarat's early history has been rewritten in recent years, with the discovery of two important Harappan sites—Dholavira and Lothal—that are thought to date from more than 4,000 years ago. These sites, both open to visitors, show evidence of large trading communities, with strong maritime traditions, that were part of what is known as the Indus Valley civilisation (*see p. 14*). Gujarat became, and still remains, something of a religious crucible. The ancient temple at Dwarka and the modern one at Somnath are among the most important Hindu shrines in India, while Palitana is as important to the Jain religion. The first Muslim invasions occurred in Gujarat in the early 11th century, and the oldest surviving mosque is in Bhadreshwar in Kutch. A succession of Muslim armies passed through Gujarat, and, in the early 14th century, the Delhi Sultanate under the Khilji Dynasty defeated the Hindu Solanki Dynasty that ruled Patan. The Solanki Dynasty was responsible for the early flowering of decorative and sacred architecture in Gujarat, and built the great Sun Temple at Modhera. The Gujarat Sultanate, which broke away from rule by Delhi in 1407, was responsible for a period of extraordinary architectural creativity that synthesised Muslim and Hindu traditions.

Under Sultan Ahmed Shah, the capital was moved to Ahmedabad. The most important of his successors was his great-grandson Mahmud Begada (ruled 1458–1511), who built Champaner. Ahmed Shah's dynasty ruled until 1573, when it was overthrown by the army of the Mughal emperor Akbar.

Throughout this period, Gujarat remained an important trading centre, attracting migrants from as far afield as east Africa and Armenia—adding to the sizeable number of Zoroastrians who had left their native Persia by the 10th century, and possibly earlier. Surat emerged as the major west Indian seaport, and part of the Gujarat coastline came under Portuguese and then British control as the European powers became more entrenched and the Mughal Empire began to shrink. The Portuguese built settlements at both Diu and at Daman, which they ruled until 1961—and which are not part of the modern state of Gujarat. Migration out of Gujarat was as important as migration into the state, and there are large, thriving Gujarati communities in east Africa and the UK.

Under the British, large areas of modern-day Gujarat were part of the Bombay Presidency, though there were many semi-independent princely states. At Independence, they all became part of Bombay state, which was bifurcated along linguistic lines in 1960 to form Gujarati-speaking Gujarat and Marathi-speaking Maharashtra. Ahmedabad became the capital of the new state, but was soon replaced, in 1970, by Gandhinagar, a newly built capital just to the north, and named after the state's most famous son. Gujarat has done relatively well economically since Independence, but more recently suffered a devastating earthquake, in 2001. There have also been decades of serious

ARCHITECTURE OF THE GUJARAT SULTANATE

The Islamic mosque architecture of the Sultanate period in Gujarat is often described as the most 'Indian' of Muslim building styles. There is a much closer attention to detail than elsewhere in India, often ornate, the building work relying heavily on Hindu and Jain craftsmen. Sometimes temples were simply adapted—as at Siddhpur—to form mosques. Elsewhere, the prayer area of a mosque was designed like the assembly hall of a temple. There is a heavy emphasis on decorative detail, particularly in the minarets, which are usually constructed on either side of the *iwan*. And there are impressive examples of *trompe l'oeil* masonry work, at the Cambay Mosque and the better-known spectacular stone tracery work at the Sidi Sayyid Mosque in Ahmedabad.

tension between some members of the majority Hindu and minority Muslim populations, and more than 2,000 people, most of them Muslim, died in riots in various parts of the state in 2002.

AHMEDABAD

Ahmedabad (*map 4 C2*), a huge industrial and commercial city (pop. 5,000,000), also contains an impressive collection of Sultanate-period mosques and tombs, a lively walled old city full of interesting buildings, as well as Mahatma Gandhi's Sabarmati ashram and one of India's best museums. The earliest surviving buildings date back to the early 15th century, though there is archaeological and documentary evidence of earlier settlement. According to a much-repeated legend, Sultan Ahmed Shah decided to build his new capital here after seeing the unlikely sight of a dog being chased by a hare. He named the new city after himself, and began building in the area around the Bhadra Fort, on the eastern bank of the Sabarmati River. His successors built the stone gates and walls that ring the old city. Most of the gates still exist, often in the middle of roundabouts, and so do large portions of the city wall. More than two dozen mosques from the Sultanate period also survive in Ahmedabad. The first of the bridges across the Sabarmati was built in British times, and it was then that the western bank of the river, now its modern centre, was first developed.

The area around the old city became the heart of Ahmedabad's most important industry, the textile trade, which still plays an important role in the city's economy. To the south of the city, important Muslim pilgrimage centres such as Sarkhej and Isanpur, which were once villages surrounded by countryside, are now being swallowed up by modern Ahmedabad.

AHMEDABAD OLD CITY CENTRE

The remains of Ahmed Shah's Bhadra Fort are on the western side of the old city, just 400m from the river, and this is a good place to orient oneself. It is easy to walk from here to several of the most important Sultanate mosques, including the main Jama Masjid (Friday Mosque), 500m to the east, and the Sidi Sayyid Mosque, 300m to the north, and famous for its superb perforated sandstone carvings, or *jali*-work. Opposite the latter building, in the House of MG Hotel, it is possible to rent an excellent audio walking guide to the centre of the city.

Bhadra Fort

The large gateways and towers of Bhadra Fort (1411) are Ahmedabad's oldest surviving buildings. They were the eastern entrance to Ahmed Shah's citadel and palace, the only other survival of which is the Ahmad Shah private mosque. Although government offices occupy some of the rooms inside the gateways, it is possible to get onto the broad ramparts of the fort by passing through the Archaeological Survey of India

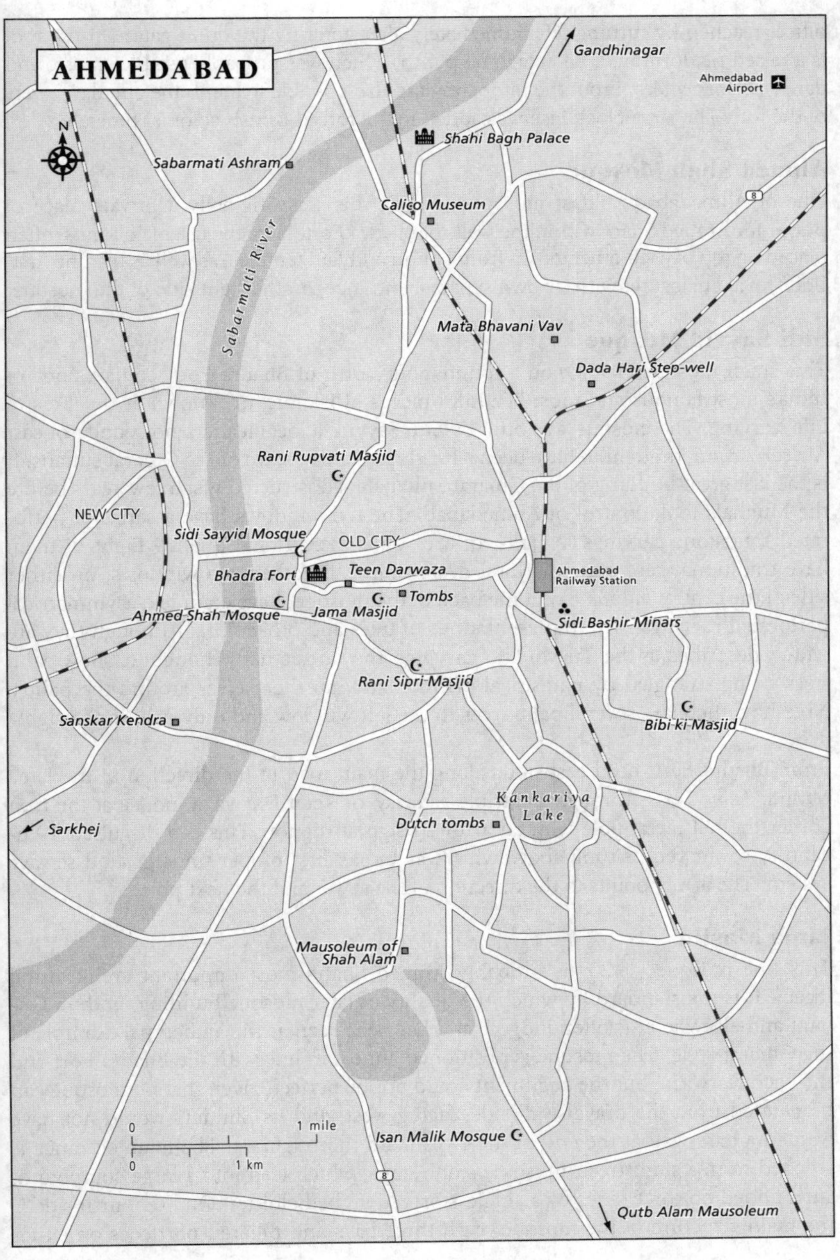
AHMEDABAD
N
Gandhinagar
Ahmedabad Airport
Shahi Bagh Palace
Sabarmati Ashram
8
Calico Museum
Sabarmati River
Mata Bhavani Vav
Dada Hari Step-well
Rani Rupvati Masjid
NEW CITY
Sidi Sayyid Mosque
OLD CITY
Bhadra Fort
Teen Darwaza
Ahmedabad Railway Station
Tombs
Ahmed Shah Mosque
Jama Masjid
Sidi Bashir Minars
Rani Sipri Masjid
Sanskar Kendra
Bibi ki Masjid
Kankariya Lake
Sarkhej
Dutch tombs
Mausoleum of Shah Alam
0
1 mile
Isan Malik Mosque
0
1 km
8
Qutb Alam Mausoleum

office, reached by turning left immediately after entering the outer gate. On the roof is a raised platform with an octagonal plinth, which was probably used for music and dance performances. From the ramparts, it is also possible to climb the circular towers of the fort. The large clock face was added to the fort in British colonial times.

Ahmed Shah Mosque

One of Ahmedabad's oldest mosques (1414), this was originally a private place of prayer for Ahmed Shah, within the walls of Bhadra Fort. Note the use of columns, often placed on top of each other, taken from Hindu and Jain temples, as well as the fine first-floor royal enclosure, with its own separate entrance, on the right side of the mosque.

Sidi Sayyid Mosque

This small mosque (1572), on a roundabout north of Bhadra Fort, contains one of India's most famous and most beautiful pieces of Islamic art, known as the 'Tree of Life' carving. The mosque was built by Sidi Sayyid, a local leader and scholar of east African origin, thought to have been a freed Abyssinian slave of the Gujarat sultans. It is the last great building of the Gujarat Sultanate, constructed just a few years before the Mughals took control of Ahmedabad. The ten windows have a series of perforated sandstone carvings, or *jali*-work, of quite exceptional quality. Eight of them have traditional geometric or floral designs, but the other two windows, on either side of the central *mihrab* bay at the back of the mosque, have complex, asymmetrical perforated carvings, with representations of trees and other flora. Although they are widely described as the 'Tree of Life' carvings, they are actually thought to show palm trees being strangled by parasitical plants that wrap themselves around the palms. Note how there are several palm trees in the left window and only one on the right.

From Bhadra Fort, head eastwards along the main road in the direction of the Jama Masjid. As you pass through the triple gateway, or **Teen Darwaza**, notice at the next corner the tall metal pole with an arrowed sign at the top. This is a disguised 19th-century sewer vent, sitting above what was India's first proper underground sewage system. The arrow points to the direction of the sewer and the next pole.

Jama Masjid

This fine mosque (1423) is probably Ahmed Shah's most important architectural legacy. It is the standard by which the quality of later mosque building, both in Gujarat and elsewhere, is often judged, and has been seen as the archetypal example of the Gujarat style. The mosque is positioned almost in line with the Bhadra Fort and the Teen Darwaza, but the alignment could not be perfect, given that no mosque can be entered from the prayer-wall side, facing west, and its builders would not have wanted a bare wall at the end of the city's main thoroughfare. The main entrance is reached from a side street, up some stone steps, which lead into a large compound, surrounded on three sides by a single-storeyed arched cloister. On the fourth side is the main structure of the mosque, with three bays and pillared porticoes on either side. The harmoniously balanced proportions of the mosque façade have drawn particular praise from architectural historians, though in fact the minarets which once stood on the carved buttresses of the central bay have long since disappeared—they were badly damaged in an earthquake in the early 19th century, and later dismantled. The interior consists of more than 200 slender columns. Unusually for this period, these were not recycled pillars from Hindu or Jain temples, but specially carved for the mosque, though the masons did use many Hindu motifs. Notice the complex way in which the main exterior archway relates to the columns that support the main roof-dome. A two-storeyed gallery sits immediately beneath the dome, and, although there is no access for the public, it is possible to see very high-quality perforated stonework on the upper levels of the mosque. At the entrance of the mosque, set into the floor, is a large piece of carved black stone which is, according to some sources, an inverted Jain statue.

Tomb of Ahmed Shah

Immediately to the east of the Jama Masjid is the tomb of Ahmed Shah, the ruler under whom so many of the important early Sultanate buildings were constructed. Ahmed Shah died in 1442, but work on the tomb probably started before then, and was completed by his son and successor Muhammad Shah, who is also buried in the tomb. The third grave is of Ahmed Shah's grandson. This square, multi-domed tomb complex, with its enclosed verandah, became the template for mausoleum design in the Sultanate period.

Rani ka Hujra and its environs

Across a small road to the east of Ahmed Shah's tomb is the Rani ka Hujra, or Tombs of the Queen. This unexpectedly peaceful enclosure, surrounded on all sides by buildings, has some finely-carved cenotaphs of female members of Ahmed Shah's family. The enclosure has well-proportioned cloisters on all four sides.

The tall 19th-century building to the south of the Rani ka Hujra tomb complex, with balconies and a pagoda-style roof, is Ahmedabad's **former stock exchange**. Beyond the stock exchange are some of the most interesting and least modernised parts of the old city, which is divided into smaller compact units known as *pols*, and contain a large number of old *havelis*, or large houses with inner courtyards. The House of MG audio guide (*see p. 362*) is a good way of exploring these areas.

There are at least a dozen other Sultanate tombs and mosques within the old walled city—of which the most interesting architecturally is the **Rani Rupvati Masjid** (1510). This small pretty mosque, on the main road from the Bhadra Fort to the Delhi Gate, has extremely ornate truncated minarets, with rich Hindu and Muslim decorative motifs, as well as a beautifully carved central *mihrab*, or prayer niche. Notice how the design of the sides of the upper storey of the main gateway allows light into the mosque. South-east of the Jama Masjid, near the Astodiya Gate, is a very small and extremely pretty mosque—the **Rani Sipri Masjid** (1514)—with delicately carved tapering minarets, and unusual Hindu-style side windows.

NORTH OF THE OLD CITY

Calico Museum

This superb museum (*open Thur–Tues; T: 079 2286 8172 or 079 2286 5995 for reservations; calicomuseum.com*) is one of the best in India. Inside is a beautifully laid-out collection of textiles, bronze sculptures and miniature paintings of high quality. The museum is in a large private house, with splendid gardens, belonging to one of Ahmedabad's best-known families, the Sarabhais. There is no open access to the museum, and it is necessary to join the organised tour that takes place at 10.30am each day. The museum also allows the first 15 visitors who do not have a reservation to join the tour. Bags and cameras are not allowed into the museum, and can be left at the gate.

Shahi Bagh Palace

This poorly-restored minor Mughal Palace is now a museum and memorial celebrating the life of Sardar Vallabhbhai Patel, one of India's most important leaders at the time of Independence and the country's first deputy prime minister. One room in the attic is kept as a memorial to the Nobel Prize-winning writer and artist Rabindranath Tagore, who stayed here in 1878. The building became the residence of the governor of Gujarat when Ahmedabad was still the state capital, and was turned into a museum in 1980.

EAST OF THE OLD CITY

Dada Hari step-well

This fascinating step-well (1499), in the Asarwa area of Ahmedabad, has six levels and is one of the finest in Gujarat. Like most Gujarati step-wells, or *vavs*, it has a series of decorated columned chambers at each level which cover the steps leading down to the well. The Dada Hari Vav has Sanskrit and Arabic inscriptions near the entrance, and floral and geometric carved stonework. There are also separate narrow spiral staircases that lead down to the well. Beyond the step-well is the fine tomb and mosque complex of Dada Hari, with finely carved stumps of what were once minarets. Notice the typically Gujarati combination of Hindu-style post-and-beam openings used for the windows and a Muslim-style arched doorway used for the entrance to the mosque. A few hundred metres away is a smaller 11th-century step-well, the **Mata Bhavani Vav**, which is a place of pilgrimage for some Hindus.

Sidi Bashir Minars

Three hundred metres southeast of Ahmedabad railway station are two circular minarets, connected by an archway, which were once part of a mosque that was destroyed by Maratha invaders in the 1750s. They are popularly known as the 'Shaking Minarets', because of how they sway in strong winds or earthquakes. Their flexibility used to be demonstrated by a man who would climb one of the minarets and give it a good shake in a way that would make the other minaret sway, but this practice is now forbidden for safety reasons. There are two other fine circular minarets, again without a mosque, adjacent to the railway station.

Bibi ki Masjid

This large mosque (1454), 1km east of the railway station, has one complete circular minaret and a second with the top two levels missing. There is fine stonework on the minaret buttresses—notice in particular the very detailed carving of trees, and the highly decorated *mihrabs*, or prayer niches.

SOUTH OF THE OLD CITY

Kankariya Lake

This large man-made lake (1451), 2km south of the railway station, appears circular from the air, but is in fact a regular 34-sided polygon. It was built in the reign of Sultan Qutbuddin, and is surrounded by stone steps as if it were an amphitheatre. A causeway leads to a small island in the centre of the lake. Notice the carved triple sluice gates to the east of the lake. On the west side of the lake, set in some pretty gardens, are some 17th-century **Dutch tombs**. The Dutch had a large trading post or factory in Surat dealing with cotton and indigo, and a number of traders were also based in Ahmedabad.

Qutb Alam Mausoleum

This impressive and unusual tomb is in the suburb of Vatva, 5km south of Kankariya Lake. The painted dome of the tomb sits on two levels of cloistered arches, partly ruined but beautifully proportioned. Unlike most Sultanate-period monuments, the building does not use any traditional Hindu post-and-beam construction techniques, and is entirely supported by arches.

The southern suburbs of Ahmedabad have a number of fine mosques, particularly in the area known as Isanpur. These include the small **Hassan Shahid ki Masjid**, which has an attached step-well with Hindu carvings and one small erotic tableau, and the early 16th-century **Isan Malik Mosque**, which was badly damaged in the Hindu-Muslim riots of 2002, and which is undergoing restoration. The **mausoleum of Shah Alam**, 2km southeast of Kankariya Lake, is set in a large complex that attracts many pilgrims and includes an assembly hall, and a mosque with very finely carved minarets.

WEST OF THE OLD CITY

Ahmedabad's main modern commercial and residential districts are on the other side of the Sabarmati River. The west bank of the Sabarmati was barely settled 100 years ago, and most of its buildings date to the 20th century. The most famous is the **Sabarmati Ashram**, set up by Mahatma Gandhi in 1917, and which remained his home and political headquarters until 1933. This was where Gandhi started his famous Salt March in 1930, a protest walk through Gujarat, at the end of which he symbolically gathered a handful of salt drying naturally on the coast, at a time when salt was a monopoly of the colonial government. The small bare rooms in which Gandhi, his wife Kasturba and their closest associates lived, can be visited within a large peaceful compound overlooking the river. There is an interesting exhibition about the life and work of Gandhi in an appropriately simple modern building designed by Charles Correa, one of India's best-known architects.

The Swiss-born architect Le Corbusier, largely responsible for the northern Indian city of Chandigarh, also designed Ahmedabad's **Sanskar Kendra**, or Cultural Centre (1957), which looks like a kind of warehouse on stilts and has not aged well. It contains the city's main public museum. Outside the entrance is a large seated marble statue of Queen Victoria, her nose and right hand broken off. The museum contains some interesting displays about the history of Ahmedabad, as well as the world's longest incense stick (4.5m tall), complete with an attestation from Guinness World Records.

AROUND AHMEDABAD

SARKHEJ

Until recently, this fascinating Muslim pilgrimage site, set around a pretty lake, was a village southwest of Ahmedabad (*map 4 C2*). Now the city has reached Sarkhej and is beginning to envelop the area around this large complex of tombs, mosques and ruined palaces. The compound containing the main buildings is on the northern side of the lake. Immediately on entering the compound, the mausoleum of Sultan Mahmud Begada is on the left; behind that is a building containing the tombs of the Sultanate queens, and beyond that is the mosque. To the left is the tomb of Shaikh Ahmed Khattu.

Tomb of Shaikh Ahmed Khattu

This tomb (completed 1473) is one of the largest in Gujarat, each side of the square mausoleum measuring more than 30m. Shaikh Ahmed Khattu, also known Gunj Bakhsh, who died in 1445, was Sultan Ahmed Shah's spiritual guide. His tomb is still a place of pilgrimage and, along with the mosque, is one of the original buildings of Sarkhej. The mausoleum has a large central dome, and rows of 13 smaller domes on each side. The tomb itself is in the inner chamber (note the unusual decorated underside of the main dome), which is surrounded by a colonnade, constructed, not of arches, but using the post-and-beam method.

Jama Masjid

The large mosque (1446–58) in Sarkhej has a spacious courtyard, surrounded by cloisters and a prayer hall topped with ten small domes. Unusually for a Gujarati mosque, the façade of the prayer hall is all at one level and includes no arches. Another unusual feature is the kink in its rectangular shape. There are windows on the south side of the mosque offering excellent views of the lake, and the ruined palaces beyond.

Mausoleum of Sultan Mahmud Begada

The mausoleum of Sultan Mahmud Begada, who died in 1511, also contains the graves of two of his successors. Some of the Gujarat sultans, like Muslim princes elsewhere in India, chose to be buried next to a place of pilgrimage. The cenotaphs themselves are larger than usual, and finely carved. Notice the three carved prayer niches, or *mihrabs*, on the western side of the mausoleum, and the prayer position on the flooring, marked with tiles. A door, now closed, led to the small quay that separates the male and female tomb compounds. It is now necessary to return to the external verandah and head to the left in order to enter the smaller **tomb of the queens**, through which it is possible to access the quay. The tomb of the queens contains several cenotaphs, including that of Rani Rajabai, who died in 1590, by which time the Gujarat Sultanate was no more, and the region was ruled by the Mughals.

Sarkhej Lake

The lake at Sarkhej was enlarged during the reign of Sultan Mahmud Begada. On the southwestern side of the lake, easily approached by road or on foot, are two fascinating ruined summer palaces, built in the time of Sultan Mahmud and used by him and his family to escape the heat of Ahmedabad. The palaces have beautiful views of the mosque and tombs of Sarkhej, and it is possible to see the carved triple sluice gates to the west of the mosque.

GANDHINAGAR

Named after Mahatma Gandhi, Gandhinagar (*map 4 C1*) is the capital of Gujarat, and lies 25km north of Ahmedabad. Work began on the city in the 1960s, and the first government offices were opened there in 1970. Its modern architecture is not particularly distinctive—the largest and most imposing buildings are the huge thermal power station and two enormous modern temples, built in a Classical style: the Akshardham and the Swaminarayan mandirs. There are the remains of a small fort, probably from the Mughal period, overlooking the Sabermati, near the Sarita Ujjain Park in the south-eastern part of Gandhinagar.

Six kilometres southwest of Gandhinagar is the very fine **Adalaj step-well** (1502). This striking and richly-decorated five-storey underground step-well, with some superb carving, was built during the Sultanate period, but commissioned by local Hindu Vaghela chieftains. Throughout the step-well are friezes showing elephants and horses. Side niches contain small idols, including one of a horse, which is still worshipped.

DHOLKA

Thirty-five kilometres southeast of Ahmedabad is the ancient town of Dholka (*map 4 C2*), with four unusual and very different mosques from the pre-Sultanate and Sultanate periods. Dholka is a treasure trove of medieval Muslim architecture, but is little visited, even though it is easily reached from Ahmedabad and Sarkhej.

Bahlol Khan Ghazi Masjid

The oldest of the mosques, the Bahlol Khan Ghazi Masjid (also known as the Hilal Khan Masjid in some older sources) was constructed in 1333, when Dholka was under the rule of a governor appointed by the Tughlaq rulers of Delhi. The main entrance to the mosque is from the east, and consists of a domed two-storey portico, with fine perforated stonework. Inside is a courtyard, without cloisters. The prayer hall has three identical arched bays and smaller arched doorways on either side. The minarets are very unusual, looking almost like ornate lampposts, and clearly the design was more influenced by Hindu rather than Muslim architectural tradition. Historians have speculated that the builders had never actually seen a minaret before, and this may also explain why they were constructed over the centre of the prayer hall rather than at the front or the sides. The interior of the prayer hall has the distinctively Gujarati mix of Muslim arcuate and Hindu trabeate architecture, as well as some fine geometrically carved stonework, both in relief and perforated. Outside the mosque are the remains of an older temple.

Tankha Masjid

The second oldest of Dholka's mosques is known as the Tankha Masjid (1361), but it is widely known, particularly by Hindus, as Bhim ka Rasola, or 'Bhima's kitchen', after one of the heroes of the Hindu epic the *Mahabharata*. The early history of the building is unclear. Unusually for a mosque, there are two separate courtyards, and the prayer area is in the connecting hall. There are two prayer areas, one in front of the other, both of course facing west, with separate prayer niches and pulpits. Again unusually, the mosque has many wooden columns—finely carved but not dated authoritatively.

Khan Masjid

The largest and grandest of Dholka's mosques, the Khan Masjid (1453), or Alif Khan Masjid, overlooks a large man-made lake to the west of the town. It was built in the Sultanate period, but is quite unlike any other mosque of that time. The Khan Masjid was probably intended as an *idgah*—a congregational building outside the city used for special occasions. There is some similarity in design to mosques in southern Iran, suggesting the architect of the building was Persian, or was at least someone who had visited Persia. Only the main entrance gate and the prayer hall have survived, while the façade of the main building has crumbled. Nevertheless, this is one of India's most distinctive and memorable mosques.

It was built on an immense scale, out of brick rather than stone, and has three huge domed congregation chambers, with arched entrance bays. Towering over the building are two lantern-like minarets at each end, one of them much ruined. Originally three huge brick arches linked the two minaret towers in a way that would have concealed the domes, but the arches have crumbled, and only stumps remain. There are remnants of fine perforated stonework and plaster decoration inside and outside the mosque. Access to the roof is possible for fine views over the lake and the town. Notice also the fine domed pavilions constructed on either side of the mosque; one of them contains a tomb.

Dholka also has an impressive **Jama Masjid** (Friday Mosque), which is very similar in design and decoration to many of the Sultanate-period mosques in Ahmedabad.

LOTHAL

The ancient deserted town of Lothal (flourished c. 2000 BC, *map 4 C2*) is one of two major Harappan sites in Gujarat. The other, at Dholavira in Kutch, is larger and more impressive—but a lot harder to reach. The site at Lothal is only 65km south of Ahmedabad, and is thought to have been a shipbuilding centre and major trading port more than 4,000 years ago. Lothal, which means 'mound of the dead', was discovered in 1954 (though in the 19th century British engineers used bricks from the site during railway building) and small-scale excavations continue. It is surrounded by a mud-brick embankment, which was, in turn, originally surrounded by water on three sides. Lothal was situated on a tidal estuary which has since dried up, and it is now 20km from the sea, on a flat desolate plain, with scorching heat at most times of the year.

The actual site at Lothal consists of a long rectangular artificial lake, widely identified as a shipyard, and the foundations of a planned town consisting of a large number of domestic and small-scale industrial buildings. On entering the site, the 'dockyard' is on the right, while the town is straight ahead.

The 'dockyard'

The lake is a brick-walled long, narrow basin, which most archaeologists believe was used as a dockyard, or possibly as a dry dock for shipbuilding. A minority argue that it was actually nothing more than an irrigation tank, but if so, it was curiously well-built. Boats are believed to have entered from the north, and been loaded, unloaded and repaired in the basin.

The upper town

Excavations in the main site at Lothal have revealed the existence of a grid-like street layout. The first building one encounters on entering the site is a raised platform which is thought to have been a warehouse situated in front of what is rather grandly called the Acropolis, or upper town. Note the extensive and still-visible drainage system, and what is thought to be the remains of a ruler's mansion at the highest point of the site. The foundations of many of the buildings have been squared off and neatened up in a way that can make it hard to visualise as a town last settled almost 4,000 years ago.

The lower town

Beyond the Acropolis is the lower town, with simpler, smaller housing and less sophisticated drainage. Note the square building with a ruined circular construction that is thought to have been a kiln. Sun-dried bricks were used for the less important structures, but kiln-fired bricks were used elsewhere. There is also archaeological evidence that Lothal was a bead-making centre, and a tentative identification has been made of some of the rearmost buildings as a bead factory.

The **museum at Lothal** (*open Sat–Thur 10–5*) includes finely painted pottery and figurines of bulls, dogs, goats and what the museum curator insists is a gorilla—which has never been native to India. There are large numbers of seals, arrowheads, blades, beads, toys, dice and shell jewellery. There are also small funerary objects recovered from a cemetery at the rear of the site, and a cast of two skeletons found in a single grave.

KHAMBAT (CAMBAY)

This old port city and former princely state sits at the head of a gulf bearing the same name (*map 4 C2*). The port is now largely silted up, and tidal bores make it unsuitable for shipping anyway. Khambat, or Cambay, as it is better known in English, was once world-famous. Marco Polo visited the port in the late 13th century, and the Tughlaq Dynasty installed a governor of Gujarat who was, for a while, based in Cambay. Queen Elizabeth I of England wrote to the Mughal emperor Akbar as the 'King of Cambay', since this was where many foreign travellers to India made first landfall. There are still a few traces of Khambat's former glory, including a splendid early mosque, which is thought to have been restored during the Sultanate period.

Jama Masjid

The Jama Masjid (1325) has a large cloistered courtyard and an impressive triple-bay façade to the prayer hall. The complex has 44 small domes in total. The interior of the mosque has some fine Gujarati-style perforated carved stonework on the upper levels of the main gateway as well as the two mezzanine prayer areas intended for women. The columns are from a Hindu temple, and have had additional column sections added to raise the interior to its full height. Large parts of the mosque have been built with layers of bricks of alternating sizes, narrow and broad—a style of building that was probably brought here by a Tughlaq architect from Delhi.

There is an unusual attached tomb and shrine, on the seaward, southern side of the mosque. From the inside, this appears to be part of the same building, but careful examination of the stonework on the outside shows that it was built separately. There is fine carving on the eastern exterior of the building. In particular notice the *trompe l'oeil* carved door, complete with handles and hinges, which is extremely realistic.

Nawab's Kothi

To the east of the tomb is the Nawab's Kothi, one of the palaces of the nawab of Cambay. The gateway is thought to have been constructed in the 14th century, and inside is a wooden hall with large coloured-glass windows, used as an *imambara*, or a place for annual ceremonies to mark the death of the Prophet Muhammad's grandsons by the Shi'a rulers of Cambay. Behind the hall are parts of the old brick walls and bastions that once enclosed the city of Cambay.

In the centre of the town is a 19th-century clock tower and gateway, with inscriptions in four languages: English, Hindi, Urdu and Persian—but not Gujarati. The English inscription includes the cost of the clock tower (10,725 rupees) and a quotation that seems particularly appropriate for Cambay: 'Time and tide wait for no man'.

NORTHERN GUJARAT

North of Ahmedabad, towards the border with Rajasthan, the terrain becomes hillier, and Islamic influence on architecture becomes less marked. Here are two of the glories of the Hindu Solanki Dynasty: the Sun Temple at Modhera and the Rani ki Vav, or step-well, at Patan; both are easily visited on day trips from Ahmedabad or en route to Udaipur or Mt Abu in southern Rajasthan.

MODHERA

Modhera Sun Temple

This shrine (1027) to the sun-god Surya, 78km northwest of Ahmedabad (*map 4 C1*), is arguably the finest piece of Hindu architecture in western India. It is also the most important surviving building of the Solanki Dynasty, which flourished in Gujarat between the 10th and 13th centuries. It is one of only three major sun temples in India (the others are at Konarak in Orissa and in Kashmir). The temple complex consists of two beautifully and richly decorated religious buildings, with lavish stone carvings of animals, gods and humans—and a remarkable stepped water tank.

The temple (*open 8–6*) is approached, past the ticket office, from the east. On the left as one enters the complex, beneath some trees, is an impressively large collection of assorted carvings and masonry which shows that the complex was once even bigger and more lavishly decorated. To the right is the tank, while the temple is straight ahead.

The temple consists of two buildings, both aligned due east so that the morning sun pours through their portals. Closest to the water tank is a free-standing unenclosed pillared pavilion, or *sabha mandapa*, which served as an assembly hall and as a shelter from the sun. On the eastern side, facing the tank, is an ornamental gateway, or *torana*. The exterior is decorated with finely-carved friezes, depicting a large variety of human and animal activities. The central interior space of the assembly hall is an octagon, surrounded by columns—and this area is just as richly decorated, with elephants and humans as the key motifs. Notice the small dwarves serving as column brackets.

The main shrine: The exterior of the main Modhera shrine is even more beautifully decorated, encrusted with carved gods and goddesses and beautiful women. Note the armless image of Surya, the sun-god, standing bolt upright while being driven through the heavens by seven horses. A frieze of elephants, their heads protruding out of the temple walls, surrounds the building at knee level. Inside, through a doorway with particularly delicate carvings, is a *mandapa*, or entrance chamber, the central area of which is an octagon. Each of the eight pillars that make up the octagon is covered in carvings, some of them erotic. On the left column nearest the shrine, there is a particularly vivid tableau showing a shocked woman covering her face as she is shown a variety of sexual acts. The shrine itself is empty, the idol allegedly removed or destroyed by Muslim invaders seven centuries ago. There is an ambulatory passage around the shrine.

The water tank: The large rectangular water tank is one of the most beautiful and richly decorated in India, and is in superb condition. It consists of double flights of stone steps at right angles to each other that lead down to the water. More than 100 small shrines, many containing miniature idols, have been built into the steps. There is also a partly ruined **step-well**, from which some Hindu carvings have been recovered, 300m to the east of the water tank. Between the step-well and the main Modhera site are a small pillared pavilion and a lake.

PATAN

Once the most important city in Gujarat, Patan lies 30km north of Modhera (*map 4 C1*). Then known as Anhilavada, it was the regional capital under the Solanki Dynasty (10th–14th centuries), but was repeatedly sacked by Muslim invaders. Ahmed Shah moved the capital to Ahmedabad in the early 15th century. This fascinating walled city is now a busy district headquarters—though the most important buildings are in fact all outside the city walls. Most visitors come to Patan to see the Rani ki Vav, which has the finest decoration of any step-well in India, but the city has several other attractions, including its ancient watercourses, and an unusual mausoleum, known as the tomb of Baba Farid.

The southern outskirts of Patan

On the southern approach to the city—on the left-hand side of the road leading from both Modhera and Ahmedabad—is the **Idgah**, or congregational mosque. While not an important building in itself, just beyond it runs an unusual **ancient canal**, with particularly fine bridges, that leads into the huge water reservoir on the other side of the road. It is possible to walk for a few hundred metres to inspect the five bridges, which are each supported by carved columns and beams. Note also the *chattris*, or tiny parasol-like pavilions, above the circular sluices at the point where the waters of the canal enter the reservoir.

About 300m north of the reservoir is the largest and most impressive of the city gates, the **Khan Sarovar Gateway**, with large reinforced bastions and Hindu idols set into the walls on either side of the gate. A Muslim cemetery is adjacent to the gate, just outside the city walls. Most of the old gates of Patan have survived relatively intact—though large parts of the wall have collapsed or been demolished.

Jama Masjid

In the centre of the old city is a 14th-century mosque, the old Jama Masjid, or Gomta Masjid, which has Hindu decorative motifs on its columns and exterior. These would either have been taken from a Hindu temple, or carved *in situ* by Hindu craftsmen.

The Rani ki Vav, or Queen's Step-well

The lower levels of this stunning piece of subterranean architecture (c. 1060) are covered with carvings of the highest quality and are in superb condition. The step-well has survived so well because, for many years, it was buried beneath mud, and so was not damaged by humans or by the climate in the way that so many other Solanki-period monuments were. It was only fully excavated in the 1980s. The step-well was commissioned in the mid-11th century by Rani Udayamati, wife of King Bhimadeva I, and was obviously intended as a water source.

The Rani ki Vav (*open 8–6*) is just beyond the outskirts of modern Patan. From a distance, the step-well looks like little more than an undistinguished rectangular hole in the ground, with steps leading downwards. The upper parts of the step-well are relatively bare, and the top two levels of pillar chambers have long disappeared. It is only when one reaches the third underground level that the full glory of the Rani ki Vav becomes visible. For here are walls where every inch is covered with some of the finest carvings to be seen anywhere in India. Many of them are of the god Vishnu, in several avatars. Look for a superb carving showing Vishnu in his tenth and last avatar, Kalki, riding a horse. Nearby is the goddess Durga killing a demon buffalo. Between the two is a glorious carved image of a beautiful woman with her hand raised to strike a monkey who is climbing up her leg.

Sahasralinga canals

Three hundred metres beyond the Rani ki Vav are canals and water features known collectively as the Sahasralinga ('thousand lingams'), which date from the 11th century. Beyond the Sahasralinga is the fascinating and little-visited Baba Farid Tomb complex, overlooking the seasonal River Saraswati. The Mughul emperor Akbar's most feared general, Bairam Khan, is said to have been murdered while visiting this site in 1561, possibly by the son of someone whose death he had ordered.

The Sahasralinga canals seem to have brought water from the Saraswati to feed a reservoir that is now dry. Take the path down into the dry water course, where there is what is probably a step-well, with the tops of dozens of stone columns, some with lintels still attached, poking out through the earth. Follow the water channel that leads to a circular stepped pool. Alongside the channel are lots of small Shiva shrines, from which the Sahasralinga got its name.

STEP-WELLS

Step-wells are found in many parts of India, but it is in Rajasthan, where they are called *baolis* or *baoris*, and Gujarat, where they are known as *vavs*, that they have a distinctive place in the architectural tradition. They are, of course, sources of water, usually built around an underground spring. Steps lead down to the water, which is carried up in buckets. But many Indian step-wells—of which the Rani ki Vav is probably the finest example in decorative terms—are also meeting places in which to escape the searing heat of the midday sun. Many of them have subterrarean rooms, while, particularly in Gujarat, step-wells were also often sacred sites, and richly decorated with images of gods, humans and animals.

One hundred metres beyond the pool is the mysterious **mausoleum of Baba Farid**, overlooking the normally dry bed of the river Saraswati. One corner of this beautifully situated tomb has entirely disappeared—and the domed roof is supported by a ceiling beam. There is an unusual roofless structure next to it, which may also once have been a domed tomb. Note how the square structure has been converted into an octagon at floor level, rather than, as usual, at the base of the dome. Lying on the ground near the mausoleum is a large range of archaeological debris, both Hindu and Muslim, roughly sorted, as if someone was beginning to put together a jigsaw puzzle.

SIDDHPUR

Siddhpur is a fascinating town, 25km east of Patan and 100km north of Ahmedabad (*map 4 C1*). Though seldom visited, it has some interesting 19th-century domestic architecture and one of India's most unusual religious buildings. This town has a high percentage of Dawoodi Bohra Muslims, a sect of Islam that has many adherents in Gujarat. A large part of the centre of the city known as **Bohravad** has many streets laid out in an almost north European fashion, with terraced two-storey buildings, painted in pastel colours, facing each other along clean, extremely well-swept streets. Bohra Muslim men are recognisable by their white hats with gold embroidery, while the women wear two-piece veils.

There are also the impressive remains of the large 12th-century **Rudramahalaya Temple**, which towers over a disputed building that can only be described as both a temple and a mosque. On approaching the site, on the eastern side of the Siddhpur, the huge ornate columns behind the disputed building become visible. Two storeys high and richly decorated with carvings, these were part of what was an enormous temple dedicated to the god Rudra, an early form of Shiva.

In front of the ruins is the disputed building itself, which has the features of both a mosque and a temple. Its rear wall faces the west, towards Mecca, but its large turrets are lavishly carved with Hindu motifs and idols. Inside, there is a Muslim ablution tank in the courtyard, a *minbar*, or pulpit, and a prayer niche, or *mihrab*, on the rear wall. However, the cusped arch of the *mihrab* has been cut through to make it a temple doorway. In two of the side chambers of the building are small Shiva lingams. The building is guarded, and photographs are not allowed.

PALANPUR

The town of Palanpur, 30km north of Siddhpur, is the capital of the former Muslim princely state of the same name (*map 4 C1*). The handsome early 20th-century **Zorawar Palace** is now the town court. On the eastern side of town are the decaying mausolea of the nawabs of Palanpur, known as the **Shahi Roza**, while to the south is the **George V Club** (1913), an unexpectedly palatial neo-Mughal building. The Neoclassical **Balaram Palace** (1930s), 14km to the north of Palanpur, is now a hotel.

TARANGA & VADNAGAR

At **Taranga** (*map 4 C1*), 40km east of Siddhpur, the 12th-century Solanki king Kumarpal converted from Hinduism to Jainism and erected the enormous **Ajitanath Jain Temple**, picturesquely situated in rocky hills. Taranga is a peaceful place, and the exterior of the building is impressively complex. It has three large porches and a series of clustered towers. The interior has finely carved ceiling panels, and its dome has 16 brackets in the form of naked women adopting a variety of different poses. In the ancient walled town of **Vadnagar**, 25km south of Taranga, are two superb 12th-century carved stone temple gateways, though the temple has long since disappeared. The fine **Pancham Mehta Vav**, or step-well, is on the southeast side of Vadnagar.

IDAR & SHAMLAJI

Idar, 98km northeast of Ahmedabad, is the capital of the former princely state of the same name (*map 4 C1*). It is overlooked by a fortified rocky hill, at the bottom of which is a crumbling palace; steps lead up to more ruins on the summit. **Shamlaji**, 42km east of Idar, is an important Hindu pilgrimage centre. The main Shamlaji Temple (16th century), dedicated to Vishnu, has fine stone carvings, and there are several other older shrines nearby.

SOUTHERN GUJARAT

Although the southern part of Gujarat is best known as the industrial and trading belt of this economically successful state, the area has several important historical buildings and an improving tourist infrastructure. **Baroda**—now officially **Vadodara**—was the capital of the large princely state of the same name, and has some superbly extravagant 19th-century architecture. Just 45km from Vadodara are the extraordinary ruins of the medieval city of Champaner, now a UNESCO World Heritage Site. Surat was the site of the first British settlement in India in the early 17th century—and it was on this coastline that the first Zoroastrians from Iran, later known as Parsis, landed in India, possibly as early as the 8th century. The southernmost part of the state borders the former Portuguese settlement of Daman, which has a fascinating double fort on either side of an estuary next to the sea. The largely tribal interior is much less developed, but there have been recent attempts to extend tourism into this area, particularly around the town of Chhota Udaipur.

VADODARA

This large industrial city (*map 4 C2*, formerly Baroda) was the capital of the large former princely state of Baroda, and has one of India's most distinctive princely palaces and a fine museum.

The modern history of Vadodara dates from 1721, when the Maratha general Pilaji Gaekwad captured the region from the declining Mughal Empire. His descendants ruled the state until Independence—and the family name, Gaekwad, became shorthand for the ruler, who would be known as 'the Gaekwad' of Baroda. Under the British, Baroda was one of just five states to be given a 21-gun salute, and its rulers gained a reputation for extravagance and for their patronage of art. Sayajirao III, who became the maharaja at the age of 12 in 1875, ruled Baroda for 64 years, and oversaw the growth of one of India's most impressive art collections. He was also a social reformer, introducing compulsory primary education for boys and girls and a network of libraries—thought to be India's first. His reputation among Indian nationalists grew, when, during the Delhi durbar of 1911, he broke with protocol by turning his back on the king-emperor George V, after having paid him symbolic homage.

The Laxmi Vilas Palace complex

The enormous royal compound, still partly occupied by the former royal family, is in the south of the city. It has a museum, the extraordinary Laxmi Vilas Palace itself, a small golf course, a cricket pitch and a huge area of parkland. Coming from the south, the first gate leads to the **Maharaja Fatehsingh Museum** (*open Tues–Sun 10.30–5.30*), which is also the place to purchase tickets for the palace. The museum, housed in a modern building, has a large collection of the paintings of Raja Ravi Varma, India's best-known 19th-century artist. It also has some 19th-century European paintings, what are presumably copies of several Titians and a Raphael, and a large collection of Wedgwood china, Lalique glassware and porcelain from China and Japan. Outside is a scaled-down, fully-functional model of the steam engine that pulled the famous British train the *Flying Scotsman*, and which used to steam its way around 3km of tracks in the palace grounds.

Laxmi Vilas Palace: This huge palace (1880–90) is approached from a separate entrance on the main road—though it is in the same compound as the museum. The palace (*open Tues–Sun 11–5; tickets need to be bought at the museum; an audio guide is available at the reception desk in the palace*) is an extraordinarily lavish Indo-Saracenic edifice, with influences from many other architectural styles. Local tradition holds that it was the most expensive private building constructed anywhere in the world during the 19th century. The building is asymmetrical, and its off-centre tower is the city's most distinctive landmark. The building is entered from the rear, from where one proceeds to the handsome garden at the front for a superb view of the main façade—dozens of spires, domes and finials give the palace a fairy-tale appearance. The original design of the building was by Major Charles Mant, who is reported to have gone mad and killed himself when he mistakenly believed that he'd made a serious architectural error. He was replaced by R.F. Chisholm, who completed the building. The tower was designed to hold a giant clock, but when it was realised that the ticking of the device would keep the royal family awake, it was replaced with a lantern, which to this day is lit whenever the maharaja is in residence. The left-hand side of the palace (viewed from the garden) was intended as the public area, while the right-hand side housed the private quarters of the royal family. The garden is very pretty, with European-style statues and urns (note the beautifully carved peacock urn), as well as lampposts with the Baroda monogram, which were commissioned from a Scottish foundry.

The palace interior: Part of the ground floor of the actual palace is open to the public. The entrance portico is superbly decorated, as is the entrance hall and the main staircase, largely in Italian marble. Note the stained-glass roof with Sayajirao III's monogram. To the right of the staircase, among the exhibits in the very impressive armoury, are a sword belonging to the last of the great Mughal emperors, Aurangzeb (labelled Exhibit 2), and a machine for throwing metal discs at the enemy (Exhibit 5). The Gadi Hall was the coronation room, with, instead of a throne, a large white mattress under a shade shaped like a peacock. Head along the corridor to the left of the staircase, past the long, narrow arcaded courtyard with an ornate pond and statues, until you reach the durbar hall. Note the Italian mosaic floor, stained-glass windows and the multicoloured patterned ceiling. The small internal balconies have brackets carved as trumpet-playing angels.

Vadodara Museum

The Sayaji Bagh park, 2km north of the Laxmi Vilas Palace, houses the enormous Vadodara Museum and Art Gallery (*open daily 10.30–5*) in what was the Victoria Diamond Jubilee Institute. The gallery has, arguably, India's best collection of European paintings, with many originals by minor Dutch masters of the 16th and 17th centuries, a wider collection of 19th-century paintings, as well as works ascribed to Rubens, Fragonard, Landseer, Turner, Constable, Degas and Cézanne. The museum also has an interesting Egyptian collection and some particularly fine Persian tiles. There are superb Jain bronzes (6th–8th centuries) from Akota, just outside Vadodara, including a large statue of Rishabnath, the first Jain *tirthankar*, or saviour, also known as Adinath.

Other sights in Vadodara

There are a number of other former royal palaces in Vadodara. The Neoclassical **Pratap Vilas** (1910), to the southeast of the Laxmi Vilas Palace, is now a railway office—staff may allow you to visit the building—while the **Nazarbagh Palace** (1721), to the east of the main palaces, is a former royal guest house that is now in a poor condition. The Nazarbagh Palace is near the distinctive pyramid-like clock tower, built on an 18th-century pavilion known as the Mandvi. The old city has several interesting 18th- and 19th-century houses built out of wood, including the four-storey **Tambekar Wada**, the former residence of the *diwan*, or prime minister, of Baroda, which has some fine 19th-century wall-paintings. The **Kothi Kacheri** (late 19th century), 1.5km west of the Mandvi, was the Gaekwad's secretariat, and is still in use as government offices. Just to the north is the **Kirti Mandir**, the 20th-century *chattris*, or memorials, to the royal family, with paintings by one of India's most important 20th-century artists, Nandalal Bose. The Renaissance-style **Markarpura Palace** (late 19th century), in the south of the city, now belongs to the Air Force and is firmly closed to visitors.

CHAMPANER

Champaner (*map 4 D2, open daily sunrise–sunset*) is an extraordinary deserted medieval city surrounded by jungle, 45km northeast of Baroda. The site, and the nearby fortified Pavagadh Hill which overlooks Champaner, were strongholds of local Rajput rulers until they was conquered by the forces of the Gujarat Sultanate in 1484. The victorious sultan, Mahmud Begada, had Champaner constructed as a southern capital—a counterpart to Ahmedabad. But Champaner was hardly used. It was captured by the second Mughal emperor Humayun in 1535, and the city went into gradual decline. In 2004, the **Champaner-Pavagadh Archaeological Park** was declared a UNESCO World Heritage Site—the first in Gujarat—and it is expected to become a major tourist destination.

Orientation: To reach Champaner, take the airport road out of Vadodara, and head northeast, beneath the elevated Delhi–Mumbai highway, towards Hilol. From Hilol ask for Pavagadh, not Champaner, as the latter name is less well known. The Champaner-Pavagadh monuments are widely spread, and there are many parts of the site that have not been excavated. Approaching from Vadodara, there are several minor monuments (*see below*) before one reaches Champaner's western gate. Beyond the gate and to the left are the major monuments, including the inner citadel, with its impressive walls and the Jama Masjid, while the hill of Pavagadh looms on the right. To ascend the hill, drive up to the first of a series of plateaux, where a cablecar takes visitors most of the way up the hill, and which is mainly used by Hindu pilgrims heading for the Mahakali Mata Temple on the hilltop (there is also a footpath). On the other side of Champaner, the road continues past a large lake, with some minor medieval ruins, towards Jambugodha (*see Accommodation, p. 409*) and Chhota Udaipur.

The approach to Champaner

There are three interesting minor ruins close to the road from Vadodara before reaching the western gate of Champaner. The **Ek Minar ki Masjid** (c. 1530), or 'One Minaret Mosque', is visible from the main road on the left, and approached along a small lane. It consists, as one might expect, of an impressive single minaret, the ruins of a mosque, and an empty tank. It is possible to climb the minaret, which has some fine carved features, and get excellent views of the surrounding countryside. Return to the main road, and 600m further ahead, also on the left, is the **Helical Step-well** (16th century), which is a brick-and-stone well, the waters of which can be reached by a spiral staircase. Just 250m beyond the well on the right is the pretty **Sakar Khan Dargah**, a small tomb structure with an over-sized dome. Note the quality of the internal decoration of the tomb, and the effect of using different coloured stones on the interior of the dome. Just behind the tomb is an old tank and beyond that is part of the old outer city walls of Champaner. Back on the road, pass through the arched Western gate and continue for another 600m to reach the city's very impressive inner walls of the Citadel—many of its bastions, merlons and balconies survive.

The Citadel

The Citadel, which served as the royal enclosure, is a rectangular walled compound, 900m from east to west and 300m from north to south. Note how the main southern gate to the Citadel is set at an angle to the walls to allow an easier defence against attack. Pass through the gate, which is decorated with bands of Arabic calligraphy and the hanging pot motif which is so common in Gujarati Muslim architecture. Immediately inside the enclosure is the fine **Sahar ki Masjid**, with its five domes and two central minarets, which probably served as the private mosque of the sultan. Note the hanging pot motif in the *mihrab*, or prayer niche, of the mosque. There are several other ruined buildings nearby, including an old customs house, or *mandvi*, and a more modern village, but there is no sign of the palace, which is thought to have been destroyed by the Mughal emperor Humayun in 1535.

Jama Masjid

The Jama Masjid (1508–09), or Friday Mosque, is just to the east of the Citadel and can be approached via the main road or by passing through the eastern gate of the Citadel. The mosque is Champaner's largest and most impressive building, and its external walls, with their carved stonework, are more attractively decorated than any comparable mosque in Gujarat. The mosque itself has its main entrance on the east, through a richly carved porch gateway. The gateway has particularly fine *jali*-work stone tracery, as well as carved stone S-brackets supporting its eaves, and an impressively detailed drum that once supported a dome. The large interior courtyard has arcades on all sides, and the impressive five-bayed façade of the assembly hall has an extended high central arch flanked by 36m-high minarets. There are also smaller towers at the four corners of the building, with clusters of large and small white domes. Note the geometric and floral carvings and the hanging pot motif on the minarets, as well as the little first-floor window, with its small balcony, overlooking the entrance arch.

The unusually large interior is 11-pillars deep, with a series of internal spaces that are capped by domes. The main central space has finely carved upper galleries, currently inaccessible to the public—note the fine carved ribs on the interior of the dome. There is a women's prayer area, with its own entrance, and a perforated screen in the northwestern part of the assembly area. The middle of the mosque's seven *mihrabs*, or prayer niches, is the most lavishly carved. Walk round the mosque to see its other entrances and the finely-carved buttresses on the rear of the mosque.

Kevda Masjid

About 500m to the northwest of the Jama Masjid is the smaller Kevda Masjid (early 16th century). There is a pretty pavilion-style cenotaph with a fluted dome roof in the compound. The mosque has fine carved stonework on its minarets and central *mihrab*. Like the Jama Masjid, it has a high central arch behind which is a gallery, accessible via the steps inside the minarets. Note the stone benches in the gallery, from where there are fine views.

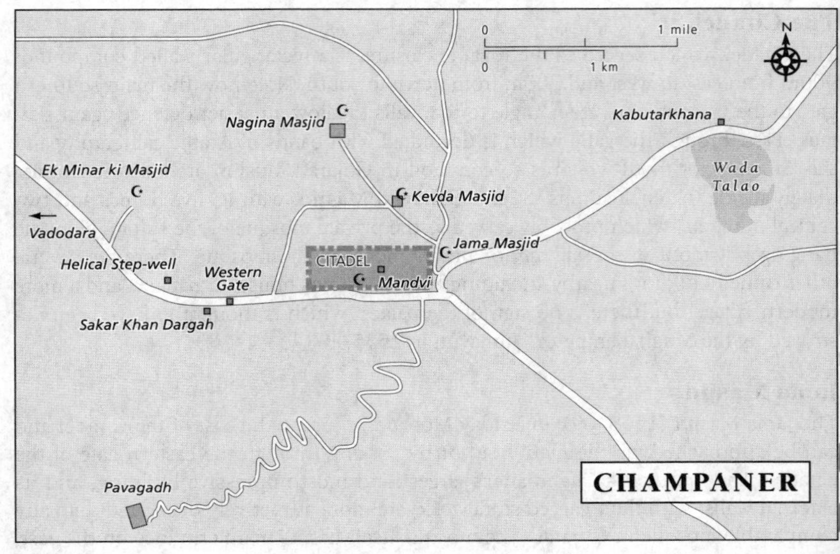

Nagina Masjid

Some 600m to the northwest of the Kevda Masjid, deep in the Champaner jungle, is another smaller mosque, the minarets of which have lost their upper tiers. This is the **Nagina Masjid** (early 16th century). It also has a cenotaph, more enclosed and smaller than the one at the Kevda Masjid, with some exquisite floral and geometric designs. The exuberantly carved central *mihrab* is probably the most impressive of the prayer niches of Champaner's many mosques. There are several other mosques and tombs in Champaner, particularly in the less-excavated eastern part of the site, of which the **Lila Gumbaz ka Masjid**, with its fluted dome, and the heavily restored **Kamani Masjid** are excellent examples of architecture of the late Sultanate period. In the most easterly part of the site, next to the large lake known as the Wada Talao, are two other buildings: the **Kabutarkhana**, a large pavilion set on a plinth, and a smaller building that directly overlooks the water.

Pavagadh

Pavagadh is reached by taking a left leading uphill from the main road, just before the Jama Masjid. The winding road passes by several minor fortifications from the Sultanate and earlier Rajput periods until it reaches the Machi Plateau. From Machi, there is a steep pilgrim path that goes past a domed granary—though many visitors prefer to take the cable car. Closer to the top is the ruined **Lakulisha Temple** (11th–12th century), with fine carving on the surviving bottom half of the building, as well as further impressive fortifications. The temples at the top of the hill are very popular with Hindu pilgrims, but the buildings are modern.

EAST OF CHAMPANER

To the east of Champaner are several minor former princely states, in a largely tribal area of Gujarat. These include **Jambughoda** (*map 4 D2*), formerly known as Narukot, 20km southeast of Champaner, where the 20th-century palace has been turned into a hotel.

About 40km further to the east is **Chhota Udaipur** (*map 4 D2*), or little Udaipur, the capital of a medium-sized princely state of the same name in a largely tribal region, not far from the border with Madhya Pradesh. The state, which was formed in the 18th century, was ruled by the descendants of the last Hindu king of Champaner. The impressive **Kusum Vilas Palace** (1934) is on the western side of the town, and has a five-storey central tower and a pretty pool with European statuary. It is possible to wander around the grounds, which house a school, and to see the entrance portico, but, as the former royal family still lives inside the palace, entry into the main building is only possible with their permission. The **old fort** is in the centre of Chhota Udaipur, between the lake and the river. Its walls are intact, but the buildings are ruined. The **durbar hall** (1913), just outside the walls, is also a romantic shell of a building, with pillars that have fallen to the floor, following a devastating fire.

DABHOI

This small town (*map 4 C2*), 30km southeast of Vadodara, has four superbly carved 14th-century city gates. They were constructed during the rule of the pre-Muslim Solanki Dynasty—which was also responsible for the extraordinary Modhera Temple and the Rani ki Vav step-well in northern Gujarat (*see pp. 373 and 374*). The town was square in shape, and once fully walled, with gates positioned at the four cardinal points.

The western one is the **Baroda Gate**, which has a superb series of carved corbelled brackets supporting the main structure of the building and further fine carvings on the interior walls of the gate. The carvings represent the ten avatars of the Hindu god Vishnu, as well as other religious and mythological themes. Note the colonnaded guard rooms on either side of the Baroda Gate.

The northern **Mahudi Gate** is also intricately carved, and has old friezes which have been set into the surviving parts of the wall. Note also the smaller outer gate set at an angle of 90° to the main gate.

The most interesting and largest of the entrances to Dabhoi is the **Hira Gate**, on the eastern side of town. The interior of the gateway is not intricately carved, but the large Kali Temple built into the northern side of the gate has Dabhoi's finest carvings. It has a superb elephant frieze and overhanging balconies. On the outer side of the walls is the unexplained carving of a man and a woman next to a tree, reminiscent of European images of Adam and Eve. Just to the left is the image of a demon. The Hira Gate also has a smaller outer gateway.

The fourth entrance to old Dabhoi was through the southern **Nandodi Gate**, which has corbelled arches showing scenes from the story of Vishnu, and which also has a smaller outer gateway.

BETWEEN VADODARA & SURAT

Rajpipla

The town of Rajpipla (*map 4 D2*), 60km south of Vadodara, was the capital of the former princely state of the same name. There is the large Neoclassical **Rajvant Palace** (1910), parts of which have been turned into a hotel and a small museum, full of equestrian trophies won by a former maharaja. There are several other royal buildings in and near the town, including the handsome **Vadia Palace** (1940s), now used by the forest department.

Bharuch

Midway between Surat and Vadodara, and formerly known as Broach, this was an ancient port city (*map 4 C3*). In the 17th and 18th centuries it was an important British and Dutch trading settlement, sitting on the northern bank of the sacred River Narmada. Little has survived from the British or early period, but there are a few pretty 19th-century buildings to the west of Bharuch, and the ruined old fort that dominated the city is still there, its river-facing walls still intact. Also in the northwest corner of the fort, amid ruined buildings and rubbish heaps, is the tomb of David Wedderburn, the British general who led an assault on the city in 1772.

SURAT

This large industrial city (*map 4 C3*) played a critical role in the early European colonial period, but, apart from two very interesting European cemeteries and a superb textile museum, there is not a great deal to see here. The old centre of Surat is situated on the southern bank of the River Tapti, about 16km from the sea. A medium-sized settlement during the Gujarat Sultanate, the city emerged as a major trading centre in the early 17th century, when the Mughal emperor Jehangir permitted the British and then the Dutch to set up 'factories' in Surat—largely for exporting cotton to the Middle East and Europe. The Mughals seemed to see this as a counterbalance to growing Portuguese influence along India's western coast, little imagining how Britain's territorial ambitions would grow over the next 200 years. The British eventually took control of the city in 1759, but natural disasters and the silting up of the river in the 19th century led to a migration of many Parsi and Jain business families to Mumbai, and Surat was set on a path of slow decline. It remained a major textile and diamond-cutting centre, but its image suffered seriously because of an outbreak of plague in the 1990s.

Surat Castle

The town's castle (1546) is a low building overlooking the Tapti in the centre of old Surat, and has been much altered since it was built in the latter days of the Gujarat Sultanate. It was captured in 1575 by the Mughal emperor Akbar. The old riverside bastions are crumbling, but there are fine views of the Tapti from the ramparts. The rest of the buildings are occupied by government offices.

European factories

The ruins of the old European factories, or trading posts, can be seen down a lane leading to the river that runs next to the Mission School in the Mughalsarai area of Surat. Go through a large red gate on the right of the lane to see the remains of some European buildings. Surat's oldest buildings, from the late Sultanate period, are a little to the east: the most interesting of these is the **Marjan Shami Roza** (1540), the tomb of Khwaja Safar Suleiman, a governor of Surat, whom locals believe was a European who converted to Islam. Unusually, this domed tomb has a variety of differently shaped arches on its external arcade.

European cemeteries

Head towards Kataragama gate for the European cemeteries, which can take some finding. The **Dutch and Armenian cemeteries** are in a single compound down a side road on the right, in the area known as Rampura. The main gate is often locked, but there is a second entrance down a side lane.

The Dutch tombs have a few inscriptions and, architecturally, are a synthesis of Indian Muslim and European architecture. Note the fine octagonal two-storey tomb (1691) of Baron Adrian van Reede, the local director of the Dutch East India Company.

On the other side of the compound is the Armenian mortuary chapel, surrounded by gravestones laid into the ground, with inscriptions in the distinctive Armenian script, some of which date back to the 16th century.

A little further on is the even more impressive **British cemetery**, with many of the oldest British graves in the country. These include the two-storey tomb (1659) of the Oxendon brothers, Christopher and George, both senior figures in the East India Company. The second largest tomb is thought to be that of Gerald Aungier, who is best known as the East India Company official who realised the potential of Mumbai as a major British settlement.

TAPI Textile Museum

Surat also has a little-visited textile museum that ranks alongside the more famous Calico Museum in Ahmedabad (*see p. 366*). The TAPI (short for 'Textiles and Art of the People of India') collection is both fascinating aesthetically and a strong reminder of India's role in producing textiles for the world. This beautifully laid-out gallery inside an old factory building, in the Garden Silk Mill Complex, has textiles that date back to the 13th century, as well as examples of cloth manufactured in India collected from as far afield as Indonesia, Africa and America. A visit is highly recommended for anyone with even a passing interest in textiles. There is also an impressive collection of modern art.

The owners of this private collection allow access to the public, but you need to contact Munira in advance (*T: 0261 3071411 or makikwala@gmail.com*). The textiles are usually not exhibited during the monsoon period because of the humidity, which can cause damage to the fabric.

BETWEEN SURAT & DAMAN

The coastal area of southern Gujarat has several small towns and villages of considerable historical importance, but with little for most visitors to see. Udwada and Sanjan were very early Parsi settlements, but the fire temples there are closed, as elsewhere, to non-Zoroastrians. For those interested in Parsi history, **Navsari** (*map 4 C3*), the largest town between Surat and Daman, is worth a visit. It has the **Dastur Meherjirana Library** (1872), in a fine Neoclassical building, with an impressive collection of Zoroastrian manuscripts and books, and a conservation room upstairs. The collection includes the original ordinance, or *sanad*, granted by Emperor Akbar to the Parsi priest Dastur Meherjirana, who attended the gathering of the faiths in Fatehpur Sikri in 1578. There is also a fire temple, or *agiary*, in the centre of Navsari. Non-Parsis are not allowed entry, but the building has a low, Neoclassical façade set in a pretty garden—and, unusually for agiaries, has an interesting exterior. Note the distinctively Zoroastrian winged angel, or *farohar* symbol, over the columned portico. There are also examples of stained-glass *farohars* at the rear of the building.

Dandi (*map 4 C3*), 16km west of Navsari, was the destination of Mahatma Gandhi's Salt March of 1930—the climax of a 23-day walk from Ahmedabad to challenge the British monopoly on salt production. There is a small **Salt March Museum** (*open Mon–Sat 10.30–5*) in the village, in the house called Saifee Villa, where Gandhi stayed, and a memorial close to the beach.

DAMAN

The interesting former Portuguese coastal settlement of Daman sits on both sides of an estuary (*map 4 C3*). It is surrounded by Gujarat, yet is not part of the state, and the Maharashtra border is only 20km away to the south. Daman is centrally administered, as part of what is known as the Union Territory of Daman and Diu—though Diu is on the other side of the Gulf of Cambay, 200km away by boat and more than 500km by road.

Daman was captured by the Portuguese in the early 16th century and, like the other Portuguese settlements of Diu and Goa, was only incorporated into India in 1961. Daman is popular with Indian tourists because of its beaches and because alcohol is widely available—unlike in surrounding Gujarat.

Moti Daman Fort

The large fort on the south side of the River Damaoganga is known as Moti Daman (1580s–90s), or 'big Daman'. It has high sloping walls, which are fully intact, are more than 2.5km in length and have ten bastions. Note the arrowhead shape of the bastions which is typical of Portuguese forts and designed to make it easy to defend from a land attack. The fort is surrounded by a deep moat. Note the Portuguese ensign and inscription over the heavily-defended land gate (1581), as well as a statue of a woman, presumably the Virgin Mary or a saint, behind a glass window. Inside are a series of sleepy, shaded streets, with a main square, churches, government buildings and private houses.

Immediately to the left of the gate are the Municipal Council Offices, beyond which is the **Chapel of Our Lady of the Rosary** (1607), with an unusually austere exterior. The interior, however, is exquisitely decorated, and it alone makes a visit to Daman worthwhile. The main altar is surrounded by carved and gilded wooden panels showing scenes from the lives of the saints and of Jesus. Note the tableau showing the circumcision of Jesus on the left and the Last Supper on the right. The vaulted ceiling of the chancel has unusual images of flying angels with gilded wings. Note also the richly carved and decorated pulpit, as well as the carved tombstone laid into the floor. The chapel is often locked, but ask in the nearby house for the *chowkidar*, or watchman, who has the key. On the eastern side of the square is the old Portuguese jail, still in use.

On the far north of the square is the **Church of Bom Jesus** (1606), with an elevated façade and an ornate altarpiece with statues of the saints in niches. Further north, beyond the Governor's House, is a small **memorial to the Maratha Light Infantry**, which led India's military operations to oust the Portuguese from Daman in 1961. There is also a garden that serves as a memorial to the Portuguese who died in earlier centuries in Daman, where old gravestones have been relaid in the ground.

On the northwest corner of the fort, on the broad walls overlooking the estuary and with good views out to sea, is the old Portuguese **lighthouse** (1888), next to a much larger new lighthouse. The **River Gate** (1593) of the Moti Daman is also decorated with Portuguese ensigns and inscriptions. The bridge over the river to the northern part of Daman is closed to motor vehicles, which have to take the road bridge a little further upstream.

Nani Daman

The northern side of the estuary is known as Nani Daman, or 'little Daman', and has the much smaller **Fort of Jerome** (1627) overlooking the river, with walls just 600m long. Over the main sea gate is a large stone image of St Jerome, accompanied by the lion from whose foot he is said to have extracted a thorn. Note the large cross over the ornate façade of the gate, as well as the lengthy inscription and ensigns. The interior of the fort contains a church, dedicated to **Our Lady of the Sea** (1903), which is now also used as a school. Like the fort at Moti Daman, St Jerome Fort has arrowhead bastions.

SAURASHTRA

Meaning 'a hundred nations', Saurashtra is the peninsula (*map 4 A2/B2/C3*) that juts out into the Arabian Sea, bordered on the west by the Gulf of Kutch and on the east by the Gulf of Khambat (Cambay). It is largely flat, but is famous for two mountains that are major Jain pilgrimage sites: at Shatrunjaya, near Palitana, and at Girnar, near Junagadh. It also has virgin grasslands and forest, which are the last natural home of the Asiatic lion, and which also host a large number of other animals, including the blackbuck antelope, leopards and marsh crocodiles.

History of Saurashtra

Saurashtra has been settled since the pre-Harappan period, and there are important Hindu, Buddhist and Jain sites that date back more than two millennia. India's earliest Muslim invaders made a series of raids on Saurashtra in the 11th century, while the 16th century saw the arrival of the Portuguese, who ruled the island of Diu, now connected to the mainland by bridges, for more than 400 years. The rest of Saurashtra was ruled by a series of local dynasties, under the control of a Mughal governor and then the Maratha Empire.

The British did not directly rule Saurashtra, but instead oversaw, and received income from, more than 200 principalities, some of them no larger than a village. Others were considerably bigger, and the subcontinent's two most important 20th-century politicians, Mahatma Gandhi and Muhammad Ali Jinnah, hailed from the neighbouring semi-independent Saurashtrian kingdoms of Rajkot and Gondal respectively (although Gandhi was actually born in Porbandar and Jinnah in Karachi). In the late 19th and early 20th centuries, there was a remarkable flurry of palace construction by the princes of Saurashtra—then more widely known as Kathiawar (after the Kathi clan which migrated to this area many centuries ago)—and the results of that building boom are evident to any traveller in the region.

At Independence, all the Saurashtrian states were merged into India, though the Muslim ruler of Junagadh attempted to accede to Pakistan, and was exiled. The former royal families have not been as successful as their Rajasthan counterparts in turning their former palaces into heritage hotels, largely because of the much lower tourist traffic. Rajkot is the main city of modern Saurashtra, with a population of more than one million. This guide starts in the far east of Saurashtra and proceeds to Diu, Junagadh, Rajkot and the western part of the peninsula.

BHAVNAGAR

Some 150km south of Ahmedabad is the coastal town of Bhavnagar (*map 4 C2*), which overlooks the Gulf of Khambat (Cambay). It was founded in the early 18th century and was the capital of the princely state of the same name. Its name is taken from Bhavsinhji of the Gohel Dynasty, who moved his capital here from nearby Sihor in the early 18th century. In the British period, Bhavnagar was often spelled Bhownuggur. Mahatma Gandhi briefly studied at Samaldas Arts College, and there is a small museum about his life: the **Gandhi Smriti** (*open Tues–Sun*). Sharing the same building, in the centre of town, is the small **Barton Museum** (1895), which has some fine stone carvings, as well as a collection of coins, inscriptions and textiles. Note in particular the first display on the left, with an unusual stone image of Garuda, the eagle-god, bent down on one knee, with a snake trapped between his legs; also in the same display are two different donor couples and a central tablet showing all 24 Jain *tirthankars*, or saviours.

About 500m northwest is the fine **Alfred High School** (1872), named after the second son of Queen Victoria, and built in a late-Mughal style, with cusped arches and ornamental domes. It is now officially the Shantilal Shah High School, but is still known by its old name. Nearby are a series of interesting late 19th-century buildings, including the primary school, just opposite, with the girls' school to its right and the high court on its left. In the heart of old Bhavnagar is the 19th-century **City Palace**, or **Darbargadh**, with many original features still visible, including some fine stone carved figures around the entrance arch. The most unusual building in Bhavnagar is the **Darbargadh Kothi** (1882), designed as a large warehouse with the second floor devoted to the state archives. A long raised corridor runs along the centre of the building, complete with lifting equipment, while up above are rooms filled with more than 200 years of land records. On the western outskirts of the town is the **Nilambagh Palace**, the former residence of the maharaja, which has been turned into a comfortable hotel.

Sihor

Roughly halfway along the road between Bhavnagar and Palitana is Sihor (*map 4 C3*), a small town surrounded by hills. It was the capital of the Gohel Dynasty before Bhavnagar, and contains a small ruined **fort**, with a three-storey **palace** that has fine carved wooden beams and columns, and some recently restored paintings on the walls and ceilings. The top storey has some excellent ceiling paintings.

SHATRUNJAYA

The extraordinary hilltop temple complex of Shatrunjaya (*map 4 C3*) is one of the most important places of pilgrimage for members of the Jain religion and, arguably, has the prettiest location of any religious site in India—high above the town of Palitana, which is 42km southeast of Bhavnagar. To reach the complex requires an uphill walk of between one and two hours—or you can be carried by porters—but the spectacular sight of the fairytale-like spires of more than 800 temples makes it more than worth the effort.

According to Jain tradition, the town of Palitana and the hill called Shatrunjaya were visited by all 24 *tirthankars*, or saviours, of Jainism. The first temple is said to have been built by the son of the first *tirthankar*, Adinath, many thousands of years ago, and has since been rebuilt 15 times. None of the existing buildings is thought to pre-date the 12th century. The town of Palitana is dominated by more than 100 Jain *dharamsalas*, or rest-houses for pilgrims. Palitana was also the capital of a princely state of the same name, and there are three palaces that belong to the former ruling Gohil Dynasty, a branch of the same royal family as nearby Bhavnagar.

Orientation: There is vehicular access to the foot of Shatrunjaya Hill, which is visible from far away. You're not supposed to wear shorts or any leather items while on the hilltop—though, in practice, many Jains are flexible on these issues. If you are carrying a camera, buy a ticket in the small office on the left, before the steps begin. Take your own water and snacks, or buy them next to the car park—unlike Hindu pilgrimage sites, no refreshments are available en route. It is best to start very early to avoid the heat. The temples themselves are open from 6am until sunset, and many pilgrims start the long walk up the hill by 5am. There are more than 3,000 well-maintained stone steps leading up the hill. Many Jain pilgrims and tourists are carried up the hill on *dhoolis*. The cheapest *dhooli* is a canvas seat attached to a long wooden pole which is carried by two porters and costs about Rs600 return, while the most comfortable chair, carried by four porters, costs twice as much.

There are several small temples on the way up. The path splits just before the summit of Shatrunjaya, and you can choose which of the two peaks of the temple-covered hill to visit first. Most visitors take the left path, which leads to the **Bari Toonk**, or main compound, on the far, southern side of the hill. The entire site is divided up into nine *tookhs*, or walled compounds, and lots of outlying temples—though, confusingly, the near-side northern peak is commonly known as Nau Tookh, or nine compounds, yet it has only six. The complex is now so large that the small valley between the two peaks has also been filled with temples, and it is possible to walk between the two peaks without returning to the junction in the steps.

It is tempting to spend many hours wandering around the Shatrunjaya complex, escaping the heat of the plains. Many pilgrims will climb the hill at sunrise and descend only at sunset. Visitors are welcome to visit all parts of the complex, and climb up the stairs onto the compound walls for spectacular views of the whole complex and the surrounding countryside. Orange-clad *poojaris*, or temple attendants, who spend most of their time washing the idols, will often guide you (they welcome, but do not demand, tips) and help identify the *tirthankar* idols, of which there are many thousands in Shatrunjaya. Most of them can be identified by the small symbol on the base of the statue: the first *tirthankar*, Adinath, is shown with a bull; Neminath, the 23rd *tirthankar*, has a shell; while Mahavir, the last *tirthankar* and founder of Jainism, has a lion symbol. In the main temples you may not be allowed to take photographs of the idols—if in doubt, check with the *poojari*.

Temples on the southern peak

The best known and most visited of all the shrines is the main **Adinath** or **Adishwara Temple**, dedicated to the first *tirthankar*, which is reached by going through to the very end of the Bari Toonk compound, through a series of gates and following the painted white path on the ground. You will pass the only temple in Shatrunjaya belonging to the smaller Digamber Jain sect—whose priests wear no clothes—before reaching a gate, where you will be asked to remove nothing more than your shoes and show your camera ticket. Then enter through the Hathi Pol, or Elephant Gate, guarded by a couple of carved stone elephants.

On the left is a temple with a tree growing through its outer wall. This is part of the very unusual **Neminath Temple**, also known as the Bhool Bhulaiyan (or labyrinth), half of which is below ground, and which is made up of a series of courtyards at different levels. On entering the first part of the temple, the smaller idol one sees is of the penultimate *tirthankar*, Parusnath, but the main idol is of Neminath, his immediate predecessor. A door, now locked, at the back used to give access to a labyrinth of passages under the temple.

Beyond the Neminath Temple is the main **Adishwara Temple**, a large shrine built in the Hindu style, with a *mandapa*, or assembly hall, with a pyramid-shaped roof leading to a sanctuary which is capped by a curvilinear layered tower, topped by a spire and with a profusion of miniature subsidiary towers. Unlike most Hindu temples, it has three doors and side porticoes, and an unusual second-floor entrance to a gallery of the assembly hall. There is an elegant frieze of buxom dancers and musicians on the exterior. Inside is a large white marble statue of the first *tirthankar*, Adinath (also referred to as Adishwar and Rishabnath), with eyes made of crystal and a gold crown. There are several other interesting temples in the Bari Tookh compound, including, on the left, the four-headed Gandaria Chaumukh shrine, with two brown and two white statues.

Temples on the northern peak

To reach the other compounds on the northern peak of Shatrunjaya, retrace your steps and follow the signs to the **Nau Tookh**, by-passing—or visiting, if you have the time—the more modern 19th- and 20th-century temples in the intermediate valley. You will pass a series of steps heading down the hill towards Adpur (5km west of Palitana)—the other pilgrim route to and from Shatrunjaya. The northern peak has a series of smaller compounds, or *tookhs*, mainly named after the wealthy Jain merchants who first had them built. The main temple in this part is the **Adinath Chaumukh Temple**, also dedicated to the first *tirthankar*. Unlike the other Adinath temple in the Bari Tookh, this one has an external colonnade, with some finely carved stonework on the upper part of the column. Pass through this temple (you'll need to carry your shoes) to take the other fork of the main path to the junction slightly below the top of the hill in order to descend. As you near the bottom of the path and the town of Palitana, note the large model of the Jantar Mantar astronomical complex, based on the originals in Jaipur and Delhi, on the left. There is another slightly shorter and steeper route up to Shatrunjaya from Adpur, 5km to the west of Palitana, close to the Vijay Vilas Palace hotel.

PALITANA

Palitana itself (*map 4 C3*) is a busy pilgrimage town, with several buildings of architectural interest. There are many fine *dharamsalas*, or rest-houses—the Digamber Jain one on the main road into the town is probably the finest. Note also the busy, covered Willingdon Vegetable Market, named after a British viceroy of the 1930s. There are two royal palaces, both called **Hawa Mahal** (Palace of Winds), in a single compound on the northern outskirts of Palitana. Ownership of the properties is disputed within the former royal family. A watchman will normally allow you to look around. The older two-storey palace, which was once used as a hotel, is on the left and in poor condition, although it was only built in 1909. Just next to it is the newer and sturdier four-storey palace, completed in the 1930s, which is in good condition. This one is locked, but it is possible to peer in through the porch windows. There is also an indoor swimming pool, behind the new palace, the roof of which has collapsed. Another palace, in nearby Adpur, which belongs to a junior branch of the family, has been turned into a hotel.

DIU

This former Portuguese island territory (*map 4 B3*), connected by two bridges to the Saurashtra mainland, is not part of the state of Gujarat, but is administered from Delhi along with another former Portuguese enclave, Daman (*see p. 386*), as a Union Territory. The island (pop. 25,000) is just 13km long and only 3km wide, and has a very fine sea-fort, some fascinating churches and the best beaches in the region. Unlike Gujarat, alcohol is widely available in Diu, and this means that the bars of Diu are very popular with young men from Gujarat, particularly at weekends.

History: Historically, Diu came to prominence in 1509, when it was the site of a major maritime battle in which a Portuguese fleet of 18 ships defeated the combined forces of the Gujarat Sultanate, the sultan of Zamorin (from Kerala) and their Egyptian Mamluk allies. By that time, the Portuguese had already built settlements further down the Indian coast, and the battle helped to consolidate their presence in the region. In 1535, as a result of a tactical alliance between the Portuguese and the Gujarat Sultanate—against the newly emerging Mughal Empire—the Portuguese were granted permission to build their great fort on the eastern tip of Diu island. It became known as the Gibraltar of the East, and was a major settlement in the 17th century. It gradually became a colonial backwater, however, overshadowed by Goa. It remained Portuguese territory until 1961, when Indian forces captured Diu after a brief battle in which the fort and the airport were bombed, and several Portuguese soldiers were killed.

Diu Fort

This was probably the best defended and most impressive sea-fort in India. It occupies the entire tip of the island and is surrounded on three sides by the sea. The fourth side is protected by two moats, one of them tidal, that have been cut through rock. The entrance is from the north, opposite the minute fortified island called Pani Kotha, which has a small lighthouse. From the car park, cross the first of two bridges, over the tidal moat. Note the Portuguese coat of arms (with the shields and castles that are on the modern Portuguese flag) and an inscription, dated to 1641, high up on the outer walls of the fort. Beyond the second bridge is a low gateway and a **jetty**, which is shown in the earliest drawing of the fort and would have been the original means of access to the fort, by boat. The jetty and access to the interior of the fort is guarded by St George's bastion. Pass through two more gateways, the second one bearing original decorations, and enter a courtyard, the buildings of which are now occupied by the inmates of Diu Jail. Visitors are not encouraged to linger in this part of the fort; the main precincts are entered through yet another gate.

From here it is possible to wander for hours, climbing up on the bastions for superb views of the of the mainland and the Arabian Sea, examining the cannon and artillery left behind by the Portuguese. The main **church** is normally closed, but there is an interesting **ruined chapel**, with a fine façade, next to the southern St Tiago Bastion. Climb up to the raised platform on which the lighthouse stands for good views over the two moats—it is also possible to reach, down a staircase and across a small bridge, the outer defensive positions that separate the moats. Between the fort and the mainland is **Pani Kotha**, or Fortim do Mar, a tiny island fort with a chapel. It was used as a prison and for unloading large ships that could not get close enough to the main fort. Small boats are available at the main Diu jetty to take you out to Pani Kotha.

THE BATTLE OF DIU

Some historians now see the 1509 Battle of Diu as an important turning point in world history. The battle marked the displacement of Venice (which was allied to the Egyptians) by Portugal as the most important European maritime power. More important in the long run, however, was that the outcome of the battle ensured domination of the Indian Ocean trade routes by European rather than Middle Eastern fleets, and this made possible the eventual European colonisation of India, as well as many other parts of Asia.

Diu City

A charming place to wander round, Diu City is really little more than a small walled town, with several churches and a few brightly coloured Portuguese-style buildings. The older generation still speak some Portuguese, but for most islanders colonial rule has been largely forgotten. **St Paul's Church**, Diu's biggest, is 400m west of the fort car park. It was originally built as a seminary, but its enormous ornamental façade was added in the 19th century. The interior has some superb carved woodwork,and a pretty wooden gallery, while the neighbouring courtyard of the former seminary—now a school—has a small garden and the remains of an old mural in the northwest corner. About 300m southwest of St Paul's is the former **Church of St Francis of Assisi**, which is now a hospital but has retained its old chapel. Note the carved and painted wooden screen behind the altar, and a sculpture of St Francis showing the stigmata, or wounds of Christ. Just 150m to the northeast of St Paul's, a small **museum** has been created in **St Thomas's Church**. It contains fine wooden carvings of the saints and some stone inscriptions taken from other churches.

At Fadum, 2km outside Diu, on the airport road, is the enormous white façade of the 17th-century **Church of Our Lady of Remedies**. Unusually, its height is greater than its length; the impressive façade houses a tiny chapel with a carved wood screen.

SOMNATH

Also known as Prabhas Patan, Somnath lies 70km west of Diu (*map 4 B3*), overlooking the Indian Ocean, and is one of the most important Hindu pilgrimage sites in India. The temple here is a modern one, begun in 1950, on the site of several previous shrines. According to tradition, the original temple was built out of gold by the moon-god Somraj, and has been rebuilt many times. The shrine has also been associated with Krishna, but is now a Shaivite temple, and the site is one of the 12 *jyotir* lingams—12 places where Shiva appeared as a column of light. Today, Somnath is used as a kind of shorthand by Hindu nationalists for Muslim iconoclasm and temple-destruction. The temple was famously destroyed in 1024 by Mahmud of Ghazni, who led the first significant Muslim invasion of India. The gates of Somnath were taken to Ghazni in Afghanistan. In the 19th century, the British found some old wooden gates in Ghazni, and brought them back to India. When it was realised that they were not from Somnath, they were dumped in a room in Agra's Red Fort, where they can still be seen in the Anguri Bagh (*see p. 216*). The modern temple is not particularly interesting, but looks very pretty at sunset (*note that no electronic equipment, including phones and cameras, is allowed in the complex*). There is a small museum near the car park, with lots of pieces of old versions of the temple.

JUNAGADH

This fascinating small city (*map 4 B3*)—once the capital of the princely state of the same name—is largely ignored by tourists, but has an unusually rich history, and contains some exceptional Buddhist, Jain and Muslim buildings. It is picturesquely situated at the foot of Mt Girnar—the highest peak in Gujarat—and its shrines attract many Hindu and Jain pilgrims. It is also just 60km from **Gir National Park**, the last home of the Asiatic lion.

The history of Junagadh really starts millions of years ago, when the extinct volcano at Mt Girnar last exploded. It created the extraordinary doughnut-shaped ridge, beneath which Junagadh sits—and in the centre of the doughnut are tall spires of rock, which have become the site of important Hindu and Jain temples. The area has been settled for more than 2,000 years, as demonstrated by the Ashoka Rock Edicts at the foot of Girnar, and a series of early Buddhist caves around Junagadh. Junagadh's citadel, known as Uparkot, is thought to date from the 10th century, when the Rajput Chudasama Dynasty ruled this region. By the 15th century Junagadh was ruled by the sultans of Gujarat, who built the great mosque in Uparkot, and, under Emperor Akbar in the late 16th century, Junagadh was controlled by a Mughal governor. In the 18th century, with the Mughal Empire in disarray, the local governor, Muhammad Bahadur Khanji, set himself up as the independent ruler of Junagadh, and founded the Babi Dynasty, which ruled the state until 1947. In 1947, the Muslim nawab of Junagadh attempted to accede to Pakistan—with which it had no territorial border, though the state did have access to the sea near Somnath. The nawab was then exiled to Pakistan, and a plebiscite confirmed Junagadh's accession to India. The authorities in Islamabad still formally consider Junagadh state to be part of Pakistan, and it is marked as such on some Pakistani maps.

Orientation: The highest point of the town is the Uparkot Fort, close to Mt Girnar. To the east of the fort is the road to the start of the Girnar footpath, which passes the

Ashoka Edict, and then a village where the footpath starts. Some 500m southwest of the fort are the old palace and the Junagadh Museum; the royal tombs are 1km to the west, near the railway station.

Uparkot

Uparkot literally means Upper Fort, and its impressively large fortifications cover a large area to the east of the city. Because of its size, it is best to take your vehicle inside the fort, the main gate of which is approached from the southwest (*open daily sunrise–sunset*). Note the small cannon protruding from the fort walls, as well as a pretty look-out balcony on the left. Once through the double off-set gates, pass through a dark tunnel into the fort. The far end of the tunnel has very fine carved stone brackets. On entering the fort precincts there is, directly ahead, a building with the words 'Entrance Tower' inscribed on the outside. Climb the stairs which lead to a series of reservoirs, with ornate waterworks buildings concealing the pumps and the pipes. From the first reservoir, there are excellent views of Mt Girnar, on which it is possible to make out the Jain temple complex close to the summit.

To the right of the reservoirs, on the battlements, is an enormous 16th-century cannon, known as the Kadanal Cannon. Almost 4m long and cast in Cairo, it is thought to have been brought here from near the coastal settlement of Diu, after a failed Turkish assault on Portuguese positions there. Return to the internal fort road and go uphill to two more foreign cannon, also cast in Cairo, up on the battlements.

Uparkot Jama Masjid: Opposite the cannon is the back of Junagadh's 15th-century Jama Masjid, or Friday mosque—note the ornate Gujarati-style carvings on the false buttresses on the rear of the mosque. The building itself is unusual in being fully covered, with three domes (now missing) supported on pillars and three *mihrabs*. Note the fine ornate carvings around the main *mihrab*. The original entrance area is on the other side of the building and at a lower level, and leads to large underground rooms beneath the mosque.

Uparkot's Buddhist caves: Further along the road are some unusually deep and complex Buddhist caves. The caves, which have been tentatively dated to as early as the 1st century, take the form of a three-storey underground building, cut out of the rock. The subterranean rooms are approached by a winding staircase. The top of the pillars in the lowest rooms are richly carved, but the actual carvings are heavily worn. Benches have been cut into the rock, and there are smaller rock-cut medallions, which seem to show donor couples. Note how the rock has been cut to allow light into the lowest level by an ancient skylight.

Uparkot's step-wells: The two remaining important buildings in Uparkot are both early step-wells, but quite different from each other architecturally. The first, the **Adi Kadi Vav**, 150m east of the caves, has simply been cut directly into the rock, without the normal post-and-beam support structure for such wells; it may date from the same period as the Buddhist caves. The second, another 250m further south and known as the

Lashkari Vav, or Army Well, is more complex and has been tentatively dated to the 2nd century, though the upper portions were restored or rebuilt in the Nawabi period. This well uses a series of stairs that work their way round the well, with large windows cut into the lower face of the well. Note how there are two separate levels for drawing water.

Baba Pyara and Khapra Kodia caves

Just outside the southern walls of Uparkot, next to the road leading to Girnar, are the 2nd-century **Baba Pyara** Buddhist caves. The caves are set over two levels and have more than 30 rooms. There are carved pillars and traces of rock-carved floral decoration around some of the door openings, but the caves are largely bare. The largest cave (Number 6, approached from the right of the complex) has the horseshoe shape that is typical of a *chaitya*, or Buddhist assembly room. About 300m north of the northern walls of Uparkot is another Buddhist cave complex, the **Khapra Kodia** caves (3rd–4th century), with five small square water tanks, approached by descending staircases, and with a colonnade on one side.

The Nawabi tombs

Two tombs and a mosque close to the railway station (pass through the gate beneath the large clock tower and turn right at the city jail) represent the exuberant flowering of a very distinctive late 19th-century architectural style that combines the European Rococo tradition with Muslim funerary architecture. The most northerly of the tombs, known as the **Mahabat Maqbara** (1892), is the most extravagant (almost kitsch) of the Babi Dynasty mausolea. It is thought to house the grave of Nawab Mahabat Khan (1851–52), as well as several other royal graves. The free-standing spiral minarets (up which one can climb) twist in different directions to retain the building's overall symmetry. Note the combination of marble and painted stucco inside the tomb. Nearby is a **second tomb**, but with even more ornate external decoration, and which is overtly modelled on a *mandapa*, or the assembly hall, of a Hindu temple. In a separate compound is the large main mosque, the minarets of which also have an external spiral staircase. Beyond the mosque is the large 19th-century City High School, now named after the best-known Gujarati medieval poet, Narsinh Mehta.

Junagadh Museum

The museum (*open 9–12 & 2.45–6; closed Wed and 2nd and 4th Sat of the month*) is in the durbar hall of the Nawab's Palace in the centre of old Junagadh, where there are several other interesting buildings from the Nawabi period. The main hall has an impressive collection of silver chairs with repoussé work. The larger, grander furniture, towards the back of the room, has lion motifs or shaped lion heads—commonly used as a symbol of the dynasty that developed the Gir sanctuary as a protected area for lions. Note the minute pistols in the third display case. In the portrait gallery is a photograph of the moustachioed Sir Shahnawaz Bhutto, the last prime minister of Junagadh and grandfather of Benazir Bhutto, as well as photographs of the royal family of Junagadh with their beloved dogs—many of which joined the family in exile in Pakistan.

Ashoka Rock Edicts

On the right (south) side of the road from Junagadh to Girnar, less than 1km east of Uparkot, are the Ashoka Rock Edicts, around which a shelter has been built. The edicts, like many others of their kind around India, were written during the reign of Ashoka the Great (304–232 BC), and were both an appeal to righteous behaviour and a declaration of the Mauryan Empire's claim over far-flung parts of the subcontinent. The large rock on which the Ashoka Edicts were written also has more recent inscriptions—from the 2nd and 5th centuries—which describe a huge lake and a burst dam that was almost certainly in the low-lying area within the Mt Girnar ridge.

Girnar

Mt Girnar (*map 4 B3*) is a major centre of pilgrimage for both Jains and Hindus, and has been an important religious site for more than 2,000 years, and probably a lot longer. The main temples are high up on Mt Girnar, and it is advisable to start walking before dawn if you want to avoid the worst of the daytime heat. The views from the mountain peak over the crater of the extinct volcano and of nearby Junagadh are spectacular.

The approach to Mt Girnar from Junagadh takes visitors and pilgrims to the bottom of a series of more than 7,000 steps to the furthest of the Hindu temples—which takes two to four hours. Many visitors go only as far as the Jain temple complex, visible from the base, which is reached after about 3,500 steps—or 1½ hours. There are plenty of small shops selling refreshments along the route. Many pilgrims and tourists are carried up the hill on *dhoolis*, or canvas seats attached to long wooden poles, carried by two porters. No tickets or permissions are needed. The steps up to the Jain temple complex are all uphill, and some parts are very steep—but the steps are well-maintained throughout.

Jain temples: The most important of the large grouping of Jain temples is similar to the Shatrunjaya temple complex at Palitana (*see p. 391*), also in Gujarat, but smaller. Here more than a dozen temples have been built on terraces set into the side of the mountain, most of them surrounded by large fortified walls. The largest and most important of the Jain temples is the one dedicated to the 22nd *tirthankar*, or saviour, Neminath. The entrance is on the left as you head up the mountain, through a small gate. Inside you'll need to deposit bags and cameras (however you can take pictures of the temple, from above, if you head a little further on uphill).

The 12th-century temple is contained within a large courtyard, with small shrines to all the *tirthankars* around the side walls. Just in front of the main temple is a small shrine to Adinath, the first *tirthankar*, marked by a small bull. Inside the temple is a large black image of Neminath, with crystal eyes and crown. Note the fine stone carving of dancing women on the roof of the domed assembly hall. Go through the door on the far side of the courtyard for an excellent view of a large group of Jain temples, some old, some modern. Note how the modern extensions and renovations to the temples use pretty mosaic patterns on their roofs—and have not been given the false antiquity treatment seen at many temples.

Hindu temples: The first and lowest of the peaks has a small Hindu temple dedicated to Ambaji, a form of the goddess Parvati. There is a brief descent, and a long climb up to the second temple, dedicated to the Gorakhnath, a Shaivite guru. Then there is a steep descent to a small ashram and an even steeper ascent up a narrow cone of rock to the last of the temples, dedicated to Guru Dev Dutt, and containing a three-headed idol riding a bull, all carved out of white marble.

GONDAL

This town (*map 4 B2*) was the capital of the former princely state of the same name. Just 35km south of Rajkot on the road to Junagadh, Gondal was ruled by the Jadeja Dynasty from the 17th century until Indian Independence, and the family continues to play a major role in the development of the town. Gondal has one of Gujarat's prettiest palaces, the Naulakha, as well as several other royal buildings.

Durbargadh

The oldest building in Gondal is the 18th-century Durbargadh, or old city fort complex, which includes the magnificent Naulakha Palace overlooking the Gondali River. The complex is entered from the main road through a cusped gateway beneath a tiered clock tower. Ahead is a long rectangular courtyard, with the Naulakha Palace at the far end. On the right is the dilapidated *zenana*, or women's quarters. Walk through the arch gateway, with a guardian statue on each side, and around the side of the *zenana* to see some fine stone tracery on the upper walls. Notice also the small Muslim shrine, to a saint known as the Gori Pir, in the main courtyard beneath the *zenana*.

Naulakha Palace: The Naulakha Palace, which dominates the Durbargadh complex, is so named because it cost *nau lakh*, or 900,000 rupees, to build. It is an unusual three-storey building, with a pretty cloistered terrace on the first floor, with some fine stone carving and striking side-towers. Note particularly the animal sculptures, real and mythological, on the eaves, emerging from the stonework above the ground-floor eaves, and the graceful, more Classical design of the third-floor façade. There is excellent stone and wood carving above the doors to the first-floor suite of rooms that now contain the museum.

Naulakha Palace Museum: Inside the museum are displays of photographs, books, trophies—and a huge collection of toy-cars belonging to the same maharaja who collected the real cars kept at the Orchard Palace (*see opposite*). The ornate balcony has fine views over Gondal. The large top-floor room is the durbar hall, and is still used by the maharaja. Make sure you go to the part of the museum in a separate building to the left (south) of the Naulakha, which contains a display of traditional kitchen equipment. It also has a pair of giant scales on which, on special occasions, the maharaja would be weighed, and the equivalent of his weight in gold would be given to the poor. Drive across the nearest bridge, just to the south of the Naulakha, to get excellent views of the palace reflected in the river.

Other Gondal palaces

The late 19th-century red-brick **Orchard Palace**, 600m east of the Naulakha, is the former royal guest house, and its garages have a very impressive collection of old cars, mainly from the 1950s, lovingly maintained and still in working order. Also note the old railway saloon carriage parked in the palace gardens, with a bedroom, dining room, bathroom suite and period fittings. Behind the Orchard Palace is the larger **Huzoor Palace**, still occupied by the former royal family. There is yet another palace, 1.25km north of the Naulakha: the **Riverside Palace**. Built in the 1880s for the crown prince, it has a large collection of royal memorabilia, photographs and wall-mounted stuffed animal heads. Both the Orchard and Riverside palaces are hotels (*see Accommodation, p. 410*).

RAJKOT

Saurashtra's largest city (*map 4 B2*) is best known as the childhood home of Mahatma Gandhi, but it was also the capital of the princely state of the same name, and is where the British political agent oversaw all the princely states of Kathiawar. The British also encouraged the opening of the palatial Rajkumar College in 1870, to provide a modern education to the princes of the region.

Gandhi's home is known locally as **Kaba Gandhi no Delo**, and is in a side street off Gheekantha Road in the old city. The house, which surrounds a small courtyard, is well maintained but over-restored, in sharp contrast to neighbouring buildings. It contains numerous photographs relating to the life of India's most venerated leader. Gandhi came here from Porbandar in 1876, when he was seven. His father had been appointed dewan, or prime minister, of Rajkot, and this remained Gandhi's home until he left to study law in Britain 12 years later. At the age of 13, he married Kasturba, also from Porbandar, and the couple lived in a now-demolished upstairs room above the entrance gateway—his father's room was on the right, inside the gate. In his autobiography, Gandhi describes how his father died while he and Kasturba were making love in the upstairs room. He refers to 'the shame of my carnal desire' as something he had 'never been able to efface or forget'. He later took a vow of chastity—after the birth of his four sons.

Alfred High School, 400m west of Gandhi's home, is a fine Victorian building, now renamed **Mohandas Gandhi School**, after its most famous pupil. The **Watson Museum** (*open 9–12.45 & 3–6; closed Wed and 2nd and 4th Sat of the month*) is just north of the high school, and has a small but important collection of Hindu and Jain sculpture, gathered from all over Gujarat. On entering the sculpture gallery you will see very fine statues of the sun-god and goddess, Surya and Suryani, opposite each other. Note the flying archers on either side of Surya and how carefully Suryani's necklaces have been draped over and between her breasts. There is a statue of Queen Victoria in white marble, looking particularly unamused, with a small copper crown resting on her head. The museum is named after Colonel John Watson, the British political agent for Kathiawar in the 1880s; it was built with funds donated by the princely families of the region.

WANKANER

This town (*map 4 B2*) is the capital of a former princely state of the same name, 35km north of Rajkot. Wankaner has several interesting palaces scattered around the town, two of which are comfortable hotels. Wankaner's former ruling Jhala Dynasty first established itself in this part of Saurashtra region in the early 17th century.

Durbargadh

The oldest and smallest of the palaces is the Durbargadh in the centre of town. It was badly damaged in the 2001 earthquake, and it is no longer possible to go inside the building. The main gate, built out of stone, is now closed, but it is possible to enter the compound, by going round the cinema—formerly the high court building—and then passing through a tin door into the complex. On the right, badly cracked, is the pretty palace building which overlooks the river. The other buildings were all part of the high courts and later used as a school until the earthquake.

Main palace complex

The main palaces are dramatically positioned on a hill overlooking Wankaner, 850m southwest of the Durbargadh. Note the distinctive Wankaner crest, with its two lions, on the entrance gate. The **old palace**, built in the 1880s, is on the left, partly obscured by trees; the new palace, the **Ranjit Vilas**, built in 1907, is the large impressive building with a clock tower, while the two-storey building on the right was built as a guest house, and is now a hotel. Guests of either of the Wankaner royal hotels can ask for a tour of the palaces, which is often given by the last maharaja's grandson, who stays in the main palace. The clock tower and the external turrets of the Ranjit Vilas were badly damaged in the earthquake, but the rest of the building remained intact. The palace has a huge, handsomely furnished main hall and side-rooms—all of the walls are decorated with ancestral portraits and animal heads. The window panes have been incised with the royal crest and 'BAZ', the initials of the maharaja who built this palace. Outside in a garage are some vintage cars, including a Rolls-Royce bearing the licence plate Wankaner-1. Up on a hill above the palace complex is a ruined tower marking the Allied Victory in the Second World War; it too was badly damaged in the earthquake.

Almost 2km north of Wankaner is another royal palace that has been converted into a hotel. The 1930s **Oasis Palace** has an unusual 20th-century step-well with underground rooms, built in traditional style. It is concealed within a modern outhouse.

MORVI

Twenty-five kilometres north of Wankaner is the town of Morvi, or Morbi (*map 4 B2*), the capital of another former princely state of the same name. In 1979 Morbi was devastated by floods in which more than 1,200 people died when a dam burst—the town was also severely affected by the 2001 earthquake. There are several former palaces, including the neo-Mughal **Willingdon Secretariat**, near the main bridge across the River Macchu. It was originally the queen's residence and incorporates the **Mani Mandir Temple**. It was converted into an administrative building in 1936 and named after the then viceroy. About 500m to the south is another palace, which has an unusual walkway bolted on its outer walls and which leads to a suspension bridge across the river.

WADHWAN

This small walled town (*map 4 C2*) was the capital of the former princely state of the same name. It is approximately midway between Ahmedabad and Rajkot. Unusually, Wadhwan's old walls and gates are intact, and there is a neglected old palace—the **Durbargadh**—at its centre, and an unfinished 20th-century palace near the railway line outside the town. The main **Wadhwan Palace** is an impressive building. It was slightly damaged during the earthquake of 2001, though, and plans to convert it into a hotel have been put on hold. It is possible to walk around the grounds. The old town also has a fine 13th-century step-well, known as the **Madhu Vav**, with six pretty pyramidal roofs, and weathered carved stones with images of Bhairava (a form of Shiva) on the right, and the monkey-god Hanuman on the left.

JAMNAGAR

Jamnagar (*map 4 B2*) is an important industrial city near the coast of northwestern Saurashtra, 75km west of Rajkot, and is the capital of the former princely state of the same name, although it was also known as Nawanagar. Its ruler in the early 20th century was the Jam Saheb K.S. Ranjitsinhji, better known as Ranji, who played cricket for England, and after whom India's oldest domestic cricket competition is named.

The **Lakhota Lake** (officially **Ranmal Lake** after a former ruler of the principality) is the main feature of the centre of Jamnagar. Two causeways lead to an island in the middle of the lake, with a 19th-century circular fortification known as the Lakhota Tower. Inside is the **Lakhota Museum** (*open 10–1 & 2–5; closed Wed and 2nd and 4th Mon of the month*), which houses a collection of stone carvings, including a fine 10th-century statue of Surya the sun-god and some miniature-style paintings of the early rulers of Jamnagar. There is also a small memorial to Ranji, and a fine painted scroll depicting the Battle of Bhuchar Mori in 1591, at which the Mughals gained control of this part of Gujarat. On the southern side of the lake is the impressive **Bhujiyo Kotho**, a heavily fortified building, badly damaged in the 2001 earthquake, and which once served as the royal arsenal.

Northern Jamnagar: The **Pratap Vilas Palace** is an enormous early 20th-century neo-Gothic building, now closed and empty, on the northern side of Jamnagar. Also in the north of the city is one of India's strangest 20th-century buildings, a rotating **Solarium**, which looks like a giant propeller resting on a large octagonal drum. The Solarium, based on a building in the French spa town of Aix-les-Bains, was used to treat patients suffering from skin ailments and tuberculosis, but is now deserted.

GOP & GHUMLI TEMPLES

On the road between Jamnagar and Porbandar are two important temples: at Gop, midway between the two cities; and at Ghumli, 25km southeast of Gop and 30km northeast of Porbandar.

Gop Temple

This 6th-century temple is one of the oldest free-standing Hindu shrines in India, and is actually situated in the village of Jinawadi, near Gop (*map 4 B2*), and should not be confused with the more modern temple on a nearby hilltop. The partly ruined temple has some worn carvings on its elaborate plinth. The upper levels of the assembly hall and the circumambulatory passage are missing but the sanctuary and the tower are largely intact. Note the two-tiered roof, with its recurring horseshoe-shaped *gavaksha* motif.

Ghumli Temple

The Ghumli Temple complex (*map 4 B2*), set in a pretty wooded valley, is dominated by the partly ruined **Naulakha Temple**, which largely dates from the 12th-century Solanki period. Like the Naulakha Palace at Gondal, it is so named because it is said to have cost *nau lakh*, or 900,000 rupees, to build. There are fine friezes around the plinth, showing elephants, horses and human figures. There is a worn image of a bearded Brahma, with his consort Saraswati and his vehicle, the goose Hamsa, on the side of the temple. Note the two-storey assembly hall, with many of the upper-level columns still standing. The smaller **Ganesh Temple**, with its curved tower, is a little older—probably from the early 10th century. Its assembly hall is now missing, though the recesses for the roof supports are visible above the entrance to the sanctuary. There are two small pools within the compound, and a much larger step-well on the far side of the compound. The more impressive **Vikia Vav** step-well is 15km away, near the village of Bhauneshwar (head first to the town of Deber). Badly damaged by lightning in 2009, it has some fine carvings on the columns that support its five underground levels, which include images of monkeys, deer and a rhinoceros.

PORBANDAR

The coastal town of Porbandar (*map 4 A3*) is best known as the place where Mahatma Gandhi was born in 1869. His father, Karamchand, was the prime minister of the princely state of Porbandar at the time.

Gandhi's birthplace

The complex known as **Kirti Mandir** (*open daily 7.30–6*), which includes the house in which Gandhi was born, is now a memorial and a museum. The actual house is an 18th-century three-storey building, with low ceilings and steep staircases. A red swastika on the ground floor marks his birthplace, and visitors can also see the rooftop room where Gandhi read as a small child. He left Porbandar for Rajkot when he was seven years old. The modern memorial next to the house is 79ft high, one foot for each year of Gandhi's life. Just beyond Gandhi's house is **Manek Chowk**, an enclosed market area with a 19th-century archway.

Porbandar's palaces

The town has two palaces to the east of Kirti Mandir, close to the sea. The **Huzoor Palace** (1927) overlooks the beach. It is still owned by the former royal family, but is empty most of the time and it is possible to walk through its grounds. The older **Daria Mahal Palace** (1903) is slightly inland and 1km to the south, between the enormous Birla cement factory and the lighthouse. It is now a teacher training college, and visitors are normally allowed to look around. The highlight is the pretty durbar hall, with chandeliers, a painted ceiling and some fine stained glass.

DWARKA

The pretty Hindu pilgrimage town of Dwarka (*map 4 A2*) is on the western tip of Saurashtra. The Hindu god Lord Krishna is said to have lived here, and the 16th-century **Dwarkadheesh Temple** draws large numbers of Krishna devotees. The temple is a pretty, multi-tiered limestone building, with half-excavated ruins of an older shrine within its compound. There are some fine friezes of elephants and other animals and humans on the plinth of the ruined shrine. Steps lead down from the temple to bathing *ghats* on the River Gomti, which enters the sea at Dwarka. On the northern outskirts of Dwarka is a 12th-century temple dedicated to Krishna's consort Rukmini; it has some fine external carvings.

Beyt Dwarka (*map 4 A2*) is a small island, 30km north of Dwarka, which is said to have been Krishna's original abode—though its main temple dates from the 19th century. There are boats to the island from the village of Okha.

KUTCH

Kutch (sometimes Kachchh or Cutch) is the most westerly district of India, and one of its largest and most remote (*map 4 A1–2/B1–2*). It has its own language, Kutchi, and distinctive cultural and historical traditions. Kutch is a peninsula surrounded in the south by the Arabian Sea and to its north by the dry salt flats of the Ranns of Kutch, which turn to water during the monsoon. The Great Rann is closer to the sea and the Pakistan border, while the Little Rann is much closer to northern Gujarat and Ahmedabad, and is the only surviving habitat of the Asiatic wild ass. It is attracting a growing number of travellers who come here to visit India's most important Harappan site, the palaces of the capital Bhuj, and the distinctive tribal arts and crafts of the villages of Kutch.

It also has what is thought to be India's oldest surviving mosque, at Bhadreshwar, near the coast. Kutch was the epicentre of a major earthquake in 2001 that caused large-scale destruction in much of the region and killed 2,300 in Bhuj alone. The River

Indus is thought to have once flowed through the Rann of Kutch, but was diverted to the west by an ancient earthquake. The Jadeja Dynasty ruled Kutch, with the title of maharao, from 1510 until 1948, when the princely state was incorporated into Independent India.

Visiting permission: Special permission is not needed to visit the capital, Bhuj, the Harappan site at Dholavira or the towns along the southern coast. However, permission is needed to visit many of the interior villages, particularly in the north and west, close to the frontier with Pakistan. Permission is normally granted very quickly and with little fuss at the office of the DSP (Deputy Superintendent of Police) in Bhuj, near the high court to the southwest of Hamirsar Lake. Take passport-sized photographs and a photocopy of the key pages of your passport.

BHUJ

Large parts of Bhuj (*map 4 A1*), the capital of Kutch, were badly damaged in the 2001 earthquake, though the most important heritage buildings were saved and are undergoing restoration. Part of the old walls were razed after the earthquake. The most important buildings are in the area around Hamirsar Lake in the centre of the old town.

The palace complex

The main palace area is on the northeastern side of the lake and consists of two buildings: the 18th-century **Aina Mahal** and the 19th-century **Prag Mahal**. The main gate has some interesting stucco statues on the exterior upper-floor **Naqqar Khan**, or Drum House. Note also how the gate abuts part of the older stone walls of Bhuj. Inside, there are older palace buildings on the right, while the European-style Prag Mahal, with its clock tower, is immediately ahead

Prag Mahal: This palace (*open daily 9–11.45 & 3–5.45*) was badly damaged in the earthquake, and large cracks are visible in several parts of the building. Note how different coloured sandstone blocks have been used to create a pattern on the exterior of the palace. As restoration work continues, the durbar hall, and the steps and verandah leading to it, have been reopened to the public. The entrance lobby has a pretty painted ceiling with floral designs, while the large double-height durbar hall has stucco figures that serve as brackets to the gallery above. Note also the painted medallions over the doorway, and the chandeliers hanging from the cloth ceiling.

Aina Mahal: The 'Palace of Mirrors' (*open Sun–Fri 9–12 & 3–6*) is less impressive externally, but contains the remarkable collection of the maharaos of Kutch and some unusual interior decoration. The long, narrow entrance chamber has, among its varied exhibits, a 15m-long finely painted 19th-century paper scroll, showing in intricate detail the annual state parade of the Kutch ruler. To the left, a doorway leads into the music room (Fuvera Mahal), with its low ceiling and a small throne with a rope-pulled fan above it. Beyond are the richly-decorated private quarters of the palace. These contain an extraordinary array of Indian and European craftwork and paintings, much of which dates to the 18th century—unlike most princely museum collections which were largely assembled in the late 19th and 20th centuries. Note in particular the Delft-style tiles, manufactured locally by an Indian craftsman who had travelled to Holland, and the fine mirror-work in various parts of the inner palace. There is also a superb early 18th-century ivory-inlay door—note the framed letter turning down a request from the V&A Museum in London to borrow it. The Hira Mahal was the official bed-chamber of the maharao, and contains a low bed with legs made of gold.

Elsewhere in Bhuj

Sharad Baug Palace: The modern, single-storey Sharad Baug Palace (*open Sat–Thur 9–12 & 3–6*) is set in its own gardens on the western side of the lake, and was the home of the last Maharao of Kutch, who ruled the state for six months until its accession to India in 1948. There is a small collection of antiques and mementoes inside, as well as the coffin in which the last maharao's body returned to Bhuj from London, prior to his cremation in 1991.

Kutch Museum: This is a purpose-built museum (1884) on the southeast side of the lake (*open 10–1 & 2.30–5.30; closed Wed and 2nd and 4th Sat of the month*). The garden outside the museum has some 19th-century gravestones with inscriptions in Hebrew and Marathi, a relic of the small Jewish community that used to live in Bhuj. Inside the museum is a Harappan seal from Dholavira—at least 3,000 years old and undeciphered—as well as some pretty decorated pottery. There are also some interesting Hindu and Jain carvings, including a fine head of the sun-god Surya. The most important exhibit is an early Buddha bronze (7th century) from Saurashtra in the *abhay-mudra* posture, with the right hand raised, palm outwards, which is meant to represent fearlessness and that one carries no weapons.

The Ramkund: This pretty, square step-well behind the Ram Temple and opposite the museum has a fine carved frieze around the lower levels. Note the images of the ten avatars of Vishnu, beginning with the fish and the tortoise, on the right of the well.

Royal *chattris*: These memorials are on a stretch of grassland 600m to the west of the lake. They were very badly damaged by the earthquake, but are under restoration. Note the unusually fine images of members of the royal family carved onto memorial stones.

The Bharatiya Sanskriti Darshan: This folk museum (*open daily 10–1.15 & 2–5*), on the Mandvi Road, has a collection of handicrafts from remote parts of Kutch. Visitors are not permitted to visit the ruined hill-fort of Bhuj, in the southeast of the town.

AROUND BHUJ

North: The largely tribal villages to the north of Bhuj contain some of the region's best examples of traditional crafts, colourful textiles and diverse architectural styles. Permission is required to visit villages near **Kalo Dungar** (Black Hill), Kutch's highest point above sea level at 462m. Permission is not needed to visit the village of **Kotay**,

20km northeast of Bhuj, which has the recently restored **Kotay Temple**. Note the stepped plinth, and a multi-faceted tower with some fine external carvings that are typical of the Solanki period (10th–14th century). It is not clear whether the temple was originally dedicated to Shiva or to Surya.

West: Permission is needed to visit most places in western Kutch. The town of **Tera** (*map 4 A1*), 85km west of Bhuj, has a pretty 19th-century fort, and is an important Jain pilgrimage centre. The town of **Lakhpat** (*map 4 A1*) was a thriving port until a branch of the River Indus was displaced by the earthquake of 1819. The 7km-long city walls were built in 1801, and are largely intact. There are fine views from the battlements of the point where the Rann of Kutch meets the tidal Kori Creek. There is also a Sikh *gurudwara* marking the site of a visit by the first guru, Nanak, as well as several interesting Muslim tombs.

South: The town of **Kera** (*map 4 A2*), 20km south of Bhuj, has an unusual **Shiva temple** from the 10th-century Solanki period, which was later incorporated into the walls of the **Fort of Kapilkot**. The temple was split vertically during the 1819 earthquake, and only the plinth and rear of the sanctuary and the tower have survived. Note the fine frieze of elephants, and the stone grilles at the back of the temple.

BHADRESHWAR & MANDVI

The little-visited town of **Bhadreshwar** (*map 4 B2*), 45km southeast of Bhuj and just 4km from the coast, has the ruins of India's oldest surviving mosque. The first mosques in India are thought to have been built in Kerala in the 7th century, but no parts of the original buildings are thought to have survived. The **Solah Khamba Masjid** (c. 1170), or 16-pillar Mosque, is largely buried in the sand, but the tops of many pillars and the ceiling slabs are still visible, as is the upper part of the *mihrab*, or prayer niche. In the undergrowth is a long stone block with a carved Arabic inscription. Nearby are two other Islamic shrines in much better condition. The **Lal Shahbaz Qalandar Dargah** (1275) is a shrine to a 13th-century Muslim saint. It has an unusual corbelled dome, pyramidal outside and hemispherical within. The semicircular *mihrab* is flanked by two windows, and several columns bear traditional Jain designs. The rectangular **Choti Masjid**, or Little Mosque, is thought to be from the same period as the Qalandar Dargah, and has an unusual internal *mihrab*, as well as the main *mihrab* at the rear of the building. To the east of the Muslim shrines is an enormous Jain temple—an important pilgrimage site—which replaced an older temple destroyed by the 2001 earthquake. On the far side of the Jain temple is a multi-storey step-well, its different levels supported by carved columns.

Mandvi (*map 4 A2*) is a pretty seaside town, known for its shipbuilding industry, which flourishes along an estuary close to the sea, and for its sandy beaches. It also became a summer retreat for the Kutch royal family, who built an impressive palace close to the sea, 6km west of the town. The domed sandstone **Vijay Vilas Palace** (1929) was built in the neo-Rajput style and set in pretty gardens. There are excellent views from the roof of the palace.

DHOLAVIRA

Dholavira (*map 4 B1*) is probably India's most remote major archaeological site. It is also the most important Harappan excavation in India, dating from the period of the Indus Valley civilisation more than 4,000 years ago. The other major Harappan sites, Mohenjo-daro and Harappa, are in Pakistan. The Dholavira site is on the western side of an island in the Rann of Kutch known as Khadir, which is surrounded by water during the monsoon, and by dry salt flats the rest of the time.

Visiting Dholavira

The island can be reached only by a dramatic 8km-long causeway across what looks like snow but is actually salt. The causeway is accessed from the town of Rapar in northeastern Kutch. It is only 90km from Bhuj as the crow flies, but 200km by reasonable roads, and the journey can be completed in less than five hours. Construction of an alternative, quicker route from Bhuj across the Rann of Kutch is underway. Food and water are not available at the site (*open daily from 9*). There is little shade at the site and it is advisable to take a hat. There is a sign at the site saying photography is not permitted—though the museum manager says that the rule is never enforced, and that visitors are welcome to take pictures.

The site at Dholavira was first discovered in the 1960s, with most of the excavation taking place in the 1990s. The site dates back to approximately 2650–1450 BC, with a small gap towards the end of this period. The River Indus is thought to have flowed nearby during this period. As with other Harappan sites, seals bearing the mysterious undeciphered symbols of the Indus Valley civilisation have been discovered here, as well as many other artefacts—some of which are on display in the small museum. Although much has been discovered about the everyday lives of the people who lived here, we know little for sure about their ethnic origins, religious beliefs and language, and it remains unclear why the civilisation collapsed.

The site is approached from the car park, with the museum on the right. The first important structure is the deep **eastern reservoir**, which sits at the foot of the citadel, and which has a staircase running down one wall. It is one of several reservoirs on the site, which had a complex water retention and drainage system.

The Citadel

Beyond the eastern reservoir is the Citadel at Dholavira, approached by steps that lead through its eastern gate. Note some fragments of columns that were once part of an entrance portal. On the summit of the Citadel are the lower levels of several circular and square buildings, a well and a drain with an underground water conduit. There are good views from the Citadel of the rest of site. To the left (south) are more reservoirs; straight ahead (west), with the salt flats in the distance, is what was probably a cemetery; and to the right is a large open area, then the lower town, with its grid of streets and houses. Immediately ahead is the area named the 'bailey', after the medieval British term for the area just outside the motte, or Citadel. It was here that senior officials of

Dholavira are thought to have lived, in larger houses than the rest of the population. On the well-defended main northern gate, the remains of what is thought to have been the world's oldest signboard were discovered, with ten undeciphered Harappan symbols—the largest example of such lettering. The symbols, each of which is about 37cm high, were made from gypsum and are thought to have originally been inlaid in wood, which then rotted away. The remains of the signboard have been reburied beneath a protective sheet of corrugated iron, but there is a photograph of them in the museum.

Outside the Citadel: On the south (left) of the Citadel is a series of reservoirs, partly dug out of the soil and partly cut out of rock, which are as deep as 7m, and have an impressively fine finish. The reservoirs are connected by channels that allow excess water to flow to the west, towards the Rann of Kutch. To the west, beyond the 'bailey', in what is thought to be the cemetery, several structures have been excavated that contain pottery, beads and jewellery of the kind that are buried next to dead bodies at similar sites. However, only one skeleton has been discovered so far. Most of ancient Dholavira lay to the right (north of the Citadel). A large open area between the Citadel and the lower town, and labelled the 'stadium' by archaeologists, may have served as a parade ground or meeting place for festivals. The lower town, with its own fortification, has a grid of narrow streets at right angles to each other, with the lower levels of dwellings still visible.

Dholavira Museum

The well laid-out small museum next to the car park has an impressive collection of objects recovered from the site during excavations. These include objects made out of shell and of copper, bangles, beads, toys and figurines. Note particularly the terracotta figurines of a bull and a peacock. There is some pretty decorated pottery, some large storage vessels and perforated jars, the purpose of which is uncertain.

PRACTICAL INFORMATION

GETTING THERE

• **By air:** Gujarat's main airport, at Ahmedabad, is well connected with the rest of the country, with several daily flights to Mumbai and Delhi, as well as a growing number of international connections. In southern Gujarat, Vadodara has daily connections to Mumbai and to Delhi. Saurashtra and Kutch are very well connected by air to Mumbai, with daily flights to six airports in the region: Bhavnagar, Diu, Rajkot, Porbandar, Jamnagar and Bhuj—but none currently to any other Indian cities.

• **By train:** There are good train services from Mumbai to Vadodara (5hrs) and Ahmedabad (6hrs). Some of the trains also stop at Surat and Bharuch. For Daman, get a slower train to Vadodara from Mumbai and get out at nearby Vapi. There are also useful services to Ahmedabad from Delhi (14hrs) and from Jaipur (12hrs).

• **By road:** There are major highways leading to southern Gujarat from

Mumbai, and from Udaipur in southern Rajasthan to Ahmedabad. Other less-used road routes lead from Mt Abu in Rajasthan to Kutch, and from western Madhya Pradesh to Champaner and Vadodara.

GETTING AROUND

There are good railway services within Gujarat, particularly from Ahmedabad to Vadodara (2hrs), Rajkot (4½hrs), Somnath (9½hrs) and Bhuj (8hrs). Gujarat's major roads are among the best in India, and are usually faster than travelling by train. Auto-rickshaws are widely available in the towns and cities, and taxis can be hired in most places.

ACCOMMODATION

• **Ahmedabad:** The most attractive hotel in Ahmedabad is the **House of MG** (*$$; T: 079 25506946; houseofmg.com*), a former family mansion built by Mangaldas Girdhardas (or MG) in 1924, in the heart of the old city; it is now run by his great-grandson. Alternatively, there is the 5-star **Meridien Hotel** (*$$$; 079 25505505; starwoodhotels.com*) near Nehru Bridge.

• **Northern Gujarat:** The best hotel in the north of the state is **Balaram Palace Resort** (*$$; T: 02742 84278; balarampalace.com*), a former royal residence just north of Palanpur.

• **Southern Gujarat and Daman:** There is a wide variety of relatively uninteresting accommodation aimed at business travellers in Vadodara. **The Taj group** has hotels in **Vadodara** (*$$$; Taj Residency; tajhotels.com; T: 0265 6617676*) and in **Surat** (*Taj Gateway; tajhotels.com; 0261 6697000*).

Jambugodha, 30km east of Champaner, has a simple friendly hotel, the **Nature Lover's Retreat** (*$; jambugodha.com; T: 02676 241258; mobile 098250 41215*) in part of a royal palace built in the 1930s, while there two other converted palaces in south Gujarat: the **Kali Niketan palace in Chhota Udaipur** (*$$; T: 02669 233577; chhotaudepur.com*), and the **Rajvant Palace** (*$; T: 02640 220345; rajvantpalace.com*) in Rajpipla.

In Daman the more comfortable hotels are near Devka Beach, 3km north of the town. The **Cidade de Daman Hotel** (*$$; cidadededaman.com; T: 0260 2250590*) is probably the best, but the grubby beach is not recommended for swimming.

• **Saurashtra Peninsula:** Eastern Saurashtra has a number of attractive heritage hotels, most of them former palaces or royal guest houses—in Bhavnagar, Palitana, Gondal and Wankaner—and there are plans to open several more. Modern hotels, often aimed at business travellers, are available in all Saurashtra's cities.

In Bhavnagar, the **Nilambag Palace** (*$$; T: 0278 2424241/2429323; nilambagpalace.com*) is a large former royal residence built in the 1860s, with comfortable rooms, an outdoor swimming pool and tennis court. In Palitana, the **Vijay Vilas Palace Hotel** (*$; T: 02848 282371; 094271 82809; vishwa_adpur@yahoo.co.in*) is comfortable but not air-conditioned. It is the former summer retreat of a Palitana prince, was built in 1906 and has passed on to his welcoming descendants, who serve superb local food. It is set in pretty gardens, 6km outside Palitana on the Adpur road, at the foot of one of the routes up to the Shatrunjaya Temple complex.

In Gondal, The **Orchard Palace** (*$$; T: 02825 220002/224550; gondalpalaces.com*) is part of the Huzoor Palace complex on the western outskirts of the town. It is also possible to stay in the old train saloon, stationed next to the palace. If the Orchard Palace is full, rooms will be made available at the pretty **Riverside Palace**.

In Wankaner, The **Royal Oasis Hotel** (*$$; T: 02828 220000; wankanerheritagehotels.com*) is another palace hotel, 2km north of Wankaner. It is set in pretty gardens, serves high-quality local food, has an indoor swimming pool and an unusual step-well. A little further north, in Morvi, is where the **Neemrana group** is, at the time of writing, about to open a hotel in a former palace in the town (*neemranahotels.com*).

The best hotels in the coastal enclave of Diu are outside the main town. **Radhika Beach Resorts** (*$$; T: 02875-252553/54/55; radhikaresort.com*) is on Nagoa Beach, 7km east of the main tourist attractions. **Magico do Mar** (*$$; T: 098242 30908, 02875 252567; magicodomar.com*) is on the mainland, close to the checkpost with Diu.

If you're staying in Junagadh, near Mt Girnar, the modern **Leo Resorts** (*$$; T: 0285 2652844-5; leoresorts.com*), on the road to Mt Girnar, is recommended, while in Rajkot **The Imperial Palace** (*$$; T: 0281 2480000; theimperialpalace.biz*) is a modern business hotel.

On the southwest coast in Porbandar, **Hotel Natraj** (*$; T: 0286 2215658; hotelnatrajp.com*) is a clean, modern hotel in the centre of town, and on the Gulf of Kutch in Jamnagar, the slightly run-down **Hotel Aram** (*$; T: 0288 2551701; hotelaram.com*) once belonged to the royal family; it is the city's best-known hotel.

• **Kutch:** The most comfortable accommodation in Bhuj is at **Hotel Prince** (*$$; T: 02832 220370; hotelprinceonline.com*), which also has the Toral restaurant for superb Gujarati *thalis*. Confusingly there is a slightly less comfortable hotel called the Hotel Prince Residency, run by the same group. The only other comfortable accommodation are the luxury tents at **The Beach at Mandvi** (*$$$; T: 02834 295725; mandvibeach.com*), very close to the Vijay Vilas Palace, outside Mandvi.

FOOD

Gujarati cuisine is largely vegetarian, though the Muslim and Parsi communities in the state are big meat-eaters. The centrepiece of a Gujarati meal is a *thali*, a plate with several dishes on it. Rice and breads are widely available, as is a large selection of vegetables. Among the best-known Gujarati dishes is *dal dhokli*, a lentil curry with dumplings; and the vegetable stew known as *oondiyo*. Saurashtran (or Kathiawadi) food is largely vegetarian, with breads made from millet (*bajra roti*). It tends to be slightly spicier than other Gujarati food. Surat is best known for *ponk*, a softened roasted green millet widely available in winter as a street food, and usually served with chutney and *sev*, a deep-fried crispy noodle. There are dozens of Gujarati snacks, including *dhoklas*, made from chick-pea flour that has been fermented and steamed, and *khandvi*, which are rolls of cooked chick-pea paste.

High quality Gujarati food is available from road-side cafés, and from some of the hotels listed above. Among the hotels whose food is highly recommended is the **House of MG** in Ahmedabad, the **Vijay Vilas Palace Hotel** in Palitana, the **Royal Oasis Hotel** in Wankaner and the **Hotel Prince** in Bhuj.

In Diu, the cuisine has a strong Portuguese and Goan influence, and spicy seafood dishes are a speciality. **Apana Restaurant** on the waterfront in Diu town is the area's best seafood restaurant, and has delicious tandoori fish and prawn curries.

Drink: *Chhaas* is a drink made from buttermilk that's widely available in Gujarat. Alcohol is banned in the state, though in some hotels foreigners may be served drinks in their rooms. When alcohol is available, legally or illegally, there is often little choice. Alcohol is widely available in the former Portuguese enclaves of Daman and Diu.

FURTHER READING & VIEWING

Gujarat by Anjali Desai (India Guide, 2009) is a good guidebook, widely available in the state. Mahatma Gandhi's autobiography is very interesting about growing up in Saurashtra in the late 19th century. Dom Moraes and Sarayu Srivatsa visit the European cemeteries in Surat in *The Long Strider* (2003), their eccentric travelogue and biography of Thomas Coryate, a 17th-century British wanderer who walked to India and died near Surat. The historian Patrick French follows Gandhi's Salt March route in *Liberty and Death* (1997).

The conclusion of the Salt March at Dandi is portrayed in the 1982 film *Gandhi*. Sooni Taraporevala's *Little Zizou* (2009), an English-language comedy about the Parsi community, has several scenes in the Gujarati coastal town of Udwada, just north of Daman.

For travel assistance and in-depth historical and cultural knowledge, the curator of the Aina Mahal in Bhuj, Pramod Jethi (*T: 093742 35379*), is extremely helpful. He's also the author of the locally published *Kutch: the people and their handicrafts*.

MADHYA PRADESH

For years, it has been a cliché of travel literature to describe Madhya Pradesh (*maps 5 and 6*) as India's best-kept secret. It is still not a major international tourist destination, but its remarkable range of heritage sites (arguably greater than any other part of India) and its rapidly improving tourist infrastructure means that domestic and foreign travellers are beginning to take this state much more seriously.

Madhya Pradesh (or MP), which literally means 'Middle State', has India's most impressive prehistoric cave paintings at Bhimbetka, the best-preserved Buddhist stupa in the country at Sanchi, the extraordinary erotic carvings at Khajuraho's Hindu temples and the enormous medieval Muslim fortress at Mandu, as well as numerous crumbling forts and palaces spread throughout the land. Until recently, the region was divided into dozens of princely states, small and large, and the palaces and memorials of Orchha form a particularly fine example of what these princedoms left behind. In the north and west of the state are the monumental palaces, shrines and fortresses of Gwalior and Indore—two of the great Maratha princely states which played such an important role in 18th- and early 19th-century India. Even the capita,l Bhopal, best remembered for one of the world's worst industrial disasters, has a fascinating Muslim old city, with one of the largest mosques in South Asia.

SOUTHERN MADHYA PRADESH

BHOPAL

It is unfortunate that Bhopal (*map 6 B1*) is best known as the location of what at the time was the world's worst industrial disaster because, to many visitors' surprise, the city is one of India's prettiest state capitals, with large lakes and leafy parks.

History: According to tradition, the city was founded by, and named after, the great Parmar king Rana Bhoj in the 11th century, and it was he who built the dam that created the Upper Lake around which Bhopal was later built. No buildings survive from the early period though, and the modern history dates back to the early 18th century, and the arrival of an Afghan adventurer in the service of the Mughals named Dost Muhammad Khan. He conquered the area, first setting up his capital in Islamnagar, 10km to the north, but then gradually fortifying and building in the area around the lakes. It became a princely state, whose rulers built the mosques and palaces of central Bhopal. Unusually, it had a series of female rulers, or begums, and Bhopal gained a reputation as one of India's more progressive principalities. After Independence, Bhopal benefited from the rivalry of the larger cities of Indore and Gwalior, and emerged as the compromise capital of Madhya Pradesh.

On 3rd December 1984, a gas leak at the Union Carbide factory in north Bhopal resulted in many thousands of deaths. Most of Bhopal was quickly made safe, but its international reputation as a place of disaster and death has hindered the growth of tourism in this interesting city.

Orientation: Bhopal is built around two lakes: the enormous **Bara Talab** (or 'Big Lake', though usually referred to in English as the Upper Lake) on the west side of the city; and the smaller **Chota Talab** ('Small Lake', or usually Lower Lake) to the east. The older parts of the city are just north of the lakes and west of the railway station, while the main palaces and two major mosques are between the old city and the Bara Talab. The Union Carbide factory lies derelict to the north of the city. Overlooking the southern banks of the Bara Talab are the leafy Shamla Hills—home to several museums and the city's best hotel. None of Bhopal's royal palaces has become a tourist site in the traditional sense; instead they have been converted into schools or government offices. However two of the palace complexes are worth visiting.

The 'Taj Mahal'

This palace (1871–84) was built, like its more famous namesake in Agra, by Shah Jahan—though this Shah Jahan was a begum and the female ruler of Bhopal. Unlike the older building, this really was a '*mahal*'—a palace—rather than a tomb. It is north of the enormous mosque, the Taj-ul Masajid, on the far side of what is, by Bhopal's standards, a small lake. The palace is a six-storey building, with more than 100 rooms built in a late-Mughal style, with cusped arches and projecting balconies on the façade. It is not officially open to the public, but a big restoration project was underway at the time of writing, and visitors are allowed to wander around the site and see the pretty courtyard with its pavilion.

Taj-ul Masajid

The red sandstone Taj-ul Masajid (begun 1881), just 500m south of the Taj Mahal, is India's largest mosque and is said to accommodate 10,000 devotees. It was commissioned by Begum Shah Jahan. She originally asked for a replica of the Jama Masjid in Delhi, and the similarities in design are striking. Its minarets are higher and less elegant, and the sides of the courtyard have dozens of rooms, used as a *madrasa*. The building was only completed in the 1980s. Note the semicircular design of the main staircase up to the mosque, as well as the separate areas for women at either end of the prayer hall.

Sadar Manzil and Gauhar Mahal

The other palace complex is close to the Upper Lake. The gates to the complex still stand, as do several of the palaces, including the **Sadar Manzil** (1898), once a public audience hall and now government offices, and with a pretty courtyard and arcades. Just to the south and closer to the lake is the **Gauhar Mahal** (1819–37), the earliest surviving city palace.

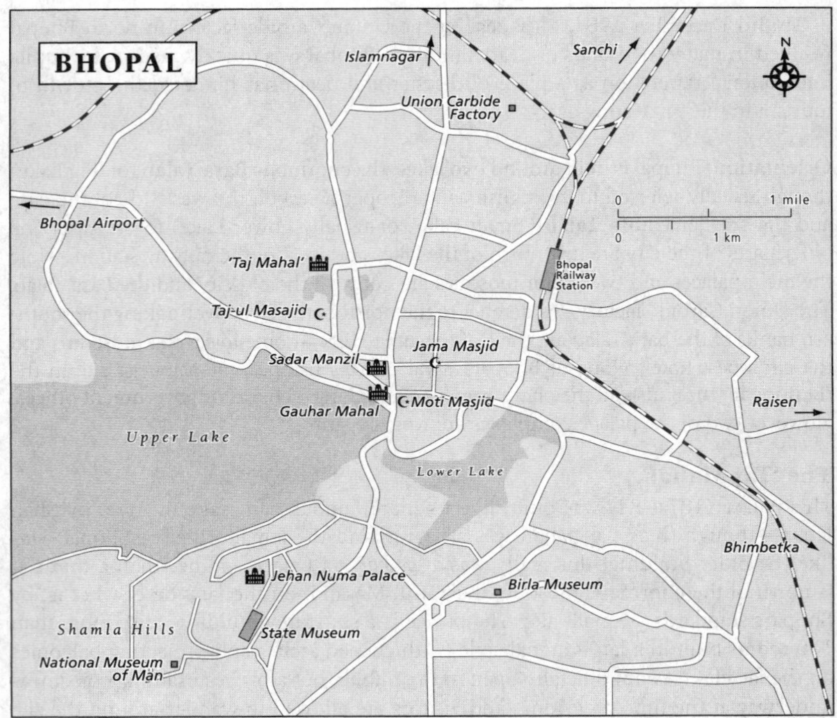

Moti Masjid and Jama Masjid

About 200m to the east of the Upper Lake palace complex is the fine **Moti Masjid** (1860). The outer structure is built from sandstone, while its prayer hall and domes are constructed from white marble. Bhopal's oldest mosque, the triple-domed **Jama Masjid** (1837), is in the geometric centre of the old city, at the crossing point, known as the Chowk, of its two main streets.

Bhopal's Museums

State Museum: Up in the Shamla Hills, in the southwest of Bhopal, the State Museum (*open Tues–Sun 10.30–5.30*) has one of the best archaeological collections in the country. It is also unusually well laid-out in a purpose-built museum that opened in 2005. The sculpture gallery contains some fine pieces of mainly Hindu temple carvings from across the state. Note in particular the statues recovered from Hinglajgarh, near the Rajasthan border, which include a superb female version of Varaha, the boar avatar of Vishnu. There is also a fine 12th-century relief carving of a recumbent mother and child, surrounded by guards, that has been identified as Krishna and his mother.

Birla Museum: The more old-fashioned Birla Museum (*open Tues–Sun 9.30–8; closed public holidays*), near the Birla Mandir, has a congested collection of fine statues in separate galleries devoted to Shiva, Vishnu, Devi (female goddesses) and Jain sculpture. There are detailed guides to the exhibits in pamphlet form, and this makes the Birla Museum a good place to learn about Hindu iconography. As in the state museum, there are superb pieces from Hinglajgarh, including an unusual carving of Vainayaki, the female form of the elephant god Ganesha, riding on an oversized mouse, and a triple-headed image of the goddess Maheshwari, stepping on the body of a naked man.

The National Museum of Man: Also known as Rashtriya Manav Sangrahalaya, this anthropological museum (*open Tues–Sun 10–5.30 Sept–Feb, 11–6.30 March–Aug*) is set in more than 200 acres of forest and scrub overlooking the Upper Lake in the Shamla Hills area. There are replica tribal villages too, and it all serves as an excellent introduction to the history, traditions and crafts of India's many tribal peoples.

AROUND BHOPAL

Islamnagar

The fortified village of Islamnagar (*map 6 B1*), just 10km north of Bhopal, off the Berasia road, was the first capital of the nawabs of Bhopal in the early 18th century, and it has three interesting palaces. The village is entered through three sets of gates, and past some impressive walls and bastions. A lane leads left to the most ruined of the palaces, the **Gond Mahal**, with its two courtyards and pretty upper-storey columned terraces. The more important palace complex is on the right of the road that runs through the village (*open daily 10–4.30*). The palace complex, consisting of the **Chaman Mahal** (1715) and the **Rani Mahal**, includes several well-maintained buildings with pretty curved roofs, and a bathhouse. There is also a Mughal-style *char-bagh* garden with fountains—one of very few to be found in central India.

Raisen

Some 30km east of Bhopal and 20km south of Sanchi is the fascinating, little-visited **Raisen Fort**, which towers above the town of the same name (*map 6 B1*). About 4km before Raisen town, on the Bhopal road, a bumpy road leads off the main highway halfway up the hill. It is then a steep ten-minute walk to the plateau, through a series of gates. The hill-fort dates to the 12th century, though the large number of surviving buildings are from later periods. On reaching the inner precincts of the fort, turn right for the palaces and other major structures. Before reaching the palace complex, note the impressive building on the left, which has served both as a mosque and a temple. The temple sanctuary, which sticks out of the back of the mosque assembly hall, has a Shiva lingam. The ruined **palace complex** is enormous, and there are lots of surviving shrines, domes, cupolas, arches and decorative features, as well as an impressive stepwell at the centre of the complex, and lots of old cannons. At the far end of the plateau (close to the television tower) are some ruined temples, storehouses, watchtowers and other gates leading down to the plains.

Raisen Museum: Almost directly opposite the road leading up to the fort is a small museum with a collection that includes a fine 9th-century statue of Hanuman with a dagger in his belt, and a large 10th-century relief of a sleeping mother and child protected by seven female guards.

Bhojpur

The enormous, unfinished 11th-century **Bhojeshwar Temple** dominates the small town of Bhojpur (*map 6 B1*), which is 20km southeast of Bhopal, 2km to the east of the road leading towards Bhimbetka. The temple, dedicated to Shiva, was commissioned by Raja Bhoj, the greatest of the Parmar kings, who fought against the early Muslim invasions led by Mahmud of Ghazni. The massive dome was never completed, and the incomplete main structure remains one of the most imposing temples in the region—the polished Shiva lingam inside the sanctuary is one of the largest in India. Note the carvings on rocks nearby, which show what the finished temple was meant to look like.

BHIMBETKA

The painted rock-shelters on Bhimbetka Hill are India's most important prehistoric site, set in a pretty location 40km southeast of Bhopal (*map 6 B1*). Take a right turning 6km after Obaidullahganj, which is on the main Bhopal–Hoshangabad road, from where you can see the distinctive boulders on the summit of Bhimbetka. The smaller road crosses a railway line, then heads uphill past a checkpost (at which cars need to show their anti-pollution certificate) to the ticket office (*open daily dawn–dusk*). Drive on to the main car park. Because some of the paintings are hard to spot and the numbering system is confusing, it is worth taking a guide. More than 600 rock shelters have been identified—more than half of which have paintings. Most visitors do not go beyond the inner group of shelters on Bhimbetka Hill—the others are much harder to visit, and warn your guide in advance if you wish to venture to them. Bring water, as there are no refreshments available at the site.

History of Bhimbetka

The sandstone geological formations on Bhimbetka have, from a distance, the appearance of a ruined fort. However, the spectacular rock formations and their surroundings are entirely natural, and the rock-shelters (they are not really caves since they are not confined spaces and have multiple access routes) have not been created by humans, but have been used by them for several millennia. The dating of the paintings and of the period of occupation of the rock-shelters themselves is not conclusive, but some paintings are thought to date back at least 10,000 years, and the shelters may have been occupied for much longer. The inhabitants were hunter-gatherers, and many of the paintings are of hunting scenes. The shelters continued to be used until at least 1,500 years ago, and more recent paintings have been superimposed on early ones.

The paintings—which use mineral-based paints—were discovered by the Indian archaeologist V.S. Wakanker as recently as 1958.

The order of rock-shelters described here is the one normally used by guides at Bhimbetka. They are all contained within a small area.

Rock-shelter 1 is at the end of a signposted path that leads into the Bhimbetka site from the car park. It has very clear white images of two elephants with upturned tusks; the smaller elephant has a rider, carrying a goad and a spear, and with a sword in his belt. Close by is an excavated site where a human skeleton was found. The nearby tunnel-like shelter known as the auditorium has lots of red paintings, with the best group showing deer, other animals and what appears to be a peacock. To the right of this is a hunting scene.

The **Zoo Rock-shelter** is so named because of different animals to be seen on its walls. The white painting, which includes elephants, deer, leopards and buffalo, as well as a man carrying a stick and a water pot, are older than the red paintings, which are more naturalistic and show horses (only introduced to India about 4,000 years ago), long-haired horsemen and archers.

Rock-shelter 8 is a raised chamber, and its paintings have survived very well. Among the images are paintings of horsemen riding (some with weapons), foot soldiers and chickens. **Rock-shelter 9** has patterns and images in green and yellow, as well as a finely painted white horse, several humans and a slightly deformed elephant on the far right. **Rock-shelter 10** has a painting of a bird sitting in a tree, with lots of figures that are hard to make out.

Rock-shelter 12 has several hunting scenes with one particularly fine representation of a startled buffalo painted in red, with decorative patterns inside the image of the buffalo. **Rock-shelter 15** has possibly the best known of the Bhimbetka images: an enormous square-jawed wild boar or bison chasing a very small human being. **Rock-shelter 11** has some of the most recent images, painted less than 2,000 years ago, showing horsemen carrying swords or spears, while **Rock-shelter 6**, the last of the main Bhimbetka group, has white, stick-like images of dancers and drummers.

For greater detail on the other caves at Bhimbetka Hill and at the nearby Bhonrawali Hill, the Archaeological Survey of India book on Bhimbetka is recommended and is available in the tent close to the ticket office—however, note that the book uses a different numbering system.

PACHMARHI

This pretty hill-station (*map 6 B1*), 5hrs drive southeast of Bhopal, was settled by the British in the early 1860s. It has the handsome neo-Gothic **Christchurch** (1875), with stained-glass panels installed as memorials by members of the congregation. There is also a **Catholic church** (1892), and a small **museum** inside the Forestry Department's Bison Lodge. The oldest structure in Pachmarhi is a **Gond shrine**, which serves as a memorial to the dead, with piles of carved wooden plaques placed in the shrine within a year of a relative's death.

SANCHI

The small town of Sanchi (*map 6 B1*), 40km northeast of Bhopal, has one of the world's great Buddhist sites—a well-preserved main stupa, with quite exceptional carvings on its gateways, surrounded by deserted shrines and monasteries, situated on top of a hill commanding magnificent views over the surrounding countryside. There is one comfortable place to stay in Sanchi, or the site can be visited on a day trip from Bhopal. Sanchi is particularly beautiful just after dawn.

History: In contrast with so many Buddhist sites in India, the Great Stupa at Sanchi has no direct connection with the Buddha. However, the wife of the greatest of the Mauryan emperors, Ashoka the Great—who converted to Buddhism in about 250 BC—came from nearby Vidisha, and their son Mahendra, who later spread Buddhism to Sri Lanka, spent some time here. The inner core of the Great Stupa is thought to date from this period. However, the stupa was extended and the magnificent gateways added in the 1st century BC during the Shunga and Satavahana dynasties. The Buddhist statues and several of the outer buildings date to the 5th-century Gupta period, while the perimeter wall dates to the 12th century—closer to the present day than to the foundation date of the stupa.

Orientation at the Sanchi site: The Sanchi site is approached by turning right (southeast) off the main Bhopal to Vidisha road. The smaller road has a ticket office near the bottom of the hill (*open daily dawn–dusk*) on the left, just before the entrance to the Archaeological Museum. The road then passes through a gate and twists steeply up the hill—note the nearby rock-cut steps, used by centuries of devotees. At the end of the road is a large car park, with a modern Buddhist prayer hall on the left and the main site in front of you. Several buildings are visible at this point, including the main stupa, with its high gateways, which is straight ahead, and the smaller Stupa 3 to the left. There are dozens of other structures on the site, including an upper level to the left of the main stupa and a lower level to the right. Beyond the lower level, down a small track, is the little-visited Stupa 2, with its fine carved railings. Refreshments are available at the site, at a small cafeteria on the left, behind the conservation office.

The Great Stupa of Sanchi (Stupa 1)

With its four superb ceremonial gateways, this is the most intact ancient Buddhist stupa in India. The core of it was first built in the 3rd century BC and expanded two centuries later; it was deserted by the 14th century. Its rediscovery was by British archaeologists in 1818—and we are all fortunate that, unlike two other great stupas, at Bharhut and Amaravati, it was not dismantled and sent to museums. The cost of sending the gates and railings to the British Museum in London was seen as prohibitive,

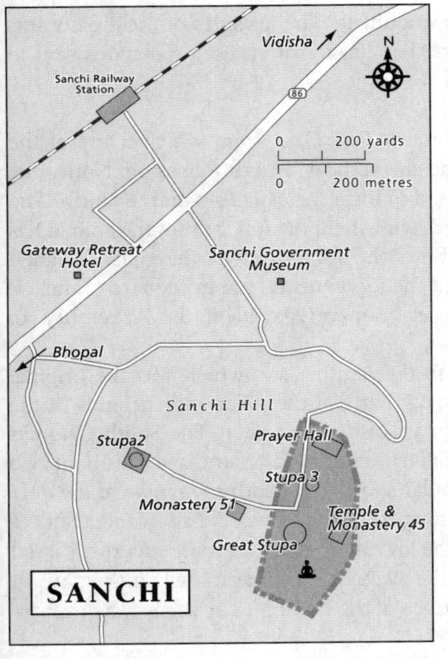

and when the French began to show an interest in having them, it was quickly decided by the British and the begum of Bhopal to keep them *in situ*.

Orientation at the Great Stupa: The first gateway, or *torana*, which faces visitors as they approach the stupa, is also the most complete: the North Gate. Visitors are recommended to walk round the stupa in a clockwise direction first, examining the outside and inside of the gate carvings before entering the circumambulatory passage—the raised balustraded walkway.

North Gate: There are more than 50 separate relief carvings on the columns and crossbars of the gate: here we will point out the highlights; for full details, see the ASI publication on Sanchi, which is available at the bookshop near the entrance. Many of the carvings show scenes from the life of the Buddha, though not the Buddha himself. The Buddha was never depicted at this stage in the development of Buddhism, and is instead represented by an empty throne or a Bodhi tree. All the gates have two pillars, with carvings on all four sides, though not on all the surfaces. The tops of the pillars are crowned with elephants (north and east), lions (south) and dwarves (west), and they support a complex superstructure with three gently curving crossbars which are in turn supported by vertical struts and finely carved brackets. The gates are connected by railings that run around the stupa.

The North Gate is the best preserved of the gateways, and, unlike the south and west gates, did not need to be reconstructed by archaeologists. Note the astonishing detail on the top part of the gate, particularly the brackets carved in the shape of women standing next to or clinging to trees. Higher up on the left pillar are images of the Buddha's mother, Maya, standing, and of her seated on a lotus and being bathed by elephants. The lowest panel on the right pillar is one of the few non-religious tableaux, showing scenes from everyday life. The lowest intact panel on the left pillar shows the Buddha, represented by a tree, preaching to his followers. The inside faces of the North Gate pillars are also richly carved, with figures of guardians at the lowest level. The top part of the inside face of the right pillar has a panel that depicts a stupa and a gateway, which might even be Sanchi itself. Note the half-human, half-bird figures known as *kinnaras*, and, at the bottom, human figures that are thought, from their unusual head-

and footgear, to represent visiting foreign Buddhists. The far sides of the crossbeams are also finely carved, and the middle one has images of gruesome demons sent to place obstacles in the Buddha's path.

East Gate: Head left to the slightly less intact East Gate, from which many of the smaller carvings between the crossbars and the vertical struts are missing. Notice the different ways four elephants have been used to form the capitals—on the North Gate only the front half of the elephant was used, while here the full form of the animal has been used. The front of the right pillar shows the six heavens of the gods, designed with pillars to look like a six-storey house. The top panel on the inside face of the left pillar has some remarkable carvings of scenes from everyday life in the 1st century BC.

South Gate: Continue round the stupa to the South Gate, which was the original main ceremonial entrance to the stupa. Many parts of the pillar and the ends of the crossbars are missing, and it is the least intact of the four gates. The South Gate has lion capitals—as did the nearby Ashoka pillar, which predates the gate by about two centuries. The top panel of the gate's left pillar shows the Buddha's sermon at the deer park in Sarnath (*see p. 247*), with a pillar crowned by the Wheel of Law—note the deer at the bottom of the panel. The far side of the lowest crossbar has some superbly carved images of a battle—thought to represent the siege of Kushinagar—when there was a violent struggle over who should get the ashes of the Buddha. The ashes were eventually divided into eight parts.

West Gate: This gate has also lost many of its features, and has been reconstructed. The capitals are supported by pot-bellied dwarves. The only surviving panel on the left pillar is possibly the most touching of the carvings at Sanchi: it shows five couples in a garden, all busily chatting or flirting. The siege of Kushinagar is repeated from the South Gate on the front of the middle crossbar.

The rest of the Great Stupa: Unlike many other stupas (including Stupa 2 at Sanchi), the railings at the Great Stupa at Sanchi are plain, though inscriptions are visible on the inside crossbars and pillars, as well as on the paving stones of the lower walkway. The architecture of the stone railings mimics a wooden railing, which it almost certainly replaced. The balustrade round the upper walkway is decorated with relief carvings of floral and animal designs. On top of the stupa is a small, square railing around a much-restored triple umbrella—one of the common Buddhist symbols.

Other buildings near the Great Stupa

Stupa 3: Slightly to the north of the Great Stupa is a small mound known as Stupa 3. It has one gateway and is thought to have been built in the same period as the other gateways. The carved images are similar, but the workmanship is less fine. Relics of two of the Buddha's closest disciples were buried here, then disinterred in the 19th century and taken to London. There are several smaller stupas nearby.

Temple 31: The nearby Temple 31 is largely an 11th-century structure, though the plinth and two of the columns date from the 5th–6th-century Gupta period. The standing image of the Buddha (probably 4th century) beside the temple has an unusual snake-hood halo. Note the stone tenon joint at the base of the statue, indicating that it has been moved here from its original location. There are several pillars nearby, though the most important is the stump of the **Ashoka pillar** (254 BC) close to the South Gate of the Great Stupa. It is the oldest visible structure at the site, though it was unfortunately broken in the 19th century and two of its pieces are now in a nearby shelter. The polished sandstone pillar was originally more than 12m high, and its carved lion capital is now in the Sanchi Museum.

Temple 17: Dating to the 5th century and positioned near the Ashoka pillar, Temple 17 is a fine example of a Gupta-period structure and is seen as a prototype for much later temple architecture. Note the lions on the capitals of the columns. The larger, horseshoe-shaped **Temple 18** is in ruins, but has several free-standing columns that are still upright—behind are a large number of ruined temples and monastic buildings.

The Vajrapani Pillar: This is another 5th-century Gupta-period relic, once topped by a statue of Vajrapani, the *bodhisattva* who symbolised the Buddha's power; the statue is now in the museum.

East and west of the Great Stupa

East: At the top of the staircase on the eastern side of the Great Stupa, are several more ruined structures, mainly monastic, largely from the Gupta and later periods. The main building here is **Temple and Monastery 45** (10th century), which consists of a square compound with cell-like rooms around the wall and a shrine at the back, part of the sanctuary of which survives, as well as the circumambulatory passage and much of its imposing tower. The plinth of the assembly hall survives, though the superstructure has disappeared, and the sanctuary retains much of its original decoration. There is a fine stone Buddha statue in the recess to the right of the sanctuary.

West: To the west of the Great Stupa are steps that lead down to a water pool and to the well-preserved foundations and lower wall of **Monastery 51**. Follow the path 250m further down the hill for **Stupa 2**, the railing posts of which are prettily decorated with floral, animal and human images, while the corner posts, close to the stupa entrance, have carved panels. These include Maya, the Buddha's mother, standing on a pedestal and being bathed by elephants.

Archaeological Museum

The Archaeological Museum (*open Sat–Thur 10–5*) is at the foot of the road leading up to the main Sanchi site—close to the ticket office. Among the exhibits are the finely carved and polished sandstone lion capital (254 BC) that once stood on top of the Ashoka pillar, next to the Great Stupa. Similarly, the heavily jewelled Gupta-period Vajrapani capital (5th century), from the pillar of the same name, is on display here. There are also several superb Buddha images from the Gupta and later periods, including a 4th-century meditating Buddha, with superbly carved pleats in his clothing.

AROUND SANCHI

Most visitors to Sanchi also go to the Udayagiri caves near Vidisha, but there are several other places worth visiting. One option is to hire a car (and driver) and make a long day trip to some of the fascinating, little-visited Hindu, Buddhist and Jain monuments in the area, including Gyaraspur, Pathara, Eran and Udayapur.

Udayagiri

The 5th-century rock temple-caves of Udayagiri (*map 6 B1*) are just 4km east of the district headquarters at Vidisha and 14km from Sanchi, and they have superb examples of late Gupta-period carvings, including a famous image of Varaha, the boar avatar of Vishnu.

The caves are cut into the side of a hill which is approached from the west, and are numbered, but not in order. Cave 19 is visible from the roadside before you reach the main gate, but visiting the site makes more sense if you continue to the official entrance, 300m further along the road, and return to Cave 19 by a different route (*see below*). There is no entry fee, but the watchman who opens the doors to some of the caves will expect a small tip.

Exploring the caves: Cave 6 (AD 402) has images of Vishnu, and of Durga killing the demon buffalo, and an inscription from the period of the Gupta ruler Chandragupta II. The Varaha Cave, or **Cave 5** (early 5th century), has a superbly modelled enormous relief carving of Varaha, the boar avatar of Vishnu, with—unlike at Eran (*see p. 424*)—a human body. One leg rests on a rock and his consort, Bhu, clings to his shoulder. Around him are sages who took shelter from great floods by hiding in Varaha's bristles. The receding waters are depicted by wavy lines cut into the lower rock. Note the musicians playing above Varaha's head and the snake-hooded figure at his feet.

Take the steps up the hill for **Cave 7**, on the left, which has two female guardian figures next to the otherwise undecorated entrance. Inside are a finely carved ceiling rose and an inscription in Pali script, describing the visit of the Gupta ruler Chandragupta II to the site. Do not go further up the hill now, but instead turn left over a boulder and head down again to visit **Cave 4**, which has badly damaged guardian figures outside the door, as well as pilasters cut from the rock. Inside is an unusual lingam, finely carved with the face of Shiva's consort Parvati. It is possible to continue from here to the little-visited **caves 3, 2 and 1**, the last of which has a columned porch and a Jain image—but which is almost 500m away.

Return to the rock-cut staircase for more caves belonging to the main group. In **Cave 13**, the second most important cave at Udayagiri, there is a sleeping Vishnu. The relief carving, partially obscured by a metal grille, shows Vishnu lying on the serpent Sesha. There are several minor caves further up the hill, and it is possible to walk to the top, past a ruined Gupta temple and the locked staircase entrance to a Jain cave cut into a cliff, and then down another set of stairs to **Cave 19**, which has the remains of a large columned portico, and some fine carving around the door. Alternatively there is access to Cave 19 from the road.

The Pillar of Heliodorus

Two kilometres north of Vidisha and across the River Betwa is a free-standing column known as the Pillar of Heliodorus. The pillar was erected in 111 BC by Heliodorus, a visiting ambassador from a Greek kingdom in what is now Pakistan, who, according to the inscription, had become a Hindu. The pillar, and a temple that once stood nearby, were dedicated to Vasudeva, a form of Vishnu. Note the floral decoration and Mauryan-style bell capital. The pillar is now venerated as Khambh Baba by villagers (*khambh* means pillar, *baba* is an honorific title similar to 'saint').

Vidisha

In the town of Vidisha itself (*map 6 B1*) is the **Bijay Mandal**, a huge 12th-century temple plinth, with a 17th-century mosque built on top. There are lots of stone-carved temple pieces lying on the plinth and in the pretty gardens—in which there is also a step-well. Parts of the temple are being restored. There is also a small **Archaeological Museum** in Vidisha, on the Sagar road, which has a fine carving of Vishnu on his 'vehicle', the man-eagle Garuda.

Gyaraspur

The village of Gyaraspur (*map 6 B1*), 44km northeast of Sanchi, on the main road between Vidisha and Sagar, has some fine temples and was an important Hindu and Jain centre during the later period (9th–10th century) of the Pratihara Empire. One of the country's most famous works of art, the *Salabhanjika*—a stone carving of a woman that is repeatedly referred to as India's *Venus de Milo*—was found here, and is now in Gwalior's Gurjari Mahal museum (*see p. 440*).

Bajra Matha: On entering the village from the Vidisha side, the partly ruined Bajra Matha on the right is an unusual triple shrine. The Matha was originally a Hindu temple, but it was later converted into a Jain shrine, and statues of Jain *tirthankars* were placed in the three sanctuaries. Some very fine Hindu carvings survive on the outside of the temple. Just beyond the Bajra Matha, on the roadside, is a small open-air compound that serves as a museum and has several interesting temple carvings.

Athstambh: In the centre of Gyaraspur, on the left (west) side of the road, is the Athstambh (c. AD 980), or 'Eight Pillars', a ruined temple once dedicated to Shiva, of which only part of the assembly hall survives. Note the beautifully carved *torana*, or archway, which emerges out of the mouths of monsters—and also the amorous couples carved on the lintel that once led to the sanctuary. The road to the left from the Athstambh leads into the countryside and to a 6th-century Buddhist stupa.

Maladevi Temple: Turn right and up the hill towards Gyaraspur's most important shrine, the Maladevi Temple. To the left on the lower slopes of the hill is the 9th-century **Hindola Toran**, or Swinging Arch—the beautifully carved entrance to the temple that lies in ruins behind. Note the carving of avatars of Vishnu on the sides of the column, including the first avatar, Matsya (a fish), the second, Kurmi (a tortoise) and the third, Varaha (a boar). There are also interesting carvings amid the ruins of the temple.

The Maladevi Temple (9th century) lies beyond the crest of the hill, with superb views over the surrounding countryside. A stone ramp leads from the car park down to the temple, which is built into the side of the rock. The temple is thought to have been used by Jains, but also has Hindu and Buddhist images. Most of the best external carvings are in the crevice in the rock on the left, including an image of the god Indra with his vehicle, an elephant. Inside the shrine are carvings of Jain *tirthankars*, or saviours, including a standing monolithic statue of Sitanath, and a particularly fine seated figure in the sanctuary that is usually identified as the first *tirthankar*, Adinath, but could possibly be a representation of the Buddha.

Pathari

The village of Pathari (sometimes called Badoh Pathari, *map 6 B1*) is 30km northeast of Gyaraspur (continue on the Sagar road, and take a left turn towards Udayapur) and has scattered Jain and Hindu ruins in a picturesque setting at the foot of a hill.

Jain temples: There is a rectangular stone compound on the south side of the hill, containing a dizzying number of small Jain temples, and some superb Jain and Hindu carvings. Enter the compound through a very low door on the hill-facing side. Inside is a small pavilion in the centre, and rows of shrines built into the compound wall, with a variety of different towers and spires. A group of Hindu carvings, including a dancing Ganesha, are on a wall on the right.

Gadarmal Temple: About 600m to the south of the Jain temples, along the road that leads away from the hill, is the Gadarmal Temple (9th century), with the ruins of a ceremonial entrance avenue that has high gates guarded by stone lions. There are particularly fine carvings round the doorway of the sanctuary, and pretty images of amorous couples on the far side of the exterior wall of the sanctuary.

Dasavatar temples: Some 600m to the east of the Jain temples is a group of ruined Hindu temples known as the Dasavatar group (9th–10th century), literally the 'Ten Avatars' of Vishnu. There is a large statue of Varaha, the boar avatar of Vishnu, as well as a lot of smaller carvings, including amorous couples and erotica involving a level of athleticism unthinkable for most. On the other side of the hill, in the village of Pathari, is a tall free-standing column (869) with an unidentified statue on top, and a small Shiva temple.

Eran

The village of Eran (*map 5 A3*), with its superb monolithic image of the boar avatar of Vishnu, is just 20km north of Pathari as the crow flies. It can, however, take well over an hour to get there along the badly surfaced and indirect roads. Ask first for Mandi Bamora station, and when you reach the railway line ask for Eran. The small village is on the banks of the Bina River, while the compound containing the 5th-century statues and temple remains from the late Gupta period are 600m east of the village. This was probably a Dasavatar group, similar to the complex in Pathari.

The Boar of Eran: This is an enormous free-standing sandstone sculpture of Varaha, the third avatar of Vishnu, in his animal form. Carved into the boar's hide are tiny human figures—the hundreds who are said to have taken shelter in Varaha's bristles during a great flood. The goddess Bhu, symbolising the earth, rests on Varaha's tusk.

Other carvings in Eran: Nearby is a fine standing statue of **Vishnu with a halo**, at the back of a later temple that is now in ruins but still has some interesting carving. Just beyond that is a broken statue of **Narasimha**, the lion avatar of Vishnu. The 13m sandstone column at the centre of the complex has a fluted capital, topped by a block carved with a lion and back-to-back images of Vishnu and his vehicle Garuda, their heads separated by a wheel. Note the fine friezes at the bottom of the nearby plinth with broken columns. An enormous carving of Varaha with a human body, which was also found at Eran, is now in the museum at Sagar University (*see below*).

Udayapur

The village of Udayapur (*map 5 A3*) is 18km west of Pathari, and has one of the most important and impressive buildings of the Parmar Dynasty, the well-preserved **Udayeshwara Temple** (1080), dedicated to Shiva. It is a particularly ornate temple, though sadly many of the lower statues have been defaced. Note how the multi-faceted shape of the sanctuary both creates more surfaces for carved images and enables it to appear almost circular. The ceiling of the assembly hall is richly decorated. A large stone sculpture of Shiva's vehicle, a Nandi bull, complete with its large gold lingam, looks into the sanctuary; it was presented by a Gwalior maharaja in the 18th century.

Sagar

The town of Sagar (*map 5 B3*), 100km east of Sanchi, was built around a large lake. It has an 18th-century fort, in which British residents sought refuge during the 1857 Uprising. The **Archaeological Museum** at Sagar University has a number of important exhibits, including a large statue of Varaha, the boar avatar of Vishnu, brought here from Eran. The large, decaying **Rahatgarh Fort**, the site of a key battle in the Uprising, is close to the main road from Sanchi, 35km west of Sagar.

SOUTHWESTERN MADHYA PRADESH

Southwestern Madhya Pradesh, known historically as Malwa, has one of India's most important and beautiful historical sites, the enormous ruined medieval city of Mandu, the capital of the Malwa Sultanate. It also has some fascinating buildings from more recent times, when this area was part of the princely state of Indore, ruled by the Holkar Dynasty. The city of Indore itself is little visited by tourists, but has some interesting palaces and museums. The Holkars' old capital at Maheshwar has, arguably, India's most spectacularly located hotel, inside the old fort high up above the river, as well as a series of interesting temples. Also in the region are two important Hindu pilgrimage towns, Ujjain and Omkareshwar.

INDORE

The most populous city in Madhya Pradesh and the state's commercial capital, Indore (*map 6 A1*) was the capital of the large princely state of the same name. Indore itself is not very old, having emerged as an important city only in the early 19th century, when it replaced Maheshwar as the capital of the princely state ruled by the Holkar Dynasty. It has some interesting 19th- and 20th-century buildings, including palaces, museums, municipal buildings and memorials.

Rajwada Palace

Indore's most distinctive building is the old Rajwada Palace (1812–34) in the centre of the city. It has a towering seven-storey façade—the top half painted brown and white—which looms over Indore's main square. Note the elephant and horse brackets made out of wood that support the balcony windows. The internal courtyard now houses offices, and the only important surviving building is straight ahead, with an open seven-bayed verandah on the ground floor and the old banqueting hall above it. Note the quality of the multi-coloured stonework of the building, and the pretty carvings on the capital and on the arch keystones. The banqueting hall is normally locked, but it is possible to go up the stairs and peer in through the window. To reach the other part of the palace, leave through the main gate—turn left and left again, and enter into another courtyard, prettily rebuilt after a fire in the 1980s. It contains the Holkar family temple, with an idol of Malhari Martand, worshipped as a form of Shiva.

Royal *chattris*

These memorials (19th century) to the Holkar rulers of Indore are on the banks of the filthy Khan River, 300m east of Rajwada Palace. There are two impressive buildings: on the left is a twin memorial to two unnamed maharajas; on the right is a memorial to a maharani. Note the carvings of guards on the plinth beside the steps up to the *chattris*. The sanctuaries are usually locked, but if you push the door it should open enough for you to see the statues inside, which are dressed in clothes that are regularly changed by family retainers. There are more royal *chattris* 1.5km to the southeast—also on the banks of the river.

Central Indore

In the centre of Indore are a large number of interesting municipal buildings from the late 19th and early 20th centuries, including the **Mahatma Gandhi Hall** (1905), originally named after King Edward VII and a fine example of Indo-Saracenic architecture. It was designed by Charles Stevens—the son of Frederick Stevens, who was responsible for Mumbai's magnificent Victoria Terminus station. Also look out for the unusual **Kanch Mandir**, a 20th-century Jain temple decorated with thousands of mirrors.

Lalbagh Palace

This enormous palace (begun 1886) is set in extensive grounds, 2.5km southwest of Rajwada Palace. Most parts of the palace (*open Tues–Sun 11–5*) and grounds are open to the public. The outer gates were based on those at Buckingham Palace in London, and have very similar lantern stands on top of the gate pillars, as well as the royal crest integrated into the ironwork of the gate. The palace itself is a long rectangular building constructed in a mixture of European styles, and was used as a home by the Holkars until the 1970s. Much of the glasswork bears the monogram TRH for Tukoji Rao Holkar III, who was forced to abdicate by the British in 1926 following the unsolved murder of his former mistress's lover.

The palace interior is lavishly decorated and furnished, with lots of veined marble and gold leaf, particularly in the main assembly room at the front of the building. There are pretty stencilled paintings of peacocks and griffins on the upper walls of the long corridor, which goes past the billiard and reading rooms to the banqueting hall. Note the coronets above the lintels in the doorways around the banqueting hall entrance. Behind the banqueting hall is a large three-storeyed dance hall, with a wooden floor, two stuffed tigers and an upper-storey gallery for spectators. Then there is a series of Western-style rooms with well-maintained ceiling paintings of Greek gods in diaphanous clothing resting on clouds. Stucco and painting are the main forms of decoration. Beyond is an Indian-style dining hall in the Rajput mode, with geometrically patterned ceiling decoration and pillars. Upstairs are simple bedrooms and a tiny planetarium, which is still in use, with ten seats in front of an umbrella-like projector screen. Just outside the palace, note the white marble statues of Queen Victoria and two courtiers standing in a formal garden.

Indore Museum

This small museum (*open Tues–Sun 10–5*) next to the zoo, in the southeast of the city, has an exceptional collection of badly-labelled Hindu carvings and sculptures from the region around Indore. There are many superb relief carvings of gods, mainly from the 10th–12th centuries, recovered from the ancient fort of Hinglajgarh, close to the Rajasthan border. Look out for a very fine panel showing Shiva playing a musical instrument called a *veena*, which is still in use today; nearby is an unusual statue of the teacher Lakulisa, believed by some Hindus to be an avatar of Shiva, who is seated in the lotus position with an erect penis. There is a fine carving of the boar-god Varaha, an incarnation of Vishnu, covered in tiny seated gods. There are also old reproductions of the great Buddhist cave-paintings of Bagh, 120km away—the originals in Bagh have now faded so much that they are barely recognisable.

UJJAIN

Ujjain (*map 6 A1*) is one of the holiest of Hindu temple towns, as one of the four venues (along with Hardwar, Allahabad and Nasik) of the Kumbh Mela (*see p. 59*). But it is also, arguably, one of the least attractive of the major Hindu religious sites, and much of the town and its holy places seems very modern. The main temple is the **Mahakaleshwar**, close to the banks of the dried-up Shipri River, and contains one of the 12 *jyotirlingams* (or 'phalluses of light') of Shiva in an underground shrine. Above is the **Omkareshwar Temple**, one of Ujjain's prettier shrines, with old carved stone pillars.

On the banks of the Shipri, 1.25km to the south of the Mahakaleshwar Temple, is one of the five astronomical observatories that are each known as **Jantar Mantar** (c. 1725). They were built in the early 18th century by the maharaja of Jaipur, and this is the only one still in regular use—by Hindu astrologers. The complex's five brick-built astronomical devices are smaller than their more famous counterparts in Jaipur and Delhi (the other two were built at Varanasi and Mathura, though the latter observatory has long since disappeared).

Eight kilometres north of Ujjain, on an island in the river, linked by bridges to the mainland, is the 15th-century **Kaliadeh Mahal**, which is shaped like a tomb. It may originally have been a temple to the sun-god Surya, and the central room has been turned into a Surya shrine in modern times. Note the water garden with small pavilions and waterside rooms. The Mughal emperor Akbar is said to have stayed here.

DEWAS

This town (*map 6 A1*), 40km northeast of Indore, is the capital of two small former princely states: Dewas Senior and Dewas Junior—which became well known through the writings of the British authors E.M. Forster (who also wrote *A Passage to India*) and J.R. Ackerley. Both of them wrote entertaining descriptions of their stays with the royal family of Dewas Junior in the 1920s: the *Hill of Devi* by Forster and *Hindoo Holiday* by Ackerley. Their accounts helped shape the view that many of India's maharajas were wastrels. Dewas is now a large industrial town. The hill in the middle of the town, after which Forster named his book, has a temple that is a popular pilgrimage site.

DHAR

This small town (*map 4 D2*), 60km west of Indore, was the first capital of the Muslim Malwa Sultanate in the early 15th century, and has two fine mosques from that period. Shortly after they were built, the Malwa sultans moved their capital to Mandu. It later became the capital of a small princely state of the same name.

The **Kamal Maula Masjid** (1400), the oldest of Dhar's mosques, is in the centre of the town, near the main market, and is a disputed site. Many local Hindus refer to it as the Bhojshala, after a temple built under the Hindu Parmar Raja Bhoj in the 11th century, and say that it was an important shrine to the goddess Saraswati. Inside, it is immediately clear that large amounts of material from one or more Hindu temples were used in building the mosque. Inscriptions in Indic scripts are still visible on the wall on the left, as you enter the pretty mosque courtyard, and on the outer side of a column adjoining the very low wall near the *mihrab*, or prayer niche. Also stored in a metal cage in the left cloister are some Hindu carvings, which have not all suffered the ritual disfigurement so often the case with reused Hindu temple debris.

The **Lat ki Masjid** (1405), or Pillar Mosque, is slightly out of town, 800m south of the first mosque, and just beyond the Fish Market (Machi Bazaar). It gained its name from the large wrought-iron metal pillar, dated to the early 10th century, that lies in three pieces outside the mosque. The building itself is similar to the Kamal Maula Masjid, with less obvious use of Hindu spolia. Note the two raised platforms within the assembly hall—one of which has a separate side entrance. Go inside the main entrance porch, locked from the outside, with its handsome domed octagonal chamber.

Dhar also has an old **fort** and several other interesting buildings, including the 20th-century **Jhira Bagh Palace**—now a hotel.

MANDU

The deserted city of Mandu (*open daily dawn–dusk, map* 6 *A2*) is one of India's great historical sites, and extraordinarily rich in fascinating medieval buildings. It is set amid ravishing countryside, inside an enormous fortified hilltop, surrounded by deep ravines, and it is particularly beautiful during the monsoon. It is about 80km from Indore (via Dhar), and 35km from Maheshwar, so it is easy to visit on a day trip, though there are also now basic places to stay within Mandu.

History of Mandu

Mandu was first settled in the 6th century, and was part of the Parmar Kingdom that was conquered by the Delhi Sultanate in the early 14th century. Following the Mongol invasion of north India, Delhi lost control of its southern territories, and the Malwa governor, Dilawar Khan, set himself up as independent sultan. His son Hoshang Shah, whose great tomb is one of the highlights of this visit, moved the capital to Mandu from Dhar. Hoshang Shah's dynasty did not long survive him—his successor was poisoned, and a new dynasty took control of Malwa, under Mahmud Khilji, and his son Ghiyath ud-Din. By the early 16th century, Malwa suffered defeats at the hands of the Gujarat Sultanate and the Mughals, and the last Malwa sultan, Baz Bahadur, famous in Indian folklore for his love of the Hindu shepherdess Rupmati, was overthrown by the Mughal emperor Akbar in 1561. Mandu became a forgotten, deserted city.

Part of Mandu—the little-visited Sonagarh Citadel (to the west of the main monuments)—was refortified in the 19th century by the Marathas, and there is an old continuously occupied village within the fort, but it is only recently that Mandu has emerged as an important tourist destination. Malwa's distinctive architectural style is best seen at Mandu, with its broad entrance stairways, pointed arches, flattened domes, strong horizontal lines and its use of stones of different types and colours. Note also the dozens of baobab trees, with their bulbous trunks; they are said to have been first brought to Malwa from East Africa by medieval Muslim traders.

Orientation: You know you are close to Mandu when you pass a large number of long-forgotten tombs and outbuildings on either side of the road, which then dips down, before rising through a series of gates to the top of the enormous fortified plateau on which this glorious hillfort, thought to be India's largest, was constructed. The dozens of surviving buildings in Mandu are normally divided into four main groups.

First, on driving into the fort, comes the **Royal Enclave**, best known for the extraordinary Jahaz Mahal, or Ship Palace, down a road to the right, and the strange Hindola Mahal, or Swinging Palace, if you go straight ahead. Beyond the Royal Enclave is the **Central Group**, containing Mandu's most important religious buildings, including the Jama Masjid and the Tomb of Hoshang Shah. Then there is the less visited, but very interesting **Sagar Talao Group** (also referred to as Lal Bagh), around a lake of the same name, consisting of the ruins of smaller mosques, palaces and tombs. The final group is known as **Rewa Kund**, after the smaller rectangular lake, and here are Mandu's main buildings from the later period: Baz Bahadur's Palace and Rupamati's Pavilion. There are many buildings that fall outside these four groups, and it is possible to spend several days wandering around Mandu—and finding other ruins, largely forgotten here but which would be major tourist attractions anywhere else. Three sets of monuments: the Jahaz Mahal, the Jama Masjid and Tomb of Hoshang Shah, and Rupmati's Pavilion and Baz Bahadur's Palace each need a separate ticket.

The Royal Enclave

The main entrance to the fort is via the long, narrow Delhi Gate (1405–07), followed by the Bhangi Gate, which is thought to be from the pre-Muslim period, since it did not use arches. Passing through further gates, one reaches the plateau and the first buildings within the Royal Enclave. It is possible to head left for the Jahaz Mahal, but the Hindola Mahal is closer and straight ahead. Just before the latter are two very different step-wells, one open to the skies, the other covered over and underground. Nearby is a ruined bathhouse.

The distinctive, cathedral-like **Hindola Mahal** (1425), or Swinging Palace, got its name from its sloping sides, at a 13° angle, converging like the ropes of a swing. It is thought to have been used by Hoshang Shah as a durbar hall, or large assembly room, though some experts believe it belongs to the later Khilji period. It is shaped like a 'T', and it seems likely that the arms of the transept are a later addition. The rest of the Royal Enclave can be reached by backtracking or heading towards the Jama Masjid and turning right alongside Hoshang Shah's Tomb.

The **Jahaz Mahal**, or Ship Palace (late 15th century), is a tall, narrow and long building that stands between two large lakes. According to tradition, the palace was staffed only by women. The famously pleasure-loving ruler of Mandu, Ghiyath ud-Din Khilji, is believed to have had a harem of 15,000 women, and it is presumed that the Jahaz Mahal was his 'pleasure palace'. Note the two bathing pools within the Jahaz Mahal, and the remains of yellow and blue tiling on the exterior and interior of the building. The terrace and its small pavilions with domed and pyramidal roofs were probably used for song and dance performances. There is a small, unimpressive museum here, with worn, pre-Sultanate Hindu carvings, and some old porcelain and crockery. The buildings continue around the northern side of the western lake and include ruined palaces that create picturesque reflections in the water.

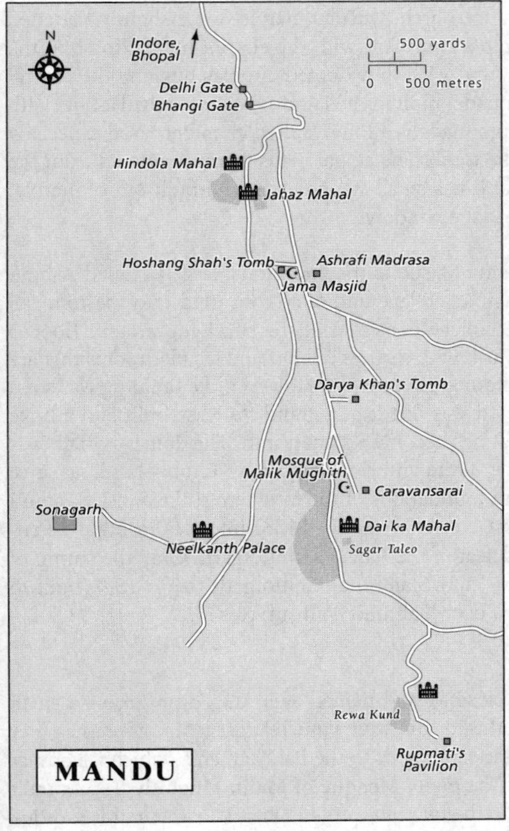

Central Group

Jama Masjid: Completed in 1454, the majestic Jama Masjid, or Friday Mosque, is on the main road opposite the Ashrafi Madrasa, and it shares its back wall with the tomb of Hoshang Shah, the founder of medieval Mandu. Construction got underway during the reign of Hoshang Shah, and the design was allegedly inspired, like several medieval Indian mosques, by the great Ummayad Mosque in Damascus. The mosque was clearly meant to impress. It was built on a 5m high arcaded plinth, with a broad staircase leading up to the main entrance porch, with its sandstone and marble doorway. Note the blue tiles on the outside and inside of the domed porch, and the use of different colours of sandstone. The large courtyard is entirely surrounded by arcades, and the main prayer hall has 11 bays. The prayer hall is five bays deep, with undecorated columns, but the main *mihrab*, or prayer niche, makes good use of blue tiling, while each of the *mihrabs*, and the *minbar* (or pulpit) uses a combination of black and white stone in a way that offsets the austerity of the rest of the mosque. There are two side entrances: one for the staff of the mosque, and one for the royal family, which leads to the raised area inside the prayer hall. Note how thick the wall is here: broad enough to allow an internal passage.

Hoshang Shah's Tomb: The western wall of the mosque forms the eastern wall of the enclosure containing Hoshang Shah's Tomb (c. 1440), which is thought to be India's first marble-clad mausoleum, and which was completed before the mosque. In conception and construction, it is probably Mandu's finest building, though it does not have the whimsical quality of the Jahaz Mahal or Rupmati's Pavilion. The tomb is now accessed from within the gated mosque compound rather than from its original entrance on the road. Note the pretty entrance porch, with its marble dome slightly flattened in the Malwa style, which leads into a courtyard with the elegant marble tomb in the centre, raised slightly on a plinth, and with four domed cupolas hugging the central large dome. On the right is a colonnade, built in the Hindu (i.e. not arched) style, with decorated pillars. Parallel to the colonnade is a long vaulted chamber, used especially in the hot months by visitors to the tomb. The actual mausoleum is entered from the south, and Hoshang Shah's cenotaph is a small stepped pyramid built out of marble. Note the fine marble tracery set into the windows.

Ashrafi Madrasa: Opposite the Jama Masjid is the enormous, largely ruined Ashrafi Madrasa (c. 1436), built as a religious college and later converted into the tomb of Mahmud Khilji (died 1469). The college consisted of the surviving ground floor, a square building set round a courtyard, with a series of halls and smaller rooms that are still visible—as are the bases of its four corner towers. However, the building was soon converted into a tomb, the courtyard was filled in, a grand staircase built and a huge domed mausoleum erected on what has become a giant plinth. The dome—which was aligned with the domes of the Jama Masjid and Hoshang Shah's Tomb—has long since collapsed, but parts of the wall and foundations of the tomb are still extant. Mahmud Khilji also converted the northwest corner tower (c. 1433) into a 50m high, seven-storey victory tower, to mark his defeat of the Rana of Chittorgarh. Only the stump of the tower survives, while the great Vijay Stambh at Chittorgarh (*see p. 189*), built to mark a previous victory by the rana over Mahmud, still survives.

Sagar Talao Group

The next group of monuments is close to, and named after, the Sagar Talao—a small water tank, 2km south of the Jama Masjid, and with a much larger reservoir on the other side of the road. Visitors will also see signboards to the Lal Bagh area, which is another name for the same part of Mandu. The pretty **Mosque of Malik Mughith** (1432), built in the early Malwa style, is similar to the two mosques in Dhar. Like them, this mosque reused carvings from Hindu temples, but, unlike them, it is built on an arcaded plinth. Malik Mughith was the father of Mahmud Khilji, the first of the Khilji rulers of Malwa. Note the fine decoration, which uses carved stone and tiles, above the ruined porch. Nearby is the large **Caravansarai** (1437), a large courtyard with vaulted halls. Two fine tombs also form part of the Sagar Talao Group, though they are referred to as palaces, or *mahals*. The **Dai ka Mahal** (literally 'the wet-nurse's palace') sits on an arcaded plinth, with a high dome and the ruins of a mosque; while the **Dai ki Chhoti Bahen ka Mahal** (literally 'the wet-nurse's younger sister's palace') also has a fine dome, but no mosque.

Rewa Kund Group

The final group of monuments, close to the small rectangular tank known as the Rewa Kund, are Baz Bahadur's Palace and Rupmati's Pavilion, both of which became important during the later period of the Malwa Sultanate. They form part of the story, much repeated by guides, of Malwa's last sultan, Baz Bahadur, and his Hindu mistress Rupmati.

BAZ BAHADUR & HIS MISTRESS RUPMATI

According to tradition, Baz Bahadur was out hunting near the Narmada River when he heard Rupmati, a shepherdess, singing. He fell in love with her beautiful voice, and she agreed to live with him in Mandu, so long as she would able to see her beloved Narmada River every day. Baz Bahadur was defeated in battle by the Mughals, and Rupmati is said to have committed suicide to avoid capture.

Baz Bahadur's Palace: Just next to the Rewa Kund is Baz Bahadur's Palace (1509), which has a large courtyard, surrounded by arcades, with a pool in its centre. There is also an octagonal pavilion that projects over the walls and has fine views over the countryside, as well as two pretty rooftop pavilions. Access to the roof is from the south side of the building. Note also the old plumbing system, which was connected to a water tower next to the Rewa Kund that has long since disappeared.

Rupmati's Pavilion: Up the winding path above the palace is the three-storey stepped building known as Rupmati's Pavilion, which was probably built as a sentry post and a water tower in the early 15th century; it was later extended. From the roof of the building, with its two small domed kiosks, there are magical views over the valley more than 350m below—and in clear weather the Narmada River, 19km away, can be seen. This is where Rupmati is said to have come each day to see the river—modern visitors can use the powerful telescope that has been installed in the courtyard. The rest of the building is less impressive, but note the huge cistern, and the long vaulted rooms that would have provided shade in the hot season.

Elsewhere at Mandu

Mandu has several dozen other monuments spread over the large plateau. Notable among them are the **Darya Khan Tomb** (1526) and the **Hathi Mahal** (or Elephant Palace) in the areas between the Sagar Talao and the Jama Masjid. Also of note are the **Lal Mahal**, or Red Palace, on the eastern side of the plateau, and the **Neelkanth Palace**, on the western side, which has now been converted into a Shiva temple.

MAHESHWAR

The picturesque town of Maheshwar (*map 6 A2*) is built on a high cliff overlooking the sacred River Narmada. It was the 18th-century capital of the Holkar rulers, who were Marathas from modern-day Maharashtra. They then moved their capital to Indore in the 19th century. Maheshwar is most closely associated with Ahilyabai Holkar, a rare female ruler of a Hindu princely state, who is still remembered for her wisdom, benevolent rule and devoutness. She became regent on the death of her father-in-law, the first maharaja (her own husband having died earlier), and ruled the Holkar dominions from 1767 to 1795. She played a major role in the revival of Hinduism in the 18th century, commissioning the building or renovation of many Hindu temples in major pilgrimage sites, including at Varanasi, Ayodhya, Ujjain and Omkareshwar.

Orientation: Maheshwar is 70km south of Indore and less than 30km southeast of Mandu, on the north bank of the Narmada River. The main visitor attractions in Maheshwar are close to the river: the fort overlooks the Narmada, and built into the steep slope beneath it, closer to the water's edge, is the memorial of Ahilyabai.

Maheshwar Fort

There is public access to the eastern part of the **Ahilyabai Fort Palace** (1766), which has a number of small buildings, including a housing estate for weavers. From this side, the fort can seem a little unimpressive, whereas the view of the fort from the riverbank is quite spectacular. On the right, a small museum is set around the courtyard, from where Ahilyabai Holkar once ruled. On the left is a small factory, where visitors can see weavers working at their looms, creating the famous Maheshwari saris with their distinctive borders—an industry originally brought to this town by Ahilyabai. The main residential part of the fort is now mainly a hotel, though Ahilyabai's descendants still live in part of the building. If you're not staying in the hotel, you will need permission to look around, particularly at the fort's spectacular views over the Narmada. Note also the small Muslim tomb on the northwest bastion of the fort, beyond the vegetable garden and the swimming pool.

Ahilyabai's *chattri* and temple

The high-walled compound containing Ahilyabai's *chattri*, or memorial, is accessed from the fort or the river banks, and consists of two large courtyards. The outer courtyard contains a domed memorial to a Holkar prince, Vithoji Holkar (died 1801), who was executed by being trampled to death by elephants on the orders of the paramount Maratha ruler, the Peshwa. Note the high-watermark plaques in the stone floor marking the great floods of the 20th century. The main courtyard contains the Ahilyabai memorial—the Ahilyeshwar Shiva temple, with a small statue of Ahilyabai clothed in a sari and with a Shiva lingam in front of her. The carvings of two figures holding hands are thought to be Radha and Krishna, on the upper part of the pillars. The large pineapple-shaped stone objects in the courtyards are used as lampholders, and on important occasions 180 lights are placed on each of them. Some of the carvings depict French soldiers who fought alongside the Holkars against the British.

Maheshwar *ghats*: Beneath the fort and the memorials are some of the prettiest *ghats* in India. The stone steps lead down to the river, and are used for bathing, the washing of clothes and ritual purification. There are several other interesting temples along the Narmada, particularly to the west, as well as the ancient **Baneshwar Temple** (5th century) on a small island in the middle of the river. Boats can be hired to take visitors to the temple and the opposite bank of the Narmada.

OMKARESHWAR

This pretty temple town (*map 6 A2*) on the banks of the Narmada is 60km east of Maheshwar and an easy half-day trip from there. The main temples are an island in the middle of the river, supposedly shaped like the Hindu holy word 'Om', giving the town its name ('omkar' means to make the sound 'Om', and 'eshwar' means god). The island, with its two hills, is approached from the mainland by one of two footbridges or by ferry. Note the strange modern building shaped like a ship on the western side of the first bridge. The most popular shrine, the **Omkar Mandata Temple,** is dedicated to Shiva, and contains one of the 12 *jyotirlingams*. It has some older carved columns, but most of the temple is modern. Further up the hill is an interesting old palace.

The most important of the Omkareshwar shrines is the very attractive half-ruined **Siddnath Temple**, high up on a hill on the east side of the island, from where there are superb views over the Narmada dam to the new lake, beneath which several villages have been controversially submerged. Note the very fine frieze of large elephants, carved almost in the round, which rings the plinth of the temple. The temple itself, dedicated to Shiva, has finely carved door frames, and, unusually for a Hindu shrine, the building has four doors. There is a huge amount of finely carved masonry around the ruins of the building, including a very pretty relief carving of an amorous couple.

BURHANPUR

Burhanpur (*map 6 A2*) was once an important Mughal city, 116km south of Maheshwar and best known as the place where Mumtaz Mahal, buried in the Taj Mahal, died in 1629. It is sometimes visited en route from Maheshwar to the painted caves of Ajanta, 100km further south in Maharashtra. The old **Mughal Fort**, or **Badshahi Qila**, is on the western bank of the River Tapti, while on the eastern side of the river in Zainabad is Mumtaz Mahal's first tomb, known as the **Ahukhana** and part of a Mughal pleasure garden. The fine 15-bayed **Jama Masjid** (1588) in the centre of Burhanpur predates the Mughal conquest of the area in 1596. The great **Asirgarh Hill-Fort**, 20km north of Burhanpur, is one of India's oldest and most well-defended. It was the scene of one of Akbar's most important victories in 1600, when he overthrew the ruler of this region, known as Khandesh. Asirgarh was later much fought over between the British and the Marathas.

NORTHERN MADHYA PRADESH

The northern part of Madhya Pradesh has a long, twisting border that almost surrounds areas of the neighbouring states of Uttar Pradesh and Rajasthan. For this reason, some destinations—Jhansi, Deogarh, Kalinjar, Samthar (all UP) and Dholpur (Rajasthan)—that are actually in those states are included in the Madhya Pradesh part of the guide. Much of northern Madhya Pradesh is hilly and arid, with the ravines of the

Chambal River and its tributaries providing the most distinctive geographical feature of the area. The west was dominated by Gwalior state, and is flatter and more fertile, while to the east, the area known as Bundelkhand has lots of smaller principalities, and many of the palaces and forts in these have survived.

GWALIOR

The former princely state of Gwalior (*map 5 A2*), with its capital city of the same name, was ruled from the early 18th century until Indian Independence by the Scindia Dynasty. Gwalior was one of the most important states during the British period, and the Scindia family has continued to play a larger role in modern-day Indian politics than any other royal dynasty. Modern Gwalior is built around and below the hill-fort that dominates the city and the surrounding countryside. The fort itself, on a long narrow plateau, dates back more than a millennium, and has some very fine Jain rock carvings, deserted palaces and unusual temples—as well as housing a well-known educational institution, the Scindia School. Below, on the plains, are a number of important palaces and tombs from the last four centuries, all of which help to make Gwalior a fascinating and under-visited city.

History: Gwalior is said to have been named after a 6th-century hermit, Gwalipa, who cured the region's ruler of leprosy. The hill appears to have been first fortified by the rulers from the Gurjara Pratihara Dynasty, probably in the 9th century. In the early 11th century, the forces of Mahmud of Ghazni—so successful elsewhere—were unable to capture the fort, but later Muslim invaders, under Sultan Iltutmish of Delhi, conquered Gwalior in 1232, and it remained under the control of the Delhi Sultanate until the end of the 14th century.

Tomar period: In 1398, with the Sultanate in chaos following the invasion of Timur, a new dynasty, the Tomars, established itself in Gwalior. The Tomars commissioned the superb Jain carvings that are found on either side of the path up to the western side of the fort. During this period, the Man Mandir palace was built, and Gwalior emerged as a major centre of Indian classical music—which it remains to this day. Gwalior was taken by the Lodi sultans in the early 16th century, before passing into Mughal hands. The first Mughal emperor Babur described Gwalior as, 'the pearl among the fortresses of Hind'. His successors used Gwalior as a prison, often jailing members of their own imperial family within the fortress.

Rise of the Scindias: As the Mughal Empire began falling apart in the 18th century, the Scindias—one of the powerful Maratha families from modern-day Maharashtra—emerged as a major regional power, capturing Gwalior in 1765 from their base more than 400km to the southwest in the city of Ujjain. Gwalior became the Scindias' capital in 1810, and a new city, known as Lashkar, was built at the southern foot of the hill-fort. Under the British, the semi-independent kingdom of Gwalior amassed great wealth and flourished as a regional centre. It was one of just five princely states granted a 21-gun salute (the others were Kashmir, Hyderabad, Baroda and Mysore).

At Independence, Gwalior was first merged into the state of Madhya Bharat, of which it became the winter capital—with Indore as the summer capital. In 1956, both of the former Maratha states were superseded, when Bhopal was made the capital of the much larger state of Madhya Pradesh.

Gwalior Fort

Orientation: There are two main ways of accessing the hill-fort, which runs north to south for 2.5km and is very narrow—less than 150m in places. Most visitors drive up from the west side of modern Gwalior, along a road that takes them past the best of the rock carvings and reaches the plateau through the Urvahi Gate. However, the more impressive old ceremonial route up to the summit is from the northeast, taking walkers past a palace that is now a museum, as well as some less impressive rock carvings, and several gateways. You could drive up, and then walk down—getting the driver of your vehicle to meet you at the bottom—or catch an auto-rickshaw to your next destination.

The road route into the fort takes visitors to a junction at the top of the steep hill. On the right is the road leading to the Teli Mandir and to the Scindia School (*visitors not normally allowed*), straight ahead and to the right is the Sikh temple, straight ahead and to the left are the Saas Bahu temples, while a left turn leads to the main palace complex. The ticket office is in the palace complex (*open dawn–dusk*), so it makes sense to start from there, and tickets are needed for the Man Mandir Palace, the Sas-Bahu temples and the Teli ka Mandir—the same ticket can be used for all three locations.

Rock carvings: The western rock carvings (6th–15th centuries) are found at various points on either side of the pretty road that leads up to Gwalior Fort. Most of them are colossal statues of Jain *tirthankars* (literally 'ford-makers' but translated as 'saviours' or 'prophets'), sculpted out of the rockface, but almost in the round. Some of these statues were damaged—defaced and castrated—in the Mughal period, but most of them are in good condition. Most statues of the *tirthankars* can be distinguished from each other only by the carving of an animal or symbol cut into the plinth, and in Gwalior the first *tirthankar*, Adinath, symbolised by a bull, is the most common subject. These statues mainly date from the 15th-century Tomar period of rule in Gwalior, but there is one carving of a seated couple that is thought to date back to the 6th century.

Man Mandir Palace: The palace (1486–1516, with major restorations in the 1890s), built by Raja Man Singh Tomar and also known as the Man Singh Palace, is perhaps the most impressive surviving pre-Mughal palace in India—and was used by the Mughals as a prison. Its richly decorated and colourful façade is an image that has been used repeatedly on tourist literature, and yet it still appears magically fresh on repeated visits. The southern wall, which most visitors see first, is particularly impressively decorated; its turquoise, yellow and green tiling is so bright that it is scarcely credible it was built

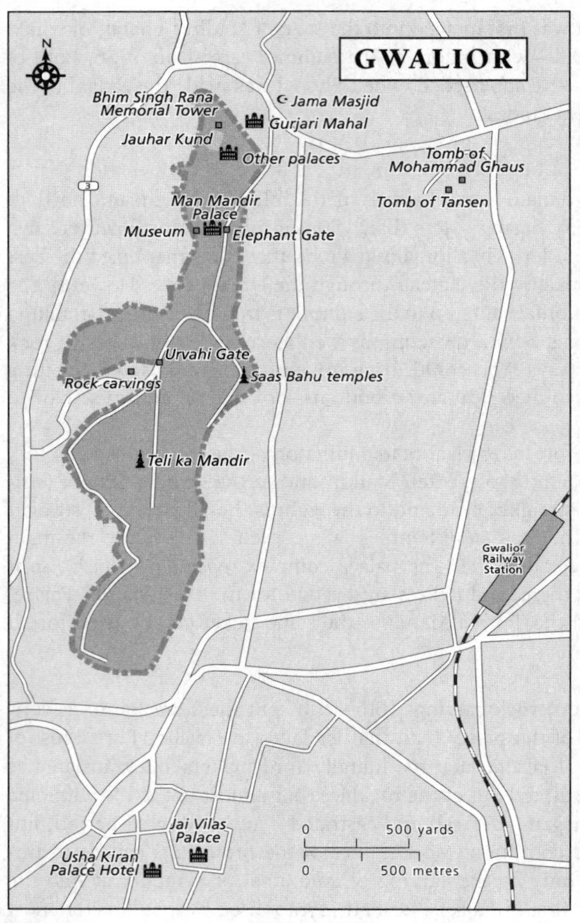

500 years ago. Note the frieze of yellow geese two-thirds of the way up the building, and the elephants on either side of the rooftop parapets. The magnificent 30m-high eastern wall—best viewed from the area overlooking the large Hathi (or Elephant) Gate that leads to the pathway down to Gwalior—is built on top of an almost sheer rock face, and has five large round towers with lots of smaller parapets and cupolas. Inside the palace are two pretty courtyards with verandahs and screened galleries at an upper level. There is a complex system of staircases leading down to the underground rooms, and it is advisable to bring a torch. There are two large 16-sided rooms, one on top of the other. In these rooms, the Mughal emperor Jehangir imprisoned the sixth Sikh guru, Hargobind Singh, and his grandson Aurangzeb imprisoned several of his own relatives in the 17th century, including one of his brothers, Murad Baksh, and his son Muhammad Sultan. Murad was eventually executed here.

North of the palace: Just north of the main palace building is a courtyard surrounded by rooms on three sides, now used as a store by the archaeology department. Beyond are several more **deserted palaces**, less interesting than Man Mandir but covering a much larger area, and providing fine views of the fort and town below. Note the secret passages that have been revealed inside the walls of the furthermost palace. These palaces have a number of different names used by guides and historians; they were built in the 15th and 16th centuries, under the Tomars, and later altered and added to by the Mughals, who also built their own smaller palaces. Near the far end of the fortress is the handsome *chattri*, or memorial tower, of Bhim Singh Rana, who briefly conquered Gwalior in the 1760s. The large square tank is known as **Jauhar Kund**, and is thought to be where the women of the fortress committed *jauhar*, or mass self-immolation, when the forces of the Delhi Sultanate conquered Gwalior in the 13th century.

Archaeological Museum: Opposite the Man Mandir Palace is the Archaeological Museum (*open daily 10–5*), which has some very fine pieces of sculpture from the Gurjara Pratihara period (c. 700–1000). In the cabinet at the end of the first room is a panel with a magnificent carving in deep relief that depicts a woman lying on her side with a child holding her breast ready to suckle, while she has her feet massaged. Note also, in the back room, a 10th-century panel showing an erotic scene that is well-worn but leaves nothing to the imagination, and, in the front verandah, a charming 18th-century statue of a maharaja, seated sideways on a bench and holding a sword.

Head south from the Man Mandir Palace for the fort's main temples: the Teli ka Mandir on the western side, and the Saas Bahu shrines on the east. You'll need to show your ticket at both places.

Teli ka Mandir: The heavily restored Teli ka Mandir (8th century), literally 'oilman's temple', is a unique architectural hybrid, combining key elements from north and south Indian temple traditions. Its tower resembles a south Indian *gopura*—a temple gateway with a series of tapering layers, with the emphasis on horizontal rather than vertical lines. It is possible that its original name was not Teli but Telangana, a word once used to describe southern Inda, but now more accurately used to refer to northern parts of the state of Andhra Pradesh. This temple's vaulted roof is also a peculiarity, with its arched ends, a shape more frequently seen in early Buddhist architecture. Notice also the very early repeated use of the horseshoe-shaped *gavaksha* motif, commonplace in later north Indian temples, and the lack of a pillared assembly hall.

Saas Bahu temples: With their open pillared assembly halls, the Saas Bahu temples (1093) are of a very different design to the Teli ka Mandir. '*Saas*' means mother-in-law and refers to the larger temple; '*bahu*' means daughter-in-law and refers to the smaller shrine next to the fort walls. The Saas Temple has been heavily restored, and both temples have lost their original sanctuaries.

Also within the walls of the fort is a modern **Sikh temple**, or *gurudwara*, built to commemorate Guru Hargobind Singh's imprisonment in the fort by Emperor Jehangir. Beyond it is the modern Scindia School. The northeastern **Hathi Gate**, with a fine tiled ceiling, leads to the old ceremonial stone path running down the hill towards the oldest parts of modern Gwalior, past a number of Jain rock carvings (many of them badly damaged) and the small 9th-century **Chaturbhuja Temple**, dedicated to Vishnu.

Gurjari Mahal

Near the bottom of the path leading down from the fort is a **museum** (*open Tues–Sun 10–5*) housed within the attractive two-storey palace known as the Gurjari Mahal (c. 1510). Raja Man Singh is thought to have built the Gurjari Mahal for his wife Mrignayani Gurjari at the foot of hill on which his own palace stood. The museum has some superb Hindu and Jain sculptures and panels, including two huge lions guarding the exterior gate. Its most famous exhibit is a much-reproduced statue of an almost naked woman, known as the *Salabhanjika*, which gets repeatedly referred to in tourist literature as India's *Venus de Milo*—the statues do have a certain armless, twisting similarity.

Mughal Gwalior

In the area of the town below the Gurjari Mahal is what is left of Mughal Gwalior. The city's **Jama Masjid** is a small, pretty Mughal mosque built out of red and white sandstone, and with tall, cylindrical minarets. Note how each paving stone inside the mosque is carved to form an individual prayer space. About 1km further east, set in pretty gardens, is the very fine 16th-century sandstone **tomb of Muhammad Ghaus**, a Muslim saint. It has some superb stone latticework, and remains a very popular shrine. Close by is the **tomb of Tansen** (late 16th century), by reputation north India's greatest ever Classical musician and singer, and founder of the Gwalior *gharana*, or school of music. Note the nearby tamarind tree, from which would-be singers pluck a leaf in the belief that chewing it will give them the vocal skills of Tansen.

Jai Vilas Palace

The 19th- and 20th-century palaces of the Scindias are to the south of the hilltop, in the area known as Lashkar—meaning military camp, which was its role before the building of what Scindias described as their new city. The Jai Vilas Palace (1874) is a large two-storeyed building, designed in the Tuscan style by Michael Filose, a British architect of Italian descent. The palace is surrounded by parkland, and encloses a large courtyard. Part of the palace is now a **museum** (*open Tues–Sun 9.30–5.30*). After entering the courtyard, turn right for the first of two areas that are open to the public. This wing of the palace contains a series of rooms with stuffed tigers, an armoury, princely regalia, palanquins and an indoor swimming pool, plus a number of other rooms with period furniture. Notice how the windows have the word 'welcome' etched into them. There is a room devoted to the life and career of Madhavrao Scindia, the only son of the last maharaja, who was a senior Indian government minister and died in a plane crash in 2001. The second area is in the central part of the palace, and contains the enormous dining rooms and durbar halls. The dining room has a silver toy train that ran on tracks along the main table, taking brandy and cigars to the guests. The enormous durbar hall is thought to have two of the heaviest chandeliers in the world, at 3.5 tonnes each. According to local tradition, the builders checked the strength of the ceiling by having ten elephants walk up a ramp and stomp about on the roof.

NORTH OF GWALIOR

The Chambal ravines

The Chambal ravines (*map 5 A2*), which one drives through on the road between Agra and Gwalior, are a maze of small valleys that have been cut deep into the soil by seasonal tributaries of the Chambal River, which runs along the border between Madhya Pradesh and Rajasthan.

THE BANDIT QUEEN

Until recently, the ravines were the home to bandits, known as *dacoits*, the most famous of whom was Phoolan Devi, the Bandit Queen. Her life story was made into a film, and Phoolan Devi later became an MP. She was shot dead at her home in Delhi in 2001. In the 19th century, the same ravines and the countryside further to the east sheltered members of the Thuggee cult: criminal gangs who robbed and murdered travellers—and gave the word 'thug' to the English language.

Morena district's Hindu temples

About 25km northeast of Gwalior in Morena district (*map 5 A2*, take the road towards Bhind and then turn left at Malanpur) are some important but little-visited Hindu temples spread over a distance of 4km. The main **Bateshwar temple complex** (c. 8th century), has more than 50 excavated shrines built under the Pratihara Dynasty, while nearby is the **Vishnu temple at Padhavali**, with some very fine carving and which was later turned into a fortress. Three kilometres to the east is the superb **Ektashwara Mahadev Temple at Mitaoli**, now dedicated to Shiva, but the unusual circular design of which suggests that it was originally a Chausath Yogini temple, dedicated to the mother goddess, like similar temples elsewhere.

Dholpur

This former princely state (*map 5 A1*) is actually in Rajasthan but is much more likely to be visited on a day trip from, or en route to, Gwalior, 60km to the south. The well-known politician and former Rajasthan chief minister Vasundhara Raje is a princess of Gwalior and married to the maharaja of Dholpur. The area is famous for its sandstone quarries, the source for the Dholpur stone used for the construction of the great buildings of New Delhi. The **Raj Niwas Palace** is on the left as one passes through the town of Dholpur—and is now a luxury hotel. Note the fine sandstone ornamentation on the exterior of this early 19th-century building, as well as the fabulous tilework in many of the rooms and passageways. Just 700m south of the palace are several interesting buildings aligned along the main road through the town: the red sandstone **Jubilee Hall Library**, built in the Indo-Saracenic style, a **16th-century tomb** which has become the town hall, and a graceful **clock tower** (1910). Visible on the left as one travels towards Gwalior are the impressive ruins of the ancient **Shergarh Fort**. To visit the fort, which has several temples inside, take the road that sweeps down into the ravine and rises up into the fort through a series of gates. The ruins of India's oldest **Mughal garden**, built by the Emperor Babur in 1527, are 3.5km west of Dholpur, near the village of Jhor.

SOUTH OF GWALIOR

Gwalior is a good base for exploring the northernmost parts of Madhya Pradesh and the surrounding states—though many visitors choose Orchha as an alternative base.

Shivpuri

This busy town (*map 5 A2*) straddling the Delhi–Mumbai highway, 100km southwest of Gwalior, is the former summer capital of the Scindias. The former palaces and Secretariat are now government buildings, but the unusual early 20th-century **royal *chattris***, in a pretty location to the east of the town, are worth visiting. They are also an unusual tribute to the devotion felt by one maharaja, Madhavrao I, for his mother Maharani Jijabai, as well as the continuing influence of the Scindia family in this part of the state. Enter the complex (*open daily 8–12 & 3–8*) from the north, next to the large **Jijabai Chattri**, which faces a pretty marble pond with four walkways that meet in the middle.

Inside the *chattri* is a seated marble statue of Jijabai, dressed in a sari. She is treated as if she is still alive: her attendants change her clothes twice a day and full meals are set before her. Each day at 3–4pm and 5–6pm, music is played by live performers in the hall of the *chattri*, which locals and tourists are welcome to attend. The only other *chattri* is to her son Madhavrao, who built the entire complex on the site of an old palace. It is built in the style of a Hindu temple and is guarded outside by Shiva's vehicle, Nandi the bull. Madhavrao's statue is also clothed and fed daily. The other Scindia family members have their *chattris* at Gwalior. Note the small Shiva lingam at the centre of the pool walkways, and the Rama and Krishna temple on either side of the pool. Beyond the pools are some pretty gardens, and an elaborate formal gate, with a *naqqar-khana*, or drum-room, above—once used to announce the arrival of visitors to the *chattri* complex. Shivpuri also has a wildlife park, with a castellated hunting lodge called **George Castle**. It was built for King George V, who was visiting Shivpuri in 1911 for a tiger shoot. However, the king changed his plans and decided not to stay the night at the castle.

Narwar

The hilltop at Narwar (*map 5 A2*), 70km southwest of Gwalior, has been fortified since the 3rd century and remains one of India's most visually impressive and romantic fortresses. It has long been deserted, and the buildings are largely derelict. Inside, however, are the ruins of many dynasties and empires, including a fine durbar hall, pavilions and, unusually, a Roman Catholic cemetery for the European mercenaries and workers employed by the Mughals and the Scindias.

Chanderi

This little-visited town (*map 5 A3*) was once a major city, the northern capital of the Malwa Sultanate during the 15th century, when one of India's greatest forts, Mandu, was the southern capital. It is not on the scale of Mandu, but Chanderi has a remarkable collection of unusual ruined buildings and a fine hill-fort, well protected by other hills and lakes. The easiest way to visit is as a long day trip from either Gwalior or Orchha, although the nearest major railway station is at Jhansi, 90km to the north. Modern Chanderi is a large, busy town that is famous in India for its traditional hand-woven saris. The ruins of the medieval city are widely spread out, with many tombs and memorials surrounded by farmland, and visitors may want to find a guide to point out some of the better-hidden ruins.

Chanderi Fort: Coming from Jhansi, visitors can first drive up the road on the left to Chanderi Fort, which was originally built in the 8th century and taken by the Delhi Sultanate in 1261. It later came under the control of the Malwa Sultanate, then the Mughals and the Marathas. The fort was held by anti-British forces during the 1857 Uprising, and was not recaptured until the following year. Most of the buildings have disappeared, but a heavily-restored palace, which was turned into a small fortified barracks in the 19th century, still stands, as do the ruins of an older mosque, thought to date from the time of Babur, the first Mughal emperor.

Jama Masjid: The Friday Mosque (c. 1450) is in the centre of Chanderi on the main road and in a walled compound. Inside is a pretty courtyard, with cloistered side walls and 11 arched bays in the assembly area, capped with three domes. It is similar in design to the main mosque in Mandu, except for the snake-like brackets, or corbels, supporting the eaves—more reminiscent of Hindu architecture.

Welcome Gate: On the other side of the road are part of the old city walls—turn left inside the walls and you will reach a tall ceremonial gate, officially called the Badal Mahal Darwaza (c. 1460) but known locally by the English name, 'Welcome Gate'. This unusual structure, 15m high, is Chanderi's best-known monument, and was presumably the gateway to a Badal Mahal, or 'Palace of the Clouds'. It is seen as a unique hybrid of Tughlaq (the sloping towers), Gujarati (the latticework) and Malwa influences. Nearby are several other medieval buildings and ruins, including a large underground building undergoing excavation, and a step-well with small pavilions called the Chakla Baoli.

Southern outskirts of Chanderi: To the south of modern Chanderi is an enormous **Jain rock carving** (c. 1300) of the first Jain *tirthankar*, or saviour, Adinath, cut into the hillside. Just beyond is the **Kati Ghat** (1430), a gate that has been cut through the hillside into the next valley through the hill—an impressive feat of engineering for the period. Further along the road leading south out of Chanderi, beyond a small **museum** (*open Sat–Thur 10–5*) and often missed by visitors, is the enormous **Kushak Mahal**, an impressive palatial structure built over four floors and in four separate blocks, connected only by bridges at roof level. This mysterious building is unlike any other in India, and it has proved hard to come up with a satisfactory explanation for why this clearly secular building should have been compartmentalised in such an unusual manner, or why it should be so far away from the other ruins of 15th-century Chanderi.

BUNDELKHAND

Bundelkhand (*map 5 A2–3/B2–3*) is the historical name of northeastern Madhya Pradesh, and is still in general use. The region stretches southeast from Gwalior, past the palaces of Datia, the magnificent former Bundelkhand capital of Orchha, as far as the temple town of Khajuraho, and the hill-forts of Ajaigarh and Kalinjar. Some parts of modern-day Uttar Pradesh, such as Jhansi, are also historically part of Bundelkhand—and are included in this part of the guide. The name Bundelkhand derives from the Bundela Rajput dynasties, which ruled over several small kingdoms in the region. These dynasties were forced to accept the suzerainty of the Mughal, Maratha and British empires, but retained a large amount of independence, nevertheless. In the British period, Jhansi was one of the key centres of the Uprising of 1857. Later the British created Bundelkhand Agency, consisting of nine royal states of which Orchha was the biggest. In 1956, the states of Bundelkhand were merged into the new state of Madhya Pradesh. The main language of the region is Bundeli, a dialect of Hindi. The countryside is hilly, with sparse vegetation, though it was once thickly forested and has several rivers that flow northwards into the Yamuna.

JHANSI

Jhansi (*map 5 A2*, pop. 500,000) is the largest city in the Bundelkhand region. It is known to all Indians as the home of Rani Lakshmi Bai, whose failed attempts to defeat the British in the 1857 Uprising turned her into a folk-hero, still venerated in a similar way to Joan of Arc in France. Jhansi is in Uttar Pradesh, but connected with the rest of that state only by a very narrow strip of land, and thus almost totally surrounded by Madhya Pradesh.

The fort at the heart of modern Jhansi was first built by the rulers of Orchha in the early 17th century, and later briefly captured by the Mughal army of Emperor Shah Jahan. In the 18th century, after a series of battles for Jhansi, the fort came under the control of the Marathas, who extended its defences and turned it into the impressively fortified building that can be visited today. A Maratha dynasty ran the state until there was no male heir to the throne, at which point the British, under what was known as the 'doctrine of lapse', annexed the kingdom. Lakshmi Bai, the wife of the last raja of Jhansi, was pensioned off.

In 1857 soldiers garrisoned in Jhansi rebelled, killing British officials and members of their families. The Rani of Jhansi took command, and for almost a full year Jhansi and its queen became the focus of the rebellion in this part of India. In June 1858, she escaped from the besieged fort on horseback, heading to the north. She fought her last battle near Gwalior, where—apparently dressed as a man, with a sword in each hand and holding the reins of her horse in her mouth—she was killed by the British. Jhansi was briefly transferred to the state of Gwalior, but then came under direct British control.

Jhansi Fort (*open dawn–dusk*) remains a fine example of 18th-century defensive military architecture, with its concentric walls built on a granite outcrop. There is a small museum inside, and a guide will point out the parapet, near the flag tower, from which the Rani of Jhansi is said to have leapt down the hillside on horseback. There is also a small **archaeological museum** on the road from the fort into Jhansi town.

SOUTH OF JHANSI

Talbehat

An attractive ruined fort on a hill overlooking a large lake, Talbehat (*map 5 A3*) is on the main highway (NH26) about 50km south of Jhansi. Like Jhansi, it is actually part of Uttar Pradesh. The 17th-century **fort** was built by Bharat Shah of Chanderi, who was from the Orchha royal family. He had been in line for the Orchha throne, but the Mughals installed another branch of the family at Orchha and gave Bharat Shah's branch Chanderi and Talbehat—which is thought to have been settled by people from the Gond tribe since at least the 7th century. Talbehat was occupied by supporters of the Uprising during 1857, and reclaimed by the British the following year. The main fort is rectangular, approximately 250m by 50m, with outer walls that extend more than 300m along the water front. Note the small isolated **bastion**, set into the lake, accessible only by boat or a narrow walled causeway. Despite its derelict state, the outer walls and the battlements of the main fort are in good condition, and many of the architectural features of the forts have survived. Particularly unusual is the complex arrangement of staircases leading down to the waterside, through a triple-arched gateway.

Deogarh

Arguably India's least visited major historical site (*map 5 A3*), the **fort** (Deogarh literally means 'fort of the gods') and its surroundings contain some of the country's most impressive Jain and Hindu sculpture—all more than 1,000 years old. Deogarh is hard to get to—at least three hours from Orchha, via Lalitpur, and on the road to nowhere—so it receives very little tourist traffic. It is in a spectacular location, on a cliff overlooking the River Betwa, and surrounded by thick jungle and partly ruined fort walls.

The **Dashavatara Temple**, dedicated to Vishnu, is one of India's oldest free-standing Hindu shrines, dating from the 6th-century Gupta period. Only the plinth and the square sanctuary survive, but there are some exceptional carved panels in the wall niches, including images of Vishnu resting on the snake Ananta, and of Vishnu riding his vehicle Garuda, and rescuing the elephant Gajendra from a king and queen who are almost fainting out of respect for the god. Note also the fine carvings around the doorway.

The **Jain temples** (9th century) within the fort area are fine examples of the Pratihara period, with tall 'curved' richly-ornamented towers. But even more interesting is the long compound wall, studded with some superb inlaid Jain images taken from old temples. Take the nearby steps down to the river for fine views and some rock-cut Jain and Hindu carvings.

ORCHHA

Orchha's riverside palaces, temples and cenotaphs are exceptional examples of 16th- and 17th-century Rajput Bundela architecture, with clear Mughal influences. Orchha (*map 5 A2*), which is still little more than a village, has become one of India's emerging tourist destinations. During the monsoon season it is one of the prettiest places in India, with the pinnacles and turrets of its magnificent decaying buildings sticking out of the lush foliage. Orchha is set in beautiful countryside, on a bend of the River Betwa, and is an easy weekend break by train from Delhi. It is also an excellent base for exploring the rest of Bundelkhand, and is just 15km southeast of Jhansi.

History: For more than two centuries Orchha was the capital of the princely state of the same name. Raja Rudra Pratap Bundela decided to move his capital from Garhkundar to Orchha in the early 16th century. He believed that by fortifying the island in the River Betwa on which Orchha's palaces now stand, he could better provide protection against invading forces than in the open hill country around Garhkundar. The walls round the island were constructed first, and, over the next 100 years, three palaces were built within these walls. The most impressive palace, the Jehangir Mahal, was built during the reign of Bir Singh Deo (1605–27), who had ousted his brother with the help of the Mughal emperor Jehangir—after whom the new palace was named. Bir Singh Deo was also responsible for the superb Lakshmi Narayan Temple which sits on the hill above Orchha, as well as for the great palace-fortress of Datia.

Bir Singh Deo's son Jhujar Singh fell out with the next Mughal emperor, Shah Jahan, and a Mughal army overran Orchha, damaging many of the buildings. In the late 17th century, stability was restored in Orchha, though the emergence of the Marathas continued to threaten the state's independence. In 1783, the capital of the state was moved to Tikamgarh, though the Bundela Dynasty continued to use the palaces of Orchha, and maintained the riverside memorials to their ancestors.

Orientation: Most visitors to Orchha approach from the eastern side, having come from either Jhansi or Khajuraho. The old stone walls of Orchha are still largely intact, and mark the boundaries of the former capital. On entering the town, one passes a few scattered memorials and temples, before reaching the fortified island citadel on the left, which is connected to the mainland by a bridge. On the island are the two main palaces, and lots of smaller buildings. To the right are the towers of the Chaturbhuj Temple, with the Lakshmi Narayan Temple high up on the hill overlooking the town. The *chattris* memorialising Orchha's rulers are a few hundred metres further along the river.

To reach the main palace complex (*open daily 8–6*), it is possible to drive across the bridge to the island, but most visitors, unless they are staying in the Sheesh Mahal, prefer to walk, as this gives the best long-distance view of the palaces. Enter the lower courtyard through the tall sandstone gateway (if the ticket office is closed, head across the courtyard and up some stairs to a second ticket office). The less ornate Raj Mahal, with its fine painted interiors is the closest large building on the right, while the spectacular Jehangir Mahal is at the back and the small Sheesh Mahal is on the left, adjoining the Jehangir Mahal.

The Raj Mahal

The Raj Mahal (1530–90), or King's Palace, is an imposing five-storey building without the large domes and tiered façade of the more recent Jehangir Mahal. The external public meeting area, or Diwan-i Am, is on the south side of the building—a large columned hall on a plinth. Note the paintings inside the vaulted ceiling. The entrance to the Raj Mahal is on the east side of the building from where one enters the first of two large courtyards. The raised area on the right would have been used for entertainment. Staircases lead to up to rooms that surround the courtyard, and down to the toilet and kitchen areas. The courtyards are separated by a two-storeyed gallery, containing some fine paintings—including an image of a king with the body of a large bird—presumably representing Garuda, Vishnu's mount. Further along the same stretch of the roof is Vishnu resting on the snake Ananta while his consort Lakshmi massages his legs.

At the far side of the second courtyard are more rooms with fine examples of Bundela painting. Note the image of an elephant (in the furthest room), which is actually a composite picture of 12 women. From this side of the Raj Mahal, there are fine views from the upper levels of the rest of Orchha. The final set of paintings is in the near right corner (northeast side) of the second courtyard, and includes an image of gods and devils pulling at either end of a giant snake, in what is known as the Samudra Manthan, or 'churning of the oceans'. Note also the brilliantly-coloured mythological Chungal bird, with the head of an elephant and the body of a lion: it has captured some small elephants, and is having its head pecked by a peacock.

Sheesh Mahal

The small Sheesh Mahal (1763), or Mirror Palace, is the most recent of the important Orchha buildings, and is on the north side of the upper courtyard, abutting the Jehangir Mahal. It is now a hotel. Note the fine tilework on the upper part of the building from where there are good views of other Orchha monuments.

Jehangir Mahal

The Jehangir Mahal (c. 1610) is architecturally the most impressive and intricate of the Orchha buildings and brings together strong Hindu and Muslim elements in a style that prefigures the Indo-Saracenic architecture of the 19th century. The building was constructed by Raja Bir Singh Deo to commemorate the visit of the Mughal emperor Jehangir to Orchha, and seems to have been used as a guest house and a place of entertainment rather than as a royal residence.

This massive square building, 67m in length and breadth, contains a single courtyard. Visitors normally enter through the small entrance closest to the Raja Mahal, thought to have been the servants' door. The original ceremonial gateway is on the

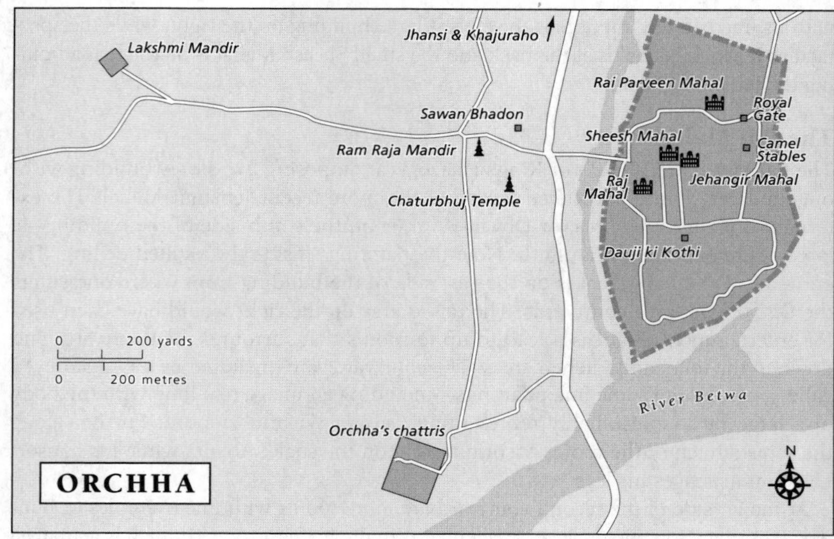

far side. Note the two tiers of balconies that surround the other three sides of the exterior.

The interior is even more impressive, with pretty water pools in the main courtyard, and an extraordinary variety of cupolas, domes, pavilions, balconies and stairways ranged around the sides of the building. Note the unusual V-shaped balcony windows on the ground floor, and the elephant and peacock brackets used to support the upper balconies. In the basement and around the courtyard are more than 200 rooms. The top storey of the palace has eight domes, in a number of different styles, with some surviving tilework. The large dome on the west side, closest to the Raja Mahal, has small statues of gods covered by cupolas. The main door is through a passageway that can be reached from the far side of the courtyard—give it a good pull; it is rarely locked. The exterior gives a superb view of the surrounding gardens and the river, as well as the Jehangir Mahal ceremonial gateway, with a finely carved entrance *torana*, or archway, and guardian elephants made of stone.

In the grounds of the palace complex are a number of other interesting buildings, including the **Rai Parveen Mahal** (late 16th century) to the left (north) of the Jehangir Mahal. The palace is named after Rai Parveen, a courtesan who was famous for her beauty. The paintings in the upper rooms are depictions of Rai Parveen in various different dance postures. Note the pretty enclosed garden next to the palace. Nearby is the **Royal Gate**, which served as the ceremonial entrance to the palace complex, and to its right are the camel stables, with high pointed arches. The **Dauji ki Kothi** (17th century), on the south side of Jehangir Mahal, close to the road, is thought to have been a nobleman's mansion.

Orchha town

The town of Orchha is dominated by the impressive spires of the **Chaturbhuj Temple** (mid-16th century). It was built on a high platform in a hybrid Hindu-Muslim style, with a central dome and a courtyard, as well as its typically Hindu curvilinear towers. Chaturbhuj means four arms, thought to be a reference to both the cross-shape of the temple and the four-armed Vishnu, to whom the shrine was originally dedicated. To the right (north) of the Chaturbhuj Temple is the heavily restored but slightly older **Ram Raja Mandir** (mid-16th century), a temple that was built as a royal palace and still looks like one. The two unusual chimney-like towers just beyond the Ram Raja Mandir are known as the **Sawan Bhadon**, after the two rainiest months in the local calendar, and are air vents for underground chambers that are closed to the public.

Orchha's *chattris*

Most of Orchha's superb royal *chattris*, or memorials, are grouped near the river to the south of the town, about 800m south of the Chaturbhuj Temple. All of them, except one, look like temples with tall spires. The exception—the memorial to Raja Bir Singh Deo—is the furthest of them, and was designed like a small palace on a plinth built into the river bank. Cross the bridge for some excellent views of the *chattris*, which are particularly picturesque during the monsoon.

Lakshmi Mandir

The distinctive Lakshmi Mandir (*open daily 9–5*), is a temple up on a hill, 1km to the west of the Chaturbhuj Mandir. Its high square walls make it look like a fort, and, most unusually, the temple is aligned diagonally, with the main entrance in the eastern corner. There is a high-domed octagonal tower over the sanctuary, and some fine paintings on its walls and vaulted roof. Some of the paintings show scenes from the *Ramayana*, while others are from the 19th century and depict British soldiers fighting against the Rani of Jhansi in the 1857 Uprising.

There are scattered *chattris*, palaces, guardhouses, wells and temples throughout the area circumscribed by the 7km walls of Orchha—a wonderful place to explore for anyone who likes visiting ruined buildings set in exceptionally beautiful countryside.

AROUND ORCHHA

Datia

Datia (*map 5 A2*) is a fascinating and little-visited town, 40km north of Orchha on the road between Gwalior and Jhansi, and it is home to one of India's most imposing 17th-century residences, the Bir Singh Palace. Datia was also the capital of a small princely state ruled by a branch of the Orchha royal family, whose descendants still occupy other nearby palaces.

The **Bir Singh Palace** (c. 1620) is an unforgettable building, more impressively intimidating and also more austere than the Jehangir Mahal, and built by the same Bundela ruler, Raja Bir Singh Deo. It is situated high on an outcrop of rock in the centre of the modern town, overlooking a lake. It was never used as a home by the royal family, and instead became a guest house and a place for music and dance performances. Like the Orchha palaces, it is an eclectic mix of Mughal and Rajput architecture—and the Datia palace was one of the few Indian buildings that the architect of British New Delhi, Edwin Lutyens, admitted to admiring.

The building is entered from the west, where the towering façade has a series of stone balconies with fine latticework. The top of the tall entrance arch is surrounded with coloured tiles and painting, and the doorway leads, rather unexpectedly, into two lower storeys, which sunlight barely reaches. On entering the main courtyard, there is the surprise of daylight in a large courtyard containing a spectacular tower-like seven-storey inner palace. Around the side of the courtyard are three levels of rooms which are joined to the palace-tower by narrow bridges. Note the pretty external tiling, in blue, turquoise and yellow, that has survived in several places. The topmost room of the tower has a very high internal dome, with paintings of different birds. Several of the other rooms are decorated, but you'll have to get the watchman to unlock them. Make sure you see the large rooms—on the east (over the gate), west and south side on the first floor of the outer palace building. The vaulted western chamber probably has the best—and least badly restored—artwork, including a picture of two elephants that appear to be floating in the branches of a tree.

There are a large number of other palaces, forts, temples and *chattris* around Datia—and it is easy to spend a day visiting this area. Some 10km to the northwest of the town is the Jain pilgrimage site of **Sonagiri** (meaning 'golden peak'). It is particularly important to the smaller Digambar sect of Jains, who believe that this was where the eighth *tirthankar*, Chandraprabha, attained salvation. There are more than 100 white temples, modern and old, spread over a hill and the nearby town.

Barua Sagar

This towering 18th-century fort (*map 5 B2*), 10km east of Orchha, is in a spectacular position overlooking a man-made lake. It played an important role in the 1857 Uprising and was used as a base by the rebel leader Tatia Tope. The defeat of Tope's army at the Battle of Betwa in April 1858 was the last major battle of the Uprising, and shortly afterwards Barua Sagar and the rebel capital of Jhansi were taken by the British. Barua Sagar was later used by the British as a rest-house and hunting lodge. Though many of the rooms in the fort have survived, parts of it have been over-restored, and some older features of this impressive fort have been plastered over.

Garhkundar

This is one of the earliest and most impressive of the Bundelkhand fortifications. It stands, almost forgotten, in desolate countryside (*map 5 B2*), 40km east of Orchha. Garhkundar (also known as Kundar) is an enormous, forbidding palace-fort, high up on a rock of black granite, with a clear view of the surrounding plains. It is thought to date back at least to the 12th century, and witnessed major battles between local Rajput rulers and the forces of the Delhi Sultanate. Garhkundar preceded Orchha as the capital of the Bundela Dynasty. Although unused for centuries, Garhkundar's basic structure, seven storeys high, is largely intact—and, for those who like going off the beaten track, it makes a fascinating half-day excursion from Orchha. Take food, water and a torch.

Samthar

This is an extraordinary 18th-century fort-palace (*map 5 B2*), surrounded by triple walls and a wide, water-filled moat. It is some 60km northeast of Orchha, across the state border in Uttar Pradesh. Samthar is still inhabited by members of the former royal family, who live in the seven-storey Italianate tower at the heart of the palace, which is not officially open to the public. However, visitors are normally welcomed—and shown around the grounds and the family's private temple, with its impressive religious and secular wall-paintings (look for the bearded gymnasts). The 19th-century tower, designed by an Italian known locally as Tonton Sahib, is one of the most unexpected buildings that one will come across in India, and is a reminder of how strong Western influences were on India's royal families. Also ask to be taken to what were the elephant stables, and, if possible, on a tour round the 1.5km-long walls—accessible, with permission, by car.

On the northern side of the road between Orchha and Samthar is the charming smaller fort of **Ammargarh**, which is also owned by the Samthar family. Although it is partly ruined, one can get excellent views of the surrounding countryside from its uppermost rooms.

Irich

Irich (or Erich, *map 5 B2*), set high on a ridge above the River Betwa, is 20km beyond Samthar—and also in Uttar Pradesh. In the Sultanate and Mughal periods, Irich was an important urban centre, but is now little more than a village. The main Friday Mosque, or **Jama Masjid** (1311), is the oldest in this part of India, and in excellent condition. Irich's once enormous city walls have mainly been swept away by floodwaters, but there are several crumbling medieval buildings in this forgotten place.

KHAJURAHO

Khajuraho (*map 5 B3*) is a remote town in eastern Bundelkhand, and its economy is almost entirely dependent on tourism. Every year many thousands of visitors fly to Khajuraho or make long overland journeys to see the superb Chandela temples, best known for their erotic carvings, but which also demonstrate an exceptional quality of stone-craft and provide an intriguing snapshot of life in 10th- to 12th-century Bundelkhand. Khajuraho is also a good base for visiting the fascinating ancient hill-forts of Ajaigarh and Kalinjar, which have their own superb rock carvings.

History: Khajuraho was ruled by the Chandela kings, who were feudatories of the Gurjara-Pratihara Empire, which controlled much of north India from Kannauj in modern-day Uttar Pradesh. The role of the town of Khajuraho in the Chandela Kingdom is not entirely clear, and no remains of secular buildings have been found. It seems most likely that it was a sacred city rather than a centre of government—which certainly at one period was at Mahoba, 50km to the north. Khajuraho and the Chandela Dynasty had fallen into decline by the 13th century, and the later temples—mainly in the southern group—are less impressive aesthetically. According to local tradition, most of the major temples were erected to commemorate military victories, though there is little other evidence to support this. It does seem likely that individual temples were associated with specific Chandela rulers. It is thought that so many of the temples escaped destruction at the hands of Muslim iconoclasts largely because Khajuraho was so remote. The 14th-century Moroccan traveller Ibn Battuta visited Khajuraho and reported that some of the temples were damaged. He described yogis with matted hair who were treated as gurus by local Muslims.

The temples were rediscovered by the British in the 19th century—accompanied by considerable moral outrage at the erotica they found there. Alexander Cunning-

KHAJURAHO'S EROTICA

The biggest mystery related to Khajuraho is why so much erotica has been carved on the temples, to which there are a number of possible answers. They have been seen simply as a reflection of less prudish times, when sex was less of a taboo subject—and so the carvings could be seen as a form of sex manual, as a companion guide to the *Kama Sutra*, or as a reflection of what was seen as a major part of normal life. Others have argued that, just as the nude became the touchstone of Western art, so the three-dimensional representation of naked or near-naked bodies became the greatest test of the skill of a medieval Indian sculptor. There is also thought to be a strong religious element to the erotica—either as a legacy of ancient fertility symbols, or as influenced by Tantric beliefs, in which skilful sexual intercourse is an element of the self-control needed for enlightenment. Note how the more geometrically-stylised and gymnastically-complex erotica are usually in the external recesses between the assembly hall and the sanctuary, which is traditionally held to be the weakest part of the temple in spiritual terms, and therefore in need of protection with powerful images. It is now most commonly argued that all of these theories may be relevant to understanding the temple erotica. There are examples—for instance along the plinth of the Lakshmana Temple—of clearly secular sexual images, including one where some observers are so shocked that they are covering their eyes, while other images are so lavishly carved that they serve as exemplars of the extraordinary artistic skills of the sculptors. For the latter images, it is more than likely that the sculptures may well have had some deeper religious symbolism, which we may never be able to decipher. It is also worth remembering that the majority of the images at Khajuraho are not erotic, but no less beautifully carved for that.

An example of the many astonishing erotic images at Khajuraho (10th–11th century).

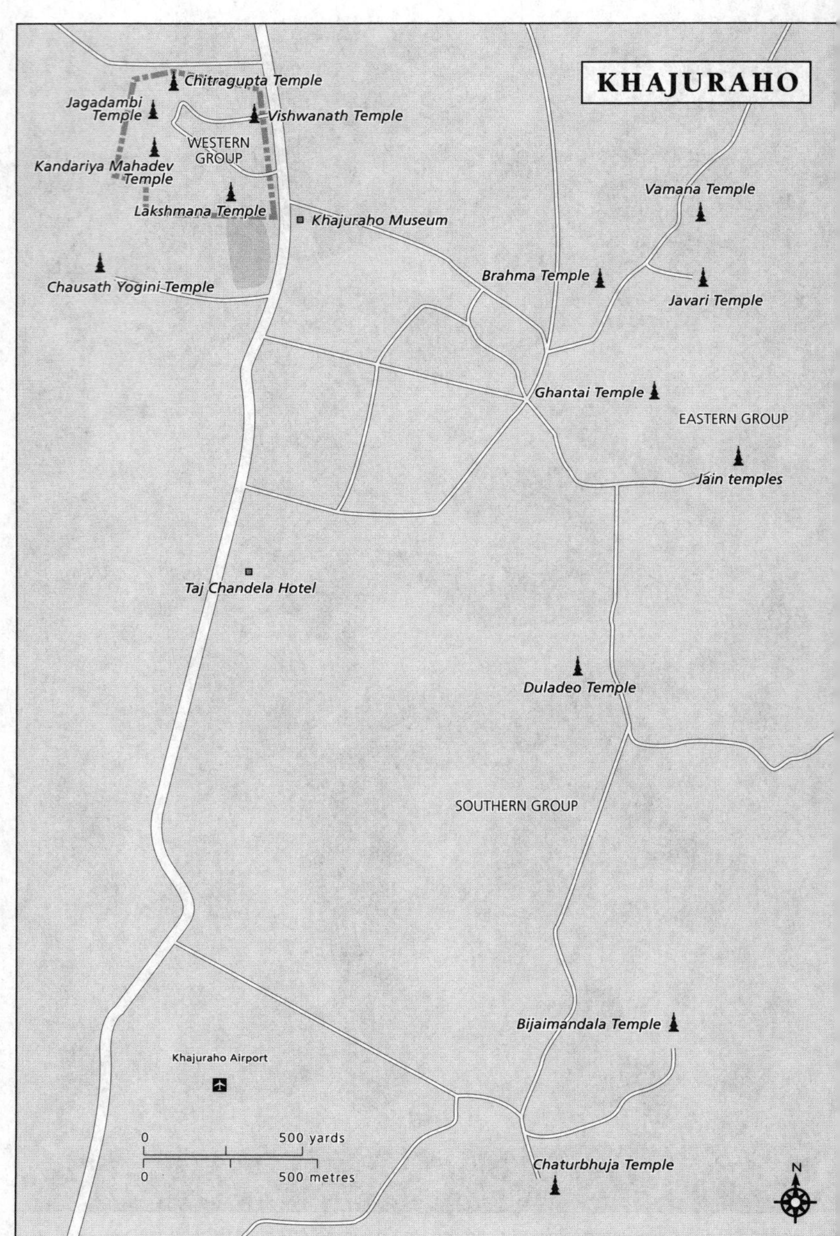
KHAJURAHO
Chitragupta Temple
Jagadambi Temple
Vishwanath Temple
WESTERN GROUP
Kandariya Mahadev Temple
Lakshmana Temple
Khajuraho Museum
Chausath Yogini Temple
Vamana Temple
Brahma Temple
Javari Temple
Ghantai Temple
EASTERN GROUP
Jain temples
Taj Chandela Hotel
Duladeo Temple
SOUTHERN GROUP
Bijaimandala Temple
Khajuraho Airport
0
500 yards
0
500 metres
Chaturbhuja Temple
N

ham, the first head of the Archaeological Survey of India, famously described them as 'disgustingly obscene', while his successor J.D.M. Beglar wrote of the 'degradation and obscene immorality' on the walls of the Khajuraho temples.

These days, guides will often attempt to embarrass their customers with frank descriptions and explanations of individual carvings. It is useful to have a guide if you do not have much time, because they can point out the most interesting carvings among the many thousands that can be seen. Their interpretations of the carvings cannot always be relied on, though.

Architecture of Khajuraho: The earliest buildings at Khajuraho were constructed out of granite, while the later, more celebrated, temples were built out of sandstone. The sandstone temples all have a roughly similar design and an east–west alignment. They are built high up on a rectangular plinth, which they sometimes share with other shrines. Each has steps leading up to an entrance porch (or *ardha-mandapa*), through which one enters the temple, followed by the assembly hall (*mandapa*) and a vestibule (*antarala*) that connects the assembly hall to the inner sanctuary (*garbha-griha*) which houses the main idol. Some of the larger temples have one or two transepts, running north–south, with balconied windows, as well as an ambulatory passage surrounding the sanctuary.

Orientation: There are three groups of temples in Khajuraho. The most important and impressive temples are known as the western group and are in the heart of the modern town of Khajuraho, just next to the main market, where many of the cheaper hotels and the archaeological museum are located. A little to the southwest, on the other side of a water tank, are the ruins of the oldest of the Khajuraho temples, the Chausath Yogini. The eastern group of temples is 1.5km to the east of the main group and includes the Jain temple complex and outlying Hindu temples close to a tank. The southern group, 3km southeast of the main temples, is the most spread out and includes the recently excavated ruins of what was probably Khajuraho's largest temple, the Bijaimandala Mandir. The more luxurious hotels are along the road from the airport to the western group of temples.

Western group of temples

The main temples (*open dawn–dusk*) of the western group are set among well-kept lawns in a large fenced compound. The ticket office is next to the entrance gate, where audio guides are available. There are six important temples in the compound and several other minor ones—this guide book describes them in clockwise order. Go straight ahead, and then left for the large Lakshmana Temple, which faces two smaller shrines to Lakshmi and Varaha.

Lakshmana Temple: This large shrine to Vishnu (930–50), is the earliest fully-developed example of a typical Khajuraho temple, complete with subsidiary temples, three transepts and an internal ambulatory passage. Though not the largest of the temples, it is many people's favourite, largely because of the range and exuberance of the carved figures on its external and internal walls.

The carvings on the side walls of the **plinth**, are—unlike almost every other temple in the town—largely intact, and have some of the best secular imagery in Khajuraho, including the most famous of the erotica, which incorporates an image of bestiality. Walk clockwise around the base of the temple to inspect these images closely, which are on the southern wall, next to the compound fence, and very close to the Shiva temple. Amid the huge variety of sexual positions on display, note the carvings of three figures apparently so shocked by what they are seeing that they have covered their eyes. The men with long beards are thought to be members of the royal family, or courtiers; and there is a kingly figure seated on a throne under a canopy, being fanned by a female attendant. The rest of the frieze, which continues around the base, shows scenes of hunting and warfare, with large numbers of finely-shaped elephants and horses, and is devoid of religious images.

On the **platform**, the emphasis becomes much less secular and more formal—and the quality of the carving, often almost in the round, is extremely fine. The erotica—largely in the recess between the external walls of the assembly hall and the sanctuary—is more acrobatic, and the images are carved to a template of complex coital positions; this is repeated in several other temples. Young, full-breasted women are shown twisting like vines, in variations of what is known the *tribhanga* position, when the upper, middle and lower sections of the body are pointing in three different directions. Note also the image of a woman pulling a thorn from her foot—a subject that is seen at other temples.

The **shrine steps** that lead up to the actual shrine are a superbly ornate series of *toranas*, or entrance gateways, as part of the outer porch, which appear to show the crocodile-like sea monsters known as *makaras* swallowing or spitting out a long line of maidens. Look back to see that the tiny Lakshmi shrine, slightly to the east on its own plinth, is in alignment with the Lakshmana Temple, and look up to see the quality and complexity of the ceiling decoration. The large stone inscription says that the temple was completed during the reign of the Chandela king Dhanga.

The assembly hall and the rest of the temple is dark, and you will need a torch—except for those parts lit up temporarily by sunlight entering through the windows of the transepts. In the sanctuary is Vishnu as Vaikuntha, with three heads: a human one in the middle, with a boar and a lion on each side.

Varaha Temple: Just to southeast of the large Lakshmana Temple be sure to visit the small open Varaha Temple (900–925), which is the oldest of the shrines within the compound. It has a superb free-standing sandstone carving of the boar Varaha, one of Vishnu's ten avatars. The finely polished Varaha is covered with a pattern of tiny gods carved in relief, and at its feet lies a penitent serpent and two disembodied feet, each carved with an anklet and thought to be the remains of a statue of a goddess.

Towards the back of the compound is the next group—three very different temples which share the same large H-shaped plinth.

Kandariya Mahadev Temple: Dating from 1025–40, this is the largest and, at 35.5m, the tallest of all the Khajuraho shrines, and is dedicated to Shiva. It has superbly elaborate carving on its external walls and entrance porch. The plinth is sparsely decorated, except where carving from other temples has been reused. On the southeast corner of the plinth is a carving of a lion-like animal, known as a *sardula*, with a human figure cowering beneath its jaws. The main spire, or *shikhara*, has 84 subsidiary spires—more than any of the other temples—and the bases of these spires cascade down the side of the building, giving it a particularly lavish and grand profile. The acrobatic erotica, particularly in the external recesses between the assembly hall and the sanctuary, are an extraordinary testament to the skills of the artisans who carved these figures. Note the deliberately asymmetrical figure of man standing on his head while engaged sexually with three women. The *torana*, or entrance gate, is very complex, with superb images of sea monsters, one of them with two women riding on its nose. Inside are further fine carvings, some of them of amorous couples. The sanctuary houses a Shiva lingam.

Next to the Kandariya Mahadev temple is the smaller, partly ruined **Shiva shrine**, which may have originally been a temple to Shiva's consort, Parvati. It also has a fine carving in the porch of a jewelled *sardula* (lion-like monster), with a woman cowering beneath it. The other large shrine on the same platform is the **Jagadambi Temple** (1000–1025), originally dedicated to Vishnu, but with Shiva's consort Parvati now installed in the sanctuary. The spire is much simpler than the Kandariya Mahadev, but the carving is of a similarly high quality. The south face has one of the few homosexual images at Khajuraho.

Chitragupta Temple: This heavily restored temple (1000–1025) sits on its own in the northwest corner of the compound, and is the only shrine in Khajuraho dedicated to Surya, the sun-god. It is of a similar design to the Jagadambi Temple, and has some carving on the northern side of the plinth. There are excellent carvings on the main temple, including an eleven-headed Vishnu (the original god as well as his ten avatars, animal and human) on the south face. Surya is almost always portrayed, as at the great Sun Temple at Konarak, riding seven horses—look carefully at the base of the statue and you can make out the horses, driven on by a whip-bearing charioteer.

Vishwanath Temple: This superb temple (1002) sits close to the eastern side of the compound, close to the road. It is similar to the Kandariya Mahadev, though with fewer spires, and both temples are dedicated to Shiva. According to the long inscription in the porch, the temple originally had two lingams, one emerald and one stone, but only the latter survives. The exterior of the temple has superb carvings of gods in the two tiers of niches that are the key feature of the lower part of each side of the building. There is also a fine panel, presumably of Shiva and Parvati, over the main entrance. Note the precariously placed carvings of elephants with unusually long trunks (and a mahout) over the rear eaves of the temple. On the north side, in the recess between two transept windows is a panel showing more acrobatic sex. Note the unusual panel in which a woman is covering her eyes in shame because of the sexual act that is taking place before her—evidence that the Chandelas did have sexual taboos. The man next to the shocked woman is enjoying himself, while in the neighbouring panel is another fine image of a woman removing a thorn from her foot.

Nandi Temple: Directly opposite the Vishwanath Temple, and sharing the same plinth, is the small open Nandi Temple, which contains a large beautifully carved statue of the bull Nandi, Shiva's vehicle. Note how the Nandi statue and the lingam in the Vishwanath Temple are in alignment. There are also finely-carved elephant and lion statues on either side of the two sets of stairs leading up to the part of the plinth occupied by the Nandi Temple.

Other temples in the complex: Also in the compound, close to the Vishwanath and Nandi plinth, is a ruined and reconstructed Parvati temple. This was almost certainly originally dedicated to Vishnu—note the figure of Vishnu over the doorway. The other nearby temple is a much more recent construction, built by the maharaja of Chhattarpur in the 19th century.

Outside the compound: There are two important temples outside the compound, both of them on the southern side. The **Matangeshwara Temple** is a large early 10th-century Shiva shrine—which is still in use and attracts many pilgrims. It is approached along a lane on the other side of the ticket office from the main entrance. The Matangeshwara Temple is in very close proximity to the Lakshmana Temple, which from a distance it closely resembles. But it is much less decorated, and without erotic carvings. Inside is an enormous Shiva lingam, more than 1m in diameter, and 2.5m high. From the platform of the temple, you can see into a locked compound containing a huge number of statues and carvings recovered from in and around Khajuraho, giving you a sense of the former scale of this temple town. About 300m southwest of the compound, on the other side of a rock-cut pool, is Khajuraho's oldest temple, the **Chausath Yogini** (c. 9th century), its name meaning '64 goddesses'. It is unlike any other shrine in the area: a rectangular building made of granite, rather than sandstone. Inside are the remains of niches that once held statues of the goddesses, none of which survives.

Khajuraho Museum: The museum (*open Sat–Thur 10–5*) is in the centre of the town and is normally visited at the same time as the western group of temples. It has some very fine sculptures, but there is little explanation and it lacks the extraordinary context and atmosphere so apparent elsewhere in Khajuraho. It does, however, remind us that despite the number of extant temples in Khajuraho, there were once many more temples—the museums' artefacts have been drawn from their ruins. Visitors enter through a carved temple doorway, guarded by lion-like figures. There are two **external side galleries**: the left one has a fine pot-bellied image of the fire-god Agni and an impassive Durga.

In the museum's **main gallery**, in the central room, is a very well-known exhibit: a large dancing Ganesha, in deep relief, with a slightly damaged mouse—the elephant god's 'vehicle'—below him. Note the larger mouse sculpture that has been placed in front of Ganesha. To the left is a gallery of Jain artefacts—note in particular the unusual figure of a Jain mother goddess carrying a baby whose hand still rests on her breast, though the baby's arm has long since disappeared. In the right gallery is a superb image of a king, bearded and impassive, making an offering to the gods, while his queen next to him is bent, and her hands pressed together in supplication. In the end room on the left is an unusual Ganesha statue of the elephant god in an embrace with Vighnesvara, as well as two chilling skeletal images of the goddess Chamunda, a particularly fearsome form of Durga. There is also a fine panel showing Vishnu's ten avatars—starting with fish and a tortoise churning the ocean (at the beginning of creation), and ending with Krishna and Kalpi (a horse), the messiah-like future incarnation of Vishnu. In the first room on the right is perhaps the most interesting carving of all—a frieze that contains what is presumably a self-portrait of a sculptor hard at work with hammer and chisel, while labourers carry a huge block of stone on a pole. None of this distracts the amorous couple at the far end of the frieze.

Eastern group of temples

This disparate group of temples is spread out over a large area to the east of the modern town, and includes a cluster of Jain shrines. Head eastwards from the museum along Khajuraho's main shopping street. On the left, note the large rock-carved figure of the monkey god Hanuman (922), housed in a modern shrine and painted a garish orange.

Brahma Temple: Beside a normally dry lake is the small Brahma Temple (c. 900), with an unusual four-headed lingam of Shiva, not Brahma, in the sanctuary. However, the god portrayed above the doorway is Vishnu, a fine carving in which he is shown riding his vehicle, the man-eagle Garuda—indicating that this was originally a Vishnu temple. It is not clear how this shrine got its current name.

Vamana Temple: A little beyond the Brahma Temple on the left is the Vamana Temple (1050–75), dedicated to the dwarf-avatar of Vishnu, Vamana. This temple has some of the finest carving in Khajuraho, including famous images of women applying makeup in front of mirrors. There is very little sexual imagery here—just one small panel high up on the left front of the building. Note the unusual headdress, almost East Asian features and broad hips of the Vamana carving in the temple's inner sanctuary; it is as if the sculptor intended the dwarf-god to look as different as possible from all the other gods.

On the right is the exquisite **Javari Temple** (1075–1100), dedicated to Vishnu, with a particularly fine *torana*, or entrance archway, several erotic carvings and a headless Vishnu in the sanctuary.

Ghantai Temple: This ruined temple is 350m southeast of the Brahma Temple on the road towards the cluster of Jain temples—and was itself probably a Jain shrine. The main features of this temple, the sanctuary of which is missing, are the very fine relief carvings in the form of hanging bells (*ghanta*) on the surviving pillars of the porch and assembly hall of the shrine.

Jain Temples: The Jain temples are in their own compound and which includes the modern Shantinath Temple, with many statues and pieces of carved stone taken from Jain shrines that no longer exist. The most interesting of the group is the **Parasnath Temple** (950–70), which clearly belongs to the Khajuraho style of sculpture and architecture, though there is none of the wilder erotica seen at the western group. Note the particularly fine image of a woman painting the sole of her foot. Although this is a Jain temple, several clearly Hindu images and gods can be seen inside and outside the shrine—which indicates the extent of the overlap between the two religions.

Only the old spire, or *shikhara*, survives of the **Adinath Temple**, which has some very pretty carving. The temple porch, though a more modern construction, also has some fine external carvings.

Southern group of temples

The southern group is the most widely spread-out of the clusters of temples at Khajuraho, and consists of just three shrines. The **Duladeo Temple** (1100–1150), dedicated to Shiva, is 700m southwest of the Jain temples, next to a small river, and is one of the most recent of the surviving temples. The carvings are profuse and include some amusingly gymnastic erotica, but they are less animated than elsewhere at Khajuraho, and this has been interpreted as indicating a decline in aesthetic creativity towards the end of the Chandela period. Another 1km further south are the ruins of what is thought to have been Khajuraho's largest shrine, the **Bijaimandala Temple**, 1m longer than the Kandariya Mahadev. This temple, dedicated to Shiva, was probably begun in the late 10th century, but was never completed and only excavated in 1999. Note the pretty elephant frieze, and the unfinished carvings on the assembly hall part of the ruins. Another 600m south, close to the airport perimeter, is the pretty **Chaturbhuja Temple** (c. 1100), dedicated to Vishnu and with unexceptional carving on the exterior. However, the large statue of Vishnu in the sanctuary is superbly carved, and is the chief reason for visiting this temple.

AROUND KHAJURAHO

There are several possible day trips from Khajuraho, including one that takes visitors to the town of Panna, and then on to the superb medieval hilltop forts of Ajaigarh and Kalinjar. The road to Panna passes close to the extraordinary 19th-century palace of Rajgarh, owned by the maharaja of Chattarpur. It is 15km from Khajuraho, and is superbly located in low, forested hills, with a very attractive series of rooftop kiosks. It is being converted into a hotel by the Oberoi group. Panna is best known in India for its diamond mines, many of them open-cast and easy to visit. There is also a national park, with the occasional tiger and the nearby Pandav waterfalls.

Panna

This town (*map 5 B3*), the former capital of the small princely state of the same name, 35km from Khajuraho, has the bizarre **Balram Temple** (1880s), a Hindu shrine supposedly built to resemble London's St Paul's Cathedral, and quite unlike any other temple in India. The main **Rajmandir Palace** (1896) was built by the same architect, and is a large, handsome building with a fine colonnaded façade—part of which is still occupied by the former royal family. In the centre of Panna is a large lake, surrounded by other royal buildings and by pretty *chattris* commemorating the former rulers of the princely state.

Ajaigarh

Ajaigarh (*map 5 B3*), 25km north of Panna, was the capital of another small princely state. The town and its palaces are nestled beneath a steep hill, on top of which is one of India's most romantic and least-visited hill-forts, with some superb rock-carvings, some very pretty half-ruined temples and great views of the surrounding countryside. The old palace at the foot of the hill is largely in ruins, but still worth a visit—note the new palace, a large white building, visible in the distance. It is a 25-minute steep walk uphill, more than 500 steps, to Ajaigarh's impressive fortifications, the 5km-long walls and bastions of which hug the edge of the triangular plateau at the summit.

History: The fort dates back to at least the 12th century, and was controlled by the same Chandela Dynasty that was responsible for Khajuraho. Ajaigarh was captured by the last Hindu ruler of Delhi, Prithiviraj Chauhan, in 1182—and then taken by the forces of the first sultan of Delhi, Qutbuddin Aibak, two decades later. There were intervening periods of independence under local dynasties, including the Gond kingdom of Rani Durgavati, but both the Mughals and the British considered Ajaigarh to be of strategic importance, and captured the fort. The last siege of Ajaigarh took place in 1809, when the British took the fort and handed it over to a local princely family.

The fort: After about 400 steps, one reaches the first of a series of gates. Note how carved stone blocks—several of which show a frieze of elephants and were presumably taken from old temple buildings—have been used as part of the fort walls. Once through the second gate, there is a large carved figure of a dancing Ganesha, the elephant-god, in bas-relief on a huge boulder that seems to have fallen from its original position. There are several smaller figures cut into the same rock. Go through the next gates and there are even more Hindu and Jain rock carvings, some exquisitely sculpted; they include an image of a resting cow and several of men on horseback. The final gate takes visitors to an open area with a few surviving buildings and a large forested plateau. It is possible to walk around the walls of the entire fort, but the temples are easiest to visit by taking the path through the forest to the two lakes. There are usually guards or archaeological department officials to point the way. Three ancient temples stand, precariously, near the southernmost lake, one of them overlooking the waters.

Eastern gateway: Ensure you go further on to Ajaigarh's second surviving entrance gateway, beyond the lakes, just below which are the best rock carvings of all. These include a man praying before a Shiva lingam, a large seated Ganesha, superb representations of a calf suckling on its mother and a woman milking a cow. There are also carved handprints marking *satis* (the immolation of widows), and superb images of terrifying female deities brandishing the heads of decapitated victims by their topknots.

Kalinjar Fort

The ancient hill-fort of Kalinjar (*map 5 B3*), just 25km northeast of Ajaigarh, has an even more important history, and was considered the mightiest fortress of medieval India. It is actually just over the state border in Uttar Pradesh, and, unlike Ajaigarh, it is possible to drive to the summit. Kalinjar also has superb rock carvings, as well as the ruins of many military, religious and secular buildings spread over a large area.

History: The fortified plateau, with its 6km-long walls, has been settled for more than 1,800 years, but its early history is most closely associated with the Chandela kings who built the Neelkanth Temple and commissioned a series of very fine rock carvings. India's first Muslim invader, Mahmud of Ghazni, made several attempts to take Kalinjar in the early 11th century, and it was briefly captured by the Delhi Sultanate in the early 13th century. One of India's most influential rulers, Sher Shah Suri, who temporarily deposed the Mughals, was killed while besieging Kalinjar in 1545, when a live shell ignited his gunpowder supplies. Sher Shah Suri's body was carried from Kalinjar to Sasaram, now in Bihar, where he was buried in a glorious lake tomb that survives to this day (*see p. 613*). In the 18th century, Kalinjar was part of the kingdom of Panna, and many of the buildings on the plateau date from that period. The fort was captured by the British in 1812, and successfully defended by a small garrison of British soldiers during the 1857 Uprising—the last time Kalinjar saw fighting.

There are two distinct parts to Kalinjar: first, the plateau with its scattered ruins, mosque, tomb, barracks and impressively evocative palaces, which date largely from the Muslim and later periods; and second, an extraordinary area between the old gateways that mark what used to be the main route up to the fort, with some superb ruins from the earlier Chandela period. The latter area has the colonnaded Neelkanth Temple, dedicated to Shiva, and with its sanctuary cut deep into the rock and containing some unusual carved lingams. All around are magnificent rock carvings, including, beyond the temple, an enormous swaggering Bhairav—the wrathful manifestation of Shiva, carrying a head in one of his many hands. Note also the garland of skulls that runs across the lower part of his body. There is also, on the near side from the temple, a superb rock-cut Shiva head, next to which is a bearded king and his queen, hands pressed together in obeisance—echoing a similarly devout royal couple on display in the Khajuraho museum.

Mahoba and Charkhari

Less extraordinary than the Panna-Ajaigarh-Kalinjar day trip from Khajuraho is an interesting journey to Mahoba and Charkhari. Prettily situated beside a series of lakes, **Mahoba** (*map 5 B2*) was the Chandela capital during part of the time when the Khajuraho temples were being built, 50km away. Little remains of the great fortifications of that period, and the most interesting Chandela monuments are the exquisite temple in the middle of one of the lakes and some lakeside pavilions. **Charkhari** (*map 5 B2*), 18km beyond Mahoba, is a small former princely state, with an impressive fort that looms over the town. There is currently no easy access to the fort, which is in use by the defence ministry, though locals are willing to guide you up the old rock-cut stairs to the top. In the town are several old gates, palaces and memorials which you can wander around freely.

EASTERN MADHYA PRADESH

JABALPUR

The main city of eastern Madhya Pradesh is Jabalpur (*map 6 C1*), seldom visited except by those travelling to the wildlife parks at Bandhavgarh and Kanha. The town, on the northern bank of the Narmada River, was the capital of the Gond Kingdom until it was conquered by the Mughals in the 16th century. The picturesque ruins of the old Gond-period Madan Mahal hill-fort are on the western side of the city, while the Rani Durgavati Museum (*open Tues–Sun 10–5*) has fine stone carving from the Gond period and the preceding Kalachuri Dynasty.

Around Jabalpur

The marble rocks on either side of the Narmada at **Bhedaghat** (*map 6 C1*), 15km west of Jabalpur, are the best-known local tourist attraction, and just above the rock is the circular **Chausath Yogini Temple** (10th century). It was originally dedicated to the goddess Durga (Chausath Yogini means '64 goddesses'), but it now has a later Shiva shrine at its centre. **Mandla**, 77km southeast of Jabalpur, has a partly ruined Gond fort situated on a bend in the Narmada.

Bandhavgarh

The wildlife park of Bandhavgarh (*map 6 C1*) was the former hunting ground of the maharajas of Rewa. It is best known for animals, but inside the park are a fine hill-fortress and an 11m-long carved figure of Vishnu asleep on the snake Anantha, which lies in the open near a forest spring, at the foot of the fort.

Rewa

The town of Rewa (*map 5 C3*), closer to Khajuraho than Jabalpur, was the capital of the former princely state of the same name and has an interesting 16th-century fort-palace overlooking the river. The unusual Gugri gate, with exuberant carvings, was brought here from a ruined Shiva temple at Gugri 19km to the east of Rewa. The large Govindgarh Palace (late 19th century), 18km south of Rewa overlooking a lake, was used as a summer retreat by the royal family.

PRACTICAL INFORMATION

GETTING THERE

• **By air:** Both Bhopal and Indore have good flight connections to the rest of the country, with regular flights from Delhi and Mumbai. Gwalior does have a little-used airport, but is best reached by train. Khajuraho, however, is well-connected by air, with at least three daily flights directly from Delhi or via Varanasi. Jabalpur also has an airport, with daily connections to Delhi, making this the easiest way of reaching the wildlife parks at Bandhavgarh and Kanha.

• **By train:** Bhopal and Gwalior are also well served by train. The 6.15am fast Shatabdi service from Delhi takes 3½hrs to Gwalior and 7½hrs to Bhopal. It is even possible to go on a long day trip to Gwalior from Delhi (the train back to Delhi leaves at 7pm). The same train service from Delhi also stops en route at Agra, and the stop after Gwalior is Jhansi (4½hrs from Delhi), which is very close to Orchha. Indore has long-distance services from Delhi (13½hrs) and Mumbai (14hrs), and there is a night train from Delhi to Khajuraho (10½hrs).

• **By road:** National Highway 3 (NH3) runs from Agra, via Gwalior, Shivpuri, Indore and on to Mumbai—and has seen major improvements in recent years. Other key roads into the state are less well-maintained, but include the important Varanasi–Khajuraho route.

GETTING AROUND

The most important rail service is the Shatabdi (*see above*) connecting Gwalior and Bhopal (3½hrs). Otherwise, lengthy road journeys are the norm. Among the main visitor routes are the roads connecting Bhopal with Indore, Orchha with Khajuraho, and some travellers also make the long road journey (approx 8hrs) from Khajuraho to the tiger reserve at Bandhavgarh. Taxis are easily available in most centres for day trips and longer journeys. Auto-rickshaws are available in the main towns. In Khajuraho, cycle-rickshaws are widely used and it is also possible to hire bicycles in the main market.

ACCOMMODATION

Madhya Pradesh has a wide selection of comfortable hotels in most parts of the state. Hotels operated by the Madhya Pradesh Tourism Department tend to be much better-run than state tourism hotels elsewhere in the country.

Southern Madhya Pradesh

• **Bhopal:** Bhopal's most luxurious hotel is the **Jehan Numa Palace** (*$$; T: 0755*

2661100; hoteljehanumapalace.com), a former 19th-century royal residence.
• **Pachmarhi:** Pachmarhi's best hotel is the heritage Rock-End Manor (*$$; T: 07578 252079; mptourism.com*).
• **Sanchi:** Sanchi has the comfortable **Gateway Retreat** (*$; T: 07482 266723; mptourism.com*), run by the state tourism department. Very light sleepers may be disturbed by the nearby railway line.

Southwestern Madhya Pradesh
• **Dhar:** In Dhar, the 20th-century **Jhira Bagh palace** is also recommended (*$$$; T: 07292 232850; jhirapalace.co.in*).
• **Indore:** Indore has several hotels aimed at business travellers, of which the most comfortable is the **Fortune Landmark** (*$$; T: 0731 2557700; fortuneparkhotels.com/hotel_indore*).
• **Maheshwar:** Maheshwar has one of India's finest heritage hotels, the **Ahilya Fort** (*$$$; T: 011 41551575 (Delhi), 07283 273 329; ahilyafort.com*) in a stunning location overlooking the Narmada River. It has excellent European and Indian food, using local produce, much of which is grown organically within the grounds of the fort.
• **Mandu:** In Mandu, the state tourism department's **Malwa Resort** (*$; T: 07292 263235; mptourism.com*) is recommended, though many visitors to Mandu prefer to stay in Maheshwar or Dhar.

Northern Madhya Pradesh
• **Gwalior:** The best hotel in Gwalior is the **Usha Kiran hotel** (*$$$; T: 0751 2444000; tajhotels.com*), which is a former Scindia palace, built in the late 19th century and now run by the Taj group. Alternatively, the **Central Park Hotel** (*$$; T: 0751 2232440; thecentralpark.net*) is recommended—and is in a central location close to the railway station.
• **Khajuraho:** Most of Khajuraho's best hotels are south of the main group of temples on the airport road. The **Taj Chandela** (*$$$; T: 07686 272 35564; tajhotels.com*) is currently the best hotel in Khajuraho, though the **Usha Bundela** (*$$; T: 07686 272386/87; ushalexushotels.com*) and the **Radisson** (*$$; T: 07686 272777; radisson.com*) also have comfortable hotels. If you prefer a more central hotel, close to the main temple, the more basic **Surya** (*$; T: 07686 274145, 274572; hotelsuryakhajuraho.com*) is recommended. Once the **Oberoi** (*oberoihotels.com*) finally opens its palace hotel, 15km away in Rajgarh, it is likely that it will become the best and most interesting hotel in the region.
• **Orchha:** In Orchha, the **Sheesh Mahal Hotel**, (*$; T: 07680 252624; E-mail: smorchha@mptourism.com*), run by the state tourism corporation, is spectacularly situated inside the palace complex. The royal suites ($$) are highly recommended, but service and food are average. The **Amar Mahal Hotel** (*$$; T: 07680 252102, 252202; Email: amarmahal@sancharnet.in*) on the southern side of Orchha, near the royal *chattris*, is a modern building constructed to look like a palace. It has good service, above-average food and a swimming pool.

Eastern Madhya Pradesh
• **Bandhavgarh:** In Bandhavgarh, a former royal guest house has been turned into the slightly run-down **Maharaja's Royal Retreat** (*$$; T: 07653 265306*).
• **Jabalpur:** Jabalpur's best hotel is the recently-modernised 19th-century

Narmada Jacksons (*$$; T: 0761 4001122; jacksons-hotel.net*).

FOOD

Because Madhya Pradesh is one of India's least homogenous states, there is no particularly distinctive cuisine that belongs to the state as a whole. Wheat-based breads rather than rice are staple foods, along with a wide variety of vegetables. The great Maratha kingdoms of Gwalior and Indore introduced Maharashtran elements into the culinary traditions of the elite, while the royal kitchens of Bhopal were well known for their non-vegetarian Nawabi Muslim cuisine. For good Nawabi cuisine try the evening street food in **Chowk Bazaar**, particularly the spicy meat stew known as *nihaari*, or slightly blander versions available at the **Jehan Numa Hotel**.

FURTHER READING & VIEWING

There are several good guidebooks, including *Discovering Madhya Pradesh* by Hugh and Colleen Gantzer, published by the state tourism department, who have also published useful short guides to Gwalior, Khajuraho, Indore, Bhopal, Sanchi and Bhimbetka in the 'Good Earth' series. *Dreaming Vishnus: A Journey through Central India* by Vikramjit Ram has an amusing account of trying to find the 'Boar of Eran' (Penguin India, 2008).

Both E.M. Forster and J.R. Ackerley, who were friends, wrote memorable books about their time as tutors of minor maharajas in the 1920s. Forster stayed at Dewas, near Indore, and wrote *The Hill of Devi*, while Ackerley stayed at Dewas and at Chhattarpur, near Khajuraho, and wrote *Hindoo Holiday* about the latter. Both books are still in print.

Animals' People by Indra Sinha, which made the Booker shortlist in 2007, contains a fictionalised account of the Bhopal gas tragedy, in which Bhopal is thinly disguised as Khaufpur, or 'city of fear'. There is also a movie set during the tragedy, called *Bhopal Express* (1999) with dialogue in English and Hindi.

CHHATTISGARH

Though a state in its own right, Chhattisgarh—to the east of Madhya Pradesh—is one of the least-visited parts of India. Large parts of the state have been affected by a Maoist insurgency, which makes it inadvisable to travel in some areas. Take local advice before going outside the capital, Raipur. Chhattisgarh—the name means '36 forts'—was formed out of the mainly tribal eastern districts of Madhya Pradesh in 2000. The heavily forested state, with several wildlife parks, has a poor visitor infrastructure, but has the potential to become an important tourist destination in years to come.

RAIPUR

The Chhattisgarh capital (*map 6 D2*) has good air connections to Delhi and Mumbai. It feels like a modern town, and a series of man-made water bodies is all that remains of a much older settlement. The **Mahant Ghasidas Memorial Museum** (*open Tues–Sun 10–5*) in Raipur, and named after a local raja who founded it in the 19th century, is near the DK Hospital, and has several interesting Buddhist bronzes from Sirpur.

OUTSIDE RAIPUR

There are important 8th-century Hindu temples, dedicated to Vishnu, at **Rajim** (*map 6 D3*) on the Mahanadi River, 40km southeast of Raipur. **Sirpur**, 70km east of Raipur, has the scattered ruins of 7th-century Hindu temples and Buddhist monasteries.

Some 100km north of Raipur, **Kawardha** (*map 6 D2*) is the capital of a former minor princely state of the same name. The 1930s **palace** has been turned into a hotel ($$; *T: 07741 232085; kawardhapalace.com*).

MUMBAI (BOMBAY)

Mumbai (*map 11 A2*, pop. 20,000,000) is the state capital of Maharashtra (*see p. 501*) and also India's financial capital—indeed, it is the most important financial centre between Frankfurt and Hong Kong. It is also a bustling, sweaty megacity, densely populated and spectacularly positioned, overlooking the Arabian Sea. Mumbai is also home to Bollywood, India's version of Hollywood, and the city contains the ostentatious residences of many of India's best-known celebrities, as well as Asia's largest slum. It is still known as Bombay to many of its older residents, even though the name was officially changed in 1995 to Mumbai—which was already used by Marathi-speakers for the city. The origins of the name of the city are disputed. Visitors are usually told that it was named after the goddess Mumba-devi, whose temple is in Bhuleswar in southern Mumbai. In the colonial period it was usually said that the name was a contraction of the Portuguese 'Bom Bahia', or 'good bay'.

HISTORY OF MUMBAI

Mumbai is built on a series of islands, the ancient outlines of which are still just traceable beneath the streets of one of the most densely populated places on earth. There were seven of these islands, all now joined by roads and bridges, and large areas of land have been reclaimed from the sea. The original inhabitants of the islands were fishing communities, belonging to the Koli tribe—and there are today small fishing villages all along the sea-coast of Mumbai (surrounded by areas of urban sprawl) known as Koliwadas, the place where the Kolis live. Sopara and Kalyan, northern suburbs of Bombay, were once—more than 2,000 years ago—major seaports. And in the 6th century, the nearby Elephanta Caves were built as a major shrine to the Hindu god Shiva.

Colonisation: The Portuguese made their claim to having founded Mumbai on the basis of the viceroy of Portuguese India, Francisco de Almeida, sailing into the deep harbour in 1508—when he declared it a 'Bom Bahia'; and the islands were ceded to Portugal by the sultan of Gujarat in 1534. Over the next 100 years the Portuguese built small settlements on the islands, including a number of churches and forts that still survive, but it was ruled from the fortified city of Bassein (Vasai) to the north. In 1661, the islands were ceded to Britain as part of the dowry of Catherine of Braganza, the daughter of the king of Portugal, when she married King Charles II. The city's second British governor, Gerald Aungier, realised the potential of Bombay, with its deep harbour, and in the 1670s he began fortifying the largest island, set up a court and built a hospital. At about this time the first Parsi and Armenian traders began to settle in the city. Its population grew rapidly, and the British East India Company moved their west Indian headquarters to the city from Surat.

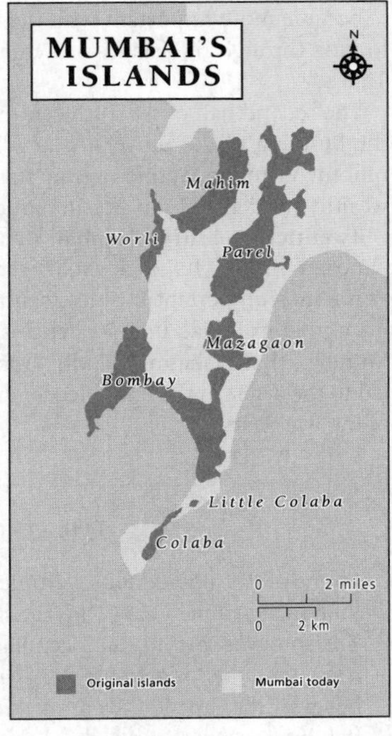

Expansion: In the 18th century, Mumbai expanded rapidly. Causeways were constructed to join some of the islands, land was reclaimed from the sea by the building of massive embankments, and the south of the city began to take on its modern shape as one landmass. Yet it remained essentially an island trading post and shipyard. It was not until the final defeat of the Marathas in the early 19th century that the city's immediate hinterland and the Deccan came under British control. The last of the original seven islands, Colaba and Little Colaba, were finally joined to the rest of the city in 1838, by the road which is still referred to as Colaba Causeway.

The northern part of modern Mumbai, home to the international airport, Bandra, Juhu Beach and the studios of Bollywood, was situated on another series of islands, the biggest of which was known as Salsette. These islands were strategically and economically important because they could provide a land route to the rest of India. The British claimed Salsette as part of Catherine of Braganza's dowry, though the Portuguese repudiated this. The latter were ultimately driven out by the Marathas, and the British did not gain control of the island until 1774. Salsette

PARSIS IN MUMBAI

The small Parsi community, Zoroastrians originally from Persia, played a major role in the early development of Mumbai. Parsis began to migrate to Mumbai from Gujarat in the 17th century. The first Tower of Silence—an enormous open-air well where Parsis leave the bodies of the dead—was built in this period, and later there would be agiaries, or fire temples, in many parts of the city. Several Parsi families came to dominate the city's economy in the 19th and early 20th centuries. The Wadia family were the main shipbuilders, while the Jeejeebhoys made a fortune from trading in cotton and opium. The Tata group, founded in the 1860s by the Parsi businessman Jamshedji Tata, remains a major world player in a wide variety of industries and services—and has specialised in buying up former British industrial giants, including British Steel, Tetley Tea, Jaguar and Land Rover.

became more important with the building of the railways in the 1850s, which had to pass through the island—though north Mumbai remained largely rural until the 1950s.

The second half of the 19th century was a period of great growth for Mumbai, with the building of the university, new docks, many municipal buildings and the magnificent Victorian Gothic railway stations. Many of the buildings were constructed by wealthy residents of the city, in particularly members of the Parsi community.

Twentieth-century Mumbai: By the early 20th century, Mumbai's population was almost a million. Its stock exchange was formed in 1875 and it had replaced Kolkata as the most important business centre in India. The city would play an important political role in India's Independence struggle, and it was from Gowalia Tank, in South Mumbai, that Mahatma Gandhi launched the 'Quit India' movement in 1942, which led to the arrest of the entire leadership of the main political party, Congress, for much of the war years.

THE DAY IT RAINED GOLD

In one of the most serious wartime incidents in India, more than 700 people were killed when a merchant ship caught fire and exploded in the city docks in 1944. The ship was carrying an incendiary combination of explosives, weapons, oil and a large number of gold ingots. The explosion was so enormous that many people believed the Japanese were invading and fled the city. The gold bars were sent flying over Mumbai, crashing through people's roofs, or landing in the streets. There are still occasional media reports of gold ingots being dredged up from Mumbai harbour.

After Independence in 1947, the city became the capital of Bombay state, which was split into Gujarat and Maharashtra in 1960, Mumbai becoming the capital of the latter. The 1970s saw a fresh influx of migrants from elsewhere in India, and the rise of the anti-migrant Shiv Sena party. Organised crime also took root in the city, and a growing nexus emerged between criminals, politicians, and the business and film worlds. In 1992 and 1993 there were major Hindu-Muslim riots in which almost 900 people, mainly Muslims, died, damaging Mumbai's reputation as a cosmopolitan and tolerant city. This was followed by a series of bomb blasts in which more than 200 people were killed. In 1995 the city was officially renamed Mumbai, the Marathi-language name for Bombay. More than 170 people were killed in terrorist attacks in 2008—among the targets was the city's best-known hotel, the Taj, overlooking the Gateway of India.

Mumbai orientation: Mumbai is one of the largest cities in the world. The city has now been effectively divided into three parts: South Mumbai is the city's historic centre with all its most important 19th-century buildings, as well as the harbour (for the ferry

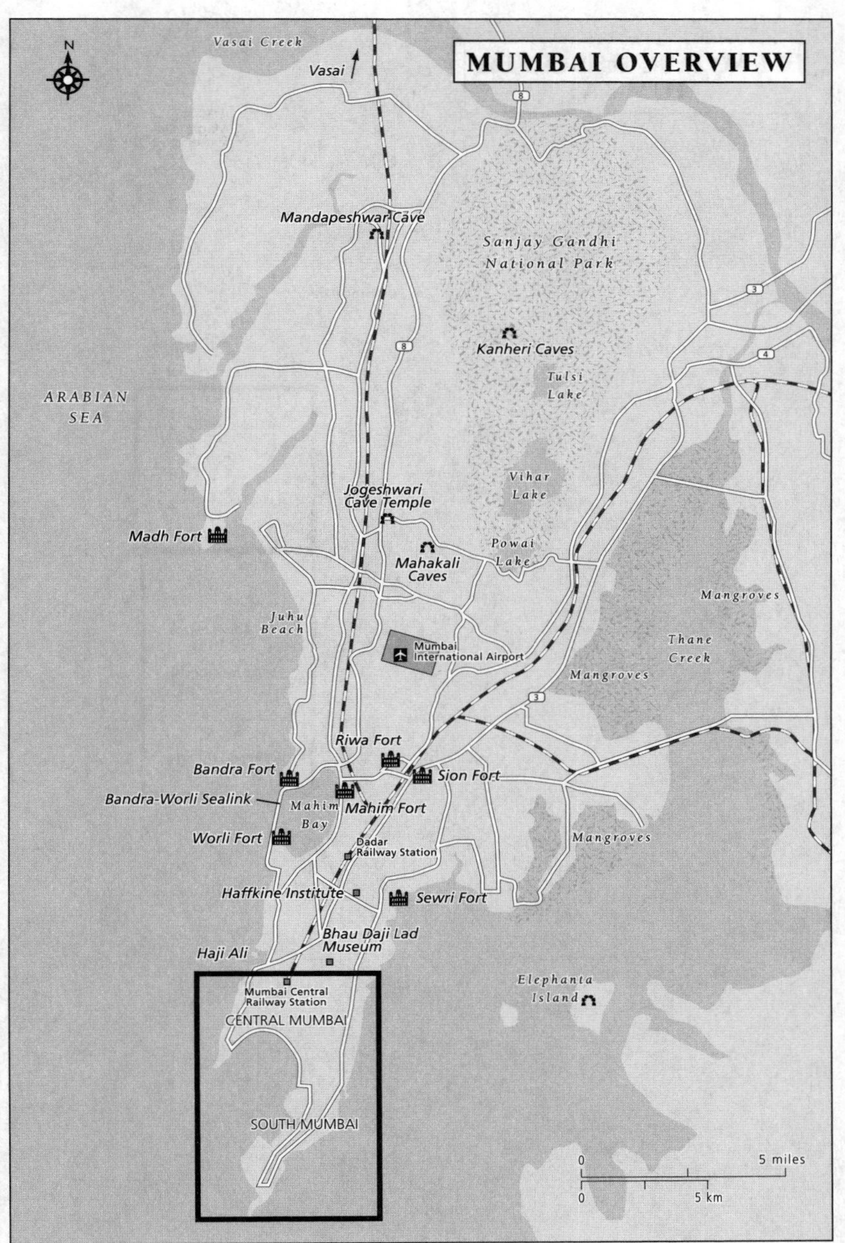

For Central and South Mumbai see next page.

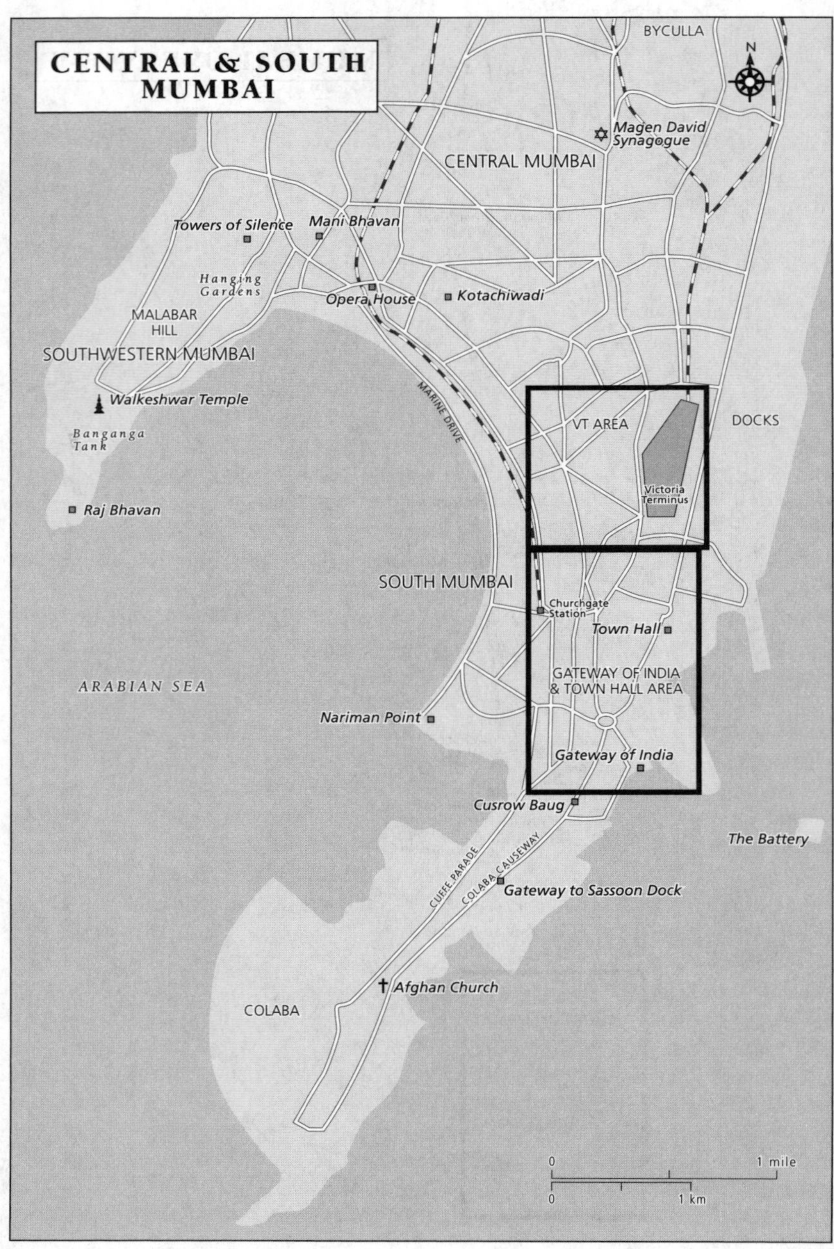

For a map of the VT area see p. 482, for the Gateway of India and Town Hall area see p. 475.

to Elephanta); North Mumbai has the best beaches, the airport and the Bollywood film studios, as well as the Kanheri Caves; Navi Mumbai (or New Bombay) is on the mainland, and is a growing commercial and industrial area, and dormitory suburb—which most travellers will only see if they are driving to Pune or into the interior of Maharashtra. The city's transport infrastructure has not kept pace with its growth, and the city has several major travel bottlenecks (also caused by Mumbai's elongated shape, surrounded by the sea) which can make driving around the city very exasperating. In peak hours, it is much quicker to use the very crowded train network for travelling between the north and south of the city. Most visitors still stay in South Mumbai, though a growing number also stay on Juhu Beach, or one of several newer hotels elsewhere in central Mumbai and the north of the city.

This part of the guide deals first with South Mumbai, starting from the southernmost point of the peninsula, Colaba, then proceeds northwards and westwards through the rest of the older parts of the city.

SOUTH MUMBAI

COLABA

Colaba and Little Colaba (also known as Old Woman's Island) were separate islands, accessible only by boat or at low tide, until 1838 when they were joined to the main island by a road that is still known as Colaba Causeway. Since then the Colaba area has been expanded through reclamation, and a second road, known as Cuffe Parade, parallel to the Causeway, was constructed on reclaimed land in 1906. The southernmost tip of Colaba is now a naval base and inaccessible to visitors, though one can see the remains of a lighthouse from the main road.

Afghan Church

There is access to the neo-Gothic Afghan Church (1858–65) with its distinctive tall, thin steeple, 60m high. It is the earliest example of the neo-Gothic architectural style in India. Officially the Anglican Church of St John the Evangelist, it was built by Henry Conybeare to commemorate the dead of the First Afghan War (1839–42), in which the British were thoroughly defeated by the Afghans. The church has a handsome, sombre interior, with Gothic arches and some fine stained glass by William Wailes. Note the many wall plaques listing the officers who died in the conflict, and the tablet declaring that the private soldiers who died were 'too many to be so recorded'. The church is still in use, and is normally open from 10am.

Heading north up Colaba Causeway, past Cusrow Baug on the left, is a 1930s Parsi housing complex, with a large arched entrance gate, and, on the right, the gateway to the **Sassoon Dock**, built in the 1870s by the Indian Jewish entrepreneur Sir Albert Sassoon, and still in use by fishing boats.

THE SASSOON FAMILY

The Sassoons were the richest and most influential members of Bombay's tiny community of Baghdadi Jews, who migrated to India in the 19th century. The head of the family, David Sassoon (b. 1792 Baghdad, d.1864 Pune), who moved to India in 1832, made a fortune from the cotton trade, and his son Sir Albert Sassoon (1818–96) invested heavily in Bombay real estate. The Sassoons were also philanthropists, building the Elphinstone schools and the Sassoon Library (*see pp. 477 and 483*), and were prominent figures in contemporary Bombay society—though David Sassoon never learned to speak English (*see also p. 73*).

NORTH FROM THE GATEWAY OF INDIA

At the northern end of Colaba is **Apollo Bunder**—an Anglicised version of an old place name meaning fish quay (the younger generation refer to the area as 'Gateway')—a large open area overlooking the bay, and which was traditionally where passengers arriving in India by ship would disembark. The **Gateway of India** (1927), Mumbai's best-known monument, is here: a large ceremonial gate built to commemorate the arrival of King George V in 1911, but not completed for another 16 years. It was through this gate that the last British military contingent left India in 1948. Originally, there were plans to build a ceremonial avenue leading up to the Gateway, but these were abandoned for economic reasons, and the gate, built in a fusion of Western and Gujarati styles, stands alone—and not aligned with the neighbouring buildings and street layout. The main structure is built out of local basalt, but the domes and galleries were constructed out of reinforced concrete.

Taj Hotel

Opposite the Gateway is another major Mumbai landmark, the impressive Taj Mahal Hotel (1904), usually referred to just as 'The Taj', and built by the Parsi industrialist Jamsetji Tata at a time when many of the best hotels were not open to Indians. It is still a luxury hotel, arguably Mumbai's best, with a superb view over the bay; it was the scene of a major terrorist attack in 2008. It is built in a busy fusion of styles, to the design of Indian and British architects, with a distinctive Italianate octagonal central dome and Moorish side domes. The high-rise **Taj Annexe** was built in 1972. Other buildings grouped around Apollo Bunder include the **Yacht Club** (1896–98), next to the new Taj, which was built as a residential annexe to the original yacht club—which is on the other side of the road overlooking the bay—a fine low-level building now occupied by the offices of the Atomic Energy Commission (1881) and not open to the public. Note the small fortified island in the bay, known as Middle Ground Coastal Battery, or **'The Battery'**, visible from the old Taj. The fortifications date back to the early period of British rule in the late 17th century, and the island is still in use as a naval base with a permanent staff of just eight sailors.

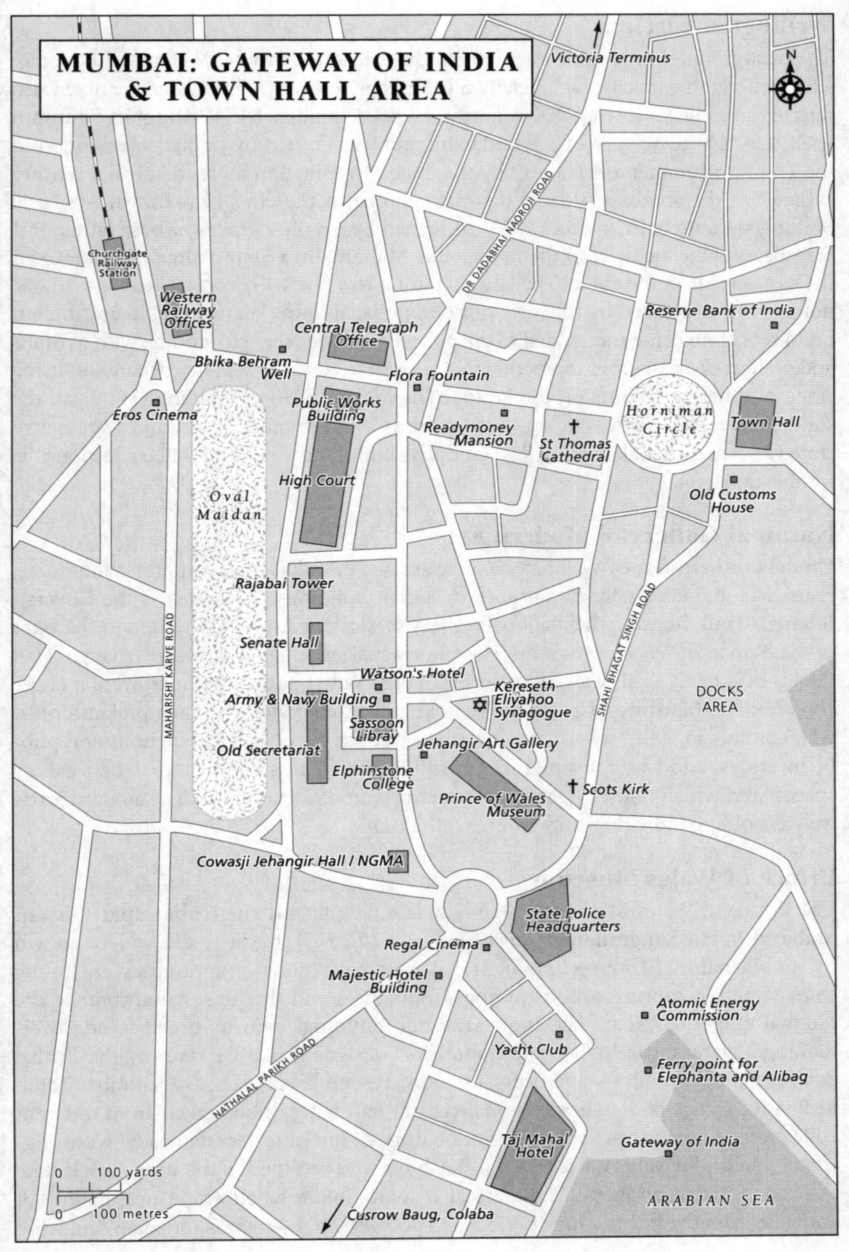
MUMBAI: GATEWAY OF INDIA
& TOWN HALL AREA
Victoria Terminus
N
Churchgate Railway Station
Western Railway Offices
DR DADABHAI NAOROJI ROAD
Reserve Bank of India
Central Telegraph Office
Bhika Behram Well
Flora Fountain
Eros Cinema
Public Works Building
Readymoney Mansion
St Thomas Cathedral
Horniman Circle
Town Hall
High Court
Oval Maidan
Old Customs House
Rajabai Tower
SHAHI BHAGAT SINGH ROAD
MAHARISHI KARVE ROAD
Senate Hall
Watson's Hotel
Kereseth Eliyahoo Synagogue
DOCKS AREA
Army & Navy Building
Sassoon Library
Jehangir Art Gallery
Old Secretariat
Elphinstone College
Scots Kirk
Prince of Wales Museum
Cowasji Jehangir Hall / NGMA
State Police Headquarters
Regal Cinema
Majestic Hotel Building
Atomic Energy Commission
Yacht Club
NATHALAL PARIKH ROAD
Ferry point for Elephanta and Alibag
Taj Mahal Hotel
Gateway of India
0 100 yards
0 100 metres
ARABIAN SEA
Cusrow Baug, Colaba

Wellington Circle

The next group of important Mumbai buildings is found around Wellington Fountain and Wellington Circle (now officially S.P. Mukherjee Chowk, but also sometimes also referred to as Regal Circle), 400m north of Apollo Bunder. The **Wellington Fountain** itself stands at the centre of a roundabout and was erected by public subscription in the 1860s to commemorate a visit by the duke of Wellington more than half a century earlier. On the southern side of the circle is one of the city's best-known Art Deco buildings, the **Regal Cinema** (1934), designed by Charles Stevens, whose father, F.W. Stevens, was the architect of the neo-Gothic **Maharashtra State Police HQ** (1876) on the eastern side of the circle. The latter building was originally constructed as a sailors' home on land donated by the maharaja of Baroda, and was later used as a government building before being transferred to the police. Note the relief of Neptune with nymphs and seahorses on the roof-top pediments, as well as some very pretty decoration using stone of different colours on the façade. The **Majestic Hotel** building (1909) on the southeastern side of the circle is now used as a government hostel and cooperative store (known as Sahakari Bhandar), and was built by the same architects responsible for the Taj Hotel.

National Gallery of Modern Art

On the northern side of Wellington Circle are two of India's most important museums, housed in architecturally significant Edwardian buildings. To the left is the **Cowasji Jehangir Hall**, housing the National Gallery of Modern Art (NGMA), and to the right is the Prince of Wales Museum. The enormous low-domed Cowasji Jehangir Hall (1911–20), or CJ Hall, was designed by George Wittet and is the fulcrum of a larger complex, the **Institute of Science**. The old hall, named after the Parsi philanthropist who commissioned it, was once used as a venue for concerts, examinations and public meetings, and was converted in the 1990s into what is one of India's best gallery spaces, and which houses an important permanent collection of Indian modern art as well as holding individual and group exhibitions.

Prince of Wales Museum

The Prince of Wales Museum (1914–22) is now officially the **Chhatrapati Shivaji Maharaj Vastu Sangrahalaya** (*open Tues–Sun 10.15–6*), but it is still widely known by its old name. It houses one of India's best collections of antiquities, including some superb sculpture, wood carvings, miniatures and the personal armour of the Mughal emperor Akbar. The Indo-Saracenic building, with its broad façade overlooking a park and a high white dome, was designed, like CJ Hall, by the British architect George Wittet—and bears a striking resemblance to the Gol Gumbaz Tomb in Bijapur (*see p. 683*). The octagonal central hall has exhibits taken from different collections—note in particular the 8th-century Akhnoor terracotta heads, with ringlets of hair and jewellery, excavated in Kashmir, and sculpted in the Indo-Greek style associated with Gandhara. There are also some fine terracotta figurines, mainly of animals, from the Indus Valley period (c. 1000 BC). To the right is the main sculpture gallery, with some superb relief panels from Aihole in Karnataka, some very fine Gandhara heads—including a 6th-century standing Shiva, found in Parel, in central Mumbai. The mezzanine houses jewellery, pottery and figurines from Indus Valley sites, including Mohenjo-daro—note the perforated clay vessels, the use of which remains unclear.

Upper floors: The **first floor** has a fine collection of miniatures, including some from the pre-Mughal period, as well as a famous painting (1620) of the Mughal emperor Jehangir distributing alms at Ajmer. There are also interesting collections of Nepalese and Tibetan art on the first floor, including some fine painted cloth from the 16th and 17th centuries. The **second floor** has the armoury, with the superb steel-and-gold personal armour of Akbar the Great, manufactured in 1581. Note the quality of the workmanship of the breastplate, which is thought to have been moulded to the shape of Akbar's torso. There is also some other fine weaponry, including a Mughal sword with a crystal hilt in the shape of a parrot. The collection of paintings by European masters includes works by Veronese, Rubens and Constable, though the authenticity of several of the attributions has been questioned. There are good examples of painting from the Bombay School of the late 19th and early 20th centuries, including a fine oil painting (1882) by Pestonji Bomanji of his daughter feeding a parrot, influenced both by the European naturalistic tradition and the murals of Ajanta. There is also India's best collection of East Asian art, donated by the Tata family and which includes some fine porcelain and jade.

The **museum extension** on the right of the main building has a good coin collection, and the small and beautifully laid-out **Karl and Meherbai Khandalawala Gallery** has some fine bronzes, including a superb 15th-century dancing Bala Krishna, the child form of Krishna, from Karnataka.

Kala Ghoda

Head around the left side of the Prince of Wales Museum to reach the area known as Kala Ghoda, or Black Horse, after an equestrian statue of King Edward VII that once stood here (it is now in the grounds of the Bhau Daji Lad Museum in Byculla—*see p. 484*). Kala Ghoda is known as the art district of Mumbai, and the **Jehangir Art Gallery** is the country's best-known commercial art gallery. Across the road from it is a row of important Victorian and Edwardian buildings. On the left is the neo-Gothic **Elphinstone College**, named after a British governor, which is one of India's oldest academic institutions; it also houses the Maharashtra state archives. This was one of a series of buildings largely funded by the Parsi philanthropist Sir Cowasji Jehangir, and a medallion bearing his image is on the front of the building. Just to the north of the college, along Esplanade Road (officially Mahatma Gandhi Marg), is the neo-Gothic **Sassoon Library** (1870), Mumbai's oldest library, built by the family of the Baghdadi Jewish merchant David Sassoon, whose image peers out of a medallion above the cusped arch of the entrance porch. Next to it is the recently restored Neoclassical **Army & Navy Building** (1900s), formerly a department store, and now housing corporate offices. The final building of this group is the crumbling **Watson's Hotel** (1867–69), the cast iron frame of which was imported from England. In 1896 this was the location for the screening of the first film ever shown in India.

Rampart Row

Rampart Row (officially Kaikhushroo Dubash Marg) marks the southern end of the old Bombay Fort, the walls of which were demolished in the 1860s. Head down the first alley on the left to the large blue Neoclassical mansion housing the **Kereseth Eliyahoo Synagogue** (1884), the finest in Mumbai. The large handsome prayer hall is on the first floor and its windows are decorated with floral stained glass. Note the Star of David motif on the cast iron brackets that support the internal balcony. A little further to the north is the old **Armenian Church of St Peter**, behind a building called, appropriately, Ararat, the mountain in historical Armenia where Noah's ark is thought to have landed. Back on Rampart Row, at the far end towards the docks and behind the Prince of Wales Museum, is the Neoclassical **Scots Kirk** (1815–18), officially **St Andrew's and St Columba's Scottish Church**, with a tall steeple erected in 1827. Note the unusual book-like memorial to a former chaplain who died of cholera in 1881—on the balcony of the assembly hall.

Around the Oval Maidan

To the west of Kala Ghoda, on a parallel street, are several institutional and government buildings overlooking a large green area known as the Oval Maidan. From Wellington Circle, head down Madame Cama Road, then left along Mayo Road (now Bhaurao Patil Marg), which runs alongside the Maidan. The large building on the right is the neo-Gothic **Old Secretariat** (1874), a four-storey structure which uses different coloured stone to great decorative effect. Note the tiled pyramid-shaped roof of the central tower.

The next block is taken up by the very impressive university complex, designed by the eminent British architect Sir George Gilbert Scott (who never visited the city) and dominated by the magnificent Rajabai Tower, one of Mumbai's best-known landmarks. The main **Senate Hall** building was completed in 1874, in the style of a French medieval church, and was financed, like so many buildings in this part of the city, by the Parsi philanthropist Sir Cowasji Jehangir. Note the fine open spiral staircases, which provide external access to the verandahs. The public are not normally allowed inside to see the fine stained glass and impressive assembly hall.

The **Rajabai Tower** was built, according to Scott's design, slightly later, and completed in 1878. The 79m-high tower, named after the mother of the main sponsor of the building, Premchand Roychand, is loosely based on the 14th-century Campanile in Florence, designed by Giotto—and its basic shape, and the narrow vertical mid-levels are quite similar. Note the two rows of statues set within niches in the walls of the tower. The lower group represents the major communities of western India. The uppermost part of the tower has an intricate lantern with further sculptures. The library has sculpted heads of Shakespeare and Homer underneath the staircase landing.

Beyond the university is **Mumbai High Court** (1871–78), the second-largest public building in the city after the Victoria Terminus. The design by Col. J.A. Fuller was based on a German castle and explains the building's fortress-like appearance. Note the statues representing Justice and Mercy on the pinnacles of the two octagonal towers on either side of the central tower. There are fine relief carvings of an extraordinary variety of flora and fauna on top of the pillars, along the cornice bands and near the windows. Outside the court is a 'mosquito-proof' well, with a stone tablet declaring it to have been constructed in 1851 by Seth Raggoondass Ramlall for the use of the public. Next to the high court is the **Public Works Building** (1872), also designed by Fuller, and on the opposite side of the road is the **Central Telegraph Office** (1874).

Turn left along the road separating the Oval Maidan from the next expanse of green, the Cross Maidan. On the north side is the **Bhika Behram Well** (1725), one of the oldest constructions in this part of the city, although the above ground structure is much more modern. It was built by a Parsi citizen, and entry remains restricted to Parsis, for whom it serves as a place of worship.

Around Churchgate Station

Beyond the well and on the far side of the Cross Maidan, near Churchgate station and the Eros Cinema, are the superb **Western Railway Offices** (1894–99) designed, like VT Station and the Police Headquarters on Wellington Circle, by F.W. Stevens. This is arguably Mumbai's most underrated Victorian building, and one of the finest pieces of Indo-Saracenic architecture in the country. Note the cluster of domed pavilions on the upper levels of the central tower, as well as the almost Byzantine appearance of the building, imparted by the use of different coloured stone and plaster on the façade. A stucco lion above the pediment of the entrance holds a shield bearing the monogram of Bombay, Baroda and Central Indian Railways. Originally, the sea reached up to the Railway Offices. The layered verticals of the central tower of the Railway Offices received an unexpected echo in the distinctive Art Deco **Eros Cinema** (1938), built on reclaimed land, like the 1930s **Art Deco residential apartments**, along the western side of the Oval Maidan.

Flora Fountain and Horniman Circle

This area, just to the north of Kala Ghoda, contains several fine buildings from the British period, including the city's old town hall and the Anglican cathedral. **Flora Fountain** (1869), officially Hutatma Chowk, was built at the road intersection at the heart of Mumbai's old commercial district. A statue of the minor Roman goddess Flora stands on four rather angry-looking dolphins, which loom over four large sea-shells. The junction has a seated **statue of Dadabhai Naoroji** (1925), the first Indian member of the British parliament, who became the Liberal MP for Finsbury Central in 1892. There is also a **'martyrs' memorial** in granite to those who died in the 1955 agitation against the division of the old Bombay presidency into Maharashtra and Gujarat.

The Flora Fountain intersection marks the site of the old Church Gate of the fort, and, 200m to the east, down Veer Nariman Road, is the city's oldest British church,

St Thomas's Cathedral (*see below*). Note, on the south side of the road, the fine wooden balconies of the **Readymoney Mansion**, the home of the Parsi philanthropist Sir Cowasji Jehangir (there is a CJ monogram over the door), who adopted the soubriquet Readymoney.

Horniman Circle was laid out in 1867 on the site of the old Bombay Green, the original open space within the fort. It consists of a circular garden, with a pond and four ornamental gates. A road rings the garden, which is in turn surrounded by Italianate buildings constructed as crescents around the circle, which was originally named after Lord Elphinstone, the governor of Bombay. It was renamed after Benjamin Horniman, a British journalist who supported the freedom movement, after Independence in 1947. Note the two-storey **fountain and well** (1873) at the western side of the circle, with its inscription in four languages: English, Hindi, Gujarati and Urdu.

St Thomas's Cathedral

The recently restored cathedral is the oldest British structure still in use in Mumbai, and is the Anglican church after which Churchgate was originally named. Construction began in 1672 but was not completed until 1718, and the tower is a 19th-century addition. Note the tribute plaque on the left of the main door to the 18th-century chaplain Richard Cobbe, who ensured that the church was completed. The interior has a huge number of wall plaques, some of them extremely ornate and carved out of marble. Most remarkable is the recumbent figure, carved in marble, of Thomas Carr, the first bishop of Bombay, who died in 1859. Note how he is covered in a sheet but is wearing shoes. The chairs used by King George V and Queen Mary when they visited the cathedral in 1911 are preserved at the front, and bear small plaques. The fine stained glass dates from the restoration of 1869. The ornate water fountain outside the church, designed, like the Rajabai Tower, by George Gilbert Scott, bears the inscription: 'Whosoever drinketh of the water that I shall give him shall never thirst.' Note the small runnel that carried water outside the church precincts to passers-by. Flying buttresses support the external walls of the chancel at the eastern end of the church.

The Town Hall area

There are some fine Victorian buildings around the circle, and at the far end is one of India's finest Neoclassical buildings, the **Town Hall** (1833), which is now the headquarters of the Asiatic Society. Designed by Colonel Thomas Cowper, it was originally both an administrative centre and an assembly hall for the elite of the city. Its broad external staircase leads up to the main portico, with eight fluted Doric columns. The side and end porticoes use similar columns, all shipped in pieces from Britain. Note how the windows and doors have projecting shades to protect them from the sun and rain. Inside is the grand assembly hall, a large library, several fine meeting rooms and an impressive collection of statues. These include a fine standing statue by one of the most successful of Georgian sculptors, Sir Francis Chantrey, of the soldier and historian Sir John Malcolm, who carries a sword and whose cloak rests on two of his own books: *A Memoir of Central India* and *A History of Persia*. The library has copies of *The Times* of London since 1801 and a 14th-century copy of Dante's *Divine Comedy*, which Mussolini is said to have attempted to purchase for £1,000,000.

To the south of the town hall is the **Old Customs House**, parts of which are thought to date back to the 17th century, when the Portuguese ruled the city—though most of the building is 19th century. The dockyard wall, south of the Old Customs House, marks the line of the old walls of Bombay Fort and leads back to Wellington Circle.

To the north of the town hall is the **Reserve Bank of India** (1939), with its grand entrance defined by two large stone columns. Further north is the 12m-high Ruttonsey **Mulji Memorial Fountain**, erected by Mulji in memory of his only son, and designed by F.W. Stevens. Note the elephant head brackets with their water spouts.

Just to the east of the fountain is the area known as **Ballard Estate**, reclaimed from the sea and laid out in the early 20th century, with George Wittet as the chief architect. There is an unusual uniformity of design and style throughout the estate which was, and still is, an important business centre. The passenger docks moved here, and it became the main maritime entry point to India.

VICTORIA TERMINUS (VT)

This enormous, magnificent station, officially the **Chhatrapati Shivaji Terminus**, but still widely known as VT, is now a UNESCO World Heritage Site—and ranks with New Delhi and Kolkata's Victoria Memorial as one of the greatest architectural creations of the British period. Designed by F.W. Stevens in the neo-Gothic style, it was partially built on reclaimed land close to the historic area known as Bori Bunder. The old public gallows once stood at the centre of the roundabout known as Nagar Chowk, in front of the station. The first railway line in India ran between here and Thane, 30km away, and predated the start of the construction of VT by 25 years.

Victoria Terminus was inspired by London's St Pancras Station, but it is far grander and has a much greater wealth of detail. Work on the station began in 1878 and was completed ten years later at a cost of more than 2.5 million rupees. The symmetrical main façade is 120m long and makes superb use of different coloured stone. Note the rooftop statues—of a large figure representing Progress on the central dome, while the gables carry figures representing Engineering, Commerce and Agriculture. The exterior also carries the monogram GIPR, which stands for the Great Indian Peninsula Railway, and has some very delicate carved stone tracery, with animal and bird motifs. Note the carved medallions showing civic dignitaries of the Victorian era and a frieze of relief carvings of human profiles, animals and symbols between the ground floor and the first. The carvings of lions and tigers are meant to symbolise Britain and India respectively.

The interior of Victoria Terminus is also lavishly decorated, with great attention to detail, though, unlike the exterior, many changes have been made over the years. The ticket hall is particularly fine, with a spectacular high vaulted ceiling supported by columns made of Italian marble and elaborate stone arches. The main part of the station has highly ornamented ironwork.

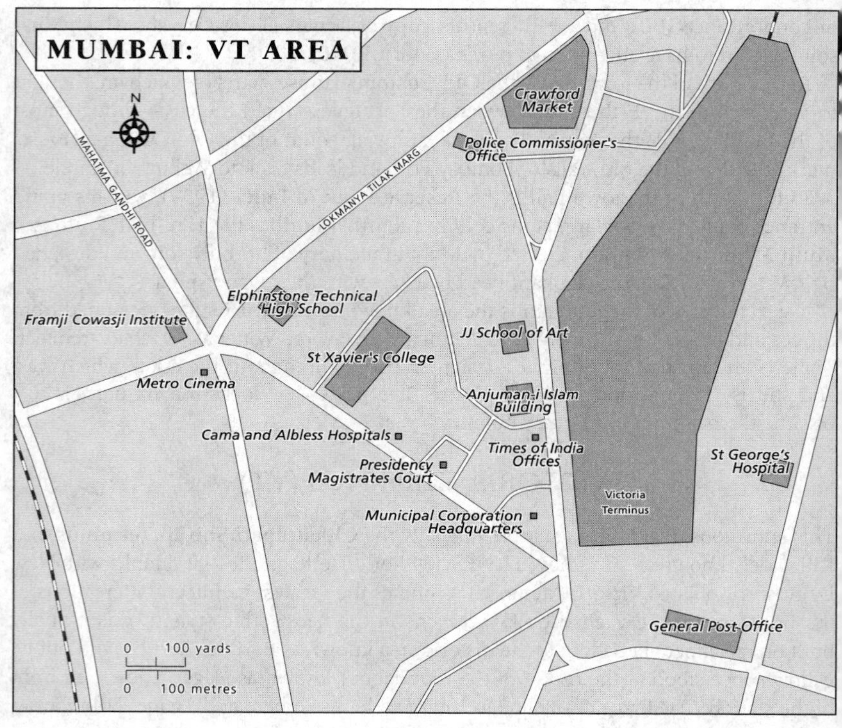

Around VT

Close to VT is another fine Victorian building, by the same architect, F.W. Stevens. The **Municipal Corporation Headquarters** (1884–93) has a distinctive 71m-high central tower, and two side towers each capped by bulbous domes. The design makes skilful use of a tightly-angled corner plot. Note the large statue on the gable roof, symbolising 'Urbs Prima in India', or the first city of India, and the winged beasts guarding the roof of the vestibule.

In front of the building is a statue of the lawyer and political activist Sir Pherozeshah Mehta, who died in 1915. Just to the east of VT, largely hidden by trees, is the **General Post Office** (1904–10), an Indo-Saracenic building designed by George Wittet and John Begg. Like Wittet's Prince of Wales Museum, it borrows from Bijapur's Gol Gumbaz Tomb. To the northeast of VT, close to the docks, is **St George's Hospital** (1892), which was built on the site of an inner fortification of the city known as Fort George. The only surviving building of the fort can be visited here, just to the east of the hospital. It is a single-storey heavily reinforced building, with narrow windows and a cavernous basement that was probably used for storing ammunition. It is now occupied by the State Department of Archaeology.

West of VT

There are also several interesting buildings on Cruikshank Road, now Mahapalika Marg, which leads northwest from VT towards the Metro Cinema. The neo-Gothic **Presidency Magistrates Court** (1884–89) has some pretty carvings forming a frieze along the cornice between the ground and first floors. Note also the unusual narrow white 'flèche' spire. The neo-Gothic **Cama Hospital** (1886) and **Albless Hospital** (1890) for women and children were both named after Parsi entrepreneurs and have founders' plaques in their entrances. **St Xavier's College** (1891) is part of the large St Xavier's complex, named after the Jesuit missionary St Francis Xavier, which extends to nearby Tilak Marg. The college, which has a pretty courtyard, also houses the **Heras Institute of Indology**, a small research-based museum which is open to the public. The neo-Gothic **Elphinstone Technical High School** (1872–79), named after a former governor of Bombay and financed by the Sassoon family, is on the corner of Tilak Marg and is approached up a broad series of steps. Note the fine cast-iron grille on the front arched doorways. The large junction just beyond the college is known as Dhobi Talao, meaning 'washerman's tank'—a reminder of the large pond that was once here. The other buildings around Dhobi Talao are the Art Deco **Metro Cinema** (1938), the fine Neoclassical **Framji Cowasji Institute** (1925), which houses the 'People's Free Reading Room and Library', previously known as the Bombay Native General Library.

Between VT and Crawford Market

The road leading north from VT towards Crawford Market has several important buildings, including the **Times of India Offices**, completed in 1903 (the newspaper's nickname is 'the Old Man of Bori Bunder', after the Bori Bunder area around VT), and the striking **Anjuman-i Islam building** (1893), now occupied by the Tyebji High School, with a high central tower and a fine decorative effect conveyed with coloured stone and floral carvings. The next plot is occupied by the sprawling campus of the **JJ School of Art**, India's best-known art school. The construction of the first building at the school in 1857 was funded by the Parsi philanthropist Sir Jamsetjee Jeejeebhoy, whose initials gave the school its name. J. Lockwood Kipling was one of the first teachers at the school, and Rudyard Kipling was born here in 1865, in a small building long since demolished. There is a bust of Kipling and a plaque on the dean's residence marking his birth; it suggests, incorrectly, that Lockwood Kipling was the school's principal.

Crawford Market

Officially renamed Mahatma Phule Market (though most people use the older name), Crawford Market is 800m to the north of VT. It was designed by William Emerson, completed in 1869 and named after Arthur Crawford, the municipal commissioner of Bombay (1865–71). It is a large distinctive neo-Gothic complex, with an unusual octagonal clock tower. There are three fine relief carvings over the main doorways, all by J. Lockwood Kipling, Rudyard's father, which show local people engaged in different occupations. The flagstones on the floor of the market were imported from Scotland. Note the ornamental fountain designed by Emerson and decorated with images of animals and river goddesses by Lockwood Kipling. Opposite Crawford Market is the vast **Police Commissioner's Office** (1896–97). About 700m northwest of Crawford Market is the **Mumbadevi Temple**, one of the city's most important Hindu shrines—and after which Mumbai is said to have been named. The temple was built in the 19th century, after the demolition of the original temple which stood near VT.

BYCULLA

Byculla, now an inner city district 4km north of VT (*map p. 472*), was developed in the mid-19th century as an upmarket residential area, and a few interesting buildings survive from that period. These include, in the southern part of Byculla, the **Magen David Synagogue** (1861), on Sir JJ Road, with a blue Neoclassical façade and a four-storey clock tower, and the Neoclassical **Christ Church** (1834) on nearby Clare Road.

Bhau Daji Lad Museum

Further north, on the eastern side of the main road and next to the city zoo, is the beautifully restored, Neoclassical **Bhau Daji Lad Museum** (*map p. 471; open Thur–Tues 10–5.30*), which looks like an English country house. Originally built in 1872 as the Victoria & Albert Museum, it was renamed after the physician and amateur archaeologist who played a major role in raising funds for the museum. The two-storey building has pedimented windows and Corinthian columns on its façade—a contrast with the large exhibition hall inside, with its iron columns and brackets that support the balustraded balcony and handsome painted wooden ceiling. Note the pretty Victorian turnstiles, manufactured by Isler & Co of Southwark, London, on entering the building.

The main hall has a large collection of antiquities and paintings. At its centre is a large standing marble sculpture (1864) of Queen Victoria's consort Prince Albert, who had died in 1861—it was a gift of the Baghdadi Jewish businessman David Sassoon, which explains why it has an inscription in Hebrew. Many of the displays reflect the interests of 19th-century museum-goers, with busts showing members of different communities and castes, and a very wide range of headgear—as well as models of craftsmen at work. The museum has a small collection of fine miniatures, old maps and examples of the late 19th-century Bombay school of pottery.

Outside the museum are a number of important statues and carvings. Most significant is a large 6th-century **stone elephant**, well-worn, which used to be near the main jetty on Elephanta Island (*see p. 490*) and gave the island its modern name. It was brought here in 1864 and fell apart en route. The other statues are from the British period and were originally on display at important junctions and buildings around the city, and moved here after Independence. These include an unusually waif-like Queen Victoria, which once stood in the Fort area, and a standing statue of the early 20th-century viceroy, Lord Hardinge, which was previously at Apollo Bunder near the Gateway of India. Note also the stone that served to mark the limits of Bombay city.

Victoria Gardens

Behind the museum are the pretty Victoria Gardens, now renamed Veermata Jijabai Bhonsle Udayan. They are entered through an ornate 19th-century gate with three arches, built in the Italian style. Inside, as well as a zoo, is the original Kala Ghoda, or Black Horse statue, which gave its name to the artistic quarter of the modern city—and which is in fact a statue of King Edward VII on horseback.

Parel

In Parel, 4km north of the Bhau Daji Lad Museum, is the **Haffkine Institute** (*map p. 471*), one of the city's oldest buildings, part of which—a Portuguese chapel—was built in the 17th century. It then served in the late 19th century as the residence of the governor of Bombay, before being turned into an infectious diseases research institute.

MALABAR HILL & SOUTHWESTERN MUMBAI

The southwestern parts of South Mumbai are largely residential, with huge apartment blocks rising from Malabar Hill (*map p. 472*). The governor's house, **Raj Bhavan** (19th century), is at the southern tip of the peninsula—but not open to the public. The 18th-century **Walkeshwar Temple**, and the pretty **Banganga Tank**, a man-made pond, are just to the north of Raj Bhavan. There are a few interesting 19th-century bungalows left on Malabar Hill, as well as the handsome **Hanging Gardens**, laid out in the late 19th century on top of large underground tanks from which the city drew its water supply. Next to the gardens are the **Towers of Silence** (*closed to the public*), large circular structures, where the bodies of dead Parsis are exposed to the elements and to the attention of birds of prey.

Just to the north of Malabar Hill, on Laburnum Lane, is **Mani Bhavan** (*open daily 9.30–6*), where Mahatma Gandhi stayed when he was in the city. There is a small museum dedicated to Gandhi's life and work. Just north of Marine Drive and east of Malabar Hill is the Neoclassical **Opera House** (1908–12), while **Kotachiwadi**, 300m east of the Opera House, was once a Christian village, almost enveloped by the city, which has a few surviving 18th- and 19th-century wooden houses with large open verandahs.

Two kilometres north of Malabar Hill, on the coast, is one of the city's best-known monuments, the **Dargah of Haji Ali** (*map p. 471*), an Islamic shrine, built in the 19th century over a 15th-century grave on an island linked to the mainland by a tidal causeway. Streams of pedestrians head out to the shrine at low tide.

THE FORTS OF BOMBAY

Bombay has a series of little-visited old forts, constructed by the British and the Portuguese. Four of them overlook the Arabian Sea, while three others are further inland. Three of the sea-forts are situated around the bay now crossed by the Bandra–Worli Sealink, a 4km bridge which opened in 2009 (*map p. 471*).

Worli Fort: This is the southernmost of the forts, at the furthest end of the peninsula known as Worli Tip, in a fishing village beyond the commercial and residential parts of Worli. It is very small, less than 30m square, and in relatively good condition. It was built by the British in the 1670s, more as a lookout point than as a military position. It is now used as a gym by villagers.

Mahim Fort: The more impressive, easily approachable Mahim Fort, at the southern end of the short stretch of sand close to Mahim Creek, has fared less well. It has become a residence for a large number of poor families and is suffering from tidal erosion. It was built on the site of a much older fort that guarded the important waterway that fed into the sea here, which is now the heavily polluted Mahim Creek. The fort was captured from the Gujarat sultans by the Portuguese in 1534, after a series of battles over 18 years. In 1661 it was ceded, along with most of the rest of Mumbai, to the British, and partially rebuilt and strengthened in the 1680s.

Bandra Fort: On the north side of the bay, just beyond the Taj Lands End Hotel, is Bandra Fort. It was built by the Portuguese as Castella de Aguada in 1640 as a defensive fortification, a watchtower and a watering station for ships (provided by nearby freshwater springs). It remained in Portuguese control after the cession of Mumbai to the British in 1661, and was brought under British control only in the 18th century, when it was partially demolished to ensure it could not be captured by the Marathas. Note the Portuguese inscription on the outer gate, which dates the foundation of the lower bastion (*balvarte*) to 1640. The upper parts of the fort were once extensive but are now in ruins, and have been converted into a garden.

Madh Fort: This is 10km as the crow flies from Bandra, and the most remote of the old coastal fortifications. It is on Madh Island, which can be approach by ferry from the suburb of Versova, or by driving a long way round via Marve. The outer walls of this 17th-century fort are in good condition and, with their circular corner bastions, are an interesting piece of Portuguese military architecture.

Sewri Fort: A small recently restored fortification, Sewri Fort is in an industrial area of the same name, overlooking the mudflats at the northern end of Mumbai Harbour. It was built by the British in 1680, and used as a watchtower. There are very pretty views over the mudflats, on which large numbers of flamingoes congregate.

Sion Fort: This fort stands on top of a hill, next to the highway as it passes through the suburb of Sion and close to Sion station. A now largely ruined building, it was built by the British in the 1670s and has fine views over northern Mumbai. It marked the northern limit of territory ceded by the Portuguese to the British.

Riwa Fort: To the east of the large area known as Dharavi and 2km west of Sion, Riwa Fort is also known as Kala Qila, or Black Fort. There is no doorway to this small fort, in a crowded area, hemmed in by shacks and houses, and you will need to borrow a ladder from local residents if you want to enter it. The old access route was by an underground staircase that is now blocked. The fort once sat at the end of a narrow spit of land that jutted out into the creek—which is now 400m to the north. The fort has a large inscription on its southern wall declaring it to have been built in 1737 by the governor of Bombay, John Horne.

NORTH MUMBAI

Northern Mumbai (*map p. 471*) is best known as the location of the city's airport and its film studios, but there are four significant sets of rock-cut caves also, one of which, Kanheri, is enormous and very impressive. Two of the others are Jogeshwari and Mahakali, both of which have important sculptures and cave design features, and are close to the Andheri region of central North Mumbai. Mandapeshwar is the last of the four, and is in the Borivli area of North Mumbai, not far from Kanheri. It has fine carvings and an unlikely Christian connection.

Jogeshwari Cave-Temple

The fascinating Jogeshwari Temple (6th century) is one of India's most unusual ancient Hindu shrines, because of its distinctive layout and out-of-the-ordinary location. The underground temple is 800m east of Jogeshwari station, and just 100m east of the Western Express Highway, down a small lane called Gufa Marg, or Cave Road, which runs parallel to the highway. The area is crowded, and homes have been built on top of, and next to, the cave complex. Two stone staircases have been cut out of the bedrock: one from the west and the other from the east lead down to the caves. The western entrance, which is the easiest to find, and which runs off Gufa Marg, leads down to what was probably the rear gate of the temple. The carvings are very worn here, and it is only just possible to make them out—but they would once have covered much of the porch.

Inside the largest cave is an inner rock-cut temple, surrounded by 20 finely-carved stone pillars. Note the distinctive squashed-cushion shape near the top of each column. The temple is now a living Hindu shrine to Jogeshwari, a form of Parvati, the wife of Shiva. To the right is a superb verandah, partially open to the skies, with ten finely-carved pillars, all in excellent condition. Adjoining the verandah area are temples to Shiva and Ganesha. Straight ahead within the main temple is a second, larger entrance porch, which contains Jogeshwari's finest carvings, with large guardians on either side of the door and a tableau showing Shiva and Parvati playing dice, and Nataraja—or Shiva as the Lord of the Dance. Beyond is an open area, most of which was once covered, and which leads to the eastern staircase and back to street level. It is also possible to get good views into the temple from above by walking along the street-level path on the side of the eastern entrance.

Mahakali Caves

The Mahakali Caves (also known as the Kondivte Caves) are a series of rock-cut Buddhist shrines, 5km to the southeast of the Jogeshwari Caves. The 18 caves are approached from the Jogeshwari–Vikhroli Link Road and are cut into the side of the summit of a hill, with some fine views over north Mumbai. The first group of less interesting caves is on the approach to the top of the hill, but the main group is just on the other side of the hilltop at the end of a short road. There are two important caves in the centre of this group: the first cave complex has a large main room with an unusual circular chamber behind it, which has a substantial decorated rock-cut stupa occupying most of its area. There are some fine Buddhist carvings of a later period than the rest of the cave, which has been dated to the 2nd century. The second main cave has a large chamber supported by four finely-carved pillars and a smaller room that contains a pedestal for a statue.

Kanheri Caves

In North Mumbai, amid the forests and lakes of the Sanjay Gandhi National Park, are the impressive Kanheri Caves. They were created, all 109 of them, as Buddhist places of worship, study and residence between the 1st and 9th centuries, during which time Kanheri was an important centre of Buddhist learning. Taxis and rickshaws are not allowed inside the park, so either take a private car, or squeeze into the public bus that runs inside the park (Borivli is the nearest railway station). The caves have been cut into the side of two hills, separated by a small ravine. Two of the best caves are close to the ticket office, so a visit need not involve a long walk. But it is also possible to wander around for several hours, exploring some of the caves on higher levels—and excellent views can be had from the top of the hills. Three separate numbering systems have been used for the caves, which makes identifying them rather difficult (except near the ticket office, where the numbering system is the same). A guide can help to point out the most interesting caves further up the hill.

Head up the main steps from the ticket area (*open Tues–Sun 9.30–5*), and the series of caves starts on the right. The two-storey **first cave** is unfinished, but does have finely-carved columns with squashed-cushion capitals similar to those at Elephanta. The second and third caves are much more impressive.

Cave 2: This is a broad unsupported incision in the hillside, and more open to the elements than most of the caves. Inside are two stupas and some small chambers. Around the first stupa are fine carvings, including, on the left of the rear wall, some that show Avalokiteshwara (who refused Buddhahood until all beings were liberated) saving his devotees from a series of perilous situations. The clearest one shows a lion attacking some humans (top left). Most of the other carvings, mainly in excellent condition, are of Buddhist teachers. The small crouching figures on the left of the stupa are devotees and donors, whose names are listed in the nearby inscription.

Cave 3: This is the most impressive and important cave in Kanheri, and was begun towards the end of the 2nd century. For all their beauty, the finely-decorated front courtyard and the carvings on the verandah do not quite prepare one for the enormous *chaitya*, or colonnaded hall, inside. Intended for Buddhist congregational gatherings, the *chaitya* stretches back a further 28m into the hillside. Notice the huge rock-carved 6th-century Buddhas in decorated niches on either side of the verandah, while the figures on the panels between the small *chaitya* entrances are donor couples. The inscriptions on the exterior columns give their names. The *chaitya* hall is domed and semicircular at the far end, where there stands a stupa. There are elephant and lion images carved on the capitals of the interior columns.

There are 100 more caves further up the rock-cut path, none of them as magnificent as Cave 3—but still worth visiting. Notice how they have rock-cut cisterns for storing water, and some have benches and seats carved out of rock. The best known of the other caves is one close to the usually dry watercourse which contains a carving of Avalokiteshwara, here portrayed with four arms and eleven heads. The remains of two dams can be seen along the bed of the watercourse.

Mandapeshwar

Suburban Mandapeshwar, less than 2km northwest of Borivli station in northern Mumbai, has one of India's most unlikely combinations of listed monuments. Cut into the side of a small hill, next to a busy road, is an ancient Hindu cave-temple, with some very fine rock carvings, and just above the caves are the ruins of a 16th-century Portuguese church. The ownership of the monuments is disputed, and this has hindered conservation work. The main cave—probably from the 6th century, and never completed—has five bays. They are separated by heavily eroded columns, with carved roof brackets. The half-columns emerging from the wall have squashed-cushion capitals like those at Elephanta. On the steps leading up to the cave are the remains of guardian lions, only a couple of paws visible on the left. Inside, the cave looks bare, with five smaller rooms leading off the large hall; in the central one is a small Shiva lingam.

The principal carvings: The main Mandapeshwar carvings are in the far right room. There are two panels: the first is badly damaged—it once showed Shiva as the King of the Yogis (now only his disciples seated beneath a lotus survive); the other is dynamic and beautiful—an image of Shiva dancing. This latter panel is remarkably similar to the iconic Shiva dancing at Elephanta, incorrectly known as Nataraja. The one at Mandapeshwar is in slightly better condition, and one needn't worry about crowds of tourists here, though a torch is useful. Notice the exceptional detail on the uppermost parts of his eight arms, as his hands grasp a cloak. The seated drummer on the left, barely discernible in Elephanta, is clearly visible here; so too is Vishnu riding the man-eagle Garuda in the top-right corner, and three-headed Brahma on his geese in the top left.

The outer walls: On the outer wall of the south side of the cave complex is another rock carving: of a large cross; on the opposite side are the remains of a roughly carved angel. From the 16th century, when the Portuguese took control of this part of the Indian coastline, the caves became a monastery, and this area became known as Mount Poinsur. A church was built on what is effectively the roof of a Shiva temple. By climbing up on the left side of the cave (next to another half-excavated cave), one can visit the ruins of the church. Amid the undergrowth, it is possible to make out parts of the pillars and decorated arches that once spanned its nave, close to where a more modern church has now been built.

ELEPHANTA

The forested island of Elephanta, located in Mumbai's enormous harbour, is home to one of India's finest cave temples, a shrine to the Hindu god Lord Shiva. It has 6th-century rock carvings that are of the very highest quality, though partially damaged by time and vandalism. Because of its proximity to Mumbai, the caves of Elephanta are many visitors' first experience of a major Indian historical or religious site—and it can be a little overwhelming. The huge temple, cut deep into the basalt rock, has inspired awe in foreign visitors since the Portuguese arrived here almost 500 years ago. And despite the damage inflicted on them over the years, the beauty and the vigour of the carvings come alive here in a way that is only matched by the slightly later Kailashnath Temple at Ellora. The carvings are also an excellent introduction to Hindu iconography—an opportunity to identify the different gods and stories portrayed in the huge carved panels.

History: The early history of Elephanta remains a mystery. The cave and the carvings probably date to the 6th century, but very little is known about the people who created them. The two most likely builders were either the Kalachuris or the Konkan Mauryas, 6th-century rulers of parts of what is now the Maharashtra coastline. In the early 16th century, the caves—then used as cattle sheds—were 'rediscovered' by the Portuguese, who controlled the island until the early 18th century. They named the island Elephanta because they found a life-size statue of an elephant with a baby elephant on its back near the southern coastline of the island (the elephant has since fallen apart—but a large chunk of it can be seen in the Bhau Daji Lad Museum in Mumbai (*see p. 484*). In 1712, a Portuguese soldier fired a large gun inside the cave—apparently 'to test the echo'—and in so doing destroyed one of the pillars.

The island was garrisoned by the British in 1774, and several drawings of the cave that survive from the early British period all show severe waterlogging, which caused extensive damage to the lower parts of many of the carvings. In 1875 the cave was spruced up and transformed into a banqueting hall for the visiting Prince of Wales (later King Edward VII). Elephanta was handed over to the Archaeological Survey of India in 1909, and regular conservation work has taken place since then. Although the cave has not been used as a temple for more than a millennium, the island attracts large numbers of Hindu visitors at key religious festivals related to Shiva.

Orientation: Elephanta is a 30-minute boat-ride from the Gateway of India (next to the Taj Hotel), and provides a pleasant contrast to the hyperactivity of Mumbai. As the skyscrapers recede into the distance, visitors get excellent views of the harbour and the docks, so critical to Mumbai's early growth. It is almost possible to imagine Mumbai as it was just a few hundred years ago, as a series of forested islands. Then, as one approaches Elephanta, India's largest container port looms in the near distance—but the island itself is largely unspoilt.

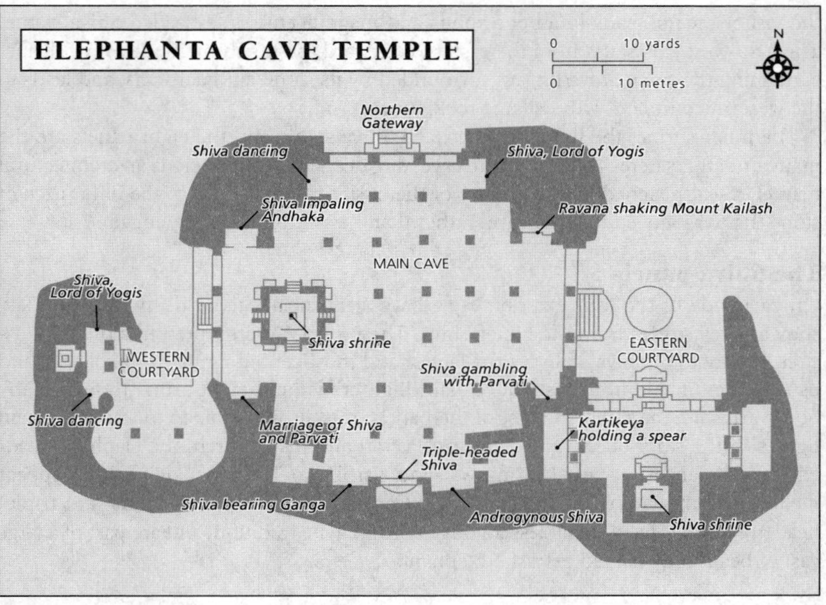

The island, known as Gharapuri by its 1,200 inhabitants, has two small hills: the one on the west has the main cave, halfway up its northern slope. From the jetty, a footpath or a miniature railway can be taken by visitors to the bottom of the hill. A broad pathway, lined with souvenir-sellers, leads up to the cave (palanquins are available for those who can't make the climb). At the top is the **ticket office**, a small **museum** and a short path to the right leading to the **main cave** (*open Tues–Sun 9–5*). Another path leads ahead to smaller, less interesting caves, and winds its way to the top of the hill—from where excellent views can be had of Mumbai harbour, and where 20th-century anti-aircraft artillery is still in position, amid the ruins of a small fortification.

Main cave

The main cave is entered from the triple-bayed northern gateway—and it is helpful to stand in the central bay to orient oneself. Ahead is a deep cave, cut more than 40m into the rock. The cave is supported by distinctive columns, with 'squashed-cushion' capitals, left in place when the rest of the rock was cleared. Each of them has a little carving of four dwarves at the point where the column stops being square and becomes cylindrical. The entire cave has a very deliberate geometrical layout. It is divided up into 37 bays, separated by the columns. The bays are laid out in an inner square of five by five, and a group of three outer bays on each side of the inner square. There are two key axes running through the cave temple. The north–south axis (on which the visitor enters) leads to an enormous and magnificent triple-headed Shiva statue. The east–west axis starts from the eastern courtyard, passes through the Shiva shrine, containing the stone Shiva lingam surrounded by its stone-cut guardians, and leads to the western courtyard with its large rock-cut cistern.

The inner shrine, the huge triple-headed Shiva statue and the eight panels are the main attractions here—but the entire cave, dug deep into solid rock, is an architectural marvel, a feat matched by the artistry of the *in-situ* carving. Indeed, the only piece of stone that was moved into the cave, rather than hewn from it, is the lingam.

The Shiva panels

On each side of the four exterior triple bays are panels, carved deep into the rock, showing key stories from the life of Shiva. These stories each represent a different aspect, or mood, of Shiva—always the largest and most central figure in the panels, and usually identifiable from his matted hair, high crown and eight arms (though many of the arms are missing). In most of the panels, it is also possible to identify the main figures in the story of Shiva: his consort Parvati and his children, the elephant-headed Ganesha and the spear-bearing war-god Kartikeya. The other deities that appear include Vishnu (riding on the man-eagle Garuda), elephant-riding Indra and triple-headed Brahma. They are all lesser gods in the Shaivite tradition, and are part of a large cast of beautifully-carved extras at Elephanta.

Northern panels

Shiva, Lord of Yogis: The first, badly damaged panel on the left of the entrance gateway shows Shiva in meditative mood as the Lord of Yogis, or Yogeshwara, seated in the lotus position. He may originally have had an erect phallus—as in a very similar carving in Ellora. Shiva is surrounded by, but unaware of, other celestial beings. Brahma, with three heads and riding some geese, is in the top left—geese or swans are the usual 'vehicle' of Brahma.

Shiva dancing: The impressive second panel on the right of the entrance gateway, directly opposite the first, is one of the most famous (and known incorrectly as Nataraja—a different dance in which Shiva plants his foot on the head of an unhappy dwarf). Shiva's angry dance symbolises the destruction of the world, and it is possible to make out seven of his eight arms all pointing in different directions. Notice his children Ganesha and Kartikeya (with the spear) watching him on the left; his consort Parvati, to the right, with the narrowest of waists, cannot bear to watch. The elephant on the right is not Ganesha, but Airavata, the 'vehicle' of Indra.

Eastern panels

Ravana shaking Mount Kailash: The first of the eastern panels is badly damaged. It depicts Shiva seated on the sacred Mount Kailash. Beneath him is the demon-king Ravana, who had dared to disturb Shiva and Parvati's love-making and was trapped by Shiva underneath the mountain. Shiva leans towards what was once a carving of a seated Parvati.

Shiva gambling with Parvati: This panel is one of the most damaged. But it is still possible to make out a slightly petulant Parvati, irritated that Shiva has once again cheated at a game of dice.

Southern panels

Androgynous Shiva: This beautiful panel shows Shiva as Ardhanarishwara—part man, part woman—a transformation, according to some ancient Hindu texts, that allowed Shiva to produce all living creatures. Notice how the male and female sides of Shiva's body are accentuated. The female side, sometimes identified as Parvati, has more jewellery, her hip is accentuated, she looks into a mirror and she has a single large breast. Notice the fine, naturalistic carving of Nandi the bull, on which the 'male' Shiva rests one of his many arms. Beside Nandi is Shiva's son Kartikeya, and above them are three-headed Brahma, riding four geese, and Indra, riding his elephant.

Shiva bearing Ganga: This panel shows Shiva, bringing the river-goddess Ganga (the Ganges) down from heaven in the tresses of his hair. Ganga is the three-headed goddess just above Shiva's crown. The postures of Shiva and the jealous Parvati appear to mimic each other. Note the snake that rears up between them, and how the dwarf at their feet is paying more attention to Shiva than Parvati.

Western panels

Marriage of Shiva and Parvati: This panel places the bride and groom at the centre of the composition, surrounded by gods and other celestial beings. Brahma kneels at Shiva's side. Parvati's father, Himavant, is at her side, gently pushing her towards Shiva.

Shiva impaling Andhaka: This badly damaged panel shows Shiva impaling his own son, the monster Andhaka, and collecting his blood in a bowl. If he were to let a single drop of blood fall to the ground, a new monster would be born. The bowl is clearly visible on the right in one of Shiva's right hands, and above it is the mutilated body of Andhaka. Shiva has a skull set into his crown.

Triple-headed Shiva

The most impressive of all the cave carvings is the huge triple-headed bust of Shiva, chiselled out of the southern wall. Six metres high and in good condition, here is Shiva alone in his contradictions, without any other gods or celestial beings looking on. The Shiva head on the left is of a furious god, who looks as if he is spitting at the snake that he holds in his hand. The central Shiva head is full-faced, a meditating, peaceful Shiva with a crown covering his matted hair. The Shiva head on the right shows the god's feminine aspect, with an ornate headdress and holding out a lotus flower. According to some Shaivite traditions, the carving should be thought of as five-headed, with two that are invisible—one above the bust, and one looking into the wall. On either side are *dwarapalas*, or door guardians, each resting an arm on the head of a dwarf attendant.

Shiva shrine

The shrine of the cave temple is an undecorated chamber with a doorway on each side. Within is a lingam, or phallus, that is modest in size compared to those in many Shiva temples. The shrine doorways also have magnificent *dwarapalas*, with crowns that almost touch the roof of the cave. They have been carved in the round, so that they almost come away from the wall against which they rest.

Eastern and western courtyards

Before leaving the cave, visit the eastern and western courtyards, where further carvings can be seen. The eastern courtyard was originally an entrance to the main cave, but has now been blocked off. It has its own smaller cave. The stone lions outside the Shiva shrine once stood outside the entrance bay, on the topmost step. The four-armed *dwarapala*, or door guardian, on the right is of a more complex design than those inside the main cave, and may have been carved later. In a side chamber next to the *dwarapala* is a badly damaged frieze of mother-goddesses, and a large statue of Shiva's son Kartikeya, holding a spear. The western court also has a small cave, with images of Shiva dancing and of Shiva, the Lord of Yogis—though neither is as beautifully carved as the similar images inside the main cave. Note the large water cistern cut into the rock on the southern side of the courtyard.

Other sights at Elephanta

There are several other caves further up the hill, though none of them bears comparison with the first one. Cave 3 is the most interesting, with a seven-bayed entrance. Note the frieze of small carved figures above the bay furthest to the right. There are damaged carvings within. On the neighbouring hill is another bare cave which the Portuguese used as a church as well as the remains of a Buddhist stupa thought to date back to the the 2nd century BC. The site museum, near the ticket office, has some other sculptures and carvings found on Elephanta, including images of Vishnu and Parvati.

VASAI (BASSEIN)

North of Mumbai, beyond the Vasai Creek (actually the rather large estuary of the Ulhas River) and easily accessible by rail or road (Vasai Road is the nearest station), is the fascinating former 16th-century Portuguese sea-fort and city of Vasai (*map 11 A1*). It was previously known as Bassein, and has some very impressive fortifications and no fewer than five beautiful ruined churches.

History: Vasai was ceded to the Portuguese by Sultan Bahadur Shah of Gujarat in 1535, and stonework from older Islamic buildings was reused by the Portuguese. Vasai was once an important Portuguese base—one of a string of Portuguese cities along the coast of western India that included Cochin, Goa, Diu and Mumbai, all of which have remained important settlements. For two centuries Vasai Fort was a place of fabled prosperity, inside which only the Portuguese aristocracy were allowed to live. However, Vasai (like Chaul, just south of Mumbai) was relinquished by the Portuguese in the 18th century, and became forgotten and overgrown—it is now a place of many ruins, wonderfully evocative and strangely under-visited, given its proximity to Mumbai.

Orientation: Most visitors enter Vasai along a road that has been broken through the western side of the fort wall, just north of the old Land Gate. The road passes west to east through the fort to the Sea Gate. All of the main surviving buildings are on the southern side of the road, closest to the sea. The 2.5km-long walls of the city are in excellent condition, and parts of them can be walked along. They are a superb example of 16th-century defensive architecture, with steeply sloping ramparts and sharply angled bastions along the sea-face of the fort.

Land Gate

The gate is 70m south of where the road cuts through the wall. Above the Land Gate is a pretty arched opening, with ornate double Corinthian columns, and a double cornice with floral and geometric medallions. Nearby is a large square building which probably served as a guardhouse, and its roof is the base for the flagstaff.

St Paul's Church

The first major building, near the Land Gate, is the large Church of St Paul, without a roof, except over the chancel. It has an unusual entrance to the vestibule, with three arches resting on Doric columns. This leads through to a smaller doorway, which opens into the nave of the church. A long low arch still spans the nave, and dozens of gravestones of Portuguese soldiers and migrants are set into the floor. Of all the churches in Vasai, this one shows the greatest sign of re-used building materials, and some local residents say it was once a mosque, pointing out pieces of pre-European patterned stonework set into the walls. Many columns and arches still stand in the church cloisters on the south side of the building.

Church of St Gonsalo Garcia

This church, just beyond St Paul's and known locally as the Church of St Gonsalo Garcia, is in good condition. It is historically the most important, and has recently been restored for use by Vasai's large Catholic population. Gonsalo Garcia was the first Indian Catholic saint. He was born in 1556 in Bassein, to a Portuguese father and an Indian mother. He was one of the 26 'Nagasaki martyrs'—Franciscan missionaries who were crucified in 1597 in Japan, having refused to renounce Christianity. The church is also dedicated to St Anthony, and was used by Jesuits. The façade is in excellent condition, with Corinthian double columns on either side of the entrance arch, an ornate rectangular window above and a small circular window on top. Notice the IHS monogram of Christ (the first three letters of Jesus's name in Greek, transliterated into Roman script), with accompanying cross and nails, on either side of the rectangular window. The chancel has a fine barrel roof, and the exterior of the four-storey tower is largely intact. The cloisters still have extensive two-storey colonnaded archways, though the roofs have largely collapsed. Traces of the original red and white paintwork can be made out above the lower arches of the cloisters.

A third, smaller **unnamed church**, 100m beyond St Gonsalo Garcia, again has double Corinthian columns on either side of the entrance arch. The walls have long lancet windows and the chancel has a barrel roof. Close by are the remains of the citadel, wildly overgrown, and with little obviously to be seen inside. There are the remains of a gate, and over the entrance arch is the Portuguese royal coat of arms with its traditional five inner shields, arrayed in an unusual way (they normally form a cross), together with an outer border containing seven towers.

A further 300m along the wall of the fort are the remains of the **Matriz**, or **Cathedral of St Joseph**, with its three-storey tower, which can still be climbed for spectacular views out to sea. Follow the walls to the well-defended Sea Gate, beyond which is a small fishing village.

Church of the Dominicans

The final important building is the Church of the Dominicans, with its four-storey tower, reached by heading back from the Sea Gate 400m towards the Land Gate along the road: the church is on the left. Notice the Dominican symbol of a dog bearing a torch above the southern gate. St Dominic's mother, while pregnant, is said to have dreamed of her child as a torch-carrying dog illuminating the world. Nearby are the remains of other unidentified non-religious buildings.

NEAR VASAI

A few kilometres north of Vasai are the remains of a much older settlement known as **Sopara** (*map 11 A1*, 5km west of Nala Sopara station). Ancient texts and archaeological discoveries indicate that it was an important town during the reign of Emperor Ashoka (3rd century BC), and inscriptions at other sites indicate that Sopara continued to be a major settlement throughout the Buddhist period. The only significant sign of Sopara's history is a huge **brick stupa** outside the modern town. It was excavated in the 19th century, and a casket was found, containing pottery fragments believed to be part of the begging bowl of Buddha (now locked away in the Asiatic Society); fragments of one of Ashoka's Edicts were also found here. Around the stupa are a few small, well-worn sculptures and pieces of carved stonework that may have been part of the *torana*, or formal gateway, to the stupa. Note the four similar figures of small fat men leaning backwards—these were probably brackets supporting one of the beams of the *torana*.

The nearby **Chakreshwar Temple**, overlooking a lake, has some fine carvings. The most impressive is a 2m-high three-headed, four-armed statue of Brahma, with his 'vehicle', a goose, at his feet. In a display case inside the temple is an exceptional stone-carved statue of a woman—probably the Hindu love-goddess Rati—holding a very lifelike carved parrot.

PRACTICAL INFORMATION

Mumbai is, along with Delhi, the main point of entry to India for most first-time visitors, many of whom report an immediate sense of intense 'culture shock'. It is one of the busiest, most populated cities in the world, and it can all seem a little bewildering at first. If you're not used to the often intense humidity, don't overdo it at the start of your trip to India. Drink lots of fluids and do not try to spend the entire day wandering about the city. It is a city most visitors return to, so there is rarely a need to attempt to see everything at one go.

GETTING THERE

• **By air:** Many world cities and most major airlines have flights to India's commercial capital. It is, with Delhi, the main hub for internal flights—with daily services to all part of the country. The international and domestic terminals are on opposite sides of the airport, 8km apart by road, and a good 20-minute drive—longer during rush hour. The airport is officially called the Chhatrapati Shivaji International Airport, but the old name for the international terminal, Sahar, and for the domestic terminal, Santa Cruz, are still in wide use. It is about 20km from the airport to South Mumbai—and during the rush hour in the monsoon period the journey can take up to 2hrs—though the new Worli–Bandra Sealink has made the trip considerably quicker.

• **By train:** Mumbai is very well-connected to the rest of the country by railway. The main stations used for cross-country travel are the spectacular neo-Gothic Chhattrapati Shivaji Terminus (still widely known as Victoria Terminus or VT) in South Mumbai, and Dadar Station in central Mumbai. Mumbai Central (in the south of the city) and Bandra Station (towards the north) are also used extensively for services to Gujarat, while Lokmanya Tilak Station (formerly known as Kurla Terminus) is used for some trains from central and southern India. There are fast inter-city services to Delhi (16½hrs), Chennai (24hrs), Ahmedabad (7hrs), Bangalore (24hrs) and Aurangabad (7hrs).

• **By road:** Some of India's best roads connect Mumbai with Pune and the cities of southern Gujarat. It is a long day's drive from Mumbai to Goa (12hrs). Bus services are also available to most major cities, and shared taxis are widely used for destinations such as Pune.

• **By sea:** Boats for Elephanta Island, and to Mandwa for Alibag and coastal Maharashtra—providing the quickest route to the former Portuguese settlement of Chaul and on to Janjira Fort—are available from Apollo Bunder, next to the Gateway of India. There are currently no boat services to Goa.

GETTING AROUND

• **By road:** Mumbai's long narrow shape means that the key north–south roads get very congested in rush hour and during the monsoon. A journey from the Taj Hotel to Juhu Beach can take half an hour late at night but more than two hours during busy periods. Taxis are widely available: the normal black and yellow ones are ubiquitous in the city and have meters. The meter reading will normally not be the actual cost of the journey—your taxi driver should produce a tariff card which will convert the figure on the meter into the true rupee cost; the rate also increases at night. More comfortable are the all-blue Cool Cabs, which are air-conditioned and which also have meters—and are approximately 50 percent more expensive. Metered auto-rickshaws are widely available in the north of the city, but are not allowed to operate in the southern part of Mumbai (south of Mahim creek).

• **By train:** Mumbai city and suburban trains can be very crowded, but are quick and reliable. First-time travellers are advised to travel first class. There are slow and fast trains operating on the main north–south lines, and it can take a while to understand how the network works. Tickets must be purchased at the booths near the entrance to each station. There are also separate women's carriages on most trains. If you are travelling second class, you need to be ready to alight early because you are likely to be blocked by a rush of people getting on to the train.

South Mumbai has two major termini: Churchgate and Chhatrapati Shivaji Terminus (still better known as Victoria Terminus or VT), and from these stations two parallel lines, known as the western and central lines, head northwards. Churchgate serves the western side of Mumbai, with slow and fast locals. They all stop at Dadar, Bandra, Andheri and Borivli (for the Kanheri Caves), and on to the Maharashtra mainland—but make sure you get the right slow train if you want to stop in between at, say, Santa Cruz (for the domestic airport), Vile Parle (for Juhu Beach) or Vasai Road (for the former Portuguese settlement at Vasai). Chhatrapati Shivaji Terminus (Victoria Terminus) serves the central line, which heads north through the middle of the city, and serves both as the most important inter-city train station and as a major city terminus—though one that is slightly less useful to tourists. But get trains from here to Byculla (for the Bhau Daji Lad Museum), as well as fast trains on the west-coast trains to Bandra and beyond.

• **Other transport:** Buses are widely available, but tourists tend not to use them—despite the fact that they are better run and less congested than in, say, Delhi. The hovercraft that used to operate between Marine Drive and Juhu is no longer in service.

ACCOMMODATION

The **Taj Mahal and Palace Hotel** (*$$$; tajhotels.com; T: 022 6665 3366*), known by everyone as the Taj and overlooking the Gateway of India, is India's best-known hotel, and one of its oldest and most luxurious. It was the scene of a terrorist attack in 2008, in which 31 staff and guests died, and during which the old building was set on fire. The hotel quickly reopened, and the building was restored. It is well placed for visiting the historic heart of Mumbai. Most major chains have hotels in Mumbai—including the **Oberoi** (*$$$; oberoimumbai.com, T: 022 6632 5757*), overlooking Marine Drive, and the **Marriott** (*$$$; marriott.com; T: 022 66933000*) on Juhu Beach in the north of the city. There are several smaller hotels close to the Taj, including the **Gordon House Hotel** (*$$$: ghhotels.com; T: 022 22894400*).

FOOD

Mumbai is a food-lover's heaven. It has superb seafood, India's best savoury street snacks, and the richly varied cuisine of a city that is home to many migrant communities. Its five-star hotels have good restaurants, but they're overpriced, and Mumbai is the city where it is worth making a real effort to visit other eating places.

Snacks: Among the city's famous street foods are *pao bhaji* and *bhelpuri*. *Pao bhaji* is the archetypal Maharashtran snack sold throughout the city—it is a potato-based vegetable curry reduced to a paste by continuous chopping on big metal plates, which is served with the small buns known as *pao* (from the Portuguese for bread). *Bhelpuri* is a savoury snack—thought to be of Gujarati origin—containing puffed rice, chopped onion and lots of other ingredients; it is even more ubiquitous than *pao bhaji*. There are lots of different varieties, available at *bhelpuri* stalls, particularly near the city's beaches. The very popular bombay duck, incidentally, known locally as *bomli*, is not duck at all, but a fish.

Seafood: Excellent seafood is widely available in Mumbai. **Trishna** (*$$; trishna.co.in; T: 022 22614991/22703213*), in the back lanes of the Kala Ghoda area of Mumbai, is probably the best-known seafood restaurant in the country, with superb crab, prawns and fish cooked in a variety of styles—it is most famous for its Mangalorean cuisine, in which spices and coconut play an important role. **Mahesh Lunch Home** (*$$; T: 022 66955554*), in north Mumbai near the Royal Tulip hotel on Juhu Tara Road, serves similar food to Trishna—and some locals say its food tastes even better. Both restaurants have a simple, functional design, and attract large numbers of customers, particularly after 9pm at weekends. Trishna also has a branch in Andheri in North Mumbai, and Mahesh has a branch in the Fort area in the south of the city.

Parsi food: The best Parsi food is had at Parsi weddings and in family homes, but there are several establishments, known as **Irani restaurants** (often little more than cafés), in the Fort area that serve tea and snacks—with delicious egg-based dishes such as *akoori* (a lightly-spiced scrambled egg concoction). For a more sophisticated Parsi menu, **Britannia Restaurant** (*$; T: 022 22615264*) in Ballard Estate, close to the docks, is excellent. *Dhansak*, a mixture of lentils with mutton or chicken, is the signature Parsi dish, and *patra-ni machhi*—fish covered in green chutney and cooked in a banana leaf—is particularly recommended.

European Food: Mumbai also has some of India's best European food. **Indigo** (*$$$; T: 66368999; foodindigo.com*), close to the Taj Hotel on Mandlik street, is beautifully laid out in a colonial building, and has superb food using local ingredients cooked in a variety of mainly European styles.

FURTHER READING & VIEWING

• **Books:** *Maximum City* by Suketu Mehta (Random House, 2004) is the best-known recent book about modern

Mumbai, and dwells on the seamier side of city life. Gillian Tindall's *City of Gold* (Penguin India, 1982) is still recommended as a history and biography of the city.

There are many superb novels set in Mumbai—including all of the works of Rohinton Mistry, a Parsi who now lives in Canada. His *Such a Long Journey* (1992) and *A Fine Balance* (1995), both set in the 1970s, are particularly recommended. Mumbai plays a central role in Salman Rushdie's *Midnight's Children* and *The Moor's Last Sigh*. Ardashir Vakil's excellent *Beach Boy* (Penguin, 2000) is about a child growing up in a house overlooking Juhu Beach in the early 1970s. John Irving's complex detective story *A Son of the Circus* (1995) is also set in Mumbai, as is Gregory David Robert's best-selling *Shantaram* (2003)—based on the author's long stay in the slums and prisons of the city.

• **Films:** *Slumdog Millionaire* (2008) is the best known and most successful of the international films that have been shot in Mumbai, winning eight Oscars and running into controversy in India for supposedly glamorising poverty. Twenty years earlier, *Salaam Bombay* (1988) also looked at poverty in Mumbai through children's eyes—in a way that was less romantic and more touching—and started off the international career of the director Mira Nair. Many of India's most successful films are set in Mumbai, including the multi-award-winning 1996 movie *Bombay*, set during the 1993 riots, or the 1989 Hindi classic *Parinda*, which deals with the city's criminal underworld.

MAHARASHTRA

Despite having India's largest city, Mumbai (*covered in its own chapter in this guide—**see p. 468*), as its capital, as well as its busiest airport, Maharashtra (*maps 11 and 6*) is less firmly on the tourist trail than many other states. Tourism has played a minor role in the state's economy, and for this reason its infrastructure has developed less rapidly. In many other ways though, Maharashtra is a traveller's dream—unspoilt and welcoming—and contains an extraordinary range of important and beautiful historical and cultural monuments. It has India's finest rock-cut temples and paintings, at Ellora and Ajanta, in the north of the state, and some of India's most impressive military architecture, in the form of the imposing Maratha sea- and hill-forts. Maharashtra also has fine, unspoilt beaches, attractive hill-stations and, in Pune, one of India's most modern cities. Also worth visiting are the forgotten Portuguese fortifications at Chaul, near Mumbai, and the Sultanate-period fortress of Daulatabad near Aurangabad. The great Shiva temple at Elephanta Island is also within the state, but is covered in the Mumbai chapter (*see p. 490*).

Proceeding inland from Maharashtra's long coastline, the terrain changes dramatically from the narrow, dry strip of coastal land known as the Konkan, to the spectacular, almost lunar hills of the Western Ghats, to the richer agricultural lands of the Deccan Plateau—which forms the bulk of the territory of India's third-largest state. The economically richest lands are the highest parts of the Deccan Plateau, near the city of Pune, known as the sugar belt of western Maharashtra. To the east of the sugar belt are Marathwada and Vidarbha—less developed parts of the state, and little visited by tourists. Two of India's most important rivers, the Krishna and the Godavari, both rise in the hills of western Maharashtra, not far from the west coast, and eventually enter the Bay of Bengal from Andhra Pradesh, on the other side of the country.

HISTORY OF MAHARASHTRA

The modern landscape of Maharashtra and the rest of the Deccan Plateau was created more than 60 million years ago by a huge series of volcanic explosions throughout this region. These explosions coated the area with a thick layer of molten lava, which in some places is as much as 2km thick. This geographical feature is known as the Deccan Traps—where traps are a stair-like geographical feature caused by huge overlapping lava flows (*see box overleaf*). This is particularly noticeable in the area close to Ajanta and Ellora.

Some prehistoric settlements have been excavated in Maharashtra which date back 40,000 years, though the strangest relic from the time of the earliest humans is the huge Lonar Lake, created about 50,000 years ago by the last massive meteorite to have hit the earth. The earliest monumental architecture dates from the 3rd century BC, when Buddhism was the dominant religion in much of India, and the Satavahanas were the ruling dynasty in the region. Kalyan and Sopara, just north of modern Mumbai, were the main sea-ports at the time—and a ruined Buddhist stupa can be visited in Sopara. Across the state are hundreds of rock-cut caves, used as monasteries and places of rest, often on key trade routes between the sea-ports and the Deccan Plateau. The caves at Bhaja are probably marginally the oldest, but work began on the famous caves at Ajanta by the 2nd century BC. The rich tradition of cave architecture continued until the 9th century, and encompasses the extraordinary decorated caves and rock-built shrines to be found at Elephanta, Kanheri, Ajanta and Ellora.

THE DECCAN & THE DINOSAURS

Some scientists believe that the scale of the volcanic eruptions that created the Deccan Traps also caused the extinction of dinosaurs and 70 percent of all animal species around the world. Palaeontologists called this the Cretaceous-Tertiary extinction event and believe that it was caused by devastating climate change. It is the cause of the climate change that is most disputed—and one school of thought believes that the Deccan Traps were responsible, because the explosions released huge amounts of carbon dioxide into the atmosphere. Many others believe the climate change was caused by a giant meteorite that struck coastal Mexico.

The Hindu Yadava Dynasty built its capital at Devagiri in the 12th century, but was defeated by the forces of the Delhi Sultanate, and Islam made its earliest appearance in the Deccan. In 1327, Muhammad Bin Tughlaq moved his capital from Delhi to Devagiri, which he renamed Daulatabad—building the dramatic fortress that still stands outside the city of Aurangabad—before moving all the way back again to Delhi. Local Muslim dynasties replaced the Tughlaqs until the arrival in the Deccan of the Mughals in the late 16th century. Emperor Akbar took control of the main city, Ahmednagar, in 1600, and over the next 50 years the Mughals conquered most parts of modern Maharashtra.

The Mughals soon came up against a new enemy, Shivaji (*see p. 508*)—who founded the Maratha confederacy which would, long after his death, in the 18th century, conquer large parts of India. Shivaji fought many battles against both the Mughal forces of Emperor Aurangzeb and the Bijapur Sultanate in modern-day Karnataka. From his headquarters in the remarkable hilltop fort of Raigad, Shivaji dominated the neighbouring countryside using guerrilla warfare techniques. He built or extended an extraordinary series of sea- and hill-forts across western Maharashtra, many of which have survived the centuries since Shivaji's death in 1680. Emperor Aurangzeb, meanwhile, moved to the Deccan to oversee the military campaign against the Maratha confederacy, basing himself in the city of Aurangabad, which he named after himself, and close to which he was later buried. Aurangzeb's forces killed Shivaji's son and heir, and reconquered large tracts of the Deccan—but at great cost to the Mughal Empire. Many historians see the Deccan campaigns as having overstretched the Mughals, leading to the gradual disintegration of the empire after the death of Aurangzeb.

The British and Maharashtra

The 18th century was dominated by a growing conflict in Maharashtra between the Maratha confederacy and the British, who became the main power along the region's coastline—although it was not finally won by them until their victory in the third Anglo-Maratha war of 1818. Mumbai, by this time, was a major seaport and trading city, and became the capital of the Bombay Presidency, which stretched from modern-day southern Pakistan to the border of Goa, and beyond into Karnataka. It excluded the west of modern-day Maharashtra, as well as a large number of princely states. The first railways over the Ghats were built in the 1850s, dramatically simplifying travel between Mumbai and the Deccan. The British years were characterised by great financial growth and architectural activity in Mumbai—which, like Kolkata, has many fascinating public and private buildings from the 19th and early 20th centuries. The rest of the region, however, remained less developed. In 1960, Bombay State was split in two: the northern part became Gujarat, the southern, Marathi-speaking areas became Maharashtra, with Mumbai as its capital. Since the 1970s, Marathi chauvinism has played a growing role in Maharashtra's politics—with the rise of the Shiv Sena party, led by Bal Thackeray, which complains that non-Maharashtrans are taking over large cities in the state.

BETWEEN MUMBAI & PUNE

There is now an expressway between the two great urban centres of Maharashtra, Mumbai and Pune, which means that many visitors fail to visit the forts, Buddhist caves and hill-stations that are scattered across the spectacular countryside of this part of the state.

MATHERAN & ENVIRONS

Matheran (*map 11 A2*), just 45km east of Mumbai and 80km northwest of Pune, is one of India's finest hill-stations, and one of the few that has managed to avoid rampant commercialisation and overcrowding. It has been able to do this partly because no motorised transport is allowed; instead visitors travel on foot, on horseback or are pulled around in an ungainly cart. It can be very crowded at holiday weekends, though.

The hill-station was first developed in the 1850s by the British, and became a favourite place to get away from the Bombay heat, particularly for the British and for members of the Parsi community. Many of the large, airy colonial homes with large verandahs and sloping roofs survive—the best preserved is Barr House, now a hotel called the Verandah in the Forest. Several others survive too, in various states of ruin, particularly on the south side of the hill, away from the crowds and the car park.

Look also for the peaceful Parsi cemetery. The views from a series of promontories known as 'Points', on the south side of Matheran, over the lunar landscape of the Sahyadri Mountains, are breathtaking. Matheran can be reached by road, or by an extremely slow mountain railway.

Twenty-eight kilometres south of Matheran, on either side of the Mumbai–Pune expressway, are two more adjoining hill-stations: **Lonavla** and **Khandala**, both of which are more commercialised than Matheran. Just beyond them, towards Pune, are the fine Buddhist caves of **Karla** and **Bhaja**—on the north and south sides of the expressway, respectively. This has been a major trade route for more than 2,000 years, which explains the Buddhist buildings here. The only expressway exit near the caves is at Lonavla.

Karla and Bhaja

The enormous 1st-century Chaitya Cave at **Karla** (*map 11 A2, also known as Karli or Karle, open daily 9–5*), the best-preserved rock-cut Buddhist prayer hall in India, is approached by a road leading 3km north from the expressway up into the hills. It is a steep uphill walk to the main cave. There is an excavated court in front of the cave—as well as a small, more recent Hindu shrine on the right of the entrance arch. On the left is a column with a four-lion capital—and there was probably once a matching column where the Hindu shrine now stands. Note how the upper part of the entrance has been designed to allow light into the hall, while there are carved images of donors between the doorways. There are dozens of small rectangular sockets on the façade that once supported a wooden superstructure. Inside is a long horseshoe-shaped chamber, with two rows of columns and a stupa at the far end, capped by an inverted pyramid and a carved wooden umbrella. There are still original pieces of teak embedded in the ceiling ribs. Note the elephants ridden by amorous couples on the capitals of the columns. The other caves at Karla have few decorative features.

The less-visited **Bhaja** (or Bhaje) Caves (*map 11 A2, open 8–6*) are 6km south of Karla, in the hills on the opposite side of the valley through which the expressway passes. The main *chaitya* hall (Cave 12), smaller than the one at Karla, is thought to be the second oldest major rock-cut Buddhist cave in the country, dating from the 2nd century BC—only the Lomas Rishi Cave in Bihar (*see p. 608*), which has no internal decoration, is older. The front of the cave is open here; unlike Karla, and it would have been protected by a wooden gateway, the sockets of which can be seen cut into the stone. Note how the pillars here slope inwards in imitation of timber buildings, and that many of the decorative carvings imitate features normally seen on wooden structures. There are several other interesting caves, including the later Cave 19, with some fine relief images of deities—including the sun-god Surya riding a chariot pulled by horses, and crushing demons beneath its wheels.

Near Bhaja

Above the Bhaja Caves is the largely ruined 18th-century **Visapur Fort**, approached by a steep track. Beyond Visapur, on the next hilltop, is the well-defended 17th-century Lohagad Fort. There are fine views of the surrounding countryside from both forts.

Bedsa Caves

There is also a third group of Buddhist caves, at Bedsa, beyond Lohagad Fort, with another fine 1st-century *chaitya* hall (Cave 7), similar in design to the one at Karla but with fine capitals on the verandah columns showing royal couples riding animals. The columns inside the hall are largely undecorated, with a tall hemispherical stupa at the end. Cave 11 at Bedsa is a monastery, with small cells and a main chamber with the horseshoe shape of a *chaitya* hall.

PUNE

The industrial and commercial city of Pune (*map 11 B2*, pop. 4,000,000) was previously called Poona—the name of the city is pronounced 'poonay', not 'pyoon', although the pronunciation 'poona' is still widely used. It is one of India's largest cities, and is situated just 120km southeast of Mumbai, along a modern highway. Pune is an attractive city, set amid the pretty hills of the Western Ghats, many of which have impressive fortresses on their summits. For most of the year it has a gentle climate—the exception is during the pre-monsoon period, when temperatures can rise dramatically.

History: The city is closely associated with Shivaji, the great Maratha leader of the 17th century, who stayed in Pune periodically—but no significant buildings survive from this period. Pune became a major centre only in the mid-18th century, when the Peshwas, the hereditary prime ministers of the Maratha Empire, moved their capital here from Satara, 95km to the south. The city was captured by the British in 1818, and the last Peshwa was deposed. His adopted heir, Nana Saheb, later became one of the leaders of the 1857 Uprising. Pune, meanwhile, became both an important military base and a major commercial centre, attracting large numbers of migrants—including many Parsis and Jews. In the 1980s, the Indian mystic Bhagwan Sree Rajneesh, also known as Osho, set up his commune here—attracting large numbers of foreign visitors, many of whom became long-term residents. Pune today is a thriving IT and new technology centre, and is one of India's most cosmopolitan and friendly cities.

Orientation: The oldest parts of Pune, including the Shaniwarwada Fort, are on the southern banks of the Mutha River, in the southwest of the modern city. Just to the east of the old city is New Pune, including the main railway station and many hotels—first built up during the British period. Further to the east is the Osho commune and the residential area known as Koregaon Park. The airport and the road to Mumbai are in the north of the city.

Old Pune

The impressive walls of the **Shaniwarwada Fort** (*open daily 8.30–6*) in the heart of Old Pune, south of Shivaji Bridge, once enclosed the palace of the Peshwa—destroyed by fire in 1836. The almost square fort (1736), with rounded bastions, now contains some very pretty gardens, and one can make out the stone foundations of the timber palace and other buildings. About 600m south of the fort is **Vishrambaug Wada** (1811), built as a palace for the last Peshwa, and which retains its original timber façade with some fine carved woodwork. Inside (*open Tues–Sun 10–8*) are three courtyards, a dance hall and a small museum dealing with the history of Pune. Some 300m to the east of the palace is **Mahatma Phule Market** (1886), one of Pune's best-known landmarks, named after a 19th-century social reformer. The market is an unusual octagonal neo-Gothic building, with eight wings radiating outwards.

The prettiest surviving bits of Old Pune are in **Tulsi Bagh**, just north of the market—in the centre of Tulsi Bagh is the 18th-century **Rama Temple**, with a multi-tiered conical spire.

The **Raja Dinyar Kelkar Museum** (*open daily 9.30–5.30*), 300m southeast of the market, has an impressive private collection of paintings, sculptures and everyday utensils in a 19th-century building. Among the exhibits is the Mastani Mahal, part of a palace built by an 18th-century Peshwa for his mistress—which was brought here from the town of Kothrud and reassembled. About 2km to the south of the market is the **Parvati Temple** (1748), on top of a small hill, from which the last Peshwa is said to have witnessed the defeat of his army. The temple itself has an unusual design and a multicoloured tower with an onion shaped dome.

New Pune

Among the interesting buildings in New Pune's Manekji Mehta Road are the **Council Hall** (1870) in multicoloured brick, with its Italianate tower, and the neo-Gothic **St Paul Church** (1860). Nearer the railway station is the neo-Gothic **Sassoon Hospital** (1867 onwards), funded by the Jewish Sassoon family, who were also responsible for the **Ohel David Synagogue** (1863), one of India's largest. The red-brick synagogue, known as Lal Deval, 1km south of the station, has a church-like tower, while the interior has a wooden ceiling and pillars. Outside is the chapel-like tomb of the Baghdad-born David Sassoon (*see p. 474*), who died in Pune in 1864.

Other sights in Pune

Pune's oldest structure is the **Pathaleswara Temple** (c. 1000), dedicated to Shiva, 1km northwest of the Shaniwarwada Fort, across the river. It consists of a large rectangular court dug out of the rock, with a central circular pavilion housing a carved image of Nandi the bull. About 4km north of the fort is **All Saints Church** (1841), with some interesting memorial tablets, which served as the main garrison church for the British military in the cantonment area. In the northeast of the city, on the way to the airport, is the **Aga Khan Palace** (*open daily 9.30–5.30*), built for the hereditary leader of the Ismaili sect of Muslims, Aga Khan III, in 1893. Mahatma Gandhi was imprisoned here in the early 1940s, and his wife Kasturba died in the palace in 1944—there is a memorial *samadhi* marking the site of her cremation. The Aga Khan later gave the palace to the Indian nation.

SOUTH OF PUNE

There are several important **hill-forts** south of Pune, of which Sinhagad, or the Lion Fort, is the easiest to visit. Two of the most important forts—Raigad and Rajgad—have very similar names, so be careful not to confuse them.

Sinhagad (*map 11 B2*), 20km southwest of Pune, is accessed by a motorable road that leads almost to the summit. It was contested many time in the decades of fighting between Shivaji and the Mughals. On one occasion, Shivaji's forces scaled its walls, using ropes to lift soldiers and animals up the steep sides of the hill—according to local tradition the first ropes were pulled up the walls by monitor lizards. The gateways and fortifications are largely intact, though most of the buildings inside are in ruins.

Rajgad (or Rajgarh (*map 11 B2*)), 45km southwest of Pune, is arguably the most spectacular and impregnable of Shivaji forts, and one of India's most impressive examples of military architecture. The fort was built by Shivaji in 1647 and functioned as his capital until it was replaced in 1672 by the better-known Raigad Fort (*see below*). Rajgad is in a remote location, close to the tiny village of Vageghar, and is a long uphill climb. There are many ruined buildings inside the fort. A further climb takes one to the citadel with the overgrown ruins of Shivaji's palace. There are long fortified spurs, known as *machis*, that overlook sheer cliffs, which gave this fort the reputation of being impregnable, and from where there are dramatic views over the surrounding countryside.

Purandhar (*map 11 B2*), 30km southeast of Pune, was one of Shivaji's most important forts, and the birthplace of his son and successor, Sambhaji, in 1657. In the British period it served as a garrison, a sanatorium and a prisoner-of-war camp for German captives in the Second World War. Among the few surviving buildings is a crumbling church from the British period. Purandhar is defended by a second, lower hill-fort, called **Vajragad**.

Sasvad (*map 11 B2*), just 9km northeast of Purandhar, has several interesting 18th-century mansions, in what was the ancestral home of the Peshwas. **Jejuri**, 42km southeast of Pune, is best known for its **Khandoba Temple**, an important Hindu pilgrimage centre, which is dedicated to a local form of Shiva.

RAIGAD

The great fortress of Raigad (*map 11 A2*), which was the capital of Shivaji's Maratha Empire during the latter years of his rule, is 54km southwest of Pune (as the crow flies) but more than twice that distance by road, and is just as easy to reach from Mumbai. Mahad is the nearest town. The views from the top of Raigad are spectacular, and because Shivaji was cremated here it has become a place of pilgrimage for admirers of Maharashtra's most renowned leader. Raigad is one of the region's oldest forts, and was captured by Shivaji from the Sidis of Janjira (*see p. 511*) in 1656. In 1672, Shivaji chose Raigad as his new capital, replacing Rajgad (*see above*). In June 1674, Shivaji was crowned as Chhatrapati, or 'Lord of the Umbrella', at Raigad—and he was cremated here six years later.

CHHATRAPATI SHIVAJI

Shivaji (1630–80) is probably the most important and revered figure in Maharashtran culture. The site of his birth at Shivneri Fort and the site of both his coronation and his death, at Raigad Fort, have become places of pilgrimage. The main airport, railway station and museum in Mumbai have all been renamed after Shivaji, together with the honorific title 'Chhatrapati', meaning 'Lord of the Umbrella'—the title he assumed at his coronation in 1674. Even though he ruled as Chhatrapati for only six years, he is honoured as the greatest Maharashtran hero, and is above criticism. A biography of Shivaji by an American academic that was accused of being disrespectful was banned, an arrest warrant was issued for its author and a Pune-based institute that helped research the book was ransacked.

It is a very steep 2½-hour climb up more than 1,400 steps to Raigad's main gate, on the north side of the summit. However, there is a cable car which takes passengers to the top in just four minutes. On top, as well as a guest house, there are several buildings and ruins from Shivaji's period. These include two large 12-sided watchtowers and the foundation walls of a large palace complex, where it is possible to make out many of the rooms. At the centre of the palace is a modern throne on the plinth where Shivaji was crowned. To the northwest are the ruins of Raigad's old shopping street—and beyond, on the northwest side of the fort, is the site of Shivaji's cremation, as well as a memorial to his favourite dog, Waghya.

SOUTHERN MAHARASHTRA

Mahabaleshwar

The state's largest hill-station—first developed by the British in the 1820s—is at Mahabaleshwar (*map 11 B2*), 120km by road southwest of Pune. **Christ Church** (1842–67), near the bus stand, has some pretty stained glass, and there is the **Beckwith Memorial**, dedicated to a British general who died here in 1831. Old Mahabaleshwar has several temples which mark this area as the source of the Krishna River.

Pratapgarh

The hill-fort of Pratapgarh (1656, *map 11 B2*), 15km west of Mahabaleshwar, commands the strategic Parghat Pass that leads down towards the coast. The fort was built by Shivaji, and it was here that he personally killed Afzal Khan, the commander of the Bijapur army, with a weapon made out of steel claws. **Afzal Khan's Tomb** is on the left on the road up to the fort. The fort has impressive defensive walls, and inside is the **Bhawani Temple**, which contains the family deity of Shivaji's family.

Satara

This town (*map 11 B3*), 95km south of Pune, on the Mumbai–Bangalore highway, was the capital of the former princely state of the same name. Previously it was the capital of the Maratha Empire, under Shivaji's grandson Shahu, who was crowned there in 1708. Pune replaced it as the Maratha capital in 1749, but Shivaji's descendants continued to live in and rule Satara.

The town has several **palaces**, and it is possible to wander round the former royal complex in the centre of town, now occupied by the Pratapsinh High School. There is a small **museum** (*open Tues–Sun 10–5*) close to the bus stand, and to the south of Satara is the ruined fort, at the foot of which is a palace still occupied by members of the former royal family.

The *chattris*, or **memorials to the royal family**, are at Mahuli, 6km east of Satara—and are considered to be among the finest examples of Maratha architecture.

KOLHAPUR & PANHALA

Kolhapur (*map 11 B3*), 115km south of Satara, is the main city of southern Maharashtra and the capital of the former princely state of the same name.

The **Old Palace** (Juna Rajwada), which was partly ruined by a fire in the 19th century, is next to Kolhapur's most important temple, dedicated to Mahalakshmi, in the centre of the old city. The impressive three-storey entrance gateway to the palace has been turned into a shrine, known as the **Bhawani Mandap**. There are several extremely ornate late 19th-century royal and municipal buildings designed by Charles Mant, who was also responsible for the main palace at Vadodara. These include the ostentatious **New Palace** (1884), on the northwest outskirts of the city, with neo-Mughal arches and domes, and a 45m-high clock tower. Inside is a **museum** (*open daily 9.30–5.30*) with royal memorabilia.

The old **town hall**, also designed by Mant, houses Kolhapur's **government museum** (*open Tues–Sun 10.30–5.30*), which displays objects excavated from nearby Brahmapuri Hill, including some Roman-style bronzes dating back 2,000 years—a reminder of Kolhapur's importance on ancient trade routes. Brahmapuri Hill overlooks the handsome royal memorials on Panchaganga Ghat next to the river. Kolhapur's most modern royal building, **Shalini Palace** (1934), is now a slightly run-down hotel in a pretty location overlooking Rankala Lake on the western outskirts of the city.

Just 18km northeast of Kolhapur is **Panhala Fort** (*map 11 B3*), occupied since at least the 12th century, but later an important base for the Bahmanid and Bijapur sultanates, and the Marathas. The fort is triangular, with high walls more than 6km long enclosing a large plateau, with lots of homes, roads and some guest houses.

The Tin Darwaza, or triple gate, near the western entrance to the fort, is a fine example of architecture from the Bijapur Sultanate, while there is an interesting step-well built into a nearby bastion.

SOUTHEAST MAHARASHTRA

The main city in this little-visited part of the state is **Solapur** (or Sholapur, *map 11 C3*), with an impressive fort in its centre, first built by the Bahmanids of Bidar but extended by the Adil Shahis of Bijapur in the 15th century.

There are several important forts in the region. The great **Fortress of Naldurg** (*map 11 C2*), 45km east of Solapur, was built in the 16th century by the Adil Shahis, for whom it was a major military base. Note how both sides of the Bori River have been fortified with a long wall, serving both as a bridge and a dam, connecting the two parts.

Parenda Fort, in the centre of the town of the same name (*map 11 C2*), 81km northwest of Solapur, is a fine example of Sultanate military architecture, and contains an interesting mosque, baths and a step-well.

The town of **Ter** (*map 11 C2*, sometimes spelled Thair), 75km north of Solapur, was an important centre in the 1st–2nd-century Satavahana period. There is a **museum** (*open Tues–Sun 10–4*) containing some fine terracotta figurines excavated in the town, as well as later sculptures. The Satavahana-period **Trivikrama Temple**, dedicated to the giant avatar of Vishnu, may once have been a Buddhist shrine, and is thought to be the state's oldest free-standing structure, though it has been much altered in the medieval period.

Pandharpur (*map 11 B3*), 62km west of Solapur, is one of Maharashtra's most important pilgrimage sites—with a large Hindu religious complex grouped round the main Vithoba Temple, dedicated to a form of Vishnu. The complex dates to the 13th century, but most of the structures were rebuilt during the 17th–18th-century Maratha period.

COASTAL MAHARASHTRA

The coast of Maharashtra, also known as the **Konkan coast**, runs for almost 400km between Mumbai and Goa. It has some of the country's best beaches—though very few luxury hotels—and some superb sea-forts.

ALIBAG

The coastal town of Alibag (*map 11 A2*) is a short ride by boat and car from the Gateway of India in Mumbai harbour, and is now full of weekend homes. Under Shivaji, Alibag was the main Maratha naval base. The small **Hirakot Fort** (early 18th century) is on the northern side of the town, while the impressive **Kolaba Fort** (17th century) is built on an island in Alibag harbour. It is possible to walk out to the fort at low tide, and boats are available at other times. There are two smaller fortified islands, **Underi** and **Khanderi**, off the coast slightly to the north of Alibag, near Nagaon beaches—from where boats are available.

CHAUL

The fascinating ruined Portuguese settlement of Chaul (*map 11 A2*, also known as Revdanda), 13km south of Alibag, is similar to Bassein (now Vasai), 90km away (*see p. 494*). Like Bassein, the high fortifications of the settlement guard an estuary and overlook a beach, and inside the walls are several churches and other crumbling buildings. Chaul was first settled and fortified in 1516 by the Portuguese, who were forced to hand it over to the Marathas in 1740—after which the fort was no longer used for military purposes.

On entering the fort through the northern gate (from Alibag), turn right along a footpath for the ruins of the **Church of the Augustinians** (1587). Beyond this, closer to the sea wall, is the surviving 30m six-storey tower of the **Church of the Franciscans** (1535), and a little further south is the **Church of the Dominicans**, where part of the vaulted roof to the chancel and nave survive. Follow the walls past a gateway and the ruined St Francis Xavier Chapel to rejoin the road next to the main sea gate. Next to the gate is the **inner citadel**, its enclosure now collapsing; it was formerly the residence of the Portuguese governor, and also contains the ruins of the Matriz, or cathedral. On the other side of the estuary, jutting out to sea, is a heavily fortified promontory known as **Korlai Fort**. There is another fortress on the hill above Chaul.

JANJIRA

Janjira (*map 11 A2*, also known as Murud-Janjira) is India's most impressive sea-fort—a heavily fortified island, 350m from the mainland and 50km south of Alibag. The island was occupied in the early 16th century by Africans from Abyssinia, known locally as Sidis, who served in several of the armies of the Deccan sultans. Neither the Marathas nor the European powers were able to capture the island, which remained under Sidi control—an unexpected African enclave on the coast of India. Eventually, Janjira—with large tracts of territory on the mainland—became a principality under an Abyssinian-origin nawab, who ruled the island during the British period.

Visiting the fort: There is a regular ferry service to the island, which leaves from the fishing village of Rajpuri and which drops passengers at the steps leading up to the fort's only gate. The enormous walls (1694–1707) with 17 semicircular bastions, encompass the entire island. Inside there are numerous overgrown palaces—including one five-storey building—a mosque and lots of cannons.

Other sights nearby: On the mainland, 5km to the north, on top of a cliff, is the extravagantly ornate 20th-century **Ahmedganj Palace**. This is the palace of the former nawabs of Janjira, and it is still occupied by members of the family.

Just to the south of the jetty for Janjira, at **Khokri**, next to the main road, are three tombs (known as **Gol Gumbaz**) of 17th- and 18th-century nawabs of Janjira. The largest of them belongs to Sirul Khan, during whose reign Janjira island was fortified.

SUVARNADRUG, JAIGAD & RATNAGIRI

There is an important coastal fortification at Harnai (*map 11 A2*), 60km south of Janjira, where it is possible to take a boat from the village out to visit the island fortress of **Suvarnadrug**, 500m off the coast. Suvarnadrug, which means Golden Fort, was built by Shivaji's forces in 1669 to counter the influence of the Sidis of Janjira. The buildings inside the fort are in ruins. Note the fortifications on the mainland opposite Suvarnadrug. A further 60km down the coast is **Jaigad** (*map 11 A3*), a small coastal fort, 15km north of the popular beach resort of Ganpatiphule. There are also minor fortifications on the promontory at **Ratnagiri** (*map 11 A3*), the largest city on the coast between Mumbai and Goa. Historically, Ratnagiri is remembered as the place to which the last king of Burma, Thibaw, was exiled by the British in 1886. The **Thibaw Palace** (1909), on the southern side of Ratnagiri, is a rather forlorn red-brick reminder of his long exile.

VIJAYADRUG & SINDHUDRUG

There are two major sea-forts between Ratnagiri and the Goan border. The first is **Vijayadrug** (*map 11 A3,* originally known as Gheriah), which lies 50km south of Ratnagiri. It was built on a peninsula jutting northwards into the sea by the Adil Shahis of Bijapur in the 16th century to protect a fine natural harbour. It became an important naval base under Shivaji, and has remarkably impressive defences. Note the three tiers of fortifications, with outer walls that rise out of the ocean. Several buildings survive inside the fort, including the long, narrow barracks and a granary divided into four chambers.

Sindhudrug (*map 13 A1*), 58km south of Vijayadrug and just 40km north of the Goa border, is the largest of the island forts, and the one most closely associated with Shivaji. It is approached by boat from the town of Malva, 1km to the north. The fort has formidable walls, in some points 4m thick, with large rounded bastions—there are handprints near the main gate, which are said to have been made by Shivaji. Inside the fort is the **Shivarajeshwar Temple**, erected by one of Shivaji's sons, which contained a much venerated sculpture of Shivaji. There are two other small temples in the fort.

The road continues south to Goa, and two more forts: **Redi** (*map 13 A1*), just over the border in Maharashtra, and **Tiracol** (*map 13 A2*), just inside Goa (*see p. 650*).

NORTHERN MAHARASHTRA

The road from Pune to Nasik goes through **Khed** (*map 11 B2*, now officially Rajgurupur), with the handsome **mosque** and **Tomb of Dilawar Khan** (1613)—a general of Ahmednagar.

Shivneri Fort: This fort, in which the Maratha leader Shivaji was born in 1627, overlooks Junnar (*map 11 B2*), 76km north of Pune and a short detour off the Pune–

Nasik road. The fort rises 300m above the plain, and a road leads part of the way to the top on the south side of the hill. At the northern end of the triangular plateau on the summit are the two-storey **pavilion** where Shivaji was born and the small **Kamani Mosque**. There are some Buddhist caves cut into the eastern side of the hillside, though there are more impressive Buddhist caves nearby, including *chaitya* halls at Tulja Hill, 2km east of Shivneri, at Lenyadri Hill, 4km to the north, and at Manmodi Hill, 2km to the south.

NASIK

Nasik (*map 11 B1*, also known as Nashik) is an important pilgrimage town, 145km northeast of Mumbai, that has also become a major industrial centre and the main home of India's growing wine industry. Just outside Nasik are the Buddhist Pandav Lena Caves, with some superb rock-cut carvings, while all around are the strange funnel-shaped hills that dominate this part of the Maharashtra countryside. Nasik's religious importance derives from its association with the *Ramayana* epic—it is said to have been one of the places where Rama and Sita stayed during their 14-year exile. The city, through which the sacred River Godavari runs, is also one of the four sites of the mass Hindu pilgrimage known as the Kumbh Mela.

Nasik city centre: The centre of Nasik contains an unusual series of pools, used by worshippers, bathers and washerwomen—which have been created by dividing the river lengthways and crossways. The largest of the ponds is called the **Ramkund**—and is where Rama is believed to have performed the funerary rites for his father. There are large numbers of temples, of which several date back to the 18th century, when this was an important centre of the Maratha Empire. These include the fine **Sundara Narayan Mandir** (1747), a large grey building overlooking the south side of the weir above the Ramkund.

Pandav Lena Caves

These fascinating Buddhist caves (2nd century BC–6th century AD) are halfway up a steep hill in the southwestern suburbs of modern Nasik, just above a memorial to Dadasaheb Phalke, a pioneering figure in the Indian film industry.

Orientation: It is a steep ten-minute walk up the hill to the **ticket office** (*open daily 8.30–5*). Ahead are 24 caves that have been cut into the hillside, and which were used as part of a monastery complex. To the right are caves 1–10, older but less decorated than caves 11–24, on the left. If you're short of time, make sure you visit caves 3, 10, 18, 20, 23 and 24; if you have more time though, start at Cave 1.

Cave 1 is a simple cave, with a frieze of cows and interior rock-cut steps leading to a niche which may have once held a statue. **Cave 2** is a smaller, pillar-less cave with some fine carvings, including a large seated Buddha and a guardian carrying a fly-whisk. Note the many rock-cut cisterns which enabled large quantities of water to be stored in the complex. **Cave 3** is one of the most important and impressive Nasik caves, with a finely carved exterior. Elephants, cows and mythological animals are carved on the unusual capitals of the six columns. Note the false rafters carved under the eaves, shaped to look as if they are made out of wood. Dwarf-like figures have been carved at ground level so that they appear to be holding up the façade as if it were a balcony. Inside the porch, there are guardians on either side and inscriptions above the door. The interior consists of a large central living area and small cells with raised platforms that were probably used as beds. There is a relief carving of a stupa on the back wall, surrounded by female worshippers.

Cave 4 is much smaller but also has a columned façade with similarly complex capitals on its pillars; note the people riding on an elephant's back. **Caves 5–9** are relatively uninteresting; though note the inscriptions above the entrance on Cave 6, the rock-cut step on Cave 8, and the carving of elephants and cows above the entrance to Cave 9. **Cave 10** is another important temple, similar in design to Cave 3, but without a balcony. There are again false rafters carved in stone under the eaves of the façade, and the porch has a heavily inscribed interior. The smaller **Cave 11** is up some stairs and has some pretty carving cut into the wall. **Caves 12–14** are almost totally bare. **Cave 15** (below) and the very fine **Cave 16** (above) are small twin caves, both circular with similar carvings, the former more weathered.

Caves 17–20 are all part of the central complex within the monastery, centred around the superb Cave 18. **Cave 17** is approached by steps on the right side of Cave 18 and is similar to Cave 4 in external design, with the same complex pillar design.

Cave 18 is arguably the most impressive of the Pandav Lena Caves, with its exquisite three-storey façade. Note the repeated use of the horsehoe-shaped arch, and the way the rock has been cut to resemble railings, windows and a balcony, with mini-stupas resting on the railing. The interior is a traditional Buddhist *chaitya* assembly hall, with a stupa at the far end. The rest of the hall is plain, apart from the pot-shaped bases to the columns. Note the post-holes in the upper parts of a wall which once supported the rafters of a wooden ceiling.

Cave 19 is a small cave, with finely carved internal door arches and railings. **Cave 20** is the slightly larger counterpart to Cave 17, approached by steps and on the other side of Cave 18—and with a fine façade. It was enlarged in later times, and the carvings at the back of the large internal room, with small side cells, date from this period. **Caves 21 and 22** are almost bare.

Caves 23 and 24 are entered through an open area cut deep into the rock—similar in scale to the main caves at Kanheri—giving a very impressive feel to the final, and most recent, of the Pandav Lena Caves. **Cave 23** is tucked into the nearest corner of the overhang, and has two finely carved columns with guardians on either side of the door that leads to the inner cave—with a proliferation of carved Buddhas, celestial beings and worshippers. Along the wall at the back of the overhang is another cell with more carvings of seated Buddhas, a guardian carrying a fly-whisk, and devotees—as well as a second fine cave, also labelled with the number 23. **Cave 24** is further along the overhang and contains carvings that are more weathered, but also has a greater depth of relief of any masonry work at Pandav Lena. A little beyond is another unnumbered cave, devoid of decoration except for a superb railing carved into the stone above the entrance.

TRIMBAKESHWAR

The sacred Trimbakeshwar mountain (*map 11 B1*) is 30km west of Nasik and is the source of the Godavari River, which flows for almost 1500km from here before it reaches the Bay of Bengal over to the east—although the nearest sea-coast is just 90km away to the west. At the foot of the mountain is the **Trimbak Temple** (1780s), which houses one of India's 12 *jyotirlingams*. There is a long, steep walk up Trimbakeshwar, which takes pilgrims past many temples. There are superb views from the top.

AURANGABAD & NORTH-CENTRAL MAHARASHTRA

The area around Aurangabad in north-central Maharashtra is one the most historically rich in all of India. The very different cave complexes at Ajanta and Ellora are the most artistically and architecturally impressive rock-cut caves in the country—and, arguably, the world. Ajanta is best known for its superb 5th-century wall-paintings, while Ellora has some quite extraordinary carvings and architecture from the 6th–10th centuries—both places are remarkable UNESCO World Heritage Sites. That's not all. Twice Delhi's rulers have moved their capital to this area: first in the 1320s, when it was sited at Daulatabad, near Ellora—and this remains one of India's greatest medieval forts; and again in the 1680s, when Aurangabad itself became the effective capital of the Mughal Empire—and there are are some important scattered remains of the Mughal period. It is usual for visitors to base themselves at Aurangabad, which has an airport and a good tourist infrastructure, though there are basic, clean hotels at Ellora and at Ajanta. The two sets of caves are not close (83km apart, in fact), and your visit will be very rushed if you try to see them both on the same day.

AURANGABAD

This city (*map 11 B1*) was once the capital of the Mughal Empire, under Emperor Aurangzeb, after whom it is named. Despite the presence of caves nearby that date back to the 1st century, the city was founded only in the early 17th century, when Malik Ambar, the African-born prime minister of the Ahmadnagar Sultanate, made it his headquarters. In 1683 the Mughal emperor Aurangzeb moved his court here, so as to be in a better position to fight his enemies in the Deccan—and changed the city's name from Fatehnagar to Aurangabad. It remained Aurangzeb's main base until his death in 1707, and he was buried in nearby Khuldabad. Apart from the Bibi ka Maqbara, nicknamed the 'Poor Man's Taj' or 'the Taj of the Deccan', there are few surviving buildings from the Mughal period—and in the 18th century the city became part of the state of Hyderabad. Aurangabad is now an important industrial city.

Bibi ka Maqbara

The most important surviving building from the Mughal period is the Bibi ka Maqbara (or 'wife's tomb') of 1650–57—an elegant white mausoleum, the reputation of which has suffered from the obvious comparisons with the Taj Mahal—it has been nicknamed the 'Poor Man's Taj'. The Bibi ka Maqbara (*open daily dawn–10pm*) is in fact the tomb of Rabia Durani, the daughter-in-law of Mumtaz Mahal—the woman for whom the Taj Mahal was built. Rabia was the wife of the Mughal emperor Aurangzeb, who was the son of Mumtaz and the emperor Shah Jahan, who commissioned the Taj Mahal. The tomb in Aurangabad, however, was commissioned by Rabia's son Azam Shah, and not by Aurangzeb—who, according to local tradition, refused sufficient funds for the construction of as grand a building as the Taj.

Nevertheless, the Bibi ka Maqbara is still a superb example of a Mughal garden tomb, set—unlike the Taj Mahal—in the centre of a rectangular formal garden. Note the fine stucco work on the interior of the large gateway. The main building is narrower and squarer than the Taj Mahal, and the interior is very different—and, unusually, the doorways do not lead to a cenotaph, but to an octagonal gallery overlooking the actual grave. Like the Taj Mahal, the Bibi ka Maqbara has four tapering minarets, but they are octagonal rather than circular. There is a mosque on the west side of the tomb. The Aurangabad Caves are visible in the hills to the north, and at night the Bibi ka Maqbara is lit up and looks very pretty.

Mughal Aurangabad

Several of the old gates of Aurangzeb's Aurangabad do survive, and so do portions of the city walls. However, the main palace compound, known as **Qila Arak** (just north of the Delhi Gate), has almost disappeared—though there are a few ruined buildings near the **Shahi Masjid**, which served as the emperor's personal mosque.

There are also the remains of Aurangabad's 17th-century **hydraulics system**, which brought water into the city. Water pressure was controlled by towers, of which the **Panchakki** is the best-known surviving example. The nearby **Dargah of Baba Musafir** is a pretty example of a 17th-century Mughal tomb complex; it still attracts devotees, who come to pay homage at the grave of one of Aurangzeb's spiritual guides, who was originally from Bukhara in Central Asia. There is also a small **museum**.

The cantonment area—on the road to Ellora—has the tiny neo-Gothic **Holy Trinity Church**, as well as the **British cemetery**, dominated by an obelisk to Colonel Richard Seyer.

Aurangabad Caves

The rock-cut cave temples at Aurangabad are nowhere near as spectacular as those at Ellora and Ajanta, but still have some interesting Buddhist carvings and architectural features, as well as commanding views over the city. The caves (*open daily sunrise–sunset*) are in two groups, 2km to the north of the Bibi ka Maqbara. Apart from the older Cave 4, they all are thought to date, like most of the Ajanta Caves, to the 5th–6th-century Vakataka period.

Western group: This group of caves, numbered 1–5, is approached by some steep steps beyond the car park and ticket office. **Cave 1** was never completed, though its verandah has some interesting carvings, including amorous couples around the door frame and on the pillars. **Cave 2** is smaller, but its interior has a walled sanctuary, protected by huge carved guardians and containing a fine statue of a seated Buddha. There is a passage round the sanctuary with many more carvings. **Cave 3** has an unimpressive exterior, largely because the verandah has collapsed, but inside are some finely detailed carvings in the large open hall supported by 12 rock-cut columns. The façade of **Cave 4** has also collapsed, revealing a fine *chaitya*-style temple, with rock-cut ceiling ribs and a stupa at the rear of the hall. This is thought to be the oldest of the caves—dating to the 1st-century Satavahana period. Little remains of **Cave 5** apart from a seated Buddha statue.

Eastern group: This group of caves, numbered 6–9, is 1km away from the western group and is approached by returning on the same road and turning left rather than going back to the city. **Cave 6** has an almost bare exterior, with square columns with tiny figures cut into them halfway up. Inside are carvings of Buddhas, celestial beings and devotees. **Cave 7** is the finest of the Aurangabad Caves—similar in design to Cave 6, but with a far richer and varied collection of carvings. Note the fine broad-hipped female deities guarding the door, as well as other female figures in the side sanctuaries. There are fragments of painting on the ceiling of the verandah. **Cave 8** is ruined and **Cave 9** unfinished, but it does have a damaged image of the dying Buddha in the state of *parinirvana*—similar to Ajanta's Cave 26—and several other carvings in better condition.

DAULATABAD

The fortress of Daulatabad (*map 11 B1*) is one of India's most remarkable examples of medieval military architecture. Daulatabad is striking from a distance—a fantasist's idea of a fairy-tale castle, perched inaccessibly on top of a huge unscalable rock that rises from the plains. It is just as impressive from close up—as the ruined city that surrounds the rock becomes visible, and as the ingenuity of the medieval masons, who cut a hidden stairway inside the rock, becomes evident.

History: Daulatabad was originally known as Devagiri, or Deogiri, the hill of the gods, and was an important centre of the 11th–12th-century Hindu Yadava Dynasty—remains of their temples can be seen in some of the more recent buildings in the area. It was captured in 1296 by the forces of the Delhi Sultanate under the Khilji Dynasty, and in 1327 Muhammad bin Tughlaq moved the capital of the Sultanate from Delhi to Devagiri, and changed its name to Daulatabad, or City of Fortune. He soon reversed his decision and moved his capital back to Delhi—and over the next two centuries Daulatabad came under the control of the Bahmanids of Gulbarga and Bidar, and the Nizam Shahis of Ahmednagar. The Mughals took the fort in 1633 without a battle, having bribed a Nizam Shahi general with more than a million rupees to open its gates. It was later fought over by the Marathas and the forces of the Nizam of Hyderabad—and Daulatabad remained part of Hyderabad state until Independence

Orientation: The road from Aurangabad (12km to the southeast) to Ellora (10km to the north) passes through the outer walls of Daulatabad. The entrance to the main buildings of the fort is on the west side of the road, where there is a car park beside the next set of defensive walls. Just inside the gateway is the ticket office (*open daily 6–6*)—and the path into the lower parts of the fort and to the upper fortress. The area between the two sets of outer walls is now largely agricultural, but there are scattered ruins that are worth exploring if you have time. It is a steep climb to reach the upper fort and involves walking through a tunnel—so take a torch and some water.

The outer defences

The walls of Daulatabad are impressive defensive fortifications—note how neither set of walls goes round the great central rock of the fortress, but instead they begin and end by abutting the rock. The outermost area, known as **Amberkot**, has walls that are 6km long and largely intact, complete with dozens of bastions. The second set of walls surrounds an area known as **Mahakot**, and consists of a double circuit of fortifications, stretching for 2.5km, with dozens of circular and square bastions; it contains most of the ruins of the old city of Daulatabad. The series of old gates that lead into the city are largely intact, with a series of blind turns to increase the defensive capability of the fort against any invader. Note the carved stonework and pillars on the walls and gates. There is an interesting collection of cannons between two of the gates.

Inside the main fort

Once inside the walls of Mahakot, a path leads straight ahead, towards the Chand Minar and on to the upper fortress. On the immediate left is a star-shaped **step-well** (1332) and a number of other ruined buildings, while a track to the right takes you to the ruins of some buildings known as the **Kacheri**, or court room, though it looks more like the ruins of a garden palace. A little further along the main track, and up some stairs on the left, is a large square water tank.

Jama Masjid

Just beyond the water tank is an even larger square building, Daulatabad's old Jama Masjid (1319), or Friday Mosque—which has been converted in recent times into a Hindu temple, dedicated to Bharatmata, or Mother India. It was one of India's largest mosques, measuring 80m by 60m. It once had cloisters running round three sides of the building, though only the columns survive. The prayer hall is largely intact, and columns from old temples have been reused here—probably from a Jain shrine.

Chand Minar

Just to the northeast of the mosque is the 40m-high Chand Minar (1435), or Moon Tower, thought to have been built as a tower of victory by the Bahmanid sultan Alaud-din to mark his conquest of the fort—though it is also believed to have served as a minaret from which the call to prayer was made for the nearby Jama Masjid. Note the circular gallery, supported by carved stone brackets, as well as a few surviving blue glazed tiles, which probably covered most of the tower. At the bottom is a small mosque. The main path is straight ahead, but a smaller path to the right goes to a small outdoor museum, next to a former palace, with some fine carved figures of Hindu gods and Jain saints, recovered from Daulatabad. Beyond and behind the museum are more ruined buildings—including a closed gateway leading out of the fort, which has a small attached mosque.

The main path through the fort continues past more ruined buildings towards another set of impressive defensive walls, with a gate leading through to the Balakot (also known as Kalakot), the inner citadel. Just to the right before the gate is a small mosque.

The citadel

Inside the citadel, the path starts going uphill past several more ruined buildings, thought to have been the royal residences during the Bahmanid and Nizam Shahi period. Note the two-storey **Chini Mahal**, or Chinese palace, so named because of the blue and white Chinese-style tiling that is still visible on parts of the building. The last Qutb Shahi ruler of Golconda, Abul Hasan, was imprisoned in the Chini Mahal by Aurangzeb and died here in 1700. Further on is a large circular bastion, on which rests a finely decorated cannon. Note the large storage jars buried in the ground next to the bastion.

The moat and the tunnel

The next defensive feature of the fort is a remarkable rock-cut moat, with sheer sides making the upper fortress inaccessible except by a drawbridge. The stone bridge that crosses the moat is a 19th-century addition. From here, the only way up to the highest levels of the fortress is by a tunnel cut deep into the rock. There are two entrances to the tunnel, which is unlit. On the right is the original full tunnel—home to many bats—which can still be used. If instead you take the steps on the left, you join the old tunnel halfway along, and the journey to the upper fort becomes a little less daunting. Guides with torches are normally available nearby. Note how windows have been cut into the rock to allow some light into the tunnel; these windows also afford good views of the moat and the fortress below.

The Baradari

At the other end of the tunnel a steep walk awaits, uphill to the Baradari (1636), the white-and-grey stone palace built by Emperor Shah Jahan near the summit of the rock. It was used as a summer retreat by both Shah Jahan and his son and successor Aurangzeb. The Baradari, which literally means '12 doors', has 12 archways grouped round a large courtyard. A little further uphill, at the summit of the rock, are more ruined buildings, an underground tank, a hermit's cave, which has become a shrine, and large cannon resting on a bastion. There are glorious views of the fort below and of the surrounding countryside.

The outer fort

Opposite the car park, outside the main fort complex, there is an interesting old bath-house, known as the **Shahi Hammam**. Note the circular roof vents that would have allowed steam to escape. Also nearby is a pretty *dargah*, or Muslim tomb-shrine.

KHULDABAD

The walled village of Khuldabad (*map 11 B1*, also known as Rauza), whose pretty domes and garden overlook a lake, along the road between Daulatabad and Ellora, is an important Islamic pilgrimage centre. It contains two *dargahs*, or shrines, to Sufi saints who attracted the following of a number of important political leaders, including the last of the great Mughal emperors, Aurangzeb—he was buried here in a simple grave in 1707.

Entering from the Daulatabad side, you pass through a large outer gate, constructed in the early 18th century. The overgrown **Lal Bagh Tomb complex** is approached through an outer courtyard on the left, with a decaying water channel. The inner courtyard contains the **Tomb of Khan Jahan**, Aurangzeb's foster-brother, which was once surrounded by water and has the remains of yellow tiling on the exterior, and pretty internal decoration. A gate next to the small mosque in the garden leads to another garden with more tombs.

Aurangzeb's grave

In the heart of the village of Khuldabad are two *dargahs*. The one on the right—to Sayyid Zeinuddin Shirazi, who died in 1370—also contains Aurangzeb's grave. Aurangzeb asked to be buried in a simple grave close to the tomb of Zeinuddin, whom he considered to be his spiritual guide. The small compound containing Aurangzeb's grave is now entered separately, immediately to the left in the main *dargah* courtyard, though it is actually part of the larger compound containing Sayyid Zeinuddin's tomb. In conformity with conservative Islamic tradition, no structure has been placed above Aurangzeb's grave, which is covered with earth and has a small tree growing in it. The pretty marble screen was added by the Nizam of Hyderabad in 1921. In the main inner compound, a sandstone screen surrounds the grave of Azam Shah, Aurangzeb's son. In the far corner is a covered area with a safe that contains what is said to be a robe worn by the Prophet Muhammad, and which is put on display once a year on the Prophet's birthday.

Other buildings in Khuldabad

The other *dargah*, on the opposite side of the road, is dedicated to Sheikh Burhanuddin Garib, who died in 1344. Nizamul Mulk, who was founder of the Asaf Jah Dynasty that produced the nizams of Hyderabad, is buried here. Behind Burhanuddin's *dargah* is a walled compound—approached by taking a left turn further north in Khuldabad village—that contains a lovely garden, with some pretty pavilions and the sunken **tomb of Bani Begum**, the consort of one of Aurangzeb's sons.

Mausoleum of Malik Amber

Continue uphill through Khuldabad's northern gate, past some minor tombs and another *dargah*, to reach the walled Mausoleum of Malik Amber (1626), an African general, born in modern-day Ethiopia, who was sold into slavery and later became prime minister of the Ahmednagar Sultanate. He was the founder of Aurangabad and one of the most feared soldiers of the Mughal period. Note the superb stonework on the exterior of the tomb, as well as the smaller tomb just outside the compound, in which Malik Amber's wife was buried. Go past the modern guest house to reach a path that leads downhill to the great Kailashnath Cave at Ellora, less than 1km away.

ELLORA

The remarkable Buddhist, Hindu and Jain caves of Ellora (*map 11 B1, open Wed–Mon dawn–dusk*), cut deep into a basalt cliff face 20km west of Aurangabad, are a stunningly original collection of architectural masterpieces. Not only are they extraordinary for the way they reverse many of our modern ideas about building—they are really enormous sculptures cut from a single rock—but also several of the caves have a quite unbelievable level of detail and complexity. While at Ajanta exquisite paintings have been added to the rock, at Ellora everything is taken away by a mason's chisel.

History: Little is known about the early history and purpose of the Ellora Caves—and there are fewer inscriptions than at similar sites. The dating of the excavation has proved problematic, though it is now thought that several of the basic caves, and probably Cave 29 (Dhumar Lena), should be ascribed to the 6th-century Kalachuri period. It seems likely that the Buddhist and Hindu caves were excavated at a similar period and were in use concurrently, as monasteries and temples respectively. The two triple-storey Hindu caves (11 and 12) are thought to date from the 7th–8th-century Early Chalukya period—while the great Kailashnath Cave (16) was created in the 8th-century Rashtrakuta period, with the building of more of the Hindu caves, and the Jain ones, continuing into the 10th-century Rashtrakuta period. Many of the caves were originally painted—and some traces of paint are still visible. But Ellora was never abandoned, and the caves' proximity to the important 18th-century Grishneshwar Temple and

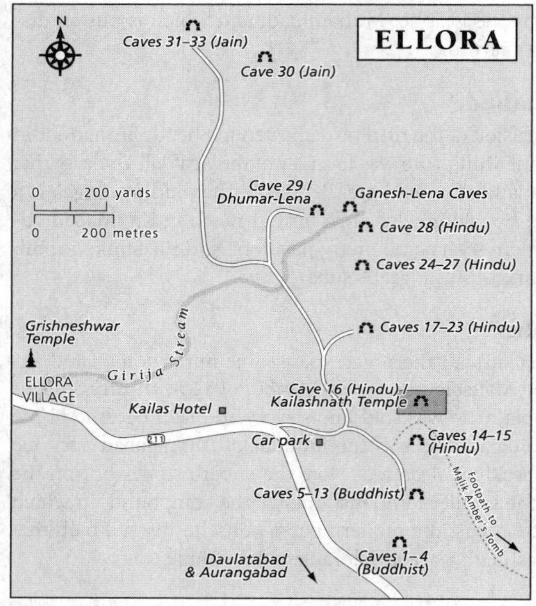

the village of Ellora means that they have little of the remoteness sensed by visitors to Ajanta. However, it remains a quiet place, especially early in the morning before the coach parties arrive from Aurangabad, or just before dusk when the fading sunlight shines directly into the caves.

Orientation: The main road from Aurangabad via Daulatabad runs parallel to, and just 200m from, the Ellora Caves. The caves themselves face westwards, and can be quite dark and cold in the early morning. There is a large car park near the ticket office—from where an auto-rickshaw can be hired to visit the more distant Jain caves (1km to the north), though it is a very pleasant walk to them. The Ellora Caves are numbered 1–34, from south to north. The southern group, 1–12, are all Buddhist, while caves 14–29 are Hindu and caves 30–34 are Jain. The nearest cave to the car park is the centrepiece of the Ellora Caves: number 16, known as Kailasa or Kailashnath. Visitors can choose any order they like. This guide starts from the southernmost of the Buddhist caves, and proceeds in numerical order. If you are in a hurry, leave out the first four caves.

Caves 1–4

The bare **Cave 1** is where, according to local tradition, the stone-cutters stayed while they were excavating the other caves. **Cave 2** is a typical *vihara*: a Buddhist monastery with a columned verandah and a large central hall. It has unadorned side cells for the use of the monks, and a Buddha shrine in the sanctuary at the rear. Most of the first nine caves are like this. Note the fine carvings on the partially ruined verandah. Most of the carved figures are of seated or standing men—either representing the historical Buddha, or *bodhisattvas* (Buddhist saviours). The female figures are usually Hariti, the Buddhist protector of children, or the *bodhisattva* Tara. Note the finely-carved cushion-shaped capitals. The more basic **Cave 3** has simpler pillars with pot-and-foliage capitals. Note the small cell between caves 3 and 4 with a carved image of a seated Buddha with his attendants. **Cave 4** has two storeys, with the upper floor now closed. It also has pot-and-foliage capitals. Note the finely carved door guardians, with their dwarf-like attendants.

Caves 5–9

Cave 5 is larger than the preceding caves and has been dug deeper into the hillside, giving it an unusual rectangular shape. The two low benches carved out of the floor were probably used for eating and studying. Note the cushion-shaped capital similar to Cave 2. The front portion of **Cave 6** is ruined, but there are fine carvings of standing *bodhisattvas* and a seated Buddha in the sanctuary, guarded by small lions carved onto the plinth. Here the numerical order of the cave is confusing. **Cave 9**, with its very pretty façade, is approached through Cave 6, while the rest of the caves are accessed by going back down the stairs. **Cave 7** was never finished, and lacks decoration. Unusually for a *vihara*-style cave, there is a passageway round the sanctuary of **Cave 8**—note also the fine guardian figures in this cave. The fine carving outside the cave is of Panchika and Harika, a semi-divine couple in the Buddhist tradition.

Cave 10

This cave, sometimes known as Vishwakarma, is a superb example of a *chaitya* hall—a horseshoe-shaped cave intended as a place for worship and with a stupa that can be circumambulated. The cave has its own courtyard, with worn rock-cut figures of animals. Like many other caves, there is a columned verandah, but the roof of this one supports a terrace, behind which is a superbly carved upper façade, designed to let light into the hall. Note the fine carvings of flying celestial beings on either side of the topmost window, and the amorous couples on the parapet wall of the terrace. Inside, the long hall is divided into three aisles by two sets of octagonal columns. Note the rock-cut ceiling ribs, thought to be an imitation of contemporaneous wooden temple ceilings. The central Buddha figure almost seems to be bursting out of the stupa, and is framed by an archway covered with relief carvings of celestial figures. Note also the fine frieze of carvings of preaching Buddhas, and of Buddhist tales between the column capital and the ceiling ribs. Stairs from the verandah lead up to the terrace, and, if the doors are not locked, onto a gallery inside the *chaitya* hall.

Caves 11–13

The three-storey **Cave 11** used to be known as Do Tal, or 'two storeys', until another, lower storey was dug out of the mud in modern times. From outside, this cave, and the similar Cave 12, look like simple excavations, with strong horizontal lines and little embellishment—almost in the style beloved by architects of modernist urban housing of the mid-20th century. But inside, on each floor, there is a profusion of Buddhist carvings, and sanctuaries with Buddha statues, guardians and relief wall-carvings. The finest sculptures are on the top floor. **Cave 12**, known as Tin Tal, or 'three storeys', has a similar façade and layout to Cave 11—but the internal carvings are of an even higher quality. Note particularly the row of seven seated Buddhas in the top-storey verandah, and the three female *bodhisattvas* beside the sanctuary. Inside the top-storey sanctuary there are traces of paintwork and a large seated Buddha. **Cave 13** was never properly excavated.

Cave 14

This is the first of the Hindu caves, and it has some fine wall-carvings of Hindu gods, and portrayals of images and stories that are repeated several times in the next few caves. The first recess on the left shows the goddess Durga, followed by the goddess Lakshmi being bathed by elephants, and Varaha, the boar avatar of Vishnu, as well as two different portrayals of a seated Vishnu. On the right side, the best-known image is of the multi-headed demon Ravana, shaking Mount Kailash, the abode of the gods. Above Ravana sit Shiva and Parvati. Note how Shiva lazily pushes the mountain back down again with his foot. There are three other Shiva images: one dancing, one killing the demon Andhaka, and a third where he is shown playing dice with Parvati. The sanctuary is protected by guardian figures, though the main idol has disappeared. Note the figures of the *saptamatrikas*, or the seven mothers, on the right wall of the sanctuary.

Cave 15

This is known as the Dasavatara, after the ten ('das') avatars of Vishnu—though there are also many Shiva images, and it has a Shiva lingam in the sanctuary and a Nandi bull amid the columns. The cave consists of a large courtyard with a monolithic assembly hall at its centre and a two-storey cave complex—similar to the previous two caves at the back. Once again the top storey has the finest carvings—some of the best in Ellora—in recesses between pilasters, around a large hall cut deep into the rock. On the left side are Shiva images, from the front: spearing the demon Andhaka; Shiva dancing; Shiva playing dice with Parvati; Shiva and Parvati's marriage; and Ravana shaking Mount Kailash. At the back of the cave on the left are carvings of: Shiva emerging from the lingam to save his devotee's son Markendeya from Yama, the god of death; and Shiva receiving the goddess Ganga in his hair. At the back, on the right, are more Shiva images, including a very fine one of Shiva still within the lingam, and of him destroying demons while riding a chariot. On the right side of the cave are Vishnu images, from the front: Narasimha, the lion avatar of Vishnu, fighting a demon; Vishnu as the giant Trivikrama striding across the world; Varaha, the boar avatar of Vishnu; Narasimha disembowelling the demon; Vishnu resting on the serpent Shesha; and Krishna lifting the town of Govardhan above his head to save the people and animals of the town from the fury of Indra. From the terrace of the upper storey, notice how the lions and other figures on the roof of the assembly hall are part of the same rock from which everything else in the compound has been cut.

Cave 16

Kailasa, or Kailashnath, the 'abode of the gods', is one of India's greatest Hindu shrines and one of its most unusual. It seems unbelievable that everything you see in the huge temple complex—all the statues, all the ornamentation, every last detail—was cut out of the hillside, particularly because the centrepiece of the complex looks exactly like a 'built' temple. The thin wall of rock that provides the complex with its façade gives an idea of the original shape of the hillside. Three deep trenches were then cut downwards from above, forming the side and back passages around the temple. In all, 200,000 tons of rock are thought to have been removed over a period of 100 years in the 8th–9th centuries.

Façade: The worn façade of Cave 16 is one of Ellora's finest, though it acts to conceal rather than advertise the extraordinary temple complex inside. On the façade are both Shiva- and Vishnu-related carvings—as if to demonstrate the non-sectarian nature of the main temple, which, although dedicated to Shiva, has many carvings of other gods. Notable is the image of Varaha, the boar avatar of Vishnu, on the right of the entrance, where its protected position has meant it is less worn that the other carvings.

Entrance area: The small entrance door emerges into a covered area under a bridge that connects the Nandi shrine to the upper storey window that has been cut into the façade. Straight ahead is a carved image of the goddess Lakshmi being bathed by elephants. To the left and to the right are open spaces that form a passage surrounding the central Kailashnath Temple. Note that on both sides, in identical places, are what were once identical elephants and columns and which—like everything else here—were cut out of the rock. They have aged differently, and the elephant on the right is barely recognisable. In the outer walls are more rock-cut cave-temples, some of them with superb carving—and too frequently neglected by hasty visitors.

Side caves on the left: Heading left (that is, clockwise) from the entrance, the first important cave is the Shrine of the River Goddesses—with its superb and well-known (there is even a life-size copy at Aurangabad airport) carvings of Saraswati, Ganga and Yamuna—the three great ancient rivers of north India (the Saraswati River has since disappeared). Note how each of the goddesses is framed by an arch emerging from the mouth of a sea monster. The next largest cave, up some stairs, is the Lankeshwara Temple, a Shiva shrine with a large Nandi bull, some fine carvings and a good view across to the main temple.

Side caves at the back: Towards the rear of the complex is a gallery of carvings cut into a deep recess that starts on the left wall, continues along it and then returns along part of the right wall. The first set of carvings is Shiva-related—including an unusual representation of the ten-headed demon Ravana chopping off his heads and presenting them to a Shiva lingam. Further on is an image of a lingam, within which there is a carving of Shiva. The second set of carvings is Vishnu-related and includes a fine image of the man-lion Narasimha tearing out the entrails of a demon.

Side caves on the right: Beyond the gallery, almost coming full circle round the main temple, is the Hall of Sacrifice, with arguably the finest carvings at Ellora—images cut almost in the round and showing the powerful female gods Durga, Chamunda and Kali seated above emaciated bodies. Close by are the *saptamatrikas*, or seven mother goddesses.

Main temple: The exterior of the main temple has a long frieze of elephants, and occasionally other animals, that goes around the entire plinth. On the left front side of the temple are the most detailed carvings at Ellora, showings scenes from the *Mahabharata*, while on the right side are scenes from the *Ramayana*. Higher on both sides of the temple are now familiar images of Shiva, or of one of the avatars of Vishnu. Note the small amounts of paintwork on the exterior of the temple. Steps lead up to the area that separates the main temple from the smaller Nandi Shrine, which contains a statue of Nandi the bull, Shiva's 'vehicle', facing towards the temple lingam. Note the detail on the roof of the Nandi shrine. Beyond it is another open area leading to a chamber which looks out over the entrance to the entire complex.

The main assembly hall of the temple is entered through a doorway flanked by stone-cut guardians and attendants, and inside are 16 decorated columns and several more Shiva carvings. There are fragments of murals on the ceiling. A lingam occupies the sanctuary. Doors lead out onto the rear terrace, offering excellent views over other parts of the complex. The terrace surrounds the tower of the sanctuary—which rises 32m above the inside of the complex—and there are subsidiary shrines on the terrace. Note how masons have been unable to complete the tower of two of the smaller shrines, presumably because of faults in the rock. The upper parts of the main temple are in fact best viewed from the hillside, and there are steps up the hill on either side of Cave 16. Notice in particular the roof of the assembly hall decorated with a large lotus leaf pattern, on which four lions appear to prowl.

Caves 17–28

Caves 17–20 are over the footbridge to the north of Cave 16. They are relatively uninteresting, especially if you have just come from Cave 16, although Cave 17 does have a finely-modelled carving of Durga killing the demon buffalo. **Cave 21**, known locally as the Rameswara Cave, is a Shiva temple with a Nandi bull carved out of the rock in the courtyard; it has some fine carving. On the left is a sinuous image of the river goddess Ganga, while Yamuna is on the right. Among the images inside the verandah are those showing Ravana shaking Mount Kailash, with Shiva and Parvati seated above, and a superb collection of the seven mother goddesses, carved almost in the round, each carefully modelled and each entirely different. **Caves 22–28** are, again, relatively uninteresting—though Cave 22 has some carvings, Cave 25 has an uncommon ceiling image of the sun-god Surya riding a chariot pulled by seven horses, and on the left of Cave 27 are fine standing images of, from left to right, Brahma (with three heads), Vishnu (with a conch) and Shiva (with a trident). A footpath behind Cave 28 leads up to the older **Ganesh-Lena Caves**, with traces of paintings on the ceiling of one of the verandahs.

Cave 29

Known also as Dhumar-Lena, Cave 29 is the last of the Hindu caves, and is approached either from the road beneath or by the rock-cut pathway under the cliff face that leads from Cave 28. It is similar in design to the great Elephanta Cave near Mumbai, with a central Shiva shrine, superbly carved columns with cushion-shaped capitals, and a series of very fine Shiva panels around the inner walls. These include a ferocious Shiva spearing his demon son Andhaka, as well as Ravana shaking Mount Kailash, with a nonchalant Shiva and Parvati sitting above. Note also the superb guardian figures around the main shrine.

Jain Caves (30–33)

It is a further 600m by footpath or road to the final set of caves, all of them Jain. The small unfinished rock-cut **Cave 30** is slightly up the hill behind Cave 32, and it is easy to miss if you go by road. It is sometimes referred to as Chota or Little Kailasa, because it is a miniature, though incomplete, replica of Cave 16—though that is actually a better description of Cave 32. In **Cave 32**, the column and the elephant in the compound and the central shrine clearly imitate Cave 16, albeit with Jain religious figures. Note the traces of paintings on the ceiling. The figure in the central shrine is Mahavir, the 24th and last of the Jain saviours. In the subsidiary shrines, cut in the side walls, are some fine carvings of semi-divine female figures, one sitting on a lion, the other on an elephant—each of them beneath a tree. **Cave 33** is the final important excavation: a two-storey Jain shrine with fine carvings of semi-divine figures, one male and one female, each signifying prosperity, and with Mahavir in the sanctuary. Note the paintings in the shrine, which are probably Ellora's best.

Grishneshwar Temple

Modern Ellora's most important place of pilgrimage is the 18th-century Ghrishneshwar Temple, almost 1km west of the caves in the heart of the village. Like so many major Hindu shrines of this period, it was commissioned by Ahilyabai, the Holkar queen who lived in Maheshwar (240km to the north in Madhya Pradesh). The shrine is dedicated to Shiva, and is a fine example of 18th-century Hindu revivalist architecture.

AJANTA

The Ajanta Caves (*map 11 C1, open Tues–Sun 9–5.30*) are spectacularly located on the side of a remote, forested hill, overlooking a horseshoe-shaped bend in the River Waghora. Inside the caves are some remarkably well-preserved paintings and carvings—the most complete representation of the early Buddhist tradition to be found in India. Some of the work is thought to date back to the early 2nd century BC, though the greater part is from the 5th century and the reign of the Vakataka ruler Harisena—whose dynasty ruled a large part of central India during the Gupta period. The caves, cut with chisels into the basalt rock, would have been used as a *vihara*, or monastery where Buddhist monks lived, studied and prayed. The caves were abandoned soon after the 5th century—and were only rediscovered in 1819, by a British hunting party led by Captain John Smith, who spotted one of the caves with external carvings from the other side of the narrow valley. The caves were filled with silt and were in use by animals at the time.

Information and orientation: The Ajanta Caves are usually approached by road from Aurangabad, 85km to the south, a journey by car of 1½–2 hours. The nearest large town, and train station, is at Jalgaon, 52km to the north. Locals sometimes pronounce and spell Ajanta as Ajinta. All visitors are dropped off at a car park, 4km from the

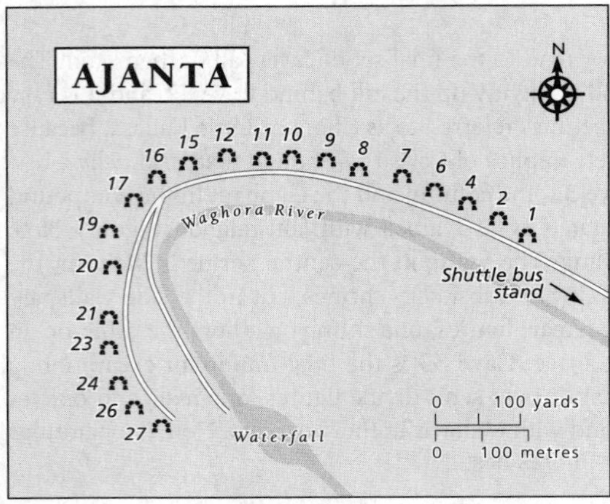

caves, where you must pay a small 'amenity fee' (retain your ticket) before walking through an open-air shopping area to a second parking area; there, a shuttle bus will take you close to the ticket office near the caves. From here it is a short steep walk up to the caves—or it is possible to be carried by porters in a chair. You will be asked to remove your shoes before entering many of the caves. The caves are weakly lit to preserve the paintings, and cameras must have their flash switched off. Take a torch, and allow your eyes to get used to the darkness before you start examining the paintings on the walls. Guides are available and are particularly helpful in pointing out some of the detail of the images. The caves are numbered in order from 1 to 27, though the older group of caves are in the middle—and Cave 10 is thought to be the oldest of them all. Caves 1, 2 and 17 have the finest paintings, while the best carvings are to be found in caves 9, 19 and 26.

Cave 1

Arguably the finest of the painted caves, Cave 1 (late 5th century) has an external courtyard, a columned verandah and two side porches. Note the fine carvings above the columns, showing animals, dancers, musicians and scenes from the life of the Buddha. Almost the entire interior is covered in paintings, faded and with missing patches in some places, but in remarkable condition elsewhere. The columns have carvings on and near their capitals, and the sanctuary of the cave is occupied by a large seated carving of Buddha. To the sides are small cells which would have been used as dormitories by the monks.

The murals, starting clockwise from the left of the entrance, depict a variety of scenes from the *Jatakas*, The first scene is from the *Sibi Jataka*, where the good king rescues a pigeon from a hawk and offers to give the hawk an amount of flesh, cut from his own body, equivalent to the weight of the pigeon. The clearest images are on this side of the cave, covering much of the left wall, where the *Mahajanaka Jataka* is depicted. In this tale, the shipwrecked King Mahajanaka is tempted by a beautiful queen and her attendants living in a city; however, he meets an ascetic, decides to renounce the world and leaves the city on horseback—the city and palace scene give us a strong idea of what urban centres of ancient India might have looked like. The large painted figure, with an elaborate headdress, just to the right of the entrance to the sanctuary, is one of Ajanta's best-known and most beautiful images. It depicts the *bodhisattva* Padmapani carrying a lotus flower and wearing a sacred cord, which has pearls threaded on to it. On the other side of the door is a less complete image of the *bodhisattva* Avalokiteshwara, grimacing slightly with his mouth open and wearing a striped cloth. Although much of the right wall of the cave is incomplete, and it is not always clear which *Jataka* stories are being illustrated, look out for some very fine depictions of human faces and bodies. Note also the rich imagery of the ceiling, with painted panels being used to divide up the enormous surface area.

AJANTA PAINTINGS

Most of the paintings depict scenes from the Buddhist *Jataka* tales, which are stories from the life of the Buddha's previous incarnations. The painting technique involved covering the stone surface with a rough plaster made from clay mixed with dung, straw and animal hair. This was then covered with a layer of smooth lime plaster, which became the actual painting surface. The subject matter would be drawn in red upon the surface, with a thin coating of grey paint, and then painted in the full range of natural colours that are still visible in Ajanta.

Caves 2 and 3

The slightly smaller **Cave 2** repeats many of the themes of Cave 1 and has a similar design. However, the presence of painting in the entrance verandahs allows visitors a better-lit view and the opportunity to get a real sense of the vibrant colours used by the artists. Note also the carved image of the female Buddhist saviour Hariti with a child on her knee, on the lintel of the left porch. Inside are dozens of repeated images of seated Buddhas, as well as further illustrations of the *Jataka* stories. Most of the right wall is given over to a depiction of the *Vidhurapandita Jataka*, which describes the courtship of Princess Indrati (shown on a swing) and General Punnaka. Indrati and Punnaka are shown together at a window. The ceiling is even more richly painted than in Cave 1. **Cave 3** is up the stone stairs and is closed to the public.

Caves 4 and 5

The enormous **Cave 4**, the largest in Ajanta, was never completed, but still has fine carvings on the verandah and inside the cave. The panel to the right of the door shows Avalokiteshwara. The sanctuary has a fine seated Buddha, with small figures of deer and humans, probably donors, around the base of the statue. To the left of the sanctuary are large relief carvings of standing *bodhisattvas*, while on the right are half-finished statues, which help us to get a clearer understanding of how the sculptors worked on the basalt rock. **Cave 5** is only partially excavated, but has some carvings round the doorframe. It was probably affected by the same weaknesses in the rock that seem to have prevented the completion of Cave 4.

Caves 6–8

Cave 6 is Ajanta's only two-storey cave, and is decorated with paintings and carvings. The lower sanctuary has a distinctive arch which emerges from the mouth of two *makaras*, or sea-monsters. The internal staircase leads to a terrace with lots of small rock-cut Buddha images, and further large carvings inside the top-storey cave. **Cave** 7 has two small porticoes, but no central hall. The dozens of large and small Buddha images show the 'miracle of Sravasti', when the Buddha levitated and showed himself in all his different forms. **Cave 8** is closed.

Caves 9–10

Cave 9 is the first of several caves that are generally thought to date to an earlier period, probably the 1st century BC. The horseshoe-shaped cave served as a *chaitya*, or religious assembly hall, and does not have the rectangular shape—or small cells, or sanctuary—of the *vihara*, seen in the previous caves. Instead there is a stupa, with a double drum and an inverted step pyramid, which is the focus of religious activity and which would be circumambulated by devotees. The façade of the cave is particularly striking—and it is probably this cave or the next one that was spotted by the 19th-century British hunters who rediscovered Ajanta. Some of the carvings and painting belong to the later period, and, inside the cave on the left, one can see 5th-century images superimposed on those from the 1st century BC. The vaulted roof would once have had wooden ribs, the sockets of which can still be seen on the side of the roof. **Cave 10** is a *chaitya* cave, similar to, and probably slightly older than, Cave 9—and here also there are signs of two phases of painting. Note the deep rock-cut side ribs, which would have been continued across the ceiling in wood. There is some fine internal painting on the columns and the side walls.

Caves 11–16

Cave 11 is a *vihara*-style monastery building, with some fine paintings on the upper parts of the verandah and on the interior ceiling, including images of animals and birds. **Caves 12 and 13** are simple caves, the façades of which have collapsed, although some fine carved decorative features survive on Cave 12. **Cave 14** is closed, but visible from the terrace of Cave 16. The verandah of **Cave 15** has collapsed, but it retains its finely-carved door frame and a large seated Buddha in the sanctuary. **Cave 15a**, down some stairs, has a large rock-cut elephant on each side of the doorway. **Cave 16** is one of Ajanta's largest, and has some fine paintings depicting *Jataka* stories and, on the right wall, tales from the life of the Buddha. An inscription on this cave allowed historians to date the later caves to the rule of King Harisena. All the caves from Cave 16 onwards belong to the later 5th-century period.

Caves 17 and 18

Cave 17 is, arguably, Ajanta's finest, with superb paintings inside the verandah and on the interior walls of the cave. The ceiling and upper walls of the verandah are richly and brightly decorated, with animals, crowd scenes and Buddha images. Note particularly the series of eight amorous couples above the main doorway, and, immediately above them, eight seated Buddhas. Turn to the left: on the far left wall of the verandah is a Wheel of Life, while in between is a series of successive images of a couple drinking wine, travelling towards a city gate and distributing alms. Towards the far end of the wall on the right of the doorway are images of the Buddha subduing a wild elephant. Inside the cave, several *Jataka* tales are depicted—including, on the immediate left of the door, the story of the *bodhisattva* Chhaddanta, who took the form of a six-tusked white elephant who cut off his own tusks. The left wall depicts the *Vishwantara Jataka*—and has an image of Prince Vishwantara, alone with his wife, telling her he has been banished from his father's kingdom. The right wall tells the *Simhala Jataka*, or the story of Simhala's conquest of Sri Lanka—note the fine image of Simhala sitting in a tent with a young woman, who is actually an ogress. Note also the very fine decoration on the ceiling of the cave. **Cave 18** is of little interest.

Cave 19

This is a very fine *chaitya* cave, one of two (Cave 26 is the other) that belong to the later period. The external carvings are particularly impressive for the quality of the carvings and for the sheer number of large and small figures—mainly the Buddha, seated and standing. The upper arch, as in the other *chaitya* cave, allows more light into the main chamber. The stupa is the most complex at Ajanta: it includes a Buddha image, surrounded by an arch that emerges from the mouths of *makaras*, or sea-monsters, and a complex tiered structure on top of the stupa. Note the vaulted ceiling with its rock-cut ribs.

Caves 20–25

Cave 20 is smaller, with some interesting carvings above the doorway, and a fine seated Buddha in the sanctuary, with two deer kneeling by the plinth. **Caves 21 and 23** are very similar in layout, with carvings and fragments of paintings—note the fine painted Buddha on the left internal wall of Cave 21, as well as the unusual circular patterns, in red and white, on the ceiling between two columns. **Cave 22** is up some stairs, and is normally closed, but it is possible to see some fine carving on either side of the sanctuary by peering through the wire door. **Cave 24** is the second largest in Ajanta and incomplete—giving visitors an idea of the way in which such huge quantities of rock were dug out of the hillside, and how the artists began planning the sculptures that can be seen in the other caves. **Cave 25** is bare and uninteresting.

Caves 26 and 27

Another large *chaitya* hall, **Cave 26** is best known for its superb carving of a 7m-long recumbent Buddha in the state of *parinirvana*—or total nirvana. The exterior, very similar to Cave 19, is covered with fine carvings, though the stupa inside is less complex. The *parinirvana* carving is on the left as you enter. Notice, beneath the Buddha's sleeping figure, how his earthly followers mourn the death of his body, while, above, heavenly figures welcome his attainment of complete nirvana. **Cave 27** is the last of the caves and has partially collapsed.

NEAR AJANTA

Five kilometres back from the Ajanta car park towards Aurangabad is the small fortified **Ajinta village**, from which the caves got their name. The village has some fine walls, gates, bastions and a bridge—all of which date from the 18th century, as well as a Mughal-style mosque with seven cusped arches, which is thought to date from the same period.

The village of **Anwa** (*map 11 C1*), with its fine 12th-century temple, is an interesting 8km detour off the Ajanta–Aurangabad road. The turning, to the east, is 10km before the Ajanta car park. The **Marha Temple** is on the far side of Anwa village, set in a compound, and should not be confused with the more modern temple which villagers may direct you to. The Marha Temple, with its assembly area open on three sides, was built under the Yadava Dynasty and originally dedicated to Vishnu. It now has a Shiva lingam in its sanctuary. Note the fine carvings on the exterior of the sanctuary, and particularly on the columns and ceilings in the assembly hall.

AHMEDNAGAR

The town of Ahmednagar (*map 11 B2*), midway between Aurangabad (107km) and Pune (110km), was once the pre-eminent city in the region. It was named after Ahmed Nizam Shah, a commander under the Bahmani Dynasty of Bidar, who formed his own state in 1496, and founded the Nizam Shahi Dynasty which ruled from Ahmednagar. The Ahmednagar Sultanate took part in the defeat of the Vijayanagar Empire in 1565, and was frequently at war with Bijapur and with the Mughals. The Sultanate survived until 1628, when the Mughals occupied the city. It became an important military base under the British, and many Indian nationalist leaders were interned here. Today the city attracts few tourists, but several historic buildings, spread out across different part of modern Ahmednagar, are worth visiting. The city is known simply as 'Nagar' by locals.

Ahmednagar Fort

Ahmednagar Fort (1550s) is on the eastern side of the modern city and was the Nizam Shahi citadel. The great 20m-high walls of the fort, more than 1.7km long and almost circular, are intact, but the palaces of the Sultanate period have long since disappeared. Visitors are allowed to drive into the fort, which is still a military area, and park just inside the modern gateway. It is possible to walk the full length of the impressive defensive wall along the battlements. If you do this heading clockwise, you will pass at one point through an unusual tunnel created when the wall was extended upwards, and then reach the old chain drawbridge across the broad moat. Just before completing the circle, you should come to the old main gate, in which there is a small *dargah*, or Muslim shrine, in the old guardroom. There is a small **museum** in the centre of the fort, in what is called the 'National Leaders Block'—where a courtyard and rooms have been preserved to honour the site in which a group of Indian nationalist leaders, including Jawaharlal Nehru (later to become the first prime minister of India), were interned from 1942 to 1945.

Ahmednagar's mosques

About 500m from the fort is the tiny **Damri Masjid** (1568), an exquisitely decorated grey mosque, with some superb carved stonework. The old city has several Nizam Shahi mosques, most of which have been modernised. The first floor of the **Mecca Masjid** (1525) has pillars that were brought from Mecca, and an unusual mixture of styles of roof vaulting.

Hawai Khana

On the northern borders of modern Ahmednagar, 5km northeast of the fort, is a small former summer palace of the Nisam Shahi period, known locally as the Hawai Khana, or House of Winds. It is a two-storey octagonal building, once surrounded by a large octagonal lake, which is now usually dry. On the south side are more ruined palace buildings surrounding an old gateway, and on the left (east side), down some steps, are the old royal baths, with circular roof vents to let out the steam. About 500m to the south, on the road side, is the ventilation tower for an underground water palace, now flooded.

Nizam Shahi tombs

On the western borders of the modern city, 3km west of the fort, is the neglected tomb complex of Ahmed Nizam Shahi (1509), the founder of Ahmednagar. The complex, known as Bagh Rauza, is surrounded by fields and has a number of lesser tombs outside the compound that have been turned into homes. The tomb of Ahmed Nizam Shahi is open on four sides and has some fine stone-carved decoration—floral, calligraphic and geometric, on the exterior and interior of the building. The other tomb, with an unusual pyramidal roof, belongs to Ahmad's prime minister, Shah Tahir.

Faria Bagh

Just 2km to the south of the city, a little to the west of the Solapur road, is the enormous water palace known as the **Faria Bagh** (1583). It is in an army area, and you need to follow signs to the Cavalry Tank Museum to reach the palace, which stands in the middle of a square dry lake, connected to the 'mainland' by a 70m causeway. Look carefully, for the shape of the building is very similar to the Taj Mahal, but without its domes; and it predates the Taj by more than half a century. Note the use of the Baghdad octagon—an octagon with alternate long and short sides—and the high central arch, with double-decker arches on each side. Climb on to the low-domed roof for excellent views of the surrounding countryside. The nearby **Cavalry Tank Museum** has a collection of old tanks and an unusual Rolls-Royce armoured car.

EAST OF AHMEDNAGAR

To east of the city, 8km along the Paithan road, is **Alamgir's Dargah**, where the last of the great Mughal emperors, Aurangzeb, died in 1707 (Aurangzeb was also known as Alamgir). Ask to be shown the tiny underground room, beneath the mosque, where

Aurangzeb is said to have stayed. About 2km further, on the summit of a hill, stands the imposing **Tomb of Salabat Khan** (late 16th century), known locally as Chand Bibi Mahal. It is a three-storey octagonal tomb, open on all sides. The graves of Salabat Khan, a prime minister of Ahmednagar, and his family can be visited underground—notice the light vents in the very flat internal dome that covers the underground chamber. There are superb views from the top of the tomb building.

The town of **Paithan** (*map 11 B1*), between Aurangabad and Ahmednagar, is an important ancient Hindu pilgrimage centre, best known now as the home the 16th-century Hindu poet-saint Eknath.

The spectacular **Lonar Lake** (*map 11 C1*), 125km east of Aurangabad, is an almost perfectly circular body of water, created by a meteorite more than 50,000 years ago. There are a number of interesting temples on the high ridge that surround the lake, some of them dating back to the 12th century.

EASTERN MAHARASHTRA

The eastern part of Maharashtra (also known as Vidarbha) is little visited by tourists, but has some important forts and pilgrimage sites.

Nagpur

Seven hundred kilometres east of Mumbai, Nagpur (*map 6 B2*) is eastern Maharashtra's largest city, and has some interesting buildings from the Maratha and British periods. The area known as Mahal (literally 'palace') is the old Maratha part of the city, with a few surviving royal buildings, now used as offices, from the period between 1743 and 1853, when it was ruled by the Bhonsle princely family. The old Bhonsle *chattris* are at Nava Sukhrawari, close to the Nag River. Sitabaldi Fort in the centre of Nagpur is closed to the public. Just to the east of the fort, near the state assembly (Nagpur serves as the state's second capital for part of the year), is the modern **Zero Point Milestone**, a large pillar that is so named because Nagpur is considered the geographical centre of India. A kilometre and a half to the west of Zero Point is the high-domed Neoclassical **Nagpur High Court** (1937–42). Designed by Henry Medd, it is one of the finest buildings of the late British period in India.

Ramtek and Wardha

The important pilgrimage centre of **Ramtek** (*map 6 C2*), 38km northeast of Nagpur, has several temples dedicated to the Hindu god Rama and other avatars of Vishnu. The temple complex is on a hilltop and consists of several shrines, some of which date back to the 11th century, and with idols that are even older.

In the other direction from Nagpur is the town of **Wardha** (*map 6 B3*; 68km southeast of Nagpur). It is best known as Mahatma Gandhi's home from 1933. He actually stayed in **Sevagram Ashram**, 5km east of Wardha, which has been turned into a memorial to Gandhi.

Achalpur

Previously known as Ellichpur, the town of Achalpur (*map 6 B2*), 200km west of Nagpur, was the capital of the former state of Berar, which broke away from the Bahmanids of Bidar in the 15th century. There is an open-air congregational mosque, or **Idgah** (1347), and the **Jama Masjid** (15th century), as well as two fine 15th-century forts in the region: **Gavilgad**, near Chikaldara, 25km to the northwest, and **Narnala**, 52km to the west.

PRACTICAL INFORMATION

GETTING THERE & GETTING AROUND

There are several airports in the interior of Maharashtra, of which Pune and Aurangabad are the most widely used by tourists. There are regular flights to both cities from Mumbai and Delhi, though many travellers heading from Mumbai to Pune, and its nearby caves and forts, travel by car along the modern highway (3½hrs from Mumbai airport) or by train (3hrs). Other airports include Kolhapur (daily flights from Mumbai) and Nagpur (daily services from Mumbai and Delhi).

The state has a good train network, with several trains each day from Mumbai to Nasik Road (3½hrs) and Nagpur (12hrs) on the Calcutta route, and a morning train to Aurangabad (6½hrs). Roads in the state have improved in recent years.

ACCOMMODATION

Pune and Western Maharashtra

• **Janjira**: The **Golden Swan Resort** ($$; *T: 0952144 274078; goldenswan.com*) near Janjira has comfortable cottages next to an enormous empty beach. Further down the coast, the state tourism department's **MTDC Holiday Resort** ($$; *T: 02357 235248*), on the beach at Ganpatipule, is in a lovely location, and comfortable but not luxurious.

• **Matheran:** Matheran has many hotels, of which the most comfortable is the Neemrana group's **Verandah in the Forest** ($$; *T: 02148 230296; neemranahotels.com*), a 19th-century former holiday home.

• **Pune:** Pune's best-known luxury hotel is the **Taj Blue Diamond** ($$$; *T: 020 66025555; tajhotels.com*) in Koregaon Park, though other comfortable accommodation includes the **Oakwood Residence** ($$$; *T: 020 25670011; tghotels.com*) near the Deccan Gymkhana Club.

Southern Maharashtra

• **Kolhapur:** The **Shalini Palace** ($$; *T: 0231 2630401; welcomheritagehotels.com*) claims to be Maharashtra's only palace hotel.

• **Nagpur:** The town's most comfortable accommodation can be found at the **Pride Hotel** ($$$; *T: 0712 2291102 pridehotel.com*), near the airport.

• **Solapur:** Here, the **City Park Hotel** ($$; *T: 0217 2729791; hotelcitypark-solapur.com*) is probably the best accommodation in town.

Northern Maharashtra

• **Ajanta:** Here there are the new cottages at the **MTDC Ajanta Tourist Complex** (*$; T: 02438 244230*).

• **Aurangabad:** There are several comfortable hotels here, including the **Taj Residency** (*$$$; T: 0240 2381106; tajhotels.com*) and the **Lemon Tree** (*$$; 0240 6603030; lemontreehotels.com*).

• **Ellora:** There is the comfortable but basic **Kailas Hotel** (*$; T: 02437 255556; hotelkailas.com*) in Ellora.

• **Nasik:** The best hotel in Nasik is the **Gateway Hotel** (*$$$; tajhotels.com; T: 0253 6604499*), on the Mumbai road, which is run by the Taj group. There is also the much simpler Taj-owned **Ginger Hotel** (*$; gingerhotels.com; T: 0253 661 6333*), on the Trimbak road.

The area around Nasik has many of India's best vineyards, and **Sula Vineyards** (*$$$; T: 0253 2230575; sulawines.com*), just outside the town, has a luxury three-bedroom bungalow, where visitors can stay.

FOOD

The food most widely associated with Maharashtra is buns stuffed with chopped cooked vegetables, known as *pao bhaji* (*see Mumbai, p. 499*), although in much of the state, breads are eaten unleavened. Coconut is widely used in cooking, and fish is a staple in coastal regions. The other food item that most Indians associate with the state are Alfonso mangoes, which come from the Konkan coastal region—they are available from April to August.

FURTHER READING

The best local guidebook to Maharashtra (as well as parts of neighbouring states) is Outlook Traveller's *Weekend Breaks from Mumbai*, while there is a superb English-language resource for fort-lovers at http://trekshitiz.com/EI/EI_DefaultUserAlpha.asp.

Two of the state's least-visited historic sites are celebrated in two popular, if very different, novels. Part of Amitav Ghosh's *The Glass Palace* is set in the Ratnagiri home of the last king of Burma, while the third of Bernard Cornwell's Richard Sharpe series, *Sharpe's Fortress*, is set in the remote fort of Gavilgad.

KOLKATA (CALCUTTA)

Kolkata (*map 8 D1*, known as Calcutta before 2001) is the capital of West Bengal (*see p. 560*). It is the youngest of India's four great cities, but often feels like the oldest—and the most charming. It divides opinion in a way that no other city does. For most Bengalis, it is India's intellectual and artistic capital. For many other Indians, it is the city that time forgot—caught up in its past and neglectful of the present. For many foreigners, especially those who have never visited India, Kolkata is the archetypal symbol of urban poverty and disease. The story of the Black Hole of Calcutta lives on in the English language as a metaphor for appalling, unsanitary conditions more than two centuries after the disputed incident, in which as many as 100 British settlers may have suffocated to death in a small unventilated room. For Rudyard Kipling, 19th-century Calcutta was the 'City of Dreadful Night', and once again the description stuck; and, of course, no one did more to call attention to Kolkata's poverty than an Albanian nun known as Mother Teresa. But Kolkata is also a megacity, with a population of more than 14 million. And, like other megacities, it has its share of modernity and affluence, its flyovers, its shopping malls and hi-tech industries; and it had an underground metro long before any other Indian city.

Large parts of the centre of Kolkata feel like an open-air museum of 19th-century colonial architecture. Many of the buildings are in desperate need of restoration, though the sight of trees growing out of the side of colonial mansions has an evocative, romantic feel that makes walking through this city a fascinating experience. When it is too hot and muggy, there are some fine museums, temples, mosques, churches and cemeteries to visit. Parts of the old riverfront have been restored, and it is possible to take a boat trip on the Hooghly.

HISTORY OF KOLKATA

According to most history books, Calcutta (with that spelling) was founded in 1690 by the British trader Job Charnock, on the site of three villages—Sutanuti, Kalikata and Gobindapur—which he purchased on behalf of the East India Company on the muddy eastern banks of the Hooghly. That, though, has been the subject of some historical revision in recent years (*see box on p. 539*).

Charnock had previously been based further upriver, at the town of Hooghly, but felt that the British positions there were too hard to defend against the Mughal army, which still formally controlled most of Bengal. Charnock died in 1693, three years after establishing a British base in the area, and so he never saw the city grow—though his mausoleum is in Kolkata, at the St John's Church cemetery. By 1707 the British had completed the building of Fort William in a part of town close to the Writers' Building and the main post office. By the middle of the 18th century, a sizeable British population—and a small Armenian community—had settled in the city.

The Black Hole of Calcutta: Plans to strengthen the city fortifications were the immediate reason for a pre-emptive attack on Calcutta in 1756 by the 20-year-old nawab of Bengal, Siraj ud-Daula. Most of the city's foreign residents escaped down the river, but 143 of them were, in the height of summer, packed into a small guard room, which would later became known as the Black Hole of Calcutta. According to one of the survivors, John Zephaniah Holwell, more than 100 people died overnight of heat exhaustion and suffocation. There were just 23 survivors. This account has been challenged by recent Indian historians, with the suggestion that Holwell inflated the figures. British forces, led by Robert Clive, later known as Clive of India, recaptured the city, which had been briefly renamed Ali-nagar, early the following year.

CLIVE OF INDIA

Robert Clive (1725–74) originally came to India as a civilian, working as a junior civil servant in Madras. He was caught up in fighting against the French in southern India, and made his reputation as a soldier. Soon after the recapture of Calcutta, Clive led the British forces to an even more important victory at the Battle of Plassey, ensuring British supremacy in Bengal. The new nawab of Bengal, who owed his position to the British, rewarded Clive handsomely. He returned to Britain as one of the richest men in the country, with the nickname Clive of India, the best-known of the 'nabobs' (a corruption of the title 'nawab') who had made their fortune in India. A parliamentary enquiry into Clive's wealth attracted huge publicity, and though he was cleared of misconduct, he fell into depression and committed suicide. Until recently, visitors to Kolkata Zoo could see one of Clive's pets, a giant tortoise that lived to be more than 250 years old. It died in 2006.

The growth of Calcutta: A new, larger Fort William was constructed on the site it still occupies, and this was a time of great financial and territorial growth for the city. The earliest colonial architecture dates from this period, including the barracks that were later converted into the city's main government offices—known as the Writers' Building. In 1773, Calcutta was made the capital of British India, and the controversial figure of Warren Hastings—who was later accused and acquitted of corruption—became the first governor-general. As the city grew in the 19th century, it was split into the 'White Town' of the rulers and the 'Black Town' of the Indians. In 1911 the British decided that Delhi would replace Calcutta as the Indian capital, a decision from which some Bengalis say the city has never recovered.

Calcutta at Independence: Just before Independence, the city was torn apart by Hindu-Muslim riots in which more than 1,000 people died. It was then swamped by migrants and lost a large part of its hinterland to East Pakistan—later Bangladesh. The city remains an enormous, congested metropolis, with high levels of poverty, but recent years have seen some improvement, as well as considerable investment in the city's infrastructure—and more recently still, in the conservation of the city's crumbling heritage buildings. It is also a city that remains understandably proud of its intellectual heritage, having been a home to two of India's greatest 20th-century cultural icons: the polymath poet, novelist, painter and lyricist Rabindranath Tagore; and the film-maker Satyajit Ray—and it remains a place where having brilliant ideas will bring you greater respect than making a business fortune.

THE FOUNDING OF 'KOLKATA'

As elsewhere in India, campaigners in 'Kolkata' fought a successful campaign to enforce the local-language version of the city's name on English speakers. But in Kolkata, they have gone further. In 2003, two years after the name change, the Kolkata High Court declared that Job Charnock was not the founder of the city, and that Kolkata would no longer celebrate its birthday on the 24th August. The court argued that the pre-existence of the village of Kalikata—from which Calcutta/Kolkata drew its name—demonstrated why Charnock should be not seen as its founder.

Orientation: The dominating geographical feature of Kolkata is the Hooghly River, heading southwards to the Bay of Bengal and the Indian Ocean. The river forms the city's western boundary, and is spanned by two giant bridges—the older Howrah Bridge (officially the Rabindra Setu), to the north, and the Vidyasagar Setu (also known as the Second Hooghly Bridge), to the south. Along the river are a number of access points, with steps leading down to the water, known as *ghats*, used by passenger ferries, bathers, pilgrims and washermen and women. The river runs north–south until just beyond the Maidan, the great open area at the heart of the city, when it turns westwards, past the once great docks of Kidderpore. The city of Howrah sits on the opposite bank of the Hooghly and is officially a separate urban area. However, for all practical purposes it is really part of Kolkata, and is home to the main railway station. To the east of the city are salt lakes and marshes—diminished by urban encroachments, but still a source of fish for the piscivorous people of Kolkata.

Two major roads run north–south through Kolkata: the Strand, which runs alongside the Hooghly; and Chowringhee Road (officially Jawaharlal Nehru Road), which runs almost parallel to the Hooghly, but further inland. The Metro line largely follows the route of Chowringhee Road. Many of the city's former colonial mansions are in the south of the city, while rich Indians in the 19th century would often live in northern Kolkata. The main government area is around Dalhousie Square (now BBD Bagh), and the old commercial parts of the city are further to the north and east, along with the city's old Chinatown, and areas once popular with other minorities, including Jews, Armenians and Parsis.

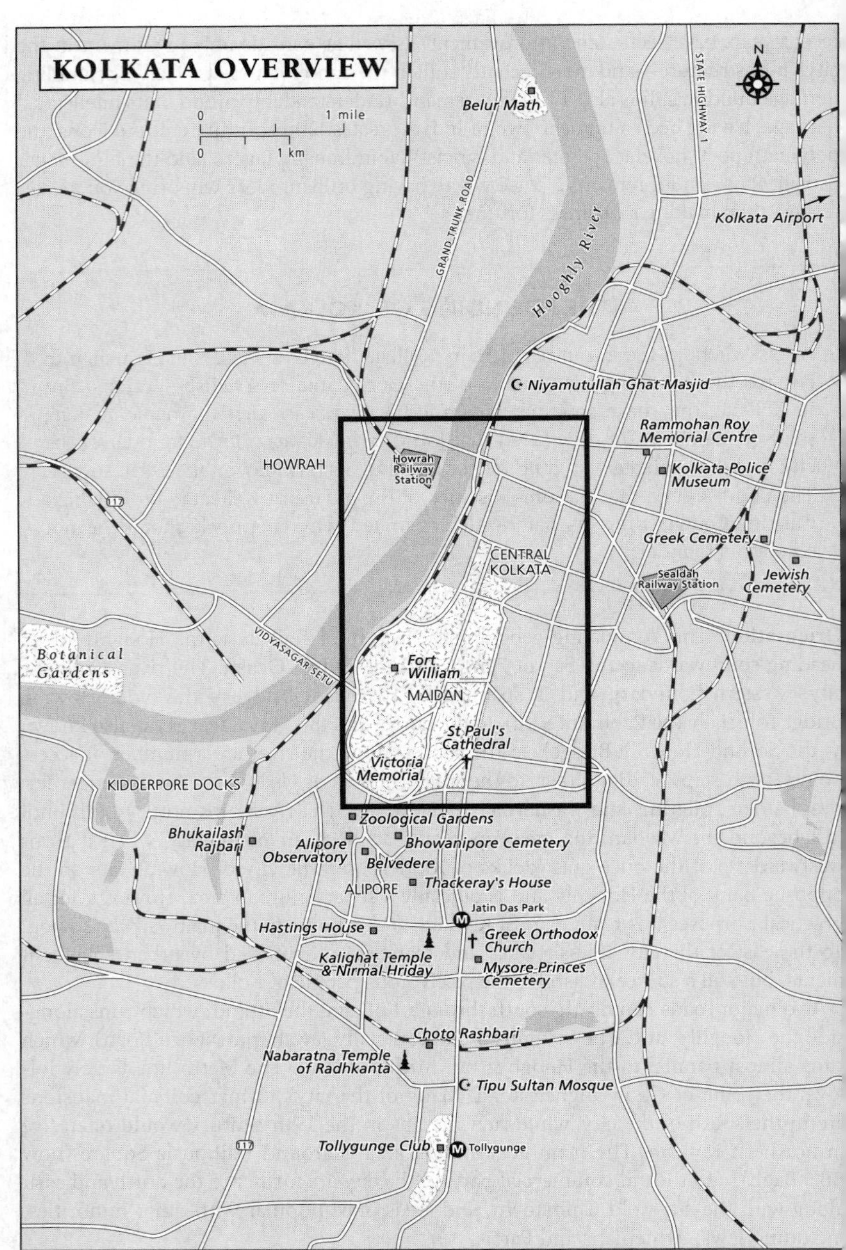
KOLKATA OVERVIEW
0
1 mile
0
1 km
Belur Math
STATE HIGHWAY 1
GRAND TRUNK ROAD
Hooghly River
Kolkata Airport
Niyamutullah Ghat Masjid
Rammohan Roy Memorial Centre
Kolkata Police Museum
HOWRAH
Howrah Railway Station
117
Greek Cemetery
CENTRAL KOLKATA
Sealdah Railway Station
Jewish Cemetery
VIDYASAGAR SETU
Botanical Gardens
Fort William
MAIDAN
St Paul's Cathedral
Victoria Memorial
KIDDERPORE DOCKS
Zoological Gardens
Bhukailash Rajbari
Alipore Observatory
Bhowanipore Cemetery
Belvedere
ALIPORE
Thackeray's House
Jatin Das Park
Hastings House
Greek Orthodox Church
Kalighat Temple & Nirmal Hriday
Mysore Princes Cemetery
Choto Rashbari
Nabaratna Temple of Radhkanta
Tipu Sultan Mosque
117
Tollygunge Club
Tollygunge

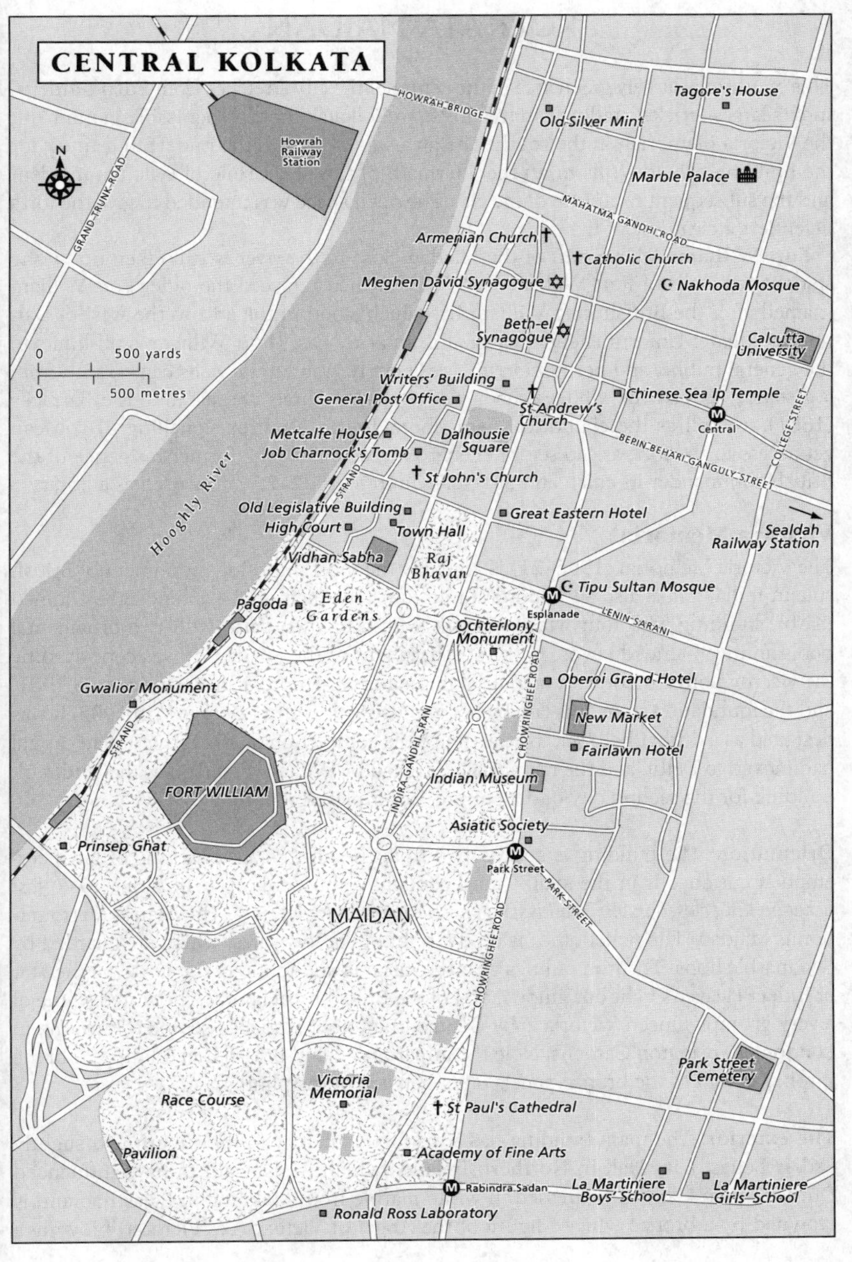
CENTRAL KOLKATA
Howrah Railway Station
HOWRAH BRIDGE
GRAND TRUNK ROAD
N
0 500 yards
0 500 metres
Hooghly River
Tagore's House
Old Silver Mint
Marble Palace
MAHATMA GANDHI ROAD
Armenian Church
Catholic Church
Meghen David Synagogue
Nakhoda Mosque
Beth-el Synagogue
Calcutta University
Writers' Building
General Post Office
Chinese Sea Ip Temple
St Andrew's Church
Central
COLLEGE STREET
Metcalfe House
Dalhousie Square
Job Charnock's Tomb
BEPIN BEHARI GANGULY STREET
STRAND
St John's Church
Old Legislative Building
Great Eastern Hotel
High Court
Town Hall
Sealdah Railway Station
Vidhan Sabha
Raj Bhavan
Tipu Sultan Mosque
Pagoda
Eden Gardens
Esplanade
LENIN SARANI
Ochterlony Monument
Gwalior Monument
Oberoi Grand Hotel
STRAND
New Market
CHOWRINGHEE ROAD
INDIRA GANDHI SRANI
Fairlawn Hotel
FORT WILLIAM
Indian Museum
Asiatic Society
Prinsep Ghat
Park Street
PARK STREET
MAIDAN
CHOWRINGHEE ROAD
Park Street Cemetery
Victoria Memorial
Race Course
St Paul's Cathedral
Pavilion
Academy of Fine Arts
Rabindra Sadan
La Martiniere Boys' School
La Martiniere Girls' School
Ronald Ross Laboratory

KOLKATA MAIDAN

This enormous, largely green area in the centre of the city stretches from Eden Gardens, India's largest cricket stadium, in the north, to Kolkata's most recognisable monument, the Victoria Memorial, in the south. The area was cleared in the mid-18th century for the building of Fort William, in the aftermath of the Black Hole of Calcutta incident and the subsequent recapture of the city. The open space was intended to give the fort's defenders a clear line of fire.

Fort William: A large part of the Maidan close to the river is still taken up by the star-shaped walls of Fort William (1757–73), which replaced the older Fort William (named after the British king William III) which stood in the area to the west of Dalhousie Square. Unfortunately, because it is an army base, Fort William is off-limits to the general public, and permission to visit is rarely granted. Its walls can be seen from a distance, as can the whitewashed, wedge-shaped three-storey Dalhousie Barracks (1861), as well as the cylindrical Semaphore Tower, used for signalling. If you can get access to the fort, ask to see Kitchener House (1780), the former residence of the British commander-in-chief, and St Peter's Church (1822–28), now used as a library.

Victoria Memorial

The Victoria Memorial (1906–21) is arguably the most imposing monument of British rule in India, and is also an important museum. The memorial—an enormous domed marble building with four wings—stands within its own park, with two ornamental pools and well-tended lawns, in the southern part of the Maidan. It was conceived by the viceroy Lord Curzon as a memorial to the former empress after her death in 1901, and the foundation stone was laid by her grandson, the future George V, in 1905. It was designed as a durbar hall, but, by the time of its completion in 1921, the Indian capital had moved to Delhi, and the memorial, designed by William Emerson as the landmark building for the second city of the empire, never played that role.

Orientation: The building is approached from the north—although the original ceremonial entrance is in the south—and contains a museum (*open Tues–Sun 10–5; last ticket at 4.30; closed public holidays; no photography allowed inside*). The nearest Metro station is Maidan. The ticket office is on the right of the low gates, which are guarded by two marble lions. The iron railings bear the insignia and motto of the Order of the Star of India ('Heaven's light our guide'), and of the British royal family. The seated statue of a very grumpy Queen Victoria is by George Frampton, who also sculpted *Peter Pan* in London's Kensington Gardens. Note the imperial sun and British lion on the rear of the throne, as well as the bronze panels on either side of the plinths.

The exterior: The main building has a distinct similarity to the superb and slightly earlier Belfast City Hall in Northern Ireland (which is also said to have influenced Durban Town Hall). It is dressed in white marble from Makrana in Rajasthan and is crowned by a bronze winged figure of the Angel of Victory (i.e. Victoria) blowing a

The Victoria Memorial was built over a 15-year period, and by the time of its completion in 1921, Calcutta was no longer the capital of British India.

bugle. The use of white marble and the side domes pay some homage to Mughal architecture, particularly the Taj Mahal, but overall the Victoria Memorial belongs very much to the Edwardian Baroque style used for civic buildings throughout Britain. The architect, William Emerson—who more than 30 years earlier had been responsible for Mumbai's Crawford Market—remained in Britain, while the supervising architect in Kolkata was Vincent Esch, who also worked for the nizam of Hyderabad and was responsible for several early 20th-century buildings there. Note how the wings are connected at the side by curved colonnades, and the original triumphal entrance to the memorial is on the southern side—the route would have passed through an archway bearing an equestrian statue of Edward VII. Closer to the original main entrance is a statue of the viceroy Lord Curzon. On the northern façade, through which visitors now enter the building, note the names of four great Indian rivers, the Ganges, Jumna, Indus and Krishna, inscribed on the wings, beneath a carved representation of rushing water.

The interior: On entering the memorial, there are rectangular galleries to the left and the right, with statues of George V and Queen Mary. Ahead is the circular central hall, with the foundation stone on the right, while at the centre of the hall is a statue of a young Victoria by Thomas Brock—he also designed her memorial outside Buckingham Palace in London. The drum of the dome has murals depicting scenes from Victoria's life. There are two further galleries at the back of the building, and one on the first floor that contains paintings of Indian political leaders of the 20th century. Among the exhibits normally on display in the downstairs galleries are oils by Thomas and William Daniell, whose prints provided 19th-century Britain with its most well-known images of India. There are also late 18th-century paintings by the Anglo-German Johann Zoffany. They include a Lucknow group portrait that incorporates the French adventurer Claude Martin (*see p. 231*) and Zoffany himself. Note also the paintings by the Irish artist Thomas Hickey, of one of the sons of Tipu Sultan (*see p. 668*) and his court eunuch, both exiled to Calcutta after the Battle of Srirangapatnam. Unmissable, if it is not still under restoration, is the enormous painting of the future Edward VII entering Jaipur in 1876, by the Russian artist Vereshchagin. There are also French cannon recovered from the Battle of Plassey and a sword owned by the Mughal emperor Aurangzeb.

St Paul's Cathedral

The Gothic square-towered St Paul's Cathedral (1839–47) lies directly to the east of the Victoria Memorial, and replaced St John's as the most important church in Kolkata. It had a tall steeple, more than 50m high, on top of the tower, which was twice destroyed by an earthquake. After the second earthquake, in 1937, it was not rebuilt. To your right on entering the church, at its western end, are the partially obscured stained-glass windows designed (1880) by Edward Burne-Jones—widely acclaimed as the finest stained glass in India. The original west window had been blown out by a cyclone, and Burne-Jones was commissioned to design a replacement as a memorial to Viceroy Lord Mayo, who had been killed by a convict while visiting a prison in the Andaman

Islands. The central figure is of Christ; on the left, David holds his harp, and on the right, Solomon holds a model of the temple of Jerusalem. Below Christ is St Michael weighing the souls of the dead. The walls of the church are cluttered with memorial plaques and marble carvings in relief, while at either side of the altar, laid into the floor, are memorials to the bishops of the cathedral.

The **Academy of Fine Arts** (*open Tues–Sun 3–6*), nearby on Cathedral Road, has a collection of Mughal miniatures and the works of Bengali artists, including Rabindranath Tagore and Jamini Roy. Also on the southern side of the Maidan is the **Race Course**, with its fine pavilion (1905–07).

Prinsep Ghat and the Gwalior Monument

The **Prinsep Ghat** (1841) is a well-restored Palladian porch with a colonnade of Ionic columns, set in pretty gardens on the riverside near the Maidan. The *ghat* was for many years the main point of disembarkation for visitors to the city, and is now overshadowed by the towers of the Second Hooghly Bridge. It was built as a memorial to James Prinsep, the assay master at the Kolkata Mint, who is now best remembered as the man who deciphered the ancient scripts inscribed on the edicts of Ashoka.

The **Gwalior Monument** (1847) is 600m north of Prinsep Ghat, close to Judges Ghat, and has fine views over the Hooghly. It commemorates the dead of the Gwalior campaign of 1843, when the British defeated the forces of the maharaja of Gwalior. The metal pillars are made from guns captured by the British during the campaign.

The Ochterlony Monument and Eden Gardens

On the northern side of the Maidan, the most distinctive building is the **Ochterlony Monument** (1828), now officially the Shahid Minar, or Martyrs' Tower. The 46m-high tower, which takes the form of a fluted column, commemorates the victory of the British, under General Ochterlony, in the Nepal war of 1814–16. It is no longer possible to climb the spiral staircase that leads to the platform at the top of the tower. Architecturally, it is said to be a combination of three Oriental styles: an Egyptian plinth, a Syrian column and a Turkish dome.

The pretty **Eden Gardens** (*open 12–5*), next to the cricket stadium of the same name, has a handsome red-and-gold pagoda that was brought from Burma in the 1850s, while the gardens themselves are named after Emily and Fanny Eden—the sisters of Governor-General Lord Auckland—both of whom wrote about their experiences in India.

NORTH OF THE MAIDAN: KOLKATA'S CIVIC CENTRE

The area immediately north of the Maidan has a number of government buildings, including the Legislative Assembly and Government House—now known as Raj Bhavan. Also here are Kolkata's high court, town hall and main post office, the Writers' Building and St John's Church, with its memorial to Calcutta's putative founder Job Charnock. The best Metro station for exploring the area is Esplanade.

Raj Bhavan

The Neoclassical Raj Bhavan (1799–1803) is the residence of the governor of West Bengal, and stands within its own gardens just to the north of the Maidan. It was originally called Government House and served as the home of Britain's governors-general and viceroys until the transfer of the capital to Delhi in 1911. It is modelled on Kedleston Hall in the English Midlands—coincidentally the home of the Curzon family, whose most famous scion would become viceroy at the end of 19th century and live in Government House. Raj Bhavan is larger than Kedleston though, with an extra floor, and all of the four wings that were originally intended for the Curzon family seat. Though closed to the public, its superb façade can be seen through the main northern gate.

West of Raj Bhavan

Just to the west of Raj Bhavan is the **Vidhan Sabha** (1931), or State Assembly—a fine example of 20th-century Neoclassical architecture. Just to its north is **Kolkata Town Hall** (1807–13). A plaque to the left of its Doric portico records the name of the architect, John Garstin, who was also responsible for arguably the oddest building of the British period, the Golghar in Patna (*see p. 599*). The town hall houses the **Kolkata Panorama** (*open Tues–Sun 11–6*), an exhibition that tells the story of the city with the help of robots.

Down a lane at the eastern side of the town hall is the **Old Legislative Council** (mid-19th century), with fluted Corinthian columns, and on the western side of the town hall is the enormous neo-Gothic **Kolkata High Court** (1864–72). The design of the High Court, by Walter Granville, borrows directly from the medieval Cloth Hall in the Belgian city of Ypres. Note the profusion of stucco figures of humans and animals in the capitals of the building's clustered columns.

East of Raj Bhavan

On the eastern side of the Raj Bhavan is the long white façade of the **Great Eastern Hotel** (1840), for years the city's main hotel, but closed at the time of writing for major rebuilding. The striking green, ten-domed **Tipu Sultan Mosque** (1842) is on the corner of Chowringhee and Lenin Sarani. It was built by Ghulam Muhammad, one of the sons of Tipu Sultan, who was exiled to Calcutta from Mysore after the defeat of his father.

St John's Church

The church (1784–87) and its grounds occupy a large area north of the town hall and high court, and contain one of the oldest British monuments in India, the tomb of Job Charnock. The church was, in fact, a cathedral, until the construction of St Paul's in the 1840s. St John's was built next to the site of the old British cemetery, prior to the opening of the Park Street Cemetery in 1767. The church, loosely modelled on St Martin-in-the-Fields in London, originally had its main entrance on the east side, closest to the entrance gate, but it was moved to the west side in 1797. The colonnaded side verandahs are later additions, designed to reduce the glare from the sun. The church steeple has a truncated ill-proportioned look, apparently because an entire tier was omitted due to the weakness of the foundations. The **tomb of Lady Canning** (1861), the wife of the first viceroy, is on the north verandah—it was designed by Sir George Gilbert Scott, the architect of London's Albert Memorial and St Pancras Station, and several buildings in Mumbai.

The interior: On the inside walls are a large number of fine carved marble memorials. Of particular interest on the right wall is a memorial to James Achilles Kirkpatrick, a British Resident in Hyderabad who married an Indian princess. Kirkpatrick—who was the central character in William Dalrymple's history of the British in late 18th-century India, *White Mughals*—died in Calcutta in 1805. There is also a Zoffany painting of the *Last Supper* in which city dignitaries have been depicted as the apostles.

The grounds: A signboard close to the main entrance to the church points to the corner of the compound where a group of memorials and tombs can be found. Visitors first pass the **Rohilla Monument**, a domed memorial to the dead of the 1794 Rohilla War. The **tomb of Job Charnock** (c. 1695), who is usually credited with founding the city in 1690 (*but see box on p. 539*), is a large octagonal pavilion. Around the mausoleum are a number of early British gravestones, and inside are several memorial stones. The one to Charnock has a Latin inscription and was erected by his son-in-law Charles Eyre, whose wife Maria, the oldest daughter of Charnock, is also commemorated in the same inscription. The type of black stone that carries the inscription, found mainly in India, is now known as Charnockite, a name given to it by a British geologist in the early 20th century. The adjacent stone commemorates another of Charnock's daughters, Catherine, while nearby is a memorial stone to William Hamilton, who cured the Mughal emperor Farrukhsiyar of a 'malignant distemper', and who, in return, received an elephant, jewels and a set of medical instruments with shafts made of gold.

The white **memorial to the victims of the Black Hole of Calcutta** in the churchyard is a replica created in the early 20th century at the behest of the viceroy Lord Curzon. It was brought from Dalhousie Square to St John's Church after Independence.

Dalhousie Square

This large square (officially BBD Bagh) is often seen as the heart of the city. It was laid our after the demolition of the Old Fort William in the mid-18th century, though the water tank at its centre appears to predate this. In the mid-19th century it was named after the Viceroy, Lord Dalhousie, and then renamed, post-Independence, after the initials of the first names of three men, Benoy Basu, Badal Gupta and Dinesh Gupta, who, in 1930, laid siege to the Writers' Building and killed the British inspector-general of prisons.

Writers' Building: The four-storey, red and white Writers' Building (1776) occupies the northern side of Dalhousie Square, and was originally built as barracks. It is now the headquarters of the West Bengal government, and many ministers have their offices inside. Access is not normally permitted to members of the public. Note the four groups of statues on the roof of the building representing from west to east: Science, Agriculture, Commerce and Justice.

General Post Office: The most important building on the western side of the square is the white-domed GPO (1868), a fine Neoclassical building designed by Walter Granville, who was also responsible for the High Court. The brass line embedded in the steps and forecourt of the post office marks the line of the wall of the old Fort William. The 'Black Hole of Calcutta' (*see p. 538*) stood close to the northern wall of the GPO.

St Andrew's Church: The northeast corner of Dalhousie Square is occupied by St Andrew's Church (1818), formerly Kolkata's Scottish Kirk. Like St John's, it is modelled on St Martin-in-the-Fields, and indeed bears a greater similarity to that London church. Note the memorials to Scottish Highland regiments inside, with the Gaelic motto meaning, 'In memory of the heroes who are no more'.

To the west of Dalhousie Square, on the Strand overlooking the river, is **Metcalfe House** (1844), one of India's finest Neoclassical buildings. It is raised up high on a plinth, with double-height Corinthian columns forming a colonnade on all sides. It used to house the National Library.

CENTRAL KOLKATA: NORTH OF DALHOUSIE SQUARE

The area immediately north and west of Dalhousie Square is a hodge-podge of government buildings, banks, shops and businesses, as well as private residences. Large parts of it are very congested, but it is a fascinating place to wander around and includes areas originally settled by some of the city's minorities, such as the Chinese, the Jews and the Armenians. The nearest Metro stations are Chandni Chowk and Central.

Catholic Cathedral

A short walk northeast of Dalhousie Square on the Brabourne Road is the twin-towered Roman Catholic Cathedral (1797–99), which is also known as the Portuguese Church. The church has been heavily and garishly restored, but note the range of nationalities represented in the wall-mounted and floor-embedded memorial stones here. They include several Armenians and one Chaldean, from Babylon, with an inscription in both Latin and Arabic.

Kolkata's synagogues

On the opposite side of Brabourne Road from the Catholic Cathedral are two synagogues. The **Neveh Shalome Synagogue** (1911) is on the site of the first synagogue built in the city in 1826. It is now derelict, but recognisable from its red brick walls and a half-hidden signboard. The second one, the **Meghen David Synagogue** (1884) has a tall, red church-like steeple and is well maintained. The grounds are entered from the side street, but it is quite difficult to get permission to go inside the building (*in order to do so, call David Nahoum on T: 033 65269936*).

JEWS OF KOLKATA

The first Jewish settler in Kolkata is thought to have come from Syria in 1797. The newcomers were known—like their fellow Arabic-speaking Jewish migrants in Mumbai—as Baghdadi Jews, though they did not come only from Baghdad. By the mid-20th century the community numbered more than 5,000 and were mainly working in business, particularly as diamond traders, but also as confectioners. There are now fewer than 50 Jews living in the city—most left after Independence and settled in Britain, the USA or Israel.

The **Beth-el Synagogue** (1856) is the oldest of the three, and is just 200m to the southeast. It is slightly harder to find and overlooks Pollock Street (*permission is also needed from David Nahoum to enter this synagogue*).

The Armenian Church

The Armenian Church (1724) is 150m northwest of the Catholic Cathedral, and is the oldest church in Kolkata. It is well maintained and surrounded by gravestones embedded in the ground, with inscriptions in English and Armenian. One gravestone is marked 1630, suggesting an earlier date for the founding of the city, but this is now thought to have been caused by a mason's error. Kolkata still has a small Armenian population, the largest in India, and members of the Armenian community have been active in the hotel trade, business and the law. There is also a **Parsi fire temple** (1839) nearby on Ezra Street, with a Neoclassical columned façade.

The main Chinese settlement, including an interesting Chinese cemetery, is in Tangra, in eastern Kolkata, but a smaller enclave exists about 500m east of St Andrew's Church. It has the **Chinese Sea Ip Temple** (1905), which welcomes visitors. North of the little Chinatown and just east of the Catholic Cathedral is the **Nakhoda Mosque** (1926–42). This is Kolkata's largest mosque, at 400m in length, and represents an interesting 20th-century effort at imitating Mughal architecture.

COLLEGE STREET

A short distance northeast of Dalhousie Square is one of Kolkata's most impressive thoroughfares, College Street, with several important 19th-century educational buildings designed in a Neoclassical style, including the **Old Medical College Building** (1852), **Hare School** (1872) and **Presidency College** (1874). Kolkata University is home to the **Ashutosh Museum of Indian Art** (*open Mon–Sat 10.30–4.30*), established in 1937, which has a large, badly kept collection of sculptures, manuscripts and paintings from the Bengal region. It includes some excellent examples of Bengali folk art, particularly the painted scrolls known as *pats*, and the Kalighat style of painting, with its poster-like use of colours, and stylised drawing of human figures and gods.

NORTHERN KOLKATA

Northern Kolkata, north of the Howrah Bridge, was the home of many rich Indian families, and several of their ancestral homes survive. Many residents of the north of the city will tell you that this is the real Bengali Kolkata.

The Marble Palace

Among the great homes that have survived is the remarkable Marble Palace (1835), the home of the descendants of Raja Rajendra Mullick, on Muktaram Babu Street—a congested lane off Chittaranjan Avenue. Much of the house has been turned into a museum and a small zoo (*open 10–4; closed Mon and Thur; no photographs; nearest Metro station: MG Road*). In order to visit, it is necessary to pick up a permission letter from the West Bengal Tourist Office in the southeast corner of Dalhousie Square, which is issued immediately—some visitors to the Marble Palace say that the watchman will allow you in without a letter for a small fee.

The façade of the palace has a portico with six monumental Corinthian columns topped by a Rococo pediment—setting the tone for the extravagant and slightly seedy interior. Inside is an elegant central courtyard, and rooms full of European antiques and bric-à-brac. The rooms on view (members of the family still live here) are the public quarters, including a billiards room and a ballroom. The floors are all marble, and there are small European-style statues and busts everywhere. There are many European paintings, including what the guide will tell you are originals by Reynolds, Rubens and Murillo. Caged birds are kept inside the palace, and there is an aviary with larger birds in the lush garden, as well as a small zoo with some deer.

Home of Tagore

Just 300m to the north of the Marble Palace, in the area known as Jorasanko, is the home of Rabindranath Tagore—probably the most important Indian cultural figure of the 20th century (*see also p. 579*). The house, officially the Jorasanko Thakurbari (1784), now functions as a university and a museum (*open Tues–Sun 10.30–4.30; nearest Metro station: Girish Park*). Many generations of the Tagore family lived here, and a number of them became well-known painters, writers, poets and scholars. Rabindranath is the best-known internationally and received the Nobel Prize for Literature in 1913, but other members of the family are also greatly revered in Kolkata. The large, well-maintained house contains an impressive collection of Bengali art and the room in which Rabindranath Tagore died in 1941.

Raja Rammohan Roy's Home and Museum

There are two houses in north Kolkata associated with Roy. About 1.5km east of the Marble Palace is the **Raja Rammohan Roy Memorial Centre** (*open 11–5; closed Mon, Wed and Fri*) on Raja Rammohan Roy Sarani. This was the house of Roy's son, and contains a well laid-out museum, with few exhibits but lots of information about Roy's campaign against the practice of *sati* and the formation of the Brahmo Samaj movement, which is still very active in Bengal. Roy's actual house, built in 1815 on nearby APC Road, has been turned into the **Kolkata Police Museum** (*open Tues–Sun 10–5*), and has an interesting collection of weapons—including a book bomb—used by Indians fighting against British rule in the first half of the 20th century.

RAJA RAMMOHAN ROY

Roy (1772–1833) was the greatest figure of the Bengali Renaissance in the early 19th century. He was the founder of the Brahmo Samaj, which aimed at reforming and modernising Hinduism, and led the successful campaign to have *sati*, the immolation of widows, outlawed; he also campaigned against child marriage. He believed in the existence of a single god. Roy died while visiting Britain in 1833, as a representative of one of the last Mughal emperors, and is buried in Bristol's Arnos Vale cemetery in an Indian-style tomb, designed like a small pavilion.

Further to the west on Nakheldanga Road (an easy side trip while going to the airport) is the **Jewish cemetery**, tightly packed with gravestones and tombs, and the slightly emptier **Greek cemetery**, with its small chapel.

Near Howrah Bridge

To the west of the Marble Palace, close to the river and 1km north of Howrah Bridge, is Kolkata's oldest functioning mosque, the **Niyamutullah Ghat Masjid** (1784). This recently restored mosque, set on a high plinth with nine domes, was once much closer to the Hooghly, which has shifted westwards. The decorated stonework used on some of the lintels and thresholds is thought to have been taken from the ruins of Gaur (*see p. 573*).

Almost at the foot of the Howrah Bridge is the magnificent Neoclassical **Old Silver Mint** (1831)—one of the city's most impressive buildings, but sadly neglected. The Doric portico of the main building is modelled on the Parthenon in Athens. The complex consists of a series of enormous Neoclassical buildings where silver coins were minted until 1952. There are plans to restore the buildings and turn them into a museum and a heritage hotel.

HOWRAH

The **Howrah Bridge** (1943), officially the **Rabindra Setu**, is probably Kolkata's best-known landmark, seen repeatedly in films set in the city. At the time of its construction it was, at 457m, the third-longest cantilever bridge in the world (after the Pont de Québec and the Forth Rail Bridge). Just next to the bridge on the western bank is **Howrah Station**, one of the biggest and oldest in India. The first train left Howrah in 1854, but the current building dates to 1905.

Belur Math (20th century) is an enormous Hindu religious complex, 5km north of the bridge on the Howrah (west) side of the river. It is dedicated to the life of Swami Vivekananda and the spiritual and philanthropic organisation that he founded, the Ramakrishna Mission. Vivekananda became a wandering monk after the death of his guru, Paramahans Ramakrishna, and he travelled widely through India. He later travelled through Asia, America and Europe in the final years of the 19th century, teaching his modernised spiritual form of Hinduism to an audience who knew little about India. A few years before his death in 1901, at the age of only 39, he moved to Belur. He remains an important figure for many Indians, and most Indian cities have a street named after him, usually contracted to SV Road. The main **temple building** (1938) here is an unusual mixture of Christian, Muslim and Hindu styles, and draws large numbers of pilgrims.

The city's **Botanical Gardens** are on the far side of the river, 3km west of the Second Hooghly Bridge, and contain a remarkable 250-year-old banyan tree, the prop roots and canopy of which stretch to more than 1km in circumference.

THE PARK STREET AREA & CHOWRINGHEE

The eastern side of the main Chowringhee Road (officially Jawaharlal Nehru Road) has a number of impressive, mainly 19th-century, institutional buildings, which overlook the Maidan. These include the long façade of the Grand Hotel (now the **Oberoi Grand Hotel**), the **Bible Society**, with its twin pediments, the **Young Men's Christian Association** (1902), with its single pediment, and the red-brick **Government College of Art and Crafts** (1892). However this stretch of Chowringhee is dominated by the Indian Museum, though the view is now partly blocked by a flyover. Behind the Oberoi Grand are the distinctive pitched roofs and spires of what is still known as the **New Market** (1875), and which remains one of the city's busiest markets.

Indian Museum

This enormous museum (*open Tues–Sun 10–4.30*) overlooking Chowringhee was designed, like the High Court and the GPO, by Walter Granville, and it was needed as a home for the large collection of antiquities that had previously been housed at the Asiatic Society. The actual collection was founded in 1814, making this effectively Asia's oldest surviving museum. During the time that Calcutta was the capital of India (until 1911), it received the most important works of art excavated by the British.

The three-storey museum building was opened to the public in 1875, and contains some superb Gandhara and Mathura sculpture, as well as the spectacular Bharhut stupa railings, which would grace any museum in the world. Be careful though: some visitors miss out on the best part of the museum, because the main door to the Bharhut antiquities is closed, and it is necessary instead to go a long way round through the archaeology gallery and pass through what looks like, but is not, a closed door. The museum also has large collections of rocks and minerals, stuffed animals (and a human embryo), a small Egyptian gallery and an impressive coin collection. The museum as a whole is not well organised and the exhibits are poorly labelled, but if you can't find something, ask at the bookshop.

Entrance area: Several important exhibits are in the main entrance area, including a polished stone lion from the Mauryan period (3rd century BC), which once stood on top of a column, and a strange column capital, shaped like a tree, that comes from Vidisha in Madhya Pradesh and dates to the Shunga period (2nd century BC). Around the colonnaded courtyard are a large number of sculptures, including some fine basalt figures from the Pala Empire (8th–11th century) in north Bengal.

The most significant collection, however, is in the long **archaeology gallery** on the south side of the courtyard. The most important exhibits from Gandhara and Mathura are largely to the left as one enters the gallery, and the Bharhut ruins are behind a door next to the Gandhara sculptures. Among the **Mathura sculptures** are a superb full-size standing Buddha (5th century), with diaphanous rippling drapery and spiral locks of hair, and some beautifully carved railing posts (2nd century) which would have surrounded a stupa. As well as the religious images on the railings, note the domestic scenes, with two individuals leaning over a window sill, shown in the top-left corner of each of the posts. The Greek-influenced **Gandhara sculptures**, which came from 19th-century British excavations in modern-day Afghanistan and Pakistan, are among the best in India. Note the superb seated *bodhisattvas*, including one showing Padmapani, the lotus-carrying avatar of Avalokiteshwara, with a huge ornamental turban and a pointed moustache. The frieze pieces are also particularly fine, and include one that shows the Buddha being born out of the side of his mother, Queen Maya, who is standing cross-legged beneath a tree.

The Bharhut Collection: Most of the surviving ruins of the Bharhut stupa (c. 2nd century BC) are in one air-conditioned room, where they have been displayed so that visitors can walk between them and around them, and see the superb quality of the workmanship. The ruins of the stupa—in Bharhut, outside Satna in the central state of Madhya Pradesh—were discovered by Alexander Cunningham, the founder of the Archaeological Survey of India, in 1873. Almost all the pieces were moved to the Indian Museum—though a few ended up in the Allahabad Museum and abroad. The site at Bharhut is now bare, though the shape of the stupa can still be made out. The stupa, surrounded by the railings and gates that are in the museum, may have been started during the Mauryan period, in the 3rd century BC, under Ashoka, but most of the carving comes from the slightly later Shunga period. The writing on the stonework is in the Brahmi script, and records the building of the railings and gate, and the people who donated money to have it built.

The Bharhut ruins consist of large sections of the 2.1m-high circular railing that surrounded the stupa, and the 6.8m-high southern gate—similar to the more recent and more complete one at Sanchi (*see p. 420*). Note the difference between the carvings on the cross-rails, which are all contained within circular medallions, and the carvings on the posts and the coping stones, which have greater freedom. Most of the post carvings are of *yakshas* and *yakshis*, or semi-divine males and females, while the coping stones carry carvings of real and mythical animals, many of them half-human. The subject matter of the medallions varies markedly, from simple floral patterns and human head-and-shoulder images, to marvellously complex relief carvings, showing monkeys riding an elephant and a typical village scene, with a step-well and bullock-cart.

Upper Galleries: Ensure you go upstairs in the Indian Museum for some superb sculptures, including more fragments from Bharhut, as well as a fine collection of bronzes from south and east India. There is also an art gallery with an impressive collection of early 20th-century Bengali paintings by Rabindranath Tagore, his nephew Abanindranath and Jamini Roy.

Asiatic Society

The Asiatic Society (*open daily 10–5*) is on the corner of Chowringhee and Park Street in an old building of 1808 that is largely concealed by inelegant modern additions. The society was founded in 1784 by Sir William Jones, the greatest of Britain's early Orientalist scholars, as a research institute and library. It has a collection of 150,000 books, including early Sanskrit manuscripts and rare copies of the Koran. There is a small museum in the building that includes an Ashoka rock edict and paintings ascribed to Rubens and Reynolds—though the bulk of the society's collection went to the Indian Museum.

Park Street Cemetery

This cemetery, which opened in 1767, is at the far end of Park Street from Chowringhee, and is a fascinating place for a stroll. The quality and variety of the funerary architecture are amazing, and there are a number of interesting individual graves. These include the grave of Rose Aylmer—the subject of Walter Savage Landor's most famous poem, which takes her name as its title—who is said to have died from a surfeit of pineapples. Her tombstone is on the far left corner of the first junction as one walks through the cemetery, and has the full text of Landor's poem. Rather bizarrely, the tomb almost takes the shape of a pineapple that has been peeled in the Indian fashion, like a spiral. Also buried here, in one of the largest tombs—the only one with a paved walkway—is Sir William Jones, the founder of the Asiatic Society. .

La Martiniere schools

La Martiniere Boys' and Girls' schools (1835 and c. 1840, respectively) sit across the road from each other about 500m south of the Park Street Cemetery. They are the city's best-known schools, and were founded, like La Martiniere School in Lucknow, by the French adventurer Claude Martin. They are both fine Neoclassical buildings—the Boys' School has a central semicircular building that juts out from the main structure and serves as a chapel.

SOUTH KOLKATA

The area south of the Maidan has a large variety of interesting buildings, including the Kalighat temples and two other less well-known Hindu shrines. It is also where some of the grandest homes of India's rulers are to be found—most of them now converted into institutional buildings—and there are also some unusual buildings erected by the exiled sons of Tipu Sultan, the defeated ruler of Mysore.

Ronald Ross Laboratory

Just to the south of the Maidan, in the grounds of the Presidency General Hospital (1901–19), now known as the SSKM Hospital, is the Ronald Ross Laboratory (late 19th century). This is where Ross, in 1898, discovered that malaria is spread by a parasite that lives in a mosquito, for which he received the 1902 Nobel Prize for Medicine. This is often claimed as India's first Nobel Prize, since Ross, like Kipling who received a Nobel Prize five years later, was born in India. The first Indian to receive the award, in 1913, was Rabindranath Tagore, born 5km north of the Ross Laboratory in Jorasanko.

Just to the south of the hospital is the enormous **Bhowanipore Cemetery**, which began as the Hospital Burying Grounds, and which houses the Commonwealth War Graves cemetery.

Kalighat Temple and Mother Teresa's Home

The **Kalighat Temple** of 1809 (nearest Metro station: Kalighat) is the most important Hindu shrine in Kolkata, and large numbers of pilgrims queue to see the icon of the goddess Kali in its inner sanctuary. The current domed building replaced an older temple, said to mark the spot where a goddess fell to earth. You are allowed to take your shoes into the complex but not into the inner sanctuary—and you do not, despite what you may be told, have to make a large donation.

Walk on a little past the temple to reach **Nirmal Hriday** (1925), the former temple rest-house, or *dharamsala*, where Mother Teresa started the Missionaries of Charity in 1952. It remains a home for the dying, and visitors are allowed to go inside, where the terminally ill lie on mattresses on the floor and are looked after by nuns.

East of Kalighat

East of Kalighat Temple, on the main road leading south (SP Mukherjee Road), near Kalighat railway station, is the fine Neoclassical **Greek Orthodox Church** (1925). It replaced a church built in 1780 that was near Dalhousie Square. Note the wall memorial in English, Urdu and Greek to the 19th-century Sanskritist Demetrius Galanos which was moved from the old church when it was dismantled.

In the backstreets behind the Greek church is one of Kolkata's strangest collections of monuments, known as the **Mysore Princes Cemetery** (early 19th century). Here, in Satish Mukherjee Road, are six tombs of descendants of Tipu Sultan, the Prince of Mysore, who was defeated by the British at the Battle of Srirangapatnam in 1799 and exiled to Calcutta. The tombs are in poor condition and have been engulfed by a slum—in fact, most of them have been subdivided and are inhabited. One of the tombs has distinctive fluted minarets, while others are built to a more traditional octagonal design. One of the tombs is still looked after, and silken cloths cover the cenotaphs.

South of Kalighat

About 2km further south of Kalighat is Kolkata's second **Tipu Sultan Mosque** (1843), better proportioned than the well-known one in the centre of the city. In the garden are the graves of the family of Ghulam Muhammad, the son of Tipu Sultan who constructed both mosques.

The **Tollygunge Club** (1781) was originally the private estate of an indigo planter who died in the cholera epidemic of 1801. The handsome Neoclassical building with paired Tuscan columns then became the temporary home of the Mysore royal family, and then a British-style club in 1895.

The **Choto Rashbari** (1846) is a fascinating private temple complex, 1.25km south of Kalighat, at the far end of Tollygunge Road. It consists of a square colonnaded courtyard with a series of small shrines dedicated to Shiva, and a large sanctuary with a Krishna shrine and an impressively fantastical traditional nine-turreted roof, in the Bengali Nabaratna style. The nearby **Nabaratna Temple of Radhakanta** (1796), on the other side of the stream known as Tolly's Nullah, is built to a similar design.

ALIPORE

The area of southwest Kolkata known as Alipore is one of the city's grandest, and was developed by the British as a leafy suburb—an escape from the bustle and grime of the city centre. It is home to the 45-acre **Zoological Gardens**, inaugurated by the Prince of Wales in 1876, and the 21-acre gardens of the **Agrihorticultural Society of India** (1872). The enormous mansion called **Belvedere** (mid-18th century), now home to the National Library, is Kolkata's grandest, and was once owned by Warren Hastings, the first British governor-general. The National Library was moved there from Metcalfe House in central Kolkata in 1948. Warren Hastings actually stayed at a building still known as **Hastings House** (1776), on Judges Court Road, which is now used by an education training institute. The wings and portico of this large European-style house were later additions.

Thackeray's House (1770s), at the back of Alipore Jail, is arguably the prettiest of the European houses in Alipore, and is now the District Magistrates Residence. It was the childhood home of the novelist Thackeray, and the view of the house from the garden with its paired Tuscan columns is particularly fine. A plaque inside the entrance to the house records that Thackeray lived here for three years. Ask the watchman to contact the district magistrate for permission to enter. The **Alipore Observatory** (1876–99) is still in use by the Meteorological Department. Ask permission at the gate to see the unusual observatory building, with its cluster of four towers.

Kidderpore, just to the west of Alipore, is home to the city's docks as well as a fine, little-visited temple complex, the **Bhukailash Rajbari** (1780). The old mansion, or Rajbari, is derelict, but two traditional Bengali-style Shiva temples overlook a pretty lake.

PRACTICAL INFORMATION

GETTING THERE

• **By air:** Kolkata has an international airport with daily connections from Dhaka, Bangkok and Dubai, and less regular connections from London, Frankfurt, Singapore and Kathmandu. However, most visitors arrive by land or by domestic airlines. There are several flights each day from Delhi and Mumbai, and good connections to most other major Indian cities.

• **By train:** The main railway station is in Howrah, on the west bank of the river, though some trains also go from Sealdah on the eastern side of the city. There are long-distance services from Delhi (17hrs) and others from Mumbai and Chennai that take more than a day. The railway is also a useful way of reaching the neighbouring state capitals—Patna (in Bihar) and Bhubaneswar (in Orissa) are both 7hrs away—and it is also the best way of reaching the interior of West Bengal. It takes about 7hrs to Malda (for the ruins of the medieval cities of Gaur and Pandua) and 10hrs to New Jalpaiguri (for Darjeeling). There are also local trains for Chandernagore and Tribeni further north along the Hooghly River.

GETTING AROUND

Kolkata had India's first Metro, which opened in 1984 and runs north–south. It is easy to use, very well placed for visitors to the city and is usually the quickest way of moving about Kolkata. A second east–west line is under construction at the time of writing. Alternatively, taxis, auto-rickshaws and cycle rickshaws are widely available—as well as hand-pulled rickshaws, despite a prolonged campaign to ban them.

Kolkata is also a good city to wander around on foot. **Calcutta Walks** (*calcuttawalks.com: T: 033 40052573/22110416*) offer tailored guided walks around the city.

ACCOMMODATION

Kolkata has several 5-star hotels including the **Park Hotel** (*$$$; T: 033 2249 9000; theparkhotels.com*), on Park Street, which is well placed for visiting the main sights in the city. So is the **Oberoi Grand** (*$$$: T: 033 2249 2323; oberoikolkata.com*), slightly to the north on Chowringhee, in a 19th-century building. The **Fairlawn Hotel** (*$$; T: 033 2252 1510; fairlawnhotel.com*) on Sudder Street, in the heart of the city, is very old-fashioned, with a colonial ambience; it is much loved by its regulars. The **Great Eastern** (*T: 033 6452 6800; thelalit.com*), close to Raj Bhavan, is thought to be India's oldest quality hotel. It is currently under renovation by its new owners, the Lalit group.

FOOD

Fish and rice are the staple foods of Kolkata, and the city also prides itself on its Bengali sweets and desserts. But, as in any of the large cities of India, food from the rest of the country, and from abroad, is widely available. Bengalis are proud of their cuisine, and are particular about what they eat. For instance, they will often eat very bony fish, arguing that the boniest is often the tastiest—and this can take some getting used to for visitors, as can the distinctive mustard flavour of much Bengali food, which comes from the use of mustard oil or paste in cooking. There is also a general mixture of five spices, known as *panch phoron*, which is used in much Bengali cooking. *Maccher jhal* is a typical Bengali fish curry, which, unlike curries elsewhere in the country, uses little or no tomato or onions. Prawns are also very popular. Most meals are eaten with yellow *cholar dal*, often cooked with coconut and rice—and sometimes a deep-fried bread called a *luchi*.

Desserts are usually very sweet. *Mishti doi* is a delicious sweetened yoghurt, usually served in a clay pot. *Rosgolla* is a syrupy cheese and semolina ball.

Kewpie's Kitchen (*$$; Elgin Lane just south of Rabindra Sadan Metro; T: 033 2486 1600; kewpieskitchen.com*) is Kolkata's best-known Bengali restaurant. It is family-run and serves *thali*-style meals. **Bhojohori Manna** (*$; bhojohorimanna.com*) is a new chain of low-price Bengali restaurants that has several branches in Kolkata. It was started by five friends, including the eminent film director Goutam Ghose, who wanted a restaurant that served traditional home-cooked Bengali cuisine of the kind that many families have stopped cooking, because it is so time consuming. The different fish curries are highly recommended—try the *Pabda Jhol* if you find *Hilsa* too bony. The most central branch is at **Hazra** (*23A Priyanath Mullick Road; T: 033 2454 5922; nearest Metro station: Jatin Das Park*).

FURTHER READING & VIEWING

• **Books:** The best guide to the city's old buildings is *Calcutta: Built Heritage Today* by Nilina Deb Lal (Intach, 2006), while Prosenjit Das Gupta's *Ten Walks in Calcutta* (Harper Collins India, 2008) is particularly useful for north and central Kolkata. Among the more general books on the city, Krishna Dutta's *Calcutta: A Cultural and Literary History* (Signal, 2003), and Geoffrey Moorhouse's *Calcutta: The City Revealed* (first published in 1971, republished Faber, 2008) are both recommended. Rudyard Kipling's series of essays *City of Dreadful Night* (first published in 1899) is still in print.

Several of India's best-known modern novelists were born in Kolkata. These include Vikram Seth, part of whose *A Suitable Boy* is set in the city. Several of Amitav Ghosh's novels are set, partially or wholly, in Kolkata—including the start of *Shadowlines* (1988), *Calcutta Chromosome* (1996) and *Sea of Poppies* (2008), all published by Penguin India. Similarly, the city plays a central role in Amit Chaudhuri's best-known novel, *A Strange and Sublime Address* (1991), while the Bengali-language novelist Sankar's best-known work, *Chowringhee* (Penguin India, 2007), set in a Kolkata hotel, has recently been published in English to critical acclaim, more than 40 years after it was written.

• **Films:** Kolkata is the home to a strong tradition of independent film-making, and the results are often more popular internationally than in the rest of India, outside Bengal. The most successful film director was Satyajit Ray, who died in 1992 and remains a cultural icon in Bengal—but there is also Ritwik Ghatak, Mrinal Sen and Aparna Sen. Ray's 1959 film *Apu Sansar* (*The World of Apu*), the third of his acclaimed Apu Trilogy, is largely set in Kolkata, as is *Mahanagar* (*The Big City*). Two fine English-language Indian films, *36, Chowringhee Lane* (1981) and *15, Park Avenue* (2005), are by the country's leading female director, Aparna Sen. Both are set in Kolkata, and the first stars Jennifer Kendal as an Anglo-Indian schoolteacher. The Bollywood classic *Howrah Bridge* (1956) was shot at many well-known locations in Kolkata, and gives an interesting insight into how the city has changed over more than 50 years. *Parineeta* (2005) is a more recent Bollywood movie that uses Kolkata's major sights as a backdrop.

Among the English-language films set in Kolkata are Roland Joffe's *City of Joy* (1992), starring Patrick Swayze and based on the 1985 novel of the same name by Dominique Lapierre, and Louis Malle's controversial 1969 documentary *Calcutta*, which was widely criticised in India for its portrayal of poverty in the city.

WEST BENGAL

Geographically, West Bengal (*maps 8 and 7*) is India's most varied state, stretching from the Himalayan mountains in the far north all the way to the sea. In between are the flood-prone plains of the Ganges and its many tributaries, the great city of Kolkata—historically known as Calcutta and covered in its own chapter (*see p. 537*)—and the maritime mangrove forests of the Sundarbans and the Indian Ocean. West Bengal has borders with no fewer than three countries—Bangladesh, Nepal and Bhutan—and only a very narrow strip of Indian territory runs between the first two of those countries. This is the so-called Chicken's Neck, a 20km-wide stretch of West Bengal that is the only terrestrial link between all of northeast India and the rest of the country. The most distinctive feature of most of West Bengal is the sheer quantity of water that is visible almost everywhere, as the mighty Ganges and its tributaries and distributaries carve their way through the rich agricultural lands of what is India's most densely populated large state. The main branch of the Ganges actually splits off into Bangladesh, but there is still a major river, the Hooghly, which goes through the state to the sea, and along which many of West Bengal's most important urban centres, including Kolkata, were built.

Besides Kolkata, the state has a large number of visitor attractions, including the hill-stations and tea estates of Darjeeling and Kalimpong, the distinctive Sultanate-period Muslim architecture of Gaur and Pandua, the terracotta temples of Bishnupur, the Sundarban National Park, and the former French, Danish, Dutch and Portuguese river-ports along the banks of the Hooghly.

West Bengal, with a population of more than 80 million, is just one part of historical Bengal. The other part, the East, is now Bangladesh. The Bengali language and culture are taken very seriously by the people of the state, and the great figures of 20-century Bengali culture, such as the Nobel Prize-winning writer and artist Rabindranath Tagore and the film director Satyajit Ray, continue to command great respect—even adoration. Food is almost as important—and the traditional diet of rice and fish remains the staple in areas near the sea and the big rivers. Bengali cuisine also makes wide use of mustard as a spice and has dozens of very sweet milk-based desserts.

HISTORY OF WEST BENGAL

There is evidence of human settlement in West Bengal that goes back at least 10,000 years, but the earliest historical ruins or monuments date from a much more recent period. The earliest important site is the ruined city of Chandraketugarh, which probably dates from the 5th-century Gupta period, but there is little else that has survived from the period of Hindu and Buddhist rule in this part of Bengal—no equivalents of the great Buddhist sites in neighbouring Bihar or Bangladesh.

Sultanate period: The earliest surviving major monuments are from the Muslim period of rule in Bengal, in which a distinctive local form of Islamic mosque and tomb architecture developed. The Delhi-based Slave Dynasty conquered Bengal in the early 13th century, bringing Islam to the region and putting in place local governors. But gradually a local Muslim elite took control and established what became known as the Bengal Sultanate. The earliest Muslim buildings are at Tribeni in the south, just 50km north of Kolkata. But the major centres were in the middle area of West Bengal, and the magnificent ruined cities of Pandua and Gaur stand tribute to the Bengal style of Islamic architecture.

Mughals and Europeans: By the late 16th century, the Mughals had conquered Bengal and European traders had also arrived in the region—with the Portuguese setting up their first trading post on the River Hooghly, north of modern Kolkata. They were followed by the Dutch, the French, the British and the Danes, each of whom set up similar small trading posts. In 1690 the British began building a new fortified settlement, further down the Hooghly towards the sea, which they named 'Calcutta' after the nearby village of Kalikata. With the Mughal Empire disintegrating, local nawabs based in Murshidabad took control of most of Bengal, and a period of intense rivalry between the nawabs and the British got underway. In 1756 the army of Nawab Siraj ud-Daula captured Calcutta, imprisoning the British residents in the infamous 'Black Hole' (*see p. 538*). But a year later, the nawab was defeated at the Battle of Plassey and Calcutta was recaptured. Ten years later, the Battle of Buxar confirmed British dominance in Bengal, and Calcutta became the administrative centre for the British East India Company, and later the capital of British-ruled India.

Under British Rule: The 19th century saw what became known as the Bengal renaissance, a movement that combined social reform and mass education with a period of rich cultural creativity. The event that sparked the failed 1857 Indian Uprising against the British, the Barrackpore Mutiny, took place in Bengal, which was relatively unaffected during the rest of the rebellion. The British decision to partition Bengal in 1905 led to an upsurge of political activity—and although the decision was reversed in 1911, the British provided Bengalis with a new grievance by transferring the capital from Calcutta to Delhi. The best-known Bengali leader in the Independence struggle was Subhash Chandra Bose, who broke away from Gandhi, and obtained German and Japanese support for his Indian National Army during World War II. During the war, Bengal suffered its most serious famine since the 1760s, with more than a million people dying of starvation.

Independence: Bengal was partitioned at Independence, with the majority-Hindu western part of the province going to India and the majority-Muslim part becoming part of Pakistan—though the Pakistan part of Bengal later achieved its own independence as Bangladesh in 1971. Many Hindus left their ancestral homes in East Bengal, and in the years since there have been large influxes of Bangladeshis—both Hindu and Muslim—into West Bengal in search of new opportunities. Although Kerala elected India's first Communist government, it is in West Bengal that Communism entrenched itself. It had a series of democratically-elected

Communist governments from 1977—though, after 34 years in power, the lost the elections of 2011. In the 1980s and 90s the mainly Nepali-speaking far north of the state, around Darjeeling, was affected by agitation for a separate Gorkhaland state. The agitation died down once greater autonomy was granted for the hill regions, but periodically the Darjeeling area is brought to a standstill by Gorkha nationalists.

HOOGHLY RIVER TOWNS

The area just north of Kolkata, on the west bank of the Hooghly River (*map 8 D1*), has a little-visited collection of historic towns, where many European nations built trading settlements in the 16th and 17th centuries—before the founding of Calcutta (Kolkata). It now feels like a sleepy backwater, a distant suburb of Kolkata, with many fascinating colonial buildings. The area can be visited on a day trip from Kolkata. An excursion to the former settlements and other important sites on the northern side of the city takes visitors first to the nearest of the former trading settlements at Serampore (Danish), followed by Chandernagore (French), Chinsura (Dutch), Hooghly Town (British), Bandel (Portuguese), and then to some very fine examples of Hindu and Muslim architecture at Bansberia (Hindu temples), Tribeni (mosque and tower), Chota Pandua (mosque and tomb) and Kalna (Hindu temples). (*All on map 8 D1.*)

THE HOOGHLY RIVER & ITS TRADING POSTS

The Hooghly (also known as the Bhagirathi) is a major branch of the Ganges, which splits in northern Bengal to create an enormous delta. Dozens of branches eventually spill into the Bay of Bengal, and the largest of these, the Padma, crosses into Bangladesh near Farakka, north of Murshidabad. The lower reaches of the Hooghly were navigable by large ocean-going ships, so the area formed a large natural harbour and base for maritime trade. Even those who came by land, such as the Muslim invaders who came from Delhi in the early 13th century, built their settlements close to the river. In the 18th century, the west bank of the Hooghly was one of the world's great international melting pots. The Portuguese, Dutch, British, French and Danes each had their own riverside settlements, with short-lived attempts by the Prussians and Austrians to build trading posts. Greek and Armenian traders also settled in the area, which already had a mixed Hindu/Muslim population. The silting up of the river in the 19th century, the building of the railway and the emergence of Calcutta as one of the world's most important trading cities ensured the gradual decline of the older settlements, which were all, except for the French settlement at Chandernagore, brought under British control, and then integrated into West Bengal at Independence.

SERAMPORE

This former Danish settlement on the Hooghly, 25km north of Kolkata, dates back to 1745. It was known officially by the Danes as Frederiksnagar (after King Frederik V), and is now officially called Srirampur. Serampore contains two important colonial buildings: the handsome Serampore College, on the south side of the town, and St Olav's Church on the north side. The Danes sold Serampore and their other Indian possession at Tranquebar (*see p. 808*) to the British in 1845 for 1,250,000 rupees.

WILLIAM CAREY

A former shoemaker from Northamptonshire, William Carey (1761–1834) arrived in Serampore on 10th January 1800 and died there 34 years later. He became the most famous and influential of many 19th-century Christian missionaries in India—a role that would be replayed by Mother Teresa in the 20th century. He learnt Bengali and Sanskrit, and published grammars of both languages. He supervised the first translation of the Bible into Bengali and other Indian languages. His first wife, an illiterate peasant woman who accompanied him very unwillingly, went mad and died; he then married a Danish aristocrat. Two American universities, in Mississippi and in Pasadena, California, have been named after him.

Serampore College

The Neoclassical Serampore College (1826), a large mansion with six well-proportioned Ionic columns supporting a fine moulded entablature, was set up by three British Baptist missionaries, William Carey, Joshua Marshman and William Ward, who were not made welcome by the mainly Anglican authorities in Calcutta, but whom the Danes allowed to operate freely. The college was set up 'for the instruction of Asiatic, Christian, and other youth in Eastern literature and European science', and today it is a theological college and a library, with an impressive collection of old manuscripts. It welcomes visitors (*Mon–Fri 10–4*).

St Olav's Church

St Olav's has an unusually tall spire, and its British architects loosely based the design on St Martin-in-the-Fields in London. Note the small, broken pediment, open in a way that is a distinctive feature of Danish architecture; and the royal insignia of King Christian VII (CRVII for Christianus Rex VII).

CHANDERNAGORE

This pretty town (also called Chandannagar), situated on a bend in the Hooghly, 35km north of Kolkata, was a French colony from the late 17th century until 1950, and the French influence is clearly visible in many of the buildings overlooking the riverside promenade.

History: The French settlement of Chandernagore was founded by the French Compagnie des Indes in 1688 on land purchased for 40,000 rupees, and fortified under the name Fort d'Orléans. However, it was not developed into an important trading post until the 1730s, and the arrival of the administrator most closely associated with France's burgeoning Indian empire, Joseph François Dupleix (*see p.787*). Chandernagore was taken in 1757 by the British at the time of the Battle of Plassey, but restored to France in 1763 under the Treaty of Paris that ended the Seven Years War. It was again taken by the British twice more, and finally returned to France in 1816 after the Napoleonic Wars. It remained under French control, administered by the French governor-general in Pondicherry until 1950, when, in a plebiscite, its inhabitants voted by 7,463 to 114 to join India. Unlike the three other French enclaves, which are still ruled from Pondicherry, Chandernagore was integrated into the surrounding territory of West Bengal.

Orientation: The main buildings from the period of French rule overlook the broad road and wide pavement that runs alongside the river, giving excellent views of the other bank of the Hooghly, which is approximately 350m wide at this point.

Dupleix Palace

The most important of the town's buildings is the former Dupleix Palace—the administrative centre of French Chandernagore—which is now a museum, library and French cultural centre. The **museum** (*open daily 11–5.30*) contains a wide range of memorabilia of the French period, including Chandernagore's last flag, lowered in 1950, and a large bust of Marianne, the emblem of Republican France. Among the other buildings along the main road—the former Quai Dupleix—are the old **Thistle Hotel** (1878), now a court building, the former **Ecole de Jeunes Filles** (1903), now an English Medium School, and a stepped **clock tower gateway** (1845). Note the French-language memorial stone on the front of the police station, inscribed to a police officer, Jules Quin-Célestin, who was killed by 'foreign terrorists' in Chandernagore in 1933. There is also a small riverside pavilion—the town's main meeting place—which leads down to a jetty. The pavilion was erected in memory of an early Indian recipient of the Légion d'honneur.

About 100m back from the main road, opposite the pavilion, is the distinctive **Church of the Sacred Heart** (1875–84), with a semicircular pediment, coupled pillars, three-storey side towers, some fine stained glass and carved wooden confessionals. The crumbling tombs and obelisks of the French cemetery are further from the waterfront, and the inner roads of Chandernagore have several more buildings from the French period.

CHINSURA

This former Dutch settlement (also called Chunchura), 40km north of Kolkata (*map 8 D1*), is just south of the former early British settlement called Hooghly, named after the river which these towns now overlook. The Dutch settled Chinsura in the early 17th century, building Fort Gustav as a small garrison in what was the most northerly of the many small Dutch settlements in India. In 1825, it was exchanged by the Dutch for the British settlement of Bencoolen (modern-day Bengkulu) on the island of Sumatra in Indonesia. It was then merged with the town of Hooghly under British rule.

The District Commissioner's Residence (*permission for access needed from the district commissioner in the large building opposite*) overlooking the river is Chinsura's oldest building, constructed in 1687 and greatly altered since. Note the monogram VOC (Verenigte Oostindische Compagnie, or United East India Company) inscribed above the sweeping double staircase.

Armenian Church

The well-maintained Armenian Church of St John the Baptist (*knock hard on the gate to gain access*), 500m north of the Commissioner's House, was built in 1695 to cater for the small community of Armenian traders who had settled in the area. The church steeple is a 19th-century addition, but the rest of this large apsidal building is thought to be original. The church is now looked after by the remaining small Armenian community in Kolkata, members of which visit on special feast days. Note the older gravestones, with inscriptions in Armenian, laid flush with the paving stones in the covered area next to the church. Among the many interesting English-language inscriptions is a memorial to the son of 'the late Freedone Melik Beglaroff, last independent prince of Karabagh, in the province of Tiflis, Caucasus'. Karabagh is now better known as Nagorno-Karabakh, the disputed territory that Armenia and Azerbaijan fought a war over in the 1990s, while Tiflis is now Tbilisi, the Georgian capital.

The old Dutch cemetery, with many Dutch and British tombs, has many interesting inscriptions, and graves that date back to 1740.

HOOGHLY

This small town (also called Hughli), next to Chinsura on the west bank of the river of the same name (*map 8 D1*), was the headquarters of the British East India Company in Bengal prior to the founding of Calcutta in the late 1680s. In the 16th century, the Portuguese built a settlement here before returning to Bandel, slightly to the north. The British built their trading settlement here in the 1650s. In 1686 the forces of the nawab of Bengal attacked British positions at Hooghly, at which point the senior British official Job Charnock decamped downstream and began building a new settlement at what became Calcutta. There are no surviving buildings from the early colonial period—though there are lots of riverside mansions and warehouses mainly dating from the 19th century.

The *imambara*

Hooghly has a very impressive *imambara* (1861), or Shia Muslim assembly hall, built in the late Mughal style, overlooking the river, 2km north of Chinsura's Armenian

Church. From the topmost windows of its enormous clock tower (nicknamed 'Big Ben' by locals), one gets superb views in every direction. Note the multi-coloured calligraphy covering much of the exterior and interior of the prayer hall, which has its own coloured chandeliers made from Belgian glass.

Behind the prayer hall is a small garden that leads down to the river. On the right is the cantilevered **Jubilee Bridge** (1887).

Bandel

Just north of Hooghly town is another settlement—this one formerly Portuguese. It was founded in the late 16th century and conquered in 1632 by the Mughal emperor Shah Jahan, who captured four Portuguese priests. The **Portuguese church** at Bandel, dedicated to Our Lady of the Rosary, is the oldest in Bengal (1660), replacing an even older church, built in 1599, but which has been so heavily restored that it looks entirely modern.

BANSBERIA

This small town, 5km north of Pandel and 50km north of Kolkata (*map 8 D1*), has two unusual temples that stand next to the dilapidated former *rajbari*, or palace, of the former raja of Bansberia. The largest is the visually stunning seven-storeyed **Hamseshwari Temple** (1814), which, with its 13 pointed domes, has a fairytale quality. It is dedicated to the goddess Kali and has several side temples with Shiva lingams. Note the pretty decoration on the roof of the entrance porch. The smaller, square **Vasudev Temple** is much older (1679) and built to a traditional Bengali design, with sloping cornices and an octagonal tower. It is dedicated to the god Vishnu and has fine terracotta decoration. Note the quality of the sculpture around the cusped entrance arches. The lowest level of decoration on the side facing the Hamseshwari Temple is thought to show Portuguese gunmen travelling in boats, presumably arriving on the banks of the Hooghly.

TRIBENI

Just 1.5km north of Bansberia, within the small town of Tribeni (*map 8 D1*), overlooking the Hooghly, is East India's oldest mosque (1298) and oldest tomb (1313) in the same complex. At the time of their construction, this area was known as Saptagram (and Satgaon) and was the largest city in south Bengal. The double-chambered **tomb of Zafar Khan Ghazi**, who conquered southern Bengal on behalf of the sultan of Delhi, is thought to have been built from the ruins of a Krishna temple. Many stones with carvings of gods, animals and humans, including a dancing girl, have been reused for the tomb and between the steps leading up to the first chamber. The five-bayed **Tribeni Mosque**, constructed 15 years before the tomb, also reused older carved stone pieces, particularly around the prayer niches. The domes are thought to have been restored in the 16th century, and the terracotta decoration is also thought to date from this later period.

PANDUA

This small town (*map 8 D1*), 16km northwest of Tribeni and 55km north of Kolkata, is sometimes known as Chota Pandua, or little Pandua, to avoid confusion with the better-known ruined city of Pandua 230km to the north. It has an unusual 14th-century mosque and *minar*, or tower. The 18m-high five-tiered *minar*, probably intended as a victory tower and minaret, stands, like the earlier Qutb Minar in Delhi, a short distance away from the mosque. Note the carved stone door frame of the *minar*, behind which a spiral staircase (*normally closed*) leads to the top. The **Bari Mosque** is unusually long and thin, with 21 bays and 21 prayer niches, and was once covered by 63 domes. Notice the raised platform on the left side, which would have been screened off and used by women and by the ruler. The *minbar*, or pulpit, is in unusually good condition for a mosque of this age.

KALNA

This town overlooking the Hooghly (*map 8 D1*), 17km north of Chota Pandua and 70km from Kolkata, has several superb temples grouped inside the old palace compound, or Rajbari, formerly belonging to the princely state of Burdwan. Ask for directions to the Rajbari, and you will be brought to a road that separates the main group of temples on the left and the unusual circular Shiva temple complex on the right.

Shiva Temple

Head first to the Shiva Temple complex (1809), consisting of two concentric circles made up of a total of 108 small temples. In the outer ring, the temples have alternating white and black lingams, while temples in the inner ring, built around a well, have only white lingams.

Rajbari compound

Next head into the Rajbari compound to visit the fascinating main group of temples. The first small **Pratapeswar Temple** (1849) has some of the richest and finest terracotta decoration to be found anywhere in India. The modelling of the figures—humans, gods and animals mainly in scenes from the *Ramayana*, particularly in the curved area above the door arches—is superb and in excellent condition. Just beyond is the octagonal, roofless **Rasa Manch**, used by the maharaja during religious ceremonies.

The **Lalji Temple** (1739), within a walled compound, is a magnificent larger temple—the oldest in Kalna. It has a fine assembly hall, and 25 roof pinnacles arranged around a central tower. Note the unusual vertical carved flanges around the fluted corners of the temple, with fine sculptures of animals and humans attacking each other. On the other side of the compound is the almost identical **Krishna Chand Temple** (1752), which also has some beautifully carved terracotta scenes from the life of Krishna. At the end of the compound are the former palace, now occupied by government officials, and the palace gate, the rooms of which are Communist Party offices.

THE EAST BANK OF THE HOOGHLY

Barrackpore

The only major historical settlement on the east bank of the Hooghly, opposite Serampore, is the former British garrison town of Barrackpore (*map 8, D1*), famous as the site of the first rebellion that marked the start of the 1857 Uprising. It was here that the mutineer Mangal Pandey, who along with many other soldiers objected to the use of animal fat in rifle cartridges, attacked a British officer, and was later executed.

Among the surviving buildings from the British period are **Government House** (1813), now a police hospital, the **Semaphore Tower** (1820), the Neoclassical **Cenotaph** (1813), built to commemorate those who died in the British victories in Java and Mauritius, and **Flagstaff House** (1863), now used by the West Bengal governor as a weekend retreat—and which has several statues of British colonial dignitaries (*apply to the controller of the governor's household, Raj Bhavan, in Kolkata for access*).

St Bartholomew's (1831), the garrison church, is easier to visit, and has some interesting memorials. Nearby are the old **British cemetery** and the **parade ground** where the events of 1857 took place.

THE MURSHIDABAD REGION

Murshidabad (*map 7 C3*), on the eastern bank of the Hooghly, 180km north of Kolkata, was the most important city in eastern India for the first half of the 18th century and contains an extraordinary treasure trove of 18th- and 19th-century architecture, reflecting both the Muslim and the British colonial styles. Confusingly, the historical name Murshidabad is now mainly used to describe the district in central West Bengal—and the former city which it originally described is usually referred to by locals as Lalbagh, or after the main palace, Hazar Duari. Baharampore, just 10km to the south, is the main city of Murshidabad district.

History: Murshidabad was founded in 1704 on the site of the older town of Maksudabad when Murshid Quli Khan, the nawab of Bengal, transferred his capital from Dhaka, now the capital of Bangladesh. For 50 years, the nawabs, officially the representatives of the Mughal Empire, but with a very large degree of independence, ruled Bengal, Orissa and Bihar from Murshidabad. But in 1757, the British, based in the fast-growing city of Calcutta, established their supremacy in Bengal by defeating the army of Nawab Siraj ud-Daula (nicknamed Sir Roger Dowlett by the British) at the Battle of Plassey, 40km south of Murshidabad. The British then installed Mir Jafar, a general who had betrayed Siraj ud-Daula.

The name Mir Jafar is still used in Bengali to describe a traitor, similar to the name Quisling in English. Mir Jafar's descendants continued to hold the position of nawab of Bengal, and built many of the impressive colonial-style buildings, such as the great Hazar Duari Palace. In the 1880s, the princely family were 'downgraded' following the abdication of one of the rulers, and became the nawabs of Murshidabad. In the 20th century the family went into debt and lost most of its estates, which were taken over by the government. Many expected Murshidabad to become part of East Pakistan at the time of Partition, because it had a Muslim majority. Its inhabitants did not learn that they would instead become part of India until three days after Independence. East Pakistan (later Bangladesh) was given Hindu-majority Khulna instead. Pakistan's first president, Iskander Mirza (1899–1969), was the grandson of the last nawab of Bengal, and was born in Murshidabad.

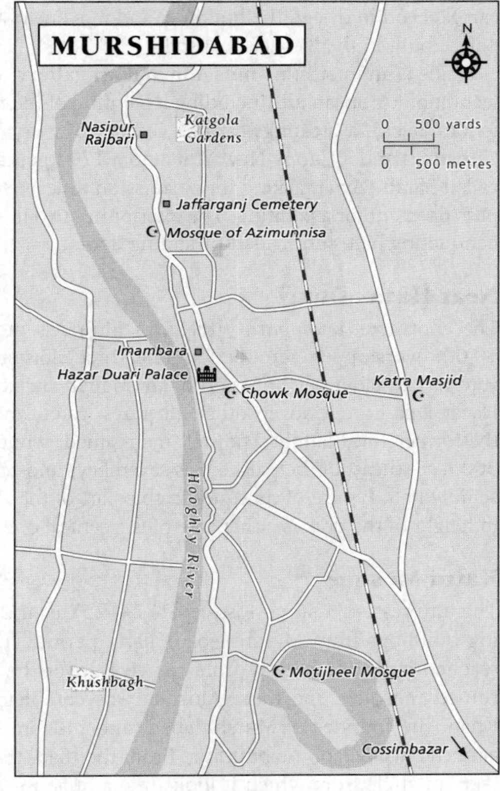

Orientation: Most of Murshidabad's important buildings are along the river front. They include the Hazar Duari Palace, and the old Nawabi cemetery and several colonial-style mansions in the northern suburb of Jaffarganj. The Katra Mosque is away from the river, 2.5km east of the palace. The Khushbagh tombs are on the other side of the River Hooghly, easily accessible by boat from Murshidabad, or by road via Baharampore.

Arriving from the south and the road from Kolkata, visitors to Murshidabad pass through an old city gate, and then the large triple-arched Tripolia Gate before reaching the palace complex at the heart of Murshidabad.

Hazar Duari

The Hazar Duari, meaning literally '1,000 doors', is a huge European-style mansion (1837) whose magnificent northern façade overlooks a park next to the Hooghly, facing the even larger *imambara*. The palace façade has a six-pillar entrance portico, with a low pediment and a steep, broad staircase—based on the design of Government House in Kolkata. Nawab Humayun Jah commissioned the British architect and general Duncan McLeod to design the building, and it is one of the earliest examples of a princely palace built in the Neoclassical style.

Inside is an interesting **museum and art gallery**, with an impressive armoury, a collection of European art (including a painting of the marquis of Spinola that is ascribed to Van Dyck), a greetings card carved out of ivory wishing one Lady Fraser 'a Merry Christmas and a Happy New Year' and a 1793 petition to the nawab by a British artist called Sarah Baxter, asking for permission to leave Murshidabad, as well as 4,000 rupees payment for a painting. The interior has two interior courtyards, and an 89m-long banqueting hall, subdivided by sliding doors.

Near Hazar Duari

The enormous ***imambara*** (1847), or Shi'a Assembly Hall, is large enough to hold 10,000 worshippers, grouped around three cloistered courtyards. The central courtyard has an older pavilion, part of an original *imambara* that burnt down. Close to the Hazar Duari are a dozen other mosques, gates, and minor palaces that belonged to the former royal family. The well-maintained, whitewashed **Chowk Mosque** (1767), 300m southeast of the palace, has seven bays and seven domes, and a long narrow assembly hall, typical of mosques in this part of the country. Note the gradual decrease in height of the domes either side of the central one.

Katra Mosque

The impressive Katra Mosque (1724–25) is the most important of the surviving buildings from Murshidabad's early period. It is 2km east of the Hazar Duari, reached by heading away from the river, over the railway line, past another pretty, ruined mosque. The Katra Mosque was completed in the reign of Murshid Quli Khan, the founder of Murshidabad, and his tomb is under the steps of the main, eastern entrance of the building. From the road, the mosque is approached from the rear, an angle from which it looks like a huge fort, with two large octagonal towers that function both as minarets and as defensive fortifications. The outer walls of the building, which entirely surround the mosque, have lots of small rooms that were used as a *madrasa*. The mosque assembly hall has five small bays and two surviving domes and is dwarfed by the rest of the complex. Note the large drainage channels under the mosque.

A little south of the mosque, in the Nakurtala area, is a large cannon, known as Jahan Kosha ('world-subduer') and forged in 1637. It is more than 5m long, weighs more than 7 tonnes and is thought to have been brought here from Dhaka, when Murshid Quli Khan transferred the capital to Murshidabad. Until recently, the branches of a pipal tree had lifted the gun several metres above the ground, but the cannon has now been set on a plinth.

Jaffarganj

The northern suburb of Murshidabad known as Jaffarganj has a number of important buildings and sites that are worthy of investigation.

Mosque of Azimunnisa Begum: Around 1.5km north of Hazar Duari are the ruined mosque and tomb of Azimunnisa Begum, daughter of Murshid Quli Khan. Like her father in the Katra Mosque, she is buried under the stairs—the intention being that she would be blessed by the footsteps of the faithful over her grave.

Jaffarganj Cemetery: Three hundred metres further north and on the right side of the road is the dilapidated but fascinating Jaffarganj cemetery, which contains several hundred royal graves from the 1760s to the current day. Unusually for a Muslim cemetery, many of the inscriptions are written in English. Note the blue Chinese tiles around some of the graves.

Nasipur Rajbari: Some 600m to the north of the cemetery, also on the right, is another European-style palace with an imposing façade. It is known as the Nasipur Rajbari, and its inner courtyards are open to the public. It was not owned by the royal family, but by a rich 18th-century merchant called Debi Singh—one of several who built large mansions in this area—and it still belongs to his descendants. Note the carved lions at the foot of the stairs, and the two terrified crowned lions in stucco on the pediment of the building. The first-floor railings have been shaped to include the initials NR, for Nasipur Rajbari. Access to the building is through the corridor on the right. The first courtyard has a covered area that was used for dances and musical performance, and there is a large Rama temple in the second courtyard, with numerous smaller side temples.

Another 200m further on from the Nasipur Rajbari is a small house containing a museum full of 19th-century household objects and furniture owned by the Jagat Seth family, whose large palace was washed away when the Hooghly changed its course. Next to the museum is a small garden with European statues and a Jain temple.

Katgola Gardens: The pretty Katgola Gardens—very popular with local tourists—contain what was once a very impressive mansion, owned by a Jain merchant. However, it has been so over-restored that it is barely recognisable. The crumbling outbuilding just behind the police post gives an indication of how the mansion must have once looked.

Other sights in Murshidabad

On the southern side of Murshidabad is Motijheel, where the small Motijheel mosque (1750), cemetery and ruined *madrasa* overlook a pretty horseshoe-shaped lake, which was once a bend in the Hooghly. On the other side of the river, easily accessed by boat, are the tombs of Siraj ud-Daula and another 18th-century nawab, set in pretty gardens known as Khushbagh.

COSSIMBAZAR

This town (*map 7 C3*, also known as Kasimbazar) on the southern outskirts of Murshidabad, just north of Baharampore, was an important early British trading settlement, founded in the mid-17th century on the site of an older town. Two well-known figures from the East India Company were based here: in the 1650s Job Charnock, traditionally seen as the founder of Calcutta; and in the mid-18th century Warren Hastings, who later became the first British governor-general.

In 1757 Cossimbazar was captured by the Siraj ud-Daula, and Hastings and other British residents were taken as prisoners to Murshidabad. There were also Dutch and Armenian communities in the 18th century—and there is a small Dutch cemetery with 47 gravestones, though very few surviving inscriptions, on the western side of Cossimbazar.

Choto Rajbari

Cross the railway to reach Cossimbazar's Choto Rajbari, or Small Palace, which is also a small museum and is still owned by the descendants of the last raja of Cossimbazar. It is an 18th-century palace with a well-maintained 19th-century neo-Gothic façade, complete with conical green roof turrets. Inside the sprawling building are three temples, and lots of rooms with 19th- and 20th-century furniture.

British Cemetery

Four hundred metres east of the Choto Rajbari is a fascinating British cemetery, which includes the grave of Warren Hastings' wife Mary and their three-week-old daughter Elizabeth.

COSSIMBAZAR'S CONNECTION WITH JANE AUSTEN

Warren Hastings later had a god-daughter called Eliza Hancock. She was named after his short-lived daughter, and thought to be his illegitimate child. Eliza was also the first cousin of Jane Austen. She married a French nobleman and took the title Comtesse de Feuillide. Their son was named Hastings after her father. Following her husband's death on the guillotine during the French Revolution, Eliza returned to England where she married her cousin Henry, Jane Austen's brother, and is thought to have been the model for several of the novelist's more strong-willed characters, including Mary Crawford in *Mansfield Park*.

Also buried here is Lyon Prager, who died at the Factory House, Cossimbazar, and was 'a diamond merchant, and Inspector of Indigo and Drugs to the Hon'ble East India Company'—a reminder of the wide range of business then being conducted by Europeans in this part of India.

Bara Rajbari

About 350m south of the British Cemetery is the decaying Bara Rajbari, or Large Palace, with a handsome Neoclassical façade and four-columned portico. The main interior courtyard is wildly overgrown with bushes and creepers, and the masonry is collapsing.

PLASSEY

This was the site (*map 7 C3*, also known as Palasi) of the 1757 battle that ensured British supremacy in Bengal and the defeat and death of Nawab Siraj ud-Daula, whose forces were responsible for the 'Black Hole of Calcutta' (*see p. 538*). The nawab's army had the support of a small contingent of French troops, but were betrayed by one of his generals, Mir Jafar, who became the next nawab. Robert Clive, later known as Clive of India, commanded the British forces—and was later ennobled as Baron Clive of Plassey. There is not much to see at the site of what was probably the most important battle of the British colonial period, although the countryside is very pretty. There is a 19th-century obelisk commemorating the battle at the end of a road near the village of Plassey (follow signposts to 'Monument'). Head 100m towards the river, and on the left are three modern obelisks marking the site where three important supporters of the nawab were killed.

THE MALDA REGION: GAUR & PANDUA

The two long-deserted and little-visited medieval cities of Gaur and Pandua, which both have some superb Muslim medieval architecture, are close to the modern town of Malda (*map 7 C3*), 300km north of Kolkata. Between the 14th and 16th centuries, Gaur and Pandua, 30km apart (south and north of Malda respectively), alternated as the capitals of the Bengal Sultanate. Gaur has an extraordinary range of ruins, and it can take a full day to visit them all; Pandua has fewer surviving buildings, but its Adina Mosque is one of the most impressive medieval buildings in east India. Modern Malda (pop. 250,000) has subsumed the old 17th-century British settlement of English Bazar, or Ingraj Bazar, by which the main town is still often known.

GAUR

The ruined medieval city of Gaur (*map 7 C3*) is one of India's best-kept secrets. It is not easy to get there, but for anyone interested in Muslim architecture, Bengali history or medieval archaeology it is worth the effort.

History: The city was once on the banks of the Ganges, which has now changed its course and flows 15km to the west. Gaur's history goes back more than a millennium, to when it was the capital of the Hindu Pala and Sena dynasties. But its main surviving buildings are from its second period as the capital of the Muslim sultanate of Bengal between 1442 and 1576 (it had previously been the capital from 1211 to 1354). It survived as a Mughal outpost until the 17th century, and the emergence of Murshidabad and Calcutta further to the south. Then Gaur became overgrown and forgotten, and stone from its buildings was taken for construction elsewhere. In the early 16th century, though, Gaur was enormous, covering more than 50km square, a long narrow rectangle running north–south along the Ganges; most of that land is now under cultivation. The ruins of Gaur straddle the India-Bangladesh border, and one of its ancient gates actually forms the frontier post. The most important buildings are in India, but if you have a Bangladeshi visa and a multiple-entry Indian visa, it is relatively easy to cross the frontier to see three fine medieval mosques.

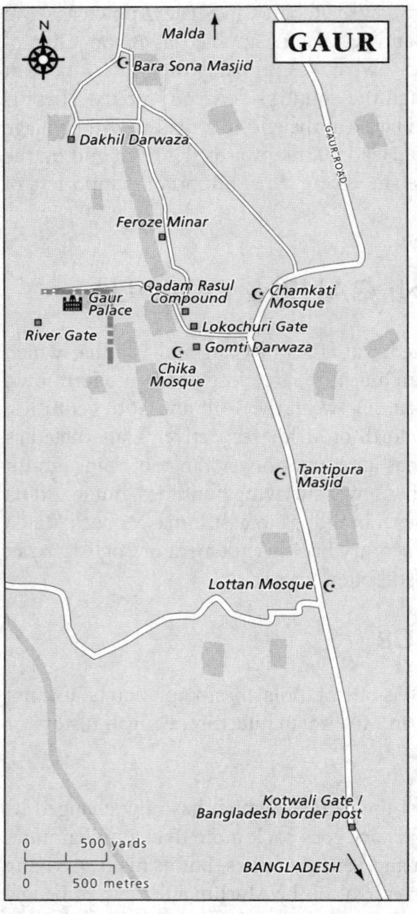

Orientation: The road to Gaur is also the main road from Malda, 13km away, to the Bangladesh border. It is best to hire a vehicle in Malda, preferably with a driver who knows the Gaur site, as there are several important buildings half-hidden in the trees, between the large fish ponds and along dirt tracks without signposts. The first significant building on approaching the site from the north is the Bara Sona Masjid, just north of the old north gate (the Dakhil Darwaza), from where it is necessary to turn right, then left past the tower or Minar to the central area, from where it is possible to walk (or drive) to several of the buildings, including the remains of the palace, and the enormous walls of the citadel. Further to the south, it is helpful to have a vehicle in order to visit two very pretty mosques closer to the Bangladesh border, as well as the ruined city gate that marks the frontier.

Bara Sona Masjid

In view of its name (Bara Sona Masjid translates as 'large golden mosque'), it is fair to presume that this building (1526) once had gilded domes, but the main assembly hall is now largely in ruins. The most impressive part of this 11-bayed mosque is the 50m-long verandah that is still intact—as are two of the three mosque gates. The pillar bases in the main assembly enable visitors to get a sense of what the mosque once looked like, and the bases of two of the *mihrabs*, or prayer niches, are still visible. Note the raised platform on the north side of the mosque, which would have been the entrance for women.

Dakhil Darwaza

This mid-15th century gateway (literally 'entry gate'), 500m southwest of the Bara Sona Masjid at the end of a short causeway, is an imposing structure that probably was the northern entrance to the city. It had five-storey lookout towers on each corner, of which the one on the southeast is the best preserved. The gate has a long arched tunnel, with two internal side corridors that each have a side door, with surviving stone rings on which the doors were hung. Note the terracotta ornamentation, particularly over the doorway arches. There are steep embankments on either side of the gate that conceal unexcavated walls.

Feroze Minar

This 25m-high five-storey brick tower (1489) overlooks a body of water, which may have once been a moat, 1km to the southeast of the Dakhil Darwaza (return back along the causeway towards the Bara Sona Masjid, turn right and right again). It is thought to have been a Victory Tower (there is no surviving mosque nearby), possibly built by an Abyssinian general who briefly ruled Gaur. Note how the lower three storeys are 12-sided, while the upper two are circular. An early 19th-century drawing of the tower shows it with an open, domed room at the top, which has since disappeared.

Some 400m beyond the Feroze Minar, the road splits. Turn left for the great walls of Gaur and the ruined palace. Go straight ahead for a series of mosques, tombs and gates that make up the rest of the city.

The city walls

There are two long stretches that remain of the enormous old city walls of Gaur, known as the Bais Gazi (meaning 22 yards), each more than 20m high and 200m long, and built out of brick with terracotta decoration. The first stretch of wall runs east–west just north of the old palace and is largely intact. There are no windows, though there are wall niches on the southern side. The second stretch of wall is southeast of the palace—it runs north–south and has a right-angle corner, but is broken in several places.

Gaur Palace

Recent excavations in what is thought to have been the palace (before 1460) have revealed unusual circular foundations, which some archaeologists believe were used to support wooden pillars. However, architectural evidence from the partial excavations indicates that this may date to a pre-Islamic phase of Gaur's development. Note the wells and steps at the centre of the complex, and the unexplained side apertures in the circular foundation cylinders.

River Gate: A short stroll west of the palace leads to a recently excavated river gate, with a complex stepped construction complete with floor tiling, thought to date to the more recent period of Gaur's development. The Ganges once flowed just beneath the gate, but the river has now moved 15km to the west. There are also unexcavated ruins just next to the large water tank, to the east of the palace.

There are two routes from the palace to the next collection of buildings, a compound that contains the Qadam Rasul and the tomb of Fath Khan, opposite some tea stalls. Either return to the road from the Minar, and turn right, or head south of the tank, past the north–south walls.

Qadam Rasul

The square Qadam Rasul building (1531), its name meaning 'foot of the messenger', contains a stone footprint of the Prophet Muhammad—but it is not, despite what the signboard says, a mosque. Note the repeated terracotta motif of a hanging lamp on the exterior of the building—the most common of the many designs at Gaur. The **tomb of Fath Khan** (late 17th century) is one of the youngest buildings in Gaur, and contains the grave of a son of one of Emperor Aurangzeb's generals. The curved *bangaldar* roof is typical of Bengali architecture but is the only example of this style at Gaur.

Chika Mosque

The square Chika Mosque (c. 1450) is less than 200m south of the Qadam Rasul, and is almost certainly not a mosque but a mausoleum, or possibly an administrative building. Some of the external terracotta ornamentation is coloured. It appears to have been part of a small complex, with a number of other buildings, the ruins of which can be seen. It has an unusual stepped dome like the smaller and very pretty **Gomti Darwaza** (1512), or Domed Gate, just 60m to the east of the Chika Mosque. Note the two pillars on the façade, made up of miniature pillars of glazed terracotta, apparently intended to resemble stacks of bangles of the kind still seen in any Indian market. The large Mughal **Lokochuri Gate** (1655) is 90m to the north, with a Naubat Khana, or drum room, above it.

Head through the gate and then turn right towards the Bangladesh border for two more mosques and part of the southern group of buildings in Gaur; while a left turn will take you to the Chamkati Mosque, 200m to the north.

Tantipura and Lottan mosques

The partly ruined and dome-less **Tantipura Masjid** (1475), 1km south of the Lokochuri Gate, on the right side of the road, is one of the oldest surviving mosques in Gaur. It was named after the Weavers' Quarter (Tantipura) that once surrounded it; and the building has very pretty floral terracotta decoration. Note the unusual corrugated effect of the brickwork on the rear of the mosque. About 700m further south on the other side of the road is the prettily decorated **Lottan (or Nattan) Mosque** (c. 1480). It is an unusual design, with three small front domes over a verandah, and a large stepped dome over the main mosque chamber. Note the fine quality of the glazed and coloured terracotta tiles, inside and outside the mosque.

The Bangladesh border

Another 1.25km south, past the customs and immigration buildings, is the ruined **Kotwali Gate**, which marks the Indian side of the border with Bangladesh.

No cameras or phones are allowed here. You can climb the southern part of the ruined gate, and you can see old bastions and the pretty terracotta niches on the Bangladeshi side. The embankments on either side of the gate are the overgrown old outer walls of Gaur.

The **Chamkati Mosque** (c. 1480), back on the road and 300m north of the turning to the Lokochuri Gate, is similar in design to the Lottan mosque. It is under restoration, and its left side is almost completely new, with a few old pieces inserted.

PANDUA

Some 15km north of Malda, close to the National Highway, are the ruins of the deserted city of Pandua (*map 7 C3*), capital of Bengal from 1344 to 1452. There are fewer monuments than at Gaur, which both preceded and succeeded Pandua as capital, but the glorious, partly ruined Adina Mosque, once the largest in India and covering an area of 14,000m square, is the most important single building that has survived from Bengal's Sultanate period.

Adina Mosque

This mosque (1364–74) is visible from the main road leading north, but it is only when one goes down the slip road on the southern side of the mosque that the enormous scale of this building becomes clear. It has been compared to the great Ummayad Mosque in Damascus, and has a similar size and layout, and was built during the reign of Sikander Shah (1358–1390), of the Ilyas Shahi Dynasty.

Outer walls and gates: The modern entrance to the site is from the southwest. Ahead is the long wall of the back of the mosque—constructed out of grey basalt at the bottom and red brick on top. Some of the blocks of stone have been taken from Hindu temples, and there are several carvings of Ganesha, the elephant-god, other deities and dancing girls embedded in the lower wall. Unusually for the rear wall of a mosque, it is pierced by entrance passages at three points. The imposing royal entrance to the mosque is two-thirds of the way along the wall, and has a columned entrance porch at a right angle to the final gateway. Note the finely carved stone door frames.

Inside the mosque: The porch leads through into the private royal area of the mosque, or *badshah-i takht*, (literally 'throne of the emperor'), on a raised platform within the main building. The floor was originally covered in stone slabs, some of which survive (the rest have been replaced with wood), and these rested on the unusually broad pillars that supported this part of the mosque. The quality of the polished black stone *mihrabs*, or prayer niches, carved in relief, is particularly fine. Descend the stairs to enter the public part of the mosque and see the superb carving around the main *mihrab*, decorated with relief carvings of hanging lamps, and the almost intact *minbar*, or pulpit. Unusually, the central area did not have a dome, but a barrel vault which has since collapsed. The dozens of *mihrabs* to the north of the platform and the south of the central assembly area are also made of carved stone, and have delicate terracotta work above each of them. Note the truncated arch just north of the platform, suggesting that the royal area of the mosque was extended at a later date.

The mosque courtyard: The true scale and splendour of the Adina Mosque only really becomes clear when one moves into the large grassy courtyard to see the partly ruined cloisters that surrounded the other sides of the building, as well as the nest of low domes that covers the platform area of the mosque. There are more entrances on the western and southern walls, two of which have carvings of Ganesha as part of the door frames.

Other buildings in Pandua

To reach the other two significant buildings in Pandua, head back south, not along the highway, but along the village road for almost 2km.

Eklakhi Tomb: This tomb (c. 1425), visible from the road, is a distinctive mausoleum with a grand dome and the slightly sloping cornice that came to distinguish much later Bengali architecture. It is thought to contain the tomb of Sultan Jalaluddin Shah, a Muslim convert from Hinduism whose Hindu father, Raja Ganesh, continued to be the *de facto* ruler of Bengal. There is a defaced carving, probably of Ganesha, over the door frame of the tomb, and a beautiful tiny carving of a crouching figure on the top right external part of the frame, thought to be Krishna—and clearly taken from a Hindu temple, where it would have been vertical rather than horizontal. There is also some fine terracotta decoration, particularly of hanging lamps—the most common motif in the buildings of Gaur and Pandua.

Qutub Shahi Mosque: Just behind the Eklakhi Tomb is the Qutub Shahi Mosque (1582), also known as the Sona (or 'golden') Masjid. It was built by a descendant of the Muslim saint Nur Qutub al-Alam, whose much rebuilt shrine is just behind. Although the roof has collapsed, the mosque is in relatively good condition and has the distinctive curved cornice of many other buildings of this period. The mosque reuses material from other buildings—probably an older mosque. Note the carved calligraphy on a piece of stone embedded on the top right exterior of the mosque gate.

The Pandua area has a number of other ruined buildings, including the remains of **Sikander Shah's Palace** (late 14th century), near the deer park on the other side of the highway from the Adina Mosque.

OLD MALDA

In Old Malda, 8km west of the modern town, is the 16th-century **Jama Masjid**, which is still in use. Note the barrel-vaulted main roof with two side domes. Across the river is a tall tower, the **Nim Serai Minar** (late 16th century), with stone projections shaped to look like elephant tusks, allegedly used to display the heads of decapitated thieves. There is a fine little **Chaitanya Temple**, and old houses with wooden doors.

SHANTI NIKETAN

Shanti Niketan (*map 8 D1*, literally 'abode of peace'), 140km northwest of Kolkata, is home to an unorthodox university set up in the early 20th century by the Nobel Prize-winning Bengali polymath Rabindranath Tagore.

History: Shanti Niketan was originally an area of infertile land which the father of Rabindranath Tagore purchased in 1863. It became a 'forest retreat' and a place of meditation to which family and friends could escape from Calcutta, and, as Tagore put it, ' be steeped in peacefulness…surrounded by the limitless sky, and the light…nursed in the arms of the primal mother'. In 1901, Tagore founded a school here, to which the rich of Calcutta would often send their errant sons. The emphasis was on simple living and an international education. In 1921 it became the Vishva Bharati University, very quickly gaining an excellent reputation in the fields of fine art, music and Indology—all subjects very dear to Tagore's heart. Much of Tagore's vision survives. The university is proud to include the great Bengali film director Satyajit Ray and the Nobel Prize-winning economist Amartya Sen among its alumni.

Visiting: The campus is largely open-air, with most classes taking place outdoors, under trees, with students seated on the ground. Shanti Niketan is an interesting place to visit, but it is no longer a rural paradise, and there are lots of buildings and too much litter. However, there are works of art everywhere, and students working hard at their studies or playing cricket. There is also a small museum called **Rabindra Bhavan** (*open Thur–Mon 10.30–1 & 2–4.30; mornings only on Tues*). It is best to hire a guide from near Rabindra Bhavan, who for about Rs200 will walk you around the campus, tell you about its history and, if you wish, introduce you to students and teachers.

RABINDRANATH TAGORE

Rabindranath Tagore (1861–1941) was the leading Indian cultural figure of the first half of the 20th century. Few have been as versatile. He is best known in the West as a writer of plays, novels and poems—most famously *Gitanjali*, subtitled 'Song Offerings', for which he won the 1913 Nobel Prize for Literature—and for which W.B. Yeats wrote an introduction. But Tagore was also a social and religious reformer, an influential artist and a composer of songs still loved throughout Bengal. Two of his songs later became the national anthems of India and Bangladesh. He was knighted by the British, but made himself a nationalist hero by returning the knighthood after the Jallianwala Bagh Massacre (*see p. 294*) of 1919. He had frequent disagreements with the other towering figure of the age, Gandhi, but it was Tagore who first honoured Gandhi with the epithet Mahatma, or 'Great Soul'. Visitors to West Bengal will see busts, statues and images of Tagore—always with a long, straggly beard—almost wherever they go.

BISHNUPUR

This small town (*map 8 C1*), 120km northwest of Kolkata, contains a dazzling collection of terracotta temples with a wide variety of curved roofs, and a trip here can easily be combined with a visit to Shanti Niketan. Bishnupur represents the apogee of the tradition of terracotta art and architecture in Bengal, and has some of the most distinctive and unusual temple designs in the country. Most of the temples were constructed in the 17th and 18th centuries, when the Malla Dynasty ruled this part of Bengal. The Mallas had been devotees of Shiva, but became Vaishnavites under Bir Hambhir (1587–1620), who named the town after Vishnu with the 'V' changed to a 'B' as is often the case in the Bengali language. The last Malla ruler sold his kingdom to the maharaja of Burdwan in the late 18th century.

Orientation: There are two large groups of temples, 1.5km apart—one to the south of the town (the southern group), the other in the centre, near the ruins of the old palace (the central group). In addition, there are three other important stand-alone buildings: the Shyama Raya Temple, tucked away down a side lane just 300m southeast of the central group; the Rasa Manch, midway between the two groups; and the Madan Mohan Temple, 800m northeast of the central group. It is possible to find a guide from the tourist shops next to the southern group who will navigate you through the town and point out interesting pieces of terracotta decoration.

Southern group

The photogenic but architecturally orthodox southern group has no fewer than seven temples, as well as the large Dalmadal cannon, used by the Malla kings against Maratha invaders in the 18th century. The two easternmost of this group, the **Kalachand Temple** (1656) and **Radhamadhab Temple** (1737), are similar in design, though the latter has a separate *mandapa*, or assembly hall. The nearby **Radhagovinda Temple** (1727) has a separate smaller side-temple with false wheels to make it resemble a chariot. The **Nand Lal Temple**, and the smaller **Jor Mandir temples** are close by. Note how the middle temple of the Jor Mandir subgroup is the only one in Bishnupur that does not face south.

Rasa Manch

The highly unusual Rasa Manch (early 17th century) building is shaped like a step pyramid surrounded by low curved domes. Ras Manch is not a temple but a royal building used for religious purposes during important festivals. It is relatively undecorated (only the east side has terracotta plaques) but it has a series of ambulatory corridors surrounding a central sanctuary, where idols would be placed at festival times.

The small **Bishnupur Museum**, near the Rasa Manch, has displays of local archaeological finds, mainly Hindu and Jain statues, as well as prehistoric stone tools, local textiles and examples of painting from the area.

Shyama Raya Temple

This temple (1643) is arguably Bishnupur's most idiosyncratic and elaborate building, with square towers on each corner and a two-storey octagonal tower in the middle. It also has some superb terracotta decoration of animals and scenes from the *Ramayana*. Note in particular the roundels showing the flute-playing Krishna surrounded by *gopis*, or shepherdesses.

Central group

On the east side of the central group are two 17th-century gates—one enormous and well fortified, the other smaller. They are at right angles to each other, and probably together formed the main entrance to the palace compound. The **Lalji Temple** (1658) is surrounded by a compound, and is similar in design to the southern group of temples. Enter the modern Durga Temple opposite to get a view of the overgrown ruins of the Malla Palace.

The **Radhashyam Temple** (1758) is the most recent of the Bishnupur buildings. It has a more rounded, dome-like roof than the others, and some fine external decoration. Look out in the lobby of the southern entrance for a tableau showing the reclining Vishnu, resting under the shade of a multi-headed snake. Just above are a cow, a horse and an elephant, each with a rider, and below are humans riding what appear to be geese.

The most easterly of the central group, the **Jor Bangla** (literally, 'joined curved roofs'), or Keshta Rai Temple (1655), is built to another unusual design, deliberately resembling two traditional Bengali huts that have been joined together at one side. It has some superb terracotta decorations, particularly on the west face, which tell stories from the Hindu epics. Note the image of Bhishma, one of the heroes of the *Mahabharata*, shown dying on a bed of arrows. The archer in this and many other images is Arjuna, the most virtuous of the epic's heroes.

Madan Mohan Temple

This shrine (1694), 800m to the northeast of the central group, is the prettiest and most impressively decorated of the single-spire temples. It is also a living temple, with effigies of Radha and Krishna in the central sanctuary. It has several fine below-knee-level friezes of geese, cows and hunting scenes. In the front verandah is a terracotta plaque of an elephant made up of nine women—one for each leg, one for the trunk, and four for the body—a popular Hindu motif.

DARJEELING & THE WEST BENGAL HILLS

In the far north of the state of West Bengal, the hill-station of Darjeeling (*map 7 C1*) is famous for its tea and superb views of the world's third largest mountain, Kanchenjunga, which is on the border with Nepal. Darjeeling is a popular destination with both foreign and domestic tourists.

History: The land on which Darjeeling was built was originally rented by the British from the king of Sikkim in the 1830s for £300 per annum, and was developed first—like so many hill-stations—as a sanatorium. The tea estates surrounding the area were planted in the 1850s, while the railway, one of the 19th-century's great engineering achievements, opened up Darjeeling as one of India's leading hill-stations—and later as the summer retreat for the government of Bengal.

In recent years, normal life has been frequently disrupted by activists of what has become known as the Gorkhaland movement—the partially successful attempts of the local Gorkha population (who prefer this spelling to the traditional English 'Gurkha') population to obtain greater autonomy from the Bengali-dominated state government. Darjeeling (which means 'Place of the Thunderbolt') is still a town with a strong British character in terms of architecture and atmosphere, but it has also been heavily influenced by Nepalese, Bengali and Tibetan migrants to the area.

Orientation: Darjeeling was built on the west-facing slope of a hill, with the Mall, its main upper thoroughfare (which is closed to vehicles), running north–south. At the northern end of the Mall is the square known as Chowrasta (literally 'four roads'), and further north still is Observatory Hill, with some fine views. Almost parallel, on the west side of the Mall at a lower level, is the Hill Cart Road, which is open to vehicular traffic. The railway station is on the south side.

Central Darjeeling

St Andrew's Church, first constructed in 1843 and then rebuilt in 1874 following an earthquake, is just to the west of Observatory Hill. It is Darjeeling's best-known building from the British period, and has some interesting memorial tablets inside. The old **Government House**, to the north of Observatory Hill, was rebuilt in the 1930s after an earthquake and is now the summer residence of the governor of West Bengal, and known as Raj Bhavan. It is normally closed to the public. Nearby is the **Bhutia Busty Gompa** (1879), a Buddhist monastery with the original copy of the classic Tibetan *Book of the Dead*.

Further north on Jawahar Road West, about 40 minutes' walk from Chowrasta, is the **Himalayan Mountaineering Institute and Everest Museum** (*open Fri–Wed 8.30–4.30*), within the grounds of Darjeeling Zoo. The museum traces the history of attempts to climb Everest, and on a nearby hilltop is a memorial marking the cremation site of Tenzing Norgay—he and Edmund Hillary were the first people to climb Everest, in 1953. There is a small observatory behind the museum with a telescope presented to a Nepalese prince by Adolf Hitler.

Almost 2km south of Chowrasta are the handsome grounds and buildings of **St Paul's School**, formed in Calcutta in 1823, and which moved to Darjeeling in 1864. The actress Vivien Leigh was born here in 1913.

The neo-Gothic **town hall** (1917) on Laden La Road, now known as the Municipality Building, was gutted by a fire in the 1990s, but has since been rebuilt. Close to the railway station is **St Columba's Kirk** (1894), with some fine stained glass. On the western side of Darjeeling are the well-maintained **Lloyd's Botanical Gardens** (*open Mon–Sat*), laid out in 1878.

Beyond Darjeeling

The village of **Ghoom**, 8km south of Darjeeling, is the penultimate stop (before Darjeeling) on the mountain railway. It is also the highest station on the line, which was completed in 1881. There is a small **railway museum** and the **Yiga Choling Gompa** (1875), the most interesting Buddhist monastery in the area, with some fine murals.

There are several other smaller hill-stations, including **Kurseong** (*map 7 C1*), on the road (and railway line) from the plains up to Darjeeling and Kalimpong, 2½ hours' drive east of Darjeeling and on the main road to Sikkim.

KALIMPONG

This hill-station (*map 7 C1*) has several interesting Buddhist monasteries, including the **Thongsa Gompa** (1692, rebuilt in the 19th century) on the northeast side of the town, beyond which is **Tharpa Choling Gompa** (1926), and the largest monastery, the **Dzongdopelri Gompa**, opened by the Dalai Lama in 1976, which sits on top of Durpin Hill. There is also the unusual **St Teresa's Catholic Church** (1929), built by Swiss Jesuit missionaries in the style of a Buddhist *gompa*, and with carved figures of the apostles that look like Buddhist monks. Just 4km to the northeast of Kalimpong is **Dr Graham's Home** (1900), an orphanage and school set up by a Scottish missionary. It has a small museum and a Scottish-style chapel, with slate roofs, a square tower and a steeple.

Most visitors to the Darjeeling Hills pass through one or more of a series of settlements in the plains to the south—including the main town of Siliguri (*map 7 C1*), the railway hub at New Jalpaiguri (*map 7 D2*) and the airport at Bagdogra (*map 7 C2*)—but none of these has buildings of great historical interest. However, the area also provides access to Gaur and Pandua. It is also the easiest way of reaching Cooch Behar.

Cooch Behar

This little-visited town (*map 7 D2*, officially Koch Bihar) was the capital of the former princely state of the same name. The enormous red-brick two-storey **Rajbari**, or New Palace (1875), with a dome modelled on St Peter's in Rome, is the town's best-known building. The Rajbari houses a **museum** (*open Sat–Thur*) in its durbar hall and other rooms of the palace—in which royal memorabilia as well as local stone carved sculptures from as early as the 8th century are on display. There are several other interesting palaces and royal buildings, most of them red-brick, in the town.

PRACTICAL INFORMATION

GETTING THERE & GETTING AROUND

• **By air:** Most visitors to the state fly either to Kolkata or to Bagdogra in the far north of West Bengal. Bagdogra—which is convenient for Darjeeling and the state of Sikkim—has regular flights from Kolkata and Delhi. There are no airports (except across the border in Bangladesh) close to the Murshidabad and Malda areas, or that serve the west of the state, and it is necessary to travel long distances by road or rail.
• **By train:** There are good train services from Kolkata to Bolpur, for Shanti Niketan (2½hrs), Murshidabad (4hrs), Malda (6hrs), and Jalpaiguri, for Darjeeling (10–12hrs).
• **By road:** Most of West Bengal's roads are badly maintained. One exception is the Grand Trunk Road (NH2), which heads north out of Kolkata, parallel to the west bank of the Hooghly. It then turns west, and provides access to the western parts of the state, close to Shanti Niketan and Bishnupur.

ACCOMMODATION

There is clean, cheap accommodation available in many of the larger centres of West Bengal.

Murshidabad region
• **Baharampore:** Near to the town of Murshidabad in Baharampore are the **Hotel Samrat** (*$; T: 03482 251147*), which has AC rooms, while the prettily located **Hotel Manjusha** (*$; T: 03482 270321*), just north of the Hazar Duari, does not have AC rooms.

Malda region
• **Malda:** the Golden Park Resort (*$; T: 03512 262251 hotelgoldenpark.com*) on the northern outskirts of the city is the best hotel.

Western districts
There are several basic hotels in Shanti Niketan, but the other option if you are visiting Shanti Niketan or Bishnupur is to stay in one of the nearest big towns, Burdwan (officially Varddhaman) and Durgapur.
• **Burdwan:** The **Hotel City Tower** (*$; T: 0342 3239700*) is at the top of a shopping mall.
• **Durgapur:** The **Ginger Hotel** (*$; T: 0343 254 3333; gingerhotels.com*) in Durgapur is clean and modern.
• **Shanti Niketan:** Basic and cheap is the **Hotel Shantiniketan** (*$; T: 03463 254434*).

Darjeeling and the West Bengal Hills
• **Darjeeling:** Here the best-known hotel is the **Windamere** (*$$$; T: 0354 2254041; windamere.com*), built in the 19th century on Observatory Hill as a guest house for British tea planters, and now converted into a comfortable if old-fashioned hotel, serving traditional Anglo-Indian food and high tea from 4pm each day. The **Mayfair Hotel** (*$$$; T: 0354 2256 376; mayfairhotels.com*) is the former summer retreat of the maharaja of Nazarganj, while the **Elgin** (*$$$; T: 0354 2254082; elginhotels.com*) is the former home of the maharaja of Cooch Behar.
• **Kalimpong:** There are several hotels from the colonial period here, includ-

ing the **Himalayan Hotel** (*$$; T: 03552 255248; himalayanhotel.biz*), still run by the McDonald family, who have lived here since the early 20th century.

FOOD

See Kolkata Practical Information (p. 557)

FURTHER READING & VIEWING

Bengal: Sites and Sights (Marg, 2003) by Pratapaditya Pal and Enamul Haque is an excellent coffee-table guide to the major historical sites of Bengal.

The best book on Tagore, the founder of Shanti Niketan, is *Rabindranath Tagore: The Myriad-minded Man* (I.B. Tauris, 2008) by Krishna Dutta and Andrew Robinson.

The Inheritance of Loss by Kiran Desai won the 2006 Booker Prize. It is a novel largely set in Kalimpong—near Darjeeling—and deals, in part, with the Gorkhaland agitation.

The critically acclaimed English-language Indian film *Mr and Mrs Iyer* (2002), directed by Aparna Sen and starring her daughter Konkona Sen Sharma, is set in the hills around Darjeeling.

SIKKIM

The small northern state of Sikkim (*map 7*), high in the Himalayas, which became part of India only in 1975, has recently begun to emerge as an important tourist destination. Most visitors go to Sikkim to spend time in the mountains relaxing and trekking, but there is also a growing interest in the state's Buddhist heritage. The Buddhist monasteries, or *gompas*, are more modern than those of Ladakh, and the art is less impressive, but it is hard not to be moved by the atmosphere and location. However, Sikkim is still relatively remote—possible to reach only by road or helicopter—and parts of the state are off-limits to most foreigners. A permit is needed to enter the state, available at the main crossing point from West Bengal and at diplomatic missions around the world.

HISTORY OF SIKKIM

Little is known about the early history of Sikkim, though Buddhism is believed to have been brought to the area by Guru Rinpoche, also known as Padmasambhava, in the 9th century—at a time when Buddhism was beginning to die out in much of the rest of India. Sikkim's history is partly the story of its three main communities: the Lepchas, the Bhutia and the Nepalese.

The Lepchas were early migrants. They are now just a small percentage of the population, but widely seen as Sikkim's aboriginals—some of whom still follow the old Bon religion, though most are Buddhist. The next group of migrants were the Bhutias, who came over the Himalayas from Tibet, and who founded the Namgyal Dynasty, which ruled Sikkim from 1641 until 1975. The Namgyal kings, known as Chogyals, expanded into neighbouring territories—including Bengal and Nepal—in the 18th century, but were then driven back in the 19th century, losing Darjeeling to the British in 1835. The 19th century saw mass migration by Nepalese Hindus into the southern part of the kingdom, partly to work on plantations created by the British, and Nepali speakers are now the majority of the state's population.

The Chogyals accepted British suzerainty, but opted not to join India when the British left in 1947. Instead, Sikkim remained officially independent—though, as in the British period, Sikkim's foreign and defence policies were run from India. In the early 1970s an anti-royalty movement emerged, which had strong support from Sikkim's Nepalese majority. India eventually stepped in, partly because of concerns about Chinese influence. A referendum was held in 1975, as a result of which Sikkim became an Indian state, and the monarchy was abolished. China recognised Indian sovereignty over Sikkim only in 2003.

Sikkim borders three other countries: Bhutan, China (Tibet) and Nepal. The main peak of the world's third-highest mountain, Kanchenjunga (officially Khangchendzonga), is on the border with Nepal.

GANGTOK & ENVIRONS

Sikkim's capital since 1894 is a largely modern town, spread over a series of hills in the southeast of the state (*map 7 C1*). There are fine views over the surrounding countryside, with spectacular dawn views of Kanchenjunga, but the town itself is a little disappointing, partly because the most important buildings from the Chogyal period are closed to the public. It is, however, a good base for making forays into the rest of the state.

The **Chogyals' Palace**, to the southeast of the town, is open briefly each year during the Pang Lhabsol festival (late Aug/early Sept), while the former **British Residency** (1890s), a handsome gabled building, is the home of the governor of Sikkim. The **Enchey Monastery** is a pleasant 3-km walk north of Gangtok's main market; it was founded in 1840 and rebuilt in 1909. The **Namgyal Research Institute of Tibetology** (*open daily 10–4, closed Sun and 2nd Sat of the month*), on the south side of Gangtok, has one of India's best specialist museums, focusing on Buddhist and Tibetan culture.

Around Gangtok

Rumtek Monastery (*map 7 C1*), 24km west of Gangtok, is one of Sikkim's best-known Buddhist complexes—largely because it is the seat in exile of the Karmapa Lama, the head of the important Kagyupa, or 'Black Hat', sect of Tibetan Buddhism. The monastery itself was built in the traditional style in the 1960s, under the direction of the 16th Karmapa Lama, as a copy of his historical seat in Tibet. There are currently two rival karmapas and a legal dispute over Rumtek, which is the reason for the heavy security at the monastery.

There are several more monasteries and other sites north of Gangtok, close to the North Sikkim highway. **Kabi Lunchok**, 17km from Gangtok, marks the traditional site of the pact of friendship between the native Lepcha and Bhutia migrants from Tibet—there are a number of memorial stones here. The recently renovated and bustling **Phodong Monastery** (early 18th century), also known as the Royal Chapel, is 40km north of Gangtok, on the north Sikkim highway. The more peaceful **Labrang Monastery** (1814) is 30mins' walk away, and the modest ruins of **Tumlong**, Sikkim's capital for much of the 19th century, are also nearby, just off the road between Phodong and Labrang.

SOUTHWEST SIKKIM: AROUND PELLING

Pelling (*map 7 C1*) is the main tourist centre in southwestern Sikkim, 120km from Gangtok and 14km from Gezing, or Gyaltshing, the main town in the west of the state. Pelling has spectacular views of Kanchenjunga, and it is a 30-min walk from here (or a short drive) to the state's finest monastery at Pemayangtse. The **monastery** (*open daily 7–4*) was built in 1705, making it one of the oldest in Sikkim, and is set on a hilltop with the ruins of the former Sikkimese capital of Rabdentse in the forest below. There are multiple shrines and other structures in the complex, while the main three-storey prayer hall has pretty painted doors and windows, with a fine carved model of the heavenly abode of Padmasambhava, who is believed to have brought Buddhism to Sikkim.

Rabdenste, Sikkim's royal capital between 1670 and 1793, lies in ruins, a short walk or drive southeast of Pemayangtse Monastery. The capital was moved away from here because of its proximity to Nepal, with which Sikkim fought several wars in the 18th century. The walls of a number of buildings, as well as a row of three small stupas known as *chortens*, have survived in this little-visited site surrounded by forests. **Sanga Choeling Monastery**, 45mins' walk west of Pelling, is slightly older than Pemayangtse and has some fine murals.

Yuksom (*map 7 C1*), 2hrs drive north of Pelling, was Sikkim's first royal capital under the Namgyal Dynasty, and is now the start of the Kanchenjunga trek. In **Norbugang Park**, what is said to be the original coronation throne, built out of stone, is under a large pine tree. A few crumbling stone ruins are all that is left of **Tashi Tenka**—the old royal palace complex, just south of the Norbugang Park, near the village of Gupha Dara, on the road back to Pelling. It is a steep half-hour uphill walk from Norbugang Park to the the picturesque **Dubdi Gompa** (1701), which is probably Sikkim's oldest monastery.

Tashiding Monastery (1717) is one of Sikkim's most popular *gompas*—and an important pilgrimage centre, in a spectacular location with superb views of Kanchenjunga. There is a full day trek to here from Yuksom—but it is easiest to reach by road from Pelling. Note the stone walls with Buddhist mantras carved onto individual rocks.

PRACTICAL INFORMATION

PERMITS

The mountains of Sikkim are largely invisible in the monsoon, so avoid June–Aug if you are hoping for spectacular views. Permits are needed for all foreigners entering Sikkim—though these are easily available at the main border crossing with West Bengal at Rangpo, as well as at Indian visa offices abroad, Sikkim House in Delhi and Kolkata, and the Sikkim Tourist Office in Siliguri. Carry passport-sized photos and passport photocopies. The permit covers all places mentioned in this guide. However, special permits are required for most of the north of the state, including the longer trekking routes.

GETTING THERE

Sikkim's international borders are closed to all foreigners and most Indians. Visitors enter Sikkim by road from West Bengal. It is about 4hrs from the nearest airport, at Bagdogra (which is well connected to Delhi and Kolkata), and about the same from the nearest major station, New Jalpaiguri, from where taxis and shared jeeps are available. It is also about 4hrs from Darjeeling by road, and 3hrs from Kalimpong.

There is a daily helicopter service (Rs3000; *T: 0353 2531959; mountain-flightindia.com*) from Bagdogra to Gangtok—usually leaving at 11am. The flight takes 30mins, but is subject to cancellation if the weather is bad or if there are not enough bookings.

ACCOMMODATION

In Gangtok, **Hotel Nor-Khill** (*$$$; T: 03592 205637; elginhotels.com*) is a former 1930s royal guest house and now Sikkim's best-known place to stay. The same group also has the comfortable **Mount Pandim Hotel** in Pelling (*$$$; T: 03592 205637; elginhotel.com*), also a former royal guest house.

FOOD

Sikkimese food is heavily influenced by both Tibetan and Nepalese cuisine, with the meat-filled Tibetan dumplings known as *momos* one of the most popular dishes. Also popular is the nettle stew known as *shishnu* or *sochhya*. Several of the hotels in Gangtok, including the **Norkhill** and **Netuk House** (*$$; T: 03592 222374*) on Tibet Road, specialise in Sikkimese food, but it is usually best to order this in advance.

FURTHER READING

Sikkim: Land of Mystique (Eicher Good Earth, 2002) is a good basic guide and widely available locally.

NORTHEAST INDIA

The seven states of northeast India attract little domestic or international tourism. Those who do visit come largely for the wildlife reserves in Assam, best known for the white rhino. Much of the countryside, though, is beautiful, and there are—albeit rather sparsely spread—some interesting historical buildings, including those of the former capital of Assam at Sibsagar. There are heavy restrictions on travel in this strategically important region, which borders China, Burma, Bangladesh and Bhutan, and special permits are needed by foreigners wishing to visit four of the states: Arunachal Pradesh, Nagaland, Manipur and Mizoram. But international tourists are encouraged to visit the other three states: Assam, Meghalaya and Tripura.

The states are a complex agglomeration of different tribal and ethnic groups. Christian missionaries were particularly active in the smaller states during the 19th century, and Nagaland, Mizoram and Meghalaya all have Christian majorities. During World War II, the Japanese army invaded the eastern part of the region, and there are several sites connected with the war. At Independence, East Pakistan—later Bangladesh—was created out of the Muslim majority areas of the region. This almost cut the northeast off from the rest of India—connected only by a narrow strip of land in West Bengal, popularly known as the Chicken's Neck and just 20km across.

ASSAM

Assam (*map 9*) is the most populous of the northeastern states, and the easiest to visit. Its main city, Guwahati, sits on the southern bank of the great Brahmaputra River, which divides the state into two. The official capital of the state is Dispur, which is actually now part of Guwahati. Assamese is the most easterly of the Indo-European languages, and is spoken in most parts of the state.

History: Assam's history, until the 19th century, was dominated by a series of independent principalities, which were united into what is usually described as the kingdom of Ahom in the 13th century (Ahom is the same word as Assam; the English letter 's' is often pronounced 'h'). The Ahom Dynasty ended when the Burmese, followed soon after by the British, occupied the Brahmaputra Valley in the 1820s. The British planted tea in many low-lying parts of Assam, and the great tea estates continue to play a major role in the local economy. At Independence in 1947, the Muslim-majority Bengali-speaking Sylhet area of Assam opted to join Pakistan. In the 1980s and 90s, Assam was badly affected by separatist violence, as Assamese nationalists, Bodo tribes and other groups all campaigned for greater autonomy. The situation is much more peaceful now, but it is still worth taking local advice before travelling to the more remote areas of the state. The two main wildlife reserves are at Manas, close to the

Bhutan border, and at Kaziranga in central Assam—they have not been affected by the insurgencies in recent times.

Guwahati

The best-known historic building in Guwahati (*map 9 B3*, previously Gauhati) is the very popular **Kamakhya Temple** complex, dedicated to different forms of the Hindu mother goddess Shakti. It is a major centre for the esoteric form of Hinduism known as Tantra. The 17th-century main shrine (*open daily 8–1, pay Rs500 to go to the head of the queue*), built on the site of an older temple, is on a hilltop 6km west of the centre of the city, surrounded by lots of smaller shrines. The temple has a distinctive beehive-shaped tower, and the extraordinary underground sanctuary is built around a rock that is said to symbolise Shakti's *yoni*, or vagina. Iron oxide in the rock means that water from a natural spring turns red, symbolising the menstrual flow of the goddess. Animal sacrifices are carried out here regularly, and visitors to the sanctuary may need to step through blood in bare feet.

There is also the attractive **Umananda Temple** (1695), dedicated to Shiva's wife Uma, on a small island in the middle of the Brahmaputra, just opposite the centre of Guwahati, and easily accessible by ferry.

The **State Museum** (*open Tues–Sun 10–4*), just north of the railway station, has an interesting collection of sculptures and terracotta panels from the Ahom period, as well as displays about tribal culture.

Around Guwahati

Hajo, 30km northwest of Guwahati, is an important pilgrimage site for Hindus, Buddhists and Muslims. The 16th-century **Hayagriva Madhava Temple**, on Manikuta Hill, is considered by some to be the place where the Buddha died, rather than Kushinagar in Uttar Pradesh. The **Poa Mecca Mosque** is said to have been built in the 12th century by a visiting Iraqi prince.

The partly ruined **Madan Kamdev** group of temples, 50km north of Guwahati, via Baihati, has some fine exterior sculptures, some of them erotic; they date back to the 10th–12th centuries.

Tezpur

The town of Tezpur (*map 9 B2*), 125km east of Guwahati, is prettily located on the north bank of the Brahmaputra. The Chinese advanced close to Tezpur during the war of 1962, forcing the city's evacuation. Around 5km to the east of the town is the extremely ruined **Da Parbatia Temple**, with a superb 5th–6th-century stone-carved gateway and a few sculptures scattered across the site.

Sibsagar and environs

The most historically important sites in Assam are in or near Sibsagar (*map 9 C2*), 62km south of the town of Dibrugarh and 52km northeast of Assam's second city, Jorhat, both of which have airports and hotels. Sibsagar was the capital of the Ahom Kingdom for most of the 17th and 18th centuries, and there are buildings from the older Ahom capitals, at Garhgaon and Charaideo, to the south and southeast of the town.

The square man-made lake in the centre of the town has three fine 18th-century Hindu temples on its southern banks, of which the largest and central one is the Sivadol, 32m high and dedicated to Shiva.

Rangpur: Just 2.5km south of Sivadol is **Rangpur** (*map 9 C2*), the royal centre of old Sibsagar. The largest surviving building is the four-storey **Talatal Ghar**, sometimes referred to as the Kareng Ghar, a mid-18th-century palace, which also has three storeys underground. Note the curved vaulted roofs, similar to those seen in neighbouring Bengal—thought be based on the shape of village huts. About 600m to the west of the Talatal Ghar is the mid-18th-century **Rang Ghar**, a large two-storey pavilion from which the royal family watched sporting events and artistic performances. Its unusual oval shape and curved roof make it one of Assam's most distinctive buildings, and it is often used on tourist literature. Note the crocodile sculptures on the roof. South of the Talatal Ghar by about 1km is another large square pond, known as **Joysagar**, on the northern bank of which is the early 18th-century **Vishnudol Temple**, with an octagonal sanctuary, and carvings of avatars of Vishnu on the outside of the building.

Garhgaon and Charaideo: Twelve kilometres southeast of Sibsagar is another older royal capital, at **Garhgaon** (*map 9 C2*)—though the main surviving structure here, known as **Ahom Raja's Palace**, also dates, like the Rangpur buildings, from the 18th century. The red-brick palace is four storeys high, each storey receding slightly to give the building a pyramidal shape.

The oldest of the Ahom capitals is at the fascinating archaeological site of **Charaideo** (*map 9 C2*), 12km east of Garhgaon and 25km east of Sibsagar. A few unusual royal burial mounds, known as *maidams* and dating from as early as the 13th century, have been excavated here. The mounds consist of a vaulted underground tomb chamber, with a small tower on top of the mound.

Majuli

Just north of the town of Jorhat is Majuli (*map 9 C2*), once the world's largest river island, but now much reduced by erosion. Majuli is easily accessible by boat from Jorhat—it is possible to visit some of the many Hindu monasteries known as *satras*, set up by devotees of Vishnu, that are an unusual feature of the island. The *satras* at Auniati and North Kamalabari are particularly recommended.

Around Dibrugarh

The largest town in the far east of Assam, **Dibrugarh** (*map 9 C2*) is at the centre of the state's main tea-growing area. The town itself was largely destroyed in an earthquake in 1950. About 70km to the east is **Digboi** (*map 9 D2*), where oil was first found in India in the late 19th century. The town is so named, according to local tradition, because of the order given by the British supervisor to a local workman: 'dig boy'. Digboi also has a well-maintained Second World War cemetery.

Some 11km south of Digboi is the railway town of **Margherita** (*map 9 D2*), named by a group of Italian railway engineers after the then queen of Italy. Just 10km beyond Margherita is **Ledo** (*map 9 D2*), the start of the **Stilwell Road**—the Second World War supply route that led through to China, and which was named after the American general 'Vinegar Joe' Stilwell.

MEGHALAYA

The small hilly state of Meghalaya, the name of which means 'Abode of the Clouds', is best known for its rains, and for the town of **Cherrapunji** (*map 9 B3*)—known to generations of geography students as the rainiest place in the world. The state was formed in 1972, from the southern hill districts of Assam, dominated by the Khasi and Garo tribes. The main tribes of Meghalaya are matrilineal, and the majority of the population is Christian. The capital, **Shillong** (*map 9 B3*), was originally developed by the British as the capital of undivided Assam, and it continued to play that role until the creation of Meghalaya. It is a pretty town but, like the rest of the state, has no major historical monuments, though there is a museum specialising in local history, the **Don Bosco Centre for Indigenous Cultures** (*open daily 9.30–4.30; Sun 1.30–4.30*), in the Mawlai area of Shillong.

ARUNACHAL PRADESH

This remote mountainous state borders Bhutan, China and Burma, and receives few foreign visitors, who need a permit to enter. Arunachal's boundary with China is disputed, and during the 1962 war the Chinese occupied a large part of the state. China continues to refer to the area as South Tibet, and does not recognise the MacMahon line—the frontier agreed by the British and Tibetans in 1914. No single tribe or ethnic group is in a majority in the state, though most of the inhabitants have one of the Tibeto-Burman languages as their mother tongue.

Tawang Buddhist Monastery: The main tourist attraction is this Buddhist monastery—high up in the mountains of western Arunachal Pradesh, close to the Tibetan border (*map 9 B2*). The monastery, more than ten hours' drive from the Assamese town of Tezpur, is closely associated with the sixth Dalai Lama, who was born nearby in 1683. It is one of the largest Buddhist monasteries in world, with dozens of buildings spread over a hillside, and is run by the Gelugpa sect of Tibetan Buddhism. The monastery was partly rebuilt in the 1990s. The main shrine has an 8m-high gilded statue of the Buddha.

Itanagar: Arunachal's capital, Itanagar (*map 9 C2*), is a largely modern city, though the ruins of the 14th–15th-century **Ita Fort** survive on the east side of the town. The town's **Nehru Museum** (*open Tues–Sun 10–5*) is mainly devoted to local culture.

Malinathan: Just to the east of Likabali in eastern Arunachal, 80km north of the Assamese town of Dibrugarh, lies Malinathan (*map 9 C2*), which has the interesting ruins of a 14th–15th century temple, with some fine carved friezes and sculptures.

NAGALAND

This small state bordering Burma has been badly affected by one of Asia's longest-running insurgencies, with members of the Naga tribes on both sides of the Burma-India border demanding self-determination. The security situation has improved in recent years, and tourists are beginning to come in larger numbers, partly to visit the traditional tribal villages in the north of the state. Nagaland is overwhelmingly Christian—most of them Baptists.

The main attraction for foreign visitors is the well-maintained **war cemetery** in the capital, **Kohima** (*map 9 C3*). The Battle of Kohima (1944) was one of the most important land battles of the Second World War, and it was here that the advancing Japanese army, which had come up through Burma, was turned back. The cemetery is built partly on the site of the British deputy commissioner's tennis court, which saw some of the fiercest fighting. Most of the exhibits at the **State Museum** (*open Tues–Sun 9.30–3.30*), 2.5km north of the cemetery, relate to Nagaland's tribal history and culture.

Dimapur (*map 9 C3*), Nagaland's largest city, on the border with Assam, has the ruins of a 14th-century palace of the Kachari Dynasty. There are some unusual monolithic sculptures in **Dimasa Park**, 4km west of the airport.

MANIPUR & MIZORAM

The former princely state of Manipur is periodically disrupted by long-running insurgencies, and it is difficult to get permission to travel beyond the capital, **Imphal** (*map 10 C1*), which was the scene of an important battle against the Japanese in the Second World War. There is a war cemetery in Imphal, as well as the partly ruined **Kangla Fort** (*open 9–4*), once home to the rulers of Manipur. The **State Museum** (*open Tues–Sun 10–4*) is on Kangla Road. The state is best known in the rest of the country for the Manipuri style of classical Indian dancing.

The small state of Mizoram has no major historical monuments, though its countryside is very pretty, and it is slightly easier to get permission to visit Mizoram than the other states bordering Burma. The vast majority of Mizos are Christians, though there is a small group who claim to be descendants of one of the lost tribes of Israel, and who practise Judaism.

TRIPURA

This interesting but little-visited former Hindu princely state is, like several of the northeastern states, disrupted by low-level insurgencies—but it is not necessary to get special permission to travel here.

Agartala: The state capital, Agartala (*map 10 B2*), has the fine **Ujjayanta Palace** (1899–1901) at its centre, built next to two large artificial lakes—with several extravagant temples on their banks. The palace is now used as the state assembly, but visitors are allowed to visit the building when the assembly is not sitting. About 2km to the north is the former **Kunjaban Palace** (1923), now the Raj Bhavan, the official residence of the governor of Tripura. The small **State Museum** (*open Mon–Fri 10–5*) is at Post Office Circle, 800m southeast of the Ujjayanta Palace, while the **royal mausolea** are on the north bank of the Howrah River, a further 1km southeast.

Udayapur: About 40km southeast of Agartala, Udayapur (*map 10 B2*) is the former royal capital, and has the **Tripura Sundari temple** (1501), the most important Hindu shrine in the region, just to the south of the town. The temple, known locally as Matabari, is dedicated to the mother goddess. The sanctuary is a square building, designed like a traditional Bengali hut, with a gently curving roof but capped by a hemispherical tower.

Neermahal Palace: Built as a summer retreat for the royal family in 1930, Neermahal Palace (*map 10 B2, open daily 9–4*) stands on an island in the large Rudrasagar Lake, 38km south of Agartala. This charming palace, built in a hybrid style, with pretty bridges and domes, is approached by boat from the Sagarmahal Tourist Lodge, near the village of Melagarh.

Unakoti Rock Carvings: This is one of the remotest important archaeological sites in the country, with enormous rock-carved images of Hindu gods that are superb and thought to date to the 7th–9th centuries (*map 10 B2*). The closest village is **Kailashahar**, on the Bangladesh border, 90km north of Agartala. There is an enormous head of Shiva, with flowing hair, cut into the bare rock, more than 8m high, as well as several images of Ganesha and numerous other carvings and ruins.

PRACTICAL INFORMATION

PERMITS

Permits are not needed for foreign visitors wishing to go to Assam, Meghalaya and Tripura—though it is common to be asked to register on arrival. Elsewhere permits are essential and must be obtained in advance. It is easiest to apply through a travel agent who regularly deals with permits for the northeast. The rules are complex and different for each state, but it is worth persisting. If you wish to do it on your own, the best place to do so is in Delhi at the Ministry of Home Affairs office at Lok Nayak Bhavan, Khan Market (*map p. 114*). If you get stuck, seek help from the state tourism offices in Delhi.

The sun rises and sets very early in India's northeast, because it is in the same time zone as the rest of the country. For this reason, many historical sites and museums close at 4pm.

GETTING THERE & GETTING AROUND

Most visitors enter the northeast through one of the region's many airports—of which Guwahati in Assam is the busiest and best-connected. There are also rail services from the rest of the country, but these take a very long time indeed: 17hrs from Kolkata to Guwahati, and 36hrs from Delhi. Trains are more useful within the region, with regular services from Guwahati to Dimapur (6hrs) and Dibrugarh (13hrs). Travelling in the mountains can be very slow, though the roads leading to the borders tend to be well maintained because they are used by the security forces. Ferries are an essential means of transport around the Brahmaputra River, which is 10km wide in places.

ACCOMMODATION

Assam

• **Dibrugarh:** Just outside the town, in the middle of a tea estate, is the 19th-century **Mancotta Chang Bungalow** (*$$; T: 03732 301120; purviweb.com*), which is recommended.

• **Guwahati:** The town's best hotel is the **Kiranshree Portico** (*$$; T: 0361 2735300; kiranshreeportico.com*) near the railway station, while the more basic **Ginger Hotel** (*$; T: 0361 6113333; gingerhotels.com*), run by the Taj group, is on the eastern side of town.

• **Jorhat:** Near Jorhat is the **Thengal Manor** (*$$; T: 03762 339519; welcomheritagehotels.com*), a large colonial house converted into a comfortable hotel and a good base for visiting Sibsagar.

It is also possible to take an **Assam Bengal Navigation cruise** (*$$$; assambengalnavigation.com; T: 0361 2602223*) along the Brahmaputra, staying on a luxury river boat. Tours lasting four, seven or ten nights start from Guwahati, Kaziranga or Dibrugarh.

Meghalaya

• **Shillong:** In Meghalaya, the best hotel is the **Tripura Castle** (*$$; T: 0364 2501111*), the former summer villa of the maharajas of Tripura on the eastern side of Shillong.

Tripura

• **Agartala:** In Tripura, the best option is to stay in Agartala at **Ginger Hotel** (*$; T: 0381 230 3333; gingerhotels.com*), run by the Taj group; it is on the airport road.

FOOD

The cuisine of the northeast is very varied, and reflects the region's heterogeneity. Rice and river fish are widely eaten, and there are strong Bengali, Tibetan and Chinese influences. Even though some of the world's hottest chillies are grown in this region, the food tends to be less spicy than in other parts of the country. For Assamese specialities, the simple **Khorika Restaurant** on GS Road in Guwahati is recommended.

FURTHER READING & VIEWING

The journalist and academic Sanjoy Hazarika has written widely about the politics of the northeast, including *Rites of Passage* (Penguin India, 2001), as has the veteran BBC correspondent Subir Bhaumik, with *Troubled Peripheries* (Sage, 2010). Also recommended is *A Game of Chess: Classic Assamese Stories*, edited by D.N. Bezboruah (Penguin India, 2010). Fergal Keane's *Road of Bones* (Harper Collins, 2010) tells the story of the Battle of Kohima. There is an interesting 1945 US propaganda film called *The Stilwell Road* about the supply route from eastern Assam to China—it is narrated by Ronald Reagan, long before he became president of the US. It was released commercially on DVD in 2001.

BIHAR

Among most Indians, Bihar (*map 7*) has a poor reputation as one of the most corrupt and backward of India's states. But historically, Bihar can be considered the crucible of Indian civilisation, as the birthplace of those least materialistic of religions, Buddhism and Jainism, and as the capital of the great Mauryan Empire, the most successful early attempt to create an all-Indian political entity. Today, Bihar is scattered with fascinating little-visited ancient monuments that bear testimony to its former greatness. Many of its foreign visitors are Buddhists from East Asia and the rest of the world; and, despite the generally poor infrastructure, there are good hotels and transport connections near the main Buddhist sites—Bodhgaya, Rajgir and Nalanda, home to one of the world's first universities. The state capital, Patna, was once a great city, but it is now used as a kind of shorthand for all that ails India. But even Patna, prettily situated on the banks of the Ganges, has some fascinating colonial buildings, while elsewhere in the state, particularly in Sasaram, are some impressive monuments from the long period of Muslim rule in Bihar.

Bihar is India's third most populous state with more than 85 million inhabitants. Bihar shares a long northern border with Nepal, and the main geographical feature of the state is the River Ganges—more than 3km wide in places—which flows west to east towards West Bengal. Much of the land is fertile and well-resourced, and there is no obvious reason why it should be one of the poorest states in the country. However, it does suffer from major floods most summers, and there was a particularly severe one in 2008, which displaced millions of people.

HISTORY OF BIHAR

The area along the Ganges has been settled since prehistoric times, but in the first half of the first millennium BC there seems to have been a clearing of lands for human settlement and the cultivation of rice. By the 6th century BC the region had a number of powerful kingdoms that had a rice-based agricultural economy—in contrast to the wheat- and livestock-based agriculture further to the west. The most powerful of these kingdoms was Magadha, with its capital at Rajgriha (modern Rajgir). Other princely states produced two of India's most influential thinkers and leaders: the Buddha (who was born outside the modern borders of Bihar in Nepal); and the prophet of Jainism, the 24th *tirthankar*, Mahavir. Bimbisara, the king of Magadha, was the Buddha's first royal patron.

The 4th century BC saw the rise of the Mauryan Empire, with its capital at Pataliputra, on the site of modern Patna. Greek ambassadors visited what was probably then the largest city in the world, and provided us with our first travellers' accounts of life in India. Ashoka the Great converted to Buddhism and enlarged his grandfather's empire so that most of what is now India was ruled from Pataliputra.

After the Mauryas, Bihar became less important politically, though it was the homeland of the Gupta Dynasty, which ruled much of north India in the middle years of the first millennium. But Bihar also emerged as a place of learning and pilgrimage—a Buddhist holy land, visited in the 5th and 7th centuries by pilgrims from China, who left detailed accounts of Bihar in these periods. Fa Xien, writing in about the year 400, saw the ruins of Ashoka's Palace in Pataliputra, while an awestruck Xuan Zang, writing more than 200 years later, described Nalanda as a thriving centre of Buddhist learning. As Hinduism regained strength, Buddhism went into slow decline—and by the arrival of the first Muslim invaders in the 13th century, it seems that Buddhism was moribund.

Muslims from the Khilji tribe took control of much of Bihar, using it as a base in their successful overthrow of the Slave Dynasty in Delhi. Later, in the 16th century, another local Muslim ruler, Sher Shah Suri—buried at Sasaram in southwestern Bihar—brought the nascent Mughal Empire to its knees. He and his family ruled Delhi for 15 years, reconstructed the Grand Trunk Road and built a series of now-forgotten forts across the more lawless parts of the Bihar countryside. After the return of the Mughals, Bihar was ruled by local governors—usually as part of the province of Bengal.

From British rule to post-Independence

In the 17th century, the first British trading post was set up in Patna, which became a centre for trade in saltpetre, sea-salt and, later, opium. The Battle of Buxar in 1764 confirmed British supremacy in Bihar which it ruled as part of Bengal until the early 20th century, when both Orissa and Bihar were split off. Patna was made the provincial capital, and was provided with many new government buildings. Bihar played an important role in the freedom struggle, and the 1917 indigo workers' agitation, in the Champaran district, was Gandhi's first major civil disobedience campaign.

At Independence, the leading Bihari lawyer and freedom fighter Dr Rajendra Prasad became India's first president, while in the 1970s the Bihari politician Jayaprakash Narayan, known as JP, led opposition to the state of emergency proclaimed by Prime Minister Indira Gandhi. The best-known contemporary Bihari is the politician Laloo Prasad Yadav, who is notorious in India for his earthy, rustic sense of humour. Since the 1980s, caste has been the dominant factor in Bihari politics—and violence has often broken out between different caste and ideological factions. In 2000, Bihar was split into two parts, with the largely tribal, mineral-rich southern districts breaking off to form the state of Jharkhand. Recent years have seen the emergence of a more stable, less corrupt government in Bihar, and the state's reputation in the rest of India has begun to improve. However, there is still sporadic criminal and political violence, and it is best not to travel on minor country roads at night. If in doubt, seek local advice.

PATNA

Patna (*map 7 B2*), the capital of Bihar, is one of the world's oldest continuously inhabited cities. It dates back at least 2,500 years and possibly much longer. In the 3rd century BC, it was described by the Greek visitor Megasthenes as the greatest city in India, with dimensions of 15km by 2km, presumably stretching along the Ganges. 'The city wall was crowned with 570 towers and had four-and-sixty gates…their king has in his pay a standing army of at least 60,000 foot-soldiers, 30,000 cavalry, and 9,000 elephants: whence may be formed some conjecture as to the vastness of his resources.' Historians believe Patna may have been the most populous city in the world. Sadly little survives from the early period—a few museum pieces and the waterlogged archaeological park at Kumrahar are all that remains of one of the great cities of the ancient world.

However, there are some fascinating buildings from almost two centuries of British rule in Patna, including the bizarre Golghar, one of the strangest of India's colonial edifices, as well as a few older monuments—and two superb museum collections.

Orientation: The medieval and early British parts of Patna are on the east side of the modern town, beyond the city's only bridge across the Ganges—and include the Jalan Museum and the old Gulzarbagh Cemetery. The central part of the city is dominated by the Gandhi Maidan, an oval-shaped park, and nearby are the Golghar and the Patna Museum. To the west are government buildings, which the British named the New Capital area—and further west still are the airport and the cantonment.

Golghar

Literally meaning 'circular house', Golghar is an extraordinary 27m-high hemispherical structure, built in 1786 during the British colonial period as a grain warehouse. It has become Patna's best-known building. Golghar is 300m west of Gandhi Maidan and is always open to the public. Climb up one of two curved external staircases for a superb view of Patna and the Ganges. The staircases were built to allow men carrying grain to walk to the top, pour the grain in through the now-covered hole and walk down the other side. Grain could be retrieved from one of the four side doors, now all closed. Note the never-completed inscription in English and Urdu declaring that, 'for the perpetual prevention of Famine in these Provinces, THIS GRANARY was erected by Captain John Garstin. Completed on the 20th of July 1786. First filled and publickly closed by…'

A prince from Nepal is once said to have ridden his horse to the top of Golghar.

Patna Museum

The state museum (1929), 1km southeast of Gandhi Maidan, is built in the Indo-Saracenic style, and has a superb and unusual—albeit poorly labelled—collection, and many of the exhibits have been shown abroad. The museum (*open Tues–Sun 10.30–4.30; additional ticket needed for the Buddha relics*) contains one of most famous examples of ancient Indian art, the lissom Didarganj Yakshi, as well as what are said to be the cremation relics of the Buddha.

The Didarganj Yakshi: This sculpture (c. 3rd century BC) is a full-sized statue of a woman carrying a fly-whisk, which was unearthed from the mud of the Ganges in

Didarganj, near Patna, in 1917. It is carved out of a single block of Chunar sandstone, and is probably the most delicately modelled and finely polished of all Mauryan sculptures—and may be roughly contemporaneous with Alexander the Great. The figure has a particularly elaborate hairstyle, with a twisted plait, and is heavily jewelled, with large earrings, a headdress and enormous anklets. She is dressed in a long cloth, draped and gathered at the front, another part of which is wrapped round her elbow, as if she intends to cover the top part of her body at a later time.

Ground-floor galleries: In the same gallery and those connected to it are many more fine pieces of sculpture, including some marvellous examples of Gandhara art from what is now Afghanistan (note the moustachioed seated Buddha from the 1st century), as well as the very pretty relief carving of a woman with a parrot from the Gupta period (5th century). There is also some fine sculpture from Orissa, and from the ruined Mundeshwari Temple near Sasaram (*see p. 614*). The room on the other side of the hall is full of stuffed animals, including an eight-legged goat—presumably conjoined twins rather than a taxidermist's invention.

Upper galleries: Upstairs is a large collection of terracotta figurines excavated in different parts of Patna and elsewhere in Bihar, largely from the Mauryan period, more than 2,000 years ago. Note also the finely moulded elongated heads of figurines from the more recent Gupta period, and an impressive collection of Buddhist and Jain bronzes from the 9th–11th centuries. There is heavy security around the most significant of the museum's exhibits: a tiny egg-like white casket that was excavated from a 5th-century BC stupa at the Buddhist site of Vaishali in northern Bihar. The casket contains a piece of a conch, some beads, a piece of gold leaf, a coin, some earth and what are thought to be the ashes of the cremated body of the Buddha. According to Buddhist sacred texts, the Buddha's ashes were split into eight parts, and one of these was sent to the rulers of Vaishali, almost 2,500 years ago.

Colonial Patna

West of the museum are the government buildings of modern Patna, largely built in the early part of the 20th century. The most striking of these are **Patna High Court** (1916), 900m west of the museum, with an unusual dome over a pediment, and the **Secretariat** (1929), with its 54m pink clock tower, at the other end of a broad avenue from the three-storey **Government House** (1920s), now known as Raj Bhavan.

Ashok Rajpath

East of Gandhi Maidan, the main road, Ashok Rajpath, runs parallel to the river for almost 10km, passing a number of interesting buildings. Almost 1.5km east of Maidan is the **Khuda Bakhsh Oriental Public Library** (*open Sat–Thur; T: 0612 2301507; kblibrary.bih.nic.in*) and the adjoining **Curzon Reading Room** (1905), which has a number of very rare old manuscripts, including one saved from the great 10th-century Muslim library of Cordoba. Phone in advance for access to the manuscripts. Casual visitors can see a walking stick said to have belonged to an unnamed British

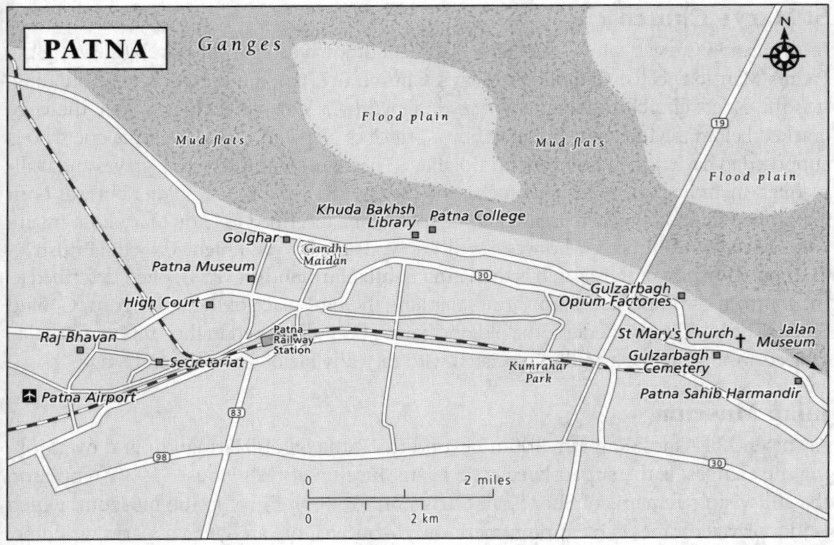

Prince of Wales, a sword of the Persian emperor Nadir Shah and some finely wrought 17th-century astrolabes. Just 200m beyond the library is the most impressive of the many university buildings, **Patna College**, a sprawling, largely 19th-century building that goes down to the water front. Part of the Ganges-facing façade of the building is an 18th-century Dutch building.

Gulzarbagh

Another 5km east along the Ganges are the old **opium factories** of Gulzarbagh, opposite the city court jail. The long, high walls and the enormous old warehouses are still there, but the complex has now been converted into a government printing press. Ask for the stationery department, where you will be shown a large room in an 18th-century building, in which Shah Alam, one of the weakest but longest-surviving of the later Mughal emperors, was enthroned in 1761. Just 1km east of the opium factory is the old British **Gulzarbagh Cemetery**. This fascinating, wildly overgrown graveyard, with dozens of ornate crumbling tombs, has one of India's oddest memorials: a tall brick tower, like a chimney, that reaches high above the trees. The inscription lists more than 40 people, all British, who were killed in what became known as the Patna Massacre of 1763. They had been taken prisoner by the nawab of Bengal, Mir Qasim, who was in dispute about taxation with the British, and were murdered by being thrown into a well by a European adventurer called Walter Reinhardt, nicknamed Samru. Reinhardt's widow, Begum Samru, became one of the wealthiest people in India in the early 19th century, owning famous palaces in Delhi (*see p. 110*) and Sardhana (*see p. 228*).

St Mary's Church

In the area 400m east of the cemetery that is still known as Padri ki Haveli (meaning the Padre's Mansion) is the Catholic **St Mary's Church** (1770s), a fine Neoclassical building. It is the oldest church in Bihar, and was designed by a Venetian architect. Note the large cracked bell in the forecourt presented by a prince of Nepal in 1782 (the same one who is supposed to have ridden his horse up Golghar). There are some interesting graves and wall-plaques, including one to Jos Jeff Finch, who died in 1815 as a British soldier but was born Giuseppe Fini in Italy. There is also a 1916 tombstone inscribed to Lady Mary Rose Imam, wife of Syed Sir Ali Imam, who was a well-known Patna lawyer, knighted by the British.

About 1km east of the church is the **Patna Sahib Harmandir** (1954), often described as the fourth most important Sikh shrine, marking the birthplace of the tenth guru, Gobind Singh. The building is modern, the old one having been destroyed in the 1934 earthquake. Objects inside include a cradle associated with the early life of Guru Gobind Singh.

Jalan Museum

At the end of Ashok Rajpath, 400m beyond the Patna Sahib Harmandir and overlooking the Ganges, is the superbly eclectic Jalan Museum at Qila House (1930s), built on the still-visible remains of Sher Shah Suri's Fort (1540s). Entry to the museum, which is in a private home, is by appointment only—but visitors are given a warm welcome, and a trip here is strongly recommended. (*Call Aditya Jalan on T: 0612 2641121 in the mornings or evenings, or 0612 2655479 in the afternoons to fix a time, or email quilahouse@hotmail.com. Mornings are usually best for an actual visit, or any time on Sun*). The Qila House must rank as one of the most richly decorated and furnished houses in the country. The collection was begun by the present owner's grandfather in the 1920s, and includes rare jade, porcelain, glass, weaponry and silverware from India, China and Europe. A family member will normally take you around, pointing out a wine cooler believed to have belonged to Marie Antoinette, Napoleon III's very short bed and a set of Crown Derby crockery chosen by George III of England.

Ruins of Pataliputra

The only visible ruins of ancient Patna, or Pataliputra, are 2km away from the river at **Kumrahar Park**, along Patna's heavily congested main east–west road. Sadly, it is one of India's most disappointing archaeological sites. The park is pretty, but the supposed **Ashoka Palace**, a hall with the stumps of more than eight pillars, is now under water, with just one half-intact pillar lying on its side nearby. At the back of the park are excavated foundations of the **Arogya Vihar**, a 5th-century hospital and monastery. The tiny **museum** has a few terracotta figurines recovered from the site.

WEST OF PATNA

Maner

This small town (*map 7 A2*), 30km west of Patna, has a Muslim tomb complex known as the **Choti Dargah** (1616), or Small Shrine, which is arguably the most impressive

Mughal monument in eastern India. The complex, which overlooks a large, pretty lake, contains the tomb of a *pir*, or saint, called Makhdoom Shah Daulat, who died in 1608. The intricate multi-layer design of the corner towers of the tomb is unusual, and the quality of the koranic calligraphy on the roof of the tomb verandah and inside the tomb chamber is particularly fine. There is a small mosque on the west side of the complex, and a cloister that runs along the rest of the west wall. Steps lead down to the lakeside. The complex also has an imposing main gate, which was built slightly later than the tomb. Opposite the Choti Dargah, on a raised area on the other side of the lake, is the **Bari Dargah**, or Large Shrine, which is less architecturally interesting, but draws many more pilgrims. It contains the older grave of the 14th-century Sufi saint Yahya Maneri, whose Maktubat (letters) remain important Sufi texts.

Dinapore

Dinapore (*map 7 B2,* also Danapore, or Dinapur) is the army cantonment area between Patna and Maner, where three regiments mutinied during the anti-British Uprising of 1857. **St Luke's Church** (1862) has a fine, well-maintained Neoclassical façade, an octagonal tower and many interesting inscriptions. There is also a large, poorly maintained **British cemetery** (mainly 19th century) near Anand Bazaar, with the graves of many railway workers—on the left side is the part of the burial ground used mainly for children.

NORTH OF PATNA

Vaishali

One spectacular piece of Mauryan art and some sparse ruins are all that is left of Vaishali (*map 7 B2*), 50km north of Patna and the capital of the ancient republic of Licchavi. Vaishali was flourishing by the middle of the first millennium BC, when the Buddha visited this city many times, as a mendicant and a preacher. But, by the time the Chinese traveller Xuan Zang came here in the 7th century, the city was already in ruins. According to some accounts, the Jain saviour Mahavir was born here.

Approaching Vaishali from Patna (the drive takes up to 2hrs), one first reaches a large excavated site, known as the **Raja Vishal ka Garh** (600 BC–AD 400) or King Vishal's Fort), on the left side of the road. The foundations of what is thought to have been a large palace are visible. Pottery, seals, glass fragments and an inscription indicate that this site was occupied for at least 1,000 years. About 1km to the northeast, around a large rectangular tank, is what is thought to have been the centre of Vaishali—with a modern Japanese-built stupa in the southeastern corner. There is a small **museum** (*open Sat–Thur 10–5*), with some excavated terracotta figurines, stone sculptures and ancient coins on the north side. Nearby, set in a pretty garden, are the unimpressive ruins of the **Buddha Relic Stupa** (5th century BC), under a dome made of aluminium sheeting, where the small egg-like casket said to contain the Buddha's ashes (now in Patna Museum) was found during an archaeological dig in 1958.

The Lion Pillar: The most interesting part of Vaishali, 2km north of the Relic Stupa, is a site called Kolhua (*open daily dawn–dusk*), which has the majestic Lion Pillar and a fine brick stupa. According to Buddhist tradition, Kolhua marks the spot where some monkeys offered a bowl of honey to the Buddha. The smooth sandstone **Lion Pillar** (3rd century BC) has been dated to the reign of Ashoka the Great, is 11m high and has as its capital a very fine carved crouching lion. Note the quality of the carving of the lion's mane, and the detail around its nose and whiskers (binoculars will give you a clearer view). The pillar, which unusually has no contemporary inscription, does have writing from the later Gupta period, as well as some 18th-century British graffiti. The pillar may have been put up by Ashoka to commemorate the Second Buddhist Council, which was held in Vaishali 100 years after the death of the Buddha. Next to it is a large **brick stupa**, its inner core constructed at the same time, but its outer layers dating from the 4th–6th-century Gupta period. All around are small votive stupas, circular and square, some with niches for statues. Towards the back of the site, to the right of the pond, are the ruins of a **monastery**, with an unusual swastika-shaped interior layout, which also dates to the Gupta period.

Kesariya, Motihari and Lauriya Nandangarh

Recent excavations near the sleepy village of **Kesariya** (*map 7 A2*), 50km north of Vaishali, has revealed one of India's most impressive stupas. The terraced brick-built stupa is one of the world's highest at 38m—with Buddha statues in many of the niches in the terraces.

Some 30km north of Kesariya is **Motihari** (*map 7 B2*), the birthplace of the British writer George Orwell (born Eric Blair in 1903); his father was serving there at the time as a civil servant in the Opium Department. Plans are underway to turn his former house into a museum. There is also a small **Gandhi Museum**, reflecting the importance of this region, known as Champaran, in Gandhi's 1917 campaign against the British control of indigo farming.

The village of **Lauriya Nandangarh** (*map 7 A1*), 62km northwest of Motihari, has two important Buddhist relics. There is a 3rd-century BC **Ashoka Pillar**, similar to the one at Vaishali, with a lion seated on a bell-shaped capital. There is also the base of an enormous stupa, more than 150m across, with the ruins of a smaller stupa inside.

Darbhanga

The town of Darbhanga (*map 7 B2*), 95km northeast of Patna, was the capital of the former princely state of the same name. Several interesting princely buildings survive, including the **Anand Bagh Palace** (1880s), which now houses a college that promotes the learning of Sanskrit.

EAST OF PATNA

The little-visited area east of Patna, along the Ganges, was once a major trade route and of critical strategic importance to the Mughals and the British. The city of **Munger** (*map 7 B2*), formerly known as Monghyr, 135km east of Patna, was an important Mughal centre on the south bank of the Ganges. The city's impressive fort was much admired, and painted, in the British period, as a fine example of Muslim military architecture—but it was seriously damaged in the earthquake of 1934.

There is an important Buddhist site at **Antichak** (*map 7 C2*), in the far east of the state, 220km from Patna and 93km from Malda in West Bengal. The site consists of the ruins of the Buddhist university of **Vikramshila** (*open daily sunrise–sunset*), built by the Pala king Dharampala in the late 8th or early 9th century. There is a large stupa designed in the shape of a cross with Buddha statues inside a prayer chamber, as well as a monastery building and a small museum.

SOUTHERN BIHAR

The southern part of Bihar has three major Buddhist sites: **Bodhgaya**, where the Buddha achieved enlightment; **Rajgir**, the site of a ruined city where the Buddha preached; and **Nalanda**, the site of a great Buddhist monastery and university. Because of the large number of Buddhist pilgrims visiting from East Asia, the area has a much better tourist infrastructure than the rest of Bihar. The region also has several other sites that are worthy of investigation.

BODHGAYA

Bodhgaya (*map 7 B3*), the most important of the many Buddhist places of pilgrimage, known in scripture as 'the navel of the earth', is situated 100km south of Patna, close to the large modern town of Gaya. It is a peaceful, friendly place, filled with Buddhist visitors from East Asia and the rest of the world. It has become a spiritual centre, where people gather to practise meditation techniques and yoga, and to study Buddhism. There are many modern temples and stupas, reflecting the wide variety of contemporary historical styles of building in Buddhist countries—note in particular the handsome Thai *wat* on the southern side of the town.

The main temple and the large Bodhi tree mark the place where Buddhism began about 2,500 years ago. The Buddha, a prince called Siddhartha Gautama, who renounced the material world and his family, travelled widely as an ascetic throughout Bihar. At Bodhgaya he stopped and meditated beneath a pipal tree (a kind of fig), where—after 49 days—he attained *bodhi* (usually translated as 'enlightenment', but arguably 'awakening' is more accurate). In Bodhgaya, signboards say that he attained enlightenment in 623 BC, but this is disputed, and some experts have made a strong case for a later date, possibly around 400 BC.

Although Bodhgaya is best known as a Buddhist site, historically it was owned and run for many centuries by Hindus, for whom the Buddha is an avatar of Lord Vishnu. To this day, the management of the temple is carried out by a committee of Hindus and Buddhists, and many Hindus come to Bodhgaya to perform the death rites of relatives, usually while visiting important Hindu temples in Gaya. In 1992, an argument between Hindu priests and Buddhist pilgrims led to fighting within the temple complex, and many Buddhists continue to insist that the complex should be entirely under their control.

The Mahabodhi temple complex

The main temple complex (*open daily 5am–9pm*), a UNESCO World Heritage Site, is in the heart of the small town. A pedestrianised street, with lots of market stalls, leads up to the main gate, where you can leave your shoes (wear socks if you are visiting on a winter morning—it can get very cold). Inside the temple complex, a second gate on the eastern side leads into the large sunken garden dominated by the towering Mahabodhi Temple (*see box opposite*). There are several walkways around the garden, on the south of which is a large pool known as the Muchalinda Lake, teeming with fish that are fed by the faithful. The Buddha, in his sixth week of meditation, is said to have been saved from a great storm by the snake-king known as Muchalinda, who lived in the lake.

Closer to the temple, on the eastern side, are some pieces of masonry, including an ancient *torana*, or entrance gateway, and parts of the original three-tiered railing that surrounded the temple. The railing (parts of which are modern replicas) is very finely carved and jointed, and is probably from the Shunga period (1st century BC), not, as previously believed, built by the Mauryans. These, and the stone bench (*see below*), are the oldest surviving parts of the complex. Note the many dozens of small votive stupas and shrines in the garden. On the northern side of the temple are the stumps of pillars that once formed a cloister, constructed by Ashoka the Great, over the path where the Buddha walked while he meditated. The lotuses on the raised platform represent the Buddha's footsteps.

The Bodhi tree: At the rear of the temple is the Bodhi tree, surrounded by a railing. It is not the original tree, but it may be in lineal descent from the one under which the Buddha sat. A cutting from the original tree was taken to Anuradhapura in northern Sri Lanka, and so when the one in Bodhgaya was destroyed, a fresh cutting was taken from the Anuradhapura tree. There is a carved stone bench covered with a gold cloth between the tree and temple, which is quite hard to see. It is the **Vajrasana** (3rd century BC), or Diamond Throne, placed here in the Mauryan period, and is said to mark the precise spot where the Buddha attained enlightenment.

The temple: The current Mahabodhi temple is 55m high—a layered building, almost triangular in shape, and with niches at all levels. Most of the niches have statues of the Buddha, and the particularly fine standing Buddhas on either side of the main door are thought to be from the 6th century. Inside is a large seated Buddha in gilded stone.

About 300m west of the temple is the **Bodhgaya Museum** (*open Sat–Thur 10–5*), which has a fine display of the original finely-decorated railings recovered from the main temple site—made from both sandstone (1st century BC) and granite (6th century AD). There are also some high-quality Buddhist and Hindu sculptures from the 9th–11th centuries.

DATING THE MAHABODHI TEMPLE

There has been considerable controversy over the age of the actual Mahabodhi Temple. We do know that the stone bench, the railing, and the pillar stumps all date to a much earlier period than the main shrine. The temple, in anything close to its current form, is not mentioned in the description given of Bodhgaya by the 5th-century Chinese traveller Fa Xien. However, the existing temple is similar in design to one described by the 7th-century Chinese traveller Xuan Zang—so the date normally given for the building is the 6th century. The temple had fallen into ruins by the 15th century, and underwent major restoration in the 19th. It has proved difficult to ascertain which parts are original—though the temple had no side towers or doorway arch in a famous 18th-century British drawing of it—these additions were funded by Burmese Buddhists in the 19th century.

Hindu temples: Just opposite the main Bodhgaya complex are a large number of Hindu temples, with triangular spires—a testament to the importance of Bodhgaya in Hinduism. These temples, mainly shrines to Shiva, are little-visited now.

BARABAR CAVES

The 3rd-century BC Barabar Caves are set in rocky hills 30km north of Bodhgaya (*map 7 B3*). To reach the Barabar Hills, head north on the Gaya–Patna road, and turn right (east) at Bela for a final 10km journey along one of India's worst roads—and take a torch. The caves are very early examples of rock-cut architecture, perhaps the earliest, and were made famous, as the 'Marabar Caves', by E.M. Forster in his 1924 novel *A Passage to India*, later made into a very successful film. Forster rhapsodises over the bare polished granite walls of the caves 'as smoother than windless water, more voluptuous than love'. The key scene in the novel happens in one of the caves, when a British woman is alone with an Indian doctor, who is later wrongly accused of assaulting her. The Barabar Caves were not used, though, for the 1984 film.

Orientation: From the car park, next to the desolate and almost empty museum, you need to find a guide—essential for once, because they have the keys to the caves.

Caves 1–2: You will be taken 200m uphill to **Cave 1**, cut directly into the rock. This cave, like the others, was thought have been used by Jain monks. This undecorated single-chamber cave is rectangular, with an arched ceiling, and cut out of solid granite. Its walls have been very finely polished, so smooth that the polishing might have been carried out yesterday. There is a stone bench at one end. **Cave 2**, known as the **Sudama Cave**, round the back of the same rock, has two chambers—an outer one that is rectangular, and an inner circular room.

Lomas Rishi Cave: Just a few metres away is **Cave 3**, known as the Lomas Rishi Cave, and this is the finest in the Barabar Hills. It has a superbly carved outer doorway, imitating in design the shape of a hut, with its curved eaves and sloping supports. Within the architrave is a finely carved frieze of elephants. Inside is a large rectangular chamber, with, like Cave 2, an attached circular room. The discovery of a flaw in the rock meant that this part of the cave was never completed.

There are several other minor caves nearby, some of which have inscriptions. On the top of the neighbouring hill, up some very steep steps, is a Shiva temple from where there are superb views over the neighbouring countryside.

RAJGIR

Rajgir (*map 7 B3*), once known as Rajgriha, meaning 'abode of the king', was a major city and the capital of the kingdom of Magadh in the 6th century BC, spread across seven hills. It is 70km south of Patna, and 55km northeast of Bodhgaya. Several of the sites are connected with the life of the Buddha, and also with his contemporary and early follower King Bimbisara of Magadh, whose capital was Rajgir, and who is said to have been imprisoned here and starved to death by his son and successor Ajatshatru. None of Rajgir's ruins is particularly special in artistic or architectural terms, but they are very widespread and give a sense of the scale of urban development in this part of India 2,500 years ago.

Orientation: Because the ruins are spread out across the rocky terrain, it is advisable to have a vehicle to travel between the sites, particularly if you are in a hurry. But it is also an interesting place to wander in, and many of the minor sites and more recent Buddhist, Jain, Hindu and Muslim shrines are not on the main road running through Rajgir.

Low walls built of stone ring and subdivide most of Rajgir, and it has been calculated that the existing outer walls extend for 48km. Most visitors, coming from Bodhgaya, enter the Rajgir area through a low pass in the hill, which was once the southern gate, sometimes known as the Bimbisara Gate.

Southern ruins

On either side of the road are the ancient walls, made of loosely fitted pieces of rock, around an inner core of smaller stones. About 300m beyond the southern gate is an excavated stupa. Just beyond is a junction. The main Rajgir sites are straight ahead. However, the road on the right is worth a detour. It leads through an excavation that has revealed the foundations of what is thought to be the **Jivakamravana Monastery** (4th–3rd centuries BC), with four apsidal (horseshoe-shaped) rooms. At the end of the road is a chairlift which takes visitors up to the modern **Japanese Shanti Stupa** on top of Gridhrakuta Hill, or Vulture's Peak. Halfway up are some undecorated caves that are said to have been used by the Buddha. Return to the junction and head north to the rest of Rajgir. On the right, 300m after the junction, are the excavated foundations of a square building, with 2m thick walls, known as **Bimbisara's Jail** (5th century BC). This is where King Bimbisara is thought to have been imprisoned by his son Ajatshatru, and where the king eventually died. An iron manacle was found during the excavation. Note the foundations of the round corner towers, for what may have been a small fort.

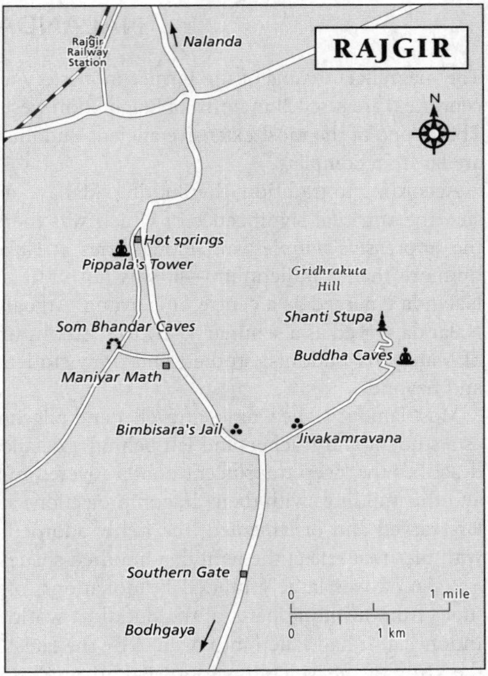

Maniyar Math and the Son Bhandar Caves

One kilometre beyond the jail is the **Maniyar Math**, Rajgir's strangest building—made even more unusual by its modern corrugated iron roof. It looks like a cross between a well and a temple, and may originally have been a stupa. Its structure suggests it has been repeatedly added to and rebuilt, and it has the remains of religious images from the 5th-century Gupta period. The shrine deity at one stage seems to have been Mani-naga, a serpent-god.

About 300m to the west of the Maniyar Math are the two **Son Bhandar Caves** (3rd–4th centuries), which were cut into the hillside by Jain monks. The roof and walls of the western cave are largely intact, and it is possible to make out an inscription and the bottom half of a torso carved in relief on the wall. The roof of the eastern cave has collapsed, but on the inside wall are some fine relief carvings of Jain saviours.

Central Rajgir

Return to the main road, and head north to Rajgir's **Hot Springs** (or Topada), possibly the reason why this area was originally settled more than 2,500 years ago. The Hot Springs, which are part of a temple complex, still attract large crowds of pilgrims and visitors, and the water is comfortably warm.

Up the hill behind the Hot Springs is a stone structure known as **Pippala's Tower** (named after the sacred pipal tree), which may have functioned as a watchtower. Buddhist tradition holds that this was the residence of the president of the First Buddhist Council, formed after the death of the Buddha, and whose meetings were held in caves on top of the hill above Pippala's Tower. Further north are more excavated foundations, including a stupa, the ruins of a walled garden, and the restored old city walls on the northern side of the city.

NALANDA

The magnificent ruins of the former monastery and university of Nalanda (5th–12th centuries) are just 12km north of Rajgir, 2km west of the Rajgir–Patna road (*map 7 B3*). This is one of the most extensive ancient Buddhist sites in the world, and excavations are far from complete.

According to tradition, the Buddha, Mahavir and Ashoka the Great all visited this site, the spiritual significance of which was therefore enormous. However, most of the impressive temples and monasteries at Nalanda actually postdate the Buddha by more than a millennium—it was not until the 5th century, at the earliest, that Nalanda emerged as a centre of learning. Arguably the first university in the world, Nalanda served as a seminary—by the 7th century, it had become the leading centre of Mahayana Buddhist studies, and drew students and pilgrims from all over India and beyond.

Most famously, the Chinese traveller and pilgrim Xuan Zuang lived here for 12 years as a student and teacher, and left behind a detailed account of Nalanda in c. 630. He describes the 'deep translucent ponds covered in blue lotus and red Kanaka flowers', and the buildings with their 'dragon projections and coloured eaves, the pearl-red pillars carved and ornamented, the richly adorned balustrades, and the roofs covered with tiles that reflect the light in a hundred shades.'

Nalanda was largely funded by donations, often from royal families, and sometimes from far-flung parts of the Buddhist world, including Sumatra in modern-day Indonesia. It had fallen into decline by the late 12th century, when it was sacked by the army of the Muslim warlord Bakhtiyar Khilji. A Tibetan pilgrim who visited in 1235 described Nalanda as damaged and looted, but met a 90-year-old Buddhist teacher—possibly Nalanda's last—with a group of students. From that time until excavations got underway in the 19th century, though, Nalanda was largely deserted.

Orientation: All the main buildings at Nalanda (*open daily 9–5.30*) are part of a large compound, more than 700m long, accessed from the main road through Nalanda town, opposite the entrance to the very interesting museum. The entrance is from what was the back of the Nalanda site, which is why the main temples are furthest from the main road.

There is a large amount to visit within the compound, and if you have limited time, just visit the three most interesting temples (3, 12 and 2), and one or two (1 and 5) of the 11 monasteries. The impressive square-shaped monastery buildings, which served as university hostels, are in fact very similar to each other, and have much less decoration than the temples. The way the buildings are numbered in Nalanda can be very confusing, since the numbering system reflects the order of excavation, and makes no distinction between the purposes of the buildings. So there is Monastery 1, but no Monastery 2 or 3, as these numbers are borne by temples; there are, though, monasteries 4–11, and then the numbers 12–14 refer to temples. Every new excavation complicates the numbering system further.

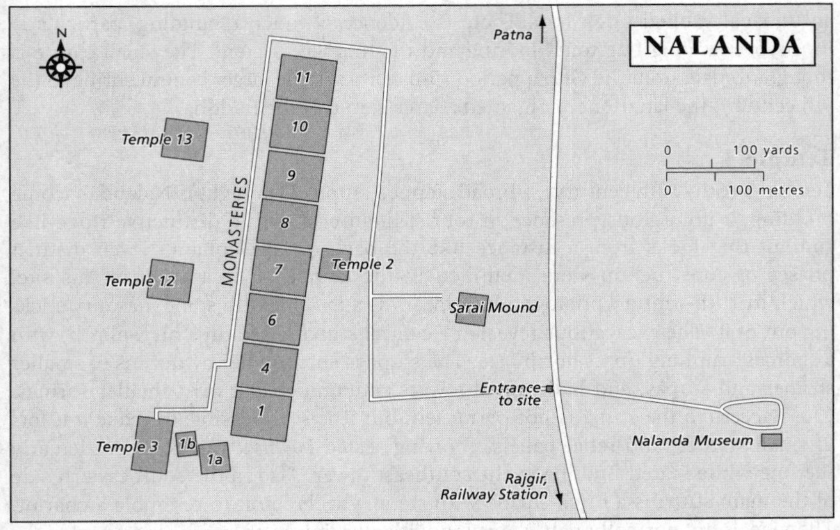

It is also sensible to resist the temptation to enter the first building you come to, and instead follow the main path through the gardens, and pass along a corridor between Monasteries 1 and 4, and then climb up the steps on the left onto the far walls of Monastery 1. From here one gets a good view of the layout of the entire site, and can see that the temples, rather than the monasteries, were the real focus of the Nalanda complex. From here the site is dominated at one end by the most impressive of all the Nalanda ruins, Temple 3, an enormous, stepped stupa surrounded by smaller votive stupas, towers and shrines, while further to the left are other stand-alone temples and the monasteries, arranged in a neat row stretching off into the distance.

Monastery 1

The most impressive and best-preserved of the monastery buildings was built, or rebuilt, during the reign of King Devapala (810–50) of the Pala Dynasty, with a donation—according to a copper plate inscription found on the site—sent by Balaputra Deva, the king of Sumatra, and endowed by Devapala with the income from five nearby villages. The layout follows the typical rectangular plan of the Nalanda monasteries, each approximately 60m by 50m, with an entrance doorway to the west, which opened into a large inner courtyard, usually with a central shrine. Surrounding the courtyard are cells used as rooms by monks. Some of the cells have a shelf for keeping manuscripts and other belongings, a niche in which a light could be kept and post-holes that would have supported ceiling beams. Monastery 1 had a grander entrance staircase than the others, leading to the upper storey and two subsidiary hostel buildings (1a and 1b on the plan). There is a surviving upper-level room with an unusual vaulted brick roof. There is evidence of much rebuilding, particularly in the overlapping flagstone flooring and the drainage system. The small shrine is thought to date from the Gupta period (5th century), the larger central shrine to the 9th century; the latter once contained a large statue of the Buddha.

Temple 3

Temple 3 (6th–12th century), a broad stepped stupa, 31m high, is Nalanda's iconic building, a ubiquitous presence in tourist literature, with a distinctive ridge-like summit that looks from a distance like the back of an elephant. Seven distinct phases of construction were identified in the course of excavation of this site, which in 19th-century photographs appears as a mound with some masonry sticking out of it. The excavations revealed a central stupa raised on a high plinth, with a staircase running up its north face. The stupa is surrounded by dozens of smaller shrines and stupas, and half-ruined towers containing their own smaller shrines. Close access to the stupa is not permitted, but it is still possible to make out lots of small statues, and relief panels, showing seated *bodhisattvas*. Note particularly the fine white seated Buddha in the southeast tower. Also in the southeastern side of the main stupa is a brick shrine with stone wheels, built to resemble a chariot. The wheels are normally partly covered with aluminium sheeting, and so you may need to crouch to see them properly.

Temples 12 and 2

Temple 12 (7th century and later) is 150m north of Temple 3 and has a small subsidiary shrine on its south side with the base of a large statue, studded with tiny Buddha images. There are also dozens of tiny stupas, many of them decorated, and two finely-carved pillars that stand on the forecourt of the temple.

Temple 2 (7th century) is approached by heading east from Temple 12, along the passage that separates monasteries 7 and 8. This ruined temple has the best surviving frieze of carvings around its base—panels carved in relief, depicting gods and goddesses, children playing, a man playing the flute, a large variety of animals, and two lovers who are not quite entwined.

Other buildings in the Nalanda complex

Other excavated buildings (there are many areas of the site which still have not been excavated) include **Monastery 4**, where it is possible to make out how a new monastery was built on the fire-damaged ruins of an older one, while the overlapping remains of **Monastery 5** are still a mystery to archaeologists because several of the cells have no doors, not even—as in some other monasteries—ones that appear to have been bricked up. **Monastery 6** has some ruined ovens in its upper courtyard, while the ruins of three successive buildings are visible in the excavations of **Monastery 7**. Back near the entrance gate is the Sarai mound, excavated in the 1970s, which revealed another temple (as yet unnumbered), in which the base of a colossal Buddha can be seen.

Nalanda Museum

The museum (*open Sat–Thur 10–5*) is opposite the entrance to the Nalanda site and has several statues and other artefacts recovered during the Nalanda excavations. The first room has two very fine and quite different Avalokiteshwaras. The first in black basalt is immediately as you enter, the second is a large sandstone statue—a very complex piece of carving in which all his arms have survived and the Buddha of compassion is surrounded by several female *bodhisattvas*. Further inside notice the unusual terracotta pot with more than 30 spouts, several stucco heads, ancient scissors, razors and a branding iron. There are also some Hindu figures, including a particularly fine panel in black of Kuber, the god of wealth, with his large protruding stomach.

Pawapuri

Some 15km to the east of Nalanda is the important Jain pilgrimage centre of Pawapuri—the place where the last of the Jain saviours, Mahavir, was cremated. There, at the centre of a lake, is a pretty marble shrine that can be reached by a pedestrian causeway.

SASARAM

The little-visited town of Sasaram (*map 7 A3*), 140km southwest of Patna and 110km southeast of Varanasi, contains one of India's finest mausolea, the lake-tomb of Sher Shah Suri, as well as some other interesting Muslim monuments from the early 16th century.

The tomb of Sher Shah Suri

Built in 1545, this spectacular tomb (*open daily 8–5*) is set on a plinth in a man-made lake in the western part of Sasaram, a little south of the railway line. Sher Shah Suri was a provincial warlord, probably born in Sasaram, who defeated the Mughal emperor Humayun and ruled in Delhi from 1540 to 1545. During his brief reign, he built much of the Purana Qila in Delhi, commissioned the construction of large parts of the Grand Trunk Road and introduced the rupee as the main currency of northern India. He died in an accident in the great hill-fort of Kalinjar. His descendants ruled only briefly, and were overthrown by Humayun.

The large domed entrance gate to the tomb of Sher Shah Suri is on the northern side of the lake and has its own unidentified tomb inside. To each side of the gate are small wall-mosques. A causeway, with a bridge in the middle, takes visitors the 110m to the actual tomb. Note how the tomb and its plinth were rotated (by 8°) to correct the misalignment of the platform on which they sit, and which did not point due west to Mecca. The platform and the plinth seem to have been constructed in a hurry, and much of the external masonry work is quite roughly finished and not carefully shaped as was normal during this period. According to an inscription, it was completed just three months after Sher Shah Suri's death, but is likely to have been commenced before he died.

The mausoleum: The octagonal tomb itself, a strikingly attractive grey sandstone building in the pre-Mughal Lodi style, has a pyramid of domes on its roof, the largest of which rises to a height of 47m above the platform. It was designed by Alawal Khan, who was later buried in a pretty tomb on the outskirts of Sasaram. At the time of its construction, in the late 1540s, Sher Shah Suri's tomb had India's largest dome. The dome rises from an octagonal base, the sides of which are then bisected to form a 16-sided and then a near-circular 32-sided drum, on which the dome rests. Note how the symmetry of the tomb is broken only on the side facing west, towards Mecca. This is where the prayer niches are inside the tomb, and the exterior water-facing wall does not have the kiosks and large staircases that are seen on the other three sides. Inside are many graves; Sher Shah Suri's is normally covered in a green cloth. Note the large inscription from 1882 describing how the British restored the tomb. There are a number of other religious buildings and tombs around the lake.

Other sights in Sasaram

The **tomb of Hassan Sur Khan** (c. 1540), Sher Shah Suri's father, is 300m to the east of the lake, its spired dome clearly visible from his son's mausoleum. This is a slightly less elegant building, smaller and without a lake, but with a similarly striking array of domes and kiosks set on an octagonal tomb. Just to the east of the tomb, and in the same complex, is an unusual stepped tank with a pavilion, and another courtyard with wall niches.

The fascinating unfinished **tomb of Salim Sher Suri** (c. 1550), Sher Shah's son and successor, is 1km northwest of the main tomb, across the railway lines. It is similar in design to his father's tomb—an octagonal plan, set on a square island in the middle of a lake connected to the mainland by a causeway.

The pretty **tomb of Alawal Khan** (c. 1550), Sher Shah Suri's architect, lies 3km to the east of modern Sasaram, near the village of **Qadir Ganj**. Very different in design to the other Suri-period tombs, it has a large yellow sandstone gate, with handsome *chattris* that lead into a walled courtyard with gravestones and a finely carved prayer wall with *mihrabs* (prayer niches) at the far end. It is probably unfinished, and was meant to have a covered area, but no plans for the building have survived.

Hill-forts near Sasaram: The Suri Dynasty also built two enormous hill-forts near Sasaram, including **Rohtas** (35km to the south) and **Shergarh** (30km to the west), which at the time of writing were said to be too dangerous to visit without a police escort, because of criminal gangs near the forts. Seek local advice before travelling to either.

Mundeshwari

The fascinating half-ruined **Mundeshwari Temple** (early 7th century)—at the top of a hill 7km southwest of the town of Bhabua and 45km west of Sasaram (*map 7 A3*)—is said to be the oldest free-standing stone temple still in use in India. It is a two-minute uphill walk from the car park. The temple is very old, and seals have been found that suggest it had previously been an important Buddhist centre. From the amount of temple debris—some of it beautifully carved—that has been found on the ground, it is clear that this was a major religious complex. The temple, of which only the base of the sanctuary survives, is built to an unusual octagonal design, rather than the traditional square plan. It also has three entrance gates and a fourth false door. Note the high-quality carving on the door-frames. Unusually, it houses both Shiva and Durga idols. The Shiva idol is at the heart of the sanctuary, while a large statue of Mundeshwari, a form of Durga, is in the right alcove.

The nearby village of **Chainpur**, further west, once had an important fort, which has almost entirely disappeared. There are the remains of a city gate, two old wells and a small shrine which was once a tomb—out of its roof grows a quite extraordinary collection of trees.

PRACTICAL INFORMATION

GETTING THERE

Bihar's main airport at Patna is well-served by daily flights from Delhi, Kolkata, Mumbai and Ranchi. The other airport, at Gaya, is mainly used for international flights bringing Buddhist pilgrims from Sri Lanka and East Asia. Varanasi, in eastern Uttar Pradesh, is the most convenient airport for Sasaram and southwestern Bihar. Both Patna and Gaya (for Bodhgaya) are well-connected by train to Delhi and Kolkata.

GETTING AROUND

Bihar's roads, once appalling, have improved in recent years, but in the more remote parts of the state can still be very bad. Private taxis are widely available for long-distance journeys, as are auto-rickshaws in the towns and cities. Hardier visitors may want to use the extensive bus network. But do not travel along small country roads at night, and get local advice—such as from your hotel—about safe travel in Bihar. In the past, tourist cars have been stopped after dark, and the occupants robbed.

The Delhi-based tour operators **Buddhapath** (*T: 0120-2511633; buddhapath.com*) organise tours of the major Buddhist sites in Bihar and eastern Uttar Pradesh, and are recommended.

ACCOMMODATION

• **Bodhgaya:** There are comfortable hotels here, largely targeted at East Asian visitors. **The Royal Residency** (*$$; T: 0631 2201156-7; theroyalresidency.net*) and the **Lotus Nikko** (*$$; T: 0631 2200700; lotustranstravels.com*) are the best in town.

• **Patna:** There is one slightly rundown five-star hotel, the **Maurya** (*$$; T: 0612 2203 04057; maurya.com*), just next to the Gandhi Maidan. The **Hotel Windsor** (*$; T: 0612 2203 2508; hotelwindsorpatna.com*) on Exhibition Road is also comfortable, and popular with younger visitors.

• **Rajgir:** The Japanese-style **Centaur Hokke** (*$$; T: 06112 55231; centaur@*

dte.vsnl.net.in) and the **Rajgir Residency** (*$$; T: 06112 255404; rajgir-residency.com*) are the best in Rajgir.

• **Sasaram:** Most towns in Bihar have basic hotels, and in Sasaram the best is the simple and noisy **Gopal Deluxe** (*$; T: 06184 224366*).

FOOD

Rice is the staple food of Bihar, though a variety of breads are also widely available. Many Hindus are vegetarian; and of the two religious faiths that were born in Bihar, Jainism is adamantly vegetarian, and Buddhism largely so. However, there is a strong non-vegetarian influence from northern India and Mughlai cuisine, and also from Bengal, where fish and mustard seeds are key ingredients. Biharis are particularly proud of their sweet dishes, and the finest sweet pastry, known as *khaja*, is said to come from Rajgir, while excellent *tilkut* wafers, made of crushed sesame seeds and sugar, are found in Gaya. After China, India is the second-largest producer of *litchis* (lychees), and Muzaffarpur in northern Bihar is the main centre for growing the fruit, which is harvested in late May and throughout June.

FURTHER READING & VIEWING

The 1924 novel *A Passage to India* (Penguin Classics) by the British writer E.M. Forster is set in the thinly-disguised Bankipore area of Patna (called Chandrapore in the book), and gives a superb picture of the late British colonial period. The climactic event of the novel occurs at the Barabar Caves—or Marabar Caves, as renamed by Forster.

The early chapters of Arvind Adiga's 2008 Booker Prize-winning *White Tiger* paint an unremittingly gloomy picture of modern Bihar. For historical context, try Arvind Das's *Republic of Bihar* (Penguin, 1992).

The film of *A Passage to India* (1984), directed by David Lean, though not actually shot in Bihar, still manages to evoke a powerful image of Bihar as it was in the 1920s.

JHARKHAND

Jharkhand (*maps 7 and 8*) is a state of almost 30 million people, which was detached from the rest of Bihar in 2000. Very few foreign or domestic tourists visit the state. A high percentage of the population of Jharkhand is tribal, and large parts of the state are covered with forest. It is one of India's least developed states, though it has some of the country's most important coal and iron ore reserves, as well as the large industrial city of Jamshedpur, named after Jamshedji Tata, the founder of the Tata business dynasty, who set up India's first steel plant here in the early 20th century. The state has been badly affected by Maoist Naxalite unrest—so take local advice before travelling outside the main centres.

The state capital is the large, modern city of **Ranchi** (*map 8 B1*), with few visitor attractions apart from the 300-year-old **Jagannath Temple**, a smaller version of the Hindu temple of the same name in Puri, in the neighbouring state of Orissa. Non-Hindus are allowed inside the temple (which they are not in Puri), which is on the outskirts of Ranchi, west of the airport. There is also a small **museum** (*open 8–6: closed Sun and Sat afternoon*) at the Tribal Research Institute, near the Morabadi Stadium. There are two interesting Christian cemeteries near the Old Hazaribagh Road, 1.5km north of the station: the **Ranchi War Cemetery** and the old **British Cemetery**.

There is a major Jain pilgrimage centre at **Parusnath** (*map 7 B3*), near Dumri on NH2, the Grand Trunk Road, 105km from Ranchi. As many as 20 of the 24 Jain *tirthankars*, or saviours, are said to have achieved salvation at Parusnath. It is a long uphill walk to the Jain temple, from where there are spectacular views over the Jharkhand countryside. There are Jain-run guest houses in the nearby village of Madhuban. It is advisable to start walking before dawn, and many pilgrims start at 4am. No leather items are allowed on the hilltop.

Rajmahal (*map 7 C3*), in the far northeast of the state, was the capital of Bengal during the early Mughal period. Its largely ruined 16th-century palaces and mosques—on the south bank of the Ganges—are now most easily visited from Malda in West Bengal (65km away via the Farakka Barrage), rather than from Ranchi, which is 315km away.

PRACTICAL INFORMATION

Jharkhand's main airport is at Ranchi, with good connections to Delhi and Bombay. Jamshedpur also has an airport but with very few scheduled flights. There is an averagely good rail network—northern Jharkhand is on the main Delhi–Kolkata route—and the famous Grand Trunk Road, which runs from Delhi to Kolkata, also runs through the state, where it is known as NH2.

The best hotel in Ranchi is the **Yuvraj Palace** (*$$; 0651 2480326; hotelyuvrajpalace.com*).

ORISSA

The eastern Indian state of Orissa (*maps 8 and 12*) has some of India's finest examples of Hindu sacred architecture, including the Sun Temple at Konarak, and a wide range of important Buddhist monuments, wildlife parks and superb beaches. Orissa can feel underdeveloped and isolated from the rest of India, but this area was once the home to great maritime empires, whose seafarers helped spread Buddhism to Sri Lanka, and Hinduism to Bali and other places in what is now Indonesia. Orissa is also India's most disaster-affected state—suffering from recurrent cyclones, floods, droughts and heat-waves—and this has affected development in the state, which is still one of India's poorest. Its enormous mineral wealth has made it attractive to mining companies, whose activities in the state are very controversial.

Orissa can be divided into two very different regions: the coastal strip, and the forested hills of the interior. The coastal strip and the delta of the Mahanadi River, where most of Orissa's great monuments are to be found, have rich agricultural lands, largely used for growing rice. Fishing and sea trading continues to play a major part in the economy. The interior is underdeveloped, largely settled by tribal peoples and partly affected by India's long-running Maoist insurgency. These lands are rich in wildlife and minerals, particularly iron ore and aluminium, and have thriving and distinctive tribal cultures, though very few major historical monuments or buildings.

HISTORY OF ORISSA

Coastal Orissa was the heart of the Kalinga Empire, which flourished more than 2,000 years ago. The ancient Greek traveller Megasthenes said the king of Kalinga had more than '60,000 foot-soldiers, 1,000 horsemen, 700 elephants keeping watch and ward in preparedness for war'. The preparations were not enough, though, and Emperor Ashoka defeated the Kalingas in 262 BC in a battle that took place just south of the modern capital Bhubaneswar. Ashoka was so appalled by the bloodshed he witnessed in Orissa that he converted to Buddhism.

Orissa became one of the heartlands of Buddhism, and there are a number of important monuments and excavations from the Buddhist era in Bhubaneswar, and in the northern part of the delta region. The most important period of Hindu temple-building began in the 7th century, with the main surviving early shrines in Bhubaneswar. The great coastal temples of Jagannath at Puri and the Sun Temple at Konarak are products of the later Ganga Dynasty. Orissa later sank into relative obscurity, a forgotten outpost of the Mughal, Maratha and British empires.

Under the British, some of its coastal towns became seaside resorts for the rich of Calcutta, further north along the Bay of Bengal. Life in the interior was little affected, though by the 20th century Orissan dance, textiles and metalwork had gained a national and then international reputation. In the 1930s, Orissa became the first Indian province (and later state) to be demarcated on linguistic grounds—with the vast majority of the state's inhabitants speaking Oriya. The recent politics of Orissa have been dominated by two members of the same family: Biju Patnaik, who died in 1997, and his son Naveen.

THE PATNAIK FAMILY

Biju Patnaik, after whom Bhubaneswar Airport (as well as many other buildings) are named, was a larger-than-life figure. He was an athletics champion and an aircraft pilot who fought against the British. He then helped Indonesia fight the Dutch, famously rescuing two Indonesian leaders and flying them to India. His son Naveen, who had lived much of his life outside Orissa, succeeded him as chief minister. His daughter, Gita Mehta, is best known as the writer of *Karma Cola*, an entertaining book about how Westerners were seduced by Indian spiritualism in the 1960s and 70s.

BHUBANESWAR

Bhubaneswar (*map 8 C3*) is unique among Indian cities. It is both a modern post-Independence state capital—and, like Chandigarh and Gandhinagar, it has numerous Modernist buildings—but it is also a fascinating old temple town, and close to the site of an ancient battle that transformed Buddhism into a major international religion.

The modern city of Bhubaneswar, largely designed by the German architect Otto Koenigsberger in the 1940s, lies close to the delta of Orissa's main river, the Mahanadi, and just 15km from Orissa's old capital, Cuttack. The main visitor attractions in the city—the Hindu temples built between the 7th and 13th centuries, the Jain caves of Khandagiri and Udayagiri, the site of the Battle of Kalinga at Dhauli, and the ruined walls of the fortress of Sisupalgarh—are to the south of the modern city, not far from the airport.

THE HINDU TEMPLES OF BHUBANESWAR

Most temples of the distinctive Orissan style have a tall, gently curving tower, in which the inner sanctum and the idol are found, and an adjoining, low-roofed, usually rectangular building that serves as porch or assembly area. A wide range of very fine Orissan temple architecture can be found in Bhubaneswar, though there is nothing as spectacular as the partly-ruined Sun Temple at Konarak, 50km to the southeast.

There are said to be about 500 old temples in Bhubaneswar, of which at least a dozen are architecturally important. Unlike some other temple towns, the main shrines are well kept, often situated in pretty parks and with small water pools nearby. The largest temple, the Lingaraj, does not allow non-Hindus into its precincts, but the others all do.

Orientation: Most of the temples are grouped around the lake, the Bindu Sagar, in the south of Bhubaneswar, and can be visited on foot. There is a small northern group, 1km away, including the Rameswar Temple, and the ruins of the city's oldest temples are close by. The charming Rajarani Temple is 1.5km to the east.

Bindu Sagar group of temples

The oldest complete shrine in Bhubaneswar (mid-7th century) is the **Parasrameshwara Temple**, 200m east of the Bindu Sagar lake. It is an archetypal early Orissan Shiva temple with a curvilinear square-towered sanctuary and a low-roofed assembly hall, or *mandapa*. Despite its age, the sanctuary has some of the finest external carvings to be seen in Bhubaneswar. The southern and eastern walls of the sanctuary have carved idols of the elephant-god Ganesha and the warrior-god Kartikeya, both sons of Shiva. Note the marvellous tiny contorted human figures set in square boxes just above both idols. The niche on the northern wall is empty, but look up for a fine carving of the goddess Durga spearing the demon buffalo. There is very early, and relatively mild, erotica in a frieze around the middle layer of the sanctuary. The assembly hall is a slightly later addition, and the two buildings have not been properly joined.

Vaital Deul Temple (late 8th century) is strikingly different from the other temples of Bhubaneswar. The sanctuary is rectangular, and this gives its roof a curious vaulted, semicircular shape, unlike the towers seen elsewhere—it is reminiscent of the *gopura* of south India. The roof is topped by three identical finials. The assembly hall, or *mandapa*, has its own miniature towers, similar to the curvilinear towers of other Bhubaneswar temples. The exterior of the sanctuary has some interesting carvings, including Shiva as the half-male, half-female Ardhanarishwara, on the west face. Note the frieze of small figures shown in a range of domestic situations halfway up the building.

The towering **Lingaraj Temple** (late 11th century) is, in religious terms, the most important in Bhubaneswar, and is part of a large walled compound just to the south of Bindu Sagar Lake. It is closed to non-Hindus. There are good views of the temple and dozens of smaller shrines from the roof of the nearby Lingaraj Hotel, access to which may require a small payment. The tower of the temple is 36.5m high, and the shrine has three assembly halls. There is an interesting, neglected ruined temple to be found in the grounds of the police station, opposite the Lingaraj Temple. It has been constructed out of brick and stone, and has a very fine tower. Unusually, access to the sanctuary is down some steps.

The **Mukteshwar Temple** (late 10th century) is on the main road leading from Puri and Konarak into modern Bhubaneswar, and 400m east of the lake. This very pretty temple is set next to a small rectangular pool, in a well-tended walled garden with several other smaller shrines. The Mukteshwar Temple has its own waist-level walled enclosure and a fine free-standing curved entrance gateway, with delicate carvings of reclining maidens and monsters' heads projecting from either side. The temple sanctuary itself consists of the traditional Orissa curvilinear tower and a lower assembly hall

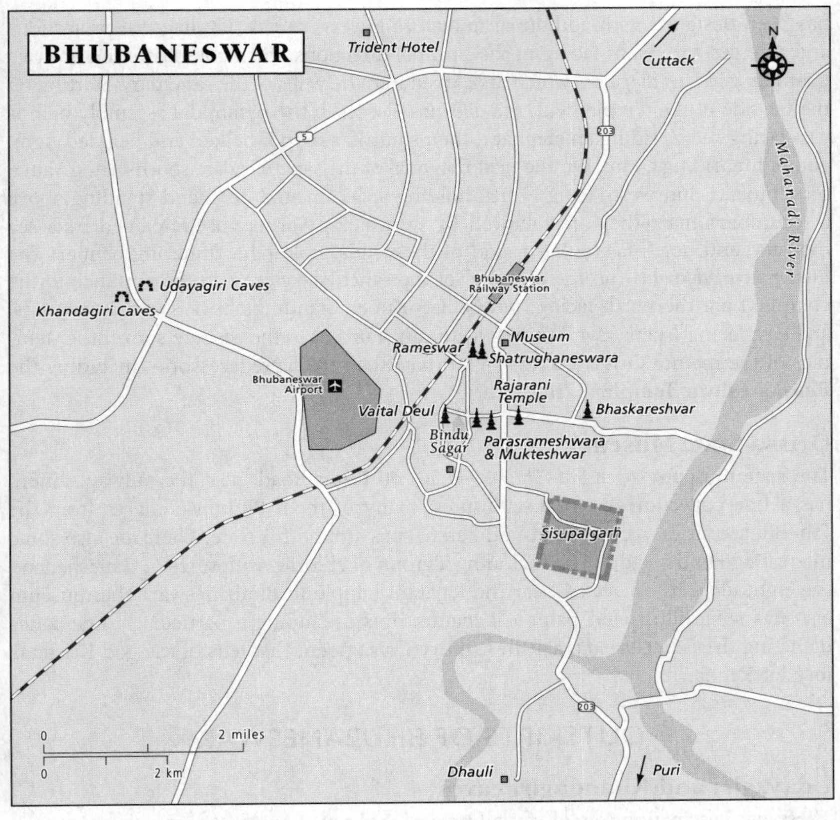

with a stepped pyramid roof. There are fine carvings on the exterior, and a much more ornately decorated interior than in most Orissa temples.

The northern and eastern groups

The most important of the northern group is the **Rameswar Temple** (13th century), 1km north of Bindu Sagar lake. Unusually among the Bhubaneswar temples, Rameswar has a separate sanctuary and entrance hall. It is the most recent of the temples and has much less decoration than the others. Across the road are the remains of three temples, known as the Shatrughaneswara group, which are the oldest of the Bhubaneswar shrines, and have some fine carvings, including some elephants fighting each other, and several Shiva images.

To the east of Bindu Sagar Lake, the **Rajarani Temple** (early 11th century) is a particularly fine example of the mature Orissan style, set in lovely, peaceful gardens, and with the most interesting carvings in Bhubaneswar. The exterior of the sanctuary has been designed with additional miniature towers, so that its diagonal projections and recesses have walls facing in the cardinal directions. Each compass point has two guardian gods, or *dikpalas*, which are carved into the walls of the sanctuary. Starting on the far side of the temple, with the *dikpalas* closest to the pyramidal assembly hall, is east-facing Indra, riding an elephant, then south-facing pot-bellied and bearded Agni, god of fire, riding a ram. On the next diagonal of the sanctuary are south-facing Yama, on a buffalo, and west-facing Nirrti, holding a decapitated head and standing above a recumbent man; they are followed by west-facing Varuna, accompanied by a sea monster, and north-facing Vayu, god of the winds, holding a fluttering banner. The final pair of *dikpalas* (on the diagonal of the sanctuary closest to the entrance to the complex) are the north-facing, pot-bellied Kuber, standing above some money-jars, and east-facing Ishana, symbolising fecundity. Further to the east are some other temples of the mature Orissan style—less ornate than their predecessors—including the **Bhaskareshvar Temple** (12th century).

Orissa State Museum

The state museum (*open Sat–Thur 10–4.30*) on Lewis Road, near the railway station, has a fine collection of stone sculptures, many of them Buddhist images from the 7th–8th centuries, recovered from different sites around the state. There are also some interesting Hindu sculptures, including a group of chlorite sculptures of Ganesha, and the eight *dikpalas* excavated near the Rajarani temple in Bhubaneswar. The museum also has some illustrated palm-leaf manuscripts, including a particularly fine series depicting the *Gita Govinda*, a 12th-century Oriya poem that tells of the god Krishna's love for Radha.

OUTSKIRTS OF BHUBANESWAR

Udayagiri and Khandagiri caves

These two fascinating sets of caves (*marked on the map on p. 621*), cut deep into the sandstone of two adjoining hills 3km west of Bhubaneswar, date back as early as the 2nd century BC. Buddhism and Jainism were the dominant religions at the time, and these caves were part of a Jain monastic complex built by the Jain ruler Kharavela, whose capital was probably Sisupalgarh (*see opposite*). The caves are thought to have served as dormitories and study areas for the monks, though later some were converted into shrines. Several of the caves have some very fine carvings, especially the Rani Gumpha cave, a spectacular early example of storytelling through rock-cut art.

Udayagiri: The easterly group of 17 caves has been cut into a large sandstone outcrop known as Udayagiri, or 'Sunrise Hill'. From the entrance gate, steps lead up to a sub-group of small caves—numbers 3, 4 and 5—which date from the 1st century BC. Cave 3 has an elephant frieze above its arched doorway and is connected to Cave 4; both of them have two storeys. Note the carved door guardians and animal sculptures on the column brackets.

Turn right past Cave 2 to the most important cave in Udayagiri, the Rani Gumpha (Cave 1), or a left up the hill past Cave 9 to the Ganesh Gumpha (Cave 10), and a hill-top structure that was probably a Jain temple.

Cave 1: The Rani Gumpha, or Cave 1 (*gumpha* or *gufa* means cave), is the largest and most elaborate of the caves. It takes the form of a three-sided open courtyard, with two levels of cells on each side. There are fine relief carvings next to and above many of the cell gateways—those on the second level are in better condition. Several doorways have carved guardians. There is a superb sequence of relief carvings on the interior of the upper level of the cells. They appear to be episodes from a mysterious, unidentified narrative—a lost epic perhaps—parts of which are also replicated in the Ganesh Gumpha and elsewhere in Udayagiri.

The left-most scene depicts an attendant, carrying so much on his tray and in his arms that he appears to be about to fall. The next scene shows a group of elephants cowering before a man with a club and a woman whose arms are raised as if to strike the animals. Further to the right are a man and woman (it is known to be a woman from similar, less-worn images at Udayagiri) fighting with swords and shields. Another woman is being abducted just to the right of the fighting scene. In the following episode, beyond the next doorway, a horse shelters under a parasol, and an archer takes aim at a winged deer; the archer is seen again next to a naked woman climbing down from a tree. In the final episode a woman is shown being pampered by female attendants.

Cave 10: Return down the steps (though it is possible to head over the rocks behind the Rani Gumpha), and take the next path up, past Cave 9, to Cave 10, known as the Ganesh Gumpha (1st century BC), with its two guardian elephants standing in the courtyard. These sculptures and the carved image of Ganesha, the elephant-god, are thought to be from a later Hindu period than the rest of cave, which was built by Jains. There are very similar relief carvings to those seen in the Rani Gumpha.

Caves 14 and 12: Head back down the hill and take the next set of steps up to see Cave 14, which has, carved into the rock, a 1st-century BC inscription in the Brahmi script, which refers to the Chedi rulers of Kalinga, who commissioned the cave complex. Beyond is Cave 12, the Bagh or Tiger Gumpha, the entrance to which is shaped like the head of an open-mouthed tiger. On the summit of the hill are the remains of an apsidal, or horseshoe-shaped, building that was probably a temple.

Khandagiri: The Khandagiri cave complex on the other side of the road has 15 excavated structures. Khandagiri, which means 'broken hill', is less interesting than Udayagiri, partly because many of the caves have been closed to the public, who have to peer through wire mesh or dirty glass. However, **Cave 3** has some good carvings, while **10 and 11** have fine relief carvings of the Jain *tirthankars*, or saviours, high up on their rear walls.

Sisupalgarh

Around 3km east of Bhubaneswar airport, and just visible from the main road to Puri, are the walls of Sisupalgarh (3rd century BC; *map p. 621*). This is thought to have been the ancient fortified capital of Orissa at the time of Ashoka's conquest of the region. The walls form a perfect square, each side 1.16km in length, and with precise right angles at each corner. The walls are overgrown and, apart from gaps where gateways were placed, there is little obvious sign that this was once a great city. Recent excavations, away from the road, have revealed a number of stone columns, and archaeologists are expecting further significant finds here.

SOUTH OF BHUBANESWAR

Dhauli

Six kilometres south of Bhubaneswar airport is Dhauli (*map 8 C3 and p. 621*), the site of the ancient battle where the armies of Emperor Ashoka defeated the local Kalinga rulers. Ashoka was so appalled by the bloodshed at Dhauli that he later saw this as the turning point in his life, which led to his conversion to Buddhism. There is a **rock-cut edict** near the bottom of the hill at Dhauli, in which Ashoka declares that the people of the region were like his children, that no one would be punished without trial, and that officials should be free from anger and from hurry. Above the edict, and part of the same boulder, is a sculpture of the front half of an elephant that has been chiselled out of the rock—this was intended to mark the site of the edict for passers-by. On the nearby hill is a large and impressive **modern stupa**, built by Japanese Buddhists, and from where there are excellent views over Bhubaneswar and the surrounding countryside.

Hirapur

The unusual **Chausath Yogini Temple** (11th century) at Hirapur (*map 8 C3*), 20km southeast of Bhubaneswar, is set amid rice fields next to a lake—like many village shrines. However, this open-air temple is dedicated to the Chausath Yogini, or '64 goddesses', and has many fascinating small statues of women, most of them symbolising female power and strength. Only in the far west of Orissa, at Ranipur Jharial, is there a temple that bears any similarity to this.

The temple itself consists of a small circular courtyard, surrounded with goddess idols inserted into niches on the external and internal walls of the shrine. There is a small central pavilion that has been rebuilt at a later date. There are nine external idols, eight of which depict benign, seductively-posed women, each carrying a cup, while the ninth (on the left of the entrance) brandishes a sword over her head.

Around the inner wall are 60 idols (one covered with cloth) showing the *yoginis* in a wide range of activities, poses, costumes and headgear—many in war-like attitudes. Among the finest statues is the fourth from the left, showing a fearsome woman riding a turtle; further on is a goddess standing on a curled-up body, and another standing on a human head. The best of the statues, though, are on the right—look out for the female elephant-goddess and the goddess of fire, with a strange rippled background to the carving. There is also a skeleton-like idol of the goddess Chamundi.

The small pavilion at the centre of the temple has a shrine with three more *yoginis*, bringing the total to 63—one of the idols is missing. The four male statues are of Bhairava—a particularly warlike form of Shiva.

Chaurasi

Thirty kilometres to the east of Hirapur is the village of Chaurasi (*map 8 C3*), home to the pretty little **Varahi Temple** (10th century), set amid the paddy fields. It is a fine example of mature Orissan sacred architecture. The temple is dedicated to Varahi, the female version of the boar-headed god Varaha, who is the third avatar of Vishnu. The richly decorated sanctuary tower is rectangular (like the Vaital Temple in Bhubaneswar), and was built separately from the *mandapa*, or assembly hall. There is some mild erotica on the tower and the frieze below the upper roof of the *mandapa*.

Note the fine image of Surya in the external niche at the back of the sanctuary, in which the sun-god is shown holding two lotus flowers and seated on a chariot, driven by seven tiny horses and a minute charioteer.

Puri

This large coastal town (*map 8 C3*), 50km south of Bhubaneswar, is an unusual mixture of the sacred and the profane. It is the site of one of Hinduism's most important places of pilgrimage, the Jagannath Temple, as well as being a British-style seaside town, used as a summer residence by the British governor during the colonial period. Later it was briefly a minor destination on what became known as the 'hippy trail' in the 1960s and 70s. There are fewer foreign visitors now, and the seaside hotels and guest houses are full of holidaymakers from Kolkata. Puri has a long sandy beach, with huge waves and strong currents.

The 12th-century **Jagannath Temple** is dedicated to Jagannath, a form of Krishna. Only Hindus are allowed inside; non-Hindus can get a view of the temple, known in British times as the 'White Pagoda', from the roof of the Raghunandan Library (for a small fee). The impressive curvilinear tower of the main sanctuary is 56m high.

JUGGERNAUT

Every summer, the Rath Yatra (or 'chariot journey') festival takes place, in which a series of decorated vehicles, or chariots—with the largest bearing an image of Lord Jagannath—go in procession through the streets of Puri. It is from the vehicles in this festival that the English word 'juggernaut' comes. Early British accounts describe how Hindu pilgrims would be killed beneath the wheels of the chariot—and that is how the English word juggernaut came to mean both a very large vehicle and something unstoppable.

KONARAK

The 13th-century Sun Temple at Konarak (*map 8 C3*, sometimes Konark), 50km south-east of Bhubaneswar, is one of the finest Hindu temples in the country. The combination of its sheer size, partially ruined condition, the exceptional quality of its mainly erotic carvings and also its picturesque setting make a visit to this magnificent building unforgettable. It is a supremely confident example of Hindu sacred architecture—an enormous stone-built monument that looks as if it floats above the ground, an effect accentuated by its being designed to resemble a chariot. It has 12 intricately carved giant wheels, pulled by a team of seven horses—all frozen in stone. It also has several exuberantly carved naturalistic colossal statues of animals, quite unlike any other sculpture that was being produced in this period anywhere else in the world.

History: Konarak is now 2.5km from the sea, but when it was built in the 13th century the coast was much closer and the temple served as a beacon for seafarers. Less than 30km further down the coast is the great Hindu pilgrimage town of Puri, and the Jagannath Temple. However, it is still not clear why King Narasimha of the eastern Ganga Dynasty chose this site for the greatest of the Orissan temples. The reason for its construction is also opaque—though it is thought likely that Narasimha commissioned it as a memorial to mark his army's victory over Muslim invaders. The temple was both admired and despoiled by later Muslim rulers of the region. Emperor Akbar's chronicler Abu Fazl wrote that, 'even those whose judgement is critical and who are difficult to please stand astonished at its sight'. By the early 19th century the British had renamed the temple the 'Black Pagoda', in contrast to the 'White Pagoda' at Puri. Part of the tower of the sanctuary was still standing in the 1830s, but collapsed soon after. The base of the temple and its famous chariot wheels were covered in sand, and 'rediscovered' during excavations in the early 20th century. At the same time the inside of the temple was filled with sand through a funnel to stop it collapsing. Unlike the great temples of Jagannath at Puri and Lingaraj at Bhubaneswar, the Konarak Temple is no longer a place of worship, and the idol of Surya the sun-god, which stood at the heart of the sanctuary, disappeared many centuries ago.

Orientation: The temple (*open daily dawn–dusk*), which is aligned on an east–west axis, is approached from the ticket office in the east. If you want every erotic scene described in clinical detail, hire one of the local guides waiting outside—they specialise in trying to embarrass visitors. The Konarak Temple complex consists of the enormous main temple building at the centre of the walled compound. The tower of the temple sanctuary has collapsed, and the tallest structure in the complex is the pyramidal roof of the *mandapa*, or assembly hall, of the temple. In front of the temple, closest to the entrance, is a separate columned building on a high plinth, known as the Bhoga Mandapa, which is believed to have served as a dance hall. In the grounds of the complex are two minor temples and the remains of the temple kitchen, as well as free-standing sculptures of elephants and horses, aligned with the temple's north–south axis.

Bhoga Mandapa

This square building, probably a dance pavilion, is raised up on a plinth, with rich carvings covering its lower walls and a staircase on each of its four sides. The eastern staircase, nearest the entrance gate, has two enormous and extraordinary sculptures, each showing a fierce lion rearing over a subdued, kneeling elephant that holds a prostrate human figure in its trunk. The quality of the rest of the carvings on the dance pavilion is not as fine as on the main temple, though still worth close inspection. There are excellent views of the upper part of the roof of the main temple from the plinth of the pavilion.

The walls of the Sun Temple plinth

The lower part of the temple, consisting of an enormous plinth, much of it buried for centuries beneath sand, consists of friezes and carvings of quite exceptional quality. At the eastern side next to the dance pavilion, at the foot of the steps leading into the temple entrance, are the remains of seven large stone horses; immediately behind each team of horses are the first two of the temple's intricately carved wheels. With this architectural innovation, the temple is converted into a colossal chariot. Each wheel has eight spokes and its own circular medallion and protruding central axle, complete with axle pin. The 4m-high lower walls have a profusion of carving: as well as the famous erotic scenes, the subject matter also covers domestic themes and depictions of animals. One small tableau on the southern side shows an old woman, presumably departing on a pilgrimage: a grandchild clings to her as she blesses her son, while her daughter-in-law touches her feet. There are also court scenes, including a famous one where the king riding an elephant appears to be receiving the gift of a giraffe, native only to Africa, from a group of petticoat-wearing foreigners. Elephants and horses are part of almost every frieze, but notice also the dragon-like mythical animals, and the half-human, half-snake creature, with its tail coiled round a pillar.

Eastern entrance door

Having walked around the entire lower wall and seen each of the 12 wheels, climb the main staircase, between the teams of chariot horses, to see the magnificent eastern entrance door of the temple. This gateway, fashioned from green chlorite stone, consists of eight architraves, each with its own distinctive motif. The motifs are broken only at the centre of the roof of the doorway, with small tableaux, and, at each end, by tiny gods carved into the stone. The interior has been bricked up, and a large stone-carved sign declares: 'To preserve this superb specimen of old Indian architecture the interior was filled by order of the Hon'ble J.A. Bourdilon, ISO Lieutenant Governor of Bengal. AD 1903'.

The temple walls

The walls of the actual temple building have large sculptures, carved in the round and much more vivid than those on the lower walls. Many of these are sexual couplings, which leave nothing to the imagination, but there are also mythical beasts, friezes and, on the higher levels of the pyramid-shaped roof, a series of finely sculpted musicians, which unfortunately are too far away to see in great detail. The area behind the pyramidal roof is the site of the tower of the temple sanctuary, now in ruins. There are, however, three large chlorite sculptures of Surya, the sun-god. On two sides, the south and the west, Surya is shown bejewelled, wearing long boots and standing in a chariot, pulled by seven tiny horses, framed in the frieze below the god's feet. The southern Surya statue has a topknot, whereas the western Surya has a crown. The kneeling figure, with a sword by his side in both sculptures, is thought to be King Narasimha. The other kneeling figure is thought to be Narasimha's chief priest. Notice how, with the southern statue, the upper torso of Surya's charioteer has survived between the feet of the god. The third statue of Surya, on the north side, shows the sun-god riding a horse—here the tiny figures of the king and his priest are standing upright, not kneeling.

Guardian animals

In the grounds of the complex, set on plinths on the north and south sides of the temple, are extraordinarily animated statues of elephants and war-horses that deserve close inspection. These statues were originally placed at the bottom of the north and south staircases, as guardians and protectors of the temple facing outwards. Now they face inwards, placed in their current positions in the 20th century. Note how much detail and action have been put into the statues of the horses, particularly the one on the right, which rears over a defeated human opponent who clings onto his sword and cowers beneath his shield. The elephants, too, are portrayed in action, each carrying the body of a lifeless soldier in its trunk. There are several other free-standing animal sculptures scattered around the complex.

Mayadevi Temple

This smaller shrine, which was excavated from the sand in the early 20th century, is known as the Mayadevi Temple, after one of the wives of Surya, and is in the southwest corner of the complex. It is thought to predate the main Konarak Temple, with which it shares several decorative and structural features. The roof of the Mayadevi Temple has entirely disappeared, though that does mean that, unlike the main temple, it is possible to enter the interior of the building. The exterior has two more Surya statues carved from chlorite, one on horseback, the other standing (now headless). Note the interesting sea-monster water-spouts carved out of chlorite near the base of the building. The one nearest the main temple has a fish in its mouth. Just beyond the Mayadevi Temple is a still smaller shrine, built out of brick, that was excavated in 1956. It is thought to have been dedicated to Vishnu.

Navagraha architrave

Outside the temple complex and slightly to its north, in a modern building, is part of the carved chlorite *navagraha* architrave from the eastern gateway to the main temple. The only part of the temple used for active worship, it is known as the *navagraha*, or nine planets, and is a relief panel carrying images of the gods associated with each planet.

Konarak Museum

A short walk to the north of the complex is the little-visited museum (*open Sat–Thur 10–5*), which has more fine carvings recovered from the main site. Note the sandstone image of a kissing couple, and a chlorite carving of the king praying to three gods. The museum garden has some excellent carved statues of mythical animals.

WEST, NORTH & EAST OF BHUBANESWAR

Simhanath

The 8th-century Simhanath Temple is on an island in the Mahanadi River, 45km west of Bhubaneswar (*map 8 B3*), and most easily approached by a short ferry ride from Baideshwar on the southern bank. This early Orissan temple—dedicated to Shiva though named after the lion avatar of Vishnu—has some very fine sculptures in its arched recesses. It is similar in design to the Parasrameshwara temple in Bhubaneswar.

Cuttack

About 30km north of Bhubaneswar (*map 8 C3*), this former capital of Orissa is almost encircled by the waters of the Mahanadi Delta—one of the reasons it was replaced by Bhubaneswar as the administrative centre of the state in 1948. Modern Cuttack is a congested city, best known for its Barabati Cricket Stadium and the ruins of a 13th-century fort of the same name. The stones of **Barabati Fort** were used in the time of British rule to build an embankment, and today only the moat, a gateway, and the ruins of what was once a nine-storey palace are still visible.

THE DIAMOND TRIANGLE

Three excavated sites (5th–13th centuries BC), nicknamed the Diamond Triangle, give a fascinating insight into the life and art of the later Buddhist period. They are easily visited on a day trip from Bhubaneswar, and are set in fertile countryside on the northern side of the Mahanadi Delta (*all on map 8 C3*). The sites have been excavated recently and, unusually, many of the finds are still *in situ* rather than in an urban museum elsewhere in India or abroad. Ratnagiri is the richest and most impressive, Udayagiri is the prettiest and most romantic, while Lalitgiri is the largest and most architecturally important.

Orientation: Udayagiri and Ratnagiri are on the same road, about 10km apart. To reach them, take the highway towards Paradeep (by turning off the main Bhubaneswar–Kolkata road) and then take the first left. Udayagiri comes first, after 10km, set in the cleft of a hill on the left, and then Ratnagiri after about 20km. For Lalitgiri, return to the Paradeep highway, head towards Paradeep and then take the first major road on the right.

Udayagiri

There are two parts to the Udayagiri site—the upper and lower excavations—and both are approached from the car park, around which some Buddhist statues have been placed.

Upper excavations: To reach the first part of the site, head to the left and uphill, where there are the ruins of two monasteries and various other buildings. There are dozens of smaller shrines, and large statues lying around the site, including a finely carved Tara (a female *bodhisattva)* and a particularly impressive seated Buddha inside the central shrine of the rearmost monastery. On the left there is also an enormous relief carving of Avalokiteshwara, the *bodhisattva* of compassion, lying on the ground. Notice also the smaller statues of lions and carved gryphons at the back of the first monastery.

Lower excavations: The most recent excavations at the Udayagiri site are to the right from the parking area, on level ground. They include an excavated stupa with a Buddha statue in the shrine, and a monastery with outbuildings. Both parts of the site have some very fine statues strewn about—including, again, images of Tara and Avalokiteshwara. The monastery building also has some superb carvings around the door frame of the shrine.

Ratnagiri

This superb site is thought to have once been the principal centre of Buddhism in Orissa. Unlike Udayagiri, the main monuments are situated around the top of a low hill. The site contains two monasteries, one of which is in unusually good condition, a stupa and a number of smaller temples and shrines. There are some extremely beautiful carvings strewn around the site, some just sticking out of the ground, unexcavated. Archaeological work is continuing here—and more Buddhist treasures are being unearthed every year. This site probably has the finest collection of *in-situ* sculpture from the late Buddhist period to be found anywhere in India.

The **main monastery** consists of a large courtyard, with smaller cells inside, and a shrine at the rear with a Buddha statue inside. The courtyard has become an impromptu museum for a quite dazzling display of Buddhist statues and carvings. Unusually, almost the entire ground floor of the monastery is intact, and there are even steps leading up to what was once a second floor. The door frame of the main gate, finely carved, is made of green chlorite and is intact. Note the sophisticated drainage system in the far left corner of the courtyard. Just next to the north door is another smaller monastery, and beyond that a recently excavated site, from which a Hindu temple had to be moved (it has been rebuilt a little further down the hill). Recovered from the temple building was a huge relief carving of the *bodhisattva* Manjushri. Grouped around the brick stupa are dozens of other shrines, half-buried statues and carvings.

The nearby **Ratnagiri Museum** has some interesting exhibits from early excavations (including two enormous Buddha heads), but the best carvings and statues are to be seen—and sometimes tripped over—on the main site.

Lalitgiri

This recently excavated Buddhist centre of learning is thought to be the oldest of its kind. There is much less decoration than at the other two sites, but there are the remains of a large apsidal, or horseshoe-shaped, hall, which was probably a temple and place of assembly for monks. There is also a monastery with the bottom half of a Buddha, a small museum with some fine Buddhist figures, and a restored hilltop stupa with some excellent views of the surrounding countryside.

BHITARKANIKA & BALASORE

Travellers to the **Bhitarkanika National Park** (*map 8 C3*), famous for its turtles and crocodiles, should visit the **Rajkanika Palace**, belonging to the minor former princely state of Kanika, 105km northeast of Bhubaneswar and 7km before Chandbali—the main access point for the park.

Much further northeast of Bhubaneswar—about 180km—is the town of **Balasore** (*map 8 C2*, also Baleswar), which was once an important European trading post on the Burabalang River. It is just 10km from the small beach resort and missile-testing site at Chandipur-on-Sea. There is an old British cemetery in the part of the town known as Dinamardinga, while there are some Dutch tombs behind the Government Girls' School.

WESTERN & NORTHERN ORISSA

The western parts of Orissa are largely tribal forest lands, and are also rich in natural resources such iron ore and bauxite—which has led to confrontation between large mining corporations and local residents. The few tourists who come to western Orissa largely do so either to visit the tribal villages, particularly around Jeypore in the far southwest of the state, or for the nature reserves, of which Simlipal, to the north, is the best known. There are also several former princely states—with some interesting palaces—including those at **Baripada** (*map 8 C2*). Beyond Baripada—which is the capital of the former princely state of Mayurbhanj and the gateway to the Simlipal National Park (*map 8 C2*)—is **Khuching** with the important, partially reconstructed 11th-century Khichakeshvari Temple.

Ranipur Jharial

In the far west of the state is one of India's most remote groups of important Hindu shrines at Ranipur Jharial (*map 8 A3*), beyond Titlagarh in the Bolangir district. The main temple is the **Chausath Yogini Shrine** (10th century), built, like the one at

Hirapur (*see above*), to a circular design. It sits on a rock outcrop and is dedicated to 64 goddesses, statues of which are kept within the small sanctuaries around the inside of the temple. A pavilion at the centre houses a three-headed statue of Shiva. On a nearby rock surface are dozens of small temples, many consisting of little more than a tower and a sanctuary. At the bottom of the outcrop is the 10th-century **Indralath Temple**.

SOUTHERN ORISSA

The road to southern Orissa and Andhra Pradesh goes past **Chilka Lake** (*map 8 B3*), an enormous coastal lagoon famous for its birds and dolphins.

Ganjam

This small coastal town (*map 12 D1*), just south of Chilka Lake, has an interesting 18th-century British **fort** and **cemetery** in a picturesque location overlooking a sandy estuary. Ganjam was once an important trading port under French and then British rule, and the British built the fort as a defensive citadel and customs office. The inner part of the fort is pentagonal, with spear-shaped bastions attached to each angle of the pentagon. The walls are largely intact, but the residential buildings inside are in ruins. Several buildings, including a temple reputedly much older than the fort, are in better condition. The fort has three entrances: a land gate, a sea gate and a 'secret' exit route marked in modern times by blue paint. About 300m away is a surreal cemetery, visible from the fort. It contains dozens of enormous funerary megaliths—in the shape of obelisks, urns and vases with a pale blue finish—that tower over the surrounding fields. The graves date from the 1780s to the 1850s.

Gopalpur-on-Sea

This small resort town (*map 12 D1*) was built in British times and has a rather jaded feel. Among the remaining British bungalows on the sea front are one called 'Waverley' and another called 'Brighton Villa'. There is also a lighthouse, which is open to the public, and some superb beaches to the south of the town.

PRACTICAL INFORMATION

GETTING THERE & GETTING AROUND

Bhubaneswar has Orissa's only commercial airport. It has daily connections to India's major cities. There are also good train connections from Kolkata to Bhubaneswar (7hrs) and Puri (9½hrs), as well as local services from Bhubaneswar to Puri (1½hrs) and Balasore (3hrs). The roads near the coast are normally in good condition, while those in the hills are often very slow. Auto-rickshaws are available in most towns.

ACCOMMODATION

• **Bhubaneswar:** There is a wide range of comfortable accommodation in Bhubaneswar. The modern **Trident Hotel** (*$$$; T: 0674 2301010; tridenthotels.com*) in the north of the city is probably the most luxurious hotel, while the Taj-run **Ginger Hotel** (*$; T: 0674 6663333; gingerhotels.com*), just opposite the Trident, provides more basic accommodation, but is highly recommended.
• **Gopalpur-on-Sea:** The existing hotels are relatively simple in this coastal town, and the best of these is the **Swosti Palm Resort** (*$$; T: 0680 2242455; swosti.com*). However, the Oberoi group is planning to reopen its old beachfront hotel in Gopalpur-on-Sea.
• **Puri:** The town has a large number of hotels on its long beachfront. The **Mayfair Beach Resort** (*$$$; T: 06752 227800; mayfairhotels.com*) is probably the best. The **Toshali Sands Resort** (*$$; T: 06752 250571; toshalisands.com*) is between Konarak and Puri.

FOOD

The local cuisine of Orissa is one of the least known in India, partly because of its similarity to Bengali cooking. In the coastal areas there is, predictably, a strong emphasis on seafood—and even in the hill areas most people are non-vegetarian. Rice is the main staple. Orissa's best-known dish is *pakhal*, rice left to ferment overnight, which is sometimes mixed with yoghurt—but it is rarely available in tourist restaurants. Many Orissans claim that the *rosgolla*, the syrupy ball of cheese and semolina that is widely seen as a typical Bengali dessert, is actually from Orissa.

The **Fish and Prawn Restaurant** (*T: 0674 2301936*) in Jaydev Vihar in Bhubaneswar is recommended for seafood.

The **Wildgrass Restaurant** (*T: 094370 23656*) in Puri has local seafood dishes, while the seafood *dhaba* (roadside café) on the main road south at Chilka Lake also does superb fish and crab.

FURTHER READING

John Beames' *Memoirs of a Bengal Civilian* (Eland, 2003) is an interesting account by a 19th-century British civil servant, a large part of which deals with his time in Cuttack and Balasore. Prafulla Mohanti's *My Village, My Life* is an account of growing up in a coastal village in Orissa.

GOA

The small western Indian state of Goa (*map 13*) has become synonymous with beach tourism, and attracts large numbers of foreign visitors, many of them on charter flights, particularly over the Christmas and New Year period. Many of them never leave the beaches. But Goa—the headquarters until 1961 of Portugal's Indian territories—has a great deal more to offer than just its beautiful coastline and excellent tourist infrastructure. It has some of India's finest churches and forts, and some superb colonial mansions. Its mixed Catholic and Hindu heritage, together with strong surviving Portuguese architectural and culinary influences, make Goa quite unlike any other place in India, allowing for fascinating trips into the lush riverine interior of the state. In fact, until recently, all the major population centres were inland or along estuaries; only with the development of mass tourism has the coastline been developed.

Goa can be divided into three distinct parts, with rather different histories and traditions. The northern part of Goa has many of the state's busiest beaches, and extends to the Maharashtra border. It is predominantly Hindu and Marathi-speaking, unlike the rest of the state, which is more Catholic and Konkani-speaking. The central part of the state, around the broad estuaries of the Mandovi and Zuari rivers, has the capital, Panjim, the evocative ruins of the earlier Portuguese settlement at Old Goa and the airport at Dabolim. It stretches back into the rivers of inland Goa; while the far south of the state, beyond Margao, is less developed for tourism, and it is still possible to walk for miles along the coast without meeting other visitors.

Tourism now plays a major role in Goa's economy, which traditionally had relied on trade, fishing, and coconut and cashew nut products. Some locals are unhappy at the way they feel the arrival of so many visitors from India and abroad has threatened Goa's distinctive culture.

HISTORY OF GOA

Little is known of Goa's early history, though it is thought to have been part of the 4th-century BC Mauryan Empire, and its coastal position would almost certainly have made it part of the Indian Ocean trading routes that predated the European arrival on western India's Malabar coastline. The oldest surviving buildings in Goa date back to the Hindu Kadamba Dynasty, which ruled parts of Goa and northern Karnataka between the 11th and 13th centuries. This was followed by periods of rule by neighbouring dynasties, including the Vijayanagar Empire based in Hampi and two Muslim sultanates, the Bahmanids of Gulbarga, who built a settlement near Pilar, south of Panjim, and the Adil Shah sultans of Bijapur, who are thought to have developed what is now known as Old Goa as a port for Muslim pilgrims making the Haj to Mecca.

The Portuguese arrival: The first Portuguese ships to arrive in India in 1498, under the command of Vasco da Gama, headed further south to Calicut and later Cochin.

Their ostensible aim was to secure the trade route to the East Indies, and bring valuable spices back to Europe. It was not until February 1510 that a Portuguese fleet, under Alfonso de Albuquerque, appointed by Lisbon as 'Governor of India', arrived off the coast of Goa. The Portuguese defeated the Bijapur forces and briefly occupied the city of Old Goa, before being driven out. They returned later in the year and, on 25th November 1510, reoccupied Goa; they would not leave for another 441 years. By 1543, the Portuguese had conquered most of Goa's heartland, which later became known as the Old Conquests. Goa became the most important of Portugal's Asian territories and the base for Catholic missionaries, of whom Francis Xavier was the most important. There were many forced conversions to Catholicism, and the Inquisition was introduced in 1560 as a way of preventing heresy. Many were tortured and executed—and the Inquisition was not discontinued until 1774. The main regional rivals to the Portuguese during the late 17th and 18th centuries were the Marathas, who briefly captured large parts of Goa in 1680.

Portuguese Goa and the British: In the latter half of the 18th century, the Portuguese acquired more territory, partly as a reward for having helped the British at the Battle of Srirangapatnam (*see p. 26*); these territories were integrated into Goa and known as the New Conquests. By the mid-19th century, with British supremacy in India undisputed, Goa's importance began to decline—and Portuguese rule was challenged by a series of peasant-led rebellions, largely in response to heavy taxation. However, Portugal was able to retain Goa as a colony (along with its other smaller coastal settlements of Daman, Diu, Dadra and Nagra Haveli) after the rest of India gained its Independence. Eventually, after some brief skirmishes, the Portuguese were expelled from Goa in 1961, and the territory became part of India.

Konkani, Marathi and English are all widely spoken in Goa. Although Portuguese is dying out as a written and spoken language, Portuguese influence over Goa's architecture, cuisine and religious practices remains very important; and most villages and all towns have churches built mainly in the Portuguese Baroque style, with large whitewashed curvilinear façades and ornate interiors. Secular Portuguese buildings tend to be long and low, with handsome white façades and red tile roofs. They are usually built out of the heavily weathered red laterite stone, which is ubiquitous in Goa.

The state of Goa has a Hindu majority, but Christians form a large minority of over 25 percent, and there is a much smaller Muslim community. Goa has a smaller area than any other Indian state, and with about 1.5 million inhabitants it has the fourth smallest population after the northeastern states of Sikkim, Arunachal Pradesh and Mizoram.

PANJIM

Panjim (*map 13 A2*, officially Panaji) is one of India's most relaxed state capitals, prettily situated on the southern bank of the estuary of the Mandovi River. It was the site of an important palace from the pre-colonial Adil Shahi period, and was one of the first places occupied by the Portuguese. It was used as the Portuguese temporary headquarters in the early 16th century, and the main church was originally built in this period. However, Old Goa soon became the Portuguese capital, and the area around Panjim declined in importance. In the 18th century, partly because of epidemics affecting Old Goa as well as the silting up of the Mandovi, key government offices, including the viceregal residence, were moved to Panjim. It became the official capital of Goa in 1843, and the headquarters of Portugal's empire in Asia.

Orientation: The city has a long waterfront on the Mandovi estuary, some of it on reclaimed land. Inland is a high ridge running north–south, which separates the western part of the city, with the main government buildings, from the eastern part, which contains the old Portuguese residential quarter known as Fontainhas. The museum and the bus station are in the most easterly part of Panjim, on the other side of the Ourem Creek, and are close to the two bridges over the Mandovi that lead to the beaches and towns of north Goa. Panjim is an easy city to walk around, and the best place to start is probably the former State Secretariat, overlooking the Mandovi River.

CENTRAL PANJIM

State Secretariat

The former State Secretariat (mainly late 18th century) is a long whitewashed two-storey building with an arched stone entrance, close to the Mandovi River in central Panjim. It was built on the site of a 15th-century palace erected by the Bijapur sultan, Yusuf Adil Shah, and which was known by the Portuguese as Idalcão's Palace—a corruption of the name Adil Khan, one of the sultan's titles. Under the Portuguese, it served successively as the viceregal palace, then the central government office, or Secretariat, and it is still used now as an office by a number of government departments.

Head inland from the State Secretariat for a large square, which has a monumental column (1898) that once supported a bust of Vasco da Gama—placed here on the 400th anniversary of his landing in India—now replaced by a copy of Ashoka's lion capital, which serves as India's national emblem. Head to the eastern end of the square for an excellent view of Panjim's most important church, described below.

ABBÉ DE FARIA

Next to the Secretariat is an unusual bronze statue (1945) of the Goan priest Abbé de Faria hypnotising a young girl. José Custódio de Faria was one of the founding fathers of hypnotism as a therapeutic treatment. Born of mixed-race parents in northern Goa in 1756, he trained to be a priest in Europe, fought in the French Revolution and became a professor of philosophy in France. He died in Paris in 1819. Alexandre Dumas' fictional priest of the same name in *The Count of Monte Cristo* was based on de Faria.

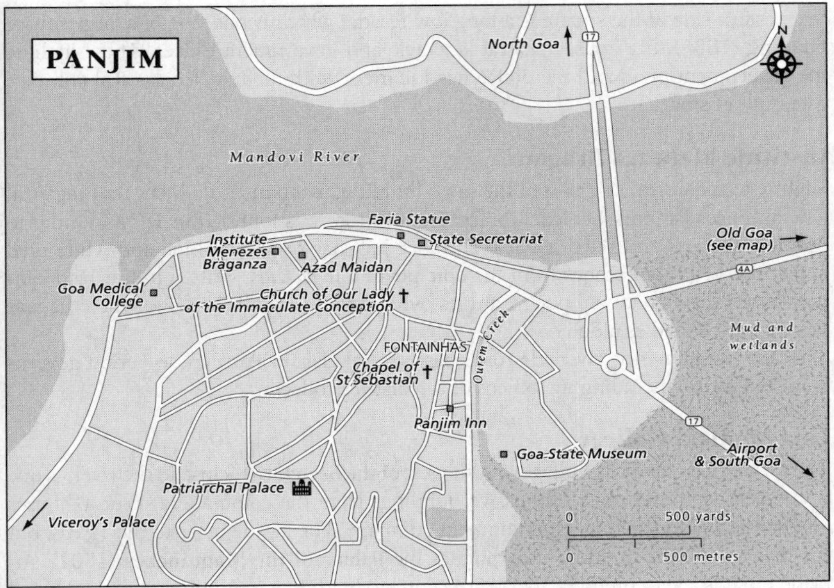

Church of Our Lady of the Immaculate Conception

This church (1540; rebuilt 1619) stands high on a ridge overlooking the western part of Panjim and is the city's best-known landmark (*officially open to visitors 10–12.30 & 3.30–5.30, but often open at other times as well—try the side door on the left*). It has impressive double flights of staircases built out of red laterite, with whitewashed balustrades that lead uphill from the street. There are two side towers, with a high bell tower, the huge bell of which once hung in the Augustinian church in Old Goa. Note the bell ropes hanging down the exterior of the building, with a notice-board imploring people not to ring them. The interior is less impressive but has a richly gilded main altar, and gravestones set into the mosaic floor. Behind the church, on top of the hill behind, is a small cross.

To the south of Our Lady of the Immaculate Conception is a road that leads to Fontainhas, and beyond that a road leads up to the imposing two-storey **Patriarchal Palace** (1894), on the summit of the hill known as Altinho, which is the home of the archbishop of Goa. Nearby is the less imposing but heavily guarded residence of Goa's chief minister.

WEST OF THE SECRETARIAT

A little to the west of the Secretariat, towards the sea and 100m from the river, is another smaller square (known as Azad Maidan, or Freedom Square) with memorials to those who died in the 'freedom struggle against Portuguese colonial rule in India'. On the western side of the square is a long low façade, which is one side of a large square building (1839) that houses several key civic and government offices. These include the government press and the police headquarters, with its fine Neoclassical entrance gate built of stone.

Institute Menezes Braganza

Slightly to the north, and part of the same building, is the Institute Menezes Braganza, which houses Panjim's Central Library. The institute was founded in 1832 in order to promote the arts and sciences. The entrance hall has some fine blue-and-white tiled depictions (1935) of scenes from the epic poem *The Lusiads*, written in the 16th century by Portugal's national poet, Camões, who visited Goa in 1553–54, where he was briefly imprisoned as a debtor.

Head west along the riverside road, past several elegant Portuguese-period government buildings, including the offices of the district collector.

Goa Medical College

The former Goa Medical College, 500m west of the Secretariat, close to the river, is one of the best-kept and most impressive buildings from the colonial era. It now houses government offices and an entertainment company. The façade dates to the 1920s, but the rear part of the building incorporates the **Palace of the Maquinezes** (1702). Attached to it is a very pretty chapel (18th century), with fine interior giltwork and wood carvings. Nearby, at Miramar Circle, near the city beach, is an old cannon, which marks the site of the dismantled Gasper Dias Fort.

FONTAINHAS

Head east from the Secretariat for Fontainhas, Panjim's Latin Quarter, with pretty Portuguese-style private residences. It is an interesting area to stroll around. One of the best examples of Portuguese domestic architecture is the **Panjim Inn** on 31st January Road, which is now a hotel (*see Accommodation, p. 655*), and was previously the home of the D'Silveira family. Nearby is the Neoclassical single-towered **Chapel of St Sebastian** (1888), on St Sebastian Road. It has an unusual wooden crucifix, showing Christ with his eyes open, which is said to have been originally in the Palace of the Inquistion in Old Goa, before being transferred to the chapel of the Secretariat in the 18th century, when it was occupied by the Portuguese viceroy.

On the other side of the Ourem Creek from Fontainhas is the **Goa State Museum** (*open Mon–Fri 9.30–5.30*), which has an interesting collection of Hindu and Christian art, as well as a wooden table used during the Inquisition in Goa.

THE VICEROY'S PALACE

The former Viceroy's Palace is on the headland at Capo Raj Bhavan, beyond Dona Paula beach, 6km southwest of Panjim. Originally a Franciscan convent and then the archbishop's residence, it is now the official home of Goa's governor and is normally closed to the public. However, if you present yourself at the gates at 9.30 on Sunday morning, you will be given a pass allowing you to attend Mass in the 16th-century chapel around which the palace was built. You can then wander around the outside area, close to the chapel and the nearby grotto. The former palace is a handsome arcaded building, with iron pillars and an enclosed wooden balcony. There are also glorious sea views, and it is possible to make out Fort Aguada to the north.

The **chapel** itself has a number of 17th-century memorial stones embedded in the wall, including that of Dona Paula (near the front on the left), after whom the nearby beach is named. According to local tradition, Dona Paula was a viceroy's daughter, who fell in love with a local fisherman and then threw herself off the cliff when prevented from marrying him. There is no historical evidence for this—and it seems that the real Dona Paula was a Portuguese benefactor married to a governor-general. At the southern end of Dona Paula Beach is the **British cemetery** (*push hard on the gate to get in—it appears locked, but is not*), which dates from the Napoleonic Wars, when British troops were based here to guard against a possible French invasion.

OLD GOA

The impressive churches and ruins of Old Goa (*map 13 A2*), 9km east of the modern city of Panjim, are the most important monuments of the early European colonial period in India. Old Goa, which overlooks the Mandovi River, was the headquarters of Portugal's Asian empire until the mid-19th century, when the capital was formally moved to Panjim, a short distance downstream. Most of the surviving buildings, which are spread over a wide area, are ecclesiastical, and represent the apogee of Baroque architecture in the Eastern hemisphere. The buildings are surrounded by well-kept gardens and lush jungle, and the overall setting is very picturesque. Almost nothing else remains of the great city that once stood here (known as the Rome of the East), and its civic buildings and great mansions have long since vanished.

History: This area was settled during the Adil Shahi period—remains of a gate from a pre-Portuguese palace have been re-erected near the Church of St Cajetan. According to some accounts, this site may have been the second capital of the Bijapur Sultanate. By the latter part of the 16th century, it was the most important Christian city of the east, with a population estimated at 200,000. However, the region was disease-prone, and suffered a number of serious epidemics in the 16th and 17th centuries, and it was nearly conquered several times by the Marathas. Gradually through the 18th century there was a shift of government and population to Panjim, and eventually in 1843 the capital was moved away. Already Old Goa was partly in ruins, and apart from some of the main churches, the Portuguese allowed the old city to decay.

Architecture: The buildings of Old Goa are almost all constructed out of laterite stone, with its distinctive red hue and weather-worn look; in most cases it was plastered over. For unadorned stone features, imported basalt was used. The architects were usually European, and though the artisans were Indian, there is little obvious trace of Indian architectural traditions. Most of the churches, particularly in their interiors, are examples of Baroque architecture, with façades that make extensive use of pediments, curving scrolls and volutes; and they often have high side towers. The interiors are usually richly decorated, often in gold, with twisted helical columns, coffered vaulted ceilings, richly painted wooden panels, statues carved from wood, and gilded wooden altars and pulpits.

Orientation: Most visitors enter Old Goa from the west, along the highway leading from Panjim, from which one can see some of the tops of church buildings peeping out through the trees. The most important group of buildings is gathered around a large central green area, which has small restaurants on its western side. On the north side of the green are the Church of St Francis of Assisi, museum and cathedral, while to the south is the Basilica of Bom Jesus, which houses the Tomb of St Francis Xavier, the most important Christian shrine in Goa. The superb ruins of the Augustinian convent are a short way up the hill to the west of the green, and two surviving hilltop churches—the Church of Our Lady of the Rosary, to the west, and the Church of Our Lady of the Mount, to the east—both provide superb views over Old Goa, the river and the surrounding countryside. (*The buildings of Old Goa are open daily 8.30 –5.30; only the museum charges an entrance fee.*)

Basilica of Bom Jesus

This church (1594–1605) dominates the southern side of the large central square of Old Goa. It is particularly distinctive because, unlike most of the other nearby buildings, its plaster finish has been removed and the red laterite, out of which all the buildings were constructed, is visible. The flying buttresses are later additions, intended to strengthen the northern wall of the church. The basilica is joined to a second large three-storey white building known as the Professed House (*see overleaf*). The name of the church literally means 'Good Jesus', but it is also widely known as the Church of St Francis Xavier, whose tomb it contains—a fact which makes it one of the most important pilgrimage sites in Asia.

The façade: The fine four-tiered façade—very austere by Portuguese standards—is built from carved basalt blocks set into laterite and has a hybrid design, drawing from Renaissance and early Baroque traditions. It makes use of the three Classical orders: Ionic, Doric and Corinthian. The highest tier bears the monogram IHS, widely used by Jesuits as a reference to Jesus—it represents either a Latin transliteration of the Greek spelling of Jesus, or is an acronym for Iesus Hominum Salvator or 'Jesus, the Saviour of Men'. Note the winged angels immediately around the monogram and in the tableau in which the monogram is set.

The interior: Apart from the richly decorated altar, the interior of the basilica is relatively plain. Immediately to the right is a painted wooden statue of a swaying St Francis Xavier with a cross in his hand. On the pillars nearby are Latin inscriptions marking

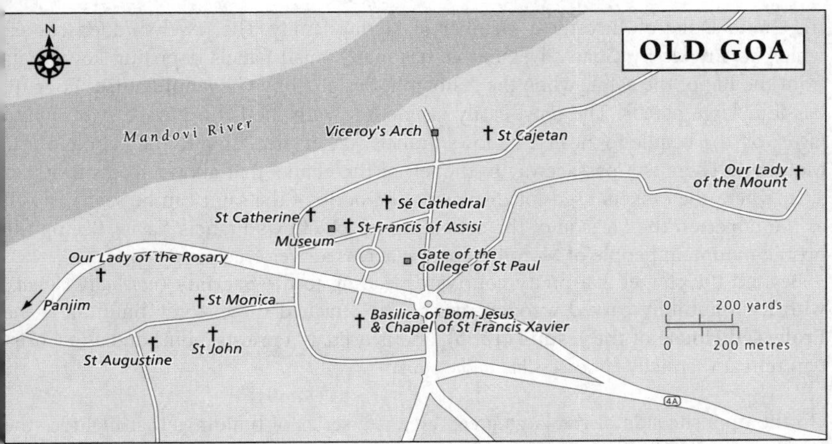

the consecration of the church in 1605 by the archbishop of Goa, and to the left is a niche with an altar dedicated to St Anthony of Padua, the 13th-century preacher who was born in Lisbon. Halfway along the nave on the northern (left) wall of the nave is the unusual gilded bronze memorial of the benefactor of the church, Jeronimo Mascarenhas, who died in 1593. On the southern wall is the richly gilded and carved pulpit, which the preacher would enter through a small door set into the wall—the carvings around the pulpit show Jesus at the centre, with the Four Evangelists and the Four Doctors of the Western Church (saints Gregory, Ambrose, Augustine and Jerome) at either side. Further on, there are side chapels in the transepts. The one on the north is the Chapel of the Blessed Sacrament, while to the south is the Chapel of St Francis Xavier (*see below*).

The altar: The richly gilded high altar, set inside a coffered and vaulted chancel, has the twisted columns and broken cornices and pediments of the Baroque style. Standing above a small central figure of the infant Jesus is a large statue of St Ignatius Loyola, the founder of the order of Jesuits, who stares devoutly upwards at the golden sunburst with its IHS monogram. Set into the upper tier of the altar are figures representing the Trinity (with the Holy Spirit depicted by a dove flying above the globe) and surrounded by cherubs. On either side of the main altar are two smaller altars: the one on the left is dedicated to the Virgin Mary; the one on the right to St Michael the Archangel.

Chapel of St Francis Xavier: This chapel (1655–98) occupies the south transept of the Basilica of Bom Jesus, and contains the body of the man who is most closely identified with the spread of Christianity to India and the Far East. He is often credited with having baptised more people than any other Christian evangelist.

The chapel is approached through a superbly decorated Baroque archway, with twisted columns and a broken pediment. The body of Francis Xavier is kept in a finely-wrought silver casket (1638) that rests on a marble cenotaph (1698) sent by Cosimo

III, Grand Duke of Tuscany, a member of Medici family. The jewel-studded casket, which was made by Goan silversmiths, has many small panels depicting key events from the life of the saint, while the cenotaph, designed by Giovanni Battista Foggini, has four large panels. The most easily visible one with the Latin phrase '*Nox inimica fugat*', or 'the hostile night flees', shows Francis Xavier preaching to the people of the Moluccas. There is a passageway to the left of the chapel that allows access to its far side, where the caskets used for displaying the body of the saint can be seen, as well as the tablet on the far side of the cenotaph, which shows Francis Xavier fleeing the hostile mountain people of Moro by floating across a river on a plank.

Beyond the chapel is a pretty courtyard, leading to the **Sacristy** (*normally closed*), with its beautifully carved wooden doors. The attached three-storey building is the **Professed House of the Jesuits** (1585), and is used as a priests' home and as a Christian retreat (*normally not accessible to the public*).

On the opposite side of the large green area is a series of buildings that includes the small Chapel of St Catherine and a complex of adjoining structures, including the Church of St Francis of Assisi, the museum and the cathedral.

Chapel of St Catherine

This chapel (1550) is the most westerly building on the northern side of the green, situated at a lower level than the other structures. It is a small, heavily restored north-facing building, and it marks the location of Goa's first church, built by Albuquerque in 1510 on the site of the gate through which he entered the former Adil Shahi city, which

ST FRANCIS XAVIER

St Francis Xavier (1506–52) was born in Spain and studied in Paris, where he met St Ignatius Loyola, whom he helped to found the Society of Jesus, better known as the Jesuits. He was appointed by King John III of Portugal to head a mission to spread Christianity in the East Indies, and arrived in Goa in 1542. Goa became his base, from where he travelled to the modern-day countries of Sri Lanka, Malaysia, Indonesia, China, Japan and possibly the Philippines. He died on the island of Sancian, off the coast of China in 1552, and his embalmed body was eventually sent back to Goa. However, his body is no longer intact. In 1614, his right arm was severed at the elbow and is now in the Church of the Gesù in Rome. Five years later, the rest of his right arm was cut off, and parts of it sent to churches he had visited in East Asia. One of his toes was bitten off by a Portuguese noblewoman who wanted to set up her own Francis Xavier Church, and though this toe was later recovered, three other toes are missing. The body of St Francis Xavier is put on display every ten years: winter 2014 and 2024 are the next scheduled public viewing dates.

he had conquered. The church was dedicated to St Catherine because Albuquerque's decisive victory over the Adil Shahis took place on St Catherine's Day—25th November 1510. The interior is bare—but notice the stone tablets set in the wall. The one on the left, marking a Portuguese victory in Diu and Cambay in 1547, shows St Martin on horseback giving half his cloak to a beggar. Nearby are parts of the ruined laterite walls that once surrounded Old Goa. The Royal Hospital and the Arsenal were both next to the Chapel of St Catherine, but nothing remains of either building.

Church of St Francis of Assisi

This large white four-storey west-facing building (1661) with octagonal side towers dominates this part of Old Goa, and has a superbly decorated interior. The Franciscans were the first of the Roman Catholic religious orders to come to Goa, having accompanied Albuquerque in 1510, and a Franciscan church was first built on this site in 1521.

The stone entrance is from the original church—it is in the Manueline, or Portuguese late Gothic, style that is rarely encountered in Goa. Manuel I (reigned 1495–1521) ruled Portugal during its great age of exploration, and the style of architecture associated with him has strong maritime and Oriental motifs—note the astrolabe on each side of the royal crest at the top of the gate, which was used as a symbol of exploration and as part of Manuel's personal coat of arms.

Inside the church is a low, painted arch that served as an internal buttress and which delays one's view of the full beauty of the altar. Note the large number of gravestones embedded in the floor of the nave. There are three small chapels on either side of the nave, including one dedicated to St Elizabeth of Portugal (Isabel in Portuguese) with a fine wood-carved altarpiece. Note that it is inscribed with the text of the *Nunc Dimittis* from the Gospel of St Luke, probably the best-known of Latin hymns. The main church altar is richly decorated in the Baroque style, filling the height of the chamber; note in particular the superb floral painted panels on the rib-vaulted ceiling. On the side walls are paintings depicting scenes from the life of St Francis, while the altar has a central arched opening that contains a tabernacle, carried by the Four Evangelists. Above, between the double-twisted columns, St Francis comforts Jesus on the cross.

Archaeological Museum

Next to the Church of St Francis of Assisi is a white two-storey building that was once a convent and is now the Archaeological Museum of Old Goa (*open Sat–Thur 10–5*). It has a fine collection of carvings, statues and paintings from both the pre-European and Portuguese periods. An enormous bronze statue of Albuquerque dominates the entrance hall, and is thought to have been cast during the lifetime of the commander who conquered Goa on behalf of the Portuguese—it stood in the main square in Panjim until Goa's independence from Portugal. There is also a more modern statue of Portugal's national poet, Camões, carrying a scroll of his poem *The Lusiads*; the statue used to stand in the central square of Old Goa. Among the pre-European exhibits are some Hindu carvings in basalt from the 9th to the 14th centuries, including a particularly fine standing Vishnu from the 13th century and an unusual 'hero stone' from the 12th century showing a king surrounded by umbrella-holding courtiers in the top panel, and a maritime invasion in the lower panel. The upstairs galleries are devoted to the Portuguese period, with a series of portraits of governors and viceroys covering the period 1505 to 1961. They were moved from the Secretariat (formerly Idalcão's Palace) in Panjim in 1962.

Heading east from the Church of St Francis towards the cathedral, one passes the old Archbishop's Palace (1608), which is actually joined to both buildings. It is a white two-storeyed building that now houses a small **modern art gallery** (*open Tues–Sun 9.30–5.30*), and it is possible to wander around inside. Note how the lower parts of the walls are painted in red, and the use of the motif of a double-headed eagle, the meaning of which is unclear here.

Sé Cathedral

The Sé Cathedral (1562–1652) is Goa's most important ecclesiastical building (the name Sé derives from the Portuguese for a bishop's see). It is dedicated to St Catherine and is one of Asia's largest churches. Work on building the cathedral began, at royal expense, during the reign of King Sebastian, in 1562, and the church was first used in 1619. However, it took another 33 years for the altars to be completed. Its east-facing whitewashed main façade is relatively austere, with only the Corinthian columns and carved stonework around the doorways and above the windows showing any real ostentation. Note the inscription over the main door marking the year when work started on the cathedral, and the Jesuit IHS monogram above the other doors. There is also the Portuguese coat of arms (which still forms part of the Portuguese flag) in the broken pediment above the first-floor window. One of the square towers collapsed after being struck by lightning in 1776. The surviving tower houses the Golden Bell, famous for its mellifluous sound.

The spacious interior of the cathedral contains eight separate chapels as well as the high altar. The largest of these is the Chapel of the Blessed Sacrament on the left, which is approached through a decorated archway and screen. The altar is richly gilded, and there are fine painted ceiling panels. Directly opposite is the Chapel of the Cross of Miracles with its superbly crafted wooden screen.

The high altar, at the end of the vaulted chancel, has some very fine sculpted wooden panels set between Corinthian pillars. The central panel on the lower level shows St Catherine of Alexandria holding a book—next to her is a wheel, the instrument on which she was tortured. The panels on either side show scenes from her life. There are six side altars including one dedicated to St Peter, in the upper panel of which Jesus is shown handing a set of keys to the apostle; beneath is the Latin *ego tibi dabo claves regni caelorum*, or 'I will give unto thee the keys of the kingdom of heaven'.

About 200m south of the cathedral is the **Gate of the College of St Paul** (1542), one of Goa's oldest Portuguese buildings, with Corinthian columns and Doric pilasters made of basalt. The actual college, which served as a training institute run by the Jesuits, was demolished in 1832.

Viceroy's Arch

To the west of the gate, in the central square of Old Goa, is the Viceroy's Arch (1599), 200m northeast of the cathedral and close to the river and the Church of St Cajetan. It was rebuilt on the site of an older gate by Governor Francisco da Gama to commemorate the centenary of the arrival in India of his own great-grandfather, Vasco da Gama. The gate would have been passed through by most new arrivals to Old Goa, just after disembarking at the river jetty 100m to the north. The arch collapsed in the 1940s and was rebuilt in 1954. The northern face of the gate has a statue of Vasco da Gama. Notice also the emblems beneath the statue: a deer, which was part of the family crest of the da Gama family, and astrolabes, which symbolised exploration.

The inner walls of the arch have two inscriptions: one that is related to the building of the arch, and another that is a stone-carved plaque set into the wall, marking the end of Spanish control over Portugal in 1656. It shows a kingly figure holding a sword above the inscription *Legitimo E Verdadeiro Rei Dom João IV Restaurador Da Liberdade Portuguesa* ('the legitimate and true King John IV, the restorer of Portuguese liberty'). Note the Portuguese coat of arms next to the sword. On the southern side of the gate there is a fine stone statue of a woman, thought to represent St Catherine; she is subduing a man who is thought to be one of the former rulers of Old Goa. The ruins of part of the old walls of the city can be seen nearby.

Church of St Cajetan

Just 200m to the east of the Viceroy's Arch is the distinctively Italianate Church of St Cajetan (1656)—which is in fact modelled on the Basilica of St Peter's in Rome, and is arguably one of India's finest churches. It was built by Italian members of the Theatine order of monks, set up in the early 16th century by St Cajetan (also known as St Gaetano), who had been sent on a papal mission to preach Christianity to the people of Golconda, near modern-day Hyderabad. They were denied entry to Golconda and stayed on in Goa, building this church and the neighbouring convent.

The high Corinthian columns and pediment of the façade, as well as the ribbed dome, are all borrowed from St Peter's in Rome, which had been completed in 1626. Statues of the Four Evangelists are in the niches on the lowest level of the façade, while there is an unusual variant of the Portuguese coat of arms over the door.

On entering, one's eyes are drawn up to the large glazed dome at the centre of the ceiling, through which light pours into the church. The drum of the dome is inscribed with the Latin words *Quaerite primum regnum Dei et justitiam ejus, et haec omnia adjicientur* (seek first the kingdom of God and his righteousness, and all other things will be given to you), from St Matthew's Gospel. Below the dome is a low stone table with the Latin phrase *filii tui in circuitu mensae tuae* inscribed around its edge—or 'thy children round about thy table', from Psalm 128. Beneath the table is a stone slab covering an old well, more than 22m deep.

The finely carved wooden altarpiece has a central image of a seated Mary, as Our Lady of Divine Providence, surrounded by angels. Behind the altar is a crypt, where the corpses of the viceroys were stored prior to being shipped back to Portugal for burial.

There are several other altars, statues in niches and oil paintings in the church—some of the paintings showing scenes from the life of St Cajetan.

In the garden in front of the church is a free-standing stone doorway, its pillars decorated with stone carvings, and the remains of a perforated screen. The doorway is thought to have been part of Adil Shah's Palace, and possibly part of a temple before that. The palace was used as the residence of the Portuguese governors until 1695, but by the 19th century the building had collapsed.

Church of St Augustine

To the west of the main square, up a steep road behind some restaurants, is a further group of impressive ecclesiastical buildings, dominated by the 42m tower of the ruined Church of St Augustine (1602), which was once thought the most impressive and beautifully decorated of Old Goa's churches. Large parts of the ruins have been excavated, and the site is well-labelled and carefully maintained.

The church, officially dedicated to Our Lady of Grace, was built by Augustinian friars in 1602 on the site of an older church. The main part of the building collapsed in 1842, but the impressive façade survived until 1931—there is a photo at the site that shows a façade very similar in design to the Basilica of Bom Jesus. The church once had eight chapels, four altars and a convent—the outlines and lower walls of which can be made out thanks to the recent excavations.

Note the gravestones embedded in the floor of what was the nave, and the fine reconstruction of tilework that once adorned the walls of the church. The main bell from the church was moved to the Church of the Immaculate Conception in Panjim.

The large plain building just to the east of the Augustinian Church is the Church and Convent of St John of God, constructed in the early 18th century and now a home for the elderly, run by Franciscan nuns.

THE GEORGIAN CONNECTION

The Church of St Augustine is believed to contain part of the body of Queen Ketevan of Georgia, who was tortured and killed on the orders of Shah Abbas I of Persia in 1624, for refusing to convert to Islam, and later canonised by the Georgian Church. One account claims that her mangled body was brought here by Augustinian friars and buried to the right of an altar—it is not clear which altar. Excavations continue, with strong interest from the Georgian Embassy in Delhi.

Church of St Monica

The still larger building to the south of the ruined tower, with flying buttresses disfiguring its façade, is the Church and Convent of St Monica (1606–37), part of which has been converted into a museum of Christian art. On the exterior, note the fine carved foundation tablet over the door, showing the bleeding Lamb of God, over the Latin words for the 'book of the life of the Lamb', a reference to the New Testament. Other parts of the façade have inscriptions and carvings, including an unusual depiction of a ship above a doorway, and different versions of the Portuguese coat of arms. There is a statue of St Monica, the 4th-century patron saint of married women and mother of St Augustine, in a high niche, partially hidden by one of the buttresses.

Inside there is a three-tiered altarpiece, with St Augustine at the centre of the lowest tier and St Monica immediately above. High above the altar, in what is known as a tribune, is the wooden figure of Jesus on a cross, known as the Miraculous Crucifix. It is said to have moved and bled in 1636, and remains one of the most venerated objects of Christian worship in Goa.

The **Museum of Christian Art** (*open daily 9.30–5.30*) has some fine examples of Indo-Portuguese craftsmanship, including silverware, ivories and wood carvings showing Christian images, some with traditional Indian motifs.

Church of Our Lady of the Rosary

The road that passes through the flying buttresses of the Church of St Monica leads up to the Church of Our Lady of the Rosary (1544–47). The church sits high on a hilltop in the most westerly part of Old Goa, and has superb views over the Mandovi River. It is one of Goa's earliest churches, and, unlike most of the other buildings of Old Goa, is built in the Manueline style, with high windows, curved turrets and a single tower. There is a 20th-century Portuguese inscription that Albuquerque witnessed the reconquest of Goa in November 1510 from these heights. Inside, the church is simply decorated, with two side chapels and three altars. Note the finely carved marble cenotaph of Catirina, the wife of the Portuguese Governor Garcia de Sá, which unusually makes use of the normally Islamic motif of the hanging vase—particularly associated with the late Sultanate and early Mughal periods.

Church of Our Lady of the Mount

On the far side of Old Goa, 1km east of the central square and up a winding road, is the hilltop Church of Our Lady of the Mount (1557), from where there are superb views of the Sé Cathedral, St Cajetan Church, the river and the lush tropical countryside. A Portuguese plaque on the external wall records that this position was occupied by the Muslim artillery while trying to defend Goa against the forces of Albuquerque in May 1510. The church itself is usually closed.

PILAR

Six kilometres to the south of Old Goa is Pilar, now an important place of pilgrimage for Roman Catholics, but which is thought to have been the original Govapuri (after which Goa was named), capital of the Kadamba Kingdom until the 14th century. Nothing remains of Govapuri. It is still widely and confusingly known as Goa Velha, meaning 'old Goa', which dates back to the time when what is now known as Old Goa was not called Velha Goa in Portuguese. The **Franciscan Capuchin monastery**

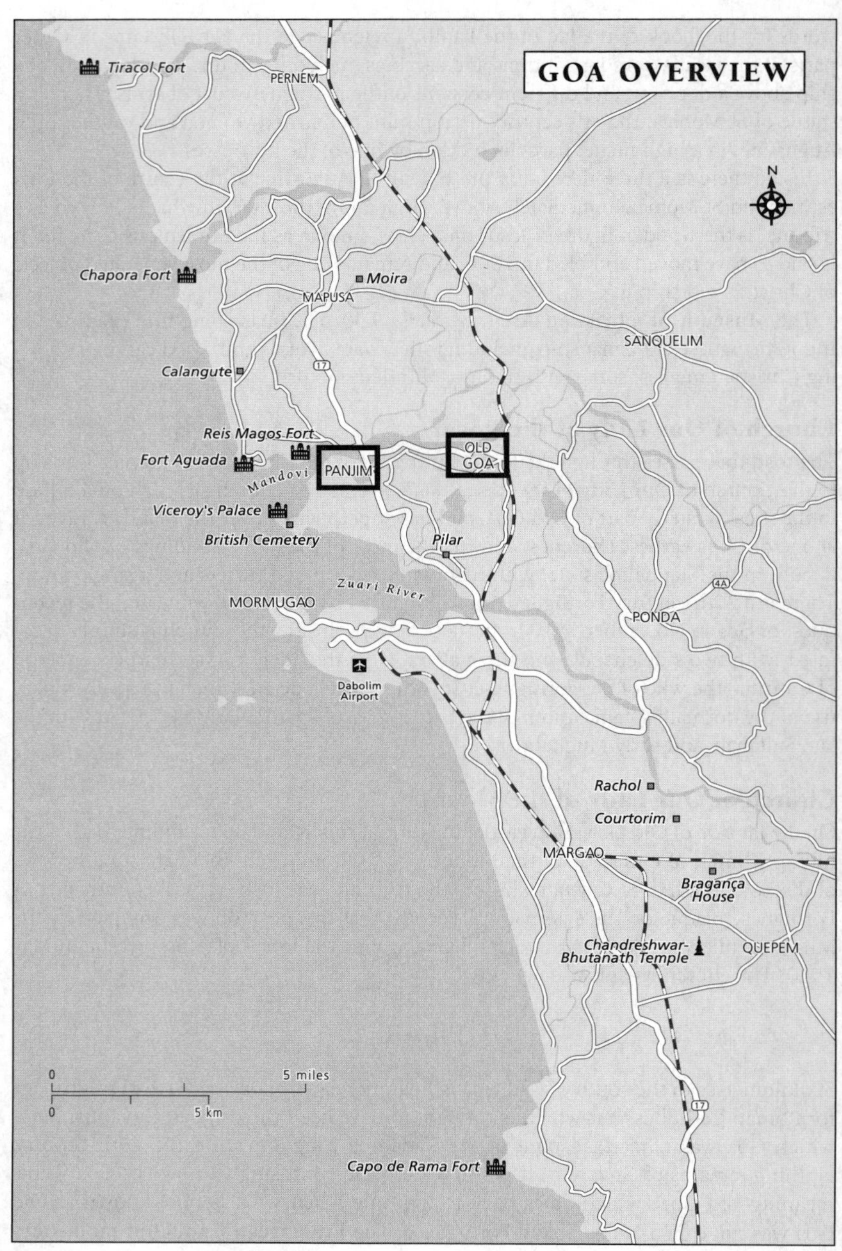

For a detailed map of Panjim see p. 637, for Old Goa see p. 641.

at Pilar was built in 1613, and has a fine carved stone doorway, with a statue of St Francis of Assisi over the portal. The main attraction for local pilgrims is the tomb of Fr Agnelo de Souza, who died in 1927, and who is now in the process of beatification. It is possible to visit the seminary and its huge blue-tiled confessional chamber, with many confession booths inside.

NORTH GOA

The coastline of north Goa is only about 30km as the crow flies, from Aguada (on the north side of the Mandovi estuary) to the Maharashtra border. In between, though, are several important forts, at least a dozen beaches and two major estuaries, one of which has to be crossed by ferry. The main inland town of the region is Mapusa, pronounced Mapsa, best known for its market.

Reis Magos Fort

This small triangular fort (1551) sits on a small headland, directly opposite Panjim's Miramar beach, overlooking the north bank of the Mandovi River. The fort, named after the nearby church, dedicated to the Reis Magos, or the Magi kings, was originally built in 1550, and rebuilt in 1707. It was one of the few places in north Goa that the Marathas were unable to conquer in the 17th and 18th centuries. The fort was later used as a prison, and is now being converted into a cultural centre. Note the circular turret, which allowed firing from all directions, and the discarded cannon with the Portuguese coat of arms. There is also a long steep defensive wall leading down to the river. Below is the whitewashed four-tiered east-facing Church of Reis Magos, which also dates from 1551 but was rebuilt in 1771.

Fort Aguada

This large fort (1609–12) sits at the end of a peninsular headland just north of Panjim, above and beside the well-known hotel resort that bears the same name. Aguada literally means 'watering-place', and during the Portuguese period many larger ships would pick up water (kept in the fort's enormous underground water tank) and other supplies from here. The main citadel of the fort sits on the hilltop, but other parts of the fort are to be found elsewhere, and include the impressive fort-like jetty found at the southern end of Candolim Beach and the inaccessible and still-functioning Aguada prison, overlooking the Mandovi estuary. The actual citadel is almost square in shape, and is surrounded on three sides by a deep rock-cut moat. The bastions are arrow-shaped, in common with many Portuguese forts, which would have made it very difficult for an invader to scale the walls. The interior of the citadel contains a small 19th-century lighthouse—there is a larger, more modern lighthouse a little to the west.

About 6km north of Aguada in Calangute is the **Church of St Alex** (1741) with towers, domes and Rococo mouldings over the arched doors and windows.

Chapora Fort

This large ruined walled fort (1717) was built at the top of a steep hill near the sea. It is situated 14km north of Aguada, overlooking the south side of the mouth of the Chapora River, and is just beyond Vagator Beach. It has superb views, particularly towards Morjim Beach on the other side of the river. The fort was originally built by the Adil Shahs, but was rebuilt by the Portuguese in 1717, at which point it marked the northern limit of Portuguese territory. It was captured by the Marathas in 1739, and was later retaken, by which time the acquisition of the territory known as the New Conquests had reduced the fort's military importance. The fort has two small gates, cannon emplacements and some ruined buildings. The church and barracks that once stood here have long since collapsed, and the interior is almost empty.

Around 4km east of Mapusa, north Goa's main town, is the **Church of Our Lady of the Immaculate Conception** (1636) in the village of Moira. The church façade, rebuilt at the end of the 18th century, is an important example of the Goan Rococo style—with its three towers, the outer one square and the middle one octagonal.

Fort Tiracol

Fort Tiracol (early 18th century), also known as Terekhol, lies 40km north of Panjim, close to Goa's border with Maharashtra (*map 13 A2*). It is possibly Goa's finest fort, set on a hilltop headland, overlooking the Terekhol estuary. The pretty 18th-century **St Anthony's Church** fills much of the interior—and the fort's sea-facing rooms have been converted into a hotel (*see Accommodation, p. 655*). Access to the fort from the beaches further south is by a public car ferry across the Terekhol, though there are land routes from Maharashtra and the interior of Goa. The fort was originally built by the Maratha rulers of Sawantwadi in southern Maharashtra, and captured by the Portuguese only in 1788. Tiracol was the scene of one of the few violent incidents of the independence struggle from Portugal, when two demonstrators calling for Goa to be integrated into India were killed by Portuguese forces in 1955. There is a small memorial outside the fort.

Just 6km north of Tiracol, across the border in Maharashtra, is the ruined **Redi Fort**, overlooking Paradise Beach. It too was built by the rulers of Sawantwadi. Close to the Maharashtra border, 14km east of Tiracol, is the town of **Pernem**, which has a largely 19th-century palace belonging to the Deshprabhu family, who were made viscounts under Portuguese rule. It is best to call in advance for access (*T: 083229 5642460*). The nearby **Mulvir Temple** at Malpem, 2km to the east, has interesting 18th- and 19th-century wall-paintings, depicting Vishnu, Krishna and various scenes from the *Ramayana*.

SOUTH GOA

The southern part of Goa, south of the Zuari River, has a longer coastline than the north, and its beaches are very busy near the airport at Dabolim, but almost empty further south towards the border with Karnataka. There is only one sea-fort, at Cabo de Rama, but the interior, around the large town of Margao, has many of Goa's most interesting buildings from the Portuguese period as well as the strange rock carvings of Usgalimol. In the east of the state, close to the road towards Londa and Hampi, is the 13th-century Mahadeva Temple of Tambdi Surla.

On the south side of the Zuari River, close to the road for the airport and Margao, is the ruined old Church of Our Lady of Health (1606) of Sancoale, the four-tiered façade of which, with its Corinthian pilasters and stucco figures over the doorways, is all that has survived.

MARGAO

Margao (*map 13 A2*), 15km south of the Zuari Bridge, is south Goa's main town and railway junction (the alternative spelling Madgaon is often used by the railways). The central square is dominated by the west-facing four-tiered **Church of the Holy Spirit**, founded in 1565 but largely rebuilt in its current form in 1675. Note the small canopied niche on the third tier showing the Virgin Mary with the Twelve Apostles, an image that is repeated in the main altar. The dove on the top tier represents the Holy Spirit.

The **Sat Burznam Gor**, literally the 'seven-towered house', 300m east of the church, is a fine example of 18th-century Goan domestic architecture. Only three of the 'towers' (really separate pyramidal roofs) survive, but the exterior of this many-windowed building is in excellent condition. Note the use of mother-of-pearl in place of glass for the windows. The da Silva family, whose ancestors built the Sat Burznam House, still occupies part of the building. There are several other old Portuguese buildings nearby.

AROUND MARGAO

Rachol

Eight kilometres to the north of Margao, close to the banks of the Zuari River, is the **Patriarchal Seminary** (1574–1610) at Rachol, still a training institute for priests. It no longer houses the Museum of Christian Art, which moved to the Church of St Monica in Old Goa. The seminary was once a fortified compound surrounded by walls and a moat. The low hill on which the seminary is built is thought to mark the site of a Muslim fort, and before that a Hindu temple. A gateway from the early colonial period survives with Doric columns and the Portuguese coat of arms. The seminary itself is built around an open courtyard; there are fine paintings and murals on the walls, many of which are in desperate need of restoration. Over the main door is King Sebastian of Portugal's coat of arms, along with an inscription recording that he founded these buildings. Note also the ubiquitous monogram IHS, used here as a symbol of the Jesuits. The chapel has a fine coffered vaulted chancel. Note the unusual side altar, with a prone statue of St Constantine, the Roman emperor who converted to Christianity, dressed as a soldier. There is also a small wooden statue of Christ, known as the Menino Jesus, or Child Jesus, which was taken from the church at nearby Colva and is thought to have miraculous properties.

Courtorim

The pretty Church of St Alex in Courtorim, 3km southeast of Rachol, between a lake and the Zuari River, has unusual octagonal side towers, capped by cupolas and lanterns. The altarpiece is a fine example of Goan Rococo, with golden Corinthian columns, an exuberant foliate arch, and cherubs and angels—while the tabernacle in front is represented as a small building.

Bragança House

The small village of Chandor is 10km east of Margao and contains one of Goa's best examples of Portuguese domestic architecture, the Bragança House (18th century). The Braganças were an aristocratic Portuguese family who later played an important role in the movement against colonial rule. This unusually long two-storey red-tiled building is now divided between the two branches of the family—the Menezes-Braganças (west wing) and the Pereira-Braganças (east wing)—but one of the apartments is usually open to the public (*10–5*). As well as having a pretty exterior, with a balcony for every first-floor window, the interiors are full of old furniture, glassware and crockery, and decorated in a traditional Portuguese style.

Quepem

The town of Quepem, 15km southeast of Margao (*map 13 A2*), has the **Palácio de Deão** (1787), or Dean's Palace—a superb mansion built at a time when the Portuguese were expanding into the territories known as the New Conquests. This region was incorporated into Goa only in 1782, when a young nobleman-priest, José Paulo de Almeida, in the service of the archbishop of Goa, set about building a settlement in the jungle. The mansion he built once overlooked a broad river, but this is now no more than a small stream because of silting and an upstream dam. After Almeida's death in 1835, the building was used as a holiday residence for the viceroys and governor of Goa. The palace has been beautifully restored, with period furniture and very pretty gardens. Its owners welcome visitors and will provide meals if booked in advance (*see p. 656*).

Chandreshwar-Bhutanath Temple

Some 4km west of Quepem, on top of a heavily forested hill, is the Hindu Shaivite Chandreshwar-Bhutanath Temple, from where there are superb views over the surrounding countryside. Most of the buildings are modern, but notice the Kadamba-period carved stone door frame, which is thought to date to the 13th century. There are also chariots for displaying the images of gods, which are kept in corrugated iron sheds. The large wooden chariot is particularly well carved and has some erotica on one side.

Rock carvings of Usgalimol

These fascinating and little-visited Stone Age rock carvings (c. 9000 BC) are in a remote area of Goa, more than 25km southeast of Margao and 6km southeast of the town of Rivona. There are also several old rock-cut Buddhist caves in the area. To reach the

Usgalimol (also known as Pansaimol) rock carvings, head south out of Rivona, past the Colamba Forest checkpoint, and follow the road until you reach a sign on the right that says 'protected site'. Then follow the marked track until you reach a small hut, occupied by a watchman, who will show you around the flat rock on which carvings were discovered in 1984 by locals who were cutting the rock for building materials. To the naked eye, the carvings are not immediately clear, but the watchman will pour water on the lines of the figures to help you see them. Among the more than 100 carvings cut into the laterite rock are representations of a dancing human, a woman giving birth, cows, deer, a peacock, fertility symbols and a labyrinth.

Cabo de Rama Fort

This is the only important sea-fort in south Goa and is situated on a headland between Mobor and Agonda beaches, about 25km southeast of Margaon (*map 13 A2*). It came under Portuguese control only in the 1760s, as part of the territorial expansion of Goa known as the New Conquests. The fort is named after the Hindu god Rama, who, according to local tradition, spent several years in exile here. This large fort is approached from inland Goa through thickly forested countryside. There is a deep rock-cut moat and a small entrance gate, the upstairs rooms of which were used until recently as a school. Inside there is a small church, dedicated to St Anthony, which is still in use at weekends. Two ruined rooms with barred windows behind the church were used as jails during the Portuguese period. Head westwards towards the sea for some superb views and another jail close to a ruined flagstaff building.

EAST GOA

The eastern parts of the state are visited by relatively few tourists compared with the western parts. The main tourist attractions here are the Spice Hills, the Bondla and Bhagwan Mahaveer nature reserves, and the Dudhsagar waterfalls. The small mosque at Ponda and the temple at Tambdi Surla are the only significant historic sites, while Hindu pilgrims visit the heavily restored and modernised old temples of this region, particularly the very popular Mangeshi Temple between Old Goa and Ponda. The **Arvalem Caves**, near Sanquelim, 21km east of Panjim, are in a pretty location and of early Buddhist construction, though unsophisticated compared to Buddhist caves found in the rest of the country.

Ponda

Ponda, 25km southeast of Panjim, has the oldest functioning mosque in Goa, the **Safa Masjid** (1560), built during the late Adil Shahi period—by which time the Portuguese were already in control of the coastal areas. The mosque consists of a small rectangular building, constructed out of laterite, with a single chamber, raised on a plinth next to a large rectangular pool. Note the arched niches around the base of the mosque and around the pond.

Tambdi Surla

The **Mahadeva Temple** at Tambdi Surla (12th–13th century) is the finest example of architecture from the Kadamba period. It has survived because of its isolation, situated in forests north of the main road from Goa to Karnataka (head north for 15km from the village of Molem on NH4a). The temple, dedicated to Shiva, is built from black basalt and has a broad low assembly hall, open to the east, covered with sloping stone slabs. The sanctuary has a multi-tiered tower with carvings of Brahma, Shiva and Vishnu on the exterior. Note the unusual carved pillars, the star-like shapes carved on the ceiling and the fine perforated screen in the porch.

PRACTICAL INFORMATION

Goa is both India's smallest state and the one with the best tourism infrastructure. Its economy is heavily dependent on tourism, particularly in the coastal areas. The beaches between Anjuna in the north and Benaulim in the south get very busy in the winter season, with large numbers of Indian and European tourists. If you're prepared to travel a little further, there are deserted beaches even in high season. Many repeat visitors to Goa say that the state is most beautiful in the monsoon, even though the sea is unsafe for swimming.

GETTING THERE

• **By air:** Dabolim Airport, near the tip of a peninsula jutting into the sea 19km south of Panjim, is the main entry route for most visitors to Goa. It is very well connected to other Indian cities, and has several daily flights from Delhi and Mumbai. It also receives many charter flights from Europe, particularly the UK and Russia during the winter season. Even the most distant parts of Goa can be reached from the airport in less than two hours. There are currently plans to build a second airport, either in north Goa or just over the border in Maharashtra.

• **By train:** Goa is not particularly well-served by trains. Its main railway station is not in Panjim, but in the southern town of Margao, though many trains go on to Vasco near Dabolim Airport. There are a number of long-distance train services (11hrs from Mumbai, 15hrs from Cochin-Ernakalum).

• **By bus:** There are several long-distance bus services to and from Goa, including buses from Mumbai (12hrs), Hampi (9hrs from Hospet) and Bangalore (12hrs); they operate from and to the Kadamba bus terminal in Panjim, and also serve some of the major beach resorts.

• **By road:** It is easy to hire a car and a driver to take you to and from your next destination, and this gives you greater flexibility in visiting places on the way than a scheduled bus. However, for visitors on a tight budget, it is cheaper to hire your car outside Goa, since local rates are higher, and foreigners are usually expected to pay more.

• **By boat:** At the time of writing there were no scheduled boat services to Goa, though some visitors do travel down the coast in hired boats.

GETTING AROUND

Goa has two major highways: the north–south NH17, which runs parallel to the coast several kilometres inland and passes through Panjim, and the NH4a, which runs east from Panjim into northern Karnataka towards Hampi. Taxis and auto-rickshaws are widely available throughout Goa, though it is best to agree a rate before heading off—and to take local advice on rates. The cost of travelling tends to be higher in Goa than elsewhere in India.

For longer journeys, hire a car and driver for a half-day or a full day; it is usually considerable cheaper to do so from the small car hire companies close to the major beaches, rather than directly through your hotel. Motorbikes and bicycles are also available for hire, particularly near the main beaches.

Car ferries still operate in some places, such as on the road to Fort Tiracol in the far north of the state. There are sea and river cruises from Panjim, and it is possible to hire a private boat for short or long trips.

ACCOMMODATION

Goa has an extraordinary range of hotels, most of them along the beaches north and south of Panjim. Some of the hotels are among the most luxurious in the country, and most major chains are represented along the beaches of Goa.

North Goa

The Taj group's **Fort Aguada Hotel** (*$$$; T: 0832 664 5858; tajhotels.com*) is in a spectacular location, at the southern end of Candolim Beach, within the old ramparts of a 16th-century Portuguese fort. However, the beach itself has suffered heavy erosion caused by a grounded ship that has been stuck in shallow waters of the sea since 2000.

The superbly located **Fort Tiracol** (*$$$; T: 02366 227631; forttiracol.com*) in the far north of Goa is one of India's most unusual hotels. The rooms are built into the walls of the fort, part of which is still occupied by a church, with local villagers attending regular Mass. It is necessary to take a ferry or private boat from Tiracol to the nearest beach.

Siolim House (*$$$; siolimhouse; T: 0832 2272138; 09822 584560*) in north Goa, inland from Anjuna Beach, is a prettily restored 17th-century colonial mansion, once used as the Goan residence of the governor of Macau and now converted into a hotel.

• **Panjim:** Fewer visitors stay in Panjim, which has three fine heritage hotels in the old Latin Quarter of Fontainhas, all under the same ownership. The **Panjim Inn** ($$) is their main property, a 19th-century colonial mansion, while **Panjim Pousada** ($$) is a smaller 20th-century residence. The most comfortable of the three is the **Panjim Peoples** ($$$), a converted former school building. (*For all three contact: T: 0832 2226523; panjiminn.com.*)

South Goa

Bhakti Kutir (*$$; bhaktikutir.com; T: 0832*

2643469), on Palolem Beach in south Goa, provides simple, clean accommodation in an eco-friendly environment, with cottages built out of local materials.

• **Rentals:** Visitors staying for a week or longer will often rent an apartment or a house. For instance, **Sunbeam House** (*$$; sunbeamgoa@gmail.com; T: 0832 226 8525*) in Assagao, near Mapusa in north Goa, is a luxurious villa with a swimming pool, and also comes with a cook.

FOOD

Goa is a food-lover's dream. Not only is there the superb local Goan cuisine and a huge range of fresh seafood, but also there are some of India's best international restaurants in this state.

Unsurprisingly fish and other seafood play a major role in Goan cuisine, but so do pork, chicken, coconut, bread rolls, desserts and the local drink, known as *feni*. The cuisine has strong Portuguese influences. Goan fish (or prawn) curry is a staple food among Catholics and some Hindus; the curry is normally cooked with coconut milk and the slightly sour fruit of the kokum tree, and eaten with rice or bread.

Other important dishes are pork vindaloo, a normally very spicy curry in which wine vinegar is used to marinate the meat. The name 'vindaloo' comes from the Portuguese *carne de vinha d'alhos*, meaning meat with wine and garlic. *Xacuti* is another curry, in which the spices are roasted and where coconut and white poppy seeds are used. *Sorpatel*, a curry made from the blood and offal of a pig, is seen as one of the most typically Goan of dishes, but is more of an acquired taste. Prawn *balchao* is a fiery marinated prawn dish, normally eaten with rice or bread, while chicken *cafreal* is a grilled chicken dish marinated with garlic and other spices.

The best-known Goan dessert is *bebinca*—a many-layered baked sweet, made of flour and coconut milk.

Goan restaurants

Goan cuisine is widely available throughout the state, but those restaurants serving a foreign clientèle, particularly in the beach areas, often make the food a little bland.

• **North Goa:** Go to a small place like **Kamlabai's** (*$; T: 09850 703341*) on the Assagao road out of Mapusa for superb local cuisine at a simple restaurant. The best-known restaurant for Goan food, though, is **O Coqueiro** ($$) in Porvorim, which is also famous as the place where the serial killer Charles Sobhraj was recaptured after his escape from Delhi's Tihar Jail.

• **Panjim:** Here, the **Panjim Inn** (*see above*) has excellent Goan cuisine.

• **South Goa:** Best of all is the food at the **Palácio de Deão** (*$$; T: 0832 2664029; 098224 80342*) in Quepem, but it is essential to call in advance.

Other restaurants

Much of the best seafood is to be found at beach shacks—it is best to visit them early if you want something special such as crab or lobster.

The basic **Amigos Restaurant** (*$: T: 0832 2401123*), under the bridge over the Nerul River, between Panjim and Calangute, has superb seafood. **Bomra's** (*$$; T: 098221 49633*) on the main road near Calangute Beach has superb and unusual Burmese food. **La Plage** ($$; *T:098221 21712*), in a series of large shacks and tents on Ashwem Beach in north Goa, is one of India's best French restaurants, and **J&A's** (*T: 098231 39488*), overlooking the Baga River, has good Italian food.

FURTHER READING & VIEWING

The most interesting and varied literary and historical introduction to Goa is the compilation of essays, poems and short stories called *Reflected on Water: Writing on Goa* (Ed. Jerry Pinto; Penguin India, 2006). Large parts of Sagarika Ghose's novel *Blind Faith* (HarperCollins India, 2006) are set in a fictionalised village on a beach in north Goa. For advice on beaches, shopping and wildlife, the frequently republished Outlook Traveller's guide to Goa is the most comprehensive.

For those who enjoy church-hopping, *Parish Churches of Goa* by José Lourenço (Amazing Goa Publications, 2005) is very detailed.

The critically acclaimed 2007 American movie *The Pool*, directed by Chris Smith, is set in Goa and was shot in and around Panjim; it concerns a young hotel worker who becomes obsessed with a swimming pool in a private house.

Many Hindi movies have been filmed on the beaches of Goa—among the better known is the 2001 romantic hit *Dil Chahta Hai* (*What the Heart Wants*), starring Aamir Khan and Preity Zinta.

KARNATAKA

Karnataka (*maps 11, 13 and 14*) is one of India's most varied states. It is best known internationally for its capital, Bangalore, which in the early years of the new millennium came to symbolise all that was modern in India. But elsewhere the state has an extraordinarily rich history—with the ruined medieval city of Hampi as one of the great tourist sites of the world. In contrast to Bangalore, the tourist and transport infrastructure in the rest of the state is underdeveloped—particularly in the north, where the great Muslim sultanates of the Deccan Plateau once flourished. In the south there is some of India's most spectacular Hindu and Jain architecture, and, in the city of Mysore, a supreme example of the flamboyance of princely India in the British period. The climate and geography of the state is similarly varied—from the mountains and nature reserves of Coorg and the far south to the forested hills of the Western Ghats, and from the great river-irrigated plains of the Deccan Plateau to one of India's least spoilt coastlines, on the west. Most of the state is very hot in April and May, but by July the monsoon rains make even the Deccan Plateau pleasant, if still quite warm—there is nowhere in the state that ever gets genuinely cold.

HISTORY OF KARNATAKA

Making historical sense of Karnataka's extraordinary artistic and architectural heritage is more of a challenge than for any other Indian state. It has had a series of geographically and chronologically overlapping dynasties—some of which were short-lived but culturally prolific. Prehistoric remains have been found in several parts of the state, and the 3rd-century BC Mauryan Empire stretched well into northern Karnataka. An inscription by the Mauryan emperor Ashoka is on display at Sannathi, near Gulbarga, where archaeologists have uncovered Buddhist ruins from the 1st century AD.

The Chalukyas and the Rashtrakutas: Several minor dynasties controlled parts of Karnataka until the emergence, in the 6th century AD, of the Chalukyas, who dominated large areas of the state and left behind the magnificent temple art and architecture in and around Badami. The greatest of the Chalukyan kings, Pulakesin II, conquered large parts of neighbouring Andhra in the early years of the 7th century, and after his death the kingdom later split into the West (Karnataka) and East (Andhra) Chalukyas.

The power of the West Chalukyas diminished as the Rashtrakutas emerged as a major power. The greatest of the Rashtrakutan monuments are at Ellora in the state of Maharashtra to the north—and little has survived from this period. The descendants of the West Chalukyas rebuilt their kingdom, and—usually referred to as the Late Chalukyas—were based at a new capital at Kalyan, in the north of Karnataka, though the most important Late Chalukyan buildings are near the central town of Gadag.

The Gangas and the Hoysalas: Large parts of the south were dominated by the Gangas, whose buried temples are being excavated at their former capital at Talkad, and who were also responsible for the Jain monolith at Shravana Belagola. They were eventually defeated c. 1000 by the Cholas from Tamil Nadu. The next major powers in southern Karnataka were the Hoysalas (1026–1343), whose superb temples at Halebid and Belur still attract large numbers of visitors. The Hoysalas were one of several long-standing dynasties forced from power by the invasion of Muslim-led forces from the Delhi Sultanate—though it was a Hoysala commander, Harihara, who in 1336 founded a new Hindu kingdom that became known as the Vijayanagar Empire.

Hindu Vijayanagar and the Muslim sultanates: By the middle of the 15th century, the Vijayanagar Empire, with its capital at Hampi, controlled much of southern India—and many of its great artistic and architectural masterpieces have survived. Just after the emergence of the Vijayanagar Empire, the Bahmanid Sultanate was founded in northern Karnataka, with its capital at Gulbarga and then Bidar. The Bahmanid Sultanate fell apart in the early 15th century, and its smaller successor sultanates combined forces to defeat the Vijayanagar Empire in 1565; what was left of the empire moved to what is now Andhra Pradesh.

The emergence of Mysore and Anglo-French rivalry: The Mysore Kingdom, ruled by the Wodeyar Dynasty, was created in the south by a former Vijayanagar governor—while in the north of the state the wars between the sultanates led, in 1619, to the defeat of Bidar by Bijapur. By the late 17th century, Bijapur had in turn been defeated by the Mughal emperor Aurangzeb, and much of Karnataka was a Mughal province. In the 18th century, the former Mysore commander Hyder Ali emerged as the most powerful force in southern Karnataka—and, with some support from the French, he and his son and successor, Tipu Sultan, fought a series of wars against the British.

The Mysore forces were finally defeated at the Battle of Seringapatam (Srirangapatnam) in 1799. The Wodeyars were restored to the Mysore throne, but British supremacy over the entire south of India was now assured. Large areas of northern Karnataka had been part of the territory of the nizams of Hyderabad since the 18th century, and remained so until Independence in 1947.

After Independence: The state, with its current boundaries, was formed in 1956 from the old princely state of Mysore and the parts of Hyderabad and the Bombay and Madras presidencies that had a majority of Kannada speakers. The state was known as Mysore until 1973, when it was renamed Karnataka.

BANGALORE (BENGALURU)

Bangalore (*map 13 C3*, officially Bengaluru) is the capital of the southern state of Karnataka and the city most closely associated with India's recent information technology and call-centre revolution. It is a relatively modern city (pop. 5,000,000), situated at the southern end of the Deccan Plateau, with excellent connections to the rest of the country, and a growing number of international flights to its smart new airport. Bangalore's altitude of 1000m gives it a milder year-round climate than many other Indian cities. Bangalore was for years known as the Garden City. However, its recent rapid growth has increased congestion and pollution, and the city is no longer the sleepy, leafy conurbation that many older visitors remember. Instead, it claims to be India's most cosmopolitan city—a 'fun' place for the young, best known now for its pub culture, multinational corporations and IT services industry. Its name was officially changed to its Kannada-language name of 'Bengaluru' in 2006, which translates as 'city of boiled beans', after the dish said to have been provided by a poor woman to a king who got lost while passing through the area. However, 'Bangalore' is still widely used.

History: The city was founded in 1537 as an outpost of the Vijayanagar Empire by Kempe Gowde, a local chieftain, though some historians argue for a much earlier date. After the collapse of the Vijayanagar Empire in 1565, a number of rulers—including the Wodeyars of Mysore, the Adil Shahis of Bijapur and the Marathas—vied for control of what was then no more than a town. By the mid-18th century Bangalore had become a base for Hyder Ali and Tipu Sultan in their growing confrontation with the British—though Mysore and Srirangapatnam were more important.

Only after the defeat of Tipu Sultan in 1799 did Bangalore begin to play a major role in the region, as the British moved their military base there from Srirangapatnam, which was deemed unhealthy. Mysore remained the official capital of Mysore state, ruled by the Wodeyars, but by the end of the 19th century Bangalore had a larger population and was a more important administrative centre. Its reputation as a modern city goes back more than a century, and it was the first important centre in India to have electric street lighting. It became the headquarters of the Indian aeronautics industry in the 1940s and then the base for the Indian Space Research Organisation. After Independence Bangalore became the capital of the state, the name of which was changed from Mysore to Karnataka in 1973.

Orientation: The old town is on the southwestern side of Bangalore, with what is left of the pre-British settlement, while the modern city centre—with many of the best hotels—is along MG Road to the east of Cubbon Park. Bangalore's famous International Technology Park is to the east of the city, beyond the old airport, though many of the high-tech industries are located elsewhere. Bangalore's new airport is well to the north of the city, near the village of Devanahalli.

OLD BANGALORE

Tipu Sultan's Palace

The best-known monument in Old Bangalore is Tipu Sultan's Palace (1781–91) on Albert Victor Road (*open 8.30–6*). It is a modest two-storey pillared pavilion, with high cusped arches, painted walls and small rooms. The palace is set in a pretty garden that is similar to, but less impressive than, Tipu Sultan's Summer Palace at Srirangapatnam. Note the carved wooden brackets supporting the roof eaves. The building stands in the grounds of the old demolished Gowda Palace, which was pulled down in the 18th century.

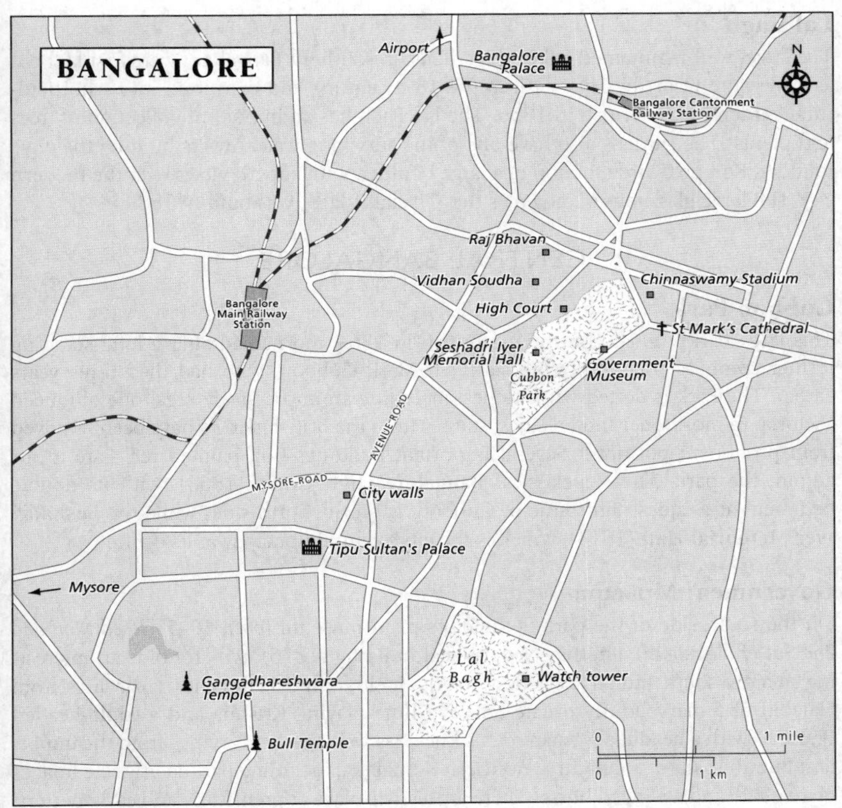

City walls

The only significant surviving part of the old city fortifications is 500m to the north, near the City Market, but on the opposite (south) side of the Mysore Road. This is a triple gateway, with an impressive barbican and pieces of stone with relief carvings taken from older buildings and embedded in the walls. Note one unexpected piece of erotica, high up on the left wall, inside the largest compound of the gateway.

Hindu temples

Two Hindu temples stand about 2km south of Tipu Sultan's Palace, in Basavangudi. The **Bull Temple** contains a large monolithic Nandi bull, 4.5m high, carved out of a boulder in the 16th century. The **Gangadhareshwara Temple**, 800m northwest of the Bull Temple, is built into a crevice in the rocks and has unusual Vijayanagar-period pillars in its courtyards—including two with large discs, said to represent the sun and the moon, and another fashioned in the shape of a trident.

Lal Bagh

The large, well-maintained Lal Bagh gardens, in southern Bangalore, were first laid out as a pleasure resort by Hyder Ali in the 18th century, and converted into a horticultural garden by the British in 1856. The Lal Bagh has an important collection of trees and plants. The gardens also have one of the surviving watchtowers built by the city's founder, Kempe Gowde, on top of a large boulder, with superb views over the modern city. The large glasshouse, known as the 'Crystal Palace', was built in 1889.

CENTRAL BANGALORE

Cubbon Park

This large park was laid out by the British in 1864 and named after a long-standing former commissioner of Mysore state, Sir Mark Cubbon, who had died three years earlier. The Park is dotted with statues, including an impressively regal one of Queen Victoria. In most other Indian cities, statues from the British period have been removed from prominent positions. Several important buildings—all painted red—are in, or adjoin, the park. The Neoclassical **Bangalore High Court** (1868), with its double pediment and equestrian statue of Cubbon, is on the north side, while the **Seshadri Iyer Memorial Hall** (1913), which is the city's central library, is at its centre.

Government Museum

On the south side of the park is the city's main museum (*open 10–5; closed Mon and 2nd Sat of the month*), another Neoclassical building (1876), which holds an interesting, mainly south Indian collection. Works include fine 12th-century carvings from Halebid of a marvellously ornate Surya, a flute-playing Krishna and a triple-headed Brahma (with a headless woman on his knee), as well as relief carvings from the important Buddhist site at Sannathi in northern Karnataka, including particularly fine images of a buffalo and a winged horse. There are also displays of prehistoric and early pottery, terracotta figurines from Hampi, miniature paintings from the Deccan, and fine Mysore paintings depicting scenes from the *Ramayana* and the story of Krishna. In the museum gardens there is an interesting collection of hero stones.

Other buildings around Cubbon Park

Just to the east of Cubbon Park is the **Chinnaswamy Stadium** (1969), home of Karnataka cricket, while to the north, facing the high court, is the enormous modern **Vidhan Soudha** (1951–56), or State Assembly, built in what has become known as the neo-Dravidian style, with the complex column bases and capitals that are part of south Indian Hindu architecture. The **Raj Bhavan** (1831), or Governor's House (the former British Residency), is next to the Vidhan Soudha, but special permission is required to visit. Bangalore's oldest church, **St Mark's Cathedral** (1808, enlarged 1901), is just east of Cubbon Park—a yellow building with a semicircular apse. A memorial plaque records the death of Sir Walter Scott of Abbotsford, who died at sea in 1847; he was the nephew of the novelist of the same name.

Bangalore Palace

This palace of 1865 (*open daily 10–6*), 2km north of Cubbon Park, is one of India's strangest royal palaces—built in the style of Windsor Castle, with high crenellated towers and turrets. The palace was originally built for a British merchant, then taken over by the maharaja of Mysore, who extended the building and whose descendants continue to occupy part of it. The interior is well maintained and richly decorated, with two pretty inner courtyards and items of furniture made out of elephant body parts. Note the small screened dais in the durbar hall, where the royal family would sit on formal occasions.

NORTH OF BANGALORE

Devanahalli

This small village (*map 13 C3*), next to the main road from Bangalore towards Hyderabad and just 6km north of the new airport, was the birthplace of Tipu Sultan. Its impressive 16th-century fortifications are visible from the main road, and 13 of the fort's bastions are intact and in good condition.

Nandi Hills

This area (*map 13 C3*), 45km north of Bangalore but just 20km north of the new airport, was used as a summer retreat by Tipu Sultan and by the British, and is now a minor hill resort. The main hill has extensive fortifications, known as Nandi Drug, or Nandi Fort. A road takes visitors to a car park inside the fort's cusped outer gateway, three-quarters of the way up the hill—it is best to walk up from here, though one can pay to be allowed to take one's car to the top. Just beyond the gateway, on the left, is Tipu Sultan's small summer palace, a two-storey building with a passageway running through it. Nearby is a large stepped pond. A little further up the hill, to the left, are some fantastic views from a spot known as Tipu's Drop, from where Tipu Sultan is said to have had his prisoners thrown down the hill. At the top of the hill are a temple and the 19th-century summer residence of the British Commissioner of Mysore—now used as a guest house.

Bhoganandishwara Temple

This superb, little-visited temple (9th–10th centuries) in Nandi village, on the plains just to the north of the hill, has an unusual mixture of different architectural styles, including Chola, Hoysala and Vijayanagar, which date back to the Nolamba period. The complex is entered through a large arcaded outer courtyard with some minor shrines mainly to *nagas*, or snake-deities. A gateway, with a pillared assembly hall on the left, leads into the main temple compound, with arcades around the centre. Twin temples here have been joined by the construction of another shrine between them. The compound and the temples have some superb relief carvings, mainly of Hindu gods, including several images of a triple-headed Brahma riding on a goose; Vishnu riding the very human-like eagle Garuda; and Shiva on his vehicle, Nandi. There are also some fine images of female water-carriers and dancers, as well as courtly scenes.

Be sure to walk around the shrines' circumambulatory passages to see some more superb, but partially hidden, relief carvings. To the north of the main temple compound is a very fine stepped pond, with statues of gods around the parapet of the courtyard.

NORTHWEST OF BANGALORE

Shivaganga Fort

This spectacular fort (*map 13 C3*), built on the side of a craggy mountain, was the 17th-century headquarters of the Gowdas after they were driven out of Bangalore, 46km to the southeast, by the Wodeyars. Two temples and part of a palace survive, and steps lead up to the top of the hill, from where there are superb views.

Sibi and Sira

About 95km northwest of Bangalore, on the NH4 towards Chitradurga, is the village of **Sibi** or Seebi (*map 13 C3*), which has the 18th-century **Narasimha Temple**, dedicated to the lion avatar of Vishnu. The temple has some very fine ceiling murals depicting both courtly and religious themes.

The town of **Sira** (*map 13 C3*), 115km northwest of Bangalore, on the NH4, was an important 17th-century Mughal outpost. It is home to the fine **tomb of Malik Rihan** (1651) and the five-bayed **Jama Masjid**, with its three small domes.

EAST OF BANGALORE

Kolar

The town of Kolar (*map 13 C3*), 60km east of Bangalore on the Chennai highway, is best known for its goldmines, but it also has an Islamic shrine, or *dargah*, closely associated with the family of the late 18th-century ruler of Mysore, Hyder Ali. It has two interesting Hindu shrines as well: the 11th-century **Kolaramma Temple**, one of Karnataka's few Chola buildings; and the 17th-century **Someshwara Temple**, probably the most elaborate building from the Gowda period.

Kurudumale

The village of Kurudumale (*map 13 C3*), 30km east of Kolar and 10km northwest of Mulbugal, has an interesting Chola-period shrine, the **Someshwara Temple** (12th century), dedicated to Shiva and with fine carvings of the god on the pillars of the assembly hall. Kurudumale also has a popular **Vinayaka Temple**, dedicated to Ganesha, from a similar date but much altered in the Vijayanagar period.

MYSORE

The pleasant city of Mysore (*map 14 B1*, officially Mysuru), 130km west of Bangalore, was the capital of one of India's most important princely states and it has a number of interesting palaces. It has also gained more recent fame as an international yoga centre and is a good base from which to visit other sights in southern Karnataka, such as the river island of Srirangapatnam, the temple at Somnathpur, the Jain pilgrimage site of Shravana Belagola, and the nature reserves at Bandipur and Nagarhole. The enormous Mysore Palace is in the centre of the town and is its best-known landmark. To the south is Chamundi Hill, with its 17th-century temple.

History: The city dates back to the late Vijayanagar period, when the Wodeyar family were appointed governors. With the collapse of the Vijayanagar Empire in 1565, the Wodeyars set up Mysore as an independent state, which they ruled—with a lengthy hiatus in the late 18th century—until Independence. Hyder Ali and his son Tipu Sultan were the 18th-century usurpers of the Mysore throne, and in 1793 Tipu Sultan levelled much of old Mysore in preparation for the building of a new capital. But construction did not get underway until the new century, by which time Tipu Sultan was dead and the British had restored the Wodeyars.

Mysore Palace

This palace (1897–1912), officially known as the Amba Vilas, is possibly the most ornate and exuberant of the many enormous palaces built by Indian maharajas during the period of British rule. It is even more dazzling when it is lit on Saturday and Sunday nights, and during the Hindu festival of Dussehra—or Dasara as it is usually spelled in the south. It stands within a fortified compound constructed by the Wodeyars in the 18th century. The palace complex is entered through the southern gate, where there is a ticket office (*open daily 1–5.30; no cameras or phones allowed in the palace but they can be used in the grounds; there is a cloakroom just inside the complex. Shoes have to be left in separate area next to the actual palace*).

The palace was built on the side of an early 19th-century palace that was destroyed by fire in 1897. The architect was Henry Irwin, who was also responsible for the Viceregal Lodge in Simla—two radically different buildings.

Façade and grounds: The façade of the Mysore Palace is a riot of red and gold domes and pinnacles, scalloped arches and pavilions—Indo-Saracenic style at its apogee. It has at its centre a five-storey tower with a golden dome, surmounted by a lantern and a smaller dome. The area in front of the palace is like an open stage, with a raised covered platform from where the great Dussehra procession was viewed by the maharaja and his guests, and which is still used during the Dussehra festival. Statues of snarling panthers are to be found in several places around the grounds and interior of the palace. There are also several shrines within the complex, including the most important, the Varahaswami Temple, with its high *gopura*, or entrance tower, next to the ticket office.

Ground floor: The entrance to the actual palace is through what is known as the Dolls Pavilion, which contains mainly European art objects. Note the wooden model of the palace that burned down in 1897, and the golden howdah on which the maharaja would sit on the back of an elephant during the Dussehra festival—it was used until 1970. Visitors then turn left into an arcaded inner courtyard, with murals (1934–45) depicting the Dussehra festivities in Mysore and a panel showing St

Philomena's Cathedral (*see below*). The following courtyard—known as the Kalyana Madtapa, or marriage pavilion—is covered by an octagonal stained-glass roof resting on eight sets of triple iron pillars, all imported from Scotland. Note the peacock motif in the stained glass, and the pretty floor tiles. Beyond the marriage pavilion is the portrait gallery, which includes pictures of the Wodeyars by India's most successful 19th-century painter, Raja Ravi Varma. There is then a furniture room with chairs made of silver and cut-glass.

Durbar hall: Visitors then head upstairs, past a plaster-of-paris statue of Krishnaraja Wodeyar IV, during whose reign the palace was built, and into the enormous and ornately decorated public durbar hall that doubles up as the Dussehra viewing area. Note the rich stucco decorations and the painting on the ceiling and walls. The nearby private durbar hall has the throne of the Wodeyars, with its golden umbrella as a canopy, which is brought out on display for the ten days of the Dussehra festival.

Jagan Mohan Palace

This smaller palace (1861) is 600m west of Mysore Palace and contains an art and sculpture gallery. The palace was used as a temporary residence for the maharaja after the burning down of the old Mysore Palace in 1897 and before the completion of the new one in 1912. The front part of the building contains a large pavilion behind the grand Hindu-style façade, while the rear of the building is Neoclassical and contains the unexciting **Jayachamarajendra Art Gallery** (*open daily 8.30–5*). The latter includes a few exhibits from the maharaja's collection, including items belonging to Tipu Sultan; a painting gallery that has works by Raja Ravi Varma and Nicholas Roerich (*see p. 321*); and some porcelain vases and bronzes. The high-domed whitewashed **Lalitha Mahal** (1921) is a large palace set in pretty grounds in the eastern suburbs of Mysore, built as a royal guest house and now a hotel (*see Accommodation, p. 710*).

St Philomena's Cathedral and Government House

On the north side of the city is the neo-Gothic **St Philomena's Cathedral** (1931–51), loosely based on Cologne Cathedral, with two enormous spires that make it one of the city's most distinctive landmarks. Between the cathedral and Mysore Palace is the Neoclassical **Government House** (1805), used by the British Resident (or representative) in the princely state during the 19th and early 20th centuries.

AROUND MYSORE

Chamundi Hill

Just to the south of Mysore is Chamundi Hill, from where there are superb views of the region. Three-quarters of the way up the hill is the 5m-high **Nandi Monolith**, a carving of Shiva's vehicle, the bull, cut from a single boulder. On the hilltop is the **Chamundeshvari Temple**, founded in the 17th century but modernised several times since. Nearby is the **Rajendra Vilas Palace**, built in the Rajput style as a summer retreat for the Wodeyars and now being converted into a hotel.

Talkad

The little-visited town of Talkad (*map 14 B1*), 50km east of Mysore, close to the northern bank of the Kaveri River, was once the capital of the Ganga Dynasty, which is now best known for the great Jain statue at Shravana Belagola (*see p. 673*). Much of the old capital is covered in sand dunes, though small parts of it have been excavated. The most interesting buildings are from the later Hoysala period (12th–13th centuries).

The main **Vaidyanatheshwar Temple** (*closed 1–4.30*) is a large and complex Hoysala shrine with some recent sandstone additions. Note the superbly carved temple guardians next to the entrance to the main shrine. To see the other temples, head up over the sand dunes. The **Pataleshwara Temple** has been dug out of the sand and belongs to the earlier Ganga period. But it and another Ganga-period temple have been over-restored. There is a large Hoysala shrine, the **Kirti Narayana Temple**, undergoing major, but more sensitive, restorations.

Somnathpur

The superb **Keshav Temple** (*open daily 9–5.30*) at Somnathpur (*map 14 B1*), 25km east of Mysore, is one of the finest examples of the Hoysala style, with quite stunning detail in much of the carving. The temple, constructed in 1268, is within a large walled compound. Visitors pass through a gate, with the distinctive lathe-turned Hoysala columns, into a courtyard dominated by the temple, and with an arcade and mini-temples around the sides. The temple has three shrines, which along with its assembly hall give the temple the shape of a cross—though each shrine has so many facets that it approximates a circle. The lower levels of the temple exterior are covered with tiers of friezes showing elephants, horses with riders, military processions and battle scenes. Higher up are images of gods—mainly avatars of Vishnu including Narasimha (the lion) and Varaha (the boar). Inside are more lathe-turned and multi-faceted columns, and some impressively intricate ceiling panels. Note the large statue of Krishna holding a flute in the left shrine, while the shrine on the right has Vishnu in the form of Janardhana. The central shrine has a more modern statue of Vishnu.

SRIRANGAPATNAM

This fortified island in the Kaveri River (*map 14 B1*) was the site of a battle that confirmed British supremacy in southern India. The Battle of Seringapatam (as the British called it) in 1799 resulted in the death of Tipu Sultan, known as the Tiger of Mysore. It also meant the end of his French allies' aspirations to play a major role in the subcontinent.

Orientation: Srirangapatnam is 15km north of Mysore, on the Bangalore–Mysore road, which cuts through the island from north to south. If approaching from Bangalore, on the northern side of the island, the main fortified area is to the right (west)—while Tipu Sultan's Summer Palace and his mausoleum are to the left (east), in the more rural, sparsely populated part of the island.

Tipu Sultan's Summer Palace

The small Summer Palace (*open daily 9–5*) is set in a pretty garden on the eastern side of Srirangapatnam. Officially the **Daria Daulat Bagh**, or Garden of the Wealth of the Sea, it was built by Tipu Sultan as a pleasure resort in 1784. After Tipu Sultan's death, Arthur Wellesley, later the Duke of Wellington and British prime minister, stayed here. The paintings on the verandah are protected by sunshades that obscure the design of the building, which has double-height ground-floor reception areas, overlooked by first-floor rooms with balconies. The well-signposted paintings on the verandah include a particularly fine depiction (western wall) of the Battle of Pollilur in 1780, when Tipu's father Hyder Ali defeated the British under Colonel Baillie, who is shown biting his nails while being carried in a palanquin.

The interior of this well-preserved and richly decorated building is devoted to drawings, paintings, maps and mementoes associated with Tipu Sultan—including paintings of his sons, who were exiled to Vellore and then Calcutta after their father's death. There is a fine oil painting by Zoffany of Tipu Sultan as a 30-year-old (1780), holding a curved sword and with a dagger in his waistband.

Gumbaz

Just 2km east of the Summer Palace is the Gumbaz (literally 'dome')—the handsome mausoleum of Tipu Sultan and his father, Hyder Ali, which stands in formal gardens entered through an arched gateway. It was built by Tipu Sultan after the death of his father in 1782. The domed tomb is surrounded by other buildings, including an ornate, seven-bayed mosque with high, thin minarets. There are dozens of graves of members of Tipu Sultan's family nearby. The actual mausoleum has three entrances and a painted interior, and contains three cenotaphs marking the underground graves of Tipu Sultan (his cenotaph is covered in a cloth with a tiger skin design), his father (in the middle) and his mother. The ebony doors with ivory inlay were donated in 1855 by Viceroy Lord Dalhousie.

Other buildings on the eastern side of Srirangapatnam

Next to the road leading east from the Gumbaz is a small domed **memorial pavilion to Colonel Baillie**, whose image appears in the painting at the Summer Palace, and who died while in Tipu Sultan's custody. Between the Gumbaz and the Summer Palace, on the north side of the road, is the over-restored **Abbé Dubois's Church** (1800), built by and named after a French missionary who lived here from 1799 to 1823, and who wrote a book on Hinduism which became the standard European text on the religion. Also on the eastern side of the road that runs through Srirangapatnam are several early European buildings, including the **Doctor's Bungalow**, next to the Mayura River View hotel, which was briefly the headquarters of the garrison commander. The old **garrison cemetery** is on the eastern side of the road just before the road crosses the river and heads towards Mysore. It has been well restored by members of the de Meuron family, whose Swiss ancestor set up the de Meuron regiment, which served both the Dutch and British East India companies.

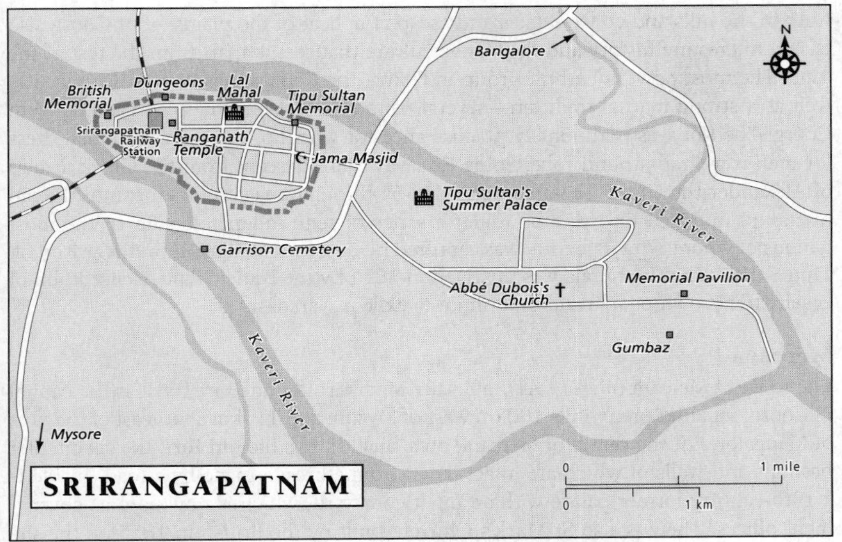

The western side of Srirangapatnam

The much more built-up western side of the island is surrounded by a moat and the old fortifications, with several impressive gateways, particularly in the Mysore Gate area. Close to the road is the attractive **Jama Masjid** (1787), with its two ornate minarets. This is Srirangapatnam's main mosque, and was built by Tipu Sultan. Note how what appears to be the roof of the mosque is in fact the raised prayer area—from where there are fine views. Just 1km to the east is the **Ranganath Temple**, dedicated to Vishnu, which is thought to date back more than a millennium to the Ganga period, though it underwent significant rebuilding in the 19th century. Note the fine Hoysala-style lathe-turned columns in the assembly hall. Nearby are the ruins of Tipu Sultan's main palace, the **Lal Mahal**.

Several key locations in Srirangapatnam are along the northern river-facing wall of the island. In the far west, beyond the railway line and amid crumbling ruins, is an **obelisk memorial** to the British forces killed at the Battle of Seringpatnam (Srirangapatnam). There are sets of underground dungeons here too, where Tipu Sultan kept his British prisoners in famously insalubrious conditions. Between the two sets of dungeons, not far from the Water Gate, is a small park and memorial marking the spot where Tipu Sultan died.

COORG

The beautiful hills and forests of Coorg (*map 14 A1*, officially Kodagu), in the far south of Karnataka, are a popular and easy-to-reach destination. Most visitors go there to walk in the hills and coffee estates and escape the heat of the plains—but Coorg also has an interesting history and distinctive culture that sets it apart from the rest of the state. The most powerful ethnic group in Coorg, the Kodava, has its own language as well as a strong martial tradition—several of India's best-known soldiers came from Coorg. The Kodavas traditionally practise ancestor worship, and the ceremonial dress for men is a wrap-around robe. Some Kodavas claim descent from the Greek armies of Alexander the Great. The area was ruled by the Vijayanagar emperor until the fall of Hampi in 1565. Coorg came under a series of semi-independent rajas, the most famous of whom, Vira Rajendra, was captured by, and then escaped from the prison of, Tipu Sultan. The Coorg raja was unseated in 1834 by the British, who accused him of cruelty to his own people and sent him into exile in Varanasi.

Mercara

The town of Mercara (*map 14 A1*), officially Madikeri, founded in 1681, is the capital of Coorg, set amid pretty hills 100km west of Mysore and 110km southeast of the port of Mangalore. At the centre of Mercara, on a small hill, is the **old fort**, the six circular bastions and walls of which are intact, apart from a breach made by a road. Inside is a 19th-century former palace with an inner courtyard, which is now used as government offices. There is also **St Mark's Church**, built by the British in 1855 on the site of a temple. It has pretty stained-glass windows and a small **archaeological museum** with some fine 13th-century Jain statues inside and some interesting hero stones in the garden. The old main gate to the fort is open, and part of the gatehouse now houses a small jail.

About 300m east of the fort is the **Omkareshwara Temple** (1820). Its dome and four turrets are more reminiscent of Muslim than Hindu architecture.

On a hillside 1.5km north of the fort are the Muslim-style **royal tombs** (1820 and 1834), known as *gaddiges*, of two Hindu rajas of Coorg. They are clearly influenced by the design of the mausoleum of Hyder Ali and Tipu Sultan in Srirangapatnam, but have Hindu carvings next to the doorways.

Southern Coorg

In the south of Coorg, close to the town of Kakkabe (*map 14 A1*), is an old royal hunting lodge, known as the **Nalnad Palace** (1792). This two-storey building inside a small compound is at the foot of Karnataka's highest mountain, Tadiyendomol. It was here that the last raja of Coorg took refuge before he surrendered to the British in 1834. In the grounds is a small marriage pavilion, with a bull on each corner of the roof. The palace has some pretty painted walls and ceilings.

BELUR & HALEBID

The Hoysala temples of Belur and Halebid, just 16km apart (*map 13 B3*), have superb examples of Hindu temple art at its most intricate. The Hoysala Dynasty ruled much of southern Karnataka between the 11th and 14th centuries, until their territories were subsumed into the Vijayanagar Empire. The use of steatite, or soapstone, which is soft when newly quarried and then hardens, enabled craftsmen to carve figures and patterns of extraordinary detail and complexity.

Belur

The great **Chennakesava Temple** (1117) at Belur (*map 13 B3*) is on the west side of this small town, 30km from the district headquarters at Hassan and 190km from Bangalore. Belur was the first capital of the Hoysala Dynasty, and the temple was built in celebration of a military victory of the Cholas. The temple (*open daily dawn–dusk; a torch is useful for the interior*) is set within a rectangular compound, entered through an entrance gate with a high Vijayanagar-style *gopura*, or tower.

Temple grounds: Inside the compound is the main temple (which has lost its tower), as well as several interesting subsidiary shrines and arcades around the side in which further shrines have been built. Note the finely-carved figures and inscriptions embedded in the right (northern) wall. There is a pretty water-filled pool in the north-east corner of the compound, and several smaller empty pools elsewhere.

Temple plinth: The main temple is dedicated to Vishnu, whose many avatars appear in the intricate carving on the exterior and interior of the building, though there are also images of Shiva. The temple is set on a plinth and has the distinctive star-like shape of many Hoysala shrines, allowing more external surface area for carving—though the front part of the temple around the assembly hall is rectangular. The best carving is at the back of the temple, around the exterior of the sanctuary. The lowest level of the temple has a continuous frieze of elephants, while the next levels have complex friezes based on decorative and figurative designs, particularly dancers and musicians. Higher up, closer to eye level, are larger deities and human figures, almost carved in the round.

Temple entrance: Above the main entrance is a very intricately carved *torana*, or door arch, with the winged figure of Garuda, the man-eagle, and Vishnu's vehicle at the centre. Just above this is Narasimha, the lion avatar of Vishnu, whose image is seen at several places around the temple, usually, as here, tearing out the entrails of a demon. Note the large carved figures of a human and a lion-like creature at each of the three entrances.

External carvings: The scene on the left of the main entrance, with a seated man holding a dagger and surrounded by numerous other people, is thought to be a representation of the Hoysala king Vishnuvardhana and his court. Note the brackets, carved in the image of women, one of them holding a parrot, the other looking into a mirror. There are also two images of a monkey trying to disrobe a woman, one on each side of the building. Heading clockwise, there are carvings of court entertainers and amorous couples. As you approach the southern entrance, there are several small panels showing Varaha, the boar avatar of Vishnu, and above them Narasimha. Among the carvings on the rear part of the temple are the ten-headed demon Ravana trying to lift Mount Kailash, the abode of the gods, with Shiva and Parvati sitting unperturbed near the mountain's summit. There is also a superb dancing Shiva, his right foot resting on the head of an elephant, and nearby is the sun-god Surya being pulled by seven horses. Note how the lower-level animal friezes are more numerous and intricate at the rear of the shrine.

Temple interior: Inside the temple is an extraordinary array of carved pillars supporting the roof of the assembly hall. Some are simply lathe-turned, others multi-faceted and covered with carvings. The roof carries carved scenes from the *Mahabharata*. The lintel above the entrance to the sanctuary shows Vishnu and Lakhsmi both seated. The 2m-high image of Chennakesava (a form of Vishnu) inside the sanctuary is still used for regular worship.

Halebid temple

The double-shrined **Hoysaleshvara Temple** at Halebid is 16km from Belur and is in a picturesque location overlooking a large lake (*map 13 B3*). Construction of the temple, dedicated to Shiva, began in 1121, slightly after the large Vishnu temple in Belur. Halebid appears to have emerged as the Hoysala capital at this time. It was a large city, and its crumbling walls can still be seen on the outskirts of the town, as can other temples.

Orientation: The temple complex (*open daily dawn–dusk*) is entered from the north, though the two shrines are east-facing, and so visitors are actually approaching the temple from the side, in alignment with a lateral passage that connects the two inner shrines. To the left, towards the lake, are separate pavilions for two monolithic Nandi bulls, Shiva's vehicle, each adorned with jewels and bells, facing towards the sanctuaries and the lingams inside. The main temple uses the typical star-shaped Hoysala design, though the plinth on which it rests has been squared off in a rectilinear fashion.

Temple exterior: The friezes of the Halebid temple are even more numerous and complex than at Belur, with tiers of animals that include elephants, lions, horses, geese, monsters, musicians and mythological scenes. Higher up the walls of the temple are dozens of standing images of Shiva and Parvati, and more complex carvings, including Shiva dancing, the lion-god Narasimha tearing out the entrails of a demon, and the elephant-god Ganesha dancing. Near the top are carvings of amorous couples. However, the best carvings of all are around the exterior of the sanctuaries. Here you will find some of the best examples of medieval Hindu art, including images of Krishna lifting Govardhan Hill to protect the livestock and people, and, next to it, Shiva dancing inside the skin of an elephant.

Temple interior: As in Belur, the interior has a remarkable variety of lathe-turned and carved columns, and some fine ceiling decoration; but the design of the interior is quite different, because of the double shrine and four entrances.

There is a small outdoor **archaeological museum** (*open Sat–Thur 10–5*) in a fenced-off area of the compound, with many Hindu and Jain carvings, inscriptions and dozens of pieces from the missing tower of the temple.

Other sights in and around Halebid

About 450m south of Halebid's main temple are the **Jain Bastis**—three 12th-century Jain shrines. The nearest, dedicated to the 23rd *tirthankar* of Jainism, Parusnath, has a large open assembly hall, with lathe-turned Hoysala columns, ornate ceiling slabs and a large image of Parusnath in the sanctuary. Note the carved images of human, animal and mythologicial figures high up on the exterior of the sanctuary walls. The small middle shrine is dedicated to Adinath, while the far one is dedicated to Shantinath, of whom there is a large statue inside. There is also a rectangular step-well in the compound.

The **Kedareshwara Temple**, 300m east of the Jain Bastis, is an interesting Hindu temple, with some superb external carvings, more expressive than those at the main Halebid shrine. Note the images of Shiva and Parvati riding the bull Nandi, a dancing image of Ganesha, which unusually shows the elephant-god in profile, and some scenes from the *Mahabharata* and the *Ramayana*.

The village of **Dodda Gaddavahalli** has a Hoysala temple, prettily located overlooking a lake, 15km north of Hassan on the road to Belur. Note the pyramidal temple towers and the fine lathe-turned columns. The main shrine in the compound is to the female goddess Kali, guarded by large statues of skeletal guardians. Three other shrines are dedicated to Shiva, Bhairava and Lakshmi.

SHRAVANA BELAGOLA

The extraordinary Jain pilgrimage town of Shravana Belagola (*map 13 B3*) is situated on and around two large granite hills, 120km west of Bangalore, just south of the main road to Hassan. The summit of the southern hill has the enormous and justly famous monolithic statue of Bahubali, known as the Gommateshwara. It is also believed to be the place where Chandragupta, the founder of the Mauryan Empire who later converted to Jainism, died in about 290 BC.

The route to the monolith

The footpath to the monolithic statue goes up the southern hill, known as Vindhyagiri, and starts close to the square water tank in the centre of town. It is a steep climb up rock-cut steps, and shoes cannot be worn (there is a cloakroom at the bottom for leaving shoes). If it is warm, the steps can get very hot—and it is advisable to wear socks. Many pilgrims and visitors get carried up on special chairs known as *dhoolies* for a fixed fee.

About two-thirds of the way up there is a wall and some lesser temples, including the triple-shrine **Odegal Basti**, with stone struts supporting its lower walls. A side path to the right leads to a pillared hall and the **Chennana Basti**, a small shrine that has been built around a rock-cut image of the eighth Jain *tirthankar*, Chandraprabha. The steps up to main shrine pass next to a series of inscriptions, protected by perspex and carrying English translations. There is also a small pavilion surrounding a single finely-carved pillar (10th century). The structure on top contains a small 13th-century statue.

The **Akhand Gateway**, with side pavilions, is at the top of the next flight of stairs and has a fine carved image of Lakshmi being anointed with oil by two elephants over the doorway, and lots of tiny carved figures on the boulder to the left. The steps pass through two more gateways, each with carved figures at the side, before reaching the high-walled temple compound—painted with orange and white stripes—on the top of the hill.

The monolith of Bahubali

Apart from the main temple, the complex also has a small shrine called the **Siddhara Basti**, with two early 15th-century commemorative columns in the antechamber and a seated Jain statue in the sanctuary. There is also the unusual **Gullekayi Ajji Mandapa**, a pavilion with a statue of an old woman, always dressed in a sari, in the upper compartment, and a statue of a young woman on the lower level. Note how pieces of stones with relief carvings of human and animal figures have been embedded in the compound walls. There is a door leading from the outer compound onto a large rock, from where there are fine views of the countryside and of the head of the Bahubali Monolith.

The **temple** consists of a series of small shrines and arcades around the remarkable 17.7m-high **monolith of a naked Bahubali** (981), the son of the first of the Jain *tirthankars*, carved during the rule of the Ganga Dynasty. Bahubali is the embodiment of renunciation in Jain thought for having refused to defeat his older brother in a contest, despite being much stronger. Every 12 years, one of the most important and colourful Jain celebrations, the Mahamastakabhisheka, is held in Shravana Belagola. Thousands of pilgrims come here, and the monolith is anointed with milk, liquid turmeric and sugar cane juice. The next Mahamastakabhishekas are in 2018 and 2030.

The smooth pale-grey granite monolith is carved in the round from the head to the knees, with quite exceptional attention to detail and scale. Note the anthills and snakes carved onto the rock out of which Bahubali emerges, as well as the leafy creeper that coils around Bahubali's limbs. Either side of the monolith are 12th-century Hoysala statues of temple guardians—while the arcades house a variety of statues of Jain *tirthankars*.

Shravana Belagola town

The small town of Shravana Belagola occupies the narrow valley between the two hills. At the eastern end of the town is the **Bhandari Basti** (1159, with later additions), a large Jain temple with the statues of the 24 *tirthankars* arranged in one long row. The nearby Jain Math, with its gold doors, is the former residence of the spiritual leader of the Jains of Shravana Belagola. Inside are some fine 18th–19th-century murals showing scenes from Jain tradition and the lives of the *tirthankars*. It also has a collection of Jain bronzes, some of which date back to the Ganga period.

Chandragiri Hill

The northern hill at Shravana Belagola, known as Chandragiri, has a large compound with many temples and other monuments, and is less high than Vindyagiri. The footpath (no shoes allowed) is slightly to the west of the pool and less steep than the steps up to the Bahubali Monolith. The compound is entered through a gateway on the south side.

To the left are several pavilions, inscribed stones and pillars, as well as an upright statue of Bahubali's brother, Bharat. To the right are more than a dozen temples, of a similar but not identical design. The most interesting is the 12th-century **Chandragupta Basti**, with an unusual stone screen, carved with small figures, telling the story of Bhadrabahu, the Jain monk who was Chandragupta Maurya's guru. In the rocks outside the compound is the **Bhadrabahu Cave**, where Chandragupta is believed to have died.

Shantinath Basadi

On the far side of Chandragiri hill, and approached by taking the road heading east from Shravana Belagola and then bearing left, is the Shantinath Basadi—a Jain shrine with its exterior richly decorated with some superb carvings in the Hoysala style. The seated statue of the 16th *tirthankar*, Shantinath, is in the sanctuary.

Near Shravana Belagola

About 30km south of Shravana Belagola, close to the Mysore Road on a ridge above the plains, is the pilgrimage town of **Melukote** (*map 13 B3*), which is associated with the 13th-century Vaishnavite philosopher Ramunuja. There are several interesting shrines here, including a hilltop **Narasimha Temple** and the large **Narayana Temple**, with its fine hall built in 1458 under Vijayanagar rulers.

MANGALORE & ENVIRONS

The city of Mangalore (*map 13 A3*) is Karnataka's main port, just north of the border with Kerala. It is an ancient city but there is not a great deal for visitors to see. It is a good base for visiting the nearby temple towns of Mudabidri and Udupi, and its airport gives access to northern Kerala, and the hills of Coorg to the east.

Mangalore city

The only part of Mangalore's old fortifications to survive is a watchtower on the north side of the city, overlooking a pretty estuary. It is known as **Sultan's Battery**, after Tipu Sultan, who is said to have built it in the late 18th century. There is a small **government museum** (*open Sat–Thur 9.30–5.30*), with some wood and stone carvings, in the hilly Bejai area of the city. The most attractive of the city's many churches is the **St Aloysius Chapel** (1895), part of St Aloysius College. The walls and ceilings of the chapel are covered in some interesting murals, painted in the late Baroque style by the Italian artist Antonio Moscheni, who died in Cochin in 1905. The **Manjunath Temple**, dedicated to Shiva, is the city's most important temple, prettily located at the foot of Kadri Hill, and surrounded by palm trees. The current building dates from the 17th-century Nayak period, and it has some interesting carved pillars.

Mudabidri

The small town of Mudabidri (*map 13 A3*), set in heavily forested hills 30km to the northeast of Mangalore, has dozens of Jain temples and seminaries, largely dating from the 15th and 16th centuries. The largest shrine, officially the **Chandranath Basti** but better known as the **One Thousand Pillar Temple** (1429), is at the end of the main street. The original stone gateway has some fine carvings of guardian figures. Inside the large compound, the two-storey temple has a sloping wooden roof coated with copper tiles. The golden image in the sanctuary is of Chandraprabha (also known as Chandranath), the eighth Jain saviour.

Take the road round the temple to reach the gates of **Chowter Palace**, the residence of the minor princely family that once ruled Mudabidri. If the palace is closed, ask for the key at the building on the left of the inner gate. The palace is a small, not very palatial building, set around a courtyard with some very fine wood carvings on the large pillars on the right. Note in particular how the artist has created the image of an elephant out of the shape of nine women. The other major shrine in Mudabidri is the **Guru Basti**, dedicated to Parusnath, the penultimate of the 24 Jain saviours. Note the wide variety of styles of stone pillars in the assembly hall.

Karkala

The town of Karkala (*map 13 B3*), 15km north of Mudabidri, is another important Jain centre. It is best known for its hilltop monolithic **Gommateshwara Statue** (1432). The impressive 13m-high stone carving is an imitation of the larger 17.7m monolith at Shravana Belagola, carved 500 years earlier. Like the larger monolith, the statue is an image of Bahubali, the son of the first Jain saviour. There are several Jain temples nearby.

Udupi

Udupi (*map 13 A3*), 50km north of Mangalore, is an important Hindu pilgrimage town, with several temples grouped round an open square. The temples date back to the 12th century, when a famous Vishnu devotee, Madhava, was born here. However, the name Udupi is best known throughout India as the birthplace of a particular kind of vegetarian cuisine (*see p. 710*).

NORTHERN KARNATAKA

Northern Karnataka has a poor tourist infrastructure yet some of the finest tourist attractions in the country. It is here that great sultanates and the Vijayanagar Empire vied for supremacy, and many extraordinary buildings survive from this period. The most spectacular are at Hampi, but Bijapur, Gulbarga and Bidar all have some impressive historical structures, while the area in and around Badami has some of India's finest early temples.

BIDAR

The little-visited town of Bidar (pronounced, approximately, 'bidder'), located in the northern tip of Karnataka (*map 11 D2*), has some quite exceptional monuments built by two Muslim dynasties, the Bahmanis and the Baridis, who ruled large parts of central India from the 15th to the 17th centuries. The Bahmani sultans moved their capital from Gulbarga to Bidar in 1424. By the late 15th century the Bahmani Empire controlled a large band of territory from the western coast of India to the east, all ruled from the great fortress at Bidar, which remains one of India's most impressive citadels. The successor Baridi Dynasty controlled a smaller area but continued to build within Bidar Fort, and, like the Bahmani, left behind a collection of distinctive mausolea. The craft of bidriware, where blackened metal is inlaid, or damascened, with another, more precious metal, often silver, is named after Bidar—and visitors can see bidriware being made in the back streets of the old town.

Orientation: Most visitors travel to Bidar from Hyderabad in Andhra Pradesh, about 3hrs away by road, and enter the old walled city through the southern gate. Head past the large watchtower, past the superb *madrasa* of Mahmud Gawan on the left, to the main southwest gate of the fortress. The Bahmani tombs are at Ashtur, 3km to the east of the fort. The Baridi tombs are 3km to the west of the fort.

Bidar Fort

This large, roughly circular fort, 1km in diameter and with two sets of walls, sits at the northern end of the town at the edge of a plateau overlooking the surrounding countryside. It is possible to drive inside most parts of the fort, which is entered through two outer gates. Note that the second gate has two bands of tiles above its balconies: the lower with Arabic calligraphy, the higher with multicoloured tiles. It is known as the Sharza ('roaring' in Persian) Gate because of the animals above the archway. The road becomes a causeway across a broad moat, with strange ridges of rock running its length, before passing through the final, low-domed Gumbad Gate.

Orientation: Once inside the fort, to the left of the Gumbad Gate you will see the pretty Rangeen Mahal, while straight ahead is the compound enclosing the museum and the mosque. To reach the main fort buildings, take the road around the compound to the right. To the far right of the Gumbad Gate is another road that leads past the Old Magazine—a bastion with a large cannon, temple and mosque.

The **Rangeen Mahal** (mid-16th century), meaning 'coloured palace', is usually locked, but the watchman will open it for visitors. It is the fort's best-preserved building. Inside is a courtyard with a small pond, leading to a series of rooms and open areas, with some superb carved wooden columns, brackets and ceilings (make sure you look up); there is also some fine plasterwork of peacocks and parrots, coloured tiling and, in the end room, some mother-of-pearl inlay. Go to the roof for fine views of the rest of the fort and of the town. The old kitchens are visible on the right (west) of the palace.

The **Fort Museum** (*open daily 9–5*) is housed in the old palace baths, inside the gated compound and next to a pretty garden. There is a fine hero stone, with a man firing an arrow which pierces all the way through his enemy's body.

The garden, known as **Lal Bagh**, has a central pond and is overlooked by the **Solah Khamba Masjid** (1327), or 'sixteen column mosque', with a high, flattish central dome. The mosque was founded during the occupation of Bidar by the forces of the Delhi Sultanate, under the Tughlaq Dynasty, but has been substantially altered since. Note the widespread use of the trefoil motif in the mosque, on the drum of the dome and above the arches, among other places. Next to the mosque is the **Tarkash Mahal** (*closed to visitors*), said to be named after a Turkish princess who lived there. Note how the water supply for the ponds and the baths comes from the Tarkash Mahal.

Main palaces: Behind the compound are two large ruined palaces. The nearest building is the **Diwan-i Am**, or public audience hall, which was the ceremonial centre of the Bahmani and Baridi dynasties. Note the large courtyard with its stone column bases, which once supported wooden pillars. The second, slightly less ruined and larger building is the **Takht Mahal**, or Throne Palace, which served as a private audience hall. There is also an attached pavilion with six domes. Note the lotus-shaped pond on the far side of the palace, and the large arched entrance area, where it is just possible to make out a sun motif superimposed with a lion or tiger in the surviving coloured tiles above the archway. If you head downhill from the palace towards the lake in the lower area of the fort, you will see that the walls of the Takht Mahal are actually much more impressive than they at first seem.

Other buildings: There are many other ruined buildings within the fort, and particularly interesting are the northeast gate, beyond the Old Magazine, which is known as the **Mandu Darwaza**, with its well-defended entrance, and the nearby **tower**, with a huge cannon, engraved with Arabic calligraphy. It is just possible to make out the distant Ashtur Tombs from the top of the tower.

Bidar town

The most important building in the town of Bidar is the enormous **Madrasa of Mahmud Gawan** (1472), a partly ruined Islamic college built in the Persian style on the main road leading up to the fort. It is named after its founder, a trader of Persian origin who became prime minister of the sultanate, the most important administrator under the Bahmanids, and who was later executed by the sultan. This unusual three-storey building was originally square, with a giant archway on each side leading into the central courtyard. Three of the arches have survived, but the one that would have overlooked the road has long since gone, making it hard to imagine the building as it originally looked. One of its pair of 40m-high cylindrical minarets survives, along with much of its multicoloured tiling, arranged in an elegant zigzag pattern. Part of the building is used as a mosque. Walk round the *madrasa* to see the fine stonework tracery in the windows, as well as projecting towers with their bulbous domes.

Other buildings in Bidar town: The distinctive circular building at a road junction 350m south of the *madrasa* is a watchtower known as the **Chaubara**. Just 60m south of the Chaubara is the **Jama Masjid** (15th century), which has been repeatedly renovated and now has an ugly modern façade that almost entirely obscures the mosque's old structure. Large parts of the old **city walls** survive, as do several well-defended gates—

and there are several old *khanqahs*, which served as Islamic monasteries and places of retreat, scattered about the town. The fine eastern gate of Bidar leads sharply downhill towards Ashtur and the Bahmani tombs.

Ashtur

Some 3km east of Bidar is Ashtur, the impressive funerary complex of the later Bahmani rulers. The first building on the right side of the road, before the royal tomb, is the unusual mausoleum, or *chaukhandi*, of a Shia Muslim saint, Khalil Ullah, who died here in 1460. Beyond the large gateway is what looks like a two-storey octagonal tomb. In fact, it is a screen for an inner single-storey domed tomb. There is superb calligraphy work on the screen, as well as some extensions to the building, which, inside and out, has a large number of lesser tombstones. A large step-well close to the road served what was once an important pilgrimage site.

The majestic **royal tombs**, six arranged in a single line, are 500m further along the road. Note the distinctive high drum and dome of the Bahmanid tombs, as well as the small finials and trefoil motif, the surviving tilework and calligraphy on some of the building, and the layers of arched recesses. The last, most easterly tomb, that of Ahmed I, who shifted the Bahmani capital from Gulbarga, is the oldest (1436) and the best-preserved. Its painted interior is particularly fine, with red and gold geometric designs covering most of the walls.

The Baridi tombs

These tombs have now been enveloped by modern Bidar, though they still stand in their own parkland in the west of the town, with two groups of tombs on either side of the Udgir Road. The more numerous smaller tombs, in an enclosed park (*closed Mon*) on the northern side of the road, include those of the first two Baridi rulers, while the largest and finest of the Baridi tombs is surrounded by trees, 400m away on the south side of the road. This is the tall open **tomb of Ali**, the third Baridi ruler, and was started in 1577, three years before his death. The tomb has no doors, just four large archways and superb blue tiling on its interior walls and on the underside of the dome. Be sure to visit the two-storey gateway on the far side of the tomb, with an attached mosque. The other similar but smaller structure to the west is the **tomb of Ibrahim**, Ali's son and successor.

AROUND BIDAR

The **Jalasanghvi Shiva Temple** (*map 11 C2*), 35km west of Bidar on the Humnabad Road (take the turning on the left, just before the Reliance gas depot), has some superb external carvings, mainly of women dancing or posing. The south side, which is seen first by visitors, has a statue of Shiva in the main recess, but notice, just to the right, a woman holding up a tablet inscribed with 'Vikramaditya', the name of the temple's royal founder. The west end recess has a statue of Narasimha, the lion avatar of Vishnu, with Durga in the north recess.

Basavakalyan Fort

This superb but little-visited citadel (*map 11 C2*), 63km west of Bidar and 60km north of Gulbarga, was the capital of the Hindu Late Chalukya and Kalachuri dynasties, between the 10th and 13th centuries. It then became an outpost for the rulers of Bijapur and Bidar, and eventually came under the control of the nizams of Hyderabad; in the 19th century it was used as an important regional base. The town and fort were known as Kalyan until the 1950s, when it was prefixed with Basava, the name of a 12th-century social reformer from this region.

Visiting Basavakalyan Fort: The fort (*open Tues–Sun 10–5.30*), on the north side of the town, is approached through a gateway that leads into a large ceremonial courtyard, now used as a school. A gate on the far left side of the courtyard leads to a causeway across a broad moat, and the entrance to the fort. Inside is an array of partially ruined buildings, in better condition than many medieval forts largely because it was still in use in the 19th century. First pass through the outer gates, with old cannon balls lining the pathway and pieces of old Hindu sculpture lying around and embedded in the walls. On the left is an old jail, with bars. After three more gates and some ruined stables and magazines, you should find yourself inside the inner citadel. The main palace rooms are straight ahead, while the Rangin Mahal (Coloured Palace), durbar hall and the three-bayed mosque are all to the right. Note the reused temple door frames in the main palace, and the empty pools in several courtyards. The inner and outer walls have some fine cannon, including one signposted Kadak Bijali Toph (or 'lightning cannon') which is moulded superbly and inlaid with coloured metal.

It is also worth walking round the full external circumference of the fort (900m) to see its strong defences and deep moat. Note the widespread use of carving from temples in the wall, and also two large step-wells in the moat—clearly a later addition. There is a **museum** just outside the fort, with some interesting but poorly-labelled Hindu sculpture, mainly from the 11th–14th centuries.

GULBARGA

The historically important city of Gulbarga (*map 11 C3*) was the first capital of the Bahmani Dynasty after they declared their independence from the Delhi-based Tughlaq Sultanate in 1347. From here they fought a series of wars against Vijayanagar (Hampi), and then moved to the strategically better-positioned fortress in Bidar, 100km to the northeast. The city was then controlled by the rulers of Bijapur and Bidar, before being captured by the Mughals and then becoming part of the territory of the nizams of Hyderabad. There are buildings from the Bahmani period scattered throughout the modern city.

Gulbarga Fort

The low broad double walls of Gulbarga Fort occupy the centre of the modern city. The entrance into the fort is from the east, across the old moat, through an arched gateway. Immediately to the left is the Bala Hissar citadel, and beyond that is the distinctive covered mosque. The Bala Hissar is almost solid, and at the top of the steep steps is an enormous cannon.

Inside the fort is the **Jama Masjid** (1367), or Friday Mosque. It has no courtyard and is fully covered, making it unique in southern India. There is one large dome over the *mihrab*, or prayer niche, four medium-sized ones at each corner, and 75 smaller domes, rounded at the centre and wedge-shaped at the edge. Its similarities to the Great Mosque at Cordoba have been exaggerated, and there is thought to be no direct connection. Note the common Bahmani trefoil motif along the roof of the mosque, and the lack of minarets. One explanation for its unusual design is that it may have been built as a palace and only later converted into a mosque. Visit the old **bazaar street** in the northwest corner of the fort, built in Bahmani times and still occupied, and, at the end of the street, the now closed **western gate** of the fort—more impressive than the eastern one by which modern visitors enter.

Haft Gumbad

Around 1.5km east of Gulbarga is a group of Bahmani tombs, known as the Haft Gumbad, or 'Seven Domes'. The group is approached from the east and has two separate twin tombs, buildings with two domes joined by an interior passage. The furthest of the twin tombs, the **mausoleum of Tajuddin Firuz** (1422), who died shortly before the move to Bidar, is the largest and most impressive, with complex external recessed niches, and some fine plaster decoration inside. Nearby is the **dargah of Hazrat Gesu Nawaz** (c. 1422), the shrine complex of a widely venerated Sufi Muslim saint, who came to Gulbarga in 1413. It consists of a series of domed tombs, and two gateways which postdate the Bahmani period. The first, near the modern entrance to the complex, has cylindrical towers, while the superb and unusual second ceremonial gate, built in the Mughal period, has square towers and stucco decoration, including two images of a lion riding an elephant. The earliest Bahmani tombs are to the west of the fort in an area now enveloped in urban sprawl.

Other buildings in Gulbarga

The **Chor Gumbad** (1420), or 'Thief's Dome', originally intended as Hazrat Gesu Nawaz's tomb, is on higher ground, 2km east of the fort, and has four small corner towers with fine internal decoration. There are excellent views of Gulbarga from its roof. About 1km northeast of the fort is the **dargah of Sheikh Sirajuddin Junaydi**, the shrine of the spiritual guide of the early Bahmani ruler. The large and impressive gateway was added by the Bijapur ruler Yusuf Adil Shah in the early 16th century.

AROUND GULBARGA

Holkonda

This largely forgotten group of fine Bahmani tombs, also known as Kolikonda (*map 11 C3*), is 30km north of Gulbarga and is well signposted from the road to Bidar. The tombs sit just over the crest of the hill, on the eastern side of the road. Visitors pass through a whitewashed ceremonial gate on the left. There are five tombs in the first compound and a ruined mosque at the back. Beyond it is the largest tomb, belonging to Shaykh Muhammad Mayshakha, the 14th-century Muslim saint to whom the complex is dedicated.

Sannathi

The village of Sannathi (*map 11 C3*), 58km south of Gulbarga on a bend in the Bhima River, is an important Hindu and Buddhist site. The **Chandralamba Temple** (11th century), dedicated to a form of the Hindu goddess Devi, has an unusual circular sanctuary. A 3rd-century BC inscription by the Mauryan king Ashoka was found here and is on display. Nearby are excavated ruins of Buddhist stupas and a citadel thought to date from the 1st-century Satavahana period.

Firuzabad

This extraordinary but little-visited ruined Bahmani city overlooking the River Bhima (*map 11 C3*), 30km south of Gulbarga, just off the main road to Bijapur (take the unpaved road opposite the dargah of Khalifat Rahman), is in poor condition and in desperate need of conservation. It is possible to make out a number of buildings, gateways and large parts of the 4.5km-long city walls. It was built in 1400 by (and named after) the Bahmani ruler Tajuddin Firuz, to commemorate his victory over the Vijayanagar forces, but it appears to have been abandoned soon after. Encourage someone from the nearby village to show you around, and ask to see the ruins of the enormous mosque, with its surviving walls and main gate, and tumble-down prayer area, complete with prayer niches. The old palace baths, or *hammam*, are closer to the river. Note the air-vents in the domes of the building.

BIJAPUR

This large city (*map 11 C3*) is home to two of the great buildings of Deccani architecture—the Gol Gumbaz tomb and the Ibrahim Rauza mausoleum—as well as numerous fascinating 16th- and 17th-century palaces, gateways and mosques. Most of the city's buildings belong to a slightly later period than those of Gulbarga and Bidar, and have examples of the Deccani style at its most developed. Bijapur, whose history predates its capture by the Delhi Sultanate in 1294, emerged as the major city of the Deccan in the early 16th century. The Adil Shahi Dynasty, formerly feudatories of the Bahmani rulers of Bidar, set themselves up as independent rulers. Bijapur then played a major role in the final defeat of the Hampi-based Vijayanagar Empire in 1565, and took large parts of Vijayanagar territory. The Adil Shahis also fought and eventually lost to the Portuguese in Goa in the 16th century, and Bijapur itself came under Mughal rule in 1686. Bijapur is an interesting city to walk around, and is full of minor ruins of the Adil Shahi period.

Orientation: The largely intact outer city walls, 10km long, form a circle around much of modern Bijapur, and enclose all the major monuments apart from the Ibrahim Rauza, which is 600m west of the western Mecca Gate. The Gol Gumbaz is to the far east of the city, but still within the old walls; the railway station is nearby but on the other side of the wall. The 2km-long inner city walls enclose the heart of old Bijapur and its former palaces.

Gol Gumbaz

The unique Gol Gumbaz (1659), meaning circular dome, is probably the single most distinctive Muslim building in the entire Deccan. It is the tomb of Muhammad Adil Shah, the ruler of Bijapur for 30 years until 1657. It is said that he wanted to eclipse his father Ibrahim's spectacular tomb—the Ibrahim Rauza. At the time of its construction, the Gol Gumbaz had one of the largest domes in the world, only slightly smaller than that of the Pantheon in Rome, and, at 37.9m, twice the diameter of the dome of the Taj Mahal, completed 15 years earlier. But it is not only the scale of the Gol Gumbaz that is so distinctive. Its unusual, octagonal tiered minarets also give it a striking appearance, criticised as inappropriate and out of proportion by some architectural historians, but which help make it one of India's most unforgettable buildings.

Visiting the Gol Gumbaz: The tomb is approached on foot from the south, from a small car park off MG Road, next to the **ticket office** (*open daily 6.30–5.30*). One's first view of the tomb is partially obscured by the two-storey Nakkar Khana, or Music Gallery, which houses a small **museum** (*open Sat–Thur 10–5*), and restrictions on access to the park around the Gol Gumbaz can make it hard to get an unrestricted view suitable for cameras without a wide-angle lens. On the left of the tomb is a five-bayed mosque, while other nearby buildings (*no public access*) are part of Bijapur's complex 17th-century waterworks.

The actual mausoleum is entered through a central stone screen, pierced with a door and windows, a dark contrast to the bright plasterwork which covers the rest of the building. Inside, the cenotaphs of Muhammad Adil Shah and his family are covered with a wooden frame resting on a large plinth—the graves are beneath the tomb. Look up to see the intricate interlocking arches that allow such a huge space to be spanned by a single dome. It is possible to climb a series of steps to the tomb's whispering gallery, where—unless you choose to visit early in the day—you are likely to be joined by hundreds of children testing the building's impressive acoustics.

Jama Masjid

To reach the Jama Masjid, head down the road directly opposite the entrance to the Gol Gumbaz, and bear right at the pretty Sufi tomb with its distinctive high bulbous dome. The Jama Masjid (1576, with later additions), or Friday Mosque, was built in the reign of Ali Adil Shah. It is entered by the northern gate, which unusually offers a choice of entrances: to the cloisters and the prayer hall, by a staircase and an upper doorway; or down some steps, past storage rooms and into the large courtyard. The basic design of the mosque is simple, with seven equal bays and cloisters around the side. However, it was never finished—the minarets planned for the eastern corners of the mosque were never built, and both the eastern gateway and the lavishly decorated *mihrab*, or prayer niche, are later additions.

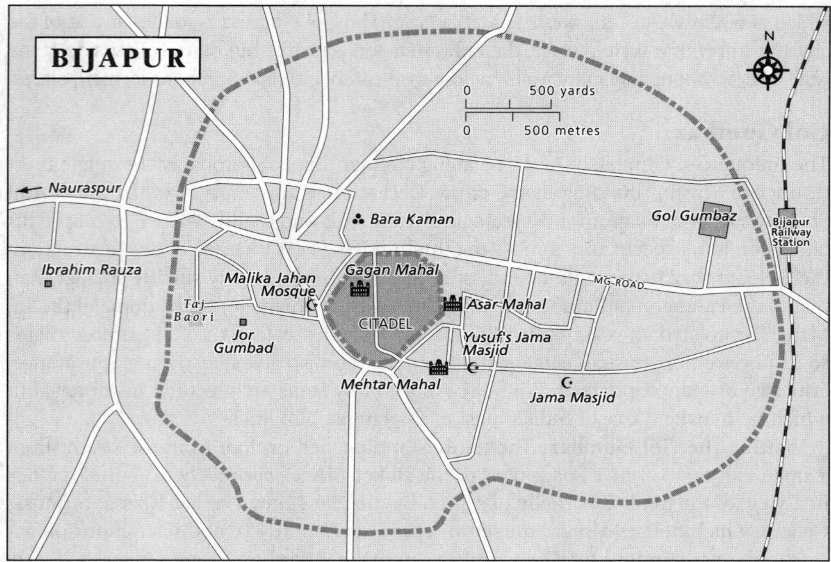

About 500m west along the same road as the Jama Masjid is the small mosque known as **Yusuf's Jama Masjid** (1513), one of the oldest Adil Shahi buildings—now sadly hemmed in by new construction. Another 150m west is a handsome, tower-like three-storey building called the **Mehtar Mahal** (c. 1620), which, despite being called a 'mahal', or palace, is in fact the entrance gatehouse to a mosque. Note the pretty balconies supported by stone struts that have been carved to resemble wood. The internal stonework is superb, particularly on the ceilings, and it is possible to climb up a narrow staircase to the roof for superb views of Bijapur.

Asar Mahal

Continue westwards to the inner walls of Bijapur. On the right, just on the outside of the walls, is the large white Asar Mahal (1646), overlooking a large pond, with its back to the moat. This large palace was converted into a reliquary for two hairs that were said to have come from the Prophet Muhammad's beard, which explains why the building is in such good condition—and also why there is a large notice, not always enforced, saying that women are not allowed inside.

The design of the building is unusual, with its double-height portico supported on four wooden pillars—which is possibly a later addition. Ask the watchman to open up the rooms in the palace, some of which have wall-paintings of plants, flowers and trees, and some unexpected Ajanta-style human figures. Look out of the rear window for a clear view of the surviving piers of a bridge that connected the palace with the citadel across the broad moat. The ruined building on the far side of the Asar Mahal is known as the Jahaz Mahal, or 'Ship Palace'.

Bijapur citadel

There are several entrances to the citadel, and large parts of its old walls are now missing. The walls are most intact at the entrance closest to the Asar Mahal, and visitors pass between high bastions, one of which has a small mosque resting on its walls, and then pass under a low arch into the eastern side of the inner precincts of the citadel. The main surviving buildings are on the citadel's western side.

Gagan Mahal: The largest of the ruined buildings is the imposing Gagan Mahal (1561), constructed as the audience hall of Ali Adil Shah, with a huge central archway and two slim, high side arches. Note the pretty fish motif used in the false stucco brackets on the front of the arch, and also what were once rooms, with dozens of little niches, presumably for lighting and storage, at the top of the building's side towers. On the other side of the road from the Gagan Mahal is the much-modified **Anand Mahal** (1589), which is now government offices. The original three-arched portico now covers a badminton court.

On the north side of the street behind the Gagan Mahal is the **Jal Mandir**, or Water Temple, a miniature pavilion consisting of one room topped with a petalled dome on stone-carved brackets and eaves, surrounded by a pond. The tall building on the opposite side of the street from the Jal Mandir is the **Sat Manzil**, or seven-storey house, only four storeys of which survive.

The Royal Quadrangle: The Sat Manzil is in the northwest corner of the Royal Quadrangle—a courtyard surrounded by buildings, and the main palace area under the Adil Shahis. Most of the buildings are now government offices, including the **Chini Mahal**, so named because of the Chinese-style tiling with which it was once decorated. On the southern side of the Quadrangle is the southern gate to the citadel, with a small mosque in the western wall. The flat-roofed larger mosque on the road near the gate is Bijapur's oldest, the **Kareemuddin Masjid** (1320), constructed by the invading army of Delhi's Tughlaq sultans, and largely built from columns and stones which were once part of Hindu and Jain temples. The nearby **Mecca Masjid** (1669) is within a walled compound with arcades—its tapering minarets may belong to an older mosque.

North and west of the citadel

Just north of the citadel is Bijapur's strangest ruin, known as the **Bara Kaman** (1650s), or 'twelve arches'. It is the unfinished tomb of Ali Adil Shah II, and intended to be larger than the tomb of his father at Gol Gumbaz—indeed the plinth covers a bigger area. Many of the first-floor arches have survived, but work is not thought ever to have begun on the second storey. The small **Malika Jahan Mosque** (1586) is just to the west of the citadel and was built by Ibrahim II in honour of his wife. It has some elaborate stonework, particularly on the brackets supporting the eaves—though the view is partly obstructed by corrugated sheeting, which covers part of the courtyard. Close by is the **Jor Gumbad**—two handsome late Adil Shahi tombs, one square, one octagonal. The tombs have become part of a shrine for one of those buried here, the Adil Shahi spiritual adviser Abdul Razzaq Qadiri. On the western side of the Jor Gumbad is Bijapur's largest water tank, the **Taj Baori** (1620s), with its handsome gateway and side towers. Just north of the main road leading towards the Ibrahim Rauza is a bastion with an unusual 16th-century cannon known as the **Malik-i Maidan**, or 'Lord of the Plains', which was brought here in 1632. Note how the muzzle of the cannon has been cast with the image of monsters swallowing an elephant.

Ibrahim Rauza

The magnificent Ibrahim Rauza complex (1626) is 600m west of Bijapur's western walls. The complex (*open daily 6.30–5.30*) consists of a large walled compound, a gate with high finial towers, some pretty gardens and two gorgeous twin buildings that are similar but not identical: the tomb of Ibrahim Adil Shah II and his family on the left, and the mosque on the right. The complex is approached from the north, along a pathway leading through the small door of the gateway. The tomb and mosque sit on the same large plinth, supported by arches and separated by a rectangular pool with a fountain. Behind are more gardens. The tomb itself is larger than the mosque, and square with a pyramid of finials and turrets on its domed roof. The external walls of the tomb chamber have some superb geometric and calligraphic designs carved in relief. Inside are six cenotaphs, the largest of which is Ibrahim Adil Shah's. The mosque is rectangular, and the necessity of its prayer niche pointing to Mecca determines the orientation of the entire complex.

NEAR BIJAPUR

Nauraspur (*map 11 C3*) is 5km west of the Ibrahim Rauza. It was begun by Ibrahim Adil Shah in 1599 as a new city, but sacked by the invading Sultan of Ahmednagar in 1624 and never completed. It has an unusual nine-sided citadel wall, at the centre of which is a building constructed to an almost identical design to the Gagan Mahal in the Bijapur citadel. There are several mosques, tombs and other buildings in the nearby fields, including one miniature tomb with an unusually high drum supporting its dome.

Five kilometres east of Bijapur, just to the north of the main road and near the village of Ainapur, is the impressive unfinished **Tomb of Jahan Begum**, wife of Muhammad Adil Shah, who is buried at Gol Gumbaz. Parts of the towers and arches survive, and it seems likely that the building was intended as a near replica of the Gol Gumbaz tomb, but on a smaller scale.

BADAMI

This small town (*map 13 B1*) is 105km south of Bijapur and 100km northwest of Hampi. Sitting at the west end of a lake that is almost surrounded by a horseshoe of sandstone hills, Badami must rank as one of the prettiest of India's great archaeological and historical sites. Its temples—rock-cut and free-standing—date from the 6th and 7th centuries, and are superb examples of early Hindu art and architecture. The town also makes an excellent base for visiting the other great temple towns of this part of Karnataka: Pattadakal and Aihole. Badami served as the capital of the Early Chalukya

Dynasty, which ruled most of Karnataka and large parts of Andhra Pradesh in the 6th–8th centuries.

Orientation: Most visitors enter Badami from the north, past the railway station and the Badami Court Hotel. As one enters the town, the Malegitti Shivalaya Temple is visible on the left. A little further on, a road to the left takes you to the museum and the north side of the lake. Continue through the town, and a well-signposted road on the left will take you to the famous cave-temples and the south bank of the lake.

The cave-temples

The four cave-temples of Badami, all cut into the sandstone outcrops that loom above the town, are approached from the car park and ticket office (*open daily dawn–dusk*) and then by steps cut into the hillside.

Cave 1: This late 6th-century cave has a porch supported by four columns and is a Shiva temple. Outside the cave on the right is a superb 18-armed dancing Shiva, with his vehicle, the bull Nandi, and his son Ganesha at his feet. Just next to the dancing Shiva is a small side shrine with a four-armed Durga killing a demon buffalo, a seated Ganesha and Kartikeya riding a peacock. Just inside the main porch on the right is another fine Shiva with Nandi, while at the far end of the porch is the figure of Harihara, who is a combination of Shiva and Vishnu and carries the former's trident and the latter's conch. Note also the presence of their respective vehicles, Nandi the bull and Garuda the dwarf-like human eagle. There are also fine carvings on the ceiling of the porch, including a coiled *naga* (snake) deity. There are monstrous beasts on the column brackets, some of them devouring other animals, while on the sides of the brackets are carvings of amorous couples. A Nandi bull stands outside the inner sanctuary, with its black Shiva lingam.

Cave 2: The second cave is similar to Cave 1 in design but is a Vishnu temple. Carved temple guardians stand outside the porch. Inside on the far left is Varaha, the boar avatar of Vishnu, carrying his consort Bhudevi in the palm of his hand, while on the right Trivikrama, the giant avatar of Vishnu, strides across the universe. On the ceiling of the porch are complex designs, one using swastikas, another using 16 fish radiating from a floral hub. The idol is missing from the inner sanctuary.

The terrace outside Cave 2 has superb views of the lake, the rock-cut temples by the waterside and on the opposite hillside, as well as of the town of Badami. Ahead are more steep steps leading up to a gate—part of the more recent Adil Shahi fortifications of the hillside. Note the steps on the right, now barred by a grille, which used to lead up to the hilltop fort, which is now closed after a series of accidents.

Cave 3: Dating to the year 578, this is the most impressive and largest of the group, with ornately carved columns, some superb relief carvings of deities and friezes of animated dwarves beneath the main carvings. On the far left of the porch is a standing Vishnu, with extra arms joined at the elbow, while just inside the porch on the left is a superb Vishnu seated on a coiled snake. On the wall, at a right angle to the seated

Vishnu, is Varaha, his boar avatar. The outermost carving on the far right of the porch is of Harihara, who is half-Shiva (carrying a trident) and half-Vishnu (carrying a conch). Note the line separating the two gods that runs down the centre of the headdress. Just inside the porch is a Trivikrama, similar to the one in Cave 2. The innermost large carving on the right is of Narasimha, the lion avatar of Vishnu. The ceilings, column brackets and eaves are also richly decorated, particularly the fine carving of Garuda, half-man half-eagle, on the underside of the overhang. The main idol in the sanctuary is missing.

Cave 4: This cave is smaller and more recent than its predecessors, and is a Jain shrine, not a Hindu temple. As such, it has some fine carvings of Jain *tirthankars*, or saviours, on the walls of the porch, as well as dozens of tiny carvings of Jain figures that have been cut into the rock at a later period. The figure in the inner sanctuary is Mahavir, the 24th and last of the Jain *tirthankars*—recognisable because of the lion beneath him.

Badami town

At the back of the car park for the cave-temples is a pretty **Adil Shahi tomb** (16th or 17th century), made of sandstone and erected by a military officer in memory of his wife. From here it is possible to walk down a stone passage and along the western bank of the lake, where pretty steps serve as the wall of a dam. Halfway along is the **Yellama Temple**, from the Late Chalukya period, overlooking the lake. A little inside the town from here is the older **Jambulinga Temple** (699), with some pretty carved ceiling panels.

Badami Museum: The temples and museum on the north side of the lake are approached by a well-signposted road. The excellent museum (*open Sat–Thur 10–5*) is unusually well laid-out, and has some fine pieces. Note in particular the carving of the fertility goddess Lajja Gauri, splaying her legs and with a lotus flower instead of a head, and two superb carved panels from Pattadakal in which Shiva spears a demon and shoots arrows while riding in a chariot. There are also some good maps of the area.

Hill temples

Behind the museum, a path leads up through a gate and a crevasse between two large rocks towards two fine Early Chalukya temples and the more recent fort. The first temple is the **Lower Shivalaya** (7th century) on a promontory overlooking the town and the lake, of which only the sanctuary and tower survive. At the top of the hill past some more fortifications is the **Upper Shivalaya** (early 7th century), which is probably the earliest free-standing Chalukya temple. Part of the assembly hall has collapsed, but the tower, sanctuary, circumambulatory passage and plinth are still intact, and there are fine carvings of elephants near the temple entrance. Despite its name, this was not originally a Shiva temple, as the carved panels with scenes from the life of Krishna indicate. The views from the temple are the best in Badami, and it is well worth exploring the ruined fortifications, including granaries shaped like giant conical bee-hives and complex waterworks, including a sluice gate.

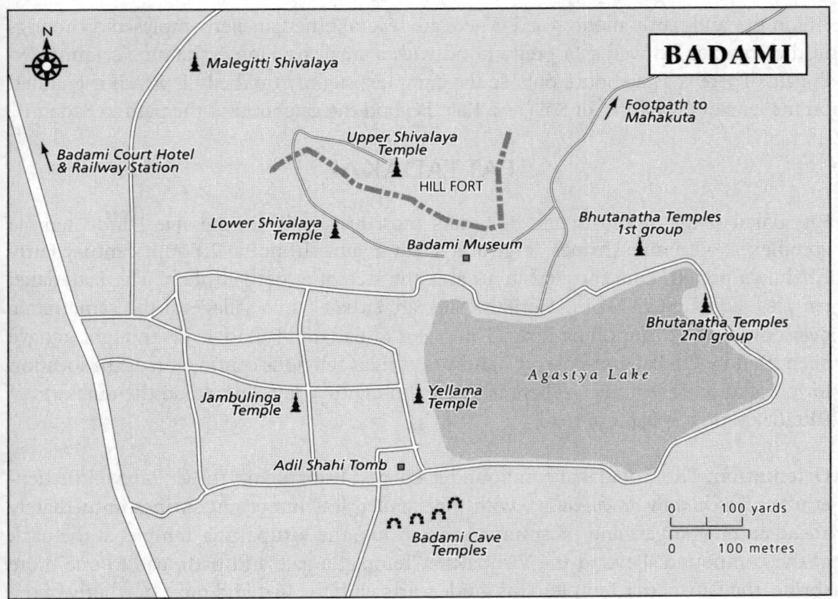

Lakeside temples

Further around from the museum are two groups of shrines known as the **Bhutanatha temples**. The first group belongs to the 11th-century Late Chalukya period, while the second group, prettily situated at the far end of the lake, belongs to the 7th-century Early Chalukya period. Beyond the second group are rocks with more carvings. There is one superb image of Vishnu resting on the snake Anantha while having one of his legs massaged by his consort Lakshmi. There is also a cave with a back-breakingly low entrance, inside which is a fine seated carving of Mahavir, the founder of Jainism.

Malegitti Shivalaya Temple

This temple (late 7th century) is approached separately by road, but sits on the side of the same hill as the other two Shivalaya shrines, and is the most complete of the three. There are fine panels of Shiva on the south face and Vishnu on the north.

Mahakuta

It is possible to walk with a guide from near the museum in Badami over the hill to the Mahakuta temple complex (*map 13 B1*)—a distance of less than 4km; by road it is 15km. On entering the main gate of the walled compound, the **Mahakuteshwara Temple** (late 7th century) is ahead of you, guarded by a small pavilion with a carving of the bull Nandi. The exterior of this Shiva temple has several fine carvings, some of them labelled, including Ardhanarishwara, the half-male and half-female form of Shiva. The interior is still in use and partly modernised. There are several other smaller temples and carvings in the complex, as well as a pretty pond with a small pavilion containing a four-faced lingam. There is a gatehouse outside the complex, slightly up the hill, which is guarded on the far side by figures of Kala and Kali. Beyond the gatehouse is the path to Badami.

PATTADAKAL

Pattadakal (*map 13 B1*) is one of India's most artistically impressive Hindu temple complexes, with nine shrines, large and small, mainly from the 7th–8th-century Early Chalukya period, concentrated in an area the size of a football pitch. The Pattadakal temples, a UNESCO World Heritage Site, are situated in a village of the same name overlooking the Malaprabha River, 15km east of Badami. Pattadakal is thought to have been used by the Badami-based Chalukyas as their religious centre, and as the location for coronation ceremonies. There is also a 9th-century Jain temple on the outskirts of Pattadakal on the Badami road.

Orientation: The Pattadakal compound is entered from the northeast, next to the ticket office (*open daily dawn–dusk*), with the smaller, less important shrines immediately ahead and the largest and most impressive shrine, the Virupaksha Temple, at the back of the compound. Beyond the Virupaksha Temple, a gate and path lead to one more shrine, the Papanatha Temple. This guide starts with the first and most northerly of the main temples, the Kadasiddheswara, and proceeds southwards. It is useful to have a torch to examine the fine carved stonework inside the main temples.

The smaller temples

The small **Kadasiddheswara Temple** consists of a simple tower, covering a sanctuary containing a Shiva lingam, and an assembly hall. Note the carving of Shiva and Parvati above the lintel of the doorway, and of Shiva dancing on the front of the tower. The nearby **Jambulinga Temple** is built to a very similar design and also has a dancing Shiva on the tower, which is in better condition than that on the first temple. The larger **Galaganatha Temple** has a high curvilinear tower, but has lost most of its assembly hall. Note the large carving of eight-armed Shiva killing the demon Andhaka. The **Sangameshwara Temple** has a distinctive square multi-storey tower, and is particularly interesting for the incomplete state of many of its external carvings, which gives a sense of work in progress. The smaller **Kashivishvanatha Temple** is probably the latest of the group, with a small Nandi bull on the plinth facing the shrine. The pillars have images from the stories of Shiva and of Krishna.

The main temples

The largest and most important shrines, the Mallikarjuna and Virupaksha temples, are at the back of the complex and were constructed by two Chalukya queens c. 745 to celebrate the victory of King Vikramaditya over the Pallavas. They were built to a very similar design, though the Virupaksha shrine has survived the centuries slightly

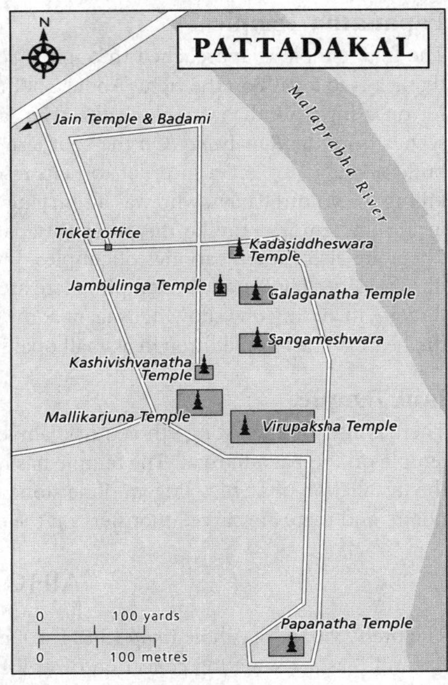

better. Both have carved figures on the exterior and superb carved stone panels inside, showing scenes from the Hindu epics.

The **Mallikarjuna Temple** is the nearer and smaller of the two shrines, and several of the carvings on the exterior are unfinished. Most of its compound wall has now disappeared, and the Nandi bull in front of the temple is partially broken. Note the worn figure of Ugra Narasimha, the lion avatar of Vishnu in his terrifying form, disembowelling a demon, on the inside of the external column on the right of the entrance. Inside are superb friezes carved onto the supporting columns of the assembly hall, as well as some finely-carved ceiling panels and column brackets.

The **Virupaksha Temple** is thought to have been used for the coronation of Chalukya rulers, and is the largest and most intact of the Pattadakal shrines. Much of its compound wall and the eastern and western gates to the temple have survived. Inside the compound is a Nandi *mandapa*, or pavilion, sheltering a large carving of the bull, Shiva's vehicle. Both the bull and the lathe-turned Late Chalukya-style internal columns are from a later period. But the exterior of the Nandi pavilion, with several carvings of amorous couples, dates back to the building of the temple in the mid-8th century. Note also the sinuous relief carving of a woman with an impossibly narrow waist allowing a parrot to eat from her hand.

The Virupaksha Temple has religious images on its exterior, including (going anticlockwise), a carving of Shiva emerging from the lingam, an eight-armed Shiva standing on the demon-dwarf, a four-armed dancing Shiva, and some damaged images of Shiva and Parvati. Beyond the southern door is a superb image of Shiva with his hair down, standing on the dwarf. On the right of the main entrance is Trivikrama, the giant avatar of Vishnu, striding, with one leg held high, through the heavens.

On the ceiling of the porch of the main temple entrance is a panel showing the sun-god Surya being pulled on a chariot by seven horses. The large square assembly area is supported by 16 columns, each with carved friezes mainly showing scenes from the *Ramayana* and *Mahabharata*. Note the fine carving of the goddess Durga killing the demon Mahishasura in the small sanctuary on the northern side, while the main sanctuary has a black Shiva lingam.

Papanatha Temple

The final temple is approached through a gate at the back of the Virupaksha Temple that leads to a path on the right. About 150m along the path is the Papanatha Temple, set on a high plinth overlooking the river, and with impressive exterior carvings of scenes from the *Ramayana*. On the southern wall are the monkeys carrying stones to build a bridge to Lanka in order to help rescue Sita from Ravana, as well as Ravana killing the vulture Jatayu who was also trying to rescue Sita. There is a large Nandi bull inside the temple—unlike the other Pattadakal shrines where the Nandi is outside. There are also superb carvings of couples, presumably temple donors, but, again unlike the other big Pattadakal temple, there are no friezes. There are fine ceiling panels, though, including one showing Nagaraja, the king of the snakes. Note how light enters the heart of the temple through a small opening at the side of the roof.

Jain Temple

There is also an interesting 9th-century Jain temple, 700m west of the main Pattadakal temple on the Badami road. The temple has been converted into a Hindu shrine, with the installation of a Shiva lingam. Fine stone elephants with riders are in the entrance porch, and there are carved monsters on the entrance to the inner sanctuary.

AIHOLE

The pretty village of Aihole (*map 13 B1*), 10km northeast of Pattadakal and 25km from Badami, has a fascinating collection of well-signposted Hindu and Jain temples scattered across a wide area, and shows an extensive variety of architectural styles used between the 6th and 12th centuries.

Orientation: The road from Pattadakal enters Aihole from the south, with the Meguti Temple on a hilltop on the right. Aihole can be a difficult place in which to orient yourself, and it is best to head first to the best-known monument, the Durga Temple, on the north side of the village, and return later to some of the lesser buildings.

The Durga Temple

This temple is set in a compound next to the ticket office (*open dawn–dusk*). It is not a temple dedicated to the goddess Durga, but is so named because of its proximity to the *durg*, or fort. It is one of India's finest and most unusual early temples, with an apsidal, or horseshoe-shaped, design like many Buddhist rock-cut temples, but with a more traditional curvilinear tower. The interior is relatively bare, but the porch and the circumambulatory passage have some superb carvings from the Early Chalukya period. Going clockwise, they are Shiva with Nandi, Narasimha (the lion avatar of Vishnu), Vishnu (with his vehicle Garuda, the man-eagle), Varaha (the boar avatar of Vishnu) with his consort Bhudevi on his shoulder, the goddess Durga killing the demon buffalo, accompanied by her vehicle (a lion) and Vishnu (note the finely carved drapery). The porch of the temple has a number of fine carvings and friezes, including several of amorous couples. Two of the ceiling panels from here are now in the National Museum in Delhi. Nearby is a stepwell and a small museum (*closed Fri*), though the best exhibits are the hero stones and several carved representations of Ganesha, the elephant god, displayed outside the building.

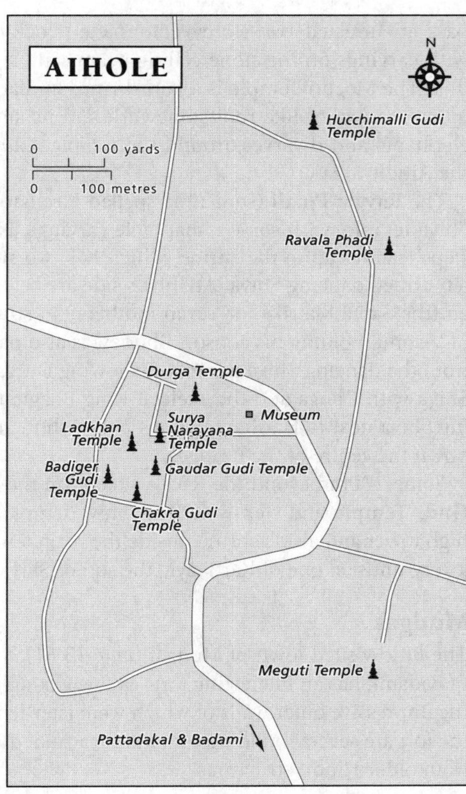

Near the Durga Temple

Just to the south of Durga Temple are several more shrines grouped around an irregularly-shaped tank. The small **Surya Narayana Temple** has a large, more recent image of Surya the sun-god (note the tiny horses at his feet) in the sanctuary. The larger **Ladkhan Temple** is based on a design usually used in wooden buildings, with a roof structure made to look like split logs, and a broad assembly hall. Unusually, there is a small chamber in the centre of the roof. There is a Nandi bull in the assembly area and a Shiva lingam in the sanctuary. The simple **Gaudar Gudi Temple** is at a lower level, indicating that it predates the Ladkhan Temple. Note the repeated use of the pot motif on the exterior. The partly ruined **Badiger Gudi Temple** is to the right of the tank and has a fine carving of Surya the sun-god on its tower, while the **Chakra Gudi Temple**, on the far side of the tank, has a high tower and a series of carvings of amorous couples around the door frame of the sanctuary.

Other temples in Aihole

There are other groups of less significant half-ruined temples in the centre of the village and along the road that circles it. However, the other most important sites are the Meguti Temple on the hilltop, approached by a footpath on the east side of Aihole, and two shrines (Ravala Phadi and the Hucchimalli Gudi) a little outside the village, also approached by a road close to the bottom of the hill.

The **Meguti Temple**, in a large fortified compound on the hill overlooking Aihole, is approached by more than 125 steps leading from the east of the village. The steps pass an unusual two-storey colonnaded rock-cut Buddhist temple (6th century), with carvings on the stone ceiling beams and a ceiling panel showing a seated Buddha. The Meguti Temple is a Jain shrine, similar in design to the Ladkhan Temple in its use of timber-like roof stonework and its small roof chamber. Note the frieze of elephants and dwarves around the temple. Climb the staircase for superb views of the Aihole area.

The **Ravala Phadi** (sometime spelled Ravanaphadi) is a small 6th-century rock-cut Shiva temple, with some remarkable carvings. Note the Nandi bull at the foot of the steps leading up to the shrine, which has two side chambers. On the left is a superb ten-armed dancing Shiva. At Shiva's side are beautifully carved groups of lissom women (the Sapta Matrika, or 'seven mothers') in strange tall hats. Varaha, the boar avatar of Vishnu, holding his consort Bhudevi is also part of this group. On the opposite side from the dancing Shiva is a group showing Durga killing the demon buffalo, as well as Shiva with Ganga and the skeletal King Bhagirath on the side. There is also a standing Shiva next to Harihara, who is half-Vishnu and half-Shiva—note the dividing line down the centre of the headgear.

Some 200m beyond the Ravala Phadi, on the same small road, is the **Hucchimalli Gudi Temple** and step-well. This Shiva temple stands in a large compound, with a high tower and a side shrine. Inside the main temple are some fine carvings, including a very unusual one of Kartikeya, the son of Shiva, riding his vehicle, a peacock.

Mudgal

The little-visited town of Mudgal (*map 13 B1*), 75km north of Hampi and 82km east of Badami, has an interesting fort—a fine example of Vijayanagar military architecture, the impressive outer walls of which were later reinforced by the Bijapur sultans. Inside the fort are several buildings, including a ruined mosque that was built using elements from older Hindu structures.

HAMPI

Hampi (*map 13 B2*), also known as Vijayanagar (literally 'city of victory), is one of India's most important historical sites, and one of exceptional beauty. This remote ruined city, with temples, palaces, avenues, statues, towers and bridges, all spread over a huge area along the Tunghabhadra River and further into the interior, is set in a gorgeous location, surrounded by water, hills and huge stone boulders. According to some Hindu traditions, it is the site of Kishkinda in the epic *Ramayana*, the forest home of the monkeys who helped rescue Rama's wife Sita from the demon king Ravana. More recently, it was the capital of the Hindu Vijayanagar Empire, which flourished from the mid-14th to the mid-16th century. It was abandoned following the defeat of the Vijayanagar kings to the Deccan sultanates in 1565. The main Virupaksha shrine, near the river, has remained an active temple, and the Hampi site has attracted foreign visitors for more than 200 years. It was made a UNESCO

World Heritage Site in 1986, and the conservation of this spectacular site has been the subject of much debate and anguish.

Set in a remarkable landscape, it remains one of the world's great ruined cities, and is worth taking several days to explore. Its remoteness and modest tourist infrastructure mean that it has not been overrun by visitors. In fact, the site is so large that it is possible to spend hours wandering around the old suburbs of Vijayanagar, away from the main tourist attractions, without bumping into any other travellers.

History: The Vijayanagar Empire was born in the mid-14th century. Two brothers, Harihara and Bukka (who are thought to have been in the service of a minor princely state), took advantage of a power vacuum caused by the invasion and departure of the forces of the Delhi Sultanate to set up their own kingdom and the Sangama Dynasty. By the mid-15th century, the empire under Devaraya I extended to both coastlines and large parts of southern India. In 1485, the Sangamas were overthrown by the short-lived Saluva Dynasty. The Tuluva Dynasty took control of Vijayanagar in 1505, and under Krishnadevaraya and Achutaraya the empire continued to grow. In its heyday, the Vijayanagar Empire was one of the richest and most powerful in India, and there are several extensive accounts of the city by European visitors, who were all amazed by the city's size and opulence.

The Vijayanagar Empire at Hampi ended in 1565 when Ramaraya, the last Tuluva emperor, was killed on the battlefield of Talikota, 100km to the north, by the forces of the four Deccan sultanates of Bijapur, Bidar, Golconda and Ahmadnagar. Surviving members of the dynasty moved the capital further south to Penugonda and Chandragiri in modern-day Andhra Pradesh, and to Vellore in Tamil Nadu. The main Virupaksha Temple remained an important shrine, and Hampi, which is actually the name of the village near the temple, continued to be settled—though the rest of the great city of Vijayanagar was deserted.

Orientation: The ruined city of Vijayanagar is on the southern side of the Tunghabhadra River. Most visitors approach from the nearest major town, Hospet, which has several hotels, though a growing number stay in guest houses on the other side of the river, which can be crossed by boat. Vijayanagar has two main areas. The Sacred Centre is close to the river and includes the main Virupaksha Temple in the west and the Vitthala Temple in the east. Cars are not allowed to travel through the Sacred Centre, and it is a great place for walking. (Cars can park close to both of these temples, though it is a long detour to go by road between them.) To the south of the Sacred Centre, away from the river, is the Royal Centre, with the *zenana* enclosure, the elephant stables and numerous residential buildings, pavilions, baths and more religious buildings.

There are also several outlying suburbs, including Anegondi, on the other side of the river (5mins by boat or 1½ hours by road), and Kamalapuram, which houses the archaeological museum and which is close to the main road to Hospet.

A ticket is required for the Vitthala and the *zenana* enclosures—though the same ticket can be used for both places.

THE SACRED CENTRE OF HAMPI

This area closest to the river contains both the oldest and newest parts of the Hampi/Vijayanagar site. The Virupaksha Temple predates the Vijayanagar Empire, as do many sites linked with the *Ramayana*, but some parts were built in the 19th century. The nearby village of Hampi has been continuously occupied, while the rest of the sacred centre was abandoned in the 16th century, and the buildings began to crumble over the intervening years, until conservation began to be taken seriously in recent decades.

Orientation: Four large temples (Virupaksha, Krishna, Tiruvengalanatha and Vitthala), each with a broad colonnaded avenue, are the main features of the Sacred Centre, around which other buildings have been constructed. The best-known location in the Sacred Centre is the Hampi Bazaar, a 700m-long colonnaded avenue running east–west, with the Virupaksha Temple and numerous small restaurants and shops at its western end. It is where many visitors begin their exploration of the ruined city. The key landmark at the other end of Hampi Bazaar is Matanga Hill, looming above the eastern end of the bazaar and visible from almost everywhere in the area. On the other side of Matanga Hill is the Tiruvengalanatha Temple, while the Vitthala Temple is further northeast, close to the river, and the Krishna Temple is further away from the river on the road from the Hampi Bazaar back towards the Royal Centre.

Virupaksha Temple

The main temple complex at Hampi (*open daily dawn–dusk; closed 1–2.30 for lunch*) stands at the end of a broad avenue. It continues to attract large numbers of Hindu pilgrims, and is thought to date back to the 7th century. The 50m-tall *gopura*, or entrance tower, is from the 19th century (though older pieces of carved stone are set into its lower levels) and leads into a large courtyard. On the far left is a large hall, with complex cut-out pillars, and ahead is a smaller *gopura*—both buildings are thought to date from the reign of Krishnaraya in the early 16th century. Footwear should be left at the smaller *gopura*, through which visitors can enter the smaller inner compound.

The entrance hall to the main shrine was added in the early 16th century, though its brick-and-plaster parapet, with statues in recesses, dates only to the 19th century. The interior of the entrance hall has ornate and complex carved columns with huge rearing monstrous animals in the distinctive Vijayanagar style. The ceilings have some fine paintings of scenes from the *Ramayana* and of Virupaksha (another form of Shiva), which are probably 19th-century reworkings of older paintings. There are several smaller shrines in the compound—and a large gate, under another *gopura*, leads to a large stepped Manamatha tank, painted red and white, and surrounded by more shrines. Beyond the tank is a path leading down to the river.

Hemakuta Hill and the Ganesha statues

Immediately to the north of the Virupaksha Temple is an enormous rockface with steps cut into it, known as **Hemakuta Hill**. Several small pavilions, temples, gateways and

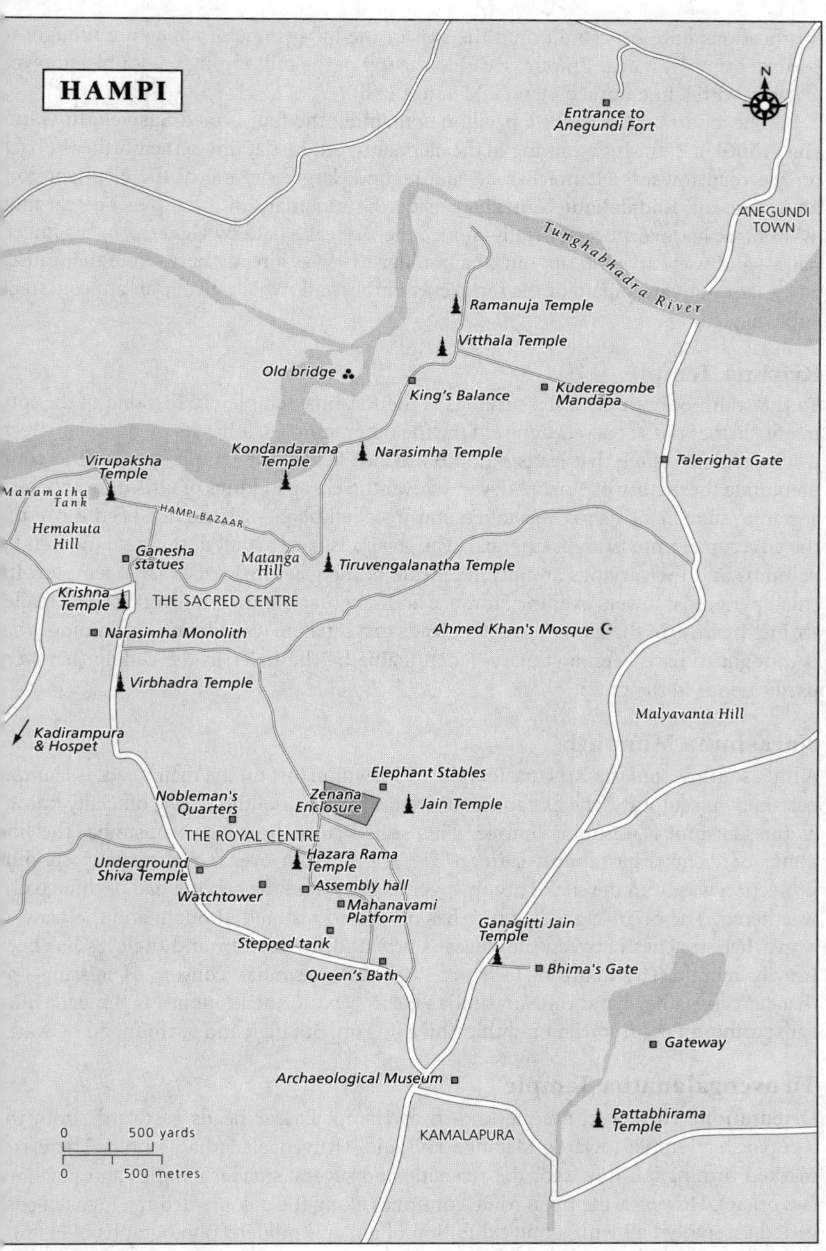
HAMPI
N
Entrance to Anegundi Fort
ANEGUNDI TOWN
Tunghabhadra River
Ramanuja Temple
Vitthala Temple
Old bridge
King's Balance
Kuderegombe Mandapa
Kondandarama Temple
Narasimha Temple
Talerighat Gate
Virupaksha Temple
Manamatha Tank
HAMPI BAZAAR
Hemakuta Hill
Ganesha statues
Matanga Hill
Tiruvengalanatha Temple
Krishna Temple
THE SACRED CENTRE
Ahmed Khan's Mosque
Narasimha Monolith
Virbhadra Temple
Malyavanta Hill
Kadirampura & Hospet
Elephant Stables
Nobleman's Quarters
Zenana Enclosure
Jain Temple
THE ROYAL CENTRE
Underground Shiva Temple
Hazara Rama Temple
Watchtower
Assembly hall
Mahanavami Platform
Ganagitti Jain Temple
Stepped tank
Bhima's Gate
Queen's Bath
Gateway
Archaeological Museum
Pattabhirama Temple
0
500 yards
KAMALAPURA
0
500 metres

fortifications have been built onto the side of the hill—some of which are thought to predate the Vijayanagar Empire. Head to the top of the hill, through a double-storeyed gateway with a fine framed view of Matanga Hill.

Just beyond the gateway is a pavilion containing the four-armed **Sasivekalu Ganesha** (1506), a 2.4m-high carving of the elephant-god. Just 200m to the northeast, back on the road towards Hampi Bazaar, is a second, larger carving of the elephant-god known as the **Kadalekalu Ganesha**, inside the sanctuary of a temple. The carving, 4.5m high, has exceptional detail—notice the rice cake held by Ganesha in his fingernails—and was carved *in situ* out of a boulder that was already here. Note the unusually narrow square pillars of the temple assembly hall, which give it an almost Greek appearance.

Krishna Temple

To the south of both Ganesha carvings is the Krishna Temple (1513), one of the four major shrines of the Sacred Centre. Like the other temples, it has its own bazaar street, a colonnaded avenue that leads out into modern fields. The temple was built to commemorate the victory of Krishnadevaraya over the Gajapati kings of Orissa, from where a granite statue of Krishna was taken and installed here—it has since been moved to the government museum in Chennai. The *gopura* is partly ruined, but note the slender columns and the carvings around the inside of the gate. Inside is a large temple with small pyramidal towers over the entrance and sanctuary, and with several other smaller shrines nearby. To the left is a gate that leads to a separate walled area, containing what is thought to have been a granary—identifiable by the holes in the ceiling that were used to pour in the grain.

Narasimha Monolith

A little southwest of the Krishna Temple, in a pavilion just off the main road, is Hampi's best-known sculpture: the extraordinary Narasimha Monolith (1528), officially known as the Lakshmi Narasimha Temple. This seated stone figure of Narasimha, the lion avatar of Vishnu, has almost cartoon-like popping-out eyes. Until recently, its only protection was from the snake canopy over its head, and the carving had become badly weathered. The 6.7m-high sculpture has now been restored, though, and the band of stone that stretches between the knees is new and the area around the eyes has been heavily rebuilt. The figure of Lakshmi, Vishnu/Narasimha's consort, is missing—all that remains is her hand on Narasimha's back. Next to the monolith is the Badavilingam shrine, an enormous monolithic Shiva lingam, 3m high and surrounded by water.

Tiruvengalanatha Temple

Orientation: The broad avenue known as Hampi Bazaar heads eastwards from the Virupaksha Temple towards Matanga Hill and Tiruvengalanatha Temple. There is a marked turning left down for the riverside and several smaller temples and pavilions (*see below*). However, the main route continues along the colonnaded road, past a converted assembly hall with a fine exhibition of old and modern photographs of Hampi until you reach its end, marked by a pavilion sheltering a damaged monolithic Nandi bull. The nearby stone steps take visitors over a small pass to the colonnaded street that leads to the Tiruvengalanatha Temple. A side path here takes visitors to the south side of Matanga Hill and the steps that lead to the summit.

The temple: Tiruvengalanatha Temple (1534), also known as the Achutaraya Temple after the king during whose reign it was built, stands at the end of a 380m-long colonnaded street oriented north–south, unlike the three other temple streets which run east–west. Note the high stone platforms on the street, close to the temple, that were used for getting in and out of chariots. The temple itself is hemmed in by hills and is arranged in concentric rectangles—a pattern best viewed from the top of Matanga Hill. The outer and inner gates each have a partially ruined *gopura*. On the right after passing through the outer gate is a multi-columned assembly hall with some finely carved columns. At the back of the outer compound is a small gateway leading to a rock-cut image of the goddess Kali—still under worship and brightly painted—from where there are steps leading up Matanga Hill. The main Tiruvengalanatha shrine is a rectangular building in the inner compound, with some more finely carved pillars. Tiruvengalanatha is a form of the god Vishnu, but the sanctuary which once housed the idol of the god is now empty.

Matanga Hill is best approached from the Tiruvengalanatha Temple. There is a small temple set in a compound on top of the hill, and some quite spectacular views of the entire Hampi-Vijayanagar site.

Near the riverside

There are a number of smaller temples, pavilions, caves and carvings along the riverside walk that takes you from Hampi Bazaar towards the Vitthala Temple. These include several sites connected with the *Ramayana*, and so attract Hindu pilgrims. The whitewashed **Kondandarama Temple** has a large relief carving of the heroes of the *Ramayana*, while the place next to the river known as the Chakratirtha marks the spot where Rama is believed to have crowned Sugriva as the king of the monkeys.

There are several rock carvings near here, including dozens of tiny lingams and a superb reclining Vishnu. **Sugriva's Cave**—in the rocks near the river, its entrance painted white—is said to have been the spot where Sugriva hid the jewels of Sita, which she had dropped to the ground when she was abducted by Ravana. There are some rock carvings inside. On the side of the nearby hill is the small **Narasimha Temple** (14th century), with a two-storey gateway and a pyramidal stone tower over the empty sanctuary.

Vitthala Temple

The superb Vitthala Temple (*open daily 8.30–5.30*) is many visitors' favourite location in Hampi. Set close to the river, it is surrounded by other smaller ruined buildings, and has a long colonnaded avenue stretching out to the east. Its magnificent assembly hall has some of the finest carving to be found anywhere in India. The temple is thought to have been built in the early 15th century, but the assembly hall dates to 1554, just 11 years before the defeat of the Vijayanagar Empire by the Deccan sultanates.

Orientation: There are a number of ways of reaching Vitthala: on foot, by bicycle along the river, by motorised vehicle from the Royal Centre or by boat across the river. The temple itself is oriented east–west, and is entered from the east, close to the 500m-long avenue that is set at a slight angle to the main shrine.

Temple compound: The main entrance to the Vitthala Temple compound is through a gateway with a partly ruined *gopura* tower, which leads into a large courtyard. Immediately ahead is a stone chariot, and behind that the main assembly hall and the Vitthala shrine. Slightly to the left and right are free-standing assembly halls, and there are further interesting buildings at the back of the compound, which is surrounded by arcades, some of them ruined. The main architectural feature of the complex is the widespread use of cut-out colonnettes—little columns cut from and therefore joined to the same stone as the main column. Guides will tap the colonnettes to produce musical notes, though there is no evidence that this was a deliberate feature—and music experts say the notes do not, despite what one may be told, form a musical scale. Note also the realistic relief carvings of lizards on the roof eaves of the assembly hall at the back left side of the compound. Friezes run around the lower levels of the entire complex, mainly comprising elephants and horses.

Stone chariot: The beautifully carved stone chariot with detachable stone wheels and miniature columns is in fact a shrine to the man-eagle Garuda, Vishnu's vehicle. It once had its own tower, still visible in 19th-century photographs. There is a small relief carving of Garuda inside.

Main assembly hall: The hall has undergone major restoration, though the structure is largely intact. The cut-out colonnette style of column design is at its most sophisticated and ornate here, with complex arrays of columns cut from a single block of granite and decorated with relief carvings of monsters, animals, dwarves and deities, as well as miniature shrines containing images of avatars of Vishnu. There are also superb friezes, including, low on the plinth on the left (north) side of the temple, some that show Portuguese horse-trainers, with European-style hats and jackets, who were in great demand in mid-16th-century Vijayanagar. The high tower over the sanctuary has carvings of deities, but the main idol, presumably of the Vitthala avatar of Vishnu, is missing.

Around the Vitthala Temple

The colonnaded ceremonial avenue that leads up to the Vitthala Temple is Hampi's finest, though the eastern part has disappeared—now marked only by a couple of surviving roadside pavilions. One of these, the **Kuderegombe Mandapa**, just south of the road, has fine columns carved in the shape of rearing horses. Just ahead, on the north side of the road, is a pretty water tank with a shrine at its centre, and as one approaches the temple there are a number of ruined buildings.

Set at right angles to the main avenue is a small ruin that leads to another shrine, the **Ramanuja Temple**, which has some fine carvings of scenes from the *Ramayana*. Behind the Vitthala Temple, on the path towards Virupaksha and the rest of Hampi, is a gateway known as the **King's Balance**. Note the stone rings on the underside of the cross beam: a chain once hung from here as part of the weighing mechanism. The Vijayanagar emperors were said to have been weighed on this balance, and the equivalent weight in precious stones was distributed to temple priests. The dramatic ruins of the **old bridge** that led across the Tunghabhadra can be seen on the western side of the Vitthala Temple.

THE ROYAL CENTRE OF HAMPI

The area of Hampi/Vijayanagar now known as the Royal Centre is further away from the river, and is still separated from the Sacred Centre by a narrow valley used for agriculture. There are minor buildings on the road that links the two centres, including the whitewashed **Virbhadra Temple**, which is still in use. The Royal Centre itself can be divided into a number of separate areas, which are surrounded by walled compounds. The two most important compounds are the *zenana* enclosure, on the northeastern side of the Royal Centre, and the Hazara Rama Temple, which is thought to have served as the private shrine of the Vijayanagara emperors.

Orientation: This description of the Royal Centre starts from the west, for visitors who have come from the Sacred Centre, or directly (not via Kamalapura) from Hospet. Vehicles are allowed to drive through most of the Royal Centre.

Western buildings

A stepped water tank marks the road that leads into the Royal Centre. Just beyond it, on the south side of the road, is the **Underground Shiva Temple** (14th century), the roof of which is level with the surrounding land. When it was built, the land was much lower, but soil movement caused by irrigation has almost engulfed the temple, which is still affected by flooding. East of the temple, on the other side of the road, is a small ruined palace, and on a side road 300m further along on the left are the excavated ruins of what has become known by archaeologists as the **Nobleman's Quarters**, with lots of walls, narrow streets, drainage channels and wells.

On the south side of the road are several other buildings, including the distinctive two-storey octagonal **watchtower** with a pyramidal roof, and nearby a three-bayed **assembly hall**—not a mosque, as indicated by the sign on the main road. It is possible to walk from here to the Hazara Rama Temple, but most visitors return to the road.

Hazara Rama Temple

The superbly decorated walls of the Hazara Rama Temple (early 15th century) make it one of Vijayanagar's most impressive monuments. Be sure to walk around the outer walls of the compound, where carvings show processions of people and animals taking part in religious festivals and military parades. Inside the temple compound, the exterior of the temple and parts of the perimeter wall are covered with relief carvings telling the story of the *Ramayana*. The story begins in the far right (northwest) corner of the temple and proceeds in sequence clockwise, with additional scenes on the perimeter wall closest to the entrance gate. Among the more distinctive figures to look for are the multi-headed demon Ravana, the monkey-god Hanuman, and Rama and his brother Lakshman—normally carrying bows. Note the long street that leads from the southern gate of the temple, and the smaller temple in the compound, which was probably dedicated to Narasimha, the lion avatar of Vishnu. There are four polished dolerite columns inside the assembly hall of the temple, with relief carvings of avatars of Vishnu (of whom Rama is one) and of figures from the *Ramayana*. The sanctuary has no idols, but the three holes in the pedestal were probably sockets for statues of Rama, Lakshman and Sita.

Zenana enclosure and nearby buildings

The *zenana* enclosure (*open dawn–dusk*) is to the northwest of the Hazara Rama Temple, down a well-signposted small road. It seems unlikely that this high-walled, almost rectangular compound was in fact the *zenana*, or female quarters, given the proximity of the elephant stables and the parade ground, and it may in fact have been the military centre of Vijayanagar. On entering the compound, there is a small museum (with some porcelain and metal objects, and Buddhist carved stone panels) on the near left side, which probably served as a treasury. A tall three-storey **watchtower** is further away to the left, and has some finely carved brackets supporting balconies. Covering a large part of the centre of the enclosure is the plinth of what is known as the **Queen's Palace**, but was a large building that almost certainly played some other role. Ahead and slightly to the right is the most important surviving building in the *zenana* enclosure, the two-storeyed **Lotus Mahal** (16th century), with its cusped arches and pyramidal roof towers—an unexpected mixture of Hindu and Muslim styles. It is thought to have been used as a council chamber. At the back of the compound are two more watchtowers, one of which is octagonal with an arcaded top storey.

Elephant Stables

A gate at the back of the enclosure leads into a large open area, probably used as a parade ground. On the far side is one of Hampi's most distinctive buildings, the Elephant Stables, with eleven arches, under each of which two elephants would be housed. Note the wide variety of roof domes and towers, and the rooftop pavilion which would have been used by drummers and other musicians. On the left (north) side of the open area is an arcaded building, also with eleven bays, that may have served as a grandstand from which parades could be viewed. Beyond the Elephant Stables are a number of partly ruined shrines, including a pretty Jain temple.

South of the Hazara Rama Temple

Beyond the Hazara Rama Temple is a large collection of ruined buildings that almost certainly served as the main palaces of Vijayanagar. The **large plinth** 120m south of

The exquisitely carved remains of the Hazara Rama Temple at Hampi.

the temple was probably an assembly hall, which would have had wooden columns resting on the dozens of pillar footings still visible on the surface of the plinth. The large ceremonial staircase led to what was a second floor. Just 50m beyond the plinth is an **underground chamber**, the roof of which has been partially exposed, and which visitors can enter. Note the schist stone slabs and columns taken from an older temple. The building is thought to have functioned as a treasury.

To the left of the underground chamber is the **Mahanavami Platform** (15th century, with later additions), an 8m-high stage on which the emperor is thought to have performed and witnessed religious rituals. There are superb carvings round the side of the platform, including images of elephants, horses, camels, geese, wrestlers and musicians. On top of the platform are column footings where wooden pillars would have been placed to support a roof. There are fine views over Vijayanagar from here.

About 100m to the south of the platform is a very pretty **stepped tank**, excavated and restored in the 1980s, as well as the small aqueduct that provided water to this part of the Royal Centre. Just beyond the stepped tank is a much larger reservoir—and along the nearby road are a number of other water-related structures. These include the **Queen's Bath**, which is square in design, with a plain exterior, extremely pretty internal arcades and ornate balconies that would have looked over the water that once filled the central area of the building. There is a much smaller octagonal bath, just beyond the small temples to the northeast of the Queen's Bath.

EAST OF THE ROYAL CENTRE

The are a number of scattered ruins to the east of the Royal Centre. They are little-visited and easiest to access from the road linking the town of Kamalapura with the Vitthala Temple. These ruins include the **Ganagitti Jain Temple** (1385), one of the oldest surviving Vijayanagar buildings, with a tall column placed in front which records that it was built by Irrugappa, a commander under Harihara II. Close by is **Bhima's Gate**, which served as an eastern entrance to the city and is named after the hero of the *Mahabharata*, whose image, bearing a mace, has been carved on a nearby slab.

Head further north towards Vitthala, to **Malyavanta Hill** with the Raghunatha Temple complex at its summit. Note how the main temple has been built against a large boulder, on which the shrine's tower rests. Just outside the west wall of the complex, there is a series of small lingams and images of the bull Nandi carved into a rock crevice.

Back on the road towards Vitthala, down a lane on the left, is **Ahmed Khan's Mosque** (1439), named after the military officer who commissioned it. It is built like the assembly hall of a Hindu temple, but oriented towards Mecca, and with a prayer niche inside. This area of Vijayanagar was set aside for the city's Muslims, and there are a number of graves and tombs nearby. The modern road to Vitthala (and the Anegundi ferry) continues through the towering **Talerighat Gate**, which marks the edge of the urban core.

HAMPI'S SUBURBS

Vijayanagar was a megacity by the standards of its time, and a number of interesting buildings have survived from several of its suburbs, particularly Anegundi.

Kamalapura

The suburb of Kamalapura is just to the south of the city, close to the Royal Centre. The **Archaeological Museum** (*open Sat–Thur 9–5*) has some excellent carvings gathered from Vijayanagar, including beautifully worked headless statues of a king and queen, a fine sandstone relief carving of the man-eagle Garuda and the monkey god Hanuman, as well as a superb resting Vishnu having his legs massaged. There is also a very helpful relief map of the area. Further along the same road is the impressively grand **Pattabhirama Temple**, dedicated to Rama, and once the nucleus of a large urban extension to Vijayanagar. Half a kilometre to the north is an unusual, high-domed gateway that is supported on four arches.

Anegundi

This interesting town, a former suburb of Vijayanagar on the northern bank of the Tunghabhadra, was once connected to the city by the ruined bridge near the Vitthala Temple. A controversial modern bridge to Anegundi collapsed before completion in 2009, killing eight people, and now the traditional coracle boats are the primary way of crossing the river—a road detour takes more than an hour. Anegundi's history predates that of Vijayanagar, and it is still the residence of a line of local gentry who claim descent from the Vijayanagar emperors. The town is entered (by road) through a 14th-century gateway and the **Gagan Mahal**, a small palace in the centre of the town, now used as an office by the local council.

The **Chintamani Temple** complex is just to the east of Anegundi, on a bend in the river, while a large fortified **citadel** is on the western side of the town. The citadel has a Durga temple and, beyond, a boulder-strewn plateau with superb views from its riverside walls of the Vitthala Temple and other Vijayanagar buildings.

Towards Hospet

Several villages on the road to Hospet (*map 13 B2*), the main modern-day urban centre closest to Hampi, have buildings that date to the Vijayanagar period. These include two fine Muslim tombs in the village of **Kadirampura**, and two gateways and a temple (later turned into a fort) in **Malpannagudi**. Just outside Hospet (on the Hampi road) is the **Anantashayanagudi Temple** (1524), with its unusual high tower.

NORTHWEST OF HAMPI: THE ROAD TO GOA

Many travellers make the long journey between Goa and Hampi in one day, but there are several interesting places to visit en route, and comfortable places to stay in Hubli.

Kuknur and Ittagi

The village of **Kuknur** (*map 13 B2*, sometime Kukkanur), 60km west of Hampi, has a fine group of 9th-century Rashtrakuta shrines, known as the **Navalinga temples**. The complex consists of nine sandstone shrines, with distinctive square towers, all now dedicated to Shiva, but which were built for the worship of female deities. The village of **Ittagi** (*map 13 B2*), 6km west of Kuknur, has the superb 11th-century **Mahadeva Temple**, next to an attractive stepped water tank. The elaborate temple carvings and architecture are often seen as the finest surviving example from the Late Chalukya period.

Lakkundi, Dambal and Gadag

The village of **Lakkundi** (*map 13 B2*), 80km west of Hampi and 10km east of Gadag, has two important shrines—one Hindu, one Jain—and a step-well on the eastern side of the village. The **Kashivishvanatha Temple** (12th century) is on the southern side of the village, with a small Surya sanctuary facing the main one, which is dedicated to Shiva. Note the superb lathe-turned pillars. Close by is the Jain Basti (11th century), with some fine external and internal carvings.

Some 12km southeast is the **Dodda Basappa Temple** (12th century), in the village of Dambal (*map 13 B2*); its star-shaped sanctuary has so many facets that it is almost circular. The main town in the area, **Gadag**, also has several shrines from the Late Chalukyan period, including the Trikuteswara and Saraswati temples (11th and 12th centuries) within the same compound in the southern part of Gadag.

Hubli and Belgaum

There is not a huge amount to see in the large Hubli-Dharwar conurbation (*map 13 B2*), roughly midway between Hampi and Goa, though it is useful for its airport and hotels. There is one impressive Hindu shrine, however: the **Chandramouleshwara Temple** (12th century) between the twin cities, at Unkal.

The village of **Kittur** (*map 13 B1*) on the Belgaum road, 27km northwest of Dharwar, has a ruined fort that was once occupied by Rani Chennamma, the queen of Kittur, who took up arms against the British and died in jail in 1829—and who has become a folk-hero. The city of **Belgaum** (*map 13 B1*) in the far northwest of Karnataka, 85km from Goa, was an important outpost under the Bahmanid and Bijapur Sultanate. The almost circular 13th-century fort, 800m in diameter, was partially rebuilt in the 17th century, when the main north gate was built.

Karwar and the northern coastal area of Karnataka

The city of **Karwar** (*map 13 A2*), just south of the Goa border and built on the estuary of the Kali River, is an important naval base and seaport. The Portuguese explorer Vasco da Gama landed at the Anjediv Islands, just off the coast of Karwar, in 1498. The islands are currently off-limits to visitors. On the northern side of the river are the ruins of the 17th-century **Sadashivgarh Fort**.

Around 35km to the south of Karwar is the temple-town of **Gokarna** (*map 13 A2*), the beaches of which are beginning to attract international tourists. Non-Hindus are not allowed to enter the main **Mahabaleshwara Temple** (18th century), which is dedicated to Shiva.

The town of **Bhatkal** (*map 13 A3*), 68km south of Gokarna, has some fine Hindu and Jain temples. The Jain temples are on the main street, while the most interesting of the Hindu shrines, the **Khetapai Narayan Temple** (16th century), dedicated to Vishnu and with fine carved stone screens that look as if they are made of wood, is 2km east of the centre of Bhatkal.

Jog Falls (*map 13 A2*) are 40km northeast of Bhatkal. They are India's highest waterfalls and are particularly impressive during and after the monsoon.

SOUTH OF HAMPI: THE ROAD TO BANGALORE

Like the route to Goa, many travellers make the long journey between Hampi and Bangalore in one day, but, again, there are several interesting places to visit en route, as well as simple places to stay in Chitradurga.

Bagali, Kuruvatti and Harihar

The small village of **Bagali** (*map 13 B2*), 65km southwest of Hampi, off the Hospet–Harihar road, has the very fine **Kallesvara Temple** (10th century), best known for the erotic carvings on the exterior walls of the sanctuary, and for the high quality of the sculpture on the 11th-century extensions to the shrine. The village of **Kuruvatti** (*map 13 B2*), 40km west of Bagali on the banks of the Tunghabhadra River, has the **Mallikarjuna Temple** (11th century), with finely modelled brackets in the shape of female dancers on the shrine's outer pillars. **Harihar** (*map 13 B2*) is a town named after its **Harihareshwara Temple** (1224), which was erected by the Hoysala king Narasimha II and built to a typical Hoysala design, with particularly fine lathe-turned pillars.

Chitradurga

The city of Chitradurga (*map 13 B2*), 120km south of Hampi and 180km north of Bangalore, has an impressive hill-fort, within which are some interesting temples. The fort has been occupied since at least the 13th century, and was controlled by the Vijayanagar Empire until 1602, when it passed into the hands of local Nayak rulers. It was captured by the forces of Mysore, then taken by the British during the defeat of Tipu Sultan.

The **fort** (*open daily sunrise–sunset*), which has a series of walls running along the hillside, is accessed from the east through massive well-defended outer gates that date from the Vijayanagar period. Note the large star-shaped pit with several grindstones. The main footpath leads through several more gates, past columns and other structures to two 13th-century Hoysala temples. The **Hidimbesvara Temple** is built on top of a large rock, with two gateways from the later Nayak period. The **Siddheshwara Temple**, to the south, has a two-storey gateway with a roof terrace.

Other parts of the old **walled city of Chitradurga** survive at the foot of the fort, including a small **museum** (*open Mon–Sat*) inside an old guardhouse. To the southeast of the fort, away from the city, are the natural Chandravalli Caves, which have traces of prehistoric settlements.

EAST & NORTHEAST OF HAMPI

Bellary

This district headquarters (*map 13 C2*) 50km southeast of Hampi has a large and impressive **fort** (*open daily dawn–dusk*), which has recently been renovated. It is built on an enormous rock, and it is a steep climb (more than 350 steps) to the top. Once there, though, you can enjoy superb views and investigate interesting military buildings, largely dating from the 18th century, when this fort became one of the strongholds of Hyder Ali of Mysore. Just outside the walls of the upper fort is an enormous rock plateau, with several pools, a temple and some cell-like buildings.

Raichur

This district headquarters (*map 13 C1*), 140km northeast of Hampi, has an old fortified city centre overlooking a lake. The fortifications largely date from the 14th and 15th centuries, as do several mosques within Raichur's walls. The citadel, Bala Hissar, is in the southwest corner.

The large ruined fortress of **Maliabad**, 5km south of Raichur, was built by the Kakatiya Dynasty (who were responsible for the great Warangal Fortress) in the 12th–13th century, and it has two fine monolithic statues of elephants

PRACTICAL INFORMATION

Southern Karnataka has a better tourist infrastructure than the north of the state. Bangalore and Mysore are easy to reach, and the main roads are in good condition. Visiting northern Karnataka involves a little more advance organisation than other parts of the country because of its less developed infrastructure. This does mean, though, that its superb historic sites, particularly Hampi, have not been swamped by tourists or ruined by development. However, several days, or longer, needs to be set aside for a visit.

GETTING THERE

• **By air:** Most visitors to southern Karnataka arrive at Bangalore's new airport, just north of the city, from where there are connections to all major Indian urban centres and a growing number of international airports. There is also an airport in Mangalore, on the coast, with connections to Bangalore, Mumbai, Goa and Cochin. Northern Karnataka is poorly served by airports, and Hampi, the most important tourist destination in the region, is not easy to reach. The airport at Hubli is 140km west of Hampi, but only has regular flights from Bangalore or Mumbai. Hyderabad is the best major airport for the northeast of the state, particularly Bidar (110km) and Gulbarga (170km), while Goa is better for Badami (200km) and Bijapur (260km).

• **By train:** There are long-distance train services to Bangalore from Delhi (33 hours) and from Mumbai (25 hours), but the shorter inter-city services—Chennai (5hrs), Coimbatore (6½hrs) and Hyderabad (10½hrs)—are more useful and time-efficient. Trains to northern Karnataka include several services from Mumbai to southern India, passing though Gulbarga.

• **By road:** Many visitors heading to Hampi travel by road from Bangalore (280km) or from the neighbouring states of Goa (280km) or even Andhra Pradesh (Hyderabad is 315km from Hampi). The roads connecting Bangalore with Chennai and Hyderabad are multi-lane highways that are normally well maintained.

GETTING AROUND

• **By train:** Among the more useful services within the state are the trains from Bangalore to Mysore (3hrs) and the night train from Bangalore to Hospet (9hrs) for visitors to Hampi, and elsewhere in northern Karnataka.

The first stretch of Bangalore's Metro is expected to open by 2012, but the disruption caused by construction is expected to last a lot longer. However, the first stations to open, in the centre of the modern city, will make city travel a lot easier. There are also plans for a rail link to the airport—but currently bus or taxi (allow at least an hour and take local advice) are the best ways of getting there.

• **By road:** Major roads in southern Karnataka are generally in good condition, and taxis can be hired in most places for long-distance travel. Intercity bus services are widely available. Autorickshaws are available in most towns, and are the best means of travelling short distances. In Hampi, bicycles can be hired at Hampi Bazaar, and small circular boats (coracles) ferry visitors and locals across the river.

• **On foot:** For walking tours of Mysore, the tour company **Royal Mysore Walks** is recommended (*T: 09632 044188; royalmysorewalks.com*).

ACCOMMODATION

Southern Karnataka

• **Bangalore:** Karnataka's capital has a large number of comfortable 5-star hotels, with many of the major chains represented. Prices tend to be higher than elsewhere in the country. The Taj group has three hotels, of which the centrally located **Taj West End** (*$$$; T: 080 66605660; tajhotels.com*), on Race Course Road, is the most luxurious—an enormous 19th-century building set in 20 acres of gardens. **The Park Hotel** (*$$$; T: 080 2559 4666; theparkhotels.com*) on MG Road is an interesting piece of modern international design by the British-based Conran & Partners. The Neemrana group has the well-restored **Villa Pottipati** (*$$; T: 080 23360777; neemranahotels.com*), a large former family house, built in 1873 in the Malleswaram area of north Bangalore.

• **Belur and Halebid:** Hotels in Belur and Halebid are very basic, and instead many visitors either stay at the **Hoysala Village Resort** (*$$; T: 08172 256065*) on the Belur Road, just outside Hassan, or at the **Taj Gateway** (*$$; T: 08262 660660; thegatewayhotels.com*) in Chikmagalur, 20km northeast of Belur.

• **Coorg:** Recommended hotels in Coorg include the **Green Hills Estate** (*$$; T:08274 254790; neemranahotels.com*), a late 19th-century mansion close to Virajpet in southern Coorg, which is part of the Neemrana group. **Orange County Resort** ($$$; T: 08274 258481), near Siddapur in southern Coorg, is set in a coffee estate and is Coorg's grandest resort hotel. More basic accommodation is available next to the Nalnad Palace, outside Kakkabe, at the **Palace Estate** (*$; T: 08272 229830; palaceestate.co.in*).

• **Mangalore:** There are a number of mid-range hotels in Mangalore, of which the best is **The Gateway** (*$$; T: 0824*

6660420; thegatewayhotels.com) on Old Port Road, operated by the Taj group.

• **Mysore:** The best hotel in Mysore is the **Lalitha Mahal Palace** (*$$$; T: 0821 2526100; lalithamahalpalace.in*), with its high central dome and pretty gardens, built by the maharaja as a royal guest house in the 1930s. There is also the **Green Hotel** (*$$; T: 0821 4255000; greenhotelindia.com*), which is a smaller former palace. A Radisson hotel is under construction.

It is possible to stay in simpler hotels in nearby Srirangapatnam, such as at the **Fort View Resort** (*$; 08236 252777; fortviewresorts.com*).

Northern Karnataka

The tourist infrastructure in northern Karnataka is underdeveloped, and there are no 5-star hotels. However, most places have adequate accommodation, and Badami and the area around Hampi have hotels or guest houses that are better than adequate.

• **Badami:** The **Badami Court** (*$$; T: 08357 220320*), just outside Badami, is a comfortable 3-star hotel.

• **Bidar:** The best hotels in Bidar are on Udgir Road, not far from the bus station. They are basic but clean, and have air-conditioned rooms. Try **Sapna International** (*$; T: 08242 220991*) or the **Krishna Regency** (*$; 08242 221991*).

• **Bijapur:** In Bijapur the **Hotel Navaratna International** (*$; T: 08352 222771*) on Station Road is comfortable and modern, though the most upmarket hotel is the **Hotel Shashinag Residency** (*$$; T: 08352 260344*).

• **Chitradurga:** Clean, simple accommodation is available in Chitradurga at the **Amogha International** (*$$; T: 08194 222762; amoghachitradurga.com*).

• **Hampi:** The most comfortable accommodation nearby is at Hospet, 15km away, where the **Shanbag Towers** (*$; T: 08394 225910*) and the **Hotel Malligi** (*$; T: 09394 228101*) are the best options.

Many visitors prefer to stay across the river in guest houses or small hotels, and then travel to Hampi by ferry. The **Kishkinda Trust** (*$; T: 08533 267791*) in Anegundi has turned traditional homes into guest houses. The Kishkinda Trust also runs **Shama's Cottages** (*$$; T: 094805 46362*), a small hotel with individual huts on the edge of the town. Hampi's **Boulders** (*$$; T: 08539 265939*), also on the north bank of the Tunghabhadra River, is recommended as well.

• **Hubli:** In Hubli, **The Hans Hotel** (*$$; T: 0836 2374770; thehanshotel.com*) is aimed at business travellers.

FOOD

Karnataka has a variety of different cuisines, of which two—Udupi and Mangalorean—are well known in the rest of India. Udupi food, which comes originally from the town of the same name in the central coastal region of the state, is wholly vegetarian and Udupi is said to have been the birthplace of the ubiquitous *dosa*, a pancake made using rice flour and lentil flour, which is available in dozens of varieties and is widely seen as the typical south Indian food.

Mangalorean food, named after the coastal city in southern Karnataka with a large Christian population, is seafood- and rice-based, and uses coconut in cooking, particularly for *gassi*, the Mangalorean form of curry. Prawn *gassi* is probably the best-known Mangalorean dish, often served with the soft *neer dosa*, made from rice flour. Many Mangaloreans migrated to Mumbai, where two of city's best-known restaurants—Trishna and Mahesh—serve Mangalorean food.

Coorg also has its own distinctive cuisine, in which rice and local hill vegetables are staple ingredients, and pork is widely eaten, unlike in most other parts of India.

Karnataka's best-known sweet dish is Mysore *pak*, a speciality of the city. A cross between fudge and cake, it is made of sugar, ghee and chick-pea flour.

FURTHER READING

Karnataka is not very well served by guidebooks. 52 *Weekend Breaks from Bangalore* in the Outlook Traveller series is useful for southern Karnataka, as well as the northern parts of Kerala and Tamil Nadu. There is an excellent short guide to Hampi by John Fritz and George Michell called simply *Hampi* (India Book House, 2003), which includes selections from accounts by early European visitors to the Vijayanagar Empire. There is also the superb coffee-table book *Silent Splendour: Palaces of the Deccan* (Marg, 2010) by Helen Philon, with fine photographs and essays relating mainly to the Sultanate period in the Deccan.

Multiple City: Writings on Bangalore, edited by Aditi De (Penguin India, 2008), is an interesting anthology of fiction and non-fiction about the city now officially called Bengaluru. R.K. Narayan (1906–2001) was one of the first Indian writers in English who was internationally successful, and his very fine Malgudi series of novels is set in a fictionalised, shrunken version of Mysore.

ANDHRA PRADESH

The large south Indian state of Andhra Pradesh (*maps 12 and 13*) receives fewer international visitors than it deserves, and most of those who do come are business travellers visiting its capital, Hyderabad. Until recently the state has made little attempt to attract international tourists, though its Hindu pilgrimage sites, such as Tirupati, have always brought huge numbers of visitors from the rest of India. In fact, it has some very fine buildings and works of art from periods of Hindu, Muslim and Buddhist dominance in the region. The main language of Andhra Pradesh is Telugu, though Urdu is widely spoken among Muslims in the north of the state.

Andhra is normally divided into three separate areas: the coastal districts of eastern Andhra; Telangana, in the northeast, which was formerly part of the princely state of Hyderabad; and the southwestern part of the state, known as Rayalaseema, which is separated from Telangana by the River Krishna.

HISTORY OF ANDHRA PRADESH

The earliest important archaeological sites in Andhra date to the early Buddhist period, in the 2nd or 3rd centuries BC. A number of major Buddhist sites have been excavated, including the great stupa of Amaravati—the most important remains of which are now in the British Museum in London—and the 3rd-century ruins of Nagarjunakonda, which were moved to an island to prevent them being flooded in the 1950s. Among the superb Hindu monuments are those at the ruined city of Warangal, in the north of the state, and the remains of several Vijayanagar settlements in southern Andhra.

Muslim dynasties: In the late 15th century, the Muslim Qutb Shahi Dynasty, based at Golconda on the outskirts of modern Hyderabad, emerged as a major power in the region. Golconda and the new capital of Hyderabad fell to the Mughal emperor Aurangzeb in 1687, though a new dynasty, the Asaf Jahis, who became known to the world as the Nizams of Hyderabad, soon became the new dominant force across large tracts of central India. Europeans, including the British, Dutch and French, founded small settlements along the Andhra coast in the early 17th century, but by the late 18th century most of southern and coastal Andhra was part of the Madras Presidency, ruled by Britain. The small coastal enclave of Yanam remained part of France, however, until 1954. Although it is surrounded by Andhra Pradesh, Yanam is now ruled from Pondicherry.

After Independence: At the time of Independence, many Telugu speakers objected to being included in the Tamil-dominated Madras state. But it was not until a politician called Potti Sreeramulu—still a hero in Andhra—fasted to death in 1952 that the central government agreed to the demands of the Telugu speakers for a separate state. Meanwhile, in 1948, the princely state of Hyderabad, through a mixture of persuasion and paramilitary force by the central government, acceded to India.

A NEW STATE OF TELANGANA?

In 1956, the Telugu-speaking parts of Hyderabad state, including Hyderabad city itself, were allowed to break away and join the rest of Andhra Pradesh. However, many of them would have preferred their own state, which was to have been called Telangana. After several decades of campaigning, the creation of such a state was agreed to, in principle, by the central government in 2009.

HYDERABAD

India's sixth most populous city, with more than four million inhabitants, Hyderabad (*map 12 A2 and p. 715*) has become a major centre for IT services and the film industry. Just outside the city, almost enveloped by its suburbs, is the great fortress of Golconda.

History: The city was founded in 1592, just south of the Musi River, as a new, less-cluttered capital by the ruler of nearby Golconda, Muhammad Quli Qutb Shah. It was he who commissioned the city's best-known building, the Charminar. During the period of Mughal rule in the late 17th and early 18th centuries, Hyderabad declined in importance, and it was not until 1763 that the nizams restored the city to its pre-eminent position in the region. During the British period, Hyderabad emerged as the largest and most populous of India's princely states, and the nizams became famous around the world for their fabulous wealth.

In the 19th century the city spread rapidly northwards, with the creation of New Hyderabad between the Musi River and the Hussain Sagar Lake. The British cantonment of Secunderabad, named after Nizam Sikander Jah, was set up after an 1853 treaty that allowed the stationing of a British garrison in Hyderabad. Locally, Secunderabad and Hyderabad are often known as the twin cities, though the former has in practice been swallowed up by the latter. After the great floods of 1908—the high-water mark is still visible on many heritage buildings—the Musi River was dammed and became today's sluggish stream. The city became the capital of the new state of Andhra Pradesh in 1956, and began to grow very rapidly. The heart of the old city is still largely Muslim and Urdu-speaking, but Telugu-speaking Hindus and migrants from the rest of the country began to settle in other parts of Hyderabad. By the early 2000s Hyderabad began to replace Bangalore as India's IT boomtown, and was nicknamed 'Cyberabad'. And in 2009 the new international airport, probably India's best, opened to the south of the old city. But the city has also been affected by the continuing agitation for a separate state of Telangana, with Hyderabad as its capital.

Orientation: Hyderabad is a large, confusing city, in which the main geographical landmarks, 4km apart, are the Musi River and the Hussain Sagar Lake. Between the river and the lake are several important buildings of the later Nizami period, and the commercial heart of modern Hyderabad, with many of the city's business hotels. The old city, on the south side of the Musi, has many of Hyderabad's most important tourist sites, including the Charminar, the Chow Mahalla Palace and the Salar Jang Museum. To the north is Secunderabad and the enormous lake of Hussain Sagar, while the plush residential areas of Banjara and Jubilee Hills are to the northwest, with the HITEC city, the heart of Hyderabad's IT industry, further to the west. To the southwest, and now practically swallowed by the city, is the great medieval Golconda Fortress and the Qutb Shahi tombs. South Hyderabad, between the old city and the new airport, also has important visitor attractions, including the Paigah tombs, as well as the city's best heritage hotel, the Falaknuma Palace.

OLD HYDERABAD

The Charminar

The Charminar (1592), literally 'four minarets', was the first building to be constructed when Hyderabad was founded. It is an unusual four-arched monumental gateway, capped with a viewing area, a small mosque and four towers. It is also one of the best-known buildings in India (probably the best-known in the south of the country) because of its association with a brand of cigarettes with the same name. The Charminar, 900m south of the river, was constructed as the hub of the new city of Hyderabad, which was sited 8km to the east of the old Qutb Shahi citadel at Golconda. Now standing at the centre of a busy roundabout, the Charminar is a square building, with minarets at each corner that tower 56m above the street. The four sides of the building are identical, except for the high arch on the upper storey of the west façade behind which is the *mihrab*, or prayer niche, of the mosque. The clocks are a 19th-century addition. The area under the Charminar, with its pretty fountain, is now fenced in, except for a small *dargah*, or Islamic shrine, on the east side.

Inside the Charminar: The entrance to the Charminar (*open daily 9–5.30*) is through a gate on the north side, and a spiral staircase inside the near right arched column leads up to the lower level of balconies, overlooking both the exterior and interior of the building. Royal proclamations were once read from here. The staircases leading up to the mosque on the next floor and inside the four minarets are now closed to the public.

Near the Charminar

About 150m to the southwest of the Charminar is the **Mecca Masjid** (1614 onwards), the city's most important mosque, built in the reign of Muhammad Qutb Shah. It is named after Mecca because bricks made from clay brought from Mecca were inserted over the central arch of the mosque. The later nizams of Hyderabad were buried here in simple graves under a long arcade which disrupts the symmetry of the building. Visitors are not usually allowed inside the prayer hall of the mosque but, despite some forbidding signboards, are normally permitted into the courtyard.

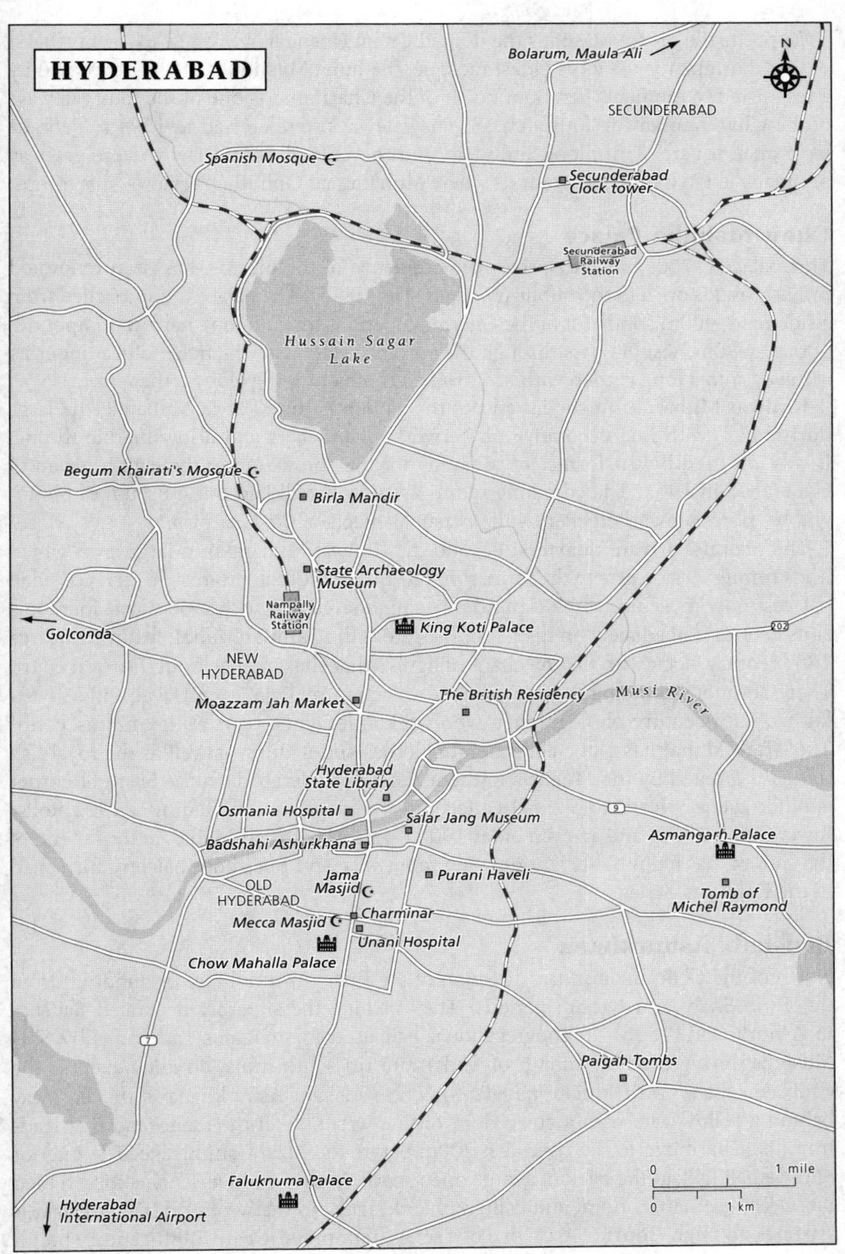
HYDERABAD
Bolarum, Maula Ali
N
SECUNDERABAD
Spanish Mosque
Secunderabad Clock tower
Secunderabad Railway Station
Hussain Sagar Lake
Begum Khairati's Mosque
Birla Mandir
State Archaeology Museum
Nampally Railway Station
Golconda
King Koti Palace
202
NEW HYDERABAD
Moazzam Jah Market
The British Residency
Musi River
Hyderabad State Library
Osmania Hospital
Salar Jang Museum
9
Asmangarh Palace
Badshahi Ashurkhana
Jama Masjid
Purani Haveli
OLD HYDERABAD
Tomb of Michel Raymond
Charminar
Mecca Masjid
Unani Hospital
Chow Mahalla Palace
7
Paigah Tombs
0
1 mile
0
1 km
Faluknuma Palace
Hyderabad International Airport

For a map of Golconda see p. 722.

Opposite the Mecca Masjid is the domed Unani Hospital, while just to the northeast of the Charminar is the city's oldest mosque, the **Jama Masjid** (1598), sadly ruined by a recent redevelopment. Just 80m north of the Charminar is one of the four gateways of the **Char Kaman** (or 'four arches'). The gateways were erected in 1594 to define a large open square, 215m long and wide, and they all still stand. The western gateway originally led to the parade grounds where Muhammad Quli Khan reviewed his troops.

Chow Mahalla Palace

This palace (1760s onwards), the main residence of the nizams, has been renovated recently and is open to the public (*open Sat–Thur 10–5*). The palace is approached from a side road, 400m southeast of the Charminar, and is inside a long narrow compound, 500m by 80m. Visitors pass through the entrance gate, with the ticket office under its archway, into a long garden with arcades and rooms running along either side.

Khilwat Mubarak: At the far end of the garden is the Khilwat Mubarak, the large durbar hall, with fine decorative plasterwork, chandeliers and a low marble throne. It was last used by the former royal family for the coronation of the eighth nizam of Hyderabad in 1967. The adjoining rooms are now a well-laid-out museum of photographs, porcelain and crockery—the personal effects of the later nizams.

The **nizams' private quarters:** Beyond the Khilwat Mubarak is a large lawn which leads through a side gate to the former private quarters of the nizams—a series of small palaces, now museums, built around a rectangular garden with a pool and fountains at its centre. Immediately on the left of the gate is the **Tahniat Mahal**, featuring a large 18th-century clock with tiny mechanical figures that enact scenes from the royal court. There are more photographs, including a collection by Raja Deen Dayal, India's best-known 19th-century photographer, who worked for some years at the nizams' court. The **Aftab Mahal** has a fine collection of clothes and textiles, as well as the royal fish standard granted by the Mughals to the nizams of Hyderabad. In the far right corner another gateway leads to a small collection of vintage cars, including a 1912 Rolls-Royce Silver Ghost, and an even older 1906 Napier. The **Afzal Mahal**, at the far end of the garden, has a double-height drawing room with an upper-floor balcony, furnished in the European style.

Badshahi Ashurkhana

North of the Charminar, in the direction of the river, are a number of buildings from the Qutb Shahi and Nizami periods. They include the superbly decorated Badshahi Ashurkhana (1596)—a congregational hall used for religious gatherings by Shia Muslims during the holy month of Muharram (in south India, an *ashurkhana* is the equivalent of a north Indian *imambara*). The Badshahi Ashurkhana is tucked away behind a yellow gate with a green door on the west side of the main road that leads from the Charminar to the river, just 200m before the Afzal Ganj Bridge. The interior of the small hall, at the back of a large open space, is covered in a richly coloured tiled mosaic of geometric, floral and calligraphic designs. To the west of the *ashurkhana* is **Hyderabad High Court** (1916), one of a series of impressive early 20th-century buildings constructed by the nizams, and designed by the British architect Vincent Esch in the Mughal style. The **Dar ush-Shifa** (1532), just behind the Salar Jang museum is Hyderabad's oldest building, predating the foundation of the city, when its central courtyard and vaulted rooms served as a caravanserai (a roadside inn). It was later turned into a hospital, and the rooms are now used as workshops, while the courtyard houses an *ashurkhana*.

Purani Haveli: Nizams' Museum

In the heart of Old Hyderabad, between the Charminar and the Salar Jang Museum, is the Purani Haveli, a former royal palace that is now the Nizams' Museum and a college. Like the Chow Mallah Palace, it is a long, narrow compound with lots of separate palace buildings—some of them inaccessible behind the European-style bungalow with a broken pediment that is at end of the main courtyard. The Nizams' Museum (*open Sat–Thur 10–4.30*) runs along the left (east) side of the compound. Among its exhibits is what is purported to be the world's longest wardrobe, built for the sixth nizam, who lived here in the 1870s and is said to have never worn any of his clothes more than once. There is also a manually operated lift, a bed made of marble and a walking stick with a handle that is studded with diamonds, rubies and emeralds.

Salar Jang Museum

This museum (*open Sat–Thur 10–5; no cameras*), on the south bank of the Musi River, 1.25km northeast of the Charminar, has one of India's oldest and most famous collections of Indian antiquities and European art. Like his father before him, Yusuf Ali Salar Jang (1889–1949) was prime minister of Hyderabad, though only for two years when he was in his 20s. He spent the rest of his life collecting *objets d'art*, which were originally housed in his ancestral home; they were moved to the current building in 1968. The building has recently been extended, and the European art and artefacts moved into a separate area. The main museum consists of 33 galleries.

Galleries 3–7: Some of the more important exhibits in **Galleries 3 and 3A** include some fine south Indian bronzes, and Hindu, Jain and Buddhist stone sculptures from south India. These include a fine limestone Buddha with broken arms, dated to the 2nd–3rd century. Note the superb north Indian lingam with the face of Shiva from the 5th-century Gupta period in the centre of the room, and the two granite Nandi bulls from nearby Warangal, next to the door. There is also a fine relief carving of Vishnu, seated on the snake Shesha, with his ten avatars represented above him. **Gallery 6** has some carved ivory, and the metal inlay-work known as bidriware (also in Gallery 29), from the nearby town of Bidar. Note also the unusual wooden kneeling sculpture of Garuda, the eagle-god, with a bronze breastplate and mask. **Gallery 7** has some fine north Indian textiles, as well as Mughal glassware. The next set of galleries is devoted to an interesting collection of old toys.

Galleries 12–28: One of the museum's best-known exhibits is in **Gallery 12**: it is the 'Veiled Rebecca', a well-crafted marble statue of the wife of Isaac by the 19th-century Italian sculptor Benzoni. **Gallery 16** has a collection of 19th- and 20th-century

Indian art, including works by Raja Ravi Varma and India's best-known contemporary painter, M.F. Husain. **Gallery 17** has a good collection of miniatures and illustrated manuscripts. The jade collection in **Gallery 28** includes a ring that belonged to the Mughal emperor Shah Jahan, as well as a dagger handle made of rock crystal that belonged to his son Aurangzeb.

European Galleries: These galleries, in a separate building, include oil paintings by Canaletto, Chardin, Constable and Landseer, though experts say several of these are of doubtful provenance and may be copies.

NEW HYDERABAD

Along the river

The commercial heart of Hyderabad lies north of the Musi River and was first developed in the 19th century. Among the buildings from the Nizami period are the multi-domed **Osmania Hospital** (1925), a fine neo-Mughal structure; like the high court, which it faces across the river, it was designed by Vincent Esch. Within the compound wall of the hospital is a large tamarind tree that saved the lives of over 100 people during the great flood of 1908 when they managed to cling to its branches until the water subsided. A memorial plaque pays homage to the tree.

Further to the east, also overlooking the river, is the distinctive arched façade of the **Hyderabad State Library** (1891), designed by Indian architects.

The Residency

The most important European-style building in Hyderabad—and arguably the finest Georgian building in India—is the former Residency (1803–06), which is now the University College for Women and also known as Koti. The building is in poor condition and can be hard to find; although it originally overlooked the Musi, the entrance is from an inside road. A watchman will try to take you around and will also expect a tip of several hundred rupees.

History: The building became the home of Colonel James Achilles Kirkpatrick, the Resident in Hyderabad from 1797 to 1805, who drove out the French and established British supremacy in the region. He married a Hyderabadi noblewoman, Khair un-Nissa—a story retold by William Dalrymple in *White Mughals* (2002)—but died before the Residency was complete. The Neoclassical building is traditionally ascribed to Samuel Russell, although an Indian architect, whose name has not survived, played a major role in its design.

Façade and interior: The façade is grandly Palladian, with a fine staircase guarded by stone lions leading up to a double-height portico with eight well-proportioned Corinthian columns supporting a pediment framing the British coat of arms—the traditional lion and unicorn on either side. The crumbling interior has a large reception hall, with an internal balcony and chandeliers, while the main staircase is similarly grand in conception. The other side of the building, which once commanded an avenue that led down to the riverside, is circular, with a covered entrance portico. The rear of the building is, in fact, part of a larger compound with three old gateways—their old names are still visible above the arches: Lansdowne (after a viceroy) to the left; Empress straight ahead; and Roberts (after a commander-in-chief) to the right.

British Cemetery: Outside the compound, to the right, along the side of Esra Hall, is a footpath that leads to the old overgrown British Cemetery. Among the tombs is a pretty circular columned kiosk, with the grave of Frances Sydenham, the wife of Kirkpatrick's successor as Resident. Near the back of the cemetery is a group of children's tombs. Back outside the cemetery, and a little further along the path, is a damaged model of the Residency that dates to the time of Kirkpatrick. It is thought to have been used as a dolls' house. Next to it is a stone tablet recording the digging of a well by Kirkpatrick in 1802. Further on, behind the cemetery, is a tall building thought to have been built as a *kabutarkhana*, or pigeon house, and which was probably part of Khair un-Nissa's Palace.

King Koti

This palace, on King Koti Road, near the area known as Abids, was the main 20th-century residence of the nizam. It is currently under dispute, and only the gate and the high walls are visible. It was originally the home of a businessman called Kamal Khan, whose initials were inscribed all over the buildings. The nizams renamed the building King Koti (or King's House) so as to be able to retain the inscription.

Twentieth-century buildings

There are several interesting 20th-century buildings in other parts of New Hyderabad, including, from south to north: the **Moazzam Jah Market** (1935), with its high-domed clock tower; the **State Archaeology Museum** (*see below*); the neo-Rajput **Andhra Pradesh Assembly Building** (1913), originally conceived as Hyderabad's town hall; and the white marble **Birla Mandir** (1976), spectacularly located on, and built into, one of the enormous boulders found all over the city and the surrounding countryside.

State Archaeology Museum

This museum (*open Sat–Thur 10.30–5*), just south of the State Assembly, has an important collection of early Buddhist, Jain and Hindu antiquities—mainly from the former nizams' dominions, including Warangal and Amaravati—which are spread out over several indoor and outdoor galleries. The most popular attraction with locals is a decrepit-looking Egyptian mummy. Near the entrance is a lovely 12th-century fragment of a frieze from Warangal, showing a woman looking into a mirror with an attendant either side of her. In the bronze gallery is a very early south Indian bronze (4th–5th century) of the Buddha of Compassion, Avalokiteshwara, and a later Chola-period (c. 12th century) Nataraja, showing Shiva as the Lord of the Dance, his foot treading on the back of a dwarf. In the main gallery is a collection of 30 pieces from Amaravati, the greatest of the south Indian Buddhist stupas—the best of the superb carved panels are now in the British Museum in London. The Jain gallery, in a separate building and compound to the left of the main museum, has some very fine statues of Parusnath, with a snake hood behind his head.

Begum Khairati's Mosque

Some 700m east of the Birla Mandir, this mosque (1633) is New Hyderabad's finest Qutb Shahi building. It is partly concealed by modern construction, but has a pretty cornice and unusually ornate minarets. It was built by Muhammad Qutb Shah for his tutor Akhund Mullah, who died while on a visit to Mecca and whose empty tomb stands just to the north of the mosque.

About half a kilometre north of the mosque is the enormous **Hussain Sagar Lake**. This is a reservoir, 2.5km across and 3.5km from north to south, built in 1562 to serve the old capital Golconda.

SECUNDERABAD

North and east of Hussain Sagar Lake is Secunderabad (*map 12 A2 and on p. 715*), Hyderabad's twin city, with which it is now contiguous. It was named after the third nizam, Sikander Jah, and was founded in the 19th century as a garrison for British troops. There is still a large cantonment area to the northeast, as well as clubs and palaces that date back to the British period.

Among the more interesting buildings are the neo-Gothic **Spanish Mosque** (1905), near the old airport, with octagonal, tapering multi-tiered spires, and the impressive brick **clock tower** (1896) just north of the railway station. Further north, in Bolarum next to the cantonment area, is the former country house of the British Resident, now known as **Rashtrapati Nilayam** (1860s)—one of three official residences of the President of India (the others are in Delhi and Simla). It is closed to the public. Also in Bolarum is the neo-Gothic **Holy Trinity Church** (1848), built with a donation from Queen Victoria—her great-great-granddaughter Queen Elizabeth came here on a state visit in 1983. Nearby is a bungalow called **The Retreat** (1875), at J-95 Allenby Lines, in which Winston Churchill stayed while playing for an army team in a polo tournament in 1897.

The **shrine of Maula Ali** is situated to the far north of the city. In the mid-16th century, a eunuch called Yaqoot had a dream in which he was led to the top of a hill where Ali, the son-in-law of the prophet, was seated on a rock at the summit; the next day Yaqoot returned to find what he believed was the mark of Ali's hand on the same rock. Today, the shrine attracts worshippers from all faiths and is an especially important place of worship for Shia Muslims. Apart from the beautiful arch at the entrance of the shrine, the views from the top of this hill are definitely worth the climb.

SOUTHERN HYDERABAD

Southern Hyderabad also has some important buildings from the Nizami period. These include the superb Paigah tombs in a compound 4km southeast of the Charminar.

The Paigah tombs

To reach these tombs, find the small lane leading to Preston Junior College near the Owaisi hospital. The Paigahs were one of Hyderabad's most important noble families, intermarried many times over with the ruling Asaf Jahi Dynasty. The tombs and the small mosque have some immaculate marble tracery-work, and richly ornamented stucco decoration. None of the tombs is the same, though the main group are based on a single template of a small, square, flat-roofed building, open at the centre so that the tomb is open to the skies, in accordance with more conservative Islamic traditions. Note the superbly ornate curved pinnacles on the rooftop of the tombs.

Around the Paigah compound are many more tombs as well as the **Old Idgah** (1610), with its large, stunted minarets and five-bayed prayer hall.

Falaknuma Palace

This palace (1884) is on a small hill 3km south of the Charminar and is now a luxury hotel (*see Accommodation, p. 742*). It is the most impressive of Hyderabad's palaces, partly because of its superb location, but also because of its fine Neoclassical façade and richly decorated interior. It was built by Sir Vicar al-Umra, a member of the noble Paigah family, whose maternal grandfather was the third nizam. He later presented it as a gift to his cousin the sixth nizam, and it remains the property of the former royal family.

The **tomb of Michel Raymond** sits on a rocky outcrop 4km east of the Charminar, in the area known as Moosaram Bagh. The place name Moosaram is a contraction of Monsieur Raymond, who was the commander of French mercenary forces in the service of the nizam, and who died in 1798. His mausoleum consists of a recently reconstructed Greek-style pavilion and a tall obelisk. A little further down the hill is the **tomb of Anne Jenkins**, who died in childbirth in 1809—nothing more is known about her. Just 300m north of the Raymond tomb is the mock-medieval **Asmangarh Palace** (1885), built by Sir Asman Jah, a prime minister of Hyderabad who belonged to the noble Paigah family. The unusual castle-like building is now a school.

GOLCONDA

The ruins of Golconda (*map 12 A2*), one of India's greatest and richest medieval cities, lie to the west of modern Hyderabad and have now been almost entirely enveloped by its suburbs. The citadel, Golconda Fort, remains one of India's most spectacular visitor attractions, built on and around a steep hill strewn with huge granite boulders. Nearby is the magnificent tomb complex of the Qutb Shahi Dynasty.

History: Golconda was a fortified outpost of the Hindu Kakatiya Dynasty, based in Warangal in the 12th–13th centuries, and was then ruled from 1364 by the expanding Bahmani Sultanate based in Gulbarga. It soon became a major diamond mining and trading centre, and the name Golconda would later be synonymous with immense wealth. But it was not until the emergence of the Qutb Shahi Dynasty in the early 16th century that Golconda became a major city and the capital of one of several Muslim sultanates in the Deccan. The founder of the dynasty, Quli Qutb al-Mulk, was a Bahmani governor who declared independence on the death of the Bahmani sultan Muhammad in 1518. He and his son Ibrahim strengthened the walls of Golconda

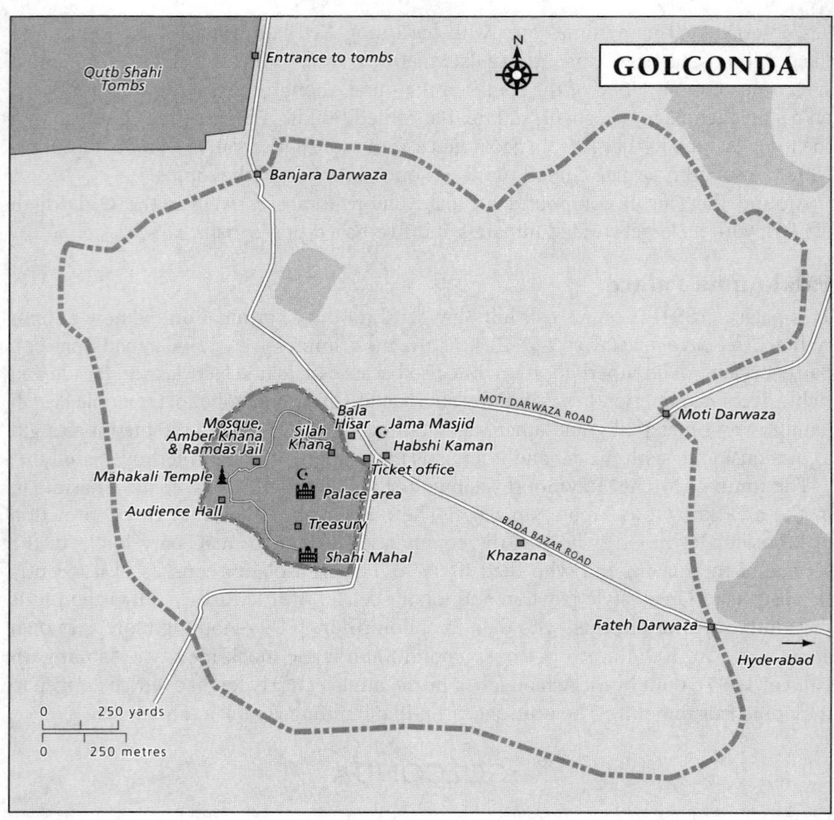

and constructed many of the surviving buildings within the fortress. Diamond mining made Golconda world famous as a place of legendary wealth. Under Ibrahim's son and successor, Muhammad Quli Qutb Shah, the decision was taken to move the capital to Hyderabad in 1592, though Golconda continued to function as a citadel—and it was here that the Qutb Shahis took refuge when the Mughals invaded. The Mughal emperor Aurangzeb eventually captured the fort in 1687, and imprisoned Tana Shah, the last of the Qutb Shahis, in Daulatabad Fort in modern-day Maharashtra. Under the early nizams, Golconda continued to be used as a treasury, though many of the older buildings were allowed to fall into disrepair.

Orientation: Golconda Fort, 8km west of Charminar, and on a hill that rises almost 100m above the plains, is visible from many parts of Hyderabad. Most visitors travelling from Hyderabad enter the old walled city of Golconda from the eastern Fateh Darwaza, or Victory Gate. This leads to a long straight avenue which culminates at the foot of the entrance to the fort. There are several other approaches to the walled city and the fort, including the northeastern Moti Darwaza, or Pearl Gate, which is used by visitors coming from North Hyderabad and Secundarabad, and the northwestern Banjara Darwaza, which leads to the Qutb Shahi tombs.

There is only one entrance to the actual fort (*open daily 9–5*), which leads through a second set of walls. Most of the palaces are to the left, while the citadel on the hilltop can be approached by a number of routes, of which the one on the right (or north) is the least steep, while the one on the far left (or south) is the most dramatic.

The fort gateways

Just outside the entrance to the fort are two enormous arched structures, known as the **Habshi Kaman**, or African Gateways, which are believed to have housed at one time the Abyssinian guards of the sultan of Golconda. Note the stucco animal figures above the external arches. The main gate, known as the **Bala Hisar**, or Citadel Gate, is hidden behind a barbican to provide 360° defensive protection—and to see the gate one has to turn right into the barbican. Above the gate are stucco figures of lion-like monsters and peacocks, while in the gateway is a small display of old weapons and pottery found inside the fort.

The citadel

Just inside the gate, guides clap their hands to show how sound echoes from the bottom of the fort to the top, enabling easy communication. To the right of the gate is the old mortuary bath, where deceased female members of the royal family were laid out and washed before being moved to the burial grounds outside the fort. Just ahead of the gateway are numerous semi-ruined buildings, which served as a garrison, stores and granaries, while to the right are gardens and one of the pathways leading up the hillside. To the left are the triple-storeyed arcades of the **Silah Khana**, or armoury, now used for exhibitions.

Palace area: Beyond the armoury are the palace buildings, many of them still intact, although they have lost most of their decoration. There is a series of enclosures, walled open areas, surrounded by buildings. These enclosures were progressively restricted to smaller and smaller groups of people, and only the royal family and their servants had access to the innermost areas. The first enclosure has on the right (west), the pretty three-bayed **Taramati Mosque**, with fine plasterwork above its parapet. Just beyond are the largest and most impressive palace buildings, including the large public audience hall. There is a pretty domed octagonal chamber with a small pool and dozens of wall niches. Steps take you to the roof of this building, which extends to the eastern side of the fort, giving a good view over parts of the fort to which there is no public access. The next enclosure has a 12-sided pool in the middle of the paved court, with modern seating for a sound-and-light show; it is surrounded by more palace buildings.

Shahi Mahal: Officially closed to the public but visible near the walls is the ruined Shahi Mahal—a small pavilion in the middle of an enclosure. The watchman may let you visit the Shahi Mahal, and other off-limits areas, and it is possible to head left along the inside of the walls of the fort and come out near the main entrance, not far from the offices of the Archaeological Survey of India.

The southern path to the summit: To the right of the enclosure with the 12-sided pool are further buildings, including another mosque and the **Treasury** (1624), which is thought to be where Golconda's famous jewels, including the Kohinoor (*see p. 289*) and the Hope diamonds, were kept. Steep steps lead up the side of the hill, past storage buildings and granaries, and alongside water tanks and channels that were part of the complex hydraulic system that took water to the buildings on top of the hill.

Golconda's hilltop: On the summit is a two-storey building used as an audience hall by the Qutb Shahi kings, and a large open area next to which is the **Mahakali Temple**, built into some boulders. There are superb views of the palace buildings, the rest of the fort and large parts of Hyderabad from the summit. Just below is the tiny **Ibrahim Mosque** (late 16th century), named after the third Qutb Shahi ruler, which has exquisite minarets and plasterwork.

A little further down the hill, by the middle group of steps, is the granary, or **Amber Khana**, a building with small holes in its roof which allowed grain to be poured in through the ceiling. Beneath the Amber Khana is the **Ramdas Jail**, said to be named after a minister of the last sultan, who was imprisoned here after having been accused of misusing public funds.

Beyond the citadel: Other buildings outside the inner citadel walls but inside the outer walls of Golconda include the whitewashed main mosque, or **Jama Masjid** (1518), near the Bala Hisar Gate. Its interior has been ruined by a modern extension. Back on the main road between the fort and the Fateh Darwaza is the **Khazana**, or Treasury, now a poorly maintained museum.

Qutb Shahi tombs

To reach the magnificent royal necropolis of the Qutb Shahis, leave Golconda through the northern Banjara gate, with its defensive fortifications and water-filled moat. The tomb compound (*open daily 9.30–5.30*), which contains some of India's finest funerary architecture, is 500m beyond Banjara gate. Most of the tombs are built to a similar design—an onion dome on a cube, often with two tiers, and ornately decorated corner minarets. Many of them were originally covered with coloured tiles, though only a few traces of these remain. Most have a separate mosque, and the whole necropolis is set in a pretty formal garden. The tombs were restored in the 19th century by Salar Jang I, a prime minister under the nizams, and provided with English and Urdu nameplates which can still be seen. The tombs get progressively older as you move from the entrance area to the back of the complex.

Abdullah Qutb Shah's tomb: One of the finest of the mausolea, the tomb of Abdullah Qutb Shah, the sixth sultan (d. 1672) is just outside the compound on the right. It is a two-tiered tomb, with a large bulbous dome on a petalled base, fine plasterwork, trefoil battlements on each tier and some surviving coloured tiles on one of the columns of the second tier. The austerely decorated interior contains an unusual cenotaph, rather like a step-pyramid, which is covered in Arabic calligraphy. Just to the left of the compound entrance is the incomplete, unplastered tomb of Prince Nizamuddin, the top of its dome missing.

First group of tombs: The tombs immediately inside the gate, to the left and right, belong to female members of the Qutb Shahi dynasty. The large mausoleum immediately to the right inside the compound is the tomb of Hayat Baksh Begum (d. 1667), the wife of Muhammad, the fifth sultan. It is similar to Abdullah's tomb, but lacks the trefoil battlements on the lower tier. Unusually there are two mosques associated with this tomb. The smaller one on the nearside is known as Aurangzeb's Mosque, because the Mughal emperor Aurangzeb is said to have prayed here during the siege of Golconda in 1687. The larger five-bayed Great Mosque (1668) behind the tomb is the biggest in the complex, and has very fine stucco decoration on the façade and minarets. Behind are two smaller tombs containing the graves of two of Abdullah Qutb Shah's consorts, Pemamati and Taramati.

Tomb of Muhammad Qutb Shah: The largest mausoleum in this part of the complex is the tomb of Muhammad Qutb Shah (d. 1626), built to a similar design, with slightly enlarged petals beneath the dome. Beyond Muhammad's tomb to the left is a ramp with spindly rough-cut columns. The ramp was used to draw water from the tank it overlooks. Note the pretty basement arcades around the water tank. On the right is the **mortuary complex**, where the bodies of members of the royal family were laid out and washed. Built during the reign of Muhammad Quli Qutb Shah, it had a hot and cold cistern. There is a large 12-sided platform, inlaid with a black basalt swirling pattern on which the bodies were placed. In the neighbouring building is a small museum with weapons, pottery and stucco decoration found at the site.

Tomb of Muhammad Quli Qutb Shah: Facing the mortuary complex is the most impressive of all the mausolea: the tomb of Muhammad Quli Qutb Shah, the fourth sultan and the founder of Hyderabad, who died in 1612. The tomb is raised on a high plinth, and there is a recess on each side for a portico supported by thin octagonal columns. Note the unusual passages that have been cut diagonally through the corners of the tomb. Next to it is an *idgah*, or large wall mosque, where congregations would pray on special occasions.

The oldest of the Qutb Shahi tombs: The tombs of the first three sultans are nearby. The most distinctive of these is the tomb of Jamshed (1550), the second sultan, an octagonal building with a first-floor balcony. The tomb of Quli Qutb ul-Mulk, the first sultan, is between those of Muhammad Quli and Jamshed. It is the simplest and oldest of the group, and formed a prototype for the later mausolea. The tomb of Ibrahim (1580), the third sultan, on the far side of the compound, closest to Golconda, has surviving coloured tilework above its arches.

NORTHERN ANDHRA PRADESH

Medak

The town of Medak (*map 12 A2*), 78km north of Hyderabad, has a large ruined hill-fort, most of the buildings of which are from the Bahmanid or Qutb Shahi periods. The fort is reached by a steep stone staircase with several elegant gateways, the uppermost of which has a carved elephant on each side of the entrance. The enormous neo-Gothic cathedral (1914–24) can accommodate 5,000 worshippers and is one of the largest churches in Asia.

Bhongir Fort

About 45km northeast of Hyderabad on the road to Warangal is Bhongir Fort (*map 12 A2*), dramatically situated on top of a huge rock, rising 120m above the plains. Parts of the fort, including its impressive walls, date to the 12th-century Kakatiya period. There is a ruined palace and other buildings on the summit.

WARANGAL

The ruins of the great medieval Hindu fortress city of Warangal (*map 12 B2*) are 135km northeast of Hyderabad, and make an interesting day trip. However, if you also want to see the superb Ramappa Temple at Palampet (*see opposite*), a further 60km northeast, it is best to stay overnight in Warangal.

History: Warangal was the capital of the Kakatiya Dynasty, which dominated large parts of Andhra Pradesh from the 12th–14th centuries. The Kakatiyas were weakened in the early 14th century following attacks by the Delhi Sultanate, and in 1366 the Gulbarga Sultanate took control of Warangal. In 1510 the Vijayanagar ruler conquered Warangal, and the fort was seized by the first of the Qutb Shahi rulers of Golconda in 1532.

The walls of Warangal

The impressive walls of the city survive largely intact and form two almost perfect concentric circles just to the south of the modern town. The 7km-long outer walls are largely made of earth, but have stone gateways. The 4km-long inner walls are built of enormous blocks of granite that rest on each other without the use of mortar, and they are surrounded by a water-filled moat. The four gateways to the fort, at the cardinal points of the compass, are inside formidable defensive bastions.

The inner walls: Most visitors enter from the western gate, where they are forced to turn sharply right and then left to enter the fort. Note the fine carved stonework from temples and other buildings that has been reused in the restoration of the gateway, probably in the period of rule from Gulbarga. The area within the walls is now largely agricultural, but there are several buildings and ruins along the main west–east axis.

The Kush Mahal: Some 400m east of the West Gateway is the Kush Mahal, or Shitab Mahal, an unusual vaulted rectangular building with huge sloping walls. It may date to the late Kakatiya period, but it is also believed to have served as the audience hall of Shitab Khan, the Gulbarga governor who declared himself independent and was then defeated by Vijayanagar forces in 1510. The building is now used as a small museum, with some superb pieces collected from the Warangal site. Note in particular the carved stone monsters used as column brackets outside the Kush Mahal. There are fine views of Warangal from the roof of the building.

The main Warangal site

The Warangal archaeological site (*open daily dawn–dusk*) is 200m east of the Kush Mahal in a large compound. The site is dominated by four impressive *toranas*, or temple gateways, with some superb detail. Note the goose at the end of each crossbar and the lions on the side brackets. The rest of the site has hundreds of often beautifully carved stone pieces of what was once a huge Shiva temple. Note particularly a large carved Nandi bull, Shiva's vehicle, as well as a carving of Shiva's son Ganesha, the elephant-god. Some parts have been crudely re-assembled, and on the near right (southeast) is the stone floor of a subsidiary shrine, as well as a temple with finely carved columns. There is also a temple on the other side of the road from the entrance to the site, which has a number of interesting carvings embedded in the concrete outside the shrine, including a Nandi bull and a fine Shiva lingam with four faces.

Warangal Rock

A little east of the archaeological site (about 200m) is the entrance to a public park with a footpath that leads up onto the enormous rock after which Warangal (derived from the Telugu word *orugallu*, meaning 'single rock') was named. The rock, which overlooks a large lake, has a temple and an octagonal pavilion on its summit, which may have served as a watchtower. There are several more temples and other buildings close to the eastern gateway of Warangal Fort.

Thousand Pillared Temple

In the town of Hanamkonda (now contiguous with modern Warangal), 6km northeast of Warangal Fort, is another major Kakatiya shrine, known inaccurately—since it has very few pillars—as the Thousand Pillared Temple (1163). It is constructed out of basalt, and has some fine carved basalt images, particularly above the entrance to the shrines and on the ceiling of the entrance hall. It is an unusual three-shrined temple, which has been laid out in a cruciform shape. The left shrine is to Shiva, the middle one to Vishnu, the right one to Surya. It is now actively worshipped as a Shiva temple, with a large lingam in the sanctuary. Note some very fine carved images, including two large deities, lying in the compound, and a large inscribed stone with carved images of donors worshipping at a Shiva lingam at the top of the temple.

RAMAPPA TEMPLE, PALAMPET

The superb Hindu temple (1213) near the village of Palampet (*map 12 B2*), 60km northeast of Warangal, is probably the finest surviving piece of Kakatiya art and architecture. The temple is dedicated to Shiva and has a subsidiary Shiva shrine within its compound. The temple complex was damaged in a 17th-century earthquake, and the original gateway on the right side of the compound was rather bizarrely affected, and now has several columns that look as though they are about to collapse.

The carvings on the exterior and interior of the main temple are of a particularly high standard. Note how the external brackets to the columns take the form of superbly sinuous carvings in basalt of women and mythical beasts. The outer walls have fine relief friezes depicting animals, amorous couples, gods, wrestlers, musicians and dancers.

The internal columns are intricate pieces, designed with a mixture of square, cylindrical and octagonal shafts. The columns and the roof panels have delicate carvings illustrating key Hindu themes and stories. Among them are the churning of the oceans at the creation of the world, when demons and gods pulled at either end of an enormous snake. There is also a charming representation of Krishna sitting in a tree, having stolen the clothes of the bathing cowgirls, as well as a large variety of images of Shiva, particularly on the ceiling panels. Note also the strangely buckled paved floor, caused by an earthquake.

NAGARJUNAKONDA

This is possibly India's strangest major archaeological site (*map 12 A3*). It is on an island created in 1960 when an enormous dam was completed on the Krishna River, flooding an area that was astonishingly rich in Buddhist and Hindu sites, unearthed by archaeologists in the 1920s. Several excavated buildings and a large collection of antiquities had been moved onto what was then the summit of a hill and is now a small island, less than 2km long and 500m wide. Most of the monuments and exhibits date to the 3rd–4th-century Ikshvaku Dynasty, which ruled large parts of Andhra Pradesh from its capital at Nagarjunakonda. The Ikshvakus were ousted by the Pallavas of Kanchipuram in the 5th century. There are also ruins from the earlier Neolithic period, about 3,000 years ago, and from the 16th and 17th centuries. The lake is called Nagarjuna Sagar, and the area is often simply referred to as Sagar.

Orientation: The island (*open Sat–Thur*) is a 45-minute boat ride from the mainland. The ferry leaves from what is known as the 'launch station' at Vijayapuri, just south of the dam. The timings of the ferry can be very confusing and are aimed at day trippers from Hyderabad, who come in large numbers in the winter months as much for the boat ride as for the monuments and the museum on the island. One ferry usually leaves at 9.30am. However, the ferry operators tend to wait until the boat fills up, though they say it will leave by 10.30, even if it is not full by then. Alternatively, if you are staying nearby, you could take the Archaeological Survey of India boat at 8.30am, which normally allows individual travellers on board but not large groups. Large bags are not allowed on the boats. If you are staying at AP Tourism's Vijay Vihar complex (*see Accommodation, p. 742*), make sure you leave plenty of time to reach the launch station, which is about 12km away. The hotel staff are happy to ring the launch station to find out when they expect the boat to leave. On arrival at the island, check the time of the return journey—you need at least two hours to see the island properly. Basic snacks and drinks are available on the island, but it is no longer possible to stay there overnight.

The ferry docks at the eastern end of the island, from where visitors walk past some minor ruins to the museum. The main relocated buildings are in the centre and western end of the island, on either side of a long walkway. The fortified walls are the only original feature of the island and are thought to date from the 16th century.

Nagarjunakonda Museum

This well-laid-out museum has some superb carvings excavated from Buddhist sites that are now underwater. Many are carved relief scenes from the railings, columns and drum-slabs of excavated stupas which depict stories from the Buddhist *Jataka* tales. Most of the best pieces are in the first part of the gallery.

Note in particular the 3m standing Buddha, which is the best-known example of Ikshvaku art. It was found in several pieces in the sanctuary of a *chaitya* temple that has been moved to a site on the island 500m west of the museum. Among the more easily recognised *Jataka* tales is the Sivi *Jataka*, in which a king protects a dove from a hungry hawk by cutting a piece of flesh from his own thigh to feed to the hawk. Note the scales with which the king's flesh is measured against the weight of the dove. There is also a fine image on a broken pillar on the right-hand side at the end of the main gallery that depicts a dwarf pulling a goat by one of its horns.

Among the non-Buddhist exhibits are a fine seated carving of Narasimha, the lion incarnation of Vishnu, and some Roman coins discovered during the excavation—a reminder of the international nature of trade in the early centuries of the first millennium.

Relocated buildings on Nagarjunakonda

Just beyond the museum, on the lakeside, are some reconstructed stone bathing *ghats* that once stood next to the river. The other relocated archaeological sites, apart from some minor Hindu temples near the *ghats*, are all to the west of the museum, past the thick stone walls—the only original features on the island. The first relocation, on the left after the walls, is a 2nd-century, pre-Ikshvaku **megalithic burial site**—a circle of stones surrounding an underground chamber that contained four human skulls.

Next on the right is a relic known as the **Simha Vihara** (3rd century), which consists of a brick-built stupa, and the lower level of a monastery with small cell-like rooms. The monastery has two horseshoe-shaped shrines which face each other. The one on the left is where the 3m Buddha that is now in the museum was found—the one at the site is a modern replica. The shrine on the left has a miniature stone-clad stupa, with a circumambulatory passage.

The next reconstruction, known as the **Bodhisri Chaitya** (3rd century), is a similar but much larger stone-clad stupa, with a horseshoe-shaped *chaitya* hall. Further ahead on the right is a monastery and temple complex known as the **Chatasri Chaitya**, named after the Ikshvaku queen Chatasri, who commissioned it. The stupa, with a diameter of 27.5 is the largest to survive in Nagarjunakonda.

Next on the right is the reconstruction of the **Aswamedh**, or royal horse sacrifice. It consists of two pools, one stepped and square where the horse was washed, and one in the shape of a turtle where part of the actual sacrifice is thought to have taken place. The last of the reconstructed monuments, a little further on the left, is the tiny **Swast ka Stupa**, so named because of the swastika pattern made by the walls inside the stupa.

Anupu

There is another set of reconstructed monuments at Anupu (*map 12 A3*) on the mainland, 8km south of the ferry terminal. On the right is a ruined **temple to Hariti**, the ogress who became a deity in some Buddhist traditions. On the left is the impressive **open-air theatre** (3rd–4th century), or stadium, which has been reconstructed on the hillside. The stage had seating on all four sides, enough for an audience of about 1,000 spectators. The acoustics of the site allow sound produced from the stage to be easily heard higher up the hill. There is no similar monument from this period in Indian history, and it is not clear what it was used for.

Further along the road, on the right, is a reconstructed **monastery and 'university' complex**, thought to have been founded by the Buddhist spiritual leader Acharya Nagarjunakonda, after whom the entire area was named. Note the two stupas, one of them clad in limestone, as well the stone columns, some of which have carvings.

Srisailam

Some 80km southeast of Nagarjunakonda is the important Hindu pilgrimage site of Srisailam (*map 12 A3*), situated in a dramatic forest location overlooking a gorge along the Krishna River. The main **Mallikarjuna Temple** (15th century), surrounded by high fort-like walls, is dedicated to Shiva. Note the fine reliefs carved on the walls, most of them images of Shiva, including the god as a wandering ascetic and as the slayer of the elephant-demon.

COASTAL ANDHRA PRADESH

The long coastline of Andhra Pradesh attracts few international tourists, largely for the reason that it has no major historical sites, and there has been almost no marketing of tourism in this region. However, it does have a large number of very interesting minor sites, particularly Buddhist ones, some lovely beaches and a good travel infrastructure, currently aimed at the business market. There are airports and good hotels at Vizag, Rajahmundry and Vijayawada.

VIZAG & ENVIRONS

The seaport and industrial centre of **Vizag** (pronounced Vye-zag), officially Visakhapatnam (*map 12 C2*), is the second most populous city in Andhra Pradesh, after Hyderabad. It is an attractive city, dominated to the south by the promontory, rising 175m from the sea, known, because of its shape, as the Dolphin's Nose. Immediately to its north is a small river and the old fort area of the city, spread over three hillocks. There is little trace of the fort, but each of the hillocks has its own place of worship (from west to east): the Church of the Virgin Mary, the Venkateswara Temple church, and the Muslim tomb-shrine, or *dargah*, of Isai. **Waltair**, once a separate European settlement, next to the beach north of Vizag, is now part of the city. There are several 19th-century churches and other sights in the vicinity.

In the forested hills of **Simhachalam** (*map 12 C2*), on the northwestern outskirts of Vizag, is the important Varaha Narasimha Temple, with some fine carved stone panels in the Orissan style, including an image of Vishnu's lion avatar, Narasimha, disembowelling a demon. The temple was constructed in the 9th century as a Shiva shrine, but was converted into a Vaishnavite temple in the 11th century.

Around Vizag

About 15km north of Vizag, on a hill overlooking the coast, **Thotlakonda** (*map 12 D2, open daily 10–3*) is a 2,000-year-old Buddhist site with several stupas, the foundations of a horseshoe-shaped prayer hall and some monastery buildings excavated in the 1980s. Slightly inland, 2km to the southwest, is **Bavikonda** (*open daily 9–6*), another Buddhist site with several ancient wells and a ruined monastery.

The former 17th-century Dutch coastal settlement of **Bheemunipatnam** (*map 12 D2*), previously known as Bhimlipatnam, 23km northeast of Vizag, was twice sacked by the Marathas in the 18th century, before being taken over—as were all Dutch settlements in the country—by the British. There is an interesting Dutch cemetery near the lighthouse on Beach Road, with lots of large obelisk-shaped tombs. The Church of St Peter (1864), with its high belfry, is 2km northeast of the cemetery.

The town of **Vizianagaram** (*map 12 D2*) was the capital of the former princely state of the same name. It is 45km north of Vizag, and has an interesting 17th-century fort in the centre of the town. Vizianagaram is best remembered in India for its last ruling maharaja, known as Vizzy, who captained the national cricket team in the 1930s.

The main road (NH5) south of Vizag heads inland past the town of **Anakapalli** before veering back towards the coast and the delta of the Godavari River and its main city, Rajahmundry. Just 3km north of Anakapalli (*map 12 C2*), on a long outcrop of rock, is the important early Buddhist site of **Sankaram**. The eastern part of the hill, known as Bojjanakonda, has the foundations of a large stupa, a monastery with a horseshoe-shaped prayer area, and rock-cut chambers, several with surviving Buddha images. The western part of the outcrop, known as Lingalakonda, has the unusual sight of numerous rock-cut stupas spread in tiers over the hillside.

SRIKAKULAM & ENVIRONS

Further up the coast towards Orissa, 15km east of the large town of Srikakulam (*map 12 D2*, known to the British as Chicacole) and overlooking a river estuary, is an important Buddhist site at **Salihundram**. Excavations have revealed two horseshoe-shaped prayer halls and several stupas built in an interesting variety of designs. Eight kilometres southeast of Srikakulam in the village of Srikurman is the **Sri Kurmanatha Temple**, built in the 10th century but remodelled by the Cholas in the 12th century. It is thought to be the only temple in the country dedicated to Kurma, the tortoise avatar of Vishnu.

Mukhalingam (*map 12 D2*), 35km north of Srikakulam, was, in the 9th century, the first capital of the Eastern Ganga Dynasty, which was later responsible for the great temples at Puri and Konarak in Orissa. Several shrines survive from Mukhalingam's heyday, of which the **Madhukeshwara Temple** (9th century), in the centre of the town, is the best-preserved and most important, with some superb stone carvings. The temple is dedicated to Shiva, but there are also fine stone images related to Vishnu. Note in particular Varaha, the boar, and Narasimha, the lion, both avatars of Vishnu, on the external left wall of the main assembly hall, as well as the several subsidiary shrine towers in the temple compound.

The later **Bhimeshwara Temple** (12th century), 200m southeast, is of a similar design but less well-preserved, while on the southern outskirts of the town is the **Someshwara Temple** (9th century), with its 15m-high curved tower and more fine carvings.

KAKINADA & ENVIRONS

The southern Jagannathapuram area of the seaport of **Kakinada** (*map 12 C3*), 50km east of the city of Rajahmundry, was once an important European coastal settlement and has an interesting cemetery from the Dutch and British periods. Thirteen kilometres northwest of Kakinada, on the southern side of the town of **Samalkot** (*map 12 C3*), is the **Bhimeshwara Temple** (11th century), the largest and best-preserved of the East Chalukyan buildings in the region, while there are several fine 9th-century temples from earlier in the East Chalukyan period at **Bikkavolu**, between Rajahmundry and Kakinada.

Twenty kilometres south of Kakinada is the tiny former French enclave of **Yanam** (*map 12 C3*) or Yanaon, still administered from Pondicherry, the former capital of French India and not officially part of Andhra Pradesh. It was originally a Dutch settlement, which by the mid-18th century was at the heart of French territory that included large parts of the coast of Andhra Pradesh. Although there are some French buildings in Yanam, it is the least interesting of the former French enclaves, largely because the older parts of the settlement were destroyed in the great cyclone of 1839.

Guntapalle

Seventy kilometres west of Rajahmundry is the important Buddhist site of Guntapalle (*map 12 B3*, also Guntupalli), which can also be visited as a day-trip from Vijayawada, 75km to the southeast. The site, which dates to the period between the 2nd century BC and the 4th century AD, and has some fine Buddhist rock-cut caves as well as dozens of stupas. It is in a pretty location in forested hills and is approached from the south by steps leading up a ravine. Set on a terrace towards the rear of the site is a fine brick stupa with a circumambulatory passage.

VIJAYAWADA & ENVIRONS

The city of Vijayawada (*map 12 B3*), known as Bezawada in the British period, is located inland at the start of the delta of the Krishna River and is Andhra Pradesh's third most populous urban area after Hyderabad and Vizag. Several of the rocky hillocks in the city have minor ancient rock-cut shrines, of which those at Mogulrajapuram are the most interesting. The **Victoria Jubilee Museum** (*open Sat–Thur 10.30–5*) is in a handsome 19th-century building on Bandar Road, and has a fine standing Buddha made of limestone, as well as a number of other Buddhist antiquities. Close to the southern bank of the Krishna River, 3km south of Vijayawada, are the **Undavalli cave-temples**—Hindu shrines from the early East Chalukyan period, with a particularly fine three-storey temple. The uppermost level has a large carving of Vishnu resting on the serpent Shesha.

Kondapalli Fort

This picturesque fort (*map 12 B3*), 15km northwest of Vijayawada, was an important stronghold of the Qutb Shahi rulers of Golconda in the 16th century, but the hilltop on which it stands was fortified much earlier. It is a steep uphill walk through three outer gates into the main fort, which has a ruined palace, known as the Tanisha Mahal, from the Qutb Shahi period, as well as granaries and other buildings.

Amaravati

The ancient Buddhist site of Amaravati (*map 12 B3*), 30km east of Vijayawada on the southern bank of the Krishna, might have been one of India's major tourist attractions. Unfortunately most of the extraordinary Buddhist carvings found here in the 19th century were taken away, with the best collection now kept in the British Museum in London. The limestone carvings, with images taken from Buddhist tales, were from an enormous stupa that was probably once the largest in south India but is now just a low earth mound; it dates back to the Satavahana (3rd–2nd centuries BC) and Ikshvaku (3rd–4th centuries AD) periods.

The nearby **Archaeological Museum** (*open Sat–Thur 9–5*) does give some idea of what Amaravati must have once looked like, and there are also many carvings retrieved during later excavations, including a fine 2m-high Buddha, and an extraordinary life-size bull reconstructed from fragments found at the site.

Kondavidu Fort

The ruins of Kondavidu Fort (*map 12 B3*), 50km southwest of Vijayawada, are spread across several hilltops and in urgent need of conservation. The fort was an important base for the Reddy Dynasty in the 14th century and changed hands many times. The lower part of the fort has a ruined temple and pillared halls, while the citadel, further up the hill, has high watchtowers and crumbling stone structures.

Chezarla

A further 44km west of Kondavidu, and 24km west of the town of Narasaopet, is Chezarla (*map 12 B3*), a small village with what was probably a 3rd-century Buddhist shrine that has since been converted into an unusual Hindu temple. The long shrine building has a vaulted roof with a semicircular stone gable, complete with carvings.

Machilipatnam

The little-visited ancient seaport of Machilipatnam (*map 12 B3*), known to the British as Masulipatnam, is 65km to the southeast of Vijayawada. It was an important coastal settlement for almost 2,000 years, and was the main seaport for Golconda; it later became a major British base. It was devastated by floods in 1864, when more than 30,000 people were killed. Apart from some Dutch graves in the cemetery, there are few signs of Machilipatnam's former importance.

SOUTHERN ANDHRA PRADESH

The southern districts of Andhra Pradesh are seldom visited by international tourists. There are several important pilgrimage sites, including Tirupati and Sri Kalahasti near the Tamil Nadu border, but also the superb temple complex at Alampur, the hillfort at Gooty and the Vijayanagar period ruins at Penukonda and Lepakshi.

The city of **Kurnool** is the most important city of central Andhra Pradesh and was briefly the capital of the state. It does not have any important historical sites but is a good base for exploring the region and is very close to the fine temples at Alampur.

ALAMPUR

This village (*map 13 C1*), 15km northeast of the city of Kurnool and 160km south of Hyderabad, has a fascinating collection of little-visited early Hindu temples, grouped together on the northern bank of the Tunghabhadra River. There are also other temples that were moved here when the Tunghabhadra was dammed in 1979.

Nava Brahma temples

The nine Alampur temples are known as the Nava Brahma (*nava* means nine), although they are all dedicated to Shiva, not Brahma. Until recent times they overlooked the river, but a high embankment now protects them from the waters of the Tunghabhadra—one can get good views of the temple complex and the river from the embankment. The temples date to the Early Chalukyan period (7th–8th centuries) and were important because of their proximity to the joining of the Tunghabhadra to the Krishna River. A Muslim shrine forms part of the same complex.

Swarga Brahma Temple: The finest of the temples, the Swarga Brahma, has some superb external carvings, many of them depicting different moods in the relationship between Shiva and Parvati, and one, on the right-hand side of the entrance to the temple, showing Shiva emerging from the lingam. The Swarga Brahma is slightly hard to find—it is behind the largest temple, the Bala Brahma, which is still used by devotees.

Bala Brahma Temple: This temple has some excellent statues inside, including a bearded representation of Muni, the temple's first high priest, as well as the statues of shrivelled elderly women, the mothers of the guardians Jai and Vijay, who stand at the entrance to the sanctuary, with its natural, uncarved lingam. The smaller **Padma Brahma**, behind the Swarga Brahma, has very fine interior carvings. Also good is the **Vira Brahma Temple**, the most northerly of the group. A watchman will open the shrines on request.

Alampur Museum

Make sure you visit the small **Archaeological Museum** (*open Sat–Thur 10.30–5*) on the site, which has some unusually fine pieces, including two dancing Shivas, a very fine Nandi (the bull) being ridden by Shiva and Parvati, a squatting fertility goddess with a lotus in place of her head, and a touching relief labelled 'a sage and his wives'.

Sangameshwar Temple

Around 700m to the east of the Nava Brahma shrines is the large Sangameshwar Temple, dedicated to Shiva, which was moved here in 1979 from its original location at the spot where the Tunghabhadra and Krishna rivers met—a site that is now permanently underwater. The temple has some fine carvings, in particular the projecting elephants on the outer compound walls, as well as a large variety of Shiva images around the walls of the temple and inside the assembly hall of the shrine.

Papanasi shrines

A kilometre southwest of the Sangameshwar Temple is the Papanasi group of shrines, also moved here from an area that is now underwater. These unusual temples with pyramidal roofs date to the 9th–10th centuries and have interesting carvings, including some fine ceiling panels.

SOUTH & WEST OF KURNOOL

Adoni

This strategically located town (*map 13 C2*), 85km west of Kurnool and 95km north-east of Hampi, was an important stronghold for the Vijayanagar Empire and then the Bijapur and Golconda sultanates. The five-bayed Jama Masjid (1660) in the centre of town has an onion-shaped dome raised on a high drum, decorated with petals. To the north of the town is an impressive hill-fort, with many ruined buildings, a mosque and a tomb.

Yaganti and Ahobilam

The remote village of **Yaganti** (*map 13 C2*), 55km south of Kurnool at the head of a rocky valley, has the important 17th-century Umamaheshwara Temple, dedicated to Shiva. There is a pretty man-made pond, with carved friezes around the edge.

Another 70km further east are the two popular pilgrimage temples at **Lower and Upper Ahobilam** (*map 13 C2*), 8km apart, both from the Vijayanagar period and both dedicated to Narasimha, the lion avatar of Vishnu. The upper temple is in a pretty location, while the lower shrine has some superb carved pillars in its assembly hall.

Gooty

The small town of Gooty (*map 13 C2*), dominated by its spectacular hill-fort (mainly 18th century), is on the highway between Bangalore and Hyderabad—roughly halfway between the two cities—and 90km south of Kurnool. The old part of the town is ringed by a large hill, and can only be entered through a narrow gate. The well-maintained footpath to the hill-fort goes past a dilapidated British cemetery (if the gate is locked, the cemetery can be entered where the wall has fallen down) and a small mosque, before heading steeply uphill and passing through more than a dozen gates.

Many of the surviving fort buildings date from the time of Murari Rao, a Maratha chieftain whose support for the British against the French at the Battle of Arcot (1751) helped ensure British supremacy in south India. Note the stable buildings halfway up the fort, which are arranged as three sides of a square. The small pavilion near the top is known as Murari's seat and is said to be where Murari Rao watched prisoners being thrown to death onto the rocks below. The view from the top is superb.

Tadpatri

Tadpatri (*map 13 C2*), 35km southeast of Gooty, has two important shrines from the Vijayanagar period, both of which have fine stone carvings. In the centre of the town is the Chintala Venkataramana Temple, which is dedicated to Vishnu and has superbly carved pillars in its assembly hall. On the north side of Tadpatri is the Bugga Ramalingeshwara Temple, which is dedicated to Shiva and has intricately carved decoration on the enormous plinth of an unfinished *gopura*.

Gandikot

About 35km east of Tadpatri is the spectacular Gandikot Fort (*map 13 C2*), perched on the southern bank of a canyon through which the Pennar River runs. The fort, 100m above the river, is largely a 16th-century Qutb Shahi structure, though the site had earlier been occupied by Vijayanagar forces. Inside the fort's impressive walls are a ruined palace, a three-storey tower, an imposing mosque, a large granary and two dilapidated temples.

PENUKONDA

The sleepy town of Penukonda (*map 13 C3*), on the Bangalore–Hyderabad highway, was once the capital of the Vijayanagar Empire. After the sacking of the old capital at Hampi in 1565, the Vijayanagar rulers moved here for about two decades before shifting further south to Chandragiri (*see p. 739*), near Tirupati. The town was then conquered by the Golconda-based Qutb Shahis in 1610. Penukonda is 120km north of Bangalore and can be easily visited as a day trip, along with the great Virabhadra Temple at Lepakshi, 30km to the south.

Orientation: The town of Penukonda is dominated by a rocky hill with a ruined fort. It is not easy to climb the hill along the overgrown footpath, but there are a number of gateways, watchtowers and shrines on the way up. Part of the walls of the old city survive, including a fine stone gateway on the south side of Penukonda. In the heart of the town are a series of temples and palaces and a mosque.

Penukonda town

The Jain temple is the most northerly of Penukonda's surviving buildings. It is dedicated to Parusnath, with a fine pre-Vijayanagar sculpture (12th–13th century) of the 23rd Jain saviour standing in front of an undulating snake. The nearby five-bayed mosque (17th century), from the Qutb Shahi period, has a small bulbous dome raised on a petalled base—a similar design to the Qutb Shahi tombs in the royal necropolis near Golconda, but with a narrower than usual neck to the dome.

Shiva and Rama temples: About 200m to the south of the mosque are twin Shiva and Rama temples from the Vijayanagar period, each of them rectangular buildings that have external panels decorated with fine relief carving similar to those at the Hazara Rama Temple in Hampi (*see p. 701*). The external walls of the smaller Shiva temple (on the right as you face the hill) are covered in images depicting Shiva-related mythology. Note in particular images of his vehicle, Nandi the bull, and of his son Ganesha, the elephant-god. The Rama temple has a large, more recent extension and a similar set of relief panels on the outside of the building. These show scenes from the *Ramayana* and from the life of Krishna—note the image of Krishna sitting in a tree, having stolen the clothes of the bathing girls, who stand below imploring him to return them.

Gagan Mahal: Just to the south is the over-restored Gagan Mahal, a palace building from the Vijayanagar period, while down a footpath on the other side of the road is a pavilion from the same period with a roof shaped like an octagonal step-pyramid. Beyond the pavilion is a *baoli*, or step-well, with an unusual gateway shaped like a bull. Nearby is a small temple, with some Vijayanagar-style pillars and relief carvings.

LEPAKSHI

Like nearby Penukonda, Lepakshi (*map 13 C3*) was an outpost of the Vijayanagar Empire. It has a fascinating 16th-century temple, notable for some fine carvings and superb painted ceilings. Lepakshi is close to the Karnataka border, and the nearest large city is Bangalore, 90km away.

On the east side of Lepakshi, on the road that leads to the town from the Bangalore–Hyderabad highway, is the enormous **Nandi Monolith**, a carved representation of the bull used by Shiva as vehicle. The 8m-long bull has been cut from the huge granite boulder on which it appears to rest. Note the detail of the jewellery which adorns the bull, as well as a lingam carved onto its back.

The Virabhadra Temple

This fine temple was constructed in the mid-16th century by two brothers who were governors of the region under the Vijayanagar emperor Achyutadeva Raya. The Virabhadra Temple contains the finest examples of Vijayanagar painting.

The temple has been built on an uneven outcrop of rock which gives the complex its irregular shape. The complex is entered through the northern gateway, capped by a tower, or *gopura*, with external carvings. Inside the gateway, to the right and left, it is possible to walk around the main temple, passing cloisters with distinctive Vijayanagar cut-out colonnettes and carved lion-like figures on the columns; there is an incomplete subsidiary shrine in the southwest corner. Note how the wall of the main temple is incomplete on the southwest side, allowing visitors to see into the raised inner compound. There is also a second entrance to the main temple on the south side. The main entrance, though, is on the north side, slightly out of alignment with the outer gateway, next to a high metal post.

Outer assembly hall: From here, steps lead up to the outer assembly hall, or *mandapa*, of the main temple. This is the most richly decorated area of the complex, with superb carvings on the columns, particularly the four unusually thick pillars, set at an angle, which define the central space of the *mandapa*. Each of these pillars has a trio of carved images. Look for the bearded three-headed Brahma, and the dancing three-legged sage and Shiva devotee Bhringi. On the ceiling of the open *mandapa* are some superb Vijayanagar paintings, richly coloured, depicting scenes from the *Ramayana* and *Mahabharata*, as well as tales from the life of Shiva. Note in particular how different racial types are depicted by using skin colour and clothes as identifying features.

Inner assembly hall: The next gate leads into an inner assembly hall, the outer wall of which has friezes with carved images of geese, elephants and humans. The poorly-lit inner assembly hall has more fine carvings and paintings, and a subsidiary shrine. A fierce image of Virabhadra, a warrior deity created by Shiva, is enshrined in the main sanctuary.

Courtyard: Ensure that you visit the courtyard of the main temple by stepping down from the raised open assembly hall. In the courtyard is a boulder out of which an image of a huge coiled snake has been carved; its rearing hood shelters a lingam made of polished granite. There is also a carved Ganesha in a small shrine. Note beneath the elephant-god a carved image of his 'vehicle', a jewelled mouse.

TIRUPATI

This is one of India's best-known and popular Hindu pilgrimage cities (*map 13 D3*). The most important of the temples—and the one that is usually just referred to as the 'Tirupati Temple'—is in fact the Tirumala Venkateshwara Temple, 22km from the city by a steep winding road.

Orientation: Vehicles are allowed to a car park 400m from the temple. Some devotees walk from the city by a footpath up to the temple, and many of them have their hair tonsured as a sign of their devotion—the hair is sold to make wigs, raising $6m for the temple each year. The temple claims to be the most visited place of worship in the world, and there are often very long queues for the main shrine. It is possible to pay extra and join a quicker queue, known as 'quick *darshan*', though this may still take as long as two hours on busy days. (*No shorts, mobiles or cameras are allowed inside.*)

Tirumala Venkateshwara Temple

The temple itself, surprisingly modest by south Indian standards, dates back to at least the 9th–10th-century Chola period, and probably earlier, but became prominent in the 15th–16th-century Vijayanagar period when Venkateshwara, a form of Vishnu, was adopted as the protective deity of the royal family. Its proximity to Chandragiri—the important Vijayanagar city which became the capital in the late 16th century—gave it added importance.

The main temple is entered through a low 13th-century *gopura*. Immediately inside is a hall with carved pillars from the Vijayanagar period, and some stone and brass statues of members of the Vijayanagar royal family. The inner shrine is from the Chola period, though the gold-covered tower, with its domed summit, was rebuilt in more recent times.

Govindaraja Temple

The most important shrine in the city of Tirupati is the important Govindaraja Temple (17th century), dedicated to Vishnu, with a 50m-high free-standing *gopura*. Note the carvings of a local chieftain, with his three wives, on the left side of the corridor leading through the *gopura*, as well as dozens of other relief carvings.

CHANDRAGIRI

This town (*map 13 D3*), 13km east of Tirupati on the Chittoor road, was an important outpost of the Vijayanagar Empire. It became the Vijayanagar capital in the late 16th century, in the dying days of the empire, after the royal family was forced to flee from Hampi and then vacate the less-well-defended city of Penukonda.

City walls and gates: Chandragiri was built in a dramatic position at the foot of a fortified rocky hillside, and large parts of the impressively broad city walls still survive. The gateway on the east side has some fine carved pillars in the later Vijayanagar style—note also the half-buried free-standing stone elephants standing guard at the gateway. The plainer gateway on the western side has relief carvings of some of the emblems of the Vijayanagar Empire—a boar, a conch and a sword—next to the main gates.

Main site: The main site at Chandragiri (*open daily 8–5; no cameras inside the Raja Mahal*) has two over-restored buildings; the larger of these, the Raja Mahal, contains a museum.

Raja Mahal

The Raja Mahal (late 16th century), literally 'King's Palace', is the best surviving example of palace architecture from the late Vijayanagar period. It is a three-storey arcaded building with many projecting balconies. There is a high pyramid-shaped tower at the centre and smaller pyramidal towers at the corners. The document granting the East India Company the land on which Fort St George was built in Chennai was signed in this building in 1639. Outside are a series of decapitated statues, labelled 'Alwar', a generic name for Hindu saints who were devotees of Vishnu. Inside is a double-height audience chamber, now housing a large number of exhibits from the Vijayanagar period and earlier. Note the fine stone carved image of Hanuman the monkey-god on the right of the entrance doors, as well as a collection of bronzes of Vishnu and his consort Lakshmi. There is also some fine carving from Gandikot, including a *sati* stone depicting a man on horseback attacking a woman. The upper floors of the building are not normally open.

The nearby **Rani Mahal**, or Queen's Palace, was almost certainly not a royal residence but stables for horses and elephants. Note the ruined temple on the other side of the road, as well the impressive fortifications, with a few pavilions, on the hillside.

AROUND TIRUPATI

Gudimallam and Sri Kalahasti

The village of **Gudimallam** (*map 13 D3*), 30km east of Tirupati, is famous for a temple that has one of the oldest and most beautiful images of Shiva. The Parasurameshwara Temple dates from the 9th century, with many later additions, but the 1.5m-high lingam in the sanctuary, with a figure of Shiva carved onto its shaft, is thought to date from the 1st century BC.

The pilgrimage town of **Sri Kalahasti** (*map 13 D3*), about 20km north of Gudimallam and 34km northeast of Tirupati, is sometimes described as the Shaivite equivalent of the latter city. However, it attracts far fewer visitors. The main shrine is the Vijayanagar-period Kalahastishwara Temple, built into the gap between the Svarnamukhi River and a large rocky outcrop. In the town is a 36.5m-high, free-standing *gopura* (1516), built by the Vijayanagar emperor Krishnadevaraya. Note the Vijayanagar emblems, including a sword and a boar.

Narayanavanam and Nagalapuram

There is an interesting temple dedicated to Vishnu in the small town of **Narayanavanam** (*map 13 D3*), 33km south of Tirupati, and just 2km east of Puttur, which is on the Tirupati–Chennai road. The Kalyana Venkateshwara Temple (1541) has unusual relief carvings in the passageway running through the main *gopura*. Note in particular the sexual scene, and the kneeling soldier who is shooting a deer.

Around 23km east of Narayanavanam is another important Vishnu temple in the town of **Nagalapuram** (*map 13 D3*). The large Veda Narayana Temple dates back to the Chola period, but was extended in the 16th century, during the rule of the Vijayanagar emperor Krishnadevaraya. The outer *gopura* was never completed, but the size of the base shows how large it was intended to be. There are interesting relief carvings in the passageways of both the outer and inner *gopura*. Inside there is a portico, with finely-carved pillars, leading to the sanctuary. Note the bronzes in cages on either side of the corridor, with gods—including a very fine Garuda—on the left and *rishis*, or saints, on the right. In the sanctuary is an image of Matsya, the fish avatar of Vishnu, rarely encountered as the principal idol in a temple.

Udayagiri and Bhairavakonda

Some 140km north of Tirupati is the little-visited **Udayagiri Fort** (*map 13 D2*), one of the most impressive in southern India. The nearest city is Cuddapah, 65km to the southwest. Udayagiri was captured from the local Reddy Dynasty by the Vijayanagar Empire in 1512, and later came under the control of the Qutb Shahis and then the Mughals. The fort is reached by steep steps rising more than 300m above the plains (take water with you). Inside the upper fort is a mosque (1643) erected by a Qutb Shahi general, a granary and several other buildings. In the village at the foot of the fort is the dilapidated 16th-century Ranganayaka Temple, with a fine *gopura* inside the main compound.

About 45km northwest of Udayagiri are the rock-cut Hindu temples of **Bhairavakonda** (*map 13 D2*), dating to the 7th–8th centuries, which are cut into the side of a forested ravine. There are handsome seated carved lions at the base of many of the shrine pillars.

PRACTICAL INFORMATION

Despite the fact that the tourist infrastructure of Andhra Pradesh is less well-developed than in India's other large states, it has many comfortable hotels and eating places. The state attracts so many business travellers and pilgrims that it is actually quite well geared up for visitors—and tourists often find the state more relaxing and hassle-free than many of the country's popular destinations.

GETTING THERE

• **By air:** Hyderabad has a modern international airport, with lots of connections to the Middle East and Southeast Asia, and a growing number of flights from Europe and the US. It is also well connected to all of the major cities of India, as well as smaller centres in the south. Other less well-connected airports in Andhra Pradesh, with flights to Hyderabad and cities in neighbouring states, include Vizag (with direct flights to Delhi), Rajahmundry, Vijayawada and Tirupati.

Because Hyderabad is in the northwest corner of the state, it is often easier to reach important sites in southern Andhra Pradesh from neighbouring state capitals, particularly Bangalore (for Lepakshi) and Chennai (for Tirupati).

• **By train:** Train services link Secunderabad (for Hyderabad) with Vijayawada (5½hrs), Vizag (8hrs), Tirupati (13hrs) and Chennai (14hrs), but the Andhra Pradesh capital is not particularly well connected by rail to the rest of the country. One exception is the night train from Aurangabad (near the caves of Ajanta and Ellora) in Maharashtra to Secunderabad (14hrs).

• **By road:** Roads are generally good, particularly the main highway from Hyderabad towards Bangalore. Taxis can be hired in most urban centres, and are often cheaper than in neighbouring states. Auto-rickshaws are widely available in towns and cities.

Hyderabad-based **Detours India** (*contact Jonty; T: 09000 850505; detoursindia.com*) runs superb tours, on foot and by car, of the city and surrounding area.

ACCOMMODATION

Hyderabad

The capital has a number of fine hotels, including the newly renovated **Falaknuma Palace** (*$$$; T: 040 6629858; tajhotels.com*), run by the Taj group. It is well located for visiting the Old City and Golconda. **The Park Hotel** (*$$$; T: 040 23456789; theparkhotels.com*), in the main commercial district, is one of Hyderabad's newest hotels. The **Taj Mahal Hotel** (*$; T: 040 24758250*), in the central Abids commercial area, is a simple, comfortable heritage hotel built in 1924.

Northern Andhra Pradesh

This area has no luxury hotels, but there is lots of clean, basic accommodation.

• **Nagarjunakonda:** The most comfortable accommodation is at **Andhra Pradesh Tourism's Vijay Vihar complex** (*$; T: 08680 277362; aptourism.in*), 15km north of the ferry terminal, with superb views over the lake.

• **Warangal:** The best place to stay in Warangal is probably the **Suprabha** (*$; T: 0870 2573888*).

Coastal Andhra Pradesh

• **Rajahmundry:** The most comfortable hotel is the **River Bay** (*$$; T: 0883 2447000; riverbay.co.in*).

• **Vijayawada:** Here there is the Taj-run **Gateway Hotel** (*$$; T: 0866 6644444; tajhotels.com*).

• **Vizag:** The city has several comfortable hotels including **The Park** (*$$$; T: 0891 2754488; theparkhotels.com*), overlooking Waltair Beach.

Southern Andhra Pradesh

• **Kurnool:** The best hotel in Kurnool (for the Alampur temples) is the **Raja Vihar** (*$; T: 0851 2820702*).

• **Tirupati:** The town has a large number of hotels aimed at pilgrims, while **Fortune Kences** (*$$; T: 0877 2255855; fortunehotels.in*) feels more like a business traveller's hotel.

FOOD

Hyderabad is the best place to sample two very different kinds of cuisine. It is the home of Hyderabadi Muslim food, famous for its *biryanis*, in which rice, meat and spices are all cooked together. The Hyderabadi *biryani* is different from the north Indian or Lucknowi version, in which the rice and meat are cooked separately. The other signature dish of Hyderbadi cuisine is *haleem*, a spiced purée made from meat, lentils and wheat, which is particularly popular as a way of breaking the Ramadan fast.

The best-known Hyderabadi desert is *qubani ka meetha*, a combination of apricots, apricot kernels and cream.

The best places for Hyderabadi food are in simple city restaurants, such as the ones at the **Mehdipatnam food court** in the west of Hyderabad or at **Shadab** on High Court Road in the Old City. Also popular are **Paradise Biryani** in Secunderabad and Masab Tank, and the several branches of **Hyderabad House**.

The other cuisine that is widely available in Hyderabad is Andhra food—a superb, normally vegetarian range of spiced curries served with rice on banana-leaf plates. The fact that Andhra is the largest exporter of chillies is evident in this cuisine, and it is known for its varieties of pickles and chutneys. Snacks include *pesarettu*, a pancake made of green lentils. You can get authentic Andhra food at several branches of **Chutneys** (at Himayatnagar, Jubilee Hills and Nagarjuna Circle) and at **Southern Spice** at Banjara Hills—as well as at roadside restaurants (*dhabas*) throughout the state.

FURTHER READING & VIEWING

The Outlook Group's *Weekend Breaks from Hyderabad* is the best local guide. For the city's history, there is the very readable *Hyderabad: A Biography* by Narendra Luther (OUP India, 2006). William Dalrymple's superb social history *White Mughals: Love and Betrayal in 18th-century India* is about the love affair and marriage between a British officer and an Indian princess in Hyderabad. There is also an interesting anthology, *The Untold Charminar: Writings on Hyderabad* (Penguin India, 2008), edited by Syeda Imam. The novel *Zohra* (1950, republished OUP India, 2008) by Zeenuth Futehally is set in pre-Independence Hyderabad.

The multilingual *The Angrez* (2006), in which many of the city's most famous buildings make frequent appearances, became an international YouTube hit.

KERALA

Over the last two decades, the state of Kerala (*map 14*) has emerged as an important international tourist destination. Although the sandy beaches and backwaters of southern Kerala remain the major attractions for visitors, the city of Cochin is one of India's most interesting historic urban centres, with an old European quarter, a fine palace and a synagogue. The north of the state attracts fewer visitors, but has a rapidly developing tourist infrastructure, some glorious beaches and a number of important buildings from the early European period, while inland are some of India's most spectacular landscapes. Kerala is educationally India's most advanced state, with very high rates of literacy, a mixed Hindu-Christian-Muslim population and a powerful Communist tradition dating back to the 1930s. The main language of the state is Malayalam, and the capital is Trivandrum.

HISTORY OF KERALA

The state's early history is dominated by the Chera Dynasty, which is thought to have ruled most parts of modern Kerala for more than 1,000 years, until the early 12th century, when they were defeated by Chola forces from what is now Tamil Nadu. Unlike that of other early southern dynasties, almost nothing has survived of Chera art and architecture, probably because wood, rather than stone, was the main construction material. Kerala's early history was also marked by its importance as a centre for international trade, particularly in pepper and other spices which grow locally. The large port of Muziris, north of Cochin, which flourished 2,000 years ago and traded with the Roman Empire and others parts of the world, has been the subject of recent archaeological excavations.

Foreign religions come to India: According to tradition, the Kerala coast is where three of India's imported faiths first arrived in the country. St Thomas the Apostle is said to have arrived in Kerala in AD 52, and converted many local people to Christianity. Many of the modern-day 'Thomas Christians', belonging to at least seven small Christian sects with strong local roots, claim to be descendants of those early converts. India's earliest Jews are thought to have come to the country at about the same time (though some accounts place their arrival much earlier), and set up important communities, now almost vanished, in central Kerala. The first Muslims are thought to have come to central and northern Kerala as preachers and traders in the 8th century—in areas that still have a large Muslim population.

European trade and rule: The Portuguese explorer Vasco da Gama arrived at Kappad, just north of Calicut in 1498, the year from which the European involvement in India is usually dated. Vasco da Gama was able to extract trading concessions from the ruler of Calicut, known as the Zamorin, and later from the rulers of Cochin, where he died in 1524. The Portuguese were soon followed by the Dutch, who were based in

Cochin—though they were defeated by the forces of Travancore in 1741 at the Battle of Kolachel. By this time the British were playing a larger role on the Malabar coast, and by the end of the 18th century were the dominant force in Kerala—though the princely states of Cochin and Travancore remained nominally independent during the British period, and the French retained the tiny enclave of Mahé, which is now ruled from Pondicherry.

Independent India: At Independence, Cochin and Travancore were united as one state, and then merged with the more northerly Calicut and Kasargod areas into the state of Kerala in 1956. The following year in Kerala, one of the world's first democratically-elected Communist governments was voted to power. The Communists and Congress have remained rivals for power in Kerala ever since.

TRIVANDRUM

Trivandrum (*map 14 B3*), officially called Thiruvananthapuram, is the capital of Kerala and its largest city. Its proximity to the beaches of Kovalam and Varkala means that most visitors only use the city for transit, but Trivandrum was once the capital of the princely state of Travancore, and has several interesting buildings from that period. The capital was moved from Padmanabhapuram (now in Tamil Nadu) by Martanda Varma, possibly the greatest of the Travancore rulers.

Orientation: Trivandrum is set slightly inland from the coast, with the city's airport hugging the seashore. The old Royal Quarter is in the south of the city, beyond the railway station and close to the Padmanabhaswami Temple. The main civic buildings and hotels are in the north of the city.

ROYAL QUARTER

The old Royal Quarter of Trivandrum consists of the large Padmanabhaswami Temple, a pretty man-made rectangular pond, the palace compound (part of which is now a museum) and some portions of the old fort walls.

Royal Palace

The entrance to the Royal Palace (*open Tues–Sun 8.30–1 & 3–5*) is down a passageway that passes through the two-storey building with a clock tower that overlooks the pond, just before the temple. Visitors are allowed into one of the 18th-century palaces, but several others remain empty. Note the superb woodwork, particularly on the ceilings of the palace. An interesting collection of palanquins and howdahs (for riding elephants) are on display, as well as thrones made of crystal and of ivory. Upstairs is a pretty octagonal room with a painted ceiling, and another partially open area, jutting out of the main building, which was used as a music room. Entry is restricted to the Padmanabhaswami Temple, dedicated to Vishnu, which dates back to the 10th century, but which was rebuilt by Maharaja Martanda Varma in the 18th century. Note the Tamil-style *gopura*, as well as the fine stone-carved animals on the entrance pillars.

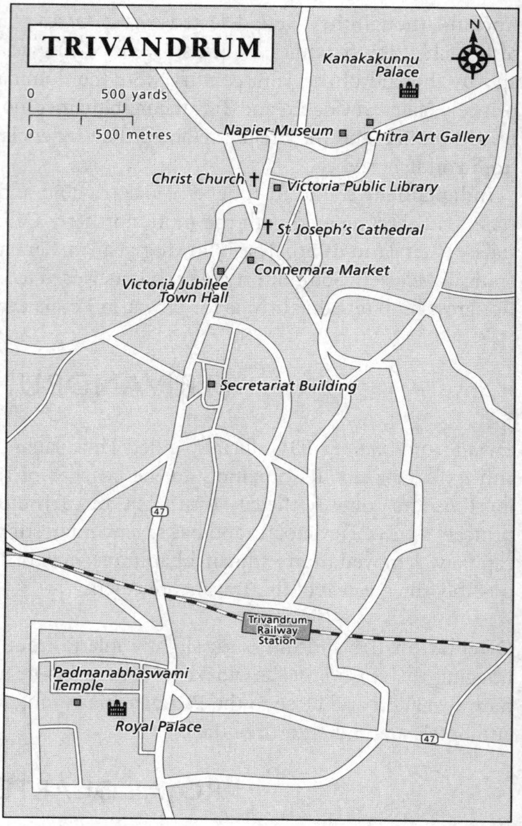

TRIVANDRUM

0 500 yards
0 500 metres

Kanakakunnu Palace
Napier Museum
Chitra Art Gallery
Christ Church
Victoria Public Library
St Joseph's Cathedral
Connemara Market
Victoria Jubilee Town Hall
Secretariat Building
47
Trivandrum Railway Station
Padmanabhaswami Temple
Royal Palace
47

City centre

Trivandrum's main north–south thoroughfare, MG Road, has several interesting buildings including, from the south: the Neoclassical **Secretariat Building** (1939) with a double pediment and a clock tower, the **Victoria Jubilee Town Hall** (1898), in a hybrid European and Kerala style, which was used for while as the state assembly, and the arched gateway of the **Connemara Market**, named after a former British governor of Madras Presidency.

Heading further north are two neo-Gothic churches: the Roman Catholic **St Joseph's Cathedral** (1873, bell tower added 1927) on the east (left); and the Anglican **Christ Church** (1859) on the west. The latter has some fine stained glass commemorating the life of a former British Resident of Travancore. Note also the 19th-century tombs in the cemetery, and, most unusually, a horse-drawn hearse kept behind glass in a display room in the church grounds. On the other side of the road from Christ Church is the twin-gabled red-brick **Victoria Public Library** (1900), which also carries the date '1000 ME', where 'ME' stands for the local Malayalam Era calendar. The initials 'VI' stand for 'Victoria Imperatrix' (Empress Victoria).

Napier Museum

Trivandrum's most important building from the British period, the Napier Museum (1872)—named after Lord Napier, a former British governor of Madras and acting viceroy—is in a large park, close to the zoo. It is an unusual fusion of Keralite and neo-Gothic architectural styles, and was designed by the British architect R.F. Chisholm, who was responsible for many late 19th-century buildings in Chennai. Note the multicoloured brickwork, and the narrow cusp-arched windows beneath a traditional Kerala tiled roof, with some fine carved woodwork. The building is now officially the **Art Museum** (*open Tues–Sun 10–4.45*), with rare Chera-period bronzes from the 9th century; there are plans, however, to move its collection to another location in Trivandrum.

Chitra Art Gallery

Also in the same park as the museum, close to the entrance to Trivandrum Zoo, is the Chitra Art Gallery, which has a large collection of paintings by Raja Ravi Varma (1848–1906), India's best-known 19th-century artist, who was born in Kilimanoor, to the north of Trivandrum. There is an annexe to the gallery, closer to the eastern entrance to the park, which has mementos of the Travancore royal family and an extravagant royal golden carriage decorated with lion motifs and cherubs carrying doves.

Just to the east of the Napier Museum is the handsome **Kanakakunnu Palace** (early 20th century), which is widely used for cultural performances.

NORTH OF TRIVANDRUM

Anjengo Fort and Janardhana Temple

The old British **Anjengo Fort** (*map 14 B3,* also known as Anjuthenga) is 26km northwest of Trivandrum, overlooking the seashore. Anjengo was an important British settlement in the late 17th century, but later fell into decline. The **Janardhana Temple**, close to the popular Varkala Beach, 36km north of Trivandrum, dates back to at least the 13th century, and is dedicated to Vishnu.

Kollam and Thangasseri

The commercial city of **Kollam** (*map 14 B3*), formerly known as Quilon, is 60km north of Trivandrum and has been identified, inconclusively, with the seaport of Nelcynda which is described in ancient Roman texts. The city has no major attractions. However, the ruins of the old Portuguese fort at **Thangasseri** (*map 14 B3*) can be visited: they are on a promontory close to the lighthouse, just 2km to the northwest of Kollam. Thangasseri was later occupied by the Dutch and the British. Dozens of 18th- and 19th-century British gravestones can be found in the rear gardens of houses on either side of the short road that crosses the promontory.

SOUTH OF TRIVANDRUM

South of the Kerala capital is the popular Kovalam Beach, but the nearest important historical sites, the palace of Padmanabhapuram and the temples at Suchindram, are over the state border in Tamil Nadu (*see p. 823*).

COCHIN

Cochin, officially known as Kochi (*map 14 B2*), is one of India's most interesting cities. It is in a spectacular location on an estuary, with several islands, and its fine historical buildings have transformed Kerala's second-largest city into a major tourist attraction over the last two decades. The main focus is Fort Cochin, on the southern side of the city, which has many interesting buildings from the European colonial period, a fine palace and India's best-known synagogue.

History: Cochin seems to have emerged as a major seaport in the 14th century, when the Periyar Tiver changed course, creating a natural harbour—and Cranganore, to the north, lost its importance. The Portuguese landed here in 1500, and Cochin became the first capital of Portugal's Indian Empire. Vasco da Gama died in Cochin in 1524, and soon after the Portuguese moved their capital to Goa, but retained a base in Cochin.

The Portuguese were ousted from Cochin in the 17th century by the Dutch, who built what is still known as the Dutch Palace for the maharaja of Cochin. The city was captured by the forces of Mysore in the 18th century, and ruled by Hyder Ali and then Tipu Sultan. The British then took direct control of the fort area of Cochin, along with all other Dutch territories. However, much of the area now occupied by the city, including Ernakulam, remained formally part of the princely state of Cochin, which accepted British suzerainty. Ernakulam was the official capital, while the maharaja's main residence was in Tripunithira, 8km southeast of the city. At Independence, Cochin was united with Travancore, to the south, to form a single state, which was then integrated into Kerala in the 1950s.

Orientation: The landscape of Cochin is dominated by water. The city consists of a series of islands, promontories and peninsulas—many of them now connected by bridges. The oldest part of the city is Fort Cochin, on the southern bank of the estuary of the Periyar River, next to the ocean. Slightly further inland, on the same peninsula, is Mattancherry, with the palace and synagogue still very close to the water. Just opposite Mattancherry is Willingdon Island, connected here by ferry, or by road further inland. It has the Taj Malabar Hotel and the old Cochin Airport. On the other side of Wellington Island is the mainland part of the city known as Ernakulam, with the main railway station. On the northern banks of the Periyar, recently connected by bridge to Ernakulam, are Bolghatty Island, with the Bolghatty Palace Hotel. Beyond that, next to the ocean and just opposite Fort Cochin, is Vypeen Island.

FORT COCHIN

Fort Cochin was the old European part of the city, overlooking the southern side of Periyar River as it enters the sea. Little is left of the actual fort, but many old European houses survive—some of which are now hotels—close to the seafront, which has a long strand for pedestrians. The main features of the waterfront are the Chinese fishing

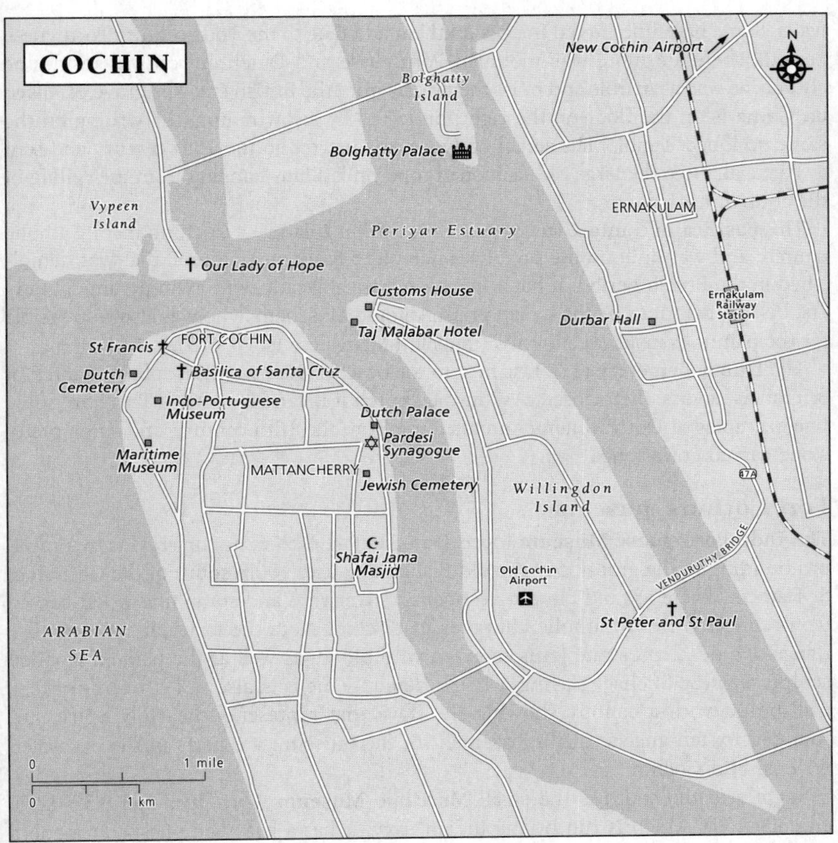

nets—huge wooden contraptions which are dipped into the water to catch fish; they can be seen throughout this part of Kerala. There are also small parts of the old seafront fortifications, with cannon still pointing out to sea.

Church of St Francis, Santa Cruz and the Dutch Cemetery

Originally dedicated to St Anthony, the **Church of St Francis** (1506) is one of India's oldest European buildings, and stands slightly inland on Church Street. It was successively a Catholic church under the Portuguese, a Protestant church under the Dutch (who sent the Catholics to nearby Vypeen Island), an Anglican church during the British period and is now part of the Protestant Church of South India. The austere façade of the church, with its small Latin inscription saying that it was renovated in 1779, is from the Dutch period. In the lobby there are a large number of gravestones—many of them removed from the nave of the church—which have been mounted on the side walls. Some have fine carved images on them and date to the 16th-century Portuguese period. There are more wall-mounted Portuguese and Dutch gravestones inside the church, as well as marble and brass memorials from the British era. The **grave of Vasco da Gama** is on the floor on the right, protected by a low railing, the writing on the stone no longer legible. His actual body was disinterred in the 17th century and sent to Portugal. Note the large old-fashioned rope-pulled fans hanging from the ceiling of the church.

The **Basilica of Santa Cruz** (1902–05), further inland, is Cochin's main Catholic church, and was built on the site of a much older Portuguese church that was demolished in the British period. It has a fine Neoclassical façade, with twin pyramidal towers. Inside are murals by the Italian priest Antonio Moscheni, who was also responsible for the paintings inside St Aloysius Chapel in Mangalore (*see p. 675*).

The **Dutch Cemetery** (1724) is next to the beach, 300m southeast of the Church of St Francis, and is often closed. Ask in the church if it can be opened. There are some fine examples of Dutch funerary architecture from the 18th century, and some pretty stone-carved gravestones.

Fort Cochin's museums

The **Indo-Portuguese Museum** (*open Tues–Sun 9–1 & 2–6; no cameras*) is in a modern building in the grounds of the old Bishop's House, 400m south of the Church of St Francis. There are old church vestments, silverware and some fine wood-carved icons collected from Catholic churches in Cochin. Note the unusual 19th-century image of a dead, prostrate Jesus smeared with blood, as well as the painted wooden sculpture of St Michael slaying a black demon. There is also a 19th-century teak wall-pulpit with a canopy showing the dove that represents the Holy Spirit surrounded by ten angels. In the basement of the museum are parts of the excavated walls of Fort Cochin.

Slightly to the south is the small **Maritime Museum** (*open Tues–Sun 9.30–12.30 & 2.30–5.30*), which is run by the Indian navy; it has a heavy emphasis on modern military history.

MATTANCHERRY

The area of Mattancherry (officially Mattancheri), 2km southeast of Fort Cochin, on the same peninsula, has two of Kerala's most popular visitor attractions: the Dutch Palace and the Cochin Synagogue.

Orientation: The sights are easiest to reach from other parts of Cochin and Ernakulam by ferry to the Mattancherry jetty, though it is a pleasant walk or short drive from Fort Cochin. The Dutch Palace is accessed from the main road, close to the jetty. The synagogue adjoins the palace compound, but can only be accessed by taking the road through a very touristy shopping street for 400m. There is also a short-cut for pedestrians through a shopping arcade sign-posted 'Ethnic Passage'.

The Dutch Palace

The palace (*open daily 8–5; no cameras inside the palace*) was originally built by the Portuguese in 1557 for the ruler of Cochin, in exchange for trading rights. It was then rebuilt in 1663 by the Dutch for a later Cochin ruler. It was constructed to a hybrid design, combining a European-style sloping stone wall, and round-arched doors and windows with a traditional Kerala roof and inner courtyard.

The palace compound is entered through a small archway with a pediment. To the left is a small low Mahavishnu temple, closed to non-Hindus, though the conical tiled roof of its sanctuary can be seen from the compound. Beyond the temple is the clock tower of the synagogue (*see below*), with three different sets of numerals—the local Malayalam and the Hebrew systems of numbering can be seen on the far side.

By Indian standards, the main palace is a modest building, of which only part is currently open to the public. The tour of the building begins on the upper floor, with a long entrance hallway which leads on the left to the royal bedchamber—and some superb, richly-coloured murals that recount the story of the *Ramayana*, and date from the 17th to 19th centuries. At the other end of the entrance hallway is another room full of fine murals—including, on the inside wall, a superb image of Vishnu resting on Shesha the snake, with Vishnu's ten avatars springing out of lotus buds. Note how the tenth avatar, Kalki, is depicted as a horse rather than the more common image of a human figure riding a horse. On the other inside wall are Shiva and Parvati, their children Ganesha riding a mouse and Murugan (also known as Kartikeya) on a peacock. Other rooms have more murals, palanquins, arms, royal portraits and an interesting photo exhibition about the history of how the royal family dressed.

Pardesi Synagogue

The synagogue (*open Sun–Thur 10–12 & 3–5; no cameras, but they can be left outside*) is at the end of Synagogue Lane in Mattancherry. It is entered through a gate on the left at the end of Synagogue Lane, close to the clock tower.

The main Jewish settlement in Kerala used to be further north in Cranganore, but in the mid-16th century many Jews moved to Cochin because of persecution by the Portuguese, and sought the protection of the Raja of Cochin. The first synagogue on this site, said to date from 1588, was destroyed by the Portuguese, but the community seems to have flourished under the Dutch. The current synagogue is largely the result of a rebuilding that took place in 1762. The clock tower dates from the same period. There are six surviving synagogue buildings in and around Cochin, but this is the only one that is still used for prayer and is open to the public. Most Cochin Jews have emigrated, mainly to Israel.

The gatehouse has a small exhibition of pictures showing scenes of Jewish life in Cochin. There are gravestones on either side of the narrow courtyard that surrounds the building. Note the Hebrew plaque taken from an older synagogue at Kochangadi, which dates to 1344. The simple, airy interior of the synagogue has some fine Chinese blue-and-white floor tiling and several glass chandeliers. The structure in the centre of the synagogue with brass balustrades is the prayer stand, and the scrolls of the Torah are kept in the golden cylinders at the rear. The Jewish Cemetery is 300m southeast of the synagogue, with several dozen tombs.

Muslim Quarter

The old Muslim quarter is just south of Mattancherry, and the oldest of the mosques, the **Shafai Jama Masjid**, also known as the Chembattapalli, dates to 1420—although it has been much altered since then.

THE REST OF COCHIN

Willingdon Island: This island, to the east of Mattancherry, is largely man-made, and named after Lord Willingdon, a 20th-century British governor of Madras and later viceroy. It is linked by bridges to the rest of Cochin. The Customs House (20th century), close to the Taj Malabar Hotel, is on the northern tip of the island, while the Church of St Peter and St Paul, with a Baroque façade, is in Venduruthy, which was once a separate island.

Ernakulam: There are few buildings of historical importance in Ernakulam, the mainland part of Cochin. The most interesting is a small 19th-century palace known as the Durbar Hall, which is now an art gallery. Now connected to Ernakulam by a bridge, **Bolghatty Island** has the Bolghatty Palace (1744), which has been much expanded and is now a hotel.

Vypeen Island: Another bridge leads to Vypeen Island (just opposite Fort Cochin and more easily reached from there by ferry), home to the Church of Our Lady of Hope (1605), built on the site of an older church. This was Cochin's main Catholic church in the Dutch period. Its Baroque façade is visible from Fort Cochin.

SOUTH OF COCHIN

The area south of Cochin is dominated by the huge Vembanad Lake which stretches to Alleppey, more than 50km away. The inland road has several interesting historical sites, and access to the lakeside resort town of Kumarakom, overlooking the backwaters. The coastal road provides access to beaches—and the quickest route to the town of Alleppey.

TRIPUNITHIRA

In the 19th century, the town of Tripunithira (*see map overleaf*), 13km east of Fort Cochin, on the inland road, became the main residence of the Cochin royal family.

Hill Palace

This palace (*open Tues–Sun 9–12.30 & 2–4.30; no cameras or phones in the main building*) is now a museum situated in pretty gardens. The car park and the ticket office are at the bottom of the hill, and it is a short walk up to the entrance. The palace consists of several low buildings, mainly constructed in the traditional Kerala style with sloping tiled roofs.

Main rooms: The main palace building has a Neoclassical façade, and the entrance leads into a hall with a pretty wooden staircase, carved with the Cochin crest. At the top of the stairs is a broad verandah. Visitors are then directed to the left, across a bridge to another building and down to a room with an interesting collection of wood carvings that date back to the 14th century. Note, in particular, the unusual wooden image of Shiva, as Nataraja, the Lord of the Dance, and some very fine panels, including familiar images of Krishna as a child sucking his toe and Krishna as a young adult lifting the Govardhan mountain. There is also a small wooden temple pavilion carved with tales from the *Ramayana*, as well some fine 19th-century ivories.

Palace Museum: The museum has an impressive jewellery collection, the centrepiece of which is a golden crown, studded with diamonds, emeralds and rubies, which was sent with Vasco da Gama in 1502 as a gift to the Raja of Cochin from King Manuel of Portugal. Another palace building on the right (south) has collections of carriages and palanquins—and a gallery with prehistoric burial urns from northern Kerala and a number of Neolithic tools.

Diamper Church

The old Diamper Church (1510) in the village of Udayamperur, 6km south of Tripunithira, was the site of the Synod of Diamper (a mispronunciation of the name of the village), at which the Portuguese attempted, partially successfully, to force the local Thomas Christians to accept the leadership of the Roman Catholic Church. The old church, which faces the opposite direction to the adjacent new one, has been disfigured by modern extensions, and it is necessary to go to the back of the site to see the original façade. There is a small museum inside the church. The carved stone cross in front of the modern church is thought to predate the European period.

VAIKOM & KADUTHURUTHI

The town of **Vaikom** (*see map overleaf*), 16km south of Udayamperur and 34km from Cochin, is famous for its Vaikkathapan Temple, dedicated to Shiva. It was in Vaikom in 1925 that Mahatma Gandhi led a peaceful and mainly successful agitation against the temple for preventing the lower castes from using the road close to the shrine. The inner sanctuary is closed to non-Hindus, but the pretty inner courtyard is open to all. Note the carved figures of devotees on the paving stones near the sanctuary entrance, and some fine carvings on the pillars of the entrance pavilion.

The village of **Kaduthuruthi**, 10km east of Vaikom, is an important Christian centre, with, confusingly, three churches dedicated to St Mary. One of these—the oldest—has an extraordinary decorated façade. Drive past the first two churches and take the first right to find it.

Old St Mary's Church

This church (also known as the *thazhathu* or 'lower' church) was built in 1599 on the site of an even older Christian place of worship.

The church has a three-storey Baroque façade, with a profusion of unusual stucco reliefs, now brightly painted. There are elephant-headed fish over the central doorway, human-headed fish with boats on their heads and numerous other images that are not usually found on a church exterior. The side of the church is more austere, but note the stone-carved cross with an inscription embedded in the wall, which is thought to have been taken from an older church. The rear of the church has a hunting scene—a man with a dog shooting a stag.

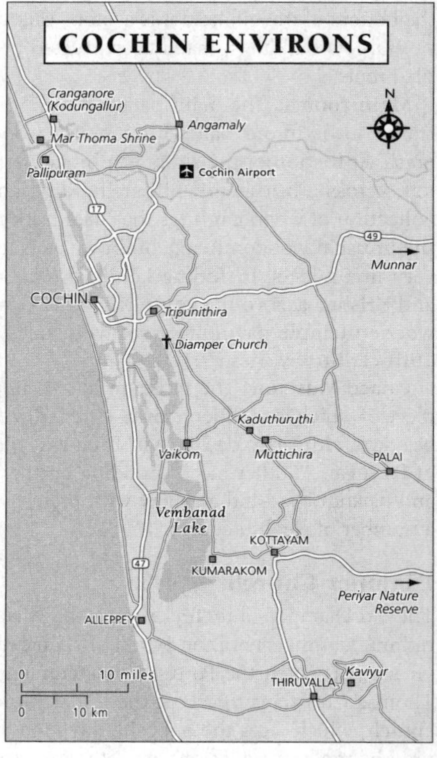

Inside the church is a restored granite font, probably from the pre-European period. The gilded wooden altar, one of India's finest, is thought to date from the 18th century, while the murals on the barrel-vaulted ceiling and wall are more recent. The large stone cross at the rear of the building is from the 16th century, or possibly earlier. Note the elephants and peacock motifs, richly carved but worn, on the plinth of the cross.

Muttichira

The village of Muttichira, 2km south of Kaduthuruthi, has the interesting Church of the Holy Ghost, which has a distinctive octagonal side-tower, with a tiled and gabled roof surmounted by a crucifix.

PALAI

The small town of Palai (*see map above*), 55km southeast of Cochin, is an Episcopal seat and home to the fine 16th-century Old Cathedral, close to the modern St Thomas Cathedral. The church has preserved its traditional character, with its central tower and sloping tiled roof. There is a fine gilded wooden altarpiece inside, with similarly ornate side altars.

KOTTAYAM

The important town of Kottayam (*see map opposite*) has two interesting churches in its western suburbs, on the Kumarakom road.

St Mary's Knanaya Church

This church, better known as Valliyapalli (or 'Big Church'), is prettily situated on a hilltop. It was founded in 1550, but the current building dates from 1588. On either side of the altar are old stone slabs with carved crosses that are similar to the one at St Thomas Mount in Chennai, and which date back to before the European period. They are believed to have been brought from Cranganore, and the main inscriptions are written in Pahlavi—used by the pre-Islamic Persian Sassanid Empire. The smaller one on the left is older, and the meaning of its inscription is disputed. Note also the fine arched entrance to the church, with relief carvings of elephants and birds carrying a cross, which is also thought to have come from an older building; there are similar but more worn carvings on the outer gate to the church compound.

St Mary's Syrian Orthodox Church

The other nearby Church of St Mary (1579), better known as Cheriapalli (or 'Little Church'), has a handsome Baroque façade, partially obscured by a modern entrance lobby. The façade has some superb stucco-work images of monsters, angels, deer and peacocks. There is a *Madonna and Child* in the niche and a double-headed bird in the pediment. Elsewhere there is a fine carved wooden gable, two snout-nosed fish over the side door and some interesting murals inside the church.

ALLEPPEY, THIRUVALLA & KAVIYUR

The port city of **Alleppey** (*see map opposite*), officially Alappuzha, 50km south of Cochin, is comparatively modern, having been developed by the Travancore Kingdom as a way of increasing trade. It is built around a series of canals, which has given it the nickname the Venice of the East. The canals are linked to the backwaters and Vembanad Lake, and there are popular beaches nearby. There is the small Revi Karunakaran Museum (*open Tues–Sun 9–5*) in the city, with an eclectic collection of glass, crystal, ivory and coir products. There are some interesting 18th- and 19th-century warehouses in the town as well.

Some 30km east of Alleppey is the town of **Thiruvalla**, which has the important Vallabha Temple, dedicated to Vishnu, with an unusual gabled tower housing Garuda, Vishnu's man-eagle mount. The town is also home to the modern St John's Cathedral, a much-heralded work of contemporary architecture, designed by the Kerala-based British architect Laurie Baker. It is a circular building with a conical roof and triangular dormer windows.

The village of **Kaviyur** is 5km east of Thiruvalla. It has the fine Mahadeva Temple, with some very fine carved woodwork, and nearby, on the northern side of the village, is a small 13th-century rock-cut cave-temple—one of Kerala's oldest surviving structures. The temple, which is probably the best-known monument from the Chera period, is dedicated to Shiva, and has carvings on its walls of Ganesha, a guardian and a chieftain.

KRISHNAPURAM PALACE

The Krishnapuram Palace (*open Tues–Sun 9–1 & 2–4.30*) is just south of the town of Kayamkulam, 42km south of Alleppey, close to the main highway to Trivandrum. Originally built for local chieftains, it became, in the 19th century, a subsidiary palace of the Travancore royal family, whose main residences were in Trivandrum and in Padmanabhapuram. The palace is built to a traditional Kerala design—a low building with sloping tiled roofs and carved wooden gables. There are some fine religious murals inside, as well as a collection of bronzes. Note the large Buddha in the garden—a reminder that Buddhism penetrated to the most southerly parts of India.

NORTH OF COCHIN

Just 2km north of Cochin Airport is the town of **Angamaly** (*map p. 754*), which has the fine St Mary Jacobite Syrian Church, recently redesignated the Soonoro Cathedral. There has been a church on this site since the year 409, but the current building dates to the 17th century. The Baroque façade, partially obscured by a modern lobby, has two strange stucco figures of smiling men resting on their sides. Inside are some fine murals, including one that shows, in extraordinary detail, the tortures of hell.

CRANGANORE

Cranganore (*map p. 754*) is now better known locally by its official name, Kodungallur. It lies 30km north of Cochin, on the north side of the estuary of the Periyar River. The area surrounding the town is one of the richest historical sites in India—though most of the buildings here are not particularly old.

History: St Thomas the Apostle is said to have landed near here in AD 52; it is also the site of what is believed to be India's oldest mosque, and Kerala's long-standing Jewish community is thought to have first settled here too. It is also held to be the site of Muziris, the ancient seaport referred to by Pliny and other Roman writers in the 1st century BC—though recent excavations suggest the site is around the village of Pattalam (*see p. 758*), 10km south of Cranganore and on the south side of the Periyar. Also on the south side of the river is India's oldest European building, a small Portuguese fort.

Cheraman Mosque

This mosque is said to be India's oldest, its age usually ascribed to the year 629, during the lifetime of the Prophet Muhammad. The current building does not predate the 18th century, and the front part of it is modern. According to local tradition, the Chera king Cheraman Perumal was persuaded by some visiting Arab traders to visit Mecca, where he met the prophet and converted to Islam. He is then said to have died on his way back to India, and the Cheraman Mosque was built in his name by Malik bin Dinar, who also built other mosques in Kerala. Other sources date the building of the mosque by Malik bin Dinar to the 8th century. The mosque is open to visitors, except on Fridays. Note the pretty wooden roof at the back of the mosque, and the fine woodwork above the pulpit.

Cranganore's Hindu temples

There are two interesting temples in Cranganore, though the sanctuaries of both are closed to non-Hindus. About 500m southeast of Cheraman Mosque is the **Mahadeva Temple**, dedicated to Shiva, which has a fine three-tiered entrance gate, with carved wooden figures placed in the gables. Behind the figures is an image of the goddess Lakshmi being bathed by elephants. The **Krishna Temple**, in fact dedicated to Vishnu, 1km to the east of the Shiva temple, is interesting because the basic building structure has barely been modified since it was constructed in the 10th–11th century. Note the pretty tiled roofs and wooden gables, as well as the smaller hut-like shrines within the compound.

Azhicode

The most important of the churches close to Cranganore is the modern Mar Thoma Pontifical Shrine (*map p. 754*) at Azhicode, 5km to the southeast of Cranganore, on the road that runs alongside Cheraman Mosque. It can also be visited by taking a ferry to Azhicode jetty. In the altar is a glass casket in which is kept a large piece of bone that is said to be part of the forearm of St Thomas, known locally as Mar Thoma. Attendants allow visitors to approach the altar under tight security. The church was consecrated in 1952, close to the place where St Thomas is said have landed 19 centuries earlier in AD 52. The relic of St Thomas was a gift from the Cathedral at Ortona in central Italy, where most of the rest of the Apostle's body is kept.

PALLIPURAM

Portuguese Fort

On the southern bank of the Periyar, in the village of Pallipuram (its old name was Palliport; *map p. 754*), is the Portuguese Fort—a small hexagonal building, with thick walls and deep-set windows, more like a watchtower. It was constructed by the Portuguese in 1503, making it the oldest European building in India.

Church of Our Lady of the Snows

Just 300m to the south of the fort, also close to edge of the water, is the Church of Our Lady of the Snows. There are two churches here: the smaller one, on the south side, has a fine Baroque façade and decrepit interior (which is about to be restored); while on the north side is a neo-Gothic church with a bell-tower that was erected in 1909. About 100m further south is a building, inside the Little Flower Convent, that was constructed as a seminary in 1600, then used as a fortress, and which is now a school.

Pattalam

The small village of Pattalam is 5km southeast of Pallipuram, and is the site of a major archaeological excavation which has unearthed huge quantities of pottery from India, the Middle East and Europe, as well as a canoe, and glass and copper beads. The site, which dates back at least 2,000 years, is thought to be the location of Muziris, a great seaport referred to by early Roman and Tamil writers. The excavation trenches are filled in after each excavation is completed, so there may not be much to see.

TRICHUR

Trichur (*map 14 B2*), officially Thrissur, is a historically important city 65km north of Cochin and 15km from the coast. It has long been a significant Christian centre and during the early European period, when the Portuguese dominated Cochin, the Cochin royal family used Trichur as a second capital. The city was captured briefly in the 18th century by Tipu Sultan, but it was soon restored to the Cochin royal family.

Vadakkunatha Temple

At the heart of modern Trichur, on a low circular hill, is the city's most distinctive building, the large Vadakkunatha Temple, dedicated to Shiva and dating back to the 9th century—though the current building is largely from the 17th century. Non-Hindus are not allowed inside. The temple's location and high walls give it the appearance of a fort, and there is some interesting woodwork on the main gate.

Trichur Catholic Church

On the southern side of the town is a series of Christian buildings, including the enormous neo-Gothic Catholic Basilica of Our Lady of Dolours (1929–40), with its 80m-high Bible Tower; it is said to be the biggest church in India. The Bible Tower (*open Tues–Sun 10–1 & 2–6*) has a collection of religious buildings and some superb views over Trichur and the neighbouring countryside.

The Surai Church

Around 300m south of the basilica is the Marth Mariam Big Church (known locally as the 'Surai Church'). This is the Indian headquarters of the Christian denomination known as the Assyrian Church of the East—the patriarch of this denomination once lived in Iraq, and has been based in Chicago since the 1940s. The church has a pretty Baroque façade, partially obscured by a modern extension. Inside there are, according to the traditions of the church, no images of Jesus, Mary or the saints. Note, however, the many chandeliers and the unusual wooden wall-pulpit, the base of which emerges from the mouth of a lion-like monster.

Shakhtananthapuran Palace

On the northern side of Trichur is the Royal Quarter, which includes the main Shakhtananthapuran Palace and several other buildings from the time when Trichur was the second capital of Cochin state. Shakhtananthapuran Palace (*open Tues–Sun 9–2 & 2–4.30*) is in a large compound 600m north of the Vadakkunatha Temple, and is entered from the west gate. The ticket office is easy to miss—on the left, inside the main compound gate. Between the gate and the ticket office, steps lead up onto the palace walls, where a flagstaff stands that was erected by Tipu Sultan in 1789 during the brief occupation of Trichur by the forces of Mysore—though the flagstaff was originally located 175m further north.

The palace is a two-storey building, constructed in the traditional Kerala style, with sloping tiled roofs. Note the Cochin crest over the lobby, which is supported by large rectangular pillars. Inside are small collections of stone sculpture and bronzes from Kerala, including one fine, rather worn image of a seated Buddha. There is also a small group of unexpectedly fine Gandhara sculptures, including parts of friezes and several Buddhas. Elsewhere, coins, arms, furniture and kitchen utensils are on display, including three toast-racks belonging to the Cochin royal family. The pretty gardens lead to a large square man-made pond.

Museums

To the east of the palace, on Town Hall Road, are two small museums. The first, the uninspiring **Government Museum** (*open 10–5.15; closed Mon and Wed mornings*), in a modern building next to the zoo, has an interesting collection of 19th-century figurines of the tribes and communities of Kerala, as well as worm-eaten stuffed animals and a fine Dutch naval sword. Just beyond the zoo is a beautifully restored minor palace, now known as the **Mural Art Museum**, with replicas of murals and paintings from elsewhere in Kerala, some interesting temple models and a fine 3rd-century head of a woman from north India.

EAST OF COCHIN

Many visitors to Kerala visit the tea estates and wildlife sanctuaries of the Western Ghats—the heavily forested hills most easily accessed from Cochin.

Periyar

The spectacular **Periyar Nature Reserve** (*map 14 B2*), 110km southeast of Cochin, and also known as Thekkady, draws many visitors to an area that was dammed in the 1890s to provide irrigation further downstream. There are still stumps of old trees sticking out of the water of Periyar Lake. The old stone Hindu temple of **Mangaladevi** is 15km away to the north, in an attractive location on a hilltop. Also in the hills southeast of Cochin is the important Hindu pilgrimage centre of **Sabarimala**, dedicated to Ayyappa—the combined form of Vishnu and Shiva, also known as Harihara.

Munnar

The town of **Munnar** (*map 14 B2*), just 90km east of Cochin, but at least three hours by road, is on an ancient trade route from Cranganore to Madurai, but is now most famous for its tea estates planted in the 19th century. It is a short walk northeast out of Munnar town to the **Tata Tea Museum** (*open Tues–Sun 10–4*) surrounded by tea estates. The High Range Club, set up by tea planters, is on the south side of the town, as is the oldest of Munnar's several churches, the single-towered Protestant **Christchurch** (1911).

Palghat

There is a pass through the Western Ghats, near the town of **Palghat** (*map 14 B2,* also known as Palakkad), on the road between Cochin and the large industrial city of Coimbatore in Tamil Nadu. Palghat has a fine fort (1768), almost square, with large rounded bastions and a moat. It is known as **Tipu's Fort**, after Tipu Sultan, the Mysore ruler whose father, Hyder Ali, had it built. The fort changed hands several times during the Mysore wars, before it was taken by the British in 1790. Part of the fort is now in use as a jail.

NORTHERN KERALA

This part of the state receives far fewer tourists than central and south Kerala. However, there are some superb beaches, forts, churches and mosques, and a growing tourist infrastructure. This part of the guide starts in Calicut and heads north towards the border with Karnataka.

CALICUT

The main city of northern Kerala is Calicut (*map 14 B1*), officially Kozhikode, 160km north of Cochin. Calicut has been an important coastal trading centre since at least the 14th century, when it was visited by the North African traveller Ibn Battuta. It was the first major settlement to be visited by the Portuguese explorer Vasco da Gama, who landed at Kappad, 20km to the north in 1498. The Hindu ruler of Calicut, known as the Zamorin, resisted Portuguese attempts to build a settlement here, and the Portuguese instead built their bases in Cochin and Goa. There followed a century of on-off fighting between the Portuguese and the Zamorin's forces, and the Zamorin was able to retain his independence during the Dutch and early British period. The invasion of Calicut by Tipu Sultan's army ended the rule of the Zamorins, and the British took control of the city in the 1790s. The English word 'calico' is derived from Calicut, which was an important centre for trading in cotton, although it is not a cotton-growing area.

Calicut's old city centre

The man-made **Mananchira Pond** in the centre of Calicut is the city's best-known landmark—and close by is the heavily modernised two-towered **Matri Dei Catholic**

Church, originally constructed by the Zamorin in 1599. Note the old gravestones placed in the outer courtyard. The more austere single-towered **Basel Mission Church** (1842) is nearby. Calicut has several fine mosques close to the large man-made pond, known as the Kuttichira. The most interesting is the multi-tiered, five-storey **Mishkal Mosque** (14th century), almost entirely built out of wood, with sloping tiled roofs; it was once Calicut's tallest building.

KAPPAD

Twenty kilometres north of Calicut is the **beach at Kappad** (*map 14 A1*), where Vasco da Gama stepped ashore in 1498, seen now—though not imagined at the time—as the beginning of the European colonial period in India. A small obelisk on the road 20m from the beach commemorates his arrival.

About 5km to the north of Kappad, near the village of **Parapalli**, is a mosque said to have been founded in the 8th century, but entirely rebuilt. On the seashore is a rock believed by local Muslims to bear the footprint of Adam, the first man. There are several shrines nearby.

MAHÉ & THALASSERY

The tiny former French enclave of **Mahé** (*map 14 A1*), administratively part of the Union Territory of Pondicherry in southeastern India, is on the banks of a broad estuary, 55km north of Calicut and just 8km south of Thalassery. It was under French rule from the 1720s until the 1950s, and retains a few French-style buildings—such as, overlooking the estuary, the former French Residency, now Government House (*closed to the public*). There is a small park along the waterfront with an iron monument, erected in 1889 to mark the first centenary of the French Revolution. Some 300m inland, on the main road, is the **Church of St Teresa of Avila** (1778), with its pyramid-shaped clock tower. The old French cemetery is 500m to the east, beyond the Lycée.

The historically important town of **Thalassery** (*map 14 A1*), formerly known as Tellicherry, 18km south of Kannur, was once a major trading settlement of the British East India Company, exporting pepper and cardamom to the West.

The small, well-maintained **Tellicherry Fort** (*open daily 8–6*), constructed by the British is 1708, is approached by steps leading up to the small eastern gate, flanked by painted guardian figures. The old main western gate on the seaward side of the fort is closed. There are several old buildings in the fort, as well as a small lighthouse.

There are two churches between the fort and the coast, of which the smaller and older **St John's Church** (1840s), to the south, is the most interesting. The cemetery has several examples of 18th- and early 19th-century funerary architecture.

Thalassery's **Odothilpalli Masjid** is a fine example of a traditional 17th–18th-century mosque, built largely out of wood, with a tiled sloping roof. Note the small octagonal turret above the front gable, as well as the way in which the *mihrab*, or prayer niche, is inside the mosque rather than forming part of its back wall.

KANNUR

The seaport of Kannur (*map 14 A1*), formerly known as Cannanore, 80km north of Calicut, is one of Kerala's most historically important cities. It has a fine early European fort, as well as the palace of Kerala's only Muslim former princely family. It became a Portuguese and then a Dutch base, its local rulers siding with Tipu Sultan against the British in the Mysore wars of the late 18th century. It later became a British garrison town.

Fort St Angelo

The well-defended Fort St Angelo (1505), built by the Portuguese with permission from the local Ali Raja Dynasty, sits on a triangular promontory overlooking the sea. The fort (*open daily 8–6*) is approached by road through the cantonment area of Kannur. A modern footbridge crosses the now dry rock-cut sea moat, alongside the well-maintained laterite walls of the fort, on a footpath leading to the main gate.

Inside the fort are a number of buildings, as well as cannons mainly pointing out to sea. On the right is the derelict church, and beyond this is a long low-level arched structure, once used as stables. Steps lead up to a small light tower and the landward walls of the fort, overlooking the moat. Note the Dutch gravestone with a carved skull-and-crossbones mounted into the fort wall, marking the death in 1745 of Susana Weyerman, the 17-year-old wife of the Dutch governor of Fort St Angelo. In the centre of the fort is another, older structure, with steps leading up to what was once the flagstaff tower and magazine—an area now used as offices. A second moat has been dug across the promontory on the seaward side.

St John's Church and the European Cemetery

About 1km north of the fort, on the other side of the cantonment, is St John's Church (1811), its exterior disfigured by later extensions. It is one of India's oldest garrison churches; the interior is more interesting and includes a memorial stone to Murdoch Brown, a controversial Scottish plantation owner, who was accused by the British of helping Tipu Sultan.

Near to the church, across a stretch of wasteland, is the old European Cemetery, with a small chapel. The Anglican graves are on the left, the Catholic graves on the right, with the oldest, most interesting structures on the far left.

The Royal Palace

To the south of the cantonment is the old Royal Palace, a simple traditional Kerala building on the main road. Part of the palace is now the **Arakkal Museum** (*closed Mon*) with a small collection of arms, glass and furniture. There is also a copy of the agreement by which the administration of the Laccadive Islands (now known as Lakshadweep), 200km off the Kerala coast, was ceded by the Arakkal royal family to the British. Note the pretty two-storey mosque just to the north of the palace, with its sloping tiled roof and two octagonal minarets.

LAKSHADWEEP

Lakshadweep is a group of islands (pop. 60,000) situated 200–300km off the coast of Kerala; the majority of the inhabitants are Muslim. Some of the islands were once ruled by the Arakkal princes of Kannur (Cannanore), who still receive an annual rental from the Indian government. Lakshadweep is administered by the central government—it is India's smallest union territory—and the only scheduled direct flights are from Cochin. The tourist infrastructure is being developed slowly, and there are no heritage structures, apart from a few old Muslim tombs.

TALIPARAMBA

The town of Taliparamba (*map 14 A1*), 18km north of Kannur, has two interesting temples that both date back to the Chera period, but were largely rebuilt in the 16th–17th centuries. The Rajarajeshwara Temple, dedicated to Shiva, has an unfinished entrance gate made of carved laterite, and a small pool nearby that is only for the use of priests. In the outer compound there is an ornately carved stone altar.

The Krishna Temple at **Trichamabaram**, just south of the town, has a pretty pond adjacent to the main compound, and some fine woodwork on the temple's gabled roof.

BEKAL FORT

The impressive 17th-century Bekal Fort (*map 14 A1*), 55km south of Mangalore (in Karnataka) and 150km north of Calicut, is in a beautiful location on a high promontory overlooking the sea. It is Kerala's largest and most interesting fort, and close to an attractive beach resort with a growing tourist infrastructure. The fort was built by the Ikkeri Nayaks, descendants of governors appointed by the Vijayanagar Empire, and whose capital was further north in Karnataka. It was captured by Mysore, under Hyder Ali, in 1763, and then taken by the British in 1792.

Orientation: Bekal Fort (*open daily 8–6*) has high laterite walls, with several rounded bastions and crenellations, and a rock-cut moat on the landward side. A causeway leads to the first gate, with some small buildings on the left, and steps that lead down into the moat. Ahead is a small temple and the ticket office.

The large main compound of the fort has been recently restored, and there are broad walkways along the walls that offer fine views over the nearby beaches. Among the surviving structure within the fort is a flagstaff tower, with a steep ramp, several stepwells and other buildings, including the magazine. Note also the underground steps that lead down to the lower levels of the fort's bastions.

Near Bekal

There is another, smaller fortification, officially called **Chandragiri Fort** (*map 14 A1, open daily 8–6*) but referred to locally as Kota, in Melperambu village, 10km north of Bekal, overlooking an estuary. The well-defended fort is empty, apart from a large step-well at the far end and a modern pavilion on the right.

About 6km north of Chandragiri Fort, in **Kasaragod** (*map 14 A1*), is the Malik Dinar Mosque, which is said to have been founded in the 7th century, but greatly modernised subsequently. Note the fine woodwork, the curved back to the *mihrab* and the way in which the entire prayer area of the mosque is raised on a plinth.

WAYANAD

The attractive hill district area of Wayanad (*map 14 B1*), northeast of Calicut, has emerged in recent years as an important destination for tourists, who largely come to see wildlife or to go trekking in the hills. The small town of **Sultan Battery** is named after a fort constructed by the Mysore ruler Tipu Sultan. The fort has now disappeared, but there is a fine 13th-century **Jain Temple** (*open daily 8–12 & 2–4*) built of stone, and 6km away the **Edakal Caves**, with some prehistoric rock carvings.

PRACTICAL INFORMATION

Southern Kerala has emerged as a major international tourist destination in recent years. The beaches at Kovalam, south of Trivandrum, and at Varkala, between Trivandrum and Cochin, are particularly popular (*both on map 14 B3*). Some visitors take package tours which often also include trips on the backwaters and to Cochin. However, Kerala remains a place that welcomes independent travellers, and there are lots of more out-of-the-way places to explore. Be aware that the names of the main cities of the state have all officially changed, though the old names are still in use.

GETTING THERE & GETTING AROUND

• **By air:** Kerala has three main airports at Trivandrum (Thiruvananthapuram), Cochin (Kochi) and Calicut (Kozhikode), all now known by their official names (in brackets here). The first two are the main points of arrival for, respectively, south and central Kerala, and are well-connected to other major cities in India, and have some flights to the Middle East and South-east Asia. Calicut in northern Kerala is less well-connected within India, and for the area around Bekal in the far north of the state, the nearest airport is actually Mangalore in neighbouring Karnataka.

There is a daily flight from Cochin to Agatti on the Lakshadweep Islands.

• **By rail:** Rail connections from other parts of India are slow, and it is usually advisable to fly. Within Kerala, there are regular trains between Trivandrum and Cochin (where the main station is called Ernakalum) which takes a minimum of 3½hrs, and several services continue to Calicut (7½hrs from Trivandrum).

• **By road:** Taxis are the main form of transport for many travellers, and there are many English-speaking drivers. As in Goa, rates are higher than neighbouring states. Most of the roads are in good condition, except during and after the monsoon.

• **By boat**: Many parts of Kerala have ferries connecting settlements along the estuaries, rivers and backwaters of the state. These are particularly useful in Cochin, and in the area between Alleppey and Kollam.

ACCOMMODATION

The main tourist areas of southern and central Kerala have some of India's most comfortable and interesting places to stay, including heritage buildings in Cochin and houseboats on the backwaters.

Southern Kerala

Most visitors to southern Kerala do not stay in the capital, Trivandrum, but close to one of the beaches.

• **Kovalam:** Among the best hotels is the **Surya Samudra Beach Garden** (*$$$; T: 0471 2267333; suryasamudra.com*), with huts built in a traditional Kerala style, close to the southern tip of the state, just beyond the longer, much busier Kovalam Beach. This is a good base from which to visit the Padmanabhapuram Palace, just inside Tamil Nadu. Kovalam also has the 5-star **Leela Kempinski** (*$$$; T: 0471 3051234; theleela.com*).

• **Trivandrum:** The more basic **Wild Palms Homestay** (*$; T: 0471 2471175*) is the closest Trivandrum has to a heritage hotel.

• **Varkala:** On Varkala Beach, north of Trivandrum, the best hotel is the **Taj Garden Retreat** (*$$$; T: 0470 2603000; thegatewayhotels.com*).

Central Kerala

Most visitors to Central Kerala either stay in Cochin, which probably has more heritage hotels than any other city in India, or on the backwaters.

• **Cochin:** Among the best hotels in Fort Cochin are two owned by the Neemrana group: the **Hotel Colonial** (*$$$; T: 0484 2217181; neemranahotels.com*), built in 1506, next to St Francis's Church, and thought to be India's oldest European residential building; and the **Tower House** (*$$; T: 0484 2216960; neemranahotels.com*), close to the Chinese fishing nets, on the main square. The neighbouring **Koder House** (*$$; T: 0484 2218485; koderhouse.com*), formerly the residence of one of Cochin's most prominent Jewish families, is also recommended. Other hotels in Cochin include the modern **Taj Malabar** (*$$$; T: 0484 6643000; tajhotels.com*), which is in a superb position overlooking the waterfront on Willingdon Island, and the state tourism-run **Bolghatty Palace** (*$$; T: 0484 2750500; bolghattypalacekochi.com*) on Bolghatty Island.

• **Vembanad Lake:** There are several luxury hotels between Cochin and Alleppey, mainly on the banks of Vembanad Lake. These include **Coconut Lagoon** (*$$$; T: 0481*

2524491; cghearth.com), near the town of Kumarakom, but only accessible by boat, and the **Park on Vembanad Lake** (*$$$; T: 0478 2584430; theparkhotels.com*).

Northern Kerala

• **Bekal:** There are luxury tents on the beach at the **Bekal Beach Camp** (*$$; T: 094626 7792*).

• **Calicut:** The best hotel in Calicut is the Taj group's **Gateway** (*$$; T: 0495 6613000; thegatewayshotels.com*), on Beach Road.

• **Thalassery:** Here, the former private residence known as **Ayisha Manzil** (*$$; T: 04902 341590 or 098470 02340*) has been converted into a comfortable guest house, above Sea View Park.

FOOD

Rice is the staple food of Kerala, both as a separate dish and as rice flour, an ingredient in many culinary dishes. Tapioca is also widely used, and to a lesser extent so too is wheat, in the Keralite version of the layered flatbread called *paratha* elsewhere in the country, and known here as *parotta*. Locally available ingredients such as seafood, coconut, pepper, cardamom and bananas are all widely used in Kerala.

The rice-flour pancakes known as *appam*, sometimes anglicised as 'hoppers', are widely eaten in Kerala, sometimes with an egg or a curry. *Idiappam*, or 'string hoppers', is a vermicelli-style rice noodle, while *puttu* are steamed rice cakes.

There is a wide variety of salt-water and freshwater fish. Fine seafood dishes are available in most parts of the state, often cooked in a mild coconut-based curry. Fish *moily* is an archetypal Keralite dish: a fish stewed in coconut milk and mild spices. Beef and pork are also more widely available than in most other parts of India. *Avial* is a mild vegetable curry cooked with coconut.

Payasam, a hot rice-based pudding, is Kerala's best-known dessert, while *ela ada* is a popular sweet snack, made from rice and coconut wrapped up in a banana leaf.

Coconut water is widely available throughout the state. Local coffee is usually fresh, though often comes with added chicory. *Toddy*, made from the sap of the coconut palm, is the main local alcoholic drink.

Unlike many hotels in the rest of the country, those in Kerala often serve high-quality local food—partly because the relative mildness of Kerala cuisine makes it more popular with Western visitors. Good seafood is available at many beach shacks.

• **Cochin:** The **History Restaurant** at the **Brunton Boatyard Hotel** (*T: 0484 2215461*) in Fort Cochin has a wide range of local food drawn from the traditional cuisines of the many different communities that have settled in Cochin. The **Menorah Restaurant** at the Koder House Hotel (*see p. 765*) often has local Jewish dishes on their menu, including *chuttuli meen* (fried fish cooked with chillis and onion). Many visitors to Cochin buy fish from the stalls near the Chinese fishing nets, and have them cooked at the small shacks nearby.

• **Trivandrum:** There is good local food at the **Wild Palms Homestay** (*see p. 765*). In central Trivandrum, **Kerala**

House, in the basement of the shopping complex next to Statue Junction on MG Road, is recommended for local food, particularly fish. The branches of the **Indian Coffee House** are also recommended for coffee and snacks.

• **Northern Kerala:** The simple **Bamboo Fresh** (*T: 0460 220075*), a restaurant on the main road near Taliparamba, north of Kannur, is recommended, while the **Ayisha Manzil Hotel** (*see opposite*) in Thalassery serves good local Muslim food.

FURTHER READING & VIEWING

Arundhati Roy's Booker Prize-winning *The God of Small Things* is set in Kerala, and so are several books by the acclaimed Keralite novelist Anita Nair.

Salman Rushdie's 1995 novel *The Moor's Last Sigh* was partly set in Cochin, while *Daughters of Kerala* (Hats Off Books, 2004) consists of 25 short stories by different women writers.

The Last Jews of Kerala (Penguin India, 2008) by Edna Fernandes tells the story of Kerala's rapidly disappearing Jewish community.

Relatively few English-language films have been set in Kerala. An exception is Santosh Sivan's historical drama *Before the Rains* (2008), set in the late colonial period with a cast of well-known British and Indian actors. Ismail Merchant's *Cotton Mary* (1999) was largely shot in Fort Cochin.

TAMIL NADU

Tamil Nadu (*map 14*) is one of India's largest and most diverse states, which is best known, from a tourist's point of view, for its remarkable range of Hindu temples and art. But the state also has India's most diverse and interesting collection of churches and Christian cemeteries, as well as the remains of former settlements of no fewer than five European nations: Britain, France, Denmark, Holland and Portugal. The ancient Hindu city of Mahabalipuram is one of India's most important and beautiful archaeological sites, in a spectacular location next to the sea, with fine beaches close by. The great living temples of central Tamil Nadu—at Tanjore, Kumbakonam, Trichy, Madurai and elsewhere—are testament to the remarkable continuities between an ancient civilisation and the modern day. The most famous of the state's many old colonial settlements is the former French enclave of Pondicherry, but less well-known settlements such as Danish Tranquebar are now firmly on the tourist route. Other under-visited locations include Chettinad—with its superb 19th-century marble and teak mansions, and the extraordinary hill-fortress of Gingee. Most parts of Tamil Nadu are warm all year round, with the heaviest rains in the autumn months. The hill-stations in the west of the state—such as Ooty and Kodai—are much cooler, and can be swathed in fog in autumn.

HISTORY OF TAMIL NADU

Early history: Tamil Nadu emerges from the mists of prehistory earlier than other parts of India because of an extraordinary collection of Tamil literature belonging to what is known as the Sangam period, from 300 BC to AD 300. Three great dynasties dominated Tamil Nadu and neighbouring areas during this period: the early Cholas, the Cheras and the Pandyas; and all three continued to play an important role for several more centuries. The early Cholas dominated central Tamil Nadu, whereas the Cheras controlled the western parts of the state and large parts of Kerala; the Pandyas were based in the southern parts of the state. Excavations at Arikamedu, near Pondicherry, have revealed evidence of a large seaport, which traded widely around the Indian Ocean and with the Roman Empire at the start of the Christian era, while in c. AD 72, Thomas the Apostle, also known as Doubting Thomas, is said to have been martyred on a spot now marked by a church on a hill close to Chennai Airport.

The Pallavas and the Cholas: The earliest of Tamil's major archaeological sites is at Mahabalipuram, where by the 7th century a fourth major Tamil dynasty, the Pallavas (who had displaced the early Cholas), had established an empire that had Kanchipuram as its capital. The Pallavas extended their territory far into modern Andhra Pradesh and Karnataka, but southern parts of Tamil Nadu around Madurai remained under Pandya control. During the Pallava period there was a major shift in architectural styles, from traditional rock-cut shrines to free-standing 'built' temples.

The Chola Dynasty re-emerged as the dominant power in much of Tamil Nadu by the 9th–10th centuries, though the extent of its connection with the early Cholas is not clear. From their capital at Tanjore—and later Gangaikondacholapuram—they built some of India's greatest temples, and the making of magnificent idols in bronze seems to have emerged at this time. The Cholas also created the largest of all Tamil empires, reaching up the eastern coast of the country, conquering the Maldives, parts of Sri Lanka and influencing large parts of southeast Asia. In the 13th century, the resurgent Pandyas defeated the Cholas, but the period of Tamil domination of what is now Tamil Nadu was coming to an end.

The emergence of new powers: Malik Kafur, a Muslim general serving the Delhi sultans, captured Madurai in 1310 and established a short-lived sultanate in the city. The Vijayanagar Empire, with its capital at Hampi in modern-day Karnataka, had become the dominant force in much of Tamil Nadu by the late 14th century. The empire ruled much of the region through local governors, known as Nayaks, several of whom would later declare independence from Vijayanagar. Important Nayak states emerged in Tanjore and Madurai in the 16th century—while the rump of Vijayanagar state remained in control of northern Tamil Nadu.

The earliest Europeans: The first Europeans to build settlements in Tamil Nadu were the Portuguese, in the 16th century, followed in the 17th century by the Dutch and by the Danish at Tranquebar. The British gained their first foothold in 1639, when one of the last Vijyanagar rulers granted them some territory in Madras, now known as Chennai. The French were the last of the Europeans to establish a settlement in the region, and for much of the 18th century battled the British for control of southern India. Other forces from northern India, including the Mughals and the Marathas, also took control of parts of Tamil Nadu, and only at the end of the 18th century was British dominance assured—by which time Madras had lost its pre-eminence to Calcutta.

Under British rule: Tamil Nadu was scarcely affected by the 1857 Uprising, and most of the princely states in the region had long since disappeared and come under direct British rule. Pudukottai in central Tamil Nadu was the only real exception, and its nominal independence lasted until 1947. The Madras Presidency under the British included much of modern Andhra Pradesh, as well as parts of Kerala, Karnataka and Orissa, and was less affected by the freedom movement than other areas of India. Caste politics did become very important from the 1920s onwards, with the formation of social movements that challenged Brahmin dominance.

The Dravidian movement and Tamil nationalism: By the 1940s there was a growing fear of north Indian domination, particularly regarding possible attempts to impose the Hindi language, and this led to the emergence of the Dravidian movement, which attempted to unite the ethnically and linguistically Dravidian southern parts of the country. But there was little unity among the different Dravidian groups, and by the 1950s the Dravidian movement had come to stand for Tamil nationalism. In the late 1950s the current state—consisting of the Tamil-speaking areas of the Madras Presidency, Pudukottai and part of Travancore—had been formed, though it did not adopt the name Tamil Nadu until 1968. This was in the aftermath of the language agitation, as a result of which Tamil Nadu became the only state where children do not have to learn Hindi at school.

Since the 1970s contemporary Tamil politics have been dominated by the two main Dravidian parties, the DMK and AIADMK, both led by important figures from the prolific Tamil-language film industry. The politics of the state were affected by the Tamil separatist movement in neighbouring Sri Lanka, and many refugees came to Tamil Nadu. In 1991 Rajiv Gandhi, the former Indian prime minister, was assassinated by a Sri Lankan Tamil separatist in Sriperumbudur, 40km from Chennai. The 2004 Asian tsunami caused greater damage in Tamil Nadu than in any other Indian state, with more than 7,000 fatalities.

CHENNAI

Chennai (formerly Madras, *map 13 D3*) is India's fourth-largest city and the capital of Tamil Nadu. It is also the oldest of the three great coastal cities of British India: Calcutta, Bombay and Madras. It was officially known as Madras until 1996, when it adopted the old Tamil literary name of the city, Chennai. The name Madras is still in wide use.

History: Traditionally, the city is said to have been founded by the British in 1639—and more specifically by the East India Company administrator Francis Day, who was responsible for building the British settlement at Fort St George on land ceded by the Vijayanagar rulers of Chandragiri, near Tirupati, in modern Andhra Pradesh. However, there are several earlier settlements and buildings within the bounds of modern Chennai. In the south of the city is the former Portuguese settlement of San Thomé, while the Kapaleeshwar Temple probably dates to the 7th-century Pallava period. Oldest of all is the site of the death of St Thomas the Apostle, who is said to have been killed in about AD 72 on the hill near Chennai airport that is named after him.

Early British Madras: The British built the walled settlement of Fort St George, which included the White Town, where the Europeans lived, on the site of the current fort; just north of it was the 'Black Town', or George Town as it later became, for the Indian residents. The city soon became the most important of the British settlements in India. In 1746, in what became known as the First Carnatic War (in fact a sideshow of the War of the Austrian Succession), the French captured Chennai from the British. When peace came in Europe with the Treaty of Aix, the French withdrew and the British retook the city in 1749. The city was nearly captured again by the French in 1759. Meanwhile Bengal had emerged as the most powerful of the British settlements in India, and in 1779 Chennai came under the direct control of Kolkata.

Madras since the 19th century: Madras continued to be South Asia's leading seaport until it was overtaken by Mumbai in the mid-19th century, and it remained the headquarters of the Madras Presidency until after Independence, when it became the capital firstly of Madras State and then, in 1968, of Tamil Nadu. It has some excellent churches, museums and civic buildings from the British era.

Orientation: The city has a long coastline, with docks on the northern side of the city, beyond Fort St George. The almost 6km-long Marina Beach stretches from just south of the fort to the Adyar River. In between are Mylapore and San Thomé, where the old Portuguese settlement was located. The city's most important thoroughfare is Anna Salai, or Mount Road, which runs from the fort to Mount St Thomas, near the airport. The modern commercial and hotel districts are mainly along Anna Salai, while many of the older institutional buildings are either on or near Poonamalee High Road, which runs west from near the fort. The older commercial district is in George Town, just north of the fort—from where this guide starts.

FORT ST GEORGE

This British fortress, first constructed in 1640, was originally rectangular. However, its old walls were dismantled following the French occupation in the mid-18th century, and the current walls, with their sharply angled bastions, were then constructed. The Fort Museum and St Mary's Church are the main visitor attractions; much of the rest of the fort is in use by the government and security forces. The construction of the new Government Secretariat near Rajaji Hall, means some other buildings may be vacated soon, and opened to the public.

Orientation: The entrance to the fort is from the road on the east, close to the sea. Members of the public can enter the fort only on foot. There is a car park on the other side of the road, and visitors then pass through a security check close to the main entrance gate. The large Neoclassical building on the left, with a first-floor raised portico, is the Tamil Nadu Legislative Assembly; beyond it is St Mary's Church, though it is currently necessary to go right round the assembly building to reach the church. Note the small park in front of the Legislative Assembly with a Rotunda (1799) in which the statue of Lord Cornwallis originally stood—it is now in the museum. There are also a number of old cannons along the walls.

Fort Museum

On the immediate right is the Fort Museum (*open Sat–Thur 10–5*) in the old Public Exchange building (1790–95), the trading centre of the British settlement. Among the exhibits on the ground floor are arms, uniforms, regimental colours and medals—as well as fragments of shells fired at Madras during the two world wars. Note the long list of battles embroidered onto the regimental colours of the 1st battalion of Madras Europeans. There are fine collections of porcelain formerly belonging to the East India Company (with its coat of arms) and the nawabs of Arcot (with Persian inscriptions). In the stairwell is an enormous statue of Lord Cornwallis, governor-general of India when Tipu Sultan was defeated at Srirangapatnam in 1799. The relief carvings on the base show two of Tipu Sultan's children being placed in his custody. Upstairs are some interesting prints, aquatints and oil paintings, mainly from the late 18th and 19th centuries.

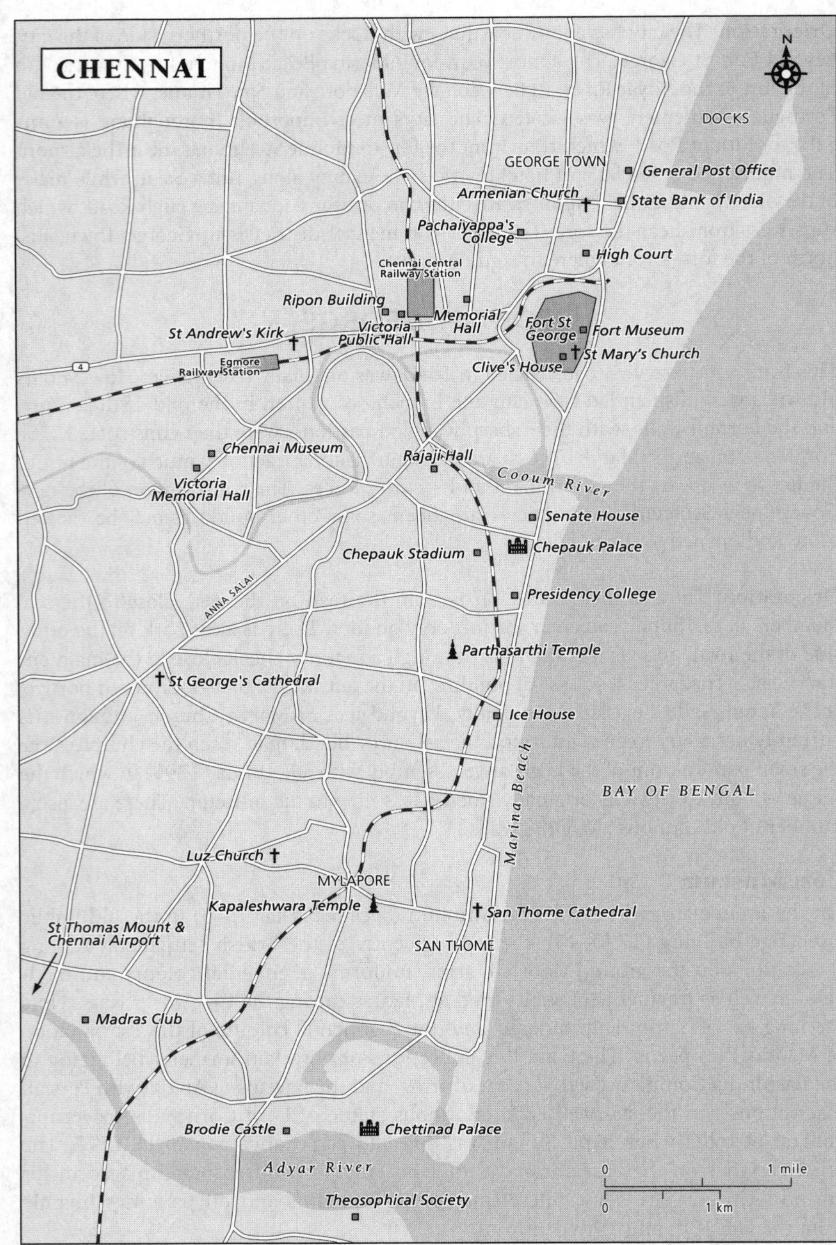
CHENNAI
N
DOCKS
GEORGE TOWN
General Post Office
Armenian Church
State Bank of India
Pachaiyappa's College
High Court
Chennai Central Railway Station
Ripon Building
Memorial Hall
Fort St George
Fort Museum
St Andrew's Kirk
Victoria Public Hall
St Mary's Church
4
Egmore Railway Station
Clive's House
Chennai Museum
Rajaji Hall
Victoria Memorial Hall
Cooum River
Senate House
Chepauk Stadium
Chepauk Palace
Presidency College
ANNA SALAI
Parthasarthi Temple
St George's Cathedral
Ice House
Marina Beach
BAY OF BENGAL
Luz Church
MYLAPORE
Kapaleshwara Temple
San Thome Cathedral
St Thomas Mount & Chennai Airport
SAN THOME
Madras Club
Brodie Castle
Chettinad Palace
Adyar River
Theosophical Society
0
1 mile
0
1 km

In order to reach St Mary's Church, go round the back of the Legislative Assembly, past the parade ground and turn left: the high steeple of the church will be visible.

Clive's House

Just before the church is the former Admiralty House, a grand Neoclassical building, now better known as Clive's House. It was originally the early 18th-century residence of an Armenian merchant, and later became the home of the British general and administrator Robert Clive, best known as Clive of India (*see p. 538*). He lived here in the 1850s, and a small room at the end of the building, signposted 'Clive's Corner', has been turned into a memorial to one of British India's most controversial figures.

St Mary's Church

St Mary's (1678–90) is the oldest building in Fort St George; indeed it is thought to be the oldest Protestant church in Asia. The walls and ceiling of the church (*open daily 9.30–5*) are unusually thick, so as to withstand both shelling and cyclones.

The church has a plain façade, but feels very open because of the series of full-length arched openings on either side. The tower (1701) and the octagonal steeple (1795) are later additions. Laid into the ground outside the church are gravestones, some with fine relief carvings. Many of them were brought here from the old graveyard in 1763.

The interior design is simple, though the walls are covered with dozens of memorials, several of them by John Flaxman and John Bacon Jr, two of the leading British sculptors of the early 19th century. Note in particular the memorial to Gericke by Flaxman, to the right of the main entrance, and to Schwartz (by Bacon) on the wall to the left. Gericke and Schwartz were both German missionaries who were particularly active in south India. Schwartz became a friend and adviser to the Raja of Tanjore, where his grave is to be found in the church named after him. The altarpiece is an oil painting of the *Last Supper* that was captured from the French in Pondicherry. It is said to have been painted by a pupil of Raphael—in fact the chalice is often said to have been painted by Raphael himself. The font near the back of the church is original, and the three daughters of Job Charnock, who founded Calcutta, were baptised in it in 1689. There is a display cabinet that includes the signature of Governor Elihu Yale in the marriage registry. Yale later became one of the benefactors of the American university that bears his name.

GEORGE TOWN

To the north of Fort St George, George Town was previously known as the Black Town, and was where, in the 17th and 18th centuries, the Indian population of the city lived.

Chennai High Court

Immediately to the north of the fort is the imposing Chennai High Court (1888–92), a large red-brick complex of Indo-Saracenic buildings with high bulbous domes and huge lobed portals. Members of the public are free to walk in the grounds, and on the northeast side, within the Law College compound, is the high spire of the tomb of David Yale (the son of Elihu Yale) and Joseph Hynmers. There is also a 38m-high Doric column on the ocean side of the compound that served as a lighthouse.

Armenian Church

On the other side of the road from main public entrance to the high court is Armenian Street, named after the fine St Mary's Armenian Church (1772), the compound of which is entered through a modest Neoclassical gateway (1712) with a pediment and semicircular recesses. Inside the compound are many dozens of gravestones, with inscriptions in English and Armenian, most of them laid flush with the ground. Note in particular the complex tomb of Reverend Haruthian Shmavonian, the editor of the world's first Armenian journal, *Azdarar*, founded in 1794. His original gravestone is underneath the steps inside the free-standing domed bell-tower. The church itself has an unusual stepped altar. The formerly large Armenian community in Chennai has now all but died out, and regular services are no longer held here.

Other buildings in George Town

Just beyond the Armenian Church is **St Mary's Catholic Co-Cathedral** (1775). There are other interesting buildings in George Town along Rajaji Salai—the road that runs parallel to the docks—including the red-brick **State Bank of India Building** (1890s), which is similar to the high court building in style. Next to it is the **General Post Office** (1884), with tall central towers and unusual roof features. Further to the west of the high court, on the main road, is the pretty **Pachaiyappas's College** (1850), with a raised Neoclassical portico of fine dimensions and six Ionic columns, and looking just a little out of place in the Chennai traffic. The building was founded to provide education for poor boys, and it is still a school. A little further to the right at the road junction is a **statue of George V**, presented to the city by an Indian resident in 1914.

POONAMALEE HIGH ROAD

This road, now officially Periyar EVR High Road, runs east–west between the city's two main railway stations, Central and Egmore, both of which are interesting pieces of Victorian architecture. The **Central Station** (1868–72) has an impressive 41m clock tower above a long two-storey arcaded façade. Nearby is the **Memorial Hall** (1857), a grand Neoclassical building intended for public meetings. Further west is the red-brick **Victoria Public Hall** (1883–89) built in commemoration of Queen Victoria's Golden Jubilee. Next to it is the huge three-storey **Ripon Building** (1913), constructed to house the city corporation and named after a former viceroy.

St Andrew's Kirk

About 1km to the east of the Ripon Building, near Egmore railway station, is one of India's finest churches, the Neoclassical St Andrew's Kirk (1818–21). This Presbyterian church has a grand pedimented Ionic portico, above which is a slender three-stage tower with an octagonal spire. The unusual feature is the circular columned hall within, with a large dome supported on Corinthian columns. There are several interesting marble memorials, and the fine stained glass is from Glasgow. Note the East India Company motto, *Auspicio Regis et Senatus Anglia* ('by command of the king and parliament of England'), on the rear pediment of the church. There are the remains of the façade of the old St Andrew's Parochial School in the church grounds.

THE PANTHEON COMPLEX

The Pantheon complex, 800m south of Egmore Station, houses one of India's most important museums, which is famous for its collection of early Hindu carvings and bronzes. It lies on the site of the Pantheon, an 18th-century place of entertainment that in the Victorian period and the early 20th century became the city's main cultural complex, with museums, a library, a technical institute and a theatre.

Orientation: The Museum is now spread over several different buildings, of which the oldest and largest is an Italianate red-brick mansion built in 1851 as the Museum of Practical Geology and Natural History. The semicircular front of this building was used as a theatre. Note the cannon on display outside, including one brought from Manila in the 18th century, when the British used Indian soldiers to fight outside their country for the first time.

Chennai Museum

Chennai's main museum (*open Sat–Thur 9.30–5*) is divided into several sections, of which the most important are the carvings in the eastern wing and the bronzes, which are held in special air-conditioned rooms at the back of the main building. This guide starts in the archaeological gallery in the east wing.

Archaeological Gallery: The layout of the gallery provides a good chronological guide to Tamil sculptural art—but only if you start on the left of the lowest gallery. This area contains carvings from the 7th–9th-century Pallava period, the best-known archaeological site of which is at Mahabalipuram (*see p. 781*). The collection includes a fine seated Vishnu, with two guardians positioned on either of the entrance door.

The early Chola statues in the next section include a superb standing Ardhanarishwara (Shiva as half-man, half-woman) leaning against a Nandi bull, as well as a seated Dakshinamurti (Shiva as a teacher). The most important of the late Chola pieces is the resting Vishnu, attended by his consorts. Also note the very fine detail on the image of Shiva emerging from the lingam.

The small Vijayanagar collection consists mainly of objects from southern parts of the empire, in modern Tamil Nadu, including a fine Durga, standing on the head of the buffalo demon Mahisha, whom she has killed. On the right side of the lower gallery are carvings mainly from southern Karnataka and Andhra Pradesh, including some unusual black stone relief panels from the 10th-century Nolamba period.

Upstairs, the collections are less well-organised, but look for some relief carvings on limestone from the great Buddist stupa at Amaravati, a carved stone from Namakkal with a maze-like twisted snake, and a good collection of Gandhara heads and some interesting pieces from the Indus Valley site at Mohenjo-daro.

Bronze Gallery: At the back of the Pantheon complex, beyond an enormous gallery of slightly moth-eaten stuffed animals, is the impressive bronze gallery, with a large collection of south Indian bronzes from the 9th century to the present. The labelling, however, is quite obscure. Most of the images on the ground floor are Shiva-related—either the god himself, in one of his many aspects, often with his primary consort Parvati or with of one his devotees (Appar, Chandikeshwara, Manikkavachakar). Particularly fine are the several Somaskanda groups—a kind of family portrait in which Shiva is shown with his wife and baby son Skanda. The first floor has several fine examples of the best-known form, in bronze, of Shiva: as Nataraja, the Lord of the Dance. There are some examples of Jain and Buddhist bronzes as well. The top floor, meanwhile, is devoted to Vishnu-related bronzes, including images of many of his avatars, and a fine group of the heroes of the *Ramayana*: Rama, Sita, Lakshman and Hanuman.

Victoria Memorial Hall

In pink sandstone on the far western side of the Pantheon complex is the strikingly ornate neo-Mughal Victoria Memorial Hall. It was used previously as an art gallery, and is now empty. The modern building on the far left, however, displays a large collection of Indian art since the late 19th century, as well as older British portraits of officials.

ANNA SALAI

St George's Cathedral

Some 2km to the south of the Pantheon, on the street known as both Anna Salai and Mount Road, is St George's Cathedral (1814–16), a large Neoclassical building with a very large portico and three rows of paired columns topped by a pediment. The octagonal spire, which reaches 42.5m above the ground, rests on a tower that is square at the bottom stage and round above. There are some fine memorials and statues inside, as well as a large cemetery in the grounds. The original entrance to the cemetery is through an unusual domed gateway (1832) which also served as a bell-tower. Some of the railings in the cemetery are said to have been made from weapons captured from Tipu Sultan at the Battle of Srirangapatnam in 1799. Note how one tomb has been totally enveloped by the hanging branches of a large banyan tree.

Rajaji Hall

Around 3km northwest of St George's Cathedral and still on Anna Salai is the enormous new Government Secretariat (2010), which dwarfs the old British-period Banqueting Hall, now known as Rajaji Hall (1802). The hall is named after C. Rajagopalachari, the last British governor-general of India, and the only Indian to hold that post. It is a large Neoclassical building, its impressive façade partly obscured by a verandah added in 1875.

SOUTH OF THE FORT

South of Fort St George is the estuary of the Cooum River, and then the long Marina Beach which starts on its southern bank. On the landward side of the road are a series of buildings connected with the city's main university.

Senate House and Chepauk Palace

The red-brick **Senate House** (1873) is the most impressive of the university buildings, with high arcades and coloured glass windows. It was designed by the most important of the architects of British Madras, R.F. Chisholm. The capitals of the pillars on the arcades have temple-style carvings. Note the distinctive domed towers, with their pretty coloured tilework and narrow, round-headed triple windows. Inside is a large hall, with some fine decoration on the staircase and ceiling, and a large *iwan*-style archway at its southern end.

Just to the south of the Senate House is **Chepauk Palace** (1768), built as the Madras residence of the nawab of Arcot and designed by the British engineer Paul Benfield. The palace has been used as government offices for more than a century, and many original features have disappeared. The palace was originally constructed as two separate long arcaded buildings. In 1870 the distinctive striped tower was added by R.F. Chisholm in order to join them together. Behind the palace is the Chepauk Stadium, the home of cricket in the city since 1916.

About 700m west (inland) from the stadium, at the northern end of Triplicane High Road, is the city's most historically important mosque, the five-bayed **Wallajah Masjid** (1795), built by the nawabs of Arcot, and with distinctive minarets that are octagonal at roof level and become fluted and then circular, topped by bulbous finials. Some royal graves are in the grounds of the mosque.

Presidency College and the Ice House

The next major building on the beachfront south of the Chepauk Palace is **Presidency College** (1860), another R.F. Chisholm building. The ribbed dome is a later addition. The interior is in need of urgent restoration, but it is possible to see some fine 19th-century woodwork on the staircase and a fine marble statue of the first principal of the college, Eyre Burton Powell.

A little further south is the distinctive horseshoe-shaped Vivekananda House, still better known as the **Ice House** (1842), reflecting the purpose for which it was built—to store ice, shipped from America. It was constructed by Frederic Tudor, a Bostonian known as the 'Ice King', who made a fortune sending ice from New England around the world. Ice would be dragged from the beach up into the building. By the 1880s the market had collapsed, however, because of the invention of the steam process for making ice.

After its period of being an ice house, the building served as a home for the poor, then as a hostel for trainee teachers. It now serves as a museum about the life and teachings of Swami Vivekananda (1863–1902), founder of the Ramakrishna Mission and one of the first Hindu gurus to be well known outside India—he stayed here for just nine days in 1887.

Parthasarthi Temple

To the northwest of the Ice House in the crowded streets of Triplicane is the Parthasarthi Temple, one the city's oldest Hindu shrines, dating back to the 9th century. However, most of the carvings date to the Vijayanagar and Nayak periods, particularly the impressive colonnade that leads to the main gateway. Inside, there is a very pretty pillared hall. The main shrine is dedicated to Krishna, though there are subsidiary shrines to one of Krishna's consorts, Rukmini; to Narasimha, the lion avatar of Vishnu; and to Garuda, the man-eagle mount of Vishnu.

MYLAPORE & SAN THOMÉ

The areas of Mylapore and San Thomé, to the north of the Adyar River, were originally under Portuguese control and integrated into the rest of the city only in the 18th century.

San Thomé Cathedral and the tomb of St Thomas

San Thomé Cathedral, just 200m from the beach, is one of India's most important Christian sites, because it contains the tomb of the apostle St Thomas, who is said to have been martyred at nearby St Thomas Mount in c. AD 72. The current neo-Gothic Catholic cathedral dates back to only 1896, but was built on the site of several previous churches, including a chapel thought to have been built by Nestorian Christians in the 7th–8th century. The Portuguese rebuilt the chapel in 1523, and it became the centre of their settlement of San Thomé, named after the apostle. Inside the church are several old gravestones, with inscriptions in Latin and Armenian embedded into the floor. Look, in particular, at the floor between the pews. Note the small window in the open area before the altar, through which one can look down into St Thomas's tomb.

The underground **St Thomas's Tomb** can be visited through the building at the back of the church, which also contains a museum. The actual tomb now looks entirely modern, with tile walls and ceiling, and a large plaster cast of St Thomas inside a glass case. A tiny piece of bone, said to be a relic of St Thomas, is on display. The small museum has several early stone crosses, human bones excavated from the area around the cathedral and a 17th-century chair used by the Bishop of Mylapore.

Kapaleshwara Temple

To the west of San Thomé Cathedral is the Kapaleshwara Temple, Chennai's largest and best-known Hindu shrine. An older temple was destroyed by the Portuguese in 1566, and the current one was built on its site 300 years ago. The temple is dedicated to Shiva in the form of a peacock, or *mayil*, which gave this area of the city the name Mylapore. The stone carvings are less interesting than those at the Parthasarthi Temple, but the main enclosure is very pretty—as is the enormous water tank at the rear of the complex.

Luz Church

Half a kilometre northwest of the Kapaleshwara Temple is Luz Church (1516), the oldest European structure in the city; indeed one of the oldest European buildings in India. There are Portuguese gravestones embedded in the ground outside the church, which has a Baroque façade, with pilasters on the lower levels and a sunburst motif above. There is a foundation plaque on the south wall erected by a Franciscan monk called Father Pedroda. Inside the church, note the decorated plaster on the barrel-vaulted roof.

ADYAR

In south Chennai, along the Adyar River, are a number of large villas set in their own grounds on both banks of the waterway.

North bank of the Adyar

Among the large buildings on the north bank of the Adyar is the sprawling **Chettinad Palace** (1902–12), still used by members of the former princely family of Chettinad. It is possible to wander around the grounds, but not normally possible to enter the building. Note the use of teak in the ceiling of the portico, and the family crest and motto above the door. Further upstream by about 800m is **Brodie Castle** (1796–98), a large Neoclassical mansion with a castellated circular tower. The East India Company administrator James Brodie, who built the castle, drowned while boating in the river in 1802. Another 2.5km upstream is the 18th-century **Madras Club**, formerly the Adyar Club, which is normally open to interested visitors. It is a Neoclassical building, constructed by an East India Company accountant called George Moubray. Note the fine octagonal dome, best viewed from the riverfront side of the building.

South bank of the Adyar: the Theosophical Society

On the south bank of the Adyar River, almost opposite the Chettinad Palace, are the **World Headquarters of the Theosophical Society**. The society was founded in New York in the 1870s, and in the early 20th century became an enormously popular spiritual sect, drawing from several religions. Its best-known leaders, the Russian mystic Helena Blavatsky and the Irish socialist and trade union leader Annie Besant, lived here.

The gardens are very pretty (vehicles are not allowed inside). They are a fine place to escape the bustle of the city, and include one of the world's oldest and largest banyan trees, as well as several small shrines. The Great Hall is a large building, partly open to the public, with plasterwork elephants' heads on the external walls. Inside is a large room with plaster reliefs related to many of the world's religions, as well as a statue of the founders of Theosophy.

TOWARDS THE AIRPORT

Little Mount

To the southwest of the city, towards the airport, just to the south of where Anna Salai or Mount Road crosses the Adyar River, is the first of two more important churches connected with the life and death of St Thomas. Little Mount is the name of the granite outcrop with a cave which St Thomas is said to have used as his place of prayer and contemplation. The place is now marked by the **Church of Our Lady of Good Health**, founded in 1551, but replaced by a largely modern building. It is possible to go into part of the cave from within the church.

Just over a kilometre south of Little Mount is **Raj Bhavan** (1817, *normally closed to the public*), which served as the country residence of the British governors of Madras and is now the residence of the Governor of Tamil Nadu.

St Thomas Mount

This hill, just 1km north of the runway at Chennai Airport and rising 90m above the plains, is said to be where the apostle Thomas was martyred in about AD 72. Steps lead up through a gate which bears the alternative name for the mount, Portuguese Mission Hill, along with an icon of St Thomas and a date, 1726. Note the two gravestones embedded in the pathway up the hill.

On the small plateau on the hilltop is the **Church of Our Lady of Expectations**, built by the Portuguese in 1523. Note the Portuguese coat of arms above the main entrance to the church, as well as a Portuguese and Armenian inscription on the west wall describing how someone called Zacarias extended the chapel in 1707. There are several Armenian gravestones embedded in the floor of the church.

Above the altar, protected by glass, is a cross that is said to have been carved by St Thomas and which was discovered by the Portuguese during the construction of the church. The inscription around the edge is in the Pahlavi script. Its meaning is disputed, but scholars now tentatively date the stone to the 7th–8th century. Above it, in a special display case, is what is said to be a fragment of one of the bones of St Thomas.

PULICAT

The small town of Pulicat (*map 13 D3*), 40km north of Chennai, was once an important seaport, but is now best known for the nearby bird sanctuary and nature reserve of the same name. The port came under Dutch control in the early 17th century and was taken over permanently by the British in 1824. All that now remains from that period is one of India's finest European cemeteries, the **Dutch Cemetery**, situated on the northern side of Pulicat, and entered through a gateway with statues of skeletons on either side. The skeleton on the left has an hourglass on its head, while the hand of the one on the right rests on a skull. Note the Latin inscription above the gate, with the date 1656 and a winged skull with an hourglass on the keystone. Immediately inside are some gravestones with fine relief carvings of family coats of arms. The more impressive tombs are further to the right.

MAHABALIPURAM

The coastal town of Mahabalipuram (*map 13 D3,* officially Mamallapuram) has an astonishing collection of rock-cut carvings and temples, as well as some of the earliest free-standing temples in southern India. Mahabalipuram is an easy day trip from Chennai—though there is good local accommodation in the town and a huge amount to see. Additionally, many visitors prefer to wander around the monuments in the morning, before it becomes too hot.

History: The main monuments date to the 7th century and the reign of Narasimha Varman I, of the Pallava Dynasty, which ruled the northern part of modern-day Tamil Nadu and briefly extended its reach as far north as Badami in Karnataka (*see p. 686*). The Pallava capital was at Kanchipuram, 60km to the west, while Mahabalipuram was its main port, trading with Cambodia, Indonesia (where a Pallava inscription has been found) and other parts of East Asia. Narasimha Varman was nicknamed 'Mamalla', or the 'Great Wrestler', from which the alternative name of Mamallapuram was derived. Building continued in Mahabalipuram into the 8th century, but the Pallava Dynasty was then in decline, and by the end of the 9th century the area had been conquered by the Cholas.

Orientation: Mahabalipuram has three major and several minor sites. In the heart of the modern town, running parallel to the sea is a long, rocky hill with a lighthouse, 700m from the water's edge, with the superb rock-cut relief carving known as Arjuna's Penance and several Pallava-period monuments built on or cut into the side of the rock. Some 800m to the east, on a spur of land sticking out into the sea, is the Shore Temple, while the free-standing Pancha Ratha temples are 1km to the south. Tickets are not needed for the hill (*open dawn–dusk*). One ticket serves for both the Shore Temple and the Pancha Ratha temples, and can be purchased at either site.

MONUMENTS ON & AROUND THE HILL

Arjuna's Penance

The enormous relief carving, more than 30m long and 14m high, cut into the side of the granite outcrop and known as 'Arjuna's Penance', is Mahabalipuram's best-known monument (*always open to the public*). It is one of India's most dramatic works of art, and is worth close inspection. The subject of the carving is disputed. Guides will nor-

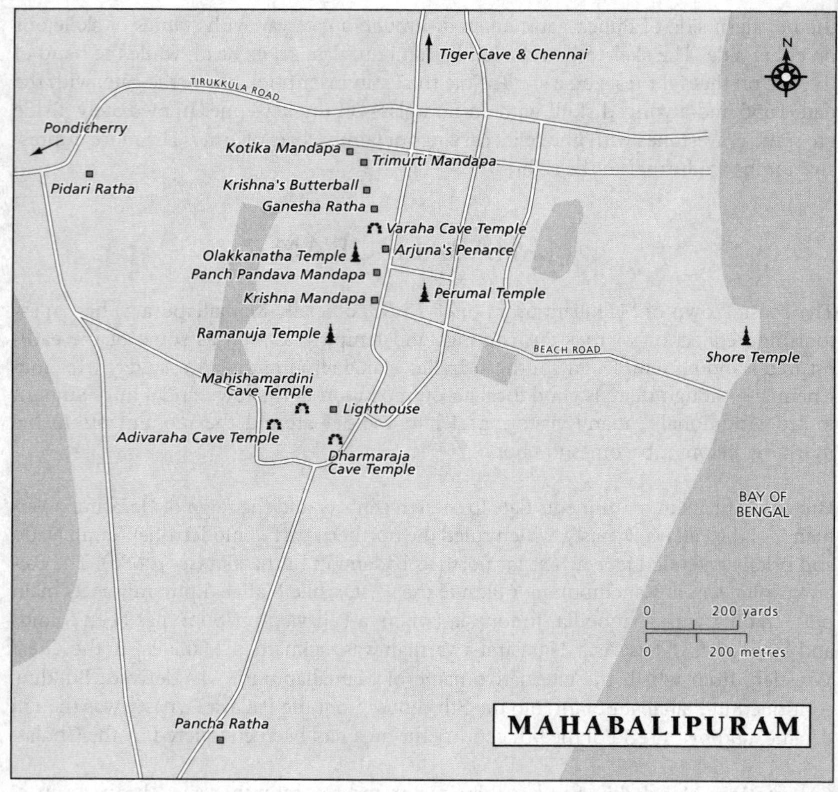

mally tell visitors that it shows Arjuna, the hero of the epic *Mahabharata* standing on one leg to win a magic weapon from the god Shiva. However, scholars believe it actually shows the ascetic Bhagiratha, who performed great acts of self-sacrifice so that Shiva would bring the heavenly River Ganga (or Ganges) down to earth. For this reason, the relief is therefore also known as Bhagiratha's Penance or The Descent of the Ganges. It is effectively divided into two parts by a cleft in the rock, down which water once flowed.

Left side of the relief: On the left of the cleft, halfway up the rock, is the figure of Bhagiratha (or Arjuna) standing in a yoga-like position on one leg, his hands raised above his head. His skeletal ribcage indicates that he has been fasting. Slightly further to the left is the taller, four-armed figure of Shiva, holding a weapon and surrounded by attendant dwarfs, known as *ganas*. Note the deer immediately beneath Shiva and Bhagirathi, which appears to be leaping from rock to rock. A little lower down, beneath the deer, is a Vishnu shrine, surrounded by animals and deities. The rest of the lower part of the left rock is unfinished. The top of the left-hand side of the left rock is covered with scenes of animals, mythical creatures and deities that are thought to represent Mount Kailash, Shiva's abode in the Himalayas.

The cleft in the rock: The carvings next to and within the cleft, down which water once ran, are of particular interest. The cleft itself is thought to represent the actual descent of the Ganges, with snake-gods, or *nagas*, playing in the water. Note the minor deities on either side staring at the miraculous appearance of the river. Just to the right of the cleft, near the base of the rock, is one of the most famous images at Mahabalipuram: it is a cat, apparently mimicking Bhagiratha's yogic pose, but actually tricking the nearby mice into a false sense of security. It has also been interpreted as an attack on fake or hypocritical ascetics of the time.

Right side of the relief: The right side of the relief has no human figures. It is dominated by finely-carved elephants and their babies, and, up above, flying celestial beings. There are many animals carved at the far right, including a separate carving, in the round, of a monkey being groomed by another monkey while it looks after its baby.

Left of Arjuna's Penance

To the left (south) of Arjuna's Penance is the incomplete **Panch Pandava Mandapa**, a rock-cut shrine with lion-shaped bases to five of the columns. Continuing left is the 7th-century **Krishna Mandapa**, with columns that were added in the 16th century. Inside is a very fine relief carving showing the god Krishna lifting Govardhan Hill above the heads of the villagers and their cows to protect them from a great storm sent by the god Indra. Note in particular the image of a cow being milked while it licks its calf.

Continue to the left, past the entrance to the lighthouse, and a second unfinished relief carving, similar in scale if not in quality to Arjuna's Penance. Note the figures of Bhagiratha and Shiva on the upper left of the rockface. Just beyond is the **Dharmaraja Cave-Temple**, consisting of three empty sanctuaries and traces of guardian figures carved on either side of the main door.

Mahishamardini Cave-Temple

At the southern end of the hill, steps lead up to the small Mahishamardini Cave-Temple, with more superb relief carvings. The temple is cut into the side of a boulder. Inside on the left is a panel showing Vishnu asleep on the coils of the snake Shesha, while on the right is a panel showing the goddess Durga astride her vehicle, a lion, and about to kill the buffalo demon Mahisha—the name of the temple means 'Mahisha-killer'. Inside the sanctuary are Shiva and Parvati seated above the bull Nandi. Note the column bases carved in the shape of lions. Above the temple, on top of the boulder, is a smaller shrine, with interesting external carvings and superb views over the town and out to sea.

Some visitors return to the southern end of the rock, and the **Adivaraha Cave-Temple** (*frequently closed*), which contains an image of Varaha, the boar avatar of Vishnu. They then return to Arjuna's Penance to visit the northern end of the rock. However, there is also a pathway that leads over the rock to the northern monuments. It passes two minor buildings: the triple-celled **Ramanuja Temple**, with fine carved columns; and the ruined **Olakkanatha Temple**, which is built on the rock above the **Krishna**

Mandapa—once a large Shiva temple, the lower walls of which survive, complete with carvings.

Varaha Cave-Temple

The first structure to the right (north) of Arjuna's Penance is the Varaha Cave-Temple. It is of a similar design to the other smaller shrines, and again has some fine wall carvings. The panel on the far left shows Varaha, the boar avatar of Vishnu, lifting his consort Bhudevi out of the ocean. The next panel shows the goddess Lakshmi being washed by two elephants, while the first panel on the right shows a devotee of Durga about to cut off his own head and give it to the goddess. The final panel shows Vishnu as the giant Trivikrama marching across the universe. Note the traces of paint on the ceiling, and the carved images of small shrines on the roof of the temple.

Ganesha Ratha and the north of the hill

Slightly further to the north is the Ganesha Ratha, a rectangular shrine cut from a single boulder. The statue of the elephant-god Ganesha in the sanctuary is a later addition. Precariously balanced on a slope further to the north is a large, almost spherical rock known as **Krishna's Butterball**. About 80m beyond the rock, facing west, is another rock-cut temple known as the **Trimurti Mandapa**, with three shrines dedicated to Brahma, Vishnu and Shiva. On the left in a recess is Durga, standing on the decapitated head of the buffalo demon Mahisha. At the back of the boulder into which the shrine has been cut is a group of rock-cut animals. The most northerly building is the small **Kotika Mandapa**, a shrine with female guardians who appear to be swaying their hips.

SHORE TEMPLE

The 8th-century Shore Temple (*open daily 6.30am–5.30pm; retain your ticket for the Pancha Rathas*) dates from the reign of Rajasimha (also known as Narasimha Varman II), and is the earliest important built (rather than rock-cut) shrine in Tamil Nadu, being slightly older than the Kailashnath Temple at Kanchipuram.

Orientation: The Shore Temple is approached by turning left along the main road through Mahabalipuram and heading towards the sea. There is a car park just outside the temple compound. The much-eroded two-towered temple is in a spectacular location and attracts large numbers of visitors.

Inside the outer compound, you pass an empty stepped water tank on your right (south) and an outer courtyard with statues of the bull Nandi placed on the walls. Just outside the temple on the north side is a pretty pool with a circular shrine in the centre and an animal, probably a boar, carved out of stone. Note the carved lions supporting the octagonal domes on the towers. The entrance to the temple is through a break in the wall on the south side.

Inside are three sanctuaries, aligned west to east. The largest is a Shiva shrine, covered by the larger of the two pyramidal towers. Inside is a multi-faceted polished lingam, behind which is a fine carved panel showing a family scene of Shiva, his consort Uma (another form of Parvati) and Skanda (another form of Kartikeya). The second, smaller shrine is thought to be the oldest, and is on the land side of the Shiva shrine; it contains an image of sleeping Vishnu. The smallest shrine, on the west and facing west, is dedicated to Shiva. Note the free-standing stone carving of a lion (with a deep recess in its chest), the vehicle of the goddess Durga, on the south side of the temple. A tiny Durga sits on the lion's knee, and the decapitated body of the demon buffalo Mahisha is on the floor.

THE PANCHA RATHA

The Pancha Ratha (literally 'Five Chariots') are a unique group of shrines cut out of boulders in the sand dunes, 800m south of the southern tip of Mahabalipuram lighthouse. Each of them is built in a different style, perhaps as architectural models for Pallava temple builders, and they are not thought to have been used for worship. They date back to the 7th-century reign of Mamalla.

Orientation: The shrines (*open daily 6–6, retain your ticket for the Shore Temple*), which for no particular reason are named after heroes of the *Mahabharata*, are approached by passing through a market at the southern outskirts of the town. The four shrines on the left (seaward side) may in fact have been cut out of one long boulder.

Draupadi Ratha: The first shrine is dedicated to the goddess Durga. It is built with a gently curving roof. The sanctuary contains a fine carved panel showing a Durga-devotee about to cut off his own head and present it to the goddess. To the landward side of the temple is a free-standing carving of a lion, Durga's vehicle.

Arjun Ratha: Immediately behind the Draupadi Ratha is the Arjun Ratha, with which it shares a plinth. The Arjun Ratha has carved pilasters, miniature roof-shrines and an octagonal mini-dome—important features of many later south Indian temples. The sanctuary of the Arjun Ratha is empty, but the nearby rock-carved image of Nandi suggests that it was dedicated to Shiva. There is a fine image of Shiva leaning against Nandi on the south side of the temple. On the east side Indra rides an elephant and on the north Vishnu is shown with Garuda, the man-eagle.

Bhima Ratha: Behind the Arjun Ratha is this unfinished rectangular building with a barrel roof and arched ends. Note the faces carved on the lower tier of the roof. The unfinished bottom part of this shrine and the Dharmaraja shrine just beyond it are a reminder that with rock-cut rather than 'built' constructions the roof is usually the first part to be completed.

Dharmaraja Ratha: This is the tallest and most elaborate of the shrines—of similar design to the Arjun Ratha, but with three rather than two storeys. Note the carving of Ardhanarishwara (Shiva as half-man and half-woman) on the east wall. The figure with a conical hat on the rear (southern wall) is Mamalla, the Pallava king.

Nakula Sahadev Ratha: The fifth shrine, known as the Nakula Sahadev Ratha, stands separately from the other four, and is shaped like a horseshoe, with a barrel roof. Note the similarity between the rear of the shrine and the rear of the nearby free-standing elephant, which has been seen as an 8th-century architectural joke.

OTHER MONUMENTS IN OR NEAR MAHABALIPURAM

Tiger Cave and Mukundanayanar Temple

The Pallava-period **Tiger Cave**, 5km north of Mahabalipuram on the beach side of the road to Chennai, has been cut from a large boulder. This extraordinary piece of almost psychedelic carving has 11 huge heads of monstrous tiger-like creatures grouped in a semicircle around a rock-cut shrine. On the left side of the boulder are two carved elephant heads, their foreheads removed to create deep recesses in the rock. There is another small rock-cut shrine just to the south, with inscriptions on the rock. Its sanctuary is very similar to the Shiva shrine at the Shore Temple, with a multi-faced lingam and a panel showing Shiva with his family. Around 300m to the north, beyond the compound containing Tiger Cave, is a recently excavated ruined temple, partially exposed during the tsunami of 2004.

Also on the beach side of the Chennai road, but on the outskirts of Mahabalipuram, is the tiny sunken **Mukundanayanar Temple**, set in its own compound. It was dedicated to Shiva, and a panel in the sanctuary shows him with his family. Note the Nandi bull on the other side of the compound fence.

Perumal Temple

Further south, on the main street through the town, close to Arjuna's Penance, is the 17th–18th-century Perumal Temple, dedicated to Vishnu, with finely carved gates. Notice also the carved gates on the other side of the road, which probably formed part of a formal avenue leading from the Perumal Temple to the Shore Temple. Further south on the main road is the **Mahabalipuram Museum** (*open Mon–Sat 9–5*).

Three more shrines

On the west side of town, close to the road that leads south towards Pondicherry, are three more small rock-cut shrines: the twin **Pidari Ratha**, close to the road, and the **Vilian Kuttai Ratha**, deeper into the compound. All three are square shrines with tiered roofs and octagonal miniature domes.

ENVIRONS OF MAHABALIPURAM

Tirukalukundaram

Some 15km west of Mahabalipuram is the town of Tirukalukundaram (*map 13 D3*), the main landmark of which is the impressive 17th-century Bhaktavatsaleshwara Temple, with Nayaa-period stone carvings. On the way up to the nearby architecturally uninteresting hilltop Vedagirishwara Temple, there is a small Shiva shrine from the

7th-century Pallava period known as the Orukal Mandapa—it contains some pretty carving and graffiti left behind by 17th- and 18th-century European visitors.

Sadras

About 10km south of Mahabalipuram, is the former Dutch fortress of Sadras (*map 14 D1*), close to the village of Kalpakkam and the sea. Sadras, which was an important textile centre, remained a Dutch settlement from 1647 to 1824, when it was ceded to the British in exchange for territory in Indonesia. Inside the recently restored fort, which has arrow-shaped bastions, is a small cemetery with several Dutch gravestones, including one that is designed like a table and has some interesting relief carvings.

Alamparai

Exactly midway between Mahabalipuram and Pondicherry (43km from each of them) is the romantically ruined 17th-century sea-fort of Alamparai (*map 14 D1*). It was a Mughal outpost, handed over to the French in 1750 and captured by the British ten years later. Parts of it were swept away in the 2004 tsunami.

PONDICHERRY

Pondicherry (*map 14 D1*, officially called Puducherry, but widely referred to as just 'Pondi') is a former French enclave on the coast of Tamil Nadu, 150km south of Chennai. It is the capital of the Union Territory of Pondicherry which includes three other much smaller former French settlements: Karaikal, also on the Tamil Nadu coast, Yanam, on the Andhra coast, and Mahé, on the Kerala coast. It has its own legislature and chief minister, and is not part of the state of Tamil Nadu. Its unusual mixture of French and Tamil traditions make it an interesting place to explore—though no visitor should go there under the impression that they are visiting a tropical version of France. Most of the modern city has a very Indian feel—though there are continuing attempts to preserve the more French parts of the city along the coast. There are several comfortable places to stay—and it is a good base for visiting the modern utopian settlement of Auroville, the great hill-fortress at Gingee and the temple town of Chidambaram.

History: Excavations in Arikamedu, in southern Pondicherry, have revealed a major seaport that flourished in the 1st century and traded with the Roman Empire. However, Pondicherry's modern history starts with the arrival of Portuguese, Danish, Dutch and French traders and settlers in the 16th and 17th centuries. The Adil Shahi rulers of Bijapur granted the French the right to set up a trading settlement at Pondicherry in 1672, and it served as the base for French expansion in the subcontinent. The territory changed hands many times, first to the Dutch in the 1690s, and to the British on several occasions in the 17th and 18th centuries. Its best-known French governor, Joseph François Dupleix, captured Madras (Chennai) from the British in 1746, but

Pondicherry was taken by the British in 1761 and was only permanently restored to France in 1817, after the defeat of Napoleon. In 1954, Pondicherry, along with the other south Indian French enclaves, became part of India.

Orientation: The grid pattern of streets, with the major roads running north–south and minor ones running east–west—a street layout originally planned by the Dutch in the 1690s and laid out by the French in the 18th century—has largely survived. The eastern part of Pondicherry close to the sea, formerly known as the White Town, was the old French Quarter, and many French colonial buildings have survived there. Along the sea runs a long promenade that is known as both Beach Road and Goubert Avenue—the latter name honouring Edouard Goubert, the Franco-Indian politician who dominated Pondicherry politics after the union with India.

THE FRENCH QUARTER

Several of the most important colonial buildings are now research institutes, government offices or hotels. They usually have colonnaded porticoes that lead on to small interior gardens, the roofs are generally flat, and the ceilings and doorway arches are unusually high. The interior streets are marked by continuous façades, with high walls that do not reveal what is inside. It is often possible to go inside, if one asks politely. It is also very interesting to wander around. This guide begins with the northern part of the French Quarter, starting at the Gandhi Memorial, halfway along Beach Road.

Gandhi Memorial

The Gandhi Memorial is of particular historical interest for the eight elegant carved granite columns that surround it, which were brought from the fort of Gingee after its capture by the French in the 1750s. The Dupleix statue now at the southern end of the promenade used to be here. This area was known by the French as the Place de la République. The nearby lighthouse (1836), set slightly in from the coast, was in use until 1979.

Bharati Park

Behind the lighthouse is Bharati Park, formerly Government Park, which served as a parade ground in the French period. There are interesting Vijayanagar-style sculptures in the park, as well as a Neoclassical monument, with a pediment on each façade and surmounted by an urn. It is known locally as the **Aayi Mandapa** (1854), and commemorates the discovery of a water source which enabled the settlement of Pondicherry. The large two-storey Neoclassical building on the north side of the park is the **Raj Niwas** (*closed to the public*), formerly the residence of the French governor—and built on the site of Dupleix's home. It now houses the lieutenant governor, Delhi's representative in Pondicherry.

Pondicherry Museum

On the east side of the Raj Niwas, on Rue St Louis, is Pondicherry Museum (*open Tues–Sun 9.40–1 & 2–5.20; no photographs*) in the former government library. It is a small but

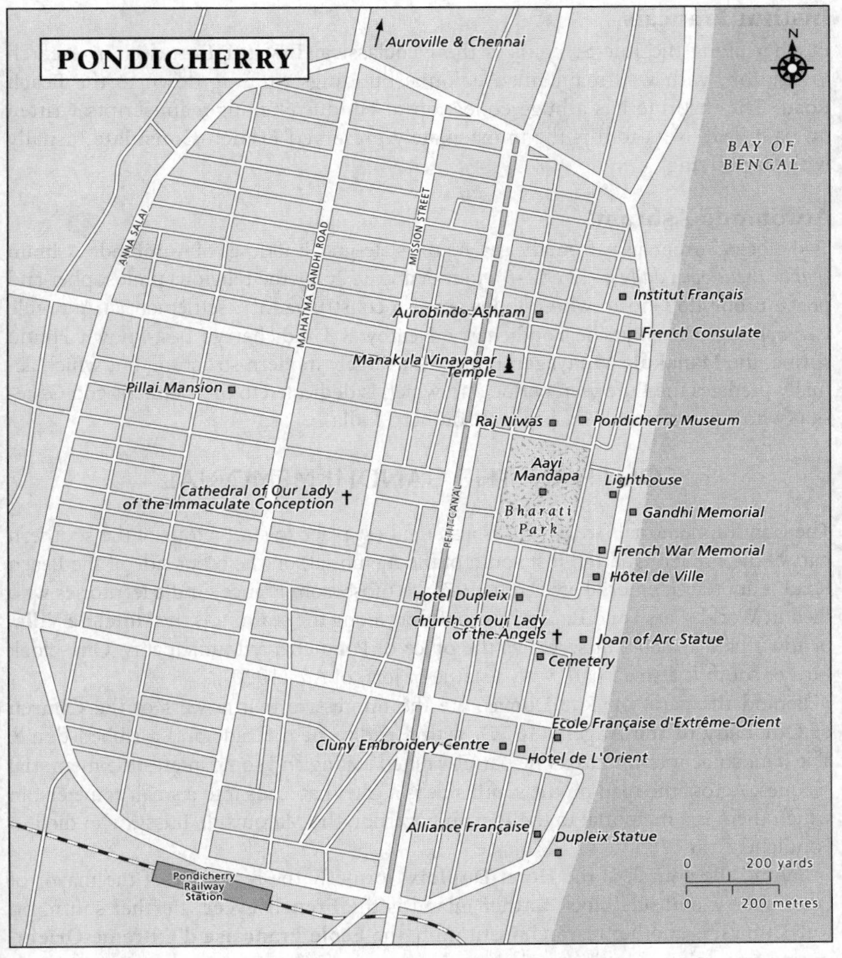

very interesting museum, partly because of the artefacts—many manufactured in the Roman Empire—recovered in Arikamedu (*see p. 791*). These include amphorae from Spain, Greece and Italy, the contents of which included wine, olive oil and fish paste. There are examples of glossy red Roman pottery known as 'Terra Sigillata'—including one small fragment from the base of a cup that can be traced, by its stamp, to a particular potter, Sertorius, based in the Tuscan town of Arezzo in the second quarter of the 1st century. There are also fine Chola bronzes, including two Natarajas, depicting Shiva as the Lord of the Dance. Among the more modern exhibits is a bed that is thought to have been used by Dupleix, the 18th-century French governor of Pondicherry.

Institut Français

Further along the Rue St Louis is the Neoclassical **Institut Français**, a research institution, with well-maintained colonial buildings running down to the Beach Road. The institute has a huge collection of Hindu religious manuscripts written on palm leaf. Next to it is the immaculately preserved **French Consulate**, usually with flags flying.

Aurobindo Ashram

Two blocks further away from the sea are the slate-grey buildings of Aurobindo Ashram (*public areas open daily 8–12 & 2–6*), founded in 1926 by the religious philosopher and poet Aurobindo Ghosh, whose followers also constructed the settlement at Auroville (*see opposite*), just outside Pondicherry. Nearby is Pondicherry's best-known Hindu shrine, the **Manakula Vinayagar Temple**—a largely modern structure, but which actually predates the European period and which is dedicated to the elephant-god Ganesha (who is often called Vinayagar in southern India).

SOUTH OF THE GANDHI MEMORIAL

The Gandhi memorial (*see p. 790*) is also the best place to start a tour of the southern part of the French Quarter. Just south of the memorial, on the other side of the Beach Road is another memorial erected in 1971, to those from France's India territories who died in World Wars I and II. The next building along the seafront is the **Hôtel de Ville**, or town hall, which still serves as the office of Pondicherry Municipality. One block further south is a small park with a statue of Joan of Arc (1920).

Behind the park, on Rue Dumas, are the impressive twin towers of the **Church of Our Lady of the Angels** (1855), with a pedimented façade and a ribbed dome. The handsome interior has a fine barrel-vaulted ceiling and some interesting memorial plaques. Across the road on the south side is a gate that leads into a small cemetery, in which there is a memorial to the French governor, the Marquis de Bussy, who died in Pondicherry in 1785.

Behind the church is the **Hotel Dupleix**, formerly the residence of the mayor of Pondicherry, and one block further inland is the **French Lycée**. Further south, on Rue Dumas, is another research institution, the **École Française d'Extrême-Orient**, in two fine colonial buildings diagonally opposite each other. On Rue Romain Rolland, one block further away from the sea, is the **Cluny Embroidery Centre**, a very pretty 18th-century former private residence that was given to the religious order known as the Sisters of St Joseph of Cluny in the 19th century. Opposite is the 18th-century **Hotel de L'Orient**, which once served as the department of Education under the French.

At the end of promenade is the Alliance Française, in the colonial **Maison Colambani**. Just opposite in a small park is the statue of the former French governor Dupleix, which was moved here to make way for the Gandhi statue further north along the Promenade. The old pier beyond the park is now closed to visitors.

THE REST OF PONDICHERRY

The French Quarter (the 'White Town') was divided from the Indian parts of the city (the 'Black Town') by a narrow waterway, now partially covered, called the Petit Canal.

Pondicherry Cathedral

The presence of Pondicherry's main church, the **Cathedral of Our Lady of the Immaculate Conception** (1770–91), on the west side of the canal, shows that the division between the two parts of the town was not absolute. The cathedral, built in the Portuguese style seen widely in Goa, with a distinctive curved outline to its façade, uses paired Doric columns on the lower level and Ionic columns on the upper level. Note the fine stucco within and below the pediment.

Pillai Mansion

About 300m northwest of the cathedral, at 69 Rue Anandaranga Pillai, is a fine example of an 18th-century Indian mansion (*no fixed opening hours; knock at the door if it is not open, or go to the other entrance at 54 Vellalar Road*). The mansion (1735) is still owned by the descendants of its first owner, Ananda Ranga Pillai, a diarist and merchant who was closely associated with Dupleix. Note the fine wood carving on the main door and in the courtyard, which is now covered, and also the heraldic crests on the railing of the balcony overlooking the courtyard.

ENVIRONS OF PONDICHERRY

Arikamedu

Excavations at this important historical site, 4km south of Pondicherry, on a river estuary beyond the village of Ariyankuppam, have revealed a major seaport that flourished 2,000 years ago. Many finds from the site are displayed at Pondicherry Museum. The British archaeologist Mortimer Wheeler, who excavated the site here in the 1940s, found so many Roman artefacts that he decided that Arikamedu was a Roman trading settlement. It is now clear that it was a major Indian port, and a centre for the manufacture of beads. The excavations have been covered up, but the views of the estuary are beautiful and the ruins of the oldest surviving church in the region, the **Church of Our Lady of Good Health** (1690), can be visited.

Auroville

Auroville (*map 14 D1*), 9km northwest of Pondicherry and just inside Tamil Nadu, is a community of 2,000 people from more than 40 countries, taking part in a social experiment aimed at developing new ways of living together. Inspired by the ideas of the Indian philosopher-poet Aurobindo and conceived by his best-known associate, 'the Mother' (a Frenchwoman called Mirra Alfassa), Auroville was established in 1969. At the heart of Auroville is the Matrimandir, or Mother's Temple, a gold-coloured spherical structure more than 15m high, inside which is a crystal globe where Aurovillians, as the citizens call themselves, meditate. First-time visitors cannot go inside the Matrimandir—but can visit the pretty gardens that surround it (*open daily 9.45–12.30 & 1.45–4, closed Sun afternoons*), as well as the extensive visitor centre (*open daily 9–6; enquiries T: 0413 26222699*).

Cuddalore

Around 25km south of Pondicherry, just over the border in Tamil Nadu is the town of Cuddalore (*map 14 D1*), an important British settlement in the 17th and 18th centuries. There is little left of Fort St David, built by the British governor Elihu Yale (who later became the benefactor of Yale University). It is possible to see one surviving bastion and part of the walls of the old fort at the back of an orphanage overlooking an estuary close to Silver Beach, on the southern outskirts of the town.

OTHER SIGHTS IN NORTHERN TAMIL NADU

Sriperumbudur

The town of Sriperumbudur (*map 13 D3*), 40km west of Chennai, was the birthplace of the 12th-century Hindu philosopher-saint Ramanuja, whose shrine is inside the important Adi Keshava Temple (16th–17th century), dedicated to Vishnu. The town is best remembered now as the location of the assassination of the former Indian prime minister Rajiv Gandhi, killed by Sri Lankan Tamil separatists in 1991. There is a large granite memorial to him on the southern outskirts of Sriperumbudur.

KANCHIPURAM

The city of Kanchipuram (*map 13 D3*), often referred to as Kanchi, is 70km southwest of Chennai on the Bangalore road and 60km northwest of Mahabalipuram. The town, which is famous for its dozens of temples and its silk saris, was the capital of the Pallava Dynasty at a time when the great carvings and temples at Mahabalipuram were being constructed. The city is less impressive than Mahabalipuram, but has a number of fine temples nonetheless. Unusually, Kanchipuram is split into two parts, with the main Shiva temples in the northwest and the main Vishnu temple in the southeast.

Ekambareshwara Temple

The largest of the Shiva shrines is the Ekambareshwara Temple (16th–17th century), close to the Chennai road, which has a 60m-high *gopura* on the south side, with unusually restrained decoration. Note the images of Shiva's sons Murugan (on a peacock) and the elephant-god Ganesha on the south side of the high pavilion in front of the *gopura*. Inside, the main sanctuary is to the left, out of alignment with the *gopura*, and immediately ahead is a large water tank. A columned hall, with Vijayanagar-style carving, leads towards the sanctuary (*closed to non-Hindus*). At the rear of the compound, behind the sanctuary, is a pretty colonnaded courtyard with a sacred mango tree—at

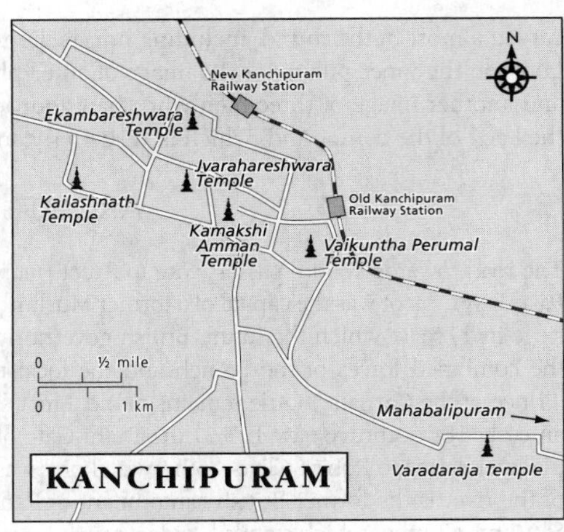

which Kamakshi, the resident goddess of Kanchi, is said to have worshipped Shiva.

About 800m to the southeast is the **Kamakshi Amman Temple** (16th century), one of the most popular in Kanchi, with some fine Vijayanagar-period carved pillars. And 500m to the south of the Ekambareshwara Temple, en route to the Kailashnath Temple, is the tiny and immaculate Chola-period **Jvarahareshwara Temple** (12th century), dedicated to Shiva and with an unusual circular sanctuary.

Kailashnath Temple

On the western outskirts of Kanchi is the city's oldest shrine, the Kailashnath Temple (early 8th century), built during the reign of the Pallava ruler Rajasimha I. Unusually, there is a line of small shrines in front of the north side of the main entrance, most of them with lingams and relief carvings of Shiva with his wife and son. Note also the lion-like monsters carved on the pilasters on the external wall of the main temple compound. There is a small, over-restored shrine just inside the main entrance, beyond which is a large colonnaded courtyard containing the main temple. Around the colonnade are dozens of subsidiary shrines with relief carvings, some of them images of Vishnu and his avatars. Note the mini-domes over the roof of each shrine. There are also fine carvings on the walls of the temple, including one of Shiva emerging from the lingam. (*The sanctuary is closed to non-Hindus.*)

Vishnu temples in eastern Kanchipuram

The **Vaikuntha Perumal Temple** (8th century), 800m east of the Kamakshi Amman Temple, dates to the reign of the Pallava ruler Nandivarman II, and is only slightly younger than the Kailashnath Temple—the external walls are of a very similar design. Inside the main complex, in a narrow open-air passage around the inner temple, are some fine carved panels showing religious and secular scenes, some of which depict historical events during the Pallava period of rule. Note in particular the pillars carved in the shape of lions. Non-Hindus are allowed to see, from a distance, the image in the sanctuary of Vishnu with arms raised.

The **Varadaraja Temple**, on the eastern outskirts of the city, is the most important of the Vishnu shrines in Kanchi. The sanctuary (*Hindus only*) was built in the 12th century, but the most remarkable feature is the 16th-century multi-pillared assembly hall, with some superb late Vijayanagar carvings. Many of the pillars have rearing animals, carved almost in the round, including horses, lion-like monsters, a swan and a parrot. Look on the inner pillars for the image of an elephant with two bodies and one head, and another image of three men who share four legs. It is possible to walk around to the back of the compound, which is very pretty and used for agricultural purposes.

ARCOT

The road towards Vellore passes close to Arcot (*map 13 D3*) on the southern bank of the Palar River. Arcot was the capital of a former Muslim princely state, and the site of a famous siege in 1751 at which the future British governor-general Robert Clive held out against the combined forces of the French and the local nawab ruler, who styled himself the 'Prince of the Carnatic'. Little remains of old Arcot except the tomb of Saadatullah Khan, an early 18th-century nawab, and the Delhi Gate of the old fort, which has a memorial plaque relating to Robert Clive—otherwise known as Clive of India. On the northern side of the river is the former British cantonment of Ranipet, which has the fine Neoclassical St Mary's Church, which stands beside a much larger modern church of the same name.

VELLORE

Vellore (*map 13 D3*) is the main city of northwest Tamil Nadu, slightly less than halfway along the road from Chennai to Bangalore. Though the city is best known in India for its Christian Medical College, it has one of the country's best-maintained urban forts, inside which is a very fine Vijayanagar-period temple, a church and a mosque.

History: The city, on the southern bank of the Palar River, emerged as an important Vijayanagar outpost in the late 16th century, by which time the capital of the empire had moved from Hampi to Chandragiri in modern Andhra Pradesh, just 80km to the north. Vellore was the last surviving Vijayanagar citadel and was eventually conquered by the combined forces of Bijapur and Golconda, then the Marathas, the Mughals and the nawabs of Arcot, before the British took control in 1780. Members of Tipu Sultan's family were kept here after his defeat and death at the Battle of Srirangapatnam. In 1806, it was the scene of the first mutiny by Indian soldiers against the British.

Vellore Fort

The almost rectangular Vellore Fort, with its intact double wall, overlooks a wide, deep moat which can only be crossed by a causeway. Note the circular castellated bastions and projecting balcony-like musket positions for the defenders of the fort. Inside the fort on the right is the large, slightly sunken Jalakantesvara Temple, abandoned soon after it was built and reconsecrated for worship as a Shiva shrine only in 1981.

Jalakantesvara Temple: The square high-walled temple compound is entered through a *gopura* on the south side, with some fine relief carving on the outward-facing stone door frame. Inside the temple to the left is the **Kalyana Mandapa**, or marriage hall, and this is one of the finest achievements of Vijayanagar architecture. The outer pillars have extraordinarily complex carvings of animals and riders, including lion-like monsters with elephants and rearing horses. Inside the hall are carvings on the pillars, some of them in deep relief, showing a wide range of gods and religious scenes connected with both Shiva and Vishnu. There are some particularly fine images of Hanuman, the monkey-god, his carved tail extending back over his head. There is also an unusual carving of the Shiva devotee Kannappa removing his own eyes with an arrow, while Shiva's hand stretches out of the lingam to stop him. There is a raised plinth, supported by human and animal figures on the platform at the back of the hall. Note how the plinth has been carved to look as if it rests on the back of a huge turtle. There are also some very fine carvings on the central ceiling panel, including some parrots carved almost in the round.

The inner temple complex is aligned at 90° to the main *gopura* and entered from the east. There is a lingam in the main sanctuary, but there are also many Vishnu-related images nearby—the temple may originally have been dedicated to both Shiva and Vishnu. Note the hundreds of tiny idols, each partly clothed, on the side of the temple.

The rest of the fort: At the centre of Vellore Fort is a large parade ground with several other buildings. On the south side is a mosque (1750, *now closed to the public*) and the **Government Museum** (*open 9.30–5; closed Fri and 2nd Sat of the month*). There is an interesting group of hero stones outside the museum, and a small collection of Hindu and Jain bronzes inside, as well as prehistoric tools, weapons and pottery. There are also some stone carvings, including a fine six-headed Murugan (labelled Arumuga), riding a peacock. On the other side of the parade ground is **St John's Church** (1846), a handsome Neoclassical church with an unusual balustraded staircase. Just beyond the church is a second museum, the **Archaeological Survey of India Museum**, with some very fine hero stones, and an interesting collection of stone carvings, mainly from the 16th–18th-century Nayak period. Note in particular the image of Narasimha, the lion avatar of Vishnu, with Lakshmi, Vishnu's consort.

Other sights in Vellore

Outside the fort, just south of the causeway across the moat, is the **British Cemetery.** It has some interesting tombs, including one to the British soldiers killed in the Vellore mutiny of 1806. To the northeast of the fort, on the road to Arcot, are the **tombs of Tipu Sultan's family** (early 19th century). To the south of Vellore, and now the city's main attraction for Indian tourists, is the **Golden Temple** (2007)—a modern Hindu shrine, dedicated to the goddess Narayani, built to a traditional south Indian design, but covered in gold-leaf and housed in a star-shaped compound.

TIRUVANNAMALAI

The ancient pilgrimage town of Tiruvannamalai (*map 14 C1*), 90km west of Pondicherry, sits at the western foot of the conical Arunachalam Mountain, an extinct volcano visible from a great distance. The mountain itself is sacred, a place where Shiva's lingam is said to have appeared as a great fire, and pilgrims walk on a marked route around the mountain. The main Arunachaleshwar Temple attracts a large number of visitors, many of them followers of Ramana Maharishi (1879–1950), who lived and died here. He was the most important 20th-century teacher of the Hindu philosophy known as Advaita Vedanta, and was one of the earliest Hindu gurus to become famous internationally. His nearby ashram, on the southern side of Mount Arunachalam, continues to draw many foreign visitors.

Arunachaleshwar Temple

The Arunachaleshwar Temple, dedicated to Shiva, can be approached from either of the four cardinal directions, with large *gopura*, or towered gateways, marking each entrance. The most attractive of the *gopura* are those on the south and east sides. The eastern *gopura* (the one furthest from the mountain) is in alignment with the temple's interior, and has a number of interesting statues in recesses on its outer façade, including: images of Shiva emerging from the lingam; Shiva as the mendicant Bhikshatana accompanied by a dog (or deer); the three-headed Brahma with his vehicle, a goose; and the three-headed Murugan riding his vehicle, a peacock. The outside of the south *gopura* has a particularly fine carving of Shiva dancing inside the skin of an elephant, on whose head he stands, and of Shiva and Parvati sitting on Mount Kailash which is shaken by the multi-headed Ravana, beneath them. Each *gopura* has interesting carvings inside its corridor, with female guardians and images of dancers running up the sides of the walls.

The north side of the outer enclosure of the temple has a large 17th-century columned hall, partially fenced in with fine carved pillars; one end has become a memorial to Ramana Maharishi. Down some stairs is an underground Shiva shrine, where Ramana lived for some time. A single *gopura* leads into the second enclosure, where there is a square water tank on the left and an audience hall immediately ahead. Beyond this is the entrance to the main temple, where there are usually long queues; it is also less aesthetically interesting than the other parts of the complex.

GINGEE

The spectacular ruined fortress at Gingee (*map 14 C1*), spread over three hillsides, 60km northeast of Pondicherry, is one of India's most under-visited major historical sites. Gingee (pronounced Jin-ji but also known locally as 'Senji') was the main southern outpost of the Vijayanagar Empire in the 15th and 16th centuries. With the decline of the Vijayanagar Empire following the sacking of Hampi in 1565, the governors of Gingee sought greater autonomy. In 1614 Gingee became independent from the rump Vijayanagar state, based in Chandragiri, near Tirupati. Later in the century Gingee succumbed to a series of invading forces: first the Bijapur sultans in 1648, the Marathas under Shivaji in 1677, and the Mughals and their feudatories at Arcot in 1698. In the 18th century the fortress was captured by the French, who took away the huge pillars that now stand on the seafront at Pondicherry. Eventually, the British forces supported the soldiers of the nawab of Arcot, who took control of Gingee. The site was abandoned in the early 19th century.

Orientation: Visitors travelling from Pondicherry pass through the western wall of the fortress on the far side of the modern town of Gingee. Close by on the right is Krishnagiri, the smaller of the three hill-forts. On the left is a well-defended hillock guarding the old eastern Pondicherry Gate, and on the hill behind, known as Chakkilidurg (also referred to as Chandrayandurg) are further fortifications. The most important of the three hills, Rajagiri, is ahead and on the left, with sheer rocky cliffs that make it look impregnable. The most important buildings are at the foot of Rajagiri, in an area known as the Palace Zone, while the main Venkataramana Temple is closer to Chakkilidurg. Most visitors climb both Rajagiri and Krishnagiri. The steps to the top of Chakkilidurg are less well maintained, and there are fewer surviving buildings.

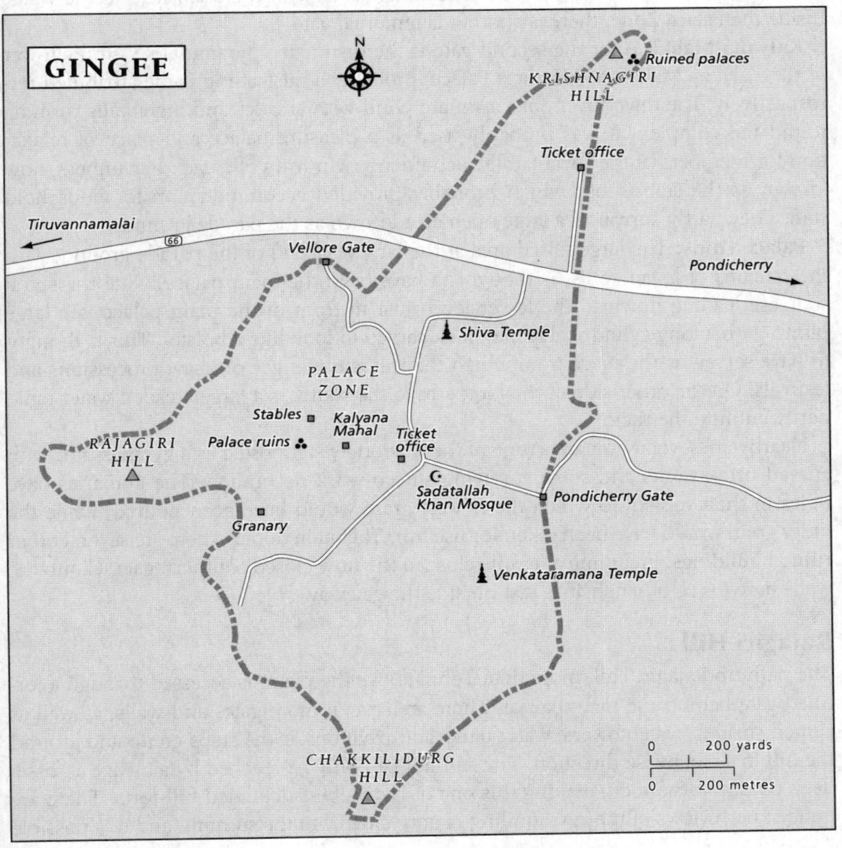

There are car parks at the foot of both Rajagiri and Krishnagiri, both of which have ticket offices (*Rajagiri open daily 9–5; Krishnagiri open daily 9–4.30; one ticket can be used for both sites*). It can be hot climbing Rajagiri, so many do so when the gates have just opened and the sun is still quite low. Take water with you. This guide starts with the Palace Zone.

Palace Zone

The entrance to the Palace Zone is through a well-defended eastern inner gateway, and just outside the gateway is the seven-bayed **Sadatallah Khan Mosque** (1703–10), erected by one of the rulers of Arcot. It is normally closed to the public, but most of its features, including the large pool in the courtyard and the pretty parapet roof with its octagonal finials, can be seen from outside. The path through the curtain walls of the southern entrance changes direction three times before the actual gateway is reached. A small collection of statues and relief carvings is kept in the open next to the walls. Inside the Palace Zone, there is another ceremonial gate.

Kalyana Mahal: After the second gate is the distinctive pyramidal six-storey tower of the Kalyana Mahal, or Marriage Palace, probably a misleading name attributed retrospectively. The tower overlooks a square pond with arcades and high walls running round the complex. It was probably used as a pleasure palace and place of relaxation for members of the royal family. Behind are twin rows of arcaded chambers, now known as the stables but which probably provided accommodation for household staff. They partly surround a large open area known as the parade ground.

Palace ruins: The large raised area at the far (west) end of the parade ground, with the remains of lower walls, is thought to have been the main palace. Note the spiral staircase leading down to the lower level. Just in front of the main palace is a large plinth with a long cylindrical stone block carved to look like a bolster. This is thought to have served as the place from which the rulers of Gingee oversaw processions and festivals. On the other side of the footpath, to the south, is a large arcaded water tank, partly cut into the rock.

Nearby are several granaries (one of them wrongly signposted as a gymnasium) with curved brick vaults and some surviving stucco-work decoration. The granaries have holes in their roofs into which the newest grain would have been poured, while the older grain would have been taken for use from the main doors. There are several other ruined buildings, including a temple close to the now closed southern gate. Climb the walls here to see other shrines just outside the gateway.

Rajagiri Hill

The path up Rajagiri Hill, more than 165m above the plain, is accessed through a fortified gate behind the main palace. There are several more gates and walls, as well as ruined shrines, watchtowers, water tanks and pavilions as the steps go up and around the hill in a clockwise direction. The summit can only be reached by a bridge across a deep chasm in the rock, making this one of India's best-defended hill-forts. There are quite superb views of the surrounding countryside from the summit, and it is possible to get a clear sense of the layout of Gingee. The old walls, with many bastions, are still largely intact and can be seen stretching across the countryside between the hilltops. The lower-level walls have broad moats.

On Rajagiri's summit are several buildings, including a small temple, several smaller shrines, a ruined flagstaff tower and several granaries.

Return to the Palace Zone, past the ticket office and the mosque. It is possible to walk further south in the gap between Rajagiri and Chakkilidurg and reach a pretty water tank, with some outlying ruined buildings. The next major attraction is Gingee's main temple, 400m to the east.

Venkataramana Temple

The abandoned and partly derelict Venkataramana Temple (16th century), dedicated to Vishnu, is a fine example of Vijayanagar architecture, and contains some fascinating relief carvings in stone. The main eastern *gopura* is intact, though its stucco-work statues are crumbling. Note the relief carvings on the lowest level of the *gopura* and on its inner walls. They show scenes from the *Ramayana*, as well as Vaishnavite deities. The monkeys from Hanuman's army can be seen on the lowest row on the right (north) wall, and Vishnu resting on the coils of the snake Shesha on the row above. Ask the watchman to take you up the stone steps to the first floor inside the *gopura* for a rare view of the inner structure of the most distinctive feature of south Indian temple architecture.

Inside the temple's first enclosure on the left is an elegant high-columned *mandapa*, or assembly hall, on which some of the lower-level carvings have been defaced. The inner part of the temple is entered through another lower *gopura*, with three shrines. The central one is dedicated to Vishnu, the others to his consorts. There are some still intact relief carvings on the columns that include images of Krishna playing his flute, and of Narasimha, the lion avatar of Vishnu.

Just to the north of the temple, guarded by a well-defended small rock-fort, is Gingee's old eastern Pondicherry Gate. It is possible to scramble over the rock-fort to the road from here. Otherwise return towards the mosque and take the vehicular route towards the main road.

Vellore Gate: On the left after 200m is a footpath that leads towards the northern Vellore Gate, though you first re-enter the inner citadel through a single-storey gate, before reaching the main gateway. Note the carving of the monkey-god Hanuman on the columns. Also between the main road and the mosque is a partly ruined Shiva temple.

Krishnagiri

The hill-fort of Krishnagiri is accessed by steps leading up from Gingee's eastern wall (it is also possible, but a little harder, to climb Krishnagiri by steps on the western wall), past the ticket office. There are a number of interesting structures near the summit, including an old oil store—a thick-walled stone building—some very pretty pavilions and a temple on top. There are some interesting relief carvings, including a frieze of elephants, and some traces of wall-paintings. Note in particular the audience hall, with projecting balconies and an unusual fluted dome.

Near Gingee

There are also some pretty pavilions and ruined shrines close to the river on the far (east) side of modern Gingee town. There is a 7th-century cave-temple at Singavaram, 3km to the north of Gingee, and the ruined Pattabhirama Temple, 2km to the south-west.

CHIDAMBARAM

The town of Chidambaram (*map 14 D1*), 60km south of Pondicherry and 60km north-east of Kumbakonam, is best known for the great Nataraja Temple, one of India's most important Hindu shrines. It is here that Shiva, as the Lord of the Dance, or Nataraja, is said to have performed the cosmic dance that marks both the creation and destruction of the world.

Nataraja Temple

The large rectangular temple complex, 470m from north to south and 340m from east to west, dates back to at least the 12th-century late Chola period, when Chidambaram served as a capital. The outermost walls and gates of the temple are modest 17th-century constructions, while the second set of walls and the four great *gopura* date from the 12th century, and form the entrance to the original temple complex. There are many later additions, some of them carried out by the Vijayanagar rulers in the 16th century. The temple can be seen from afar because of the four *gopura*—the highest are on the north and south, and measure 45m in height. (*The inner parts of the temple complex are closed daily 12–4.30.*)

The temple gateways: The main entrance to the temple is from the eastern gate, though the other gates are also open. Note the large wooden temple chariots used to carry idols through the streets during festivals. Each of the four great *gopura* is built to a similar design, the lowest two levels cut from stone, and with fine old stone carvings of deities, while the upper storeys have coloured stucco figures of the gods. In the interior passageway of the *gopura* are stone-carved relief panels showing women dancers in a range of different postures, each with an identifying inscription in Tamil. Both the south gate (interior, east side) and the west gate (exterior, north side) have fine carvings of Shiva within his own lingam. Note also the carving of Vishnu riding his vehicle, the eagle-god Garuda, on the west gate (interior, south side). The inner passage of the north gate has a fine carved stone image of the Vijayanagar emperor Krishnadevaraya, his hands pressed together, his cape blowing in the imaginary wind—the image was added to the temple after his visit in 1516.

Middle compound: The middle compound of the temple is dominated on the north side by the Raja Sabha, a large columned hall (*normally closed to the public*) that is thought to have been used for royal ceremonies. Note the life-size elephants, with their attendants, sculpted out of the east and west sides of the steps leading up the high plinth. On the east is the large Shivaganga water tank, with a basement arcade—and beyond that is the Shivakamasundari Temple (also known as the Sri Sivaganga Amman

Temple) with pretty Vijayanagar-style cut-out colonnettes, and some fine ceiling paintings on the side aisles that date from the 17th-century Nayak period—a sharp contrast to the modern mural in the main part of the ceiling.

Inner compound: The south side of the middle compound is taken up by the main temple compound, an almost square construction entered from the east. Inside, the space is filled with columned halls, subsidiary shrines and small gaps where sunlight reaches in. On the south side is the 13th-century Nritya Sabha, which served as a dance hall and has fine carved columns—though the wheels and prancing horses around the plinth are now partially buried in concrete. The innermost enclosure of all is again entered from the east, and contains two shrines, which are designed in the style of traditional village huts with curved roofs—only these roofs are covered in gilded copper. The Kanaka Sabha shrine, on the right, has a lingam made of crystal, while the Chit Sabha shrine, on the left, has a bronze of Shiva in the form of Nataraja. Men who remove the clothes from the upper part of their body are allowed to enter, but may be encouraged to pay a considerable sum of money to do so. This is entirely voluntary. In the southwest corner of the enclosure is a shrine to Vishnu, a reminder of the non-exclusive nature of Shaivite worship.

KUMBAKONAM

The town of Kumbakonam (*map 14 C1*) in the Kaveri Delta, 32km northeast of Tanjore, is one of Tamil Nadu's most important religious centres, and contains several fine temples from the Chola and later periods.

Orientation: The Nageshwara and Sarangapani temples in the city centre are particularly recommended, as is the Airateshwara Temple in Darasuram, just beyond the eastern boundary of the city. It is an easy day trip from either Tanjore (Thanjavur) or Tranquebar (55km), on the coast, but remember that most of the temples are closed between noon and 4pm. This guide starts from the Mahamakam Tank, which is next to the main road bringing travellers from Tranquebar and the coast. Visitors from Tanjore (Thanjavur) may wish to start their visit from Darasuram.

Mahamakam Tank

Kumbakonam's most popular religious site is not a temple but the large man-made water body known as the Mahamakam Tank (also known as Mahamaham), on the southeast side of the city. According to tradition, it draws its water via underground springs from the holy rivers of India. This is the location of a major Hindu festival that takes place every 12 years (the next dates are in 2016 and 2028), when pilgrims come to bathe in the tank to wash away their sins—thereby obviating the need to visit all the holy rivers. Note the small shrines and pavilions surrounding the tank. The Nayak-period pavilion to the northwest corner of the tank has a fixture on the ceiling from which the Nayak king would be weighed against treasure, usually gold—and there are relief carvings of the weighing ceremony on ceiling beams.

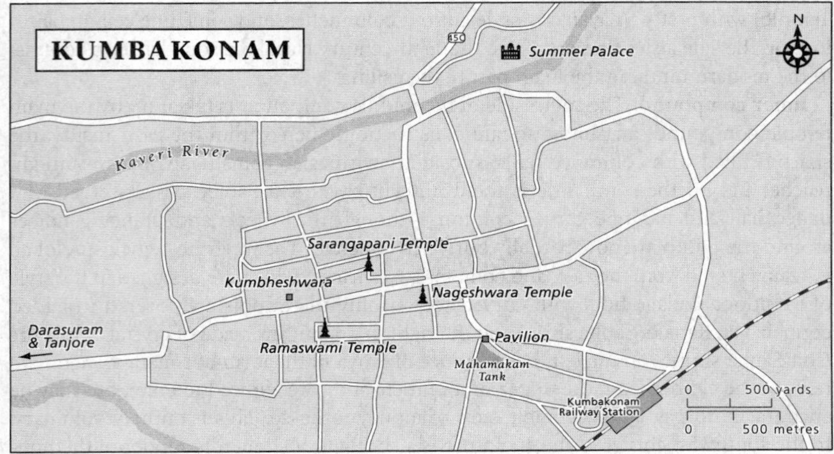

Nageshwara Temple

The Nageshwara Temple, 350m northwest of the Mahamakam Tank, is Kumbakonam's earliest religious structure, founded by the Cholas in 886; its main entrance is marked by a tall multicoloured *gopura*. A second smaller *gopura* leads into a smaller compound, with the main temple and a large assembly hall on the right (north) that has been modernised—but the side walls have older features in the form of wheels and prancing horses, as if the building were really a chariot. The exterior of the main temple, dedicated to Shiva, has some fine early Chola sculptures of sages and gods. These include, at the back of the temple, Ardhanarishwara—Shiva as a half-man, half-woman—the sculpture draped tastefully to cover his/her single breast. There is also a triple-headed Brahma above the water spout on the north side.

Sarangapani Temple

The Sarangapani Temple is 300m to the west of the Nageshwara Temple, its entrance marked by a 45m-high ten-storey *gopura* (do not mistake it for the smaller temple slightly to the south on the main road) with temple chariots parked outside. The Sarangapani is Kumbakonam's most important shrine to Vishnu, and the inner temple dates to the late Chola period.

Note the stone-carved dancing figures on the lower levels of the *gopura* and the small recess sculpture, inside the *gopura* passageway on the right, showing Krishna (an avatar of Vishnu) playing the flute. Inside, there is a large columned hall to the north and another smaller *gopura* straight ahead that leads to the walled inner temple. Walk round the outside of the inner temple walls to see some pretty carving at the rear of the building, as well as the large water tank beyond.

Inside the temple (*no photography*) a perforated stone screen conceals the sanctuary (which is entered from the side), protected by enormous guardians, while little crouching figures support a low parapet which juts out at knee level. The exterior of the sanctuary has a series of niches containing carved panels inserted in the 17th century. Going clockwise, the panels represent: Narasimha (the lion avatar of Vishnu), Trivikrama (Vishnu as a giant striding across the universe), a seated Vishnu with a cobra hood, Vishnu riding the eagle-god Garuda, and Krishna with a flute. Inside the actual sanctuary are 12 finely-carved columns, and an elegant ceiling design shows a lotus surrounded by rings of geese, lions and interlocked acrobats and dancers.

OTHER SIGHTS IN & NEAR KUMBAKONAM

Other temples in Kumbakonam include the **Kumbheshwara Temple** (17th–18th century), 400m west of the Sarangapani shrine. It is said to mark the spot where the waters of the cosmic pot, or *kumbh*, fell to earth, broken by Shiva's arrow—giving the temple, and the city of Kumbakonam, its name. Just to its south is the **Ramaswami Temple** (1620), dedicated to Rama, with some fine sculptures from the Nayak period, and some lively modern paintings of scenes from the *Ramayana*. On the northern banks of the Kaveri is the former 19th-century **Tanjore Summer Palace**, with pretty cylindrical and rectangular roof towers. It is now the government arts college, at which the greatest of modern Indian mathematicians, S. Ramanujan, studied in 1904–05.

Airateshwara Temple

The superb and little-visited Airateshwara Temple, one of the most important of the late Chola period, lies 3km to the west of Kumbakonam in Darasuram. Built during the reign of Rajaraja II (1146–72), this temple—unlike the shrines of Kumbakonam—is now an archaeological monument, and so has not been subject to modern additions and repainting, though it is still under worship. The temple is set in a pretty park which was once the outer compound, with a huge ruined *gopura* at its eastern end.

Outer precincts: The high stone walls of the temple are surmounted by a carving of the bull Nandi, marking it as a shrine dedicated to Shiva. There is a sunken entrance area with a small pavilion housing another image of Nandi, facing into the temple. Note the animals and musicians carved on the steps of the pavilion. Inside the walls is a paved courtyard with arcades around the sides. In the northeast corner of the courtyard is the Nataraja Mandapa—a covered area with fine wall-paintings that has been turned into a small sculpture gallery. Note the particularly fine, slightly damaged stone image of Shiva's many-armed son Murugan riding his vehicle, a peacock.

Exterior of the main shrine: Walk clockwise around the outside of the temple to see the painted walls (from the 17th century) and fine carvings in the wall recesses, particularly towards the back of the temple, on the outside of the sanctuary. Among the images is a covered statue of a seated Shiva as Dakshinamurti, the teacher holding a book, with modern steps leading up to the recess. At the rear of the temple is a black stone carving of Shiva emerging from the lingam. On the north side is a carving of Durga killing the demon Mahisha, and to the left is small relief panel showing the many-headed demon Ravana trying to shake Mt Kailash, the abode of Shiva.

Interior of the shrine: Steps lead up to the assembly hall of the main shrine. Note how the stones next to the step have been carved in the shape of a horse pulling a chariot wheel, with elephants carved in the same manner at the end of the wings of the assembly hall. The lower parts of the columns of the assembly hall have been carved in the form of lions with elephants' trunks.

The interior of the main temple is very dark and a bit of a disappointment after the extraordinary artwork visible outside—but note some fine carved columns, and the guardians on either side of the inner doorway.

The smaller **Daivanayaki Temple** is just to the north, within its own walled compound; there are fine carvings of animals on the steps leading up to the assembly hall.

GANGAIKONDACHOLAPURAM

The gloriously imposing Brihadishwara Temple, in the small village of Gangaikondacholapuram (*map 14 C1*), 35km north of Kumbakonam, was the most important shrine in what became the Chola capital in the early 10th century. The name Gangaikondacholapuram literally means 'the city of the Chola who conquered the Ganges', and it was built to celebrate the Chola ruler Rajendra I (reigned 1012–44), who is said to have crossed the Ganges as part of a military expedition into northern India. Large vats of holy water from the Ganges were carried from the north and poured into an enormous man-made lake, long since disappeared. There are few other remains of the Chola capital other than this huge temple, which is only slightly smaller than the similar temple built by Rajendra's father Rajaraja in the old capital of Tanjore. Like the one in Tanjore, this temple is called Brihadishwara, another name for Shiva.

Brihadishwara Temple

The temple compound is entered from the east, through a large ruined gateway flanked by enormous guardian figures. Note the circular bastion on the left, probably a late Chola addition, that gives the temple complex a fort-like appearance. The large Nandi bull immediately inside the walls is not carved from stone, but made of stone blocks that have been plastered over. The same is true of a strange lion-like figure on the right, which actually marks the entrance to a well.

Ahead is the main temple, with its six-storey tower almost 60m high. Note its slightly concave profile. In front of the assembly hall is an incomplete extension which, like the sculptures on the tower, are 17th-century additions.

External carvings: Walk clockwise round the temple to the side steps on the south side, where huge guardians flank the door. To the left is the first in a series of remarkable carvings on the external walls of the sanctuary. The first shows Shiva as Bhikshantana, a mendicant accompanied by a dog, and it is followed by carvings of Ganesha the elephant-god, Ardhanarishwara (Shiva as half-man, half-woman), Harihara (half-Shiva, half-Vishnu) and Shiva as Nataraja, the Lord of the Dance. The rear wall shows Shiva with the river-goddess Ganga, Shiva emerging from the lingam, Vishnu with his consorts Lakshmi and Bhudevi, Shiva's son Murugan, and Vishnu with Lakshmi. The north wall shows Shiva killing the demon Durga, the triple-headed Brahma with consorts, Bhairava, the most fearsome aspect of Shiva, and a seated Shiva. The final image on the wall next to the steps is the most famous at Gangaikondacholapuram, and one of the greatest pieces of Chola art: it shows Shiva bestowing a wreath on his follower Chandesha.

The interior: The temple is entered from the steps at the eastern end, where there is a small stone statue of Nandi and a long colonnade with cages on both sides, inside which are dressed Chola bronzes, including a superb standing Parvati. At the end of the hall are two huge fanged guardians, and a small columned ante-chamber with carvings on the inner wall. Note the large square columns with carvings on the capitals and two more giant guardians protecting the entrance to the sanctuary and its huge lingam.

There are several other shrines in the compound, including two Kailashnath temples, to the north and south of the main building. They were erected by King Rajendra's queens and have some fine but worn external carvings.

The only other remains of Rajendra's capital are 2km to the southwest, in the village of Maligaimedu, where the stone-and-brick foundations of what is thought to have been a palace have been excavated.

TANJORE

Tanjore (*map 14 C2*), officially called Thanjavur, is historically the most important city in central Tamil Nadu. It served as the capital of the Chola Empire from the 9th century, and was later subsumed into the Vijayanagar Empire, which appointed governors, known as Nayaks, to rule the southern parts of their territory. With the collapse of the Vijayanagar Empire in the 16th century, the Tanjore Nayaks established their own dynasty which lasted until 1675 when the Maratha warlord Ekoji (the half-brother of the great Maharashtran leader Shivaji) set up his own dynasty. The Tanjore Maratha Kingdom survived until 1855, when it was annexed by the British, who were already in *de facto* control of the region. The British tore down the old city walls, though the moat has survived, as has the fascinating Nayaka Palace, with its remarkable collection of Chola bronzes. The British also reinforced the fortifications around the great Chola-period Brihadishwara Temple to the southwest of the old city.

NAYAKA PALACE

This large palace complex is in the heart of old Tanjore and can be a confusing place to visit. The palace was founded by Shevappa Nayak in the late 16th century, but has been altered and enlarged many times since.

Orientation: There are two durbar halls—one Nayak, one Maratha. Then there are four different tickets, none costing more than Rs50, needed to visit all the public areas: two tickets for minor museums; one for the palace and one of the towers;

and another ticket for the main museum, known as the 'Art Gallery', and the other tower; entry to the marvellously eccentric collection in the library is free. The fort is entered through a series of fortified gates which lead to a large enclosure where cars are allowed to park.

The 'Art Gallery'

This museum (*open daily 9–1 & 3–6*) contains one of the best collections of southern Indian art in the country, housed in rooms surrounding a courtyard in an old Nayak-period part of the palace. Note the multi-tiered *gopura*-style tower that overlooks the courtyard. The lobby of the art gallery contains a number of stone carvings from the late Chola period, including a fine four-headed Brahma and an unusual image of Agni, the god of fire. There are also charming statues of the Chola king Rajaraja II and his queen brought from the Airateshwara Temple at Darasuram, near Kumbakonam.

Nataraja collection: The first room on the right is devoted to bronzes of Shiva as Nataraja, the Lord of the Dance, and those of his consort Parvati, sometimes referred to in this context as Sivakami. The wide range of Nataraja bronzes gives a rare opportunity to compare small differences in posture, style and iconography—and to see how the quality of the bronzes declined over the centuries. Note in particular the depiction of Shiva's flying hair and his halo of flames, the portrayal of the dwarf (representing ignorance) on which Shiva stands, of the drum in Shiva's right hand and the fire in his left.

Nayak's Durbar Hall: The next room, the pretty Nayak's Durbar Hall, with its lobed arches, has a much wider selection of bronzes—including some very finely modelled ones from Tiruvengadu, near the coast, that were buried in the 18th century to hide them from plundering armies and disinterred in 1952. There is a superb 12th-century wedding group, labelled Kalyanasundara (a word used to described Shiva as a bridegroom, but literally meaning 'beautiful wedding'), with Parvati and Shiva as the bride and groom holding hands, and Vishnu and Lakshmi on either side of them. The durbar hall has a black granite platform, with relief carvings round its side. The large standing statue on the platform is of Serfoji II, the penultimate Maratha ruler of Tanjore, who helped make the city a major cultural centre in the early 19th century. The painted plaster composition on the wall above the platform shows the coronation of Rama.

The next room in the art gallery has more bronzes, and has two fine stone statues of Ardhanarishwara (Shiva as half-man, half-woman) on either side of the entrance.

Upper rooms: The next passageway leads to stairs that go to the top of the *gopura*-style tower, once used as an arsenal by the rulers of Tanjore. On the first floor is a balcony overlooking the courtyard, as well as the skeleton of a whale washed up near Tranquebar in 1952. From the top of the building there are good views of the rest of the palace complex, as well as of the city, including the great Brihadishwara Temple, 1km to the southwest.

Bell-tower: It is also possible to climb the Maratha-period bell-tower just outside the entrance to the art gallery, but you'll need to show a ticket for the Maratha Durbar Hall.

Maratha Palace area

The Maratha part of the palace is slightly to the east of the Art Gallery, back towards the main entrance. The **Maratha Durbar Hall** is a covered area at the end of a large courtyard, with slender wooden columns and some pretty 19th-century wall-paintings. The side arcades of the courtyard have been used to exhibit sculptures. There are two other small museums nearby: the **Royal Museum**, with some old headgear and arms, and the **Serfoji Memorial Hall**, which overlooks another pretty courtyard.

Saraswati Mahal Library: The main attraction in this part of the palace complex, however, is this library (*open 10–1 & 1.30–5.30*), founded by the Nayaks in the 16th century but expanded by the Maratha rulers of Tanjore. There is one room crammed full of often rather eccentric exhibits—fine illustrated Indian manuscripts, prints showing different kinds of Chinese tortures, physiognomical drawings of humans who look like animals and a collection of 19th-century ophthalmology records.

BRIHADISHWARA TEMPLE

The Brihadishwara Temple in Tanjore is one of India's most important Shiva shrines and perhaps the greatest architectural achievement of the Chola Dynasty; it is also a UNESCO World Heritage Site. It is very much a living temple, in use continuously since its construction by the Chola king Rajaraja I in the early 11th century. It has served as the template for the temple of the same name built a generation later by Rajaraja's son in Gangaikondacholapuram—and it was, at the time of its construction, one of the largest buildings in the world.

Orientation: Entry to the temple is from the east, where a gateway, with stucco statues overhead, is part of the later Nayak-period fortifications, with flattened European-style battlements constructed by the British, and an outer moat. The fortified area encloses the temple, the large Sivaganga water tank, a church, some gardens and buildings that were used by the British as a garrison. There is a car park on the other side of the road from the entrance to the temple.

Outer precincts: The temple itself is entered through two *gopura*, much lower and less ostentatious than those built during the later Chola period in Kumbakonam and elsewhere. Both have sets of guardian figures and upper-level stucco-work images of Shiva and other deities. The temple itself only becomes fully visible after the second *gopura*. It has a long rectangular assembly hall, an antechamber between the assembly hall and sanctuary, with floors added in the Nayak period, and finally a square sanctuary with a 60m-high 13-storey tower, capped by an octagonal mini-dome and a pointed finial. It is situated in a large compound, with several interesting minor shrines and hundreds of small sculptures of Nandi bulls on the walls. There are raised colonnades on the inner walls of the compound, now used as a small museum of carvings and a modest but helpful interpretation centre. The rear colonnade has a series of linga and some fine paintings from the Nayak period.

Temple exterior: There is a large pavilion in front of the temple for the 16th-century monolithic Nandi bull, Shiva's vehicle. Note the inscriptions running round the base of the temple. The most important sculptures are on the external wall of the sanctuary. Start from the south steps, flanked by two guardians: in the recess immediately to the left is a carving of Shiva emerging from the lingam. Continuing clockwise, among the carvings on the south wall is one of Shiva as Bhikshantana the mendicant, while on the rear, west wall is Harihara (half-Shiva, half-Vishnu) followed by another image of Shiva emerging from the lingam. On the north wall there is a carving of Shiva as Ardhanarishwara (half-man, half-woman) leaning on Nandi the bull, while just beyond it, at a lower level, is one of the best-known carvings in Tanjore—of a dwarf supporting a water spout on his head while he blows a conch.

Assembly hall and sanctuary: The main entrance to the temple is by the steps at the eastern end of the assembly hall, which is partially open and has some finely-carved columns with cut-out colonettes. The walls and ceilings of the interior have paintings from the Chola and Nayak periods, but the light is poor and it is difficult to see much detail. There is an enormous lingam, almost 4m high, in the sanctuary, and there are often long queues of pilgrims lining up outside.

Christ Church

Within the outer fortifications surrounding the Brihadishwara Temple is the interesting Christ Church (1777–79), which can be reached on foot by heading north from between the inner and outer *gopura* of the fort, or alternatively by road by heading from the temple back towards the palace and then taking a left along a tunnel-like gateway through the fort walls. The church was built by a Danish missionary of Prussian origin, C.F. Schwartz, and is also known as Schwartz's Church. The entrance is at the back of the church (do not be put off by the locked side gate). Note the original inscriptions of the Creed and the Lord's Prayer over the altar. There is also a fine relief sculpture by John Flaxman, one of the great Neoclassical sculptors, a work commissioned (with an interesting inscription) by Raja Serfoji of Tanjore.

COASTAL TOWNS OF CENTRAL TAMIL NADU

Along the coast of central Tamil Nadu is a series of old European settlements. Danish Tranquebar is the most famous, but the former French settlement of Karaikal and the older Dutch enclave of Nagapattinam are worth exploring too.

TRANQUEBAR

Tranquebar (*map 14 D1*), officially Tharangambadi, is a former Danish settlement on the coast of Tamil Nadu. It has a number of interesting buildings from the Danish period, one of which has been converted into a comfortable hotel, making this small coastal town an excellent base from which to explore the area.

History: Tranquebar was one of two important Danish settlements in India—the other smaller Danish colony was at Serampore, north of Kolkata. Tranquebar was founded by the Danish East India Company in 1620, on land purchased from the Nayak kings of Tanjore, and became the property of the king of Denmark in 1624. In the 18th century it became an important base for Protestant missionaries, of whom the earliest and most famous was Bartholomäus Ziegenbalg; memorials to him are found throughout the town. It was here, under Ziegenbalg's supervision, that the Bible was translated and printed in an Indian language, Tamil, for the first time.

When Britain attacked Copenhagen in 1807, during the Napoleonic Wars, Tranquebar was also seized—although it was restored to Denmark in 1814. Denmark's main Indian possessions (except for the Nicobar Islands, which they retained until 1869) were sold to the British in 1845 for £20,000.

Tranquebar was badly damaged by the 2004 tsunami, which washed away several houses close to the shore and killed dozens of people.

Orientation: The main road into Tranquebar is through a gateway, which is all that is left of the walls that once surrounded the settlement. Ahead is Tranquebar's main thoroughfare, King's Street, with two churches. At the end on the right, next to the sea, is the old Danish citadel. To the left is the former Collector's Bungalow, now a hotel, and further north along the coast is the partly ruined Masillamani Hindu Temple. Tranquebar is an easy place to wander around—and *Reminiscences of Tranquebar* by M.A. Sultan is a good guide to its streets and buildings; it is available at the Collector's Bungalow hotel and in local shops.

The Town Gate and Gatehouse

The main Town Gate (1792), built of brick and plaster, carries numerous Danish heraldic emblems, including, on the town side of the gate, just below the date, the letter 'C' enclosing the number '7'. This stood for Christian VII, the late 18th-century Danish king; note the tiny figure of an elephant at the bottom of the 'C'. Just inside the gate on the right (south) is the Danish-period Gatehouse, now used as additional overspill accommodation by the hotel at the former Collector's Bungalow.

New Jerusalem Church

On either side of King's Street are religious and educational institutions, including, halfway up on the right, the New Jerusalem Church (1718). Note the 'F4' monogram of King Frederick IV of Denmark and its mirror image in the pediment of the church, above the date and below the crown. There are several interesting gravestones in the church compound, and inside the building is the grave of the German-born Lutheran missionary Ziegenbalg, who founded the church in October 1718 and who died in Tranquebar less than six months later. The rear wall is covered in memorial plaques and lists of pastors.

Zion Church

A little further towards the sea, on the left, is the slightly older Zion Church (1701, with later additions), which was the main place of worship for Europeans. Enter the compound through the small side gate on King's Street. There are several Danish and British gravestones outside the church. Inside the church, note the pretty relief memorial to Catharine Top, who died in 1789, in 'childbed' at the age of 19. At the end of King's Street is a modern memorial to Ziegenbalg.

Dansborg Fort and its environs

The small **Dansborg Fort** (1620), square in shape, is one of India's finest examples of early colonial military architecture. The fort (*open Sat–Thur 9.45–1 & 2–5*) was built by the Danish commander Ove Gedde to protect the new trading settlement, and its 90m-long walls are intact. Walk around them for fine views over Tranquebar, the beach and the Bay of Bengal. The main building, with its distinctive conical decorative features, now houses a small museum. Note the old jail built into the southern wall of the fort.

To the north of Dansborg Fort, overlooking the sea, is the **Collector's Bungalow**, a two-storey building that is now a hotel. On the foreshore stands the pretty half-ruined **Masillamani Temple**, which is thought to date from the 14th century; part of its assembly hall was swept away by the 2004 tsunami. Note the stucco statues on the tower of the temple. Several fallen pillars can be seen on the shoreline. Just beyond is the derelict **Pillayar Temple**, which is still used for worship. There are several other buildings from the Danish period nearby, some of them marked with plaques, and a walk through the backstreets of Tranquebar is recommended.

KARAIKAL

This small former French settlement (*map 14 D1*), 12km south of Tranquebar and 115km south of Pondicherry, forms a coastal enclave within Tamil Nadu but is, in fact, administratively part of Pondicherry Union Territory. It is a small town, the centre of which retains a French feel. Karaikal was originally leased from the rulers of Tanjore in 1739 and officially remained French territory until the 1950s, though it had two periods under British occupation in the late 18th and early 19th centuries.

The French colonial Government House in the centre of town, with its original columned verandah, is now the District Collector's House. Just to the south of the main square, which has a French war memorial (1953), is the enormous neo-Gothic Church of Our Lady of Angels (1828), its impressively high tower an addition of 1891.

NAGORE

The next town along the coast, 12km south of Karaikal, is Nagore (*map 14 D2*), famous for its distinctive 16th-century *dargah*, or Islamic shrine, with no fewer than five multi-tiered minarets, which have been compared to wedding cakes. A Muslim saint known as Qadir Wali, who is said to have saved the life of the son of the Hindu ruler of Tanjore, was buried here in 1570, and the *dargah* has become an important place of pilgrimage, for Muslims in particular. Four seven-tiered minarets stand at the corners of the original shrine complex, while the taller 43m fifth minaret, with nine tiers—built in 1753 with funds from the ruler of Tanjore—stands separately in front of the building. Note the fine embossed silver doors at the entrance to the shrine.

NAGAPATTINAM

The coastal town of Nagapattinam (*map 14 D2*, formerly Nagapatnam), just 6km south of Nagore, briefly became world famous in 2004 as the area in India worst hit by the Asian tsunami. Historically, though, Nagapattinam was an important Buddhist centre as late as the 13th century—rare so far south in India—and became a Portuguese settlement between 1554 and 1657, after which the Dutch took over, developing it into an important seaport. It was taken by the British in 1781, in retaliation for Dutch support for the American Revolution.

Nagapattinam's churches

The large neo-Gothic **Catholic Church**, dedicated to Our Lady of Lourdes, is near the lighthouse. On the floor inside the church is an unusual bilingual Tamil-English 19th-century memorial stone to a Jesuit priest. **St Peter's Church** (1774), north of the railway station, dates back to the Dutch period, and its curved façade is reminiscent of early Dutch churches in South Africa. The crossed keys on the façade are the symbol of St Peter, to whom Jesus is said to have given the keys to the kingdom of heaven.

The **Old Dutch Cemetery**—near Salt Road, behind the Pondian cinema, on the south side of Nagapattinam—is one of the most romantically overgrown European cemeteries in India. Note the fine funerary architecture and surviving stucco-work, as well as the relief carving of a naked woman, probably representing Venus, on the gravestone of a tomb belonging to the family of the early 18th-century governor Van Steelant, dated 1709.

Velanganni: 9km to the south of Nagapattinam in the village of Velanganni, is the modern **Basilica of Our Lady of Health**, one of the most important Christian shrines in southern India. It is here, in the 16th century, that the Virgin Mary is said to have appeared to local boys and then helped Portuguese sailors in distress.

TRICHY

The city of Trichy (*map 14 C2*, officially Tiruchirappalli) is an important city in central Tamil Nadu, on the south bank of the Kaveri River. At its centre is a huge conical rock, surmounted by a temple. The fortified rock rises more than 83m above the plains—and has a series of shrines that date back to the late 6th century. It was later the second capital of the Madurai Nayaks, before it became an important military base and missionary centre in the British period.

The Rock Fort

The Rock Fort is the primary focal point of Trichy, and is approached by steps that lead from the southern part of the rock to its summit. The steps lead through a cavernous but poorly-lit corridor, with carved stone columns and roofing slabs. Vehicles can reach a midway level on the staircase via a circuitous route from the northeast, but it is easier to get dropped at the bottom of the staircase, just to the right (east) of the large water tank.

At the bottom of the rock is the **Lower Cave-Temple** (8th century) from the Pandya period, with side shrines dedicated to Shiva and Vishnu. The next important shrine is the Pallava-period **Upper Cave-Temple** (late 6th century; *closed to non-Hindus*). The steps pass a small shrine with a fine relief panel showing Shiva allowing Ganga to come to earth through his hair.

The next shrine, on the right, is the **Rock Temple** (*also closed to non-Hindus*), and the final steps lead up to a small open **temple to Ganesha**, the elephant-god. It is partially clad in granite, but the old carved columns from the Chola period are still visible. There are superb views from the top—particularly of the roof of the Upper Cave-Temple and the Catholic Cathedral to the east, and the towering *gopura* of the Srirangam Temple to the north, on a large island in the Kaveri River.

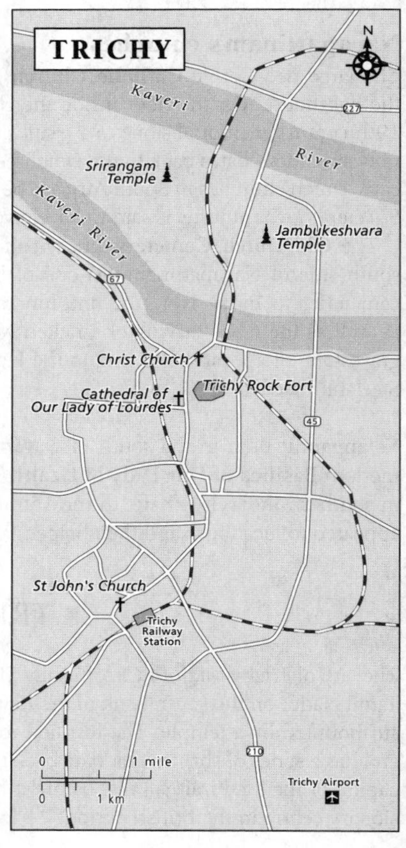

Government Museum

Just to the south of the rock is the museum (*open 9.30–5; closed Fri and 2nd Sat of the month*) in the early 17th-century Nayak Audience Hall, opposite the fort police station. It has a small collection of wood and stone carvings from the area, which are displayed in a pretty domed hall.

Trichy's churches

To the west of the water tank, on the other side of the main road, is the large neo-Gothic **Cathedral of Our Lady of Lourdes** (1841), the spire of which was added in 1895. On the northwest side of the rock is **Christ Church** (1766), associated, like the church of the same name in Tanjore, with the Prussian missionary

C.F. Schwartz. Further south, on the Madurai Road, is the **Church of St John** (1816), in the cantonment area, with a fine portico, its pediment partly obscured by a later porch. The long-standing Bishop of Calcutta, Reginald Heber, drowned in his bath while visiting Trichy in 1826, and there is a small memorial, with a bishop's mitre over one of the windows, and a more impressive brass gravestone to the right of the communion table. Today Heber is best-known as a writer of hymns, among them *Holy, Holy, Holy, Lord God Almighty*. Outside is a large cemetery, with a wide range of funerary architecture from the colonial period.

SRIRANGAM

The Ranganatha Temple at Srirangam (*map 14 C2*), a large island in the Kaveri River, is just 4km north of the Trichy Rock Fort, and is one of India's largest and most important temples. The temple, which is dedicated to Vishnu, dates back to the Chola period, but its buildings were constructed under several dynasties, including the Hoysalas and Nayaks. It has some quite superb carvings from the Vijayanagar period, and construction has continued until recent times.

Orientation: The full Ranganatha Temple complex consists of no fewer than seven concentric rectangular enclosures, of which the inner four contain only temple buildings. The outer enclosures have houses and shops, and the streets are used for chariot processions during festivals. Most visitors approach the temple from the south, passing through a series of gateways, the outermost and tallest being a 77.5m 13-storey *gopura*, started by the Madurai Nayaks in the mid-17th century and only completed in the late 20th century. Its composition is relatively restrained by the standards of most south Indian temples. To the right of the fourth *gopura*, which marks the beginning of the sacred centre of the temple, is a shoe deposit room where camera tickets can also be bought.

Rangavilasa Mandapa

Immediately inside the fourth *gopura* is the fourth enclosure of the Srirangam Temple complex. There is a courtyard with a small pavilion, behind which is the late 17th-century Rangavilasa Mandapa—an assembly hall with fine carved columns and a modern image of Vishnu seated on the serpent Shesha on its roof façade. Note in particular the rearing monsters—a cross between a tiger and an elephant, on the first set of pillars. There is an information centre on the left, where one can buy tickets to go on the low-level roof of this part of the temple complex. From the roof one can get a clearer view of the layout of the temple, including the golden roof of the innermost shrine, with its golden image of a standing Vishnu.

Venugopala shrine: A little further ahead on the left is the Venugopala shrine (early 17th century), with some fine external carvings from the Nayak period, including images of female musicians and Krishna playing the flute.

Just before the fifth *gopura*, turn right (east) for the small, interesting museum and the superb Vijayanagar carvings on the Sheshagiri Mandapa (signposted 'art/sculpture pillars'), or go through the *gopura* into the next (fifth) enclosure.

Museum

The museum (*open daily 9–1 & 2–6*) has some very fine carved ivory figurines from the Nayak period, as well as copperplate inscriptions, weapons and bronzes of the Nayak rulers with their distinctive lopsided headdresses.

Sheshagiri Mandapa

Around the next corner is the Sheshagiri Mandapa (late 16th century), a pillared assembly hall, the almost bare south-facing columns of which do not prepare one for the magnificent artistry of the columns on the north side of the building. The carvings on the two sets of four outer north-facing columns are of rearing horses, carved almost in the round, surrounded by a variety of other figures, animal and human, also chiselled out of the same stone. Each of the carvings is a variation on a theme, with some quite extraordinary detail—a triumph of both expression and animation. Note in particular how the swords and spears appear to pierce and come out the other side of the animals. There are fine, though more traditional relief carvings on the lower parts of the pillars, including images of the 'churning of the ocean', in which demons and gods perform a kind of tug-of-war using a giant snake as a rope. These carvings at Srirangam are arguably the high point of Vijayanagar art, and ironically are thought to have been completed after the fall of their main capital at modern-day Hampi, in northern Karnataka.

Beyond the Sheshagiri Mandapa is the hyperbolically named **Thousand Columned Mandapa** (*closed to the public*); it is possible to see the wheels and prancing horses on the side of the plinth. From here, either enter the fifth enclosure from the east gate or return (via the museum) to the fifth *gopura* on the south side.

Garuda Mandapa

On the inside of the fifth *gopura* is a courtyard and the Garuda Mandapa, a 17th-century assembly hall with a shrine to Garuda, the man-eagle vehicle of Vishnu. There are also statues of donors on the pillars, thought to be representations of the Nayak rulers of Madurai. Non-Hindus are not allowed to enter the sixth and seventh enclosures, which contain the main shrine with a reclining image of Vishnu. However, it is possible to go into the shrines on the north side of the middle enclosures. These are more peaceful than the others, and you pass by pretty circular water tanks near a large shrine to Narasimha, the lion avatar of Vishnu, raised on a high plinth with painted images of the god.

Jambukeshwara Temple

About 2km to the east of the Ranganatha Temple, still on Srirangam Island, is the Jambukeshwara Temple, often referred to by the name of the nearest village, Tiruvannakoil, and which is dedicated to Shiva.

PUDUKOTTAI

The small city of Pudukottai (*map 14 C2*), 50km south of Trichy and 55km southwest of Tanjore, was the capital of the former princely state of the same name. The Thondaiman rulers of Pudukottai supported the British against the forces of France and Mysore in the 18th century, and emerged as one of the few princely states in this part of India that were formally recognised as independent by the British.

The New Palace

This palace (1913–29), set in its own grounds in the centre of Pudukkottai, is an impressive princely residence that is now used as government offices. It is a three-storey building, with arcades running across the façade and an octagonal dome rising from its centre. Note the unusually fine stonework for this period, with the Pudukottai coat of arms, with its two rampant lions, carved in the round. Note also the stucco images of camels and deer.

Gokarneshwara Temple

This large temple, 1km northwest of the New Palace, was originally constructed in the 7th century but much extended in the Thondaiman period. The long, covered entrance corridor is supported by carved stone columns. There are some fine 18th-century paintings on the ceiling, showing scenes from the *Ramayana*. Note the fine statue of a nine-headed Vishnu on the right. The small shrine on the left in the innermost enclosure is to Brihadambal, the protective goddess of the Thondaiman family. The doorway in the far corner of the temple leads out on to the rock, and a small rock-cut shrine that is thought to date to the Pallava period.

Pudukottai Museum

The nearby museum (*open 9–5; closed Fri and 2nd Sat of the month*) has some royal mementoes, an interesting collection of stone carvings, including a striking 15th-century statue of Parvati, some other images of female goddesses from the nearby temple complex at Narttamalai, and Chola and later bronzes, which are not always on public view.

THIRUMAYAM

The walled village of Thirumayam (*map 14 C2*), 16km southeast of Pudukottai on the road to Karaikkudi, has an interesting hill-fort (*open 9–5.30*), surrounded by concentric walls. The inner fort has no buildings except for a large plinth with a British-era cannon on a large plinth.

Just outside the inner walls, metal steps lead up to a small rock-cut Shiva shrine. Beneath the fort on its southeastern side is an octagonal water tank and very pretty twin Vishnu (east) and Shiva (west) temples; the sanctuaries of both have been cut into the rock.

CHETTINAD

As well as being the name of a small town in the region (*map 14 C2*), Chettinad also refers to an area of central Tamil Nadu between Pudukottai and Madurai, named after the Chettiar community, many of whom made fortunes in the 19th century from trading with southeast Asia. For most Indians, however, Chettinad is best known as the name of the distinctive cuisine of this part of Tamil Nadu.

In the 19th century many Chettiar families built fabulous mansions out of Burma teak and marble in this area. Some of these homes are now open to the public. The typical design is a long narrow compound, with a columned verandah. Inside the house there is normally a formal room used for marriages and other public occasions. Beyond this is a rectangular two-storey courtyard, sometimes covered, usually lavishly decorated, with small side rooms normally used for storage, and often containing small family shrines. Beyond are the living quarters, eating areas and kitchens.

Karaikkudi

The main town in the area is Karaikkudi (*map 14 C2*), which has dozens of Chettiar mansions, most of which are private residences. Guests of the Bangala Hotel (*see Accommodation, p. 827*) can visit one of the more modern mansions, the MSMM house, which is the home of the Bangala's owner; it is superbly maintained and has some fine tile-work. On the same street, west of the Senjai Pond, are several other mansions, with some fine stucco-work statues on the outside.

Athangudi

The village of Athangudi (*map 14 C2*), 11km northwest of Karaikkudi, has several fine mansions and is also the centre of the local hand-produced tile industry—and the workshops welcome visitors. The biggest mansion is commonly referred to as the 'big house', though its owners like to call it a palace (*open daily 9–5*). It is lavishly decorated, with European-style painted images of the countryside—including a steam train and a temple. Note the pictures above the door frames in the first courtyard, which depict stories from the life of Krishna.

Chettinad

The village of Chettinad itself (*map 14 C2*), 5km east of Athangudi, has a number of impressive houses near the water tank. The **Chettinad Palace** is the largest of them, and is open only when the family is not in residence. The palace is owned by members of a former minor princely family, and the living room is full of royal memorabilia. Note above the doors of the rooms in the main courtyard the images of the goddess Lakshmi being bathed by elephants. The **MRM House**, next to the palace, has a 'life style' museum, with cooking implements and local crafts on display. The **Chettinad Mansion**, behind the palace, is now a hotel with two pretty interior courtyards.

MADURAI & SOUTHERN TAMIL NADU

The large city of Madurai (*map 14 C2; see also p. 820*), known as Madura in the British period, is the main urban centre in southern Tamil Nadu. It is home to the Meenakshi Temple, one of India's most important and busiest Hindu shrines. Madurai's history goes back more than 2,000 years, to when it was the capital of the Pandya Dynasty. However, no buildings have survived from before the early 14th century, when Madurai was captured by the forces of the Delhi Sultanate. Madurai then became an independent sultanate, before it was absorbed in 1378 by the Vijayanagar Empire.

As was the case with several other cities in Tamil Nadu, the Vijayanagar emperor appointed local governors, or Nayaks, who, when the Vijayanagar Empire disintegrated, set themselves up as independent rulers. The most famous of the Madurai Nayak rulers was Tirumala (1623–60), who was closely associated with the expansion of the Meenakshi Temple. The British took control of the city in 1763.

Orientation: Madurai's most important landmark is the Meenakshi Temple. It stands, with its high *gopuras*, at the centre of the modern city, on the south side of the Vaigai River. The railway stations and many mid-range hotels and restaurants are to the west of the city, while the airport is to the south. The Gandhi Museum and tombs of the Madurai sultans are on the north side of the river.

MEENAKSHI AMMAN TEMPLE

The main Madurai temple is one of the few major Hindu temples in southern India dedicated to a female deity. The goddess Meenakshi (literally the 'fish-eyed') is a form of Parvati, the consort of Shiva. According to Hindu tradition, Meenakshi was born with three breasts, one of which miraculously disappeared when she saw her future husband, Shiva (in the form of Sundareshwara). The Meenakshi Temple was founded by the Pandya Dynasty but largely destroyed by the Madurai sultans, before being rebuilt in the Nayak period. It is one of India's most interesting and lively temples, with some superb stone carvings and a small museum.

Orientation: The temple has five entrances, marked by *gopuras*: two on the east side, and one on each of the other sides of the large, almost square compound. The original main entrance is to the east, but many tourists are taken to the west gate because of the ease of parking and because it is less crowded—though it means a longer walk to the main areas of interest within the temple. Helpfully in terms of orientation, the *gopuras* have English inscriptions identifying them. (*The temple is open daily 5–12.30 & 4–9.30; shorts and socks are not allowed; cameras are permitted and there is an entrance fee for foreigners to be paid inside the temple—which also allows access to the museum.*)

This guide starts from the east side, with two related buildings outside the main compound, the Raya Gopura (or gateway) and the Pudu Mandapa (or assembly hall).

Raya Gopura

This unfinished ceremonial gateway, 150m east of the main entrance gate, was conceived in the reign of the great Nayak ruler Tirumala. Only its lower levels were built, but its dimensions are twice those of the next largest *gopura* in the temple.

Pudu Mandapa

The Pudu Mandapa, literally the 'new assembly hall', is a long, rectangular, covered pavilion that leads from the Raya Gopura to the eastern gate. It is now occupied by a large number of tailors, whose small booths often block one's view of some of Madurai's finest carvings. Among the carvings on the outside of the building are superb images of Shiva dancing inside the skin of an elephant he has killed (northeast corner), and Shiva and Parvati seated on Mount Kailash, with the many-headed Ravana trying to shake the mountain (southwest corner). Note also the series of prancing horses with riders at both ends of the building. Inside the assembly hall, note the magnificent three-breasted image of Meenakshi towards the eastern end of the southern passage, and the marriage of Meenakshi and Shiva (attended by Vishnu) at the western end of the same passage, close to the main temple.

The high east *gopura* leads into a covered hallway, known as the **Viravasantaraya Mandapa**, with several more finely carved pillars; again, it is full of small shops.

The Thousand Pillar Hall

A corridor and steps to the right (north) lead to the Thousand Pillar Hall, which contains what are perhaps the finest examples of Nayak sculpture, and which also houses the Temple Museum. The hall, which actually has 985 pillars, has its finest carvings on either side of the entrance. Note in particular, on the left, the image of Murugan riding on a peacock, and, on the right, a long-trunked Ganesha dancing with a woman on his shoulder. The central walkway of the hall also has very fine carved pillars, and a small shrine with a large bronze of Shiva as Nataraja, the Lord of the Dance. Cabinets contain a fine collection of smaller bronzes and ivories.

Return to the Viravasantaraya Mandapa, and head towards the middle compound of the temple, past the place where the temple elephant normally stands, blessing devotees on the forehead with a gentle touch of the tip of his trunk. A low *gopura* has an image of a dancing Ganesha on the left wall, and Murugan riding a peacock on the right.

The Viravasantaraya Mandapa leads into another assembly hall, the **Kambattadi Mandapa**, with a shrine to Nandi the bull, surrounded by some very fine carved pillars and a large gilded flagpole. Among the carvings here are Shiva dancing inside the skin of the elephant demon, Shiva emerging from the lingam, and Ardhanarishwara, the form of Shiva which is half-man and half-woman. Straight ahead is the **Sundareshawara shrine**, dedicated to Shiva, one of two sanctuaries in the temple, into which only Hindus can enter.

The fantastically carved *gopura*, or entrance tower, of the Meenakshi Amman Temple in Madurai.

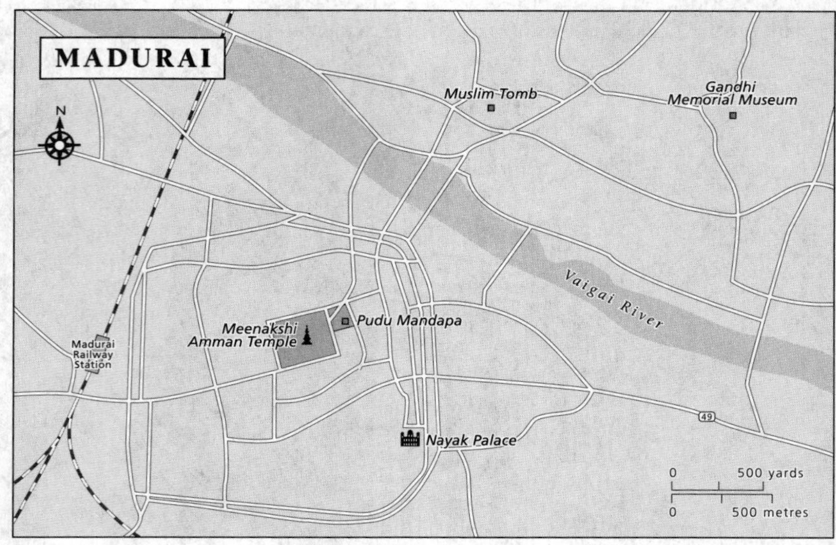

Golden Lily Tank and the Ashta Shakti Mandapa

Turn left (south) in the Kambattadi Mandapa to reach the **Golden Lily Tank**—a square, stepped pond with a large flagpole at the centre and a covered walkway around the edge. The eastern wall of the walkway has murals which illustrate the 64 miracles that Shiva is said to have performed in and around Madurai. On the western side of the tank is the entrance to the **Meenakshi shrine**, the holiest part of the temple (*to which only Hindus are admitted*). Also on the western side is a small covered area jutting out over the Golden Lily Tank, with a fine painted ceiling showing the marriage of Meenakshi and Shiva.

Ashta Shakti Mandapa: There are passageways from the Golden Lily Tank leading back into the outer compound and the southern *gopura*—as well as to a smaller assembly hall, the Ashta Shakti Mandapa, and another gateway on the eastern side of the temple compound.

The Ashta Shakti Mandapa, or 'Hall of the Eight Goddesses', has several fine carvings of female deities, and one of Shiva as Bhikshatana, the mendicant or beggar, accompanied by a dog.

NAYAK PALACE

Tamil Nadu's most important surviving example of palace architecture from the pre-British period, the Nayak Palace (1636), is 800m southeast of the Meenakshi Temple. It was part of a much larger palace complex, built by the Nayak ruler Thirumala, most of which has now disappeared.

Orientation: Officially the Thirumalai Nayakkar Mahal, the palace (*open daily 9–5*) has been heavily restored, and is now the location for an evening sound-and-light show (*daily at 6.45pm*). Visitors enter the building from the east, through an archway leading to a large courtyard.

The **courtyard** is surrounded by pillared halls on all four sides, with exuberant stucco decoration on the upper levels. The outer pillars, 12m high, support scalloped arches, and there are animal-shaped brackets under the eaves. On the far (western) side of the courtyard is the high-domed **throne hall**, where the Nayak ruler would have met his subjects and watched public performances. Note the stone-carved prancing horses embedded in the ground near the steps up to the throne hall. A doorway on the right of the throne hall leads into another large room, with similar stucco decorative features; it was thought originally to have been a dance hall, and is now a museum.

Among the exhibits in the museum is a fine 8th-century stone carving of Narasimha, the lion avatar of Vishnu, and several images of seated female deities. A doorway leads outside to a courtyard, where further carvings are on display—including Jain and Buddhist images—a reminder of how far south both religions penetrated.

NORTH MADURAI

In north Madurai, just across the Vaigai River, is the city's oldest surviving building, the shared 14th-century **Muslim tomb** of two of the Madurai sultans, Alauddin and Shamsuddin. It has become a *dargah*, or Islamic shrine.

Also on the northern side of the river is the **Gandhi Memorial Museum** (*open Tues–Sun 10–1 & 2–5.45*) in an 18th-century mansion. Among the exhibits is the blood-spattered *dhoti*, or loincloth, that Gandhi was wearing when he was killed. There is also a small **government archaeological museum** (*open Sat–Thur 9.30–5*) in the same complex with some fine examples of hero stones and memorial pillars.

TIRUPPARANKUNRAM & DINDIGUL

Just 7km to the southwest of Madurai is the town of **Tirupparankunram** (*map 14 C2*), with its distinctive granite hill rising high above the plains. At the base of the hill is the **Murugan Temple**, built during the Nayak period. It incorporates a Pandya-period cave-temple, which contains carvings of Durga and Ganesha. On the summit of the hill is the **tomb of Sikander Shah**, the last Madurai sultan, who lost his life here in 1378 as he attempted to fight off the invading Vijayanagar forces.

On the other side of Madurai—52km north of the town, in fact—is the great rock fort of **Dindigul** (*map 14 C2, open daily 7.30–5.30*), which was built by the Madurai Nayaks in the 17th century and later extended, first by Tipu Sultan and then by the British. The fort is located on an enormous bare rock on the west side of the town. It is a steep uphill walk to visit the ruined buildings, but worth it, in part for the magnificent view of the surrounding area from the hilltop.

RAMANATHAPURAM & RAMESHWARAM

The town of **Ramanathapuram** (*map 14 C2,* previously known as Ramnad), 100km southeast of Madurai, was the capital of a minor princely state. The palace complex, dating back to the 17th century and parts of which are still occupied by descendants of the Setupati royal family, is on the west side of town. The most interesting of the palaces, the Ramalinga Vilas, has some fine wall-paintings depicting religious and courtly scenes.

Road and rail bridges 40km east of Ramanathpuram connect the mainland to Pamban Island, better known by the name of its main town, **Rameshwaram** (*map 14 C2–3*). This important Hindu pilgrimage centre is very close to Sri Lanka, and, according to Hindu tradition, Rama—with the help of an army of monkeys—built a bridge across the sea to rescue his wife Sita. The main **Ramanatha Temple**, which dates back to the Pandyan period, was extended under the Setupatis in the 16th–18th centuries. Pilgrims normally bathe in the sea before entering the temple, passing through an enormous pillared corridor to reach the inner sanctuary.

TUTICORIN & ITS ENVIRONS

The little-visited area around **Tuticorin** (*map 14 C3,* officially Thoothukudi), 125km southeast of Madurai, has a number of interesting coastal settlements. Tuticorin was once an important Dutch settlement, and the Dutch built what is now known as the English Church in 1750. There is an interesting cemetery nearby. The Catholic Church of Our Lady of the Snows dates from the 17th century, but has been modernised.

Kayalpattinam, Tiruchendur and Manapad

Twenty kilometres further south along the coast is the mainly Muslim town of **Kayalpattinam** (*map 14 C3*). It has many mosques, some of which date to the 14th century. The Al-Kabir Mosque (1337), in the middle of the town, is thought to be the oldest.

About 6km to the south is the important Hindu pilgrimage town of **Tiruchendur** (*map 14 C3*). Its Subrahmanya Temple, dedicated to Murugan, dates back to the 9th century, but it has been heavily modernised in recent times. Note the older rock-cut shrines and caves near the seashore.

On a promontory 15km further south is **Manapad** (*map 14 C3*) and its Church of the Holy Cross (founded 1581). The church is an important place of Christian pilgrimage because it contains what is said to be part of the cross on which Jesus was crucified.

Kalugumalai

The 8th-century Vattuvan Kovil Temple at Kalugumalai (*map 14 C3*), about 60km northwest of Tuticorin and 100km south of Madurai, is a rare example of Pandyan architecture—an unfinished monolithic Hindu shrine cut out of a large granite outcrop. Nearby are some fine Jain relief carvings.

KANYAKUMARI & SUCHINDRAM

Kanyakumari (*map 14 B3*), formerly known as Cape Comorin, is the southernmost tip of mainland India and a popular destination among Indian tourists and pilgrims—many of whom bathe in the rocky seashore pools close to the Kanyakumari Temple. There is a Gandhi memorial marking the spot where part of his ashes were brought for immersion in the sea. There is also a memorial to the Hindu revivalist philosopher Swami Vivekananda on a small rocky island 350m from the coast—Vivekananda swam out to the rock in 1892 and meditated there for three days. The enormous statue on the even smaller neighbouring island is of the ancient Tamil poet Tiruvalluvar, and was erected in 2000. Boats leave regularly for the very short trip to the islands.

The nearby town of **Suchindram** (*map 14 B3*), 12km northwest of Kanyakumari, has the important Sthanumalaya Temple, unusually dedicated to both Vishnu and Shiva. It was originally built in the 13th century, but largely rebuilt in the 17th–18th centuries. There is a pretty man-made pond on the north side of the temple.

PADMANABHAPURAM

This small town (*map 14 B3*), prettily nestled at the foot of a range of hills, with an impressive royal palace complex, was the capital of the princely state of Travancore until the 1790s. Trivandrum, now the capital of Kerala, took its place. The Padmanabhapuram Palace is built in the Kerala architectural style, with sloping roofs and with the widespread use of timber for structural as well as decorative purposes. Although the palace is in Tamil Nadu, it is administered by the Kerala government because of its historical connections with Travancore. The nearest big city and airport is in Trivandrum, 55km to the northeast, and many tourists come on day trips here from the beaches of southern Kerala.

Padmanabhapuram Palace

The palace (*open Tues–Sun 9–4.30*) is entered through a large gate which leads into a courtyard. The ticket office is on the immediate right, close to the entrance to the museum, while the palace entrance is straight ahead. There is some fine carved woodwork over the entrance to the inner palace compound, which leads through to the main palace building, with its wooden roof and pillars. Note the wooden brackets in the form of prancing horses. This part of the complex, known as the *poomukham*, was used for public purposes, while the rest of the buildings were part of the private residence of the royal family. The lobby of the front part of the palace has a large bedstead made of granite.

The Council Chamber: Steep steps on the left lead up to the Council Chamber, where the maharaja would meet his ministers, and into an enormous empty dining hall. Steps lead back down into the open and to the palace's oldest building, the two-storey **Thai Kottaram** (early 16th century), constructed almost entirely from timber, and with a traditional small courtyard at its centre. Note the fine carved single wooden column in the downstairs room, and the pretty shuttering designed to allow cross-ventilation but keep the sunlight out.

The maharaja's private quarters: The next building, on the left, is the distinctive four-storey **Uppirikka Malika** (1750), with overhanging balconies and verandahs on the upper two floors. This served as the private shrine of the maharaja. Steep steps lead up to a small square room, and a finely carved wooden bed in which the maharaja would rest while fasting. The upper two floors have some fine religious murals but are currently closed to the public. A passage leads from the first floor into the palace apartment for female members of the royal family. These rooms are hung with pictures telling stories from the life of Krishna. Visitors are directed through a series of largely empty rooms that served as an armoury and as government offices.

The palace compound: There is a large projecting balcony, the **Ambari Mukhappu**, towards the back of the palace compound, from which the royal family would watch chariot races in the streets outside. Beyond this is a **gallery of historical paintings**, and a small palace that was used as a guest house for distinguished visitors.

Dance hall: Return towards the entrance via the **Navaratri Mandapa** (1744), a dance hall named after the religious festival of Navratri which was celebrated here. Note the fine stone pillars, carved with female images, almost in the round.

Archaeological Museum

The museum in Padmanabhapuram is on the south side of the palace compound and has a traditional Kerala-style façade, although the building is entirely modern. The lobby of the museum is dominated by the large 10th-century stone carving of a seated Kuber, the always plump god of wealth, and an even fatter 16th-century Ganesha. There are lots of wooden carvings of guardians and gods dating back to the 16th century, and, in the armoury, an extraordinary human-shaped cage that was used for punishing criminals.

WESTERN TAMIL NADU

The hill areas of Tamil Nadu known as the Western Ghats were very popular in the British period, and several hill-stations were built here, most of them easily accessible from the large industrial city of Coimbatore, or from Madurai.

Ooty

Ooty (*map 14 B1*), formerly Ootacamund, nicknamed 'Snooty Ooty' and now officially Udhagamandalam, is the best-known and largest hill-station in Tamil Nadu. It is set in a magnificent location, more than 2000m above sea level in the Nilgiri Hills. The British began settling Ooty in the 1820s, and by the 1860s it functioned as the summer capital of the Madras Presidency. The town has a fine botanical garden, a lake, a narrow-gauge railway and a racecourse, as well as several interesting 19th-century buildings. These include **St Stephen's Church** (1831), the roof timbers of which were said to have been taken from Tipu Sultan's Palace at Srirangapatnam. Also of note is the red-brick **Nilgiri Library** (1885)—designed, like many of the 19th-century buildings in Chennai, by R.F. Chisholm—and the **Ooty Club** (1830), where the game of snooker is said to have been invented. There are two much smaller hill-stations in the Nilgiris—**Coonoor** and **Kotagiri**—and many visitors go on a tour of tribal villages in the area.

Other hill-stations in Tamil Nadu include **Kodai** (*map 14 B2,* officially Kodaikanal and pronounced 'Cody'), which is high in the Palani Hills, south of the Nilgiris, and was settled by American missionaries in the 1840s. There are several 19th-century churches and an interesting observatory there.

Environs of Salem

To the north of the Nilgiris, in the Shevaroy Hills, is **Yercaud** (*map 14 C1*), the oldest and sleepiest of Tamil Nadu's major hill-stations. Yercaud is accessed from the industrial city of **Salem** (*map 14 C1*), which also has two interesting hill-forts in the vicinity.

The impressive **Sankari Fort** (*map 14 C1*), known as Sankaridrug, 36km southwest of Salem, is reached from the town below by climbing 500m uphill, passing through no fewer than ten gates. There are several ruined temples and storage buildings on the way up, and spectacular views from the top. Take your own water.

Namakkal Fort (*map 14 C1*) is 48km south of Salem, on a large outcrop of rock in the centre of Namakkal town. In the lower part of the fort is the 18th-century Narasimha Temple, within which there is an 8th-century cave-shrine with fine stone images of Narasimha, the lion avatar of Vishnu, and several other gods.

PRACTICAL INFORMATION

Tamil Nadu has a relatively well-developed visitor infrastructure, but it is also easy to escape to places where you won't see many other tourists.

VISITING TEMPLES

The state is best known for its old temples, most of them still busy places of worship. Non-Hindus are not normally allowed into the inner sanctuaries—though there are exceptions, such as Chidambaram. Shoes are not allowed, and it is wise to wear socks to protect your feet if you're visiting at the hottest times of the day. Temples normally open before dawn and close after sunset, but are usually closed from lunchtime until mid-afternoon (sometime from 12–4), so plan your trips accordingly. However, some temples leave their outer compounds open all day. Cameras are normally allowed in the outer compounds, and sometimes photography incurs a fee. Do ask if in doubt. Most temples allow visitors wearing shorts, but not the Meenakshi Temple in Madurai.

GETTING THERE & GETTING AROUND

• **By air:** Chennai in the far north of Tamil Nadu has the main airport of the state, with excellent connections to the rest of the country and a growing number of international flights. There are also airports at Coimbatore, Madurai, Trichy and Tuticorin—though the last three are served mainly by flights from Chennai and are poorly connected to the rest of India. For the far south of the state, the nearest airport is Trivandrum, in neighbouring Kerala.

• **By rail:** Tamil Nadu has a well-developed railway network, and among the most useful services are the ones to Chennai from Bangalore (5hrs) and Cochin (14½hrs). There are also overnight sleeper trains from Chennai to Tanjore (8hrs), Trichy (7hrs) and Madurai (9hrs).

• **By road:** The road network is one of India's best, and many travellers hire a taxi to take them around, particularly down the coast to Mahabalipuram and Pondicherry, which are less well-served by other means of transport.

ACCOMMODATION

Tamil Nadu has comfortable hotels close to most major sites, although, apart from Pondicherry, Tranquebar and Chettinad, there is little heritage accommodation.

Chennai and northern Tamil Nadu

• **Chennai:** There is a wide range of luxury hotels in Chennai, including three owned by the Taj group—of these the **Connemara** (*$$$; T: 044 66000000; tajhotels.com*) is the closest the city has to a heritage hotel. **The Park Hotel** (*$$$; T: 044 42676000; theparkhotels.com*), on Anna Salai, is the best of the modern hotels, a fine example of contemporary design, built on the site of the old Gemini film studios. For a mid-range hotel, try the modern **Royal Regency** (*$$; T: 044 25611777; regencygroupch.com*), on Poonamalee High Road, close to central Chennai.

• **Mahabalipuram:** For Mahabalipuram, There is the **GRT Temple Bay Beach Resort** (*$$$; T: 044 27443636; grthotels.com*), just to the north of the town. If you want to stay in the town, within walking distance of the main archaeological sites, try the mid-range **Hotel Mamalla Heritage** (*$$; T: 044 27442060; hotelmamallaheritage.com*). There is also **Fisherman's Cove** (*$$$; T: 044 67413333; tajhotels.com*), a Taj group hotel on the beach, 20km north of Mahabalipuram, back towards Chennai.

• **Tiruvannamalai:** The best hotel in Tiruvannamalai (for Ginjee) is the **Arunai Anantha** (*$$; T: 04175 237275; arunaianantha.com*) close to the ashram.

• **Vellore:** The best hotel is the **Darling Residency** (*$; T: 0416 2213001; darlingresidency.com*), very close to the fort.

Pondicherry and Tranquebar

• **Pondicherry:** The town has a wide range of comfortable hotels in the old French Quarter, several of them interesting heritage buildings. The superb **Hotel de l'Orient** (*$$; T: 0413 2343067; neemranahotels.com*), in an 18th-century building that once housed the French department of education, is now run by the Neemrana group. The partly modernised **Le Dupleix** (*$$; T: 0413 2226001; sarovarhotels.com/le_dupleix*) is a comfortable hotel, and was formerly the residence of the French general of the same name.

• **Tranquebar:** The Neemrana group of hotels has no fewer than three heritage properties in Tranquebar. The best of these is the **Bungalow on the Beach** (*$$; T: 04364 288065; neemranahotels.com*). It is possible to visit Kumbakonam and Tanjore from here on day trips.

Central Tamil Nadu

The area around Karaikkudi and Chettinad now has several heritage hotels that can be used as a base to explore both Trichy and Madurai.

• **Chettinad:** The **Chettinadu Mansion** (*$$; T: 04565 273080; chettinadumansion.com*) is in the village of Chettinad, just behind the palace.

• **Karaikkudi: The Bangala** (*$$; T: 04565 220221; thebangala.com*) is a comfortable former private residence in Karaikkudi, and guests are allowed to visit other private Chettinad mansions.

• **Tanjore:** If you wish to stay close to Tanjore, the most comfortable hotel is the **Ideal River Resort** (*$$; T: 04362 250533; idealresort.com*).

• **Trichy:** Trichy's best hotel is the **Breeze Residency** (*$$; T: 0431 2414414; breezehotel.com*).

Madurai

The **Heritance** (*$$$; T: 045223 85455; heritancemadurai.com*) is the former Madurai Club, designed using traditional materials by the 20th-century Sri Lankan architect Geoffrey Bawa.

The western hill-stations

• **Kodai:** The hill-station's only 5-star hotel is the colonial-period **Carlton** (*$$; T: 04542 240056; krahejahospitality.com*), overlooking the lake.

• **Ooty:** The hill-station has several heritage hotels, including the Taj-run **Savoy** (*$$$; T: 0423 2444142; tajhotels.com*), with several 19th-century cottages in its grounds, and **Fernhills Palace** (*$$$; T: 0423 2443910; fernhillspalace.co.in*), still owned by the Mysore royal family.

FOOD

Rice is the staple food in Tamil Nadu, and is served with most meals, usually accompanied by *rasam* (a peppery soup), *sambar* (curried vegetables) and a dry vegetable dish, traditionally eaten on a banana leaf. The rice-flour pancakes known as *dosas* are traditionally eaten at breakfast, but their popularity throughout India, and abroad, has led to them being served in some places throughout the day. *Idlis* are another popular breakfast dish: steamed balls of rice and lentil flour, served with chutney and *sambar*.

Chettinad cuisine is the best-known non-vegetarian Tamil food, served throughout the state but originating from around Karaikkudi. Chettinad chicken is the best-known dish, in which pieces of chicken are cooked in a spicy onion gravy with curry leaves. Seafood is widely available in coastal areas.

• **Chennai:** The **Saravana Bhavan** chain of restaurants, with at least 20 branches in Chennai, are the best places to get simple, cheap Tamil vegetarian food in the city. The **Annalakshmi** (*044 28525109*) on Chennai's Mount Road is probably the city's best-known upmarket vegetarian restaurant, while **The Raintree** restaurant in the **Taj Connemara Hotel** (*T: 044 66000000*) serves good Chettinad food.

• **Karaikkudi: The Bangala** (*see previous page*) in Karaikkudi serves high quality authentic Chettinad food.
• **Pondicherry**: Some of India's best French food is served at **Le Club** (*T: 0413 2339745*), on Dumas Street in Pondicherry, while the Neemrana hotels in Pondicherry and Tranquebar serve excellent fusion food—a mixture of south Indian and European influences.

FURTHER READING

Michael Wood's *A South Indian Journey* (Penguin, 1995) is a fine piece of travel writing, and serves as an excellent introduction to Tamil Nadu's culture and its many temples, while the Indian journalist S. Muthiah has written several books about Chennai, including the largely historical *Madras Rediscovered* (East West, 1999).

There are relatively few English-language novels set in Tamil Nadu. However, the Booker Prize-winning *Life of Pi* by Yann Martel is partly set in Pondicherry. *The Rapids of a Great River* (Penguin India, 2009) is an anthology of Tamil poems from the last 2,000 years. If you want to get a flavour of modern Tamil popular fiction try *The Blaft Anthology of Tamil Pulp Fiction* (Blaft, 2008).

THE ANDAMAN & NICOBAR ISLANDS

This archipelago of more than 300 islands is geographically part of southeast Asia (*see overview map on first page of the Atlas*). The islands are much closer to Burma (300km north of the Andamans) and Indonesia (200km south of the Nicobars) than to mainland India—the nearest large Indian city is Chennai, more than 1300km away. Some of the native population live an almost Stone-Age existence, and tourists are not allowed to visit the more remote islands. The British took control of the islands in the 18th century, using them as a penal colony in the aftermath of the 1857 Uprising. They were occupied by the Japanese in World War II, and there was an influx of migrants from the mainland after Independence. The Andaman and Nicobars suffered badly in the tsunami of 2004, with more than 1,000 fatalities. Tourism has concentrated on beaches, diving and wildlife in the northern Andaman group.

The capital, Port Blair, on South Andaman Island, is named after a British officer, Lieutenant Archibald Blair, who surveyed the harbour in 1788. The most interesting building in the capital is the **Cellular Jail** (*open Tues–Sun 9–12.30 & 1.30–5*), built in 1910, largely for political prisoners. The jail is on a small hill north of the town centre, and was built with tiny cells arranged in seven wings radiating from a central tower. Three of the wings survive. There is a small **Anthropological Museum** (*open Fri–Wed 9–1 & 1.30–4.30*) in the centre of Port Blair, and **Chatham Sawmill** (1836), which has been turned into a **Forest Museum** (*open Mon–Sat 8–2.30*), on Chatham Island, 3km northeast of Port Blair and connected to South Andaman by a road bridge.

Ross Island, a 1.5km boat trip from Port Blair, has the ruins of the former British administrative headquarters, but it was damaged by an earthquake in 1941 and then used as a prisoner of war camp by the Japanese in World War II. **Viper Island**, 3km to the west of Port Blair, has another disused jail from the British period, and a strange 19th-century tomb-like domed building that used to house the gallows. None of the other Andaman islands has buildings of historical importance.

PRACTICAL INFORMATION

There are daily flights from Chennai and Kolkata to Port Blair. There are also irregular, but usually weekly, passenger boats from Chennai (60hrs) and sometimes Kolkata and Vizag—for more information call **Shipping Corporation of India** (*T: 044 5231401; shipindia.com*). All foreigners are required to register on arrival, and will receive a free permit allowing them to stay for a maximum of 30 days. Visitors are not normally given permission to visit the Nicobar Islands.

The best hotel in Port Blair is **Fortune Resort Bay Island** (*$$$; T: 03192 234101; fortunehotels.in*).

PRACTICAL INFORMATION

PLANNING YOUR TRIP

It makes sense to plan a visit to India around one or two places that you definitely want to see, and add on additional locations depending on time, budget, ease of travel, weather and interest. Some first-time visitors try to cram too much into one visit; others ignore the weather when making preparations, then practically suffocate in the heat of Rajasthan in June or freeze in Ladakh in February. Some visitors come to India as part of a tour group, a few of which specialise in historical and cultural holidays and may include less well-known places in their itineraries. But independent travel in India has also become much easier and can be highly recommended, though be prepared for frustrations. There are now decent hotels in all cities and many towns; internal flights are much more reliable and frequent; and it is possible to rent a car and driver, and still travel more cheaply—mile for mile—than one would on public transport in many places in the West.

There are several well-travelled tourist routes, of which the Delhi–Agra–Jaipur triangle is the most famous. The palaces and forts of Rajasthan, and the beaches of Goa and Kerala have also been popular with international visitors for several decades. Such locations have a good tourist infrastructure, but travellers sometimes complain that they are herded around like cattle and have few genuine opportunities for interacting with Indians, or of seeing the 'real' India, in any of its multifarious incarnations. This makes it all the more worthwhile, when you are visiting famous Indian sites, to make a side-visit to somewhere less well-known. And if you are feeling more adventurous, head for states that are not on the busiest tourist routes, such as Madhya Pradesh, Gujarat or Maharashtra.

TRAVELLING TO INDIA

By air

Most visitors enter India through the airports of either Delhi or Mumbai (or possibly Kolkata, Chennai or Bangalore), although there are a growing number of international airports across the country. Delhi is better for trips to the north; Mumbai for the south. But the two cities are connected by more than 20 flights a day, and both are well-connected to the rest of the country, so there is no huge advantage of choosing one over the other. Many travellers want to visit places in the north and the south—and so might get an incoming flight routed via Delhi, and leave from Mumbai, or vice versa. A growing number of international airlines have flights to India, and there is also a burgeoning charter flight market that can provide cheap travel directly to popular destinations such as Goa or Kerala. Relatively new India-based airlines, such as Jet and Kingfisher, fly from Europe and often provide better value for money than Western airlines, as well as excellent hospitality. Many travellers also use Middle Eastern airlines such as Emirates or Gulf, which often provide the best connections to a wide range of other cities in Europe, the Middle East and Africa. From east coast America it is best to fly to India via Europe; from the west coast it is usually quicker and cheaper to fly via Southeast Asia, from where there are many shorter onward flights to India. From Australia—though there are direct flights—many travellers fly via Singapore or Thailand.

By land

There are road and rail crossings into India, but few foreign travellers use these. These land crossings are often affected by political tensions between India and its neighbours. The only border posts between India and Pakistan that are open to foreigners are the road and rail crossings at Wagah (*map 1 B3*) in Punjab, just 30km from Amritsar. There are several border posts with Nepal that are open (*see box below*). They attract little tourist traffic because of their remoteness, and most travellers fly from Kathmandu.

The land borders between India and both China and Burma are closed to tourists, but there are crossing points from Bangladesh to India. The most popular one links Kolkata and Dhaka via Benapole (*map 8 D1*). The main access route to the Himalayan kingdom of Bhutan is by land through the town of Phuntsholing (*map 7 D1*).

LAND ROUTES FROM NEPAL

The most westerly crossing point is also the shortest land route from Nepal to Delhi; it is via the western Nepalese town of Mahendranagar (*map 2 D2*). However, the journey from the India border town of Banbassa to Delhi takes at least 9hrs. The main route from Nepal to central and eastern Uttar Pradesh is via the Nepalese town of Bhairawa and the Indian border town of Sanauli (*map 5 D1*), which is about 3hrs drive from the Indian city of Gorakhpur. This is probably the most popular crossing for tourists, and it runs close to the putative birthplace of the Buddha, at Lumbini, just inside Nepal. There is another crossing at Raxaul (*map 7 A1*) in the state of Bihar, which is the quickest route from Kathmandu into India. There is one more crossing, which goes from eastern Nepal into the northern part of West Bengal, very close to Bagdogra Airport (*map 7 A2*) and the Darjeeling area.

Visas

Almost all visitors to India need a visa. Most travellers come on tourist visas, which are easiest to obtain at the Indian Embassy, High Commission or Consulate in your home country. Some Indian missions have outsourced visa services, and the regulations governing the issuing of visas change frequently. Tourist visas normally take up to a week to be issued, and are usually valid for six months. From 2010, on a trial basis, the nationals of some countries are being issued visas on arrival. Up-to-date information about vi-

sas, as well as downloadable application forms, are available on the Internet—check the website of your local Indian mission. It is extremely hard to get tourist visas extended within India. Only foreigners staying longer than six months need to register in India—so this normally affects those on business, spouse or student visas. The main cities each have a Foreigners Regional Registration Office, where visa issues are dealt with:
• **Delhi:** East Block-VIII, Level-II, Sector-1, R.K. Puram, 110066. T: 011 26711443;
• **Mumbai:** 3rd floor, Special Branch Building, Badruddin Tayabji Lane, behind St. Xavier's College, 400001. T: 022 22621169;
• **Kolkata:** 237, Acharya Jagdish Chandra Bose Road, 700020. T: 033 224700549;
• **Chennai:** Shastri Bhawan, 26, Haddows Road, 600006. T: 044 23454970;
• **Bangalore:** MHA, No. 55, Double Road (near ESI Hospital), Indira Nagar, 560038. T: 080 25297683.

Special permission is required for certain restricted areas, mainly in the northeast and along India's external borders—enquire when applying for your visa. Carry photocopies of your key documents in case of theft or loss.

CLIMATE

India is a country of climatic extremes, with some of the hottest, coldest, wettest and driest places on the planet. All the severely cold places are in the Himalayas, where winter temperatures in Ladakh, for instance, fall as low as -30°C. The hottest places are in the west—in the desert in Rajasthan and, during May and June, in Gujarat, where the temperatures regularly reach above 45°C; and parts of Rajasthan can go several years without a drop of rainfall. By contrast, the hilly northeastern state of Meghalaya has several of the rainiest places in the world, each with a yearly average of over 11m of rain. However, for most of India, it is possible to divide the climate into three seasons: the cool, the hot and the wet.

The cool season: November to March is the best time to visit most parts of India. However, the Himalayan hill-stations are then cold and snow-bound, and Ladakh is bitterly cold and inaccessible by road. In the plains of northern India, the temperatures around New Year can dip down to less than 5°C at night, and it is advisable to take warm clothing. Delhi can be extremely foggy over the New Year period. The south never really gets cold by European or North American standards, and visitors rarely need warm clothing, except in the hill-stations.

The hot season: From mid-March until the arrival of the monsoon rains in June and July is the hottest part of the year in most parts of the country. This is an excellent period to visit India's many hill-stations. It is possible to travel in other parts of the country, but it can be extremely hot in the middle of the day, with temperatures in many places well over 40°C. One advantage is that the crowds at the major tourist locations are much smaller. Air-conditioned accommodation and transport are advisable—as are sunhats. Try to visit unshaded sites in the early morning or just before sunset.

The wet season: The dominant feature of the Indian weather system is the monsoon, on which so much of the largely agricultural economy depends. The monsoon rains, which start in early June in Kerala, are often torrential and regularly flood parts of the country.

The monsoon gradually moves north and west across India, covering most of the subcontinent by mid-July, and begins to peter out by late August. Humidity is very high throughout this period; always carry lots of water, and wear light cotton clothing. Travelling is slower and more difficult at this time, and it is not possible to swim in the sea, but India during the monsoon is at its most lush and beautiful—some returning travellers say that this has become their favourite time to visit. As the monsoon ends, the country has a second, slightly cooler, hot season. Then the eastern states have a second monsoon, between mid-October and early December, while temperatures dip in the rest of the country.

WHAT TO TAKE

Loose-fitting cotton clothing, comfortable walking shoes and a sunhat are essential for travellers to most parts of India. Slip-on shoes or sandals are useful if you plan to visit lots of mosques and temples, where you have to remove your footwear. A wraparound piece of cloth, such as a sarong or a *lungi*, easily purchased in India, is useful as a protection against the sun, or as a makeshift skirt, or a towel. Women will sometimes attract unwelcome attention from local men if they have bare arms or legs, so long skirts and long-sleeved blouses are useful. Getting clothes cleaned is usually quick and cheap—therefore you do not need to carry too much clothing for your entire trip.

Most toiletries and medicines can bought in India, but there are usually only a limited variety of brands available. Some travellers report problems buying tampons, inhalers and contact lens solution in smaller towns. Other useful items that you may wish to take with you are ear-plugs, face-masks (available on airlines) and, if you plan to stay at basic hotels, an impregnated mosquito net, a multi-size bathplug and a small flashlight. Indian electric plugs normally have two or three round pins, and it is possible to buy adaptors locally. Suncream is available in India, but some travellers complain that it is of a poor quality and there is a more limited range of sunscreen factors than in many other countries.

Seek medical advice before you travel. It is important to check that your immunisations are up-to-date. Many travellers get vaccinated against hepatitis A, and take anti-malarial tablets. Your doctor or travel clinic should be able to advise which anti-malarial you should take. It is also advisable to carry a simple first-aid kit.

Most mobile phones with a roaming facility work in India, which has a wide network across towns and cities; and many hotels have wireless Internet connections for laptops.

Many travellers now use international credit and debit cards in India, and get Indian rupees from ATMs, which can be found in most large towns and cities. Indian rupees are hard to find outside India, and most travellers change some money (or travellers' cheques) on arrival at the airport, where exchange rates are usually better than at hotels. US dollars, euros and British pounds are the best currencies to bring to India, and they can be changed at most hotels and some banks.

ARRIVING IN INDIA

Visitors to India are allowed to carry two litres of alcoholic drink and 200 cigarettes. There are no restrictions on how much foreign currency a tourist may bring to India, but anyone carrying more than the equivalent of $10,000 needs to fill in a currency declaration form on arrival. All visitors fill out disembarkation cards with attached customs declarations—these are normally handed out on the plane but are also available in the arrivals area at the airport. Passengers first go through immigration, where there are sometimes very long queues, before picking up their luggage and passing through customs. Hang onto the small tear-off customs declaration form, which you will usually be asked for before you leave the main part of the airport building. After customs, there are small booths with money-changing facilities.

Many hotels will send a car and driver to pick you up from the airport. The driver will normally be waiting for you, carrying a board with your name written on it. Alternatively, hire a pre-paid taxi from one of the booths before you leave the airport building. It is not advisable to take a private taxi from outside the airport. Travellers have reported a variety of taxi scams in which passengers are told that their pre-booked hotels have closed down or been affected by riots—so that the taxi drivers can get a commission from an alternative hotel. Buses are also available from some airports, but their timings are unreliable and they are seldom used by foreign visitors.

TRAVELLING IN INDIA

By air

Air travel in India has become easier and cheaper in recent years. The country has more than 70 commercial airports running scheduled internal flights operated by a growing number of private airlines, as well as the state-owned Air India. Jet and Kingfisher, both privately owned, are the biggest airlines, with a wide selection of routes linking the major cities and some smaller ones; they each have no-frills subsidiaries, JetLite and Kingfisher Red. The cheaper airlines tend to have tighter restrictions on baggage weight (sometimes 15kg), and some do not provide any free refreshments on board. Alcohol is not served on any internal flights in India.

Internal flights can be booked at the same time as your international flights. It is also easy to book tickets in India. If you want to avoid queuing at airline offices, local travel agencies can book your ticket for a small fee, as can many hotel travel desks. It is also fairly simple to book your tickets online, via airline websites or www.yatra.com, but you will normally be expected to print your e-ticket. Most airlines have ticket offices just outside the terminal building, and it is often possible to pick up pre-booked tickets by quoting the six-character reference number (the PNR) and showing your passport. This is particularly useful for last-minute bookings, if you are travelling directly to the airport from somewhere remote, or if you have been unable to find a printer for your e-ticket. All non-resident foreigners pay 'dollar fares', which are significantly higher than the local rate.

Some flights are heavily booked, particularly those to Ladakh, where the land alternatives are either very long or closed because of snow. In late December and early January there are often severe delays on flights in and out of Delhi because of fog.

By rail

India has a large, well-run railway network linking most parts of the country, and many regular visitors to India insist on travelling by train wherever possible. Travelling by train is cheaper than flying, and often more interesting. One gets to see the Indian countryside and meet lots of other travellers, and, best of all, it is an excellent opportunity to meet Indians. Particularly for longer journeys, though, trains are a lot slower than planes. It can also be slightly more complicated getting a ticket, and the popular routes are often booked up weeks in advance. Tickets can be obtained at most railway stations, and not just for trains that leave from that station. Travel agents can also book tickets, and it is also possible to book online (and check on wait-lists) at www.indianrail.gov.in and www.irctc.co.in, where train timetables are also available. A booklet called *Trains at a Glance* is widely available and has details of all the main inter-city services. Major stations in the main cities have special booking counters for foreign travellers called 'tourist bureaux', which can speed up the process of obtaining tickets and reservations.

There are separate quotas for tourists (as well as a number of other quotas), and, if your travel plans are flexible, it is often still possible to turn up at the station and get a ticket on a train that you've been told is fully booked. There is usually a separate, much shorter queue for women. You can confirm your booking and check your seat numbers on passenger lists which are pinned up on platform notice-boards and stuck next to the door to your carriage. If you are unable to get a reserved seat, you can buy a cheap unreserved third-class ticket and speak to the conductor, who will often be able to find you a seat for a small extra fee.

Inter-city and sleeper services: Most foreign visitors use one of two types of train: fast daytime inter-city services, called **Shatabdis**, and inter-city sleeper trains. The best-known Shatabdi service is the Delhi–Bhopal service, which leaves New Delhi station at 6.15am, passes through Agra at 8.15, and reaches Bhopal just after 2pm. Other popular Shatabdi services include trains from Delhi to Chandigarh and Kalka (for Simla), Delhi to Lucknow, Mumbai to Ahmedabad, and Chennai to Bangalore and Mysore.

The best-known sleeper trains are those that leave from Delhi, known as **Rajdhani** (or capital). The Rajdhani trains are long-distance sleeper services between Delhi and major cities, such as Delhi–Mumbai (16½hrs), Delhi–Kolkata (17hrs), Delhi–Bangalore (33hrs) and Delhi–Trivandrum (43hrs). There are also other popular sleeper services on the Mumbai–Hyderabad (15hrs) and Mumbai–Chennai (24hrs) routes. Travellers who travel on first class AC or second class AC tickets are provided with bedding. First class AC normally consists of a two-bed cabin. There are two types of second class AC: two-tier, with four beds in an open cabin; and three-tier, with six beds in an open cabin. There are also beds that run alongside the corridor. The beds are turned back into seats during the daytime.

On-board services: Food and drink are regularly available on all major train services and are brought to your seat. Meals are free on Shatabdi and Rajdhani services, though the food may be too spicy for some Western tastes. Many travellers also bring their own food and drink. At some stations there is usually plenty of time to visit small shops on the platforms. Basic **toilet facilities** are available on the trains—the Indian-style hole-in-the-floor toilets are often cleaner than the Western-style toilets.

Usually wearing red shirts, **licensed porters** are available at all major stations. They will carry your luggage (for up to 50 rupees per bag, depending on the weight), and find your train and seat.

Metro systems: Delhi and Kolkata have metro systems, both of them recommended as efficient means of travelling through these busy cities. Several other cities are constructing their own metro systems. Mumbai also has a well-run suburban train network, which is best avoided at rush hour.

CELEBRATED TRAIN LINES & STATIONS

There are a number of railway lines and stations that have become tourist attractions in themselves. This includes the narrow-gauge mountain railways (known as 'toy trains') to Simla in Himachal Pradesh, Darjeeling in West Bengal and to Ootacamund (Ooty) in Tamil Nadu which together form a UNESCO World Heritage Site. Chattrapati Shivaji Terminus—better known as Victoria Terminus station—in Mumbai is also on the UNESCO list. There are also special luxury trains, such as the Palace on Wheels in Rajasthan, which cater mainly to foreign visitors.

By bus

Travelling by bus tends to be the cheapest, slowest and least comfortable method of getting around in India. Often, though, buses provide the only form of public transport in the hill areas, beyond the reach of trains. Some buses play Hindi movies or music at high volume throughout the journey, so you may want to take an eye-mask and ear-plugs. For greater comfort, try to get seats between the axles in the middle area of the bus. Toilets en route are often rudimentary, and you should take your own toilet paper. Drivers and conductors will often cram in as many people as possible, so don't be surprised if you find yourself sharing what you thought was your seat, and if some of your fellow passengers are on the roof or hanging out of the door. However, Indian bus travellers will often attempt to make you as welcome and comfortable as possible in the circumstances, as well as sharing their food with you.

New luxury air-conditioned buses are being introduced on some tourist and business routes, including Delhi–Jaipur and Mumbai–Pune, these leave more frequently than trains and are less booked-up in advance.

City bus services are normally overcrowded and uncomfortable, and drivers (particularly in the urban centres of north India) are known for their reckless driving.

By car

Many independent travellers in India hire a car and a driver. This is still relatively cheap, especially if several people are travelling together. It is an excellent way of getting to remote places quickly and visiting less well-known sites. It is possible to hire a car for just a few hours or for several days. For the short hires, there is usually an hourly rate, plus an agreed limit to the number of kilometres driven—after which an excess is payable. Air-conditioned cars are more expensive, and it is usually possible to choose from a number of different sizes of car.

For longer journeys, the cost depends on the kilometres travelled, with a daily minimum—usually between 200 and 300km. Always write down the kilometre reading, though note that most hire firms will add the distance from their office. The full payment is normally made at the end, and covers everything except tolls and state road taxes. However, you may be asked to give an advance, so the driver can pay for fuel—and not have to carry large sums of money on him. Overnight charges, known as *batta*, are usually payable direct to the driver—usually between 100 and 200 rupees—and are intended to cover the driver's lodgings and evening meal. However, many drivers prefer either to stay in the car overnight or find a free bed in the hotel in which you are staying, in order to save money. It is normal practice for you to ask the hotel if they have a driver's room—many do. Remember when you are travelling that your driver needs breaks for meals and to use the toilet. If you do not return to the place you hired the car, you will need to pay for the journey back, according to the shortest return route.

Hotels will normally provide contacts for local car hire firms, and there are usually car hire booths at airports. The luxury hotels will often have their own in-house hire cars, which can prove a lot more expensive. Ask for a driver with good local knowledge, particularly if you are travelling to less well-known places. Most drivers will speak a small amount of very basic English.

It is possible to hire self-drive cars in India, but these tend to be more expensive than hiring a car and driver. India is a difficult country to drive in, partly because so many drivers do not obey the rules. Unless you are very experienced at driving in similar conditions, it is best to avoid self-drive cars. As with many former British colonies, driving is on the left, with right-hand drive cars.

By taxi

Most cities have metered taxis, coloured yellow and black, which can be hailed on streets, at taxi stands, and at major transport hubs, such as stations, airports and bus terminals. At many airports and railway stations, prepaid taxis are available. First go to the prepaid booth, and say where you want to go. Pay them the full fare, for which they will give you a slip of paper and, usually, the number of the taxi. Then go to the head of the taxi queue and find your taxi, which should be near the front. When you finish your journey, hand the driver the slip of paper with which he can reclaim the fare.

In many cities, the taxi fares have gone up since the meters were last calibrated. Therefore, drivers carry charts that show the new fare payable against the old meter reading. A supplement is usually added for night rides, or for lots of luggage. Do make sure that the taxi driver puts his meter on at the start of the journey. Some taxi drivers will claim their meter does not work, in which case it is best to look for another taxi. If there isn't one, make sure you agree the fare in advance.

By auto-rickshaw and cycle rickshaw

Partially covered three-wheeled motorised vehicles known as auto-rickshaws are found in most parts of India. They usually have meters, and are a quick and cheap way of travelling. They do not have doors, just a canvas roof, and are not really comfortable for more than two people—though three can usually be squeezed in. They can get very cold in winter, and the roof does not always keep out the monsoon rain. They are also known as scooters and autos. As with taxis, the drivers will often say that their meter does not work—if that happens, agree the fare before you set off.

Ordinary rickshaws are tricycles with a raised backseat on which two passengers can sit. They are normally open, but have a basic rain/sun cover, which can be pulled over the passenger seat. They do not have meters, so agree a fare in advance.

By motorcycle and bicycle

It is possible to rent motorbikes and bicycles in some tourist locations, but they can be dangerous in the big cities and on national highways. Some travellers actually purchase motorbikes and bicycles and sell them at the end of their trip.

Road names and maps

In several of the large cities, and particularly in Mumbai and Kolkata, many streets are best known by their old colonial names. However, maps and written documents (such as hotel reservation confirmation slips) usually carry the new, less well-known names. The spelling of place names can differ enormously in different sources. If all this causes a problem, it is best to stop and ask. Pharmacies are good places to find English-speakers who can help you out.

Good multi-page city maps published by Eicher are available from bookshops throughout India. Eicher also publishes a useful all-India road map. Detailed maps of the Indian countryside are not widely available. TTK publishes fold-up state maps. Large parts of India are well covered by Google Maps, and this can be a useful tool for planning trips or getting precise locations.

ACCOMMODATION

There is a huge variety of accommodation available to travellers in India. The choice ranges from some of the most luxurious and beautiful hotels in the world to some of cheapest backpacker hostels. In some places, particularly in Rajasthan, the hotels can be tourist attractions in themselves.

There are a number of well-known national and international hotel groups, including the Taj, Oberoi, Sheraton, Park, Neemrana and Hyatt, with a reputation for high-quality rooms and service. The Taj and the Oberoi often have at least two hotels in the large cities—one aimed at business travellers, the other for tourists. The Taj group has started a separate chain of modern, clean, cheap hotels under the name Ginger. The Neemrana group is known for converting heritage properties into beautiful hotels, which are very luxurious—but which don't have all the trappings of many modern international hotels, such as TVs or room service.

Many travellers get their travel agents back home to make their bookings, but if you want greater flexibility it is usually possible to make your booking directly by phone or email. It is normal, even in the most expensive hotels, to bargain—and the rate you get will normally depend on occupancy levels. Room rates will also vary dramatically over the year, depending on the season. The same room in a good Goa hotel during the monsoon might be several times more expensive at New Year. Most hotels accept international credit cards, and provide (often expensive) currency exchange facilities. You may often be quoted prices without taxes, and the full rate will be significantly more.

Many mid-range hotels do not have central air-conditioning, and will instead often have a quite noisy AC unit in the room. Almost all rooms will have a fan, and an attached bathroom. Ensure that the electronic equipment (TV, AC, fridge, telephone) works when you check in. Also try to avoid rooms overlooking driveways or that are next to a mosque or a temple, to avoid noise in the early mornings. Keep a torch with you in case of power cuts. Most hotels provide a laundry service. Luxury hotels will have business centres, and even some mid-range hotels now have wireless Internet connections. Some hotels have exorbitant rates for international phone calls, so check before you dial.

EATING & DRINKING

India has a great many cuisines, similar in diversity to what one might encounter in a trip across Europe. Many hotels provide buffet meals that are often good value, and have a large range of different foods—usually with Indian, European and Chinese selections. The Indian food in these buffets tends to be less spicy (blander to the Indian palate). Don't eat anything that does not look freshly cooked, and if in doubt order from the *à la carte* menu. It is best to avoid green salads and cut fruit, unless you can be sure they have been washed with clean water.

If you want to eat real Indian food, try local restaurants. Look for the popular ones, which are more likely to have very fresh food because of the turnover of customers. In many places, a *thali*—a complete meal served on a steel plate, with lots of different dishes in small steel bowls—is a very good way to sample the local cuisine.

When travelling in the countryside, roadside cafés, known as *dhabas*, offer simple meals. *Dhaba* food is often superb, with delicious fresh breads, rice, vegetables, dal and sometimes meat. They also serve refreshing sweet milky tea. Fruit that is easily peeled, such as bananas and local soft-skinned oranges, is also recommended for journeys.

Drinking

Dirty water is a major source of disease in India. Do not drink water from a tap or a well or a stream. It is advisable to carry bottled mineral water wherever you go, though it is also safe to drink 'Aquaguard' water, which is tap water that has been filtered and cleaned. Do not have ice unless you are sure it has been made from mineral or properly filtered water.

Fresh fruit juice is widely available, but make sure it has not been mixed with unsafe water. Hot tea and coffee are safe, as is the wide range of bottled soft drinks available throughout the country. Coconut water, usually drunk through a straw from a freshly opened coconut, is also safe.

Alcohol can be purchased in many restaurants and in 'wine and beer' shops across the country. Locally brewed beers such as Kingfisher and Cobra are widely available, and better value than imported beers. High-quality Western wines and spirits can be found in luxury hotels and restaurants. There is a rapidly growing Indian wine industry—in which Sula and Grover have a reputation for quality. There are also several Indian whiskies, brandies and rums (of variable quality), as well as a wide range of local alcoholic beverages.

Some states have 'dry' days, on which no alcohol is sold. Election days and public holidays are often dry, while no alcohol is served at all in Gujarat, except inside bedrooms in luxury hotels.

Smoking: It is illegal to smoke in many public places in India, particularly restaurants, although some Indians ignore these rules.

HEALTH

There is a wide range of health issues that travellers to India could potentially face, though most visitors actually suffer little more than a sore throat or a mild stomach upset. However, it is essential to take health issues seriously. This means protecting yourself from dirty food and water, from diseases carried by mosquitoes, and from the sun. Ask your hotel to find you an English-speaking doctor if you fall ill. If you have any doubt at all about what is wrong with you, do not self-medicate. Local doctors and pharmacists are more likely to recognise your symptoms than you are. Most medicines are easily available over the counter in India, and it is easy and quick to get blood and stool tests. Private clinics tend to be more reliable than government-run clinics.

If you feel a little unwell, eat simple plain food such as rice, breads, yoghurt and bananas—these are widely available, even in remote areas. Eat only cooked food, or food that you can peel. You could also ask for *kichri*, a safe and unspiced mixture of rice and lentils, traditionally fed to sick people in India. Eggs are also available in most places. Do not try to live off biscuits. Take lots of fluids, and carry oral rehydration tablets or sachets. For more serious stomach problems consult a doctor, who may recommend a stool test, as well as a course of antibiotics. Among the more serious illnesses—fortunately developed by only a small minority of travellers—are dysentery, giardia and tapeworms. Seek medical advice for all these conditions. Hepatitis A (widely known as jaundice in India, though this actually describes only one of the symptoms) is widespread in the region, and it is advised that you get a vaccination before you travel.

Malaria, Japanese encephalitis, dengue fever and chikungunya are serious diseases carried by mosquitoes. A vaccination for Japanese encephalitis is available and is recommended. Most travellers use anti-malarial tablets, but you should seek medical advice on which tablets are most appropriate. It is best of all, though not always easy, to avoid being bitten. Use anti-mosquito sprays or roll-ons; citronella oil is a very good local substitute. Cover your arms and legs close to sunset, when you have the greatest chance of being bitten. Mosquito coils are widely available and very effective at keeping insects away outdoors, although they can be a little pungent and smoky. Electronic plug-in devices such as 'All-Nite' are used by many hotels to keep mosquitoes away, and are widely available at household stores. Some travellers who plan to stay in basic hotels carry their own insecticide-impregnated mosquito nets.

Travellers often underestimate the strength of the scorching summer sun in India, and may consequently suffer from sunburn or heat stroke. Wear a sunhat, use sun cream and drink plenty of fluids to counter the effects of the heat and sunlight. Avoid tight clothing and artificial fabrics as these can encourage the spread of fungal infections. If you are travelling at altitude, make sure you rest on arrival. Lack of acclimatisation to lower oxygen levels at altitude can lead to the syndrome known as acute mountain sickness (AMS), causing severe headaches and dizziness.

RESPONSIBLE TOURISM

India has many people living in poverty. A small minority of them are beggars, and most foreign visitors can expect to encounter beggars early on in their trip. Beggars often congregate at major tourist sites, knowing that foreigners who are new to the country are not always aware of the value of the currency. Often, a foreigner who gives money to one person will then be mobbed by many more beggars, all demanding money. There are cases where beggars have deliberately harmed themselves, knowing that visible injuries will increase their earnings from soft-hearted visitors. There are also reports of children who have been maimed as a way of increasing their income as beggars. Travellers are therefore advised not to give money directly to people who are begging. Instead, give nutritious local food or donate money to NGOs who work with the poor in India.

Child labour is officially illegal in India, but also very widespread—particularly at smaller hotels and restaurants frequented by travellers. You can help reduce the acceptability of child labour by calmly telling the hotel or restaurant manager that you disapprove of the practice.

Several India-based NGOs accept online donations; they include Save the Children India (savethechildren.in), Child Relief and You, better known as CRY (cry.org) and Helpage (helpageindia.org).

MONEY

The unit of currency is the Indian rupee. There are 100 paisa in a rupee, but paisa are of such low value that you are unlikely to encounter them except as a 50 paisa coin. One, two, and five rupee coins are in wide circulation, as are banknotes worth 5, 10, 20, 50, 100, 500 and 1,000 rupees. Do not accept damaged banknotes as you will have trouble getting shops or taxis to take them. If you obtain money from a bank or money changer, you will often be given a large stack of notes that are stapled together. Open them carefully, or ask for help, so that you don't tear them. The 100 and 500 rupee notes look similar, so take care when using them.

Travellers' cheques and cash—particularly in US dollars, pounds and euros—can be changed at most good hotels (check the exchange rate, though), banks and specialist currency exchange bureaux. If you think you may need to reconvert rupees at the end of your visit, make sure you keep your encashment certificates. Banks are best visited in the morning (9–12), and are usually open every day except Sunday and public holidays. It is possible to have money wired to you via money changers affiliated with Western Union or other international agencies for remitting funds.

International credit and debit cards can be used in larger establishments frequented by tourists and other foreigners. ATM machines are available in all cities and many large towns, and accept international credit and debit cards. If you are travelling in rural areas, take plenty of cash in Indian rupees.

Tipping

In many places, a service charge is already added to your bill. If not, add 10 percent. It is normal to give hotel porters and doormen a tip of 20 rupees, though some richer Indians will give significantly more. Carry small change for tips, particularly for the people who guard visitors' shoes outside many religious buildings. Anyone who cuts your hair or gives you a massage will expect a tip. It is normal to give a substantial tip to servants at the end of a stay in a private house in India—ask your host for advice on how much.

COMMUNICATIONS

Mobile phones work in all major cities, most towns and in many parts of the countryside. Many mobiles brought from Western countries are locked into a particular network, and it is usually possible to get these unlocked in India (though this may break your user agreement with your phone company). Otherwise, purchase a local phone and local SIM card. There are sometimes places, particularly in Delhi, where the phone signal is blocked or cut temporarily for security reasons. There are also privately-run call booths throughout the country which are much cheaper than hotel telephones.

The international code for India is +91. When dialling India from abroad drop the 0 at the start of the local city/district code. To make an international call from India dial 00 and then the country code. To dial an Indian mobile number (normally 10 digits starting with a 9) outside the city you are in—prefix the number with a 0. To dial an Indian landline number (usually 8 digits) from a mobile phone, add the local city/district code.

Most cities have Internet cafés, with cheap access to high-speed connections. In smaller places, power cuts are common, so be careful that you do not lose long pieces of unsaved text. Wireless connections for laptops are common in urban hotels, and it is possible to purchase a roaming Internet service, via a plug-in card or stick, from local ISPs.

Time zones: All of India is in one time zone, 5½hrs ahead of GMT, 10½hrs ahead of EST, and 2½hrs behind Singapore Standard Time.

Media

India has a large number of English-language newspapers and magazines, widely available in urban areas. There are several local English-language TV news channels (CNN-IBN and NDTV both have a good reputation), and BBC World Service radio is available on shortwave throughout the country and on the Internet.

SOCIAL ETIQUETTE & VISITING PLACES

Most Indians are extremely helpful to travellers, and will often go out of their way to provide assistance and hospitality to foreigners. They also expect to be treated with respect. When faced—as you undoubtedly will be—with frustrating situations, unexplained confusion or delays, be determinedly polite and do not lose your temper. Also, do not be surprised if people ask you very personal questions within minutes of meeting you.

Although many men now shake hands, the Indian traditional greeting involves the pressing of the upright palms together at chest level. Most Indians will be pleased to see that you have learnt this greeting. Use your right hand for giving or receiving, since traditionally in India the left hand is seen as less clean, because it is used for washing after going to the toilet.

It is advisable not to wear revealing or tight clothing, particularly for women, for whom it will draw unwanted attention from some Indian men. Nudity is not allowed on beaches. Displays of public intimacy are not usually considered appropriate.

Visiting places of worship

Different places of worship have different rules about clothing, but on the whole it is advisable to dress conservatively. In temples and mosques, and even some churches, you will be expected to take off your shoes at the entrance. At some temples you may be asked to remove all leather garments such as belts or watch straps. In some mosques and Muslim religious complexes, women and men have segregated areas of worship—and these should be respected. In some places, non-Hindus are not allowed into functioning temples (particularly in Kerala and Orissa), and mosques are often closed to non-Muslims during times of prayer. Most places of worship do not charge visitors for entry, but it is normal practice to put some money in the donation box.

Visiting monuments and museums

Most of the important historical monuments are run by the Archaeological Survey of India and charge a two-tier entry fee: one for Indians (and resident foreigners); and one that is much higher for non-resident foreigners. At the most popular sites, there are separate queues as well. In some places, you will be charged a separate fee for a camera. Guides are normally available at the entrance to monuments. It is best to agree a fee in advance. Opening hours for monuments vary across the country and are often subject to change at short notice.

India's main cities and state capitals all have museums, with impressive collections of antiquities that are often very poorly displayed or labelled. They are usually closed on one day a week, normally either Monday or Friday, as well as on public holidays.

PUBLIC HOLIDAYS & FESTIVALS

India has three fixed national holidays and many other religious and regional holidays, most of the dates of which vary each year. The official national holidays are Republic Day (26th Jan), Independence Day (15th Aug) and Gandhi's birthday (2nd Oct).

The many major religious festivals (*see pp. 59–70*) include Diwali (Oct/Nov), Dussehra (Sept/Oct) and Holi (Feb/March) for Hindus, Bakr Eid and Eid ul Fitr for Muslims; Guru Nanak's birthday for Sikhs (Nov); Mahavir's birthday for Jains (March/April), Buddha's birthday for Buddhists (May/June); Christmas and Easter for Christians, and Navroz, or Parsee New Year.

There is also a large number of cultural festivals, fairs and events. These include film festivals in Delhi, Mumbai and Kerala; theatre festivals in Delhi and Mumbai; the famous snake-boat races in Kerala; and a large number of dance and music festivals in different parts of the country. Jaipur has an annual book festival in January, while Delhi even has a mango festival in July. The dates of these vary each year, and can be checked online or with the Tourist Information Bureaux.

OTHER INFORMATION

Shopping

The big cities have large air-conditioned shopping malls, with many Western brand names, and where international credit and debit cards will be accepted. Smaller places may have a central market area. Shops selling a particular kind of item are often concentrated in one part of a city or town—for instance, there may be a big market that is particularly good for, say, electronic items or clothing. Chemists or pharmacies can usually be found near hospitals and clinics.

It is normal to bargain in many shops, particularly those selling handicrafts, and most sellers will set out to get higher prices from foreigners. Decide first whether you really want an item, and the maximum you are willing to pay, before you start bargaining; if you are not sure, check the prices at other shops. Shopkeepers will often serve you tea or soft drinks—and hope that their hospitality will make it hard for you to leave empty-handed. Be aware that tourist guides and taxi drivers who take you to a particular shop will often get a commission from the shop owner. If prices are fixed, as at many government shops, there will normally be a notice saying so, or you will be told.

Photography

You must not take pictures of military installations, and there are often restrictions on photography in train stations and airports. Ask before you take a photograph in a place of worship—sometimes this is not allowed or sometimes a fee has to be paid—and before you photograph individuals. Some people, particularly women in rural areas, do not want to be photographed. Elsewhere, especially near major tourist sites, you will find people who will demand a payment if you photograph them. Many tourist attractions charge an extra fee for the use of cameras, with higher rates for video cameras.

Simple photographic accessories such as memory cards and traditional film are widely available throughout the county. Many Internet cafés will back up your photos onto CD for you. The printing of photographs in India is relatively cheap and, in the big cities, of high quality.

Electricity

The electric current is 220–240 volts AC. India uses round two- or three-pin plugs, and adaptors are widely available. In many places the electricity supply is erratic, with frequent power surges and cuts, particularly in summer. Most good hotels have back-up power. It is still best to carry a small torch for emergencies.

Toilets

Toilet facilities outside the cities are often very rudimentary—and where they exist are often of the hole-in-the-floor variety. There is usually a supply of water, but no paper, so bring your own. In rural areas, most people use the fields.

GLOSSARY

Amalaka, disc-like shape, often ribbed, at the top of a *shikhara* (*qv*) tower

Apsara, a celestial nymph

Ashram, spiritual centre or retreat; usually Hindu

Ashurkhana, congregational hall used by Shia Muslims during Moharram (*qv*) (*see also Imambara*)

Avatar, another form of a god; mainly used of the Hindu god Vishnu, who according to many traditions had ten avatars (*see Dasavatar*)

Azan, the Muslim call to prayer

Bagh, a garden

Bangala, bangaldar, a gently curved roof like those used on thatched huts and many buildings in Bengal

Baoli, baori, a large well, with steps leading down to the water; a step-well

Baradari, a pavilion, traditionally rectangular, with twelve openings

Basti, 1) a Jain temple; 2) a low-income urban settlement or slum

Begum, a Muslim woman, usually of high rank

Bharat, the Hindi word for India

Bhavan, building, but sometimes used as a synonym for palace

BJP, the Bharatiya Janata Party (or Indian People's Party), one of India's largest political parties

Bodhisattva, a Buddhist saviour; in Mahayana Buddhism, one who has achieved enlightenment

Brahmin, a member of the Brahmin caste; traditionally priests and scholars by occupation

Cenotaph, literally 'empty tomb'; often used in India to describe the more elaborate 'upper' tomb, designed for public access, at Muslim mausolea. The body is normally buried in a lower chamber, accessible by a separate underground passage

Chaitya, a vaulted, horseshoe-shaped Buddhist prayer hall

Char-bagh, a Mughal-style formal garden taking the form of a square or rectangle divided into four parts

Chattri, literally umbrella; used to describe 1) a small ornamental pavilion or kiosk with a domed roof; 2) a memorial to a Hindu ruler, often in the form of a small pavilion

Chorten, a mound, normally a hemisphere, used by Buddhists as a reliquary and a memorial; the term *chorten* is normally used in Ladakh, while the word stupa (*qv*) is normally used elsewhere in India

Chowk, a courtyard in a palace; a traffic intersection; a town square or meeting place

Dargah, a shrine containing the tomb of a Muslim holy man

Darshan, the act of seeing, and therefore venerating, a Hindu god

Darwaza, a door

Dasavatar, the ten avatars, or forms, of Vishnu—often shown together in Hindu art

Dev, devi, god and goddess, respectively

Dhaba, roadside café

Dharamsala, rest-house for pilgrims

Diwan-i Am, public audience hall of a ruler

Diwan-i Khas, private audience hall of a ruler

Du-khang, Buddhist assembly hall and temple in Ladakh

Durbar, royal court or royal gathering; the room for this in a palace is known as the durbar hall

Dwarapala, painted or sculpted door guardian

Firman, royal ordinance

Garbha-griha, literally 'womb-chamber'; the inner sanctuary of a Hindu temple, housing the main icon

Garh, a fort

Gavaksha, the horseshoe-shaped motif used on many Hindu temples

Ghat, 1) a (usually broad) flight of steps on the side of a lake or river; 2) a range of hills

Gompa, Buddhist monastery in Ladakh

Gon-khang, a Ladakhi Buddhist temple housing guardian deities or protectors

Gopura, a towering pyramid-shaped gateway to a southern Indian Hindu temple

Gufa, a cave

Gumbad, a dome

Gurudwara, Sikh temple

Hammam, a bath-house

Haveli, a large house with one or more inner courtyards

Hero stone, a memorial stone, often with images of the dead person

Idgah, in Islam, a large prayer area, normally open-air, used at times of major festivals such as Eid

Imambara, congregational hall used by Shia Muslims during Moharram (*qv*) (*see also Ashurkhana*)

Indo-Saracenic, a syncretic style of architecture bringing together elements of Hindu, Muslim and European Gothic styles

Iwan, the high-arched vaulted central prayer area in a mosque

Jali, latticed or pierced screen, usually made of stone

Jama Masjid (normally translated as Friday mosque), usually the main mosque in an urban area, and the most important location for the weekly congregational prayers held on a Friday

Jataka tales, popular tales based on the lives of the Buddha's previous incarnations

Jauhar, the mass suicide, usually by burning, of women belonging to the court of a ruler defeated in battle

Jharokha, a decorated overhanging balcony

Jyotirlingam, literally, a 'phallus of light'; used to refer to one of twelve temples containing a special Shiva lingam, said to have materialised out of light

Kalasha, a pot-like shape on the spire of the tower on a Hindu temple

Kshatriya, a Hindu caste; traditionally described as the warrior caste

Kund, a lake

Lha-khang, Buddhist temple in Ladakh

Lingam, a phallus-shaped representation of the Hindu god Shiva

Madrasa, literally 'a place of study', though normally used to describe an Islamic religious school

Mahabharata, one of the two great Hindu epics (*see p.57*)

Mahal, a palace

Makara, a sea-monster used in Hindu sculpture and paintings

Mandala, a wheel-like circular diagram that is used by Buddhists as an aid to meditation

Mandapa, the assembly hall to a Hindu temple

Mandir, a Hindu temple

Mantra, a chant or saying used by Hindus and Buddhists

Masjid, a mosque

Maulana or Maulvi, an Islamic religious scholar

Mihrab, prayer niche facing Mecca on the interior wall of a mosque

Minar, a tower

Minbar, the pulpit of a mosque

Mohalla, used to describe a particular area or neighbourhood of a city

Moharram, the month of mourning for Shia Muslims

Mudra, the symbolic hand gesture made by gods and *bodhisattvas* (*qv*) in Hindu and Buddhist art

Muezzin, the person who makes the call to prayer at a mosque

Naga, a snake—often used in reference to representations of traditional snake-gods

Nataraja, the form of Shiva as 'Lord of the Dance', widely used in south India bronzes

Om, a sacred syllable and symbol used by Hindus and Buddhists

Parikrama, the clockwise circumambulation of a Hindu or Buddhist temple or religious site

Pietra dura, from the Italian 'hard stone'; used in India to denote the inlay of precious and semi-precious stones into marble, as at the Taj Mahal

Pol, a gate

Rajput, from Sanskrit, meaning originally 'sons of kings'; a north Indian caste with strong martial traditions, to which most of Rajasthan's former royal families belong

Ramayana, one of the two great Hindu epics (*see p. 56*)

Rigveda, the earliest of the Hindu sacred texts see (*see p. 56*)

Sagar, a lake

Samadhi, a memorial built on or near the site of the funeral pyre of a prominent Hindu

Sati, previously known as 'suttee' in English; the supposedly voluntary suicide by burning traditionally carried out by Hindu widows; the practice is now illegal. Sati stones and sati handprints are memorials marking the occurrence of sati; widely seen at old forts and palaces in Rajasthan

Serai, sometimes 'sarai' and 'caravansarai'; a resting place for travellers, pilgrims and armies

Shahadah, the first of the five pillars of Islam, the declaration that 'there is no God but God, and that Muhammad is the messenger of God' (*see p. 69*)

Shaivite, dedicated to the worship of Shiva

Shikhara, the tower of a Hindu temple

Stupa, a Buddhist memorial mound; usually a hemisphere

Sultanate, in architecture, pertaining to the pre-Mughal Muslim style

Thali, a dining plate, normally made of steel, with several different food items, often in small bowls or saucers

Thangka, an illustrated Buddhist scroll, usually depicting religious scenes and often used as a wall-hanging

Tirtha, literally 'a ford', but also used to describe places of pilgrimage for Hindus and Jains

Tirthankar, literally 'ford-maker'; one of the 24 Jain saviours, or prophets

Torana, ornate gateway leading to a temple or ceremonial site

Trimurti, the Hindu trinity: Brahma, Vishnu and Shiva (*see p. 47*)

Vaishnavite, pertaining to the worship of Vishnu

Vav, a step-well (*see baoli*)

Yakshi, a female attendant; often depicted in Hindu and Buddhist art

Yogini, a goddess, usually a minor deity, who sometimes attends a more important female god

Zenana, the women's quarters in a palace or other residence

INDEX

Major or explanatory references, where many page numbers are cited, are given in bold; picture references are rendered in italics. Gods, *bodhisattvas*, avatars and *tirthankars* are referenced only to pages where their role or general significance is explained.

D

ATLAS OF INDIA

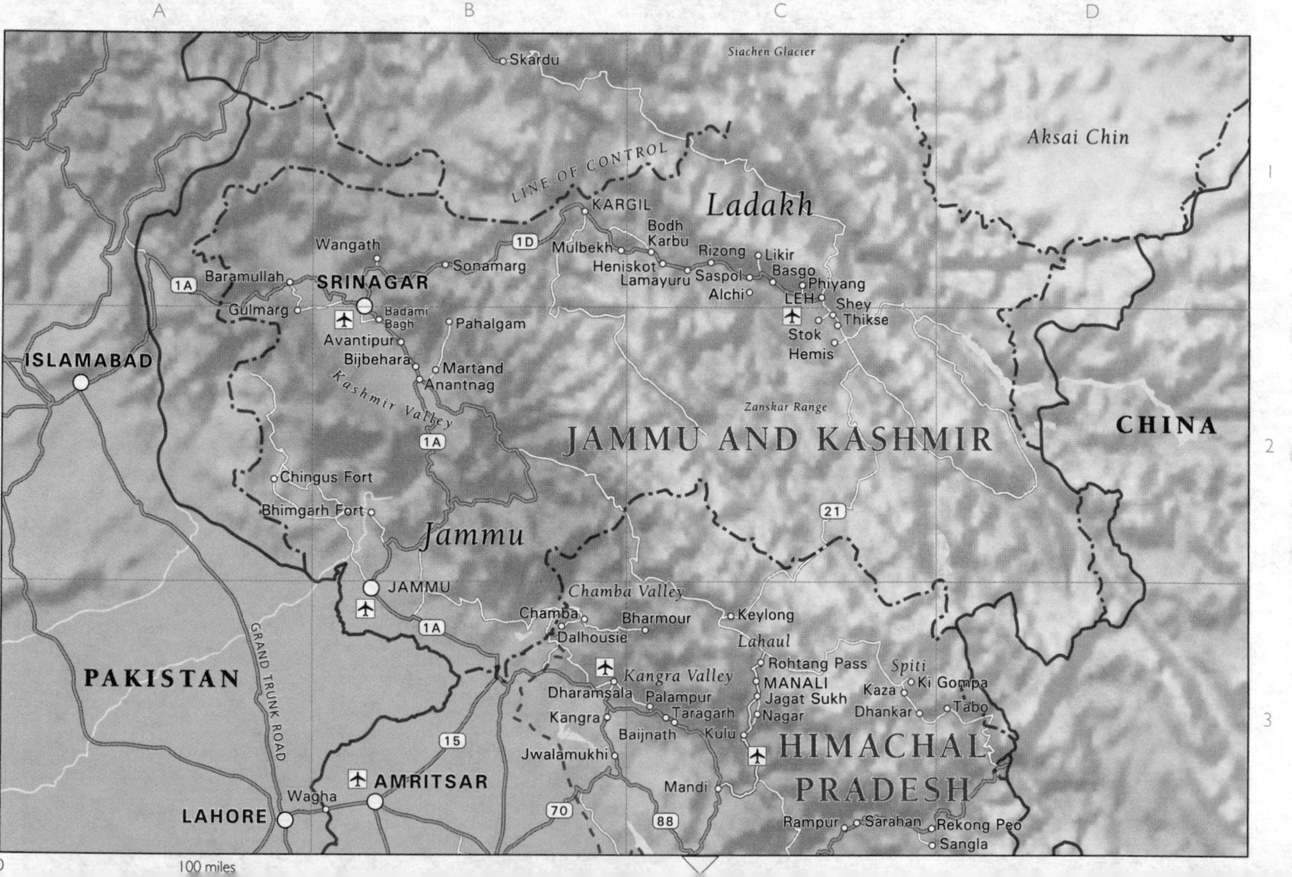
A
B
C
D
1
2
3
Siachen Glacier
Skardu
Aksai Chin
LINE OF CONTROL
KARGIL
Ladakh
Bodh Karbu
Wangath
1D
Mulbekh
Heniskot
Lamayuru
Rizong
Likir
Basgo
Phiyang
Saspol
Alchi
LEH
Shey
Thikse
Stok
Hemis
Sonamarg
1A
Baramullah
SRINAGAR
Gulmarg
Badami Bagh
Pahalgam
Avantipur
Bijbehara
Martand
Anantnag
Kashmir Valley
ISLAMABAD
Zanskar Range
CHINA
JAMMU AND KASHMIR
1A
Chingus Fort
Bhimgarh Fort
21
Jammu
JAMMU
Chamba Valley
Chamba
Bharmour
Keylong
Dalhousie
Lahaul
1A
Rohtang Pass
Spiti
Kangra Valley
MANALI
Kaza
Ki Gompa
Dharamsala
Palampur
Jagat Sukh
Dhankar
Tabo
Kangra
Taragarh
Nagar
Baijnath
Kulu
PAKISTAN
GRAND TRUNK ROAD
15
HIMACHAL PRADESH
Jwalamukhi
AMRITSAR
Mandi
Wagha
LAHORE
70
88
Rampur
Sarahan
Rekong Peo
Sangla
0
100 miles

MAP 2

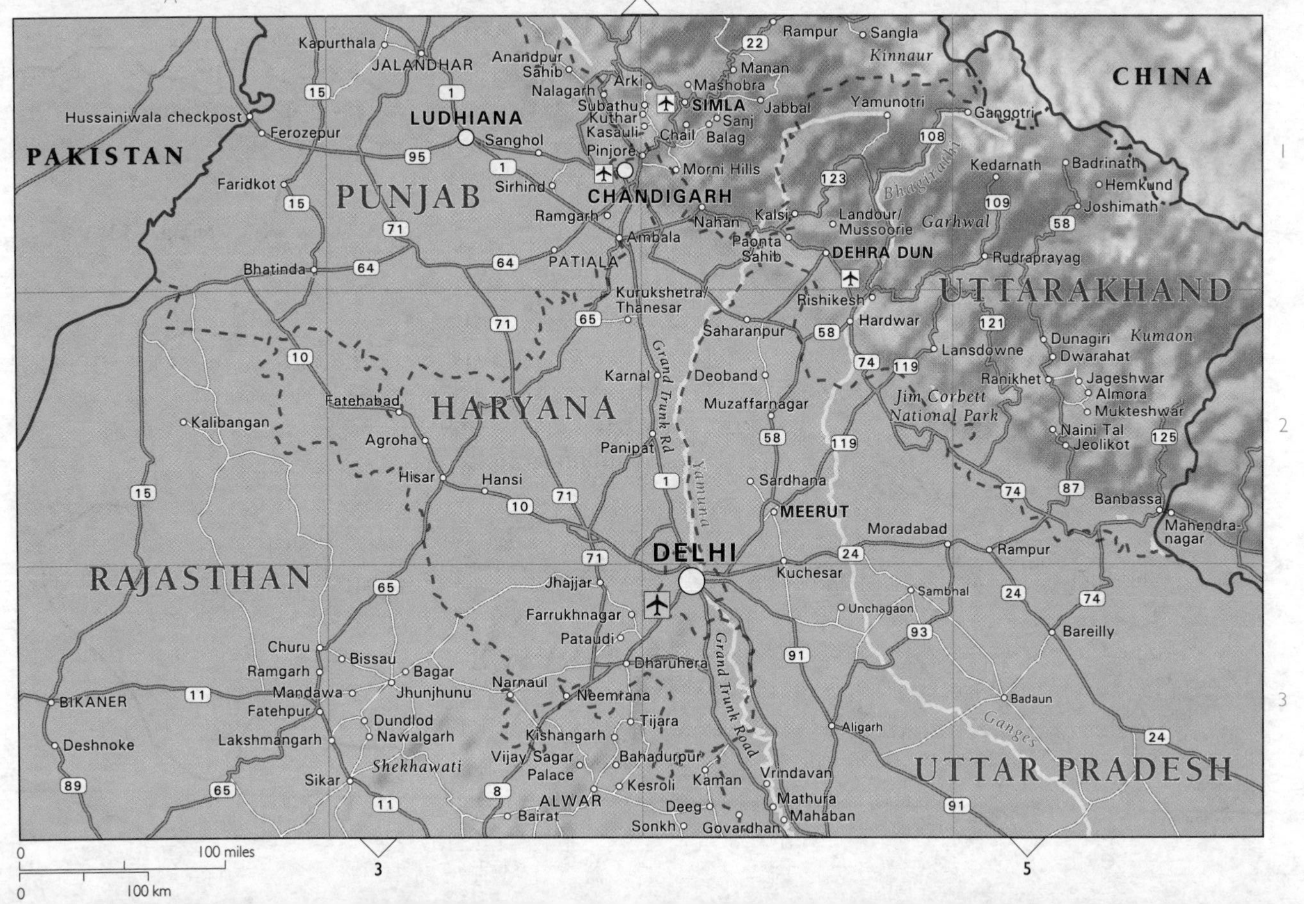

CHINA
PAKISTAN
PUNJAB
HARYANA
RAJASTHAN
UTTARAKHAND
UTTAR PRADESH
DELHI
CHANDIGARH
LUDHIANA
SIMLA
DEHRA DUN
MEERUT
JALANDHAR
PATIALA
BIKANER
ALWAR
Kapurthala
Hussainiwala checkpost
Ferozepur
Faridkot
Bhatinda
Anandpur Sahib
Nalagarh
Arki
Subathu
Kuthar
Kasauli
Pinjore
Sanghol
Sirhind
Ramgarh
Ambala
Mashobra
Manan
Rampur
Sangla
Kinnaur
Jabbal
Sanj
Chail
Balag
Morni Hills
Nahan
Kalsi
Paonta Sahib
Landour/ Mussoorie
Garhwal
Yamunotri
Gangotri
Bhagirathi
Kedarnath
Badrinath
Hemkund
Joshimath
Rudraprayag
Rishikesh
Hardwar
Kurukshetra/ Thanesar
Saharanpur
Deoband
Muzaffarnagar
Karnal
Grand Trunk Rd
Panipat
Yamuna
Sardhana
Lansdowne
Dunagiri
Kumaon
Dwarahat
Ranikhet
Jageshwar
Almora
Mukteshwar
Jim Corbett National Park
Naini Tal
Jeolikot
Banbassa
Mahendra-nagar
Moradabad
Rampur
Kuchesar
Sambhal
Unchagaon
Bareilly
Badaun
Ganges
Aligarh
Kalibangan
Fatehabad
Agroha
Hisar
Hansi
Jhajjar
Farrukhnagar
Pataudi
Dharuhera
Grand Trunk Road
Neemrana
Tijara
Narnaul
Kishangarh
Bahadurpur
Vijay Sagar Palace
Kesroli
Kaman
Vrindavan
Mathura
Mahaban
Deeg
Govardhan
Sonkh
Bairat
Churu
Bissau
Bagar
Ramgarh
Mandawa
Jhunjhunu
Fatehpur
Dundlod
Nawalgarh
Lakshmangarh
Shekhawati
Sikar
Deshnoke
22
15
1
95
1
15
71
64
64
71
65
10
71
10
71
65
15
11
89
65
11
8
1
58
58
119
74
119
121
108
123
109
58
125
87
74
24
24
74
93
91
24
91
0
100 miles
0
100 km
1
2
3
5

MAP 3

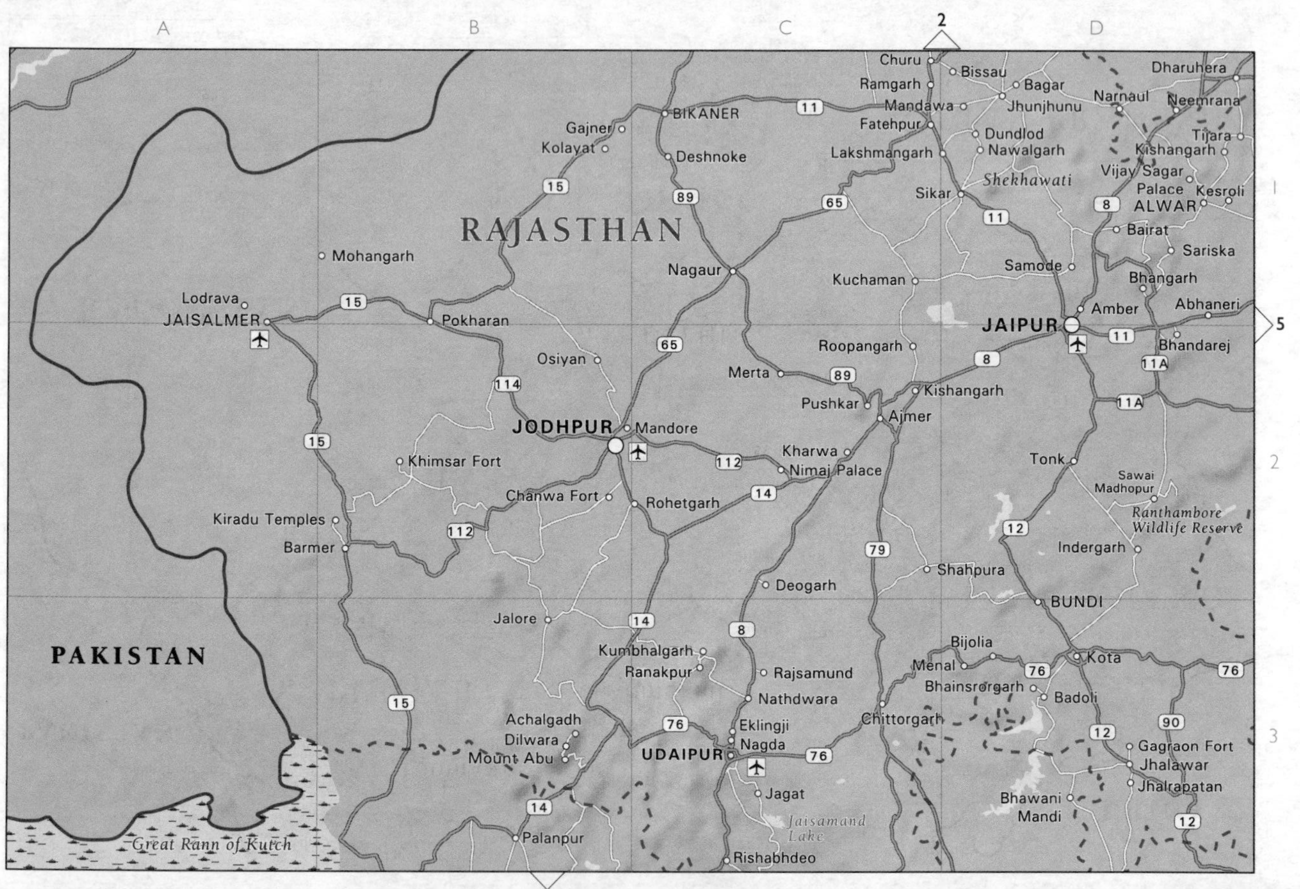
RAJASTHAN
PAKISTAN
Great Rann of Kutch
JAISALMER
Lodrava
Mohangarh
Pokharan
Gajner
Kolayat
BIKANER
Deshnoke
Nagaur
Osiyan
JODHPUR
Mandore
Khimsar Fort
Chanwa Fort
Rohetgarh
Kiradu Temples
Barmer
Jalore
Kumbhalgarh
Ranakpur
Achalgadh
Dilwara
Mount Abu
Palanpur
UDAIPUR
Eklingji
Nagda
Jagat
Jaisamand Lake
Rishabhdeo
Rajsamund
Nathdwara
Deogarh
Chittorgarh
Merta
Pushkar
Ajmer
Kishangarh
Kharwa
Nimaj Palace
Roopangarh
Kuchaman
Churu
Ramgarh
Mandawa
Fatehpur
Lakshmangarh
Bissau
Bagar
Jhunjhunu
Dundlod
Nawalgarh
Shekhawati
Sikar
Samode
JAIPUR
Amber
Bhangarh
Abhaneri
Bhandarej
Bairat
Sariska
ALWAR
Palace
Kesroli
Vijay Sagar
Kishangarh
Tijara
Narnaul
Neemrana
Dharuhera
Tonk
Sawai Madhopur
Ranthambore Wildlife Reserve
Indergarh
Shahpura
BUNDI
Bijolia
Menal
Bhainsrorgarh
Kota
Badoli
Gagraon Fort
Jhalawar
Jhalrapatan
Bhawani Mandi
15
89
65
11
8
11A
114
112
14
79
12
76
90
A
B
C
D
1
2
3
5

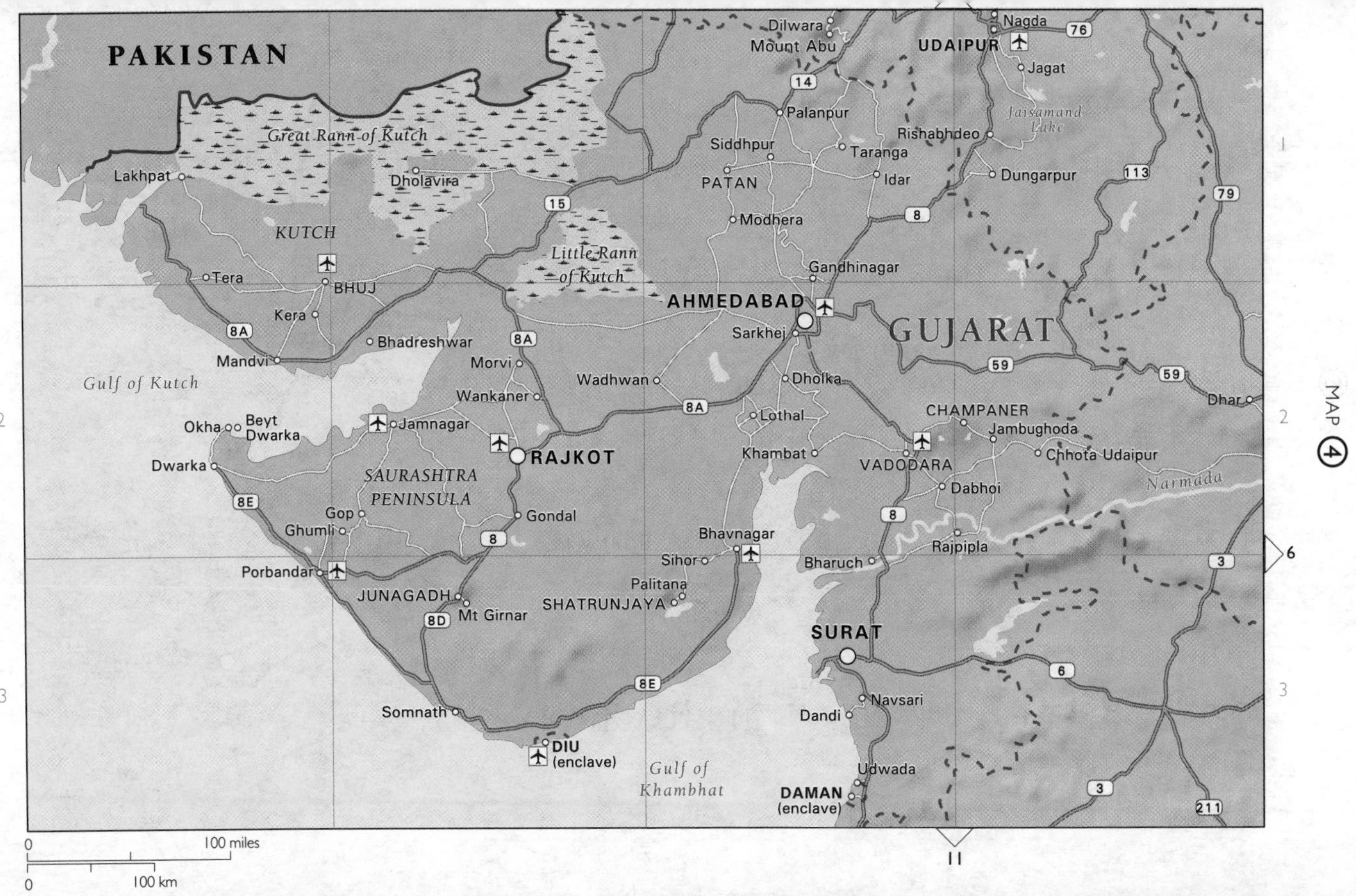

MAP 4
PAKISTAN
GUJARAT
Great Rann of Kutch
Little Rann of Kutch
KUTCH
Gulf of Kutch
Gulf of Khambhat
SAURASHTRA PENINSULA
Jaisamand Lake
Narmada
Dilwara
Mount Abu
Nagda
UDAIPUR
Jagat
Palanpur
Rishabhdeo
Siddhpur
Taranga
Dungarpur
PATAN
Idar
Lakhpat
Dholavira
Modhera
Gandhinagar
Tera
BHUJ
AHMEDABAD
Kera
Sarkhej
Bhadreshwar
Mandvi
Morvi
Wadhwan
Dholka
Wankaner
Dhar
Okha
Beyt Dwarka
Jamnagar
Lothal
CHAMPANER
Jambughoda
RAJKOT
Khambat
VADODARA
Chhota Udaipur
Dwarka
Dabhoi
Gop
Gondal
Ghumli
Bhavnagar
Rajpipla
Sihor
Bharuch
Porbandar
Palitana
JUNAGADH
SHATRUNJAYA
Mt Girnar
SURAT
Navsari
Somnath
Dandi
DIU (enclave)
Udwada
DAMAN (enclave)
76
14
113
79
15
8
8A
59
8E
8D
3
6
211
1
2
3
6
11
0
100 miles
100 km

MAP 5

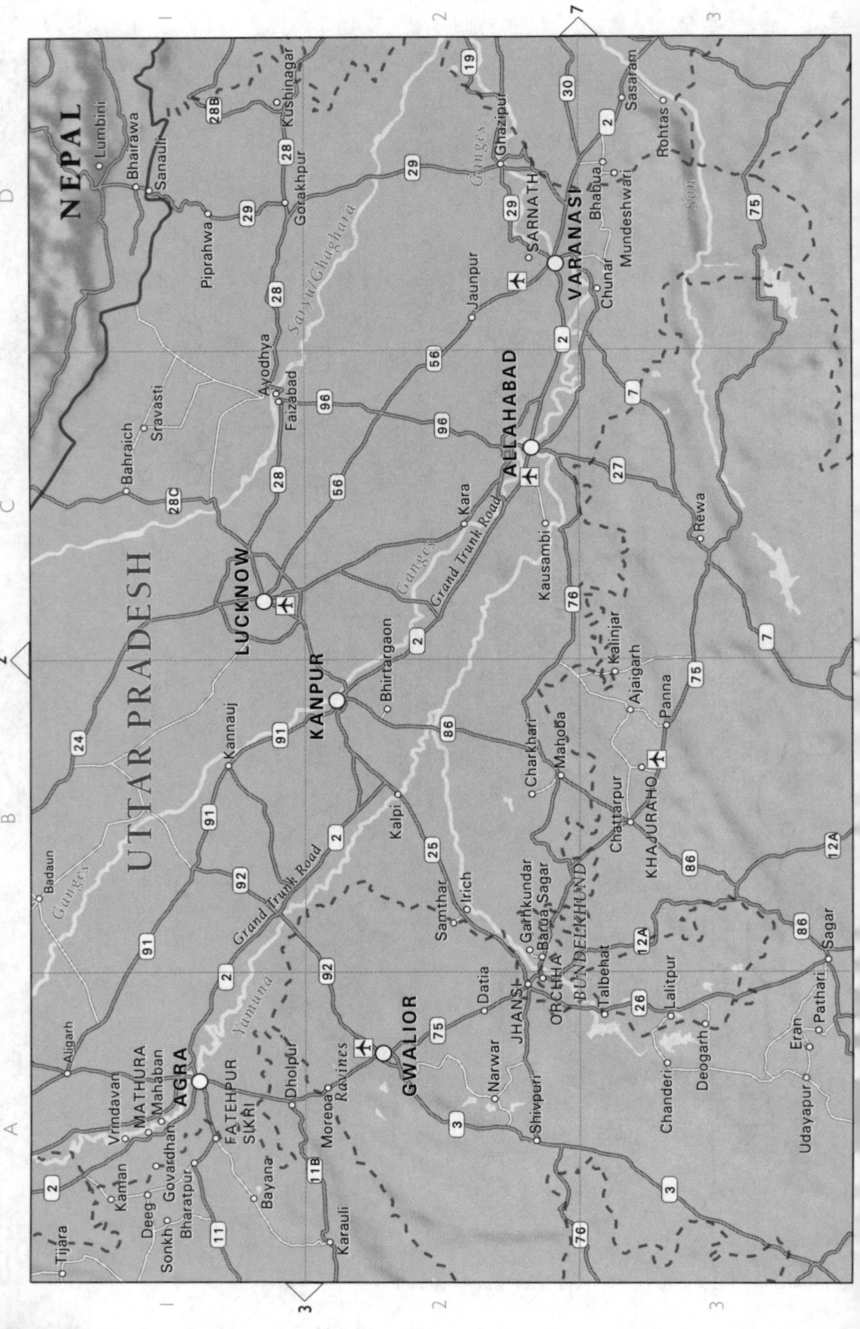

NEPAL

UTTAR PRADESH

Tijara
Aligarh
Badaun
Ganges
Kaman
Vrindavan
MATHURA
Mahaban
Deeg
Sonkh
Govardhan
AGRA
Bharatpur
FATEHPUR SIKRI
Bayana
Yamuna
Dholpur
Karauli
Morena
Ravines
GWALIOR
Grand Trunk Road
Kannauj
LUCKNOW
KANPUR
Bhirtargaon
Kalpi
Samthar
Irich
Datia
Narwar
JHANSI
Shivpuri
Garhkundar
Barua Sagar
ORCHHA
BUNDELKHUND
Talbehat
Chanderi
Lalitpur
Deogarh
Udayapur
Eran
Pathari
Sagar
Charkhari
Mahoba
Chattarpur
KHAJURAHO
Kalinjar
Ajaigarh
Panna
Bahraich
Sravasti
Ayodhya
Faizabad
Kara
Kausambi
ALLAHABAD
Rewa
Lumbini
Bhairawa
Sanauli
Piprahwa
Gorakhpur
Kushinagar
Saryu/Ghaghara
Jaunpur
Ghazipur
SARNATH
VARANASI
Chunar
Bhabua
Mundeshwari
Sasaram
Rohtas
Son

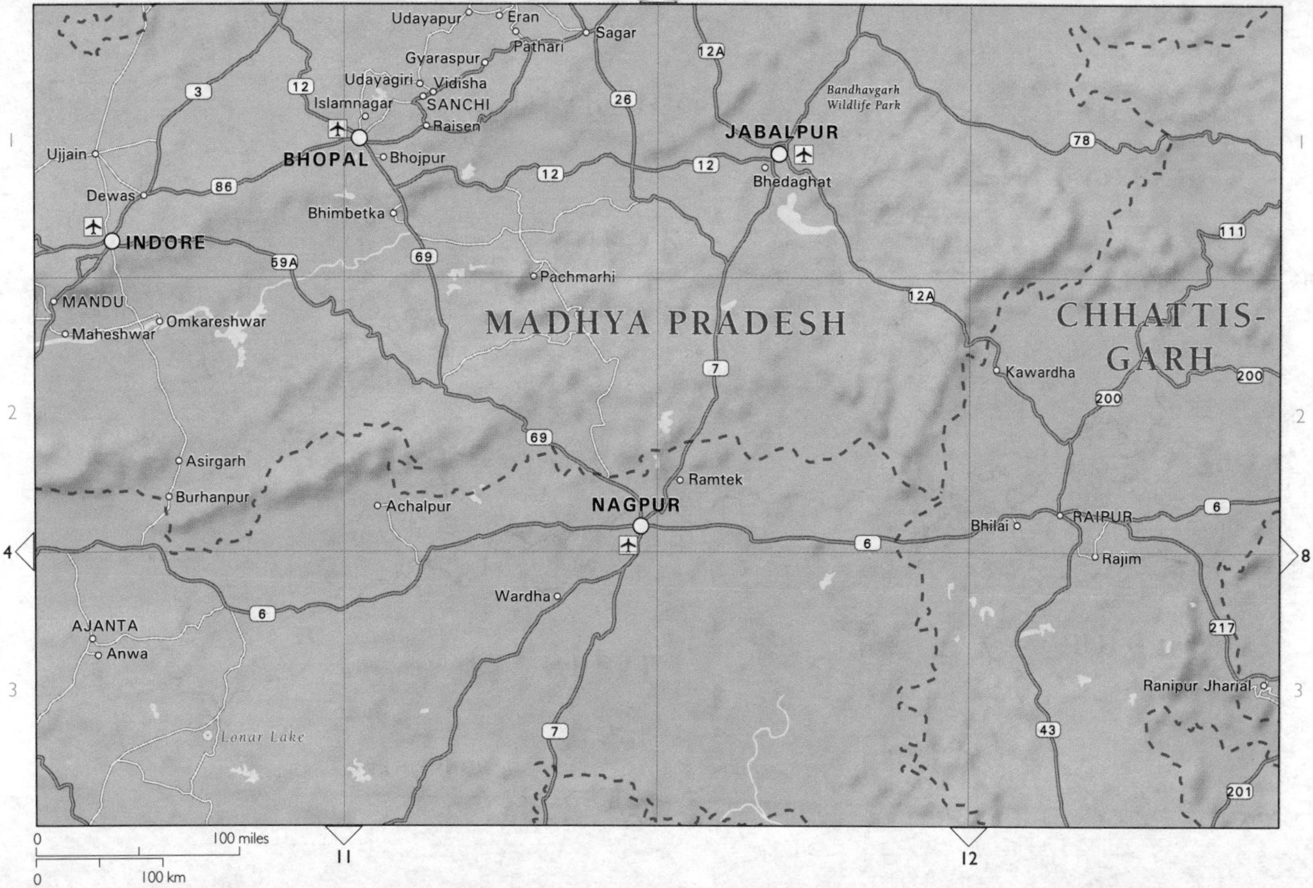

MAP 6

MADHYA PRADESH
CHHATTIS-
GARH
Udayapur
Eran
Sagar
Pathari
Gyaraspur
Udayagiri
Vidisha
Islamnagar
SANCHI
Raisen
BHOPAL
Bhojpur
Ujjain
Dewas
Bhimbetka
INDORE
MANDU
Maheshwar
Omkareshwar
Pachmarhi
JABALPUR
Bhedaghat
Bandhavgarh Wildlife Park
Kawardha
Asirgarh
Burhanpur
Achalpur
Ramtek
NAGPUR
Wardha
Bhilai
RAIPUR
Rajim
Ranipur Jharial
AJANTA
Anwa
Lonar Lake
3
12
12A
26
78
86
12
12
111
59A
69
12A
7
200
200
69
6
6
6
217
7
43
201
0
100 miles
0
100 km
1
2
3
1
2
3
4
8
11
12

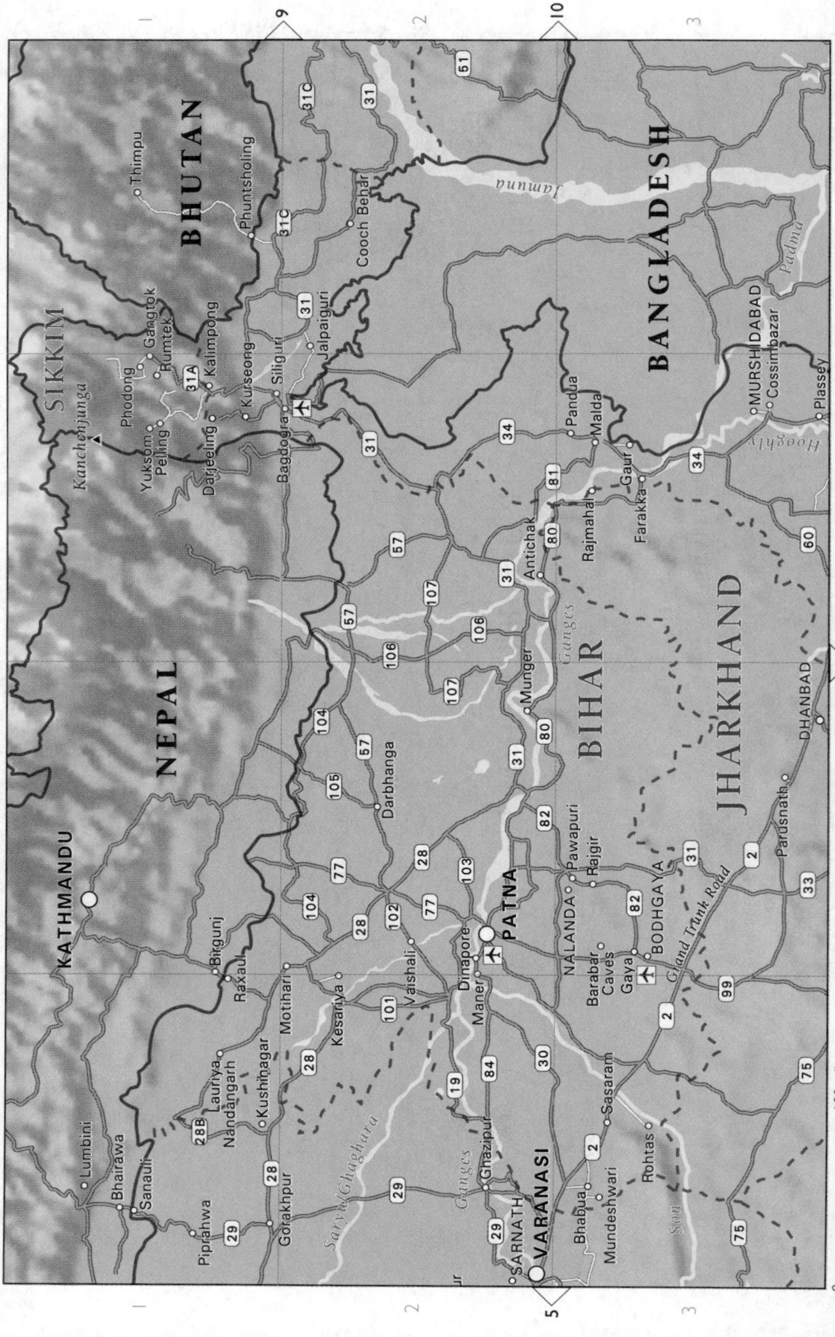

NEPAL
SIKKIM
BHUTAN
BANGLADESH
BIHAR
JHARKHAND
KATHMANDU
PATNA
VARANASI
SARNATH
Kanchenjunga
Lumbini
Bhairawa
Sanauli
Piprahwa
Lauriya Nandangarh
Kushinagar
Gorakhpur
Birgunj
Raxaul
Motihari
Kesariya
Vaishali
Dinapore
Maner
Ghazipur
Bhabua
Mundeshwari
Sasaram
Rohtas
NALANDA
Pawapuri
Rajgir
Barabar Caves
Gaya
BODHGAYA
Darbhanga
Munger
Antichak
Rajmahal
Farakka
Gaur
Malda
Pandua
Parusnath
DHANBAD
MURSHIDABAD
Cossimbazar
Plassey
Yuksom
Pelling
Phodong
Gangtok
Rumtek
Darjeeling
Kalimpong
Kurseong
Siliguri
Bagdogra
Jalpaiguri
Thimpu
Phuntsholing
Cooch Behar
Saryu/Ghaghara
Ganges
Son
Grand Trunk Road
Jamuna
Padma
Hooghly

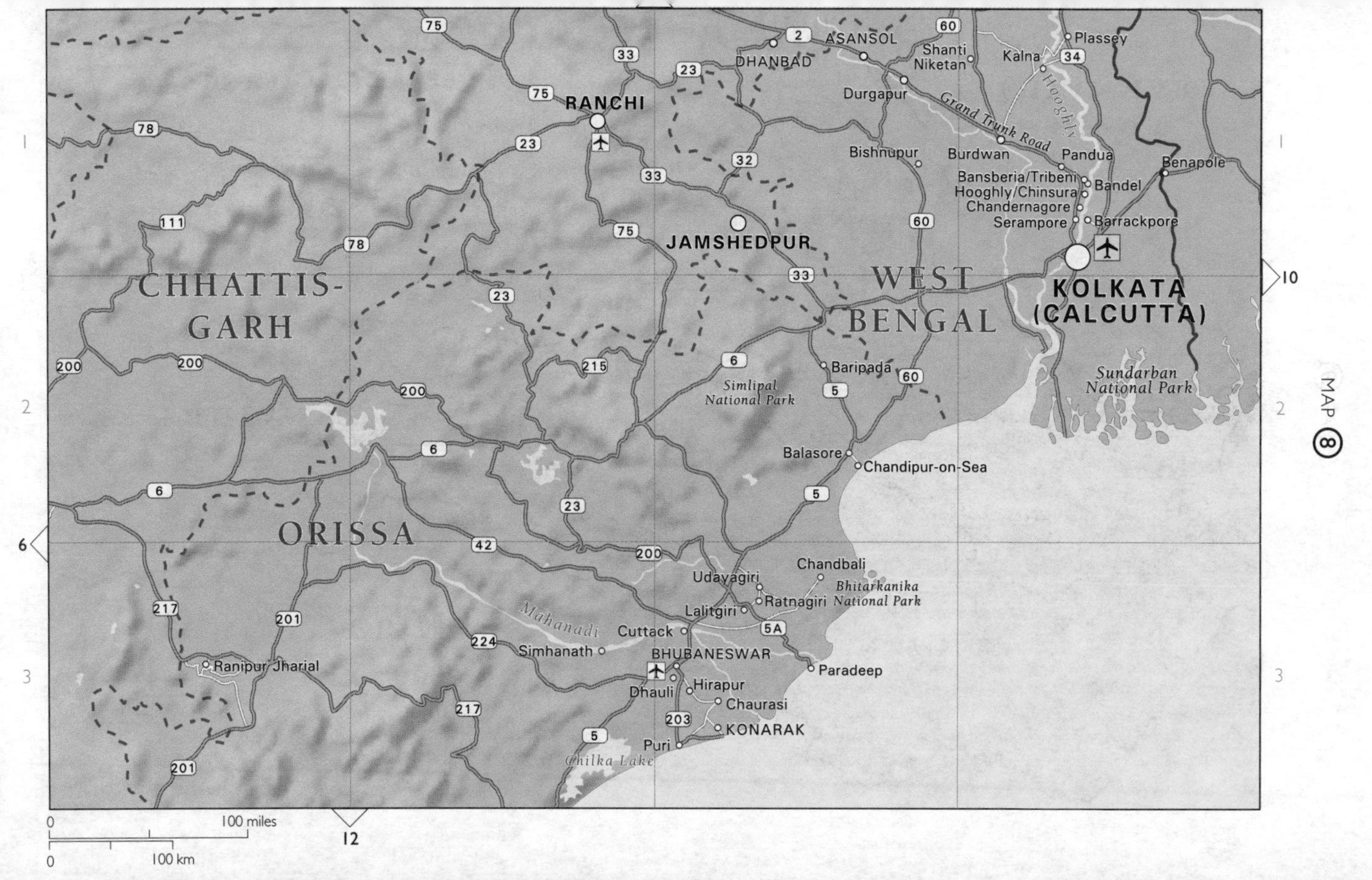
MAP 8
RANCHI
DHANBAD
ASANSOL
Durgapur
Shanti Niketan
Kalna
Plassey
Hooghly
Grand Trunk Road
Bishnupur
Burdwan
Pandua
Benapole
Bansberia/Tribeni
Hooghly/Chinsura
Chandernagore
Serampore
Bandel
Barrackpore
JAMSHEDPUR
WEST BENGAL
KOLKATA (CALCUTTA)
CHHATTIS-GARH
Sundarban National Park
Baripada
Simlipal National Park
Balasore
Chandipur-on-Sea
ORISSA
Chandbali
Udayagiri
Ratnagiri
Bhitarkanika National Park
Lalitgiri
Mahanadi
Cuttack
Simhanath
BHUBANESWAR
Paradeep
Dhauli
Hirapur
Chaurasi
KONARAK
Puri
Chilka Lake
Ranipur Jharial
100 miles
100 km

MAP 9

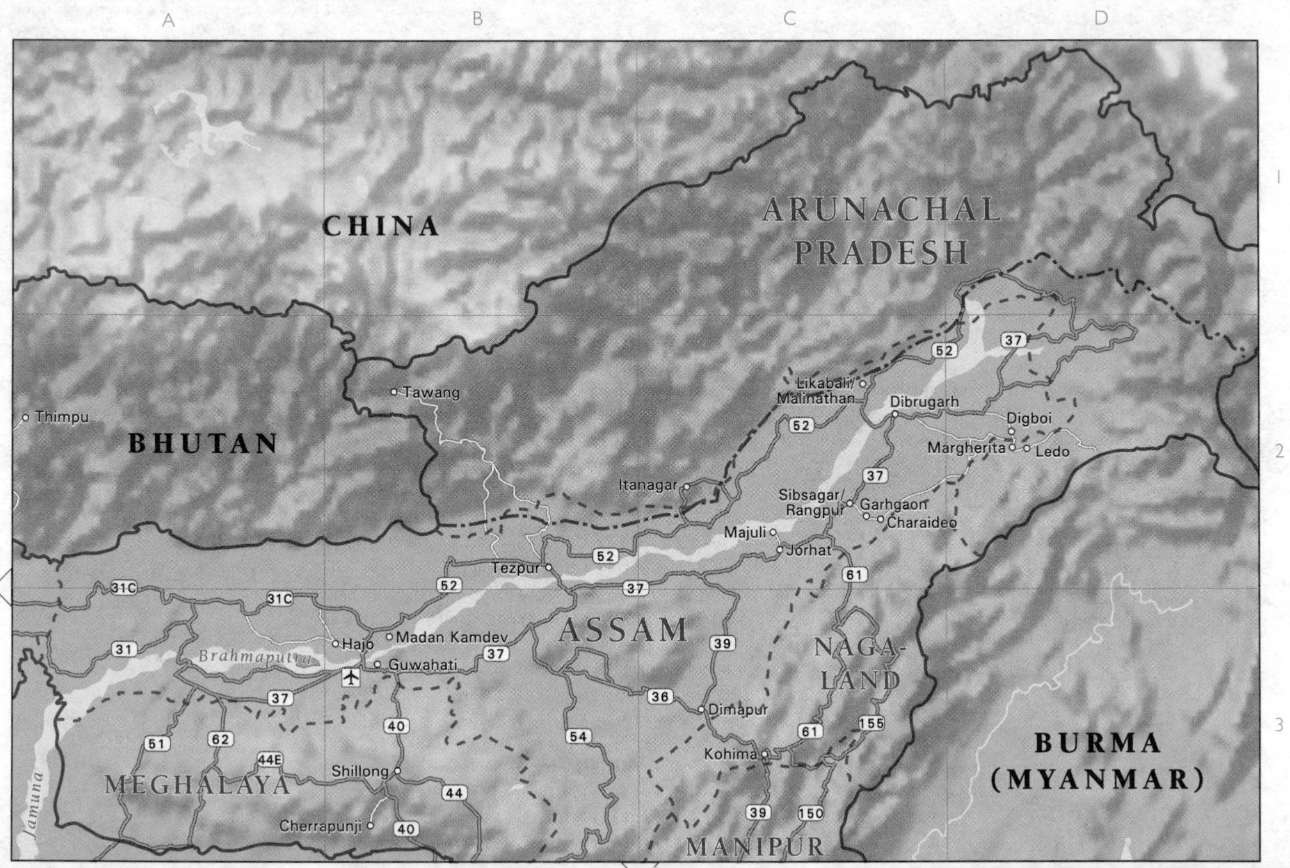

A
B
C
D
1
2
3
CHINA
ARUNACHAL PRADESH
BHUTAN
ASSAM
NAGA-LAND
MEGHALAYA
MANIPUR
BURMA (MYANMAR)
Thimpu
Tawang
Itanagar
Likabali/Malinathan
Dibrugarh
Digboi
Margherita
Ledo
Sibsagar/Rangpur
Garhgaon
Charaideo
Majuli
Jorhat
Tezpur
Hajo
Madan Kamdev
Guwahati
Brahmaputra
Dimapur
Kohima
Shillong
Cherrapunji
Jamuna
37
52
61
155
150
39
36
54
44
40
44E
62
51
31
31C
7

MEGHALAYA
51
62
44E
40
Shillong
44
Cherrapunji
40
54
Kohima
39
150
MANIPUR
53
Imphal
44
BANGLADESH
Jamuna
54
39
150
Unakoti Carvings
TRIPURA
Padma
Agartala
44A
DHAKA
Udayapur
Neermahal Palace
MIZORAM
54
BURMA (MYANMAR)
Mouths of the Ganges
0
100 miles
0
100 km
1
2
3
8

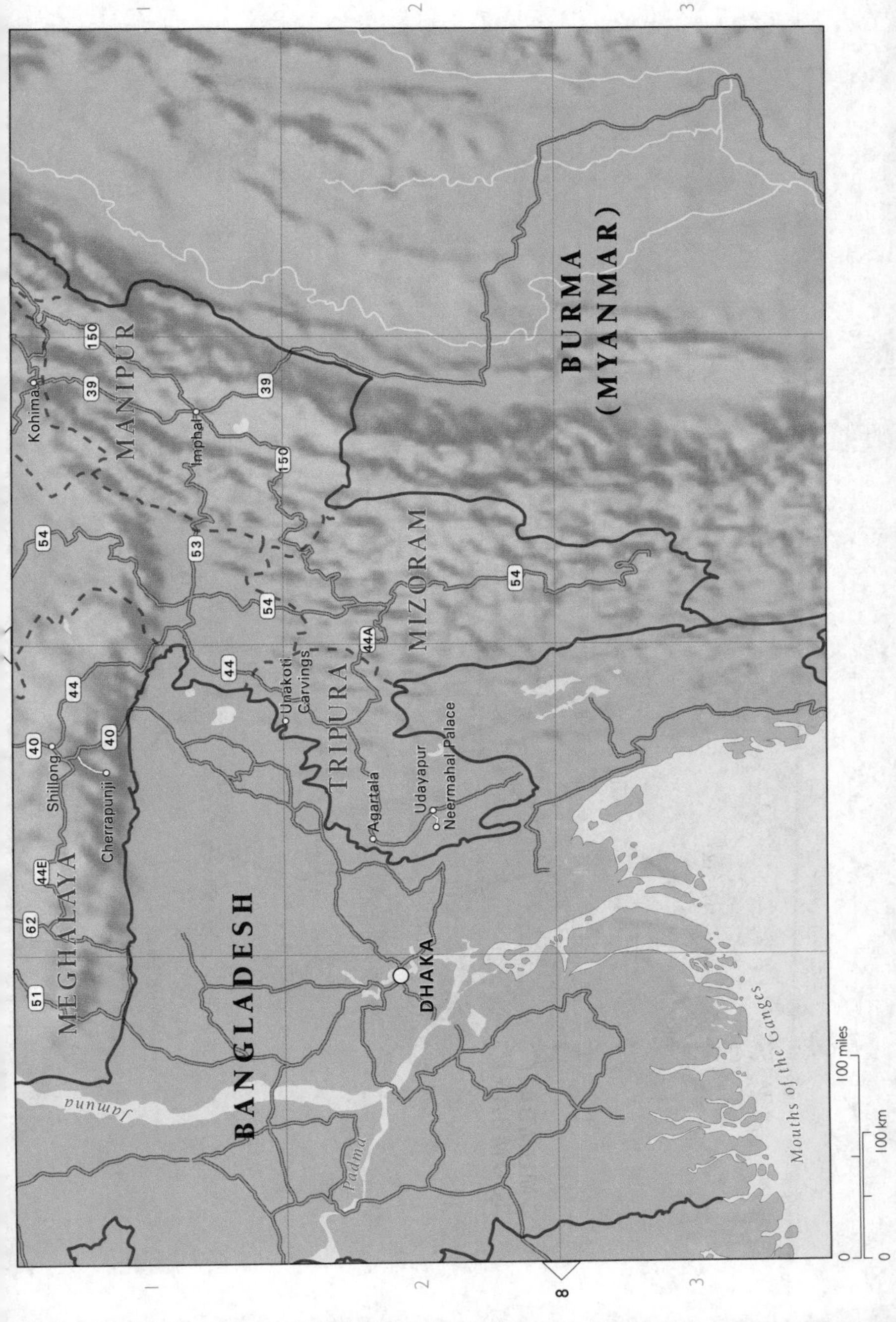

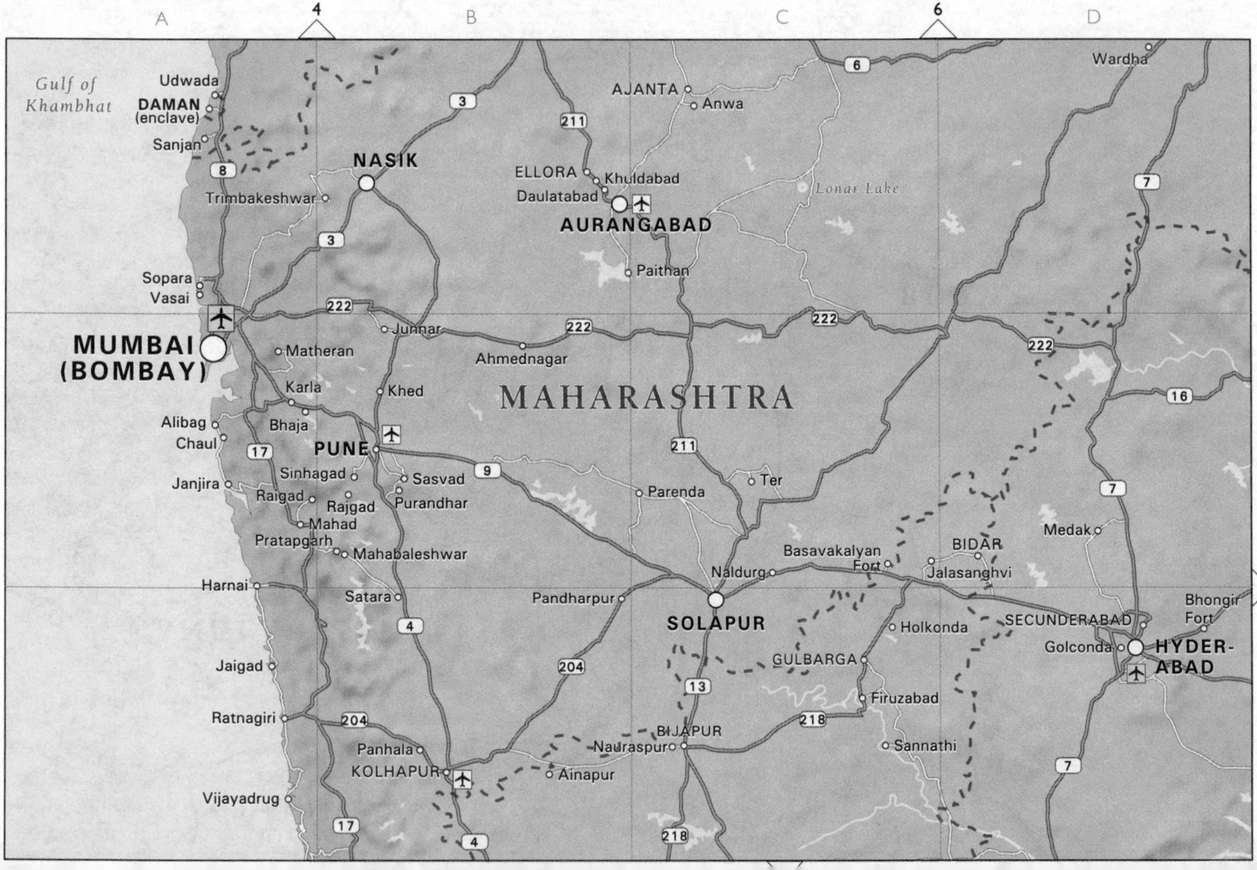

MAP 11

Gulf of Khambhat
Udwada
DAMAN (enclave)
Sanjan
Trimbakeshwar
NASIK
Sopara
Vasai
MUMBAI (BOMBAY)
Matheran
Junnar
Karla
Bhaja
Khed
Alibag
Chaul
PUNE
Sinhagad
Sasvad
Purandhar
Janjira
Raigad
Rajgad
Mahad
Pratapgarh
Mahabaleshwar
Harnai
Satara
Jaigad
Ratnagiri
Panhala
KOLHAPUR
Vijayadrug
AJANTA
Anwa
ELLORA
Khuldabad
Daulatabad
AURANGABAD
Paithan
Lonar Lake
Ahmednagar
MAHARASHTRA
Parenda
Ter
Pandharpur
Naldurg
SOLAPUR
Basavakalyan Fort
BIDAR
Jalasanghvi
Holkonda
GULBARGA
Firuzabad
BIJAPUR
Nauraspur
Sannathi
Ainapur
Wardha
Medak
SECUNDERABAD
Golconda
HYDER-ABAD
Bhongir Fort

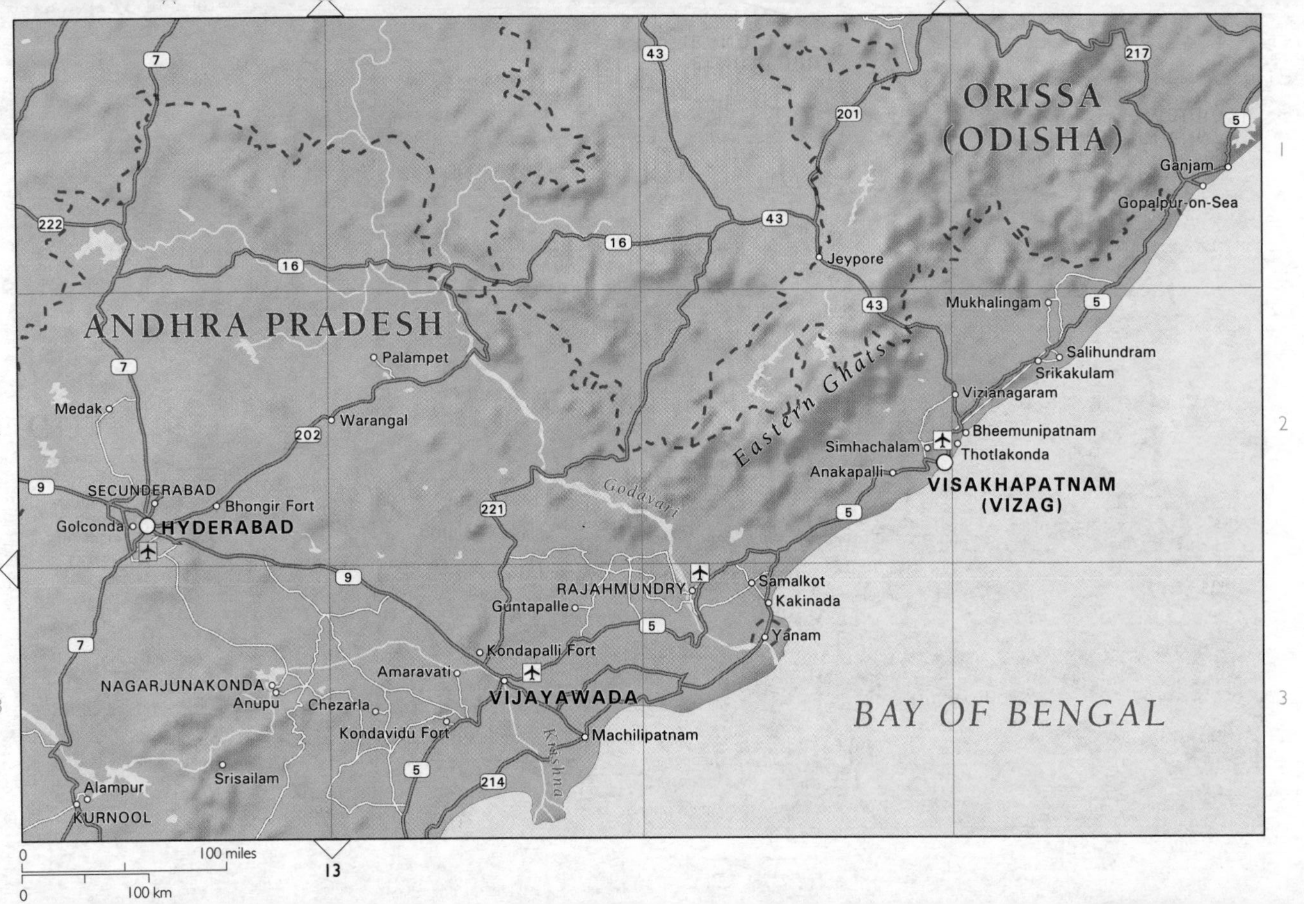
ORISSA
(ODISHA)
ANDHRA PRADESH
BAY OF BENGAL
Eastern Ghats
Godavari
Krishna
VISAKHAPATNAM
(VIZAG)
HYDERABAD
SECUNDERABAD
VIJAYAWADA
RAJAHMUNDRY
NAGARJUNAKONDA
KURNOOL
Ganjam
Gopalpur-on-Sea
Salihundram
Srikakulam
Mukhalingam
Vizianagaram
Bheemunipatnam
Thotlakonda
Simhachalam
Anakapalli
Jeypore
Samalkot
Kakinada
Yanam
Machilipatnam
Guntapalle
Kondapalli Fort
Amaravati
Kondavidu Fort
Chezarla
Anupu
Srisailam
Alampur
Palampet
Warangal
Bhongir Fort
Golconda
Medak
5
217
201
43
16
221
214
9
202
7
222
100 miles
100 km
0
1
2
3
11
13

A
B
C
D
11
12
1
2
3
Ratnagiri
Panhala
KOLHAPUR
Vijayadrug
Sindhudrug
Redi
Tiracol
Pernem
Chapora
OLD GOA
PANJIM
Mormugao
Ponda
Margao
Quepem
Cabo de Rama
GOA
Karwar
Gokarna
Jog Falls
Bhatkal
Udupi
Karkala
Mudabidri
MANGALORE
Nauraspur
BIJAPUR
Firuzabad
Sannathi
Belgaum
Kittur
HUBLI-DHARWAR
Gadag
Lakkundi
Dambal
Ittagi
Kuknur
Mahakuta
BADAMI
AIHOLE
PATTADAKAL
Mudgal
Raichur
Deccan Plateau
HAMPI / VIJAYANAGAR
Hospet
Bellary
Guntakal
Adoni
Kuruvatti
Harihar
Chitradurga
Sira
Sibi
KARNATAKA
Western Ghats
Halebid
Belur
Hassan
Shivaganga
Shravana Belagola
Melukote
Alampur
KURNOOL
Yaganti
Gooty
Tadpatri
ANANTAPUR
Ahobilam
Gandikot
Penukonda
Lepakshi
Nandi
Devanahalli
BENGALURU (BANGALORE)
Kolar
Kurudumale
NAGARJUNAKONDA
Anupu
Srisailam
Chezarla
Amaravati
Kondapalli Fort
Kondavidu Fort
Eastern Ghats
Bhairavakonda
Udayagiri
Tirupati
Sri Kalahasti
Chandragiri
Gudimallam
Narayanavanam
Nagalapuram
Pulicat
CHENNAI (MADRAS)
Sriperumbudur
Vellore
Arcot
Kanchipuram
Tirukalukundaram
Mahabalipuram
204
17
4
4A
63
13
218
7
9
5
214
205
18
206
48
46
0
100 miles

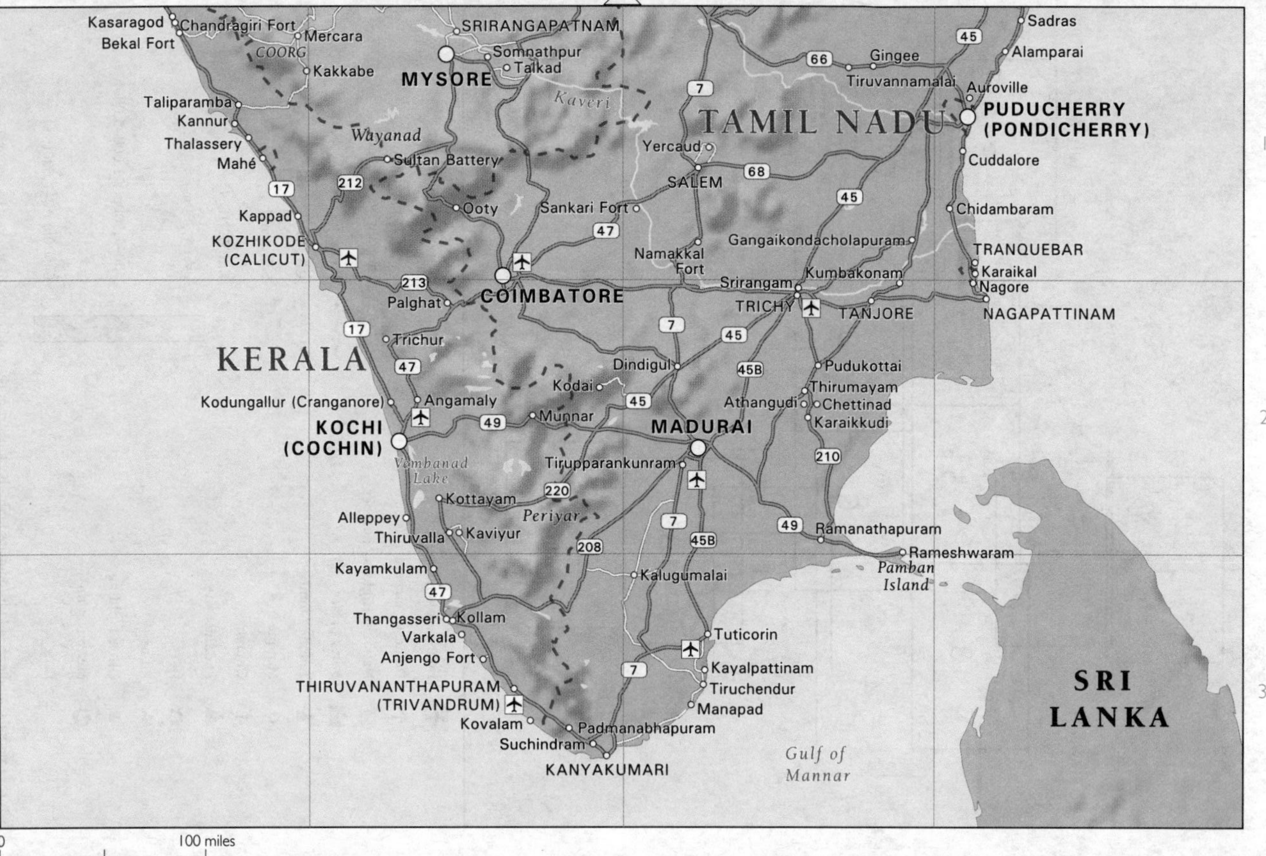

MAP 14
Kasaragod
Bekal Fort
Chandragiri Fort
Mercara
COORG
Kakkabe
Taliparamba
Kannur
Thalassery
Mahé
Kappad
KOZHIKODE (CALICUT)
Wayanad
Sultan Battery
MYSORE
SRIRANGAPATNAM
Somnathpur
Talkad
Kaveri
Ooty
COIMBATORE
Palghat
Trichur
KERALA
Kodungallur (Cranganore)
Angamaly
KOCHI (COCHIN)
Vembanad Lake
Kottayam
Alleppey
Thiruvalla
Kaviyur
Kayamkulam
Thangasseri
Kollam
Varkala
Anjengo Fort
THIRUVANANTHAPURAM (TRIVANDRUM)
Kovalam
Suchindram
Padmanabhapuram
KANYAKUMARI
Munnar
Kodai
Periyar
Dindigul
MADURAI
Tirupparankunram
Kalugumalai
Tuticorin
Kayalpattinam
Tiruchendur
Manapad
Gulf of Mannar
TAMIL NADU
Yercaud
SALEM
Sankari Fort
Namakkal Fort
Gangaikondacholapuram
Srirangam
TRICHY
Kumbakonam
TANJORE
Pudukottai
Thirumayam
Athangudi
Chettinad
Karaikkudi
Ramanathapuram
Rameshwaram
Pamban Island
Gingee
Tiruvannamalai
Sadras
Alamparai
Auroville
PUDUCHERRY (PONDICHERRY)
Cuddalore
Chidambaram
TRANQUEBAR
Karaikal
Nagore
NAGAPATTINAM
SRI LANKA
17
212
213
47
49
220
208
7
45
45B
68
66
210
0
100 miles
100 km
1
2
3

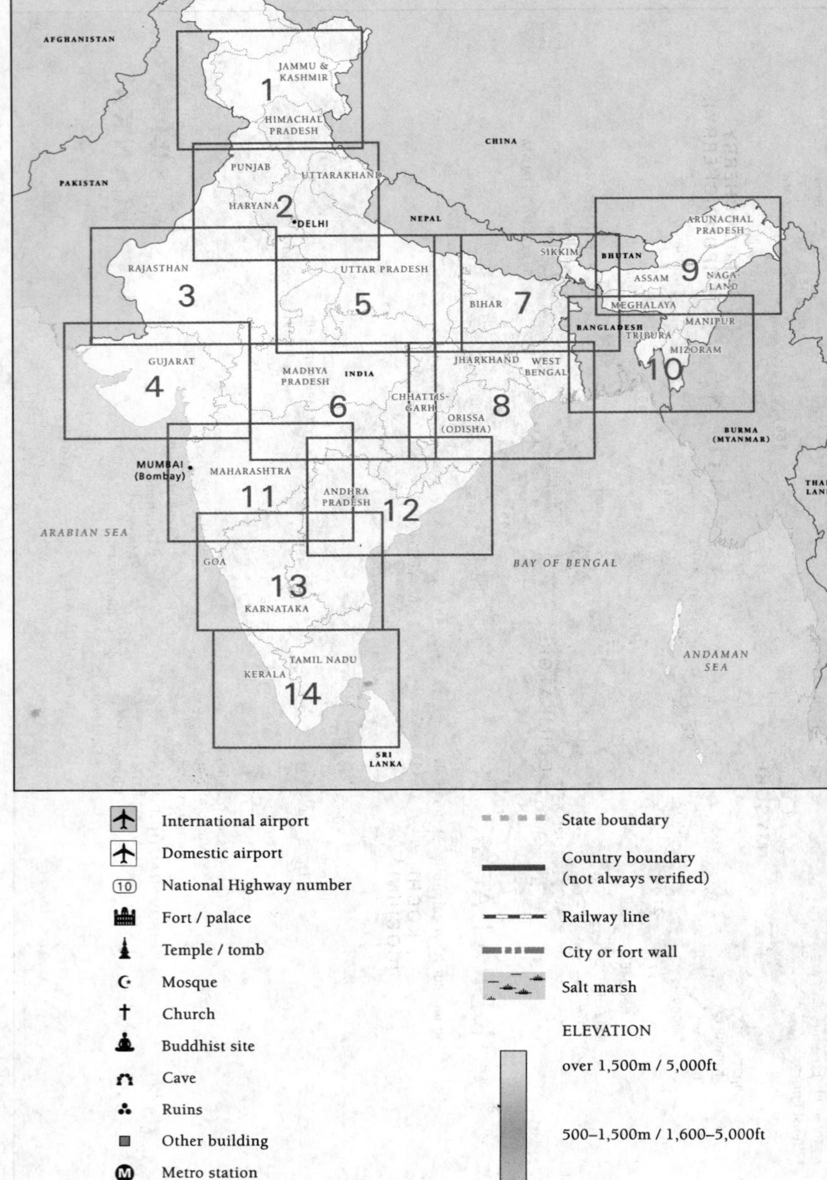

International airport
Domestic airport
10 National Highway number
Fort / palace
Temple / tomb
Mosque
Church
Buddhist site
Cave
Ruins
Other building
Metro station
Park

State boundary
Country boundary (not always verified)
Railway line
City or fort wall
Salt marsh

ELEVATION

over 1,500m / 5,000ft

500–1,500m / 1,600–5,000ft

0–500m / 0–1,600ft

NB: The external boundaries of India on maps in this book have not been authenticated and may be incorrect.